# Western Civilizations

## *Their History & Their Culture*

ARCTIC
NUNAVUT
On April 1, 1999, Canada will establish the new territory of Nunavut–meaning "our land"
GREENLAND (KALAALLIT NUNAAT) (Denmark)
Beaufort Sea
Baffin Bay
Davis Strait
NORTHWEST TERRITORIES
ALASKA (U.S.)
YUKON TERRITORY
CANADA
Hudson Bay
Labrador Sea
Reykjavik
ICELAND
ARCTIC CIRCLE
Bering Sea
Anchorage
Date Line
Monday
Sunday
RUSSIA
BRITISH COLUMBIA
ALBERTA
SASK.
MANITOBA
ONTARIO
QUEBEC
NEWFOUNDLAND
Vancouver
Seattle
Calgary
Edmonton
Winnipeg
Montréal
Ottawa
Toronto
Boston
NORTH
PACIFIC
OCEAN
UNITED STATES
San Francisco
Los Angeles
San Diego
Phoenix
Dallas
Chicago
Denver
NEW YORK
Philadelphia
Washington, D.C.
Atlanta
Houston
New Orleans
Miami
San Antonio
Gulf of Mexico
MEXICO
Monterrey
Guadalajara
Havana
CUBA
BAHAMAS
Nassau
HAITI
DOMINICAN REPUBLIC
Santo Domingo
Port-au-Prince
Puerto Rico (U.S.)
JAMAICA
Kingston
BELIZE
Belmopan
GUATEMALA
Guatemala
HONDURAS
Tegucigalpa
EL SALVADOR
San Salvador
NICARAGUA
Managua
COSTA RICA
San José
PANAMA
Panama
Caribbean Sea
ST. KITTS AND NEVIS
ANTIGUA AND BARBUDA
DOMINICA
ST. LUCIA
BARBADOS
ST. VINCENT AND THE GRENADINES
TRINIDAD AND TOBAGO
Port of Spain
GRENADA
Maracaibo
Caracas
VENEZUELA
Georgetown
GUYANA
SURINAME
Paramaribo
FRENCH GUIANA (France)
Medellín
BOGOTÁ
Cali
COLOMBIA
Quito
ECUADOR
Guayaquil
GALÁPAGOS ISLANDS (Ecuador)
Belém
Manaus
Fortaleza
Recife
BRAZIL
PERU
LIMA
Salvador
Brasília
La Paz
BOLIVIA
Sucre
Belo Horizonte
RIO DE JANEIRO
SÃO PAULO
PARAGUAY
Asunción
Curitiba
Pôrto Alegre
CHILE
ARGENTINA
Córdoba
Rosario
SANTIAGO
URUGUAY
Montevideo
Buenos Aires
Falkland Islands (Islas Malvinas) (U.K.)
TIERRA DEL FUEGO
South Georgia (U.K.)
Drake Passage
South Shetland Islands
Weddell Sea
ANTARCTICA
Ronne Ice Shelf
Ross Sea
Ross Ice Shelf
HAWAII (U.S.)
POLYNESIA
Line Islands
Phoenix Islands
KIRIBATI
Tokelau (N.Z.)
SAMOA
Apia
American Samoa (U.S.)
TONGA
Nuku'alofa
Cook Islands (N.Z.)
Society Is.
French Polynesia (France)
Marquesas Islands (France)
Tuamotu Archipelago
Austral Islands
Easter Island (Chile)
Isla Sala y Gómez (Chile)
Archipiélago Juan Fernández (Chile)
Kermadec Islands (N.Z.)
Chatham Islands (N.Z.)
SOUTH
ATLANTIC
OCEAN
TROPIC OF CANCER
TROPIC OF CAPRICORN
EQUATOR
Bermuda Islands (U.K.)
Azores (Portugal)
Madeira Islands (Portugal)
Canary Islands (Spain)
PORTUGAL
Lisbon
Casablanca
WESTERN SAHARA (Morocco)
MAURITANIA
Nouakchott
CAPE VERDE
Praia
Dakar
SENEGAL
GAMBIA
Banjul
GUINEA-BISSAU
Bissau
GUINEA
Conakry
Freetown
SIERRA LEONE
LIBERIA
Monrovia
Tristan Da Cunha Group (U.K.)
ANTARCTIC CIRCLE
Longitude West of Greenwich
150°
120°
90°
60°
30°

O C E A N
Franz Josef Land (Russia)
Svalbard (Norway)
Barents Sea
Novaya Zemlya
Kara Sea
North Land
Laptev Sea
New Siberian Is.
East Siberian Sea
R U S S I A
FINLAND
SWEDEN
NORWAY
Oslo
Helsinki
Tallinn
Lake Ladoga
St. Petersburg
Stockholm
ESTONIA
LATVIA
Riga
Baltic Sea
LITHUANIA
Vilnius
Nizhniy Novgorod
Perm'
Kazan'
MOSCOW
Yekaterinburg
Omsk
Novosibirsk
Chelyabinsk
Ufa
Samara
Minsk
BELARUS
POLAND
Berlin
GERMANY
Warsaw
Prague
Kiev
Kharkiv
UKRAINE
Dnipropetrovs'k
Donets'k
Rostov
Vienna
Budapest
MOLDOVA
Chişinău
HUNGARY
ROMANIA
Odesa
Belgrade
Bucharest
Black Sea
BULGARIA
Sofia
ISTANBUL
ITALY
Rome
Naples
Sicily
GREECE
Athens
Ankara
T U R K E Y
Izmir
Adana
Crete
Mediterranean Sea
Nicosia
CYPRUS
SYRIA
Beirut
LEBANON
ISRAEL
Jerusalem
Damascus
Amman
JORDAN
TUNISIA
Tunis
MALTA
Tripoli
Alexandria
El Giza
CAIRO
L I B Y A
E G Y P T
Lake Nasser
Red Sea
GEORGIA
T'bilisi
ARMENIA
Yerevan
AZERBAIJAN
Baku
Caspian Sea
TURKMENISTAN
Ashgabat
Mashhad
TEHRAN
I R A N
IRAQ
Baghdad
Euphrates
Kuwait
KUWAIT
Persian Gulf
Manama
BAHRAIN
QATAR
Doha
Abu Dhabi
UNITED ARAB EMIRATES
Oman
Muscat
Gulf of Oman
S A U D I A R A B I A
Riyadh
Jeddah
OMAN
YEMEN
Sanaa
Gulf of Aden
DJIBOUTI
Djibouti
Socotra (Yemen)
ERITREA
Asmara
K A Z A K H S T A N
Astana
Lake Balkhash
Almaty
Bishkek
KYRGYZSTAN
Tashkent
UZBEKISTAN
Aral Sea
Dushanbe
TAJIKISTAN
AFGHANISTAN
Kabul
Lahore
Faisalabad
PAKISTAN
KARACHI
DELHI
New Delhi
NEPAL
Kathmandu
Lucknow
Kanpur
I N D I A
Bhopal
Indore
Calcutta
Ahmadabad
Vadodara
Ganges
BHUTAN
BANG.
Dhaka
Chittagong
MUMBAI (Bombay)
Hyderabad
Bay of Bengal
Arabian Sea
Bangalore
Chennai (Madras)
Coimbatore
Cochin
Madurai
Lakshadweep (India)
SRI LANKA
Colombo
Male
MALDIVES
Andaman Islands (India)
Nicobar Islands (India)
Andaman Sea
MYANMAR (BURMA)
Rangoon
THAI.
BANGKOK
LAOS
Vientiane
CAMBODIA
Phnom Penh
VIETNAM
Hanoi
Ho Chi Minh City
Ulaanbaatar
M O N G O L I A
Ürümqi
Baotou
Lanzhou
Xi'an
C H I N A
Chengdu
CHONGQING
Kunming
Nanning
Guiyang
Wuhan
Changsha
Nanchang
Zhengzhou
Nanjing
SHANGHAI
Hangzhou
East China Sea
Taiyuan
Jinan
Tai'an
Qingdao
BEIJING
TIANJIN
Shenyang
Jilin
Changchun
Harbin
Guangzhou
HONG KONG
MACAU (Portugal)
TAIWAN
Taipei
Kaohsiung
TAIWAN
The People's Republic of China claims Taiwan as its 23rd province.
NORTH KOREA
Pyongyang
SEOUL
SOUTH KOREA
Taegu
Pusan
Sea of Japan
JAPAN
Sapporo
Kyoto
TOKYO
Nagoya
Osaka
Hiroshima
Fukuoka
Lake Baikal
Amur
Lena
Yenisey
Ob'
Irtysh
Kolyma
Sea of Okhotsk
Kuril Islands
Bering Sea
Aleutian Is. (U.S.)
Sunday
Monday
Date Line
NORTH PACIFIC OCEAN
Philippine Sea
Northern Mariana Islands (U.S.)
Guam (U.S.)
South China Sea
Duezon City
Manila
PHILIPPINES
Sulu Sea
PALAU
Koror
BRUNEI
Bandar Seri Begawan
Celebes Sea
MALAYSIA
Kuala Lumpur
SINGAPORE
Medan
Molucca Sea
I N D O N E S I A
Palembang
Greater Sunda Islands
JAKARTA
Semarang
Surabaya
Bandung
Lesser Sunda Islands
Banda Sea
Arafura Sea
PAPUA NEW GUINEA
Bismarck Sea
Port Moresby
Solomon Sea
SOLOMON ISLANDS
Honiara
M I C R O N E S I A
FEDERATED STATES OF MICRONESIA
Palikir
Caroline Islands
MARSHALL ISLANDS
Majuro
Tarawa
KIRIBATI
NAURU
M E L A N E S I A
TUVALU
Funafuti
Coral Sea
VANUATU
Port-Vila
FIJI
Suva
New Caledonia (France)
NORTHERN TERRITORY
QUEENSLAND
WESTERN AUSTRALIA
A U S T R A L I A
SOUTH AUSTRALIA
NEW SOUTH WALES
VICTORIA
TASMANIA
Perth
Adelaide
Brisbane
Sydney
Canberra, A.C.T.
Melbourne
Great Australian Bight
Tasman Sea
SOUTH PACIFIC OCEAN
North Island
NEW ZEALAND
Wellington
South Island
N I G E R
CHAD
Lake Chad
NIGERIA
Abuja
S U D A N
Khartoum
Djamena
CENTRAL AFRICAN REPUBLIC
Bangui
CAMEROON
Yaoundé
Malabo
ETHIOPIA
Addis Ababa
Lake Turkana
SOMALIA
Mogadishu
KENYA
Nairobi
UGANDA
Kampala
Lake Victoria
RWANDA
Kigali
BURUNDI
Bujumbura
DEMOCRATIC REPUBLIC OF THE CONGO
Kinshasa
CONGO
Brazzaville
GABON
Libreville
CABINDA (Angola)
Luanda
TANZANIA
Lake Tanganyika
Dar es Salaam
SEYCHELLES
Victoria
ANGOLA
ZAMBIA
Lusaka
Lake Malawi
MALAWI
Lilongwe
COMOROS
Moroni
MOZAMBIQUE
Harare
ZIMBABWE
MADAGASCAR
Antananarivo
Port Louis
MAURITIUS
NAMIBIA
Windhoek
BOTSWANA
Gaborone
Pretoria
Maputo
SWAZILAND
Mbabane
LESOTHO
Maseru
SOUTH AFRICA
Cape Town
Chagos Archipelago (British Indian Ocean Territory)
I N D I A N O C E A N
Prince Edward Islands (South Africa)
Crozet Islands (France)
Kerguélen Islands (France)
Ross Sea
Ross Ice Shelf
T I C A
STATUTE MILES
0 400 800 1200 1600 2000
0 800 1600 2400 3200
KILOMETERS
Scale at the Equator
Longitude East of Greenwich
30° 60° 90° 120° 150°

NORTH POLAR REGION
ARCTIC OCEAN
NORTH AMERICA
ASIA
GREENLAND
North Pole
Svalbard
Novaya Zemlya
ARCTIC
QUEEN ELIZABETH ISLANDS
Baffin Bay
Hudson Bay
ALEUTIAN TRENCH
NORTH AMERICA
NORTH PACIFIC OCEAN
NORTH ATLANTIC OCEAN
GULF OF MEXICO
CARIBBEAN SEA
CENTRAL AMERICA
TROPIC OF CANCER
Hawaii
POLYNESIA
EQUATOR
Amazon Basin
SOUTH AMERICA
ANDES
MID-ATLANTIC RIDGE
TROPIC OF CAPRICORN
SOUTH PACIFIC OCEAN
SOUTH ATLANT
OCEA
Falkland Islands
Cape Horn
Drake Passage
ANTARCTIC PENINSULA
WEDDELL SEA
ANTARCTIC CIRCLE
Marie Byrd Land
ANTA
THE
SATEL
GLOBAL SATELLITE MOSAIC
The beauty and complexity of Earth's landscapesñabove and below the oceansñis revealed with the Global Satellite Mosaic. The mosaic was produced for the National Geographic Society by NASA's Jet Propulsion Laboratory, using more than 500 satellite images from the National Oceanic and Atmospheric Administration. The cloud-free images show Earth in its natural colors as it would be seen from space. One can easily identify the world's major glaciers, deserts, mountain ranges, and rain forests. For example, follow the green ribbon of lush vegetation along the Nile into the stark, dry Sahara. The mountain ranges seem to rise off the map thanks to digital elevation databases from the Department of Defense. The deepest areas of the ocean realm are colored dark blue in contrast to the light blue areas highlighting continental shelves, submarine ridges, and underwater mountains.
BIOSPHERE
Thousands of satellite images are
combined to show a picture of biospheric
productivity. In the oceans, red, yellow, and
green indicate waters rich in phytoplankton. On land,
green areas show high-potential plant productivity; tan areas
suffer from productivity limitations due to aridity and temperature.

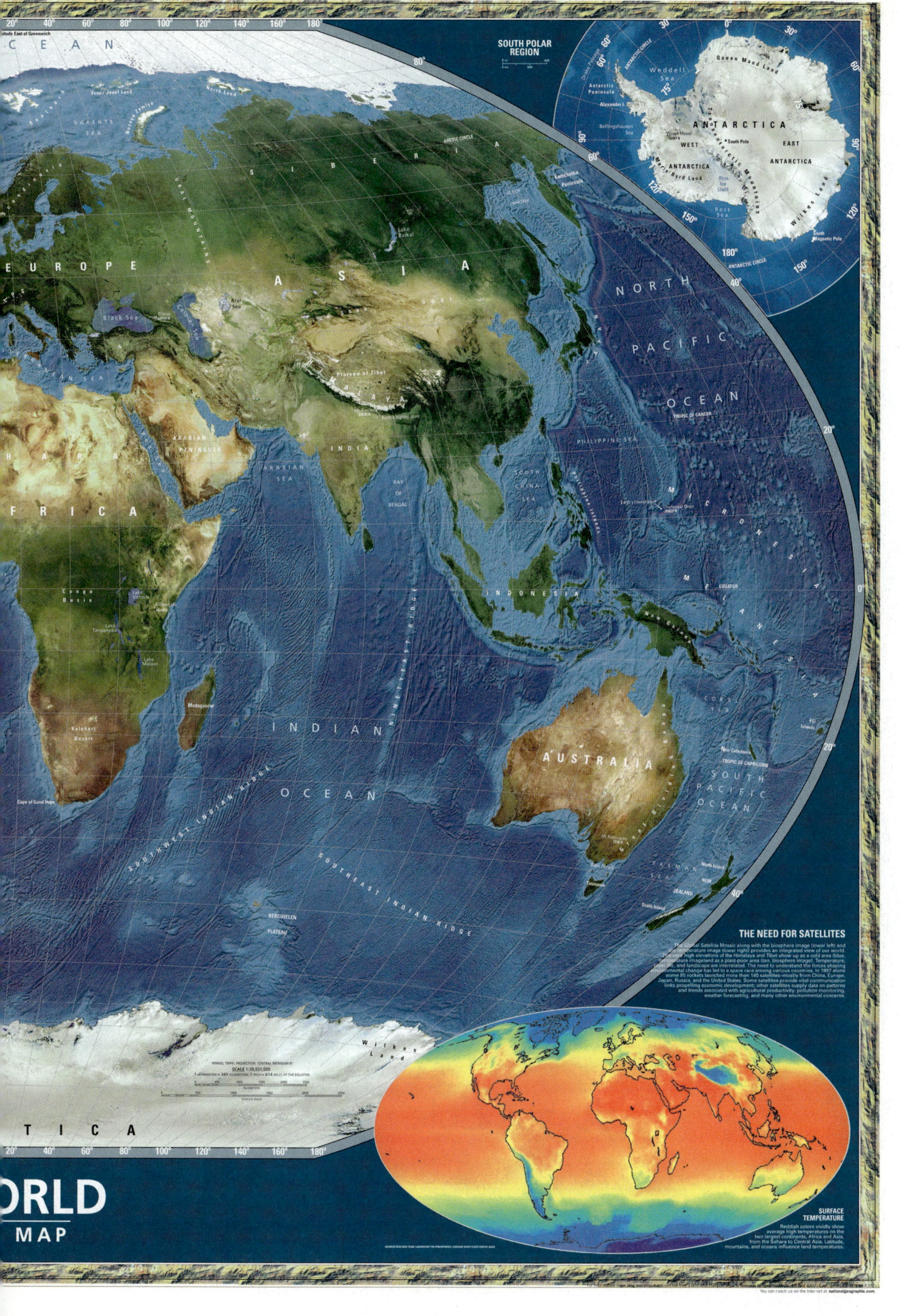
SOUTH POLAR REGION
ANTARCTICA
Queen Maud Land
Weddell Sea
Antarctic Peninsula
WEST ANTARCTICA
EAST ANTARCTICA
South Pole
Ross Ice Shelf
Ross Sea
Marie Byrd Land
Wilkes Land
ARCTIC OCEAN
Franz Josef Land
BARENTS SEA
Novaya Zemlya
SIBERIA
Ural Mountains
Lake Baikal
EUROPE
ASIA
Black Sea
Caspian Sea
Aral Sea
Plateau of Tibet
HIMALAYA
ARABIAN PENINSULA
SAHARA
AFRICA
INDIA
ARABIAN SEA
BAY OF BENGAL
SOUTH CHINA SEA
PHILIPPINE SEA
INDONESIA
New Guinea
NORTH PACIFIC OCEAN
TROPIC OF CANCER
MICRONESIA
MELANESIA
EQUATOR
Congo Basin
Lake Tanganyika
Lake Malawi
Madagascar
Kalahari Desert
Cape of Good Hope
INDIAN OCEAN
NINETYEAST RIDGE
SOUTHWEST INDIAN RIDGE
SOUTHEAST INDIAN RIDGE
KERGUELEN PLATEAU
AUSTRALIA
CORAL SEA
New Caledonia
TROPIC OF CAPRICORN
SOUTH PACIFIC OCEAN
TASMAN SEA
North Island
NEW ZEALAND
South Island
Fiji Islands
Wilkes Land
ANTARCTICA
WORLD
MAP
THE NEED FOR SATELLITES
The Global Satellite Mosaic along with the biosphere image (lower left) and the temperature image (lower right) provides an integrated view of our world. The very high elevations of the Himalaya and Tibet show up as a cold area (blue, temperature image) and as a plant-poor area (tan, biosphere image). Temperature, plant life, and landscape are interrelated. The need to understand the forces shaping environmental change has led to a space race among various countries. In 1997 alone some 85 rockets launched more than 140 satellites–mostly from China, Europe, Japan, Russia, and the United States. Some satellites provide vital communication links propelling economic development; other satellites supply data on patterns and trends associated with agricultural productivity, pollution monitoring, weather forecasting, and many other environmental concerns.
SURFACE TEMPERATURE
Reddish colors vividly show average high temperatures on the two largest continents, Africa and Asia, from the Sahara to Central Asia. Latitude, mountains, and oceans influence land temperatures.

Judith Coffin

Robert Stacey

Joshua Cole

Carol Symes

# Western Civilizations

## *Their History & Their Culture*

SEVENTEENTH EDITION

VOLUME 1

W. W. NORTON & COMPANY ▪ NEW YORK ▪ LONDON

W. W. Norton & Company has been independent since its founding in 1923, when William Warder Norton and Mary D. Herter Norton first published lectures delivered at the People's Institute, the adult education division of New York City's Cooper Union. The firm soon expanded its program beyond the Institute, publishing books by celebrated academics from America and abroad. By midcentury, the two major pillars of Norton's publishing program—trade books and college texts—were firmly established. In the 1950s, the Norton family transferred control of the company to its employees, and today—with a staff of four hundred and a comparable number of trade, college, and professional titles published each year—W. W. Norton & Company stands as the largest and oldest publishing house owned wholly by its employees.


Printed in the United States of America

*Editor:* Jon Durbin
*Project editor:* Kathleen Feighery
*Managing editor, College:* Marian Johnson
*Copyeditors:* Candace Levy and Michael Fleming
*E-media editor:* Steve Hoge
*Ancillary editor:* Lorraine Klimowich
*Editorial assistant:* Jason Spears
*Photo editor:* Junenoire Mitchell
*Photo research:* Donna Ranieri
*Senior production manager, College:* Benjamin Reynolds
*Design director:* Rubina Yeh
*Book designer:* Judith Abbate / Abbate Design
*Composition:* TexTech, Inc.—Brattleboro, VT
*Cartographers:* Mapping Specialists—Madison, WI
*Manufacturing:* R. R. Donnelley & Sons—Jefferson City, MO

The Library of Congress has Cataloged the one-volume edition as follows:

Coffin, Judith G., 1952–
Western civilizations : their history & their culture / Judith G. Coffin ... [et al.]. — Seventeenth ed.
p. cm.
Includes bibliographical references and index.

**ISBN 978-0-393-93481-6 (hardcover)**
1. Civilization, Western—Textbooks. 2. Europe—Civilization—Textbooks. I. Title.
CB245.C65 2011
909'.09821—dc22

2010038141

This edition:
ISBN: **978-0-393-93482-3 (pbk.)**

W. W. Norton & Company, Inc., 500 Fifth Avenue, New York, N. Y. 10110
wwnorton.com

W. W. Norton & Company Ltd., Castle House, 75/76 Wells Street, London W1T 3QT

1 2 3 4 5 6 7 8 9 0

To our families:

Willy, Zoe, and Aaron Forbath
Robin, Will, and Anna Stacey
Kate Tremel, Lucas and Ruby Cole
Tom, Erin, and Connor Wilson

with love and gratitude for their support.
And to all our students, who have also been
our teachers.

# About the Authors

**JUDITH COFFIN** (Ph.D. Yale University) is an associate professor at the University of Texas, Austin, where she won University of Texas President's Associates' Award for Teaching Excellence. Previously, she taught at Harvard University and the University of California, Riverside. Her research interests are the social and cultural history of gender, mass culture, slavery, race relations, and colonialism. She is the author of *The Politics of Women's Work: The Paris Garment Trades, 1750–1915.*

**ROBERT STACEY** (Ph.D. Yale University) is professor of history, Dean of the Humanities, and a member of the Jewish Studies faculty at the University of Washington, Seattle. A long-time teacher of Western civilization and medieval European history, he has received Distinguished Teaching Awards from both the University of Washington and Yale University, where he taught from 1984 to 1988. He has authored and coauthored four books, including a textbook, *The Making of England to 1399.* He holds an M.A. from Oxford University and a Ph.D. from Yale.

**JOSHUA COLE** (Ph.D. University of California, Berkeley) is Associate Professor of History at the University of Michigan at Ann Arbor. His publications include work on gender and the history of the population sciences, colonial violence, and the politics of memory in 19th and 20th century France, Germany, and Algeria. His first book was *The Power of Large Numbers: Population, Politics and Gender in Nineteenth-Century France* (Ithaca, NY: Cornell University Press, 2000).

**CAROL SYMES** (Ph.D. Harvard University) is Associate Professor of history and Director of Undergraduate Studies in the history department at the University of Illinois, Urbana-Champaign, where she has won the top teaching award in the College of Liberal Arts and Sciences. Her main areas of study include medieval Europe, the history of information media and communication technologies, and the history of theatre. Her first book was *A Common Stage: Theater and Public Life in Medieval Arras* (Ithaca: Cornell University Press, 2007).

# Brief Contents

# Contents

## Chapter 3 ▪ THE CIVILIZATION OF GREECE, 1000–400 B.C.E. 73

## Chapter 4 ▪ THE GREEK WORLD EXPANDS, 400–150 B.C.E. 107

## Chapter 5 ▪ THE CIVILIZATION OF ANCIENT ROME 141

## Chapter 9 ▪ THE CONSOLIDATION OF EUROPE, 1100–1300 275

## Chapter 10 ▪ CRISIS, UNREST, AND OPPORTUNITY, 1300–1500 311

## Chapter 11 ▪ COMMERCE, CONQUEST, AND COLONIZATION, 1300–1600 347

## Chapter 12 ▪ RENAISSANCE IDEALS AND REALITIES, c. 1350–1550 373

## Chapter 13 ▪ THE AGE OF DISSENT AND DIVISION, 1500–1600 399

## Chapter 14 ▪ RELIGION, WARFARE, AND SOVEREIGNTY: 1540–1660 427

## Chapter 15 ▪ ABSOLUTISM AND EMPIRE, 1660–1789 457

# Maps

# Documents

# Preface

The motivating principle for this edition of *Western Civilizations* is a relatively simple idea: that history students will be inspired to engage more effectively with the past if they are given a flexible set of tools to use as they approach their readings. *Western Civilizations* has always been known for its clear and vigorous account of Europe's past, and previous editions have been noteworthy for their selection of primary sources and visual images. As the authors of this new edition, we have made a special effort to bring greater unity to the pedagogical elements that accompany each chapter, so that students will be able to work more productively with the textbook in mastering this rich history. This pedagogical structure is designed to empower the students to analyze and interpret the historical evidence on their own, and thus to become participants in the work of history.

Undergraduates today have more choices in introductory history courses than they did only twenty or thirty years ago. As public awareness of the importance of global connections grew in the late twentieth century, many colleges and universities enriched their programs by adding courses in world history as well as introductory surveys in Latin American, African, and Asian history alongside the traditional offerings in the history of the United States and Europe. These developments can only be seen as enormously positive, but they do not in any way diminish the need for a broad-based history of European society and culture such as that represented in *Western Civilizations*. The wide chronological scope of this work offers an unusual opportunity to trace the development of central human themes—population movements, economic development, politics and state-building, changing religious beliefs, and the role of the arts and technology—in a dynamic and complex part of the world whose cultural diversity has been constantly invigorated and renewed by its interactions with peoples living in other places. As in previous editions, we have attempted to balance the coverage of political, social, economic, and cultural phenomena, and the chapters also include extensive coverage of material culture, daily life, gender, sexuality, art, and technology. And following the path laid out by the book's previous authors, Judith Coffin and Robert Stacey, we have insisted that the history of European peoples can be best understood through their interactions with people in other parts of the world. The portrait of European society that emerges from this text is thus both rich and dynamic, attentive to the latest developments in historical scholarship and fully aware of the ways that the teaching of European history has changed in the past decades.

Given the general consensus about the importance of seeing human history in its broadest—and if possible, global—context, Europeanists who teach the histories of ancient, medieval, and modern societies have been mindful of the need to rethink the ways that this history should be taught. For good reasons, few historians at the dawn of the twenty-first century uphold a monolithic vision of a single and enduring "Western civilization" whose inevitable march through history can be traced chapter by chapter through time. This idea, strongly associated with the curriculum of early twentieth-century American colleges and universities, no longer conforms to what we know about the human past. Neither the "West" nor "Europe" can be seen as distinct, unified entities in space or time; the meanings attributed to these geographical expressions have changed in significant ways. Most historians now agree that a linear notion of "civilization" persisting over the centuries was made coherent only by leaving out the intense conflicts, extraordinary ruptures, and dynamic processes of change at the heart of the societies that are the subject of this book. Smoothing out the rough edges of the past does students no favors—even an introductory text such as this one should present the past as it appears to the historians who study it—that is, as an ever-changing panorama of human effort and creation, filled with possibility, but also fraught with discord, uncertainty, accident, and tragedy.

## New Pedagogical Features

Our goals as the new authors of this dynamic text are to provide a book that students will read, that reinforces your course objectives, that helps your students master core content, and that provides tools for your students to use in thinking critically about our human past. In order to achieve these primary goals, the traditional strengths of the book have been augmented by several exciting new features. The most revolutionary is the new pedagogical framework that supports each chapter. Many students in introductory survey courses find the sheer quantity of information to be a challenge, and so we have created these new pedagogical features to help them approach their reading in a more systematic way. At the outset of every chapter, a ***Before You Read This Chapter*** box offers three preliminary windows onto the material to be covered: *Story Lines*, *Chronology*, and *Core Objectives*. The *Story Lines* allow the student to become familiar with the primary narrative threads that tie the chapter's elements together, and the *Chronology* grounds these *Story Lines* in the period under study. The *Core Objectives* provide a checklist to ensure that the student is aware of the primary teaching points in the chapter. The student is then reminded of these teaching points on completing the chapter, in the ***After You Read This Chapter*** section, which prompts the student to revisit the chapter in three ways. The first, *Reviewing the Core Objectives*, asks the reader to reconsider core objectives by answering a pointed question about each one. The second, *People, Ideas, and Events in Context*, summarizes some of the particulars that students should retain from their reading, through questions that allow them to relate individual terms to the major objectives and story lines. Finally, questions about long-term *Consequences* allow for more open-ended reflection on the significance of the chapter's material, drawing students' attention to issues that connect the chapter to previous chapters and giving them insight into what comes next. As a package, the pedagogical features at the beginning and end of each chapter work together to empower the student, by breaking down the process of reading and learning into manageable tasks.

A second package of pedagogical features is designed to help students think about history and its underlying issues more critically. For us as teachers, good pedagogy and critical thinking begin with good narrative writing. Each chapter starts with an opening vignette that showcases a particular person or event representative of the era as a whole. Within each chapter, an expanded program of illustrations and maps has been enhanced by the addition of **Guiding Questions** that challenge the reader to explore the historical contexts and significance of the maps and illustrations in a more critical way. The historical value of images, artifacts, and material culture is further emphasized in a new feature, ***Interpreting Visual Evidence***. We anticipate that this section will provide discussion leaders with a provocative departure point for conversations about the key issues raised by visual sources, which students often find more approachable than texts. Once this conversation has begun, students will further be able to develop the tools they need to read the primary texts. In this new edition, the selection of primary source texts, ***Analyzing Primary Sources***, has been carefully revised and many new questions have been added to frame the readings. The dynamism and diversity of Western civilizations is also illuminated through a look at ***Competing Viewpoints*** in each chapter, in which specific debates are presented through paired primary source texts. Finally, the bibliographical ***For Further Reading*** section has been edited and brought up-to-date and is now located at the end of the book.

### REVISED CHAPTER TOURS

There are significant changes to each chapter of the book, as well. In Chapter 1, the challenges of locating and interpreting historical evidence drawn from nontextual sources (archaeological, environmental, anthropological, mythic) is a special focus. Chapter 2 further underscores the degree to which recent archeological discoveries and new historical techniques have revolutionized our understanding of ancient history, and have also corroborated ancient peoples' own understandings of their past. Chapter 3 offers expanded coverage of the diverse polities that emerged in ancient Greece, and of Athens' closely related political, documentary, artistic, and intellectual achievements. Chapter 4's exploration of the Hellenistic world is more wide-ranging than before, and it includes an entirely new discussion of the scientific revolution powered by this first cosmopolitan civilization.

With Chapter 5, the unique values and institutions of the Roman Republic are the focus of a new segment, while the account of the Republic's expansion and transformation under the Principate has been sharpened and clarified. Chapter 6's treatment of early Christianity has been deepened and expanded, and more attention has been paid to the fundamental ways in which this fledgling religion itself changed as a result of its changing status within the Roman Empire. This chapter also draws on cutting-edge scholarship that has significantly revised our understanding of the so-called "Crisis of the Third Century" and the question of Rome's fragmentation and "fall."

Beginning with this chapter, the chronological structure of Volume 1 has been adjusted in order to make the periodization of the Middle Ages more conceptually manageable and the material easier to teach. Chapter 6 therefore ends with the reign of Theodoric in the West and the consolidation of Christian and pagan cultures in the fifth century. Chapter 7 now begins with the reign of Justinian; and while it still examines Rome's three distinctive successor civilizations, it no longer attempts to encapsulate all of Byzantine and Islamic history down to the fifteenth century. Instead, these interlocking histories and that of northwestern Europe are carried forward to about 950 C.E. in this chapter, and continue to intersect with one another in subsequent chapters. And whereas Chapters 8 and 9 used to cover the period 1000–1300 from two different angles (political, social, and economic *versus* religious and intellectual), the new structure interweaves these forces, with Chapter 8 covering the period 950–1100 and Chapter 9 extending from 1100 to 1300.

Chapters 10–12 all assess the transition from medieval to nearly modern. Chapter 10 looks at Europe in the years 1300 to 1500, the centuries of "Crisis, Unrest, and Opportunity." Chapter 11 explores the simultaneous expansion of Europe through "Commerce, Conquest, and Colonization" between 1300 and 1600. And Chapter 12 examines the "Renaissance Ideals and Realities" that stemmed from, and contributed to, these same events. All three chapters have been revised and expanded for this edition. Thereafter, Chapter 13 characterizes the sixteenth century as "The Age of Dissent and Division," while Chapter 14 surveys the religious, political, and military struggles that arose in the era of confessional difference, contested sovereignty, and military escalation between 1540 and 1660.

Chapters 15–17 cover the history of early modern Europe between the sixteenth and eighteenth centuries, a time that saw powerful absolutist regimes emerge on the continent; the establishment of wealthy European trading empires in Asia, Africa, and the Americas; and successive periods of intense intellectual and philosophical discussion during the Scientific Revolution and the Enlightenment. Chapter 15 has been reorganized to better relate the emergence of absolutist regimes on the continent with the alternatives to absolutism that developed in England, and to clarify the differences between the colonial empires of France, Britain, and Spain. Chapter 16 emphasizes the many facets of scientific inquiry during the Scientific Revolution and introduces a new section on women scientists. Meanwhile, Chapter 17 adds new emphasis to the ways that Enlightenment figures dealt with cultures and peoples in the parts of the world that Europeans confronted in building their empires.

Chapters 18–19 cover the political and economic revolutions of the late eighteenth and early nineteenth centuries. Chapter 18 covers the French Revolution and the Napoleonic empires in depth, while also drawing attention to the way that these central episodes were rooted in a larger pattern of revolutionary political change that engulfed the Atlantic world. Chapter 19 emphasizes both the economic growth and the technological innovations that were a part of the Industrial Revolution, while also exploring the social and cultural consequences of industrialization for men and women in Europe's new industrial societies. The ***Interpreting Visual Evidence*** box in Chapter 19 allows students to explore the ways that industrialization created new perceptions of the global economy in Europe, changing the way people thought of their place in the world.

Chapters 20–21 explore the successive struggles between conservative reaction and revolutionaries in Europe, as the revolutionary forces of nationalism unleashed by the French Revolution redrew the map of Europe and threatened the dynastic regimes that had ruled for centuries. In all of these chapters, new visual images have been added to focus students' attention on the many ways that "the people" were represented by liberals, conservatives, and revolutionaries, and the consequences of these contesting representations.

Chapter 22 takes on the history of nineteenth-century colonialism, exploring both its political and economic origins and its consequences for the peoples of Africa and Asia. The chapter gives new emphasis to the significance of colonial conquest for European culture, as colonial power became increasingly associated with national greatness, both in conservative monarchies and in more democratic regimes. Meanwhile, Chapter 23 brings the narrative back to the heart of Europe, covering the long-term consequences of industrialization and the consolidation of a conservative form of nationalism in many European nations even as the electorate was being expanded. The chapter emphasizes the varied nature of the new forms of political dissent, from the feminists who claimed the right to vote to the newly organized socialist movements that proved so enduring in many European countries.

Chapters 24 and 25 bring new vividness to the history of the First World War and the intense conflicts of the interwar period, while Chapter 26 uses the history of the Second World War as a hinge for understanding European and global developments in the second half of the twentieth century. The ***Interpreting Visual Evidence*** box in Chapter 24 allows for a special focus on the role of propaganda among the belligerent nations in 1914–1918, and the chapter's section on the diplomatic crisis that preceded the First World War has been streamlined to allow students to more easily comprehend the essential issues at the heart of the conflict. In Chapter 25 the ***Interpreting Visual Evidence*** box continues to explore the theme touched on in earlier chapters, political representations of "the people," this time in the context of fascist spectacles in Germany and Italy in the 1930s. These visual sources help students to understand the vulnerability of Europe's democratic regimes during these years as they faced the dual assault from fascists on the right and Bolsheviks on the left.

Chapters 27–29 bring the volumes to a close in a thorough exploration of the Cold War, decolonization, the collapse of the Soviet Union and the Eastern Bloc in 1989–1991, and the roots of the multifaceted global conflicts that beset the world in the first decade of the twenty-first century. Chapter 27 juxtaposes the Cold War with decolonization, showing how this combination sharply diminished the ability of European nations to control events in the international arena, even as they succeeded in rebuilding their economies at home. Chapter 28 explores the vibrancy of European culture in the crucial period of the 1960s to the early 1990s, bringing new attention to the significance of 1989 as a turning point in European history. Finally, a completely new set of primary documents and questions accompanies Chapter 29, which covers the benefits and tensions of a a newly globalized world. The chapter's conclusion now covers the financial crisis of 2008 and the subsequent election of Barack Obama, as well as recent debates within Islam about Muslims living as minorities in non-Muslim nations.

# A Few Words of Thanks

Our first year as members of *Western Civilizations*' authorial team has been a challenging and rewarding one. We are honored to be the partners of two historians whose work we have long admired, and who have been formative influences on us in our careers as students, scholars, and teachers of history. We would also like to thank a number of our colleagues around the country who provided in-depth critiques of large sections of the book: Paul Freedman (Yale University), Sheryl Kroen (University of Florida), Michael Kulikowski (Pennsylvania State University), Harry Liebersohn (University of Illinois, Urbana-Champaign), and Helmut Smith (Vanderbilt University). We are very grateful for the expert assistance and support of the Norton team, especially that of our editor, Jon Durbin. Kate Feighery, our fabulous project editor, has driven the book beautifully through the manuscript process. Jason Spears has skillfully dealt with a myriad of issues pertaining to the preparation of the text. Junenoire Mitchell and Donna Ranieri did an excellent job finding many of the exact images we specified. Lorraine Klimowich did an expert job developing the print ancillaries. Ben Reynolds has efficiently marched us through the production process. Steve Hoge has done a great job developing the book's fantastic emedia, particularly the new Author Insight Podcasts and Euro History Tours powered by Google Maps. Michael Fleming, Candace Levy, Robin Cook, and John Gould were terrific in skillfully guiding the manuscript through the copyediting and proofreading stages. Finally, we want to thank Tamara McNeill for spearheading the marketing campaign for the new edition. We are also indebted to the numerous expert readers who commented on various chapters and who thereby strengthened the book as a whole. We are thankful to our families, for their patience and advice, and to our students, whose questions and comments over the years have been essential to the framing of this book. And we extend a special thanks to, and hope to hear from, all the teachers and students we may never meet—their engagement with this book will frame new understandings of our shared past and its bearing on our future.

## NEW EDITION REVIEWERS

Donna Allen, Glendale Community College
Ken Bartlett, University of Toronto
Volker Benkert, Arizona State University
Dean Bennett, Schenectady City Community College
Patrick Brennan, Gulf Coast Community College
Neil Brooks, Community College of Baltimore County, Essex
James Brophy, University of Delaware
Kevin Caldwell, Blue Ridge Community College
Keith Chu, Bergen Community College
Alex D'erizans, Borough of Manhattan Community College, CUNY
Hilary Earl, Nipissing University
Kirk Ford, Mississippi College
Michael Gattis, Gulf Coast Community College
David M. Gallo, College of Mount Saint Vincent
Jamie Gruring, Arizona State University
Tim Hack, Salem Community College
Bernard Hagerty, University of Pittsburg
Paul T. Hietter, Mesa Community College
Paul Hughes, Sussex County Community College
Kyle Irvin, Jefferson State Community College
Llana Krug, York College of Pennsylvania
Guy Lalande, St. Francis Xavier University
Chris Laney, Berkshire Community College

Charles Levine, Mesa Community College
Michael Mckeown, Daytona State University
Dan Puckett, Troy State University
Dan Robinson, Troy State University
Craig Saucier, Southeastern Louisiana University
Aletia Seaborn, Southern Union State College
Victoria Thompson, Arizona State University
Donna Trembinski, St. Francis Xavier University
Pamela West, Jefferson State Community College
Julianna Wilson, Pima Community College

## PREVIOUS EDITION REVIEWERS

Eric Ash, Wayne State University
Sacha Auerbach, Virginia Commonwealth University
Ken Bartlett, University of Toronto
Benita Blessing, Ohio University
Chuck Boening, Shelton State Community College
John Bohstedt, University of Tennessee,Knoxville
Dan Brown, Moorpark College
Kevin Caldwell, Blue Ridge Community College
Jodi Campbell, Texas Christian University
Annette Chamberlain, Virginia Western Community College
Jason Coy, College of Charleston
Benjamin Ehlers, University of Georgia
Maryann Farkas, Dawson College
Gloria Fitzgibbon, Wake Forest University
Tina Gaddis, Onondaga Community College
Alex Garman, Eastern New Mexico State University
Norman Goda, Ohio University
Andrew Goldman, Gonzaga University
Robert Grasso, Monmouth University
Sylvia Gray, Portland Community College
Susan Grayzel, University of Mississippi
Timothy Hack, University of Delaware
Hazel Hahn, Seattle University
Derek Hastings, Oakland University
Dawn Hayes, Montclair State University
John Houston, Fordham University
Michael Hughes, Wake Forest University
Bruce Hunt, University of Texas, Austin
Ahmed Ibrahim, Southwest Missouri State University
Kevin James, University of Guelph
Lars Jones, Florida Institute of Technology
John Kearney, Cy Fair Community College
Roman Laba, Hudson Valley Community College
Elizabeth Lehfeldt, Cleveland State University
Thomas Maulucci, State University of New York, Fredonia
Amy McCandless, College of Charleston
John McGrath, Boston University
Nicholas Murray, Adirondack College
Charles Odahl, Boise State University
Bill Olejniczak, College of Charleston
Jeffrey Plaks, University of Central Oklahoma
Peter Pozesky, College of Wooster
Rebecca Schloss, Texas A&M University
James Shedel, Georgetown University
Rebecca Spang, Indiana University, Bloomington
Patrick Speelman, College of Charleston
Robert Taylor, Florida Institute of Technology
Paul Teverow, Missouri Southern State University
James Vanstone, John Abbott College
Kirk Willis, University of Georgia
Ian Worthington, University of Missouri, Columbia

# Western Civilizations

*Their History & Their Culture*

# Before You Read This Chapter

## STORY LINES

- Historians gather and interpret evidence from a diverse array of sources, many of them environmental, visual, and archeological.
- All civilizations emerge as the result of complex historical processes specific to a time and place, yet all share certain defining features.
- Prominent individuals can come to power through the use of force, but maintaining power requires legitimacy.
- Those wielding power in ancient Mesopotamia and Egypt responded in different ways to the challenge of establishing legitimacy.

## CHRONOLOGY

| | |
|---|---|
| 11,000 B.C.E. | Neolithic Revolution begins |
| 7500–5700 B.C.E. | Çatalhöyük flourishes |
| 6500–3000 B.C.E. | Jericho flourishes |
| 4300–2900 B.C.E. | The rise of Uruk in Sumer |
| c. 3200 B.C.E. | Development of writing |
| c. 3100 B.C.E. | King Narmer unites Upper and Lower Egypt |
| 2900–2500 B.C.E. | Early Dynastic Period in Sumer |
| c. 2700 B.C.E. | Reign of Gilgamesh |
| c. 2686–2160 B.C.E. | Old Kingdom of Egypt |
| c. 2650 B.C.E. | Imhotep engineers the Step Pyramid for King Djoser |
| c. 2350 B.C.E. | Sargon of Akkad consolidates power in Sumer |
| 2160–2055 B.C.E. | First Intermediate Period in Egypt |
| 2100–2000 B.C.E. | Ziggurat of Ur constructed |
| 2055–c. 1650 B.C.E. | Middle Kingdom of Egypt |
| c. 1792–1750 B.C.E. | Reign of Hammurabi |

## CORE OBJECTIVES

- **UNDERSTAND** the challenges involved in studying the distant past.
- **DEFINE** the key characteristics of civilization.
- **IDENTIFY** the factors that shaped the earliest cities.
- **EXPLAIN** how Hammurabi's empire was governed.
- **DESCRIBE** the main differences between Mesopotamian and Egyptian civilizations.

# Early Civilizations

There was a time, the story goes, when all the peoples of the earth shared a common language and could accomplish great things. They developed new technologies, made bricks, and aspired to build a fortified city with a tower reaching to the sky. But their god was troubled by this, so he destroyed their civilization by making it hard for them to understand one another's speech.

We know this as the legend of Babel. It's a story that probably circulated among peoples of the ancient world for thousands of years before it became part of the Hebrew book we call by its Greek name, Genesis, "the beginning." The story lets us glimpse some of the conditions in which the first civilizations arose, and it also reminds us of the ruptures that make studying them hard. We no longer speak the same languages as those ancient peoples, just as we no longer have direct access to their experiences or their beliefs.

Such foundational stories are usually called *myths*, but they are really an early form of history. For the people who told them, myths helped to make sense of the present by explaining the past. The fate of Babel conveyed a crucial message: human beings are powerful when they share a common goal, and what enables human interaction is civilization. To the peoples of the ancient world, the characteristic benefits of civilization—stability and safety, government, art, literature, science—were always products of city life. The very word "civilization" derives from the Latin word *civis*, "city." Cities, however, became possible only as a result of innovations that began around the end of the last Ice Age, about 13,000 years ago, and that came to fruition in Mesopotamia 8,000 years later. The history of civilization is therefore a short one. Within the study of humanity, which reaches back to the genus *Homo* in Africa, some 1.7 million years ago, it is merely a blip on the radar screen. Even within the history of *Homo sapiens sapiens*, the species to which we belong and which evolved about 40,000 years ago, civilization is a very recent development.

The study of early civilizations is both fascinating and challenging. Historians still do not understand why the first cities should have developed in the region between the Tigris and the Euphrates rivers, in what is now Iraq. Once developed, however, the basic patterns of urban life quickly spread to other parts of the Near East, both by imitation and by conquest. A network of trading connections linked these early cities, but intense competition for resources made alliances among them fragile. Then, around the middle of the second millennium B.C.E. (that is, "Before the Common Era," equivalent to the Christian dating system B.C., "Before Christ"), emerging powers began to shape these fiercely independent cities into empires. How this happened—and how we know that it happened—is the subject of Chapter 1.

## BEFORE CIVILIZATION

More than 9,000 years ago, a town began to develop at Çatalhöyük (*sha-tal-HOO-yuk*) in what is now south-central Turkey. Over the next 2,000 years, it grew to cover an area of thirty-three acres, within which some 8,000 inhabitants lived in more than 2,000 separate houses. If this seems small, consider that Çatalhöyük's population density was actually twice that of today's most populous city, Mumbai (India). It was so tightly packed that there were hardly any streets. Instead, each house was built immediately next to its neighbor, and generally on top of a previous house. People entered their houses by walking across their neighbors' rooftops and climbing down ladders into their own living spaces.

The people of Çatalhöyük developed a highly organized and advanced society. They wove wool cloth; they made kiln-fired pottery; they painted elaborate hunting scenes on the plaster-covered walls of their houses; they made weapons and tools from razor-sharp obsidian imported from the nearby Cappadocian mountains. They honored their ancestors with religious rites and buried their dead beneath the floors of their houses. Settled agriculturalists, they grew grains, peas, and lentils and tended herds of domesticated sheep and goats. But they also hunted and gathered fruits and nuts, like their nomadic ancestors, and their society was egalitarian, another feature common to nomadic societies; both men and women did the same kinds of work. But despite their relatively diverse food supply, their life spans were very short. Men died, on average, at the age of thirty-four. Women, who bore the additional risks of childbirth, died around age thirty.

The basic features of life in Çatalhöyük are common to all subsequent human civilizations. But how, when, and why did such settlements emerge? And how do we have access to information about this distant past? The era before the appearance of written records, which begin to proliferate around 3100 B.C.E., is of far greater duration than the subsequent eras we are able to document—and no less important. But it requires special ingenuity to identify, collect, and interpret the evidence of the distant past. In fact, historians have just begun to explore the ways that climatology, neuroscience, and evolutionary biology can further illuminate this period, augmenting the older findings of paleontology, archeology, and historical anthropology.

### *Societies of the Stone Age*

Primates with human characteristics originated in Africa 4 to 5 million years ago, and tool-making hominids—species belonging to the genus *Homo*, our distant ancestors—evolved approximately 2 million years ago. Because these early hominids made most of their tools out of stone, all human cultures flourishing before the fourth millennium B.C.E. (that is, the thousand years ending in 3000 B.C.E.) are designated as belonging to the Stone Age. This vast expanse of time is divided into the Paleolithic ("Old Stone") and the Neolithic ("New Stone") Eras, with the break between them falling around 11,000 B.C.E.

Long before modern humans made their appearance, recogizable human traits had already begun to leave traces on the landscape. Hominids in Africa were kindling and controlling fire as early as 164,000 years ago, using it to make tools. The Neanderthals, a hominid species that flourished about 200,000 years ago, made jewelry, painted on the walls of caves, and buried their dead in distinctive graves with meaningful objects such as horns (blown to

**CAVE PAINTINGS FROM LASCAUX.** These paintings, which date to between 10,000 and 15,000 B.C.E., show several of the different species of animals that were hunted by people of the Ice Age. The largest animal depicted here, a species of long-horned cattle known as the *auroch*, is now extinct.

make music) and, in one case, flowers. Could these hominids speak? Did they have a language? At present, there is no way that archeology can answer such questions.

However, archeology has shown that in the last phase of the Paleolithic Era, around 40,000 B.C.E., the pace of human development began to accelerate dramatically. Human populations in Africa expanded, suggesting that people were better nourished, perhaps as a result of new technologies. In Europe, *Homo sapiens sapiens* began to produce finely crafted and more effective tools such as fishhooks, arrowheads, and sewing needles made from wood, antler, and bone. The most astonishing evidence of this change was produced by these new tools: cave paintings like those at Lascaux (France), discovered in 1940. These amazing scenes were purposefully painted in recesses where acoustic resonance is greatest, and were probably intended to be experienced as part of multimedia musical ceremonies. (Flutes made from bone and ivory, dating to around 33,000 B.C.E., were found in a cave in southern Germany in 2008.) This is almost certain evidence for the development of language.

Despite these extraordinary changes, the basic patterns of human life altered very little. Virtually all human societies before 11,000 B.C.E. consisted of hunter-gatherers, bands of a few dozen people who moved incessantly in search of food. As a result of this constant movement, these groups have left no continuous archaeological record. Their lifestyle had social, economic, and political limitations which help to explain the structural differences—both positive and negative—between subsistence societies and those that can be called "civilizations." Early humans had no domestic animals to transport goods, so they could have no significant material possessions aside from basic tools. And because they could not accumulate goods over time, the distinctions of rank and status created by disparities in wealth could not develop. Hierarchical structures were therefore uncommon. When conflicts arose or resources became scarce, the solution was probably to divide and separate.

Although scholars once assumed that men did the hunting and women the gathering, such gendered presumptions do not reflect the complex realities of modern hunter-gatherer societies and they are probably not applicable to the Paleolithic Period, either. It is more likely that all members of a band (except for the very young and very old) engaged in the basic activity of acquiring food. Specialization would have been nearly impossible, since this requires the accumulation of storable surpluses.

## THE BUILDING BLOCKS OF CIVILIZATION

What changes allowed some hunter-gatherer societies to settle and build civilizations? The historical divide between the Paleolithic ("Old Stone") and Neolithic ("New Stone") Age, around 11,000 B.C.E., reflects very evident developments brought about by changes in the climate, which led to the development of managed food production, which in turn fostered settlements that could trade with one another, both locally and over long distances. For the first time, it became possible for individuals and communities to accumulate and store wealth on a large scale. The results were far-reaching. Communities became more stable, and human interactions more complex. Specialization developed, along with distinctions of status and rank. Both the rapidity and the radical implications of these changes have given this era its name: the Neolithic Revolution.

## The Neolithic Revolution

The artists who executed the cave paintings at Lascaux were conditioned to survive in harsh climatic conditions. Between 40,000 and 11,000 B.C.E., daytime temperatures in the Mediterranean basin averaged about 60° F (16° C) in the summer and about 30° F (–1° C) in the winter. These are very low compared to today's temperatures in the city of Marseilles, not far from Lascaux, which average about 86° F (30° C) in summer and 52° F (11° C) in winter. Cold-loving reindeer, elk, wild boars, bison, and mountain goats abounded in regions now famous for their beaches and vineyards. But as the glaciers receded northward with the warming climate, these species retreated with them, all the way to Scandinavia. Some humans moved north with the game, but others stayed behind to create a very different world.

Within a few thousand years after the end of the Ice Age, the peoples living in the eastern Mediterranean accomplished the most momentous transformation in human history: a switch from food-gathering for subsistence to food production. The warmer, wetter climate allowed wild grains to flourish, geometrically increasing the food supply and making settlements possible. People began to domesticate animals and cultivate plants. Stable settlements grew

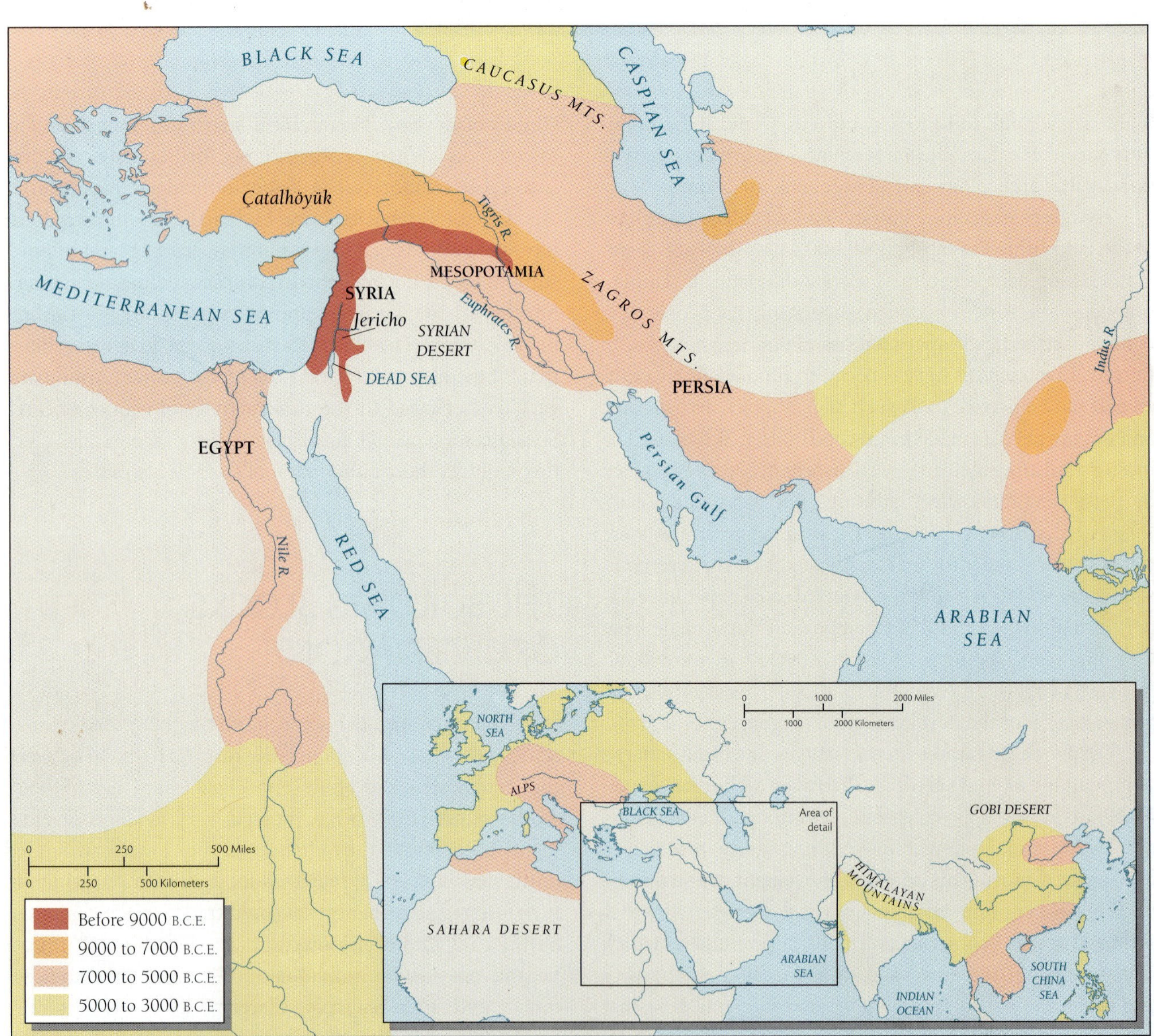


**THE GROWTH OF AGRICULTURE.** Examine the chronology of agriculture's development in this region. ▪ ***What areas began cultivating crops first, and why?*** ▪ ***In what period did agriculture spread the most rapidly, and why?*** ▪ ***How might rivers have played a crucial role in the spread of farming technologies?***

into cities. This process took several thousand years, but it still deserves to be called "revolutionary." In a relatively short time, people living in this area fundamentally altered patterns of existence that were millions of years old.

This revolution produced new challenges and inequalities. Well-nourished women in sedentary communities can bear more children than women in hunter-gatherer groups, and so the women of this new era became increasingly sequestered from their male counterparts, who in turn gave up an equal role in child care. The rapid increase in population was countered by the rapid spread of infectious diseases, while dependence on carbohydrates resulted in earlier deaths than were typical among hunter-gatherers.

But eventually, increased fertility and birthrates outweighed these limiting factors, and by about 8000 B.C.E. human populations were beginning to exceed the wild food supply. They therefore had to increase the food-growing capacity of the land and to devise ways of preserving and storing grain between harvests. Some peoples had learned how to preserve wild grain in storage pits as early as 11,500 B.C.E., and eventually they discovered that they could use this seed to produce even more grain the following year. The importance of this latter discovery cannot be overstated: once humans began deliberate cultivation, they could support larger populations and could also compensate for disasters (such as flooding) that might inhibit natural reseeding. Even more important, intensified seeding and storage provided humans with the stable and predictable surpluses needed to support domestic animals. This brought a host of additional benefits, not only guaranteeing a more reliable supply of meat, milk, leather, wool, bone, and horn, but also providing animal power to pull carts and plows and to power mills.

## *The Emergence of Towns and Villages*

The accelerating changes of the Neolithic Revolution are exemplified by towns like Çatalhöyük and by the simultaneous rise of trade and warfare—sure signs of increased specialization and competition. Hundreds, and probably thousands, of settlements grew up in the Near East between 7500 and 3500 B.C.E. Some of these can even be classified as cities: centers of administration and commerce with a large and diverse population, often protected by walls. Among the earliest of these was Jericho, in the territory lying between modern Israel and Jordan. Jericho emerged as a seasonal, grain-producing settlement, and by 6800 B.C.E. its inhabitants were undertaking a spectacular building program. Many new dwellings were built on stone foundations, and a massive dressed stone wall was constructed around the western edge of the settlement. It included a circular tower whose excavated remains still reach to a height of thirty feet, a powerful expression of its builders' wealth, technical prowess, and political ambitions.

This wall and its tower served an impressive population: Jericho covered at least eight acres and supported 3,000 people, so it was even more densely settled than Çatalhöyük. It was sustained by the intensive cultivation, made possible by irrigation, of recently domesticated strains of wheat and barley. Jericho's inhabitants also produced some of the earliest-known pottery, which allowed them to store grain, wine, and oils more effectively. Pottery's most important benefits, however, were in cooking. For the first time, it was possible to produce nourishing stews, porridges, and ales. (The capacity to produce beer is a sure sign of civilization.) Pottery production was not only vital to ancient civilizations, it is vital to those who study them. As the techniques for making pottery spread throughout the Near East and Asia, identifiable regional styles also developed. By studying the different varieties, archaeologists can construct a reasonably accurate chronology and can also trace the movements of goods and people.

Jericho and Çatalhöyük illustrate the impact that stored agricultural surpluses have on human relations. For the first time, significant differences began to arise in the amount of wealth individuals could stockpile for themselves and their heirs. Dependence on agriculture also made it more difficult

**EARLY POTTERY.** This shallow bowl from a village site in western Asia dates from about 5000 B.C.E. Distinctive design features make it possible to track the shipment of commodities throughout the ancient world.

for individuals to split off from the community when disputes and inequities arose. The result was the emergence of a much more stratified society, with more opportunities for a few powerful people to become dominant. The new reliance on agriculture also meant a new dependence on the land, the seasons, and the weather, which led to new speculations about the supernatural. Different life forces were believed to require special services and gifts, and the regular practice of ritual and sacrifice ultimately produced a priestly caste of individuals or families who seemed able to communicate with these forces. Such spiritual leadership was allied to more worldly forms of power, including the capacity to lead war bands, to exact tribute from other settlements, to construct defenses, and to resolve disputes. Through their command of the community's religious, military, economic, and political structures, certain clans could establish themselves as a ruling class.

Trade was another important element in the development of early settlements. Local trading networks were already established around 9000 B.C.E., and by 5000 long-distance routes linked settlements throughout the Near East. Exotic goods and luxury items were the most frequent objects of exchange, including marine shells and semiprecious stones like turquoise and lapis lazuli. Long-distance trade accelerated the exchange of ideas and information throughout the Fertile Crescent, and it further increased social stratification. Because status was enhanced by access to high-prestige goods, local elites sought to monopolize trade by organizing and controlling the production of commodities within their own communities and by regulating their export. For certain people could now devote at least a portion of their labor to pursuits other than agriculture: making pottery or cloth, manufacturing weapons or tools, building houses and fortifications, or facilitating trade. The elites who fostered and exploited the labor of others eventually became specialized themselves, as full-time speculators and organizers, with the leisure and resources to engage in intellectual, artistic, and political pursuits. The building blocks of civilization had been laid.

## URBAN DEVELOPMENT IN MESOPOTAMIA

The Greeks called it Mesopotamia, the "Land between Rivers." It was a land that received only about eight inches (20 cm) of rainfall per year. Its soils are sandy and summer temperatures exceed 110° F (44° C). The two rivers supplying water—the Tigris and Euphrates—are noted for their violence and unpredictability. Both are prone to flooding, and the Tigris was liable to jump its banks and change its course from year to year. It was in this challenging environment that the first urban society, the civilization of Sumer, flourished.

### *The Ubaid Culture*

The earliest cities of Mesopotamia were founded by the Ubaid peoples, so called because of their settlement at al-Ubaid (now in Iraq), which dates from around 5900 B.C.E. In this era, the headwaters of the Persian Gulf extended at least 100 miles further inland than they do today, so some Ubaid settlements bordered on fertile marshlands, which enabled them to develop irrigation systems. Although these began as relatively simple channels and collection pools, Ubaid farmers quickly learned to build more sophisticated canals and to line some pools with stone. They also constructed dikes and levees to control the seasonal flooding of the rivers and to direct the excess water into irrigation canals. Despite the hostility of the environment, Ubaid communities were soon producing surpluses sufficient to support specialists in construction, weaving, pottery making, metalwork, and trade: the typical attributes of Neolithic village life.

Yet there is also early evidence of something quite new: central structures that served religious, economic, and administrative functions, something not found in Çatalhöyük. Starting out as shrines, these structures soon became impressive temples built of dried mud brick, like the bricks described in the story of Babel—and unlike the plentiful stone used at Jericho; the scarcity of stone meant that builders in this region had to be more resourceful. Each large settlement had such a temple, from which a priestly class acted as managers of the community's stored wealth and of the complex irrigation systems that would make the civilization of Sumer possible.

### *Urbanism in Uruk, 4300–2900 B.C.E.*

After about 4300 B.C.E., Ubaid settlements developed into larger, more prosperous, and more highly organized communities. The most famous of these sites, Uruk, became the first Sumerian city-state. Its sophistication and scale is exemplified by the White Temple at Uruk, built between 3500 and 3300 B.C.E. Its massive sloping platform looms nearly forty feet above the surrounding flatlands, and its four corners are oriented toward the cardinal points of the compass. Atop the platform stands the temple proper, dressed in brick and originally painted a brilliant white.

**THE WHITE TEMPLE AT URUK, c. 3400 B.C.E.** This temple may have been dedicated to the sky god, An, or designed to provide all the region's gods with a mountaintop home in a part of the world known for its level plains.

Such temples were eventually constructed in every Sumerian city, reflecting the central role that worship played in civic life. Uruk in particular seems to have owed its rapid urban growth to its importance as a religious center. By 3100 B.C.E. it encompassed several hundred acres, enclosing a population of 40,000 people within its massive brick walls. The larger villages of Sumer were also growing rapidly, their teeming economic activity attracting immigrants just as the great cities did. Grain and cloth production grew tenfold. Trade routes expanded dramatically. And to manage this increasingly complex economy, the Sumerians invented the technology on which most historians rely: writing.

## *The Development of Writing*

In 4000 B.C.E., the peoples of the Near East were already using clay tokens to keep inventories. Within a few centuries, they developed a practice of placing tokens inside hollow clay balls and inscribing, on the outside of each ball, the shapes of all the tokens it contained. By 3300 B.C.E., priests (or their scribes) had replaced these balls with flat clay tablets on which they inscribed the symbols representing tokens. These tablets made keeping the tokens themselves unnecessary, and they could also be archived for future reference or sent to other settlements as receipts or requests for goods.

Writing thus evolved as a practical recording technology to support economic pursuits. Because it existed to represent real things, its system of symbols—called pictograms—was also realistic: each pictogram resembled the thing it represented. Over time, however, a pictogram might be used not only to symbolize a physical object but to evoke an idea associated with that object. For example, the symbol for a bowl of food, a *ninda*, might be used to express something more abstract, such as "nourishment" or "sustenance." Pictograms also came to be associated with particular spoken sounds, or *phonemes*. Thus when a Sumerian scribe needed to employ the sound *ninda*, even as part of another word or name, he would use the symbol for a bowl of food to represent that phoneme. Later, special marks were added to the symbol, so that a reader could tell whether the writer meant it to represent the object itself, or

**CUNEIFORM WRITING.** The image on the left shows a Sumerian clay tablet from about 3000 B.C.E. Here, standardized pictures are beginning to represent abstractions: notice the symbol *ninda* (food) near the top. On the right, carvings on limestone from about 2600 B.C.E. reveal the evolution of cuneiform. ▪ ***Why would such standardized pictograms have been easier to reproduce quickly?***

a larger concept, or a sound used in a context that might have nothing to do with food.

By 3100 B.C.E., Sumerian scribes also developed a specialized tool suited to the task of writing, a durable stylus made of reed. Because this stylus leaves an impression shaped like a wedge (in Latin, *cuneus*), this script is called *cuneiform* (*kyoo-NAY-i-form*). Cuneiform symbols could now be impressed more quickly into clay. And because the new stylus was not suited to drawing pictograms that accurately represented things, the symbols became even more abstract; eventually they barely resembled the original pictograms at all. Meanwhile, symbols were invented for every possible phonetic combination in the Sumerian language, reducing the number of necessary pictograms from about 1,200 to 600. But whereas the earliest pictograms could have been written and read by anyone, writing and reading now became specialized, abstract, powerful skills accessible only to a small and influential minority who were taught in special scribal schools called Houses of the Tablet.

Despite the complicated nature of the script, cuneiform proved remarkably durable. For over 2,000 years it remained the principal writing system of the ancient Near East, even in societies that did not speak the Sumerian language. Documents using the script were still being produced as late as the first century C.E. ("Common Era," equivalent to the traditional Christian practice of designating dates by A.D., for *Anno Domini*, "in the Year of the Lord"). By about 2500 B.C.E., Sumerians were using writing for a wide variety of economic, religious, political, and artistic purposes. Tens of thousands of clay tablets still survive and this makes it possible for us to know a great deal more about the Sumerians than we do about any other human society before this time. We can better understand the social structures that shaped their lives, their attitudes toward their gods, and their changing political circumstances.

## THE CULTURE OF SUMER

The great centers of Sumerian civilization—the cities of Uruk, Ur, Lagash, Eridu, and Kish—shared a common culture and a common language. They also shared a set of beliefs. However, this common religion did not produce peace. The residents of each city considered themselves to be the servants of a particular god, whom they sought to glorify by exalting their own city above others. The result was intense competition that frequently escalated into warfare. There was also an economic dimension to this conflict, since water rights and access to arable land and trade routes were often at stake.

Much of the economic production of a city passed through the great temple warehouses, where priests redistributed the city's produce. During the third millennium, these great temples also began to control the production of textiles, employing thousands of servile women and children. Temple elites also played a key role in long-distance trade, as both buyers and sellers of goods. So for any city-state to surrender its independence would not only offend the conquered city's god, it would jeopardize its entire economy and the power of its ruling class.

Each Sumerian city therefore had its own aristocracy, the group from which priests were drawn. As much as half

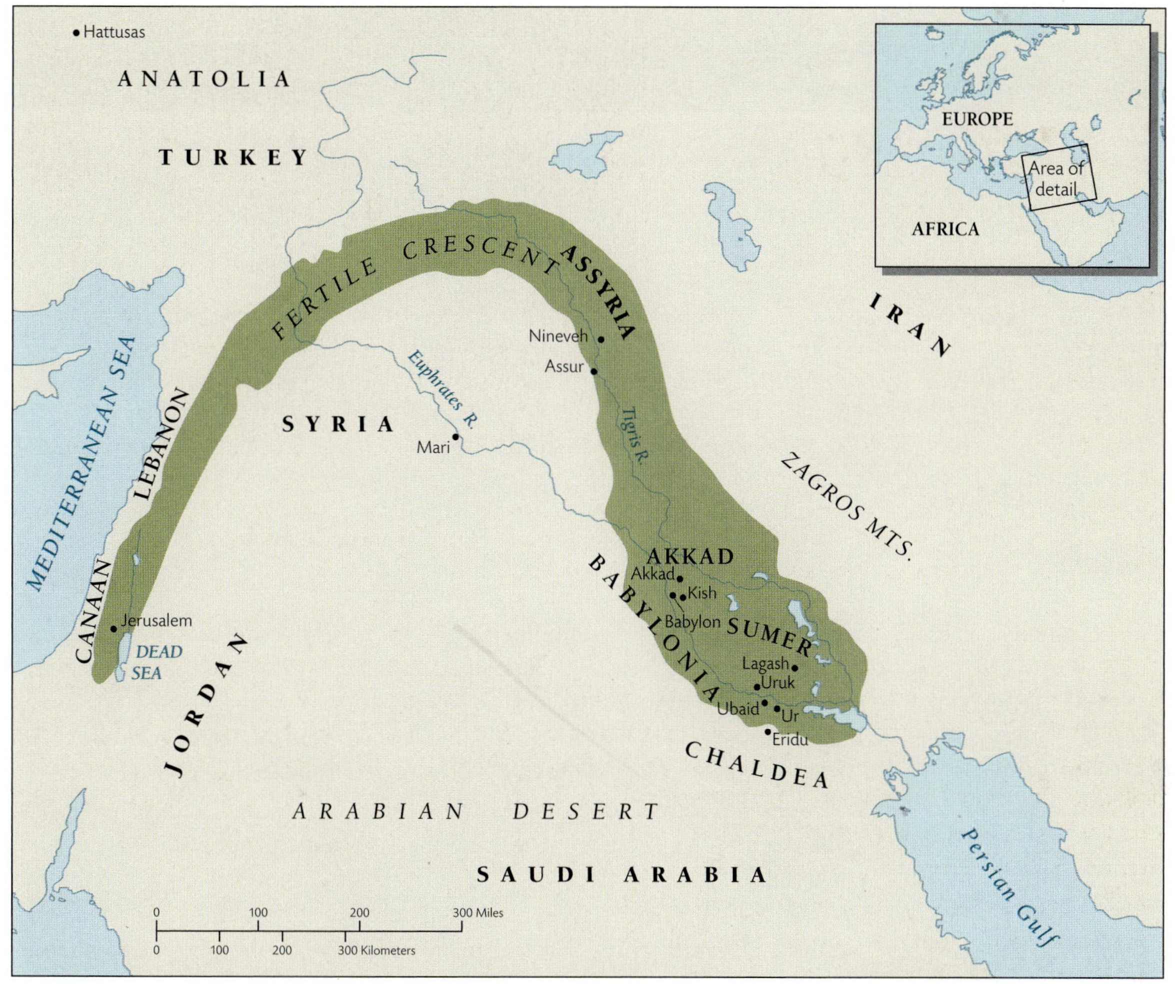


**THE FERTILE CRESCENT.** Notice the proximity of Sumerian cities to rivers; consider the vital role played by the Tigris and Euphrates in shaping the Mesopotamian civilizations. ▪ ***How many Sumerian city-states can you identify on the map?*** ▪ ***Why would Sumerian city-states have been clustered so closely together?*** ▪ ***What challenges and opportunities did this present?***

the population consisted of free persons who held parcels of land sufficient to sustain themselves, but the rest were dependents of the temple who worked as artisans or as agricultural laborers on its lands, and many of these dependents were slaves. Most of the slaves in Sumer were prisoners of war from other city-states whose bondage was limited to three years, after which time a slave had to be released. But non-Sumerians could be held indefinitely, although a few might manage to buy their freedom. In either case, slaves were the property of their owners. They could be beaten, branded, bought, and sold like any other form of merchandise. Perhaps the only positive thing to say about slavery in antiquity is that it was egalitarian: anyone could become a slave. It was not until the beginning of the modern era that slavery became linked to race (see Chapter 11).

## The Early Dynastic Period, 2900–2500 B.C.E.

Around 2900 B.C.E., conflicts among the growing Sumerian city-states became more acute. Competition for resources intensified and warfare became more frequent and destructive, leading to the eradication of many urban centers. During this period, a new type of military leadership began to emerge and eventually evolved into a form of kingship. Historians refer to this phase as the Early Dynastic Period because it was dominated by families, each headed by a war leader, whose prestige earned him the title *lugal:* "big man." Unlike the priestly rulers of the Uruk Period, lugals did not see themselves as humble servants of the city's god. Rather,

# Competing Viewpoints

## *The Flood: Two Accounts*

*One of the oldest stories in the world tells of a great flood that decimated the lands and peoples of the earth, an event that can be traced to the warming of the earth's climate at the end of the last Ice Age. Many ancient cultures told versions of this story, and two of these are excerpted below. The first, included in the* Epic of Gilgamesh, *was written down during the first half of the third millennium* B.C.E., *making it at least 1,500 years older than the similar account in the Hebrew Bible. But both are probably the products of much older storytelling traditions. The hero of the Sumerian story is Utnapishtim. The Hebrew story's hero is Noah.*

### *The Epic of Gilgamesh*

Utnapishtim spoke to Gilgamesh, saying: "I will reveal to you, Gilgamesh . . . a secret of the gods. . . . The hearts of the Great Gods moved them to inflict the Flood. Their Father Anu uttered the oath (of secrecy). . . . [But the god] Ea . . . repeated their talk [to me, saying]: 'O man of Shuruppak, son of Ubartutu: Tear down the house and build a boat! . . . Spurn possessions and keep alive living beings! Make all living beings go up into the boat. The boat which you are to build, its dimensions must measure equal to each other: its length must correspond to its width. Roof it over like the Apsu.' I understood and spoke to my lord, Ea: 'My lord, thus is the command which you have uttered. I will heed and will do it.' . . . On the fifth day I laid out her exterior. It was a field in area, its walls were each 10 times 12 cubits in height. . . . I provided it with six decks, thus dividing it into seven (levels). . . . Whatever I had I loaded on it. . . . All the living beings that I had I loaded on it. I had all my kith and kin go up into the boat, all the beasts and animals of the field and the draftsmen I had go up.

I watched the appearance of the weather—the weather was frightful to behold! I went into the boat and sealed the entry. . . . All day long the South Wind blew . . . , submerging the mountain in water, overwhelming the people like an attack. . . . Six days and seven nights came the wind and flood, the storm flattening the land. When the seventh day arrived . . . [t]he sea calmed, fell still, the whirlwind and flood stopped up. . . . When a seventh day arrived, I sent forth a dove and released it. The dove went off, but came back to me, no perch was visible so it circled back to me. I sent forth a swallow and released it. The swallow went off, but came back to me, no perch was visible so it circled back to me. I sent forth a raven and released it. The raven went off, and saw the waters slither back. It eats, it scratches, it bobs, but does not circle back to me. Then I sent out everything in all directions and sacrificed (a sheep). I offered incense in front of the mountain-ziggurat. . . .

The gods smelled the savor . . . and collected like flies over a sacrifice. . . . Just then Enlil arrived. He saw the boat and became furious. . . . 'Where did a living being escape? No man was to survive the annihilation!' Ea spoke to Valiant Enlil, saying . . . How, how could you bring about a Flood without consideration? Charge the violation to the viola-

they believed that success in battle had earned them the right to exploit the city's wealth for their own glory. This gave them a new and frightening degree of power.

The most striking expression of this development is the *Epic of Gilgamesh*, a series of stories recited over many generations and eventually written down on cuneiform tablets: the first literary monument in world history. It recounts the exploits of a lugal named Gilgamesh, who probably lived in Uruk sometime around 2700 B.C.E. Gilgamesh earns his legendary reputation through military conquest and personal heroism, particularly in campaigns against uncivilized—that is, nonurban—tribes. But he becomes so powerful that he ignores his own society's code of conduct: we hear at the start of the epic that his people complain about him because he keeps their sons away at war and shows no respect for the nobles, carousing with their wives

tor, charge the offense to the offender, but be compassionate lest (mankind) be cut off, be patient lest they be killed.' Enlil went up inside the boat and, grasping my hand, made me go up. He had my wife go up and kneel by my side. He touched our forehead and, standing between us, he blessed us. . . ."

Source: Maureen Gallery Kovacs, trans., *The Epic of Gilgamesh*, Tablet XI (Stanford, CA: 1985, 1989), pp. 97–103.

## *The Book of Genesis*

The Lord saw that the wickedness of humankind was great in the earth and . . . said "I will blot out from the earth the human beings I have created . . . for I am sorry I have made them." But Noah found favor in the sight of the Lord. . . . God saw that the earth was corrupt and . . . said to Noah, "I have determined to make an end to all flesh. . . . Make yourself an ark of cypress wood, make rooms in the ark, and cover it inside and out with pitch. . . . Make a roof for the ark, and put the door of the ark in its side. . . . For my part I am going to bring a flood on the earth, to destroy from under heaven all flesh. . . . But I will establish a covenant with you, and you shall come into the ark, you, your sons, your wife, and your sons' wives with you. And of every living thing you shall bring two of every kind into the ark, to keep them alive with you. . . . Also take with you every kind of food that is eaten." . . . All the fountains of the great deep burst forth, and the windows of the heavens were opened. . . . The waters gradually receded from the earth. . . . At the end of forty days, Noah opened a window of the ark . . . and sent out the raven, and it went to and fro until the waters were dried up from the earth. Then he sent out the dove from him, to see if the waters had subsided from the face of the ground, but the dove found no place to set its foot, and it returned. . . . He waited another seven days, and again sent out the dove [which] came back to him . . . and there in its beak was a freshly plucked olive leaf, so Noah knew the waters had subsided from the earth. Then he . . . sent out the dove, and it did not return to him anymore. . . . Noah built an altar to the Lord . . . and offered burnt offerings. And when the Lord smelled the pleasing odor, the Lord said in his heart, "I will never again curse the ground because of humankind . . . nor will I ever again destroy every living creature as I have done." . . . God blessed Noah and his sons.

Source: Genesis 6:5–9:1, *The New Oxford Annotated Bible* (Oxford: 1994).

### *Questions for Analysis*

1. What are the similarities and differences between these two accounts?
2. What do these differences or similarities reveal about the two societies that told these stories? Does one seem to derive from the other? Why or why not?
3. How did the geography and climate of Mesopotamia affect the Sumerian version of the story?

and compromising their daughters; he also disrespects the priesthood and commits acts of sacrilege. So the people of Uruk pray to the gods for retribution, and the gods fashion a wild man named Enkidu to challenge Gilgamesh.

The confrontation between Gilgamesh and Enkidu reveals the core values of Sumerian society. Gilgamesh is a creature of the city; Enkidu is a creature of the past, a hunter-gatherer. But then Enkidu has a sexual encounter with a beguiling woman and is unable to return to the wilderness: his urban initiation has civilized him and allowed him to befriend the lord of Uruk. Together they have many adventures. But Enkidu is eventually killed by the goddess Inanna, who punishes the friends for mocking her powers. Gilgamesh, distraught with grief, attempts to find a magical plant that will revive his friend. He finds it at the bottom of a deep pool, only to have it stolen from him by a water snake. In the end, he is forced to confront the futility of all human effort. He becomes "The One Who Looked into the Depths," the name by which his story was known to Sumerians. The larger message seems to be that not even civilization can shield humans from the forces of nature and the inevitability of death.

## Sumerian Religion

In the Uruk Period, the Sumerians identified their gods with the capricious forces of the natural world. In the Early Dynastic Period, however, they came to imagine their gods as resembling the powerful lugals who now ruled the city-states as kings. Like them, the gods desired to live in the finest palaces and temples, to wear the costliest clothing and jewels, and to consume the tastiest foods. According to this new theology, which clearly reflects changes in Sumerian society, humans exist merely to provide for their gods. This was, indeed, why the gods had created people in the first place; for if humanity ever ceased to serve the gods, the gods themselves would starve. There was thus a reciprocal relationship between humanity and divinity. The gods depended on their human servants to honor and sustain them; and in return, the gods occasionally bestowed gifts and favors.

As the gods' representatives on earth, kings bore special responsibilities and also enjoyed special privileges. Kings ruled by divine sanction and were thus set apart from all other men, including priests. But kings were also obliged to honor the gods through offerings, sacrifices, festivals, and massive building projects; their obligations were greater, just as their power was greater. Kings who neglected these duties, or who exalted themselves at the expense of the gods, were likely to bring disaster on themselves and their people. And even kings would could not evade death, when the human body returned to clay and the soul crossed into the underworld, a place of darkness and silence.

## Science, Technology, and Trade

The Sumerians' world-view was colored by their adversarial relationship with the environment. Precisely because neither their gods nor their environment were trustworthy, Sumerians cultivated a high degree of self-reliance and ingenuity. These qualities made them the most technologically innovative people of the ancient world.

For example, despite the fact that their land had no mineral deposits, the Sumerians became skilled metallurgists. By 6000 B.C.E., a number of cultures throughout the Near East and Europe had learned how to produce weapons and tools using copper. Mesopotamia itself has no copper, but by the Uruk Period (4300–2900 B.C.E.), trade routes were bringing this raw element into Sumer, where it was processed into weapons and tools. Shortly before 3000 B.C.E., perhaps starting in eastern Anatolia (now Turkey), people further discovered that copper could be alloyed with arsenic (or later, tin) to produce bronze. Bronze is almost as malleable as copper, and it pours more easily into molds; when cooled, it also maintains its rigidity and shape better than copper. For almost two thousand years, until about 1200 B.C.E. and the development of techniques for smelting iron, bronze was the strongest metal known to man—the most useful and, in war, the most deadly. Following the Greeks (see Chapter 3), we call this period the Bronze Age.

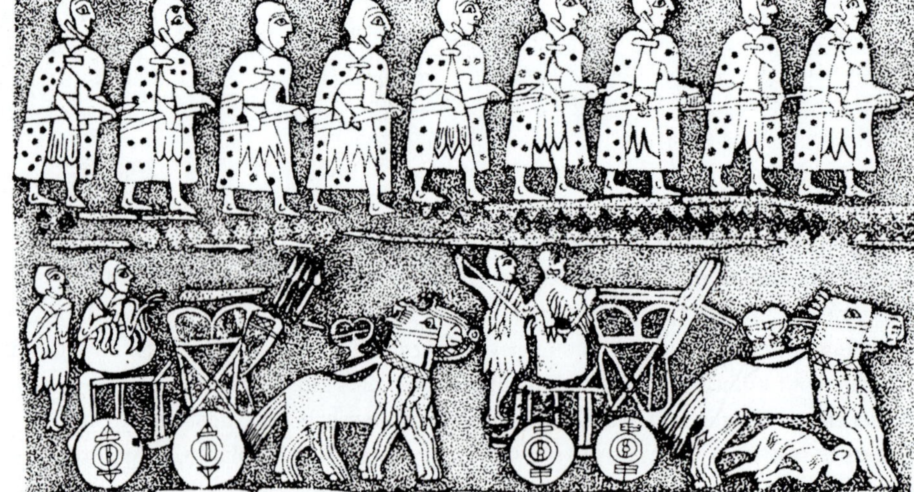

**SUMERIAN WAR CHARIOTS.** The earliest known representation of the wheel, dating from about 2600 B.C.E., shows how wheels were fashioned from slabs of wood. (For a later Mesopotamian wheel with spokes, see the illustration on page 40.)

Alongside writing and the making of bronze, the invention of the wheel was the fundamental technological achievement of the era. The Sumerians were using potter's wheels by the middle of the fourth millennium B.C.E. and could produce high-quality clay vessels in greater quantity than ever before. By around 3200 B.C.E., the Sumerians were also using two- and four-wheeled chariots and carts drawn by donkeys. (Horses were unknown in the Near East until sometime between 2000 and 1700 B.C.E.). Chariots were another new and deadly military technology, giving warriors a tremendous advantage over armies on foot: the earliest depiction of their use, dating from 2600 B.C.E., shows one trampling an enemy. At the same time, wheeled carts dramatically increased the productivity of the Sumerian workforce.

The use of the wheel in pottery making may have suggested its use for vehicles, but such a connection is not inevitable. The ancient Egyptians were using the potter's wheel by at least 2700 B.C.E., but they did not use the wheel for transport until a millennium later, when they learned the technique from Mesopotamia. In the Western Hemisphere, wheeled vehicles were unknown until the sixteenth century C.E., although the Incas had a sophisticated system of roads and probably used iron rollers to move huge blocks of stone for use in building projects. These two points of comparison help to explain why the wheel was probably invented by nomadic peoples living on the steppes of what is now Russia: civilizations that can rely on the manpower of thousands, or that can transport heavy cargo by water, do not feel the same necessity for invention.

The Sumerians can also be credited with innovations that made the most of their scarce resources. An example is the the seed drill, in use for two millennia before it was depicted on a stone tablet of the seventh century B.C.E. Strikingly, this was a technology unknown to any other Western civilization until the sixteenth century C.E., when Europeans adopted it from China, and it would not be in general use until the nineteenth century of our era. Other, more widespread inventions derived from the study of mathematics. In order to construct their elaborate irrigation systems, the Sumerians had to develop sophisticated measuring and surveying techniques as well as the art of map making. Agricultural needs may also lie behind the lunar calendar they invented, which consisted of twelve months, six lasting 30 days and six lasting 29 days. Since this produced a year of only 354 days, the Sumerians eventually began to add a month to their calendars every few years in order to predict the recurrence of the seasons with sufficient accuracy. The Sumerian practice of dividing time into multiples of sixty has lasted to the present day, not only in our notions of the 30-day month (which corresponds approximately with the phases of the moon) but also in our division of the hour into sixty minutes, each comprised of sixty seconds. Mathematics also contributed to Sumerian architecture, allowing them to build domes and arches thousands of years before the Romans would adopt and spread these architectural forms throughout the West.

Sumerian technology depended not only on ingenuity but also the spread of information and raw materials through trade. Because their homeland was almost completely devoid of natural resources, Sumerian pioneers traced routes up and down the rivers and into the hinterlands of Mesopotamia, following the tributaries of the Tigris and Euphrates. They blazed trails across the deserts toward the west, where they interacted with and influenced the Egyptians. By sea, they traded with the peoples of the Persian Gulf and, directly or indirectly, with the civilizations of the Indus Valley (modern Pakistan and India). And, along with merchandise, they carried ideas: stories, art, the use of writing, and the whole cultural complex that arose from their way of life. The elements of civilization, which

**A SUMERIAN PLOW WITH A SEED DRILL.** Seed drills control the distribution of seed and ensure that it falls directly into the furrow made by the plow. By contrast, the method of sowing seed practiced elsewhere in the world—and as late as the nineteenth century in Europe and the Americas—was to broadcast the seed by throwing it out in handfuls. Such plows were developed during the third millennium B.C.E. and were still being used in the seventh century B.C.E., when this black stone tablet was engraved.

- ***Based on what you have learned about the Sumerians and their environment, why would they have developed this technology?***

had fused in their urban crucible, would thus come together in many other places throughout the world of the Near East and Mediterranean.

## THE FIRST EMPIRES

Evidence shows that competition among Sumerian city-states reached a new level around 2500 B.C.E., as ambitious lugals vied to magnify themselves and their kingdoms. This aggrandizement of royal power was made possible by the growing complicity of the aristocracy and the priesthood, and also by the growing marginalization of commoners, whose lives and property were increasingly exploited. It was also facilitated by the new technologies discussed above.

The Royal Tombs of Ur showcase the wealth of the city's ruling families during this period. The dazzling armor and jewelry uncovered by excavations also reveal a shift in Sumerian ideas about the afterlife, since they presuppose a belief that one could enjoy such goods in perpetuity. The tombs further demonstrate how powerful the lugals had become. Still, it seems that no Sumerian lugal ever attempted to create an empire by imposing centralized rule on the cities he conquered. As a result, Sumer remained a collection of interdependent but mutually hostile states whose rulers were unable to forge any lasting structures of authority. This pattern would ultimately make the people of Sumer vulnerable to a new style of imperial rulership imposed on them from the north, in the person of Sargon the Akkadian.

### *Sargon and the Akkadian Empire, 2350–2160 B.C.E.*

The Akkadians were the predominant people of central Mesopotamia. Their Sumerian neighbors to the south had greatly influenced them, and they had adopted cuneiform script along with many other elements of Sumerian culture. Yet the Akkadians preserved their own Semitic language, part of the linguistic family that includes Hebrew, Arabic, Aramaic, Ethiopic, and Assyrian. Sumerians tended to regard them as uncivilized, but in the case of the lugal whom the Akkadians called "great king," this probably meant not being bound by the conventions of Sumerian warfare. For Sargon initiated a systematic program of conquest designed to subject all the neighboring regions to his authority. By 2350 B.C.E., he had conquered the cities of Sumer and then moved to establish direct control over all of Mesopotamia.

From his capital at Akkad, Sargon installed Akkadian-speaking governors to rule the cities of Sumer, ordering

**OBJECTS FROM THE ROYAL TOMBS AT UR.** On the left, a helmet made from an alloy of gold and silver. Its cloth lining would have been attached through the holes visible around the edges of the helmet. On the right, a queen's headdress made of gold leaf, lapis lazuli, and carnelian.

them to pull down existing fortifications, collect taxes, and impose his will. Sargon thus transformed the independent city-states of Sumer and Akkad into a much larger political unit: the first known empire, a word derived from the Latin *imperium*, "command." This enabled him to manage and exploit the network of trade routes crisscrossing the Near East. So although his political influence was felt only in Mesopotamia, his economic influence stretched from Ethiopia to India. Sargon's capital became the most splendid city in the world, and he exercised unprecedented power for a remarkable fifty-six years.

Sargon's imperialism also had an effect on Sumerian religion. To unite the two halves of his empire, Sargon merged the Akkadian and Sumerian divinities, so that (for example) the Akkadian fertility goddess Ishtar became the Sumerian goddess Inanna. He also tried to lessen the rivalry of Sumerian cities by appointing a single Akkadian high priest or priestess, often a member of his own family, to preside over several temples. His own daughter Enheduanna (*en-he-doo-Atl-nah*) was high priestess of both Uruk and Ur, and her hymns in honor of Ishtar/Inanna are the earliest surviving works by a named author in world history. The precedent she and her father established would continue even after their Sargonid dynasty finally fell; for several centuries thereafter, the kings of Sumer continued to appoint their daughters as high priestesses of Ur and Uruk.

Sargon's successor, his grandson Naram-Sin, extended Akkadian conquests and consolidated trade, helping to stimulate the growth of cities throughout the Near East and binding them more closely together. By 2200 B.C.E., most people in central and southern Mesopotamia would have been able to converse in the language of either the Sumerians or the Akkadians. Indeed, the two civilizations became virtually indistinguishable except for these different languages.

## *The Dynasty of Ur and the Amorites, 2100–1800 B.C.E.*

After Naram-Sin's death, Akkadian rule faltered. For a brief period, evidence shows that invaders from the Iranian plateau gained control of the region, which once again dissolved into a collection of rival city-states. Around 2100 B.C.E., however, a new dynasty came to power in Ur under its first king, Ur-Nammu, and his son Shulgi. Ur-Nammu was responsible for the construction of the great ziggurat at Ur, which originally rose seventy feet above the surrounding plain, and for many other architectural marvels. Shulgi continued his father's work, subduing the lands up to the Zagros Mountains northeast of Ur and demanding massive tribute payments from them; one collection site accounted for 350,000 sheep per year. Shulgi built state-run textile-production facilities to process the wool. He promulgated a code of law, calling for fair weights and measures, the

**THE ZIGGURAT OF UR.** Built around 2100 B.C.E., this great temple is the best-preserved structure of its kind. It is located at Nasiriyah, in what is now Iraq. Archeological investigations (see diagram) reveal that its central shrine, the most sacred part of the temple, was reached by climbing four sets of stairs and passing through a massive portal.

protection of widows and orphans, and limitations on the death penalty for crimes. He also pursued military conquests, the centralization of government, commercial expansion and consolidation, and the patronage of art and literature.

Shulgi established a pattern of rule that influenced the region for centuries to come, and that could even survive the much less competent rule of his grandson, Ibbi-Sin, who was eventually deposed by his own general. This man, Ishbi-Irra, was a chieftain of Amorite descent. The Amorites, like the Akkadians, were a Semitic people. Until this period they had largely been nomads and warriors, but now they came to control the ancient cities of Mesopotamia. For the next two hundred years, they used these cities as bases for the wars they fought among themselves.

## The Empire of Hammurabi

In 1792 B.C.E., a young Amorite chieftain named Hammurabi (*hah-muh-RAH-bee*) became the ruler of Babylon, an insignificant city in central Mesopotamia. By this time Babylon was precariously wedged among a number of powerful Amorite kingdoms. Its site on the Tigris and Euphrates had great potential, but it was also dangerous, because it lay in the path of mighty antagonists.

Hammurabi may have been the first ruler in history to understand that power need not be based on force. He recognized that military intelligence, diplomacy, and strategic planning might accomplish what his small army could not. A rich archive of tablets found at the city of Mari (which eventually fell under his rule) testifies to his talents and cleverness, for Hammurabi used writing itself as a weapon. He did not try to confront his mightier neighbors directly. Rather, through letters and embassies, double-dealing and cunning, he induced his stronger counterparts to fight each other. While other Amorite kings exhausted their resources in costly wars, Hammurabi fanned their mutual hatred and skillfully portrayed himself as a friend and ally to all sides. Meanwhile, he quietly strengthened his kingdom, built up his army, and, when the time was right, fell on his depleted neighbors. By such policies, he transformed his small state into what historians call the Old Babylonian Empire.

Under Hammurabi's rule, Mesopotamia achieved an unprecedented degree of political integration. Ultimately, his empire stretched from the Persian Gulf into Assyria. The southern half of the region, formerly Sumer and Akkad, would henceforth be known as Babylonia. To help unify these territories, Hammurabi introduced another innovation, promoting the worship of the little-known patron god of Babylon, Marduk, and making him the ruler-god of his entire empire. Although he also paid homage to the ancient gods of Sumer and Akkad, Hammurabi made it clear that all his subjects now owed allegiance to Marduk.

The idea that political power derives from divine approval was nothing new, but Hammurabi's genius was to use Marduk's supremacy over all other gods to legitimate his own claim to rule, in Marduk's name, because he was king of Marduk's home city. Hammurabi thus became the first known ruler to launch wars of aggression justified in the name of his primary god. This set a precedent for colonial expansion that would become a characteristic feature of Near Eastern politics, as we will see in Chapter 2, and that lies behind nearly all imperial ventures down to the present day.

Yet Hammurabi did not rely solely on religion to bind his empire together. Building on the precedents of past rulers, he also issued a collection of laws, copies of which were inscribed on stone and set up in public places throughout his realm. The example that survives is an eight-foot-tall *stele* (*STEH-luh*) made of gleaming black basalt, erected in the central marketplace of Babylon. The upper portion shows Hammurabi consulting with Marduk. The phallic form on which the laws were inscribed would have been immediately recognizable as a potent symbol of Hammurabi's authority, obvious even to those who could not read the laws themselves. (It still makes a strong impression on visitors to the Louvre museum in Paris.)

It is impossible to overemphasize the importance of Hammurabi's decision to become a lawgiver. By collecting and codifying legal precedents, like those of Shulgi, Hammurabi declared himself to be (as he stated in the code's preamble) "the shepherd of the people, the capable king"—not a lugal ruling through fear and caprice. This was setting a new standard of kingship, and expressing a new vision of empire as a union of peoples subject to the same laws.

## Law and Society Under Hammurabi

The code of Hammurabi reveals a great deal about the structure and values of Babylonian society. The organization of its 282 pronouncements offers insight into the kinds of litigation that Hammurabi and his officials regularly handled, and the relative importance of these cases. It begins with legislation against false testimony (fraud or lying under oath) and theft; followed by laws regulating business deals; laws regulating the use of public resources, especially water; laws relating to taverns and brothels, most of which appear to have been run by women; laws relating to debt and slavery; many laws dealing with marriage, inheritance, divorce, and widows' rights; and finally laws

**WOMEN AND TEXTILES.** Women were the principal producers of textiles throughout the ancient world. Even upper-class women were almost continuously engaged in spinning thread and weaving cloth for their household. Here a servant fans this elegant lady at work with her spindle.

punishing murder, violent assault, and even medical malpractice. What emerges is a fascinating picture of a complex urban society that required more formal legislation than the accumulated customs of previous generations.

Most of these laws appear to be aimed at free commoners, who made up the bulk of the population. Above them was an aristocratic class, tied to the king's court and active in its bureaucracy, who controlled a great deal of the community's wealth: palace officials, temple priests, high-ranking military officers, and rich merchants. Indeed, even legally free individuals were probably dependents of the palace or the temple in some way, or leased land from the estates of the powerful. They included laborers and artisans, small-scale merchants and farmers, and the minor political and religious officials. At the bottom of Babylonian society were the slaves, and these were far more numerous than they had been in the older civilizations of Sumer or Akkad. Many, indeed, had become slaves not because of war but through trade: either sold as payment for debts or to the profit of a family with too many children, or because they had been forced to sell themselves on the open market. Others had been enslaved in punishment for certain offenses. Slaves in the Old Babylonian Empire were also treated much more harshly, and were more readily identifiable as a separate group: whereas free men in Babylonia wore long hair and beards, male slaves were shaved and branded.

The division among classes in this society was marked. As Hammurabi's code indicates, an offense committed against a nobleman carried a far more severe penalty than did the same crime committed against a social equal, or against a dependent or slave; nobles were also punished more severely than were commoners for crimes they committed against other nobles. Marriage arrangements also reflected class differences, with bride-prices and dowries depending on the status of the parties involved. That said, Hammurabi's code also provides evidence as to the status of women in Babylonian society, and shows that they enjoyed certain important protections under the law, including the right to divorce abusive or indigent husbands. If a husband divorced a wife "without cause," he was obliged to provide financial support for her and their children. However, a wife who went around the city defaming her spouse was subject to severe punishment, and she would risk death, along with her lover, if she were caught in adultery. The sexual promiscuity of husbands, by contrast, was protected under the law.

## Hammurabi's Legacy

Hammurabi died around 1750 B.C.E. Although some contraction of the Babylonian Empire followed under his successors, his administrative efforts created a durable state in Mesopotamia. For another two centuries the Old Babylonian Empire played a significant role in the Near East, until invaders from the north sacked the capital and occupied it. But even for another thousand years thereafter, Babylon remained the region's most famous city.

# Analyzing Primary Sources

## *The Code of Hammurabi*

*The laws of Hammurabi, published on the authority of this powerful king and set up in central places throughout Old Babylonian Empire, were influenced both by the needs of an urban society and by older ideas of justice and punishment common among Semitic peoples. In its entirety, the code comprises 282 laws, beginning and ending with statements of Hammurabi's devotion to the gods, his peace-keeping mission, and his sense of his duties as king. The following excerpts are numbered so as to show the order in which these provisions appear on the stele that publicizes them.*

When the god Marduk commanded me to provide just ways for the people of the land in order to attain appropriate behavior, I established truth and justice as the declaration of the land. I enhanced the well-being of the people.

* * *

**1.** If a man accuses another man and charges him with homicide but cannot bring proof against him, his accuser shall be killed.

**2.** If a man charges another man with practicing witchcraft but cannot bring proof against him, he who is charged with witchcraft shall go to the divine River Ordeal, he shall indeed submit to the divine River Ordeal; if the divine River Ordeal should overwhelm him, his accuser shall take full legal possession of his estate; if the divine River Ordeal should clear that man and should he survive, he who made the charge of witchcraft against him shall be killed; he who submitted to the divine River Ordeal shall take full legal possession of his accuser's estate.

If a man comes forward to give false testimony in a case but cannot bring evidence for his accusation, if that case involves a capital offense, that man shall be killed.

* * *

**6.** If a man steals valuables belonging to the god or to the palace, that man shall be killed, and also he who received the stolen goods from him shall be killed.

**7.** If a man should purchase silver, gold, a slave a slave woman, an ox, a sheep, a donkey, or anything else whatsoever, from a son of a man or from a slave of a man without witnesses or a contract—or if he accepts the goods for safe-keeping—that man is a thief, he shall be killed.

**8.** If a man steals an ox, a sheep, a donkey, a pig, or a boat—if it belongs either to the god or to the palace, he shall give thirtyfold; if it belongs to a commoner, he shall replace it tenfold; if the thief does not have anything to give, he shall be killed.

* * *

**15.** If a man should enable a palace slave, a palace slave woman, a commoner's slave, or a commoner's slave woman to leave through the main city-gate, he shall be killed.

* * *

**53.** If a man neglects to reinforce the embankment of the irrigation canal of his field and then a breach opens and allows the water to carry away the common irrigated area, the man in whose embankment the breach opened shall replace the grain whose loss he caused.

* * *

**104.** If a merchant gives a trading agent grain, wool, oil, or any other commodity for local transactions, the trading agent shall collect a sealed receipt for each payment in silver that he gives to the merchant.

* * *

**128.** If a man marries a wife but does not draw up a formal contract for her, she is not a wife.

**129.** If a man's wife should be seized lying with another male, they shall bind them and throw them into the water; if the wife's master allows his wife to live, then the king shall allow his subject (i.e., the other male) to live.

* * *

**142.** If a woman repudiates her husband, and declares, "You will not have marital relations with me"—her circumstances shall be investigated by the authorities of her city quarter, and if she is circumspect and without fault, but her husband is wayward and disparages her greatly, that woman will not be subject to any penalty; she shall take her dowry and she shall depart for her father's house.

Source: Martha T. Roth, ed., *Law Collections from Ancient Mesopotamia and Asia Minor* (Atlanta, GA: 1995), pp. 76–135 (excerpted).

**The Code of Hammurabi.** The laws of Hammurabi survive on an eight-foot column made of basalt. The top quarter of the column depicts the Babylonian king (standing, at left) being vested with authority by Shamash, the god of justice. Directly below one can make out the cuneiform inscriptions that are the law code's text. How would the very format of these laws send a powerful message about Hammurabi's kingship?

## *Questions for Analysis*

1. Based on these excerpts, what conclusions can you draw about the values of Old Babylonian society? For example, what types of crimes are punishable by death, and why?

2. In what ways does the code of Hammurabi exhibit the influences of the urban civilization for which these laws were issued? What are some characteristics and consequences of urbanization? What, for example, do we learn about economic developments?

3. Examine the photographs of the *stele* preserving the code. What is the significance of the image that accompanies the laws, Hammurabi's conference with the enthroned god Marduk? What is the si gnificance of the *stele* itself as the medium that conveyed these laws to the people?

Hammurabi's legacy also extended well beyond the borders of his own kingdom. His success in achieving political stability was instrumental in shaping conceptions of kingship in the ancient Near East. After Hammurabi, unifying state religions would play an increasingly important role in the techniques that Near Eastern kings used to annex and subjugate diverse territories and peoples. Hammurabi had also demonstrated the effectiveness of writing as a political tool. Diplomacy and the keeping of archives would be essential to all subsequent empires. So too would the claim that rulers should be the protectors of the weak and the arbiters of justice.

## THE DEVELOPMENT OF CIVILIZATION IN EGYPT

At about the same time that Sumerian civilization was transforming Mesopotamia, another civilization was taking shape in a very different part of the world and in very different ways. Unlike the Sumerians, the Egyptians did not have to wrest survival from a hostile and unpredictable environment. Instead, their land was renewed every year by the flooding of the Nile River. The fertile black soil left behind every summer made theirs the richest agricultural region in the entire Mediterranean world.

The distinctiveness of Egyptian civilization rests on this fundamental ecological fact. It also explains why ancient Egypt was a narrow, elongated kingdom, running along the Nile north from the First Cataract (a series of rocks and rapids near the ancient city of Elephantine) toward the Mediteranean Sea for a distance of more than 600 miles (1,100 km). Outside this narrow band of territory—which ranged from a few hundred yards to no more than 14 miles (23 km)—lay uninhabitable desert. This contrast, between the fertile Black Land along the Nile and the dessicated Red Land beyond, deeply influenced the Egyptian worldview, in which the Nile itself was the center of the cosmos and the lands beyond were hostile and beyond the pale of habitation.

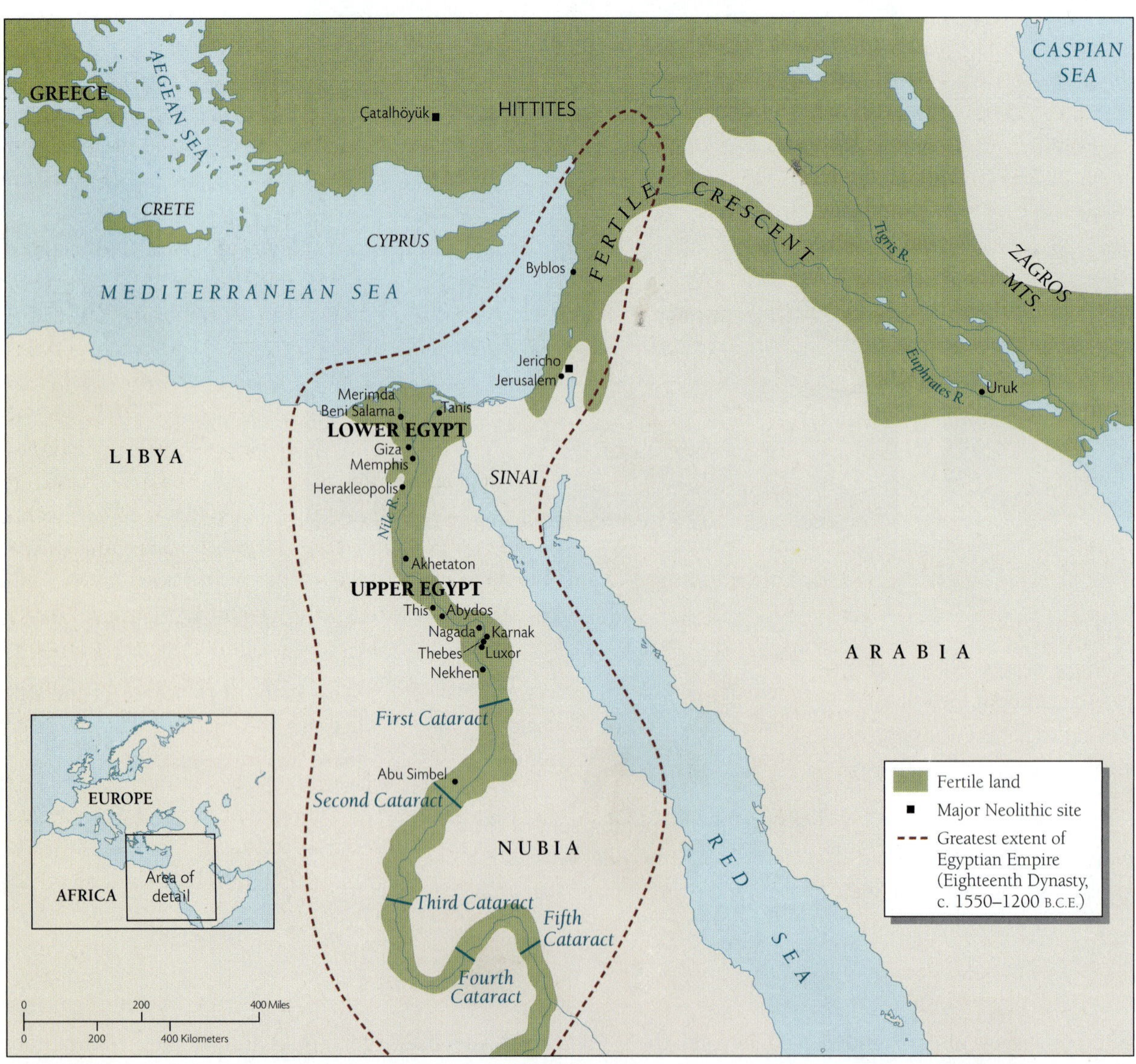


**ANCIENT EGYPT AND THE NEAR EAST.** Notice the peculiar geography of ancient Egypt and the role played by the Nile River. Identify the Nile on the map. ▪ ***In what direction does the Nile flow?*** ▪ ***How did the lands on either side help to isolate Egyptian culture from outside influences?*** ▪ ***Consider how the Nile helped forge Egypt into a unitary state under a powerful centralized government. Yet how might Egypt's relationship to the Nile be potentially hazardous, as well as beneficial?***

Ancient Egyptian civilization enjoyed a remarkable continuity. Its roots date back to 5000 B.C.E. at least, and Egypt would continue to thrive as an independent and distinctive entity even after it was conquered by Alexander the Great in 331 B.C.E. (see Chapter 4), until its assimilation into the Roman Empire after 30 B.C.E. (Chapter 5). From about 3000 B.C.E. the defining element of this civilization would be the pervasive influence of a powerful, centralized, bureaucratic state headed by pharaohs who were regarded as living gods. No other civilization in world history has ever been governed so steadily, for so long, as ancient Egypt.

For convenience, historians have traditionally divided ancient Egyptian history into distinctive "kingdoms" and "periods." Following ancient Egyptian chroniclers, modern historians have also tended to portray these Old, Middle, and New Kingdoms as characterized by unity and prosperity, punctuated by chaotic interludes when central authority broke down: the so-called Intermediate Periods. Like all attempts at periodization, these divisions do not capture the complexities of human experience or even the real pace of historical development. In this case, the periodization still used by historians reflects the conservative perspective of the ancient Egyptian state, which prized continuity and feared change. As we will see, though, the "First Intermediate Period" in particular looks like a positive development if viewed from the perspective of individual communities and commoners, rather than from the viewpoint of the pharaoh's court.

## *Predynastic Egypt, c. 10,000–3100 B.C.E.*

The phrase "Predynastic Egypt" refers to the period before the emergence of the pharaohs and their royal dynasties—an era for which archeological evidence is difficult to find and interpret. Many predynastic settlements were destroyed long ago by the waters of the Nile and are now buried under innumerable layers of silt. Furthermore, the very abundance of naturally occurring foodstuffs in the Nile Valley made the need for settlement and cultivation less pressing than in the Fertile Crescent, where (as we have seen) Mesopotamian peoples were already living together in villages during the eighth millennium B.C.E. In Egypt, by contrast, a growing population was able to sustain itself by hunting and gathering until the fifth millennium B.C.E.

The first-known permanent settlement in Egypt, situated at the southwestern edge of the Nile Delta near the modern town of Merimde Beni Salama, dates to approximately 4750 B.C.E. It was a farming community that may have numbered as many as 16,000 residents, and this number (based on burial remains and open to contention) suggests that some Egyptian communities were much larger than those of a comparable period in Mesopotamia. Thereafter, evidence shows that the Egyptian economy rapidly became more diversified: by around 3500 B.C.E. the residents of Ma'adi, just three miles away from Merimde Beni Salama, had extensive commercial contacts with the Sinai Peninsula, the Near East, and the upper reaches of the Nile, some several hundred miles to the south. Copper was a particularly vital import, since it enabled residents to replace stone tools with metal ones.

Many other Neolithic farming centers have also been discovered in or near the Nile Delta, where a degree of cultural cohesiveness was already developing, fostered by shared interests and trade. In later centuries, this northern area would be known as Lower Egypt, so called because it was downstream. Comparable developments were also occurring upstream. By the end of this Predynastic Period, Egyptian culture was more or less uniform from the southern edge of the delta to the First Cataract, a vast length of the Nile known as Upper Egypt.

Although towns in Lower Egypt were more numerous, it was in Upper Egypt that the first Egyptian cities developed. By 3200 B.C.E. (when the Sumerian city of Uruk had been thriving for a thousand years), important communities such as Nekhen, Naqada, This, and Abydos had all developed high degrees of occupational and social specialization. They had encircled themselves with sophisticated fortifications and had begun to build elaborate shrines to honor their gods. Indeed, the establishment of permanent sites of public worship may be key to explaining the growth of these towns into cities. As in Mesopotamia, a city's role as the center of a prominent religious cult attracted travelers and encouraged the growth of industries. Yet travel in Upper Egypt was relatively easy compared to Mesopotamia. The Nile bound cities together, and almost all Egyptians lived within sight of it.

It was due to the Nile, therefore, that the region south of the delta was able to forge a cultural and eventually a political unity, despite its enormous length. The Nile fed Egypt and was a conduit for people, goods, and ideas. Centralizing rulers could project their power quickly and effectively up and down its course. Within a remarkably short time, just a century or two after the first cities' appearance in Upper Egypt, they had banded together in a confederacy under the leadership of This. The pressure exerted by this confederacy in turn forced the towns of Lower Egypt to adopt their own form of political organization. By 3100 B.C.E., the rivalry between these competing regions had given rise to the two nascent kingdoms of Upper and Lower Egypt.

## *The Power of the* Pharaoh, *c.* 3100–*c.* 2686 B.C.E.

With the rise of powerful rulers in these two kingdoms, Egyptian history enters a new phase, one that can be chronicled with unusual precision. The system for numbering the ruling dynasties that emerged in this era—known as the Archaic Period—was actually devised nearly three thousand years later by an historian named Manetho (*mahn-EH-thoh*), who wrote in the third century B.C.E. By and large, Manetho's work has withstood the scrutiny of modern historians and archaeologists, although recent research has added a "Zero Dynasty" of early kings who were instrumental in bringing about the initial unification of Egypt.

Manetho did not record these rulers because he didn't know about them; we know them almost exclusively from archaeological evidence. Among them was an Upper Egyptian warlord known to us as King Scorpion, because the image of a scorpion accompanies engravings that assert his authority over most of Egypt. Another warlord, King Narmer, appears to have ruled both Upper and Lower Egypt. His exploits, too, come down to us in powerful pictures (see ***Interpreting Visual Evidence*** on page 25). Both of these kings probably came from Abydos in Upper Egypt, where they were buried. Their administrative capital, however, was at Memphis, the capital city of Lower Egypt and an important center for trade with the Sinai Peninsula and the Near East.

Following the political unification of Upper and Lower Egypt, the basic features of Egypt's distinctive centralized kingship took shape along lines that would persist for the next 3,000 years, down to Manetho's own day. The title used to describe this kingship was *pharaoh*, a word that actually means "great household" and thus refers not only to an individual king but to the whole apparatus that sustains his rule. This fact, in turn, helps to explain the extraordinary stability and longevity of Egyptian civilization, which could survive even a dynastic takeover by Macedonian Greeks in the century before Manetho wrote his chronicle. Indeed, it is comparable to some modern forms of government—none of which has yet lasted so long. As we have seen, kingship in Mesopotamia tended to be a form of personal rule, dependent on the charisma of a particular individual; the empires of Sargon and Ur-Nammu scarcely survived another generation or two after their deaths. But in Egypt, the office of the pharaoh was durable enough to survive the deaths of many individual successors, facilitating the peaceful transition of power to new rulers and withstanding the incompetence of many.

This was accomplished, as we shall see, by the efficiency of palace bureaucracy, but it was also a function of the pharaoh's close identification with the divine forces credited with renewing Egypt every year. Like the seasons, the pharaoh died only to be born again, renewed and empowered. Egyptian rulers thus laid claim to a sacred nature quite different—and much more benign—than that governing Sumeria. And they were more powerful than any Sumerian lugal, who was never more than a mortal who enjoyed (an all too temporary) divine favor.

How the earliest kings of Egypt came to be distinguished as pharaohs and to establish their claims to divinity is still not well understood. We do know, however, that legitimating their rule over all Egypt was difficult. Local civic and religious loyalties remained strong, and for centuries Lower Egyptians would continue to see themselves as distinct in some respects from their neighbors to the south. Efforts to create a unified Egyptian identity began very early, however, as the Narmer Palette may indicate. Indeed, it seems probable that the centralization of government in the person of the pharaoh and his association with divinity were related approaches to solving the problem of political unity. And together they had astonishing success. By the end of the Second Dynasty, which coincides with the end of the Archaic or Early Dynastic Period (2686 B.C.E.), the pharaoh was not just the ruler of Egypt, he *was* Egypt: a personification of the land, the people, and their gods.

## *Language and Writing*

Among the many facets of Egyptian culture that have fascinated generations of scholars is the Egyptian system of pictographic writing. Called *hieroglyphs (HI-eroh-glifs)* or "sacred carvings" by the Greeks, these strange and elaborate symbols remained completely impenetrable and thus all the more mysterious until the nineteenth century, when a French scholar named Jean François Champollion deciphered them with the help of history's most famous decoding device, the Rosetta Stone. This *stele* preserves three versions of the same decree issued by one of the Ptolemaic rulers of Egypt in 196 B.C.E., written in ancient Greek, demotic (a later Egyptian script), and hieroglyphics—still in use after more than 3,000 years. Because he could read the text in Greek, Champollion was eventually able to translate the demotic and hieroglyphic texts as well. From this beginning, generations of scholars have added to and refined the knowledge of ancient Egyptian language.

The development of hieroglyphic writing in Egypt dates to around 3200 B.C.E., when pictograms begin to appear in Mesopotamia. But the two scripts are so different that they probably developed independently; and the uses of writing for government and administration developed far

# Interpreting Visual Evidence

## *The Narmer Palette*

The Narmer Palette (c. 3100 B.C.E.) is a double-sided carving made of green siltstone. Palettes were used to grind pigments for the making of cosmetics, but the large size (63 cm, over 2 feet) of this one is unusual. It was discovered in 1897 by archeologists excavating a temple dedicated to the god Horus at Nekhen, the capital of Upper Egypt. Found nearby were other artifacts, including the so-called Narmer Macehead, thought to depict the marriage of Narmer, king of Upper Egypt, to a princess of Lower Egypt.

On the left, dominating the central panel, Narmer wears the White Crown of Upper Egypt (image A). He wields a mace and seizes the hair of a captive kneeling at his feet. Above the captive's head is a cluster of lotus leaves (a symbol of Lower Egypt) and a falcon representing the god Horus, who may be drawing the captive's life force (*ka*) from his body. The figure behind Narmer is carrying the king's sandals; he is depicted as smaller because he is an inferior. The two men in the lower panel are either running or sprawling on the ground, and the symbols above them indicate the name of a defeated town. On the right, the other side of the palette shows Narmer as the chief figure in a procession (image B). He now wears the Red Crown of Lower Egypt and holds a mace and a flail, symbols of conquest. Behind him is the same servant carrying his sandals, and in front of him are a man with long hair and four standard-bearers. There are also ten headless corpses. Below, the entwined necks of two mythical creatures (serpopards, leopards with serpents' heads) are tethered to leashes held by two men. In the lowest section, a bull tramples the body of a man whose city he is destroying.

A. Namar wearing the White Crown of Egypt.

B. Namar wearing the Red Crown of Egypt.

### *Questions for Analysis*

1. This artifact has been called "the first historical document in the world," but scholars are still debating its meanings. For example, does it represent something that actually happened, or is it political propaganda? In your view, is this proof that Narmer has united two kingdoms? Why or why not?
2. Do the two sides of the palette tell a coherent story and, if so, on which side does that story begin?
3. What might be significant about the site where the palette was found? Should the palette be interpreted as belonging with the mace, found nearby? If so, how might that change your interpretation of the palette's significance?

more quickly in Egypt than in Sumer. But unlike Sumerian cuneiform, Egyptian hieroglyphics never evolved into a system of phonograms. Instead, the Egyptians developed a faster, cursive script for representing hieroglyphics called *hieratic*, which they employed for the everyday business of government and commerce. They also developed a shorthand version of hieratic that scribes could use for rapid note taking. Little of this hieratic script remains, however, due to the perishable nature of the medium on which it was usually written, papyrus. Produced by hammering, drying, and processing river reeds, papyrus was much lighter, easier to write on, and more transportable than the clay tablets used by the Sumerians. When sewn together into scrolls, papyrus also made it possible to record and store large quantities of information in very small packages. Production of this versatile writing material remained one of Egypt's most important industries and exports throughout antiquity and into the Middle Ages. Yet even in the arid environment of Egypt, which has preserved so many ancient artifacts that would have perished in wetter, colder climates, papyrus is fragile and subject to decay. Compared to the huge volume of papryrus documents that would have been produced, therefore, the quantity that survives is small, and this significantly limits our understanding of Old Kingdom Egypt.

The origins of the ancient Egyptian language in which these texts were written has long been a matter of debate, and it can be plausibly linked to both the Semitic languages of the Near East and a number of African language groups. Some historical linguists have postulated that early Egyptian might represent the survival of a root language from which the other languages of the Afro-Asiatic group evolved. The movements of people through the Nile Valley makes this theory a distinct possibility. Whatever its origins, the Egyptian language has enjoyed a long history. Eventually, it became the tongue known as Coptic, which is still used today in the liturgy of the Coptic Christian church in Ethiopia.

**EGYPTIAN WRITING.** Egyptian scribes used a variety of scripts: hieroglyphs for inscriptions and religious texts (top), a cursive hieratic script for administrative documents (middle), and a more informal shorthand for note taking (bottom). ▪ ***What are the relationships among these three forms of writing?***

**THE ROSETTA STONE.** This famous stone, carved in 196 B.C.E., preserves three translations of a single decree in three different forms of writing: hieroglyphs (top), demotic Egyptian (middle), and classical Greek (bottom). ▪ ***Why would scholars be able to use the classical Greek text to decipher the hieroglyphic and demotic scripts?***

## *The Old Kingdom, c. 2686–2160 B.C.E.*

Because so few routine business documents of the Old Kingdom survive, historians have to rely on surviving funerary texts from the tombs of the elite in order to reconstruct the achievements of particular individuals. These sources are hardly representative, and they have tended to convey the impression that Egyptians were obsessed with death; they also tell us little about the lives of ordinary people. Further complicating the historian's task is the early Egyptians' own belief in the unchanging, cyclical nature of the universe. In this early period, there appears to have been little interest in maintaining a record of key events arranged in chronological order. This makes it difficult for us to reconstruct their history in detail.

However, the surviving inscriptions, papyri, and art of the Third Dynasty (c. 2686–2613 B.C.E.) do tell us a great deal about the workings of the "great household" that undergirded individual rulers' power. This power was vast because the pharaoh, as the embodiment of Egypt, was considered to be the intermediary between the land, its people, and their gods, so all the resources of Egypt belonged to him. Long-distance trade was entirely controlled by the pharaoh, as were systems for imposing taxation and conscripting labor. To administer these, the pharaohs installed provincial governors, known to the Greeks as *nomarchs*, many of whom were members of the pharaoh's own family.

Old Kingdom pharaohs kept tight control over the nomarchs and their armies of lesser officials in order to prevent them from establishing local roots in the territories they administered. Writing was therefore critical to internal communication and the management and exploitation of Egypt's vast wealth. This gave rise to a whole class of scribal administrators who enjoyed the power, influence, and status that went along with literacy, a skill few people could command—especially in Egypt, since few could master the intricacies of hieroglyphic reading or writing. Even a child just beginning his scribal education was considered worthy of great respect because the training was so difficult. But it carried great rewards. Indeed, the scribal author of a document from the Middle Kingdom called "The Satire of the Trades" exhorted the beginning student to persevere by reminding him how much better off he would be than everyone else.

**STEP PYRAMID OF KING DJOSER.** This monument to the pharoah's power and divinity was designed by the palace official Imhotep around 2650 B.C.E.

## *Imhotep and the Step Pyramid*

One of the greatest administrative officials in the history of Egypt exemplifies both the skills and the possibilities for advancement that the consummate scribe could command. Imhotep (*im-HO-tep*) rose through the ranks of the pharaoh's administration to become a sort of prime minister, the right-hand man to Djoser (*ZOH-ser*), a pharaoh of the Third Dynasty (c. 2686–2613 B.C.E.). Imhotep's learning included medicine, astronomy, theology, and mathematics, but above all he was an architect. Earlier pharaohs had already devoted enormous resources to their burial arrangements at Abydos. It was Imhotep, however, who designed the Step Pyramid, the first building in history constructed entirely of dressed stone. It was not only to be the final resting place of Djoser but an expression of his transcendent power as the pharaoh.

Built west of the administrative capital at Memphis, the Step Pyramid towers over the desert to a height of 200 feet. Its design was based on an older form of burial monument, the *mastaba*, a low rectangular structure built entirely of brick with a flat top and sloping sides. Imhotep probably began with the *mastaba* pattern in mind, but he radically altered it by stacking one smaller *mastaba* on top of another and constructing each entirely of limestone. Surrounding this structure was a huge temple and mortuary complex, perhaps modeled after Djoser's palace. These buildings served two purposes. First and foremost, they would provide Djoser's *ka*, his spirit, with a habitation and sustenance in the afterlife. Second, the design of the buildings, with their immovable doors and labyrinthine passageways, would (it was hoped) thwart tomb robbers, a chronic problem as pharaonic burials became more and more tempting to thieves.

Imhotep set a precedent to which all other Old Kingdom pharaohs would aspire. The pyramids on the plain of Giza, built during the Fourth Dynasty (2613–2494 B.C.E.), are a case in point. The Great Pyramid itself, built for the pharaoh Khufu (*KOO-foo*, called Cheops by the Greeks), was originally 481 feet high and 756 feet along each side of its base, constructed from more than 2.3 million limestone blocks and enclosing a volume of about 91 million cubic feet. In ancient times, the entire pyramid was encased in gleaming white limestone and topped by a gilded capstone, as were the two massive but slightly smaller pyramids built for Khufu's successors. During the Middle Ages, the Muslim rulers of nearby Cairo had their builders strip off the pyramid's casing stones and used them to construct and fortify their new city. (The gold capstones had probably disappeared already.) But in antiquity these pyramids would have glistened brilliantly by day and glowed by night, making them visible for miles in all directions. The Greek historian Herodotus (*heh-RAH-duh-tuhs*), who toured Egypt more than 2,000 years after the pyramids were built, estimated that it must have taken 100,000 laborers 20 years to build the Great Pyramid. This is probably an exaggeration, but it is a measure of the impression these monuments made.

Once thought to have been the work of slaves, the pyramids were in fact raised by tens of thousands of peasant workers, who labored most intensively on the pyramids while their fields were under water during the Nile's annual flood. Some workers may have been conscripts, but most probably participated willingly, since these projects glorifed the living god who served as their link to the cosmic

**PYRAMIDS AT GIZA.** The Great Pyramid of Khufu (Cheops) is in the center, and was completed c. 2560 B.C.E.

order. Still, the investment of human and material resources required to build the great pyramids put grave strains on Egyptian society. Control over the lives of individual Egyptians increased and the number of administrative officials employed by the state grew ever larger. So too did the contrast between the lifestyle of the pharaoh's splendid court at Memphis and that of Egyptian society as a whole. At the same time, a gap was opening between the pretensions of the pharaohs and the continuing loyalties of Egyptians to their local gods and local leaders.

## THE SOCIETY OF THE OLD AND MIDDLE KINGDOMS

The social pyramid of Old Kingdom Egypt was extremely steep. At its apex stood the pharaoh and his extended family, whose prestige and power set them entirely apart from all other Egyptians. Below them was a class of nobles, whose primary role was to serve as priests and officials of the pharaoh's government; scribes were usually recruited and trained from among the sons of these families. All of these Egyptian elites lived in considerable luxury. They owned extensive estates, exotic possessions, and fine furniture. They kept dogs and cats and monkeys as pets, and hunted and fished for sport.

Beneath this tiny minority was everyone else. Most Egyptians lived in crowded conditions in simple mud-brick dwellings. During a period of prosperity, master craftsmen—jewelers, goldsmiths, and the like—could improve their own conditions and those of their familes by fulfilling the needs of the wealthy, but they did not constitute anything like a middle class. Other skilled professionals—potters, weavers, masons, bricklayers, brewers, merchants, and schoolteachers—also enjoyed some measure of respect as well as a higher standard of living. The vast majority of Egyptians, however, were laborers who provided the brute force necessary for agriculture and construction. Beneath them were slaves, typically captives from foreign wars rather than native Egyptians.

Yet despite the enormous demands the pharaohs placed on Egypt's wealth, Egyptian society does not appear to have been particularly oppressive. Commoners' belief in the pharaoh's divinity made them willing subjects, as did the material benefits of living in a stable, well-governed society. Even slaves had certain legal rights, including the ability to own, sell, and bequeath personal property.

### *Women in the Old Kingdom*

Egyptian women also enjoyed unusual freedoms by the standards of the ancient world. Female commoners were recognized as persons in their own right and were allowed to initiate complaints (including suits for divorce), to defend themselves and act as witnesses, to possess property of their own, and to dispose of it: all without the sanction of a male guardian or representative, as was typically required in other ancient societies—and in most modern ones until the twentieth century. Women were not allowed to undergo formal scribal training, but surviving personal notes exchanged between high-born ladies suggest at least some degree of female literacy.

Women were also barred from holding high office, apart from that of priestess and also, importantly, queen. Queens are often represented as the partners of their royal husbands and were certainly instrumental in ruling alongside them: note the proud, confident bearing of Queen Khamerernebty II (*kah-mehr-en-EB-tee*, see image on page 29). And occasionally, a woman from the royal family might assume pharaonic authority for a time, as Queen Khasekhemwy (*kah-sehk-KEM-wee*, d. 2686 B.C.E.) did for her son Djoser before he came of age. Some may even have ruled in their own right; this was certainly the case under the New Kingdom (see Chapter 2).

Gender divisions were less clearly defined among the peasantry. Peasant women often worked in the fields during the harvest alongside men, and carried out a number of vital tasks in the community. The limitations of our sources, however, means that we can only glimpse the lives of these peasants through the eyes of their social superiors.

**THE PHARAOH MENKAURE AND HIS QUEEN, KHAMERERNEBTY II.** A sculpture from the Fourth Dynasty, c. 2500 B.C.E., shows this queen as her husband's royal partner.

Whatever their status, it seems that women did not enjoy sexual equality. While most Egyptians practiced monogamy, wealthy men could and did keep a number of lesser wives, concubines, and female slaves; and any Egyptian man, married or not, enjoyed freedoms that were denied to women, who would be subject to severe punishments under the law if they were viewed as guilty of any misconduct.

## Science and Technology

Given the powerful impression conveyed by their monumental architecture, it may seem surprising that the ancient Egyptians lagged far behind the Sumerians and Akkadians in science and mathematics, as well as in the application of new technologies. Only in the calculation of time did the Egyptians make notable advances, since their close observation of the sun for religious and agricultural reasons led them to develop a solar calendar that was far more accurate than the Mesopotamian lunar calendar. Whereas the Sumerians have bequeathed to us their means of dividing and measuring the day, the Egyptian calendar is the direct ancestor of the Julian Calendar adopted for Rome by Julius Caesar in 45 B.C.E. (see Chapter 5) and later corrected by Pope Gregory XIII in 1582 C.E: this is the calendar we use today. The Egyptians also devised some effective irrigation and water-control systems, but they did not adopt such labor-saving devices as the wheel until much later than the Sumerians, perhaps because the available pool of peasant manpower was virtually inexhaustible, so that the necessity for such innovations was not felt. Nor did the written laws and other documentary practices produced by the lugals of Mesopotamia have any Old Kingdom parallels. The Egyptians of this era apparently had no need for written laws beyond what was customary in their communities, or what was proclaimed as law by their pharaoh.

## Egyptian Religion and Worldview

As noted above, the special environment of Egypt and the special benefits it conferred on its inhabitants were construed as peculiar divine gifts, renewed each year through the mediation of the pharoah, who was god on earth. From what we can discern, this meant that Old Kingdom Egyptians saw themselves as superior to all other civilizations. A person was either an Egyptian or a foreigner, and the lines between the two were absolute. For Egyptians, it was simply self-evident that their country—nurtured by the Nile and guarded by the deserts and seas that surrounded it—was the center of the universe.

Although the Egyptians told a variety of stories that dealt with the creation of their world, these were not greatly concerned with how humanity came to exist. Rather, what mattered was the means by which all life was created and re-created in an endless cycle of renewal. Unlike the peoples of Mesopotamia, who were constantly faced by new and terrible challenges, both environmental and political, Egyptians experienced existence as predictably repetitive, and this was mirrored in their perception of the cosmos. At the heart of Egyptian religion lay the myth of the gods Osiris and Isis, not only brother and sister but husband and wife, two of the gods most fundamental to Egyptian belief. Osiris was, in a sense, the first pharaoh: the first god to hold kingship on earth. But his brother, Seth, wanted the throne for himself. So Seth betrayed and killed Osiris, sealing his body in a coffin. But his loyal sister Isis retrieved the corpse and managed to revive it long enough to conceive her brother's child, the god Horus. Enraged by this, Seth seized Osiris' body and hacked it to pieces, spreading the remains all over Egypt. (All of Egypt could therefore claim to be part of Osiris, a belief witnessed by shrines dedicated to him throughout the land.) Still undeterred, Isis sought the help of Anubis, the god of the afterlife. Together, they found, reassembled, and preserved the scattered portions of Osiris' body, thus inventing the practice of mummification. Then Horus, with the help of his mother, managed to defeat Seth. Osiris was avenged and revived as god of the underworld. Like Egypt itself, he could not be killed, and the cycle of his death, dismemberment, and resurrection was reflected in the yearly renewal of Egypt itself.

## Life and Death in Ancient Egypt

In addition to embodying Egypt's continual regeneration, Osiris exemplified the Egyptian attitude toward death, which was very different from the Sumerians' bleak view. For the Egyptians, death was a rite of passage, a journey to be endured on the way to an afterlife that was more or less like one's earthly existence, only better. To be sure, the journey was full of dangers. After death, the individual body's *ka,* or life force, would have to roam the Duat, the underworld, searching for the House of Judgment. There, Osiris and forty-two other judges would decide the ka's fate. Demons and evil spirits might try to frustrate the ka's quest to reach the House of Judgment, and the journey might take some time. But if successful and judged worthy, the deceased would enjoy immortality as an aspect of Osiris.

Egyptian funerary rites aimed to emulate the example set by Isis and Anubis, who had carefully preserved the parts of Osiris' body and enabled his afterlife. This is why the Egyptians developed their sophisticated techniques of embalming, whereby all of the body's vital organs were removed and then treated with chemicals—except for the heart, which played a key role in the ka's final judgment. A portrait mask was then placed on the mummy before burial, so that the deceased would be recognizable despite being wrapped in hundreds of yards of linen. To sustain the ka on his or her journey, food, clothing, utensils, weapons, and other items of vital importance would be placed in the grave along with the body.

"Coffin texts," or books of the dead, also accompanied the body and were designed to speed the ka's journey. They contained special instructions, including magic spells and ritual incantations, that would help the ka travel through the underworld and prepare it for the final test. They also described the "negative confession" the ka would make before the court of Osiris, a formal denial of offenses commited in life. The god Anubis would then weigh the deceased's heart against the principle of *ma'at*: truth, order, justice. Because *ma'at* was often envisioned as a goddess wearing a plumed headdress, in the judgment a feather from this headdress would be placed in the scales with the heart; only if the heart was light (empty of wrongdoing) and in perfect balance with the feather would the ka achieve immortality.

Throughout era of the Old Kingdom, the privilege of undergoing these preparations (and thus of ensuring immortality) was reserved for the royal family alone. By the time of the Middle Kingdom (see page 32), it was becoming possible for most Egyptians to ensure that their bodies would participate in these rituals, too.

This manner of confronting death has often led to the erroneous assumption that the ancient Egyptians were pessimistic, but in actuality their practices and beliefs were

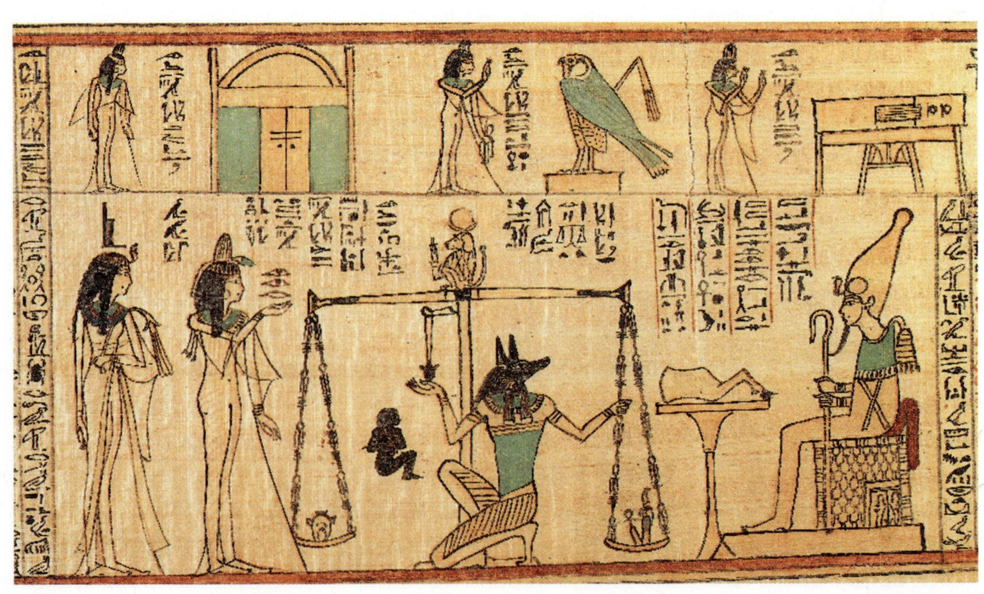

**FUNERARY PAPYRUS.** The scene, inscribed on a papyrus scroll dating from the Twenty-First Dynasty (c. 1000 B.C.E.), shows the heart of the princess for whom this book was prepared being weighed in a balance before the god Osiris. On the other side of the balance are the symbols for life (the *ankh*) and the feather of the goddess Ma'at.

# Analyzing Primary Sources

## *The Instruction of Ptah-Hotep*

*Egyptian literature often took the form of "instructions" to or from important personages, offering advice to those in public life. This document declares itself to be the advice of a high-ranking official of the Old Kingdom to his son and successor, perhaps composed around 2450 B.C.E. However, the earliest surviving text dates from the Middle Kingdom period.*

Be not arrogant because of your knowledge, and be not puffed up because you are a learned man. Take counsel with the ignorant as with the learned, for the limits of art cannot be reached, and no artist is perfect in his skills. Good speech is more hidden than the precious greenstone, and yet it is found among slave girls at the millstones.

. . . If you are a leader commanding the conduct of many seek out every good aim, so that your policy may be without error. A great thing is *ma'at*, enduring and surviving; it has not been upset since the time of Osiris. He who departs from its laws is punished. It is the right path for him who knows nothing. Wrongdoing has never brought its venture safe to port. Evil may win riches, but it is the strength of *ma'at* that endures long, and a man can say, "I learned it from my father." . . . If you wish to prolong friendship in a house which you enter as master, brother, or friend, or anyplace that you enter, beware of approaching the women. No place in which that is done prospers. There is no wisdom in it.

A thousand men are turned aside from their own good because of a little moment, like a dream, by tasting which death is reached. . . . He who lusts after women, no plan of his will succeed. . . . If you are a worthy man sitting in the council of his lord, confine your attention to excellence. Silence is more valuable than chatter. Speak only when you know you can resolve difficulties. He who gives good counsel is an artist, for speech is more difficult than any craft.

Source: Nels M. Bailkey, ed., *Readings in Ancient History: Thought and Experience from Gilgamesh to St. Augustine*, 5th ed. (Boston, MA: 1995), pp. 39–42.

### *Questions for Analysis*

1. According to Ptah-Hotep, what are the most important attributes of a man engaged in public life? What are the most dangerous pitfalls and temptations he will encounter?
2. Why does Ptah-Hotep emphasize the importance of acting in accordance with *ma'at*? How does this idea of *ma'at* compare to that in "the Prophecies of Neferty"?
3. Based on what you have learned about the changes in Egyptian politics and society, what might indicate that Ptah-Hotep lived during the time of the prosperous Fifth Dynasty of the Old Kingdom? How might these instructions have resonated differently with later readers of the Middle Kingdom?

inherently life affirming, bolstered by confidence in the resilience of nature and the renewal of creation. Binding together this endless cycle was *ma'at*, the serene order of the universe with which the individual must remain in harmony, and against which each person's ka would be weighed after death. And embodying *ma'at* on earth was the pharaoh, the earthly manifestation of all gods. For most of the third millennium, thanks to a long period of successful harvests and peace guaranteed by Egypt's geographic isolation from the outside world, the Egyptians were able to maintain their belief in this perfectly ordered paradise and the pharaoh that ensured it. But when that order broke down, so too did their confidence in the pharaoh's power.

## *The End of the Old Kingdom*

For reasons that are not entirely clear, the Fifth and Sixth Dynasties of the Old Kingdom (2494–2181 B.C.E.) witnessed the slow erosion of pharaonic power. Although pyramid construction continued, the monuments of this period are less impressive in design, craftsmanship, and size, perhaps mirroring the diminishing prestige of the pharaohs who ordered them built. Instead, the priesthood of Ra at Nekhen, which was the center of worship for the god Horus and the place where Narmer's unification of Egypt was memorialized, began to assert its own authority over that of the pharaoh. Ultimately, it declared that the pharaoh was not an incarnation of Horus or Ra, but merely the god's earthly son. This was a blow to the heart of Egyptian political theology. More practically threatening was the growing power of the pharaoh's nomarchs, whose increased authority in the provinces allowed them to become a hereditary local nobility: precisely what the vigorous kings of earlier dynasties had refused to permit. These nobles became so influential that one Sixth Dynasty pharaoh, Pepy I, even married into their ranks and produced half-caste successors by these marriages.

Scholars are uncertain as to how certain priests and local officials were able to take power away from the pharaonic center. It may be that the extraordinarily costly building efforts of the Fourth Dynasty had overstrained the economy, while the continued channeling of resources to the royal capital at Memphis increased shortages and resentments in the provinces. Other evidence points to changing climatic conditions that may have disrupted the regular inundations of the Nile, leading to famine in the countryside. Meanwhile, small states were beginning to form to the south in Nubia, perhaps in response to Egyptian aggression against its neighbors. With better organization and equipment, the Nubians may have restricted Egyptian access to precious metal deposits in and around the First Cataract, further crippling the Egyptian economy.

As a result of these calamities, the pharaoh's claims to be in harmony with *ma'at* ceased to be credible, and his power diminished accordingly. Local governors and religious authorities began to emerge as the only effective guarantors of stability and order. By 2160 B.C.E., which marks the beginning of what historians call the First Intermediate Period, Egypt had effectively ceased to exist as a united entity. The central authority of the pharaoh in Memphis collapsed, and a more ancient distribution of power reemerged: a northern center of influence based at Herakleopolis was opposed by a southern regime headquartered at Thebes, with families from each region claiming to be the legitimate pharaohs of all Egypt.

Compared to the centralized authority of the Old Kingdom, this looks like chaos. But redistribution of power always leads to some important developments in any society. In Egypt, wealth became much more widely and evenly diffused than it had been, as did access to education, the opportunities for the creation of art, and the possibilities for personal advancement. Resources that the pharaoh's court at Memphis had once monopolized now remained in the provinces, enabling local elites to emerge as both protectors of society and as patrons of local artisans. The result was a much wider and more rapid dispersal of cultural forms and goods throughout Egyptian society than had been possible under the old regime. Many of these arts and luxuries—including elaborate rites for the dead—had been developed originally at the pharaoh's court, and limited to it. Now, however, they became available to Egyptian society as a whole.

## *Life in the Middle Kingdom (2055–c. 1650 B.C.E.)*

Warfare between the two competing pharaonic dynasties would continue for over a century until 2055 B.C.E., when the Theban king Mentuhotep II conquered the northerners and declared himself the ruler of a united Egypt. His reign marks the beginning of Egypt's Middle Kingdom and the reestablishment of a unified government, but this time centered in Thebes rather than Memphis. The architect of this new government was Mentuhotep's chief supporter,

**FOOD FOR THE JOURNEY OF THE KA.** These wooden models show peasants plowing, grinding grain, baking bread, brewing beer, and slaughtering a steer. Bread and beer were the staple foods of ancient Egypt; beef was too expensive for ordinary consumption, but cattle were frequently sacrificed as funeral offerings. Such models were placed in Middle Kingdom tombs to provide food for the afterlife.

# Analyzing Primary Sources

## *The Prophecies of Neferty*

*This text presents itself as a prophecy foretelling the disasters that would strike Egypt during the First Intermediate Period. In fact, it was composed during the Middle Kingdom, shortly after the death of the pharaoh Amenemhet I, the founder of the Twelfth Dynasty. By contrasting the disorders that preceded Amenemhet's reign with the peace that he established, the document seeks to justify Amenemhet's usurpation of the throne and perhaps to legitimize his son's succession.*

Arise, oh my heart! Weep for this land wherein you were born! Falsehood is as the flood, and behold, evil is spoken with impunity. . . . The land perishes, and there is no one who cares for it. There is no one who speaks out, no one who makes lament. . . . Perished and gone are those joyful places, the fish ponds where dwell fish-eating birds, ponds alive with fish and fowl. All joy has been driven out, and the land is plunged into anguish by those voracious Asiatics who rove throughout the land. Foes have appeared in the east, Asiatics have entered Egypt. We have no (border) fortress, for foreigners now hold it, and there is no one to heed who the plunderers are. One may expect attack by night, the fortress will be breached and sleep driven from all eyes. . . . The land is destitute, although its rulers are numerous, it is ruined, but its taxes are immense. Sparse is the grain, but great is the measure, for it is distributed as if it were abundant.

But then there shall come a king from the south. His name will be Ameny, justified. He will be the son of a woman of Ta-Sety [Nubia], an offspring of the royal house of Nekhen. He shall receive the White Crown, he shall wear the Red Crown, he shall unite the Two Powers. . . . The people of his time will rejoice, for this son of a man will establish his name for ever and eternity. . . . The Asiatics will fall before his sword, the Libyans will fall before his fire, rebels will fall before his wrath, and enemies will fall through awe of him. . . .

Then Ma'at will return to her throne, and Chaos will be driven off. Joyful will he be who will see (these things), he who will serve the king.

Source: William Kelly Simpson, ed., *The Literature of Ancient Egypt: An Anthology of Stories, Instruction, Stelae, Autobiography, and Poetry*, 3rd ed. (New Haven, CT: 2003), pp. 214–220.

### *Questions for Analysis*

1. In what ways does the "Prophecies of Neferty" highlight the anxieties felt by Middle Kingdom Egyptians? What caused these anxieties?
2. Why would the author of this document choose to present it as a prophecy about the future, rather than as a description of current events?

Amenemhet (*ah-meh-NEHM-het*), who seized power after the king's death and established himself and his descendants as Egypt's Twelfth Dynasty. This succession of remarkable pharaohs remained in power for nearly 200 years, and under them the Egyptians began to exploit more thoroughly the potential for trade to the south. They secured their border with Nubia and began to send mounted expeditions to the land they called Punt, probably the coast of Somalia. By the middle of the nineteenth century B.C.E., Nubia was firmly under Egypt's control. Meanwhile, diplomatic relations with the smaller states and principalities of Palestine and Syria led to decisive Egyptian political and economic influence in this region. These lands were not incoroporated into Egypt; instead, Amenemhet constructed the Walls of the Prince in Sinai to guard against incursions from the Near East.

These huge fortifications built along Egypt's new frontier demonstrate the great resourcefulness of the Twelfth Dynasty, and their very different ways of allocating resources and expressing ambition. As such, they also display a marked shift in the Egyptian outlook on the world. Gone was the placid serenity epitomized by *ma'at* and the shared devotion to the pharaoh that had built the pyramids. Egyptians could no longer be dismissive of outsiders or disregard the world beyond their borders. Egypt was not yet an imperial power; the pharaohs of the Middle Kingdom made no attempt to absorb conquests into their kingdom. But unlike their Old Kingdom counterparts, the Egyptians of the Middle Kingdom were not turned in on themselves. Their attitiude to the pharaoh also seems to have changed. Although he continued to enjoy a special

**SESOSTRIS III (1870–1831 B.C.E.).** This powerful Twelfth Dynasty pharaoh led military campaigns into Nubia, constructed massive, garrisoned fortresses along the Nile, and dug new waterways near Aswan. More than 100 portrait busts of Sesostris survive, all with similar features. His overhanging brow, deep-set eyes, and drawn-down mouth are intended to communicate the enormous burden of responsibility the pharaoh bore as the ruler of all Egypt.

position as a divine representative, his authority did not derive solely from this source. Rather, the pharaohs of the Middle Kingdom represented themselves as what they were expected to be—good shepherds, tenders of their flock. Only by diligently protecting Egypt from a hostile outside world could a pharaoh provide the peace, prosperity, and security desired by his subjects; his alignment with *ma'at* was now conditional, and it had to be earned.

Portraits of the great pharaohs of the Twelfth Dynasty mirror this anxious outlook on the world. The literature of the Middle Kingdom also expresses the general change in attitude. Among the most popular literary forms were manuals ostensibly written by or for kings, detailing the duties and perils of high office and offering advice for dealing with difficult situations. These include the *Instruction of Amenemhet*, which purports to be life lessons handed down by the pharaoh to his son from beyond the grave, and *The Instruction of Ptah-Hotep* (see ***Analyzing Primary Sources*** on page 31), an example of Egyptian "wisdom literature" attributed to a court official of the Old Kingdom, which achieved a wider readership in this new era—much as Machiavelli's *The Prince* (see Chapter 12) has become a "self-help" book for business executives and politicians in our own time. Ptah-Hotep's teaching is upbeat and practical; by contrast, the examples of this genre produced under the Middle Kingdom are bleakly pragmatic. A pharaoh must trust no one: not a brother, not a friend, not intimate

# After You Read This Chapter

Visit StudySpace for quizzes, additional review materials, and multi-media documents. **wwnorton.com/studyspace**

## REVIEWING THE OBJECTIVES

- The study of the distant past is challenging because written sources are rare. What other sources of information do historians use?
- All civilizations require the same basic things and share certain characteristics. What are they?
- The cities of Mesopotamia remained largely independent from one another, yet shared a common culture. Why was this the case?
- Hammurabi's empire created a new precedent for governance in Mesopotamia. How did he achieve this?
- The civilizations of ancient Mesopotamia and Egypt differ in profound ways. What were the major causes of their differences?

companions. He must crush the ambitions of local nobles with ruthless ferocity. He must always be on the lookout for potential trouble. In return for his exertions on behalf of his people, he should expect neither gratitude nor reward; he should expect only that each new year will bring new dangers and more pressing challenges. Reading between the lines, we discern that Egyptians' sense of their own superiority—a product of their isolation and their comparatively benign environment—had been shattered. They saw themselves being drawn into a much wider world, and in the course of the next millennium, they would become more fully a part of it.

## CONCLUSION

While the story of Babel records the legendary loss of communication, this chapter shows that people of the distant past can still communicate with us. The marks they have left on the landscape, the remains of their daily lives, their written records, and their very bodies make it possible for historians to piece together the evidence and to make sense of it. And every year new sources come to light, meaning that we have to be ready to revise, constantly, our understanding of what happened in the past.

Although this chapter has emphasized the differences between the early civilizations of Mesopotamia and Egypt, it is worth noting some significant similarities. Both developed the fundamental technologies of writing at about the same time, and this facilitated political alliances, long-distance trade, and the transmission of vital information to posterity. During the third millennium, both underwent a process of political consolidation, an elaboration of religious ritual, and a melding of spiritual and political leadership. Both engaged in massive building and irrigation projects, and both commanded material and human resources on an enormous scale. At the same time, each of these civilizations cultivated an inward focus. Although they had some contact with each other, and some transfers of information and technology probably took place, there were few significant political or cultural interactions. For all intents and purposes, they inhabited separate worlds. This relative isolation was about to change, however. The next millennium would see the emergence of large-scale, land-based empires in the Near East that would transform life in Mesopotamia, Egypt, and the lands that lay between them. These are the developments we examine in Chapter 2.

### PEOPLE, IDEAS, AND EVENTS IN CONTEXT

- What fundamental changes associated with the **NEOLITHIC REVOLUTION** made early civilizations possible?
- What new technologies allowed the **SUMERIANS** to master the environment of **MESOPOTAMIA**, and how did these technologies contribute to the development of a new, urbanized society?
- By contrast, why did the Nile River foster a very different civilization and enable the centralized authority of the **PHARAOH**?
- How do the differences between **CUNEIFORM** and **HIEROGLYPHS** reflect the different circumstances in which they were invented and the different uses to which they were put?
- In what ways are the ***EPIC OF GILGAMESH*** and the ***CODE OF HAMMURABI*** rich sources of information about the civilizations of Sumer and **BABYLON**?
- How do the **ZIGGURATS** of Mesopotamia and the **PYRAMIDS** of Egypt exemplify different forms of power, different ideas about the gods, and different beliefs about the afterlife?
- Why was the worldview of ancient Egyptians, which was strongly reflected in the concept of ***MA'AT*** during the **OLD KINGDOM**, altered in significant ways by the time of the **MIDDLE KINGDOM**?

### CONSEQUENCES

- How do the surviving sources of any period limit the kinds of questions that we can ask and answer about the distant past? In your view, are there sources for this early era that have been undervalued? For example, if writing had not been developed in Mesopotamia and Egypt, what would we still be able to know about the civilizations of these two regions?
- What features of ancient civilizations do modern civilizations share? What might be the implications of these shared ideas, social structures, and technologies?

# Before You Read This Chapter

## STORY LINES

- During the second millennium B.C.E, new peoples settled in the Near East, spreading a related set of languages known as Indo-European, the ancestor of several major modern language groups.
- In Egypt, the rise of the Eighteenth Dynasty fostered imperial expansion beyond the Nile Valley for the first time.
- During the late Bronze Age an interconnected network of alliances bound peoples together in new ways. But this civilization was eventually destroyed by the raids of mysterious Sea Peoples.
- In the wake of these invasions, both oppressive new empires and smaller-scale states emerged.
- The worship of Yahweh among the Hebrews and of Ahura-Mazda among the Persians fostered a new view of the world, one in which a single creator god ruled over all peoples.

## CHRONOLOGY

| | |
|---|---|
| 1900–1500 B.C.E. | Minoan civilization flourishes |
| 1800–1400 B.C.E. | Creation of the Hittite Empire |
| 1792 B.C.E. | Rise of Babylon under Hammurabi |
| 1650–1550 B.C.E. | Hyksos invasion of Egypt and Second Intermediate Period |
| 1600–1200 B.C.E. | Mycenaean civilization flourishes |
| 1550–1075 B.C.E. | New Kingdom of Egypt established |
| c. 1200 B.C.E. | Invasions of the Sea Peoples begin |
| 1100–1000 B.C.E. | Philistine dominance in Palestine |
| 1000–973 B.C.E. | Hebrew kingdom consolidated |
| 924 B.C.E. | Israel and Judah divided |
| 883–859 B.C.E. | Neo-Assyrian Empire founded |
| 722 B.C.E. | Kingdom of Israel destroyed |
| 612–605 B.C.E. | Fall of the Neo-Assyrian Empire |
| 586 B.C.E. | Fall of the kingdom of Judah |
| 539–486 B.C.E | Persian Empire consolidated |

## CORE OBJECTIVES

- **DESCRIBE** the impact of new migrations and settlements on the ancient Near East.
- **DEFINE** the differences between Egypt's New Kingdom and the previous Old and Middle Kingdoms.
- **EXPLAIN** the workings of transnational networks in the late Bronze Age.
- **IDENTIFY** the new empires and kingdoms that emerged in the Iron Age.
- **UNDERSTAND** the historical importance of monotheism.

# Peoples, Gods, and Empires: 1700–500 B.C.E.

According to Hesiod, a Greek poet who flourished during the eighth century B.C.E., all of human history falls into five ages. The dawn of time was a golden age, when men lived like gods. Everything was good then, food was plentiful, and work was easy. The next age was silver, when men took gods for granted, killed one another, and lived in dishonor. So the gods destroyed them, sending a mighty flood that spared only the family of Deucalion, the son of wily Prometheus, who built an ark. Then came the age of bronze, when everything was made of bronze—houses and armor and weapons and tools—and giants fought incessantly from huge strongholds, causing destruction so great that no man's name survives. The time following was short but bright, a heroic age, the time of men who ventured with Theseus and fought beside Achilles and sailed with Odysseus, men whose names will live forever. But Hesiod's own age was iron—a dull age, a time of tedium and strife and bickering and petty feuds.`

Hesiod's periodization captures an understanding of history that had evolved with humanity itself and that reflects actual developments. The stories he knew told of a time before cities and the need for agriculture. They recalled a time when the harmony between gods and men broke down, and the human race was saved by one man's ingenuity: Utnapishtim-Noah-Deucalion. They chronicled the wars of the age we still call Bronze, when the enormous abandoned palaces visible in Hesiod's day were built. And they remembered the race of heroes whose glory was measured by their abiding fame, and who bequeathed to us a further round of stories. Thanks to new archeological finds, new linguistic discoveries, and new efforts at decoding the historical record, we can both confirm and correct Hesiod's perspective on the past.

In the second millennium B.C.E. the ancient Near East was transformed by the arrival of new peoples and by the emergence of expansive [illegible] through systematic military conquest. These migrations and conquests caused upheaval, but they also led to cultural contact and economic integration that encompassed most of the Mediterranean. The last few centuries of the Bronze Age (1500–1200 B.C.E.) were a period of intense diplomacy, trade, and exchange. By the thirteenth century B.C.E., nations from the southern Balkans to the western fringes of Iran had been drawn into a wide-ranging web of relationships.

This extraordinary system proved more fragile than its participants could have imagined. Around 1200 B.C.E., a wave of mysterious invasions led to the destruction of nearly every Bronze Age civilization. As a result, around the turn of the first millennium B.C.E. we enter a new world organized along profoundly different lines. In this new age, iron would slowly replace bronze as the primary component of tools and weapons. New and more brutal empires would

**Transformations in the Ancient Near East**

| | |
|---|---|
| Semitic peoples invade Sumer | 2000 B.C.E. |
| Indo-European peoples arrive in the Near East | 2000 B.C.E. |
| Assyrians organize trade networks | 1900 B.C.E. |
| Rise of Old Babylonian Empire | 1800 B.C.E. |
| Creation of Hittite, Kassite, and Mitanni kingdoms | 1800–1400 B.C.E. |

**THE BRONZE AGE NEAR EAST, 2000–1400 B.C.E.** Notice the geographical relationship among the older centers of Sumer and Egypt and among the newer civilizations such as Babylonia, Assyria, Phoenicia, and the Hittite Empire. ▪ ***Which of these emerging cultures would be most likely to come into contact with Egypt, and why?*** ▪ ***Where did the Indo-European peoples come from?*** ▪ ***What was the impact of the Indo-European invasions?***

come to power, while new ideas about the divine and its relationship to humanity would emerge. Two of the Western world's most enduring religious traditions—Judaism and Zoroastrianism (*zoh-roh-AHS-tree-nism*)—were born, fundamentally altering conceptions of ethics, politics, and the natural world. This Iron Age would prove a fateful historical crossroads, as elements both old and new combined to reconfigure the ancient world.

## INDO-EUROPEAN LANGUAGES AND PEOPLES

In 1786, a British judge serving in India made a discovery that transformed the understanding of history. Turning his spare time to the study of Sanskrit, the ancient language of South Asia, Sir William Jones discovered that it shares the same grammar and vocabulary as ancient Greek and Latin, to an extent inexplicable by sheer coincidence. His interest piqued, he then examined the early Germanic and Celtic languages of Europe and the Old Persian language of the Near East, and found that they also exhibit marked similarities. He concluded that all of these languages must have evolved from a common source. Within another generation, the ancient language whose existence Jones had hypothesized, and the later languages derived from it, would be labeled Indo-European, reflecting their wide distribution from India to Ireland. The Biblical story of mankind's shared language, the story of Babel, turns out to be partly true.

Since then, scholars have greatly enlarged our understanding of Indo-European languages and their speakers. Yet much remains controversial. Was an original form of the language spoken by a single population at some point in time? If so, when and where? How did it spread? Can the diffusion of its speakers be determined archaeologically, by tracing characteristic pottery types and burial rites, or are such practices distinct from language? At the moment, we have no clear answers to any such questions. It is certain, however, that Indo-European linguistic forms begin to appear in the Near East and eastern Mediterranean shortly after 2000 B.C.E. Around this same time, a group of Indo-European speakers also moved into the Aegean basin, where the resulting language became an early form of Greek. Other Indo-European speakers went east; some may have reached western China.

These were not the only new peoples moving into the Near East. As we noted in Chapter 1, Semitic-speaking peoples were also making their mark, beginning with the Akkadians and the Amorites, from whose ranks Hammurabi came. The Assyrians, the Phoenicians, and the Canaanites would also become prominent. These newcomers did not wipe out existing cultures; rather, they built on established patterns of urban life and organization. But their collective impact was enormous.

### *New Settlers in Anatolia*

By 1900 B.C.E., the nomadic Assyrians had become caravan merchants whose extensive trade networks stretched across Anatolia and Mesopotamia. They did not seek military dominance over the region; instead, they relied on the protection of local rulers and, in turn, they made these rulers rich. They also served as advisers and officials, and married into important urban families. In the process, they carried Mesopotamian civilization and its trappings into far-flung regions.

In the wake of Assyrian-assisted urbanization, new population groups were attracted to Anatolia, northern Syria, and Mesopotamia. The most formidable of these were the Hittites, an Indo-European-speaking people who arrived around 2000 B.C.E. In contrast to the Assyrians, the Hittites were conquerors and colonists who imposed themselves and their language on the peoples they vanquished. By 1700 B.C.E., they had integrated many Hittite-dominated city-states into a larger kingdom. About fifty years later, they captured a strategic mountain stronghold, Hattusas, from which their king took a new name, Hattusilis.

Under Hattusilis and his successors, the Hittites' warrior aristocracy fielded the most fearsome army of the Bronze Age. They were quick to adopt the latest technologies, including the chariot and (eventually) the use of iron for weaponry. But the Hittites also adopted the more peaceful practices of those they conquered, using cuneiform to record their own language and laws. They also sought to control trade routes, particularly the overland trade in copper and arsenic, the raw materials for making bronze. By 1595 B.C.E., they had moved southeastward into Mesopotamia, capturing and sacking Babylon.

A century later, the Kassites, another new people, moved into the devastated city and took control of it. For the next 500 years, they presided over a largely peaceful and prosperous Babylonian realm. The Hittites, however, continued to destabilize the region, until they were themselves checked by the arrival of a people known as the Mitannians, who moved into Syria around 1550 B.C.E. The Mitannians' initial advantage was their use of horses, hitherto unknown outside the steppes of Asia. Their light, horse-drawn chariots became terrifying death-machines, transporting archers rapidly around the battlefield. The

**A NEAR EASTERN WAR CHARIOT.** A light, spoke-wheeled chariot, developed for warfare, is here being used for lion hunting by the Assyrian king Assurnasirpal II (883–859 B.C.E.). See page 58.

Mitannians also pioneered cavalry tactics which devastated the foot soldiers of their rivals. Eventually, however, the Mitannians' opponents borrowed these same technologies, and the Hittites once again achieved the advantage. By the mid-fourteenth century, they had subjugated the Mitannians and were turning their attention to Egypt.

## THE NEW KINGDOM OF EGYPT

As we have seen, Egypt's Middle Kingdom had been formed by the many internal changes of the First Intermediate Period, chiefly the redistribution of wealth and power. Now it was further transformed by external forces, through the dynamic movement of new peoples from western Asia and Nubia. Some of these came to Egypt as immigrants; others were hired as mercenaries. And for a while, a strategy of accommodation preserved Egypt from large-scale armed attack and fostered commercial exchange with neighboring regions. But around 1700 B.C.E., Egypt was invaded for the first time since the unification of the Upper and Lower Kingdoms. The invaders' origins and identity remain mysterious; the Egyptians called them simply Hyksos (*HIHK-sohs*), "rulers of foreign lands." From their power base in the eastern delta of the Nile, the Hyksos began to project their authority over most of Lower Egypt.

With this conquest, the central authority of the pharaoh once again dissolved and Egypt entered into the Second Intermediate Period (c. 1650–1550 B.C.E.). Significantly, however, the Hyksos took over the machinery of pharaonic government in Lower Egypt and took steps to legitimize their rule in accordance with Egyptian precedents. Some Hyksos rulers even incorporated the name of the sun-god Ra into their own names. In Upper Egypt, by contrast, Hyksos power was weak. Here, a native pharaonic regime maintained a tenuous independence at the traditional capital of Thebes, although it sometimes had to acknowledge the suzerainty of the foreigners to the north.

This relatively short period of Hyksos domination was regarded by later Egyptians as the greatest shame of their history. Although the Hyksos established Lower Egypt as the most significant power in the Near East, filling the temporary power vacuum left by the Hittites, their conquest also weakened the dominion of Upper Egypt over the Nubians, who eventually founded an independent kingdom called Kush. This Nubian kingdom posed a much greater threat to the native dynasty at Thebes than to the Hyksos in Lower Egypt—but it also provided additional incentive to southern pharaohs determined to oust the Hyksos usurpers and reunify Egypt. Ultimately, they succeeded. By the end of the sixteenth century B.C.E., the pharaoh Ahmose had driven out the Hyksos, establishing the Eighteenth Dynasty and the New Kingdom of Egypt.

### *The Pharaohs of the Eighteenth Dynasty*

Under the Eighteenth Dynasty, Egyptian civilization reached the height of its magnificence and power, which it now exercised more widely than ever before. Although many Egyptian traditions were renewed and strengthened, the dynamism of the New Kingdom—particularly its new focus on imperial expansion—changed the very fabric of Egyptian life, which had never before looked beyond the narrow world of the fertile Nile Valley.

The Eighteenth Dynasty ruled Egypt for more than two and a half centuries, and striking developments took place during this period. Most important was the rise of a new aristocracy whose wealth was acquired through warfare and the winning of lands (with slaves to work them) which they received from the pharaoh as rewards for service. The Eighteenth Dynasty itself was forged in battle, something that had not been true of a ruling family since the time of King Narmer, over a millennium and a half earlier. Ahmose, the man who expelled the Hyksos, had been reared by the warrior queen Ahhotep, who had ruled Upper Egypt in her own right. His eventual successor, Thutmose I (c. 1504–1492 B.C.E.), was the son of an unknown warrior who married Amhose's daughter.

Under Thutmose's leadership, the Egyptians subdued the Nubians to the south, seizing control of their gold mines and securing the wealth needed to finance expanded commerce in the Near East. They also penetrated beyond their northeastern frontier, driving deep into Palestine and Syria. By the time of his death, Thutmose could claim to rule the land from beyond the Nile's Fourth Cataract in the south to the banks of the Euphrates in the north. Never had Egypt held sway over so much territory, or so clearly declared its imperial ambitions. Nor was this success fleeting. The Egyptians would sustain a strong military presence in the Near East for the next 400 years, using the new

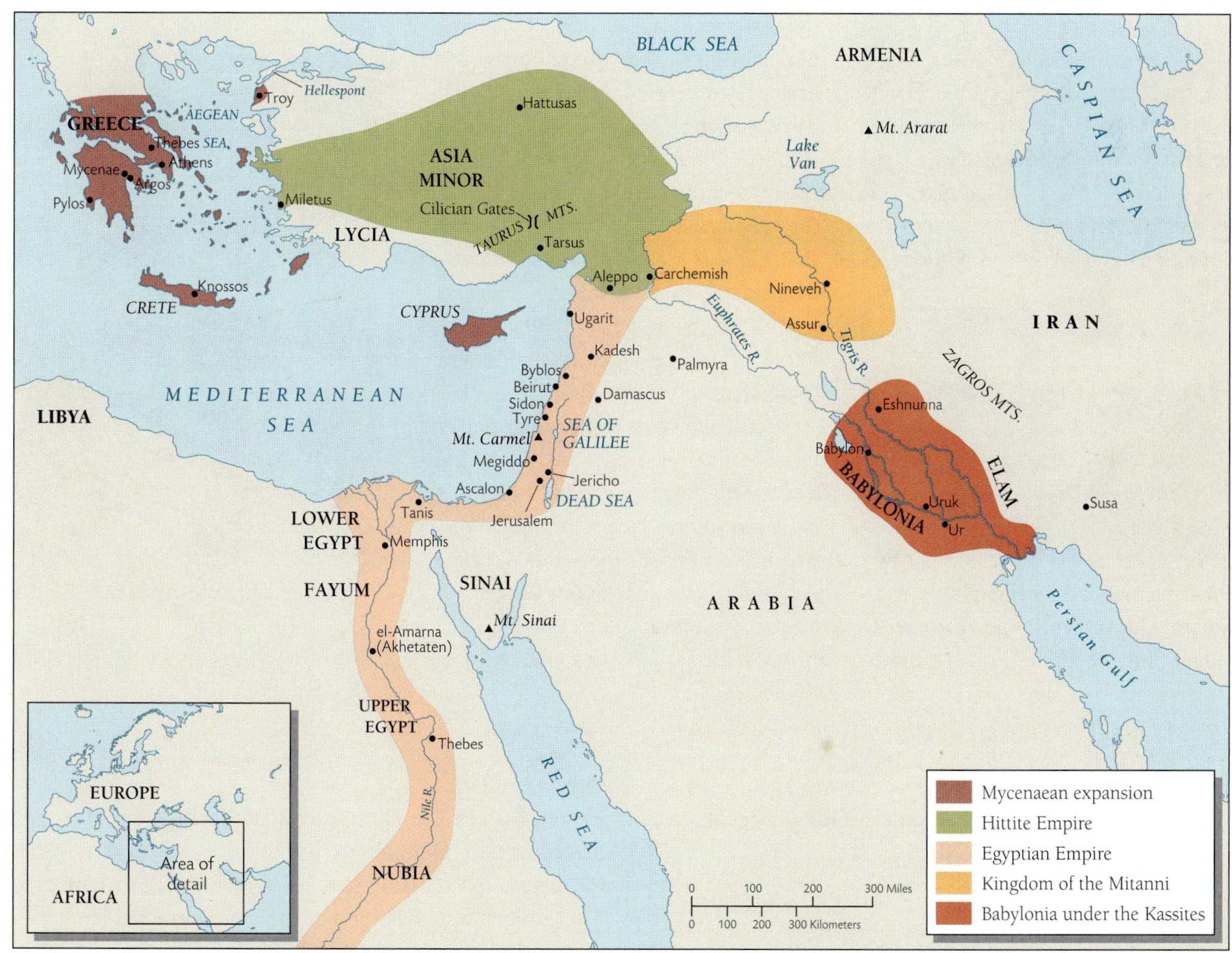


**EGYPT AND ITS NEIGHBORS, c. 1400 B.C.E.** ▪ *What is the major change on this map compared to the previous map of the Bronze Age Near East (page 38)?* ▪ *What factors appear to shape patterns of conquest and settlement in the Mediterranean?* ▪ *What developments would have enabled trade to flourish during this period?*

# Interpreting Visual Evidence

## *Remembering Hatshepsut*

The pharaohs of Egypt's New Kingdom were obsessed with self-representation and they carefully controlled their public images. The visual language they used was highly symbolic, an iconography (vocabulary of images) intended to make each successive pharaoh look as much like his royal predecessors as possible: godlike, steadfast, virile, authoritative—even when the pharaoh was a woman, Hatshepsut (1479–1458 B.C.E., images A and B). So many statues and portraits of her survive that nearly every major museum in the world has at least one (the Metropolitan Museum of Art has a whole room set aside for them). But many of these images show signs of having been defaced during the reign of her successor, Thutmose III, who was also her nephew and stepson. Until very recently, scholars assumed that Hatshepsut must have usurped his powers, and that this was his revenge. Yet the evidence clearly shows that Hatshepsut was Egypt's legitimate ruler. Why, then, would Thutmose III or his heirs have tried efface to her memory?

These two unblemished *steles* depict Hatshepsut and Thutmose III. In the *stele* on the left (image C), Hatshepsut is placed in the center of the frame, wearing a royal helmet; she is offering wine to the god Amun. Behind her stands Thutmose III, wearing the crown of Upper Egypt. In the *stele* on the right (image D), Thutmose III wears the warrior's crown, while Hatshepsut wears the double crown of Upper and Lower Egypt and wields a mace.

A. Defaced head of Hatshepsut.

B. Undefaced statue of Hatshepsut.

horse-powered battle chariots to devastating effect against their enemies.

## The Legacy of Hatshepsut

The early death of Thutmose's son and successor could have resulted in a crisis for the Eighteenth Dynasty. Instead, it led to one of the most remarkable reigns in Egypt's history, for Thutmose II (1492–1479 B.C.E.) passed the power of pharaoh to his sister, wife, and co-ruler Hatshepsut (*haht-SHEHP-soot*, 1479–1458 B.C.E.). Such brother-sister unions were common in the Egyptian royal family, although they do not appear to have been the routine way to produce royal children: pharaohs customarily kept a harem of subsidiary wives and concubines for this purpose. However, Thutmose II and Hatshepsut did conceive at least one child together, Neferure; in fact, she may have been their des-

*Questions for Analysis*

1. Bearing in mind that few Egyptians could read the hieroglyphs accompanying these images, how might they have "read" the relationship between these two royal relatives? Does this evidence support the hypothesis that Thutmose was slighted by Hatshepsut?
2. What can these images tell us about gender roles? What else would we need to know before making a judgment about masculine and feminine characteristics in ancient Egypt?
3. Given that Hatshepsut was Egypt's legitimate pharaoh, what might have motivated either Thutmose III or his son Amenhotep II to deface her image many years after her death?

C. Stele of Hatshepsut and Thutmose.

D. Stele of Thutmos and Hatshepsut from the Red Chapel at Karnak.

ignated heir. For 21 years, Hatshepsut ruled as pharaoh in her own right, while her daughter took on the usual duties of queen.

Like her great-grandmother, Ahhotep, Hatshepsut was a warrior. Moroever, she was routinely protrayed on monuments and in statuary with the masculine figure and ceremonial beard characteristic of pharaohs. She did not pretend to be a man; inscriptions almost always indicate her gender, and she herself claimed to be the most beautiful woman in the world. But it was important to Egyptians that she use the conventional iconography of power and locate herself firmly within a long history of dynastic rule.

Hatshepsut's statecraft proved crucial to the continuing success of Egypt. With her stepson/nephew, Thutmose III (son of one of her brother's lesser wives), she launched several successful military campaigns and extended trade and diplomacy. The arts also flourished, setting standards that would be emulated for a thousand years. Indeed,

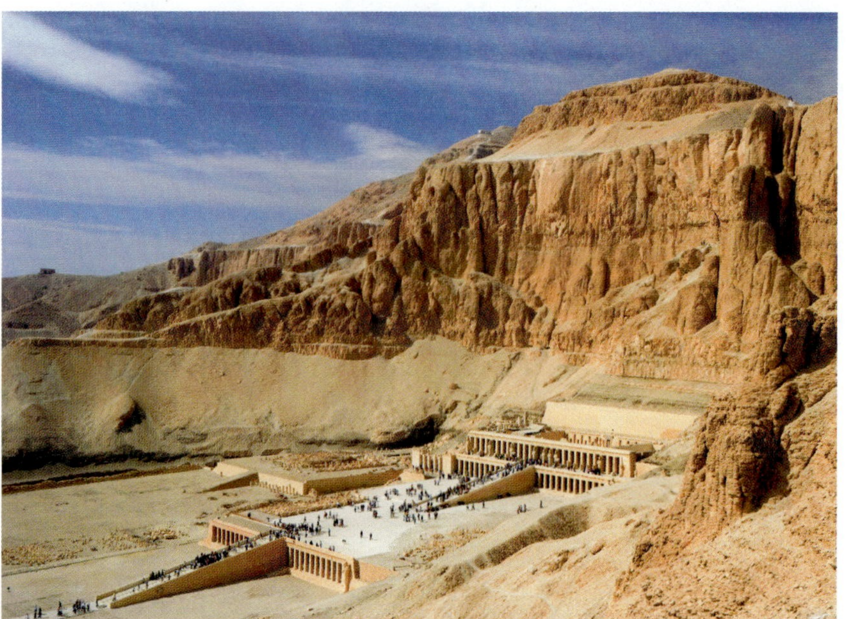

**THE MORTUARY TEMPLE OF HATSHEPSUT.** Unlike the pharaohs of the Old Kingdom, those of the Eighteenth Dynasty chose to be buried in specially built temples rather than in separate pyramids. The innovative architecture of Hatshepsut's temple, which was built into a hillside and set off by rows of columns, was widely imitated by her successors.

Hatshepsut was one of the most ambitious builders in Egyptian history, which is saying something. Her own mortuary temple, which housed the remains of her father and herself, was probably the first tomb constructed in the Valley of the Kings, the New Kingdom's answer to the pyramids.

Yet after Hatshepsut's death in 1458 B.C.E. her legacy was called into question. At some point late in her nephew's reign, attempts were made to remove her name from inscriptions and to destroy her images (see ***Interpreting Visual Evidence*** on page 42). Scholars used to assume that Thutmose himself was responsible, that he resented his stepmother/aunt's power over him. But more recent research has suggested that the culprit was his son, Amenhotep II (1427–1400 B.C.E.), who was thereby blocking the claims of royal rivals, possibly the descendants of Hatshepsut or her daughter Neferure.

## Religious Change and Political Challenge

The great conquests of the Eighteenth Dynasty brought mind-boggling riches to Egypt. Much of this wealth went to the glorification of the pharaoh in the form of grand temples, tombs, and other monuments, including the thousands of *steles* that provide us with so much information about this era. Another significant portion of the plunder went to the military aristocracy that made such conquests possible. But the lion's share went to the gods as offerings of thanks for Egypt's success. As the temples became wealthy and powerful, so too did their priests. But no temple complex was so well endowed as that of Amon at Thebes.

Thebes was not only the capital of New Kingdom Egypt, it was also the capital of the Eighteenth Dynasty and the place most sacred to Amon (or Amun), the god of creation. He therefore played an important role in the dynasty's self-image, and he is evoked in the dynastic name Amenhotep ("Amon Is Pleased") and on the *stele* of Hatshepsut shown on page 43. But Amon was more than a local god. He had come into prominence when the political center of gravity shifted to Thebes during the Middle Kingdom, and his cult had steadily increased in status and popularity. By 1550 B.C.E., he had become identified as another manifestation of the sun god Ra, and as Amon-Ra he was believed to be the divine force behind the Eighteenth Dynasty's triumph over the Hyksos. This accounts for the favor shown to his priests at Thebes, who became a formidable political and economic force. Eventually, the priesthood of Amon surpassed even the military aristocracy in importance and influence. And since the dynasty's prestige was intertwined with that of Amon, the priests had seemingly gained the controlling voice in Egypt.

## The Reign of Akhenaten (1352–1336 B.C.E.)

All of these factors are important when we consider the reign of Amenhotep IV, who inherited the vast, well-governed kingdom assembled by his predecessors. This young pharaoh showed an early inclination toward the worship of the sun, but not as an aspect of Amon. Instead, Amenhotep exalted Ra as a discrete divinity and he laid aside the traditional iconography of this god as a falcon (or a falcon-headed man), replacing it with the symbol *Aten*, the hieroglyph representing the sun's rays. He then went farther, changing his own name to Akhenaten (*AH-keh-NAH-ton*), "He Who Is Profitable to the Aten," and building a new capital to honor the god. Located halfway between Memphis in the north and Thebes in the south, it was called Akhetaten ("The Horizon of the Aten").

Although the priesthood of Amon exalted Amon-Ra, it had continued to recognize all the other gods of the Egyptian pantheon. Akhenaten's theology, by contrast, was closer to monotheism. Unlike traditional Egyptian deities, the Aten could not be imagined as taking on human or animal form. As if this were not controversial enough, Akhenaten also celebrated his new religion by representing himself in a very unconventional way. In a complete departure from the divine virility of his ancestors—which even his ancestor Hatshepsut had emulated—Akhenaten had himself pictured as a human being with distinctive features, and as a family man enjoying the company of his wife, Nefertiti, and their children. This emphasis on his own humanity might have been an extension of his theology, which honored the life force within every being. But it was also dangerous to the ideology of royal power. The pharaoh was not supposed to approachable and affable, a man with quirky personality. He was supposed to be a god on earth.

Akhenaten's spiritual revolution therefore had enormous political implications. Indeed, some scholars have suggested that it was part of a cunning attempt to undermine the influence of Amon's priests. Whatever the motives behind it, Akhenaten did not succeed in converting many Egyptians to his new religion. Not surprisingly, the priesthood of Amon also put up strenuous resistance. To make matters worse, Akhenaten did not balance his theological enthusiasm with attention to Egypt's security or interests abroad. This cost him the support of his nobility and may even have led to his deposition. He was ultimately succeeded by one of his younger sons, Tutankhaten ("Living Image of Aten"), a child of nine whose name was quickly changed to reflect his rejection of Akhenaten's beliefs and the restoration of the god Amon and his priesthood. He became Tutankhamun (1333–1324 B.C.E.), the boy king whose sumptuous tomb was discovered in 1922. After his early death, he was succeeded by a general called Horemheb, a man unrelated to the royal family who nonetheless reigned as the last pharaoh of the Eighteenth Dynasty and managed

**AKHENATEN, HIS WIFE NEFERTITI, AND THEIR CHILDREN.** The Aten is depicted here as a sun disk, raining down power on the royal family. ▪ ***What messages might this image have conveyed to contemporary Egyptians?*** ▪ ***How does this depiction of the pharaoh differ from earlier precedents?***

**THRONE OF TUTANKHAMUN.** Dating from about 1330 B.C.E., this relief in gold and silver is part of the back of the young pharaoh's throne. Although the reign of the boy king marked the rejection of Akhenaten's theology, the informal artistic style favored by his father is still detectable here in the relaxed, lounging position of the pharaoh and the intimate, confiding gesture of his queen, Ankhesenamen.

to maintain stability for nearly three decades. When he died, he passed his office to another general. This was Ramses, the founder of the Nineteenth Dynasty, who would restore Egypt to glory in the Near East.

## TRANSNATIONAL NETWORKS OF THE LATE BRONZE AGE

After 1500 B.C.E., Bronze Age history must be understood within the context of what we might call international relations. Yet it is more accurate to call the political and economic networks of this period *transnational*, because this web of alliances and relationships transcended boundaries and any idea of national identity.

The Late Bronze Age was an age of superpowers. The great pharaohs of the Eighteenth Dynasty had transformed Egypt into a conquering state, and the Hittites had created an empire out of the disparate city-states and kingdoms of Anatolia. The Assyrians controlled Near Eastern trade, and the Kassite kingdom of Babylonia remained a significant force in economic and military relationships. In addition to these imperial entities, numerous smaller states also flourished and extended their influence westward into the Mediterranean.

### *Transnational Diplomacy*

Although warfare remained the fundamental mode of interaction in the late Bronze Age, a balance of power among the larger empires gradually helped to stabilize the region and encourage trade. The archives discovered by archaeologists at Akhenaten's abandoned capital of Aketaten (modern el-Amarna) provide us with a clear picture of this process. By the fourteenth century B.C.E., a wide-ranging correspondence was binding leaders together and promoting a set of mutual goals and understandings. This is reflected in the letters' vocabulary: the most powerful rulers address one another as "brother," while lesser princes and chieftains show their deference to the pharaoh, the Hittite king, and other sovereigns by using the term "father." Breach of this protocol could cause great offense. When a thirteenth-century Assyrian king presumed to address the Hittite ruler as "brother," he received a stern rebuke: "What is this you keep saying about 'brotherhood'? Were you and I born of the same mother? Far from it! Just as my father and grandfather were not in the habit of writing about 'brotherhood' to the king of Assyria, so you should stop writing to me about 'brotherhood!'"

Rulers of this period also exchanged lavish gifts and entered into marriage alliances with each other. Professional envoys journeyed back and forth between the centers of power, conveying gifts and handling politically sensitive missions. Some of these emissaries were also merchants, sent to explore the possibility of trading opportunities as well as to cement alliances.

### *Transnational Trade*

Indeed, it was trade that allowed smaller communities to become integral parts of this transnational network. Seaside centers such as Ugarit and Byblos became powerful merchant city-states and centers for the exchange of dazzling commodities. A single vessel's cargo might contain scores of distinct items originating anywhere from the interior of Africa to the Baltic Sea, as demonstrated by the contents of a merchant ship discovered at Uluburun off the Turkish coast in 1982. At the same time, the region was supplied with goods brought in overland, via contacts reaching into India and the Far East.

Trade was not only the basis for a new economy, but also the conduit for art, ideas, and technology. In the past, such influences spread slowly and unevenly; now, though, the societies of the late Bronze Age could keep abreast of all the latest developments. Egyptians delighted in Canaanite glass, Greeks prized Egyptian amulets, and the merchants of Syria admired Greek pottery and wool. Examples of avid desire for the products of other cultures could be endlessly enumerated.

This trend was particularly marked in large coastal towns. At Ugarit, on the coast of modern-day Syria, the swirl of commerce and the multiplicity of languages spoken by traders even propelled the development of a simpler form of writing than the cuneiform still current throughout most of the Near East. The Ugaritic alphabet consisted of about thirty symbols representing the sounds of consonants. (Vowels had to be inferred.) This system was far more easily mastered and more flexible than cuneiform, and it would become the model for the development of all modern alphabets.

The search for markets, resources, and trade routes also promoted greater understanding among cultures. After a great battle between Egyptians and Hittites near Kadesh (c. 1275 B.C.E.), the pharaoh Ramses II realized that more was to be gained through peaceful relations with his northern neighbors than through warfare. The treaty he established with the Hittites fostered geopolitical stability in the region and allowed further economic exchanges to flourish. But greater integration also meant greater mutual dependence. If one economy suffered, the effects of that decline were sure to be felt elsewhere. And the farther this transnational system spread, the more fragile it became. Many of the new markets depended on emerging societies in regions far less stable, where civilization was also new.

## AEGEAN CIVILIZATION: MINOAN CRETE, MYCENAEAN GREECE

Greek poets like Hesiod described a heroic age when great men mingled with gods and powerful kingdoms contended for wealth and glory. For a long time, modern scholars dismissed these stories as fables. Tales of Theseus and the Minotaur, the Trojan War, and the wanderings of Odysseus were regarded as reflecting no historical reality. Greek history was assumed to begin in 776 B.C.E., when the first recorded Olympic Games occurred. Greece in the Bronze Age was considered a primitive backwater that played no significant role in the Mediterranean world or in the later, glorious history of classical Greece.

But in the late nineteenth century, an amateur archaeologist named Heinrich Schliemann became convinced that these myths were really historical accounts. Using the epic poems of Homer as his guide, he found the site of Ilium (Troy) near the coast of northwest Anatolia. He also identified a number of once-powerful citadels on the Greek mainland, including the home of the legendary king Agamemnon at Mycenae *(MY-seh-nee)*. Soon afterward, the British archeoleogist Sir Arthur Evans took credit for discovering the remains of a great palace at Knossos on the island of Crete that predated any of the major citadels on the Greek mainland. He dubbed this magnificent culture—which no modern person had known to exist—"Minoan," after King Minos, the powerful ruler whom the ancient Greeks described as dominating the Aegean, and the man for whom the engineer Daedalus had designed the Labyrinth. Although some of their conclusions have proven false, the discoveries of Schliemann and Evans forced scholars to revise, entirely, the history of Western civilizations. It is now clear that Bronze Age Greece—or, as it is often termed, Mycenaean Greece—was an important and integrated part of the Mediterranean world during the second millennium B.C.E.

**MYCENAEAN DEATH MASK, c. 1550–1500 B.C.E.** When the archeologist Heinrich Schliemann discovered this gold funeral mask in a burial shaft at Mycenae, he immediately declared it to be that of Agamemnon. Although it is certainly royal, this mask is too old to have been made for that legendary king, who would have lived several centuries later.

### *The Minoan Thalassocracy*

In the fifth century B.C.E., the Athenian historian Thucydides wrote that King Minos of Crete had ruled a *thalassocracy*, an empire of the sea. We now know that he was correct, that a very wealthy civilization began to flourish on the island of Crete around 2500 B.C.E. Thereafter, for about a millennium, the Minoans controlled shipping around the central Mediterranean and the Aegean, and may have exacted tribute from many smaller islands. At its height between 1900 and 1500 B.C.E., Minoan civilization was the contemporary of Egypt's Middle Kingdom and the Hittite Old Kingdom. And unlike them, it was virtually unassailable by outside forces, protected by the surrounding sea. Astonishingly, neither the great palace at Knossos nor the other palaces on the island were fortified.

Thanks to its strategic position, Crete was not only a safe haven but also a nexus of vibrant economic exchange. In this it did resemble its counterparts in the Near East because it acted as a magnet for the collection of resources which were then redistributed by its rulers and their emissaries. Knossos was also a production center for textiles, pottery, and metalwork. Minoan merchants traded these

**MINOAN FRESCO, c. 1500 B.C.E.** A stylized representation of bull-leaping, painted into the plaster of a wall at Knossos. ▪ ***Is this likely to represent real practices?*** ▪ ***Why or why not?***

with Egypt, southwest Anatolia, and Cyprus for a range of exotic goods. Through Cyprus, the Minoans had further contacts with the Levantine coast of modern-day Lebanon and Syria. Artistic influences also traveled along these routes; among much else, Minoan-style paintings from this period appear regularly in the Nile Delta and the Levant.

Traces of the bright colors and graceful lines of these paintings are still evident on the ruined walls of the palace at Knossos. Endowed with indoor plumbing, among other luxuries, it covered several acres and comprised hundreds of rooms joined by an intricate network of winding hallways that surely inspired the famous story of the Labyrinth, where the terrible Minotaur lurked in the center. The Minoans probably worshiped a god in the form of a bull or bull-man, and they appear to have devised an elaborate ritual sport known as bull-leaping, similar to bull-fighting but involving an element of athletic dance. There is some evidence that they practiced human sacrifice (possibly facilitated by the dangers of bull-dancing) as a religious rite.

Despite all these fascinating remains, Minoan culture remains mysterious because its language has yet to be decoded. Its script is called Linear A, to distinguish it from Linear B, used in Mycenaen Greece, a script that *has* been deciphered: in the early 1950s, the Englishmen Michael Ventris and John Chadwick joined their linguistic skills to expertise gained during the Second World War, when many classically trained scholars were employed in cracking enemy codes. Although Linear A and Linear B represent different languages, the formal relationship between them reflects the fact that Minoan commercial activity engaged the mainland of Greece. The presence of a wide variety of Minoan objects on the Greek mainland corroborates this.

Yet the dynamics of the relationship between Minoans and Mycenaeans remains debatable. Before 1600 B.C.E., the Minoans were clearly much more sophisticated and may have dominated their Greek neighbors. One story told of Theseus describes how the hero was sent to Crete as a hostage, intending to free Athens from the heavy tribute imposed by King Minos. Given what we have already learned about the close relationship between myth and history, it is probable that this story preserves ancient memory, just as the story of Daedalus is an attempt to explain the technological marvels of the palace at Knossos.

## Mycenaean Greece

When Linear B was deciphered, the texts written in this script forced scholars to reconsider the history of ancient Greece, proving that it stretched well back into the Bronze Age. Since then, new research shows that the Indo-

**LINEAR B TABLET FROM KNOSSOS.** Unlike cuneiform, whose characters are formed using the wedge-shaped tip of a reed, the scripts of Linear A and B used a sharp stylus that incised fine lines in clay or soft stone.

Europeans whose language became Greek entered the region in several waves after the turn of the second millennium, dominating and displacing the indigenous inhabitants. By 1500 B.C.E., huge citadels dotted the Greek landscape, ruled by warriors whose epitaphs boast of their martial prowess and who were buried with their weapons. The power of these rulers was based on their leadership and their ability to reward followers with plunder. The most successful of them gained control of strategic sites from which they could exploit major trade routes, engaging in both trade and piracy. (The line between the two has always been fine.)

Over time, and perhaps under the influence of Minoan culture, the Mycenaean citadels developed into much more complex societies. They served as both centers of government and warehouses for the storage and redistribution of goods and plunder. By the thirteenth century B.C.E., some rulers had carved out territorial kingdoms with as many as 100,000 inhabitants, dwarfing the city-states of the later classical age; Hesiod imagined their citadels to have been built by giants. Indeed, these palace centers were adapted from Near Eastern models and their massive size was not ideally suited to the Greek landscape. In war also, Mycenaean imitation of Near Eastern examples had its limits. For example, Mycenaean kings cherished the chariots used by their contemporaries on the plains of Anatolia, yet such chariots were highly impractical on rocky terrain.

Despite these and other differences from their Mediterranean neighbors, the Mycenaean Greeks played an important role in Bronze Age networks. By about 1400 B.C.E., they had subjugated Crete, taking over Knossos and using it as a Mycenaean center. When the pharaoh Amenhotep III mentions a place called "Keftiu" in his correspondence, he is probably negotiating with Crete's Mycenaean conquerors. In western Anatolia, not far from fabled Troy, at least one Mycenaean king exercised enough influence for a Hittite ruler to address him as "my brother." This evidence suggests that the Mycenaeans earned prestige as warriors and mercenaries, just as the Greeks' heroic poems attest.

The basic political and commercial unit of the Mycenaean world—a powerful king and war leader, a warrior aristocracy, a palace bureaucracy, a complex economy, large territorial kingdoms—differs markedly from the Greek city-state of the classical age (Chapter 3). However, we can trace some features of this later civilization back to the Mycenaeans, including the Greek language. Linear B tablets speak of a social group with considerable economic

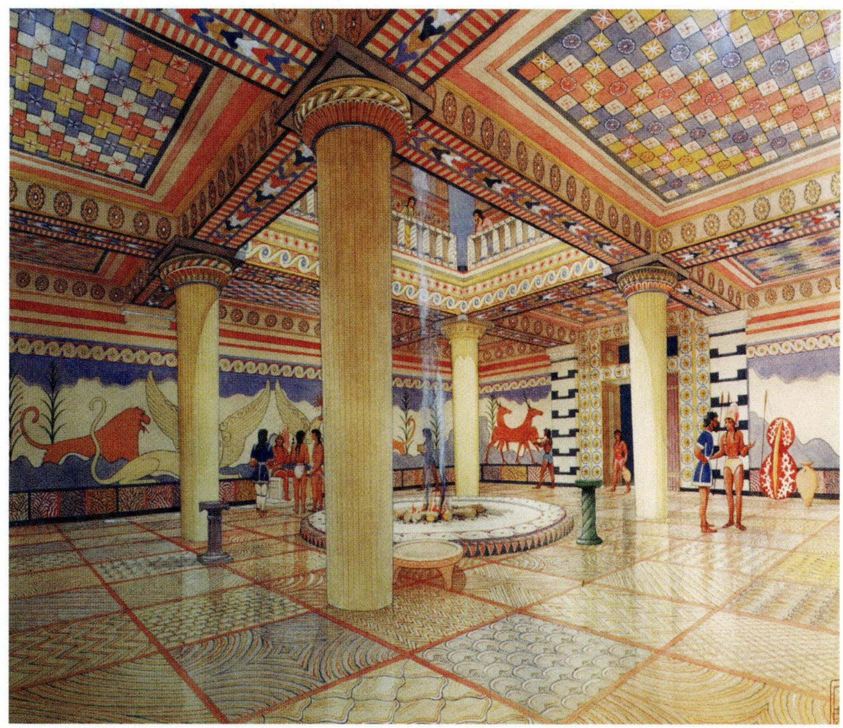

**AN ARTIST'S RECONSTRUCTION OF THE GREAT HALL AT PYLOS.** Located on the western coast of the Greek Peloponnesus, Pylos was excavated in 1952 by the archeologist Carl Blegen and his team. The principal feature of its Bronze Age palace was a large, brightly painted hall with a central hearth.

**MYCENAEAN GREECE.** ▪ ***What stands out about the geographical landscape of Greece on the map?*** ▪ ***Why was Mycenaean culture able to spread so widely?*** ▪ ***How might this dry, mountainous country surrounded by the sea determine the nature of Greek civilization and economic interests?***

and political rights, the *damos*; this may be the precursor of the *demos*, the urban population that sought political empowerment in many Greek cities. The tablets also preserve the names of several gods familiar from the later period, such as Zeus, Poseidon, and Dionysos. Perhaps most important, the later Greeks believed themselves to be descended from these legendary forebears, whom they credited with superhuman achievements. Although later Greeks knew little about these Mycenaean ancestors in fact, the impact of what they imagined about them was considerable.

## The Sea Peoples and the End of the Bronze Age

The civilization of Mycenaean Greece seems to have collapsed around the end of the thirteenth century B.C.E. What triggered this cannot be determined with any certainty: drought, famine, disease, and social unrest have all been posited. But the consequences of the collapse are clear. Because Mycenaean Greece was an integrated part of a transnational network, the effects of its demise were felt

# Analyzing Primary Sources

## The Diplomacy of the Mycenaeans and the Hittites

*Around 1260 B.C.E., the powerful Hittite king Hattusilis III sent the following letter to a "King of Ahhiyawa," identifiable as a leader of the Mycenaean Greeks, who often called themselves Akhaiwoi, Achaeans. This fascinating document exemplifies the tangle of close ties that bound powerful men together within the transnational system of the Late Bronze Age, as well as the problems and misunderstandings that could arise from the misbehavior of men under their command. The events referenced here all occur in western Anatolia (Turkey), a region controlled partly by the Hittites and partly by the Greeks, the same region in which Troy (Ilium) was located.* *(See the map on page 50.)*

I have to complain of the insolent and treacherous conduct of one Tawagalawas. We came into contact in the land of Lycia, and he offered to become a vassal of the Hittite Empire. I agreed, and sent an officer of most exalted rank to conduct him to my presence. He had the audacity to complain that the officer's rank was not exalted enough; he insulted my ambassador in public, and demanded that he be declared vassal-king there and then, without the formality of an interview. Very well: I order him, if he desires to become a vassal of mine, to make sure that no troops of his are found in Iyalanda when I arrive there. And what do I find when I arrive in Iyalanda?—the troops of Tawagalawas, fighting on the side of my enemies. I defeat them, take many prisoners . . . scrupulously leaving the fortress of Atriya intact out of respect for my treaty with you. Now a Hittite subject, Piyamaradus by name, steals my 7,000 prisoners, and makes off to your city of Miletus. I command him to return to me: he disobeys. I write to you: you send a surly message unaccompanied by gift or greeting, to say that you have ordered your representative in Miletus, a certain Atpas, to deliver up Piyamaradus. Nothing happens, so I go fetch him. I enter your city of Miletus, for I have something to say to Piyamaradus, and it would be well that your subjects there should hear me say it. But my visit is not a success. I ask for Tawagalawas: he is not at home. I should like to see Piyamaradus: he has gone to sea. You refer me to your representative Atpas: I find that both he and his brother are married to daughters of Piyamaradus; they are not likely to give me satisfaction or to give you an unbiased account of these transactions. . . . Are you aware, and is it with your blessing, that Piyamaradus is going round saying that he intends to leave his wife and family, and incidentally my 7,000 prisoners, under your protection while he makes continual inroads on my dominion? . . . Do not let him use Achaea [in Greece] as a base for operations against me. You and I are friends. There has been no quarrel between us since we came to terms in the matter of Ilios [the territory of Troy]: the trouble there was my fault, and I promise it will not happen again. As for my military occupation of Miletus, please regard it as a friendly visit. . . . [As for the problems between us], I suggest that the fault may not lie with ourselves but with our messengers; let us bring them to trial, cut off their heads, mutilate their bodies, and live henceforth in perfect friendship.

Source: Adapted from Denys Page, *History and the Homeric Iliad* (Berkeley, CA: 1959), pp. 11–12.

### Questions for Analysis

1. Reconstruct the relationship between Hattusilis III and the Achaean king, based on the references to people and places in this letter. What picture emerges of their interactions, and of the connections between the Hittite Empire and Mycenaean Greece?
2. Why is Hattusilis so concerned about the disrespect shown to him by the Achaeans? Reading between the lines, what do you think he wanted to accomplish by sending this letter?
3. Based on this letter, what you can you deduce about the standards of behavior expected of civilized participants in the transnational system of the Late Bronze Age? Within this code of conduct, what sanctions or penalties could be imposed on individuals or their nations?

throughout the Near East. Thereafter, a wave of devastation swept from north to south, caused by a group of people so thoroughly destructive that they obliterated everything in their path. We might know nothing at all about them were it not for a narrow victory by the pharaoh Ramses III around 1176 B.C.E.

In the *stele* set up to commemorate his triumph near the modern city of Luxor on Egypt's West Bank, Ramses III referred to these invaders as the "Sea Peoples" and named several groups as part of a coalition. Some were familiar to the Egyptians, who had employed them as mercenaries. From Ramses' description of their battle gear, it seems that many were from the Aegean. Most notable were the Philistines who, after their defeat, withdrew to populate the coast of the region named after them: Palestine.

Because the Sea Peoples' arc of annihilation started in the north, it may have been one of the factors contributing to the collapse of Mycenaean Greece. Disruption of northern commercial networks would have devastated the Mycenaean kingdoms, which could not support their enormous populations without trade. Suddenly faced with an apocalyptic combination of overpopulation, famine, and violence, bands of desperate refugees would have fled the Aegean basin. Meanwhile, the damage to commerce devastated the economy of the Hittites, whose ancient kingdom rapidly disintegrated. Along the Mediterranean coast we find other clues. The king of Ugarit wrote a letter to a "brother" king on the island of Cyprus, begging for immediate aid because he had sent all his own warriors to help the Hittites. Poignantly, however, we have his letter only because the clay tablet on which it was written baked hard in the fire that destroyed his palace. The letter was never sent.

In the end, the Sea Peoples destroyed the civilizations that had flourished in the Near East and Mediterranean for over two thousand years. The devastation was not total; not all cities disappeared, and trade did not cease entirely. But the Hittite Empire was gone, leaving behind it many weak, short-lived principalities. The great cosmopolitan cities of the eastern Mediterranean lay in ruins, and new groups—sometimes contingents of Sea Peoples like the Philistines—populated the coast. The citadels of Mycenaean Greece were depopulated by as much as 90 percent over the next century, and Greece entered into a period of cultural and economic isolation that would last for 250 years.

The victorious Egyptians survived, of course, but with their major trading partners diminished or dead, their civilization suffered. The Assyrians, the original architects of the networks that had undergirded the transnational system, had to fight for their very existence. In Babylon, the peaceful and prosperous rule of the Kassites withered. In the vacuum left behind, new political configurations took shape and a new metallurgical technology began to supplant the use of bronze. Out of the ashes arose the culture of the Iron Age.

## THE STATES OF THE EARLY IRON AGE

With the destruction of transnational networks, the geopolitical map of the Near East changed significantly. In Anatolia, a patchwork of small kingdoms grew up within the territories once controlled by the Hittites. Similar developments took place in the Levant—the eastern Mediterranean coastline that today comprises Israel, Lebanon, and parts of Syria. For centuries, this region had been controlled either by the Egyptians or the Hittites. With the collapse of these empires, new states began to emerge there, too. They were small, but they had a huge impact on the history of Western civilizations.

### *The Phoenicians*

The most intrepid colonists of this period were a people whom the Greeks called Phoenicians. They are also known as Canaanites, and were speakers of a Semitic language closely related to Hebrew, Amorite, and Ugaritic. Each Phoenician city had its own hereditary royal government, and every Phoenician's first loyalty was to his or her own city. In the Phoenicians' overseas colonies, however, a new type of political system emerged in which power was shared among a handful of elite families. This aristocratic form of government would become a model for many other Western societies, including those of Greece and Rome.

During the Late Bronze Age, most Phoenician cities had been controlled by Egypt. But the erosion of Egyptian imperial power after 1200 B.C.E. gave these cities the opportunity to forge a new independence and to capitalize on their commercial advantages. One Phoenician city, Gubla, was a clearing house for papyrus, the highly prized Egyptian writing material. This explains why the Greek name for this city, Byblos, became the basis for the Greek word *biblion*, meaning "book." (The Bible is so called from the plural *biblia*, "the books.") Another valuable commodity came to be the name by which the Phoenicians themselves were known: a rare purple dye derived from the shells of snails culled from seabeds off the Levantine coast. So as far as the Greeks were concerned, those who suppled this rich dye were *phoinikeoi*, "purple people." Phoenician textiles commanded a high price everywhere. So did timber from the Levant, especially cedar, and Canaanite glass. The Phoenicians also became expert metalworkers, ivory carvers, and shipbuilders.

## Phoenician Colonies and Cultural Influence

Phoenicians became famous as merchants and seafarers, but they were also aggressive colonists. By the end of the tenth century B.C.E., they had planted settlements from one end of the Mediterranean to the other and their merchants had begun to venture out into the Atlantic Ocean. We have good evidence that they traveled as far as Cornwall (southwest Britain) during this period. Indeed, the Greek historian Herodotus later claimed that Phoenician merchant-explorers even circumnavigated Africa. At the end of the ninth century B.C.E., Phoenicians from the city of Tyre established Carthage in modern-day Tunisia (North Africa). Carthage would ultimately become the preeminent power in the western Mediterranean, bringing it into conflict with Rome centuries later (see Chapter 5).

The widespread colonial and mercantile efforts of the Phoenicians meant that they influenced cultures across the Mediterranean. Among their early overseas trading partners were the Greeks, and the Phoenicians may have played an important role in reintroducing urban life to Greece after the collapse of the Mycenaean citadels. They also brought with them a number of Near Eastern artistic and literary influences. Without question, however, the most important contribution of the Phoenicians was their alphabet.

As we noted earlier, a thirty-character alphabet had evolved at Ugarit by the end of the Bronze Age. Around 1100 B.C.E., the Phoenicians refined this writing system to twenty-two characters. This simpler system further facilitated trade and accounting, and the Phoenicians may have wanted to encourage similar practices among their partners, to safeguard their own interests. The Greeks certainly remained aware of their debt to the Phoenicians: their

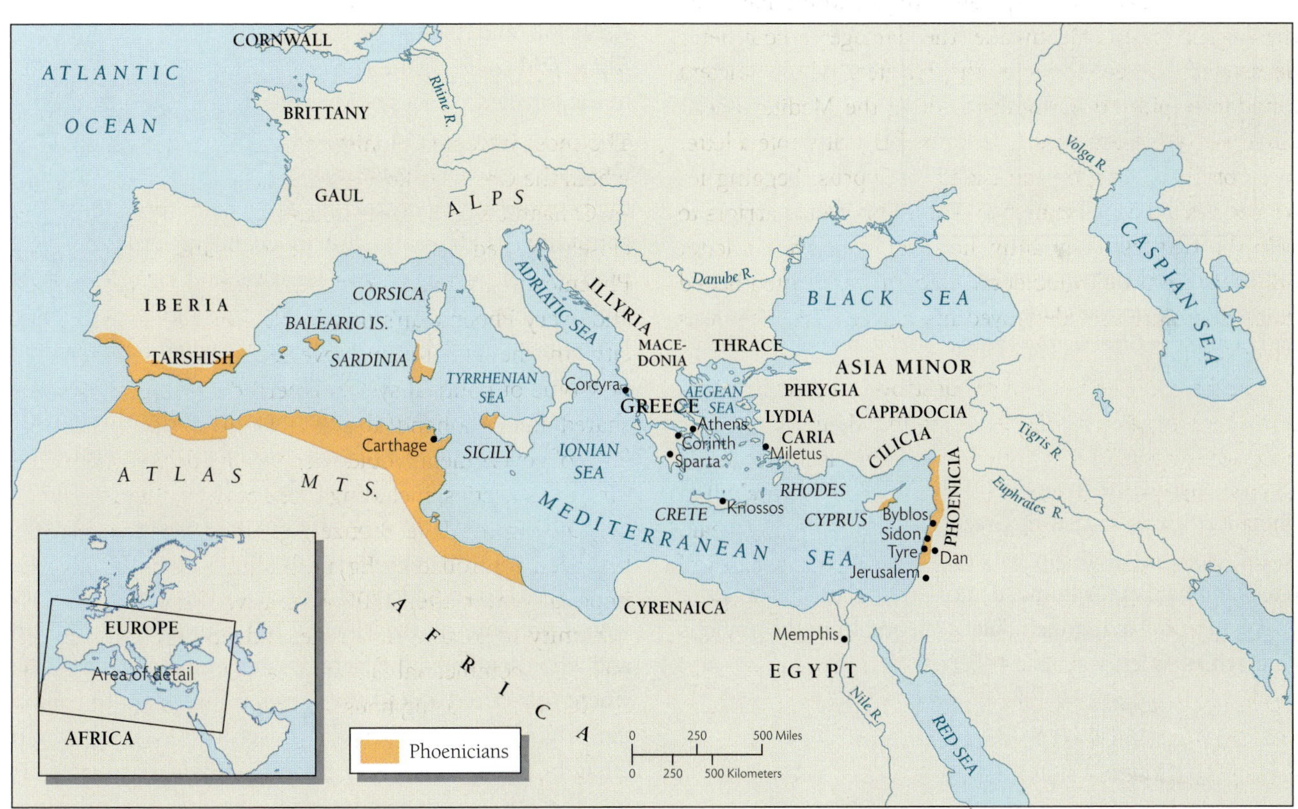


**PHOENICIAN COLONIZATION.** Compare this map to the more detailed one of Palestine on page 58. ▪ ***What part of the Mediterranean serves as the homeland for the Phoenician city-states, and where did Phoenicians establish colonies?*** ▪ ***Why would overseas colonization be of such crucial importance to Phoenician city-states?*** ▪ ***What does their westward colonization imply about the Phoenicians' aims and about the different opportunities available in the West as compared with the East?***

| Phoenician | Hebrew | Classical Greek | Modern Alphabetic |
|---|---|---|---|
| 𐤀 | א | A | A |
| 𐤁 | ב | B | B |
| 𐤂 | ג | Γ | G |
| 𐤃 | ד | Δ | D |
| 𐤄 | ה | E | E |
| 𐤅 | ו | Y | V |
| 𐤆 | ז | Z | Z |
| 𐤇 | ח | H | H |
| 𐤈 | ט | Θ | T |
| 𐤉 | י | I | Y |
| 𐤊 | כ | K | K |
| 𐤋 | ל | Λ | L |
| 𐤌 | מ | M | M |
| 𐤍 | נ | N | N |
| 𐤎 | ס | Ξ | S |
| 𐤏 | ע | O | O |
| 𐤐 | פ | Π | P |
| 𐤑 | צ | | TZ |
| 𐤒 | ק | | Q |
| 𐤓 | ר | P | R |
| 𐤔 | ש | Σ | S |
| 𐤕 | ת | T | T |

**THE EVOLUTION OF THE ALPHABET.** This table shows how the shapes of letters changed as the Phoenician alphabet was adapted by the Hebrews, the Greeks, and eventually the Romans (from whom our modern alphabet derives).

legends ascribe the invention of the alphabet to Cadmus, a Phoenician who settled in Greece. Their debt is also clear in the close relationship between the names of letters in Greek (alpha, beta, gamma, delta . . .) and Phoenician letter names (aleph, bayt, gimel, dalet . . .), and from the obvious similarities in letter shapes.

## The Philistines

Southward along the Levantine coast from Phoenicia lay the land of the Philistines, descendants of the Sea Peoples defeated by Ramses III. Their bad reputation is the result of their dominance over their pastoral neighbors, the herdsmen known as the Hebrews, who used writing as an effective weapon: the Philistines are the great villains of the Hebrew scriptures, and the word *philistine* has accordingly come to mean a boorish, uncultured person. Unfortunately, the Philistines do not appear to have made use of the same powerful technology to record their own outlook on the world, and almost everything we know about them comes from the work of archeologists, or has to be sifted through the bad press of their detractors.

The Philistines occupied a unique position in the Levant and retained a separate identity for several generations; each new archaeological discovery roots this identity more firmly in their Aegean past. We know little about their language, but their material culture, behavior, and organization all exhibit close affinities with Mycenaean Greece. For example, the Philistines introduced grapevines and olive trees to the Levant from the Aegean basin. With the profits from these industries, they created powerful armies that dominated the region in the twelfth and eleventh centuries B.C.E. They also established a monopoly over metal smithing, making it virtually impossible for their enemies to forge competitive weaponry.

Philistine power was based on five great strongholds, the so-called Pentapolis (Greek for "five cities"): Gaza, Ashkelon, and Ashdod on the coast, and the inland cities of Ekron and Gath. Again, these citadels are strikingly similar to the fortified palaces of Mycenaean civilization, and they appear to have served many of the same functions. From these strongholds, the Philistines dominated the surrounding countryside by organizing agricultural production and controlling trade routes. An independent lord ruled over each citadel, and no doubt tensions and rivalries existed among them. But much like the heroes of Greek epic, the Philistines could set aside differences when facing a common enemy.

Because we see the Philistines primarily through the eyes of their Hebrew enemies, we must be careful about drawing conclusions about them from the stories of Goliath's brutality or Delilah's sexual treachery, to name the two most infamous Philistines of the Hebrew sciptures. Yet the Hebrews had good reason to fear the Philistines, whose pressure on the Hebrew hill country was constant and who threatened the Hebrews' holy sanctuary at Shiloh, where the sacred Ark of the Covenant was said to contain the original tablets of the law given to Moses on Mount Sinai. In Hebrew tradition, the tribes of Israel had once carried the Ark before them into battle against the Philistines, only to lose it in the fray and to witness thereafter the destruction of Shiloh. The Philistines then established garrisons throughout the land of the Hebrews and exacted tribute, denied them access to weapons, and engaged in the typical abuses of an occupying people.

## *The Hebrews and Their Scriptures*

The central feature of Hebrew culture, their conception of and relationship to their god, will be discussed at greater length toward the end of this chapter. In this section, we focus our attention on the development of Hebrew society in the Iron Age Levant—while acknowledging that religion is always related to politics, as well as to economic conditions and the concerns of everyday life. Indeed the Hebrews, like all ancient peoples and many people today, could not have distinguished among these phenomena.

In reconstructing the early history of the Hebrews, we are indebted to an unusual textual source: a series of scriptures (literally "writings") that comprise mythology, laws and ritual practices, genealogical records, books of prophecy, proverbs, poetry, and royal chronicles. These are collectively known as the Hebrew Bible (from the Greek word "books") or (among Christians) as the Old Testament. They are full of information about cultural practices and key events, and they are also a guide to the intellectual unfolding of the most important religious tradition of the West. They do not, however, constitute a unified history. The books of the Bible were assembled over many centuries, mostly by unknown authors, copyists, and editors. Like other sources, they have to be treated as artifacts produced by particular historical circumstances, which also governed the way that certain texts were preserved and put together.

The first five books of the Hebrew Bible are traditionally attributed to the Hebrew leader Moses, but most of the materials in these books were borrowed from other Near Eastern cultures, including the stories of creation and the flood, which parallel those of Sumer (as we saw in Chapter 1). The story of Moses' childhood draws on a legend told about the Akkadian king Sargon the Great. The laws and rituals of the patriarchs can be found in other traditions, too. Meanwhile, the story of the exodus from Egypt is fraught with problems. Although the later Book of Joshua claims that the Hebrews who returned from Egypt conquered and expelled the native Canaanites, archaeological and linguistic evidence suggests that the Hebrews were essentially Canaanites themselves. They may have merged with scattered refugees from Egypt in the aftermath of the Sea Peoples' invasions, but for the most part they had been continuously resident in Canaan for centuries. In other words, the first five books of the Bible constitute a retrospective history whose purpose was to justify Hebrew traditions and claims to power.

Among the other writings included in the Hebrew Bible are a group of texts which record events of the more recent past, those of the period we are considering now. These historical books are more straightforwardly verifiable, even if many details are difficult to confirm. According to the Book of Judges, the Hebrews were wandering herdsmen who had just begun to establish permanent settlements around the time of the Philistines' arrival in the Levant. They had organized themselves into twelve tribes—extended clan units whose families owed one another mutual aid and protection in times of war, but who frequently fought over cattle and grazing rights. Each tribe was ruled by a patriarch known as a judge, who exercised the typical functions of authority in a clan-based society: war leadership, high priesthood, and dispute settlement. By the middle of the twelfth century B.C.E., these tribes occupied two major territories, with those settled in the south calling themselves the tribes of Judah, and those in the north the tribes of Israel.

## *The Struggle for Hebrew Identity*

The Hebrew tribes of this period had few occasions to work together as a group and little experience of organized activity. This made them highly vulnerable, especially when the Philistines conquered the Levantine coast, around 1050 B.C.E. Faced with the threat of extinction, the Hebrews put up desperate resistance from their bases in the hilly interior. To counter the Philistine threat effectively, however, they needed a leader. Accordingly, around 1025 B.C.E., an influential tribal judge called Samuel selected a king to lead the Hebrew resistance against the Philistines. His name was Saul. However, Saul proved to be an ineffective warleader. Although he blocked Philistine penetration into the hill country, he could not oust the Philistines from the valleys or coastal plains. So Samuel withdrew his support from Saul and threw it behind a young warrior in Saul's entourage, Saul's son-in-law David. Waging his own independent military campaigns, David achieved one triumph after another over the Philistines. By contrast, the armies of Saul met frequent reverses—that is, according to the chroniclers responsible for the historical books of the Bible, who wrote their accounts under David's patronage.

These same books reveal that David was not initially motivated by patriotism. He was a man on the make; and when Saul finally drove him from his court, he became an outlaw on the fringes of Hebrew society and then a mercenary in Philistine service. It was as a Philistine mercenary that David fought against Saul in the climactic battle in which Saul was killed. Soon thereafter, David himself became king, first over the tribes of Judah, his home territory, and later over Saul's territory of Israel as well.

# Competing Viewpoints

## *Two Accounts of Saul's Anointing*

*When the charismatic judge Samuel chose Saul as the first king of the Hebrews, he opened a new chapter in the political history of Israel. But Saul's kingship was not a success, and Samuel ultimately turned against him, supporting Saul's rival (and son-in-law), David. These two quite different accounts of Samuel's anointing of Saul reflect the tensions that later arose between them—and were probably written down during the later kingship of David, Saul's challenger and successor. The first account also suggests the ambivalence some Hebrews felt about having a human king at all, doubts which may have been shared by Saul himself.*

### 1 Samuel 8:4–22, 10:20–25

All the elders of Israel gathered together and [said to Samuel]: "You are old and your sons do not follow in your ways; appoint for us, then, a king to govern us, like other nations." But the thing displeased Samuel [who] prayed to the Lord, and the Lord said to Samuel, "Listen to the voice of the people in all that they say to you; for they have not rejected you, but they have rejected me from being king over them. Just as they have done to me, from the day I brought them up out of Egypt to this day, forsaking me and serving other gods, so they are also doing to you. Now then, listen to their voice; only—you shall solemnly warn them, and show them the ways of the king who shall reign over them." So Samuel reported all the words of the Lord to the people who were asking for a king. "These will be the ways of the king who will reign over you: he will take sons and appoint them to his chariots . . . he will take your daughters to be perfumers and cooks and bakers . . . he will take one-tenth of your grain and your vineyards and give it to his officers and courtiers . . . and one-tenth of your flocks, and you shall be his slaves." But the people refused to listen, and Samuel said to the people, "Each of you return to his home."

Then Samuel brought all the tribes of Israel near, and the tribe of Benjamin was chosen by lot. He brought the tribe of Benjamin near, [organized] by its families . . . and Saul the son of Kish was chosen by lot. But when they sought him, he could not be found. So they inquired again of the Lord . . . and the Lord said, "See, he has hidden himself among the baggage." Then they ran and brought him from there. When he took his stand among the people, he was head and shoulders taller than any of them. Samuel said, "You see the one whom the Lord has chosen? There is no one like him among the people." And the people all shouted, "Long live the king!" Samuel told the people the rights and duties of the kingship; and he wrote them in a book and laid it up before the Lord.

## *The Consolidation of the Hebrew Kingdom*

After David's victory around 1000 B.C.E., he strove to strengthen his authority within and beyond his kingdom. He took advantage of the opportunity afforded by Egypt's decline to expand his territory southward, eventually confining the Philistines to an inconsequential strip of coastal land. David also defeated the neighboring Moabites and Ammonites, extending his control to the Dead Sea. By the time of his death in 973 B.C.E., his kingdom stretched from the middle Euphrates in the north to the Gulf of Aqaba in the south, and from the Mediterranean coast eastward into the Syrian deserts. Israel was now a force to be reckoned with, although it owed that status to the temporary weakness of its imperial neighbors, Egypt and Assyria.

## 1 Samuel 9:1–10:1

There was a man of Benjamin whose name was Kish . . . [who] had a son whose name was Saul, a handsome young man . . . he stood head and shoulders above everyone else. Now the donkeys of Kish had strayed. So Kish said to his son Saul, "Take one of the boys with you; go and look for the donkeys." . . . As they were entering [a] town, they saw Samuel coming out toward them on his way up to the shrine. Now the day before Saul came, the Lord revealed to Samuel, "Tomorrow about this time I will send you a man from the land of Benjamin, and you shall anoint him to be ruler over my people Israel. He shall save my people from the hand of the Philistines; for I have seen the suffering of my people, because their outcry has come to me." . . . Saul approached Samuel inside the gate and said, "Tell me please, where is the house of the seer?" Samuel answered Saul, "I am the seer, go up before me to the shrine. . . . As for your donkeys that were lost three days ago, give no further thought to them, for they have been found. And on whom is all Israel's desire fixed, if not on you and your ancestral house?" Saul answered, "I am only a Benjaminite, from the least of the tribes of Israel, and my family is the humblest of all the families of the tribe of Benjamin. Why then have you spoken of me this way?" . . . As they were going down to the outskirts of town, Samuel said to Saul, "Tell the boy to go on before us . . . that I may make known to you the word of God." Samuel took a vial of oil and poured it on [Saul's] head and kissed him; he said: "The Lord has anointed you ruler over his people Israel. You shall reign over the people of the Lord and you will save them from the hand of their enemies all around."

Source: *The New Oxford Annotated Bible* (Oxford: 1994) (slightly adapted, source for both documents).

### *Questions for Analysis*

1. Do these two accounts fit together? How do they differ? Why would both have been preserved in the Book of Samuel?
2. What view of kingship emerges in the first account? What are the attributes of a king, and what is the relationship between the king, his god, and the priest anointing him? What is the role of the people in his selection?
3. The writers of Jewish scripture judged kings by their observance of the law, their zeal in fighting against competing religious cults, and their support of centralized worship at the temple in Jerusalem. How did this form of theocracy in ancient Israel compare to that in Egypt and Mesopotamia?

As David's power and prestige grew, he was able to impose on his subjects a highly unpopular system of taxation and forced labor. His goal was to build a glorious capital at Jerusalem, a Canaanite settlement that he designated as the central city of his realm. It was a shrewd choice. As a newly conquered city, Jerusalem had no previous affiliation with any of Israel's twelve tribes and so stood outside the ancient rivalries that divided them. Geographically too, Jerusalem was a strategic choice, lying between the southern tribes of Judah (David's people) and the northern tribes of Israel. David also took steps to exalt the city as a religious center by making Jerusalem the resting place of the sacred Ark of the Covenant and reorganizing the priesthood of the Hebrew god, Yahweh. By these measures, he sought to forge a new collective identity centered on his own family and its connections to Yahweh. To this end, he also encouraged the writing of histories and prophecies that would affirm this identity and his central role in forging it.

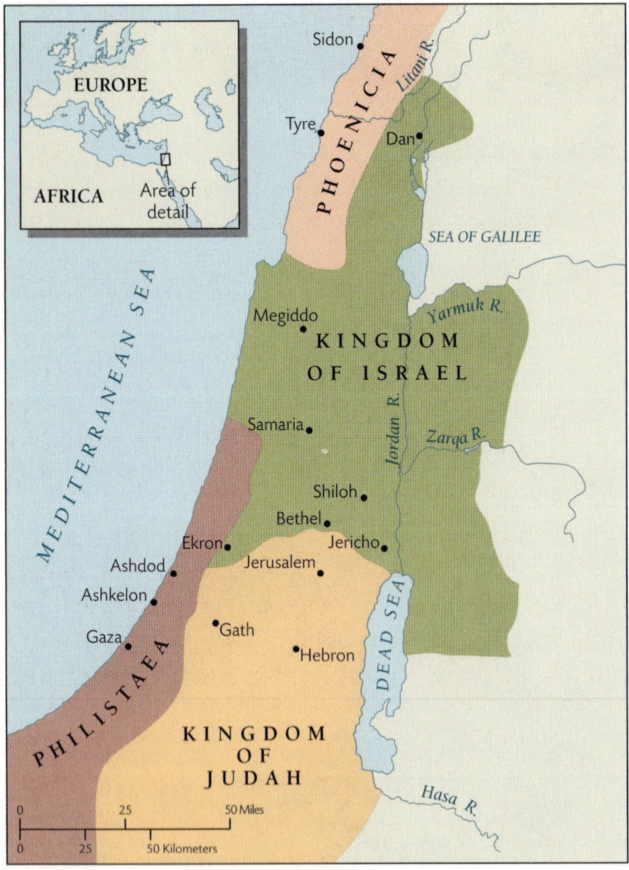


**THE HEBREW KINGDOM, c. 900 B.C.E.** Notice the scale of the map and consider the comparatively small size of the Hebrews' world. ▪ ***What advantages did the Philistines and Phoenicians possess, geographically and otherwise?*** ▪ ***Why did they present such a challenge to the Hebrews?*** ▪ ***What political and religious consequences might have resulted from the division of the kingdom after the death of King Solomon, given the location of Jerusalem?***

### *The Reign of King Solomon (973–937 B.C.E.)*

Continuing his father's policies, but on a much grander scale, David's son Solomon built a great temple complex at Jerusalem to house the Ark. Such visible support of Yahweh's cult was approved by the historians whose works are included in the Bible, and which portray Solomon's reign as a golden age. Despite his proverbial wisdom, however, Solomon was a ruthless and often brutal ruler whose promotion of Yahweh coincided with a program of despotism. Solomon kept an enormous harem of some 300 wives and 700 concubines, many of them drawn from subject or allied peoples. His palace complex—of which the Temple was a part—allowed him to rule in the grand style of ancient Near Eastern potentates. To finance his expensive tastes and programs, Solomon instituted oppressive taxation and imposed customs duties on the lucrative caravan trade that passed through his country. With the help of the Phoenician king of Tyre, Solomon also constructed a commercial fleet whose ships plied the waters of the Red Sea and beyond, trading—among other commodities—the gold and copper mined by Solomon's slaves.

Israel's new wealth was bought at a high price. Solomon maintained a large standing army of unwilling conscripts from his own people, equipped with chariot and cavalry squadrons and powered by horses purchased abroad. To undertake his ambitious building projects, Solomon also required many of his subjects to perform forced labor four months out of every year. This level of oppression was too much for many Israelites, and the north seethed with rebellion against the royal capital. Within a decade or so of Solomon's death, in fact, the fragile monarchy split in two. The dynasty descended from David continued to rule the southern kingdom of Judah with its capital at Jerusalem, but the ten northern tribes banded together as the kingdom of Israel, with their capital at Shechem. Archaeology and other accounts included in the Bible reveal that the cult of Yahweh was not yet dominant in either the north or the south, so major cultural differences also made reunification more difficult. In the meantime, the changing political situation of the Near East made the Hebrew kingdoms increasingly vulnerable.

## THE REVIVAL OF THE ASSYRIAN EMPIRE

As we have already seen, the Assyrians had long played an important role in spreading trade and promoting urban settlements. But like the other great powers of the Near East, their civilization had been devastated by the Sea Peoples. For several centuries afterward they struggled for survival. Then, in the ninth century B.C.E., a brilliant but brutal ruler laid the foundations of what historians call the Neo-Assyrian Empire. Under the leadership of Assurnasirpal II *(ah-sur-NAH-sur-PAHL,* 883–859 B.C.E.), the Assyrians began to conduct aggressive military campaigns against their neighbors on an annual basis. Those whom they defeated either had to pay tribute or face the full onslaught of the Assyrian war machine, which under Assurnasirpal acquired a deserved reputation for savagery.

Despite their military successes, Assurnasirpal and his son, Shalmeneser III (*SHAHL-meh-NEE-zehr,* 853–827

B.C.E), inspired stiff resistance. The northern kingdom of Israel formed an alliance with other small states to halt Assyrian expansion. This coalition ultimately forced Shalmeneser III to settle for smaller victories against the Armenians to his northwest and the Medes to his northeast, until a great revolt within Assyria itself ended his reign. Thereafter, a usurper named Tiglath-Pileser III seized the Assyrian throne in 744 B.C.E. and immediately demanded tribute from various kingdoms that had not paid up for generations. Those who refused fell victim to his armies.

When Tiglath-Pileser III died in 727 B.C.E., many of these recently conquered states rebelled, but Tiglath-Pileser's son, Shalmeneser V, energetically crushed them. When he died in battle, he was quickly replaced by one of his military commanders, who took the name Sargon II (722–705 B.C.E.) and claimed to be the direct successor of Sargon of Akkad, the great king of Sumer and the first great king in Mesopotamian history, nearly 1,500 years earlier (Chapter 1). Like the Hebrews, Sargon and his successors skillfully deployed history as a political tool. Eventually, they extended the frontiers of the Assyrian Empire from western Iran to the shores of the Mediterranean. Briefly, they even subjugated parts of Egypt. Sargon himself put an end to the kingdom of Israel in 722, enslaving and deporting most of the population, and he terrified the southern kingdom of Judah into remaining a loyal and quiet vassal. The ancient kingdom of Elam on the Iranian plateau—a civilization almost as old as Sumer—also fell during this period. By the seventh century B.C.E., Assyria was the unrivaled power of the ancient Near East.

## Neo-Assyrian Government and Administration

The Neo-Assyrian Empire was a military dictatorship, built on the ability of its army to spread terror and oppress both enemies and subjects alike. At its head was a hereditary monarch regarded as the earthly representative

**THE ASSYRIAN EMPIRE, C. 700 B.C.E.** ▪ *What were the territorial boundaries of the Assyrian Empire?* ▪ *Why would the Assyrians concentrate their efforts in the river valleys and along the coast, neglecting the Syrian interior?* ▪ *Notice the location of the Assyrian capitals of Nineveh and Assur; how was their situation in Mesopotamia likely to affect the Assyrians' sense of their own historical identity?* ▪ *Consider the position of Egypt. Why might the Assyrians find it difficult to subjugate Egypt permanently?*

of the Assyrians' patron god, Assur. When his army was not in the field, the king's time was taken up with elaborate sacrifices and rituals to appease the "great god." Divination and the consultation of oracles were central features of this religion, because the Assyrian king, as chief priest, had to be able to discern the will of Assur through the portents of nature.

Supporting the empire's centralized authority was an extensive bureaucracy of governors, high priests, and military commanders—professions by no means mutually exclusive. These administrators formed the highest class in Assyrian society and exercised local authority on behalf of the king. They maintained lines of transport and communication, which were the engines of Assyrian hegemony, and they oversaw construction of an extensive network of roads across the Near East that served these needs for centuries. The Assyrians also deployed a system of spies and messengers to report to the royal court on the activities of subjects and provincial governors.

Provincial governors collected tribute, recruited for the army, and administered the king's law. Not surprising for a people so mindful of historical precedent, the Assyrians modeled their laws on the code of Hammurabi, though many of their penalties were more severe. The Assyrians reserved the harshest punishments for practices deemed detrimental to human reproduction; the penalties for homosexuality and abortion were particularly harsh. Assyrian law was also rigidly patriarchal, which entailed substantial revision of Hammurabi's code: now only husbands had the power of divorce, and they were legally permitted to inflict a variety of penalties on their wives, ranging from corporal punishment to mutilation and death.

## The Assyrian Military-Religious Ethos

The Assyrians' religious, political, and military ideology took shape during the long centuries when they fought for survival, and it then became the foundational ethos for their empire's relentless conquests. Its two fundamental tenets were the waging of holy war and the exaction of tribute through terror.

The Assyrians were convinced that their god demanded the constant expansion of his worship through military conquest. Essentially, the Assyrian army belonged to Assur, and all who did not accept Assur's supremacy were, by that fact alone, enemies of Assur's people. Ritual humiliation of a defeated city's gods was therefore a regular feature of Assyrian conquests. Statues of conquered gods would be carried off to the Assyrian capital, where they would remain as hostages at the court of Assur. Meanwhile, an image of Assur himself—usually represented as a sun disk with the head and shoulders of an archer—would be installed in the defeated city, and the conquered people would be required to worship him. Although conquered peoples did not have to abandon their previous gods altogether, they were made to feel their gods' inferiority. The Assyrians were therefore strict henotheists, meaning that they acknowledged the existence of other gods but believed that one god should be the supreme deity of all peoples.

For the Assyrians, "receiving tribute" initially meant the taking of plunder. Rather than defeating their foes once and imposing formal obligations, the Assyrians raided even their vanquished foes each year. This strategy kept the Assyrian military machine primed for battle, but it did little to inspire loyalty among subject peoples, who often felt that they had nothing to lose through rebellion. Moreover, annual invasions toughened the forces of

**ASSYRIAN ATROCITIES.** Judean captives whose city has fallen to the Assyrian king Sennacherib (704–681 B.C.E.) are shown being impaled on stakes. This triumphal carving comes from the walls of Sennacherib's palace at Nineveh. ▪ ***What would be the purpose of advertising these captives' fates?***

the Assyrians' subjects. To counter them, Assyrian battle tactics became notoriously savage—even by the standards of ancient warfare, which regarded the mutilation of prisoners, systematic rape, and mass deportations as commonplace. Assyrian artwork and inscriptions actually celebrate the butchering and torture of their enemies. Smiling Assyrian archers are shown shooting fleeing enemies in the back while remorseless soldiers impale captives on stakes.

The Assyrian army was not a seasonal army of part-time conscripts or peasants, but rather a massive standing force of more than 100,000 soldiers. Because the Assyrians mastered iron-smelting techniques on a large scale, they could equip their fighting men with high-quality steel weapons that overwhelmed opponents still reliant on bronze. The organization of this army also contributed to its success. At its core were heavily armed and armored shock troops, equipped with a variety of thrusting weapons and bearing tall shields for protection. They were the main force for crushing enemy infantry in the field and for routing the inhabitants of an enemy city once inside. To harass enemy infantry and break up their formations, the Assyrians deployed light skirmishers with slings and javelins, and they combined archery and chariotry as never before. The Assyrians also developed the first true cavalry force in the West, with individual warriors mounted on armored steeds, wielding bows and arrows or heavy lances. They even trained a highly skilled corps of combat engineers to undermine city walls and to build catapults, siege engines, battering rams, and battle towers.

## The Legacy of Assyrian Power

The successors of Sargon II continued Assyrian military policies while devoting great energy to promoting an Assyrian cultural legacy. Sargon's immediate successor Sennacherib (*sen-AH-sher-ib*, 704–681 B.C.E.) rebuilt the ancient Assyrian city of Nineveh, fortifying it with a double wall for a circuit of nine miles. He constructed an enormous palace there, raised on a giant platform decorated with marble, ivory, and exotic woods, and he ordered the construction of a massive irrigation system, including an aqueduct that carried fresh water to the city from thirty miles away. His son rebuilt the conquered city of Babylon along similar lines, and was also a patron of the arts and sciences. His grandson Assurbanipal (*ah-sur-BAHN-en-pahl*, r. 669–627 B.C.E.) was perhaps the greatest of all the Assyrian kings. For a time, he ruled the entire delta region of northern Egypt. He also enacted a series of internal reforms, seeking ways to govern his empire more peacefully.

By Assyrian standards, Assurbanipal was an enlightened ruler, and one to whom all students of history owe a tremendous debt. Like Sargon II before him, he had a strong sense of the rich traditions of Mesopotamian history and laid claim to it. But he did this much more systematically: he ordered the construction of a magnificent library at the great capital of Nineveh, where all the cultural monuments of Mesopotamian literature were to be copied and preserved. This library also served as an archive for the correspondence and official acts of the king. Fortunately,

**ASSURBANIPAL FEASTING WITH HIS WIFE IN A HANGING GARDEN.** Even in this peaceful, domestic scene, the severed head of the king's recently-defeated enemy, the king of Elam, can be seen hanging from the pine tree on the left.

this trove of documentation has survived. Our knowledge of history, not to mention all modern editions of the *Epic of Gilgamesh*, derive from the library at Nineveh.

When Assurbanipal died in 627 B.C.E., the Assyrian Empire appeared to be at its zenith. Its borders were secure, the realm was largely at peace with its neighbors, its kings had adorned their capitals with magnificent artwork, and the hanging gardens of Babylon were already famous: these were artificial slopes whose cascading flowers and trees were fed by irrigation systems that pumped water uphill, an amazing marriage of engineering and horticulture. The end of Assyria is therefore all the more dramatic for its suddenness. Within fifteen years of Assurbanipal's reign, Nineveh lay in ruins. An alliance had formed between the Indo-European Medes of Iran and the Chaldeans, a Semitic people who controlled the southern half of Babylonia. By 605 B.C.E. the Chaldeans had occupied Babylon and destroyed the last remnants of Assyrian power on the upper Euphrates, becoming the predominant imperial power in Mesopotamia and the Levant. In 586 B.C.E. they captured Jerusalem, destroyed the Temple, and deported the population of Judea to Babylon. Meanwhile, the Medes retired to the Iranian Plateau to extend their suzerainty there.

## THE RISE OF THE PERSIANS

The Persian Empire emerged as the successor state to the Assyrians. This was after the region was ruled for a few decades by the Chaldean Empire (612–539 B.C.E.) and the Lydian kingdom. Once the Persians had thrown off the Chaldean yoke, they would in turn construct the largest empire known to humanity up until that time.

### *The Persian Empire of Cyrus the Great*

The Persians emerge from obscurity suddenly, under an extraordinary prince named Cyrus who succeeded to the rule of a single Persian tribe in 559 B.C.E. Shortly thereafter, Cyrus made himself ruler of all the Persians and then, around 549 B.C.E., threw off the lordship of the Medes and began to claim dominion over lands stretching from the Persian Gulf to the Halys River in Asia Minor.

This brought the Persians into close contact with the kingdom of Lydia. The Lydians had attained great prosperity as producers of gold and silver and as intermediaries for overland commerce between Mesopotamia and the Aegean. Most important, they were the first people in the ancient Near East to use precious-metal coinage as a medium of exchange for goods and services. When Cyrus came to power, their king was Croesus *(CREE-suhs)*, a man whose reputation as the possessor of untold riches survives in the expression "rich as Croesus." Distrusting his new neighbor, Croesus decided to launch a preventive strike against the Persians to preserve his own kingdom from conquest. According to the Greek historian Herodotus, he took the precaution of asking the oracle of Apollo at Delphi whether this strategy was a good one, and was told that if he pursued it he would destroy a great nation. The oracle's pronouncement was both ambiguous and true: the nation Croesus destroyed was his own. Cyrus defeated his forces in 546 B.C.E.

Cyrus then invaded Mesopotamia in 539 B.C.E., striking so quickly that he took Babylon without a fight. Once he was in Babylon, the entire Chaldean Empire was his, and his imperial policies proved very different from those of his predecessors in that region. Cyrus freed the Hebrews who had been held captive in Babylon since 586 B.C.E. and sent them back to Jerusalem, helping them to rebuild their temple and allowing them to set up a semi-independent vassal state. Cyrus also allowed other conquered peoples considerable self-determination, especially with respect to cultural and religious policies, a marked reversal of Assyrian and Chaldean policies. When Cyrus died in battle in 530 B.C.E., he left behind the largest empire the world had yet seen. Persian expansion continued even after his death when his son conquered Egypt in 525 B.C.E. Two hundred years later, a young Macedonian king, Alexander, would emulate many of his exploits and build an empire sustained by many of the same strategies (see Chapter 4).

**AN EARLY LYDIAN COIN.** Probably struck during the reign of Croesus, this coin was one of many that facilitated long-distance trade by making wealth portable.

## The Consolidation of Persia

Cyrus' son was a warrior king like his father, but after his death he left the Persian Empire a cumbersome and poorly organized collection of rapid conquests. After a short period of civil war, the aristocratic inner circle that had served both Cyrus and his son settled on a collateral member of the royal family as the new king. This was Darius, whose long reign of 35 years (521–486 B.C.E.) consolidated his predecessors' military gains by improving the administration of the Persian state. Darius divided the empire into provinces, each of which was administered by an official called a *satrap*. Although satraps enjoyed extensive powers and considerable political latitude, they owed fixed tributes and absolute loyalty to the central government, as did vassal states such as the technically autonomous Hebrew kingdom.

Adhering to the tolerant policy of Cyrus, Darius allowed the various peoples of the empire to retain most of their local institutions while enforcing a standardized currency and a system of weights and measures. Beyond this, he had little interest in imposing onerous taxes, martial law, or the Persians' own religious practices on subject peoples. After centuries of Assyrian and Chaldean tyranny, the light hand of Persian rule was welcomed throughout the Near East.

Darius was also a great builder. He erected a new royal residence and ceremonial capital which the Greeks called Persepolis ("Persia City"). He ordered a canal dug from the Nile to the Red Sea to facilitate trade with the Egyptian interior, and installed irrigation systems on the Persian plateau and on the fringe of the Syrian desert to increase agricultural production. Darius also expanded the existing Assyrian road system to enhance trade and communications throughout his huge realm. The most famous artery was the Royal Road, stretching 1,600 miles from Susa, near the Persian Gulf, to Sardis (the old Lydian capital) near the Aegean. Government couriers along this road constituted the first postal system, carrying messages and goods in

**THE PERSIAN EMPIRE UNDER DARIUS I, 521–486 B.C.E.** Consider the location of the Persian heartland and the four administrative centers of Persepolis, Susa, Ecbatana, and Sardis. ▪ ***What older kingdoms and empires did the Persion Empire contain?*** ▪ ***Why is the Royal Road especially noted on this map?*** ▪ ***How did Darius I successfully rule such a large and complex empire?***

# Competing Viewpoints

## *Two Perspectives on Imperial Rule*

*These two inscriptions exemplify two very different attitudes toward imperial power and two very different methods of achieving it. The first glorifies the victories of the Assyrian king Esarhaddon in Syria, and is one of the most important records of his reign (681–669 B.C.E.). The second commemorates the taking of Babylon by the Persian king Cyrus the Great (c. 559–530 B.C.E.), whose empire came to encompass and surpass that of the Assyrians.*

### The *Stele* of King Esarhaddon at Senjirli, c. 680 B.C.E.

To Assur, father of the gods, lover of my priesthood, Anu mighty and preeminent, who called me by name, Ba'al, the exalted lord, establisher of my dynasty, Ea, the wise, all-knowing . . . Ishtar, lady of battle and combat, who goes at my side . . . all of them who determine my destiny, who grant to the king, their favorite, power and might . . . the king, the offering of whose sacrifices the great gods love . . . their unsparing weapons they have presented him as a royal gift . . . [he] who has brought all the lands in submission at his feet, who has imposed tribute and tax upon them; conqueror of his foes, destroyer of his enemies, the king, who as to his walk is a storm, and as to his deeds, a raging wolf; . . . the onset of his battle is powerful, he is a consuming flame, a fire that does not sink: son of Sennacherib, king of the universe, king of Assyria, grandson of Sargon, king of the universe, king of Assyria, viceroy of Babylon, king of Sumer and Akkad. . . . I am powerful, I am all-powerful, I am a hero, I am gigantic, I am colossal, I am honored, I am magnified, I am without an equal among all kings, the chosen one of Assur . . . the great lord [who], in order to show to the peoples the immensity of my mighty deeds, made powerful my kingship over the four regions of the world and made my name great.

. . . Of Tirhakah, king of Egypt and Kush, the accursed . . . without cessation I slew multitudes of his men, and him I smote five times with the point of my javelin, with wounds, no recovery. Memphis, his royal city, in half a day . . . I besieged, I captured, I destroyed, I devastated, I burned with fire. . . . The root of Kush I tore up out of Egypt and not one therein escaped to submit to me.

Source: Daniel David Luckenbill, ed., *Ancient Records of Assyria and Babylonia,* Vol. 2 (Chicago: 1926–27), pp. 224–27.

### Inscription Honoring Cyrus, c. 539

He [the god Marduk] scanned and looked (through) all the countries, searching for a righteous ruler who would lead him. (Then) he pronounced the name of Cyrus, king of Anshan [Persia], declared him to be the leader of the world. . . . And he (Cyrus) did always endeavor to treat according to justice the black-headed [people] whom he (Marduk) made him conquer. Marduk, the great lord, a protector of his people/worshipers, beheld with pleasure his good deeds and his upright mind, (and therefore) ordered him to march against his city Babylon. He made him set out on the road to Babylon, going at his side like a real friend. His widespread troops—their number, like the water of a river, could not be established—strolled along, their weapons packed away. Without any battle, he made them enter his town Babylon, sparing Babylon any calamity. He delivered into his hands Nabonidus, the king who did not worship him. All the inhabitants of Babylon as well as of the entire country of Sumer and Akkad, princes and governors (included), bowed to him and kissed his feet, jubilant that he (had received) the kingship, and with shining faces. Happily they greeted him as a master through whose help they had come (again) to life from death (and) had all been spared damage and disaster, and they worshiped his name.

I am Cyrus, king of the world, great king, legitimate king, king of Babylon, king of Sumer and Akkad, king of the four rims (of the earth), son of Cambyses, great king, king of Anshan, grandson of Cyrus, great king, king of Anshan, descendent of Teipes, great king, king of

Anshan, of a family (which) always (exercised) kingship; whose rule Bel and Nebo love, whom they want as king to please their hearts.

When I entered Babylon as a friend and (when) I established the seat of the government in the palace of the ruler under jubilation and rejoicing. . . . My numerous troops walked around Babylon in peace, I did not allow anybody to terrorize (any place) of the (the country of Sumer) and Akkad. I strove for peace in Babylon and in all his (other) sacred cities. . . . I abolished the . . . [yoke] which was against their (social) standing, I brought relief to their dilapidated housing, putting (thus) an end to their (main) complaints. . . . All the kings of the entire world from the Upper to the Lower Sea, those who are seated in throne rooms, (those who) live in other (types of buildings as well as) all the kings of the West living in tents, brought their heavy tributes and kissed my feet in Babylon.

Source: Excerpted from James B. Pritchard, ed. *Ancient Near Eastern Texts Relating to the Old Testament*, 3rd ed. (Princeton, NJ: 1969), pp. 315–16.

### *Questions for Analysis*

1. Both of these inscriptions constitute propaganda, but of different kinds. How do they differ? What audience(s) are they addressing? What function(s) does each inscription serve?
2. Each of these rulers claims to have a close relationship with the divine. How do those relationships differ, and what do those differences reveal about their attitudes to kingship and its sources of power?
3. Both of these kings boast of their royal lineage and their connections to past rulers. How different or similar are these perspectives? What do they reveal about these kings' awareness of history?

relay stages from one post to another. Each post was a day's horseback ride from the next, where a fresh horse and rider would be ready to carry the dispatches brought by the postman before him. An extensive imperial spy network also used this postal system, famed throughout Persia as "the eyes and ears of the king."

Darius was an extraordinarily gifted administrator, but as a military strategist he made an enormous mistake when he attempted to extend Persian hegemony into Greece. Cyrus's conquest of Lydia had made Persia the ruler of some long-established Greek-speaking cities on the western coast of Asia Minor, a region called Ionia. But these cities resisted even the easy terms of Persian rule, desiring instead to model themselves on the self-governing city-states across the Aegean. Consequently, between 499 and 494 B.C.E., the Greeks of Asia waged a war for independence and briefly gained the support of troops from Athens, who joined the Greeks of Ionia in burning the Persian administrative center at Sardis. Darius quelled this uprising, and then decided to send a force to punish Athens and serve notice of Persian dominion over all Greek states. But at the battle of Marathon in 490 B.C.E., the Athenians dealt Darius the only major setback of his reign. And when his son and successor, Xerxes (*ZEHRK-zees*), attempted to avenge this humiliation in 480 B.C.E., a resistance led by both Athens and Sparta forced him to retreat and abandon his plans a year later. (We will discuss these events at greater length in Chapter 3.)

The Persians were thus compelled to recognize that they had reached the limits of their expansion. Thereafter, they concentrated on their Asian possessions and used money and diplomacy to keep the Greeks in check. This was not difficult, because the Greeks' hasty union in the face of Persian hegemony was short-lived, and they were too embroiled in wars with one another to pose any threat to Persia.

The richness of their culture and the general tolerance they exhibited served the Persians well in maintaining their enormous empire. Unlike the Assyrians or Chaldeans, the Persians could count on the loyalty and even the affection of their subjects. In fact, their imperial model—the accommodation of local institutions and practices, consistent administration through a trained bureaucracy, and rapid communications between center and periphery—would be the one adopted by the great and lasting empires of the near and distant future.

## *The Legacy of Zoroastrianism*

Persia's political and cultural achievements were paralleled by a spiritual one, Zoroastrianism. This important religion was one of the three major universal faiths known to the world before Christianity and Islam, along with Buddhism and Judaism (see below). Its founder was Zarathustra, known to the Greeks as Zoroaster, a Persian who probably lived shortly before 600 B.C.E. Zarathustra sought to reform the traditional customs of the Persian tribes by eradicating polytheism, animal sacrifice, and magic. That is, he wanted to redefine religion as an ethical practice common to all, rather than as a set of rituals and superstitions that caused divisions among people.

Zoroastrianism teaches that there is one supreme god in the universe, whom Zarathustra called Ahura-Mazda, "Wise Lord." Ahura-Mazda is the essence of light, truth, and righteousness; there is nothing wrathful or wicked about him, and his goodness extends to everyone, not just to one people or tribe. How, then, can there be evil and suffering in the world? Because, Zarathustra posited, there is a counter deity, Ahriman, treacherous and malignant, who rules the forces of darkness. Yet he also posited that Ahura-Mazda must be vastly stronger than Ahriman. Later teachers and priests of Zoroastrianism, the magi, placed greater emphasis on the dualism of these divine forces; they insisted that Ahura-Mazda and Ahriman are evenly matched, engaged in a desperate and eternal struggle for supremacy. According to them, light will not triumph over darkness until the Last Day, when the forces of Ahura-Mazda vanquish those of Ahriman forever. This vision of the universe would prove enormously influential, informing the developing theologies of Christianity and Islam—not to mention the plots of much modern science fiction, fantasy literature, and film.

The devotion of the Persian imperial dynasty to Zarathustra's teachings made Zoroastrianism important to the conduct of Persian government and helps to explain the tolerance of Persian rule. Unlike the Assyrians, the Chaldeans, or even the Egyptians, the Persian kings saw themselves as presiding over an assemblage of different nations whose customs and beliefs they were prepared to tolerate. Whereas Mesopotamian potentates characteristically called themselves "true king," Persian rulers took the title "king of kings" or "great king," implying that they recognized the legitimacy of other kings who ruled under their canopy. This same spirit is reflected in Persian architecture, which drew freely and creatively on Mesopotamian, Babylonian, Assyrian, Egyptian, and Greek influences, yet nonetheless created a distinctively Persian style.

**A CYLINDRICAL SEAL OF DARIUS THE GREAT (522–486 B.C.E.).** Seals were used in place of signatures to authenticate documents and correspondence. The cylindrical matrix (right) was rolled in soft wax to create an impression. This finely wrought example shows the king in a chariot, hunting lions with a bow. A winged representation of the god Ahura-Mazda rises above the scene.

Unlike other ancient religions, then, Zoroastrianism did not exalt the power of a godlike king or support any particular regime. It was a personal religion, making private, spiritual demands as opposed to public, ritual ones. Its Wise Lord supports neither tribes nor states, but only individuals who serve the cause of truth and justice. These individuals possess free will and can choose to sin or not to sin; they are not compelled by an array of conflicting gods to act in particular ways. Zoroastrianism thus urges its adherents to choose good over evil, to be truthful, to love and help one another to the best of their powers, to aid the poor, and to practice generous hospitality. Those who do so will be rewarded in an afterlife, when the dead are resurrected on Judgment Day and consigned either to a realm of joy or to the flames of despair. In the scriptures of the Zoroastrian faith, known as the Avesta (compiled, like the Bible, over the course of many centuries), the rewards for righteousness are great, but not immediate. They are spiritual, not material.

## THE DEVELOPMENT OF HEBREW MONOTHEISM

Of all the important developments that we have traced in our study of the Iron Age Near East, perhaps none is of greater significance to the civilizations of the West than monotheism: the belief in a single god, the creator and ruler of all things. This development is traditionally associated with the Hebrews, but even the Hebrews were not always monotheists. Those who argued for the exclusive worship of Yahweh were a minority within Hebrew society, albeit a vocal and assertive one. How the Hebrews came to regard Yahweh as the only divine being in the universe, and to root their identity in such an exclusive religious outlook, is a phenomenon that can only be understood within its historical context.

### *From Monolatry to Monotheism*

For those who later advocated the exclusive worship of Yahweh, the early history of the Hebrews was full of embarrassments. Even the Hebrew scriptures reveal their propensity for the worship of many gods. Yahweh himself, in commanding that his people "have no other gods before me," acknowledged the existence of other gods. The older, polytheistic Hebrew religion honored nature spirits such as Azazel and the Canaanite deity El, whose name is an important element in many Hebrew place-names (for example, Bethel) and soon became a synonym for "God." The temple built by Solomon at Jerusalem included altars to Ba'al and his wife Asherah, a fertility goddess. Later Hebrew kings continued such practices, overriding the protests of religious purists devoted to Yahweh.

By the beginning of the first millennium, however, the Hebrews living under the rule of David began to practice monolatry, meaning that they worshiped one god exclusively without denying the existence of others. Although the legendary prophet Moses is often credited as the first promoter of Yahweh's cult, sometime around the middle of the second millennium B.C.E., the ascendancy of Yahweh took place much later under the influence of the Levites, a tribe who claimed unique priestly authority and sought to enhance their own power and prestige by discrediting other gods.

The success of their campaign rested on the Levites' access to writing. The written word was especially potent in the ancient world because the skills necessary for its mastery were rare. In an age of constant threats to Hebrew religious and political sovereignty, the literacy of the Levites thus helped to preserve and promote Yahweh's worship. So did the political supremacy of the House of David, which bolstered its own legitimacy by allying itself with the Levites. The result was a centralized cult situated in the new royal capital of Jerusalem, which linked the political and the religious identity of the Hebrews to the worship of Yahweh as the supreme god.

Nevertheless, the worship of other gods actually increased in the eighth and seventh centuries B.C.E., perhaps in reaction to the austere morality demanded and imposed by the Yahwists. Thus religious figures like Jeremiah (c. 637–587 B.C.E.) railed against "foreign" cults and warned of the disastrous consequences that would arise if Yahweh's people did not remain faithful to him. Moreover, Yahweh remained a somewhat conventional god, even in the eyes of his promoters. He was conceived as possessing a physical body and was often capricious and irascible. Further, he was not omnipotent; his power was largely confined to the territory occupied by the Hebrews.

Some of the Hebrews' most important contributions to subsequent Western religions crystallized by the middle of the eighth century B.C.E. One was their theology of Yahweh's transcendence: the teaching that God is not part of nature but exists outside of it. God can therefore be understood, in purely intellectual or abstract terms, as entirely separate from the operations of the natural world. Complementing this principle was the belief that Yahweh had appointed humans to be the rulers of nature by divine mandate. When Yahweh orders Adam and Eve to "replenish the earth and subdue it, and have dominion over . . . every living thing," his injunction stands in striking contrast to other accounts of creation in which humans are made to serve the gods. Finally, Hebrew religious thought was moving in this period toward the articulation of universal ethics—a universal theory of justice and righteousness. According to the Babylonian flood story, for example, a particularly petulant god destroys humanity because their noise deprives him of sleep. In Genesis, Yahweh sends a flood in punishment for human wickedness but saves Noah and his family because "Noah was a just man."

The Hebrews honored Yahweh during this period by subscribing to certain moral precepts and taboos. The Ten Commandments in the exact form as they now appear in Exodus 20:3–17 may not have existed, but they certainly reflect earlier ethical injunctions against murder, adultery, lying, and greed. In addition, the Hebrews observed an array of ritual practices unusual in the ancient world, such as infant circumcision, adherence to strict dietary laws, and refraining from labor on the seventh day of the week.

**THE GODDESS ASHERAH.** The Canaanite fertility goddess, Asherah, was the wife of the god Ba'al (or his father, El), but she also figures in some inscriptions as the wife of the Hebrew god Yahweh. One Hebrew king even placed an image of her in the temple of Yahweh at Jerusalem. ▪ ***Why would this be viewed as controversial?***

Yet the moral standards imposed by Yahweh on the Hebrew community were not binding when the Hebrews dealt with outsiders. Lending at interest, for example, was not acceptable among Hebrews, but was quite acceptable between a Hebrew and a non-Hebrew. Such distinctions applied also to more serious issues, such as the killing of civilians in battle. When the Hebrews conquered territories in Canaan, they took "all the spoil of the cities, and every man they smote with the sword . . . until they had destroyed them." Far from having any doubts about such a brutal policy, the Hebrews believed that Yahweh had inspired the Canaanites to resist so that the Hebrews could slaughter them: "For it was the Lord's doing to harden their hearts that they should come against Israel in battle, in order that they should be utterly destroyed, and should receive no mercy but be exterminated" (Joshua 11:20).

With the political fragmentation of the Hebrew kingdoms after Solomon's death, important regional distinctions arose within Yahweh's cult. As we noted above, the rulers of the northern kingdom discouraged their citizens from participating in ritual activities at Jerusalem, thereby earning the disapproval of the Jerusalem-based Yahwists who shaped the biblical tradition. The erosion of a cohesive Hebrew identity was further accelerated by the Assyrians, who under Sargon II absorbed the northern kingdom as a province and enslaved nearly 28,000 Hebrews. The southern kingdom of Judah survived, but political collaboration with the Assyrians meant acceptance of the god Assur.

This was the whetstone on which the Yahwist prophets sharpened their demands for an exclusive monotheism that went beyond monolatry. Hebrew prophets were practical political leaders as well as religious figures, and most of them understood that military resistance to the Assyrians was futile. So if the Hebrews were to survive as a people, they had to emphasize the one thing that separated them from everyone else in the known world: the worship of Yahweh and the denial of all other gods. The prophets' insistence that Yahweh alone should be exalted was thus an aggressive reaction to the equally aggressive promotion of Assur by the Assyrians.

The foremost Hebrew prophets of this era were Amos and Hosea, who preached in the kingdom of Israel before it fell to the Assyrians in 722 B.C.E.; Isaiah and Jeremiah, who prophesied in Judah before its fall in 586 B.C.E.; and Ezekiel and the "second Isaiah" (the Book of Isaiah had at least two different authors), who continued to preach "by the waters of Babylon" during the exile there. Despite some differences

**RECONSTRUCTION OF THE ISHTAR GATE.** This is a reconstruction of one of the fifty-foot-high entrance gates built into the walls of Babylon by King Nebuchadnezzar around 575 B.C.E. About half of this reconstruction is original.

in emphasis, these prophets' messages consistently emphasize three core doctrines.

1. Yahweh is the ruler of the universe. He even makes use of peoples other than the Hebrews to accomplish his purposes. The gods of other nations are false gods. There has never been and never will be more than this one god.
2. Yahweh is exclusively a god of righteousness. He wills only the good, and evil in the world comes from humanity, not from him.
3. Because Yahweh is righteous, he demands ethical behavior from his people. Over and above ritual and sacrifice, he requires that his followers "seek justice, relieve the oppressed, protect the fatherless, and plead for the widow."

The prophet Amos summarized these teachings when he expressed Yahweh's resounding warning in the eighth century B.C.E.:

> I hate, I despise your feasts, and I take no delight in your solemn assemblies. Even though you offer me your burnt offerings and cereal offerings, I will not accept them, and the peace offerings of your fatted beasts I will not look upon. Take away from me the noise of your songs; to the melody of your harps I will not listen. But let justice roll down like waters, and righteousness like an ever-flowing stream. (Amos 5:21–24)

## *Judaism Takes Shape*

Through their insistence on monotheism as the cornerstone of Hebrew identity, the Yahwists made it possible for the Hebrews to survive under Assyrian domination. And as the Assyrian threat receded in the late seventh century B.C.E., so the Yahwists triumphed religiously and politically. The king of Judah during the waning years of the Assyrian Empire, Josiah (621–609 B.C.E.), was a committed monotheist whose court employed prominent prophets, including Jeremiah. With Assyrian power crumbling, Josiah found himself in a position to pursue significant reforms. He presided over the redrafting and revision of the "Law of Moses" to bring it into line with current policies, and it was during his reign that the Book of Deuteronomy was "discovered" and hailed as Moses' "Second Law." Deuteronomy is the most stridently monotheistic book of the Hebrew Bible, and it lent weight to this new political program.

But within a generation of King Josiah's death, the Chaldeans under Nebuchadnezzar conquered Jerusalem, destroyed the Temple, and carried thousands of Hebrews off to Babylon in 587/586 B.C.E. This Babylonian Captivity brought many challenges, paramount among them the maintenance of the Hebrews' identity. The leading voices in defining that identity continued to be the patriotic Yahwists, the same people who would later spearhead the return to Palestine after Cyrus captured Babylon and liberated the Hebrews two generations later. Among the Yahwists, the prophet Ezekiel stressed that salvation could be found only through religious purity, which meant ignoring all foreign gods and acknowledging only Yahweh. Kingdoms and states and empires came to nothing in the long run, Ezekiel said. What mattered for those living in exile was the creature God had made in his image—man—and the relationship between God and his creation.

The period of captivity was therefore decisive in forging a universal religion that transcended politics. Just as Yahweh existed outside creation, so the people who worshiped him could exist outside of a Hebrew kingdom. In

Babylon, the worship of Yahweh therefore became something different: it became Judaism, a religion that was not tied to any particular political system or territory, for after 586 B.C.E. there was neither a Hebrew ruling class nor a Hebrew state. Outside of Judah, Judaism flourished. This was an unparalleled achievement in the ancient world: the survival of a religion that had no political power to back it and no holy place to ground it.

After 538 B.C.E., when Cyrus permitted the Hebrews of Babylon to return to their lands and to rebuild the Temple, Jerusalem became once again the central holy place of Hebrew religious life. But the new developments that had fashioned Judaism during captivity would prove lasting, despite the religious conflicts that soon erupted. These conflicts led to ever more specific assertions about the nature of Judaism, and to religious teachings that focused on ethical conduct as an obligation owed by all human beings toward their creator, independent of place or political identity. The observance of ritual requirements and religious taboos would continue, but not as the essence of religious life; rather, they would be symbolic of the special relationship binding Yahweh to the Hebrews. Eventually, the transcendental monotheism that emerged from these historical processes would become common to the worldview of all Western civilizations.

## CONCLUSION

The centuries between 1700 and 500 B.C.E. were an epoch of empires. While the two great powers of the second millennium were New Kingdom Egypt and the Hittite Empire in Anatolia, a host of lesser empires also coalesced during this period, including Minoan Crete, Mycenaean Greece, and the trading empire of the Assyrians. All were sustained by a sophisticated network of trade and diplomacy. But between 1200 and 1000 B.C.E. the devastation wrought by the Sea Peoples brought this integrated civilization to an end. These invasions cleared the way for many new, small states, including those of the Phoenicians, the Philistines, the Hebrews, and the Lydians. Many crucial cultural and economic developments were fostered by these small states, including alphabetic writing, coinage, mercantile colonization, and monotheism. But the dominant states of the Iron Age continued to be the great land empires centered in western Asia: first the Neo-Assyrians, then briefly the Chaldeans, and finally the Persians.

On the surface, it may therefore appear as if nothing essential had changed. But the empires of the early Iron Age were quite different those that had dominated the Near East a thousand years before. These new empires were much

## After You Read This Chapter

Visit StudySpace for quizzes, additional review materials, and multi-media documents. **wwnorton.com/studyspace**

### REVIEWING THE OBJECTIVES

- The settlement of Indo-European peoples in the Near East had marked effects on the older civilizations there. What were some major consequences?
- Egypt's New Kingdom differed profoundly from the Old and Middle Kingdoms that preceded it. Why was this the case?
- The civilizations of the late Bronze Age were bound together by transnational networks. What were the strengths and fragilities of these relationships?
- What kingdoms and empires emerged in the Near East after the devastation caused by the Sea Peoples?
- Monotheism was a significant historical development of the first millennium B.C.E. Why is it so important?

more highly unified. They had capital cities, centrally managed systems of communication, sophisticated administrative structures, and ideologies that justified their aggressive imperialism as a religious obligation imposed on them by a single, all-powerful god. They commanded armies of unprecedented size, and they demanded from their subjects a degree of obedience impossible for any Bronze Age emperor to imagine or enforce. Their rulers declared themselves the chosen instruments of their god's divine will.

At the same time, we can trace the emergence of more personalized religions. Zoroastrian dualism and Hebrew monotheism added an important new emphasis on ethical conduct, and both pioneered the development of authoritative written scriptures that advanced religious teachings. Zoroastrianism, despite its radical re-imagining of the cosmos, proved fully compatible with imperialism and became the driving spiritual force behind the Persian Empire. Judaism, by contrast, was forged in the struggle to resist the imperialism of the Assyrians and Chaldeans. Both systems of belief would exercise enormous influence on future civilizations. In particular, they would provide the models on which Christianity and Islam would ultimately erect their own traditions, just as models of imperial governance forged in this period would become the template for future empires. In Chapter 3, we will look at the ways in which the city-states of ancient Greece both built on and departed from these models.

## PEOPLE, IDEAS, AND EVENTS IN CONTEXT

- How did the Hittite Empire integrate the cultures of **INDO-EUROPEAN PEOPLES** with the older civilizations of this region?
- What do the reigns of **HATSHEPSUT** and **AKHENATEN** tell us about the continuities and limitations of pharaonic power?
- What factors produced the transnational networks of the Late **BRONZE AGE**?
- How did the civilizations of **MINOAN CRETE** and **MYCENAEAN GREECE** differ from one another, and from the neighboring civilizations of the Near East?
- In what ways do the **PHOENICIANS**, the **PHILISTINES**, and the **HEBREWS** exemplify three different approaches to state-building at the beginning of the first millennium B.C.E.?
- What was new about the **NEO-ASSYRIAN EMPIRE**? How do its methods of conquest and its military-religious ethos compare to the **PERSIAN EMPIRE** that followed it?
- How and why did monotheism develop in the Hebrew kingdoms? In what ways might **JUDAISM** have been influenced by **ZOROASTRIANISM**?

## CONSEQUENCES

- In the religions of Akhenaten, the Persians, and the Hebrews we see a rejection of polytheism. What cultural factors may have contributed to this? What would you consider to be the long-term effects of montheism as a motivating force in history?
- What patterns of success or failure appear to be emerging when we consider the empires that flourished in the Iron Age, particularly those of the Assyrians and the Persians? Are similar patterns visible in other periods of history, including our own?

# Before You Read This Chapter

## STORY LINES

- The emergence of democracy was dependent on the historical circumstances of the ancient Greek world, including slavery and the exclusion of women from public life. It therefore differs markedly from the political system(s) described as democratic today.
- The Greeks were united only through a shared language and culture. The lack of a common political structure made it difficult for them to work toward a common goal except when faced with annihilation.
- The Athenians' leadership in the Persian Wars enabled them to dominate the Mediterranean, and also to control our understanding of their role in history.
- The cultural achievements of the fifth century B.C.E. glorified the individual male and his role in the community, and also valorized Athenian imperial ambitions.

## CHRONOLOGY

| | |
|---|---|
| 800–400 B.C.E. | Rise of the polis |
| c. 750 B.C.E. | Homeric epics transcribed |
| 725–650 B.C.E. | Hoplite tactics become standard |
| c. 600 B.C.E | Militarization of Sparta |
| 600–500 B.C.E. | Emergence of the Milesian School (pre-Socratic philosophy) |
| 594 B.C.E. | Solon's reforms in Athens |
| 546 B.C.E. | Cyrus of Persia conquers Lydia and controls the Greek cities of Ionia |
| 510 B.C.E. | Overthrow of the Peisistratid tyrants in Athens |
| 499–494 B.C.E. | Ionian Revolt |
| 490 B.C.E. | Battle of Marathon |
| 480 B.C.E. | Battles of Thermopylae and Salamis |
| 479 B.C.E. | Battle of Plataea |
| 478 B.C.E. | Formation of the Delian League |
| 431 B.C.E. | Peloponnesian War begins |
| 404 B.C.E. | Defeat of Athens by Sparta |
| 399 B.C.E. | Death of Socrates |

# The Civilization of Greece, 1000–400 B.C.E.

## CORE OBJECTIVES

- **DESCRIBE** the factors that led to the emergence of the Greek polis.
- **DEFINE** hoplite warfare and its effects on democracy.
- **EXPLAIN** the key differences among the poleis of Athens, Sparta, and Miletus.
- **IDENTIFY** the ways in which Athenian culture, philosophy, and art reflect democratic ideals.
- **UNDERSTAND** the impact of the Persian and Peloponnesian Wars.

In the fifth century B.C.E., a Greek-speaking subject of the Persian Empire began to write a book. He had been to Egypt and along the African coast, to the Greek colonies of Italy, the cities of Persia, the wilds of Thrace and Macedonia, and all over the Aegean. He had collected stories about peoples and places even farther afield: Ethiopia, India, the Black Sea. We have already met this intrepid traveler, Herodotus (c. 484–c. 425 B.C.E.), who marveled at the pyramids of Giza (Chapter 1) and who told how the king of Lydia lost his power to the Persians (Chapter 2). His reason for compiling this information was timely: he wanted to write a history of recent events. As he put it, "Herodotus of Halicarnassus here sets forth the results of his research, with the aim of preserving the remembrance of what men have done, and of preventing the great and wonderful deeds of both Greeks and barbarians from losing their glory; and in particular to examine the causes that made them fight one another."

Herodotus' fascination with the Persians, Phoenicians, and Egyptians underscores the extent to which all Greek-speakers regarded themselves as different. In fact, they had responded

**THE ACROPOLIS OF ATHENS AND THE PARTHENON.** Many Greek cities were built upon mountain strongholds, but the most famous of these is the Acropolis of Athens. First settled in the Neolithic Period, it was a fortified palace during the Bronze Age—allegedly that of the hero Theseus—and then a precinct sacred to the goddess Athena, for whom the city was named. The Parthenon, its most important surviving structure, was built on the site of an older temple after the Athenian victory over the Persians at Marathon in 490 B.C.E., and then rebuilt after the Persians sacked Athens ten years later. Most of the damage it sustained thereafter occurred during modern wars. ▪ ***Why was this site the focal point of so much activity?*** ▪ ***What do these successive events tell us about the relationship between place and identity in Greece?***

very differently to the Bronze Age collapse. While they struggled to cooperate politically, they were able to unite around a common language and culture, and their shared values were distinct from those of the people they called *barbarians:* peoples whose speech, to Greek ears, sounded like jibberish ("bar-bar-bar"). They cherished individual liberty, participatory government, artistic innovation, scientific investigation, and confidence in the creative powers of the human mind. Although the practical implementation of these ideals would prove problematic—and continues to be so—our own civilization would be unimaginable without the political experiments and cultural achievements of ancient Greece.

## FROM CHAOS TO POLIS

By the end of the twelfth century B.C.E., Mycenaean civilization had vanished. Except at Athens, the great citadels that had crowned the heights of mainland kingdoms were destroyed. But even at Athens the population steadily declined, with severe effects on the economy and on social organization. Settlements shrank in size and moved inland, away from vulnerable coastlines, thus cutting themselves off from trade and communication. Indeed, the use of writing declined to such an extent that the knowledge of Linear B disappeared. Archeological evidence suggests a world in stasis, isolated from the centers of civilization that were reemerging in the Near East.

The material realities of life in this era profoundly shaped the civilization that emerged from it. This civilization would emphasize political equality and modest display, the importance of domestic economy and self-sufficiency: these were the principles that formed the basis of early democracies. At the same time, these values affected Greek attitudes toward the divine, which had similar long-term affects on religion and philosophy. The hardships of daily life, which contrasted sharply with the stories of a heroic and opulent past, made the Greeks suspicious of their gods. They came to rely far more on the power of individual human beings than on divine intervention in human affairs. They also developed an awareness that excessive pride in one's own accomplishments could be dangerous, because such *hubris* attracted the adverse attention of the gods. While the gods favored those who showed initiative and daring, they would punish the *hubris* of those who failed to acknowledge their own limitations.

## Homer and the Heroic Tradition

By the year 1000 B.C.E., the chaotic conditions that had contributed to the isolation of Greece were alleviated by a period of relative peace. The standard of living improved, artisans developed their crafts, and increased contact among individual settlements fostered trade. Greek pottery, in particular, became a sophisticated and sought-after commodity, which Greek merchants could exchange for luxury goods from abroad.

As trade became an increasingly important feature of the new economy, the personal fortunes of those who engaged in trade increased accordingly, leading to a new kind of social stratification based on wealth. The men who controlled that wealth were aware that their status was not founded on warfare or noble birth, as had been the case in the distant past. Instead, they began to justify their preeminence as a reflection of their own superior qualities as "best men" (*aristoi*). Wealth was one sign of this superiority, but it was not sufficient in itself as a claim to aristocracy, which literally means "the rule of the best." Those who aspired to this status were expected to emulate, as far as possible, the heroes of old, whose stories lived in the prodigious memories and agile voices of the singers of tales.

These singers, the guardians of a rich oral history that had never been written down, were part poets in their own right and part *rhapsodes*, "weavers of songs." The most famous of these is Homer, the poet credited with having woven together the mesh of stories that we know as the *Iliad* and the *Odyssey*. These epics, which, like *Gilgamesh*, preserve longstanding traditions, appear to have crystallized around 800 B.C.E. This was about the time that Hesiod was working on a series of much shorter lyrics that capture a more contemporary perspective (see Chapter 2). By contrast, the epics ascribed to Homer are vast encyclopedias of lore set at the end of the Bronze Age, the time Hesiod called "the Age of Heroes." These were the days when Agamemnon had ruled in Mycenae and launched a vast expedition to conquer Troy, where the prince Paris had taken Helen, the ravishing wife of Agemernnon's brother, Menalaus; it was the age of Achilles and his Trojan rival, Hector; it was the age of Odysseus.

But these stories were not fixed in that time. Over centuries of retelling, the social and political relationships portrayed in the poems changed to reflect the assumptions and agendas of later ages. As a result, the Homeric epics are of tremendous value to historians. They also offer significant analytical challenges. For although the great events and many of the material objects described in the epics date from the late Bronze Age, the society is that of Homer's contemporaries, half a millennium later. Treating these epics as historical sources, therefore, requires the historian to work like an archeologist, carefully peeling back layers of meaning and sifting through the accumulated dust of generations.

For example, Homer depicts a world in which competition and status are of paramount importance to the warrior elite, just as they were of vital concern to the aristocrats of his own day. Through the exchange of expensive gifts and hospitality, men aspiring to positions of power sought to create strong ties of guest friendship (*xenia, zeh-NEE-ah*) with one another, and thus to construct networks of influence that would support their economic, social, and political ambitions. Indeed, it is almost impossible to overestimate the importance of guest friendship as a sacred institution, something that is well illustrated by the encounter between the Trojan warrior Glaucus and the Greek Diomedes in the *Iliad* (see page 76). It suggests that aristocrats in the Greek world conceived of themselves as having more in common with each other than they did with the local societies they dominated, something that is also reflected in the essential similarity of Trojans and Greeks in the *Iliad* and the lack of perceived differences among various Greek tribes.

However, the practice of guest friendship and the shared sense of a common culture among artistocratic households did not lessen the competition among them that frequently led to violence. (The Trojan War, after all, is supposed to have begun when Paris violated the holy ties of hospitality by seducing the wife of Menalaus while he was a guest of the Spartan king.) It also led to competition over the epic past, as fledgling aristocratic clans vied to claim descent from one or another legendary hero. A hero cult might begin when an important family claimed an impressive Mycenaean tomb as that of their own famous ancestor, someone named in the *Iliad* said to come from that place. They would then develop a pious tradition of practicing dutiful sacrifices and other observances at the tomb. This devotion would extend to their followers and dependents; eventually, an entire community might come to identify itself with the famous local hero. The heroic ideal thus became a deeply ingrained feature of Greek society, as did the stories that the epics preserved and propagated.

# Analyzing Primary Sources

## *Greek Guest Friendship and Heroic Ideals*

*Before the emergence of the Greek poleis, relations among communities depended largely on the personal connections made among leading families of different settlements. Often founded on the exchange of gifts or hospitality, the resulting bonds of guest friendship imposed serious obligations on those involved in such relationships—and on their heirs. Honoring these ties was an important part of the heroic ideal, even among those fighting on opposing sides. In this episode from the* Iliad *(Book VI), the fierce Greek warrior Diomedes encounters Glaucus of Lykia, fighting for Troy, on the field of battle.*

hen Glaucus, son of Hippolochus,
Met Diomedes in no-man's-land.
Both were eager to fight, but first Tydaeus' son
Made his voice heard above the battle noise:
"And which mortal hero are you? I've never seen you
Out here before on the fields of glory,
And now you're here ahead of everyone,
Ready to face my spear. Pretty bold.
I feel sorry for your parents . . ."
And Glaucus, Hippolochus' son:
"Great son of Tydaeus, why ask me about my lineage? . . .
But if you really want to hear my story,
You're welcome to listen. Many men know it.
Ephyra, in the heart of Argive horse country,
Was home to Sisyphus, the shrewdest man alive,
Sisyphus son of Aeolus. He had a son, Glaucus,
Who was the father of faultless Bellerophon,
A man of grace and courage by the gift of the gods. . . .
*[Here, Glaucus relates the adventures of his grandfather, Bellerophon, and how he came to Lykia and fought many battles for its king.]*
When the king realized that Bellerophon had divine blood,
He kept him there and gave him his daughter,
And half his royal honor. . . .
His wife, the princess, bore him three children,
Isander, Hippolochus, and Laodameia. . . .
His son Isander was slain by Ares,
As he fought against the glorious Solymi,
And his daughter was killed by Artemis
Of the golden reins. But Hippolochus
Bore me, and I am proud he is my father.
He sent me to Troy with strict instructions
To be the best ever, better than all the rest,
And not to bring shame on the race of my fathers. . . .
This, I am proud to say, is my lineage."
Diomedes grinned when he heard all this.
He planted his spear in the bounteous earth
And spoke gently to the Lykian prince:
"We have old ties of hospitality!
My grandfather Oeneus long ago
Entertained Bellerophon in his halls
For twenty days, and they gave each other
Gifts of friendship. Oeneus gave
A belt bright with scarlet, and Bellerophon
A golden cup, which I left at home.
I don't remember my father Tydeus,
Since I was very small when he left for Thebes
In that great war that killed so many Achaeans.
But that makes me your friend and you my guest
If ever you come to Argos, as you are my friend
And I your guest whenever I travel to Lykia.
So we can't cross spears with each other. . . .
And let's exchange armor, so everyone will know
That we are friends from our fathers' days."
With this, they vaulted from their chariots,
Clasped hands, and pledged their friendship.

Source: Excerpted from the *Iliad* of Homer, trans. Stanley Lombardo (Indianapolis, IN: 1997), pp. 115–18 (vv. 120–241).

### *Questions for Analysis*

1. Why would Glaucus and Diomedes place such emphasis on lineage, and on the stories of their ancestors?
2. What are the attributes of heroism in this passage? Why is respect for the sacred ties of hospitality so important?
3. Why do these two men exchange armor? What might be the symbolic significance of this action? What might be its consequences on the battlefield?

## *The Rise of the Polis*

The ninth century B.C.E. saw dramatic changes throughout the Aegean basin. Contacts between Greeks and Phoenicians intensified. Most crucially, the Greeks adopted the Phoenician alphabet, which replaced the long-disused Linear B of the Myceneans. Indeed, the Greeks improved on this alphabet by assigning some unneeded consonantal symbols to vowels. The Greeks also incorporated many artistic and literary traditions of the Near East, reshaping them to suit their own purposes.

At the same time, the Phoenicians also pointed the way to the revival of a lost art among the Greeks: seafaring. After the devastation of the late Bronze Age, Greek vessels hugged the shoreline and traveled only short distances, and Greeks traders waited at home for the Phoenicians to come to them. By the tenth century, however, Greeks were copying Phoenician designs for merchant vessels, which allowed them to set out on trading ventures of their own. As commercial activity increased, significant numbers of Greeks began to move to the shores of the mainland, to outlying islands, and to the coast of Anatolia.

These economic and cultural developments were accompanied by dramatic growth in the Greek population. Around Athens, the population may have quadrupled during the ninth and early eighth centuries. Such rapid growth placed heavy demands on the resources of Greece, a mountainous country with limited agricultural land. And as smaller villages grew into towns, inhabitants of rival

**THE ATTIC PENINSULA.** This map highlights the numerous poleis that dotted the Attic peninsula. It also shows the surrounding territories of Euboea, Boeotia, and Megaris. Consider the scale of the map and the geography of the peninsula. ▪ ***Where is Athens located?*** ▪ ***How do natural boundaries appear to affect patterns of settlement?*** ▪ ***Why would citizens of the other Attic poleis be regarded as citizens of Athens also, even though they did not live in the city itself?***

communities came into more frequent contact with each other. Soon, some degree of economic, political, and social cooperation among the inhabitants of these towns became necessary. But the values that had developed during centuries of isolation did not make such cooperation easy. Each local community treasured its autonomy and independence, celebrated its own rituals, and honored its own heroes. On what basis could such communities unite?

The Greek solution to this challenge was the *polis*, the root from which we derive the words *politics* and *political*. Yet Greeks considered the polis to be a social collectivity, first and foremost—not a state. For this reason, our sources speak of groups of people—"the Athenians," "the Spartans," or "the Thebans"—rather than places (Athens, Sparta, Thebes). *Poleis* (the plural of *polis*) came to be considered so essential to Greek identity that Aristotle would later define man as "a political animal," someone who participates in the life of the polis and who cannot survive outside it.

In practice, poleis combined both formal institutions and informal structures that could differ widely according to the size of the population and its material and historical circumstances. Most poleis were organized around a social center known as the *agora*, where markets and important meetings were held and where the business of the polis was conducted in the open air. Surrounding the urban settlement, the *asty*, was the *khora*, "land." The khora of a large polis might support several other towns or smaller poleis, as well as numerous villages; for example, all the residents of the entire territory of Attica were considered to be citizens of Athens. Thus the vast majority of Athenian citizens were farmers, who might come to the asty to participate in the affairs of their polis though they did not reside in the urban center.

The Greeks described this early process as the "bringing together of dwellings" (*synoikismos*, synoecism). What spurred synoecism is a matter of debate. Polis formation could come about through the conquest of one settlement by another and/or through the gradual alliance of neighboring communities. Some poleis took shape around fortified hilltops, such as the Athenian acropolis, which suggests that the initial impetus may have been defensive. Other communities may have borrowed a Near Eastern (and particularly Phoenician) practice of orienting the urban center around a temple precinct. In Greece, however, the main temple of a polis was not always located within the city's walls; at Argos, for example, the massive temple to Hera was located several miles away from any sizable settlement. In many Greek cities, moreover, temple building may have been a consequence of polis formation rather than a cause, as elites competed with one another to exalt their poleis and glorify themselves.

## THE CULTURE OF ARCHAIC GREECE, 800–500 B.C.E.

Scholars date the Archaic Period of Greek history to the emergence of the polis and the return of writing, which the Greeks would put to a wide variety of practical, artistic, intellectual, and political uses. The Athenians, in particular, used writing as a way of establishing their cultural dominance over other Greek poleis, controlling the inscription of the Homeric canon, promoting the work of contemporary poets, and fostering the writing of prose histories, which allowed them to pass on a narrative of Greek history in which they themselves played the central role. It is therefore important to bear in mind that much of what we know about this early period derives from the work of later authors who wrote from this Athenian perspective: these include the Ionian-born Herodotus, who spent much of his later life in Athens; the historians Thucydides (c. 460–c. 395 B.C.E.) and Xenophon (430–354); and the philosophers Plato (c. 428–348) and his pupil Aristotle (384–322).

### *Colonization and Panhellenism*

In the eighth and seventh centuries B.C.E., small-scale Greek trading ventures and settlements had developed into a full-fledged colonial enterprise which, like their mercantile efforts, followed the example of the Phoenicians. Many larger poleis competed with one another to establish colonies, with Athens and Corinth being particularly successful in such ventures. Although each colony was an independent foundation, it sustained familial and emotional ties to its mother polis; so even if it had no formal obligations to that city, it was often called upon to support the polis and could become entangled in the political and military affairs of the mainland. At the same time, these Greek colonies were united by their shared language and heritage, which was exported to far-flung reaches of the known world, creating a Panhellenic ("all-Greek") culture that eventually stretched from the Black Sea (parts of modern Romania, Ukraine, and Russia) to the coastline of modern France and Spain.

In fact, Greek colonization permanently altered the cultural geography of the Mediterranean world. The western shores of Anatolia would remain a stronghold of Greek culture for the next two thousand years, until the end of the Middle Ages. At the same time, so many Greeks settled in southern Italy that later Romans called the region Magna Graecia, "Greater Greece"; Greek-speaking enclaves would survive there into the twentieth century of our era. By the

**GREEK COLONIZATION, c. 550 B.C.E.** Compare this map with that on page 53. ▪ ***How do you account for the differences in Greek and Phoenician patterns of colonization?*** ▪ ***Were Greek colonies likely to compete with Phoenician colonies?*** ▪ ***Where were such conflicts most likely to erupt?***

fourth century B.C.E., more Greeks lived in Magna Graecia than in Greece itself.

Motives for colonization varied. Some poleis, such as Corinth, were blessed by their strategic location on the land bridge between Attica and the Peloponnesus (*pel-oh-poh-NEE-suhs*; the large peninsula of mainland Greece), but cursed by the poverty of their land. Trade therefore became the lifeblood of this polis and of the ruling aristocracy who bankrolled the ambitious planting of colonies up the coast of the Adriatic and into Sicily during the eighth century B.C.E. Other poleis, confronted by the pressures of growing populations and political unrest, sponsored new colonies as outlets for undesirable elements or unwanted multitudes. These colonial projects parallel, in many ways, those of modern nation-states.

Colonial expansion intensified Greek contacts with other cultures. Phoenician pottery brought new artistic motifs and mythological figures into Greece, while Egypt profoundly influenced early Greek sculptural representations of the human form (see ***Interpreting Visual Evidence***). At the same time, however, intensified contact with other cultures sharpened Greeks' awareness of their own identity as Hellenes (the Greeks' name for themselves). Such self-conscious Hellenism did not necessarily lead to greater political cooperation, but it did encourage the establishment of Panhellenic festivals, such as the Olympic Games, and holy sites. The most important of these was the temple of Apollo at Delphi, home to the oracle of the sun god on the slope of the sacred mountain of Parnassus. People from all over the Greek world (and beyond) came to seek advice from the prophetic spirit embodied in Apollo's priestess, who lived in a state of trance induced by fumes rising from a fissure in the earth and enhanced by the chewing of eucalyptus leaves. Suppliants who sought to have their questions

# Interpreting Visual Evidence

## The Ideal of Male Beauty

The Greek word *kouros* ("young man" or "youth") is now applied to a whole series of life-sized statues from the Archaic Period. The one shown here comes from Anavyssos in Attica, and was made between 540 and 515 B.C.E. (It is now in the National Archeological Museum of Athens.) Although scholars used to believe that such statues were meant to represent the god Apollo, further research has shown that most were made to commemorate the dead, especially young warriors who had fallen in battle. This one appears to be walking forward, smiling, but his eyes are closed. The accompanying inscription reads: "Stop and show your pity here for Kroisos, now dead, who once fighting in the foremost ranks of battle was destroyed by raging Ares."

### Questions for Analysis

1. What aspects of the body does the kouros emphasize? If this is intended to be a model of Greek manhood, what values would it convey to contemporary youths?
2. Is this a representation of the young man as he was when living, or in death? How do your conclusions about the ideal of male beauty change if this is a glorification of death?
3. Compare this image to the values expressed in the verses by Tyrtaeus of Sparta on "The Beautiful and the Good" (page 82). How do these two perspectives complement one another?

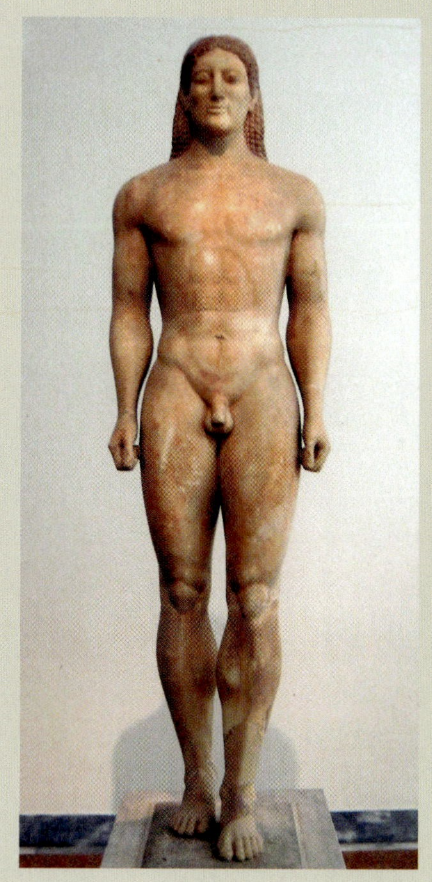

answered by the oracle would offer gifts to the shrine and then wait while the god spoke through the priestess, whose mysterious answers would be translated by an attending priest into enigmatic Greek verse. The resulting advice was essentially a riddle that called for further interpretation on the part of the recipient—who often misconstrued it: as we noted in Chapter 2, Croesus of Lydia thought that he was following the advice of the oracle when he attacked the Persians, but the great nation he destroyed turned out to be his own.

At the Olympic Games, Greeks honored the king of the gods, Zeus, near the giant temple dedicated to him at Olympia. The Greeks took great pride in these athletic competitions, and Greek historians even dated events by Olympiads, the four-year periods between games, traditionally believed to have begun in 776 B.C.E. Only Hellenes were permitted to participate in these sacred contests, and all wars among Greeks ceased while they took place. A victory in the games brought great prestige to the victor, who could be catapulted to a position of social and political power within his polis. Like colonization, these games did little to alleviate rivalry among the poleis; in fact, they often increased it. But at the same time, they strengthened the Greeks' awareness of their common culture, an awareness that could be harnessed when they faced a common threat.

## Hoplite Warfare

In the centuries immediately following the calamities of the late Bronze Age, the defense of surviving Greek communities rested with the few elite warriors who had the resourc-

**HOPLITE INFANTRY ADVANCING INTO COMBAT.** This Corinthian vase, dating from around 650 B.C.E., displays the earliest-known depiction of hoplites fighting in a phalanx formation.

es to invest in armor, chariots, and weaponry—and the leisure to emulate the heroic ideals of the past. Commoners fighting on foot played a very secondary role. This monopoly on military prowess gave the aristocracy tremendous political and social leverage. As a result, aristocrats dominated political offices and priesthoods in the poleis, as well as economic life.

But during the Archaic Period, a revolution in military tactics brought aristocratic military dominance to an end. Increasingly, the effective defense of a polis required that it be able to call on a standing militia, not just an ad-hoc band of elite warriors. Accordingly, able-bodied citizens began to equip themselves for battle and to train alongside one another. These citizen-soldiers became known as *hoplites*, from the large round shield (*hoplon*) carried by each, the chief element in a panoply that also consisted of spear, short sword, breastplate, helmet, and sometimes leather greaves and wrist-guards. In battle, hoplites stood shoulder to shoulder in a close formation called a *phalanx,* several columns across and several rows deep, with each hoplite carrying his shield on the left arm to protect the unshielded right side of the man standing next to him. In his right hand, each hoplite carried a thrusting weapon, the spear or sword, so that an approaching phalanx presented a nearly impenetrable wall of armor and weaponry to its opponents. If a man in the front rank fell, the one behind him stepped up to take his place; indeed, the weight of the entire phalanx was literally behind the front line, with each soldier aiding the assault by leaning with his shield into the man in front of him.

This tight formation and heavy armor (as much as seventy pounds including the shield) required only one shared skill: the ability to stay together. As long as the phalanx remained intact, it was a nearly unbeatable formation. But like the polis itself, it could fall apart if its men did not share a common goal. The hoplite revolution was therefore bound up with a parallel revolution in politics. As a polis came increasingly to draw upon the resources of more and more citizens, it was forced to offer them a larger share in political power. By the seventh century B.C.E., every polis needed a hoplite force to protect its independence, so any town-dweller or farmer who could afford the requisite panoply became a person with political and social standing. Together, these citizen-soldiers formed a hoplite class, which could demand a share in decision-making and thereby challenge the hegemony of old elites. Sometimes, too, they could be co-opted by an aristocratic faction or persuaded to throw support behind an aspiring tyrant.

## Aristocracy, Tyranny, and Democracy

For the better part of the seventh and sixth centuries B.C.E., aristocrats continued to dominate the Greek poleis. Struggles for influence among competing families were commonplace, and factions often attempted to checkmate rivals by passing new laws which favored their interests, or by sponsoring building projects or colonial expeditions. These differences affected polis government at every level, not least because aristocrats were the only members

# Analyzing Primary Sources

## "The Beautiful and The Good"

*The poet known as Tyrtaeus of Sparta flourished during the middle of the sixth century B.C.E. He may originally have come from Athens, but whatever his origins he expressed ideas of honor, beauty, and virtue that were universal among the hoplite warriors of the new poleis. The key terms he uses in the following verses cannot be adequately translated into English, since these short Greek adjectives are freighted with ancient meanings:* kalos *(beautiful, honorable),* agathos *(good, brave, manly). They stand in opposition to the term* aischros *(shameful, ugly, mean).*

*alos* it is for an *agathos* warrior to die, fallen among the foremost fighters, in battle for his native land; but to leave his polis and rich fields and beg—that is most painful of all, as he wanders with his dear mother and aged father, his small children and his wedded wife. Detested he will be in the eyes of all those to whom he comes, constrained by need and hateful poverty. He shames his birth and belies his glorious appearance; dishonor and misery are his companions. If no account is taken of a warrior who is a wanderer, if there is no respect for him or his family in the future, then let us fight with all our hearts for this land and die for our children, no longer hesitating to risk our lives. Young men, stand firm beside each other and fight. Do not begin shameful flight or fear. Rather, create a mighty, valorous spirit in your breasts, and show no love for your lives when you are fighting. Do not flee, abandoning the older men, whose knees are no longer nimble. For *aischros* it is for an older warrior to fall among the foremost fighters and lie out ahead of the young men—a man whose hair is already white and his beard grey—as he breathes out his valorous spirit in the dust, holding his bloody guts in his own hands, his body laid bare. *Aischros* is this to the eyes, and a cause of resentment to look upon. But to the young men all is seemly, while the glorious flower of lovely youth is theirs. To men the young man is admirable to look upon, and to women lovable while he lives and *kalos* when he lies among the foremost fighters. So let a man take a firm stance and stand fast, with both feet planted upon the ground, biting his lip with his teeth.

Source: Excerpted and modified from *The Greek Polis*, eds. W. H. Adkins and Peter White (Chicago: 1986), pp. 23–24.

### Questions for Analysis

1. How does Tyrtaeus characterize defeat? How does this poem exemplify the values and tactics of hoplite warfare?
2. Why is so much emphasis placed on physical beauty and youth? What other qualities are associated with the word *kalos*? Why is old age potentially *aischros*?
3. How does this ideal of male beauty compare with that made visible in the kouros of Anavyssos (page 80)? How does it compare to the heroic ideal expressed in the exchange between Diomedes and Glaucus (page 76)?

of society who could afford to hold unpaid and time-consuming political offices.

The aristocrats of this period pursued not only wealth, power, and fame; they also cultivated a distinctive lifestyle. Participating in politics and holding office was part of this lifestyle. So too was the *symposium*, literally a "drinking party," an intimate gathering at which elite men would enjoy wine (sometimes in large quantities), poetry and poetic competition (ranging from epics to love lyrics to drinking songs), performances by trained dancers and acrobats, and the company of *hetaeras* (courtesans) who provided witty conversation, music, and the promise of sex. Respectable women were excluded from such meetings, as they were from all other aspects of social and political life (see below). So too were non-aristocratic men. The symposium was thus an arena for the display of aristocratic masculinity.

The glorification of male sexuality was another important aspect of this homosocial aristocratic culture, and was regulated by strict social custom. Typically, a man in his late twenties to late thirties, who had just begun to make his career in political life, would take as his lover and protégé an aristocratic youth in his early to mid-teens. The two would form an intimate bond in which sexual intercourse played an important role. This intimacy benefited both partners and their familes, and allowed the younger partner to learn the workings of politics while making valuable social connections. Many later philosophers, including Plato, argued that true love could only exist between two such lovers, because only within such a relationship could a man find a partner worthy of his affections. Other types of sexual relationships were deemed ignoble, including those between men of unequal social status.

A whole complex of values, ideas, practices, and assumptions thus shaped aristocratic identity. As a result, it was impossible for those outside this elite world to participate fully in the public life of the polis. By the middle of the Archaic Period, moreover, the circle of the aristocratic elite tightened even further as smaller and smaller groups came to dominate higher offices. Many aristocrats were left on the outside of their own culture, looking in.

For these men, one remedy lay close at hand: they could form an alliance with the rising class of hoplites, who had complaints of their own about exclusion from political power. Occasionally, a single aristocrat with the backing of the hoplites would succeed in setting up an alternative form of government, a *tyranny*. The word *tyrannos* was actually foreign to the Greeks, and had been borrowed from the Lydians; it signified someone who ruled outside the traditional framework of the polis.

But a tyrant in Archaic Greece was not necessarily an abusive ruler. Indeed, tyranny often led the way to wider political enfranchisement. This is because a would-be tyrant who had sought the support of the hoplite class would then have to appease that class by extending further rights of political participation, while all the time striving to keep the reins of power in his own hands. This was an inherently unstable state of affairs, because after the original tyrant had fulfilled the wishes of the hoplites, the continuance of tyranny became an obstacle to even greater power for this segment of population. For this reason, tyrannies rarely lasted for more than two generations and could serve as a stepping-stone from aristocracy to a more broadly participatory form of government, democracy.

It is important to stress that our notion of democracy is quite different from that of the Greeks. In fact, Aristotle denegrated this form of government as "mob rule," because it gave too much power to the *demos*, a word meaning "neighborhood" or "affinity group." He saw it as a system too easily controlled by a particular faction. Our ideal of democracy is closer to what Aristotle would have called a polity, governance by the polis as a whole.

**AN ARISTOCRATIC MAN AND HIS YOUNG LOVER.** An illustration from a red-figure drinking cup, c. 480 B.C.E. ▪ ***As suggested by this image, what are the differences between these two male lovers?*** ▪ ***What relationship(s) are being depicted here?***

## The Power of Poetry

Although the aristocracy of the Archaic Period were deeply invested in the heroic ideal enshrined in the epics of an earlier age, they also strove to express their unique culture and outlook in newer poetic forms. The most characteristic of these is the lyric, a series of rhythmic verses sung to the music of the lyre. Because these songs would have been composed orally, or even improvised, relatively few survive. But those that do are valuable historical sources because they concentrate on themes of immediate interest to poets and their audiences: beauty, love, sorrow, ambition, or an important life event. And because they were the focus of entertainment at gatherings, they are often politically charged, sexually explicit, or daringly subversive of accepted norms. For example, the poet Archilochus of Paros (c. 680–640 B.C.E.) flouts the conventions of epic poetry by mocking his own failures on the battlefield: "Some barbarian waves my shield, since I had to abandon it / . . . but I escaped, so it scarcely matters / . . . I can get another just as good." So much for the heroic ideal of returning either with one's shield, or on it! In another lyric, Archilochus castigates his faithless (female) lover and his even more faithless (male) lover with whom she has run off.

# Analyzing Primary Sources

## *Songs of Sappho*

*Although Sappho of Lesbos (c. 620–550 B.C.E.) was a prolific poet and skilled musician, we know very little about her life, and only a few examples of her extraordinary verse survive. Of the nine books collected in the third century B.C.E., we now have just one complete lyric and a series of fragments, some consisting of only two or three words, often preserved because they were quoted admiringly by other authors. Astonishingly, though, a papyrus scroll containing a previously unknown part of a poem was identified as recently as 2004.*

### *Fragment 16*

Some say thronging cavalry, some say
foot soldiers,
others call a fleet the most beautiful of
sights the dark earth offers, but I say it's
whatever you love best.

And it's easy to make this understood by
everyone, for she who surpassed all
human
kind in beauty, Helen, abandoning her
husband—that best of

men—went sailing off to the shores of
Troy and
never spent a thought on her child or
loving
parents: when the goddess seduced her
wits and left her to wander,

she forgot them all, she could not
remember
anything but longing, and lightly straying
aside, lost her way. But that reminds me
now: Anactória,

she's not here, and I'd rather see her
lovely
step, her sparkling glance and her face
than gaze on
all the troops in Lydia in their chariots
and glittering armor.

Source: Translated by Jim Powell, *The Poetry of Sappho* (New York: 2007), pp. 6–7.

### *The New Fragment (2004)*

Live for the gifts the fragrant-breasted
Muses
send, for the clear, the singing, lyre, my
children.
Old age freezes my body, once so lithe,
rinses the darkness from my hair, now
white.
My heart's heavy, my knees no longer
keep me
up through the dance they used to
prance like fawns in.
Oh, I grumble about it, but for what?
Nothing can stop a person's growing
old.
They say that Tithonus was swept away
in Dawn's passionate, rose-flushed arms
to live
forever, but he lost his looks, his youth,
failing husband of an immortal bride.

Source: Translated by Lachlan Mackinnon, *Times Literary Supplement*, July 15, 2005.

### *Questions for Analysis*

1. How does Sappho use stories from the older tradition she has inherited to address her own concerns? How does the perspective of the female poet transform masculine ideas about heroism, beauty, warfare, aging?
2. What are the challenges of working with such fragmentary sources as these? If these were the only pieces of evidence to survive from Archaic Greece, what conclusions could you draw about the society and its values?

It is paradoxical, given the male domination of Greek culture, that the most famous lyric poet of this age was not a man. Rather, it was Sappho (*SAF-foh*, c. 620–550 B.C.E.), who lived in the polis of Mytilene on the island of Lesbos. Revered by her contemporaries as the Tenth Muse, Sappho composed songs for a wide array of occasions and a range of moods: songs of courtship and marriage, longing and desire, loss, old age, and death. Sometimes her lyrics seem to be addressed to men, but more often they are passionately dedicated to women: both the women whom Sappho loved and the historical women who occupy the margins of masculine epic. Frequently, they take some image or incident from that inherited tradition and give it a distinctive spin. In one song, Sappho compares herself to Agamemnon, who was only able to return from Troy after he prayed to Hera, a goddess worshiped at Lesbos; Sappho now prays that her beloved will arrive safely with the goddess's help. In another, she imagines a scene not included in the *Iliad*, the joyous wedding of the Trojan Hector and his bride, Andromache. Like later tragedies, the poignancy of this bridal song (just like the ones Sappho herself would have sung at the marriage feasts of her friends) derives from the listeners' foreknowledge of the legendary couple's terrible fate: Hector's death at the hands of Achilles, Andromache's enslavement at the hands of the victorious Greeks, and the murder of their infant son. The intimacy of lyric thus reveals something that few sources from antiquity are able to convey: the feelings and desires of individuals who were often at odds with the dominant culture of their time.

**OSTRACISM.** This political practice takes its name from the pot shards (in Greek, *ostraka*) on which the names of unpopular citizens were scratched. Many of the ballots have survived. Here we see the names of Aristeides, Kimon, and Themistocles: prominent citizens of the fifth century B.C.E. who had fallen out of favor.

## PORTRAITS OF THREE POLEIS

The poleis of the Archaic Period developed in very different ways. To illustrate this diversity, we examine three particularly well-documented examples: Athens, Sparta, and the Ionian city of Miletus. None of these, however, can be considered typical. There were approximately one thousand poleis in Greece, and about most of them we know almost nothing. But at least we can survey some of the features that, with variations, made each polis unique—and yet comparable, in some ways, to its neighbors.

### *Athens*

The Athenians liked to boast that their city had been a great metropolis since the Bronze Age described by Hesiod: a claim integral to their identity and their sense of self-importance within the larger Greek world. But although Attica had long been a populous and prosperous region, Athens itself was of no great significance during the Mycenaean Era. Moreover, it continued throughout the Archaic Period to be overshadowed by Corinth, the leading commercial city; Sparta, the preeminent military power; and the leading cultural centers of the Aegean islands and the coast of Anatolia.

When Athenians first came together to form a polis, theirs was a distinctly agricultural economy. Whatever profits aristocrats acquired through trade, they reinvested in land on the Attic Peninsula. Indeed, Athenian elites came to regard commerce as a disreputable means of earning a living, a mentality that persisted even when the city's excellent harbors and orientation toward the Aegean made Athens famous as a mercantile polis.

In the Archaic Period, aristocratic dominance over the polis rested on monopolization of elected offices and control of the city's council, the Areopagus (*ah-ree-OP-ah-guhs*), which was composed of former office-holders. By the early seventh century B.C.E., an even smaller group of aristocratic officials wielded executive authority in Athens: the *archons* or "first men." Ultimately, nine archons presided over the entire governance of the polis, including its military, judicial, and religious affairs. Although each served for only one year, all became lifetime members of the Areopagus. And because the Areopagus appointed the archons, it could therefore control its own future membership. It also served as a kind of high court, with tremendous influence over the hearing of cases.

As power was consolidated by this small group, deep economic and social divisions developed in Athenian society. A significant proportion of the population fell into slavery through debt, while struggles among aristocratic families destabilized the government and fomented cycles of revenge killings. Finally, this situation inspired Athens' first attempt to promulgate a set of written laws. In 621 B.C.E., an aristocrat named Drakon was charged with this task, and he sought to control civic violence through harsh punishments: hence our term "draconian" to describe any severe penalty, policy, or regime. This attempt failed, but its effects ultimately led both aristocrats and hoplites to an agreement.

**HARMODIUS AND ARISTOGITON.** These two aristocratic lovers helped to kill Peisistratos' son Hipparchus, and so helped bring the tyranny of Peisistratos' family to an end. Athenians celebrated them as popular liberators. This statue is a Roman copy of an original carved around 500 B.C.E. ▪ ***How does this pair of lovers compare to that on page 83?***

In 594 B.C.E., they elected one man, the poet Solon, as the sole archon for one year, and they gave him sweeping powers. Solon was an aristocrat, but he had made his fortune as a merchant and did not hold that vocation in contempt; this meant that he was not allied with any single interest.

Solon's political and economic reforms laid the foundations for the later development of Athenian democracy. He forbade the practice of debt slavery and set up a fund to buy back Athenian slaves who had been sold abroad. He encouraged the cultivation of olives and grapes, thus spurring cash-crop farming and urban industries such as oil and wine production, and the manufacture of pottery storage jars and decorative drinking cups. He also broadened rights of political participation and set up courts in which a range of citizens served as jurors and to which any Athenian might appeal. He based eligibility for political office on property qualifications, thus making it possible for someone not born into the aristocracy to gain access to power. Moreover, he convened an Athenian assembly, the *ekklesia* (*eh-KLAY-see-a*) and gave it the right to elect archons. Now, all free-born Athenian men over the age of eighteen could participate in government.

Yet Solon's reforms were not widely accepted. The aristocracy thought them too radical; the people of the demos, not radical enough. In the resulting generation of turmoil, an aristocrat named Peisistratos (*pi-SIS-trah-tohs*) succeeded in establishing himself as tyrant in 546 B.C.E. Somewhat ironically, Peisistratos then proceeded to institute Solon's reforms, and he also launched a massive campaign of public-works projects, including the collection and codification of various versions of Homer's epics. But the apparent mildness of his rule was undergirded by the quiet, persistent intimidation of Athenians by his foreign mercenaries and the ruthlessness with which he crushed any dissent. Still, by enforcing Solon's laws, he strengthened the political role of the demos and remained a popular ruler until his death. His sons, however, were less able to control the various factions that threatened their rule. One son, Hipparchus, was assassinated by a pair of devoted lovers, Harmodius and Aristogiton, aristocrats who were later remembered as liberators. The other son, Hippias, was ousted with the help of the Spartans in 510 B.C.E.

The following period of Spartan-sponsored oligarchy ("rule of the few") was brief. Two generations of increasing access to power had left the Athenian demos with a taste for self-government. For the first time in recorded history, a group of commoners can be credited with the overthrow of a regime. They rallied behind Cleisthenes (*CLIE-sthen-ees*), an aristocrat who had championed the cause of the demos after the fall of tyranny. Once voted in as archon in 508/7 B.C.E., Cleisthenes took steps to limit aristocratic power. By reorganizing the Athenian population into ten voting districts, he suppressed traditional aristocratic loyalties tied to regional Attic identities. He further strengthened the Athenian assembly and extended the machinery of democratic government to the local level throughout Attica. He also introduced the practice of ostracism, whereby Athenians could decide each year whether they wanted to banish someone for a decade and, if so, whom. With this power, Cleisthenes hoped that the demos could prevent the return of a tyrant and quell factional strife if civil war seemed imminent.

By 500 B.C.E., the political struggles of the sixth century had given Athens a far more populist temper than any other Greek polis and had strengthened its institutions of central government. In the meantime, Athens had become the principal exporter of olive oil, wine, and pottery in the Greek world. It was poised to assume the role it would claim for itself during the fifth century B.C.E. as the exemplar of Greek culture and the proponent of democracy.

## Sparta

Located in the southern part of the Peloponnesus, the polis of the Spartans represented everything that Athens was not. Athens was sophisticated, cosmopolitan, and creative; Sparta was practical, defensive, and conservative. Depending on one's point of view, either set of adjectives might indicate admiration or criticism.

Sparta took shape when four villages (and ultimately a fifth) combined to form a single polis. Perhaps as a relic of the unification process, Sparta retained a dual monarchy throughout its history, with two royal families and two lines of succession. Although seniority or ability usually determined which of the two ruling kings had more influence, neither was technically superior to the other, a situation that often led to political in-fighting among their respective supporters.

According to local tradition, Spartan hegemony in the surrounding region of Laconia began with the conquest of Messenia, one of the mainland's few agriculturally viable

**THE PELOPONNESUS.** Located on the Peloponnesian peninsula, the highly militarized society of Sparta dominated the region known as Laconia. ▪ ***Where is Sparta located?*** ▪ ***How might Sparta's location have influenced its outlook on foreign affairs?*** ▪ ***Did geography make conflict between Athens and Sparta inevitable?***

territories. Around 720 B.C.E., the Spartans subjugated and enslaved the indigenous people there, the *helots*, who now became an unfree population tied to the land and forced to work under Spartan lordship. Around 650 B.C.E., however, the helots revolted, gaining support from several neighboring poleis and briefly threatening Sparta with annihilation. Eventually, Sparta triumphed; but the shock of this rebellion brought about a permanent transformation.

Determined to prevent another uprising and to protect its superior position, Sparta became the most militarized polis in Greece. By 600 B.C.E., everything was oriented to the maintenance of its hoplite army, a force so superior that Spartans confidently left their city unfortified. The Spartan system made every male citizen a professional soldier of the phalanx. At a time when Athenian society was becoming more democratic and when citizens spent more time legislating than fighting, Spartan society was becoming increasingly devoted to an older aristocratic ideal of perpetual warfare, with personal freedom mattering less than the collective honor and security of the polis.

At birth, every Spartiate child was examined by officials who determined whether it was healthy enough to raise; if not, the infant was abandoned in the mountains. This was a custom observed elsewhere in the ancient world, but only in Sparta was it institutionalized by the state. If deemed worthy of upbringing, the child was placed at age seven in the polis-run educational system. Boys and girls trained together until age twelve, participating in exercise, gymnastics, and other physical drills and competitions. Boys then went to live in barracks, where their military training would commence in earnest. Girls continued their training until they became the mates of eligible Spartiate males, usually around the age of eighteen. No such thing as "marriage" was possible under the Spartiate system, or even desirable, for it would merely create a domestic unit and a new set of loyalties and interests that would compete with the Spartan state.

Barracks life was rigorous, designed to accustom youths to physical hardship. At age eighteen, the young man who survived this training would try for membership in a brotherhood whose sworn comrades lived, ate, and fought together. Failure to gain acceptance would mean that the young man could not become a full Spartiate and would lose his rights as a citizen. If accepted, however, he remained with his brotherhood until he was thirty years of age. Between the ages of twenty and thirty he was also expected to mate with a Spartiate woman, but occasions for this were few, a fact that partially accounts for the low birthrate among Spartan citizens. After age thirty, a Spartiate male could opt to live with his family, but he was still required to remain on active military duty until he was sixty.

All Spartiate males over the age of thirty were members of the citizens' assembly, the *apella*, which voted on matters proposed to it by a council consisting of twenty-eight elders (the *gerousia*) and the two kings. This gerousia (*gher-oo-SEE-ah*) was the main policymaking body of the polis and also its primary court. Its members were elected for life, but had to be over the age of sixty before they could stand for office. Meanwhile, five *ephors* (overseers), elected annually, supervised the educational system and acted as guardians of Spartan tradition. In the latter role, ephors could even depose an errant king from command of the army while on campaign. The ephors also supervised the Spartan secret service, the *krypteia*, recruiting agents from among the most promising young Spartiates. Agents spied on citizens, but their main job was to infiltrate the helot population and identify potential troublemakers.

Spartan policy hinged on the precarious relationship between the helots and the Spartiates. The helots outnumbered the Spartiates ten to one, and Messenia routinely seethed with revolt. Helots accompanied the Spartans on campaign as shield bearers, spear bearers, and baggage handlers. At home, however, the helots were a constant security concern. Every year the Spartans ritually declared war on them as a reminder that they would not tolerate dissent. Moreover, the constant threat of unrest at home meant that the polis was notoriously reluctant to commit its army abroad. So helot slavery made the Spartan system possible, but Sparta's reliance on a hostile population of slaves was also a serious limitation.

This system also limited Spartan's contact with the outside world. Spartiates were forbidden to engage in trade or commerce, because wealth might distract them from the pursuit of martial glory. Nor did Spartiates farm their own lands as Athenians did. Economic activity in the Spartan state fell either to the helots or to the free residents of other Peloponnesian cities who were known as *perioikoi*, "those dwelling round about." The perioikoi enjoyed certain rights and protections within Spartan society, and some grew rich handling its business concerns. But unlike the residents of Attica, in the hinterland of Athens, the perioikoi exercised no political rights within the Spartan polis. Spartiates who lost their rights as citizens also became perioikoi.

The Spartans self-consciously rejected innovation or change. They styled themselves as the protectors of the "traditional customs" of Greece, by which they meant old, aristocratic regimes and a strict observance of heroic ideals. In this role, Sparta tried to prevent the establishment of tyrannies in neighboring states and tried to overthrow them when they arose: hence their willing intervention in the affairs of Athens under the Peisistratids. Indeed, Sparta's stern defense of tradition made it an object of admiration throughout the Greek world, even though few Greeks had any desire to live as the Spartans did.

The fatal flaw in the Spartan system was demographic. There were many ways to fall from the status of Spartiate, but the only way to become one was by birth—and the Spartan birthrate simply could not keep pace with the demand for trained warriors. As a result, the number of full Spartiates declined from perhaps as many as 10,000 in the seventh century to only about 1,000 by the middle of the fourth century B.C.E. Another flaw is historical: because the Spartans placed little value on the written record of their traditions, almost everything we know about them (including the summary offered here) must be gleaned from archeological investigations or the propaganda of their enemies, notably the Athenians.

## Miletus and the Ionian Revolution in Thought

Across the Aegean from the Greek mainland lay the Greek cities of Ionia, located on a narrow strip dominating the central part of the Anatolian coast. Here, Miletus was the foremost commercial and cultural power. Long a part of the Greek world (see ***Analyzing Primary Sources*** in Chapter 2, page 51), it had also been shaped by Mesopotamian and Egyptian influences. Ionia was, for example, the birthplace of Greek epic, although debate continues over the extent to which Near Eastern models might have influenced the Homeric poems. Other creative endeavors certainly exhibit Near Eastern influences. Fantastic animals, a long-standing

**IONIA, LYDIA, AND THE PERSIAN EMPIRE.** During the seventh and sixth centuries B.C.E., the Greek cities of the Ionian coast were the cultural and commercial leaders of Greece. But during the fifth century B.C.E., after the Persians conquered Lydia, they lost this position to Athens. ▪ ***Where are Ionia, Lydia, and Miletus on this map?*** ▪ ***How does Ionia's geographical position help to explain the change in its fortunes?*** ▪ ***How might this change have influenced Ionian attitudes toward the Persian Empire?***

theme of the decorative arts, were frequently represented on Milesian pottery; and Milesian intellectuals were well aware of Near Eastern literature and learning. Some even echoed the vaunting rhetoric of Persian imperial decrees ("thus speaks Darius the Great King. . . .") to make their own, quite different observations ("thus speaks Hecataeus of Miletus: the sayings of the Greeks are many and foolish").

The relationship between the Ionians of the coast and the interior kingdom of Lydia—and its Persian successor state—were close but difficult. It was through the Ionians that the Lydian invention of coinage was introduced to the Greek world, where it revolutionized trade, made wealth portable for the first time, and introduced a host of new philosophical and ethical problems. The Ionians, in turn, played a crucial role in Hellenizing Asia Minor while at the same time insisting on their independence from it. Under the pressure of the Lydians—who sought the excellent ports of the Anatolian coast for themselves—the major cities of Ionia ultimately banded together to form the Ionian League, a political and religious confederation of poleis pledged to support each other. This was the first such organization known in the Greek world.

The Milesians founded many colonies, especially in and around the Black Sea. They were also active in Egypt, where the main Greek trading outposts were Milesian foundations. These colonial efforts, combined with its advantageous position for trade with the rest of Asia Minor, brought Miletus extraordinary wealth. At the same time, it also became a center for speculative thinking, what the Greeks called *philosophia*, "the love of wisdom." Beginning in the sixth century B.C.E., a series of intellectuals now known as the pre-Socratics (because they came before the great philosopher Socrates) raised new and vital questions about the relationship between the natural world (the *kosmos*), the gods, and men. And often, their explanations moved the direct influence of the gods to the margins or removed it altogether, something that other Greeks regarded as blasphemous. For example, Milesian philosophers built on older traditions of Near Eastern learning, such as Babylonian astronomy, but reversed older conclusions. They sought physical explanations for the movements of the heavens, and did not presume that heavenly bodies were divine. By making human observations the starting point for their knowledge, they began to formulate scientific explanations for the working of the universe.

Stimulated by the cultural diversity of their city, Milesian philosophers also began to rethink their place in the cosmos. When Hecataeus (*heck-ah-TAY-us*) remarked that "the sayings of the Greeks are many and foolish," he was deriding his contemporaries' unquestioning acceptance of a narrow world-view. He set out to expand their horizons by mapping the world, traveling extensively and studying the customs and beliefs of other cultures. Xenophanes (*zee-NOFF-uh-nees*) also posited that all human knowledge is relative and conditioned by human experience: he observed that the Thracians (a people living north of Greece) believed that the gods had blue eyes and red hair as the Thracians themselves did, whereas Ethiopians portrayed the gods as dark skinned and curly haired, as they were. He concluded that human beings always make gods in their own image, not the other way around. If oxen could pray, Xenophanes declared, they would pray to gods who looked like oxen.

Such theories would become a distinctive strand in later Greek philosophy, yet they would continue to be regarded as disturbing and dangerous—dangerous enough to warrant the execution of Socrates in Athens, where the struggle between religion and philosophy would ultimately be fought more than a hundred years after Xenophanes' bold proclamation (see below). By that time, the Persian conquest of Lydia had made Miletus and its sister cities subject to that great empire. Ultimately, Ionian resistance to Persian rule would trigger the greatest clash the Greek world had yet known.

## THE CHALLENGE OF THE PERSIAN WARS

The two major wars fought between the uneasily unified Greeks and the vast empire of the Persians were construed as defining events by those who witnessed and looked back on them. From the first, the contest was unequal. Persia was the largest and most efficient state the world had ever seen, capable of mustering over a million armed men. The Greeks, by contrast, remained a collection of disparate communities, fiercely competitive and suspicious of one another. An exceptionally large polis, such as Athens or Sparta, might put 10,000 hoplites in the field; but the vast majority of Greek states could only provide a few hundred each. So the threat of Persian conquest loomed large on the Greek horizon, after which the experience of international warfare changed the Greek world immeasurably.

### *The Ionian Revolt (499–494 B.C.E.)*

For the first time in the history of Western civilizations, we can follow the unfolding of events through the narrative of a contemporary historian: Herodotus, the first person who self-consciously set out to write an account of his own times in careful, unambiguous prose, rather than in the form of heroic poetry or the boastful language of victorious inscriptions. And luckily for us, Herodotus was uniquely qualified to probe the long-term and more immediate causes of the Persian Wars. Raised in the Ionian polis of Halicarnassus, he was a keen observer of human nature and human diversity. He regarded both the Greeks and the Persians as great peoples. Yet, as a Greek himself—albeit one born within the Persian dominion—he was not impartial. Indeed, his surviving account reflects many of the intellectual currents of mid-fifth-century Athens, where he spent the better part of his career, as well as many Athenian prejudices. This is something that must be borne in mind when reading his work.

**A MODERN REPLICA OF AN ATHENIAN TRIREME.** These versatile warships were much more powerful than the old fifty-oared pentakonters that had been in use for centuries. As the name suggests, a trireme featured three banks of oars on each side, 170 oars in total. These were manned by citizen rowers seated on benches at three different levels in the vessel's hold. In battle, rowers could help power a ship forward, turn it, and keep it on course in a chase, even when sailing into the wind. In favorable winds, sails could be used to add speed. ▪ ***How does this new military technology build on some of the same strategies as hoplite warfare?***

Herodotus was careful to show that the war between the Persians and Greeks had ancient roots and could be traced back to longstanding differences, but his narrative also shows that the catalyst was a political conflict in Miletus. In 501 B.C.E., the city was governed by Aristagoras, a tyrant who owed his power to the backing of the Persian emperor, Darius. But apparently, Aristagoras came to believe that his days as the emperor's favorite were numbered. So he turned abruptly from puppet to patriot, rousing the Milesians and the rest of Ionia to revolt against Persian rule. As a safeguard, he also sought military support from the sympathetic poleis on the Greek mainland. The Spartans refused to send their army abroad, but Athens and Eretria, on the island of Euboea, agreed to send twenty-five ships and crews. This small force managed to capture the old Lydian capital of Sardis (by then a Persian administrative center) and burn it to the ground. Then the Athenians and Eretrians went home, leaving the Ionians to their own devices. In 494 B.C.E., the rebellious poleis were finally overwhelmed by the vastly superior might of Persia.

Darius realized, however, that so long as his Greek subjects in Asia Minor could cast a hopeful eye to their neighbors across the Aegean, they would forge alliances. He therefore decided to launch a preemptive strike against Athens and Eretria, to teach these upstart poleis a lesson. In the summer of 490 B.C.E, a punitive expedition of 20,000 soldiers under two of Persia's finest generals crossed the Aegean and landed on the coast of Euboea. Their forces sacked and burned Eretria to the ground, sending its population into captivity in Persia. They then crossed the narrow strait to Attica, landing on the plain of Marathon, approximately 26 miles from Athens.

## *Marathon and Its Aftermath*

The danger was palpable, and Athenians quickly sought help from the only polis that could conceivably help them forestall annhilation by the Persians: Sparta. But the Spartans responded that they were unable to assist—they were celebrating a religious festival. Only the small, nearby polis of Plataea offered the Athenians aid. The Athenian phalanx would have to engage the mighty Persians on its own.

Heavily outnumbered and without effective cavalry to counter that of the Persians, the Athenian hoplites took a position between two hills blocking the main road to the polis. After a standoff of several days, the Athenian general Miltiades *(mil-TIE-uh-dees)* received word that the Persians were watering their horses, and that the Persian infantry was vulnerable to attack. Miltiades led a charge that smashed the Persian force and resulted in crippling losses. Almost unbelievably, the Athenians had defeated the world's major imperial power, and they had done it without Spartan help. It was a vindication of hoplite tactics and a tremendous boost to Athenian confidence.

Yet the Athenian politician Themistocles *(the-MIS-toh-klees)* warned that the Persians would not suffer such humiliation quietly, and that they would retaliate with an even larger force. So when the Athenians discovered a rich vein of silver ore in the Attic countryside a few years later, Themistocles persuaded them not to divide the windfall among themselves (the customary practice) but to finance a fleet of 200 triremes, state-of-the-art warships. Athens thereby transformed itself into the preeminent naval power of the Greek world just in time to confront a new Persian onslaught.

## Xerxes' Invasion

Darius the Great died in 486 B.C.E. and was succeeded by his son Xerxes, who almost immediately began preparing a massive overland invasion of Greece designed to conquer the entire territory, thus eradicating any future threats to Persian hegemony and avenging his father's shame.

**THE PERSIAN WARS WITH GREECE.** Imagine that you are the Persian emperor Xerxes, planning the conquest of Greece in 480 B.C.E. ▪ *What are the two possible routes that you could take to attack Greece?* ▪ *What geographical considerations would dictate your military strategy?* ▪ *Bearing in mind that Xerxes' attempt failed, what would you have done differently?*

Supported by a fleet of 600 ships, this grand army (which numbered at least 150,000 men and may have been as large as 300,000) set out from Sardis in 480 B.C.E., crossing the narrow strait separating Europe from Asia on pontoon bridges. Unlike his father, who had dispatched talented generals against Athens, Xerxes led this campaign himself.

Many Greek poleis capitulated immediately. But Athens, Sparta, Corinth, and some thirty others refused to surrender. Instead, they hastily formed a Hellenic League, an unprecedented alliance in the face of an unprecedented external threat. In August of 480, a major Persian offensive was held at bay when the outnumbered Greek allies, under the military leadership of Sparta, confronted Xerxes at the mountain pass of Thermopylae *(ther-MO-pih-lie)*. For three days, they valiantly held off the Persian multitude, whose way through the narrow pass was effectively blocked. Meanwhile, a Greek fleet led by Athens and guided by Themistocles engaged a Persian flotilla. The Spartans' defense of Thermopylae ultimately failed, but their sacrifice allowed the new Athenian warships to inflict heavy losses on the Persians.

However, these engagements left Athens without any men to defend their city. Themistocles therefore persuaded the entire population to abandon Athens for the island of Salamis. From there, the Athenians watched the Persians torch their city. Time, however, was on their side. Xerxes' massive army depended on his damaged fleet for supplies, and the Persians' military tactics—which included a heavy reliance on cavalry and chariots—were not adapted for the rocky terrain of Greece. Bad weather also made sailing the Aegean in autumn a risky business; the Persians were now desperate to force a decisive battle and return home before the season turned against them.

In late September, the numerically superior Persian fleet sailed into the straits of Salamis, believing that the Athenians were preparing to flee the island. The report turned out to be false, but so confident was Xerxes that he had a throne placed on the headland above the bay, where he would have a good view of his victory. Instead, he watched as the battle-ready Athenian triremes demolished the Persian fleet. This was the turning point of the war. Xerxes returned with the majority of his army to Persia, while an elite force stayed behind. But when the allied Greek army met the Persians on favorable terrain the next spring—an open plain near Plataea, which had been razed the year before—the Greeks prevailed. Against all odds, the small, fractious poleis had defeated the mightiest army of the known world.

**GREEK FORCES DEFEAT PERSIANS.** This detail from a bowl commemorating the defeat of Xerxes' army depicts an Athenian hoplite poised to strike a death-blow to his Persian opponent. The artist has carefully delineated the differences between the enemies' dress and weaponry. To the Greeks, the Persian preference for trousers over short tunics seemed particularly barbaric and effeminate.

## THE GOLDEN AGE OF CLASSICAL GREECE

In the half century after the Persian Wars, Athens enjoyed a meteoric rise in power and prestige, becoming the premier naval power of the eastern Mediterranean and the military rival of Sparta. Athens emerged as leader of the Delian League, a group of poleis whose representatives met on the sacred island of Delos and pledged to continue the war against Persia, which was now being fought in the Aegean. As the league's leader, Athens controlled its funds and resources. The fifth century B.C.E. also witnessed the greatest achievements in Athenian culture and politics. These were complicated, however, by the increasingly awkward relationship of Athens with its allies, who began to feel more like Athenian subjects than free poleis.

### *Periclean Athens*

The reforms of Cleisthenes in the decades before the Persian Wars continued to encourage further experiments in democracy, including the selection of major officeholders by lot. Only one key position was now filled by traditional voting: the office of *strategos*, or general. And because a man could be elected strategos year after year, this office became the career goal of Athens' most ambitious figures. Themistocles had been strategos, as was Cimon (*KEY-mohn*), who led the Delian League to victories over Persia in the 470s and 460s B.C.E. But Cimon also used the league to punish poleis who tried to opt out of membership, even suppressing revolts in these cities by force of arms and so turning the league into an instrument of Athenian policy.

By then, the political mood in Athens was changing. New voices were demanding a greater role in government; most prominent were the *thetes*, the lowest class of free men and the class that provided the triremes' rowers, the backbone of the all-important Athenian fleet. Like the hoplites of the Archaic Period, who had achieved citizenship because they were indispensible to the defense of the poleis, they wanted higher status and equal representation. The man who emerged to champion their cause was Pericles (*PEHR-eh-klees*), an aristocrat from one of Athens' most prestigious families. Pericles made the enfranchisement of the thetes the main plank of the platform that defeated Cimon, and also advocated a foreign policy that was oriented away from cooperation with Sparta. In 462–461 B.C.E. he was elected strategos and immediately used his position to secure the ostracism of Cimon. He then pushed through reforms that gave every Athenian citizen the right to propose and amend legislation, not just to vote yes or no in the citizen assembly. And by paying an average day's wage for attendance, he also made it easier for poorer citizens to participate in the assembly and in courts of justice. Through such measures, the thetes and other free men of modest means became a dominant force in politics—and loyal to the man who had made that dominance possible.

Pericles also glorified Athens with an ambitious scheme of public building and lavish festivals honoring the gods, especially Athena. Personally, too, he was a generous patron of the arts and sciences, attracting the greatest minds and talents of the day to Athens. His populist stance, combined with his charisma and his promotion of the Athenians' sense of superiority, ensured his reelection as strategos for the next three decades. During these years Athens flourished, but it also alienated much of the Greek world by its arrogance and aggression.

## Athenian Literature and Drama

Periclean Athens was not the only city to produce great works of art during this period, but our knowledge of classical Greek culture is dominated by the dramas produced at its great religious festivals. The most important of these was the Dionysia, a great spring feast devoted to the god Dionysius, which became a celebration of democratic ideals. From the beginning, therefore, drama was closely connected to the political and religious life of the state that sponsored it. Indeed, the very format of classical tragedy replicates the tensions of democracy, with its complex cast of characters and its conflict among opposing perspectives. This format was perfected under the great tragedian Aeschylus (*EYE-skihl-uhs*, 525–456 B.C.E.) and his younger contemporary, Sophocles (496–406 B.C.E.). Their dramas made use of two and eventually three professional actors (each of whom could play numerous roles) and a chorus of Athenian citizens, which represented collective opinion and could comment on the action.

Although Aristotle would later declare that the purpose of tragedy was to inspire pity and fear and so to purge these emotions through a process called *katharsis* ("purification"), this definition does not capture either the variety or impact of tragedy. Tragedies were almost always set in the distant or mythical past, but they were intended to address the cutting-edge issues of their day. Indeed, the very earliest of all surviving tragedies, Aeschylus' *The Persians*, represents events of the playwright's own lifetime; we know for certain that he fought at Marathon, because he had this fact proudly recorded on his tomb. Performed for the first time in 472, this contemporary tragedy tells the story of the great Athenian victory at Salamis, but through the eyes of the defeated Xerxes, who thus becomes its tragic hero.

But even when its subject matter was derived from the epics of Homer, the fundamental themes of tragedy—justice, the conflicting demands of personal desire and public duty, the unforeseen consequences of human actions, the brutalizing effects of power—addressed problems of immediate concern to Athenians. For example, Aeschylus' trilogy the *Oresteia* (458 B.C.E.) is ostensibly about the legendary family of the Mycenaean king Agamemnon, and traces the long-term consequences of the king's sacrifice of his daughter, Iphigenia; his subsequent murder at the hands of his grieving wife, Clytemnestra; and the vengeance taken by the couple's son, Orestes, on his own mother. But the court of law which eventually tries Orestes is actually that of Periclean Athens, and the plays' debates over the rational application of law are debates that resonated with Aeschylus' contemporaries. *Oedipus at Colonus*, one of Sophocles' later tragedies, used the story of the mythical king of Thebes to comment bitterly on Athens' disastrous war with Sparta (see below). Similarly, the *Trojan Women* of Euripides (485–406 B.C.E.), presented in 415, marks the tragic turning point in the Athenians' march toward defeat in this war. By looking back at the capture, rape, and enslavement of Troy's defeated women, Athenians were forced to look at the consequences of their own imperial policies.

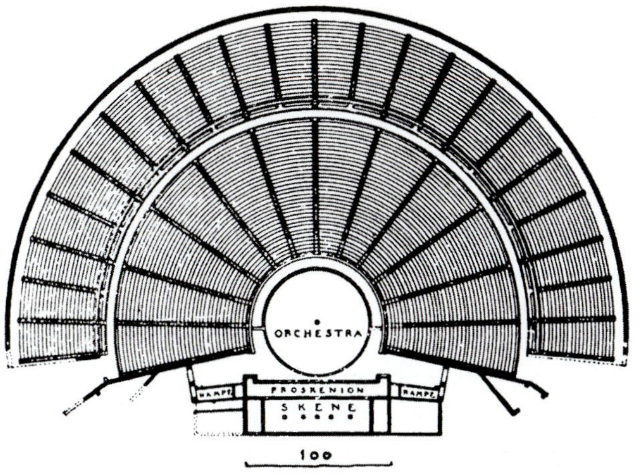

**THE THEATER AT EPIDAUROS.** Greek dramas were invariably presented in the open air, usually at dawn. Since these were civic spectacles, theaters had to be large enough to accommodate all citizens. Most, like this one at Epidauros (right), took advantage of the natural slope of a hill. The plan for the theater is shown above (left). The acting area would have been backed by a high wall, the *skene*, which housed stage machinery and enhanced the acoustics. A trained actor standing in the *orchestra* would have been audible even to those seated in the top tier. ▪ ***How would the size and setting of such a theater enhance the political character of the plays performed within it?***

Comedy was even more obviously a genre of political commentary and social satire, and could deal openly with the absurdities and atrocities of current events. Not only was it unconstrained by any poetic framework, comedy—then as now—could be effectively and safely deployed to deal with issues that were too hot to handle in any other form: sexual scandals, political corruption, moral hypocrisy, intellectual pretension, popular fads. Aristophanes (*EHR-ih-STOFF-ah-nees*, c. 446–386 B.C.E.), the greatest of the Athenian comic playwrights, lampooned everything from the philosophy of Socrates to the tragedies of his contemporary Euripides, and was an especially outspoken critic of Athenian warmongers and their imperialist aims. He regularly savaged the powerful figures whom he saw as leading Athens to its doom, and he was repeatedly dragged into court to defend himself against the demagogues he attacked. But the power and popularity of comic theater was such that politicians never dared to shut it down for long. It was too much an expression, and outcome, of Athenian ideals.

Periclean Athens was also fertile ground for the development of new literary forms. Even though the Greeks of this age were becoming more dependent on writing for legal and commercial transactions, they valued highly the arts of memory and oral debate; intellectuals had long been used to expressing themselves through poetry, which was always intended to be sung and enjoyed in performance, not to be read. The Milesian philosophers had conveyed their ideas in verse, and Solon had used poetry in justifying his political reforms. In the fifth century B.C.E., though, the rise of functional literacy in Athens encouraged the emergence of prose as a distinct literary form. Herodotus found a ready market for his histories in Athens. His younger contemporary Thucydides (*thu-SID-ih-dees*) followed suit, using his time in exile to write a masterful—and scathingly critical—history of the war between his polis and Sparta.

Between them, these two historians developed a new approach to the study of the past, emphasizing the need to collect and interpret multiple sources and focusing on human agency as the driving force of history (rather than divine intervention or divine will). Although in different ways, both conceived the historian's role as distinct from that of a storyteller. The word *historia* would continue to mean both "story" and "history" in Greek, but for Herodotus and Thucydides the historian's task was to investigate and critically reflect on the events of his own time, as well as to illuminate those of the past. These methods and goals would increasingly come to inform other prose genres, including the philosophical writings of Plato and Aristotle (see Chapter 4).

## Art and Architecture

The artists of fifth-century B.C.E. Greece revealed the same range of talents in the visual arts as poets did in their dramas. Their comic gift is exhibited in vessels made for festive use at symposia, which often depict the delights of sensuality, sexual encounters, and scenes from bawdy tales. By contrast, the heroic but humane mode of tragedy corresponds to the marble statues and sculptured reliefs made for temples and public places. Athenian sculptors in particular were drawn to the challenges of repesenting the human form accurately, while at the same time celebrating an ideal of physical beauty.

Perhaps the most striking development in fifth-century Greek sculpture was the new attention paid to the crafting of naturalistic figures, both clothed and nude. This happened first in Athens. Nothing like it had ever been seen before, although it is a trend already discernible in the figure of the *kouros* examined above (page 80) and in the successive refinements of the sculptor's art made in the previous century. What hastened the acceptance of naturalism in art is a matter of intense debate, but scholars have long wanted to link this innovation to the triumphant victories over the Persians in those key decades. Greeks tended to regard the Persian male's modesty of dress, preference for trousers, fondness for jewelry, and luxurious long hair as proofs of effeminacy (see the vase painting on page 93), whereas Greek men took pride in sculpting their physiques, and excercising and participating in athletic contests in the nude. A Greek might have said that only barbarians bowed down to their rulers like slaves and covered their shameful bodies in constricting clothes; free men celebrate their individuality not only in politics but in the care of the body and its representation.

The Athenians also made exceptional contributions to architecture in this period. All Greek temples sought to create an impression of harmony, but the Parthenon of Athens, built between 447 and 438 B.C.E., is generally considered the finest example of this. Construction of this stunning,

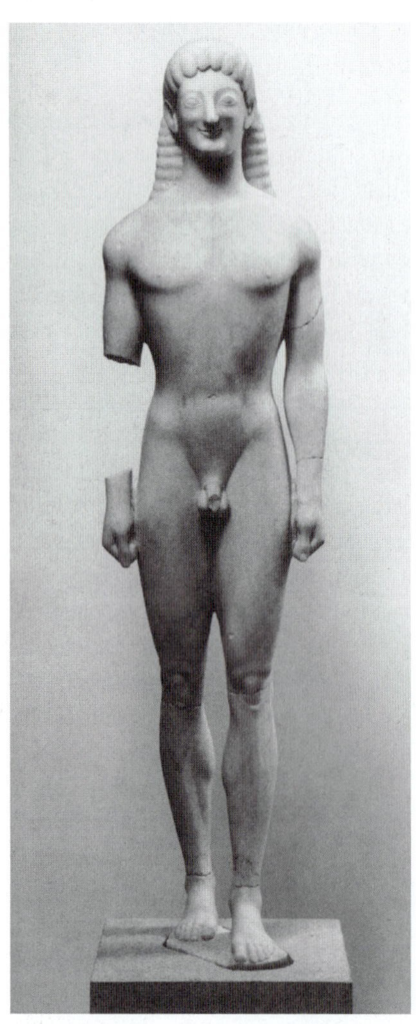

**APOLLO OF TENEA, APOLLO OF PIOMBINO, AND THE CRITIAN BOY.** These three statues, dating from about 560, 500, and 480 B.C.E., respectively, display the development of Greek statuary art. The first rather stiff and symmetrical statue (left) is imitative of Egyptian sculpture (see the statue of the pharaoh Menkaure, page 29). Roughly half a century later, the second representation (middle) of Apollo begins to display motion, not unlike the kouros on page 80. The last figure (right), showing a boy standing in a relaxed posture with his weight resting on one leg, displays even greater naturalism.

**THE SHRINE OF ATHENA IN THE PARTHENON.** This is a replica of the statue of Athena that once stood inside the Parthenon dedicated to her (see also the image on page 74). Made of gold and ivory and designed by the great sculptor Phidias, who was updating a more archaic style, the statue stood forty feet high and was visible to viewers oustide the temple and some distance away. Its image would have been reflected in a shallow pool of water located in front of the statue.

expensive, and structurally ambitious building was urged on the Athenians by Pericles as a tribute to their patron goddess, Athena Parthenos ("Athena the Virgin"), and as a symbol of their own power, confidence, and genius.

## *Women and Men in the Daily Life of Athens*

Toward the end of his famous funeral oration, which Thucydides quotes in his history, Pericles addresses only a few brief remarks to the women of Athens who mourn their fallen fathers, husbands, and sons in 430 B.C.E., the first year of the disastrous war with Sparta. He urges them to do three things: rear more children for the support of Athens and its wars, show no more weakness than is "natural to their sex," and attract no attention to themselves. For as he says, the greatest glory of a woman is not to be spoken of at all, whether for good or ill. His remarks reveal widely held attitudes toward women in classical Greece, especially in Athens.

The growth of democracy did not lead to greater equality between the sexes; in fact, it had the opposite result. In Mycenaean Greece, women were viewed as possessing extraordinary funds of courage and wisdom, as well as beauty and virtue. They were prized for their shrewd advice on political and military matters, and they played an active role in the world. Sometimes they ruled kingdoms in their own right. Indeed, this was still the case in the northern territories of Macedon and Epirus, as we shall see (Chapter 4), as well as in some Ionian poleis. But as aristocratic ideals gave way to more democratic ones, Greek women increasingly spent their lives in the shadows. The importance of the hoplite infantry and its spirit of shared purpose encouraged men to train together and to develop close relationships, something that was also sanctioned by the political system. At the same time, that spirit of equality discouraged displays of wealth, especially by women. Instead, the rearing of children to supply the infantry became the female imperative. Public spaces were restricted to male activities, while domestic, private spaces were reserved for female endeavors such as child care and weaving. Respectable women lived in seclusion, rarely (if ever) venturing forth from their homes.

In Athens, girls could be married at age fourteen to husbands more than twice their age. (Younger men were supposed to devote themselves to war.) A girl's father arranged her marriage without concern for her preferences and provided a dowry that her husband could use for her support. Legally, wives became the property of their husbands. And shortly after a wife entered her new home, a regular schedule of childbirth would begin. Typically, the interval between births was two to four years, meaning that the average young wife would bear between four and six children before she died, usually around the age of thirty-five. Her place might then be taken by another, younger woman.

Because respectable women seldom went out of doors, since it was thought immodest for them to be seen by men other than those in their families, slaves did whatever shopping or marketing the household required. Even at home, women were expected to withdraw into private rooms if visitors arrived. But they were not supposed to sit around idly, and their main occupation—this was true of all women, from royalty to slaves—was spinning and weaving. And since women's work was basically menial, men looked down on them for it, even though their own livelihoods and comfort depended on it. Available evidence even suggests that husbands were not encouraged to form emotional

**WOMEN AND WEAVING.** Wool-working and weaving were gender-specific activities in ancient Greece, in which women of all social ranks were expected to participate. On this red-figure vase, dating from 460–450 B.C.E., we see the woman on the left carding wool, and the two women on the right preparing fibers for spinning into threads, which could then be woven into cloth.

attachments to their wives, although some obviously did. In a revealing passage, Herodotus reports of a certain Lydian king that he "fell in love with his own wife, a fancy that had strange consequences." By contrast, an Athenian orator remarked that "we have prostitutes for pleasure, concubines for daily physical attendance, wives to bear us legitimate children and be our faithful housekeepers."

In addition to depending on the faithful labor and fertility of its "free" women, Athenians were as reliant on slaves as Spartans were on helots. Without slavery, none of the Athenian accomplishments in politics, thought, or art would have been possible. The Athenian ideal of dividing and rotating governmental duties among all free men depended on slaves who worked in fields, businesses, and homes while free men engaged in politics. In fact, the Athenian democratic system began to function fully only with the expansion of Athenian mining and commerce around 500 B.C.E., which enabled the Athenians to buy slaves in larger numbers. Freedom and slavery were thus inescapably, and paradoxically, linked in this democracy—much as they would be many centuries later in the United States.

Although widespread, Athenian slavery was modest in scale. Slaves did not ordinarily work in teams or in factories; the only exceptions were the state-owned silver mines, where large numbers of slaves toiled in miserable conditions. Most slaves were owned in small numbers by a wide range of Athenian families, including the relatively poor. As domestic servants and farm laborers, slaves might even be considered trusted members of the household, although their masters were legally empowered to beat them or abuse them; concubines were often drawn from among this class of slaves. Yet slaves could never be entirely dehumanized, as they were in modern slaveholding societies: the misfortune of becoming a slave through debt was a reality of Athens' recent past, and the real possibility of being enslaved in war would become a widespread consequence of Athens' overreaching ambitions.

## "THE GREATEST WAR IN HISTORY" AND ITS CONSEQUENCES

Athenian freedom rested on the servitude of others. Slaves performed much of the labor at home, while Athens' allies in the Delian League provided the resources that supported Athenian greatness. Without the surplus wealth flowing into Athens from the league, none of the projects Pericles undertook—pay for political participation, massive building projects, the patronage of Athenian drama—would have been possible. These projects kept Athens rich, its democracy vibrant, and Pericles in power. But ultimately, Athens' foreign policy and imperial ambitions undermined these achievements.

Since the 470s, as we noted above, Athens had begun crushing those allies who attempted to break from its control. By the early 440s, its only rival for supremacy in the Greek world was Sparta. Rather than attempting to maintain a balance of power, however, Pericles determined on a more aggressive policy. In order to ensure that military resources would be directed toward any Spartan opposition, he concluded a formal peace with Persia. Yet the sole purpose of the Delian League had been the defense of Greece against Persian aggression, so Athens now had no justification for compelling its members to maintain their allegiance. Many remained loyal nonetheless, paying their contributions and enjoying the economic benefits of warm relations with Athens. Others, however, did not, and Athens found itself increasingly having to force its allies back into line, often installing Athenian garrisons and planting Athenian colonists—who retained their Athenian citizenship—to ensure future loyalty.

In the context of recent history and longstanding Greek values, such behavior was disturbing. The Delian League had been established to preserve Greek independence. Now Athens itself was becoming an oppressive, imperial power. Foremost among its accusers were the Corinthians, whose own economic standing was threatened by Athenian dominance. The Corinthians were close allies of the Spartans, who in turn were the dominant power in what historians call the Peloponnesian League. (The Greeks called it simply the "Spartans and their allies.") When war finally erupted between Athens and Sparta, Thucydides—himself an Athenian—ascribed it to the growing power of Athens and the anxiety this inspired in other poleis. No modern historian has improved on Thucydides' thesis. Yet for the Athenians and their leaders, there could be no question of relinquishing their empire, or the dream of dominating the Mediterranean world. For Sparta and its allies, meanwhile, the prospect of relinquishing their independence was equally unthinkable. Two very different ideas of Greek superiority were about to fight to the death.

### *The Peloponnesian War Begins*

When the Athenians and Spartans found themselves at war with one another in 431 B.C.E., both sides believed a conclusion would come quickly—a delusion common to many of history's pivotal contests. Instead, the war dragged on for twenty-seven years. Thucydides, writing about it in exile, recalled that he knew from the time of its outbreak that it was going to be "the greatest war in history," amounting to the first world war, because by the time it was over it would involve the entire Mediterranean. He also meant that it was the worst, so devastating to both sides that it partially destroyed the proud heritage of freedom that the Greeks had treasured. By the time Athens was forced to concede defeat, all the poleis were weakened to such an extent that they would never again be able to withstand outside threats.

From the beginning, Athens knew that it could not defeat Sparta on land; and neither Sparta nor its allies had a fleet capable of facing the Athenians at sea. Pericles therefore developed a bold strategy: he would pull the entire population of Attica within the walls of Athens and its harbor and not attempt to defend the countryside against Sparta. For sustenance, Athens would rely on supplies shipped in by its fleet, which would also be deployed to ravage the coasts of the Peloponnesus.

The Spartans duly plundered the farms and pastures of Attica, frustrated that the Athenians would not engage them in battle. Meanwhile, the Athenians inflicted significant destruction on Spartan territory in a series of raids and by successfully encouraging rebellion among the helots. Time appeared to be on Athens' side, but in 429 B.C.E. the crowded conditions of the besieged city gave rise to a typhus epidemic that killed over a third of the population, including the aged Pericles. Pericles' death revealed that he had been the only man capable of managing the political forces he had unleashed. His successors were mostly demagogues, ambitious men who played to the worst instincts of the demos. The most successful of these was Cleon, a particular target of Aristophanes' ridicule, who refused a Spartan offer of peace in 425 B.C.E. and continued the war until his own death in battle four years later. It was under Cleon that Thucydides was given the impossible task of liberating a city under Spartan control; his failure in 423 led to his exile.

After the death of Cleon, a truce with Sparta was negotiated by an able Athenian leader named Nicias. But Athenians continued to pursue a "dirty war" by preying on poleis that it feared might support the Spartans. This led to atrocities like the destruction of the entire city of Melos, an island that had been colonized by the Spartans but had maintained its neutrality since the beginning of the war. When the inhabitants of Melos refused to compromise this position by accepting Athenian rule, Athens had the entire male population slaughtered and every woman and child sold into slavery. Thereafter, Athens' policy of preemptive warfare proved destructive to itself. In 415 B.C.E., a charismatic young aristocrat named Alcibiades convinced the Athenians to attack the powerful Greek city of Syracuse in Sicily, which was allegedly harrying Athenian allies in the western Mediterranean. The expedition failed disastrously, with the death or enslavement of thousands of Athenian warriors.

News of the Syracusan disaster shattered the Athenians. Many political leaders were driven from the polis as scapegoats, and in 411 B.C.E. a hastily convened assembly of citizens voted the democracy out of existence, replacing it with an oligarchy of 400 members, many of whom had been present at this vote. The remains of the Athenian fleet, then stationed in Samos on the Ionian coast, responded by declaring a democratic government in exile under the leadership of none other than Alcibiades. The oligarchy proved to be brief, and democracy was restored to Athens by 409. But a pattern of self-destruction had been established, making it difficult for anyone in Athens or outside it to believe in the possibility of restored greatness.

## THE FAILURE OF ATHENIAN DEMOCRACY

The Spartans too despaired of bringing the war to an end. Even in its weakened condition, the Athenian fleet was still invincible. Finally, Sparta turned to the Persians, who were glad to avenge themselves on Athens and agreed to supply the gold and expertise necessary to train an effective Spartan navy. Meanwhile, Athenians were turning against

**THE PELOPONNESIAN WAR.** This map shows the patchwork of colonies and alliances that bound together the supporters of Sparta and Athens at the outbreak of the Peloponnesian War. ▪ ***Which side had the geographical advantage?*** ▪ ***Which neutral powers might have been able to tip the balance by entering the war on one side or the other?*** ▪ ***What strategic and military choices did geography impose on the two combatants and their allies?***

each other and making the Spartans' task easier. In 406, a rare Athenian naval victory at Arginusae *(ar-geh-NOO-si)* ended in a sudden storm, which prevented Athenian commanders from rescuing the sailors whose ships had been wrecked. A firestorm of protest was fanned by demagogues who insisted on making an example of those generals brave enough to return to Athens. One of these was Pericles' son Pericles, who died a victim of his father's policies. Through such measures, the Athenians killed or exiled the last of their able commanders.

The result was tragic. The poorly led Athenian fleet was destroyed in 404 B.C.E. Without ships, the Athenians could neither feed themselves nor defend their city. The Spartans sailed the Aegean unopposed, installing pro-Spartan oligarchies. Finally, they besieged Athens, which surrendered. Corinth and Thebes, remembering the ruthless treatment of Melos, called for Athens' destruction. The Spartans refused, but imposed harsh terms: the dismantling of Athens' defensive walls, the scrapping of its fleet, and the acceptance of an oligarchy under Spartan supervision. These so-called Thirty Tyrants confiscated private property and murdered their political opponents. Their excesses drove committed democrats to plan a desperate coup, a bloodbath averted only through the intervention of the Spartan king.

By the end of 401 B.C.E., Athens had restored a semblance of democratic governance, but it was never more than a shadow of its former self.

With its victory, Sparta succeeded Athens as the arbiter of the Greek world. But this was a thankless job, made worse by the losses the Spartans had suffered during the war and by the fact that they were even more aggressive in their control of the Aegean than the Athenians had been. In fact, the Spartans found themselves in a position they had avoided throughout their history, because their far-flung interests now sapped their manpower and undermined their control over the helots. They also faced a reinvigorated Persian Empire, which took advantage of the Greeks' fratricidal struggles to increase its naval presence in the Aegean.

These were the circumstances in which the Athenian philosopher Socrates (469–399 B.C.E.) attempted to reform his city's ethical and political traditions. To understand something of his accomplishments, and to assess the reasons for his tragic death, we must trace briefly the history of philosophical speculation in the half century before his birth.

**SOCRATES.** According to Plato, Socrates looked like a goatman but spoke like a god.

## *The Pythagoreans and the Sophists*

After the Persian conquest of Ionia, many Milesian philosophers fled to southern Italy. Philosophical speculation thus continued in the Greek "far west." A major proponent was Pythagoras, who founded a philosophical community in the city of Croton. Pythagoras and his followers regarded the speculative life as the highest good, but they believed that one must be purified of fleshly desires in order to achieve this. Just as the essence of life lay in the mind, they believed that the essence of the universe was to be found not in the natural world but in the study of abstracts, and so they concentrated on mathematics and musical theory. The Pythagoreans established the key properties of odd and even numbers and also proved an old Babylonian hypothesis in geometry, known today as the Pythagorean theorem. Even though they shunned the material world, they still exhibited the characteristic Greek quest for regularity and predictability in that world.

Meanwhile, philosophy as it developed in mainland Greece was more attuned to questions of ethics and politics. The increasing power of individual citizens begged the question of how a man should conduct himself, in public and private life, so as to embrace "the beautiful and the good"—or at least to advance himself by the use of his wits. To answer this latter need were a new group of teachers known as Sophists, a term simply meaning "wise men." Unlike the Milesian philosophers or the Pythagoreans, however, the Sophists made their living from selling their knowledge. Their teachings are best exemplified by Protagoras, an older contemporary of Socrates. His famous dictum, "man is the measure of all things," means that goodness, truth, and justice are relative concepts, adaptable to the needs and interests of human beings. They are not moral absolutes, established by the gods. Indeed, Protagoras declared that no one could know whether the gods existed or, if they did, what they wanted. He thus concluded that there could be no absolute standards of right and wrong. Empirical facts, established by the perception of the senses, were the only source of knowledge. And because each man experienced the world in a different way, there could be only particular truths valid for the individual knower.

Such teachings struck many Athenians as dangerous. Sophists like Protagoras made everyday life a subject for philosophical discussion, but their relativism could too easily degenerate into a conviction that the wise man (or the wise state) is the one best able to manipulate others and gratify individual desires. Both personally and collectively, this conviction could rationalize monstrous acts of brutality—like those committed by Athens in the case of Melos. Indeed, the lessons of the Peloponnesian War went a long way toward demonstrating the disastrous consequences of this self-serving logic: if justice is merely

# Competing Viewpoints

## *Two Views of Socrates*

### Socrates as a Sophist

*Most people regard Socrates as the sage thinker who challenged the prevailing prejudices of his day. During his own time, however, he was not so universally admired. In Aristophanes' comedy* The Clouds, *the protagonist, Strepsiades, goes to Socrates and his "Thought Shop," asking that Socrates make him and his son, Pheidippides, orators capable of winning lawsuits and growing rich. Aristophanes implies throughout that Socrates is a charlatan who teaches word games and tricks for hire.*

**STREPSIADES:** See that he [Pheidippides] learns your two Arguments, whatever you call them—oh yes, Right and Wrong—the one that takes a bad case and defeats Right with it. If he can't manage both, then at least Wrong—that will do—but that he must have.

**SOCRATES:** Well, I'll go and send the Arguments here in person, and they'll teach him themselves.

**STREPSIADES:** Don't forget, he's got to be able to argue against any kind of justified claim at all.

**RIGHT:** This way. Let the audience see you. . . .

**WRONG:** Sure, go wherever you like. The more of an audience we have, the more soundly I'll trounce you.

**RIGHT:** What sort of trick will you use?

**WRONG:** Oh, just a few new ideas.

**RIGHT:** Yes, they're in fashion now, aren't they, [*to the audience*] thanks to you idiots. . . . [*to Pheiddipides*] You don't want to be the sort of chap who's always in the agora telling stories about other people's sex lives, or in the courts arguing about some petty, filthy little dispute. . . .

**WRONG:** People here at the Thought Shop call me Wrong, because I was the one who invented ways of proving anything wrong, laws, prosecutors, anything. Isn't that worth millions—to have a really bad case and yet win? . . . Suppose you fall in love with a married woman—have a bit of fun—and get caught in the act. As you are now, without a tongue in your head, you're done for. But if you come and learn from me, then you can do whatever you like and get away with it . . . and supposing you do get caught with someone's wife, you can say to him. . . . "What have I done wrong? Look at Zeus; wasn't he always a slave of his sexual passions? And do you expect a mere mortal like me to do any better than a god?" . . .

**STREPSIADES** [*to Socrates*]: I wonder if you'd accept a token of my appreciation? But my son, has he learned that Argument we were listening to a moment ago?

**SOCRATES:** Yes, he has.

**STREPSIADES:** Holy Fraud, how wonderful!

**SOCRATES:** Yes, you'll now be able to win any case at all.

Source: Aristophanes, *The Clouds*, trans. Alan H. Sommerstein (New York: 1973), pp. 148–50, 154, 159–60 (slightly revised).

### Socrates and the Laws of Athens

*According to his pupil Plato, Socrates spent the last days of his life in conversation with his friends and followers, some of whom urged him to escape from captivity and live in exile. In the dialogue* Crito, *a young aristocrat of that name argues that the very laws that have condemned Socrates are unjust, and that by choosing to obey them Socrates is giving them a legitimacy they do not deserve. Halfway through the debate, Socrates turns the tables on him.*

**SOCRATES:** I should like you to consider whether we are still satisfied on this point: that the really important thing is not to live, but to live well.

**CRITO:** Why, yes.

**SOCRATES:** And that to live well means the same thing as to live honorably, or rightly?

**CRITO:** Yes.

**SOCRATES:** Then in light of this agreement we must consider whether or not it is right for me to try to get away without an official pardon. If it turns out to be right, we must make the attempt; if not, we must let it drop. . . .

**CRITO:** I agree with what you say, Socrates. . . .

**SOCRATES:** Well, here is my next point, or rather question. Ought one to fulfill all one's agreements, provided they are right, or break them?

**CRITO:** One ought to fulfill them.

**SOCRATES:** Then consider the logical consequence. If we leave this place without first persuading the polis to let us go . . . are we or are we not abiding by our just agreements?

**CRITO:** I can't answer your question, Socrates. I am not clear in my mind.

**SOCRATES:** Look at it this way. Suppose that while we were preparing to run away (or however one should describe it), the Laws of Athens were to come and confront us with this question: "Now, Socrates, what are your proposing to do? Can you deny that by this act which you are contemplating you intend, so far as you have the power, to destroy us, the Laws, and the whole polis as well? Do you imagine that a city can continue to exist and not be turned upside down, if the legal judgments which are pronounced in it have no force but are nullified and destroyed by private persons?"—How shall we answer this question, Crito, and others of the same kind? . . . Shall we say, "Yes, I do intend to destroy the laws, because the polis has wronged me by passing a faulty judgment at my trial"? Is this to be our answer, or what?

**CRITO:** What you have just said, by all means, Socrates.

**SOCRATES:** Then supposing the Laws say, "Was there provision for this in the agreement between you and us, Socrates? Or did you pledge to abide by whatever judgments the polis pronounced? . . . [I]f you cannot persuade your country you must do whatever it orders, and patiently submit to any punishment it imposes, whether it be flogging or imprisonment. And if it leads you out to war, you must comply, and it is right that you should do so; you must not give way or retreat or abandon your position. Both in war and in the law courts you must do whatever your city and your country commands."

Source: Plato, *Crito*, excerpted (with modifications) from *The Last Days of Socrates*, trans. Hugh Tredennick (New York: 1969), pp. 87–91.

### *Questions for Analysis*

1. Socrates actually refused to teach the art of "making the weaker argument defeat the stronger." But in *The Clouds*, Aristophanes shows him teaching how "to win any case at all." Why were the powers of persuasion considered potentially dangerous in democratic Athens? Why would Aristophanes choose to represent Socrates in this way?
2. How do the arguments of Plato's Socrates compare to those of Aristophanes' character?
3. How does Socrates' sense of honor and his duty toward the polis compare to that of Tyrtaeus of Sparta (page 82)?

relative, then neither individual morality nor society can survive. This conviction led to the growth of a new philosophical movement grounded on the theory that absolute standards do exist, and that human beings can determine what these are through the exercise of reason. The initiator of this trend was Socrates.

## *The Life and Thought of Socrates*

Socrates was not a professional teacher, as the Sophists were. He may have trained as a stonemason, and he certainly had some sort of livelihood that enabled him to maintain his status as a citizen and hoplite. Having fought in three campaigns as part of the Athenian infantry during the war with Sparta, he was both an ardent patriot and a sincere critic of Athenian policy. His method of instruction was conversation: through dialogue with passers-by, he submitted every presumed truth to examination in order to establish a firm foundation for further inquiry. Everything we know about Socrates' teachings comes from the writings of younger men who considered themselves his pupils, and who participated in these conversations. The most important of these followers was Plato.

According to Plato, Socrates sought to show that all supposed certainties are merely unexamined prejudices inherited from others. Socrates always said that he himself knew nothing, because this was a more secure place from which to begin the learning process. He sought to base his speculations on sound definitions of key concepts—justice, virtue, beauty, love—which he and his pupils could arrive at only by investigating their own assumptions. And he focused his attention on practical ethics rather than the

**SOCRATES GAINING WISDOM FROM THE WISE WOMAN DIOTIMA.** In Plato's *Symposium*, Socrates learns the philosophical meaning of love from Diotima, an ethereal female being, wiser than he. In this sculptural representation of the scene, the winged figure between Diotima and Socrates is probably a personification of love (Eros).

study of the physical world (like the Milesians did) or abstractions (like the Pythagoreans). He urged his listeners to reflect on the principles of proper conduct, both for their own sakes and for that of society as a whole. One should consider the meaning and consequences of one's actions at all times, he taught, and be prepared to take responsibility for them. According to one of his most memorable sayings, "the unexamined life is not worth living."

It is bitterly ironic that such a man, the product of Athenian democracy, should have been put to death by democratic processes. Shortly after the end of the Peloponnesian War, in 399 B.C.E., when Athens was reeling from both the shock of defeat and violent internal upheavals, a democratic faction decided that Socrates was a threat to the state. A democratic court agreed, condemning him to death for denying the gods, disloyalty to the polis, and "corrupting the youth." Although his friends made arrangements for him to flee the city and thus evade punishment, Socrates insisted on abiding by the laws, thus proving himself true to his own principles and setting an example for future citizens. He died calmly by the prescribed method, self-administered poison.

According to Socrates, the goal of philosophy is to help human beings understand and apply standards of absolute good, rather than to master a series of mental tricks that facilitate personal gain at the expense of others. The circumstances of his death, however, show that it is difficult to translate this philosophy into principles that can be widely accepted. This would be the task of Plato, who would lay the groundwork for all subsequent Western philosophy (see Chapter 4).

# After You Read This Chapter

Visit StudySpace for quizzes, additional review materials, and multi-media documents. **wwnorton.com/studyspace**

## REVIEWING THE OBJECTIVES

- The Greek polis was a unique form of government. What factors led to its emergence?
- Hoplite warfare had a direct effect on the shaping of early democracy. Why?
- Poleis could develop in very different ways. What are some of the reasons for this?
- In what ways did Athenian culture, philosophy, and art reflect democratic ideals?
- The Persian and Peloponnesian Wars affected Greek civilization in profound ways. Describe some of the consequences of Athens' victory in the former and its defeat in the latter.

## CONCLUSION

There are many striking similarities between the civilization of ancient Greece and our own–and many stark differences. Perhaps the most salient example of both is the concept of democracy, which the people of ancient Greece would have defined as rule by a class of propertied male citizens supported by slavery. In theory and in practice, this amounted to only a small percentage of the population in Athens, whereas in Sparta the vast majority were subject to the rule of an even smaller class of Spartiates. Moreover, the growth of Athenian power meant, increasingly, the exploitation of other poleis and the spread of imperialism, a ruinous policy of preemptive warfare, and increased intolerance and paranoia. Socrates was not the only man put to death for expressing his opinions. Finally, the status of women in this "golden age" was lower than it had been in earlier periods of Greek history, and women had fewer personal rights than in any of the ancient societies we have studied so far.

And yet the profound significance of Greek experiments with new forms of governance and new ideas about the world is undeniable. This can be seen with particular clarity if we compare the Greek poleis with the empires and kingdoms of Mesopotamia and ancient Egypt. The typical political regime of the ancient Near Eastern world was, as we have seen, that of an absolute monarch supported by a powerful priesthood. In this context, cultural achievements were mainly instruments to enhance the prestige of rulers, and economic life was controlled by palaces and temples. By contrast, the core values of the Greeks were the primacy of the human male and the principles of competition, individual achievement, and human freedom and responsibility. (The very word for freedom—*eleutheria*—cannot be translated into any ancient Near Eastern language, not even Hebrew.) In his history, Herodotus records a conversation between a Greek (in this case a Spartan) and a Persian, who expresses surprise that the Greeks should raise spears against the supposedly benign rule of his emperor. The Spartan retorts, "You understand how to be a slave, but you know nothing of freedom. Had you tasted it, you would advise us to fight not only with spears but with axes." How the Greeks came to turn those spears on one another within a few generations of their united victory is a story worthy of one of their own tragedies.

Another way of appreciating the enduring importance of Greek civilization is to recall the essential vocabulary we have inherited from it: not only the word *democracy* but *politics*, *philosophy*, *theater*, *history*. How would we think without these concepts? The very notion of humanity comes to us from the Greeks. For them, the fullest development of one's potential should be the aim of existence: every free man is the sculptor of his own monument. This work of growing from childishness to personhood is what the Greeks called *paideia*; the Romans called it *humanitas*. How this and other ideas came to be disseminated beyond Greece, to be adopted by the peoples and places of a much wider world, is the subject of Chapter 4.

### PEOPLE, IDEAS, AND EVENTS IN CONTEXT

- How did the epics of **HOMER** transmit the values of the Bronze Age to the **ARISTOCRACY** of the new Greek **POLEIS**?
- How did the spread of **GREEK CULTURE** transform the Mediterranean, even as the adoption of **HOPLITE** military tactics transformed Greek politics?
- Compare and contrast the historical circumstances that led to the development of **ATHENS**, **SPARTA**, and **MILETUS.** What were the main differences among them?
- What were the different motives for the invasions of **DARIUS** and **XERXES**? By what methods did the Greek poleis manage to emerge victorious from the **PERSIAN WARS**?
- What were the triumphs and limitations of **DEMOCRACY** in **PERICLEAN ATHENS**?
- How did the **PELOPONNESIAN WAR** transform Athens and affect the balance of power in the Mediterranean?

### CONSEQUENCES

- The trial and execution of Socrates can be seen as a referendum on the relationship between the individual and the state. What does this incident reveal about the limitations of personal power and individual rights? To what degree was this incident a product of Athenian losses during the Peloponnesian War? To what extent does it reflect long-term trends in the Greek world?
- We like to think that we can trace our democratic ideals and institutions back to Athens, but does this mean that the failings of Athenian democracy also mirror those of our own? What parallels can you draw between the cultures of fifth-century Athens and today's United States? What are some key differences?

# Before You Read This Chapter

## STORY LINES

- In the wake of the Peloponnesian War, divisions within and among the Greek states eventually made them vulnerable to the imperial ambitions of King Philip II of Macedonia and his son, Alexander the Great.
- Alexander's conquest of the Persian Empire and Egypt united the civilizations of antiquity under Greco-Macedonian rule. Even after his untimely death, a shared language and culture continued to bind these civilizations together in a new Hellenistic ("Greek-like") world.
- Ease of travel, trade, and communication in this Hellenistic world fostered urbanization on an unprecedented scale. The resulting cosmopolitan culture challenged traditional social, economic, and political norms, giving rise to new social classes, forms of wealth, and technological innovations.
- The unique art forms and intellectual inquiries of Greece were thus disseminated throughout this world, and transformed by it.

## CHRONOLOGY

| | |
|---|---|
| 404 B.C.E. | Sparta defeats Athens in the Peloponnesian War |
| 401 B.C.E. | Xenophon and the Ten Thousand begin their Persian expedition |
| 395–338 B.C.E. | The struggle for Greek hegemony (Thebes, Athens, Sparta) |
| 371 B.C.E. | Epaminondas of Thebes defeats the Spartans at Leuctra |
| 356 B.C.E. | Philip II becomes king of Macedonia |
| 338 B.C.E. | Macedonia defeats Thebes and Athens at Chaeronea |
| 336–323 B.C.E. | Reign and campaigns of Alexander |
| 323–c. 275 B.C.E. | Formation of the Hellenistic kingdoms |
| 323–c. 225 B.C.E. | The Greek diaspora |
| c. 300 B.C.E. | Formation of the Aetolian and Achaean Leagues |
| 300–270 B.C.E. | Rise of Stoicism and Epicureanism |
| c. 300–200 B.C.E. | The Hellenistic scientific revolution |
| 203–120 B.C.E. | Lifetime of Polybius |

## CORE OBJECTIVES

- **EXPLAIN** Macedonia's rise to power and its triumph over the Greek poleis.
- **DESCRIBE** Alexander's methods of conquest, colonization, and governance.
- **IDENTIFY** the three main Hellenistic kingdoms and their essential differences.
- **DEFINE** the main characteristics of the Hellenistic world.
- **UNDERSTAND** how new philosophies and artistic movements reflect historical changes.

# 4 The Greek World Expands, 400–150 B.C.E.

When the young Alexander of Macedonia set out for Persia in 334 B.C.E, he brought along two favorite books. The first was a copy of the *Iliad*, which his teacher Aristotle had given him. The second was the *Anabasis*, "The Inland Expedition," by an Athenian called Xenophon (*ZEN-oh-fon*, 430–354 B.C.E). Both choices are significant. The *Iliad* recounts the story of a much earlier Greek assault on Asia, and its protagonist is the hero Achilles—a figure with whom Alexander identified: consummate warrior, favorite of the gods, a man who inspired passionate loyalty. It is also full of information useful to someone planning a long campaign in foreign lands against a formidable enemy, with a fractious army drawn from all parts of Greece and little prospect of bringing them home safely or soon. The *Anabasis* was an even more practical choice. Its author had been one of 10,000 Greek mercenaries hired by a Persian prince to overthrow his older brother, the Great King. The attempted coup failed, but Xenophon's book made the prince, Cyrus, another role model for Alexander. It also told, in detail, how Persians fought, how they lived, how they were governed, and what the terrain of their vast empire was like. Moreover, it showed what a dedicated army of hoplites could accomplish on Persian soil. This book would be Alexander's bible for the next ten years as he cut a victorious swath through the ancient civilizations of the Near East.

An avid student of history, Alexander recognized that the golden age of the Greek polis had ended in the war of attrition between Athens and Sparta. The fifty years prior to his own birth in 356 B.C.E. had merely continued this trend on a smaller scale, as the dominant poleis—first Sparta, then Thebes, then Athens—jockeyed for prominence. Meanwhile, social and economic problems were mounting. Faith in the old ideals of democracy decayed as a vast gulf opened up between the rich and the poor. Increasingly, the wealthy withdrew from politics altogether, while free citizens were reduced to debt slavery. As the poleis decayed, a new generation of intellectuals argued about what had gone wrong, and they tried to imagine how Greece could be saved. One was Aristotle, pupil of Plato and Alexander's own tutor.

Under the circumstances, no one would have been able to predict that the era of greatest Greek influence lay ahead. For rather suddenly, the stalemate of the weakened poleis was shattered by the rise to prominence of a tiny kingdom on their northern borders. Beginning in the reign of King Philip II, Macedonia came to control the Greek mainland. Then, under Philip's remarkable son, a united Greek and Macedonian army extended Greek culture and Greek governance from Egypt to the frontiers of India.

This personal empire, the empire of Alexander, could not last. But a cultural empire built upon it did. For a thousand years, a Hellenistic ("Greek-like") civilization united the disparate lands and peoples of a vast region, forming the basis of the more lasting Roman Empire and mirroring, in uncanny ways, the cosmopolitan world of our own time. How this happened is the subject of Chapter 4.

## THE DOWNFALL OF THE GREEK POLIS

The Peloponnesian War had left Sparta as the dominant power in the Greek world, but the Spartans showed little talent for their new preeminence. At home, Spartan politicians remained deeply divided over the wisdom of sending forces beyond their frontiers; abroad, Spartan armies showed even less restraint than the Athenians had done in subduing cities that should have been their allies. In 395, a significant portion of Greece—including such sworn enemies as Athens, Argos, Corinth, and Thebes—were aligned against Sparta in the so-called Corinthian War (395–387 B.C.E.). Eventually, the Spartans could bring the war to a conclusion only by turning once again to Persia, as they had done in the final stages of the Peloponnesian War. The Persians brokered a peace which they were also prepared to enforce, one which left Sparta in control. This pattern of Greek-on-Greek violence, temporarily halted by the intervention of Persia, was repeated time and again over the next fifty years, during which the advantage shifted steadily toward Persia.

### *The Struggle for Hegemony*

After the Corinthian War, the Spartans punished the most dangerous of their rivals, Thebes, by occupying the city for four years. This subjugation to a military garrison was intended and received as an act of humiliation, and

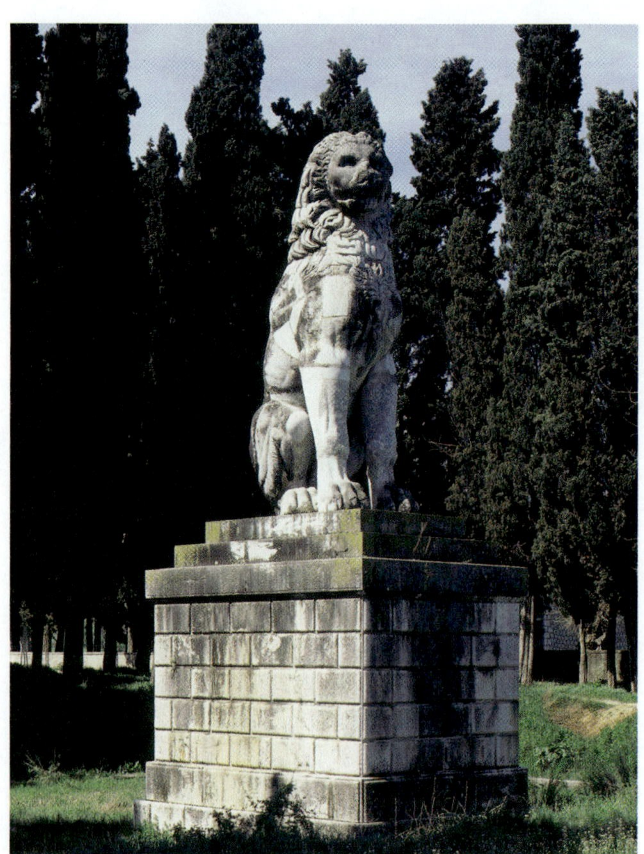

**HONORING THE THEBAN SACRED BAND.** According to ancient historians, all 300 of the Band's sworn lovers fell at the Battle of Chaeronea in 338 B.C.E., when Thebes was defeated by Macedonian forces led by King Philip II and his son, Alexander. An excavation undertaken at this site in 1890 uncovered the remains of only 254 warriors, but is possible that some were buried elsewhere. This monument is a modern reconstruction of the one originally erected by the citizens of Thebes toward the end of the fourth century B.C.E.

when the Thebans regained their autonomy they elected as their leader a fierce patriot who was also a military genius, Epaminondas (*eh-pa-min-OHN-das*, c. 410–362 B.C.E.). For decades, various poleis had been experimenting with the basic form of the hoplite phalanx, adding light skirmishers and archers to enhance its effectiveness. Epaminondas now went further. In imitation of the Spartan system, he formed an elite hoplite unit known as the Theban Sacred Band, made up of 150 couples, sworn lovers who had pledged to fight to the death for their polis and for each other's honor. Epaminondas also trained a corps of lighter-armed, fast-moving infantry. By the early 370s, he was ready for another trial of strength with the Spartans.

The Theban and Spartan armies met at Leuctra in 371 B.C.E.. Epaminondas defied convention by placing his best troops (the Sacred Band) on the left-hand side of his formation, and by stacking this phalanx fifty rows deep, making a narrow wedge of ten men abreast whose hidden strength he further disguised under a cover of arrows and javelin attacks. When the two sides met, the weight of the Theban left drove through the Spartan right flank, breaking this key phalanx in two and collapsing it. Epaminondas followed his victory by marching through Messenia and freeing the helots. Spartan power—and the unique social system that had supported it—was at an end. Overnight, Epaminondas had reduced Sparta to a small, provincial polis and launched what has often been called the Theban Hegemony.

But as Theban power grew, so did the animosity of the other Greek poleis. In 371, Athens had supported Thebes against Sparta, its ancient enemy, but when the Thebans and Spartans squared off again in 362 at the Battle of Mantinea, the Athenians allied themselves with the weaker Spartans. Although the Theban army again carried the day,

**THE INLAND EXPEDITION OF THE TEN THOUSAND.** This map shows the route taken by Xenophon and his fellow Greek mercenaries during their Persian campaigns, when they supported the failed coup of Cyrus against his brother Artaxerxes II, and then fought their way home through enemy territory (as the *Anabasis* records). Follow Xenophon's route with your finger. ▪ ***Where did it start and end?*** ▪ ***Compare this route with that of Alexander on page 121. How closely was Alexander following it?*** ▪ ***When and how did he diverge from it?*** ▪ ***Why would this journey of Greek mercenaries have provided Alexander with an important model?***

# Analyzing Primary Sources

## *Xenophon Describes an Ideal Leader*

*In his history of "The Inland Expedition" undertaken by the Ten Thousand, Xenophon (430–354 B.C.E.) mourns the death of Cyrus the Younger, whom he believes would have made a better Great King of Persia than the brother he challenged, Artaxerxes II. The following description of the prince's character and leadership became very famous in its time, often circulating as a separate booklet. It is likely to have influenced the young Alexander.*

Thus then died Cyrus, a man who, of all the Persians since Cyrus the elder, was the most princely and the most worthy of rule, as is agreed by all who appear to have had personal knowledge of him. In the first place, while he was yet a boy, and when he was receiving his education with his brother and other youths, he was thought to surpass them all in everything. For all the sons of the Persian nobles are educated at the gates of the king, where they may learn many a lesson of virtuous conduct, but can see or hear nothing disgraceful. Here the boys see some honored by the king, and others disgraced, and hear of them, so that in their very childhood they learn to govern and to obey.

Here Cyrus, first of all, showed himself most remarkable for modesty among those of his own age, and for paying more ready obedience to his elders than even those who were inferior to him in station; and next, he was noted for his fondness for horses, and for managing them in a superior manner. They found him, too, very desirous of learning, and most assiduous in practicing, the warlike exercises of archery, and hurling the javelin. When it suited his age, he grew extremely fond of the chase, and of braving dangers in encounters with wild beasts. On one occasion, he did not shrink from a she-bear that attacked him, but, in grappling with her, was dragged from off his horse, and received some wounds, the scars of which were visible on his body, but at last killed her. The person who first came to his assistance he made a happy man in the eyes of many.

When he was sent down by his father, as satrap of Lydia and Great Phrygia and Cappadocia, and was also appointed commander of all the troops whose duty it is to muster in the plain of Castolus, he soon showed that if he made a league or compact with anyone, or gave a promise, he deemed it of the utmost importance not to break his word. Accordingly the states that were committed to his charge, as well as individuals, had the greatest confidence in him; and if anyone had been his enemy, he felt secure that if Cyrus entered into a treaty with him, he should suffer no infraction of the stipulations. When, therefore, he waged war against Tissaphernes, all the cities, of their own accord, chose to adhere to Cyrus in preference to Tissaphernes, except the Milesians; but they feared him, because he would not abandon the cause of the exiles; for he both showed by his deeds and declared in words that he would never desert them, since he had once become a friend to them, not even though they should grow still fewer in number, and be in a worse condition than they were.

Whenever anyone did him a kindness or an injury, he showed himself anxious to go beyond him in those respects; and some used to mention a wish of his that he desired to live long enough to outdo both those who had done him good, and those who had done him ill, in the requital that he should make. Accordingly to him alone of the men of our days were so great a number of people desirous of committing the disposal of their property, their cities, and their own persons.

Source: Excerpted from Xenophon, *Anabasis*, ed. M. I. Finley in *The Portable Greek Historians* (New York: 1959), pp. 383–84.

### *Questions for Analysis*

1. According to Xenophon, what are the attributes of a great leader? How would Alexander have applied these to his own situation?
2. What seems to be Xenophon's attitude toward the Persians? How might his portrayal of them have been influenced by his travels among them? How might it have been colored by his attitude toward his own countrymen?
3. In what ways does Cyrus the Younger appear to have followed the example of his ancestor, Cyrus the Great (Chapter 2, page 64)?

the brilliant Epaminondas fell in battle, crippling Thebes' leadership. Athens then attempted to fill the vacuum by establishing a naval confederacy, organized more equitably than the Delian League had been. But the Athenians quickly reverted to abusing their allies, and the naval confederacy dissolved in rebellions. Greece thus remained a constellation of petty warring states, which were increasingly debilitated by their struggles with one other.

### *Social and Economic Crises*

Meanwhile, the poleis were also riven by internal turmoil. Athens was spared the political revolutions many other cities suffered, mostly because the memory of the Thirty Tyrants had discredited the cause of oligarchy there; but elsewhere in the Greek world, strife between democrats and oligarchs worsened. Incessant warfare, combined with these political struggles, profoundly affected the Greek world's economic and social infrastructures. Many ordinary people were driven from their homes or reduced to slavery. Country towns had been ravaged, some repeatedly, as had farmlands throughout Greece. The destruction of orchards and vineyards was particularly devastating because of the long time it takes grapevines and olive trees to mature: 40 or 50 years in the latter case. So when an invading army cut down an olive grove, it was destroying a staple crop for two generations. Even arable land was exhausted and less productive than it had been earlier. As a result, prices rose around 50 percent while standards of living declined because wages remained more or less stagnant. Taxes increased. In Athens, the wealthiest citizens now became the sponsors of public theaters and buildings, as well as the patrons who maintained roads and warships. Even so, the kind of ambitious civic spending undertaken by the tyrants or by Pericles was unknown in the fourth century B.C.E.

Unemployment was also widespread, especially among the growing population of the cities, which were swollen with refugees from the political collapse of the countryside and colonies. During wartime, men might find employment as rowers or soldiers in the service of their city; but when their city was at peace, many turned instead to mercenary service. The Greek states of Sicily and Italy began to hire mercenaries from the mainland, as did Sparta to supplement its own campaigns. As we have already noted, the brother of the Persian emperor Artaxerxes II, Cyrus, even hired a Greek mercenary force of 10,000 men in an attempt to seize the throne in 401 B.C.E.—although he did not reveal this aim until the army was deep in Persian territory and suddenly confronted with an enemy far more formidable than the tribal bands it had originally agreed to fight. Cyrus was killed in battle, at Cunaxa. Shortly thereafter, the Ten Thousand's Spartan general was murdered by agents of Artaxerxes, and the army—marooned in a hostile country—had to fight its way out under elected leaders, one of whom was Xenophon, who later wrote an account of these adventures. Finally, the veterans reached the Black Sea and made their way back to Greece, where many (including Xenophon) settled in Sparta. Despite all these hardships, this episode was a stunning demonstration of what a Greek army could achieve on a foreign campaign.

## RE-IMAGINING THE POLIS: THE ARTISTIC AND INTELLECTUAL RESPONSE

399 B.C.E., the year of Socrates' execution, might be taken to mark the end of an era—that of the polis. This basic engine of Greek life had continued to drive innovation and cultural production even during the Peloponnesian War, both in support of the war and in opposition to it. In Athens alone, the historians Herodotus (in his final years) and Thucydides were at work, as were the tragic poets Sophocles and Euripides, the comic playwright Aristophanes, and scores of talented statesmen, poets, sculptors, and artisans. But it's hard not to see the death of Socrates as symbolic of democracy's failure. Thereafter, the evident breakdown of society during the fourth century had a profound impact on the arts, philosophy, and especially political thought.

### *The Arts of the Fourth Century*

As we observed in Chapter 3, the painters and sculptors of the fifth century B.C.E. were already working to achieve a heightened appearance of realism. This experimentation continued in the fourth century, especially in the relatively new art of portraiture. Increasingly, artists and sculptors tried to render both objects and people as they actually looked—for better or for worse—and to convey the illusion of movement, trends that would continue in subsequent centuries. They also grew bolder in their use of tricky techniques, like the casting of full-size statues in bronze, a technology that combined high levels of artistry with sophisticated metallurgy. This was a medium in which the era's most famous sculptor, Praxiteles, excelled. Praxiteles was bold, too, in his choice of subjects, and he is widely regarded as the first artist to create full-size female nudes,

# Interpreting Visual Evidence

## *Reconstructing an Ideal of Female Beauty*

The lost statue known as the Aphrodite of Knidos was considered the most beautiful in the ancient world, but we can only study it by looking at later copies. It was the work of the fourth century's most renowned sculptor, Praxiteles (*prak-SIT-el-ezz*), who was reputed to have modeled it after the Athenian courtesan known as Phryne, a renowned beauty who inspired several contemporary artists and a whole series of apocryphal stories. The most reliable of these concerns the riches she accrued: apparently she became so wealthy that she offered to finance the rebuilding of Thebes in 336—on the condition that the slogan "destroyed by Alexander, restored by Phryne the Courtesan" be prominently displayed on the new walls. (Her offer was rejected.)

Praxiteles' original statue is thought to have been the first monumental female nude fashioned in antiquity. According to one authority, Praxiteles had initially received a commission from the island of Kos, for which he fashioned both clothed and naked versions of Aphrodite. Apparently, the scandalized citizens approved only the draped version and refused to pay for the nude. It was purchased instead by the city of Knidos on Cyprus, where it was displayed in an open-air temple so that it could be seen from all sides. It quickly became a tourist attraction and was widely copied and emulated. Two of the more faithful replicas, made by artists working in Rome, are pictured here.

A. Roman copy of the Aphrodite of Knidos.

B. Second century C.E. copy of the Aphrodite of Knidos.

### *Questions for Analysis*

**1.** As we have seen, the male nude was a favorite subject of Greek artists from the Archaic Period onward. Based on your knowledge of contemporary Greek culture and society, why was it only in the fourth century B.C.E. that a life-size female nude could be publicly displayed? Are there any precedents for statues like this?

**2.** Compare and contrast the ideal of female beauty suggested by the Knidian Aphrodite with the male ideals discussed in Chapter 3. What can you conclude about the relationship between these ideals and the different expectations of male and female behavior in Greek society? Why, for example, would ancient sources insist that the model for this statue was a courtesan?

**3.** Among the Romans, a statue like the Knidian Aphrodite was called a *Venus pudica*, a "modest Venus" (image A). Yet the citizens of Kos were allegedly shocked by its indecency, while old photographs of the copy in the Vatican Museum (image B) show that it was displayed until 1932 with additional draperies made of tin. How do you account for these very different standards of decency? To what degree do they suggest that concepts of "beauty" or "modesty" are historically constructed?

an innovation that sparked controversy in his own day and in other eras as well (see ***Interpreting Visual Evidence***).

In contrast to the visual arts, the forms and functions of drama changed considerably. In large part, this was because tragedy and comedy were no longer mounted as part of publicly funded festivals, but were instead paid for by private individuals who could exercise greater control over the content of performances. As a result, fourth-century playwrights did not have the freedom to use drama as a vehicle for political and social critique. Nor did the comic genius of Aristophanes have any true fourth-century successors. His biting, satirical wit gave way to a milder, less provocative style that bears some resemblance to modern television sitcoms. It was this "New Comedy" that laid the groundwork for comedy as it developed over the next several centuries. It came to rely more and more on mistaken identities, tangled familial relationships, humorous misunderstandings, and breaches of etiquette. The most famous comic playwright of the age was Menander (c. 342–292 B.C.E.), whose work survives today only in fragments but who directly inspired the comedians of the later Roman theater, which in turn inspired medieval and then early modern playwrights like Shakespeare. Similar trends toward escapism and frivolity are also apparent in a new literary genre that emerged during the fourth century: the prose novel, in which star-crossed lovers undergo extraordinary trials and perilous adventures before reuniting happily after a long separation. These pleasant fictions targeted an increasingly literate audience, including (like modern romance novels) an audience of women.

**BRONZE YOUTH.** This lithe statue, dating from the years 340–330 B.C.E., was found in the sea near Marathon and has been identified as a work by the master sculptor Praxiteles (or one of his pupils). Compare this male nude to those discussed in Chapter 3. ▪ ***How might changes in the style of sculpture parallel cultural changes in society at large?***

## *Philosophy after Socrates: The Schools of Plato and Aristotle*

The intellectual and political work undertaken by Socrates was carried forward by his most talented student, Plato. Born in Athens to an aristocratic family around 429 B.C.E., Plato joined Socrates' circle as a young man and witnessed at first hand the persecution, trial, and death of his mentor. For the next fifty years, to the time of his own death around 349 B.C.E., he shunned direct political involvement and strove instead to vindicate Socrates by constructing a philosophical system based on his precepts. But Socrates had taught through dialectical conversation and by example; he mistrusted writing and resisted developing a coherent set of principles. Plato's mission was therefore to transmit his legacy in a way that captured the liveliness and charm of the Socratic method, but within a more structured framework.

He did this in two ways: first by founding an informal school called the Academy (which had no buildings, tuition, or set curriculum), and later by writing a series of dialogues that wrapped weighty philosophical content in a witty and accessible dramatic format, with Socrates as the central character. Most dialogues are known by the names of Plato's contemporaries, the students who had engaged Socrates in discussion (like Crito, whose imagined dialogue with Socrates is excerpted in Chapter 3). One dialogue, the *Symposium*, actually recreates the conversation at a drinking party, where a tipsy Socrates, the comedian Aristophanes, and other Athenian worthies debate the nature of love.

The longest and most famous of Plato's dialogues is now known by its Latin title, the *Republic*. In Greek, it is

**PLATO AND ARISTOTLE.** Although many artistic representations of Plato and Aristotle were made in antiquity, the image that best captures the essential difference between their philosophies is this one, the focal point of a fresco by the Renaissance painter Raphael Sanzio (1483–1520 C.E., to be discussed further in Chapter 12). Plato is the older man to the viewer's left, who points with his right hand to the heavens; Aristotle is the younger man, gesturing with an open palm to the earth. ▪ ***How does this double portrait reflect these philosophers' teachings and perspectives?***

the *Politeía* ("Polis-governance" or even "Policy"), the first treatise on political philosophy written in the West. In it, Plato argues—through the character of Socrates—that social harmony and order are more important than individual liberty or equality. He imagines an ideal polis in which most of the people—farmers, artisans, traders—are governed by a superior group of "guardians" chosen in their youth for their natural attributes of intelligence and character. These prospective guardians would serve the polis first as soldiers, living together without private property. Those found to be the wisest would then receive more education, and a few would ultimately become "philosopher-kings." These enlightened rulers would in turn choose the next generation of guardians. This system actually bears an intriguing resemblance to the social order of Sparta, as well as containing elements of a benign tyranny, and is clearly a response to the failures of Athenian democracy in Plato's youth. But whether Plato himself believed in this system—he never voices his own opinion—is open to interpretation. Indeed, the students of Socrates who are represented as discussing it with him voice many objections. The most obvious of these is "Who will guard the guardians?" Such a system presumes that properly educated rulers will never be corrupted by power or wealth, a proposition that has yet to be sustained in practice.

The practical application of philosophy would be the preoccupation of Plato's own student, Aristotle (384–322 B.C.E.). Aristotle, the son of a physician, learned from his father the importance of observing natural phenomena. Although receptive to Plato's training, his own philosophical system was geared toward understanding the workings of the world through the rational analysis of empirical knowledge—that is, information about reality gained through sensory experience. In contrast to Plato, who taught that everything we see and touch is an untrustworthy reflection of some intangible ideal, Aristotle advocated the rigorous investigation of real phenomena, in order to uncover the natural order of the universe and of human beings' place within it. His method of instruction was also different. Unlike Socrates and Plato, whose dialogues were often playful, Aristotle delivered lectures on which his students took detailed notes, and eventually these notes became the basis of separate but interrelated treatises on politics, ethics, logic, metaphysics, and poetics. Aristotle also established rules for the syllogism, a form of reasoning in which certain premises inevitably lead to a valid conclusion, and he developed precise categories that could be used to further philosophical and scientific analysis.

With respect to morality, Aristotle taught that the highest good consists in the harmonious functioning of the individual human mind and body. Since humans differ from animals by virtue of their rational capacities, they find happiness by exercising these capacities appropriately. Good conduct is therefore rational conduct, and consists in acting moderately: showing courage rather than rashness or cowardice, temperance rather than excessive indulgence or ascetic denial. And whereas Plato conceived of politics as a means to an end which could never be achieved in this life, Aristotle thought of politics as an end in itself: the collective exercise of moderation.

But Aristotle also took it for granted that some people—like barbarians—were not fully human, and so were intended by nature to be slaves. He also believed that women were not endowed with a full measure of humanity, and so could never achieve the good life either as individuals or as participants in the public sphere of the polis. So when Aristotle asserted that "man is by nature a political animal" (or, to be more faithful to the Greek, "a creature of the polis"), he meant only Greek males of privileged status. Nor did he believe that the best form of government is a democracy. Like Plato, Aristotle saw that as a "debased" form of government. What he preferred was the polity, in which monarchical, aristocratic, and democratic elements are combined by means of checks and balances. Only this form of government, he posited, would allow free men to realize their rational potential.

### *Men of Action*

For all their brilliance and originality, Plato and Aristotle offered few prescriptions for reforming their own societies. Both imagined the perfect polis as one made up of a few thousand households, largely engaged in agriculture and living together in a single community. Although Greek civilization had begun in such a world, the realities of fourth-century political life were very different. Plato and Aristotle recognized this, to an extent, yet for both the answer was a reorganization of existing institutions, not something entirely new.

But there were other intellectuals at this time who were considering more radical alternatives. Xenophon, a veteran of the Ten Thousand, was actually another product of the Socratic tradition and an exact contemporary of Plato. He then went on to fight for the Spartan king Agesilaus (*ah-geh-si-LA-uhs*), who became a trusted friend. Thoroughly disillusioned by the failures of Athenian democracy, Xenophon spent most of his adult life in exile, and it is mostly thanks to his admiring account that we know anything about the Spartiate system described in Chapter 3. He intended his description to be a rebuke to Athens. We also have his own view of Socrates' teaching, which he related in a series of memoirs and which informs his treatises on kingship and on household management (the *Oikonomikos*, the root of our word *economics*). He also loved horses and dogs, and wrote a treatise on training them for the hunt. All the while, he watched as Epaminondas crippled the state he so admired, Sparta. So contemptuous was Xenophon of this Theban leader that he refused to mention his name in the history he was compiling.

The Athenian orator Isocrates (436–338 B.C.E.) was another direct contemporary of Plato and was also convinced that something had gone horribly awry as a result of the Peloponnesain War. Rather than imagining that a solution lay in the reform of the polis, he proposed instead that the Greeks rediscover their lost unity by staging a massive invasion of Persia. This assault, he prophesied, would be led by a man of vision and ability, someone who could unite the Greek world behind his cause. Isocrates spent most of his life casting about to find such a leader. Finally, he began to think that the man for the job was someone whom most Greeks considered no Greek at all: the king of Macedonia, Philip II.

## THE RISE OF MACEDONIA

Iscocrates had a point. By the middle of the fourth century, the Greek poleis had become so embroiled in military, political, and socioeconomic turmoil that they barely noticed the powerhouse on their northern frontier. Until the fourth century, Macedonia (or Macedon) had been a weak kingdom, regarded as a throwback to the "dark ages" before the emergence of enlightened poleis, ruled by a royal dynasty barely strong enough to control its own nobility and beset by intrigue and murderous ambition. As recently as the

# Analyzing Primary Sources

## *Aristotle's Justification of Slavery*

*Like* The Republic *of his teacher, Plato, Aristotle's treatise on* Politics *attempts to define and rationalize various methods of governance. Early in this work, Aristotle must grapple with the fact that all ancient societies were highly dependent on slave labor, and he must answer objections that the forcible subjugation of some men to the will of others goes against the laws of nature and the ideals of his own society.*

But is there anyone thus intended by nature to be a slave, and for whom such a condition is expedient and right, or rather is not all slavery a violation of nature? There is no difficulty in answering this question, on grounds both of reason and of fact. For that some should rule and others be ruled is a thing not only necessary, but expedient; from the hour of their birth, some are marked out for subjection, others for rule. . . .

But that those who take the opposite view have in a certain way right on their side, may be easily seen. For the words *slavery* and *slave* are used in two senses. There is a slave or slavery by law as well as by nature. The law of which I speak is a sort of convention—the law by which whatever is taken in war is supposed to belong to the victors. But this right many jurists impeach, as they would an orator who brought forward an unconstitutional measure: they detest the notion that, because one man has the power of doing violence and is superior in brute strength, another shall be his slave and subject.

Even among philosophers there is a difference of opinion. The origin of the dispute, and what makes the views invade each other's territory, is as follows: in some sense virtue, when furnished with means, has actually the greatest power of exercising force; and as superior power is only found where there is superior excellence of some kind, power seems to imply virtue, and the dispute to be simply one about justice (for it is due to one party identifying justice with goodwill while the other identifies it with the mere rule of the stronger). If these views are thus set out separately, the other views have no force or plausibility against the view that the superior in virtue ought to rule, or be master. Others, clinging, as they think, simply to a principle of justice (for law and custom are a sort of justice), assume that slavery in accordance with the custom of war is justified by law, but at the same moment they deny this. For what if the cause of the war be unjust?

And again, no one would ever say he is a slave who is unworthy to be a slave. Were this the case, men of the highest rank would be slaves and the children of slaves if they or their parents chance to have been taken captive and sold. Wherefore Hellenes [Greeks] do not like to call Hellenes slaves, but confine the term to barbarians. Yet, in using this language, they really mean the natural slave of whom we spoke at first; for it must be admitted that some are slaves everywhere, others nowhere.

The same principle applies to nobility. Hellenes regard themselves as noble everywhere, and not only in their own country, but they deem the barbarians noble only when at home, thereby implying that there are two sorts of nobility and freedom, the one absolute, the other relative. . . .

We see then that there is some foundation for this difference of opinion, and that all are not either slaves by nature or freemen by nature, and also that there is in some cases a marked distinction between the two classes, rendering it expedient and right for the one to be slaves and the others to be masters: the one practicing obedience, the others exercising the authority and lordship which nature intended them to have. The abuse of this authority is injurious to both; for the interests of part and whole, of body and soul, are the same, and the slave is a part of the master, a living but separated part of his bodily frame. Hence, where the relation of master and slave between them is natural they are friends and have a common interest, but where it rests merely on law and force the reverse is true.

Source: Excerpted from Aristotle, *Politics*, Book I: v–vi, trans. Benjamin Jowett (Oxford: 1920), pp. 32–37.

### *Questions For Analysis*

**1.** According to Aristotle, how does one become a slave? Why is the question of slavery's justice related to that of the just war?

**2.** Aristotle posits that some people are slaves by nature, others by some unfortunate circumstances (such as being captured in battle). For example, he says that Hellenes (Greeks) do not admit that they can be slaves; that is possible only for barbarians. What are the implications of this argument?

360s, Macedon had teetered on collapse, nearly succumbing to the even smaller kingdoms and predatory tribes that surrounded it.

Despite the efforts of a few Macedonian kings to add a bit of Hellenic culture to their court—one had successfully invited Euripides and Sophocles to his palace—Greeks considered them nearly as barbaric as their neighbors. It is still not known whether the ancient Macedonians were Greek-speaking during this period, although the royal family and nobility would at least have spoken Greek as a second language; and Macedonians seem to have participated in the Olympic Games, which were open only to Greeks. But they were definitely outsiders. Therefore, when a young and energetic king named Philip consolidated the southern Balkans under his rule, many Greeks saw it as a development no less troubling than the approach of the Persians in the fifth century.

## *The Reign of Philip II (359–336 B.C.E.)*

Philip II of Macedonia was not supposed to be its ruler. Born in 382, he was the third and youngest son of King Amyntas III, and was considered so dispensable that he was sent to Thebes as hostage when he was fourteen, at the time of the Theban Hegemony. This turns out to have been the making of him: he become the protégé of the brilliant Epaminondas and may even have trained alongside the general Pelopidas in the Theban Sacred Band. By the time he returned to the Macedonian capital of Pella in 364, three years later, he had received a more thorough education in Greek culture and military tactics than any Macedonian before him. He was also ambitious, and may already have laid great plans for the future. So when both of his older brothers died in battle, one after the other, Philip was not content with the role of regent for an infant nephew. By 356, he supplanted this nephew and was reigning as king, the same year that his queen, Olympias, bore him an heir. The boy was given the dynastic name Alexandros, meaning "a leader of men."

The first problem of Philip's reign was the fragility of Macedonia's northern borders. Through a combination of warfare and diplomacy, he subdued the tribes of the southern Balkans and incorporated their territory into his kingdom, losing an eye in the process. His success in this had much to do with his reorganization of Macedonian warriors into a hoiplite infantry along Theban lines. The mineral resources to which he now had access also helped, since Philp used that new wealth to pay and equip a standing professional army; just one of his gold mines produced as much in one year as the Delian League at its height had collected annually. Philip also organized an elite cavalry squad—the Companions—who fought with and beside the king, an innovation that may have been designed to emulate the esprit de corps of the Sacred Band, and was further intended to counter the Persian reliance on cavalry. These young men were drawn exclusively from the nobility, and Philip thereby hoped to inspire their deeper loyalty: under the guise of recruiting future Companions, he gained valuable young hostages to ensure the good conduct of fractious men. Their sons were now being brought up alongside Alexander and sharing his lessons with Aristotle, who had arrived at the Macedonian court in 343 B.C.E. Through a series of strategic marriages, Philip also managed to gain the good will and alliance of many neighboring kingdoms—although his frank polygamy was, in Greek eyes, another barbarity that called to mind the harems of Persia.

**PHILIP II OF MACEDONIA.** This tiny ivory head was discovered in a royal tomb at Vergina and is almost certainly a bust of the king himself. Contemporary sources report that Philip the Great had his right eye blinded by a catapult bolt, a deformity visible here—and testimony to the unflinching realism of Greek portraiture in the fourth century B.C.E.

Eventually, the increasing strength of Macedonia began to impinge on the consciousness of some Greeks, most notably the Athenians. But whereas Isocrates saw in Philip a potential savior of Greece, many Athenians believed that Philip's ultimate aim was to conquer and subjugate them. They may have misunderstood Philip's goals: his northward expansion was designed to secure his frontiers and the resources necessary to support an invasion of Persia, not of Greece. From 348 B.C.E. on, he was actually trying to forge an alliance with Athens, whose fleet could facilitate such an invasion by sea; in return, Philip promised to support Athens' old claim to hegemony over Greece. But the Athenians took the advice of an orator called Demosthenes, and refused to cooperate with Philip. This miscalculation would prove disastrous. Philip's inability to reach an understanding with Athens, despite strenuous diplomatic efforts, ultimately led to war, which sent the Athenians scrambling to ally with Thebes and a number of smaller poleis. Their fate was sealed at the battle of Chaeronea in 338 B.C.E., when an army led jointly by Philip and Alexander (aged 18) won a narrow victory, decimating the Athenian forces and destroying the Theban Sacred Band. In the aftermath, Philip called delegates from around mainland Greece to Corinth, where he established a new league. By and large, he left the independence of the Greek poleis unaffected. The main purpose of the League of Corinth was to provide forces for the invasion of Persia and to maintain peace among the rival poleis.

Philip never realized his dream of Persian conquest. Two years later, in 336 B.C.E., he was assassinated by a disgruntled (male) lover during a festival at Pella. The kingship now fell to Alexander. Among the Greeks, he would be known as Alexander, the Sacker of Cities. To the Romans, more impressed by military genius than the Greeks, he was Alexander the Great.

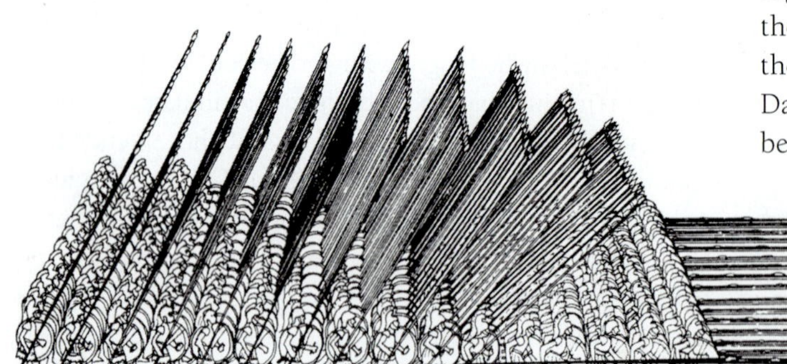

**MACEDONIAN PHALANX.** Philip of Macedonia's hoplite infantry—the model for Alexander's—was armed with two-handed pikes of graduated lengths, from 13 to 21 feet, and was massed in squares sixteen rows deep and wide. Members of the phalanx were trained to wheel quickly in step formation and to double the width of their front rank as needed, by filing off in rows of eight. The reach of their spears, called *sarissas*, extended the phalanx's fighting range.

## THE CONQUESTS OF ALEXANDER (336–323 B.C.E.)

By the time of Alexander's early death at the age of 32, a monumental legend had already built up around him. This makes it all the more ironic and frustrating that no contemporary account of his life and achievements survives. The great library assembled in his capital of Alexandria in Egypt—the repository of all Greek learning and literature—was destroyed centuries later, and with it a great portion of assembled knowledge. So when we try to reconstruct the history of Alexander, we are depending on the writings of men who lived and worked under the Roman Empire, notably Plutarch (46–120 C.E.) and Arrian (c. 86–160 C.E.), both of whom were separated from their subject by a distance of four hundred years. Luckily, there is good reason to believe that they were basing their histories on sources derived from two first-hand accounts, one written by Alexander's general (and purported half-brother) Ptolemy (c. 367–c. 284 B.C.E.), who founded a new dynasty of Egyptian pharaohs, and another by Æschines Socraticus (c. 387–322 B.C.E.), an Athenian statesman. Neverthless, it is a salutary reminder of how fragile the historical record of antiquity is, that the sources for the life of the era's most famous man are so hard to come by.

### *The Conquest of Persia*

When Alexander succeeded his father in 336 B.C.E, he could not begin to carry out his plans of conquest until he had put down the revolts that erupted immediately after Philip's death—notably at Thebes, which he punished by destroying its famous walls. Two years later, he was crossing the Hellespont at the head of a hoplite army to challenge the Great King of Persia, Darius III. From the beginning, Darius was no match for Alexander. He was a minor member of the royal family who had taken the dynastic name when he was placed on the throne after a palace coup, at the relatively old age of 45, in the same year that Alexander himself became king at 20. Darius and his advisors failed to take the Macedonian threat seriously, despite the Persians' past history of defeat at the hands of Greek armies—even on Persian soil and within living memory. Perhaps they assumed that the enormous forces they could rally in defense of their empire would easily overwhelm a comparatively small army of 42,000; perhaps they misunderstood Alexander's aims, which would reveal themselves over time to be far-reaching indeed. In any event, the Persian army was made up of mercenaries or poorly paid conscripts under the command of inexperienced generals.

Alexander achieved a series of extraordinary victories, beginning in northwest Anatolia, near the epic field of Troy, and continuing down the Ionian coastline. In 333 B.C.E. Darius was persuaded to engage Alexander personally, at the head of a force that significantly outnumbered that of his opponent. But the chosen site, on the banks of a river near Issus, favored Alexander's fast-moving infantry, not the heavy cavalry and chariots of the Persians, which had no room to maneuver and were hampered by mud. No warrior himself, Darius disgraced himself by fleeing the battlefield, abandoning not only his army but his entire household, which included his wife and his mother. (They were captured by Alexander's troops, and treated by him with great deference and respect.) Darius spent the remainder of his life running from Alexander's advancing army, until his decisive defeat at Gaugamela (near Mosul in modern Iraq) in 331, when he was killed by a local chieftain who hoped to win Alexander's favor. Instead, Alexander—acting as the new Great King—had the chieftain executed for treason. The next spring, Alexander destroyed the royal capital of Persepolis, lest it serve as a rallying point for Persian resistance.

**MARBLE HEAD OF ALEXANDER.** Alexander the Great was reported to have been very striking in appearance, although sources vary in their assessment of his physical beauty. This portrait bust was made in 180 B.C.E., about 150 years after his death. ▪ ***Given the trends in sculpture during that period (see page 135), is this likely to have been an accurate portrait?***

Meanwhile, in the two years that had passed since Darius' humiliation at Issus, Alexander had completed his conquest of Asia Minor. One by one, the cities of Syria and Palestine surrendered after Alexander made a powerful statement by destroying the wealthy Phoenician capital at Tyre. Following the example of Cyrus the Great, whose tactics he came increasingly to emulate, Alexander had developed a policy of offering amnesty to cities that submitted peacefully—but dealing mercilessly with those that resisted. The fortified city of Gaza, the last Persian stronghold on the Egyptian border, provides an example: its commander, Batis, not only refused to surrender but seemed determined to fight to the death, inflicting severe losses on the troops besieging his city and seriously wounding Alexander himself. When the fortress was finally taken,

**ALEXANDER DEFEATS KING DARIUS OF PERSIA AT THE BATTLE OF ISSUS (333 B.C.E.).** This Roman mural, discovered at Pompeii, shows Darius fleeing from the battlefield in his chariot (right), pursued by Alexander, the mounted figure on the left. Note the reflection of Alexander and his horse in Darius' large round shield.

Alexander's troops slew all the adult males and enslaved the women and children. According to a later Roman historian, Alexander also dragged the body of Batis around the city's walls behind his chariot, imitating Achilles' treatment of his fallen rival Hector.

**ALEXANDER'S WORLD.** This view of the world, modeled on maps made in antiquity, represents what intellectuals of Alexander's own time knew about geography. ▪ ***Comparing it to the map of Alexander's campaigns on page 121, how do you think this worldview affected the planning of his route?*** ▪ ***Based on available knowledge, why would he have traveled down the Indus river (near the marking* India*) and traveled overland to Susa?*** ▪ ***What similarities and differences do you find more generally, comparing this ancient map with the other maps that appear in this book?***

## Alexander in Egypt

After this, Alexander marched into Egypt unopposed. In fact, he was welcomed as a liberator: Egypt had been governed as a Persian satrapy since 525 B.C.E., when Cambyses, son of Cyrus the Great, had deposed the last pharaoh of the reigning dynasty (Chapter 2). Now Alexander himself was hailed as pharaoh and given the double crown of Upper and Lower Egypt, becoming the latest in a succession of rulers reaching back three thousand years to the time of King Narmer (Chapter 1). Something about this feat seems to have amazed even Alexander himself. The "barbarian" chieftain of a backwater kingdom in the Balkan foothills had become pharaoh of the oldest civilization on earth and heir to its immense riches and extraordinary history—a history that the Greeks knew well, thanks to the writings of Herodotus. While the Persians and (before them) the Medes had long been the Greeks' traditional enemies, the Egyptians had always been too far away to pose a threat; indeed, they were an object of awe and source of inspiration.

This may help to explain Alexander's response to the oracle of Ammon, the name the Greeks gave to the Egyptian sun god Amun-Ra, whom they identified with Zeus. At the oracle's desert oasis of Siwa, Alexander was reportedly told that he was "son of Ammon" and a god himself, a pronouncement that gave weight to a story already in circulation among his men, that he had been fathered not by Philip but by Zeus. Alexander, ever mindful of historical precedent and the historical significance of his own actions, seems to have decided at this point that Egypt should be the capital of his new empire. Persia had been the goal, and it still remained to be conquered, piece by piece; but it was in Egypt that he would build his shining new city of Alexandria. In the end, he had time only to lay out a plan for the streets and central spaces before he marched north to a reckoning with Darius at Gaugamela. When he finally returned, he was in his sarcophagus.

## Alexander's Final Campaigns

Over the ensuing five years, Alexander campaigned in the far reaches of the Persian Empire, in the mountainous regions that had been only loosely yoked together with the more settled lands of Mesopotamia. This is the region encompassed today by Afghanistan, a terrain famous for defeating every attempt at imperial conquest. There, in the mountains of Bactria, Alexander and his army experienced the hardest fighting of their long campaign. Indeed, they never succeeded in getting more than a tenuous hold on the territory, despite Alexander's marriage to Roxane, daughter of a Bactrian chieftain. Thereafter, Alexander moved down through what is now Pakistan to the Indus Valley, meeting stiff resistance from its warlords but eventually defeating their leader, Porus, at the Battle of Hydaspes in 326 B.C.E.

This was to be the last major battle of his career, and the one in which his famous warhorse, Bucephalus, was killed. (He was buried nearby, and a city was founded in his name.) And it was here in India that Alexander's exhausted army refused to go on, thousands of miles and eight years from home. He was forced to turn back, and

**THE CAMPAIGNS OF ALEXANDER.** The conquests of Alexander the Great brought Greek culture to the vast expanse of the former Persian Empire, as far east as the Indus River. Trace Alexander's route with your finger. ▪ ***Where did he start and end?*** ▪ ***What was the farthest point east that he traveled on his conquests?*** ▪ ***Why might Alexander have chosen to found so many cities named after him, and what can you conclude about the purposes of these cities, based on their locations?***

rather than attempting to recross the mountains of the Hindu Kush or the foothills of the Himalayas, he pressed southward to the shores of the Arabian Sea—what was then known as Ocean, and the end of the world. The ensuing march through the Gedrosian Desert, combined with a decade of continuous fighting, weakened him and his army considerably.

But Alexander still had great plans for the future, and when he reached the royal palace of Susa he took steps that indicate how would have tried to combine his Greco-Macedonian Empire with that of Persia, had he lived. He announced that he would begin training Persian youths to fight alongside Greeks and Macedonians, so as to begin an integration of the two armies. He arranged a mass marriage between hundreds of his officers and a corresponding number of Persian noblewomen, and he made an example of men who had been caught desecrating the nearby tomb of Cyrus the Great. Most controversially, he showed respect for his Persian subjects by adopting Persian dress—considered by Greeks to be symbolic of their enemies' barbarism—and by encouraging those around him to perform the ritual of *proskynesis* (*pros-kin-EE-sis*). According to Herodotus, who gave the practice its Greek name, this was a gesture of bodily submission performed by those of lesser social standing when they met their superiors, and by all Persians—even those of royal rank—to honor the Great King. The person paying homage would bow deeply and kiss his hand to the emperor, in some cases prostrating himself entirely. To the Greeks, this practice was not only humiliating but blasphemous: it suggested that the Persians worshiped their emperor as a god. To Alexander and his close advisors, *proskynesis* may

**LESSER KINGS OF PERSIA APPROACH THE GREAT KING TO PERFORM THE *PROSKYNESIS.*** ▪ ***Why would Alexander's Greek and Macedonian soldiers have balked at the suggestion that they show their solidarity with Persians by performing this ritual?***

have seemed an appropriate tribute to his status as "son of Ammon," but it was more likely intended to level cultural differences. In any case, it was not a success, and it fueled a mutiny among the Macedonians, which Alexander himself had to quell.

## *Alexander's Death*

Apart from these attempts to create cross-cultural cohesion, which he was not able to realize fully, Alexander took no realistic steps to create an administration for his vast empire. How he planned to govern it effectively and bequeath it intact remains a mystery; he seems to have fixed his sights more clearly on further conquests, perhaps in Arabia, perhaps toward "Greater Greece"—Italy and Sicily. We will never know. In late May of 323 B.C.E., he began to show signs of what may have been malarial fever. Some ancient sources suggest he was poisoned; his closest friend and longtime lover, Hephaistion, had died the year before at Ecbatana, leaving Alexander without his most able and vigilant bodyguard. (Emulating Achilles' passionate grief at the death of Patroclus, the mourning Alexander is reported to have built an enormous funeral pyre and "sacrificed" the residents of a nearby town to appease Hephaistion's ghost.) But he ignored the advice of his doctors and continued to play the part of a Homeric hero, drinking late and exerting himself incautiously. His condition worsened, and he died on June 10 or 11, 323 B.C.E., in the palace built by the Chaldean king Nebuchadnezzar in Babylon, the ancient capital of Hammurabi. He was not yet thirty-three years old.

# THE HELLENISTIC KINGDOMS

According to one account—by a later Roman historian—Alexander's friends and officers gathered around his bed as he lay dying and asked to whom he wished to leave his empire. He had replied, "To the strongest." According to Plutarch and Arrian, though, he was actually incapable of speech. According to still other late sources, he silently gave his signet ring to a Macedonian general called Perdiccas, the leader of his cavalry.

It was certainly Perdiccas who attempted to arrange a settlement among all the possible claimants for the throne, albeit unsuccessfully. Alexander's own son and heir was born to Roxane after his death, and eventually it was decided that the baby, Alexander IV of Macedonia, should rule jointly with Alexander's half-brother, Philip, the son of Philip II by one of his lesser wives, who may have been both mentally and physically disabled. This solution did not last, and eventually both the child and his uncle were murdered, as was Perdiccas.

# Analyzing Primary Sources

## *Alexander Puts Down a Mutiny*

*The following account comes from the history of Alexander's campaigns by the Greek-speaking Roman historian Arrian (c. 86–160 C.E.), who lived in the Roman province of Bythinia in northern Anatolia. This is the closest thing we have to a primary source, since histories written by Alexander's own contemporaries have not survived. The following passage describes Alexander's response to a mutiny among his troops after his return from India, in 324 B.C.E.*

y countrymen, you are sick for home—so be it! I shall make no attempt to check your longing to return. Go wherever you will; I shall not hinder you. But if go you must, there is one thing I would have you understand—what I have done for you, and in what coin you have repaid me. . . .

"[M]arching out from a country too poor to maintain you decently, [I] laid open for you at a blow, and in spite of Persia's naval supremacy, the gates of the Hellespont. My cavalry crushed the satraps of Darius, and I added all Ionia and Aeolia, the two Phrygias and Lydia to your empire. . . . I took them and gave them to you for your profit and enjoyment. The wealth of Egypt and Cyrene, which I shed no blood to win, now flows in your hands; Palestine and the plains of Syria and Mesopotamia are now your property; Babylon and Bactria and Susa are yours; you are the masters of the gold of Lydia, the treasures of Persia, the wealth of India—yes, and the seas beyond India, too. You are my captains, my generals, my governors of provinces.

"From all this that I have labored to win for you, what is left for me myself except the purple and the crown? I keep nothing for my own. . . . Perhaps you will say that, in my position as your commander, I had none of the labors and distress which you had to endure to win me what I have won. . . . Come now—if you are wounded, strip and show your wounds, and I will show mine. There is no part of my body but my back which does not have a scar; not a weapon a man may grasp or fling, the mark of which I do not carry on me . . . and all for your sakes: for your glory and your gain. Over every land and sea, across river, mountain, and plain, I led you to the world's end, a victorious army. I marry as you marry, and many of you will have children related by blood to my own. . . . But you all wish to leave me. Go then! And when you reach home, tell them that Alexander your king, who vanquished the Persians and Medes and Bactrians . . . tell them, I say, that you deserted him and left him to the mercy of barbarian men, whom you yourselves conquered. . . ."

On the Macedonians, the immediate effect of Alexander's speech was profound. . . . But when they were told [three days later that] . . . command was being given to Persian officers, foreign troops drafted into Macedonian units, a Persian corps of Guards called by a Macedonian name, Persian infantry units given the coveted title of Companions . . . every man of them hurried to the palace . . . and [they] swore they would not stir from the spot until Alexander took pity on them.

Source: Arrian, *The Campaigns of Alexander*, trans. Aubrey de Selincourt (New York: 1958), pp. 360–65 (slightly modified).

### *Questions for Analysis*

1. What qualities of leadership does Alexander display in this speech? How do these qualities compare to those of Cyrus the Younger, in Xenophon's description of him (page 110)?
2. Given the circumstances that precipitated this mutiny, why does Alexander use the term *barbarians* to describe the Persians and other conquered peoples? What does he hope to convey by using this word, and then by reorganizing his forces to replace Macedonians with Persians?
3. Histories written well into the nineteenth century of our era feature speeches that were allegedly spoken by historical characters on momentous occasions. How closely do you think Arrian's reconstruction of this speech reflects historical reality? How might you go about arguing that it is, in fact, an accurate reflection of what Alexander actually said?

**THE HELLENISTIC WORLD.** Each of the three successor kingdoms to Alexander's empire was based in one of the three major civilizations we have studied so far: Egyptian, Mesopotamian, and Greek. ▪ ***Based on the map above, what were the names of the three main successor states and where were they located?*** ▪ ***What might the division of Alexander's empire along such lines suggest about the lasting cultural differences among these regions?*** ▪ ***What might it suggest about the likelihood of forging a united empire, had he lived?***

Meanwhile, the satrapies that had been alloted to various leaders of Alexander's armies became the bases from which they attempted to seize control. The turmoil lasted for two generations. By about 275 B.C.E., however, three separate axes of military and political power had emerged, each with a distinctive character but headed by a Greco-Macedonian ruling class that shared a similar background. Indeed, a striking feature of this period is the renewal of ancient political patterns, especially in the Near East and Egypt. But more striking is the fact that a common culture continued to unite Alexander's fragmented empire, which is why the era after his death is called Hellenistic, "Greek-like."

## Ptolemaic Egypt

By far the most stable of the three successor states was Egypt, thanks in large part to the canny governance of Alexander's former general Ptolemy *(TOHL-eh-mee)*, possibly an illegitimate son of Philip II and one of Alexander's most trusted advisors. Ptolemy decided to withdraw from the contest over the larger empire and asked only to be given Egypt as his satrapy. This might have been construed as a modest request by potential rivals, but Ptolemy had ulterior motives. Clearly, he recognized Egypt's virtual invulnerability to attack. He also seems to have appreciated, as Alexander did, its historical cachet. And he may already have been planning to make Egypt an independent monarchy and a shrine to Alexander's memory. It was thanks to Ptolemy, in fact, that Alexander's embalmed body was returned to Egypt in 323 B.C.E.. It was supposed to have gone to the royal burial ground of Aigai in Macedonia, but Ptolemy hijacked the funeral cortege and brought it to Memphis. Later, his son Ptolemy II moved the sarcophagus to a tomb in Alexandria, where it became a pilgrimage site and an object of veneration, especially by Romans with imperial ambitions of their own.

The Ptolemies ruled for the next 300 years, until Egypt became a Roman province in 30 B.C.E. This dynasty, the thirty-second since the unification of the Upper and Lower Nile in the fourth millennium B.C.E., would be the last. The male heirs of the line all took the name Ptolemy (hence the term "Ptolemaic Egypt"). Many of their sisters were called

Cleopatra, the name of Alexander's own sister and a dynastic name among Macedonian royal women. Beginning in the reign of Ptolemy II Philadelphus ("sibling-lover"), the Ptolemies even began to follow ancient Egyptian custom by marrying their sisters. And in many other ways, they showed reverence for the culture of their kingdom while at the same time bringing it within the ambit of the wider Hellenistic world.

They achieved this, in part, by ruling from the new city of Alexandria on the Mediterranean coast, rather than from the older pharaonic capitals. In Alexandria, they acted as Macedonian kings toward their Greek and Macedonian citizens; outside of Alexandria, they played the role of pharaohs, surrounding themselves with the trappings and symbols of Egypt's heritage. But until the last Ptolemaic ruler, Cleopatra VII (69–30 B.C.E.), none of them bothered to learn the Egyptian language—although, as the Rosetta Stone attests (Chapter 1), they surrounded themselves with able administrators who could communicate effectively with their multilingual and multicultural subjects.

**TWO PORTRAITS OF PTOLEMY I OF EGYPT.** The Ptolemaic rulers of Egypt represented themselves as pharaohs to their Egyptian subjects (as in this bust) and as Greeks to their Macedonian and Greek subjects (as on this gold coin). ▪ ***Why would it have been important to project these two very different images?***

For the Ptolemies, as for the ancient pharaohs, all of Egypt was basically crown land, to be exploited for the benefit of the royal house. Supporting this tradition was the Macedonian idea that conquered land—land won by the spear—was plunder, to be used for personal enrichment and glorification. Accordingly, the Ptolemies exploited the wealth of the Egyptian countryside to the fullest. Most of this wealth ended up in Alexandria, which became the brilliant hub of the Hellenistic world. But there was little interest in improving the lives of the Egyptian peasantry whose bread-winning labors made their rulers rich. So although the third century was a prosperous and relatively peaceful one in Egypt, future pharoahs would face regular and dangerous revolts from the native populations of the countryside.

Nevertheless, Ptolemaic Egypt was the most succesful of the Hellenistic kingdoms. It was also the most influential, not only in its own day but for posterity, because of its key role in preserving and transmitting the accumulated heritage of the civilizations that had preceded it: Egyptian, Mesopotamian, and Greek. The Ptolemies used their wealth to patronize science and the arts, and they established a great Museum ("home of the Muses") and library which attracted the greatest minds of the Hellenistic world and eventually displaced Athens. Many breakthroughs in astronomy, mechanical engineering, and physics occurred in Alexandria. In particular, the study of medicine advanced greatly under Ptolemaic rule: freed from the taboos of their homeland, Greek researchers were permitted to perform autopsies on the bodies of dead criminals and vagrants, making it possible for anatomy to become a scientific discipline in its own right. It was also here that the texts of Greek poetry, drama, history, and philosophy were copied and preserved in the forms in which we know them, and here that the Hebrew scriptures were translated into Greek for a wider audience.

## Seleucid Asia

The vast possessions that Alexander had accumulated in Asia—both within the Persian Empire and outside of it—eventually fell to another Macedonian, Seleucus (*seh-LOO-kus*). Seleucus had not been a senior officer during Alexander's lifetime, but he had navigated the turmoil after Alexander's death successfully and exploited the connections he made through his Persian wife. At his death in 281 B.C.E., his half-Persian son Antiochus inherited an expansive realm, but despite his best efforts he could not extend it beyond the city named after him, Antioch, into Egypt.

Throughout its history, the Persian dynasty founded by Seleucus (known as the Seleucids) struggled with the problem of holding the disparate parts of their realm together. Their hold on the easternmost provinces was especially tenuous, but Seleucus solved part of this problem by ceding much of the Indus Valley to the great Indian warrior-king Chandragupta in exchange for peace and a squad of war elephants. By the middle of the third century B.C.E., the Seleucids had also lost control of Bactria, where a series of

Indo-Greek states were emerging with a uniquely complex culture of their own. (One Greco-Bactrian king, Menander, is remembered in Buddhist tradition and may have had Buddhist sympathies.) The Seleucid heartland now became northern Syria, parts of Anatolia, Mesopotamia, and the western half of Persia: still a great, wealthy kingdom, but far less than what Alexander had left.

Like the Ptolemies, the Seleucids presented two faces to their subjects, one looking to ancient Near Eastern tradition, another looking to Greece. In his proclamations, Antiochus used terms reminiscent of Sargon, Hammurabi, and Cyrus: "I am Antiochus, Great King, legitimate king . . . king of Babylon, king of all countries." But on his coins, he wore his hair short in the fashion of the Greeks and styled himself *basileus*, the Greek word for "king." Although the Seleucids' bureaucracy was less organized than that of the Ptolemies, even haphazard tax collection could reap huge rewards in an empire of 30 million inhabitants. However, the Seleucids did not convert their gains into public-works projects or capital investments. Instead, they hoarded their wealth in great state treasuries. All the same, they had more than enough cash to defend their borders through the third century, a period of regular warfare with Egypt. It was not until the second century, when Antiochus III lost a costly war with the Romans, that he had to plunder temples and private wealth to pay off the indemnity imposed on him.

## *Antigonid Macedon and Greece*

The Macedonian homeland did not possess the vast wealth of the new kingdoms carved from Alexander's conquests in Egypt and the Near East. It also remained highly unstable from the time of Alexander's death until 276 B.C.E., when a general named Antigonus was finally able to establish his rule over the area and his own dynasty (known as the Antigonids). Thereafter, Macedonia drew its strength from considerable natural resources and from its influence over Aegean trade, as well as its status as overlord of Greece. The Macedonians also continued to field the most effective army of any of the successor states, and its warriors had coveted bragging rights as the heirs of Alexander's unconquered army.

Antigonus was influenced by a philosophical outlook called Stoicism (discussed later in this chapter) and viewed kingship as a form of noble servitude, an office to be endured rather than enjoyed. This perspective, combined with his modest resources, convinced him not to compete with the Seleucids and Ptolemies for dominance. Instead, Antigonid policy was to keep these other two powers at war with one another and away from the Macedonian sphere of influence. Antigonus and his successors thus pursued a strategy more reminiscent of Philip II than of his son. They secured the northern frontiers, maintained a strong, standing army, and kept the fractious Greeks at heel.

The Greeks, however, were restive under the Antigonids, and two emergent powers within the Greek world served as rallying points for those who resented "barbarian" rule. These two forces, the Aetolian League and the Achaean League, were a departure in Greek political organization. Unlike the defensive alliances of the classical period, each of these two leagues represented a real political unification, with some centralization of governance. Citizens of the member poleis participated in councils of state that dealt with foreign policy and military affairs, trials for treason, and the annual election of a league general (also the chief executive officer) and his second in command. New members were admitted on an equal footing with existing members, and all citizens of the various poleis enjoyed joint citizenship throughout the league. The same laws, weights and measures, coinage, and judicial procedures also applied throughout each federation. So impressive was this degree of cooperation and unification that James Madison, John Jay, and Alexander Hamilton employed the Achaean League as one of their models in advocating federalism in the United States.

# FROM POLIS TO COSMOPOLIS

So what became of the polis, that building-block of classical Greece? As we have seen, the changes of the fourth century B.C.E. were already disrupting the traditional patterns of social and political life before Alexander's conquests. But these conquests hastened the process of transformation, and they also opened up a wider world—a world that, within a few generations, came to admire all things Greek. By 300 B.C.E., a common Hellenistic culture encompassed the eastern Mediterranean and western Asia, transcending political and geographical boundaries. It was fueled by the hundreds of thousands of adventurers who joined the Greek *diaspora* ("dispersion"), and whose emigration reduced the population of the Greek mainland by as much as fifty percent in the century between 325 and 225 B.C.E.

This exciting, urbane world was made up of interconnected cities whose scale dwarfed anything imaginable in Periclean Athens. In the fifth century B.C.E., direct participation in government had meant that every male citizen had some share and stake in his society, its institutions, its gods, its army, and its cultural life. If we transpose this outlook onto the cosmopolitan Hellenistic city, which would have been three times larger, we can appreciate the magnitude of the change: two centuries later, all these ways of defining oneself were no longer relevant. The individual male's intimate connection with the political life of the state was broken, as was his nexus of social and familial relationships. An average Greek in one of the Hellenistic kingdoms might have only his immediate family to rely on, if that. Very often, he was alone. What resulted was a traumatic disjunction between the traditional values and assumptions of Greek life and the social and political realities of the day—and a host of entirely new opportunities.

## Commerce and Urbanization

The Hellenistic world was prosperous, owing to the freedom of long-distance trade, the development of international finance, and the enormous growth of cities. Alexander's conquests had opened up a vast trading area stretching from Egypt to the Persian Gulf, dominated by Greek-speaking rulers and well-established merchant communities. These conquests also stimulated the economy by putting into circulation hoards of Persian gold and silver coins, jewelry, and other commodities acquired through plunder. Industries also benefited, because autocratic rulers found manufacturing to be a further means of increasing their revenues through trade and taxation.

**HELLENISTIC EARRINGS.** These exquisite pieces of jewelry illustrate the enormous wealth and extraordinary craftsmanship available to the elites of the Hellenistic world.

New trading ventures were particularly encouraged in Ptolemaic Egypt and the area of western Asia ruled over by the Seleucid monarchs, the heartland of which was Syria. Every facility was provided by the Ptolemies and the Seleucids for the encouragement of commerce. Harbors were improved, warships were sent out to police the seas, roads and canals were built. The Ptolemies even employed geographers to discover new routes to distant lands and thereby opened up valuable markets. As a result of such methods, Egypt developed a flourishing commerce in the widest variety of products obtainable. Into the port of Alexandria came spices from Arabia, gold from Ethiopia and India, tin from Britain, elephants and ivory from Nubia, silver from Spain, fine carpets from Asia Minor, and even silk from China. Profits for the government and for some of the merchants were often as high as 20 or 30 percent.

The rapid growth of cities had both political and economic causes. Greek rulers imported Greek officials and especially Greek soldiers to maintain their control over non-Greek populations, making many new settlements necessary. Alexander himself had founded some 70 cities as outposts of domination; in the next two centuries, his successors founded about 200 more. Urbanization also increased due to the expansion of commerce and industry, as well as the proliferation of government offices. But the most significant factors were the Greek diaspora and the migration of workers from rural areas. Population growth in some centers was explosive. At Antioch, the population quadrupled during a single century. Seleucia on the Tigris grew from nothing to a metropolis of several hundred thousand in less than two centuries. Alexandria in Egypt had half a million inhabitants. Only imperial Rome would have surpassed it in size, and it would not be until the eighteenth century of our era that European cities like London and Paris were as large. Alexandria was not only populous, it was magnificent and spacious—which Rome never was. Its wide streets were paved and laid out in an orderly grid. It had splendid public buildings and parks, the great Museum, and the famous library containing half a million books. It was the storehouse and showcase of Greek culture.

Despite the overall growth of the Hellenistic economy, not everyone enjoyed prosperity. Agriculture remained the major occupation and primary source of wealth, and small farmers in particular suffered severely from exploitative taxation. Although industrial production increased, it continued to be based on manual labor by individual artisans, most of whom lived in poverty. Among the teeming populations of Hellenistic cities, unemployment was a constant concern. Those who could not find work were forced to beg, steal, or prostitute themselves to survive.

Even those who prospered in the new economy were often subject to drastic fluctuations in their fortunes, owing to the precarious nature of mercantile endeavors. A trader who did very well selling a luxury cloth might invest heavily in it, only to find that tastes had changed or that a ship full of his wares had sunk. Merchants were also vulnerable to the boom-and-bust syndrome all too familiar to us today: an investor, thinking he could make a fortune during an upward price spiral, might go into debt to take advantage of the trend, only to find that supply in the commodity he traded suddenly exceeded demand, leaving him nothing with which to pay back his creditors. The economic landscape of the Hellenistic world was therefore one of contrasting extremes. In many ways, this was also the case with respect to its culture.

## HELLENISTIC WORLD VIEWS

Life in the Hellenistic boomtowns produced new world views and new philosophies that differed significantly from those of Plato and Aristotle. Two opposing trends ran almost parallel with one another. The first, exemplified by Stoicism and Epicureanism, promoted rational thought as the key to alleviating the anxieties of modern life. This trend was a manifestation of Greek influence, although a major departure was the new separation of philosophy from scientific inquiry, which now became its own field of study. The second trend, exemplified by the Skeptics and various religious cults, tended to deny the possibility of attaining truth through the exercise of human reason alone, and in some cases turned toward mysticism and reliance on divine revelation. Despite these stark differences, however, the philosophers and religious teachers were motivated by the same thing: the need to make human existence meaningful in a new age that lacked traditional civic structures and social values.

### *Two Paths to Tranquility: Stoicism and Epicureanism*

The two strains of philosophy that dominated the Hellenistic world both originated in Athens around 300 B.C.E. Their promoters were Epicurus (c. 342–270 B.C.E.) and Zeno (fl. after 300 B.C.E.), and their teachings had several features in common. Both were concerned with the well-being of the individual, not with the welfare of society as a whole. Both were also firmly rooted in the material world, denying the existence of any purely spiritual beings; even the soul was considered to be part of the mortal body. Stoicism and Epicureanism also responded to the new cosmpolitan age by promoting universal values: both taught that people are the same the world over, and both recognized no distinctions between Greeks and the peoples hitherto known as "barbarians."

But in other ways the two systems were radically different. The Stoics who followed Zeno of Citium (c. 335–c. 263 B.C.E.)—they took their name from the *stoa* ("colonnade") in which he regularly taught—believed that the cosmos is an ordered whole in which all contradictions are resolved for ultimate good. Evil is therefore relative; the particular misfortunes that befall human beings are merely incidents that will lead to the final perfection of the universe. Everything that happens is therefore predetermined, which means that no individual is master of his or her fate. People are free only in the sense that they can accept fate or rebel against it; that is, one is free to choose how to respond to adversity or prosperity. By freely submitting to the workings of the universe, and by acknowledging that whatever happens must be for the best, one can attain true happiness: tranquility of mind. Through the exercise of reason and emotional restraint, Stoics strove to adjust their responses to the cosmic purpose, and to purge their souls of all bitterness or regret.

The Stoics' theory of ethics and social responsibility grew out of this personal philosophy. Believing that the highest good is serenity of mind, they emphasized self-discipline and the fulfillment of one's duties. They taught tolerance and forgiveness, and they also urged participation in public affairs as a special responsibility for those with able minds. They condemned slavery and violence, although they took no real actions against these evils because they saw them as inevitable—and because extreme social change might be worse.

With some some later modifications, Stoic philosophy became the driving force behind the values of the Roman Republic and of early Christianity, and can be considered one of the most important products of the Hellenistic Age. Even those who do not embrace its tenets or its perspective may find that they have been influenced by its egalitarian and humanitarian ethos.

The teachings of Epicurus (341–270 B.C.E.) were based on the atomic theory of an earlier Greek philosopher called Democritus, who lived in the latter part of the fifth century B.C.E. and who is often called "the father of modern science." According to his central thesis, the universe is made up entirely of atoms, infinite in number, indestructible, and indivisible. Every individual object or organism is therefore the product of a combination of atoms.

Studying Democritus' writings, Epicurus and his followers reached a conclusion exactly opposite to that of the Stoics: they interpreted the atomic theory to mean that there is no ultimate purpose in the workings of the universe, that these workings are entirely random. So the highest good cannot come of submitting oneself stoically to the endurance of hardship, because it is not part of a larger plan; it is merely the chance by-product of random atomic actions. The highest good, then, must be pleasure: the moderate satisfaction of bodily appetites, the intellectual pleasure of contemplating excellence and remembering past enjoyments, and serenity in the face of death. Indeed, an individual who understands that the soul itself is material and will not survive the death of the body, that the universe operates at random, and that no gods intervene in human affairs will have no fear of death or any other supernatural phenomena. The Epicureans thus came by a very different route to the same general conclusion as the Stoics: nothing is better than tranquility of mind.

The moral teachings and political goals of the Epicureans therefore reflected their worldview. In contrast to the Stoics, however, they did not insist on virtue as an end in itself, or on the fulfillment of one's duties. For an Epicurean, the only duty a person has is to the self, and the only reason to act virtuously is to increase one's own happiness. Similarly, Epicureans also denied that there is any such thing as justice: laws and political institutions are "just" only insofar as they contribute to the welfare of the individual. Yes, certain rules have been found necessary in every society for the maintenance of order, but these rules should be obeyed solely because that is to one's advantage. The state is, at best, a mere convenience, and the wise man should take no active part in politics. Instead, he should withdraw to study philosophy and enjoy the fellowship of a few congenial friends. Modern libertarian and anarchic movements share many characteristics with Epicureanism.

## Extreme Doubt: Skepticism

The most pessimistic philosophy generated by the Hellenistic era was propounded by the Skeptics, whose named derives from a Greek word meaning "those on the lookout" or "the spies." Skepticism reached the zenith of its popularity in the second century under the influence of Carneades (c. 214–129 B.C.E.), a man born in the Greek city of Cyrene, in North Africa, who spent his youth in Athens. The chief source of his inspiration was the teaching (filtered through Aristotle) that all knowledge is based on sense perception and is therefore limited and relative. From this, the Skeptics concluded that no one can prove anything. Moreover, because the impressions of our senses can deceive us, we cannot even be certain about the truth of whatever empirical knowledge we think we have gained by observation of the world. All we can say is that things *appear* to be such and such; we do not know that they really *are* that way. It follows, furthermore, that we can have no definite knowledge of the supernatural, of the meaning of life, or of right and wrong.

The only sensible course for the Skeptic is therefore to suspend judgment: this alone can lead to happiness. If we abandon the fruitless quest for truth and cease to worry about good conduct and the existence of evil, we can at least attain a certain peace of mind, the highest satisfaction that an uncertain life affords. Needless to say, the Skeptics were even less concerned than the Epicureans with political and social problems, from which they felt wholly alienated. Their ideal was one of escape from an incomprehensible world. In some key respects they anticipated modern existentialism and nihilism.

## The Varieties of Religion

Like Epicureanism and Skepticism, Hellenistic religion tended to offer vehicles of escape from political commitments. When we think back to how close was the link between Greek selfhood and politics down to the middle of the fourth century B.C.E.—"man is a creature of the polis"—we can begin to appreciate what a radical change had occurred in just a few generations. In the classical age of the polis, as in all the societies we have studied so far, religion was wholly interconnected with politics. Divine worship centered on the gods who protected a community and furthered its interests. Hence, the most serious of the charges brought against Socrates was that he had "denied the gods of the polis" and thus committed treason. Religious crimes were political crimes, and piety was the same as patriotism.

Although this sense of a vital connection between a place and its gods persisted to a certain extent during the Hellenistic period, civic-oriented worship was compromised by the rootless multiculturalism of the third and second centuries B.C.E. In its place, some elite members of society gravitated toward one of the philosophies discussed above. Ordinary people, though, were more likely to embrace religious cults that offered emotional gratification or the diversion of colorful rituals, as well as some assurance of an afterlife, which the new philosophies did not.

# Competing Viewpoints

## *Debating the Education and Role of Women*

*The drastic political, social, and economic changes of the fourth century led philosophers to re- imagine the traditional structures of the polis, and to debate the proper role of women within these structures. Meanwhile, the cosmopolitan culture of the expanding Hellenistic world made it increasingly difficult to limit women's access to public spaces. The following excerpts represent two philosophical responses to these problems. The first comes from Plato's treatise on "Polis-matters"* (Politeía), *known to us as* The Republic, *the longest of his philosophical dialogues and the most influentical work of political thought in history. Its conceptual narrator and protagonist is Socrates, who engages in a series of debates with his pupils. The second excerpt is taken from a philosophical treatise attributed to a female follower of Pythagoras (see Chapter 3), but it was really written around 200* B.C.E. *in Hellenistic Italy, and by a man.*

### Plato, *The Republic*, c. 380 B.C.E.

**SOCRATES:** For men born and educated like our citizens, the only way, in my opinion, of arriving at a right conclusion about the possession and use of women and children is to follow the path on which we originally started, when we said that the men were to be the guardians and watchdogs of the herd.

**GLAUCON:** True.

**SOCRATES:** Let us further suppose the birth and education of our women to be subject to similar or nearly similar regulations; then we shall see whether the result accords with our design.

**GLAUCON:** What do you mean?

**SOCRATES:** . . . The education which was assigned to the men was music and gymnastic[s].

**GLAUCON:** Yes.

**SOCRATES:** Then women must be taught music and gymnastic[s] and also the art of war, which they must practice like the men?

**GLAUCON:** That is the inference, I suppose.

**SOCRATES:** I should rather expect . . . that several of our proposals, if they are carried out, being unusual, may appear ridiculous.

**GLAUCON:** No doubt of it.

**SOCRATES:** Yes, and the most ridiculous thing of all will be the sight of women naked in the palaestra, exercising with the men, especially when they are no longer young; they certainly will not be a vision of beauty, any more than the enthusiastic old men who in spite of wrinkles and ugliness continue to frequent the gymnasia. . . . . [Yet] not long ago, as we shall remind them, the Hellenes were of the opinion, which is still generally received among the barbarians, that the sight of a naked man was ridiculous and improper; and when first the Cretans and then the Lacedaemonians [Spartans] introduced the custom, the wits of that day might equally have ridiculed the innovation.

**GLAUCON:** No doubt. . . .

**SOCRATES:** First, then, whether the question is to be put in jest or in earnest, let us come to an understanding about the nature of woman: Is she capable of sharing either wholly or partially in the actions of men, or not at all? And is the art of war one of those arts in which she can or cannot share? That will be the best way of commencing the enquiry, and will probably lead to the fairest conclusion. . . .

**GLAUCON:** I suppose so. . . .

**SOCRATES:** And if . . . the male and female sex appear to differ in their fitness for any art or pursuit, we should say that such pursuit or art ought to be assigned to one or the other of them; but if the difference consists only in women bearing and men begetting children, this does not amount to a proof that a woman differs from a man in respect of the sort of education she should receive; and we shall therefore continue to maintain that our guardians and their wives ought to have the same pursuits.

**GLAUCON:** Very true.

**SOCRATES:** Next, we shall ask . . . how, in reference to any of the pursuits or arts of civic life, the nature of a woman differs from that of a man? . . .

**GLAUCON:** By all means.

**SOCRATES:** . . . [W]hen you spoke of a nature gifted or not gifted in any respect, did you mean to say that one man will acquire a thing easily, another with difficulty; a little learning will lead the one to discover a great deal; whereas the other, after much study and application, no sooner learns than he forgets? Or again, did you mean, that the one has a body which is a good servant to his mind, while the body of the other is a hindrance to him? Would not these be the sort of differences which distinguish the man gifted by nature from the one who is ungifted?

**GLAUCON:** No one will deny that.

**SOCRATES:** And can you mention any pursuit of mankind in which the male sex has not all these gifts and qualities in a higher degree than the female? Need I waste time in speaking of the art of weaving, and the management of pancakes and preserves, in which womankind does really appear to be great, and in which for her to be beaten by a man is of all things the most absurd?

**GLAUCON:** You are quite right . . . in maintaining the general inferiority of the female sex: although many women are in many things superior to many men, yet on the whole what you say is true.

Source: Excerpted from Plato, *The Republic*, Book V, trans. Benjamin Jowett (New York: 1982), pp. 170–76.

## Treatise attributed to Phintys, Third/Second Century B.C.E.

Now some people think that it is not appropriate for a woman to be a philosopher, just as a woman should not be a cavalry officer or a politician. . . . I agree that men should be generals and city officials and politicians, and women should keep house and stay inside and receive and take care of their husbands. But I believe that courage, justice, and intelligence are qualities that men and women have in common. . . . Courage and intelligence are more appropriately male qualities because of the strength of men's bodies and the power of their minds. Chastity is more appropriately female.

Accordingly, a woman must learn about chastity and realize what she must do quantitatively and qualitatively to be able to obtain this womanly virtue. I believe that there are five qualifications: (1) the sancitity of her marriage bed, (2) the cleanliness of her body, (3) the manner in which she chooses to leave her house, (4) her refusal to participate in secret cults . . . , (5) her readiness and moderation in sacrificing to the gods.

Of these, the most important quality for chastity is to be pure in respect of the marriage bed, and for her not to have affairs with men from other households. If she breaks the law in this way she wrongs the gods of her family and provides her family and home not with its own offspring but with bastards. . . . She should also consider the following: that there is no means of atoning for this sin; no way she can approach the shrines or the altars of the gods as a pure woman. . . . The greatest glory a freeborn woman can have—her foremost honor—is the witness her own children will give to her chastity toward her husband, the stamp of the likeness they bear to the father whose seed produced them. . . .

As far as adornment of her body is concerned . . . [h]er clothes should not be transparent or ornate. She should not put on silken material, but moderate, white-colored clothes. In this way, she will avoid being over-dressed or luxurious or made-up, and not give other women cause to be uncomfortably envious . . . She should not apply imported or artificial coloring to her face—with her own natural coloring, by washing only with water, she can ornament herself with modesty. . . .

Women of importance leave the house to sacrifice to the leading divinity of the community on behalf of their husbands and their households. They do not leave home at night nor in the evening, but at midday, to attend a religious festival or to make some purchase, accompanied by a single female servant or decorously escorted by two servants at most. . . . They keep away from secret cults . . . particularly because these forms of worship encourage drunkenness and ecstasy. The mistress of the house and head of the household should be chaste and untouched in all respects.

Source: From Mary R. Lefkowitz and Maureen B. Fant, eds. *Women's Life in Greece & Rome: A Source Book in Translation*, 2nd ed. (Baltimore, MD: 1992), pp. 163–164.

### *Questions for Analysis*

1. Follow the steps of the argument made by Socrates. How does he go about proving that women and men are different, and should have different roles in society? Are there flaws in this argument? What are they?
2. How does the author of the treatise seem to define "chastity," and why does she (or he) say that it corresponds to more masculine qualities of courage and intelligence? Why would this author have wanted to attribute these reflections to female members of the community founded by the philosopher Pythagoras (c. 570–c. 495), three centuries earlier? How might this treatise be responding to the changes brought about by the expansion of the Greek world in the fourth and third centuries B.C.E?
3. What are main points on which these two perspectives agree? How might ideas like those expressed here have influenced contemporary ideas of female beauty and modesty (see ***Interpreting Visual Evidence***, page 112)?

# Analyzing Primary Sources

## *A Jewish Response to Hellenization*

*Greek culture became a powerful force throughout the Hellenistic world, even in Israel. In the second century* B.C.E.*, the Hellenized ways of the Jewish elites in Jerusalem led to a revolt by a native Hebrew dynasty known as the Maccabees, who decried the effects of Hellenization on Jewish life. These events are recorded in two apocryphal books of the Hebrew Bible. In the passage that follows, note that even the High Priest of the Temple bears a Greek name, Jason.*

In those days, lawless men came forth from Israel and misled many, saying, "Let us go and make a covenant with the Gentiles [Greeks] round about us, for since we separated from them many disasters have come upon us." . . .

[This happened when] Antiochus [IV, 175–164 B.C.E.] who was called Epiphanes had succeeded to the kingdom, [and] Jason the brother of Onias obtained the high priesthood by corruption. . . . [H]e at once shifted his countrymen over to the Greek way of life . . . and he destroyed the lawful ways of living and introduced new customs contrary to the law. For with alacrity he founded a gymnasium right under the citadel, and he induced the noblest of the young men to wear the Greek hat [and not the traditional head covering]. There was such an extreme of Hellenization and increase in the adoption of foreign ways . . . that the priests were no longer intent upon the services of the altar. Despising the sanctuary and neglecting the sacrifices, they hurried to take part in the unlawful proceedings in the wrestling arena after the signal for the discus-throwing, disdaining the honors prized by their ancestors and putting the highest value upon Greek forms of prestige. . . . When the quadrennial games were being held at Tyre and the king was present, the vile Jason sent envoys . . . to carry three hundred silver drachmas for the sacrifice to Heracles. . . .

Not long after this, the king sent an Athenian senator to compel the Jews to forsake the laws of their fathers and cease to live by the laws of God, and also to pollute the temple in Jerusalem and call it the temple of Olympian Zeus. . . . Harsh and utterly grievous was the onslaught of evil. For the temple was filled with debauchery and reveling by the Gentiles, who dallied with prostitutes and had intercourse with women within the sacred precincts, and besides brought in things for sacrifice that were unfit. The altar was covered with abominable offerings that were forbidden by the laws. A man could neither keep the Sabbath nor observe the feasts of his fathers, nor so much as confess himself to be a Jew.

Source: Excerpted from 1 Maccabees 1:11; 2 Maccabees 4:10–18 and 6:1–6, in *The New Oxford Annotated Bible* (Oxford: 1973).

### *Questions for Analysis*

1. Given the history of the Hebrew kingdoms (Chapter 2), why would Hellenistic culture be particularly threatening to the Jews?
2. What, specifically, are the offensive actions and activities described here? Why, for example, would the building of a gymnasium (a Greek academy and athletic facility) in Jerusalem be problematic?

In Greek-speaking communities especially, cults that stressed extreme methods of atonement for sin, ecstatic mystical union with the divine, or contact with supernatural forces attracted many followers. Among these mystery religions—so called because their membership was select and their rites secret—one of the most popular was the cult of Dionysus, which celebrated the cyclical death and resurrection of that Greek god. The Egyptian cult of Isis, drawing on the story of Osiris (Chapter 1), also revolved around rituals of death and rebirth. So too did Zoroastrianism (Chapter 2), which became increasingly dualistic: its magi taught that the material world was entirely evil and urged believers to adopt ascetic practices that would purify their souls and prepare them for ethereal joy in the afterlife.

Like the peoples who worshiped them, the gods of the Hellenistic world were often immigrants from other lands. Temples to Greek gods and goddesses were dedicated throughout the Near East and Egypt; conversely, temples to Near Eastern divinities were constructed in the cities of the

Greek homeland. In Alexandria, scholars of religion collected Egyptian and Near Eastern mythologies, which were recorded and reformulated for Greek-speaking audiences. Here, as elsewhere in the Hellenistic world, there was a dazzling variety of religious choices.

Even among the Jews of Palestine, who resisted assimilation and the adoption of foreign customs, Hellenistic culture put down deep roots. This was especially true among the elites and among Jews living outside Palestine, who outnumbered the Palestinian population by a considerable margin by the end of the second century B.C.E. To meet the needs of these Greek-speaking Jews, and to satisfy the curiosity of Gentiles interested in Jewish beliefs, scholars working in Alexandria even produced a Greek version of the Hebrew scriptures. It is still known as the Septuagint, from the Greek word meaning "the seventy": legend has it that seventy scribes, each working independently, produced individual translations from Hebrew to Greek that were identical in every respect. This meant that the Septuagint was no less a product of divine inspiration than the original books that made up the Hebrew Bible, and could be treated as an authoritative text in its own right. For Jews concerned about their social and cultural standing vis-à-vis their Greek neighbors, it was also proof of their cultivation and their acceptance of Hellenistic values—although, ironically, some of the very portions of scripture that were now written in Greek disapproved strongly of those values.

## THE SCIENTIFIC REVOLUTION OF ANTIQUITY

The Hellenistic period is the most brilliant age in the history of science before the seventeenth century of our era. There are three major reasons for this. First, there was the enormous stimulus to intellectual inquiry caused by the fusion of Mesopotamian and Egyptian science with the philosophical methods of the Greeks. Second, as in the more famous scientific revolution of modernity, the use of a common language (in the seventeenth century it was Latin) and the ease of communication facilitated by quick, affordable travel also made the circulation of knowledge and sharing of ideas easier (in the seventeenth century, ease of communication was increased by the printing press and an international postal system). Finally, as in the seventeenth century, the competition among patrons of science was intense, which ensured the availability of ample funding. Every autocrat wanted to be thought enlightened and to be associated with new discoveries. And it might even be profitable to subsidize research that led to the development of new technologies, especially ones with military applications. But most of all, the rulers who financed scientific endeavors did so primarily for motives of prestige: they could show off a scientific gadget just as they could show off a sculpture. Even purely theoretical advances were so much admired that a Hellenistic prince who had bankrolled such a breakthrough would share the glory of it.

The arts were also transformed by the economic and political conditions of the Hellenistic world. Writers and artists working in various media strove to demonstrate their mastery of difficult techniques and so to attract the notice of potential patrons. New markets for art also changed *what* was being made, how, and for whom. In all of the civilizations we have studied so far, artists worked directly for royal or civic patrons, who were often very particular in their demands. In the Hellenistic world, art became commodified. Sometimes a work would be made expressly for a particular patron, but many works of art were fashioned for the open market. They were also designed to suit the tastes and lifestyles of urbane men and women, especially those of the merchant classes and the elite who had disposable income and wanted to increase their social standing through conspicuous consumption. This was as true of literature as of sculpture or the decorative arts: we know the names of over a thousand Hellenistic authors, either because their work survives in multiple copies sold in bookshops, or because they are mentioned in other writings (letters, pamphlets) as being in fashion. Indeed, the number of texts and *objets d'art* that exist from this period is huge, compared to earlier eras.

### *Measuring and Mapping: Astronomy, Geography, and Mathematics*

Hellenistic scientists took a major interest in measurements and map-making, whether of the heavens (astronomy) or the earth (geography) and the forms occuring in nature (geometry). The most renowned—and most wronged—of the Hellenistic astronomers was Aristarchus of Samos (310–230 B.C.E.), whose major discovery anticipated that of Copernicus by 1,700 years: he deduced that the earth and other planets revolve around the sun. Unfortunately, however, this view was not accepted by many of his contemporaries or successors because it conflicted with the teachings of Aristotle and with the Greek conviction that humanity, and therefore the earth, must be at the center of the universe. The sad fate of his discovery was sealed in the second century C.E., when the Alexandrian scholar Claudius Ptolemaeus (known as Ptolemy) published an astronomical treatise called the *Almagest*, which unequivocally argued that Aristotle was correct, and that all heavenly bodies revolve around the earth. This misinformative book was then handed down to posterity as the authoritative work of ancient astronomy. It would not be overturned until a much later scientific revolution occurred—and after the condemnation of theories made by Copernicus and Galileo that were identical to that of Aristarchus (see Chapter 16).

Closely allied with astronomy were geography and mathematics, especially geometry. The most influential Hellenistic mathematician was Euclid, whose *Elements of Geometry* (c. 300 B.C.E.) codified the work of others, including pre-Socratic philosophers like Pythagoras (Chapter 3). It remained the basic textbook for the study of that subject until the twentieth century of our era. Euclid's successor Hipparchus (second century B.C.E.) then laid the foundations of both plane and spherical trigonometry. In the field of geography—and in a host of other pursuits, too—the most original thinker was Eratosthenes of Alexandria (*air-ah-TOS-then-ees*, c. 276–c. 196 B.C.E.). Not only did he accurately calculate the circumference of the earth (within a tiny margin of error, less than 200 miles), he also developed a system of latitude and longitude, and he was the first to suggest the possibility of reaching eastern Asia by sailing west. In addition, he founded the science of chronology by attempting to establish the dates of major events reaching back to the siege of Troy. Students of history are forever in his debt.

## *Medicine and Mechanics: The Sciences of Physiology and Physics*

Before the third century B.C.E., physics had been a branch of philosophy. It became a separate, experimental science thanks to the single-handed genius of one man, Archimedes of Syracuse (c. 287–212 B.C.E.). It was he who discovered the law of floating bodies, or specific gravity, now known as "Archimedes' principle." According to legend, the idea came to him quite suddenly when he was in his bath, pondering possible theories. The stunning insight so excited him that he lept from the water and dashed out naked into the street, shouting "*Eureka!*" ("I found it!"). He also established the principles of the lever, the pulley, and the screw, and he invented both a compound pulley and a propeller. All of these discoveries had numerous practical uses in the construction of buildings, ships, and military machinery.

Other extaordinary advances of Hellenistic science were made in the field of medicine. Especially significant was the work of the Alexandrian scholar Herophilus of Chalcedon (c.335–c.280 B.C.E.), the greatest anatomist of antiquity and probably the first to practice human dissection. Many of his discoveries directly challenged the orthodoxy of Aristotelian teaching—and rightly, since Aristotle's understanding of physiology (like his knowledge of astronomical and natural science) has not stood the test of time as well as his grasp of logic and politics. Herophilus' achievements included a detailed description of the brain, which allowed him to prove that the brain was the engine of human intellect (Aristotle thought that it was the heart), as well as the discovery that the arteries contain blood alone (not a mixture of blood and air, as Aristotle had taught), and that their function is to carry blood from the heart to all parts of the body. He also understood the significance of the pulse and its use in diagnosing illness. His colleague Erasistratus (*air-ah-sis-STRAH-tus*) made allied discoveries, establishing that the heart was a pump and not an organ of emotion, explaining the working of its valves, and distinguishing between motor and sensory nerves. Erasistratus also rejected the widely held theory of the physician Hippocrates (c. 460–c. 370), who had posited that the body consists of four "humors" which need to be kept in balance through bloodletting and other invasive practices. Unfortunately, this discovery went the way of the heliocentric universe posited by Aristarchus: another encyclopedist of the second century C.E., Galen, preferred the erroneous theory of Hippocrates. His baleful

**SURGICAL INSTRUMENTS.** Tools like these were used by both Hellenistic and Roman doctors to perform surgical procedures, but they also had a variety of nonmedical uses. Shown here are a grinding stone, spoons, probes, depressors, and tongs. The large, flat-headed tool may have been used for cauterizing wounds. The inscription visible on the stone in the upper left-hand corner is probably a recipe for eye medicine.

**THE CITADEL OF PERGAMON.** An artist's reconstruction of Pergamon in the second century B.C.E., based on the work of nineteenth-century German archeologists. High atop the hill is the massive altar of Zeus (now in the Pergamon Museum in Berlin) and below it slope the tiers of the theater. Other features include fortifications, terraces, and artificial landscaping for public gardens. ▪ ***How does this complex of buildings compare to that of another citadel, the Acropolis of Athens (see Chapter 3, page 74)?***

influence, and the practice of bloodletting, thus persisted into the nineteenth century of our era.

## Urban Architecture and Sculpture

Hellenistic architecture drew on Greek models, but it was also influenced by standards and tastes more characteristic of Egypt and Persia. Two examples (both of which no longer survive) are the great lighthouse of Alexandria, which rose to a height of nearly 400 feet and which was daringly composed of three diminishing stories topped by eight slender columns supporting the light; and the citadel of Alexandria, built of stone and covered with blue-tinted plaster, described by a contemporary as seeming to float in mid-air. The best-surviving example, though, comes from Pergamon, a city on the coast of Anatolia that became the capital of a new kingdom wrested from the control of the Seleucids in the second century B.C.E. It boasted an enormous altar dedicated to Zeus that crowned the heights of the city, below which an open-air theater was built into the steep slope of the hill. In Ephesus, not far away, the streets were not only paved, but paved with marble.

But the most influential of all Hellenistic arts was sculpture, which represents a further movement away from classical ideals and even more emphasis on realism than the fourth-century sculptures discussed earlier in this chapter. Sculptors now prided themselves on faithfully reproducing facial furrows, muscular distensions, and complex folds of drapery. Awkward human postures offered the greatest technical challenges, to the degree that sculptors might prefer to show people stretching themselves or balancing on one leg in ways that hardly ever occur in real life. Because monumental sculpture of this kind was executed for wealthy

**THE MARBLE STREETS OF EPHESUS.** Ephesus was already a splendid city when it was incorporated into the Persian Empire along with other Greek settlements in Ionia. In the Hellenistic era, it became more splendid still.

private patrons, it is clear that the goal was to create something unique in both conception and craftsmanship—something a collector could show off as the only one of its type. It is not surprising, therefore, that complexity came to be admired for its own sake, and extreme naturalism sometimes teetered on the brink of distortion. Yet to modern eyes such works frequently appear familiar, because of the influence they exerted on later sculptors like Michelangelo (see Chapter 12) and Auguste Rodin. Three of the most famous examples are pictured here, each exhibiting different aesthetic qualities and artistic techniques: the *Dying Gaul*, made in Pergamon around 220 B.C.E.; the *Winged Victory of Samothrace*, dating from around 200 B.C.E.; and the *Laocoön* group, from the first century B.C.E.

## Literary Fantasy and Historical Reality

In the sixth century B.C.E. it was the lyric, in the fifth century it was tragedy, and in the fourth century it was the novel; but in the Hellenistic era, the new literary genre was pastoral verse. These poems tapped into a strong vein of nostalgia for rural pastimes and simple pleasures, a make-believe world of shepherds and wood nymphs. The most important pastoral poet of the age was Theocritus, who flourished around 270 B.C.E. in the big-city environment of Alexandria. Theocritus was a merchant of escapism. In the midst of urban bustle and within sight of overcrowded slums, he celebrated the charms of country life and lazy summer afternoons, putting into the mouths of his rustic characters unlikely sentiments expressed in ornate language. He thereby founded an enduring tradition that would be taken up by poets from the Roman Virgil to the Englishman (and classical scholar) A. E. Houseman, and that has continuously provided a wealth of themes for the visual arts. Even composers like Beethoven and Debussy owe a debt to Theocritus.

By contrast, Hellenistic prose literature was dominated by historians and biographers who consciously modeled their work on earlier pioneers, especially Thucydides. By far the most important was Polybius (c. 203–120 B.C.E.), a wellborn Greek from the mainland whose father was a prominent politician active in the Achaean League. Polybius himself was trained as a horseman and cavalry officer, and both his vocation and his family connections gave him ample opportunity to observe the workings of government, diplomacy, and military strategy. This was at a time when the Achaean League was trying to position itself favorably in ongoing wars between the rising republic of Rome and the various fractious kingdoms of northern Greece, notably

**DYING GAUL.** The original (now lost) statue on which this Roman copy was based was sculpted in Pergamon around 220 B.C.E. The sculptor clearly wished to exhibit skill in depicting an unusual subject: the Gauls were a Celtic people about whom very little was known in this era. ▪ ***How does this sympathetic representation of a "barbarian" express the new values of Hellenistic philosophy?***

**THE WINGED VICTORY OF SAMOTHRACE (left).** This marble sculpture of the goddess Nike (Victory) may originally have been displayed on the prow of a monumental ship. It formed part of a temple complex on the island of Samothrace in the northern Aegean, and dates to around the year 200 B.C.E. It is now in the Louvre Museum, Paris. **LAOCOÖN AND HIS SONS (right).** In sharp contrast to the serene and confident *Winged Victory* is this famous sculpture group from the first century B.C.E. According to legend, Laocoön warned the Trojans not to accept the wooden horse sent by the Greeks and was accordingly punished by the sea-god Poseidon, who sent two serpents to kill him and his sons. The intense physicality of this work was an important influence on Michelangelo, a millennium and a half later.

Macedon and Epiros. In 168 B.C.E., the Romans became suspicious of the Achaeans' declared neutrality and demanded that a thousand noble hostages be sent from Greece to Rome as a guarantee of the League's good behavior. Polybius was one of those hostages, and he spent the next seventeen years living in Rome. There, he became a fervent admirer of Roman customs and especially of its unique form of government. He also formed warm friendships with high-ranking Roman families, including the descendents of Scipio Africanus, a prominent Roman general. He kept up these contacts after his release, traveling to North Africa during the Third Punic War and witnessing firsthand the destruction of Carthage in 146 B.C.E. (see Chapter 5).

The result of this colorful career was a series of histories that glorified the achievements of Rome and its political system. Polybius also attempted to account for the patterns that he discerned in the history of Greece since the Peloponnesian War. He argued that historical developments follow regular cycles, and that nations pass inevitably through stages of growth and decay. Hence, it should be possible to predict exactly where a given state is heading if one knows what has happened to it in the past. Yet he also argued that the special character of Rome's constitution would allow it to break the cycle, because it combined all of the different forms of government that Aristotle had outlined in his *Politics*. This view of history galvanized the framers of the United States Constitution, directly influencing their conception of our own political institutions.

## CONCLUSION

Judged from the perspective of classical Greece, Hellenistic civilization seems strange. The autocratic governments of the age that followed Alexander's conquests would probably appear repugnant to a staunch proponent of Athenian democracy, and the Hellenistic love of extravagance and display can contrast strikingly with the tastes of the fifth century B.C.E.. Yet Hellenistic civilization had its own achievements that the classical age could not match, achievements that make it in some ways more familiar to us. Most Hellenistic cities offered a greater range of public facilities than any Greek cities of the previous period, and the numerous advances in science and technology are astonishing when compared to anything that came before, or even after.

But the most important contribution of the Hellenistic era to subsequent historical developments was its role as an intermediary between the nascent empire of Rome and the older civilizations of Mesopotamia, Egypt, and Greece. The example set by Alexander, in particular, was one that the Romans would emulate, and the economic and political infrastuctures that were put in place after his conquests would form the framework of Roman imperial government. The Romans would also take advantage of the common language and cultural expectations that bound the far reaches of the Greek-speaking world together. Their own Latin language would only become acceptable for cultivated conversation and literary expression toward the very end of the first century B.C.E., and it would never supplant Greek as the preeminent language of scholarship and administration in the eastern portions of their empire.

The Hellenistic era must also be recognized as the bridge that connects us to the earlier ages of antiquity: most of what is contained in the first four chapters of this book is known to us because older texts and inscriptions and arti-

## After You Read This Chapter

Visit StudySpaces for quizzes, additional review materials, and multi-media documents. **wwnorton.com/studyspace**

### REVIEWING THE OBJECTIVES

- Macedonia's successful conquest of the Greek poleis can be attributed to several factors. What are they?
- Alexander the Great's imperial policies were influenced by his own upbringing, the different cultures he encountered, and some key historical precedents. Give at least one example of each type of influence.
- Explain how the three Hellenistic kingdoms reflect the differences among the three main civilizations we have studied so far.
- Why is the Hellenistic world described as "cosmopolitan"? How did this urban culture differ from that of the Greek poleis?
- The philosophies of Plato and Aristotle both derive from the teachings of Socrates, but they diverge in some important ways. What are those main differences?

facts were collected and copied by the scholars of Alexandria and other Hellenistic cities. It also bridges the gap between the tastes and ideals and customs of classical Greece and those that would be more characteristic of Rome. It was Hellenistic art and architecture, Hellenistic city planning and civic culture that the Romans strove to emulate and export to their own colonies, not those of Periclean Athens. The same can be said of drama and poetry.

For us, two further aspects of Hellenistic culture deserve special mention: its cosmopolitanism and its modernity. The word *cosmopolitan* itself comes from a Greek word meaning "universal city," and it was the Greeks of the Hellenistic period who came closest to turning this ideal of globalization into reality. Around 250 B.C.E. a Greek tourist could have traveled from Sicily to the borders of India—the two ends of the earth—and never have found himself among people who did not speak his language or share his basic outlook. Nor would this tourist have identified himself in ethnic or nationalist terms, or felt any exclusive loyalty to a city-state or kingdom. He would have considered himself a citizen of the world. He would also have considered himself a modern man, not bound by the old prejudices and superstitions of the past. It is for these reasons that Hellenistic civilization seems so closely related to our own. It was a world of stark contrasts and infinite possibilities, where economic instability, extremism, and authoritarian regimes existed side by side with unprecedented prosperity, rational inquiry, and extraodinary freedoms. In Chapter 5, we will see how this world adapted itself to the dominion of a single Italian city.

## PEOPLE, IDEAS, EVENTS IN CONTEXT

- In what ways were the military strategies of **PHILIP II OF MACEDON** variations on older forms of hoplite warfare? How did the rise of mercenary armies and of **THEBES** further change military strategies in the fourth century?
- How did the philosophies of **PLATO** and **ARISTOTLE** respond to the crisis of the polis?
- To what degree did the conquests of **ALEXANDER THE GREAT** unite Mesopotamia, Egypt, and Greece?
- Why and how did the three **HELLENISTIC KINGDOMS** emerge? How were the **AETOLIAN AND ACHAEAN LEAGUES** new models for governance and cooperation in Greece?
- In what ways were **STOICISM**, **EPICUREANISM**, and other new philosophies a response to **COSMOPOLITANISM** and the breakdown of traditional societies and values?
- What were the driving forces behind the **SCIENTIFIC REVOLUTION OF ANTIQUITY**? What were its main achievements?
- What are some essential characteristics of **HELLENISTIC ART**? In what ways did it differ from that of the fifth century B.C.E. (Chapter 3)?

## CONSEQUENCES

- "The history of the world is but the biography of great men": so the Scottish historian Thomas Carlyle (1795–1881) summarized the impact of figures like Alexander the Great. How would you construct an argument in support of this proposition, using what you've learned in this chapter? How would you refute it?
- In what ways do Alexander's actions demonstrate his own knowledge of history, as well as a capacity to apply that knowledge to his own circumstances? Can you identify leaders of our own day who have mobilized their understanding of history in similar ways?
- In your view, which civilization more resembles our own: classical Athens or the Hellenistic world? Why? What characteristics make an era seem "modern"?

# Before You Read This Chapter

## STORY LINES

- Romans were proud of their unique history, especially the legend that they had overthrown their kings. They clung to this story even when individual men came to wield kingly powers.
- Roman identity, religion, and politics were intimately bound up in the worship of ancestors, especially male ancestors. As a result, fathers (living and dead) wielded extraordinary power in early Rome.
- Roman women enjoyed many more freedoms than women of ancient Greece, but they were still subject to the authority of their male relatives.
- The Roman army had unprecedented strength and importance in this civilization, but the army's relationship to Roman politics and society changed drastically as Rome's empire grew.
- Paradoxically, the Romans celebrated their farming heritage even as they built a highly urbanized society. At the same time, they regarded Greek culture as both superior and dangerous.

## CHRONOLOGY

| | |
|---|---|
| 753 B.C.E. | Legendary founding of Rome |
| c. 509 B.C.E. | Roman Republic established |
| c. 450 B.C.E. | Law of the Twelve Tables |
| 287 B.C.E. | "Struggle of the Orders" ends |
| 264–146 B.C.E. | Punic Wars |
| 134–104 B.C.E. | Slave revolts in Sicily |
| 133–122 B.C.E. | Reforms of the Gracchi |
| 107–86 B.C.E. | Consulship of Marius |
| 82–79 B.C.E. | Dictatorship of Sulla |
| 73–71 B.C.E. | Rebellion of Spartacus |
| 52–48 B.C.E. | Struggle of Pompey and Caesar |
| 48–44 B.C.E. | Dictatorship of Casear |
| 44–30 B.C.E. | Rivalry of Octavian and Antony |
| 27 B.C.E.–14 C.E. | Principate of the Emperor Augustus |
| 27–180 C.E. | Flowering of the *Pax Romana* |
| 79 C.E. | Eruption of Mount Vesuvius destroys (and preserves) Pompeii |
| 117 C.E. | Roman Empire reaches its greatest extent under Trajan |

# The Civilization of Ancient Rome

## CORE OBJECTIVES

- **IDENTIFY** the factors that influenced the formation of the Roman Republic.
- **UNDERSTAND** the basic elements of Roman identity.
- **DEFINE** the classes of people who struggled for power in Rome.
- **DESCRIBE** the impact of territorial expansion on Roman society.
- **TRACE** the events leading up to the establishment of the Principate.

Could anyone be so indifferent or slow-witted as not to care how, and under what system of government, the Romans managed to bring nearly the whole inhabited world under their rule? Can anything be more important than understanding this?" So the Greek soldier Polybius (c. 203–120 B.C.E.) addresses Greek readers in a history celebrating the achievements of the Roman Republic. Polybius had witnessed some of these firsthand: on the battlefield, in Rome itself as a hostage and a guest, and on a visit to newly conquered Carthage. What better testament could there be to the success of a small Italian city than the admiration of a cultivated Greek aristocrat who, having been subjected to Roman authority, wholeheartedly embraced it? None, unless we cite the equally enthusiastic endorsement of the same Jews who had rebelled against Greek influence in 164 B.C.E. They, too, could not say enough in praise of the Romans, and they willingly placed themselves under Roman protection.

> Those whom they wish to help and to make kings, they make kings, and those whom they wish they depose; and they have been greatly exalted. Yet for all

> that, not one of them has put on a crown or worn purple as a mark of pride, but they have built for themselves a senate chamber and every day three hundred and twenty senators constantly deliberate concerning the people, to govern them well. (1 Maccabees 8:12–15)

The only people who could say more in praise of Rome were the Romans themselves. To them, the enormous success of their empire meant that they were divinely chosen to colonize the world. This was the message conveyed by the poet Virgil (70–19 B.C.E.), commissioned by the Emperor Augustus to tell the story of Rome's rise to glory in a manner imitating the epics of Homer. In one key passage, the father of Aeneas, Virgil's epic hero, "foretells" the future and addresses posterity: "Remember, Roman, you whose power rules / all peoples, that these are your arts: plant peace, / make law, spare subjects, and put down the proud" (*Aeneid*, Book VI, lines 851–3).

While the Greeks struggled against the Persians and against each other, a new civilization emerged beyond the northern fringes of the Greek world, on the banks of the river Tiber in central Italy. By 300 B.C.E. Rome was the dominant power on the Italian peninsula. Two centuries later, it had conquered Greece itself. For the next three centuries after that—an unprecedented period of sustained expansion—its power steadily increased. In the first century of our era, it ruled the Hellenistic world as well as a vast region that Greek culture had never touched: northwestern Europe. Eventually, Rome's empire united the entire Mediterranean and most of Asia Minor, while at the same time embracing provinces that are now parts of France, Spain, Portugal, Britain, Belgium, Germany, Switzerland, and the Balkans. Rome thus built a historical arch that enabled Europe to share in a rich heritage reaching back to ancient Mesopotamia and Egypt. Without Rome, European culture as we know it would not exist, and neither would the political and legal institutions that formed the United States. To echo Polybius: "Can anything be more important than understanding this?"

## THE TIME OF THE KINGS

Romans looked back uneasily on their early history, for this was the time when they were ruled by kings. It may have been necessary in those days: Romans had never been peaceful settlers, and their land did not yield an easy living. Although Italy had sizable forests and much more fertile land than Greece, it has few mineral resources aside from excellent supplies of marble. Its extensive coastline boasts only a few good harbors, and most of these are on the western side, away from the commercial hubs of Greece and the Near East. Nor does the length of this coastline offer secure natural defenses. In short, Italy was rich enough to be attractive, but not rich enough to be easily defended. So the Romans were a warlike people from the first, continually forced to defend their own conquests against other invaders.

### Early Influences

When the Romans arrived in Italy, the dominant inhabitants of the peninsula were a people whom the Greeks called Tyrrhenians. To the Romans, they were Etruscans; and to us they remain mysterious, despite the rich archeological record they left behind. This is because their language (not a branch of Indo-European) has never been fully deciphered, even though the Etruscans used an alphabet borrowed from the Greeks, with whom they were in frequent contact. By the sixth century B.C.E., the Etruscans had established a confederation of independent city-states in north-central Italy. They were skilled metalworkers, artists, and architects, from whom the Romans later took their knowledge of the arch and the vault, among much else, including the bloody sport of gladiatorial combat and the practice of foretelling the future by studying the entrails of animals and the flight of birds.

The two most important foundation myths told by the Romans were also derived from Etruscan tradition: the story of Aeneas' escape from Troy, which became the basis of Virgil's *Aeneid*, and also the story of the infant twins Romulus and Remus, abandoned at birth and then raised by a maternal wolf, afterward founding a city on the slopes of the Palatine Hill. Both legends would be mined by Rome's historians for their metaphorical significance, and further details would be added to increase their relevance for a changing audience. For example, Aeneas' seduction and abandonment of Dido, queen of Carthage, reflected Rome's defeat of that powerful North African civilization. And for many Roman commentators, the murder of Remus at the hands of his brother Romulus encapsulated an all-too-familiar pattern in Roman politics.

One aspect of Etruscan culture was of more limited influence. In marked contrast to Greek society, Etruscan women enjoyed a very high status and played important roles in public life. They participated in politics and sporting events, they attended dramatic performances and athletic competitions (forbidden to Greek women), and they danced

**AN ETRUSCAN COUPLE.** This sarcophagus lid dates from middle of the fourth century B.C.E. and depicts a deceased couple as they lie together naked, emphasizing by their embrace the closeness of their marital bond.

in ways that shocked both Greeks and Romans. Etruscan wives also ate meals with their husbands, another departure from both Greek and Roman custom, and reclined with them on the same couch at banquets. After death, these devoted couples were buried together in the same mortuary vaults, and their tombstones and sarcophagi often emphasize mutual affection. Etruscan families even traced their descent through the female line. Some of these practices certainly affected the Romans, whose women were less sequestered than their Greek counterparts. Yet they did not enjoy the same freedoms as Etruscan women until very late in Roman history, and by then these freedoms were condemned as signs of Rome's decadence (see below).

The Romans also borrowed ideas from the Greek settlers who had begun to colonize southern Italy and Sicily in large numbers during the eighth century B.C.E. From them, Romans derived their alphabet, many of their religious beliefs, and much of their art. But the Romans downplayed Greek influence in their founding mythology, preferring to emphasize their alleged descent from Trojans and also tracing their ancestry back to an Italic people called the Sabines, from whom (according to legend) Romulus and his men had forcibly abducted their wives. This was a practice Romans would continue, in one form or another, as the legions who planted new colonies intermarried with indigenous populations from the Persian Gulf to the lowlands of Scotland.

## *The Founding of Rome*

The real founders of Rome were a tribe called the Latins, descendents of a cluster of Indo-European-speaking peoples who crossed the Alps into Italy during the second millennium B.C.E. Recent archaeological research has pushed the origins of the city back to at least the tenth century, several centuries earlier than 753 B.C.E., which the Romans themselves calculated as the year of their city's foundation.

Rome's position on the Tiber was advantageous. Trading ships (but not large war fleets) could navigate the river as far as the city, but no farther; Rome could thus serve as a commercial port but was not threatened by attack from the sea. Rome also sat astride the first good ford across the Tiber, making it a major crossroads. This was particularly important in its early years, when all roads did *not* lead to Rome and the city was just a trading post on the frontier between Latium (the territory of the Latins) and Etruria (the Etruscan homeland). There were also strategic advantages to the seven hills that ringed the settlement, among which Rome was nestled. Eventually, its central markeplace—the *forum* or "open space"—would become the beating heart of the world's most populous and powerful city, with approximately a million people crowded into an area of five square miles.

The topography of Latium—a broad, flat plain with few natural obstacles—also influenced the way the Romans dealt with neighboring communities. At an early date, they negotiated a series of agreements with their neighbors which were collectively known as the Latin Right: a trading pact called the *commercium*, provisions for intermarriage called the *connubium*, and the *migratio* that allowed a Latin resident of one settlement to emigrate to another and, after a year's residence, to have the full rights of a citizen there. These privileges contrast strongly with the rigid particularism and mutual suspicion that divided the cities of Sumer or Greece. Indeed, the Romans' later willingness to extend the Latin Right far beyond Latium was a key factor in the success of their empire.

According to their own legends, the Romans' early government was a monarchy that mirrored the structure of Roman households, with a patriarchal king who exercised power that was checked only by a council of elders, the Senate (a word derived from the Latin *senex*, "old man"). Seven kings, including Romulus, are said to have ruled in succession. The last, Tarquinus Superbus (Tarquin the Arrogant), is reputed to have been an Etruscan who paved the way for Rome's imperial expansion by dominating Latium and the agriculturally wealthy district of Campania to the south. But his power came at the price of Roman freedom and dignity, as was made clear when Tarquin's son raped a virtuous Roman wife, Lucretia, around 510 B.C.E. When she commited suicide to avoid dishonor, the Romans—led by Lucretia's kinsman, Lucius Junius Brutus—rose up in rebellion, overthrowing not only the Etruscan dynasty but rejecting the very idea of monarchy as a legitimate form of government. Henceforth, any claim to royal authority in Rome was considered anathema, and the very word "king" (*rex*) was a term of insult. The Brutus who would be instrumental in the assassination of Julius Caesar nearly five centuries later was a descendant of that same Brutus who had driven out the Tarquin kings, something he and his contemporaries never forgot.

## THE TRIUMPH OF THE EARLY REPUBLIC

The story of Lucretia's defilement and death, whether or not it occurred as it was remembered, remained a rallying theme of patriotic myth and was also a potent statement of Roman attitudes toward female chastity and family honor. And it coincided with a radical change in Roman governance. This change was so radical, in fact, that it did not match any of Aristotle's political categories (see Chapter 4), but instead combined elements of them all. The Romans themselves didn't know what to call their political system: they spoke of it merely as *res publica*, "the public thing."

The early republic was marked by almost constant warfare, initially defensive but soon aimed at stitching together a patchwork of valuable territiories that could support Rome's growing population. Gradually, Romans came to control all of the Latin hinterland and the valuable port of Ostia at the mouth of the Tiber, about twenty miles from their city. They also pushed northward toward Etruscan territory, and southward to Naples, another good port. By 300 B.C.E. Rome had absorbed or allied itself with all of central Italy and began to look even further south, to the wealthy Greek colonies of Sicily. Their rapid success is remarkable when compared to the patterns familiar to us from our study of classical Greece, the only corollary (and not a close one) being Philip II of Macedonia's subjugation of the poleis earlier in that same century. What was the secret of it? For one thing, the Romans did not impose heavy burdens of taxation and tribute on the settlements they conquered. More often, they demanded that their allies contribute only soldiers to the Roman army. Rome also extended the Latin Right to many of these conquered territories, giving them a further stake in its continued political and military expansion.

Rome thus gained for itself nearly inexhaustible reserves of fighting men. By the middle of the third century B.C.E, its army may have numbered as many as 300,000—a huge force even by modern standards, and all the more formidable due to the soldiers' rigorous training. As we have seen, the Greeks had eventually turned to paid soldiering out of economic necessity, but they fought in smaller numbers; Xenophon's army was 10,000 and Alexander's 100,000. The Great King of Persia, at the height of his powers, could claim to muster a million men, but these were private or tribal armies commanded by his satraps, not a standing army loyal to him. The Romans clearly devoted themselves to the discipline of warfare in ways the Greeks (except for the Spartans) and the Persians did not. In this, although not in their tactics, they resemble the Hittites of the late Bronze Age and the Neo-Assyrians of the eighth century B.C.E. (Chapter 2).

Although the Romans originally used the phalanx formation borrowed from the Greeks, they quickly replaced it with smaller, more flexible divisions that could adjust to the hilly conditions of central Italy. While the major unit of the Roman army was always the legion (5,000 men), the combat unit was the *maniple* ("handful"), a group of 120 infantrymen who trained together and who often performed specialized tasks or used special weaponry. The Greek Polybius could not say enough in praise of this system, which made the army adaptable to climate, terrain, and new techniques.

The republic's early history reinforced not only the military character of the Roman nation but its commitment to agriculture as the only proper peacetime employment for a Roman. The acquisition of new lands made it possible for needy citizens to maintain themselves as farmers in the new colonies around Rome. By accommodating an increasing population in this way, Romans were able

**ROMAN EXPANSION IN ITALY, 485–265 B.C.E.** This map illustrates early Roman expansion in central and southern Italy. ▪ ***What is the geographical relationship between Roman and Etruscan territory?*** ▪ ***What seem to have been the most attractive avenues for Roman expansion?*** ▪ ***What powers might have threatened Rome after its transformation into the dominant power on the peninsula after 265 B.C.E.?***

to remain staunchly agricultural for a surprisingly long time. As a result, they developed an interest in shipping and commerce fairly late when compared with the Greeks or Phoenicians. And they would continue—even at the height of their empire—to valorize rural life over that of the city.

The paragon of Roman heroism in this era was Lucius Quinctius Cincinnatus (519–c. 430 B.C.E.), a stout-hearted citizen-farmer who reluctantly accepted political office when Rome was threatened by attack. According to legend, he was found plowing his fields when a delegation of senators arrived to bring him to Rome. When in the city, he

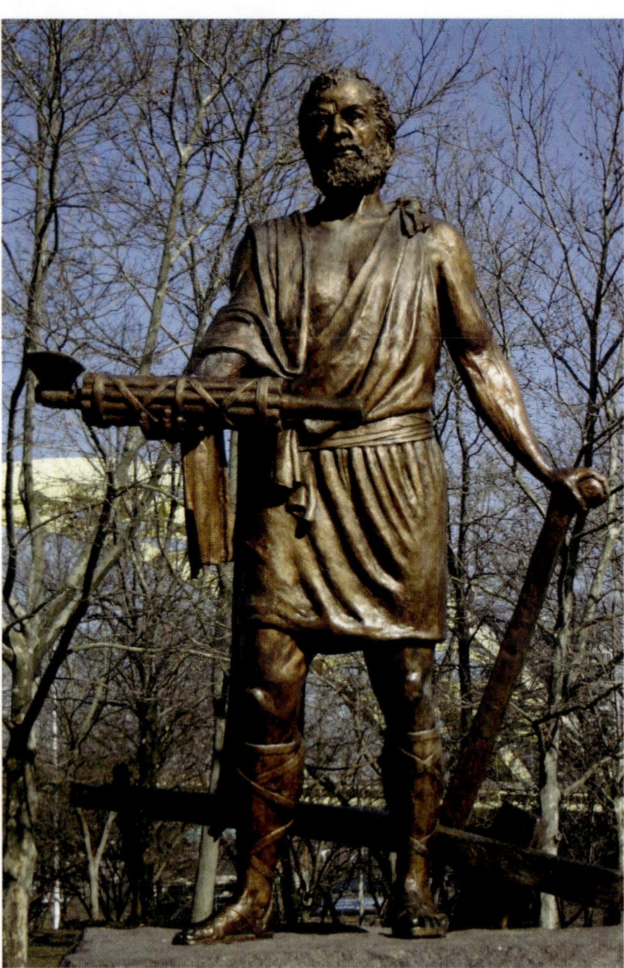

**CINCINNATUS THE STATESMAN-FARMER.** This bronze statue of Cincinnatus is prominent in Cincinnati, Ohio, which was named after the Roman dictator (and in honor of George Washington) in 1790. In his right hand he holds the *fasces*, symbolizing his powers as dictator. In his left, he grasps the handle of a plow. ▪ ***Why would this figure have fired the imagination of Americans after their War of Independence?***

found that he had been named *dictator*: a word that originally (like *tyrant* in Greece) had neutral connotations. This was a position of power to which the Romans elected one man during times of crisis. And as the term implies, the dictator's job was to tell everyone what they should do in a tough situation requiring decisive leadership. As legend has it, Cincinnatus dutifully performed this role, led Rome in its wars with hostile neighbors—and then went back to his farm. If Lucretia was the Roman epitome of matronly fortitude, Cincinnatus was the paradigm of manly virtue: willing to put his hand to politics or warfare, but preferring to put it to the plow. George Washington was frequently compared to him, to his own satisfaction.

## The Constitution of the Early Republic

During this period of expansion, Rome's political system evolved accordingly. Initially, the overthrow of the monarchy had resulted in only moderate changes; instead of a king, the government was headed by two elected officers called *consuls*. Although the consuls of the infant republic were supposedly chosen by all citizens, the Roman assembly of this period actually voted in affiliated blocs with shared interests, economic or territorial. And since groups consisting of the wealthiest citizens voted first, a majority could be reached even before the votes of the poorer groups were cast. Consequently, the consuls were inevitably members of aristocratic families, known in Rome as *patricians* because they traced descent from a famous ancestor or "father" (*pater*). During his term of office, which lasted for one year, each consul exercised essentially the same power as a king: dealing justice, making law, and commanding the army. The only limit on consular power was the right of each consul to veto the actions of the other, which often led to stalemate or violent conflict. In such cases, the Senate might have to arbitrate. In times of grave emergency (like that resulting in Cincinnatus' election), a dictator might be appointed for a term not longer than six months.

Within a generation after the establishment of the republic, patrician dominance of the government began to be challenged by the *plebs* ("people"). This was the first stage in a centuries-long contest known as the Struggle of the Orders. The plebeian classes made up nearly 98 percent of the Roman population, and they were a diverse group. Some had grown wealthy through trade or agriculture, but most were smallholding farmers, artisans, or the urban poor. Their causes for grievance were numerous. Although they were forced to serve in the army, they were nevertheless excluded from holding office. They were also the victims of discriminatory decisions in judicial trials, which were judged by patricians. They did not even know what legal rights they were supposed to enjoy, because Rome had as yet no established laws: there were only unwritten customs and practices whose meaning was interpreted by the patricians to their own advantage. The plebians were also, like the poorer citizens of Greek poleis, threatened with debt slavery.

These wrongs prompted a rebellion in the early fifth century B.C.E., when plebeians refused to join in the military defense of Rome and instead seceded from the city, camping out on the Aventine hill (see the map of Rome on page 170). This general strike of military labor forced the patricians to allow the people to elect of their own officers, who were known as *tribunes* (tribal leaders). The job of each tribune was to protect his constituents from patrician injustice. Moreover, the plebeians guaranteed the safety of these officers by vowing to kill any person who hindered them in the exercise of their powers.

The plebs' victory led to the codification of the Law of the Twelve Tables, issued around 450 B.C.E. and inscribed on wooden tablets (hence "tables"). Although this law would be regarded by later Romans as a charter of liberties, it was really a perpetuation of ancient custom. Nevertheless, the fact that the law was now *defined* made it a significant improvement. Plebeians were made eligible to hold elected offices and they gradually gained access to the Senate. A further victory came in 287 B.C.E., when the plebeians succeeded in passing a law that made decisions enacted in their own assembly, the *concilium plebis*, binding on the Roman government—whether the Senate approved them or not. It was at this time that the phrase *Senatus Populusque Romanum* came into regular use, abbreviated *SPQR* and designating any decree or decision made by "the Roman Senate and People." (Visitors to Rome will still find *SPQR* emblazoned on everything from public buildings to the manhole covers of Rome's sewers.)

These reforms had several important consequences over the long term. Successful plebeians could now work their way into the upper reaches of Roman society, which loosened the hold of patrician families. At the same time, laws preventing wealth from becoming a controlling factor in Roman politics barred senators from engaging directly in commerce. This restriction had the effect of creating a new social order, that of the equestrians ("horsemen" or knights): men who chose a life of business rather than politics and whose wealth made it possible for them to own and equip warhorses, and thus to provide Rome's cavalry.

**SENATUS POPULUSQUE ROMANUM.** The proud stamp of "the Roman Senate and People" can be found even on public works and buildings in modern Rome. It is displayed here on a manhole cover.

But the equestrians and the senators were never wholly distinct. Often, some members of an important family would stay aloof from politics while underwriting the political careers of their brothers and cousins. Those families who managed to win election by such means, generation after generation, became increasingly prestigious and influential. Meanwhile, patricians who chose politics over wealth became impoverished and resentful. By the first century B.C.E., many felt excluded from political influence and were tempted to pursue their private agendas by styling themselves champions of the people (see below).

Later Roman patriots would regard this as a golden age of shared government, but Rome was never a democracy. A republic differs from a monarchy only because power is exercised by officers who are in some way responsible to citizens, and whose offices are not (at least in theory) hereditary. It is essentially a system for reserving power to an oligarchy or privileged group. This is what the republic had been founded to achieve: kings were driven out, but patricians reigned. The constitution that emerged in these key centuries therefore broadened and stabilized oligarchy by the balance it struck between competing governmental institutions: the assembly, the Senate, and executive officeholders. Thanks to this distribution of powers, no single individual or clique could become overwhelmingly strong; but neither could direct expressions of the popular will (that is, democracy) affect Roman policy.

For the Greek historian Polybius, this was an ideal system, combining elements of the monarchy (executive officeholders, the consuls), the aristocracy (the Senate), and the polity (the people's assembly and the tribunes). For the framers of the United States Constitution, it was a model for the three branches of a new government designed to *prevent* the vast majority of Americans from participating directly in politics, while allowing some citizens (white men with sufficient property) a say in choosing their representatives. Polybius prophesied that such a system would break the political cycle that had destroyed the Greek poleis, and that it would last forever. He was wrong.

## THE ESSENCE OF ROMAN IDENTITY

The slow unfolding of the early republic ensured, in part, its success: Romans were conservatives who accepted new things reluctantly but then preserved them fiercely. The prevailing force was the *mos maiorum*, "the code of the elders" or "the custom of the ancestors" or even—to use the word derived from the Latin *mos*—"morality." This unwritten code was sacrosanct and essential to Roman identity. It accounts for the remarkable coherence of Roman culture, religion, and law, all of which rested on ancestor worship. The Latin word *pietas* ("piety") meant reverence for family traditions and for one's fathers—living and dead. What made the legendary Aeneas "pious Aeneas" was his devotion to his father, Anchises, whom he carried to safety on his back while Troy burned. Metaphorically, this meant that Aeneas was the carrier of tradition, a man willing to shoulder the burdens of his ancestors and carry them forever.

This helps to explain why the Romans, in the ensuing centuries of their world domination, continued to identify so strongly with their homeland and its customs. To a Roman, "going native" in a foreign place was a terrible betrayal of the *mos maiorum*; patriotism, after all, is dedication to the fatherland. It also explains the extraordinary maxim of *patria potestas* ("fatherly power") upheld by the Twelve Tables. A Roman father, no matter what his social class, had absolute authority within his household, including the powers of life and death. If he was too poor to raise a child, he could expose it (leaving it to perish or to charity) or sell it into slavery. If his wife or child dishonored him, he could kill with impunity. We begin to understand why Lucretia killed herself: otherwise, her father would have killed her with his own hands.

These values set the Romans apart from everyone in the Hellenistic world. The Greeks, for example, never condoned anything like *patria potestas*: when fathers kill their children in Greek mythology, they are inevitably killed in revenge by another member of their own family or by the gods. And while pride in one's ancestry is a very human attribute, and patriarchy common to nearly every civilization, the Romans' contemporaries were awed by their extreme devotion to these principles. It was one of the things that made the Romans so admirable in the eyes of those Jews disgusted by the loose morals of Hellenistic civilization (Chapter 4). For Polybius, it was the key to Roman success. In addition to describing the workings of the Roman government and army in minute detail, he reports (with anthropological interest) on the conduct of Roman funeral processions and the Romans' practice of wearing the deathmasks of their ancestors, which on other days would be hung in special household shrines.

In some respects, to be sure, Roman religion resembled that of the Greeks: Jupiter corresponded to Zeus as god of the skies, Neptune to Poseidon as god of the seas, Venus to Aphrodite as goddess of beauty and sexuality, Mars to Ares as god of war. But in keeping with the Roman equation of religion with family, this entire pantheon functioned as the family gods of the Roman state. The republic was essentially

**A ROMAN PATRICIAN OF THE FIRST CENTURY B.C.E.** This man, who wears the toga of an aristocrat, displays his piety by holding the busts of his ancestors. Busts, like the funerary masks described by Polybius (see page 149), commemorated the dead and served as the focus for family worship in household shrines. ▪ ***How does the Roman attitude toward age and death differ from that of the Greeks (see the image on page 136)?*** ▪ ***What do these differences suggest about the broader values of these two societies?***

# Analyzing Primary Sources

## *Polybius Describes the Romans' Worship of Their Ancestors*

*The Law of the Twelve Tables forbade excessive display at funerals, especially displays of wealth and grief on the part of women. Instead, funerals were supposed to be occasions for the display of family piety. In the following passage, the Greek historian Polybius—who had spent a formative fourteen years of his life in Rome—describes Roman burial customs and these rites' relationship to the strength of republican ideals.*

I'll quote just one example to illustrate the pains taken by the Roman state to produce men who will endure anything to win a reputation for valor in their country. Whenever one of their celebrated men dies . . . his body is carried with every kind of honor into the Forum, . . . sometimes in an upright position so as to be conspicuous, or else, more rarely, recumbent. The whole mass of the people stand round to watch, and his son, if he has one of adult age who can be present, or if not some other relative, then . . . delivers an address which recounts the virtues and successes achieved by the dead man during his lifetime. By these means the whole populace . . . are involved in the ceremony, so that when the facts of the dead man's career are recalled . . . their sympathies are so deeply engaged that the loss seems . . . to be a public one which affects the whole people. Then, after the burial of the body and the performance of the customary rites, they place the image of the dead man in the most conspicuous position in the house, where it is enclosed in a wooden shrine. This image consists of a mask which is fashioned with extraordinary fidelity . . . to represent the features of these dead men. On occasions when public sacrifices are offered, these masks are displayed and decorated with great care. And when any distinguished member of the family dies, the masks are taken to the funeral, and are worn by men who are considered to bear the closest resemblance to the original, both in height and their general appearance and bearing. . . .

It would be hard to imagine a more impressive scene for a young man who aspires to win fame and practice virtue. For who could remain unmoved at the sight of the images of all these men who have won renown in their time, now gathered together as if alive and breathing? What spectacle could be more glorious than this?

Source: Polybius, *The Rise of the Roman Empire*, trans. Ian Scott-Kilvert (New York: 1979), pp. 346–47.

### *Questions for Analysis*

1. Why does Polybius place so high a premium on the Romans' conduct of funerals? How can such rites be related to republican ideals?
2. Compare this analysis of Roman funerary rites to the image of a Roman patrician and his ancestors on page 148. How do they complement one another?

a giant, timeless household run by "elders" (senators) and "father figures" (patricians), some of whom traced their ancestry back to gods; the mother of Aeneas was Venus. Like a Roman household, the Roman state could flourish only if these father- and mother-gods lent their continuing and active support. Committees of priests therefore functioned as branches of the government and tended to the worship of the city's temples. But in stark contrast to other ancient societies, these priests were not full-time professionals who formed a special caste, but prominent men who rotated in and out of office while serving as leaders of the Senate. Their dual roles made Roman religion even more integral to political life than it had been in Greece (Chapter 3), similar in some ways to the integration of religion and politics in ancient Mesopotamia (Chapter 1).

The Roman man's primary duty to honor his ancestors also bolstered the prestige of the Roman army, because soldiers were supposed to sacrifice themselves for the public good and to fear disgrace above all things. The all-important sense of ancestral duty is further reflected in Roman naming practices, another custom that separated them from other cultures. Most free men in antiquity were known by a given name and their father's name only: Alexander, before he was "the Great," was "son of Philip." A free-born Roman, by contrast, had at least two names. The name by which he was known—the name that mattered—was the name of his earliest ancestor, the man from whom his family descended. Gaius Julius Caesar, to take a famous example, would have entered public life as Julius, a member of the family of the Julii, who claimed ancestry from Iulus, the son of Aeneas. His forename, Gaius, was the most common name in Rome, the equivalent of "Joe" or "John," and he would never be addressed by this name in public, except perhaps by very intimate friends or family members. His third name, Caesar, was a nickname he acquired in the course of his career: "hairy head." And because it was the most distinctive of his names—the name he didn't share with an ancestor or with average Romans—it became the name by which he was universally known. The same goes for Marcus Tullius Cicero (Cicero means "chickpea"). The illustrious Cincinnatus was actually "Curly."

What's in a name? Everything, if you were a Roman man. And nothing, at least nothing of personal significance, if you were a Roman woman. Lucretia's name was not her own, but her father's—or forefather's: the feminine version of Lucretius. If she had a sister, they would both be called Lucretia, differentiated only as Major and Minor ("big/elder" and "little/younger") Lucretia. If there were two more girls, they would be Tertia and Quarta ("Third" and "Fourth") Lucretia, and so on. The only people in Rome who had personal names were slaves (who were named by their masters, like pets) or very low-born Romans and immigrants who had no lineage that mattered.

## FROM REPUBLIC TO EMPIRE

For more than two centuries after the founding of the republic, warfare and agriculture remained the chief occupations of most Romans. A few artisans could be found in cities, and some minor attempts were made to establish trading networks. But the fact that Rome had no standard system of coinage until 289 B.C.E suggests strongly that commerce was an insignificant component of its economy. Apparently, Romans didn't rely on portable wealth; when they weren't fighting, they wanted to be home on the farm, not gadding about the world. If they had money, they put it into real estate: land or slaves.

All of this changed rapidly when Romans began to look beyond Italy. In 265 B.C.E., they completed their absorption of Etruscan territory and could claim to control most of the peninsula. A year later, they were already embroiled in a war overseas. For a home-loving people who had now secured ample resources for their own support, this seems paradoxical. Indeed, historians continue to argue about the motives for Roman expansion. Did Rome constantly seek to extend its rule as a matter of policy, to feed a collective appetite for warfare and plunder? Or was it an accidental empire, built up in a series of reactions to changing pressures at home, as well as in response to threats—real and imagined—from abroad? No definitive answer is possible, but it is in this crucial period that the Roman Republic began to transform Western civilizations, and to transform itself into the Roman Empire.

### *The Punic Wars, 264–146 B.C.E.*

In 265 B.C.E., Roman territory extended to the tip of Italy's "boot," but there it ended. Just off its coast, the large islands of Corsica and Sardinia and the western half of Sicily were part of another state, much older and far wealthier. This was the great maritime empire of Carthage, which stretched along the northern coast of Africa from modern-day Tunisia through the Straits of Gibraltar and into modern Spain. Carthage itself was a port city at the northeastern tip of Africa, founded around 800 B.C.E. as a Phoenician colony (see Chapter 2), but now independent and powerful. It had the largest and most effective navy of its day, and it commanded the vast resources of commercial networks that reached as far north as Britain and deep into Egypt and the Near East. In almost every respect but one it was far superior to Rome. Yet that one factor was decisive: while the Carthaginian fleet was unrivalled, Carthage had no standing army. It relied on mercenaries bankrolled by the enormous profits of its merchants.

The epic struggle between Rome and Carthage for dominance of the Mediterranean lasted well over a century. It crystallized in three periods of concentrated warfare known as the Punic Wars, because the Romans called their enemies Poeni, "Phoenicians." The first of these wars began in 264 B.C.E., when Rome sent a garrison to occupy the independent city of Messina (originally a Greek colony) on the eastern tip of Sicily, directly across from the Italian mainland. Carthage, in response, took advantage of the local enmity between Messina and Syracuse, another Greek city, and sent warships to protect Syracuse from what it saw as Roman aggression. Twenty-three years of bitter fighting ensued, protracted because the Carthaginians only needed to suffer one defeat in a land battle before resolving to engage the Romans solely at sea. There, they had the advantage—until the Romans built their own navy, virtually from scratch. In 241 B.C.E., Carthage was beaten down and forced to cede all of her Sicilian lands to Rome and to pay a large indemnity. Sicily thus became Rome's first overseas province. It was shortly followed by Corsica and Sardinia, which the Roman Senate contrived to seize on the grounds that Carthage had defaulted on the payment of its indemnity.

Thereafter, the Carthaginians had ample reason to harbor resentment against Rome, while the Romans were determined not to let Carthage revive its maritime power. So when Carthage attempted to expand its presence in Spain, Rome intepreted this as a threat to Roman interests and declared a new war that lasted for sixteen years: the Second Punic War. This time, however, Rome was thrown entirely off its guard by the brilliant exploits of the Carthaginian commander Hannibal (247–183 B.C.E), who very nearly defeated the Romans at their own game and on their own soil. No one had imagined that a Carthaginian attack could come by land, from the north. But daringly, Hannibal raised an army in Spain, heavily manned by cavalry in order to counter the superior infantry of Rome, and equipped it with dozens of war elephants and siege engines. He then led this entire force across the Pyrenees into Gaul (now southern France) and then over the Alps into Italy. There, he harried Roman forces in their own territories for nearly sixteen years, from 218 to 202 B.C.E.

In the end, Hannibal was challenged more by the rigors of campaigning and the difficulty of supplying his army in hostile terrain than by the Romans themselves (he had lost many of his elephants and some important equipment in the icy mountain passes of the Alps). He also seems to have counted on winning the support of the Italian territories that Rome had conquered, but Rome's generous treatment of its Latin allies kept them loyal. As a result, Rome could call on vast human resources while Hannibal had only his exhausted army, and no reserves forthcoming from Carthage. Nevertheless, he won several amazing victories in Italy before retreating—technically undefeated—in 203. He also won the admiration of the Romans themselves, whose own histories frankly acknowledge his tactical genius. Indeed, this phase of warfare ended only when a Roman general, Publius Cornelius Scipio, took a leaf out of Hannibal's book. He had been campaigning in Spain against the army of Hannibal's brother, Hasdrubal, and having seized a number of key Carthaginian strongholds he crossed into Africa and met Hannibal at Zama, near Carthage, in 201 B.C.E. His victory ended the Second Punic War and won him a new name, "Africanus," in honor of his conquest.

Carthage was now compelled to abandon all of its possessions except the city itself and its immediate hinterlands, and to pay an indemnity three times greater than the already crippling reparations demanded after the First Punic War. Yet Roman suspicion of Carthage remained obsessive, and warmongers in the Senate read every sign of recovery as a threat. By the middle of the second century, some hardliners were urging a preemptive strike. Among the most vocal was an elderly patrician called Marcus Porcius Cato, famous for his stern obedience to Roman custom and his virulent xenophobia. Cato ended every speech he gave—no matter what the topic—with the words: "And furthermore, I strongly advise that Carthage be destroyed." This won him the nickname Cato the Censor, from the Latin verb meaning "to advise."

Eventually, the Senate was persuaded. In 149 B.C.E., it seized on a minor pretext to demand that the Carthaginians abandon their city and settle at least ten miles from the coast, where they would have no access to the sea. Of course, this absurd mandate amounted to a death sentence for a city dependent on commerce, and it was refused—as the Romans knew it would be. The result was the Third Punic War and the siege of Carthage, which ended in 146 B.C.E. when the Romans breached the walls and butchered the population. Those who survived the massacre were sold into slavery,

**CARTHAGINIAN COIN.** This coin was issued by Hannibal's family around 230 B.C.E. and circulated in Hispania (Spain). Its face shows the Carthaginian god Melqart in the guise of Hercules (notice the club over his shoulder). The reverse features a war elephant with a mounted rider, like the ones that would be used by Hannibal against Rome.

and their once-magnificent city was razed to the ground. The legend that the Romans sowed the land with salt (to make it infertile) is a myth, but a poetic way of describing the successful eradication of an entire civilization. It would stand as a warning to Rome's other potential enemies.

## Roman Control of the Hellenistic World

Rome's victories over Carthage enormously increased Roman territory, leading to the creation of new colonial provinces in Sicily, North Africa, and Hispania (Spain). This not only brought Rome great new wealth (above all, access to Sicilian and African grain supplies and to the silver mines of the Iberian Peninsula), it was also the beginning of the westward expansion that became Rome's defining influence on the history of Europe.

At the same time, Rome's expansion brought it into conflict with eastern Mediterranean powers, paving the way for further conquests. During the Second Punic War, Philip V of Macedonia had entered an alliance with Carthage; soon afterward, he moved aggressively into Greece and was rumored to have designs on Egypt. Rome sent an army to stop him, and later foiled the plans of the Achaean League (see Chapter 4). This was when Polybius was sent to Rome as a hostage, and became a guest-friend in the family of Scipio

**THE EXPANSION OF ROME, 264–44 B.C.E.** The rapid increase of Rome's territories opened up new opportunities and challenges. ▪ *Looking at the phases of expansion on this map, in what directions did Roman dominion move?* ▪ *Why was this the case?* ▪ *What particular problems might have been created by the eventual extension of Roman rule into Gaul, well beyond the "Roman lake" of the Mediterranean?*

Africanus, later witnessing the destruction of Carthage. Rome also thwarted similar efforts by the Seleucid monarch Antiochus III. In neither of these cases did Rome set out to conquer the eastern Mediterranean. By 146 B.C.E., however, both Greece and Macedonia had become Roman provinces, Seleucid Asia had lost most of its territories, and Ptolemaic Egypt had largely become a pawn of Roman commercial and political interests.

## THE CONSEQUENCES OF IMPERIALISM

Rome's inadvertent conquest of Greece and Asia Minor transformed the economic, social, and intellectual life of the republic. New wealth poured in, increasing the inequalities within Roman society and challenging traditional values of frugality and self-sacrifice. Small farmers left the land and swelled the impoverished urban population, unable to compete with the huge plantations owned by aristocrats and worked by gangs of slaves. Slaves also played an increasing role in Roman cities as artisans, merchants, and household servants. Roman rule over the Hellenistic world had a particularly pervasive impact on cultural life—so much so that many Romans considered themselves to have been "conquered" by Greece. Hitherto self-assured and self-satisfied, they now felt their own language, history, and customs to be uncouth and barbaric compared to those of their cultivated colonial subjects.

### *Economic Change and Social Upheaval*

Like all peoples of the ancient world, Romans took slavery for granted. Nothing in Rome's earlier experience prepared it, however, for the huge increase in the number of slaves that resulted from its western and eastern conquests. In 146 B.C.E., 55,000 Carthaginians were enslaved after the destruction of their city; not long before, 150,000 Greek prisoners of war had met the same fate. By the end of the second century B.C.E., there were a million slaves in Italy alone. Rome's became one of the most slave-based economies in history, rivaling ancient Egypt or the antebellum South.

The majority of Roman slaves worked as agricultural laborers on the vast (and growing) estates of the Roman aristocracy. Some of these estates were the result of earlier Roman conquests within Italy itself. But others were constructed by aristocrats buying up the holdings of peasant farmers. Soldiers in particular, who might now be required to serve for years at a time on foreign campaigns, often found it impossible to maintain their farms. Instead, they moved to the city—where there was no way for free men to sustain themselves except through trade or violence. With abundant, cheap slaves to do all the rough work, moreover, there was no incentive for technological innovation. Meanwhile, expensive slaves did the specialized jobs: they were secretaries, bookkeepers, personal assistants, playwrights, musicians, sculptors, artists. There was no reason to employ paid labor at all, or even to train oneself in these arts, as the Greeks had. By the first century B.C.E., as a result, a third of Rome's one million inhabitants were receiving free grain from the state, partly to keep them alive and partly to keep them quiet. The poet Juvenal (see page 166) would later satirize the plebs as needing only "bread and circuses."

As we have seen, the Roman economy had remained fundamentally agrarian until the mid-third century B.C.E. During the following century, however, Rome's eastern conquests brought it fully into the sophisticated commercial hub of the Hellenistic world. The principal beneficiaries of this were the equestrians. As overseas merchants, they profited handsomely from Rome's voracious appetite for foreign luxury goods. And as representatives of the Roman government in the provinces, they operated mines, built roads, and collected taxes, always with an eye toward their own profits. They were also the principal moneylenders to the Roman state and to distressed individuals. Interest rates were high, and when the state could not pay its bills, it would often allow the moneylenders to repay themselves by exploiting the populations of the provinces.

Commoners who lost their lands suffered from these economic changes, but the principal victims of Rome's transformation were its slaves. Even though some were cultivated foreigners—mainly Greek-speaking—taken as prisoners of war, the standard policy of their owners was to get as much work out of them as possible until they died of exhaustion or were "freed" in old age to fend for themselves. The same irascible Cato the Censor who demanded the destruction of Carthage even wrote a "how-to" book on this subject. The ready availability of slaves made Roman slavery a far more impersonal and brutal institution than it had been in other ancient civilizations. Of course, there were exceptions. Some domestic slaves were treated as trusted family members, and slave secretaries vital to the business of Roman governance and literature could even win fame or earn enough to buy their freedoms. Some slave artisans were permitted to run their own businesses, keeping some of the profits.

But the general lot of slaves was horrendous. Some businessmen owned slaves whom they trained as gladiators, to be mauled by wild animals or by other gladiators for the amusement of a paying public. The luxurious lifestyles of the wealthy meant that dozens of slaves in every household were trapped in a cycle of menial tasks, as doorkeepers, litter-bearers, couriers, valets, wet-nurses, and child-minders. In some great households, designated slaves had no other duties than to rub down the master after his bath or to keep track of the mistress's social engagements. It was a life that debased both slave and owner, and undermined the values of the republic.

## New Money, New Values

In the early republic, as we have seen, Roman men had nearly absolute powers over their individual households. During the second century B.C.E., however, two innovations greatly altered this pattern of patriarchal control. One was the introduction of new laws that allowed married women to control their own property, instead of handing that wealth over to their husbands; if a married woman died, her possessions would then revert to her father or her father's heirs if she had no children of her own. Alongside this new law came more liberal laws that allowed women to initiate divorce proceedings.

These changes were intended to safeguard family wealth, but they also resulted in greater independence for women. A wife now had much more authority within the household because she contributed to its upkeep. If her husband did not show respect, she could leave him and deprive him of income. Ironically, the growth of Rome's slave system also gave women greater freedom, for slaves took over the traditional work of child rearing, household maintenance, and the endless tasks of spinning and weaving. Women from well-to-do families now spent more time away from the home and began to engage in a range of social, intellectual, and artistic activities. Indeed, women were among the chief consumers of the new Hellenistic fashions, commodities, and ideas available in Rome.

In earlier centuries, Romans had taken pride in the simplicity of their lives, their language, and their moral code. Now, however, elite Romans began to indulge in creature comforts and to cultivate Hellenistic habits as proof of their refinement. Bilingualism became increasingly common, and Greek literature became the standard against which Roman authors measured themselves. For Latin was not yet a literary language. It was fine for business or politics or farming, but if one wanted to express lofty or beautiful thoughts one did so in Greek, which was far more flexible and sophisticated. Well-educated Greek slaves were therefore at a premium, to lend social cachet, to write letters, and to tutor Roman children. The popularity of Greek plays, mostly comedies, was such that they quickly spawned Latin imitations, like those of Plautus (257?–184 B.C.E.) and Terence (195/185–159 B.C.E). Terence's career path is suggestive of a larger pattern: a Greek-speaker of Libyan descent, he was sold as a slave-boy in Carthage and bought by a wealthy Roman called Terentius, who took him back to Rome and cultivated his talents, which he marketed under his own name. Six of Terence's Latin adaptations of Greek comedies survive, and they enjoyed enormous popularity well into the Middle Ages, eventually influencing the plays of Shakespeare.

In short, many Romans nursed an inferiority complex with respect to Greek culture. But others regarded these foreign influences with disgust. For them, the good old ways of paternal authority and stern military discipline were giving way to effeminacy and the decadence of soft living. Increasingly, hard-line conservatives deplored these new trends and passed laws that would restore "family values" and regulate the conspicuous consumption of luxuries, especially by women. These measures were ineffectual. Rome was being irreversibly transformed from a republic of self-reliant farmers into a complex metropolitan empire reliant on foreign slaves, foreign grain, and foreign luxuries, in which a vast gulf was widening between rich and poor, and where traditional behavioral constraints were giving way to new freedoms for both men and women.

## Philosophy and Spirituality in the Late Republic

The late republic was also deeply influenced by Hellenistic philosophy, and both Epicureanism and Stoicism found strong adherents in Rome. The former was popularized by Lucretius (98–55 B.C.E.), author of a book-length philosophical poem, *On the Nature of Things*. But more congenial to Roman values was Stoicism, which soon numbered among its converts many powerful public figures. The most influential of these was Cicero (106–43 B.C.E.), famous in his day as an orator, statesman, and staunch defender of republican virtues. Cicero based his ethical teachings on the Stoic premises that virtue is happiness and tranquillity of mind the highest good. The ideal man is rational, indifferent to sorrow and pain. Yet Cicero diverged from the Stoics in his approval of the active, political life. He became an advocate for the revival of Roman tradition through service to the state. His elegant prose style also advanced the use of Latin as a language of eloquence and became the standard model for Latin composition: students learning Latin today still begin with Cicero.

The religious practices of Rome also changed markedly in this era. The most pronounced innovation was the spread of Eastern mystery cults, which satisfied a need for more emotionally intense spiritual experiences than did traditional forms of Roman worship—again, especially for women, who were largely excluded from the rites of the patriarchal state religion. From Egypt came the cults of Isis and Osiris, while from Asia came the worship of the Great Mother, all emphasizing the power of female sexuality and reproduction. Despite the attractions of these new cults, Romans continued to honor their traditional gods alongside these new, exotic deities. Roman polytheism could absorb them all, so long as the ancestor gods of the household and of the city were paid due reverence.

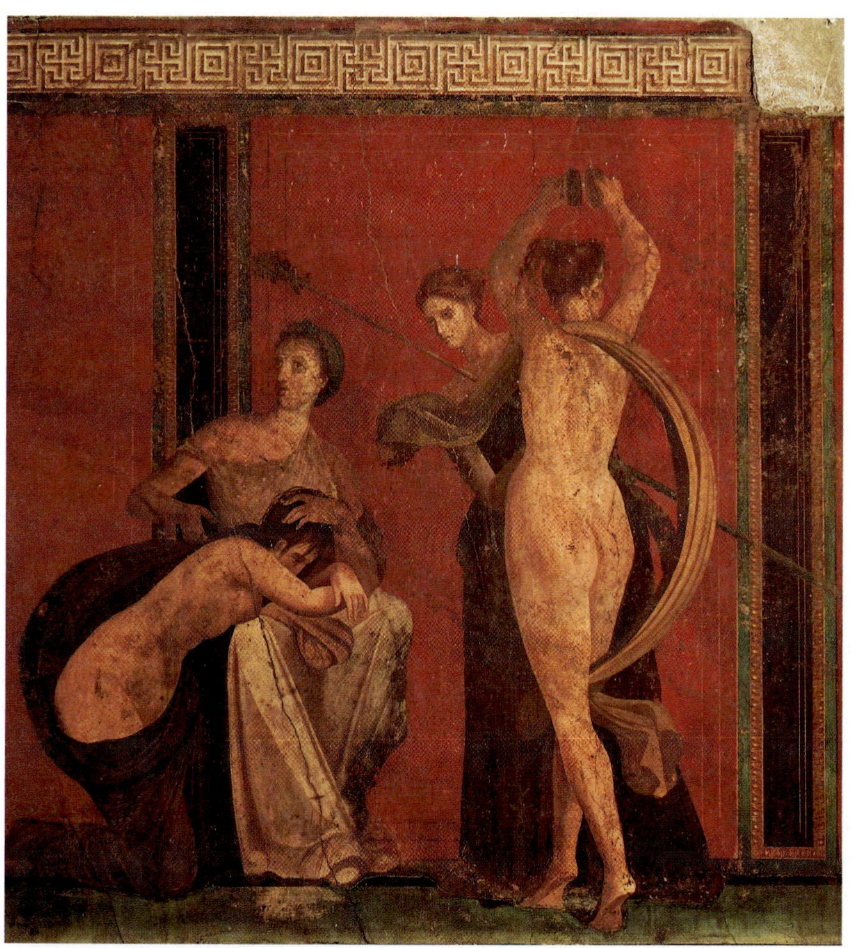

**ROMAN MYSTERY RITES.** One of the Roman houses preserved at Pompeii features an astonishing cycle of wall paintings, executed around 50 B.C.E., which give the house its name: Villa of the Mysteries. The exact meaning of these images is still debated, but some scholars have argued that they depict a succession of ritual practices. Here a young woman is being whipped, perhaps as part of an initiation ceremony, while another woman performs a dance.

## "RESTORING THE REPUBLIC": THE STRUGGLE FOR POWER

In Rome itself, the period from the end of the Third Punic War in 146 to about 30 B.C.E. was one of turbulence. Politically motivated murders, bloody competition among rival dictators, wars, and insurrections were common occurrences. Slave uprisings also added to the general disorder. In 134 B.C.E, some 70,000 slaves defeated a Roman army in Sicily before being put down by emergency reinforcements. Slaves ravaged Sicily again in 104 B.C.E. But the most threatening revolt of all was led by Spartacus, a Thracian captive who was being trained as a gladiator. Along with a band of 200 fellow slaves from a gladiatorial training camp—they had all been bought by a wealthy entrepreneur—they escaped from Capua (near Naples), heavily armed, to the slopes of Mount Vesuvius, where their cause attracted a huge host of other fugitives. From 73 to 71 B.C.E. this desperate army defeated trained Roman forces of as many as 10,000 men, and they overran much of southern Italy before Spartacus himself was killed. The Senate, terrified of the precedent set by the near-victory of the rebels, ordered 6,000 of the captured slaves to be crucified along the length of the road from Capua to Rome (about 150 miles) as a warning to future insurgents. Crucifixion was a form of punishment reserved for slaves and non-Roman rebels, and it meant a slow, terrible, and public death from gradual suffocation and exposure.

### *The Reforming Efforts of the Gracchi*

Meanwhile, these waves of rural rebellion were being mirrored by urban unrest in various forms, and the poorer classes were finding new champions among some progressive aristocrats. In 133 B.C.E., a grandson of Scipio Africanus, Tiberius Gracchus, was elected a tribune of the people. He took his office seriously and proposed to alleviate social and economic stress by instituting major reforms, chiefly the redistribution of property. As we have noted, small farmers had been losing their lands to patricians and equestrians whose new wealth allowed them to amass giant estates. To counter this, Tiberius Gracchus invoked old laws that had, under the early republic, limited the amount of land that could be held by a single person. His motives were not entirely populist. There was a grave manpower shortage in the Roman army, which had been forced to expand its presence in the far reaches of the world and had left Rome itself prey to uprisings like that of Spartacus. Since a man had to meet certain property qualifications to serve in the Roman army, the available pool of citizen soldiers was contracting. So Tiberius Gracchus aimed to refresh the reserves by creating new citizens.

With the support of his brother Gaius, Tiberius Gracchus proposed a law that would restrict estates to a maximum of 300 acres per citizen, plus 150 acres for each child in his family, with the excess land to be divided among poor settlers. Not surprisingly, most senators stood to lose from this legislation, and so engineered its veto by Gracchus's fellow tribunes. But Tiberius retaliated, arguing that tribunes who opposed the people's interests were betraying their offices, and he announced plans to stand for reelection when his term expired. A conservative faction in the Senate then alleged that Gracchus had his sights set on a dictatorship, and with this excuse they attacked and murdered him and his supporters on the day of the elections.

Ten years later, Gaius Gracchus renewed his older brother's struggle after being elected to the same office. Although a version of Tiberius's land reforms had finally been enacted by the Senate, Gaius believed that the campaign had to go further. In 123 B.C.E. he enacted several laws for the benefit of the poor, stabilizing the price of grain in Rome by building public granaries along the Tiber and checking the administrative abuses of the senatorial class by giving the equestrians greater powers. He also imposed controls on provincial governors suspected of exploiting their subjects for personal gain. Most controversially, Gaius proposed to extend full Roman citizenship to all the allied states of Italy, a move that would have kept the army well supplied with new soldiers, but which would also alter the political landscape of Rome to the detriment of the existing elite. Accordingly, the Senate proclaimed Gaius Gracchus an outlaw and authorized its consuls to deal ruthlessly with his supporters. In the ensuing conflict, Gaius and about 3,000 of his followers became the victims of a purge.

## Rivalry among Rome's Generals

Although the reforms of the Gracchi were ultimately unsuccesful, they exposed the weakness of the Senate and increased the power of the plebs, whose favor was now courted by a succession of ambitious men. Most of these were were professional soldiers who controlled one or more legions of the Roman army and who traded on military victories abroad to win the confidence of the people and access to power. The first of these was Gaius Marius, a man from an obscure provincial family who fought a successful campaign against Jugurtha of Numidia, a small kingdom that threatened Rome's hard-won supremacy in North Africa. In 107 B.C.E. Marius's popularity catapulted him to the consulship, despite the protests of the Senate's aristocracy, and he would be elected to that office six more times in the course of his life.

Marius was no statesman. But he set a powerful precedent by demonstrating how easily a general with an army behind him could override opposition, and that an army command could be an alternative path to political power. He also changed the course of Rome's history by reorganizing and expanding the army. Desperate for more men to fight in Africa and in Gaul, which Rome was slowly infiltrating, Marius abolished the property qualification that had hitherto limited military service; the potential pool of soldiers now included the urban poor and landless peasants. As a result, a career as a Roman legionnaire became an end in itself, and a soldier's loyalty was directed toward his commander—whose success would win rewards for his men—rather than to an abstract ideal of patriotism. Moreover, this change meant that factional fighting could lead to full-blown civil war, as legions loyal to one general were pitted against those of another.

This happened in Marius's own lifetime. The aristocratic general Lucius Cornelius Sulla had fought with distinction in the so-called Social War of 91–88 B.C.E., a conflict between Rome and her Italian allies that resulted in the extension of Roman citizenship throughout the peninsula. Therafter, Sulla seemed the likely person to lead Rome's army to war in Asia Minor. Marius, however, did not agree; he forced the Senate to deny Sulla's claim. Sulla's response was to rally the five victorious legions that had just fought under his command and, with a Roman army at his back, to march on Rome.

This was a disturbing move, since strong taboos had long prevented any armed force from entering the city limits. But Sulla argued that his actions were in keeping with the *mos maiorum*, which Marius and the Senate had betrayed. He was then given the coveted command in Asia Minor, after which Marius again seized control of the city. When Marius died soon afterward, a conservative backlash led the aristocracy to appoint Sulla to the office of dictator—but not for the traditional six months. Instead, Sulla's term had no limits, and he used this time to exterminate his opponents.

He extended the powers of the Senate (whose ranks, depleted by civil war, he packed with men loyal to himself) and curtailed the authority of the peoples' tribunes. Then, after three years of rule, he decided that his job was done and retired to a life of luxury on his country estate.

## Caesar's Triumph—and His Downfall

The purpose and effect of Sulla's dictatorship was to empower the aristocracy and terminally weaken the power of the plebs. Soon, however, new leaders emerged to espouse the people's cause, once again using the army as their tool of influence. The most prominent of these were Gnaeus Pompeius Magnus (106–48 B.C.E.) and Gaius Julius Caesar (100–44 B.C.E.). Initially, they cooperated in a plot to gain control of the government and to "restore the republic" by forming an alliance with a third general, Marcus Junius Crassus, the man credited with finally defeating Spartacus. This alliance was known as a *triumvirate*, meaning "rule of three men," but it soon dissolved into open rivalry. Pompey (as generations of English-speaking historians have called him) had won fame as the conqueror of Syria and Palestine, while Caesar devoted his energies to a series of campaigns in Gaul. It was under his authority that the territories of modern France, Belgium, and western Germany were added to the Roman Empire, extending its northern border along the length of the Rhine.

Caesar himself advertised these conquests in a series of self-congratulatory dispatches published in book form—*On the War in Gaul*—which secured his reputation at home and cemented the loyalty of his army. These victories also put him in a strong political position. It had become accepted that the best general should be the leader of Rome, and the example of Sulla had made it possible for that leader to be a dictator for life, a king in all but name. But it was Pompey, not Caesar, who was actually in Rome and in a position to influence the Senate directly. Indeed, in the face of tremendous popular protest and even some opposition from the aristocracy, Pompey had himself elected sole consul. Essentially, this meant that he could act as dictator. Using this authority, he declared that Caesar, who was still stationed in Gaul, was an enemy of the republic, and that his ambition was to make himself king.

The result was a pervasive and deadly civil war. In 49 B.C.E. Caesar took up Pompey's challenge and crossed the Rubicon River, the northern boundary of Rome's Italian territories, thereby signalling his intention to take Rome by force. Pompey fled to the east in the hope of gathering an army large enough to confront Ceasar's legions. Caesar pursued him, and in 48 B.C.E. the two Roman armies met at Pharsalus in Greece. Pompey was defeated and then fled to Alexandria, where he was murdered by a Roman officer attached to the court of Ptolemy XIII (62/61–47? B.C.E.).

This young pharaoh, a descendent of Alexander's general Ptolemy, was then about fourteen years old and engaged in a civil war of his own—against his elder sister and co-ruler, Cleopatra VII (69–30 B.C.E.). He must have thought that he could curry favor with Caesar by encouraging the murder of Pompey, but instead Caesar threw his support on the side of the twenty-one-year old queen. The two must have become lovers soon after their first meeting, since their son Caesarion ("Little Ceasar") was born nine months later. After a brief struggle, Ptolemy was defeated and was drowned in the Nile. Cleopatra then took as consort her even younger brother, known as Ptolemy XIV, but she ruled as pharaoh of Egypt in her own right, as Hatshepsut had done nearly a millennium and a half before.

**BUST OF JULIUS CAESAR.** Caesar's nickname meant "Hairy," but it has come to be synonymous with imperial rule. It was the title preferred by modern German rulers, who called themselves *kaisers*, and by the tsars of Russia. In classical Latin, the "C" sound is hard, which means that the pronunciations of *caesar*, *kaiser*, and *tsar* are very similar.

After that, Caesar returned to Rome in triumph—literally. A *triumph* was a spectacular honor awarded to a victorious Roman general by the Senate, and was the only legal occasion on which (unarmed) soldiers were allowed to parade in the streets of Rome. Triumphs had been celebrated since the earliest days of the republic, and they featured columns of prisoners and spoils of war, chained captives (often enemy kings) led in humiliation to their public executions, floats featuring live tableaux commemorating the achievements of the triumphant man, and thousands upon thousands of cheering Romans, who received extra rations of grain and gathered up coins thrown by the handful. Through it all, Caesar would have ridden in a chariot with a golden wreath held above his head while a slave stood behind him, murmuring in his ear the words *Memento mori*, "Remember: you will die." A triumph was so glorious and—under the republic—so rarely granted that those thus honored might forget their own mortality.

Caesar may well have done so. His power seemed absolute. In 46 B.C.E. he was named dictator for ten years; two years later, this was changed to a lifetime appointment. In addition, he assumed nearly every other title that could augment his power. He obtained from the Senate full authority to make war and peace and to control the revenues of the state. He even governed the reckoning of time, something that was regarded as controversial. In imitation of the Egyptian calendar (slightly modified by a Greek astronomer) he revised the Roman calendar so as to make a 365-day year with an extra day added every fourth year. This Julian calendar (as adjusted by Pope Gregory XIII in 1582) is still observed, and the seventh month is still named after Julius.

Caesar also took important steps toward eliminating the distinction between Italians and provincials within the empire by conferring citizenship on residents of Hispania (Spain) and the newly annexed provinces in Gaul. By settling many of his army veterans and some of the urban poor in these lands, moreover, he relieved economic inequities and furthered colonization. Even more important was Caesar's farsighted resolve to focus his efforts in northwestern Europe. Whereas Pompey, and before him Alexander, went East to gain fame and fortune, Caesar followed only the Phoenicians in recognizing the potential of the wild West. By incorporating Gaul into the Roman world he brought in a much-needed source of food and natural resources and created a new outlet for the spread of Roman settlement and culture.

In the eyes of many contemporaries, however, Caesar's achievements were signs that he intended to make himself king: a hateful thought to those who still cherished the *mos maiorum* and glorified the early days of the republic. Indeed, it was around a descendant of Lucretia's avenger, Lucius Junius Brutus, that a faction of the Senate crystallized into conspiracy. On the Ides of March in 44 B.C.E.—the midpoint of the month, according to his own calendar—Caesar was

**CLEOPATRA VII AS EGYPTIAN PHARAOH AND HELLENISTIC RULER.** Like her ancestor, Ptolemy I, Cleopatra represented herself as both enlightened Greek monarch and as Pharaoh. It was perhaps due to her example that Julius Caesar was the first Roman leader to issue coins impressed with his own image. ▪ ***How does Cleopatra's self-representation compare to that of Hatshepsut (see Chapter 2) or Ptolemy (Chapter 4)?***

**IDES OF MARCH COIN.** This coin celebrates the assassination of Julius Caesar by Marcus Junius Brutus. Brutus is shown on the face; on the reverse, a cap of liberty (customarily worn by freed slaves) is flanked by two daggers. Below is the legend *EID-MAR*, the Latin abbreviation for "the Ides of March." ▪ ***Given that Caesar drew criticism for depicting himself on Roman coinage, what do you think is the significance of using Brutus's image in this way?***

attacked on the floor of the Senate's chamber and stabbed to death by a group of men. His body would later be autopsied, the first such examination in recorded history. It was found that he had sustained 23 wounds.

## THE PRINCIPATE AND THE *PAX ROMANA*, 27 B.C.E.–180 C.E.

In his will, Caesar adopted his grandnephew Gaius Octavius (or Octavian, 63 B.C.E.–14 C.E.), then a young man of eighteen serving in Illyria, across the Adriatic Sea. On learning of Caesar's death, Octavian hastened home to claim his inheritance and to avenge his slain "father," whose name he took: he was now Gaius Julius Caesar the younger. He soon found that he had rivals among those supporters of Caesar who had not been implicated in the plot to kill him, most notably Marcus Antonius (or Mark Antony, 83–30 B.C.E.), who had served under Caesar's command in Gaul and was determined to make himself governor of that whole province.

Octavian engineered his own election to the office of consul (though he was far too young for this honor) and used his powers to have Caesar's assassins declared outlaws. He then pursued Antony to Gaul, at the head of an army. Antony's forces were overwhelmed, and in 43 B.C.E. he and Octavian reconciled and formed an alliance, bringing in a third man, a senator called Marcus Aemilius Lepidus, to make up a triumvirate. They then set about crushing the political faction responsible for Caesar's murder. The methods they employed were brutal: prominent members of the opposition were hunted down and their property confiscated. The most notable of these victims was Cicero, who was murdered by Mark Antony's thugs. (This was a revenge killing: Cicero had actively sought to undermine Antony and had branded him a public enemy.) Meanwhile, the masterminds behind Caesar's assassination, Brutus and Gaius Cassius, fled Rome and raised an army of legions from Greece and Asia Minor. But they were defeated by the united forces of Antony and Octavian on a battlefield near the Macedonian town of Philippi (founded by Alexander's father, Philip II) in 42 B.C.E. There, both Brutus and Cassius committed suicide.

With the opposition effectively destroyed, tensions mounted between Antony and Octavian, whose friendship had never been firm. Antony went to the East and made an alliance with Cleopatra, plotting to use the resources of Egypt against Octavian. Octavian, meanwhile, reestablished himself in Rome, where he skillfully portrayed Antony as having been seduced and emasculated by his foreign lover, the Egyptian queen. For ten years, Antony played the king in Egypt, fathering three of Cleopatra's children and making big plans for annexing Rome's eastern provinces. Eventually, he went too far, and Octavian had him declared a traitor while the Senate declared war on Cleopatra–not on Antony, lest Octavian be accused of starting another civil war. In 31 B.C.E. Rome's superior forces defeated those of Antony and Cleopatra in the naval battle of Actium, off the coast of Greece. Soon afterward, both Antony and Cleopatra committed suicide. Their children were taken back to Rome, and although their lives were spared they were paraded through the streets as captives. This marked the end of Egypt's independence: Cleopatra had been its last pharaoh. After more than three thousand years of self-rule, Egypt was now another province in Rome's empire.

### *The Government of Augustus*

The victory at Actium ushered in a new period of Roman history, the most prosperous and the most peaceful that

# Analyzing Primary Sources

## *Antony and Cleopatra*

*In his* Parallel Lives, *the Greek intellectual Plutarch (c. 46–120 C.E.) paired the biographies of famous Greeks with those of famous Romans, always to the disadvantage of the latter; for example, Julius Caesar suffers in comparison to Alexander the Great, as Romulus does when set up against Theseus. The following excerpt is from Plutarch's* Life of Mark Antony, *in which the Hellenistic ruler of Egypt, Cleopatra, plays a starring role.*

Caesar and Pompey knew Cleopatra when she was] still a girl, and ignorant of the world, but it was a different matter in the case of Antony, because she was ready to meet him when she had reached the time of life when women are most beautiful and have full understanding. So she prepared for him many gifts and money and adornment, of a magnitude appropriate to her great wealth and prosperous kingdom, but she put most of her hopes in her own magical arts and charms. . . . For (as they say), it was not because her beauty in itself was so striking that it stunned the onlooker, but the inescapable impression produced by daily contact with her: the attractiveness in the persuasiveness of her talk, and the character that surrounded her conversation was stimulating. It was a pleasure to hear the sound of her voice, and she tuned her tongue like a many-stringed instrument expertly to whatever language she chose, and only used interpreters to talk to a few foreigners. . . . She is said to have learned the languages of many peoples, although her predecessors on the throne did not bother to learn Egyptian, and some had even forgotten how to speak the Macedonian dialect.

She took such a hold over Antony that, while his wife Fulvia was carrying on the war in Rome against Octavian on his behalf, and the Parthian army . . . was about to invade Syria, Antony was carried off by Cleopatra to Alexandria, and amused himself there with the pastimes of a boy . . . and whether Antony was in a serious or a playful mood she could always produce some new pleasure or charm, and she kept watch on him by night and day and never let him out of her sight. She played dice with him and hunted with him and watched him exercising with his weapons and she roamed around and wandered about with him at night when he stood at people's doors and windows and made fun of people inside, dressed in a slave-woman's outfit; for he also attempted to dress up like a slave. He returned from these expeditions having been mocked in return, and often beaten, although most people suspected who he was. But the Alexandrians got pleasure from his irreverence . . . enjoying his humor and saying that he showed his tragic face to the Romans and his comic one to them.

Source: Plutarch, *Life of Marcus Antonius*, cc. 25–29, excerpted in *Women's Life in Greece and Rome: A Sourcebook in Translation*, eds. Mary R. Lefkowitz and Maureen B. Fant (Baltimore, MD: 1992), pp. 147–49.

### *Questions for Analysis*

1. How do Cleopatra's behavior and accomplishments, in Plutarch's description of her, compare to those of Roman women?
2. Given what you have learned about the values of the Roman Republic, how would a Roman reader respond to this description of Antony's behavior under the influence of the Egyptian queen? What do you think were Plutarch's motives in portraying him in this light?

Rome—or the West—ever experienced. The new Gaius Julius Caesar was now the only man left standing, and with no rivals for power he had no further need for political purges. For the first time in nearly a century, Rome was not embroiled in civil war. But it was no longer a republic, even though Octavian maintained the fiction that he was governing as a mere citizen. For four years he ruled as sole consul, until he accepted the titles of *imperator* (emperor) and *augustus*. Although these honorifics had been in use under the republic—*imperator* meant "victorious general" and *augustus* meant "worthy of honor"—they now became attached to the person of the sole ruler. So although Rome had long been an empire, it was only now that it had a single emperor. To avoid confusion, historians therefore refer to this phase of Rome's history as the Principate, from the title Augustus himself preferred: *princeps*, or "first man."

Because Augustus was determined not to be regarded as a tyrant or (worse) a king, he left most of Rome's republican institutions in place—but emptied them of their power. In theory, the emperor served at the will of "the Roman Senate and People," *SPQR*. In practice, though, he controlled the army, which meant that he also controlled the workings of government. Fortunately, Augustus was an able ruler. He introduced a range of public services, including a police force and fire brigade; he reorganized the army; and he allowed cities and provinces more substantial rights of self-government than they had enjoyed before. He instituted a new system of coinage throughout the empire, and he abolished the old, corrupt system of taxation, whereby tax collectors were compensated by being allowed to keep a portion of the monies they collected, which inevitably encouraged them to collect more than were legally due. Instead, Augustus appointed his own representatives as tax collectors, paid them regular salaries, and kept them under strict supervision. He also conducted a census of the empire's population for this purpose, and it was during one of these "enrollments" that the birth of Jesus is said to have taken place, according to the gospel of Luke (see Chapter 6). Augustus also established new colonies in the provinces, encouraging the emigration of Rome's urban and rural poor, thereby removing a major source of social tension and promoting the integration of the Roman heartland with its far-flung hinterland.

Although his rule had definitively ended the republic, Augustus represented himself as a stern defender of the *mos maiorum* and traditional Roman virtues. He rebuilt many of the city's ancient temples and prohibited the worship of foreign gods. In an attempt to increase the birthrate of Rome's citizens, he penalized men who failed to marry, required widows to remarry within two years of their husbands' deaths, and rewarded women who gave birth to more than two children. He also introduced laws punishing adultery and making divorces more difficult to obtain. To hammer the message home, Augustan propaganda portrayed the imperial family as a model of domestic virtue and propriety. Yet these portrayals were only moderately successful because the emperor's own extramarital affairs were notorious, and the sexual promiscuity of his daughter Julia finally forced Augustus to have her exiled.

**OCTAVIAN.** Caesar's adopted heir was later granted the title "Augustus" by the Senate, and was also known as *princeps*, "first man." Eventually, he would be worshiped as a god in Rome's provinces, and idealized statues like this one would be erected in temples and public places throughout the empire.

Meanwhile, more land was gained for Rome in the lifetime of Augustus than in that of any other ruler. His generals advanced into central Europe, conquering the modern-day territories of Switzerland, Austria, and Bulgaria. Only in Germania did Roman troops meet defeat, when three legions were slaughtered in the Teutoburg Forest in 9 C.E., a devastating setback that convinced Augustus to hold the Roman borders at the Rhine and Danube rivers. Subsequently, though, the Emperor Claudius would begin the conquest of Britain in 43 C.E., while the Emperor Trajan (91–117 C.E.) would push beyond the Danube to add Dacia (now Romania) to the empire. Trajan also conquered territories in the heartland of Mesopotamia, but in so doing

# Competing Viewpoints

## *Two Views of Augustus's Rule*

### Augustus Speaks for Himself

*The emperor Augustus was a master propagandist with an unrivaled capacity for presenting his own actions in the best possible light. This list of his own deeds was written by Augustus himself and was displayed on two bronze pillars set up in the Roman forum.*

Below is a copy of the accomplishments of the deified Augustus by which he brought the whole world under the empire of the Roman people, and of the moneys expended by him on the state and the Roman people. . . .

1. At the age of nineteen, on my own initiative and at my own expense, I raised an army by means of which I liberated the Republic, which was oppressed by the tyranny of a faction.

2. Those who assassinated my father I drove into exile, avenging their crime by due process of law.

3. I waged many wars throughout the whole world by land and by sea, both civil and foreign. . . .

5. The dictatorship offered to me . . . by the people and by the Senate . . . I refused to accept. . . . The consulship, too, which was offered to me . . . as an annual office for life, I refused to accept.

6. [T]hough the Roman Senate and people together agreed that I should be elected sole guardian of the laws and morals with supreme authority, I refused to accept any office offered me which was contrary to the traditions of our ancestors.

7. I have been ranking senator for forty years. . . . I have been *pontifex maximus*, augur, member of the college of fifteen for performing sacrifices, member of the college of seven for conducting religious banquets, member of the Arval Brotherhood, one of the *Titii sodales*, and a *fetial* [all priestly offices].

9. The Senate decreed that vows for my health should be offered up every fifth year by the consuls and priests. . . . [T]he whole citizen body, with one accord, . . . prayed continuously for my health at all the shrines.

17. Four times I came to the assistance of the treasury with my own money . . . providing bonuses for soldiers who had completed twenty or more years of service.

20. I repaired the Capitol and the theater of Pompey with enormous expenditures on both works, without having my name inscribed on them. I repaired . . . the aqueducts which were falling into ruin in many places . . . I repaired eighty-two temples . . . I reconstructed the Flaminian Way. . . .

34. [H]aving attained supreme power by universal consent, I transferred the state from my own power to the control of the Roman Senate and people. . . . After that time I excelled all in authority, but I possessed no more power than the others who were my colleagues in each magistracy.

35. At the time I wrote this document I was in my seventy-sixth year.

Source: "Res Gestae Divi Augusti," in *Roman Civilization, Sourcebook II: The Empire,* eds. Naphtali Lewis and Meyer Reinhold (New York: 1966), pp. 9–19.

aroused the enmity of the Parthians, who now ruled in Persia. His successor, Hadrian (117–138 C.E.), accordingly halted Rome's expansion and embarked on a defensive policy epitomized by the construction of Hadrian's Wall in northern Britain. The empire had now reached its greatest extent; in the third century, as we shall see (Chapter 6), the tide would turn and these limits would recede.

When Octavian died in 14 C.E. he was not only Caesar, Imperator, and Augustus; he was *pontifex maximus* (high priest) and "father of the country" (*pater patriae*). He was

## The Historian Tacitus Evaluates Augustus's Reign

*Writing in the first decades of the second century C.E., the senatorial historian Tacitus (c. 56–117) began his chronicle of imperial rule, the* Annals, *with the death of Augustus a century earlier.*

Intelligent people praised or criticized Augustus in varying terms. One opinion was as follows. Filial duty and a national emergency, in which there was no place for law-abiding conduct, had driven him to civil war—and this can be neither initiated nor maintained by decent methods. He had made many concessions to Antony and to Lepidus for the sake of vengeance on his father's murderers. When Lepidus grew old and lazy, and Antony's self-indulgence got the better of him, the only possible cure for the distracted country had been government by one man. However, Augustus had put the State in order not by making himself king or dictator but by creating the Principate. The empire's frontiers were on the ocean, or on distant rivers. Armies, provinces, fleets, the whole system was interrelated. Roman citizens were protected by the law. Provincials were decently treated. Rome itself had been lavishly beautified. Force had been sparingly used—merely to preserve peace for the majority.

The opposite view went like this. Filial duty and national crisis had been merely pretexts. In actual fact, the motive of Octavian, the future Augustus, was lust for power. Inspired by that, he had mobilized ex-army settlers by gifts of money, raised an army—while he was only a half-grown boy without any official status—won over a consul's brigade by bribery, pretended to support Sextus Pompeius [the son of Pompey], and by senatorial decree usurped the status and rank of a praetor. Soon both consuls . . . had met their deaths—by enemy action; or perhaps in the one case by the deliberate poisoning of his wound, and in the other at the hand of his own troops, instigated by Octavian. In any case, it was he who took over both their armies. Then he had forced the reluctant Senate to make him consul. But the forces given him to deal with Antony he used against the State. His judicial murders and land distributions were distasteful even to those who carried them out. True, Cassius and Brutus died because he had inherited a feud against them; nevertheless, personal enmities ought to be sacrificed to the public interest. Next he had cheated Sextus Pompeius by a spurious peace treaty, Lepidus by spurious friendship. Then Antony, enticed by treaties and his marriage with Octavian's sister, had paid the penalty of that delusive relationship with his life. After that, there had certainly been peace, but it was a bloodstained peace. . . . And gossip did not spare his personal affairs—how he had abducted [Livia] the wife of Tiberius Claudius Nero, and asked the priests the farcical question whether it was in order for her to marry while pregnant. Then there was the debauchery of his friend Publius Vedius Pollio. But Livia was a real catastrophe, to the nation, as a mother and to the house of the Caesars as a stepmother.

Source: Tacitus, *Annals* i.9–10. Based on *Tacitus: The Annals of Imperial Rome*, trans. Michael Grant (New York: 1989), pp. 37–39.

### *Questions for Analysis*

1. How does Augustus organize his list, and why? What does he leave out and what does he choose to emphasize?
2. Tacitus presents two contrasting views of Augustus's motives. Which does he himself seem to believe? How does his account complement or undermine that of Augustus himself?
3. Could you write a new account of Augustus's life making use of both sources? How would you strike a balance between them? What would your own conclusion be?

even deified by the Senate, which had also deified Julius Caesar at Augustus's urging. These titles and trends would be passed on to his successors, as would the system of government he had devised. And even those who mourned the passing of the republic and loathed these displays of imperial *hubris* had to admit that the system worked. Rome enjoyed nearly two centuries of peace, prosperity, and stability because of it.

The true test of any political institution is its capacity survive incompetent officeholders. Aside from one brief period of civil war in 68 C.E., the transition of power between emperors was generally peaceful and the growing imperial bureaucracy could manage affairs competently even when individual emperors proved vicious and ineffectual, as did Caligula (37–41 C.E.). Nevertheless, the fact that Rome had become an autocratic state became harder and harder to conceal. Many of Augustus's successors were heavy-handed and had difficult relationships with the Senate; and because the historians of this era were invariably members of the senatorial elite, they had a vested interest in sullying the reputations of these emperors. Hence the skilled administrators Tiberius (14 –37 C.E.) and Claudius (41–54 C.E.) were accused by their biographers of sexual perversion on the one hand and idiocy on the other. Nero (54–68 C.E.) and Domitian (81–96 C.E.) were also reviled by the aristocracy but popular among the Roman people and in the provinces; indeed, Domitian's needed reforms of provincial government and his blatant disregard for senatorial privilege account for both the Senate's hostility and his subjects' approval.

The height of the Augustan system is generally considered to be the era between 96 and 180 C.E., often known as the reign of the "Five Good Emperors": Nerva (96–98 C.E.), Trajan (98–117 C.E.), Hadrian (117–138 C.E.), Antoninus Pius (138–161 C.E.), and Marcus Aurelius (161–180 C.E.). All were capable politicians, and since none but the last had a son that survived him, each adopted a worthy successor—a policy that allowed this generation of rulers to avoid the messy family dysfunctions that absorbed Augustus and his immediate heirs. They also benefited from the fact that Rome had few external enemies left. The Mediterranean was under the control of a single power for the first time in history. On land, Roman officials ruled from Britain to Persia. A contemporary orator justly boasted that "the whole civilized world lays down the arms which were its ancient burden, as if on holiday. . . . [A]ll places are full of gymnasia, fountains, monumental approaches, temples, workshops, schools." The continual bloodshed of civil wars and of Augustus's reign of terror had abated. Now was the *Pax Romana*, the Roman Peace.

## MAKING THE WORLD ROMAN

Occasionally, the Roman Peace was broken. In Britannia, Roman legions had to put down a rebellion led by the Celtic warrior queen Boudica (d. 60/61 C.E.), which ended in a massacre of the island's inhabitants; thousands of Britons lost their lives. Another rebellion was violently quashed in Judea, the most restive of all Roman provinces, leading to the destruction of the Temple at Jerusalem in 70 C.E. In 135 C.E., a second rebellion completed the destruction of the city. Although it was refounded by Hadrian as Aelia Capitolina, a colony for veterans of Rome's army, Jews were forbidden to settle there (see Chapter 6).

Such rebellions were not the norm, however. Although the Roman Empire had been gradually achieved by conquest, it was not maintained by force. Instead, Rome controlled its territories by offering incentives to assimiliation. Local elites were encouraged to adopt Roman modes of behavior and dress in order to gain entrance to political office. Local gods became Roman gods and were adopted into the Roman pantheon of divinities. Cities were constructed on a set Roman model of urban planning, and the amenities of urban life were introduced: baths, temples, amphitheaters, aqueducts, and

**HADRIAN'S WALL.** Stretching 73.5 miles across northern England, this fortification (begun in 122 C.E.) marked the frontier of Britain as established by the emperor Hadrian. (A later wall, built further north by Antoninus Pius in 142, was quickly abandoned.) Long stretches of the wall still exist, as do many of the forts built along it. The tree in this photograph stands on the site of a "mile castle," one of the smaller watchtowers built at intervals of a Roman mile and garrisoned by sentries.

**SPOILS FROM JERUSALEM.** A bas-relief inside the triumphal Arch of Titus in the Roman Forum shows plundered treasures of the Temple at Jerusalem, including the Menorah, being carried in triumph through Rome.

paved roads (see ***Interpreting Visual Evidence*** on page 170). Rights of citizenship were extended, and able provincials could rise far in the imperial government. Some, like the emperors Trajan and Hadrian—both raised in Hispania—came to control it. Meanwhile, tens of thousands of army veterans were settled in the provinces, marrying local women and putting down local roots. It was common for soldiers born in Syria or North Africa to end their days peacefully in northern Gaul or Germania. In Camulodunum (now Colchester, England), the gravestone of a legionnaire called Longinus sketches a typical career: born in Serdica (modern Sofia, in Bulgaria) to a local man named Szdapezematygus, he rose through the ranks to become sergeant of the First Thracian Cavalry under Claudius and one of the first Roman colonists of Britannia.

Even the outer fringes of the empire need to be understood as part of Rome's orbit. Although historians speak of the empire's "borders" for the sake of convenience, these were in fact frontiers: highly fluid and permeable zones of intensive interaction. Roman influence reached far beyond these zones, into the heartland of Germania and lands further to the east. By the middle of the third century C.E., when some frontier garrisons were withdrawn to take part in civil wars within the empire itself, many of these peoples moved southward, too, sometimes as plunderers but more often as settlers and aspiring Romans (see Chapter 6).

## *The Entertainments of Empire*

The cultural and intellectual developments that began in Rome during the late republic came to fruition during the Principate, and are richly reflected in its literature. For the first time in its already long history, Latin began to replace Greek as a language of learning and poetry. Roman literature of this era is conventionally divided into two periods, the Golden Age of writings produced under the more or less direct influence of Augustus, and the Silver Age of the first and early second centuries C.E. Most Golden Age literature is, not surprisingly, propagandistic: its purpose was to advertise and justify Augustus's achievements. The poetry of Publius Virgilius Maro (Virgil, 70–19 B.C.E.) is typical, and we have already noted his strategic use of "prophecy" in the story of Aeneas (see page 142). Other major poets of this age were Quintus Horatius Flaccus (Horace, 65–8 B.C.E.) and Publius Ovidius Naso (Ovid, 43 B.C.E.–17 C.E.): the former a master of the lovely, short lyric and the latter our major source for Greek mythology, which he retold in a long poem called the *Metamorphoses* ("Transformations"). Ovid was also a satirist, and his frank advice to his readers on the best way to attract women at the race course and his own (probably fictional) strategy for conducting an adulterous affair with the wife of a senator resulted in his banishment.

# Analyzing Primary Sources

## *Rome's Party Girls*

*The* Satires *of the poet Juvenal circulated around the year 100 C.E. and attacked everything from the general erosion of public morality to the effete tastes of the elite. Some of his most pointed criticism was directed at contemporary women.*

hat conscience has Venus, when she is drunk? Our inebriated beauties can't tell head from tail at those midnight oyster suppers when the best wine's laced with perfume, and tossed down neat from a foaming conch-shell, while the dizzy ceiling spins round, and the tables dance, and each light shows double. Why, you may ask yourself, does the notorious Maura sniff at the air in that knowing, derisive way as she and her dear friend Tullia pass by the ancient altar of Chastity? And what is Tullia whispering to her? Here, at night, they stagger out of their litters and relieve themselves, pissing in long hard bursts all over the goddess's statue. Then, while the Moon looks down on their motions, they take turns to ride each other, and finally go home. So you, next morning, on your way to some great house, will splash through your wife's piddle. Notorious, too, are the ritual mysteries of the Good Goddess, when flute-music stirs the loins, and frenzied women, devotees of Priapus, sweep along in procession, howling, tossing their hair, wine-flown, horn-crazy, burning with the desire to get themselves laid. . . . So the ladies, with a display of talent to match their birth, win all the prizes. No make-believe here, no pretense, each act is performed in earnest, and guaranteed to warm the age-chilled balls of a Nestor or a Priam.

Source: Juvenal, *Sixth Satire* 301–26; based on *Juvenal: The Sixteen Satires*, trans. Peter Green (New York: 1974), pp. 138–39 (modified).

### *Questions for Analysis*

1. Compare Juvenal's account of female behavior to the legend of Lucretia, on the one hand, and Plutarch's description of Cleopatra, on the other. What can you conclude about attitudes to women, and to sexual morality? Why and on what grounds would men living under the Principate hold women responsible for society's ills?
2. What are the benefits and the drawbacks of the *Satires* as a historical source?

After Augustus's death, Roman authors had more license and became important cultural critics. The tales of Petronius and Apuleius describe the more bizarre and sometimes sordid aspects of Roman life, and the satirist Juvenal (60?–140 C.E.) wrote with savage wit about the moral degeneracy he saw in his contemporaries. A similar attitude toward Roman society characterizes the writings of Tacitus (55?–117? C.E.), an aristocratic historian who describes the events and people of his age largely for the purpose of passing judgment on them. His *Annals* offer a subtle but devastating portrait of the political system constructed by Augustus and ruled by his heirs; his *Germania* contrasts the manly virtues of northern barbarians with the effeminate vices of the decadent Romans. Like Juvenal, Tacitus was a master of ironic wit. Referring to Rome's conquests, he has a barbarian chieftain say, "They create a wilderness and call it peace."

To many people today, the most repellant (and most fascinating) aspect of Roman culture during the Principate was its spectacular cruelty, exhibited (literally) in the public arenas erected in every Roman town. Gladiatorial contests were not new, but they were now presented in ampitheaters built to hold thousands. Everyone, even emperors, attended these events, and they became increasingly bloody and brutal as people demanded more and more innovative violence. Individual gladiators fought to the death with swords or the exotic weapons of their homelands. Teams of gladiators fought pitched battles, often simulating historic Roman victories. Occasionally, a wealthy entrepreneur would fill an arena with water and stage a naval battle. Hundreds of men would die in these organized slaughters. On other occasions, hundreds of half-starved animals imported from Africa, India, or the forests Germania would tear one another—or their human victims—apart. When a fighter went down with a disabling wound, the crowd would be asked to decide whether to spare his life or to kill him. If the arena floor became too slippery with blood, a fresh layer of sand would be spread over the gore so that the performance could continue.

**FEMALE GLADIATORS.** Like men, enslaved women also fought as gladiators. This marble relief commemorates the freeing of two such fighters, "Amazon" and "Achilia," presumably as a reward for their successes in the arena.

## *Roman Art, Architecture, and Engineering*

Like Latin literature, Roman art assumed its distinctive character during the Principate. Before this time, most artworks displayed in Roman homes and public places were imported from the Hellenistic East. Conquering armies brought back wagonloads of statues, reliefs, and marble columns as plunder from Greece and Asia Minor. These became the property of the wealthy, and as demand for such works increased, hundreds of copies were made by Roman artisans. In many cases, these copies proved more durable than their originals: in Chapter 3, we noted that the statue group of the Athenian tyrannicides, Harmodius and Aristogeiton, was a Roman copy; and in Chapter 4, we were able to examine the lost Aphrodite of Knidos, courtesy of Roman sculptors.

Encouraged by the patronage of Augustus and his successors, artists began to experiment with more distinctively Roman styles and subjects. The relief sculpture of this period is particularly notable for its delicacy and naturalism, and sculptors also became adept at portraiture. Even on their coins, emperors were portrayed very much as they looked in real life; and since the matrices for coins were recut annually, we can trace on successive issues a ruler's receding hairline or his advancing double chin. Painting, however, was the Romans' most original and most intimate art. Romans loved intense colors, and those who could afford it surrounded themselves with brilliant wall paintings and mosaics made of tiny fragments of glass and stone, which were often set into the floors of houses and public baths or which formed the centerpieces of gardens. Lavish mosaics have been found in the remains of Roman villas in all the territories of the empire, and similar design features suggest that many were mosaic "kits" that could be ordered from a manufacturer, who would ship out all the necessary components along with a team of workmen to assemble them.

Augustus liked to boast that he had found Rome a city of clay and left it a city of marble. It is certainly true that

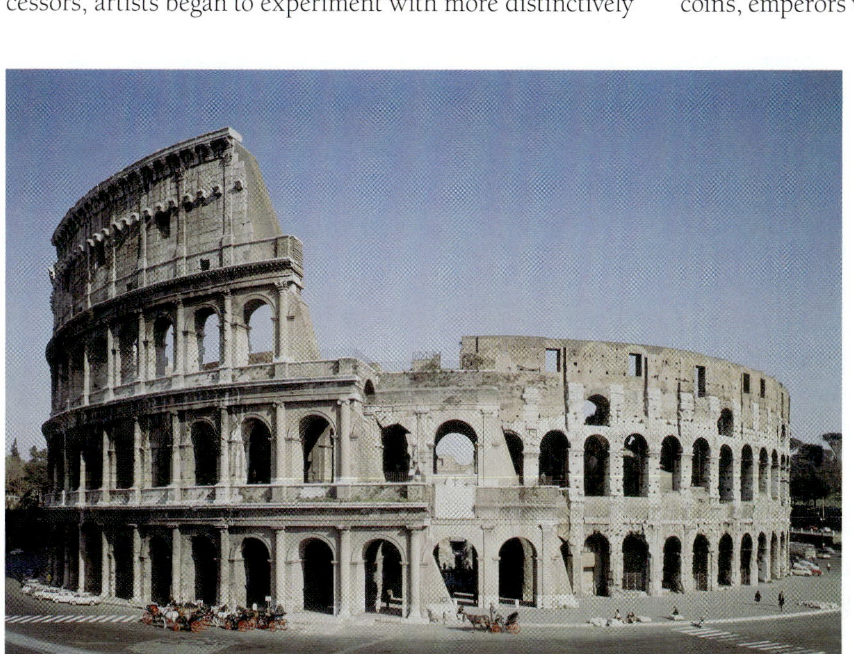

**THE COLOSSEUM.** Constructed between 75 and 80 C.E., this was the first ampitheater in Rome purposely built to showcase gladiatorial combats. Prior to this, gladiators would often fight in improvised arenas in the Forum or in other public places. ▪ ***How does this fact change your perception of Roman history?***

**THE ROMAN EMPIRE AT ITS GREATEST EXTENT, 97–117 C.E.** ▪ ***How much farther north and west does the empire now reach compared to its earlier extent (see map on page 152)?*** ▪ ***How did geography influence the process of expansion?*** ▪ ***How did it dictate its limits?*** ▪ ***For example, what role do major river systems seem to play?***

ambitious public works projects were initiated under the Principate, but in reality marble was too precious to be used in common construction. Instead, marble panels or ornaments were added to the facings of buildings that were otherwise built of concrete. For the Romans had discovered how to make a hard and reliable building material from a mixture of quicklime, volcanic ash, and pumice, and it was this—along with superior engineering skills—that allowed them to build massive structures like the Colosseum, which could accommodate 50,000 spectators at gladiatorial combats. Romans engineers also excelled in the building of roads and bridges, many of which were constructed by Rome's armies as they moved into new territories. Like the Persian Royal Road of the sixth century B.C.E. or the German Autobahn of the 1930s and the interstate highways of the United States begun in the 1950s, roads have always been, first and foremost, a device for moving armies and then, secondarily, for moving goods and people. Many of these Roman roads still survive, or form the basis for modern European highways. In Britain, for example, the only major thoroughfares before the building of the high-speed motorways were Roman roads, to which the motorways now run parallel.

The inhabitants of Roman cities also enjoyed the benefits of a public water supply. By the early decades of the second century C.E., eleven aqueducts brought water into Rome from the nearby hills and provided the city with 300 million gallons per day, for drinking and bathing and for flushing a well-designed sewage system. These amenities were common in cities throughout the empire, and the homes of the wealthy even had indoor plumbing and central heating. Water was also funneled into the homes of the rich for private gardens, fountains, and pools. The emperor Nero built a famous Golden House with special pipes that sprinkled his guests with perfume, baths supplied with medicinal waters, and a pond "like a sea." In addition, a

**ROMAN AQUEDUCT IN SOUTHERN GAUL (PROVENCE).** Aqueducts conveyed water from mountains and lakes to the larger cities of the Roman Empire. The massive arches shown here span the river Gardon and were originally part of a 31-mile-long complex that supplied water to the city of Nemausus (Nîmes). It is now known as the Pont du Gard (Bridge of the Gardon), reflecting the use to which it was put after the aqueduct ceased to function, some eight centuries after its construction in the first century C.E. Some Roman aqueducts remained operational into the modern era: the one at Segovia, Spain was still in use at the end of the twentieth century. ▪ ***What does the magnitude and longevity of such projects tell us about Roman power and technology?***

**A ROMAN FLOOR MOSAIC.** This fine mosaic from the Roman city of Londinium (London) shows Bacchus (Dionysus), the god of wine and revelry, mounted on a tiger. Tigers, native to India, were prized by animal collectors and were also imported for gladiatorial shows.

spherical ceiling in the banquet hall revolved day and night like the heavens. "At last," said Nero on moving day, "I can live like a human being."

## *The Reach of Roman Law*

As impressive and ingenious as Roman architecture and engineering are, the most durable and useful of this civilization's legacies was its system of law. Over the course of several centuries, the primitive legal code of the Twelve Tables was largely replaced by a series of new precedents and principles. These reflect the changing political climate of Rome and the needs of its diverse and ever-growing population. They also show the influence of new philosophies, especially Stoicism; the decisions of judges; and the edicts of magistrates called *praetors*, who had the authority to define and interpret law in particular cases, and to issue instructions to judges.

The most sweeping legal changes occurred during the Principate. This was partly because the reach of Roman law had to match the reach of the empire, which now extended over a much wider field of jurisdiction. But the major reason for the rapid development of Roman legal thinking during

# Interpreting Visual Evidence

## *Roman Urban Planning*

Prior to Roman imperial expansion, most cities in the ancient world were not planned cities—with the exception of the new settlements established by Alexander the Great, notably Alexandria in Egypt. Rome itself was not carefully planned, but grew up over many centuries, expanding outward and up the slopes of its seven hills from the nucleus of the Forum. By the time of Augustus, it was a haphazard jumble of buildings and narrow streets. Outside of Rome, however, the efficiency of Roman government was in large part due to the uniformity of imperial urban planning. As their colonial reach expanded, Romans sought to ensure that travelers moving within their vast domain would encounter the same amenities in every major city. They also wanted to convey, through the organization of the urban landscape, the ubiquity of Roman authority and majesty.

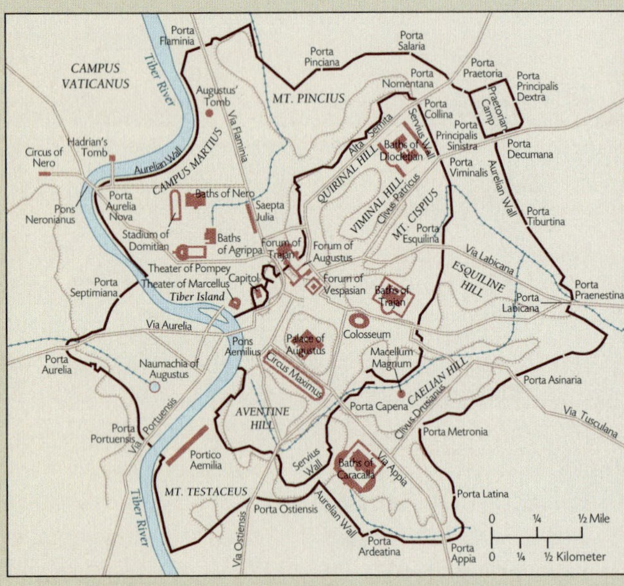


A. Imperial Rome

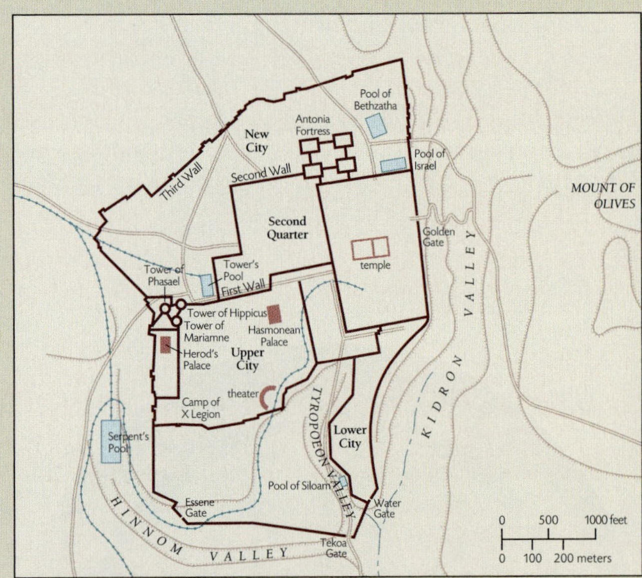


B. Roman settlement in Jerusalem after 135 C.E.

these years was the fact that Augustus and his successors appointed a small number of eminent jurists to deliver opinions on the issues raised by cases under trial in the courts. The five most prominent of these jurists flourished in the second century C.E.: Gaius (only this most common of his names is known), Domitius Ulpianus (Ulpian), Modestinus, Aemelianus Papinianus (Papinian), and Paulus. Although most of them came to hold high offices, they gained their reputations primarily as lawyers and commentators. Taken together, their legal opinions constitute the first philosophy of law and the foundation for all subsequent jurisprudence, a word derived from the Latin phrase meaning "legal wisdom."

As it was developed by the jurists, Roman law comprised three great branches or divisions: civil law, the law of nations, and natural law. Civil law was the law of Rome and its citizens, both written and unwritten. It included the statutes of the Senate, the decrees of the emperor, the edicts of magistrates, and ancient customs that had the force of law (like the *mos maiorum*). The law of nations was

*Questions for Analysis*

1. Looking closely at the map of Rome (map A), how have topographical features—like the river Tiber and the seven hills—determined the shape and layout of the city? What are the major buildings and public areas? What were the functions of these spaces, and what do they reveal about Roman society and values?

2. Compare the plan of Rome to those of Roman London (map C) and Jerusalem (map B). What features do all three have in common, and why? What features are unique to each place, and what might this reveal about the different regions of the empire and the needs of the different cities' inhabitants?

3. Given that all Roman cities share certain features, what message(s) were Roman authorities trying to convey to inhabitants and travelers through urban planning? Why, for example, would they have insisted on rebuilding Jerusalem as a Roman city after the rebellion of 135 C.E.?

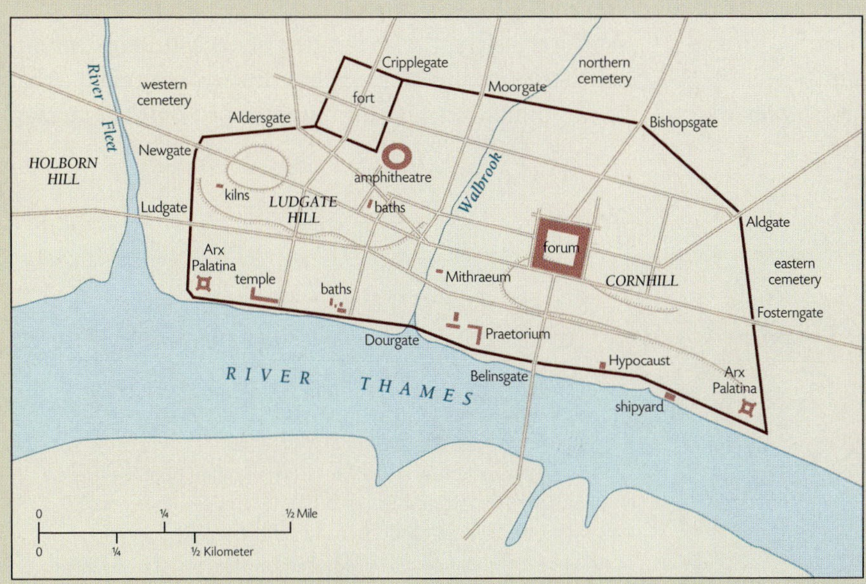


C. London under the Romans, c. 200 C.E.

not specific to Rome but extended to all people of the world regardless of their origins and ethnicity: it is the precursor of international law. This law authorized slavery; protected the private ownership of property; and defined the mechanisms of purchase and sale, partnership, and contract. It was not superior to civil law but supplemented it, and it applied especially to those inhabitants of the empire who were not citizens, as well as to foreigners.

The most interesting (and in many ways the most important) branch of Roman law was natural law, a product not of judicial practice but of legal philosophy. Roman Stoics, following in the footsteps of Cicero, posited that nature itself is rationally ordered, and that careful study will reveal the laws by which the natural world operates, including the nature of justice. They affirmed that all men are by nature equal, and that they are entitled to certain basic rights that governments have no authority to transgress. "True law," Cicero had said, "is right reason consonant with nature, diffused among all men, constant, eternal." Accordingly, no person or institution has the authority to infringe on this law, repeal it, or ignore it. This law supersedes any state or ruler; a ruler who transgresses it is a tyrant.

Although the jurists did not regard the philosophical concept of natural law as an automatic limitation on the workings of civil law, they did uphold it as an ideal. The practical law applied in local Roman courts often bore little resemblance to the law of nature, yet the development of a concept of abstract justice as a fundemantal principle was one of the noblest achievements of Roman civilization. It has given us the doctrine of human rights, even if it could not end abuses of those rights.

## CONCLUSION

The resemblances between Rome's history and that of Great Britain and the United States have often been noted. Like the British Empire, the Roman Empire was founded on conquest and overseas colonization intended to benefit both the homeland and Britain's colonial subjects, who were seen as the beneficiaries of the metropolis' "civilizing mission." Like America's, the Roman economy evolved from agrarianism to a complex system of domestic and foreign markets, problems of unemployment, gross disparities of wealth, and vulnerability to financial crisis. And like both the British and the American empires, the Roman Empire justified itself by celebrating the peace its conquests allegedly brought to the world.

Ultimately, however, such parallels break down when we remember that Rome's civilization differed profoundly from any society of the modern world. It was not an industrialized society. Its government never pretended to be representative of all its citizens. Roman class divisions are not directly comparable to ours. The Roman economy rested on slavery to a degree unmatched in any modern state. As a result, technological advances were not encouraged, social stratification was extreme, and gender relations were profoundly unequal. Religious practice and political life were inseparable.

Nevertheless, the civilization of ancient Rome continues to structure our everyday lives in ways so profound that they go unnoticed. Our days are mapped onto the Roman

## After You Read This Chapter

Visit StudySpace for quizzes, additional review materials, and multi-media documents. **wwnorton.com/studyspace**

### REVIEWING THE OBJECTIVES

- The founding of the Roman Republic was both a cherished myth and a series of events. What factors contributed to this unique system of government?
- The shared identity and values of the Roman people differed in many ways from those of other ancient cilivilizations. What were some of these major differences?
- Rome's population was divided among classes of people who often struggled with one another for power. Identify these classes and their points of contention.
- The expansion of Rome's empire had a profound impact on Roman society. Why?
- The establishment of the Principate ushered in a new era in the history of Rome. What events led to this?

calendar. The constitution of the United States is largely modeled on that of the republic, and Roman architecture survives in the design of our public buildings. Roman law forms the basis of most European legal codes and American judges still cite Gaius and Ulpian. Virtually all modern sculpture is inspired by Roman sculpture, and Roman authors continue to set the standards for prose composition in many Western countries. Indeed, most European languages are either derived from Latin—Romance languages are so called because they are "Roman-like"—or have borrowed Latin grammatical structures or vocabulary. As we shall see in the following chapters, the organization of the modern Roman Catholic Church can be traced back to the structure of the Roman state: even today, the pope bears the title of Rome's high priest, *pontifex maximus*.

But perhaps the most important of all Rome's contributions was its role as mediator between Europe and the civilizations of the ancient Near East and Mediterranean. Had Rome's empire not come to encompass much of Europe, there would be no such thing as the concept of Western civilization and no shared ideas and heritage to link us to those distant places and times. Although we shall pursue the history of Rome's fragmentation and witness the emergence of three different civilizations in the territories once united by its empire, we shall see that they all shared a common cultural inheritance. In that sense, at least, the Roman Empire did not collapse. But it was transformed, and the factors driving that transformation will be the subject of Chapter 6.

## PEOPLE, IDEAS, AND EVENTS IN CONTEXT

- In what ways were the early Romans influenced by their **ETRUSCAN** neighbors and by their location in central **ITALY**?
- What were the components of the **REPUBLIC'S CONSTITUTION**? What was the relationship between **ROMAN CITIZENSHIP** and the **ROMAN ARMY** in this era?
- How do the stories of **AENEAS, LUCRETIA**, and **CINCINNATUS** reflect core Roman values? How did those values, summarized in the phrase ***MOS MAIORUM***, set the Romans apart from the other civilizations we have studied?
- Why did the Romans come into conflict with **CARTHAGE**? How did the **PUNIC WARS** and Rome's other conquests change the balance of power in the Mediterranean?
- How did **IMPERIALISM** and contact with **HELLENISTIC CULTURE** affect the core values of Roman society, its economy, and its political system? What role did **SLAVERY** play in this civilization?
- What were the major crises of the late republic, and what were the means by which ambitious men achieved power? How did **JULIUS CAESAR** emerge triumphant, and why was he assassinated?
- In what ways did the **PRINCIPATE** differ from the **REPUBLIC**? What were the new powers of the **EMPEROR**, and how did **AUGUSTUS** exemplify these?
- How did the Romans consolidate their **EMPIRE** during the ***PAX ROMANA***? By what means did they spread Roman culture?

## CONSEQUENCES

- Polybius believed that the Roman Republic would last forever, because it fused together aspects of monarchy, aristocracy, and polity. What were the chief factors that led to its demise in the first century B.C.E.? Could these have been avoided—and if so, how?
- In what ways does the Roman Empire share the characteristics of earlier empires, especially that of Alexander? In what ways does it differ from them?
- The Roman Empire could be said to resemble our own civilization in different ways. What features does today's United States share with the republic? With the Principate? What lessons can we draw from this?

# Before You Read This Chapter

## STORY LINES

- In a little over three centuries, Christianity grew from obscure beginnings in a small Roman province to become the official religion of the empire.
- It became clear during the first three centuries of the common era that the Roman Empire was too large and diverse to be governed by a single centralized authority. Significant political, military, and economic changes occurred during the third century.
- In the fourth century, the founding of a new capital at Constantinople shifted the focus of imperial administration to the East. At the same time, mass migrations of frontier peoples created new polities within the western half of Rome's empire.
- Christianity's new association with political power changed the religion in profound ways. At the same time, Christian intellectuals adapted Rome's traditional culture to meet Christian needs.

## CHRONOLOGY

| | |
|---|---|
| c. 4 B.C.E.–c. 30 C.E. | Lifetime of Jesus |
| 46–67 C.E. | Paul's missionary career |
| 66–70 | Jewish rebellion |
| 132–135 | Expulsion of Jews from Jerusalem |
| 203 | Death of Perpetua at Carthage |
| 235–284 | Rule of the "barracks emperors" |
| 284–305 | Diocletian divides the empire |
| 312 | Constantine's victory |
| 313 | Edict of Milan |
| 325 | Council of Nicaea convened |
| c. 370–430 | Careers of Jerome, Ambrose, and Augustine |
| c. 376 | Frontier migrations begin |
| 391 | Pagan religion outlawed |
| 410 | Visigoths sack Rome |
| 476 | Odovacar deposes Romulus Augustulus |
| 493–526 | Rule of Theodoric the Ostrogoth |
| c. 500–583 | Careers of Boethius, Benedict, and Cassiodorus |

# The Transformation of Rome

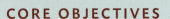

## CORE OBJECTIVES

- **IDENTIFY** the historical factors that shaped early Christianity.
- **DESCRIBE** the crises that faced Roman imperial administration during the third century.
- **TRACE** the ways that Christianity changed after if became a legal religion.
- **EXPLAIN** how the mass migrations of the fourth century affected the empire.
- **UNDERSTAND** the difference between the traditional Roman and Christian worldviews.

In the year 203 C.E., a young woman called Vivia Perpetua was brought before the Roman governor at Carthage. She was twenty-two years old, well educated, from a respectable family. At the time of her arrest she had an infant child who was still nursing. She also had two brothers (one of whom was arrested with her) and a father who doted on her. She must, one presumes, have had a husband, but he is conspicuously absent from the firsthand account of her experiences. Perpetua herself says nothing about him, though she says a great deal about her father's grief and the efforts he made to intercede on her behalf. Not only did he beg the judge for mercy, he begged his daughter to confess so that her life could be spared. He admitted to having loved her more than her brothers and blamed himself for the liberal education he had given her. Clearly, he had failed as a father: a Roman *paterfamilias* should never suffer humiliation through the conduct of a daughter, and he should kill her with his own hands if she disgraced the family. For Perpetua's crime was terrible. It was not only treason against the Roman state but an act of gross impiety toward her father, her family, and her ancestors. Worse, it was punishable by a death so debasing that it was reserved for slaves, barbarian prisoners, and hardened criminals. How could a respectable Roman matron be stripped naked before a holiday crowd and mauled by wild beasts in the arena of her own city? That was the death Perpetua died. Perpetua was a Christian.

Early Christianity posed a challenge to the Roman Empire and its core values at almost every level, a challenge exemplified by Vivia Perpetua. To be a Christian was to be, by definition, an enemy of Rome, because Christians refused to worship the emperor as the embodiment of Rome's gods; denying his divinity meant denying his authority. Moreover, the Christ whom Christians worshiped had himself been declared a criminal, a political insurgent, and had been duly tried and put to death by the Roman state. Also disturbing was the way that Christians flouted the conventions of Roman society. Perpetua was young, yet she was disobedient to her father and ancestors. She was well born, yet she chose to endure the filth of a common jail. She was a woman, yet she denied the authority of men and renounced her femininity, dying in the dust like a gladiator. If this was what it meant to be a Christian, then being a Christian was incompatible with being a Roman.

How, then, did a Roman emperor become a Christian just a few centuries after Christ's death—and just a century or so after Perpetua's? What changes did both Rome and Christianity have to undergo in order for this to happen? And what other forces were at work, within the empire and beyond its borders, that helped bring this about?

The Rome in which Perpetua was raised stretched from central Asia to the British Isles, from the Rhine to her own province of North Africa. But as we shall see, the governance of this enormous state and its diverse population was straining the bureaucracy that had been built on the foundations of the old republic. By the end of the third century, it was increasingly obvious that Rome's western and eastern provinces could not be controlled by a single centralized authority. In the fourth century, Rome itself ceased to be the capital and hub of the empire; it now shared prestige with the new city of Constantinople, named by the Christian emperor who founded it. At the same time, Rome's settled provinces were coming under increased pressure from groups of people who had long lived beyond its borders, but who were now moving from the periphery to the center. These peoples, too, would challenge what it meant to be Roman, and would contribute to the transformation of the Roman world.

**JUDEA AND GALILEE IN THE TIME OF JESUS.** ▪ ***What are the major cities in first-century C.E. Judaea?*** ▪ ***What do they indicate about the effects of Roman occupation on the lives of Jews?*** ▪ ***Given what you have learned about their history, why would some Jews resist Roman rule?***

## THE CHALLENGE OF CHRISTIANITY

Even faiths have histories. Like the Hebrew monotheism that undergirds Judaism or the central tenets of Zoroastriansm (Chapter 2), Christianity was (and is) the product of historical processes. It began with the teachings of Jesus, who lived and worked among his fellow Jews in rural Judea and Galilee around the year 30 C.E. It took root, however, in the Hellenistic world we studied in Chapter 4: the cosmopolitan, Greek-speaking cities around the eastern Mediterranean, which had now been absorbed into the Roman Empire.

## The Career of Jesus

Yeshua bar Yosef (Joshua, son of Joseph), known to the Greeks as Jesus, is one of the few figures of the ancient world—certainly one of the few commoners—about whose life we know a great deal. The earliest writings that mention Jesus specifically are the letters of his follower, Paul of Tarsus, a Hellenized Jew and Roman citizen who was active during the 50s and 60s C.E. These are closely followed by many different narratives of Jesus's life and teachings, most written between c. 70 and 100 C.E. Four such accounts were eventually included in the New Testament, a collection of Christian writings appended to the Greek text of the Hebrew Bible around the third century C.E. In their original Greek, these accounts were called *evangelia* ("good messages"); we know them as *gospels*, an Old English word that means the same thing.

Jesus was born around the year 4 B.C.E., a generation or so after Augustus came to power in Rome. (He was not born precisely in the first year of the Common Era as we now reckon it. When the monk Dionysius Exiguus first calculated time "in the year of Our Lord" during the sixth century, he made some mistakes.) When Jesus was around thirty years old, he was endorsed by a Jewish preacher of moral reform, John the Baptist, whom some considered to be a prophet. Thereafter, Jesus traveled widely around the rural areas of Galilee and Judea, preaching and displaying unusual healing powers. He accumulated a number of disciples, some of whom had political ambitions.

Around the year 30 C.E., Jesus staged an entry into Jerusalem during Passover, a major religious holiday that brought large and excitable crowds to the city. This move was interpreted as a bid for political power by both the Roman colonial government and the high-ranking Jews of the Temple. Three of the gospel accounts say that Jesus also drew attention to himself by physically attacking merchants and moneychangers associated with the Temple. The city's religious leaders therefore arrested him and turned him over to the Roman governor, Pontius Pilate, for sentencing.

Pilate's main concern was to preserve peace during a volatile religious festival. He also knew that his authority depended on maintaining good relations with local Jewish elites and with Herod, a recent convert to Judaism who ruled the province of Galilee in collaboration with Rome, as a client king of the empire. Because Jesus was a resident of Galilee, not a citizen of Roman Judea, Pilate sent Jesus to Herod for sentencing. But Herod sent him back to Pilate, politely indicating that dealing with Jesus fell under Roman jursidiction. So Pilate chose to make an example of Jesus by condemning him to death by crucifixion, the standard criminal penalty for those judged guilty of sedition. It had been rumored that Jesus planned to lead a rebellion, and something similar had happened in the second century B.C.E., when the Maccabbees overthrew Seleucid rule. Indeed, the Roman occupation of the region had only begun in 67 B.C.E. and was still resented by many Jews. Pilate would have been mindful of all this.

That might have been the end of the story. But soon after Jesus's execution, his followers began to assert that he had risen from the dead before being taken up into Heaven. Moreover, they said that Jesus had promised to return again at the end of time. Meanwhile, he had promised spiritual support to his followers in their own preaching missions. His entire career now had to be rethought and reinterpreted by his followers: in life, he had been a teacher and healer; in death, he had been revealed as something more. The evidence of this reinterpretation has come down to us in the letters of Paul and in the gospel narratives.

## Jesus and Second Temple Judaism

In 1947 an extraordinary cache of parchment and papyrus scrolls was discovered in a cave near Qumran on the shores of the Dead Sea. Over the course of the next decade, eleven more caves were found to house similar texts dating from the first century C.E. Only since the mid-1980s, however,

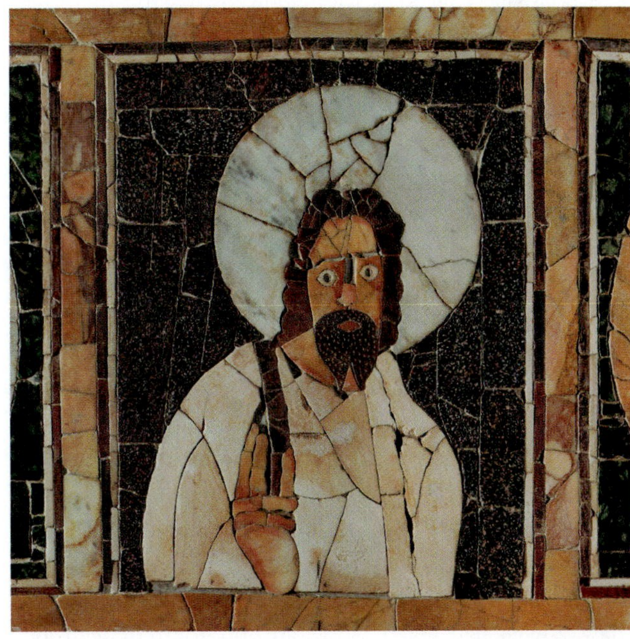

**JESUS.** This depiction of Jesus is from a third-century C.E. stone inlay.

have the texts of the Dead Sea Scrolls been widely available to scholars. Written in Hebrew, Greek, and Aramaic at various times between 100 B.C.E and 70 C.E., they have revolutionized our understanding of Judaism in the lifetime of Jesus, a period known as Second Temple Judaism. What these documents show, overwhelmingly, is the diversity of religious practice in this period, and the intense competition among groups of believers.

When Jesus was born, Roman rule in this region was still inspiring extreme responses. While many Jews were content to live under Rome's protection—especially the urban elite, who reaped the rewards of participation in the Roman economy and administration—there was talk of rebellion among rural communities and the urban poor. Many of those disadvantaged by Roman rule hoped for a messiah who would establish Jewish autonomy and a new Jewish kingdom. The most extreme of these were the Zealots, whose activities eventually led to two disastrous revolts. The first, between 66 and 70 C.E., ended in the Romans' destruction of the Temple that had been rebuilt when Cyrus the Great released the Jews from captivity in Babylon, 600 years earlier (Chapter 2). The second, in 132–35 C.E., caused the destruction of Jerusalem itself and prompted the Romans to expel the entire Jewish population. Whereas the first exile of the Jews had ended after fifty years, this new diaspora would not be reversed until the controversial establishment of the modern state of Israel in 1948. For over 500 years, Jerusalem even ceased to exist; on its ruins the Romans built the colony of Aelia Capitolina (Chapter 5). It was only in 638, when the Islamic Caliphate established Arab rule in the region and restored Jerusalem as a holy site, that Jews were allowed to settle there (see Chapter 7).

This political context is essential to understanding the circumstances of Jesus' death and the different messages conveyed by his words and actions. The Dead Sea Scrolls reveal that significant divisions had arisen among Jewish communities, and that Jesus participated in several key debates. In his lifetime, the hereditary Temple priesthood was controlled by a group known as the Sadducees, elite Jews who collaborated closely with Rome; the high priest of the Temple was even appointed by the Roman Senate. As a result of their overt political agenda, the Sadducees were regarded with suspicion by many. Their chief rivals were the Pharisees, preachers of religious doctrine who were heirs to the prophetic tradition of the First Temple period of the sixth century B.C.E. In contrast to the Sadducees, who claimed the right to control the interpretation of the Torah, the five books attributed to Moses, the Pharisees argued that Yahweh had given Moses an oral Torah as well as a written one, which explained how these books should be applied to daily life. This oral tradition had been handed down from teachers to students and was now claimed as the special inheritance of the Pharisees.

**PAUL OF TARSUS.** Many ancient images of Paul survive, and all depict him with the same features: a gaunt face, balding head, pointed black beard, and intense dark gaze. In the summer of 2009, archeologists working in the catacombs of Thekla (named after a holy woman and follower of Paul) discovered this faded fresco. It has been identified as the oldest known portrait of this formative Christian figure and can be dated to the fourth century C.E.

The Pharisees were accordingly quite flexible in the practical application of religious law. For example, in order to allow neighbors to dine together on the Sabbath (when Jews were forbidden to work, and could not even carry food outside their homes), the Pharisees ruled that an entire neighborhood could constitute a single household. They also believed in a life after death, a day of judgment, and the damnation or reward of individual souls. They actively sought out converts through preaching, and looked forward to the imminent arrival of the messiah whom God (through the prophets) had long promised. In all these respects they differed significantly from the Sadducees, who interpreted the Torah more strictly, who considered Judaism closed to anyone who had not been born a Jew, and who had a vested interest in maintaining the political *status quo*. Even more radical than the Pharisees was a faction known as the Essenes, a quasi-monastic group that hoped for spiritual deliverance through repentance, asceticism, and sectarian separation from their fellow Jews.

Although some scholars see Essene influence behind the career of Jesus, his Jewish contemporaries probably saw him as some sort of Pharisee. Jesus's emphasis on the ethical requirements of the law rather than its literal interpretation is reflected in many of his teachings. Jesus's apparent belief in life after death and the imminent coming of "the kingdom of God" also fits within a Pharisaic framework, as does his willingness to reach out to people beyond the Jewish community. Nevertheless, he seems to have carried these principles considerably further than did the Pharisees.

For most Jews at this time, Judaism consisted of going up to the Temple on holy days; paying the annual Temple tax; reciting the morning and evening prayers; and observing certain fundamental laws, such as circumcision (for men), ritual purity (especially for women), and prohibitions on the consumption of certain foods. Jesus de-emphasized such observances, and it may have seemed to some that he wished to abolish them. But what made him most controversial was his followers' claim that he was the messiah sent to deliver Israel from its enemies.

After Jesus's death, such claims grew more assertive, yet they never persuaded more than a small minority of Jews. But when Jesus's followers began to preach to non-Jewish audiences, they found many willing listeners. They began to represent Jesus in terms that made sense to the Greek-speaking communities of the Hellenistic world. Jesus, his followers now proclaimed, was not merely a messiah for

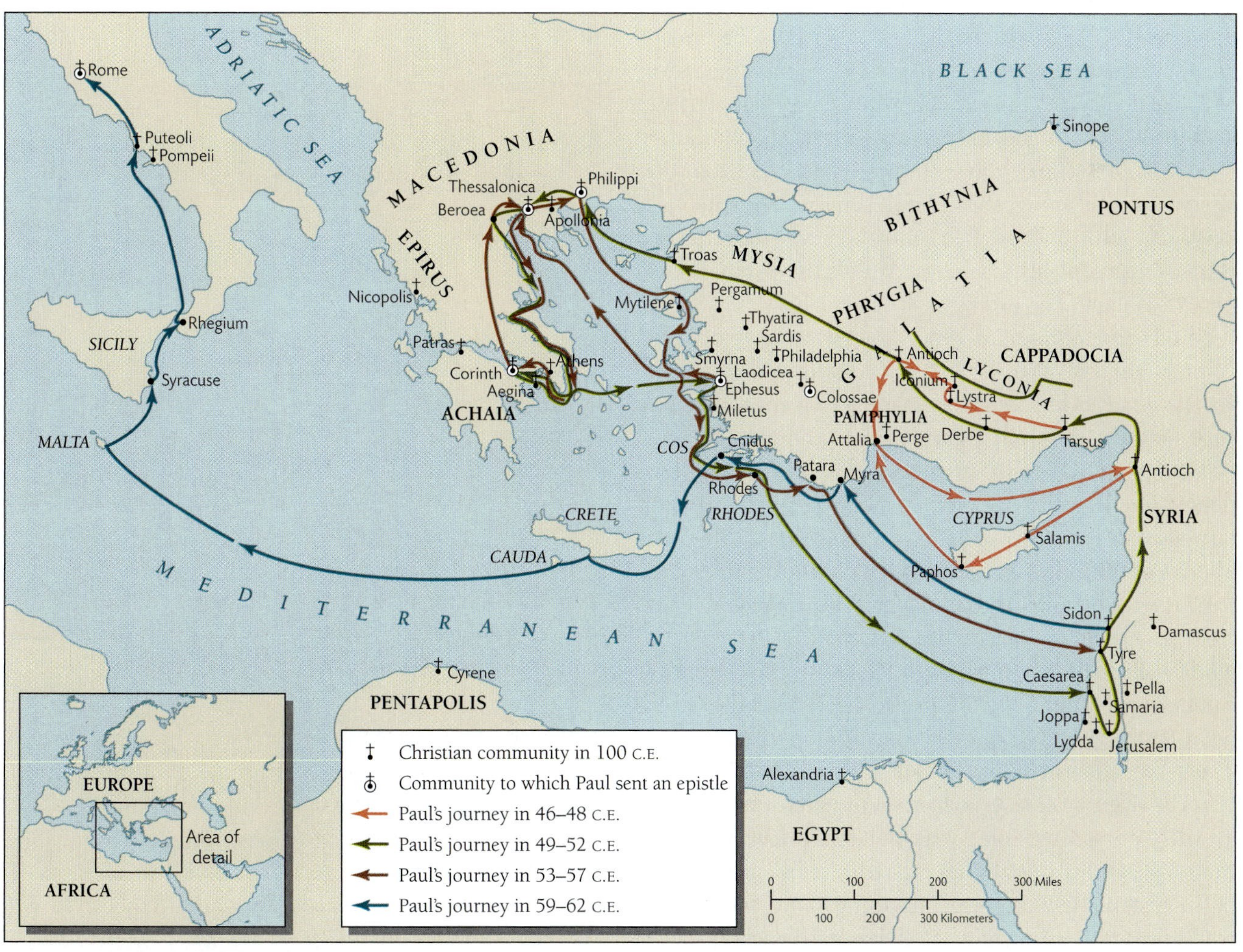


**PAUL'S MISSIONARY JOURNEYS.** Quite apart from its theological importance, Paul's career offers fascinating glimpses into the life of a Roman citizen from one of the empire's eastern provinces. ▪ ***What were the main phases of Paul's travels in the eastern Mediterranean?*** ▪ ***How were his itineraries shaped by geography and by various modes of transport?*** ▪ ***What conclusions about his mission can you draw from the extent of his travels and his major destinations?***

the Jews. He was the "anointed one" (in Greek, *Christos*), the divine representative of God who had suffered and died for the sins of all humanity. He had now risen from the dead and ascended into Heaven, and he would return to judge all the world's inhabitants at the end of time.

## Christianity in the Hellenistic World

The key figure to develop this new understanding of Jesus's divinity was his younger contemporary, Paul of Tarsus (c. 10–c. 67 C.E.). Named Saul when he was born in the capital city of the Roman province of Cilicia (now south-central Turkey), he was the son of a Pharisee and was staunchly sympathetic to that cause. The *Acts of the Apostles*, the continuation of Luke's gospel and a major source for Saul's early life, says that he was dedicated to stamping out the cult that had grown up around the crucified Jesus. But at some point in his mid-twenties—a few years after Jesus's death—he underwent a dramatic conversion experience, changed his name to Paul, and devoted the rest of his life to spreading the new faith to Greek-speaking, mainly non-Jewish communities.

Unlike Peter and some other early apostles (from the Greek word meaning "one who is sent forth"), Paul had never met Jesus. Instead, he claimed to have received a direct revelation of his teachings. This led to a number of major disputes. For example, Peter and his companions believed that followers of Jesus had to be Jews or converts to Judaism. Paul declared that Jewish religious law was now irrelevant; Jesus had made a new covenant possible between God and humanity, and the old covenant between God and the Jews no longer applied. This position was vehemently opposed by the Jewish Christians of Jerusalem, a group led by Jesus's brother, James. But after a series of difficult debates that took place around 49 C.E., Paul's position triumphed. Although some early Christians would continue to obey Jewish law, most of the converts who swelled the movement were Gentiles. Paul began to call this new community of believers an *ekklesia*, the Greek word for a legislative assembly convened by a public crier. The Latinized form of this word is translated as "church."

The earliest converts to Christianity were attracted for a variety of reasons. Some were Hellenized Jews like Paul himself. Jewish communities existed in most major cities of the eastern Mediterranean, including Rome, and had already begun to adapt their lifestyles and beliefs through contact with other cultures. Christianity also appealed to groups of non-Jews known as "God-fearers," who gathered around these Greek-speaking Jewish communities. God-fearers did not follow all the precepts of Jewish law, but they admired the Jews for their loyalty to ancestral tradition and their high ethical standards. Christianity was also attractive to ordinary cosmopolitan Greeks. Some saw Jesus as living by Stoic principles or as the embodiment of Ahura-Mazda, the good god of Zoroastrianism. Others were already devotees of mystery religions, like the very old cult of the Egyptian goddess Isis or the newer worship of the warrior-god Mithras, popular among Rome's professional soldiers. Both of these religions also revolved around stories of sacrifice, death, and regeneration and would have prepared their adherants to embrace the worship of Jesus. It was largely for the benefit of these converts that Christians began to practice elaborate initiation ceremonies such as baptism, a ritual purification common to many ancient religions and exemplified among Jews in the ministry of John the Baptist.

**A FRECSO FROM THE CATACOMBS OF ROME.** This image shows a catachumen (Greek for "instructed one") being baptized by the Holy Spirit in the form of an eagle. It is one of many paintings to be found in the ancient catacombs around Rome, subterranean burial and meeting places where Christians also hid during times of persecution. ▪ ***Why would such images have been important?***

**A CHRISTIAN LOVE FEAST.** This fresco, another image from the catacombs, shows Christians celebrating a feast. The inscription above it reads, "I join with you in love." ▪ ***How would a Roman viewer interpret this scene?*** ▪ ***How might this interpretation differ from that of a Christian?***

At the same time, there were significant differences between Christianity and these other religions. Most mystery cults stressed the rebirth of the individual through spiritual transformation, but Christianity emphasized the importance of community. By the middle of the second century, the Christian church at Rome had a recognizable structure, headed by a bishop (in Greek, *episcopos* or "overseer") and lesser officeholders, including priests, deacons, confessors, and exorcists. Women were extremely prominent in these churches, not only as patrons and benefactors (a role Roman women often played in religious cults) but also as officeholders. This high status accorded to women was unusual: in other ancient religions, women could be priests and officeholders but only in cults open solely to women; they never took precedence over men. Many cults, like Mithraism, denied them access entirely. The fact that Christianity drew its adherents from a broad range of social classes also distinguished it from other cults, which were accessible mainly to those with money and leisure. In time, these unusual features were distorted by Christianity's detractors, who alleged that Christians were political insurgents like the Jesus they worshiped, that they engaged in illict acts during their "love feasts," or that they practiced human sacrifice and cannibalism.

As both Christianity and Judaism redefined themselves during the second and third centuries, they grew further apart. Judaism was adapting to the destruction of the Temple and the mass exile of Jews from Jerusalem and surrounding provinces. By and large, the scholars who reshaped it during these difficult years ignored Christianity. It simply did not matter to them, any more than did the cults of Mithras or Isis. Christians, however, could not ignore Judaism. Their religion rested on the belief that Jesus was the savior promised by God to Israel in the Hebrew Bible. The fact that so few Jews accepted this claim was a standing rebuke to their faith, one that threatened to undermine the credibility of the Christian message.

More Christians could have responded as did Marcion, a second-century Christian scholar who declared that Jewish religious practices and the entire Hebrew Bible could be ignored. Most Christians, however, refused to abandon their religion's Jewish foundation. For them, the heroes of Jewish scripture prefigured Jesus, while the major events of Hebrew history could be read, allegorically, as Christian paradigms. Christ was the new Adam, reversing man's original sin: wood from the fateful Tree in Eden became the wood of the Cross. Christ, like Abel, had died at the hands of a brother and his blood continued to cry out from the ground. Christ was the new Noah, saving creation from its sins. Christ was prefigured in Issac, in Joseph, in Moses. All the words of the Hebrew prophets point to Jesus, as do the Psalms and the Proverbs. In short, Christian theologians argued that the Christian church is the true Israel, and that when the Jews rejected Jesus, God rejected the Jews and made Christians his new chosen people. The Hebrew Bible was henceforth the Old Testament, vital to understanding Christianity but superceded by the New Testament. At the end of time, the Jews would see the error of their ways and convert. Until then, their only reason for existing was to testify to the truth of Christianity. According to Christians, the Jews' own impiety had caused their exile from the Holy Land and would continue to bring suffering down on their descendants.

## Christianity and the Roman State

So long as Christianity remained a minority religion within the Roman Empire, such attitudes had no effect on the

# Analyzing Primary Sources

## *The Prosecution of a Roman Citizen*

*The* Acts of the Apostles *was written by the same author as Luke's gospel, and was intended as a continuation of that book. It recounts the adventures and ministry of Jesus' original disciples and also follows the career of Paul, a Hellenized Jew who became apostle to Gentiles throughout the Roman world. It offers fascinating glimpses into the workings of the Roman legal system because Paul, as a Roman citizen, had special rights under Roman law (as Jesus had not). In this passage, Paul has been accused of treason against the emperor by a group of Pharisees and has been sent to Felix, the governor of Judea. These events took place between 57 and 59 C.E.*

So the soldiers, according to their instructions, took Paul and brought him by night to Antipatris. The next day, they let the horsemen go on with him, while they returned to the barracks. When they came to Caesarea and delivered the letter to the governor, they presented Paul also before him. On reading the letter, he asked what province he belonged to, and when he learned that he was from Cilicia he said, "I will give you a hearing when your accusers arrive." Then he ordered that he be kept under guard in Herod's headquarters.

Five days later the high priest Ananias came down with some elders and an attorney, a certain Tertullus, and they reported their case against Paul to the governor. When Paul had been summoned, Tertullus began to accuse him, saying: "Your Excellency, because of you we have long enjoyed peace, and reforms have been made for this people because of your foresight. We welcome this in every way and everywhere with utmost gratitude. But, to detain you no further, I beg you to hear us briefly with your customary graciousness. We have, in fact, found this man a pestilent fellow, an agitator among all the Jews throughout the world, and a ringleader of the sect of the Nazarenes. He even tried to profane the temple, and so we seized him. By examining him yourself you will be able to learn from him concerning everything of which we accuse him." The Jews also joined in the charge by asserting that all this was true.

When the governor motioned to him to speak, Paul replied: "I cheerfully make my defense, knowing that for many years you have been a judge over this nation. As you can find out, it is not more than twelve days since I went up to worship in Jerusalem. They did not find me disputing with anyone in the temple or stirring up a crowd either in synagogues or throughout the city. Neither can they prove to you the charge that they now bring against me. But this I admit to you, that according to the Way, which they call a sect, I worship the God of our ancestors, believing everything laid down according to the law or written in the prophets. I have hope in God—a hope that they themselves also accept—that there will be a resurrection of both the righteous and the unrighteous. Therefore I do my best always to have a clear conscience toward God and all people. . . ."

But Felix, who was rather well informed about the Way, adjourned the hearing with the comment, "When Lysias the tribune comes down, I will decide your case." Then he ordered the centurion to keep him in custody, but to let him have some liberty and not to prevent any of his friends from taking care of his needs.

When some days Felix later came with his wife Drusilla, who was Jewish, he sent for Paul and heard him speak concerning faith in Christ Jesus. And as he discussed justice and self-control and future judgment, Felix was alarmed and said, "Go away for the present; when I have an opportunity I will summon you." At the same time he hoped that money would be given him by Paul. So he sent for him often and conversed with him. But when two years had elapsed, Felix was succeeded by Porcius Festus; and desiring to do the Jews a favor, Felix left Paul in prison.

Source: *Acts of the Apostles* 23:31–24:27, in *The New Oxford Annotated Bible*, New Revised Standard Version, eds. Bruce M. Metzger and Roland E. Murphy (New York: 1994).

### *Questions for Analysis*

1. Based on this account, what legal procedures are in place for dealing with any Roman citizen accused of a crime?
2. What seems to be the relationship between the Jewish elite of Judea and the Roman governor? What is the role of their spokesman, Tertullus?
3. What is the nature of the accusation against Paul, and how does he defend himself?

position of Jews under Roman rule. Judaism remained a legally recognized religion and many Jews were further protected by their Roman citizenship. Because of this, Paul could not be summarily put to death (as the noncitizen Jesus had been) when brought up on charges of treason. Instead, the *Acts of the Apostles* follows his progress through the Roman judicial system, until he was finally brought to trial at Rome and executed (by beheading) under Nero. Even the Jews of the diaspora were allowed to maintain the special status they had always had under Roman rule and were not required, as other subject peoples were, to offer sacrifices to the emperor as a god. As we have seen, nothing was more important to the Romans than *pietas* and respect for one's ancestors, and the Romans understood the Jews' traditions as a form of ancestor worship.

Christianity, by contrast, was a novelty religion. It carried neither the patina of antiquity nor the sanction of tradition. Quite the contrary. It raised suspicions on many levels: it encouraged women and slaves to hold office and therefore to rise above their proper stations; it revolved around the worship of a criminal condemned by the Roman state; its secret meetings could be breeding grounds for seditious activities. Nevertheless, the official attitude of the Roman state toward Christians was largely one of indifference. There were not enough of them to matter, and few of them had any political power. During the first and second centuries C.E., therefore, Christians were tolerated by Roman officials, except when local magistrates chose to make an example of someone who flagrantly flouted authority.

## THE CHALLENGE OF IMPERIAL EXPANSION

The emergence of Christianity within the Roman Empire coincided with the empire's most dramatic period of growth and, as a result, with a growing variety of challenges. For a long time, Rome's emperors and administrators clung to the methods of governance that had been put in place under Augustus, which were based on a single centralized authority. The reality, however, was that Rome's empire was no longer centered on Rome, or even on Italy. It embraced ecosystems, linguistic groupings, ethnicities, cultures, economies, and political systems of vastly different kinds. More and more people could claim to be Roman citizens, and more and more people wanted a share of Rome's power. This placed enormous stress on the imperial administration as the centrifugal forces of Rome's own making constantly pulled resources into her far-flung provinces, where cities had to be built, people governed, and communications maintained. The fact that the empire had no defensible borders was another problem. Hadrian had attempted to establish one after 122, by building a wall between Roman settlements in southern Britannia and the badlands of northern tribes (Chapter 5); but this act was more symbolic than defensive.

For much of the second century, such stresses were masked by the peaceful transfer of power among the so-called "Five Good Emperors": Nerva, Trajan, Hadrian, Antoninus Pius, and Marcus Aurelius. This harmonius state of affairs was partly accidental. None of these first four rulers had a surviving male heir, and so a custom developed whereby each adopted a young man of a good family and trained his successor in the craft of government. This sensible practice changed with the death of Marcus Aurelius in 180 C.E. Although he was the closest Roman equivalent to Plato's ideal of the philosopher-king, Marcus was not wise enough to recognize that his own son, Commodus, lacked the capacity to rule effectively. After his father's death, Commodus alienated the army by withdrawing from costly wars along the Danube. This move was also unpopular with the Senate, as were Commodus's violent tendencies and his scorn for the traditional norms of aristocratic conduct, including his appearing as a gladiator in the Colosseum. In 192, a conspiracy was hatched inside his own palace, where he was strangled by his wrestling coach.

### *The Empire of the Severan Dynasty*

Because Commodus had no obvious successor, the armies stationed in various provinces of the empire raised their own candidates. Civil war ensued, as it had during the crises of the late republic and in 68 C.E., when three men had struggled for imperial power. In this case, there were five major contenders. The eventual victor was a North African general called Septimius Severus (r. 193–211 C.E.).

Under Severus and his successors, the administration of Rome's empire changed to a greater extent than it had since the time of Augustus. In many respects, these changes were long overdue. Even the "Five Good Emperors" had been somewhat insulated from the realities of colonial rule. Many of them were able commanders, but they were not professional soldiers as Severus was. Another major difference was that fact that Severus had been born and raised in the North African town of Leptis Magna (now in Libya) and identified strongly with his father's Punic ancestors, seemingly more so than with his mother's patrician family. Unlike Trajan and Hadrian, who had also grown up in the provinces, Severus did not regard Rome as the center of the

# Competing Viewpoints

## *The Development of an Imperial Policy toward Christians*

*It was not until the third century that the Roman imperial government began to initiate full-scale investigations into the activities of Christians. Instead, the official position was akin to a policy of "don't ask, don't tell." Local administrators handled only occasional cases, and they were often unsure as to whether the behavior of Christians was illegal or criminal. The following letter was sent to the Emperor Trajan by Gaius Plinius Caecilius Secundus (Pliny the Younger), the governor of Bithynia-Pontus (Asia Minor), around 112 C.E. Pliny was anxious to follow proper procedures in dealing with the new sect and wanted advice about this. His letter indicates what Romans did and didn't know about early Christian beliefs and practices.*

### From Pliny to Trajan

It is my regular custom, my lord, to refer to you all questions which cause me doubt, for who can better guide my hesitant steps or instruct my ignorance? I have never attended hearings concerning Christians, so I am unaware what is usually punished or investigated, and to what extent.... In the meantime, this is the procedure I have followed in the cases of those brought before me as Christians. I asked them whether they were Christians. If they admitted it, I asked them a second and a third time, threatening them with execution. Those who remained obdurate I ordered to be executed, for I was in no doubt . . . that their obstinacy and inflexible stubbornness should at any rate be punished. Others similarly lunatic were Roman citizens, so I registered them to be sent back to Rome.

Later in the course of the hearings, as usually happens, the charge rippled outwards, and more examples appeared. An anonymous document was published containing the names of many. Those who denied that they were or had been Christians and called upon the gods after me, and with incense and wine made obeisance to your statue . . . and who moreover cursed Christ . . . I ordered to be acquitted.

Others, who were named by an informer, stated that they were Christians and then denied it. They said that they had been, but had abandoned their

universe, and the time he spent in the imperial capital as a young man seems to have convinced him that little could be accomplished there.

In fact, Severus represents the degree to which the Roman Empire had succeeded in making the world Roman—succeded so well that Rome itself was becoming irrelevant. One could be as much a Roman in Britannia or Africa as in central Italy. Severus's second wife, Julia Domna, exemplifies this trend in a different way. Descended from the Aramaic aristocracy who ruled the Roman client kingdom of Emesa (Syria), her father was the high priest of its sun-god Ba'al. She was highly educated and proved an effective governer during her husband's almost perpetual absence from Rome.

Severus largely ignored the politics of the Senate and slighted what remained of its powers. He preferred to rule through the army, which he reorganized and expanded. Two of his reforms had long-term consequences. The first was a drastic raise in army pay, probably as much as 100 percent, which had the effect of securing the soldiers' absolute loyalty and diminishing their need to augment their wages through plunder. The other was a relaxation of the longstanding rule forbidding soldiers to marry while still in service. This dispensation encouraged men to put down roots in local communities, but it also made them reluctant to move when their legion was called up. On the one hand, this domesticated the army (hitherto a highly mobile fighting machine) and may have made it less effective.

allegiance some years previously. . . . They maintained, however, that all that their guilt or error involved was that they were accustomed to assemble at dawn on a fixed day, to sing a hymn antiphonally to Christ as God, and to bind themselves by an oath . . . to avoid acts of theft, brigandage, and adultery. . . . When these rites were completed, it was their custom to depart, and then reassemble again to take food, which was, however, common and harmless. They had ceased, they said, to do this following my edict, by which in accordance with your instructions I had outlawed the existence of secret brotherhoods. So I thought it all the more necessary to ascertain the truth from two maidservants [i.e., slaves], who were called deaconesses, even by employing torture. I found nothing other than a debased and boundless superstition. . . .

## From Trajan to Pliny

You have followed the appropriate procedures, my Secundus. . . . [N]o general rule can be laid down which would establish a definite routine. Christians are not to be sought out. If brought before you and found guilty, they must be punished, but in such a way that a person who denies that he is a Christian, and demonstrates this by his action . . . may obtain pardon for his repentance, even if his previous record is suspect. Documents published anonymously must play no role in any accusation, for they give the worst example, and are foreign to our age.

Source: Exerpted from *Pliny the Younger: The Complete Letters*, trans. P. G. Walsh (Oxford: 2006), pp. 278–79 (X.96–97).

### *Questions for Analysis*

1. How does Pliny's treatment of Christians differ according to their social class? How does it differ from Felix's treatment of Paul (above)?
2. Why would Trajan insist that anonymous accusations, like those discussed by Pliny, should not be used as evidence? Why is this "foreign to our age"?
3. What do you conclude from this exchange about the relationship between religion and politics under the Roman Empire?

On the other, it gave the army a stake in the peaceful governance of Rome's colonies and further contributed to the decentralization of power.

Severus spent most of his imperial career with his army. He died at Eboracum (York) in 211, after conducting a series of successful negotiations with Pictish tribes north of Hadrian's Wall. On his deathbed, he is reported to have said to his sons, "Get along together, you two, keep the soldiers rich, and don't bother about anyone else." His elder son, Caracalla, didn't heed the first of these injunctions for long: by the end of the year, he had assassinated his brother, Geta. He then attempted to erase his brother from the historical record by declaring a *damnatio memoriae* (literally, "a condemnation of memory") that banned the

**THE EMPRESS JULIA DOMNA.** This Roman coin, dating from about 200 C.E., is one of several issued in the name of Severus's powerful wife. As the coin's legend shows, she ruled as "Julia Augusta," names associated with the imperial family since the time of Augustus Caesar.

mention of Geta's name and defaced his image on public monuments. The second of his father's orders he did obey, by extending the rights of Roman citizenship to everyone in the empire. This not only included the entire army in the franchise but increased the tax base. This was beneficial in some respects, but it may also have cheapened Roman citizenship, which was no longer a prize to be won through service or the adoption of Roman values and manners. Another indication of his populism was Caracalla's sponsorship of the largest public baths ever constructed in Rome, an enormous complex that would rival St. Peter's Basilica had it survived (the sprawling remains can still be seen). His father's final piece of advice helped to shorten Caracalla's reign significantly, since it exacerbated his already pronounced tendency to alienate everyone who disagreed with him. He was assassinated in 217.

**THE EMPEROR SEPTIMIUS SEVERUS.** This statue, carved during the emperor's lifetime, emphasizes his career as a military commander, showing him in the standard-issue uniform of a Roman legionnaire. How does this image of Severus compare to that of Augustus (see Chapter 5, page 161)? ▪ ***What do their differences suggest about the emperor's new role in the third century?***

Caracalla's true successor was his mother's sister, Julia Maesa, who ruled through his nominal heir and cousin, her adolescent grandson. This youth was known as Heliogabalus (or Elagabalus, r. 218–22) because of his devotion to the Syrian sun-god Ba'al. But when Heliogabalus caused controversy by attempting to replace Jupiter, Rome's patron god, with a Latinized version of this eastern deity, Sol Invictus ("Invincible Sun"), his own grandmother engineered his assassination. Another of her grandsons, Alexander Severus (r. 222–35 C.E.), took his place. Alexander, in turn, was ruled by his mother Julia Mamea, the third in a sucession of strong women behind the Severan dynasty, who even traveled with her son on military campaigns. This eventually proved fatal. The new prominence of the army made Rome's legions engines of political advancement even more so than under the dictators of the late republic. Many aspiring generals could harness this power, and with it the support of their legions' provincial bases. In 235, in consequence, Alexander and his mother were murdered at Moguntiacum (Mainz) in Upper Germania, when the army of the region turned against them. Nearly fifty years of civil unrest ensued. The Pax Romana was over.

## *The End of the Roman Peace*

From 235 to 284 C.E. there were no fewer than twenty-six "barracks emperors" in Rome: military commanders who, backed by a few loyal legions, struggled with one another and an array of problems. This period is sometimes called the "Third-Century Crisis" and interpreted as the time when the Roman Empire was nearly destroyed. It is more accurately interpreted as a time when the consequences of Roman imperialism made themselves acutely felt. Those aspects of the empire that were strong survived. Those that had always been fragile gave way.

The disruptions of the mid-third century exposed weaknesses in economic and administrative infrastructures. Inflation, caused by the devaluation of currency under Severus, nearly drained Roman coinage of its value.

Aspiring emperors levied exorbitant taxes on civilians in their provinces, while warfare among rival claimants and their armies destroyed crops and interrupted trade, causing food shortages. Because Rome itself was almost entirely dependant on Egyptian grain and other goods shipped in from the East, its inhabitants suffered accordingly. Poverty and famine led to a new form of slavery in Italy, as free artisans, local businessmen, and small farmers were forced to labor on the estates of large landholders in exchange for protection and food.

In 251, a terrible plague, probably smallpox, swept through the empire's territories and recurred in some areas for almost two decades. A similar plague had ravaged Rome a century earlier, but its effects had been mitigated by sound governance. Now, with an estimated 5,000 people dying every day in the crowded city, people sought local scapegoats. Christians were among those targeted. Beginning in the short reign of Decius (r. 249–51), all Roman citizens were required to swear a public oath affirming their loyalty to Rome, which meant worshipping Rome's gods. Those who did so received a certificate testifying to this fact, which they had to produce on demand. Large numbers of Christians were implicated when this edict was put into effect. The enlightened policies of earlier emperors were abandoned.

## The Reorganized Empire of Diocletian

As it happens, the most zealous persecutor of Christians was also responsible for reining in these wider destructive forces. Diocletian (r. 284–305) was a cavalry officer from the Roman province of Dalmatia (modern Croatia) who had risen through the ranks. He could have been another "barracks emperor," but he was determined not to be a victim of the cycle. Instead, he embraced the reality of Rome as a multicultural entity that could not be governed from one place by one person with one centralized bureacracy. He appointed a fellow officer, Maxentius, as co-emperor, putting him in charge of the western half of the empire and retaining the wealthier eastern half for himself. In 293, he delegated new authority to two junior emperors or "caesars," Galerius and Constantius. The result was a tetrarchy, a "rule of four," with each man governing a quarter of the empire, further subdivided into administrative units called *dioceses*. This system not only responded to the challenges of imperial administration, it was designed to secure a peaceful transfer of power, since the two young "caesars" were being groomed to take the place of the two senior "augusti."

Diocletian recognized that disputes over succession had been a fatal flaw of the Augustan system. Also unlike Augustus, who had cloaked the reality of power in the trappings of the republic, Diocletian presented himself as an undisguised autocrat. His title was not *princeps* ("first man"), but *dominus* ("lord"). In fact, his style of imperial rule borrowed more from the Persian model than it did from the Roman. Gone were the days of republican simplicity and the scorn of kingly pomp. Diocletian wore a diadem and a purple gown of silk interwoven with gold, and he introduced Persian-style ceremonies at his court.

**THE TETRARCHY: DIOCLETIAN AND HIS COLLEAGUES.** This grouping, carved from a valuable purple stone called porphyry, shows the two augusti, Diocletian and Maximian, embracing their younger ceasars, Galerius and Constantius. ▪ ***Why do you think that these rulers are portrayed with identical facial features and military regalia?*** ▪ ***What message does this convey?***

Under the Principate, the emperor's palace had been run like the household of any well-to-do Roman, only on a large scale. Diocletian, however, remained physically removed behind a maze of doorways, rooms, and curtains. Those lucky enough to gain an audience with him had to prostrate themselves, while a privileged few could kiss his robe. Too much familiarity with their soldiers had bred contempt for the "barracks emperors." As a soldier-turned-emperor himself, Diocletian was able to avoid this mistake.

Although Diocletian retained close personal control over the army, he took steps to separate military from civilian chains of command; never again would Roman armies make and unmake emperors. To control the devastatingly high rates of inflation that were undermining the economy, Diocletian stabilized the currency and attempted to fix prices and wages. He reformed the tax system. He even moved the administrative capital of the empire from Italy to Nicomedia in the Roman province of Bithynia (modern Turkey). Rome remained the symbolic capital of the empire, not least because the Senate continued to meet there. But Diocletian had little need for the Senate's advice. The real power lay elsewhere.

## THE CONVERSION OF CHRISTIANITY

By the beginning of the fourth century, the number of Christians living within the jurisdiction of Rome was statistically insignificant, probably no more than 5 percent of the total population in the West and possibly 10 percent of the Greek-speaking East. Still, it was making an impact,

**DIOCLETIAN'S DIVISION OF THE EMPIRE, c. 304 C.E.** ▪ *What areas did each of the four divisions of the empire cover?* ▪ *What seems to be the strategy behind the location of the four major capitals, both within their respective quarters and in relation to one another?* ▪ *What is the status of Rome itself, according to this map?*

and one of Diocletian's methods for promoting unity within the empire was to take a proactive stance against any group perceived as subversive. This meant reviving the policies of Decius and Valerian, but taking an even harder line. Those who could not show proof of their loyalty to Rome's gods were stripped of their rights as citizens. Christians who had been serving in the army or in government offices were dismissed. So were Manicheans, followers of the Persian prophet Mani (c. 216–276), whose teachings paralleled Zoroastrianism by positing an eternal struggle between the forces of good and evil. Indeed, Christianity and Manichaeism must have seemed very similar to outsiders, and both were implicated in a full-scale purge of religious dissidents in 303. This was the Great Persecution, a time when many Christians became martyrs—a Greek word meaning "witnesses"—to their faith.

## Christianity and Neoplatonism

Ironically, the very crises that prompted Diocletian's Great Persecution were contributing to a growing interest in Christianity. Its message of social justice and equality before God was attractive to those suffering from the breakdown of political, economic, and social structures. It also appealed to followers of a new and influential philosophical system called Neoplatonism ("New Platonism"), which drew upon the more mystical aspects of Plato's thought. Its founder was Plotinus (204–270 C.E.), a Hellenistic philosopher from Egypt who had many followers among the Roman upper classes.

Plotinus taught that everything has its source in a single supreme being. The material world, too, is part of this creation, but it is merely the residue of the divine, from which all spirituality has been drained. Human beings are thus composed of matter (bodies) and emanations of the divine (souls). This means that the individual soul, originally a part of God, is now separated from its divine source by the fact of its embodiment. The highest goal of life is therefore to attain spiritual reunion with the divine, through contemplation and acts of self-denial that will help to liberate the soul from its earthly bondage. Asceticism (from the Greek word meaning "exercise" or "training") was therefore a major focus. Plotinus and his followers believed that the body could be tamed by fasting and other forms of self-denial, and thus made a more fitting vessel for the soul.

Neoplatonism became so popular in Rome that it almost supplanted Stoicism. (Although the two philosophies shared some fundamental characteristics, Stoicism did not hold out the hope of union with the divine.) Neoplatonism also struck a blow at traditional Roman precepts, including the worship of ancestors and the devotion to the empire's gods. It was thus a natural ally of Christianity, and many important Christian theologians would be influenced by it, while many educated Romans found their way to Christianity because of it. This was not, however, the path by which Christianity's first imperial convert reached it.

## Constantine's Vision

In 305 Diocletian built a palace near his hometown of Split and retired there to raise cabbages—the first time a Roman ruler had voluntarily removed himself from power since Sulla had resigned his dictatorship, nearly four hundred years earlier (Chapter 5). Diocletian obliged Maximian to retire at the same time, and the two caesars Galerius and Constantius moved up the ladder of succession, becoming augusti of the East and West, respectively. But the transfer of power was not as orderly as Diocletian had intended. One of the candidates to fill the vacant post of ceasar was Constantius's son, Constantine, who was being trained at Galerius's court. But he was passed over, perhaps so that Galerius could pursue his own imperial agenda. So Constantine left Nicomedia and joined his father in Gaul. From there, father and son went to Britannia and campaigned on the northern borders until 306, when Constantius died and named Constantine as his successor. This infuriated Galerius, but with Constantine in control of a large army (the legions of Gaul and the Rhineland, as well as Britannia) he was forced to concede.

Meanwhile, war broke out among several other claimants to imperial authority, reducing Diocletian's tetrarchy to chaos. Constantine remained aloof from this struggle, waged mostly in Italy, and concentrated on securing his quarter of the empire. Beginning around 310, he also began to promote himself as a favored devotee of the sun-god Sol Invictus, whose cult had been revived by the emperor Aurelian (r. 270–75). This was a smart move. Increasingly, the "Invincible Sun" was associated not only with the Roman gods of light and war, Apollo and Mars, but also with Mithras, the cult popular with soldiers. It was increasingly popular in Rome as well, where the feast long dedicated to the sky-god Saturn, the Saturnalia, was now being celebrated as the rebirth of the sun after the winter solstice, on December 25.

From the worship of Sol Invictus to the worship of Christ was, at least for Constantine, a small step (see ***Interpreting Visual Evidence*** on page 190). In 312, Constantine decided to march on Italy, which was now in the hands of a man called Maxentius, who had declared himself emperor in the West and was trying to build up a coalition of supporters.

# Interpreting Visual Evidence

## *The Power of the Invincible Sun*

Roman emperors often linked their power with those of Rome's traditional gods, and they were also worshipped as gods in their own right. Look carefully at the following images and consider the visual language of power that came to be associated with Sol Invictus, "the Invincible Sun," and eventually with Jesus Christ.

A. This gold medallion was issued by Constantine in 313, a year after his victory at the Battle of the Milvian Bridge. The legend calls him "Invincible Constantine."

### *Questions for Analysis*

1. How did Constantine invoke the iconography of Sol Invictus (image A)? What messages did this imagery convey?
2. How might Constantine's use of this imagery after his initial conversion to Christianity have been interpreted by Christians? How might it have been interpreted by followers of Rome's other religions? Do you think it was designed to be ambiguous?
3. Scholars dispute both the dating and the significance of the mosaic found beneath St. Peter's Basilica (image B). Is it likely that this is a representation of Jesus as Sol Invictus? If not, how would you explain the later association of this pagan deity with the Christian God?

B. This mosaic comes from a necropolis (cemetery) found beneath St. Peter's Basilica in Rome. Its precise dating is in dispute, but it was made sometime between the mid-third and mid-fourth century.

Among them was the Christian community of Rome. It may have been this that gave Constantine the idea of currying favor in the same way, or it may have been divine inspiration that led him to emblazon Christian symbols on his banners and the shields of his soldiers the night before a major battle north of Rome, at the Milvian Bridge over the Tiber. According to later legend, Constantine had seen a vision of two intertwined letters inscribed on the sky, the first two letters in the name of Christ, and was told that "In this sign, you will conquer." He did.

In gratitude for his victory, Constantine showered benefits on the Christian clergy of Rome and patronized the construction of churches throughout the empire. He also forced Licinius, the augustus of the East, to join him in promoting religious tolerance when they met at Milan in 313. Their Edict of Milan guaranteed freedom of worship to all Rome's citizens, Christian and non-Christian. But it soon became apparent that Christianity was the favored faith of the imperial family and thus the pathway for anyone with political ambitions. Almost overnight, Christians ceased to be members of an illegal and often despised cult and became affiliates of a prestigious and profitable religion, one that was now attractive to the ruling classes. The entire basis of Christianity's appeal had changed.

**CONSTANTINE'S CHRISTIAN SYMBOL.** This fourth-century fresco shows the chi-rho symbol that Constantine claimed to have seen in the sky before his victory at the Milvian Bridge. Chi and rho are the first two letters in the Greek word *Christos.* Flanking this monogram are the first and last letters of the Greek alphabet, alpha and omega, which also refer to Jesus.

## From Illegal Sect to Imperial Institution

In his letters, Paul of Tarsus had addressed small Christian assemblies that he called churches (*ekklesiae*). Sometimes, he had even spoken of the whole Christian community as a church. But it is doubtful that Paul could have imagined a day when representatives of an official Church could meet openly, or a time when his letters to separate churches in Corinth, Ephesus, Rome, and elswhere would be gathered together in a single book.

Early Christianity had grown organically; it had not been designed as a religious system. It had no absolute teachings, apart from the words of Jesus reported in the gospels, which do not always agree on those teachings. And not all Christian communities had access to the same scriptures. Some churches had a few of Paul's letters, some had none. Some had bishops, priests, deacons, and other officeholders; some had only a handful of believers. Some counted women as their leaders; others disapproved of women in authority. Some had come under the influence of Neoplatonism or Manichaeism; others considered Neoplatonism and Manichaeism to be perversions.

In every respect, then, the Christianity that emerged after Constantine's conversion had to reinvent itself. Rituals and doctrines that had been formulated to suit the needs of small, scattered communities now had to be reconciled. Members of this new Church needed to agree on a shared set of beliefs. They needed a shared set of scriptures. They needed a chain of command. All of these fundamental structures had to be hammered out in a painful process that never quite managed to forge a common understanding. Historically speaking, this is hardly surprising. The varieties of Christianity had been too separate for too long, and they were the products of the same diversity that made the Roman Empire hard to govern. Indeed, the degree to which the Christians of the fourth century were able to agree on so many things is remarkable, given these challenges.

## The Hierarchy of the Church

When it came to organization, Rome's imperial administration provided practical models. Because the empire's basic unit of governance was the city, the city became the basic unit of ecclesiastical administration, too. Each major city now had a bishop who oversaw all the churches and also the rural areas of his diocese, a term borrowed from Diocletian's reorganization. Bishops of the empire's largest cities were called *metropolitans*, and those who ruled over the oldest and most prestigious Christian communities were called *patriarchs*. These patriarchal cities also jockeyed for preeminence: among the main contenders were Rome, whose inhabitants longed to be at the center of the world again; Alexandria, the capital of the Hellenistic world; and Constantinople, a new city founded by Constantine on the Hellespont between Europe and Asia. Which of these Roman cities should be the capital of the Roman Church?

The patriarch of Rome's claim rested on several foundations. Rome had long been venerated as the place where both Peter and Paul were martyred. And according to one of the gospels (Matthew 16:18–19), Jesus had designated Peter as his representative on earth. Peter's successors, the subsequent bishops of Rome, thus claimed to exercise the same powers. Rome's bishop also enjoyed some political advantages over other patriarchs. Unlike the bishop of the new imperial capital at Constantinople, he could act with more freedom because he didn't have to deal directly with the emperor. But as far as eastern bishops were concerned, the patriarch of Constantinople should exercise control over the entire Church. This division of opinion, the product of cultural differences and contemporary politics, would continue to affect the development of Christian institutions. In time, it would lead to a very real division within Christianity, one that has never been resolved.

## Orthodoxy, Heresy, and Imperial Authority

Christianity's new prominence also raised the stakes of disputes over its basic teachings. While followers of Jesus had disagreed about such matters almost since the time of his death, these disagreements were of little political consequence so long as Christianity remained an illegal movement. Under Constantine, however, doctrinal disputes had the potential to ignite riots and to undermine the credibility of the emperor. It was imperative, therefore, that these disputes be resolved, and through the active intervention of Constantine himself.

The most divisive theological issue of the early Church concerned the nature of God. Jesus had taught his followers that he was the Son of God, and that after his death he would leave behind him a comforting Spirit that would also be an emanation of God. Accordingly, many Christians believed that God encompassed a Trinity of equal persons: Father, Son, and Holy Spirit. But other Christians, influenced by Neoplatonism, rejected the idea that Jesus could be equal with God. Instead, they maintained that Jesus was part of God's creation and shared in his divine essence; but he was not equal to God, or eternal. This latter school of thought was called Arianism, after the Christian teacher Arius who espoused it. (It should not be confused with Aryanism, a modern racial concept.) After protracted struggles, Arianism was condemned as a heresy, a word that comes from the Greek verb meaning "to choose for oneself" and which became the Church's term for false beliefs punished with damnation. Yet many Christians continued to adhere to the Arian view.

This new emphasis on orthodoxy (Greek for "correct teaching") was another major consequence of Christianity's conversion. The beliefs of early Christians had been fairly simple: there is one God; Jesus is the anointed one who suffered and died for the sins of mankind and who was raised from the dead; in order to be saved, his followers must renounce sin. But now, beginning in the fourth century, Christian theology would become ever more complex. Christian intellectuals had to demonstrate that their beliefs could withstand intense philosophical scrutiny and that Christianity was superior to Hellenistic philosophy. Just as there were many different schools of Greek and Roman thought, so there arose many different interpretations of Christian doctrine. Before Christianity became a legal religion, any doctrinal disputes could only be addressed informally, by small groups of bishops meeting at local councils that had no power to enforce their decisions. In the fourth century, doctrinal disputes had real political consequences.

As a result, the Roman state became increasingly enmeshed in the governance of the Church. Constantine began this process in 325 C.E., when he summoned Christian representatives to the first ecumenical ("worldwide") meeting of the Christian community, the Council of Nicea, where Arianism was condemned and discrepancies over the canon of the Christian Bible were resolved. Constantine's successors carried this intervention much further. Gradually, they claimed to preside over Church councils as Christ's representatives on earth, which entitled them to decide what Christian doctrine should be. Some even violently suppressed Christian groups who refused to accept imperial mandates, labeled them heretical, and subjected them to ecclesiastical penalties—condemnation and excommunication from the Church—and to criminal penalties, too. Essentially, these imperial interventions were an extension of Augustan policies, which had made the emperor *pontifex maximus*, Rome's high priest. In the fourth century, it began to look as though this trend would continue, and that secular and spritual authority would be combined in the person of the emperor.

## New Attitudes toward Women and the Body

Women were conspicuously absent from the new hierarchy of the Church and were also barred from the decision-making process at Nicea. Even though they had long been deacons and may even have performed priestly duties, women were now firmly and completely excluded from any position of power. This was an enormous change, more fundamental than any other aspect of Christianity's conversion. Jesus had included many women among his close followers, and one of the early gospels now rejected from the biblical canon was ascribed to Mary Magdalene. Paul had relied on women to organize and preside over churches, and to finance his missionary journeys; he had declared in one letter (Galatians 3:28) that there should be no distinctions of gender, rank, or ethnicity among Christians. Women had been leaders of many early churches. Women like Perpetua were prominent among the martyrs, and were often regarded as prophets. These strong roles had always been controversial because they set Christianity apart from the traditional values of Roman society. But that had also been one of Christianity's main attractions.

What acounts for this drastic change? Three factors can be clearly identified. When Christianity was absorbed into the staunch patriarchy of Rome, it could no longer promote the authority of women effectively. As the Church came to mirror the imperial administration, it replicated the structures of governance that had been the province of men since the founding of the republic. The Church now had the capacity to exclude or censor writings that represented women as the companions of Jesus and founders of the religion based on his teachings. These efforts were so successful that it was not until after the Dead Sea Scrolls were discovered in 1947 that a gospel attributed to Mary Magdalene and other writings were known to exist.

The second factor leading to the marginalization of women was the growing identification of Christianity with Roman cults that emphasized masculinity, particularly the worship of Sol Invictus and the soldier-god Mithras. This was a deliberate strategy on the part of the Church. It is easier to convert people to a new religion if that religion is not wholly new, and embraces elements of other religions. In common with these two cults, as well as with many Eastern religions we have studied (like the worship of Osiris in Egypt), Christianity emphasized the heroic suffering and death of a male god and his eventual victory over death itself. Christ was increasingly identified with Sol Invictus and his birthday came to be celebrated on December 25, which marked the passing of the winter solstice and the return of lengthening days.

The third factor contributing to women's exclusion from power was the new emphasis on asceticism, which changed attitudes toward the body. As we noted above, Neoplatonism taught that the goal of life was to liberate the soul from the tyranny of bodily desires, a teaching that it shared with Stoicism. None of this was emphasized in the teachings of Christ. Quite the contrary: the body was celebrated as God's creation, and Christ himself had encouraged feasting, touching, bathing, and marriage. His followers insisted that he had been bodily resurrected, and that the bodies of all the faithful would be resurrected, too. Although early Christians had to be willing to sacrifice their lives for their faith, if need be, they were not required to renounce pleasures.

After Christianity became legal, however, there were few opportunities to "bear witness" to the faith through martyrdom. Instead, some Christians began to practice asceticism as an alternative path to sanctity. This meant renunciation of the flesh, especially sex and eating, activities both associated with women, who were in charge of any household's food supply and who were (obviously) sexual partners. A new spiritual movement called monasticism also took hold, providing an alternative lifestyle for men who wanted to reject the world entirely; the word for this movement and its followers comes from the Greek word *monos*, "alone." Early monks lived as hermits and practiced extraordinary feats of self-denial and self-abasement. Some grazed in the fields like cows, others penned themselves into small cages, while others hung heavy weights around their necks. A monk named Cyriacus would stand for hours on one leg, like a crane. Another, Simeon "the Stylite," lived on top of a high pillar for thirty-seven years, punishing his lice-infested flesh while crowds gathered below to marvel.

This extreme denial of the body was a departure not only from previous Christian practices but from the practices of nearly all civilizations up to this point—not to mention the realities of human existence. All ancient religions celebrated sexuality as a delight, as well as a necessity. Even Roman religion had a place for priestesses and female prophets. Moreover, marriage was so important a marker of social respectability that unmarried men were objects of deep suspicion. Furthermore, Romans had regarded citizens' bodies as being at the service of the state: men as soldiers and fathers, women as mothers and wives. Now, however, some Christians were asserting that their bodies belonged not to the state but to God, and that to serve God fully meant no longer serving the state—or posterity—by bearing children.

This was a revolutionary shift. Virginity for both men and women began to be preached as the highest spiritual standard, with celibacy for those who had once been married valued almost as highly. Marriage remained acceptable for average people, the laity, but was often represented as a second-best option whose purpose was to prevent weak-minded people from being consumed by desire. Moreover, because pseudo-scientific theories stemming back to Aristotle posited that women were inherently more lustful than men, the denigration of sexuality had a disproportionately negative effect on attitudes toward women.

## Christians and Pagans

The urban focus of Christianity is reflected in the Latin word referring to a non-Christian: *paganus*, meaning someone who lives in the countryside, a rustic. The implication is that only someone with a hopelessly ignorant outlook would cling to the old Roman religion and so spoil his chances of advancement in society. As Christians came to occupy positions of power within the empire, men with political ambitions were increasingly forced to convert—or at least conform—to Christian norms.

Constantine had retained both pagan and Christian officials in his court, and was careful to speak in terms that embraced a non-Christian audience. But his successors were less inclined to tolerate competing faiths. An interesting exception was Julian "the Apostate" (r. 360–63), Constantine's nephew, who abandoned Christianity and

**SAINT SIMEON THE STYLITE.** This gold plaque dating from the sixth century depicts the exertions of the ascetic saint who defied the devil (shown as a huge snake) by abusing his own body. Admirers wishing to speak to the saint could climb the ladder shown on the left. ▪ ***What do you make of the relationship between the luxurious medium of this image (gold) and the message it conveys?***

attempted to revive traditional Roman piety. But when Julian was killed in a battle with the Persians, his pro-pagan edicts were revoked. By 391, the emperor Theodosius (r. 379–95 C.E.) had prohibited pagan worship of any sort within the empire. Within three generations, then, Christianity had gone from being a persecuted faith to a persecuting religion. Theodosius even removed the sacred altar of the goddess Victory from the Senate house in Rome, prompting pagan loyalists to prophecy the end of the empire. Fifteen years later, Rome fell to a barbarian army.

## SHIFTING CENTERS AND MOVING FRONTIERS

In 324, Constantine broke ground for the capital city he named after himself. It was built on the site of a settlement called Byzantium, chosen for its strategic location at the mouth of the Black Sea and at the crossroads between Europe and Asia. This site gave Constantinople commanding advantages as a center for communications and trade. It also made the city readily defensible, because it was surrounded on three sides by water and protected on land by walls. It would remain the political and economic center of the Roman Empire until 1453, when the city was conquered by the Ottoman Turks (see Chapters 11 and 12).

### *East and West*

The founding of Constantinople epitomizes the shift in Rome's center of gravity from west to east. It signalled Constantine's intention to abandon the political precedents set by Diocletian, including the institution of the tetrarchy. Instead, the imperial succession became hereditary. Constantine thus embraced a principle of dynastic monarchy that Romans had rejected 800 years earlier. Even more ominously, he divided the empire among his three sons. Civil war ensued, made more bitter because each of these men represented a different faction within the Christian Church. In the meantime, the empire became more and more fragmented. The last ruler who could claim to govern a united Rome was the same Theodosius who outlawed its venerable religion. Then he, too, divided the empire between his sons.

As we have seen, there had always been linguistic and cultural differences between the Greek- and Latin-speaking peoples under Roman rule. Now, however, these differences were heightened. The East was becoming more populous, more prosperous, and more central to imperial policy; the West was becoming poorer and more peripheral. Many western cities now relied on transfers of funds from their eastern counterparts to keep them going and they suffered when these funds dried up, when trade or communication failed, or when Roman legions were transferred elsewhere. Rome itself, which had been demoted to provincial status under Diocletian, now lost even its symbolic position: the Italian city of Ravenna on the Adriatic coast became the new capital of the region and a more convenient stopping-place for emperors and ambassadors traveling from Constantinople to the administrative centers of Milan and Trier. Only two of Constantine's successors ever visited Rome, and none of them lived there.

# Analyzing Primary Sources

## *A Senator Defends the Traditional Religion of Rome*

*In 382 the Emperor Theodosius ordered the removal of the ancient altar dedicated to the goddess of Victory from the Senate chamber in Rome, as part of his efforts to make Christianity the dominant religion in the empire. This controversial move sparked heated debate and elicited strong protests from Rome's senatorial elites. The following statement of their case was made by Quintus Aurelius Symmachus (c. 345–402), who was at that time prefect of the city of Rome. It is principally addressed to the young Western emperor, Valentinian.*

To what is it more suitable that we defend the institutions of our ancestors, and the rights and destiny of our country . . . than to the glory of these times, which is all the greater when you understand that you may not do anything contrary to the custom of your ancestors? We demand then the restoration of that condition of religious affairs which was so long advantageous to the state. . . . Who is so friendly with the barbarians as not to require an Altar of Victory? . . . But even if the avoidance of such an omen were not sufficient, it would at least have been seemly to abstain from injuring the ornaments of the Senate House. Allow us, we beseech you, as old men to leave to posterity what we received as boys. The love of custom is great. . . . Where shall we swear to obey your laws and commands? By what religious sanction shall the false mind be terrified, so as not to lie in bearing witness? All things are indeed filled with God, and no place is safe for the perjured, but to be urged in the very presence of religious forms has great power in producing a fear of sinning. That altar preserves the concord of all, that altar appeals to the good faith of each, and nothing gives more authority to our decrees than that the whole of our order issues every decree as it were under the sanction of an oath. . . .

Let us now suppose that Rome is present and addresses you in these words: "Excellent princes, fathers of your country, respect my years to which pious rites have brought me. Let me use the ancestral ceremonies, for I do not repent of them. Let me live after my own fashion, for I am free. This worship subdued the world to my laws, these sacred rites repelled Hannibal from the walls, and the Senones [Gauls] from the capitol. Have I been reserved for this, that in my old age I should be blamed? I will consider what it is thought should be set in order, but tardy and discreditable is the reformation of old age." We ask, then, for peace for the gods of our fathers and of our country. It is just that all worship should be considered as one. We look on the same stars, the sky is common, the same world surrounds us. What difference does it make by what pains each seeks the truth? We cannot attain to so great a secret by one road; but this discussion is rather for persons at ease, we offer now prayers, not conflict.

Source: Excerpted from *A Select Library of the Nicene and Post-Nicene Fathers,* 2nd Series, Vol. X, (New York: 1896), pp. 411–14.

### *Questions for Analysis*

1. How does Symmachus' defense exemplify the traditional values of the Roman Republic?
2. How does Symmachus justify the coexistence of Christianity and Rome's state religion? How would a Christian refute his position?
3. Less than a decade after the altar's removal, Theodosius outlawed all religions but Christianity. Based on your reading of this letter, how would that edict have affected Romans like Symmachus?

## *Internal and External Pressures*

The shifting center of the empire and the widening gap between East and West were not the only fault lines emerging in this period. There were secessionist movements among many residents of Britannia, Gaul, Hispania, and Germania. The residents of Egypt were particularly affected by high levels of taxation, which targeted their rich agricultural lands. Meanwhile, North Africans and other citizens living in the empire's interior regions were increasingly ignored by authorities. Italians resented their new status as provincial subjects of Constantinople. Beneath the surface of imperial autocracy, the fourth-century empire was slowly dissolving into its constituent parts.

Rome was also coming under renewed pressure from its borders. Since the third century, the growing power of a new Persian dynasty, the Sassanids, had shifted military weight to the eastern frontier, reducing the number of troops stationed elsewhere. Partly as a result of this, the western empire suffered a devastating series of raids along the porous frontier of Germania. During the fourth century, relations between Romans and their non-Roman neighbors were generally peaceful, owing in part to the active presence of Constantius and Constantine in these territories. But starting in the early fifth century, a new wave of settlers moved into the empire's oldest provinces, permanently altering their histories and cultures.

## From the Periphery to the Center

In the eyes of their Roman neighbors, the tribes that lived along the empire's northern frontiers were barbarians in the pure sense of that (Greek) term: they did not speak either of the empire's civilized languages and they did not live in cities. But in no sense were they a savage people. They were settled agriculturalists and sophisticated metalworkers who had enjoyed trading relationships with the Roman world for centuries. Legionnaires from the hinterlands of Germania were core components in Roman armies. In some frontier areas, entire tribes had become Roman *foederati*, allied troops who reinforced Roman garrisons or took their places when legions were withdrawn. By the end of the fourth century, many of these tribes had even adopted the form of Christianity preached by disciples of Arius. Although this made them heretics from the perspective of the institutional Church, it also tied them more closely to Roman civilization. One general of mixed descent, Flavius Stilicho (359–408), was the military leader of the western empire under Theodosius.

What altered this relatively peaceful coexistence? Our study of many previous civilizations has prepared us to answer this question: the arrival of new peoples, and the subsequent struggle for land and resources. During the mid-fourth century, a group of nomadic herdsmen known as the Huns began to migrate westward from central Asia, into the region north and east of the Black Sea. Around 370, their arrival forced a number of other groups, notably the Goths, to migrate south and west—and in a hurry. Within a few years, they had reached the Roman frontier along the Danube River. The Goths had been clients of the Roman state for several centuries. But now they were refugees, and too numerous and too desperate to repel by force. The Romans therefore permitted them to cross the Danube and settle within the empire. In return for food and other supplies, they were to guard the region against other migrant groups.

Local officials, however, failed to uphold their end of the bargain. Instead, they forced the starving Goths to sell themselves and their children into slavery in return for food. In 378, the Goths revolted and the Roman army sent to suppress them was defeated at the battle of Adrianople. Peace was restored by accommodating the Goths' demands for goods and farmland and by enrolling them in the Roman army under their own military leaders. But when Theodosius divided the empire between his two young sons, their military advisors—including Stilicho, the de facto ruler of the West—constantly undermined one another. This provided an opening for Alaric, a young leader of the Goths, to advance his own agenda. Targeting the wealthier East, he led his army into Greece, looting or capturing many ancient cities, including Athens.

In a desperate attempt to halt these incursions, Alaric was offered a Roman military command and encouraged to move into Italy: the price of peace in the East was the West. Meanwhile, the Huns had arrived in the region corresponding to modern-day Hungary, forcing several other peoples westward toward the Rhine. On New Year's Eve in the year 406, a people known as the Vandals crossed the frozen Rhine and invaded Gaul. To repulse them, Stilicho (whose own father had been a Vandal) made an alliance with Alaric and his Goths. But Stilicho was deposed just a few months later, and he could no longer exercise any restraint on Alaric's actions.

Like Stilicho, Alaric seems to have wanted to win a permanent place for himself in the imperial hierarchy. But unlike Stilicho—and many Roman generals before him—he did not understand how to use violence as a means toward that end. His assault on Rome did not make him Rome's conqueror, it made him its destroyer. In 410, after a protracted period of siege, Alaric's army captured and sacked the city. But by now, Rome had little to offer in the way of either food or spoils. So many of the Goths moved on, eventually settling in southern Gaul and Hispania, where they established what came to be known as the Visigothic ("West Gothic") kingdom. Others, known as the Ostrogoths ("East Goths") remained in Italy. The Vandals set out for the Iberian peninsula, too, but ultimately crossed the Strait of Gibraltar to settle in North Africa. Other tribes, including the Franks and the Burgundians, followed the Vandals across the Rhine into Gaul and established kingdoms of their own.

A generation later the Huns—whose migrations had set all of these gears in motion—themselves invaded Roman territory under the leadership of their warlord, Attila. Britannia,

**THE MIGRATIONS OF ROME'S FRONTIER PEOPLES.** ▪ *What do the routes followed by these different peoples suggest about their identities and motives?* ▪ *Why did so many converge on Rome, even though the city was no longer the capital even of the western Roman Empire?* ▪ *Why did the Romans refer to them as "barbarians"?*

meanwhile, had been abandoned when its remaining legions were hastily withdrawn in 410. There, a mixed population of Romans and Celts were eventually overcome by invaders from northwestern Germania and Scandinavia: Angles, Saxons, and Jutes. These conquering tribes were so efficient that they dominated all but the westernmost and northern portions of the island within a few generations. Many Celts settled in the regions where Celtic languages are still spoken today, including Wales and Scotland. The rest of Britain became Angle-land: England.

The last Roman emperor in the West was an ineffectual usurper derisively known as Romulus Augustulus ("Little Romulus Augustus"). In 476, he was deposed by Odovacar, a chieftain who headed a mixed band of barbarians, Huns, and disgruntled Romans. Viewed from the perspective of Constantinople, this event was decisive: now it was not only "New Rome," it was the only Rome. And the only way its imperial agenda could be carried forward in the West was through a strong barbarian ruler. Luckily, the emperor Zeno (r. 474–91) knew just the man: Theodoric, the son an

**THEODORIC THE OSTROGOTH.** This coin shows the king in Roman dress but with the long hair characteristic of a barbarian nobleman. The inscription reads *Rex Theodericvs pivs princis*, "King Theodoric, pious prince." ▪ ***How does this image compare to that of Constantine (see page 190)?***

Ostrogothic king who had been sent to Constantinople as a hostage and raised in the civilized surroundings of the imperial court. After a decade of fierce fighting, Theodoric and his imperially equipped Gothic army managed to drive the Huns from Italy and establish an Ostrogothic kingdom based in Ravenna, which he ruled (with imperial support) until his death in 526.

## The Impact of the Fifth-Century Migrations

The events of the fifth century exposed the fragility of the empire's northern boundaries but penetrated to its core provinces: Italy, Gaul, Hispania, North Africa. Yet the groups that moved through these territories were small. They were joined by refugees and desperados, but they were never more than war-bands. So why couldn't long-established imperial cities sustain themselves?

By the beginning of the fifth century, many Roman armies in the West were already weakened. The best legions had been withdrawn from frontier provinces to protect the richer East. Those that remained tended to be integrated into local civilian populations, staffed by married men who grew their own food and lived with their families, making it difficult to move troops even in an emergency. Furthermore, there was no mechanism for increasing the revenues needed to support the army. And even if the citizens of Rome's western provinces had been able to maintain a crack fighting force on the frontier, there would have been little reason for them to think that such expenditure was necessary. Their "barbarian" neighbors hadn't seemed threatening for generations. Many were so Romanized that cultural differences are difficult to trace.

In the eastern Roman Empire, a thriving economy made it easier to equip and maintain a strong fighting force. Cities remained centers of commerce and industry, which meant that citizens possessed greater taxable wealth and could sustain the burdens of the imperial bureaucracy more easily. Moreover, potential invaders could be bought off or bribed to direct their attention elsewhere—as Alaric had been. For all these reasons, the eastern empire prospered during the fifth century, while the western empire floundered. After the fifth-century migrations, these differences were exacerbated. Every territory that was plundered or occupied represented tax revenues lost, and the scale of these losses was enormous. Ten years after the Goths sacked Rome, the area was capable of producing only 15 percent of the revenues it had generated in 407. Similar reductions in revenues resulted from attacks on Gaul and Hispania. After 420 or so, as the newcomers began to set up their own kingdoms, these areas ceased to pay any taxes at all to imperial authorities. When the Vandals captured North Africa in 439, the richest of all Rome's western provinces was lost.

The consequences of these structural changes were far-reaching. In the year 400, the economy of the western Roman Empire was characterized by the mass production of low-cost, high-quality consumer goods that circulated in massive quantities. Although regional and local systems of exchange continued after 500, long-distance trade in bulk goods could be sustained only in the East. As markets disappeared in the West, skilled artisans had to find other ways to make a living, or had to emigrate. Standards of living declined and so did the overall population. It is likely that the population of western Europe did not return to its fourth-century levels for a thousand years, until just before the Black Death (see Chapter 10).

Other aspects of Roman life in the West changed, too, but more gradually—almost imperceptibly. Roman bureaucracies often survived, although the proceeds from taxes now went into the purses of the new barbarian rulers or Christian bishops. Roman agricultural patterns continued in most areas, frequently under the same landlords. Roman aristocrats continued to dominate civic life, and Roman cities continued to dominate their surrounding regions, especially in southern Gaul and Hispania. Nor did the invasions bring an end to Roman culture or to the influence of Roman values. As King Theodoric the Ostrogoth was fond of remarking: "An able Goth wishes to be like a Roman; but only a poor Roman would want to be like a Goth."

## THE SHAPING OF A NEW WORLDVIEW

Throughout these upheavals, Christian intellectuals were formulating a new outlook on the world that would remain dominant until the sixteenth century. As the empire succumbed to attack from external forces, it seemed clearer than ever that a new age was beginning. Christ had promised to come again at the end of time, when all human souls would be judged. How, then, should Christians live in this new world and prepare for that imminent event? The men who forged answers to this question were contemporaries who knew and influenced one another, though they did not always agree. They are now regarded as saints and "fathers" of the Church: Jerome (c. 340–420), who came from the northeastern edge of Italy, near the port of Aquilea; Ambrose (c. 340–397), who grew up in Trier and was eventually named bishop of Milan; and Augustine (354–430), born and raised in North Africa, where he became a bishop in later life.

### *Jerome: Translating the Christian Message*

Jerome's signal contribution to the culture of the West was his translation of the Bible from Hebrew and Greek into Latin. Known as the Vulgate or "common" version, it was not the first attempt to produce a Latin Bible, but it quickly became the standard—and remained so until the sixteenth century (see Chapter 13). Jerome's translation is vigorous, colloquial, and clear; its powerful prose and poetry would influence Latin authors for a thousand years. Jerome was also an influential commentator on the Bible's interpretation, encouraging readings that emphasized a passage's symbolic or allegorical significance, as well as its literal or historical meaning.

Jerome was not a notably original thinker, but he was an eloquent and effective translator of others' ideas, as well as of others' words. He was among the first to argue that pagan learning could and should be studied by Christians, so long as it was thoroughly adapted to Christian aims. The perennial problem, of course, was that one was always tempted to appreciate literature for its own sake, and not for the light it shed on Christian truths. Jerome himself never succeeded in subordinating his love for classical authors to his love for God. He liked to tell a story about a dream he'd experienced, in which he arrived at the gates of Heaven and was asked by God if he were a Christian. When he replied that he was, God retorted, "You're not a Christian; you're a Ciceronian." Perhaps in an effort to compensate for this, Jerome became a rigorous ascetic and a fervent promoter of monasticism. He also held a narrow view of women's roles that exercised a strong influence on some later Christian teachers.

### *Ambrose and the Authority of the Church*

Jerome was primarily a scholar. Ambrose, by contrast, was an aristocrat and man of the world who helped to define the relationship between the sacred authority of the Church and the secular authority of worldly rulers. As patriarch of the administrative capital at Milan, he fearlessly rebuked the pious emperor Theodosius for massacring innocent civilians in one of his periodic purges of pagan communities. Theodosius may have been the emperor, but until he did penance for his sins Ambrose refused to admit him into his church. On matters of faith, he declared, "The emperor is within the Church, not above the Church." Eventually, Theodosius capitulated and begged forgiveness of God's representative, Ambrose, in his cathedral at Milan.

Ambrose was also an admirer of Cicero, but because of his Stoicism, not his prose. He wrote an ethics handbook, *On the Duties of Ministers*, that drew heavily on Cicero's treatise *On Duties*, written nearly four centuries earlier for the senatorial elite of the Roman Republic. Unlike Cicero, however, Ambrose argued that the motive and goal of human conduct should be reverence for God, not social or political advancement. Even more fundamentally, Ambrose argued that God assists all Christians by sharing with them the power of divine grace, but extends more grace to some Christians than to others. Ambrose's emphasis on the necessity and mystery of grace (Why does God give more grace to some than to others?) would be refined and amplified by his disciple, Augustine.

### *The Salvation of Saint Augustine*

Apart from Jesus, Augustine is often considered the greatest of all Christianity's founders. He may be the most important Christian thinker of all time. His theology is essential to the doctrine of the medieval Church and thus to modern Catholicism, and it also had a profound effect on Martin Luther and on the development of Protestant Christianities (see Chapter 13). In the twenty-first century, many Christian philosophers of various denominations describe themselves as neo-Augustinians.

Augustine's understanding of Christianity was the result of a long process of self-discovery that he described

# Analyzing Primary Sources

## Roman or Barbarian?

*These two letters from Sidonius Apollinaris (c. 430–c. 480) illustrate the ways in which cultural assimilation was rapidly blurring the distinctions between "Roman" and "barbarian" in the West. Sidonius was himself the descendant of an illustrious Roman provincial family in Gaul. He was one of the most admired Latin stylists of his day, and although he eventually became a bishop and was regarded as a saint, his letter collection (from which these extracts are taken) tells us much more about the literary culture of Romano-Visigothic Gaul than it does about his Christianity. His two correspondents also exemplify this new hybrid culture. Arbogastes was the Frankish governor of the Roman city of Trier (in what is now Germany). Syagrius was from an ancient Roman family and became, effectively, the king of a large region now corresponding to northern France and Belgium.*

### *Letter 4:17: Sidonius to his Friend Arbogastes*

My honored Lord, your friend Eminentius has handed me a letter written by your own hand, a really literary letter, replete with the grace of a threefold charm. The first of its merits is certainly the affection which prompted such condescension to my lowly condition, for if not a stranger I am in these days a man who courts obscurity; the second virtue is your modesty. . . . In the third place comes your urbanity, which leads you to make a most amusing profession of clumsiness, when as a matter of fact you have drunk deep from the spring of Roman eloquence and, dwelling by the Moselle, you speak the true Latin of the Tiber: you are intimate with the barbarians but are innocent of barbarisms, and are equal in tongue, as also in strength of arm, to the leaders of old, I mean those who were wont to handle the pen no less than the sword. Thus the splendor of the Roman speech, if it still exists anywhere, has survived in you, though it has long been wiped out from the Belgian and Rhenic lands: with you and your eloquence surviving, even though Roman law has ceased at our border, the Roman speech does not falter. For this reason . . . I rejoice greatly that at any rate in your illustrious breast there have remained traces of our vanishing culture. If you extend these by constant reading you will discover for yourself as each day passes that the educated are no less superior to the unlettered than men are to beasts.

in a remarkable book, the *Confessions*, a series of autobiographical reflections addressed to God. Augustine was not, as Jerome and Ambrose were, a confident Christian from the cradle. His father was a pagan, and although his mother was a Christian he scorned her influence and refused baptism. Full of ambition and eager to make his mark, he left North Africa for Italy as a young man, winning early fame as a teacher and charismatic orator. All the while, he gravitated from one philosophical system to another without finding intellectual or spiritual satisfaction. He regarded Christianity as a religion for fools, and only his increasing doubts about the alternatives (notably Manichaeism) and the appeal of Ambrose's teachings drove him to enquire further. After a spiritual epiphany described in his *Confessions*, Augustine decided at the age of thirty-three to embrace Christianity. Yet his struggle to grasp and explain its paradoxes occupied him for the rest of his life. His skills as a preacher and commentator led to his rapid advancement in the Church hierarchy, and he returned to North Africa as the bishop of Hippo Regis in 395.

Although he led an extremely active life—when he died in 430, he was defending Hippo against the Vandals—Augustine still found time to write more than a hundred profound, complex, and powerful treatises analyzing the problems of Christian belief. All of these grapple with a basic question: if humanity is the creation of an omnipotent God whose nature is entirely good, why are human beings so profoundly sinful? Augustine was convinced of humans' capacity for evil, and he believed this tendency was evident even in babies. He adduced himself as a supreme example.

*Letter 5:5 Sidonius to his Friend Syagrius*

You are the great-grandson of a consul, and in the male line too—although that has little to do with the case before us; I say, then, you are descended from a poet, to whom his literary glory would have brought status had not his magisterial glories done so . . . and the culture of his successors has not declined one whit from his standard, particularly in this respect. I am therefore inexpressibly amazed that you have quickly acquired a knowledge of the German tongue with such ease.

And yet I remember that your boyhood had a good schooling in liberal studies and I know for certain that you often declaimed with spirit and eloquence before your professor of oratory. This being so, I should like you to tell me how you managed to absorb so swiftly into your inner being the exact sounds of an alien race, so that now after reading Virgil under the schoolmaster's cane and toiling and working the rich fluency of [Cicero] . . . you burst forth before my eyes like a young falcon from an old nest.

You have no idea what amusement it gives me, and others too, when I hear that in your presence the barbarian is afraid to perpetrate a barbarism in his own language. The bent elders of the Germans are astounded at you when you translate letters, and they adopt you as umpire and arbitrator in their mutual dealings. . . . And although these people are stiff and uncouth in body and mind alike, they welcome in you, and learn from you, their native speech combined with Roman wisdom.

Only one thing remains, most clever of men: continue with undiminished zeal, even in your hours of ease, to devote some attention to reading; and, like the man of refinement that you are, observe a just balance between the two languages: retain your grasp of Latin, lest you be laughed at, and practice the other, in order to have the laugh of them. Farewell.



### *Questions for Analysis*

1. For what qualities does Sidonius praise Arbogastes? What might have been the motive behind his extravagant compliments?
2. For what different qualities does Sidonius praise Syagrius? Given that Syagrius controlled much of the former Roman province of northern Gaul, what would have been his reasons for learning the local language?

In the *Confessions*, he remembers that he and a few other boys once stole some pears from a neighbor's garden, not because they were hungry or even because the pears were beautiful, but simply for the sake of doing something bad. He also recounted his many sexual adventures as a young man, and recalled that rather than asking God's help in suppressing his desires he prayed, "O God, give me chastity—but not just now!" In short, he argued that the human inclination toward evil is innate. But how, if we are the creatures of a good God?

Augustine traced the origin of evil back to the Garden of Eden, where God had given Adam and Eve, the first human couple, the freedom either to follow his will or their own. Thereafter, God simply left Adam and Eve's descendants to do the same, by withdrawing from human beings the divine power (grace) by which they might overcome their own wills in order to follow his. All the evils that plague the world are thus the result of the human propensity to place their own desires ahead of God's. This fact alone would justify God's condemnation of all mankind. But because God is merciful, he chose instead to save some human beings through the sacrifice of his son, Jesus.

Why only some? Because human beings are inherently sinful, Augustine reasoned, they cannot achieve salvation on their own; they need to be led to accept Jesus by an act of God's grace. (Hence the power of Augustine's own transformative experience, which led him to embrace Christianity *against his own will* but in accordance with God's.) God alone makes this choice, and by granting grace to some and not to others he predestines a portion of the human race to salvation and sentences the rest to be damned. If this seems unfair, Augustine would answer that strict fairness would condemn everyone to Hell. Moreover, he would say that the basis for God's choice is a mystery shrouded in his omnipotence—far beyond the realm of human comprehension.

**THE CITY OF MAN.** This image illustrating a late-medieval manuscript of Augustine's *City of God* displays the violence that characterizes the City of Man by showcasing one example from the Old Testament and another from Roman mythology: Cain kills his brother, Abel, while Romulus murders his brother, Remus. Its message is that all human forms of government are the product of human sin.

### *Defending the City of God*

Augustine's audience consisted of converted Christians and intelligent skeptics like himself. And after the sack of Rome in 410, he knew that some staunch Romans blamed Christianity for it. According to them, the attack on their city was the consequence of gross impiety, exemplified by the removal of the altar of Victory from the Senate chamber. In reponse, Augustine wrote one of his most famous works, *On the City of God*, a new interpretation of human history. He argued that mankind has always been divided into two opposing societies: those who live for the world and those who seek eternal life. The former belong to the City of Man, and their rewards are the riches, fame, and power they may win on earth, all of which are tainted by sin. Only those predestined to salvation, members of the City of God, will be saved on Judgment Day.

Although Augustine is the architect of much Christian theology, he believed that he was doing no more than drawing out truths from the Bible. But he also knew that many biblical texts are obscure and that a certain amount of education is needed to understand them. In consequence, he approved of some Christians' acquiring a classical education, as he himself had done, so long as they directed their learning toward its proper end: the study of the Bible. Along with Jerome, Augustine thus formulated the rationale for Christianity's preservation of the pagan past.

## CLASSICAL LEARNING AND THE CHRISTIAN LIFE

Jerome, Ambrose, and Augustine were members of the first generation to grow up in a world where Christianity was legal, even normal. For three centuries there had been no such thing as a Roman Christian: this was a contradiction in terms. Now, however, many Romans *were* Christians. How could these identities be reconciled? As we have seen, none of these influential teachers wanted to discard the heritage of the past. But for all of them it posed serious challenges. Many new converts thought they could embrace both Christian and pagan beliefs simultaneously—and why not? Since the time of Socrates, philosophy had been characterized by its capacity to absorb and blend many competing ideas. Christian intellectuals wanted to be regarded as philosophers, but they also wanted to replace the doctrines of pagan philosophy with the doctrine of Christ. To do this, they needed to make classical learning applicable to a Christian way of life.

### *Preserving and Recycling the Classics*

Reinterpreting classical culture for a Christian audience involved careful selection, something made easier by the fact that a gradual winnowing of Greek texts had already occurred in Alexandria and continued in Rome. Roman readers had little interest in the scientific works of an earlier age, and by the third century many extraodinary advances made by Hellenistic scientists (Chapter 4) were ignored, simplified, or suppressed by popular authors like Galen and

Ptolemy. Nor did the Romans have much interest in Greek philosophy, drama, or epic. Later Roman tastes ran toward comedies, novels, and pastiches of Latin classics. One favorite pastime consisted of rearranging the verses of Virgil's *Aeneid* so that they described sexual exploits. Christians, too, could play at this game. In the fourth century, Faltonia Betitia Proba (c. 322–c. 370), the wife of a Roman senator, used Virgil's poetry to replace Aeneas with Christ.

Those pagan authors whose works were most immediately useful to Christians, like Cicero and Virgil, therefore enjoyed continued celebrity. Those texts that had long educated students in the liberal arts were also preserved, as were major classics of Latin poetry as well as histories that recorded the errors of Rome's pagan past. But texts that could not be readily adapted were subjected to careful editing. One of the men who undertook this task was Anicius Manlius Severinus Boethius (*boh-EE-thee-us*, c. 480–524), an aristocrat attached to the court of Theodoric. He is often described as the "last of the Romans," and his goal was to preserve the best aspects of ancient learning by compiling a series of handbooks and anthologies which packaged and explained classical texts in ways appropriate for Christian readers.

Boethius devoted special attention to logic, translating several of Aristotle's treatises from Greek into Latin. Because Roman philosophers had never been much interested in logic, Boethius thus forged a crucial link between classical Greek thought and the new intellectual culture of Christianity. This is most evident in *The Consolation of Philosophy*, which he wrote in prison after Theodoric condemned him to death for treason. (The justice of the charge is unclear.) In this treatise, Boethius concludes that happiness is not found in earthly rewards such as riches or fame but in the "highest good," which is God. Yet he comes to this realization not through any reference to Christian revelation but through a series of imaginary conversations with "Lady Philosophy," the embodiment of wisdom. For the next millennium, Boethius's *Consolation* was one of the most read and imitated books in the West: the ultimate example of classical philosophy's absorption into the Christian worldview.

## Monastic Education

The vital work of preserving selected classics and interpreting their meaning was increasingly done by monks, whose way of life had undergone some significant changes during the fourth century. Leaders of the monastic movement recognized that few men were capable of ascetic feats, and some disapproved of such showmanship. Rather, they advocated a more moderate approach and emphasized the benefits of communal life. In the East, the most important figure in this new monasticism was Basil of Caesarea (c. 330–379). Basil's guidelines prohibited monks from engaging in prolonged fasts or extreme discipline of the flesh. Instead, he encouraged useful work and silent meditation.

In the West, the most influential proponent of the monastic movement was a contemporary of Boethius, Benedict of Nursia (c. 480–c. 547), the son of a Roman nobleman. Benedict founded a monastery at Monte Cassino, southeast of Rome, where he urged his followers to adopt "a simple rule for beginners." Adapted from a much harsher set of precepts called *The Rule of the Master*, Benedict's *Rule* is notable for its brevity, flexibility, and practicality. It established a carefully defined cycle of daily prayers, lessons, and communal worship. It laid down guidelines for what monks should eat (a sufficiency of simple food, a small amount of wine, meat only for the sick or on special occasions) and how the work of the monastery should be performed. Physical labor was encouraged—idleness, Benedict declared, was "an enemy of the soul"—but there was also time for private study and contemplation. In all such matters, Benedict left much to the discretion of the leader of the monastery, whom all the monks were expected to obey without hesitation. This man was the abbot, from the Syriac word *abba*, "father."

## Cassiodorus and the Classical Canon

Benedict was no admirer of classical culture, but he did believe that monks must study the Bible, in order to perform their daily cycle of prayers properly and to participate fully in a life of worship. This meant they had to be educated along the lines prescribed by Augustine. And because many monks entered religious life as children, the monastery would need to provide schooling. Through this somewhat roundabout path, classical learning entered the monastic curriculum.

The man largely responsible for this was Flavius Magnus Aurelius Cassiodorus Senator (c. 490–c. 583), a younger contemporary of Benedict. Like Boethius, Cassiodorus was attached to Theodoric's court and was for many years the secretary in charge of the king's correspondence. He also wrote a *History of the Goths*, which depicted Theodoric's people as part of Rome's history. After Theodoric's death, Cassiodorus founded an important monastery at Vivarium in southern Italy. There, he composed commentaries on the Psalms as well as his most influential work, the *Institutes*. Inspired by Augustine and his own classical education, Cassiodorus believed that study of classical literature was an essential preliminary to a proper understanding of the

**CASSIODORUS.** This frontispiece from a Bible, produced in a monastery in Britain around the year 700, depicts Cassiodorus as a copyist and keeper of books. Monasteries were instrumental in changing the form of the book from the ancient scroll to the modern codex. Because their parchment pages were heavy, codices were customarily stored in cupboards, lying flat, as we see them here.

Bible. The *Institutes* is essentially a syllabus, a list of readings arranged so that a monk would begin with simpler, straightfoward works of pagan literature before moving on to more difficult works and finally to the demanding study of theology. Cassiodorus thereby defined a classical canon that formed the basis of Christian education in the West for a thousand years.

In order to ensure that his monks had access to the necessary readings, Cassiodorus encouraged the copying of books. He argued that this was precisely the sort of manual labor that Benedict had advocated. Under his influence, monasteries thus became engines for the collection, preservation, and transmission of knowledge. Nearly all the Greek and Latin texts on which we rely for our study of Western civilizations survive because they were copied in monasteries. Monasteries also developed and disseminated an important new information technology: the codex. For millennia, the book had been a scroll, a clumsy format that made searching for a particular passage difficult and confined the reader to one passage at a time. The codex facilitates indexing (from the Latin word for "finger") because a reader can flip back and forth among various pages and keep a finger in one place while looking at another. Codices also store information more safely and efficiently, because they compress many hundreds of pages within protective bindings. They are less wasteful, too, because texts can be copied on both sides of a page. They make finding a

## After You Read This Chapter

Visit StudySpace for quizzes, additional review materials, and multi-media documents. **wwnorton.com/studyspace**

### REVIEWING THE OBJECTIVES

- A number of historical factors shaped the way that Jesus's teachings were received. Describe the most important of these.
- The expansion of Rome and the strain on its central government posed significant challenges in the third century. How did Roman emperors respond?
- Christianity's acceptance as a legal religion changed it in profound ways. Why was this?
- In the fourth and fifth centuries, a new wave of migrations penetrated to the very heart of the empire. What made this possible?
- The differences between traditional Roman and Christian cultures were gradually reconciled through the efforts of Christian intellectuals. Why was this considered necessary?

given book easier, since titles can be written on the codex's spine. It's arguable, in fact, that the invention of the codex was more revolutionary than the invention of printing a thousand years later. Your copy of *Western Civilizations* is a codex.

## CONCLUSION

Since the English historian Edward Gibbon published the first volume of *The Decline and Fall of the Roman Empire* in 1776 (a year when Britain's own empire suffered a setback) more has been written about "the fall of Rome" than on the passing of any other civilization. Gibbon himself blamed Christianity, depicting it as a debilitating disease that sapped the empire's strength. Others have accused the barbarians whose movements put pressure on Rome's frontiers. But even in the time of Augustus, Roman moralists had already declared that Rome was in decline. Indeed, any self-respecting republican would say that Rome fell when Augustus came to power.

More recent scholarship has influenced the narrative offered in this chapter, which views transformation as a more accurate way of understanding this period. No civilization is static and unchanging; civilizations, like human beings, are living organisms. Indeed, any evidence of Rome's decline can also be read as evidence of its adaptability. The imperial policies of Septimius Severus and Diocletian responded to the realities of Rome's size and diversity. The settlement of frontier peoples in Rome's western provinces gave rise to hybrid polities that found new uses for Roman buildings, political offices, and laws. Through Christianity, the language, adminstrative structures, and culture of ancient Rome were preserved and extended. The flexibility of the Roman political system made this possible, because it was inclusive to a degree no modern empire has ever matched.

This transformation changed what it meant to be Roman, to the extent that historians now call this period "late antiquity" to distinguish it from the classical world that preceded it. By the seventh century, indeed, so much had changed that the contours of three distinctive civilizations can be discerned, each one exhibiting different aspects of Roman influence and crystallizing around different regions of the former empire. We will explore each of these civilizations in Chapter 7.

### PEOPLE, IDEAS, AND EVENTS IN CONTEXT

- What were the main differences between **JESUS** and other Jewish leaders of his day?
- How did **PAUL OF TARSUS** reach out to the peoples of the **HELLENISTIC WORLD**? How did his teachings influence the development of early Christianity?
- In what ways did **DIOCLETIAN**'s division of the empire and his institition of the **TETRARCHY** respond to longstanding problems?
- How and why was Christianity changed under **CONSTANTINE**? What effects did this have on attitudes toward women and their role in the Church?
- How did the relocation of the imperial capital to **CONSTANTINOPLE** contribute to the growing divide between the **GREEK EAST** and the **LATIN WEST**? How did the mass migrations of frontier peoples then transform the Latin West?
- What were the key contributions of **JEROME**, **AMBROSE**, and **AUGUSTINE** to the development of a specifically Christian outlook by the end of the fourth century?
- How did **BOETHIUS**, **BENEDICT**, and **CASSIDORUS** reshape classical culture in the fifth century?

### CONSEQUENCES

- In your opinion, which phenomenon had a more profound impact on Rome: the over-extension of imperial power or the mass migration of peoples from Rome's frontier? Why?
- Few historians would now agree with the judgment of Edward Gibbon, who posited that Christianity destroyed the Roman Empire. But to what extent did Christianity alter the traditional values and infrastructure of the Roman state? Were these alterations inevitable?

# Before You Read This Chapter

## STORY LINES

- Justinian's attempt to reconquer the Western Roman Empire was actually more destructive than the mass migrations of the previous centuries.
- Byzantine culture combined Roman legal and political systems with the learning of classical Greece, but was most acutely shaped by Orthodox Christianity.
- The close connections between religion, politics, and commerce helped to drive the rapid expansion of Islam in the eighth century.
- In western Europe, the disintegration of Roman political and economic infrastructures had a destabilizing effect, but this was countered by the success of the Frankish kingdom and the spread of monasticism.
- The empire of Charlemagne unified vast portions of northwestern Europe under a single centralized government, fostering unprecedented administrative, economic, and cultural developments.

## CHRONOLOGY

| | |
|---|---|
| 481–511 | Reign of Clovis, king of the Franks |
| 527–565 | Reign of Justinian |
| 570–632 | Lifetime of Muhammad |
| 590–604 | Papacy of Gregory the Great |
| 636–651 | Arab conquests of Persia, Palestine, Egypt, and North Africa |
| 661–750 | Hegemony of the Umayyad dynasty in the Islamic world |
| 717–787 | Iconoclast Controversy in Byzantium |
| 717–751 | The Carolingian dynasty shares power with Merovingian kings |
| 730 | The Venerable Bede completes his history of the English church |
| 750–930 | Hegemony of the Abassid dynasty in Baghdad and the Umayyad dynasty in Al-Andalus (Spain) |
| 751 | Pepin becomes king of the Franks |
| 768–814 | Reign of Charlemagne |
| 800–1000 | Period of Viking invasions |
| 871–899 | Reign of Alfred the Great in England |

# Rome's Three Heirs, 500–950

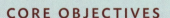

## CORE OBJECTIVES

- **EXPLAIN** why Justinian's efforts to reunite the Roman Empire proved destructive.
- **IDENTIFY** the distinctive features of Byzantine culture.
- **UNDERSTAND** the reasons for Islam's rapid expansion.
- **DEFINE** the relationship between monasticism and secular power in early medieval Europe.
- **DESCRIBE** the importance of the Carolingian Empire.

Around the year 600, Anglo-Saxon tribes who had settled on the island of Britain were approached by missionaries sent from Rome. These Latin-speaking Christians faced an enormous challenge: they had to find a way to convert tribal leaders, and also to translate the central ideas of their fath into languages and concepts that made sense in a new cultural context. They also needed to look for ways to meld Roman practices with Anglo-Saxon ones, building churches on sacred sites and gradually turning the worship of pagan gods into the rituals of Christianity. An account of these negotiations comes down to us in a remarkable history written several generations later. In *The History of the English Church and People*, a monk named Bede (c. 672–735) describes how Celtic and Anglo-Saxon peoples were united under the Roman Church and came to adopt Latin as a language of learning and worship. In so doing, he shows how Roman ideals were changed and adapted to meet new needs and to express a new worldview.

This is but one example of the ways in which the legacy of Rome was transmitted and transformed during the pivotal period known as the Middle Ages. This term is an unfortunate one, and it doesn't begin to express contemporaries' awareness of their own times. "The Middle Ages" is a modern invention: in the seventeenth century, intellectuals began to argue that an intermediate, "medieval period" (*medium ævum*) separated their own "modern age" from the glorious accomplishments of classical Greece and the empire of ancient Rome, which many European states were trying to emulate by establishing empires of their own. But in fact, it is arguable that the period between 500 and 1500 was the beginning of that "modern age." In this era, the foundations of modern political institutions were laid. In this era, the relationships among Judaism, Christianity, and Islam were first articulated, relationships that continue to affect our daily lives. In this era, three new civilizations became heirs of the Western civilizations formerly encompassed by the Roman Empire: the New Rome of Byzantium, the new empire of Islam, and the western European territories that looked increasingly to the Roman Church for leadership. Each preserved and modified different aspects of their shared inheritance, and our world is still being shaped by the interactions among them.

## JUSTINIAN'S IMPERIAL AMBITIONS

As we observed in Chapter 6, the eastern and western portions of Rome's empire were divided along linguistic, cultural, and economic lines. By the end of the fourth century, this division also became political. The Ostrogothic conquest of Italy under Theodoric (r. 493–526)—which was supported by the imperial government—briefly placed Constantinople in a position to influence affairs in the old

**THE MEDITERRANEAN WORLD UNDER JUSTINIAN, 527–565.** Compare this map with the one on page 188. (Here, the green shading represents those regions controlled by Justinian.) ▪ ***What was the geographical extent of Justinian's empire?*** ▪ ***Which areas of the former Roman Empire did Justinian not attempt to reconquer?*** ▪ ***What may have been the strategy behind these campaigns?***

Roman heartland. But none of Theodoric's short-lived successors was able to rule this territory effectively, and in 535 the Ostrogothic kingdom was overthrown in an attempt reunify the Roman Empire.

The man responsible for this was Justinian (r. 527–65), the most ambitious emperor since Constantine. Although the empire that he ruled was largely Greek-speaking, Justinian himself came from the Latin-speaking province of Dardania (now Serbia). A student of history, he saw himself as the heir to the Principate established by Augustus, and like Augustus he was aided by an astute and determined wife, Theodora, who played an influential role in his reign. Although his efforts ultimately failed, they had a lasting influence on the entire Mediterranean world.

## *The Codification of Roman Law*

Justinian's most positive and lasting accomplishment was his codification of Roman law. This was a necessary project, and long overdue: since the time of the third-century jurists (Chapter 5), the number of statutes and legal decisions had multiplied, and the resulting body of law was both massive and self-contradictory. Moreover, conditions had changed so radically that many legal principles could no longer be applied. When Justinian came to the throne in 527, one of his first initiatives was to bring existing precedents into harmony with new historical conditions and thereby to restore the prestige and power of the imperial office.

To carry out this work, Justinian appointed a team of lawyers under the supervision of a jurist called Tribonian. Within two years, this commission published the first result of its labors: the Code, a systematic compilation of imperial statutes which was later supplemented by another book, the Novels (*Novellae*, "new laws"), containing the legislation of Justinian and his immediate successors. By 532 the commission had also completed the Digest, a summary of the writings of Rome's great legal authorities, including the jurists of the Principate. The final product was the Institutes, a textbook of legal principles. Together, these four volumes constitute the *Corpus Juris Civilis*, or the "body of civil law."

Justinian's *Corpus* was a brilliant achievement. In Byzantium, it immediately became the foundation on which all subsequent legal developments would rest. Although little known in western Europe for centuries, it eventually influenced the legal systems of many nations. The nineteenth-century Napoleonic Code—still the basis of law in France, Spain, much of Latin America, and the state of Louisiana—is essentially the *Corpus* of Justinian.

The *Corpus* also had a profound impact on political philosophy. Starting from the maxim that "what pleases the prince has the force of law," it granted unlimited powers to the emperor and was therefore adopted by early modern rulers as a foundation for absolutism (see Chapter 15). But the *Corpus* also provided some theoretical support for constitutional forms of government, because it maintained that a sovereign's powers are delegated to him by the people, and that what is mandated by the people can also be taken away by them. Equally important is the fundamental principle that the state is a corporate body, not the extension of an individual's private property. The modern conception of the state as a public entity derives from the legal maxims of the *Corpus*.

## *Justinian's Attempted Reconquest*

Justinian's initial efforts to reunite the Roman Empire seemed successful. In 533 his general Belisarius conquered the Vandal kingdom of northwest Africa, thereby facilitating campaigns in Ostrogothic Italy and Visigothic Spain. By 536 Belisarius appeared poised to occupy Rome's old homeland, where he was welcomed as a savior by the former subjects of the Ostrogoths. But these early victories were illusory. When Justinian died in 565, the Mediterranean was under Roman control but the human and financial costs of these campaigns had drastically strained imperial resources. Belisarius's army in Italy was overextended, and Justinian's need to levy soldiers had led to oppressive taxes on vitally important regions like Egypt and Syria, which undermined support for his imperial project. The Romans of Italy and North Africa also resented the costs their own "liberation" imposed on them.

Justinian's campaigns also distracted attention from dangers closer to Constantinople: in particular, the developing strength of Persia under the Sassanid dynasty. To respond to the Persians' advances, Justinian's successors were eventually forced to withdraw their troops from Italy and North Africa. This left both regions dangerously exposed to further invasions and yet still failed to guarantee the safety of the eastern frontier. Only a heroic reorganization of the empire's resources after 610 saved Constantinople, but it put an end to Justinian's dream of reunification.

## *Justinian's Impact on the West*

Justinian's wars proved more devastating to Italy than the previous incursions of barbarian peoples. Around Rome, the vital supply lines of the aqueducts were cut and the

**JUSTINIAN AND THEODORA.** These sixth-century mosaics from the Church of San Vitale in the imperial capital of Ravenna show the emperor and empress processing toward the main altar of the church carrying the holy vessels used for the consecration of bread and wine. ▪ ***What do these images convey about the sacred and secular powers of both figures?***

elaborate system of conduits, drainage ditches, and reservoirs were destroyed. Parts of the Italian countryside returned to marshland, and some areas would not be drained again until the twentieth century. In 568 a new people, the Lombards, took advantage of the chaos to conquer the northern third of the peninsula. Thereafter, Italy would be divided between Lombard territories in the north and imperial territories in the southeast, with Rome and its region precariously sandwiched between them. The controlling forces within these territories would change greatly over time, but this tripartite division remained the essential political configuration of Italy until the nineteenth century. In fact, it still divides Italian politics to this day.

Constantinople's control over North Africa lasted only a few generations longer. Weakened by religious conflict and heavy taxation, this area fell easily to invading Muslims in the seventh century, along with Egypt and the rest of Roman Africa (see below). When it did, Christianity in North Africa largely disappeared, although a vibrant Christian community continued to flourish in Ethiopia. Meanwhile, tensions between Arian Visigoths and their Latin subjects continued even after after the Visigothic king officially converted in 587. This mutual hostility would subsist until the Visigothic kingdom, too, was largely absorbed by Islam. By the end of the eighth century, Christian rulers controlled only the northernmost parts of the Iberian peninsula, and Al-Andalus (Muslim Spain) became part of a new Islamic world.

## THE ROMAN EMPIRE OF BYZANTIUM

With the failure of Justinian's imperial project, the history of the Eastern Roman Empire can be said to enter a new phase. Indeed, many historians regard it as a new empire, the Byzantine Empire, an adjective derived from the name of the ancient port where Constantinople was situated. Byzantium thus became *one* of Rome's three heirs, not the sole heir of Roman authority, as Justinian had claimed. But according to the inhabitants of this empire, it never ceased to be Rome, and they were never anything but Romans. They saw themselves as carrying forward Roman traditions, values, and institutions under new circumstances.

As a result of Justinian's policies, however, this new Rome was struggling for survival. By 610 the Greek-speaking imperial dynasty that began with Heraclius (r. 610–41) was unable to extend its influence farther west than the Adriatic. Meanwhile, the Persians had conquered almost all of the empire's eastern and southern territories in Syria and Palestine. They had even plundered Jerusalem and carried off a precious relic believed to be part of the original cross on which Jesus had been crucified. With an enormous effort, Heraclius rallied his remaining military powers and routed the Persians, recapturing Jerusalem and retrieving the relic in 627.

But these gains were short-lived. Arab armies, inspired by the new religion of Islam, were able to profit from the empire's exhaustion. They soon occupied the newly reconquered Byzantine territories and claimed Jerusalem as a holy site for Muslims, too. They also absorbed the entire Persian Empire and rapidly made their way westward to North Africa. They then took to the sea, and in 677 attempted a naval conquest of Constantinople. Repulsed, they made another attempt in 717 by means of a concerted land and sea operation. This new threat was countered by the emperor Leo III (r. 717–41). Deploying keen strategy and a secret incendiary mixture now known as "Greek fire" (of course, the Byzantines called it "Roman fire"), Leo's forces were able to defeat the Arabs. Over the next few decades, moreover, Byzantium reconquered most of Asia Minor, which remained the imperial heartland for the next 300 years.

## *Sources of Stability*

In many ways, the internal politics of the Byzantine Empire were as tumultuous as the history of its changing neighborhood. Because all power was concentrated in the imperial court at Constantinople and because emperors followed their predecessors in claiming autonomous rule, opposition usually took the form of intrigue, treason, and violence. Indeed, Byzantine politics is now so famous for its cloak-and-dagger complexity that the word *byzantine* has come to denote devious machinations or elaborate systems of courtship and bureaucracy. In reality, though, many able rulers wielded their powers very effectively, while a centralized government continued to function even in times

**THE SECRET WEAPON OF BYZANTIUM: "GREEK FIRE."** This depiction of Greek fire in action illustrates a chronicle by John Skylitzes, a Byzantine historian who flourished in the eleventh century. This manuscript was copied in Sicily during the twelfth century and is now preserved in the Biblioteca Nacional de España in Madrid.

of upheaval. No polity in western Europe had anything resembling such mechanisms of government until a much later period.

Strong, self-perpetuating political institutions thus constituted a major source of stability in Byzantium and offer an explanation for the extraordinary longevity of the empire's core provinces: nearly a thousand years. The imperial bureaucracy in Constantinople regulated prices and wages, maintained systems of licensing, and controlled exports and trade. Its highly educated officials also supervised many aspects of social and cultural life, overseeing schools, the organization of the Orthodox Church, and the observance of religious rites and holidays. Even the popular sport of chariot racing—New Rome's answer to gladiatorial combat—fell under strict supervision, as did the regulation of the various teams' fiercely competitive fans. Established bureaucracies also regulated the army and navy, the courts, and the diplomatic service, endowing these agencies with organizational strengths incomparable for their time.

Another source of stability was Byzantium's sound and well-managed economy, which was far superior to that of western Europe. Commerce and cities continued to flourish as they had done in late antiquity. Constantinople became a central emporium for Far Eastern luxury goods and western raw materials. The empire also nurtured and protected its own industries, most notably the manufacture and weaving of silk, and it was renowned for its stable gold and silver coinage. Nor was Constantinople the only great urban center. The Hellenistic capital Antioch and the bustling cities of Thessalonica and Trebizond were very large and prosperous. Any one of them would have dwarfed any western European city; Constantinople may have had a population of close to a million. In the West at this time, Paris was a village and Rome may have had a few thousand people living among the ruins.

This emphasis on Byzantine trade and industry is justified because both were advanced and both provided most of the surplus wealth that sustained the state. But agriculture lay at the heart of the Byzantine economy, so much so that peasant farmers struggled to maintain their independence from large estates owned by wealthy aristocrats and monasteries. And as in the final centuries of the Roman Republic, they were only able to do so with the help of legislation. When the aristocracy eventually gained control during the eleventh century, however, free peasants were transformed into impoverished tenant-farmers, as had been the case in Rome during the third century C.E. This was one of the less fortunate ways in which Byzantium resembled its ancient predecessor.

## *Orthodoxy, Iconoclasm, and Identity*

Law, strong governance, and a thriving economy: viewed from our perspective, these seem to be the basis of Byzantine civilization. Yet the inhabitants of Byzantium cared more about religious orthodoxy. Their intense preoccupation with questions of doctrine could be a catalyst for political and social dissension, but it was also essential to Byzantine identity and endowed the empire's inhabitants with a sense of shared purpose. In old Rome, the *mos maiorum* had undergirded Roman pride and superiority (Chapter 5); in New Rome, Orthodox Christianity occupied the same fundamental place. The stakes of Byzantine doctrinal disputes were further heightened by the fact that emperors took an active role in them.

The most contentious issue, and one that came to a head in the eighth century, was a violent clash over the meaning and use of religious images, known as the Iconoclast ("image-breaking") Controversy. As we have seen (Chapter 6), Christians had long been accustomed to expressing their devotion to Christ and the saints through the making and veneration of images. There was even a legend that the author of Luke's gospel had been a painter, the maker of the first icon. At the same time, however, there was always an awareness that any representation of a holy person came close to being a form of idolatry, something that Jewish tradition strongly condemned and something that made Christians look like idol-worshippers in the eyes of pagans. Although both Latin and Orthodox Christians insisted that images were only *aids* to worship, not *objects* of worship, the line between the two was always fine.

In Byzantium, where the veneration of icons was an especially potent part of daily devotion, any suggestion that such images should be suppressed or destroyed was bound to be contentious. But that is precisely what the Iconoclasts advocated. They argued that honoring images was blasphemous because nothing made by human beings should be worshiped, an injunction expressed in the Ten Commandments given to Moses (Exodus 20:4). Moreover, they contended that Christ's divinity could not be represented artistically; it was beyond the power of even the most skilled craftsman. For their part, traditionalists responded that the images themselves were never objects of worship; rather, icons were windows through which a glimpse of Heaven might be granted to human beings on earth.

The Iconoclast movement was initiated by the same Emperor Leo III who had saved Constantinople from invasion by Muslims, and it is even possible that the iconoclasm so central to Islamic belief (Qu'ran, V. 92) played an influential role in his thinking. In other words, it may have been his attempt to answer one of Islam's greatest criticisms of Christianity. There may also have been political and financial considerations behind the campaign: by proclaiming a radical new religious movement, the emperor may have intended to reassert control over the Orthodox Church and thus to combat the growing strength of monasteries. And indeed, the great monasteries of Byzantium were major producers of icons as well as books: the manufacture of both was considered a labor especially suited to the monastic life. So when the monasteries rallied to the cause of images, they were bitterly persecuted by Leo's successors, who took this opportunity to confiscate much of their wealth.

**DEVOTIONAL IMAGE—OR DANGEROUS IDOL?** This icon of *Christos Pantokrator* ("Christ the Almighty") was painted in the sixth century and is one of the oldest such images. It is preserved at the Orthodox monastery of St. Catherine on Mount Sinai (Egypt). ▪ ***According to the proponents of iconoclasm, why would such an image be considered blasphemous?***

The Iconoclast Controversy was resolved toward the end of the eighth century, and in favor of the iconodules, the promoters of religious imagery. But it had some long-lasting effects. One was the unfortunate fact that much of the art produced or preserved in Byzantium was destroyed by imperial edict. This means that examples of Christian artistry from these first eight centuries are very rare and can be found only in Italy, Palestine, or Egypt, which were beyond the reach of the Iconoclast emperors. A second consequence was the opening of another religious and political breach between the Greek East and the Latin West. Prior to Emperor Leo's iconoclastic initiatives, the patriarch of Rome—known familiarly as "papa" in Latin slang—had often been a close ally of Byzantium's rulers. But iconoclasm called into question not only the veneration of images but the cult of the saints, and by extension the claims of papal primacy that were based on the Roman patriarch's claim to be Saint Peter's successor.

The ultimate defeat of iconoclasm also crystallized some aspects of belief and practice that came to be characteristic of Byzantine identity. One was a renewed emphasis on the Orthodox faith of the empire as the key to its political unity and military success. Religious tradition became the touchstone of political legitimacy, and vice versa. This emphasis on tradition helped orthodoxy gain new adherents in the ninth and tenth centuries, but it also reinforced the hegemony of Constantinople's own Christian traditions, marginalizing those of Syria and Armenia. Fear of heresy also tended to inhibit freedom of thought, and not just in religious matters. Although the Byzantine emperors eventually founded a university in Constantinople, its students and faculty were never permitted to express dissenting opinions or to engage in any significant degree of intellectual speculation—in marked contrast to the freewheeling intellectual atmosphere cultivated by the universities of western Europe (see Chapters 8 and 9).

## Tradition and Innovation

Although religion was central to the identity of Romans in Byzantium, so was their direct link with the Hellenistic past and the heritage of ancient Greece. Byzantine schools based their instruction on classical Greek literature to a degree that might seem surprising given the more tentative attitude toward classical learning in western Europe (Chapter 6). Educated people around the Byzantine court who quoted only a single line of Homer could expect their listeners to recognize the entire passage from which it

# Competing Viewpoints

## *Debating the Power of Icons*

*The Iconoclast Controversy of the eighth century divided Byzantine society and was a factor in the growing division between the Latin Church of Rome and the Eastern Orthodox Church. The excerpts below are representative of the two main arguments voiced at the time. The first is from a treatise by John of Damascus (c. 675–749), a Christian in the service of the Muslim Umayyad caliphs. The second is an official report issuing from the synod convened by the emperor Constantine V (r. 741–75) in 754. Constantine was carrying forward the iconoclastic policies of his father, Leo III.*

### John of Damascus, *on Holy Images*

Now adversaries say: God's commands to Moses the law-giver were, "Thou shalt adore the Lord thy God, and thou shalt worship him alone, and thou shalt not make to thyself a graven thing that is in heaven above, or in the earth beneath." . . .

These injunctions were given to the Jews on account of their proneness to idolatry. Now we, on the contrary, are no longer in leading strings . . . We have passed the stage of infancy, and reached the perfection of manhood . . . and know what may be imaged and what may not. . . . An image is a likeness of the original with a certain difference, for it is not an exact reproduction of the original. Thus, the Son is the living, substantial, unchangeable Image of the invisible God, bearing in Himself the whole Father, being in all things equal to Him, differing only in being begotten by the Father. . . . That which is divine is immutable; there is no change in Him, nor shadow of change. . . . God has noted and settled all that He would do, the unchanging future events before they came to pass. In the same way, a man who wished to build a house, would first make and think out a plan. Again, visible things are images of invisible and intangible things, on which they throw a faint light. Holy Scripture clothes in figure God and the angels. . . . If, therefore, Holy Scripture, providing for our need, ever putting before us what is intangible, clothes it in flesh, does it not make an image of what is thus invested with our nature, and brought to the level of our desires, yet invisible? . . . For the invisible things of God since the creation of the world are made visible through images. We see images in creation which remind us faintly of God, as when, for instance, we speak of the holy and adorable Trinity, imaged by the sun, or light, or burning rays, or by a running fountain, or a full river, or by the mind, speech, or the spirit within us, or by a rose tree, or a sprouting flower, or a sweet fragrance. . . .

Source: Excerpted from *St. John Damascene on Holy Images*, trans. Mary H. Allies (London: 1898), pp. 6–12.

came. In the English-speaking world, only the King James Bible has ever achieved the same degree of cultural saturation. For the Romans of Byzantium, indeed, Homeric epics were a kind of sacred text: a literary model, an instructional textbook, and a guide to personal morality and wisdom.

Byzantine scholars also studied the philosophy of Plato and the historical prose of Thucydides intensively. By contrast, Aristotle's works were less well known, while many other philosphical traditions of antiquity were deemed dangerous to orthodox belief. Even Justinian, who had presided over the codification of ancient Roman (and thus pagan) law, registered his distrust of philosophy by shutting down the Athenian academies that had existed since Plato's day. Eventually, the emperor Alexius Comnenus (d. 1118) would ban the teaching of Aristotelian logic. The traditions of Greek scientific inquiry and the advances of Hellenistic science were also neglected. Tradition was more highly prized than originality, as was preservation over innovation. The benefit of this, for posterity, is that Byzantium rescued Greek and Hellenistic writings for later ages. The

## *Canons of the Synod of 754*

It is the unanimous doctrine of all the holy Fathers and of the six Ecumenical Synods, that no one may imagine any kind of separation or mingling in opposition to the unsearchable, unspeakable, and incomprehensible union of the two natures in the one hypostasis or person. What avails, then, the folly of the painter, who from sinful love of gain depicts that which should not be depicted—that is, with his polluted hands he tries to fashion that which should only be believed in the heart and confessed with the mouth? He makes an image and calls it Christ. The name *Christ* signifies *God and man.* Consequently it is an image of God and man, and consequently he has in his foolish mind, in his representation of the created flesh, depicted the Godhead which cannot be represented, and thus mingled what should not be mingled. Thus he is guilty of a double blasphemy—the one in making an image of the Godhead, and the other by mingling the Godhead and manhood . . . like the Monophysites, or he represents the body of Christ as not made divine and separate and as a person apart, like the Nestorians.

The only admissible figure of the humanity of Christ, however, is bread and wine in the holy Supper. This and no other form, this and no other type, has he chosen to represent his incarnation. Bread he ordered to be brought, but not a representation of the human form, so that idolatry might not arise. And as the body of Christ is made divine, so also this figure of the body of Christ, the bread, is made divine by the descent of the Holy Spirit; it becomes the divine body of Christ by the mediation of the priest who, separating the oblation from that which is common, sanctifies it. . . .

Source: Excerpted from *The Seven Ecumenical Councils of the Undivided Church*, trans. H. R. Percival, in *Nicene and Post-Nicene Fathers*, 2d Series, eds. P. Schaff and H. Wace (repr. Grand Rapids, MI: 1955), pp. 543–44.

### *Questions for Analysis*

1. To what other phenomena does John of Damascus compare the making of images? How do these comparisons help him to make his argument in favor of them?
2. To what phenomena do the theologians of the synod compare the making of images? Why do they declare the bread and wine of the Eucharist to be the only legitimate representations of Christ?
3. What is the significance of the fact that John of Damascus did not fall under the jurisdiction of the emperor of Byzantium, but that of the Muslim Umayyad caliph? What conclusions can you draw about the relative freedoms in these two realms?

vast majority of ancient Greek texts known today survive because they were copied by Byzantine scribes.

Also in contrast to the West, as we shall see, Byzantine classicism and learning were the products of an educational system that extended to the laity and was open to women as well as to men. Byzantine commitment to the formal education of women was especially unusual. Although most girls from aristocratic or prosperous families were educated at home by private tutors, they nevertheless mingled freely with their male counterparts at court or on social occasions, and many learned women were praised for being able to discourse like Plato or Pythagoras. There were also female physicians in the Byzantine Empire, another extraordinary departure both from ancient tradition and from the practices of western Europe until the latter part of the nineteenth century.

Byzantine achievements in the realms of architecture and art are also remarkable. The finest example of both may be the church of Hagia Sophia (Greek for "Holy Wisdom") in Constantinople, constructed at enormous cost under the patronage of Justinian. It quickly came to define an architectural style unique to Byzantium. Its purpose was not to express pride in human accomplishment, but rather to symbolize the mysteries of the Christian religion and the holy knowledge imparted by Christ to the soul of the believer. For this reason, the architects paid little attention to the external appearance of the building. The interior, however, was decorated with richly colored mosaics, gold leaf, colored marble columns, and bits of tinted glass set on edge to refract rays of sunlight like sparkling gems. Light appeared to be generated from within. The magnificent dome over its central square represented an unprecedented engineering feat, and was upheld by four great arches springing from pillars at the four corners of the square. The result was an architectural framework that is marvelously strong, but delicate. Its effect is heightened by the many windows placed around the dome's rim, which convey the impression that it floats in midair.

**HAGIA SOPHIA.** This great monument to the artistry, engineering skill, and spirituality of Byzantium was built during the reign of Justinian. The four minarets at its corners were added in 1453, after Constantinople was absorbed into the empire of the Ottoman Turks. Hagia Sophia is now a mosque and a museum.

Many apsects of Byzantine arts and learning exerted strong influence on the craftsmen and scholars of western Europe through New Rome's continued economic and cultural contact with portions of Italy. The basilica of San Marco in Venice (c. 1063) reflects this influence, as do medieval mosaics in such cities as Ravenna and Palermo. Greek-speaking monasteries in southeastern Italy also maintained close ties with their counterparts in the eastern empire, and many were allowed to practice the rituals of the Orthodox Church. Greek books—including the comedies of Aristophanes—were copied and preserved. But much of the heritage of Western civilizations that was cultivated in Byzantium was largely inaccessible elsewhere in Europe, as the knowledge of Greek became increasingly rare.

## MUHAMMAD AND THE TEACHINGS OF ISLAM

In many ways, the civilization that formed around the religion of Islam mirrors the Roman Empire in its global reach and longevity; in this, it is truly one of Rome's heirs. Islam (Arabic for "submission") also resembles the early republic of Rome, in that it demands from its followers not just adherence to common forms of worship but also to certain social and cultural norms. But whereas the Roman Empire undergirded Christianity and elevated it to the status of a major faith by legalizing it, the Islamic faith was itself the engine of imperial expansion. Indeed, Islam is unique among the major religions in the way it has *created* political empires rather than relying on them.

### *The Revelations of Muhammad*

Islam had its beginnings in Arabia, a desert land considered so forbidding that neither the Romans nor the Persians sought to conquer it. Arabian society was tribal, and did not revolve around urban settlements. Many Arabs were herdsmen, living off the milk of their camels and the produce of desert oases. But like the Hittites in the second millennium B.C.E., their very mobility, ingenuity, and pioneering spirit made them excellent explorers and long-distance traders. In the second half of the sixth century, when protracted wars between Byzantium and Persia made travel too dangerous for merchants, the Arabs quickly established themselves as guides, couriers, and guardians of transit routes between Africa and Asia.

As part of this process, towns began to emerge. The most prominent of these was Mecca, an ancient sacred site

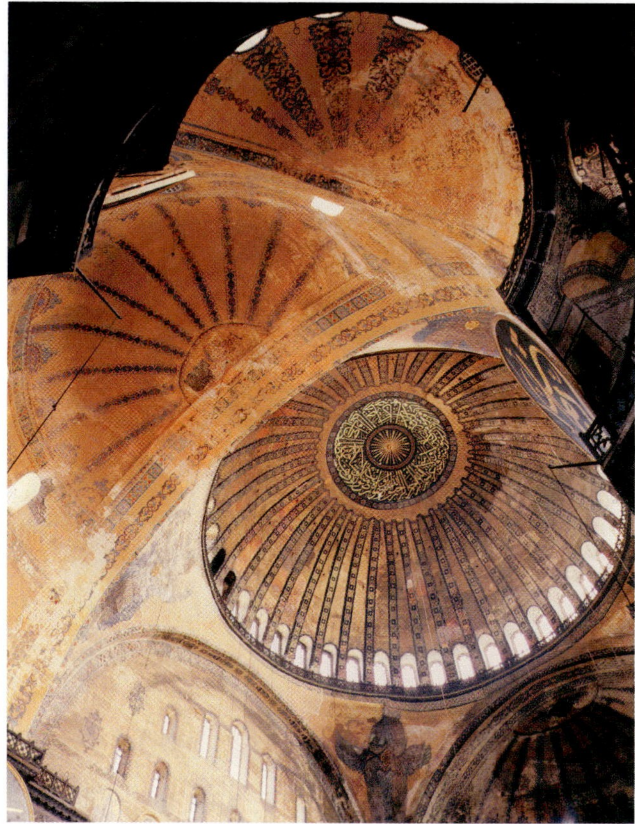

**INTERIOR OF HAGIA SOPHIA.** The revolutionary structure of the church, shown here, made it appear as if the enormous dome floated on light and air.

that lay at the crossroads of major caravan routes. Mecca was home to the Kaaba, a shrine housing the Black Stone worshiped by many Arabian tribes. (It may be a meteorite, and hence of heavenly origin.) The tribe that controlled this shrine, the Quraish (*kur-AYSH*), thus came to direct the economic life of the whole region, forming an aristocracy of traders and entrepreneurs.

Muhammad, the founder of Islam, was a member of this tribe. He was born in Mecca about 570. Orphaned early in life, he entered the service of a rich widow whom he later married, thereby attaining financial security. Until middle age he lived as a prosperous trader, little different from his fellow townsmen. But around 610, he experienced a spiritual epiphany. At this time, the Arabs worshipped many gods. Yet like the ancient Hebrews they also acknowledged one god as more powerful. For the Hebrews, God was Yahweh; for the Arabs, Allah. But whereas the Hebrews' embrace of monotheism was a long and gradual process, Muhammad's conversion was sudden, the immediate consequence of revelation. Thereafter, Muhammad received further revelations that became the basis for his teachings, and by which he was commanded to accept the calling of a prophet and to proclaim the new faith to his tribe.

At first, he was not very successful in gaining converts. Perhaps tribal leaders feared that his teachings would diminish the importance of the Kaaba, and thus of Mecca. The town of Yathrib to the north, however, had no such concerns. Its representatives invited Muhammad to live among them, and to serve as judge and arbiter in local rivalries. Muhammad and a few loyal friends accepted this invitation in 622. Because this migration—in Arabic, the Hijrah (*HIJ-ruh*)—marks the beginning of Muhammad's wider influence, Muslims regard it as the beginning of time. Just as Christians date all events according to the birth of Jesus (see Chapter 6), so Muslims begin their dating system with the Hijrah.

Muhammad changed the name of Yathrib to Medina ("City of the Prophet") and established himself as the town's ruler. In so doing, he consciously organized his followers into a political community held together by shared economic ambitions as well as by a shared set of beliefs and rituals. Yet he did not abandon his desire to exercise political and prophetic authority among his own people, the Quraish. Accordingly, he and his followers began raiding Quraish caravans traveling beyond Mecca. The Quraish defended themselves, but they could not continue to operate an extensive commercial enterprise in the face of such violent threats. By 630 Muhammad had worn down the opposition and was invited back to Mecca. His kinsmen submitted themselves to his authority and accepted his teachings. Muhammad, for his part, ensured that the Kaaba was established as Islam's holy place, a status it maintains today. And because Mecca had long been a pilgrimage site and gathering place for tribes throughout Arabia, many people were exposed to Muhammad's teachings. At the time of his death in 632, Islam had become an established faith.

## Muhammad and the Qu'ran

As its name indicates, the faith of Islam calls for absolute submission to Allah, the same God worshiped by Jews and Christians. Hence, the Muslim saying "there is no god but Allah" is more accurately translated as "there is no divinity but God." For Muslims, the history and prophecies of the Hebrews are important components of their religion, as are the teachings of Jesus, who is venerated as a great prophet. But they consider Muhammad to be the last and greatest prophet, and the closest to God.

Muhammad's teachings are essential because they establish the rituals and practices that help to ensure salvation. These teachings are preserved in the sacred scripture of Islam, the Qu'ran (*kuhr-AHN*), an Arabic word meaning "recitations." This is because Muhammad recited his revelations to his listeners, and these were eventually gathered

# Analyzing Primary Sources

## *A Sura from the Qu'ran*

*The Qu'ran preserves the teachings of Muhammad in a series of suras, or chapters. Composed in verse forms that draw on much older traditions of Arabic poetry, they are meant to be sung or chanted. Indeed, the word Qu'ran means "recitations," referring both to Muhammad's method of revealing divine truths and to the Muslim practice of memorizing and repeating portions of this sacred scripture.*

### *Sura 81: The Overturning*

In the Name of God the Compassionate the Caring

When the sun is overturned
When the stars fall away
When the mountains are moved
When the ten-month pregnant
camels are abandoned
When the beasts of the wild
are herded together
When the seas are boiled over
When the souls are coupled
When the girl-child buried alive
is asked what she did to deserve
murder
When the pages are folded out
When the sky is flayed open
When Jahím [the Day of Reckoning]
is set ablaze
When the garden is brought near
Then a soul will know what it
has prepared
I swear by the stars that slide,
stars streaming, stars that sweep
along the sky
By the night as it slips away
By the morning when the fragrant
air breathes
This is the word of a messenger
ennobled,
empowered, ordained before
the lord of the throne,
holding sway there, keeping trust
Your friend [Muhammad] has
not gone mad
He saw him on the horizon clear
He does not hoard for himself
the unseen
This is not the word of a satan
struck with stones
Where are you going?
This is a reminder to all beings
For those who wish to walk straight
Your only will is the will of God lord
of all beings

Source: From *Approaching the Qu'ran: The Early Revelations*, trans. Michael Sells (Ashland, OR: 1999), pp. 48–50.

### *Questions for Analysis*

1. What impressions of Arab culture emerge from this *sura*? What does the litany of unlikely or mystical events reveal about the values of Muhammad's contemporaries?
2. How does Muhammad speak of himself and his role in society?

together and transcribed, a process that continued after Muhammad's death. Unlike the Christian gospels, which offer different perspectives on Jesus' ministry and which were recorded a generation or two after his crucifixion, the Qu'ran is considered a direct link with Muhammad. It is also unlike most books of the Bible because it takes the form of poetry, drawing on ancient genres of Arabic song.

Like Christianity, Islam teaches that a day of judgment is coming—and soon. On this day, the righteous will be granted eternal life in a paradise of delights, but wrongdoers will be damned to a realm of eternal fire. Every person is therefore offered a fundamental choice: to begin a new life of divine service or to follow their own path. If they choose to follow God, they will be blessed; if they do not, God will turn away from them. Thus the only sure means of achieving salvation is observance of the Five Pillars of the faith: submission to God's will as described in the teachings of Muhammad, frequent prayer, ritual fasting, the giving of alms, and an annual pilgrimage to Mecca (the Hajj).

Unlike Christianity, Islam is a religion without sacraments or priests. It more closely resembles Judaism as it developed after the Diaspora, when Jews no longer had access to the Temple and no need for a Temple priesthood, but instead gathered around a master teacher (*rabbi*). Similarly, Muslims often rely on a community leader (*imam*) or scholar qualified to comment on matters of faith, who may also act

**THE KAABA.** This holy shrine remains the focus of worship for all Muslims, especially during the annual pilgrimage to Mecca. According to legend, Muhammad resolved a dispute among several tribes as to which should have the honor of lifting the Black Stone into place when the Kaaba was rebuilt. Muhammad's solution was to invite representatives of the tribes to hold the four corners of a carpet and to lift the stone together, while he himself directed its placement. ▪ ***What is the significance of this story?*** ▪ ***What message does it convey about the Prophet's important role in his own society?***

as a judge in disputes (as Muhammad had done in Medina). Although Muslims value the opportunity to come together for prayer, there is no prescribed liturgy as in the Roman and Orthodox Churches. Like Judaism, Islam emphasizes the inextricable connection between religious observance and daily life, between spirituality and politics. There is no opposition of sacred and secular authority, as in Christianity. But in marked contrast to Judaism, Islam is a religion that aspires to unite the world in a shared faith. This means that Muslims, like Christians, consider it their duty to engage in the work of conversion. This further means that there will inevitably be competition between the followers of these faiths, as both try carry out this mission.

# THE WIDENING ISLAMIC WORLD

As we have frequently noted, the death of any charismatic leader preciptates a series of crises. Muhammad and Alexander the Great represent very different types of leadership, but both created communities whose very survival seemed to depend on that leadership. Neither designated his own successor, and both left behind a number of close followers who disagreed as to the proper uses of the power they had inherited. Although the very survival of Islam seemed unlikely after Muhammad's death, within a generation it had come to encompass much of the ancient Near East.

## *The Arabic Conquest of the West*

Muhammad's closest followers were his father-in-law, Abu-Bakr *(ah-BOO-BAK-uhr)*, and an early convert named Umar. After Muhammad's death, these two men took the initiative by naming Abu-Bakr *caliph*, a word meaning "deputy" or "representative." In this capacity, Abu-Bakr began a campaign to subdue various tribes that had been loyal to Muhammad but were not willing to accept his own authority as Muhammad's successor. In the course of this, Abu-Bakr's forces began to move northward beyond the borders of Arabia, where they met only minimal resistance from Byzantine and Persian armies.

When Abu-Bakr died two year later, he was succeeded as caliph by Umar, who continued to direct his growing warrior bands against Byzantium and Persia. In the following years, Arab victories were virtually continuous. In 636 the Arabs routed a Byzantine army in Syria and then quickly swept over the entire area, occupying the leading cities of Antioch, Damascus, and Jerusalem. In 637 they destroyed the main army of the Persians and took the Persian capital of Ctesiphon. The rest of the realm offered little resistance. By 651, the Arabian conquest of the entire Persian Empire was complete.

Islamic forces now turned westward toward North Africa, capturing Byzantine Egypt by 646 and extending their control throughout the rest of North Africa during the following decades. Attempts to capture Constantinople in 677 and 717 were not successful, as we noted earlier, but in 711 the Arabs crossed from North Africa into Visigothic Spain and quickly absorbed most of that territory, too. Within less than a century, the forces of Islam had conquered the ancient Near East and much of the Roman Mediterranean, while the desert-dwelling Arabs had transformed themselves into the world's most daring seafarers.

How can we explain this prodigious achievement? On a basic level, what motivated the Arabs had motivated the Sumerians, the Neo-Assyrians, the Greeks, the Macedonians, and the Romans: the search for richer territory and new wealth. There is little evidence that Arab Muslims attempted to convert subject peoples to the faith of Islam at this time. Instead, they aimed to establish themselves as a superior ruling class. Yet religious enthusiasm certainly played a crucial role in forging a shared identity among tribes hitherto at war with one another. This identity and sense of superiority must have been further strengthenend by the absence of any serious opposition. Indeed, many of the local populations living within the Persian and Byzantine empires were restive and exhausted by the demands of these far-reaching imperial bureaucracies. To them, conquest brought deliverance. The Arabs did not demand that Jews or Christians convert to Islam, and because they exacted fewer taxes than the Byzantines and the Persians, they were often preferred to the old rulers. For all these reasons, Islam quickly spread over the territory between Egypt and Iran, and has been rooted there ever since.

## The Shi'ite–Sunni Schism

As the Arab conquests widened the world of Islam, disputes continued to divide the Muslims of Mecca. When the caliph Umar died in 644, he was replaced by a member of the Umayyad (*oo-MY-yad*) family, a wealthy clan that had resisted Muhammad's authority. Opponents of this new caliph, Uthman, rallied instead around Muhammad's cousin and son-in-law, Ali, whose family ties to Muhammad made him seem a more appropriate choice. When Uthman was murdered in 656, Ali's supporters declared him the new caliph. But Uthman's powerful family refused to accept this. Ali was murdered and another member of the

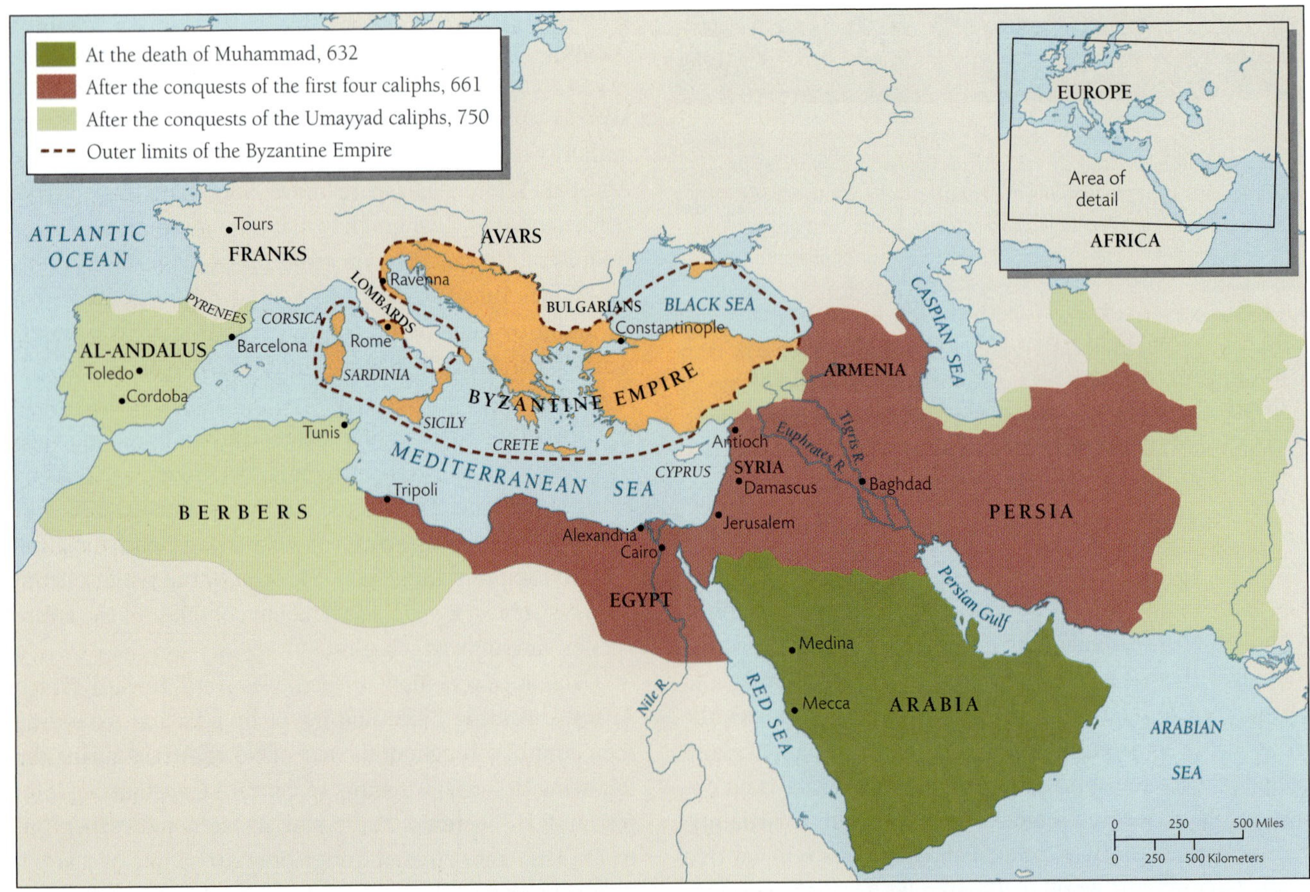


**THE EXPANSION OF ISLAM TO 750.** This map shows the steady advance of Islam from the time of Muhammad to the middle of the eighth century. ▪ ***What was the geographical extent of Islam in 750?*** ▪ ***What role did the Byzantine Empire play in the expansion of Islam?*** ▪ ***What conclusions can you draw regarding the period of especially rapid expansion in the generation after Muhammad's death?***

Umayyad family replaced him. From 661 to 750 this Umayyad dynasty ruled the Islamic world, establishing its capital at Damascus in Syria.

Ali's followers, however, did not accept defeat. They formed a separate group known as the Shi'ites (from *shi'a*, the Arabic word for "faction"). The Shi'ites insisted that only descendants of Ali and his wife, Muhammad's daughter Fatimah, could legitimately rule the Muslim community. Moreover, the Shi'ites did not accept the customary religious practices (*sunna*) that had developed under the first two caliphs who succeeded Muhammad—his father-in-law Abu-Bakr and his disciple Umar. Hence those Muslims who supported the Umayyad family and who *did* regard these customs as binding were called Sunnis. This division between Shi'ites and Sunnis has lasted until the present day. Often persecuted by the Sunni majority as heretics, Shi'ites consider themselves the only true exponents of Islam. Today, Shi'ites predominate in Iran and are the largest single Muslim group in Iraq, yet they constitute only one-tenth of the world's Muslims.

**THE GREAT UMAYYAD MOSQUE AT DAMASCUS.** This mosque was built by Caliph al-Walid between 705 and 715. Byzantine influence is apparent in its arched colonnades, its mosaics, and its series of domes, all of which was replicated in much subsequent Islamic architecture. The mosaic over the central doorway, shown here, indicates that the visitor is entering paradise. The mosque was constructed on the foundations of a Roman temple and also incorporates a later Christian shrine dedicated to Saint John the Baptist. ▪ ***Why would the caliph have chosen this site for his mosque?***

## The Umayyad and Abbasid Dynasties

The political triumph of the Umayyads in 661 and the military conquests of their supporters created a strong state centered on Damascus, formerly an administrative capital of the Roman Empire. And in many ways, the Umayyad caliphate functioned as a Roman successor state; it even continued to employ Greek-speaking bureaucrats trained in the techniques of Byzantine governance. Through these means, the Umayyads dominated the Mediterranean for several generations.

But the failure of their two massive attacks on Constantinople checked their power, which was also being challenged by a rival dynasty, the Abbasids, who claimed descent from one of Muhammad's uncles and who regarded the Umayyads as usurpers. In 750 the Abbasids led a succesful rebellion with the help of the Persians, forcing the Umayyads to retreat to their territories in Al-Andalus (Spain). In contrast with the Umayyads, the Abbasid Caliphate stressed Persian elements over Roman ones. Symbolic of this change was the shift in capitals from Damascus to Baghdad, where the second Abbasid caliph, al-Mansur (r. 754–75) built a new city near the ruins of the old Persian capital. The Abbasid caliphs also modeled their behavior on that of Persian princes and their administration on the autocratic rule of the former Persian Empire, imposing heavy taxation to support a large professional army and presiding over an extravagantly luxurious court. This is the world described in the *Arabian Nights*, a collection of stories written in Baghdad under the Abbasids. The dominating presence in these stories is Harun al-Rashid, who ruled from 786 to 809. His reign marked the height of Abbasid power.

Meanwhile, the Umayyad dynasty continued to rule in Spain and continued to claim that it was the only legitimate sucessor of Muhammad. Relations between the Umayyads of Al-Andalus and Abbasids of Persia were therefore very cold; but because their realms were far apart, the hostility between them rarely erupted into war. Instead, the two courts competed for preeminence through literary and cultural patronage, much as the Hellenistic kingdoms had done. Philosophers, artists, and especially poets flocked to both. The *Arabian Nights* was one product of this rivalry in Baghdad. Not to be outdone, the caliphs at the Spanish capital of Córdoba amassed a library of more than 400,000 volumes—at a time when a monastery in western Europe that possessed 100 books qualified as a major center of learning. Nothing remotely comparable had been seen in the Mediterranean since the time of the Ptolemies in Alexandria.

## Islamic Commerce and Industry

Alongside its political and military triumphs, the transformation of tiny settlements into thriving metropolitan commercial centers is one of Islam's most remarkable achievements. So is the Arabs' capacity to adapt themsleves to life in highly urbanized regions and to build on the long-established commercial infrastructure of Egypt, Syria, and Persia. Conversion to Islam actually increased the economic reach of this infrastructure, as trading contacts grew in tandem with the growth of the Islamic world. By the tenth century, Muslim merchants had penetrated into southern Russia and equatorial Africa and had become masters of the caravan routes that led eastward to India and China. Ships from the Muslim world established new trade routes across the Indian Ocean, the Persian Gulf, and the Caspian Sea, and for a time dominated the Mediterranean as well.

The growth of Muslim commerce in this period was also driven and sustained by a number of important new industries. Mosul, in Iraq, was a center for the manufacture of cotton cloth; Baghdad specialized in glassware, jewelry, pottery, and silks; Damascus was famous for its fine steel and for its woven-figured silk known as "damask"; Morocco and Al-Andalus were both noted for leatherworking; Toledo produced excellent swords. Drugs, perfumes, carpets, tapestries, brocades, woolens, satins, metal goods, and a host of other products turned out by Muslim artisans were carried throughout the Mediterranean world by Muslim merchants. They were also carried into central Asia, along the road to China that came to be known as the Silk Road, after the most prized commodity for which these goods were traded. With them went the Islamic faith, which took root among some peoples of modern India, Pakistan, and Afghanistan.

**ARABIC CALLIGRAPHY.** Muslim artists experimented with the art of calligraphy to make complex designs, sometimes abstract but often representing natural forms. This ink drawing on paper dates from the seventh century, and also represents the Muslim mastery of papermaking.

One commodity in particular deserves special mention: paper. Muslims learned papermaking from the Chinese and became became masters of the art in their own right. By the end of the eighth century, Baghdad alone had more than a hundred shops where blank paper or books written on paper were sold. Paper was cheaper to produce, easier to store, and far easier to use than papyrus or parchment. As a result, paper replaced papyrus in the Islamic world by the early eleventh century—even in Egypt, the heartland of papyrus production for almost 4,000 years.

The ready availability of paper brought about a revolution in the Islamic world. Many of the characteristic features of Islamic civilization—bureaucratic record keeping, high levels of literacy and book production (especially copies of the Qu'ran), even the standard form of cursive Arabic script known as Kufic—would have been impossible without the widespread availability of paper. Only in the thirteenth century would western Europeans master papermaking, but they would still continue to rely on the more durable parchment made from animal hides for the copying of most books and documents. It was not until the advent of print that paper began to replace parchment as the reading and writing material of western Europe.

## Mobility, Opportunity, and Status

As the reach of Islam extended through conquest and commerce, so Muslim culture became highly cosmopolitan, tapping into the civilizations of Byzantium and Persia, which were themselves the heirs of ancient empires stretching back to the time of Hammurabi's Babylon. The preeminence of trade and ease of travel also increased geographical mobility, and therefore social mobility. Muhammad's teachings further encouraged social mobility because the

Qu'ran stressed the equality of all Muslim men. At the courts of Baghdad and Córdoba, therefore, careers were open to men of talent, regardless of birth or wealth. Because literacy was remarkably widespread, many could rise through education and achieve top offices through enterprise and skill.

For those men wishing instead to embrace the religious life alone, Islam offered two main alternatives. One was that of the *ulama*, a learned man whose studies qualified him to offer advice on aspects of religious law and practice. These men often exerted great influence on the conduct of public life. Complementary to them were the Sufis, mystics who might be equated with Christian monks were it not for the fact that they seldom withdrew from the life of the community. While the *ulama* stressed adherance to religious law, the Sufis stressed individual contemplation and the cultivation of spiritual ecstasy. Some Sufis were "whirling dervishes," so known in the West because of their characteristic dances; others were *faqirs*, associated in the West with snake charming; still others were quiet, meditative men. Sufis were usually organized into brotherhoods and eventually made many succesful efforts to convert the peoples of Africa and India to Islam. Sufism also provided a channel for the most intense religious impulses. The ability of the *ulama* and the Sufis to coexist is testimony to the cultural pluralism of the Islamic world.

The absence of comparable careers for religious women, even comparable to those available to Christian nuns (see below), is a reminder of the limits often imposed by gender. There are significant exceptions, of course. For example, Muhammad's favored wife, Aisha (*ah-EE-sha*, d. 678), was revered as a scholar and played an important role in the creation and circulation of *hadith* (Arabic for "narrative"), comprising stories and sayings that shed light on the Prophet's life and teachings. But in general, women did not benefit from Muslim egalitarianism and opportunity. They were considered valuable, but mostly as indicators of a man's wealth and status. The Qu'ran allowed any Muslim man to marry as many as four wives, which often meant that the number of women available for marriage was far smaller than the number of men who desired to marry. This made for intense competition, and those men who had wives and daughters needed to ensure that their prized assets were safeguarded. So women were usually kept from the sight of men who were not members of the family or trusted friends. Along with female servants and the concubines also owned by a wealthy man, they were housed in a segregated part of the residence called the *haram* ("forbidden place"), guarded by eunuchs (men, usually sold as slaves, who had been castrated prior to adolescence). Within these enclaves, women vied with one another for precedence and worked to advance the fortunes of their children. But this was often the only form of power they could exercise.

## *Islam's Neighbors*

For the inhabitants of Byzantium, the triumph of the Abbasid caliphate in the eighth century released the Mediterranean from the pressures of Umayyad expansion. Farther west, the Franks of Gaul also benefited from the advent of the Abbasids. Because an Umayyad dynasty still controlled Al-Andalus, the great Frankish ruler Charlemagne (*SHAHR-leh-mayn*, r. 768–814) could counter their power by maintaining strong diplomatic and commercial relations with the Abbasid caliphate. The most famous symbol of this connection was an elephant called Abul Abbas, a gift from Harun al-Rashid to Charlemagne. More important, however, was the flow of silver that found its way from the Abbasid Empire north through Russia and the Baltic into the Rhineland, where it was exchanged for Frankish exports of furs, wax, honey, leather, and especially slaves—western Europeans who were captured and sold for profit by other western Europeans. Through these channels, jewels, silks, spices, and other luxury goods from India and the Far East also flowed north and west into Frankish territory. These trading links with the Abbasid world helped fund the extraordinary achievements of Charlemagne's own empire, which had a lasting effect on the culture and politics of Europe.

# THE CONVERSION OF NORTHWESTERN EUROPE

At the end of the sixth century, the Frankish chronicler Gregory of Tours (c. 538–594) considered himself to be a Roman, living in a Roman world of towns, trade, and local administration. Gregory was proud of his family's senatorial status and took it for granted that he and his male relatives should be bishops who ruled, by right of birth and status, over their cities and the surrounding countryside. Like others of his class, Gregory still spoke and wrote Latin—a rather different Latin from the polished prose of Cicero, but a Latin that would certainly have been comprehensible to the Romans of the republic. Although Gregory was aware that the western territories of the Roman Empire were now ruled by Frankish, Visigothic, and Lombard kings, he regarded at least some of these kings as Roman successors because they ruled in accordance with Roman models. In the case of the Franks, the king even ruled with the approval of the Roman emperor in Constantinople. It was also a source of satisfaction to Gregory that all these barbarian kings had converted to Roman Christianity and no longer embraced the heresy of Arianism. This, too, reinforced their *romanitas* and lent legitimacy to their rule.

Two hundred years later, the greatest of all Frankish kings, Charlemagne (742–814), was crowned as a new kind of Roman emperor in the West. By this time, there was no longer a sense of direct continuity with the earlier Roman world or a sense of obligation to the Roman emperor in Byzantium. When intellectuals at Charlemagne's court set out to reform the political, religious, and cultural life of his empire, their goal was to revive a Roman Empire from which they considered themselves estranged. They sought a *renovatio Romanorum imperii*, "a renewal of the empire of the Romans." This awareness of a break with the Roman past developed during the seventh century and was the consequence of profound economic, religious, and cultural changes.

## Economic and Political Instability

Even though the economy of the Roman Empire had become increasingly regionalized from the third century C.E. onward (Chapter 6), the Mediterranean remained an effective nexus of trade and communication. Gold coinage continued to circulate in both the eastern and the western provinces; a luxury trade in silks, spices, swords, and jewelry continued to move west; and slaves, wine, grain, and leatherwork still moved east from Gaul, Hispania, and North Africa toward Constantinople, Egypt, and Syria. By about 650, however, this Mediterranean world became more disintegrated. This was partly a result of Justinian's failed efforts to reconquer the Western empire, but imperial overtaxation of agricultural land, especially in Egypt and North Africa, also played a role. So did the temporary disruptions to traditional trade routes caused by Muslim raiders—temporary, because the merchants and rulers of Islam would soon do much to reconstruct and encourage patterns of commerce.

The most significant causes of economic instability in northwestern Europe were therefore internal, not external. The cities of Italy, Gaul, and Hispania could no longer maintain their walls, their public buildings, and their urban infrastructures as they had done under the Roman Empire. Although bishops and their aristocratic kinsmen still governed from these cities and continued to provide a market for certain kinds of luxury goods, barbarian kings and their nobles were moving to the countryside during the seventh century, living as much as possible from the produce of their own estates rather than purchasing their supplies in the marketplace. At the same time, much agricultural land was passing out of cultivation. The slaves or servile peasants who had farmed the large plantations for hundreds of years had no state to enforce their obedience; they were able to become more independent—yet they were also less effective, working just a few acres by themselves. Productivity declined, as did revenues from tolls and taxes.

The coinage systems of western Europe were also breaking down, which meant that wealth ceased to be portable, hindering long-distance exchange. The Arab conquests may have further reduced the supply of gold available in western Europe, because it was now being channeled eastward. But in any case, gold coins were too valuable to be useful in a local market economy. When we find evidence of such coins in western Europe at this time, they are more likely to have been plundered, hoarded, or given as gifts. By the 660s, those western European rulers who were still in a position to mint coins and guarantee their value had shifted from a gold to a silver coinage. Indeed, Europe would remain a silver-based economy for the next thousand years, until the supply of gold from European conquests in Africa and America once again made a gold standard viable (see Chapter 11).

As a result of these processes, western Europe came to rely on a two-tier economy of a kind that had not been necessary in any Western civilization since the Lydians introduced a standardized currency in the sixth century B.C.E. (Chapter 3). Gold, silver, and luxury goods circulated among the very wealthy, but most people relied on barter and various substitute currencies to facilitate transactions. Lords collected rents from their peasants in food or labor, but then found it difficult to convert these in-kind payments into the weapons, jewelry, and silks that brought prestige in aristocratic society. This was problematic not only for social reasons but for political ones: the power of lords depended on their ability to bestow such gifts on their followers (see ***Interpreting Visual Evidence***). When they could not acquire these items through trade, they had to win them through plunder and extortion. Either way, the process led to violence.

The successful chieftains of this era therefore tended to be those whose areas of influence adjoined wealthy but poorly defended territories that could be easily attacked or blackmailed. Such "soft frontiers" provided warlords and kings with land and booty, which they could then distribute to their followers. Successes of this sort would bring more followers to a lord's service, allowing him to further extend his influence; and so long as more conquests were made, the process of amassing power and wealth would continue. But power acquired through plunder and conquest was inherently unreliable. A few defeats might speedily reverse the fortunes of the lords reliant on it, leaving their followers to seek plunder elsewhere.

Another factor contributing to the instability of power in this world was the difficulty of ensuring its peaceful transfer. The rulers who established themselves during the mass migrations of the fifth and sixth centuries did not come from the traditional royal families of their peoples, and thus they faced opposition from many of their own warriors. Moreover, the groups who took possession of territories within the Western Roman Empire during these years were rarely (if ever) composed of a single affinity group; they were usually made up of many different tribes, including a sizable number of displaced Romans. Such unity as they possessed was largely the creation of the charismatic chieftain who led them, and this charisma was not easily passed on by inheritance.

## *The Merovingian Kingdom of the Franks*

Of all the groups that set up kingdoms in western Europe during the fifth and sixth centuries, only the Franks succeeded in establishing a single dynasty from which leaders would be drawn for the next 250 years. This dynasty reached back to Clovis (r. c. 481–511), a warrior-king, who established an alliance between his family and the powerful bishops of Gaul by converting to Roman Christianity—emulating the example of Constantine on many levels. Clovis's family came to be known as the Merovingians, after his legendary grandfather Merovech, who was said to have been sired by a sea monster (meaning, in effect, that no one really knew who Clovis's grandfather was). Clovis's own name proved even more long-lasting than the dynasty he founded. As the language of the Franks merged with the Latin of Gaul to become French, the name "Clovis" lost its hard "C" while the pronunciation of the "V" was softened. Thus "Clovis" became "Louis," the name borne by French kings up to the time of the French Revolution over 1,200 years later (see Chapter 18).

The Merovingians were not the only noble family in Gaul with a claim to kingship, but they were more successful in defending it than their counterparts in Visigothic Spain, Lombard Italy, and both the Anglo-Saxon and Celtic territories of Britain. In part, this was due to their capacity to transfer power from one generation to another. In medieval Europe, as at other times and places, the right of inheritance was not limited to the eldest male claimant of each competing royal family. When it came to property or power, all the sons of a king—and frequently all his male cousins and nephews, and even his daughters—could consider themselves the rightful heir. So even when the hegemony of any family was not threatened by outsiders, the transfer of power was almost always bloody.

In Gaul, however, the often brutal conflicts between rival Merovingian kings did not materially disrupt the strength and sophistication of their governance. Many elements of late Roman local administration survived throughout this period. Latin literacy, fostered by a network of monasteries linked to the Frankish court, remained an important element in this administration, providing a foundation on which Charlemagne would later build. Even the cultural revival associated with the reign of Charlemagne really began in the late seventh century at the monastic foundations fostered by members of the Merovingian family and other powerful lords.

Such monasteries grew remarkably during the seventh century and became the engines that made Merovingian Gaul wealthier and more stable than other regions of northwestern Europe. Approximately 550 monasteries were thriving by the year 700, more than 300 of which had been established in the preceding century alone. The cities of Frankish bishops also prospered, amassing most of their landed possessions by the end of the seventh century, possessions from which they would continue to profit until the time of the French Revolution.

This massive redistribution of wealth reflected a fundamental shift in the economic gravity of the Frankish kingdom. In the year 600, the wealth of Gaul was still concentrated in the south, where it had been throughout the late Roman period. By the year 750, however, the economic center of the kingdom lay north of the Loire, in the territories that extended from the Rhineland westward to the North Sea. It was here that most of the new monastic foundations of the seventh century were established.

Behind this shift in prosperity lay a long and successful effort to bring under cultivation the rich, heavy soils of northern Europe. This effort was largely engineered by the new monasteries, which harnessed the peasant workforce and pioneered agricultural technologies adapted to the climate and terrain. The most important were heavy, wheeled plows capable of cutting and turning grassland sod and clay, soils very different from those of the Mediterranean. This innovation in turn necessitated the development of more efficient devices for harnessing animals (particularly oxen) to these plows. Gradually warming weather also improved the fertility of the wet northern soils, lengthening the growing season and so making possible more efficient

# Interpreting Visual Evidence

## *The Ship Burial of Sutton Hoo*

The two most impressive finds in the history of British archeology have been made by amateurs. The most recent, in the summer of 2009, was the largest hoard of worked gold and silver ever found in one place (more than 5 kilograms of gold and 2.5 kilograms of silver; image A), discovered by a man in Staffordshire walking over a neighbor's farm with a metal detector. The hoard's extraordinary value and range of artifacts—and their historical implications—can only be guessed at now; even the dating is inconclusive.

The other find, made in 1939, was a royal gravesite dating from the seventh century (image B), which many scholars believe to be the tomb of King Redwald of East Anglia, described by Bede as a baptized Christian who refused to give up the worship of his ancestral gods. The king's body was placed in a wooden structure in the middle of a 90-foot-long ship that had been dragged to the top of a bluff (a *hoo*), eleven miles from the English Channel. The ladder in the photograph of the original excavation reaches into the burial chamber.

The contents of the grave included:

- a lamp and a bronze bucket that had been suspended from a chain
- a ceremonial helmet (image C) modeled on those worn by Roman cavalry

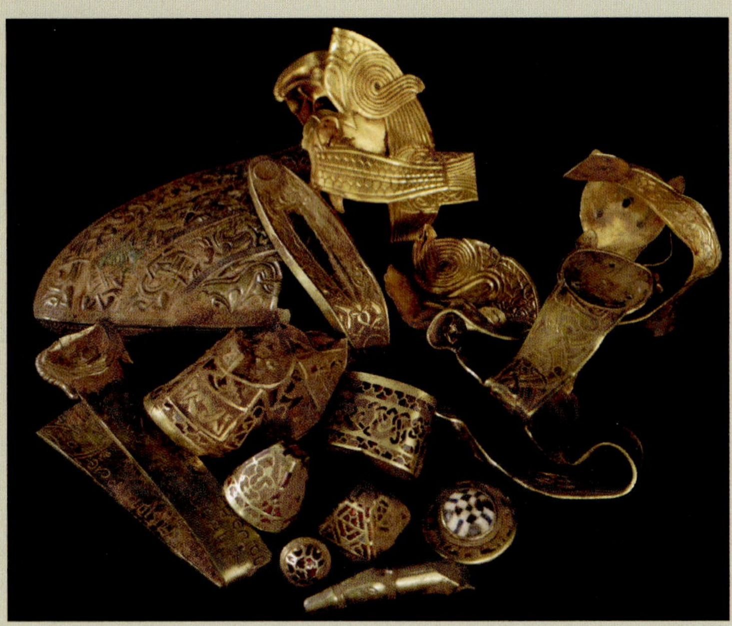

A. The Straffordshire Hoard, found in 2009.

B. The original excavation of the Burial Chamber at Sutton Hoo, 1939.

crop-rotation systems. As food became more plentiful, the population began to expand. Although much of Frankish Gaul remained a land of scattered settlements separated by dense forests, it was far more populous by 750 than it had been in the time of Clovis. All these developments would continue during the reign of Charlemagne and beyond.

## *The Power of Monasticism*

As we just noted, the seventh century witnessed a rapid increase in the foundation of monastic houses all over northwestern Europe. Although monasteries had existed in Gaul, Italy, and Hispania since the fourth century, most were

officers just before the withdrawal of the legions from Britain in 410—but decorated like helmets found in eastern Sweden

- a sword and a large, circular shield, resembling those found in Swedish burial sites
- exquisitely crafted belt buckles and shoulder clasps (image D), made of gold and garnet, and worked with designs.
- a pair of silver spoons with long handles, possibly crafted in Byzantium, and inscribed in Greek with the names PAULOS and SAULOS (Paul and Saul)
- a large silver dish (72 cm in diameter) made in Byzantium between 491 and 518
- a bronze bowl from the eastern Mediterranean
- a six-stringed lyre in a bag made of beaver skin, similar to lyres found in Germany
- a purse containing 37 gold coins, each from a different Merovingian mint, the most recent datable to the 620s
- heaps of armor, blankets, cloaks, and other gear.

C. A Sutton Hoo Helmet.

### *Questions for Analysis*

1. What do these artifacts, and the context in which they were found, reveal about the extent of Anglo-Saxon contact with the rest of the world? Which regions are represented, and why?
2. Based on this evidence, what conclusions can you draw about Anglo-Saxon culture and values?
3. Do any of these grave-goods indicate that the occupant was a Christian king? Why or why not?

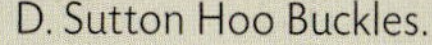

D. Sutton Hoo Buckles.

located in highly Romanized areas. In the fifth century a powerful monastic movement began in Ireland, as well, and eventually spread to the Celtic regions of Britain and from there to the Continent. The Irish missionary Columbanus (540–615), for example, was the founder of Merovingian monasteries at Luxeuil and Fontaine. Important monasteries were also established on the island of Iona, off the western coast of what is now Scotland, and at Lindisfarne, off Britain's northeastern coast. In all of these cases, close ties were forged between monks and local tribal leaders or powerful families, much to the political and economic gain of all parties.

**ABBEY CHURCH, ISLAND OF IONA.** This tiny island off Scotland's west coast is the site of many Iron Age forts and has been home to a monastic community since the sixth century. Missionaries from Iona were instrumental in converting the Celtic tribes of northern Britain, and under their influence Iona become the burial place of Scottish kings.

Most monastic foundations of the seventh century were deliberately located in rural areas, where they played a crucial role. Indeed, the material advantages of monastic innovation were a powerful incentive toward conversion in the communities directly affected by improved living conditions. Prosperity was also a powerful advertisement for authority: a lord or chieftain who had the support of a monastery and the beneficient Christian God was obviously worthy of loyalty. Because monasteries played such a key role in economic development and political order, lords often granted them special privileges, freeing them from the control of local bishops and giving them jurisdiction over their own lands. Thus, monasteries became politically powerful not only because they had been founded by powerful men, but because they were lordships in their own right.

Frequently, these new foundations were double monasteries that accommodated women as well as men. Often they were established for women only. In either case, they were often ruled by abbesses drawn from noble or royal families. Monasticism thus became a road to political power for women. It also gave women—commoners as well as queens—freedoms they did not have elsewhere, or at any other time in history up to this point. Within the monastery, women had more control over their own minds and bodies. They could wield enormous influence, promoting their families' diplomatic and dynastic interests but without the dangers and uncertainties of pregnancy. And they were also guaranteed salvation, at a time when salvation outside the cloister seemed a perilously uncertain prospect. Moreover, the prayers of holy women were regarded as particularly effective in securing divine support or retribution. This further enriched convents through donations of land and wealth, although it could not always safeguard them from violence, or their inhabitants from abduction and rape.

Convents and double monasteries also served the interests of men, which is why kings and lords supported them. They were dynamic repositories of prayer, which could further the ambitions of their male benefactors and protect them from harm. They provided a dignified place of retirement for inconvenient but politically powerful women, such as the sisters and daughters of rivals or the widow of a previous ruler. And by limiting the number of powerful women who could reproduce, convents helped reduce the number of male claimants to power. Establishing aristocratic and royal women in convents was thus an important way of controlling successions and managing political disputes.

Monasticism played an important role in missionary activity, too. As noted above, the work of Irish monks was crucial to the spread of Christianity in northern parts of Britain and in other areas of northern Europe virtually untouched by the Roman Empire. Missionaries were also sponsored by the fledgling papacy in Rome and by the Merovingian royal family—especially its women. The best example of this is the conversion of Britain's Anglo-Saxon tribes, which we glimpsed in the opening paragraph of this chapter. In 597 a group of forty Benedictine monks were sent by Pope Gregory I (r. 590–604) to the southeastern kingdom of Kent, where their efforts were assisted by Frankish translators—and by the fact that the local king, Æthelbehrt, had married a Frankish princess who was already a Christian. This pattern of influence repeated

# Analyzing Primary Sources

## *An Anglo-Saxon Slave Girl and Frankish Queen*

*The Anglo-Saxon Saint Balthild became the wife of the Merovingian king Clovis II (r. 639–57), but she began life as a slave. After the king's death, she was left in a precarious position at the Frankish court as regent for her son, Clothar III, and was eventually forced to enter the convent she had founded at Chelles, near Paris. The following excerpt from her Latin vita ("life") describes her rise to a position of power. It was probably written by a nun of Chelles.*

[P]raise should first be sung of Him Who made the humble great and raised the pauper from the dunghill and seated him among the princes of his people. Such a one is the woman present to our minds, the venerable and great lady Balthild the queen. Divine Providence called her from across the seas. She, who came here as God's most precious and lofty pearl, was sold at a cheap price. Erchinoald, a Frankish magnate and most illustrious man, acquired her and in his service the girl behaved most honorably. . . . For she was kind-hearted and sober and prudent in all her ways, careful and plotting evil for none. . . . And since she was of the Saxon race, she was graceful in form with refined features, a most seemly woman with a smiling face and serious gait. And she so showed herself just as she ought in all things, that she pleased her master and found favor in his eyes. So he determined that she should set out the drinking cup for him in his chamber and, honored above all others as his housekeeper, stand at his side always ready to serve him. . . . She gained such happy fame that, when the said lord Erchinoald's wife died, he hoped to unite himself to Balthild, that faultless virgin, in a matronal bed. . . .

[But] when she was called to the master's chamber she hid herself secretly in a corner and threw some vile rags over herself so that no one could guess that anyone might be concealed there. . . . She hoped that she might avoid a human marriage bed and thus merit a spiritual and heavenly spouse. . . . Thereafter it happened, with God's approval, that Balthild, the maid who escaped marriage with a lord, came to be espoused to Clovis, son of the former king Dagobert. Thus by virtue of her humility she was raised to a higher rank. . . .

Source: Excerpted from *Sainted Women of the Dark Ages*, eds. and trans. John E. Halborg, Jo Ann McNamara, and E. Gordon Whatley (Chapel Hill, NC: 1992), pp. 268–70.

### *Questions for Analysis*

1. Based on what you have learned about the prevalence of the slave trade in early medieval Europe, what might you speculate about Balthild's actual role in Erchinoald's household?
2. Balthild would have been a contemporary of the king buried at Sutton Hoo. Is it likely that she would have been a Christian when she was sold into slavery in England? Why or why not?
3. In light of Balthild's later status as a queen and regent for her son, why would her biographer stress that she was "careful and plotting evil for none"? To what allegations or incidents might the author of this life be responding?

itself all over southern and eastern Britain. Writing a hundred years later in the monastery of Monkwearmouth in Northumbria, the historian Bede could claim that the tribes of England were now united in their shared allegiance to the Roman Church and its English archbishop, whose seat was the cathedral in Æthelbert's capital at Canterbury. Bede credited the Roman pope for initiating this remarkable feat, and the monastic rule under which he lived for bringing it to fruition.

## *The Papacy of Gregory the Great*

Pope Gregory I, also known as Gregory the Great, was the first bishop of Rome to envision a new role for the papacy in northwestern Europe. We have seen that the Roman "papa" frequently asserted his superiority over other patriarchs; but in reality, he was subordinate to the emperors in Constantinople and to the greater prestige of the Christian East. As Byzantine power in Italy declined, however, Gregory

THE LINDISFARNE GOSPELS. This page from one of the astonishing illuminated ("light-filled") books produced by the monastery at Lindisfarne shows the opening of the gospel of John. ▪ ***Why would monastic scribes have devoted so much time, energy, and skill to the decoration of a text? How do these artistic motifs compare to those featured on the metalwork found at Sutton Hoo (pages 226 and 227)?*** ▪ ***What conclusions can you draw from these similarities?***

THE COVER OF THE LINDAU GOSPELS. This book, bound in gilded silver and encrusted with jewels and ivory cameos, was presented by Pope Gregory the Great to a Lombard queen around the year 600. ▪ ***Given what you have learned about the cultures of northern Europe, what is the significance of this rich gift?*** ▪ ***What would Gregory have been attempting to achieve by giving it?***

sought to create a more autonomous Latin Church by focusing attention on the untapped resources of the wild West. An influential theologian, he is considered the successor of Jerome, Ambrose, and Augustine (Chapter 6) because he greatly extended the applicability of their teachings to the world outside the Romanized Mediterranean. Among his doctrinal contributions were an emphasis on the necessity of penance for the forgiveness of sins and the concept of Purgatory as a place where the soul could be purified before it was admitted into Heaven—instead of being sent immediately to perpetual damnation. Alongside this emphasis on penance, Gregory emphasized the importance of pastoral care: the proper instruction and encouragement of the laity. He also sought to increase the affective power of Christian worship by promoting the performance of music. Song has always been essential to religious ritual, but Gregory encouraged it to such a degree that the very style of singing that emerged in this period is known as "Gregorian chant."

Gregory was also a statesman and leader in the model of his Roman forebears. Within Italy, he ensured the survival of the papacy against Lombard invaders by clever diplomacy and expert management of papal estates and revenues. He maintained good relations with Byzantium while asserting his authority over the other bishops of the Latin Church. His support of communities living under the *Rule* of Saint Benedict (Chapter 6) helped make Benedictine monasticism the predominant monastic force in the West. Yet Gregory's influence was not always benign. He was among the first theologians to articulate the Church's official policy toward the Jews, which became increasingly strident: building on Gregory's example, later popes would insist that the Jews' alleged role in Christ's crucifixion and their denial of his divinity had deprived them of their rights in a Christian world.

## THE EMPIRE OF CHARLEMAGNE

Toward the end of the seventh century, tensions among noble families in the Merovingian heartland of Neustria and those in the border region of Austrasia were increasing. The Austrasian nobles had profited from their steady push into the "soft frontier" areas east of the Rhine, acquiring wealth and military power in the process. The Merovingians, based in Neustria, had no such easy conquests at their disposal. Moreover, a considerable portion of their land had been given to monasteries in the course of the seventh century, which decreased their wealth and their capacity to attract followers. A succession of short-lived kings then opened the door to a series of civil wars, and finally to a decisive challenge to the Merovingian dynasty.

### *Kings and King-Makers*

In 687 an Austrasian nobleman called Pepin (635/45–714) succeeded in forcing his way into power by making himself the king's right-hand man. He took the title *maior domus*, "big man of the house," and began to exercise royal authority while maintaining the fiction that he was merely a royal servant. He did this effectively for more than twenty-five years. After his death, his illegitimate son Charles Martel ("the Hammer," 688–741) further consolidated control over both the Merovingian homeland and the royal administration. For the next two generations, the Merovingian kings were largely figureheads in a realm ruled by Charles Martel and his sons.

Charles Martel is sometimes considered the second founder (after Clovis) of the Frankish kingdom. His claim to this title is twofold. First, in 733 or 734 he repelled a Muslim force that had ventured into Frankish territory, meeting them in battle at Tours, some 150 miles from the Merovingian capital at Paris. Although the Muslim contingent was a raiding party rather than a full-scale army, this incursion may have been regarded as an attempted conquest on the part of the Umayyad dynasty of Al-Andalus; in any case, Charles' victory won him great prestige. More important, Charles had developed an alliance with Benedictine missionaries from England, who were attempting to convert the Low Countries and central Germany to Christianity. Charles' family had long been active in the drive to conquer and settle these areas, and he understood clearly how missionary work and Frankish expansion could go hand in hand. Charles assisted these conversion efforts. In return, the leader of the English Benedictines, Boniface (c. 672–754), brought him into contact with the papacy and assisted him in his efforts to reform—and control—Frankish churches.

Although Charles never sought to become king himself, he was so clearly the effective ruler of Gaul that the Franks did not bother to choose a new king when the reigning Merovingian died in 737. But then Charles himself died in 741, and his sons Carloman and Pepin were forced to allow the election of a new king while they continued to exercise power behind the scenes. This compromise did not last long, however; in 750 Carloman had withdrawn from public life by entering a monastery, and Pepin decided to seize the throne for himself. This turned out to be harder than he may have expected. Even though the reigning king was ineffectual, Frankish identity was bound up with loyalty to Clovis's descendants; even though tribal leaders had the power to elect a new king, they were reluctant to do so. Pepin therefore turned to the Frankish bishops, who were unwilling to support him without backing from the pope. To gain this, Pepin was able to trade on his family's support of the Benedictines. The pope, for his part, saw that a powerful leader of the Franks could be a potential ally in his political struggle with the Byzantine emperors over iconoclasm (which the papacy opposed) and in his military struggle against the Lombard kings for control of central Italy.

So Boniface, acting as papal emissary, anointed Pepin king of the Franks in 751. This was a new ritual, but it had a powerful Biblical precedent: the ceremony by which the prophet Samuel had made Saul the first king of Israel, by anointing him with holy oil (Chapter 2). Indeed, the significance of the Old Testament association would grow under Pepin's son Charlemagne (associated with David) and his grandson Louis the Pious (associated with Solomon). To contemporary observers, however, the novelty of these proceedings underscored the uncertainty of the process by which a legitimate king had been deposed and a new king created. And as we will see, this king-making process was the first step on a long road that would ultimately limit the power of later medieval kings and modern constitutional monarchs alike: the principle that kingship is an office and can be occupied, at least theoretically, by anyone—and that if a king is ineffectual or tyrannical, he can be deposed and replaced by a new king.

### *The Reign of Charlemagne*

Pepin's position as king was a tenuous one, and when he died it seemed likely that the Frankish kingdom would break up into mutually hostile regions: Austrasia, Neustria, and Aquitaine. That it did not was the work of Pepin's son,

Charles, known to the French as Charlemagne and to the Germans as Karl der Grosse—"Charles the Great." It is from him, as well as from his grandfather Charles Martel, that this new Frankish dynasty takes the name "Carolingian" (from *Carolus*, the Latin form of "Charles").

When Charlemagne came to power in 768, he managed to unite the Franks by the tried and true method of attacking a common, outside enemy. In a series of conquests, the Franks succeeded in annexing the Lombard kingdom of northern Italy, most of what is now Germany, portions of central Europe, and Catalonia. These conquests seemed to set a seal of divine approval on the new Carolingian dynasty. More important, they provided the victorious Franks with the spoils of war and vast new lands that enabled Charlemagne to reward his closest followers. Many of the peoples whom Charlemagne conquered were already Christians. In Saxony, however, Charlemagne's armies campaigned for twenty years before subduing the inhabitants and forcing their conversion. This created a precedent with momentous consequences, because it linked military conquest with conformity of belief. In time, the assumption that the subjugation of a vanquished people should be accompanied by their conversion would become ingrained in the philosophy and practice of most Western civilizations.

To rule his vast new empire, Charlemagne enlisted the help of the Frankish warrior class he had enriched and elevated to positions of prominence. These counts (in Latin, *comites*, "followers") supervised local governance within their territories. Among their many duties was the administration of justice and the raising of armies. Charlemagne also established a network of other local officials who convened courts, established tolls, administered royal lands, and collected taxes. To facilitate transactions and trade, he created a new coinage system based on a division of

**THE EMPIRE OF CHARLEMAGNE IN 814.** When Charlemagne died in 814, he had created an empire that embraced a large portion of the lands formerly united under the Western Roman Empire. ▪ ***What were the geographical limits of his power?*** ▪ ***How were these limits dictated by the historical forces we have been studying?*** ▪ ***Along what lines was Charlemagne's empire divided after his death?***

# Analyzing Primary Sources

## *The Capitularies of Charlemagne*

*Charlemagne's careful governance of his domains would set a high standard for other rulers far into the future. One of the means by which this governance was carried out was through capitularies (a Latin word denoting a document divided into chapters), which contained instructions issued by the central administration of the court to local counts and other authorities. The following are directives addressed in 785 to the administrators of Saxony, a region recently conquered by Charlemagne, whose inhabitants were forcibly converted to Christianity.*

### *Capitulary Concerning the Parts of Saxony*

**1.** Decisions were taken first on the more important items. All were agreed that the churches of Christ which are now being built in Saxony and are consecrated to God should have no less honor than the temples of idols had, but rather a greater and more surpassing honor.

**2.** If anyone takes refuge in a church, let no one presume to drive him out of that church by force; rather let him be in peace until he is brought to plead his case, . . . and after this let him be brought to the presence of our lord the king. . . .

**3.** If anyone makes forcible entry to a church, and steals anything from it by violence or stealth, or if he sets fire to the church, let him die.

**4.** If anyone in contempt of the Christian faith should spurn the holy Lenten fast and eat meat, let him die; but let the priest enquire into the matter, lest it should happen that someone is compelled by necessity to eat meat.

* * *

**6.** If anyone is deceived by the devil, and believes after the manner of pagans that some man or some woman is a witch and eats people, . . . let him pay the penalty of death.

**7.** If anyone follows pagan rites and causes the body of a dead man to be consumed by fire, . . . let him pay with his life.

**8.** If there is anyone of the Saxon people lurking among them unbaptized, and if he scorns to come to baptism, . . . let him die.

**9.** If anyone sacrifices a man to the devil, . . . let him die.

* * *

**12.** If anyone rapes the daughter of his lord, he shall die.

**13.** If anyone kills his lord or his lady, he shall be punished in the same way.

* * *

**18.** On Sundays there are to be no assemblies or public gatherings, except in cases of great need or when an enemy is pressing; rather let all attend church to hear the word of God. . . .

* * *

**33.** With regard to perjury, the law of the Saxons is to apply.

**34.** We forbid the Saxons to come together as a body in public gatherings, except on those occasions when our *missus* [messenger] assembles them on our instructions; rather, let each and every count hold court and administer justice in his own area. And the clergy are to see to it that this order is obeyed.

Source: From *The Reign of Charlemagne: Documents on Carolingian Government*, eds. and trans. H. R. Lyon and John Percival (New York: 1975), pp. 31–34.

### *Questions for Analysis*

1. What types of behavior does this capitulary attempt to regulate? What seem to be the major challenges faced by Charlemagne's administrators in this new territory?
2. In only one case does this capitulary mention the law of the Saxon people themselves, in the clause relating to perjury (number 12). Why would Charlemagne's administrators consider it advisable to punish this particular crime in accordance with Saxon custom?
3. How would you characterize Charlemagne's method of dealing with a conquered people? In your estimation, is this policy likely to be effective?

the silver pound into units of twenty shillings, each worth twelve pennies—a system that would last in parts of Europe and in Britain into the 1970s, when it was replaced by a decimal-based currency. As we noted above, much of the silver for this new coinage originated in the Abbasid Empire and was payment for furs, cloth, and especially slaves captured in Charlemagne's wars, who were now transported to Baghdad. The silver, in turn, circulated as far as north as Scandinavia, Russia, and the Baltic Sea.

Like Carolingian administration generally, this new monetary system depended on the regular use of written records, which means that the sources supporting historical research on Charlemagne's empire are numerous. But Charlemagne did not rely on the written word alone to make his will felt. Periodically, his court sent special messengers, known as *missi*, on tours through the countryside to relay his instructions and report back on the conduct of local administrators. This was the most thorough system of governance known in Europe since the height of the Roman Empire, reaching many parts of the Continent that the Romans had never occupied. It set the standard for royal administration in Europe for centuries.

**CHARLEMAGNE'S IMAGE OF AUTHORITY.** A silver penny struck between 804 and 814 in Mainz (as indicated by the letter *M* at the bottom) represents Charlemagne in a highly stylized fashion, as a Roman emperor with a military cloak and laurel wreath. The inscription reads *Karolus Imp Avg* (Charles, Emperor, Augustus). Charlemagne's portrait is closely modeled on both Hellenistic and Roman coins.

## Christianity and Kingship

In keeping with the traditions established by his father and grandfather, Charlemagne took his responsibilities as a Christian king seriously. As his empire expanded, moreover, he came to see himself as the leader of a unified Christian society, Christendom, which he was obliged to defend. Like his contemporaries in Byzantium and Islam—as well as his Roman predecessors—he recognized no distinction between religion and politics. Indeed, he conceived kingship as a sacred office created by God to protect the Church and promote the salvation of his Christian people. Religious reforms were therefore no less central to proper kingship than were justice and defense. In some ways, indeed, a king's responsibilities for his kingdom's spiritual welfare were more important than his other, secular responsibilities.

These ideas were not new in the late eighth century, but they took on a new importance because of the extraordinary power Charlemagne wielded. Like other rulers of this period, Charlemagne was able to appoint and depose bishops and abbots, just as he did his counts and other officials. But he also changed the liturgy of Frankish churches, reformed the rules of worship in Frankish monasteries, declared changes in basic statements of Christian belief, prohibited pagan practices, and imposed basic Christian observances on the conquered peoples of Saxony. As the dominant political power in central Italy, Charlemagne was also the protector of the papacy. Although he acknowledged the pope as spiritual leader of western Christendom, Charlemagne dealt with the bishop of Rome much as he did with other bishops in his empire. He supervised and approved papal elections, and he also protected the pope from his many enemies. To Charlemagne, such measures were clearly required if God's new chosen people, the Franks, were to avoid the fate that befell biblical Israel whenever its people turned away from their obedience to God.

## The Carolingian Renaissance

Similar ideals lay behind the Carolingian Renaissance, a cultural and intellectual flowering that took place around the Carolingian court. Like their biblical exemplars David and Solomon, Charlemagne and his son Louis the Pious considered it a crucial part of their role to be patrons of learning and the arts. In doing so, they created an ideal of the court as an intellectual and cultural center that would profoundly influence western European cultural life until the First World War (Chapter 24).

Behind the Carolingians' support for scholarship was the conviction that learning was the foundation on which Christian wisdom rested and that such wisdom was essential to the salvation of God's people. Charlemagne therefore recruited intellectuals from all over Europe. Foremost among these was the Anglo-Saxon monk Alcuin, whose

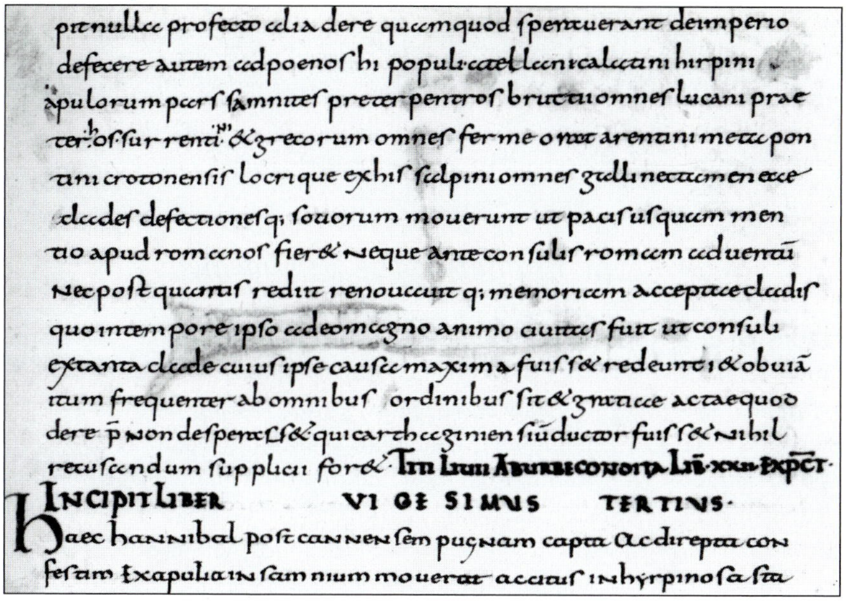
ptnullæ profecto cladere quamquod sperauerant deimperio
defecere autem adpoenos hi populi atellani calatini hirpini
apulorum pars samnites praeter pentros bruttii omnes lucani prae
ter os surrentini & graecorum omnes ferme ora tarentini metapon
tini crotonensis locrique et cisalpini omnes galli nectamen eae
clades defectionesq; sociorum mouerunt ut pacis usquam men
tio apud romanos fieret & neque ante consulis romam aduentũ
nec postquam is rediit renouauit q; memoriam acceptae cladis
quo intempore ipso adeo magno animo ciuitas fuit utconsuli
extanta clade cuius ipse causa maxima fuisset redeunti & obuiã
itum frequenter ab omnibus ordinibus sit & gratiae actae quod
de r.p. non desperasset quicarthaginiensium ductor fuisset nihil
recusandum supplicii foret· TITI LIUII AB URBE CONDITA LIB. XXII. EXPLICIT·
INCIPIT LIBER VICESIMUS TERTIUS·
Haec hannibal post cannensem pugnam capta ac direpta con
festim ex apulia in samnium mouerat accitus in hirpinos a sta

**ROMAN HISTORY IN CAROLINGIAN MINISCULE.** The very survival of Livy's history of the Roman Republic, originally written during the reign of Augustus Caesar, is a product of the Carolingian Renaissance. Furthermore, the clear layout and beautifully formed script of this manuscript copy helped readers without knowledge of Latin to make out the words. For example, the first two words of the heading near the bottom are *Incipit Liber* ("[Here] begins the book") and the sentence following it begins with a reference to the Carthaginian general Hannibal.

command of classical Latin established him as the intellectual leader of Charlemagne's court. Under Alcuin's direction, Carolingian scholars produced much original Latin poetry and an impressive number of theological and pastoral tracts. But their primary efforts were devoted to collating, correcting, and recopying classical Latin texts, including, most importantly, the text of the Latin Bible, which had accumulated many generations of copyists' mistakes in the four hundred years since Jerome's translation (Chapter 6). To detect and correct these errors, Alcuin and his associates gathered as many different versions of the biblical text as they could find and compared them, word by word. After determining the correct version among all the variants, they made a new, corrected copy and destroyed the other versions. They also developed a new style of handwriting, with simplified letter forms and spaces inserted between words that reduced the likelihood that subsequent copyists would misread the corrected texts. Reading was further facilitated by the addition of punctuation. This new style of handwriting, known as Carolingian miniscule, is the foundation for the typefaces of most modern books—including this one.

## The Revival of the Western Roman Empire

On Christmas Day in the year 800, Charlemagne was crowned emperor by Pope Leo III. Centuries later, popes would cite this epochal event as precedent for the political superiority they claimed over the "Holy Roman Empire," as it came to be called (see Chapter 9). In the year 800, however, Pope Leo was entirely under Charlemagne's thumb. And Charlemagne's biographer, Einhard, would later claim that the coronation was planned without the emperor's knowledge. For one thing, it was certain to anger the true Roman emperor in Byzantium, with whom Charlemagne had strained relations. Nor did the imperial title add much to Charlemagne's position; he was already a de facto emperor in his own right. Why, then, did he accept the title and, in 813, transfer it to his son Louis?

Historians are still debating this question. What is clear, in any case, is the symbolic significance of the action. Although the Romans of Byzantium no longer influenced western Europe directly, they continued to regard it (somewhat vaguely) as an outlying province of their empire. Moreover, the emperor in Constantinople claimed to be the political successor of Caesar Augustus. Charlemagne's assumption of the imperial title was a clear slap in the face, and it deepened Byzantium's suspicion of his cordial relationship with Byzantium's enemy, Harun al-Rashid, the Abbasid caliph in Baghdad. But for Charlemagne's followers—and for all the medieval rulers who came after him—it was a declaration of independence and superiority. With only occasional interruptions, western Europeans would continue to crown Roman emperors until the nineteenth century, while territorial claims and concepts of national sovereignty continued to rest on Carolingian precedent. Whatever his own motives may have been, Charlemagne's revival of the Western Roman Empire was crucial to the developing self-consciousness of western Europe.

## DISPUTED LEGACIES AND NEW ALLIANCES

When Charlemagne died in 814, his empire descended intact to his only surviving son, Louis the Pious. Under Louis, however, the empire disintegrated, and it was divided among his three sons in 840. Western Francia (the core of modern France) went to Charles the Bald; Eastern Francia (which became the principalities of Germany) went to Louis the German; and a third kingdom (stretching from the Rhineland to Rome) went to Lothair, along with the imperial title. But when Lothair's line died out in 856, this fragile compromise dissolved into open warfare, as the East and West Franks fought over Lothair's former territories and the imperial power that went with them. The heartland of this disputed domain, known to the Germans as Lotharingia and to the French as Alsace-Lorraine, would continue to be a site of bitter contention until the end of the Second World War (See Chapter 26).

### *The Collapse of the Carolingian Empire*

Louis faced an impossible situation of a kind we have studied many times before: the task of holding together an artificial constellation of territories united by someone else. Charlemagne's empire had been built on successful conquest. By 814, however, Charlemagne had pushed the borders of his empire beyond the practical limits of his administration. To the southwest, he now faced the Umayyad rulers of Al-Andalus; to the north, the pagan inhabitants of Scandinavia; and in the east, his armies were too preoccupied with settling the territories they had already conquered to secure the Slavic lands that lay beyond. At the same time, the pressures that had driven these conquests—the need for land and plunder to cement the allegiance of followers—had become ever more pronounced as a result of their very success. The number of counts had tripled, from approximately 100 to 300, and each of them wanted more wealth and power.

Frustrated by their new emperor's inability to reward them, the Frankish aristocracy turned against him and on each other. Smoldering hostilities between Austrasians, Neustrians, and Aquitanians—which Charlemagne had stifled by directing their energies elsewhere—flared up again. As centralized authority broke down, the vast majority of the empire's free inhabitants found themselves increasingly dominated by local lords who treated them as if they were unfree serfs. At the same time, internal troubles in the Abbasid Empire caused a breakdown in the commercial system through which Scandinavian traders brought Abbasid silver into Carolingian domains. Deprived of their livelihood, these traders turned to raiding, which is what the Norse word "Viking" means. Under these combined pressures, the Carolingian Empire fell apart, and a new political map of Europe began to emerge.

### *The Impact of the Viking Invasions*

Scandinavian traders were already familiar figures in the North Sea and Baltic ports of Europe when Charlemagne came to power. They had begun to establish strategic settlements in what is now Russia, from which they navigated down the rivers to Byzantium (through the Black Sea) and the Abbasid caliphate (through the Caspian Sea). But when the power of the Abbasids declined, Viking raiders turned to plunder, ransom, tribute collection, and slaving. At first, these were small-scale operations. But soon, some Viking attacks involved organized armies numbering in the thousands. The small tribal kingdoms of the Anglo-Saxons and Celts made the British Isles easy targets, as were the the kingdoms of divided Franks.

By the tenth century, the Vikings controlled independent principalities in eastern England, Ireland, the islands of Scotland, and the region of France that is still called "Norseman-land," Normandy. The Viking people known as the Rus' established the beginnings of a kingdom that would become Russia. At the end of the tenth century, Vikings ventured farther west and colonized Iceland, Greenland, and a distant territory they called Vinland (Newfoundland, Canada). In 1016 a Viking army placed a Danish king on the English throne.

The threat of Viking attacks then began to lessen with Scandinavia's conversion to Christianity, which proceeded rapidly from the late tenth century onward. It was also mitigated by the fact that Viking populations quickly assimilated into the cultural and political world of northwestern Europe. By 1066, when the "Norsemen" of Normandy conquered England, the English—many descended from Vikings themselves—perceived them to be French. Driving this rapid assimilation may have been the raids of the Magyars, a non-Indo-European people who crossed the Carpathian Mountains around 895 and carried out a number of devastating campaigns throughout Continental Europe before settling in what is now Hungary. The disparate inhabitants of the new Viking colonies may have been forced to unite against this common enemy, and thus have come to share a common identity.

The overall effect of the Vikings on Europe continues to be a matter of scholarly controversy. The destruction they caused is undeniable, and many of the monasteries of Merovingian, Anglo-Saxon, and Celtic lands were destroyed—along with countless precious books and historical artifacts. Yet the Vikings were not the only source of disorder in the ninth and tenth centuries. The civil wars and local political rivalries that had replaced the centralized states of Charlemagne and the Islamic caliphates contributed mightily to the chaos of the post-Carolingian world and made the Vikings' successes easily won. Nor were the Vikings a source of disorder alone. In Ireland and eastern England, Vikings founded a series of new towns. As long-distance traders, Vikings transported large quantities of silver into western Europe, fueling the European economy.

In those few regions where people did succeed in fending off Viking attacks, the unifying force of victory was strong. The best example of this phenomenon is England, which had never been part of Charlemagne's empire and which had remained divided into small kingdoms at war with one other—despite Bede's wishful history of "an English church and people." But as a direct response to the Viking threat, a loosely unified kingdom emerged for the first time under Alfred the Great (r. 871–99). His success in defending his own West Saxon kingdom from Viking attacks, combined with the destruction of every other competing royal dynasty, allowed Alfred and his heirs to assemble effective armed forces, institute mechanisms of local government, found new towns, and codify English laws. In addition, Alfred established a court school and fostered a distinctive Anglo-Saxon literary culture. While the Anglo-Saxon vernacular had been a written language since the time of the Roman missions, it now came to rival Latin as a language of administration, history, scholarship, and spirituality. Moreover, oral traditions of poetic composition and storytelling were preserved and extended, as exemplified by the epic *Beowulf*. Until the the eleventh century,

**PATTERNS OF VIKING ACTIVITY AND SETTLEMENT, c. 800–1100.** The Vikings were instrumental in maintaining commercial contacts among northern Europe, Byzantium, and Islam until the eighth century, when changing historical forces turned them into raiders and colonists. ▪ ***What area was the original homeland of the Vikings?*** ▪ ***What geographic region did the Vikings first conquer, and why?*** ▪ ***The areas marked in green show territories that were later targeted by pillagers. Why would the Vikings have avoided settlement in these areas?***

Anglo-Saxon was the only European vernacular used for regular written communication.

## The Disintegration of the Islamic World

As we noted above, the declining power of the Abbasid dynasty in Persia was one of the forces that contributed to the escalation of Viking raids. A major cause of this decline was the gradual impoverishment of the Abbasids' economic base, the agricultural wealth of the ancient Tigris-Euphrates basin, which resulted from ecological crises and a devastating revolt by the enslaved African workforce there. Tax revenues from the Abbasid Empire were also declining, as provincial rulers in North Africa, Egypt, and Syria retained larger and larger portions of those revenues for themselves. As their sources of income became depleted, the Abbasids were unable to support either their large civil service or the mercenary army on which they relied for defense. This army was manned largely by slaves and mercenaries whose loyalties lay with the individual rulers who employed them, not with the caliphs. Massively expensive building projects, including the construction of the new Abbasid capital at Baghdad, further exacerbated the fiscal, military, and political crisis.

Behind the Abbasid collapse lay two fundamental developments of great significance for the future of the Islamic world: the growing power of regional rulers and the sharpening religious divisions between Sunnis and Shi'ites, and among the Shi'ites themselves. In 909 regional and religious hostilities came together when a local Shi'ite dynasty known as the Fatimids seized control of the Abbasid province of North Africa. In 969 the Fatimids succeeded in conquering Egypt also. Meanwhile, another Shi'ite group, rivals of both the Fatimids and the Abbasids, attacked Baghdad in 927 and Mecca in 930, seizing the Kaaba. Although an Abbasid caliphate continued to exist in Baghdad until 1258, when invading Mongol armies dispatched it, the Abbasid Empire had effectively disappeared by the 930s. In its place a new order began to emerge in the eastern Muslim world, centered around an independent Egyptian kingdom and a new Muslim state based in Persia.

In Al-Andalus, disputes over succession within the Umayyad dynasty were matched by new external pressures. Beginning in the mid–ninth century, the small Christian kingdoms of northern and eastern Iberia began to encroach on Muslim territory, increasing the internal difficulties of the Umayyad caliphate. By the opening years of the eleventh century, the caliphate had dissolved, to be replaced by a host of smaller kingdoms, some of which paid tribute to the Christian rulers of the north.

The fractured political unity of the Islamic world deepened the divisions that had always existed among Muslim

## After You Read This Chapter

Visit StudySpace for quizzes, additional review materials, and multi-media documents. **wwnorton.com/studyspace**

### REVIEWING THE OBJECTIVES

- Justinian's attempted reunification of the Roman Empire proved destructive. What were its effects in the East? In the West?
- Byzantine culture was distinctive in many ways. What are some of its important features?
- The rapid expansion of Islam can be explained with reference to several historical factors. What were they?
- What accounts for the close relationship between monasticism and secular power in early medieval Europe?
- What was the Carolingian Empire, and why is it important?

groups. While Islamic rulers were extremely tolerant of religious and cultural differences when dealing with Jews and Christians, dissent within Islam itself was another matter. Under the strong rule of the caliphates, some different groups had learned to coexist; but with the disappearance of these centralized states it would be difficult to reconcile the ideal of universality with the realities of regional and ethnic differences.

## CONCLUSION

The three civilizations that emerged as Rome's heirs each exhibit aspects of Roman civilization, which was itself a product of older civilizations. Which was Rome's true successor? It depends on the criteria used to make this evaluation. If imperial Rome's most fundamental characteristics were the maintenance of legal and political institutions, the answer is Byzantium. If one is looking for a civilization that combines the rich legacies of the ancient Near East, Egypt, and the Hellenistic world, the answer is Islam, which also emulated Rome in promoting commerce and cultural exchange. If one associates Rome chiefly with the city itself and the Latin language of the first Romans, or with the Christian patriarch of Rome, the answer is northwestern Europe.

There are also many connections to be drawn among these three successors. All took on their defining characteristics in the sixth and seventh centuries and, by the eighth century, had developed unique strengths and weaknesses. Moreover, they had fruitful—if uneasy—relationships with one another, and many mutual dependencies. Italian traders were active in Constantinople, and Muslim traders were common in the ports of southern Italy and Gaul. Anglo-Saxon merchants were regular visitors to the Mediterranean. Jewish merchants in the Rhineland were carrying on an active trade with the communities of Muslim Egypt, while Viking traders had opened trade routes from the Baltic through Russia to the Black Sea and were busily founding cities from Novgorod to Dublin.

But the crises of the ninth and tenth centuries disrupted these networks and created new centers of power. Western Europeans began to share a sense of common identity: within the vast territory that extended from the Baltic to the Mediterranean, and from the Pyrenees to Poland, every ruler was (or would soon be) looking to the Roman Church for spiritual guidance and to his fellow rulers for aid and alliance. At the same time, western Europe became a society mobilized for war to a degree unmatched in either Byzantium or the Islamic world. In the centuries to come, this militarization was to prove a decisive factor in the shifting relationship among Rome's heirs.

### PEOPLE, IDEAS, AND EVENTS IN CONTEXT

- In what ways do **JUSTINIAN'S CODE OF ROMAN LAW** and the building of **HAGIA SOPHIA** reflect his desire to revive the glories of ancient Rome?
- What were **BYZANTIUM'S** sources of stability, and of dissent? What effect did the **ICONOCLAST CONTROVERSY** have on Byzantine society?
- What factors contributed to **MUHAMMAD'S** rise to power? What are the **FIVE PILLARS** of **ISLAM** and what is the role of the **QU'RAN**?
- To what extent were the **UMAYYAD** and **ABBASID CALIPHATES** heirs of Rome? What made Islamic culture of this period distinctive?
- How did the **MEROVINGIAN** kings of the Franks acquire and hold power? How did **BENEDICTINE MONASTICISM** contribute to the economy of western Europe and how was it linked to politics?
- How did **CHARLEMAGNE** build an empire, and how did the **CAROLINGIAN RENAISSANCE** revive and extend **CLASSICAL LEARNING**?
- How did the **VIKING INVASIONS** contribute to the disorder of the ninth and tenth centuries?

### CONSEQUENCES

- Arguably, each of these three civilizations could claim the mantle of the Roman Empire. In your view, which one has the strongest claim to carrying forward the legacies of the classical past?
- How do the historical circumstances in which Islam emerged compare to those that shaped early Christianity? What are some key similarities and differences?

# Before You Read This Chapter

## STORY LINES

- Around the year 1000, new agricultural technologies and new social groupings transformed the economy of Europe.
- The rejuvenation of towns and trade created new opportunities for advancement. But at the same time, the decentralization of political power led to the violent rule of lords who could harness human and material resources to their own advantage.
- A reforming movement within the Church increased the authority of the papacy, which attempted to assert its supremacy over secular rulers and to control rampant violence by directing it against Europe's neighbors.
- One manifestation of this Church-sanctioned violence was the First Crusade, which began when a Muslim attack on Byzantium became the pretext for a holy war.
- Crusading broadened cultural and economic contacts with the East, but it also led to increased intolerance of "others," both outside Europe and within it.

## CHRONOLOGY

| | |
|---|---|
| 900–1050 | Monastic reform movement |
| 911–989 | The peoples of Russia are converted to Orthodoxy |
| 936–973 | Reign of Otto I "the Great" |
| 1050 | Medieval agricultural revolution at its height |
| 1066–1087 | Reign of William the Conqueror in England |
| 1073–1085 | Papacy of Gregory VII |
| 1075–1122 | Investiture Conflict |
| 1081–1118 | Reign of Alexius Comnenus in Byzantium |
| 1095–1099 | First Crusade |
| c. 1100 | The *Song of Roland* is written down |
| 1126–1198 | Lifetime of Averroès |
| 1187 | Recapture of Jerusalem under Salah ad-Din |
| 1204 | Sack of Constantinople |

# The Expansion of Europe, 950–1100

## CORE OBJECTIVES

- **EXPLAIN** the reasons for the fragmentation of political power throughout most of Europe in ninth and tenth centuries.
- **IDENTIFY** the most important outcomes of the medieval agricultural revolution.
- **DESCRIBE** the effects of the reforming movement with the Church.
- **UNDERSTAND** the motives behind the crusades.
- **TRACE** the political, economic, social, religious, and cultural effects of the crusades.

In the version of history popularized by medieval minstrels, Charlemagne and his knights are able to defeat an Islamic army on Spanish soil. Then they face only one remaining obstacle: the castle of a Muslim king whose stalwart courage commands the Christians' respect. So when ambassadors from the king promise his conversion in exchange for the safety of his people, Charlemagne readily agrees. One of his men must now negotiate the terms of surrender. Roland, Charlemagne's noblest knight, suggests that his stepfather Ganelon be the chosen messenger. But Ganelon is furious, certain that the mission is dangerous and will end in his death. Secretly, he resolves to betray his stepson and his liege lord: he convinces the Muslim king that Charlemagne only intends to trick him into converting, and thus he incites the king to attack the Christian warriors as they travel homeward through the mountain pass. Because Roland is the bravest knight, Ganelon knows that he will volunteer to command the rear guard.

And so it happens. Roland's men are ambushed and his sworn companion, Olivier, urges him to call for help. But Roland refuses: he will never endanger his lord by any such dishonorable deed. Instead, he will fight to the death and, with his last ounce of strength, break his sword, Durandal. For it would never do to have this sacred gift of Charlemagne—made holier still by the relic in its pommel—fall into the hands of heathens. As Roland reminds Olivier, "We must not be the theme of mocking songs." The worst thing imaginable is shame; the best, to become the hero of just such an epic.

Like Homer's *Iliad*, the *Song of Roland* is the product of an oral storytelling tradition that took shape over hundreds of years. Written down around the year 1100, it reflects the many ways in which the world had changed since the time of Charlemagne. Its very language exemplifies one such change: the language we call French, no longer the Frankish tongue of Charlemagne. In Charlemagne's time, moreover, there was no such thing as knighthood or chivalry, there were no major castles, there was no holy war against Muslims. All of these features were added over time, to mirror a new reality and, most immediately, the ethos of the First Crusade (1095–99).

In this chapter, we will begin to trace the processes that transformed western Europe from an economic backwater and political patchwork into the premier power among the three successor civilizations of the Roman Empire. With the increased authority and prestige of the Roman Church, European Christendom came to embrace the formerly outlying provinces of Scandinavia, Hungary, Poland, and Bohemia. Christian colonists and missionaries would also push eastward into Prussia, Lithuania, Livonia, and the Balkans. Allied Christian armies would come to dominate Muslim Spain and Constantinople. They would also establish (and eventually lose) a Latin kingdom centered on Jerusalem and come to control commerce in the Mediterranean as well as trade routes to Central Asia and China. This expansion would be accompanied by a revolution in agricultural production, significant urbanization, a rising standard of living, and a growing population. It would foster the growth of territorial monarchies, create a wealthy but highly stratified new social order, and spur remarkable intellectual and cultural achievements.

## WESTERN EUROPE AROUND THE YEAR 1000

In the aftermath of the Viking invasions, new political entities began to emerge in western Europe. Some, on the farflung fringes of the known world, were formed when the Vikings themselves became colonists: Iceland, Greenland, and (briefly) Newfoundland. Indeed, Iceland can claim to be Europe's oldest state and the world's first parliamentary democracy. Its political institutions date back to the year 930, when settlers formed a legislative assembly called the Althing, a Norse word with the same meaning as the Latin *res publica*. In regions where Vikings settled among more established groups—the British Isles, Scandinavia, Russia, and the Low Countries—they both absorbed and affected these cultures. In Normandy, for example, the descendants of Vikings maintained marriage alliances and ties of kinship with the rest of the Norse world, while at the same time intermarrying with the Franks and adopting their language.

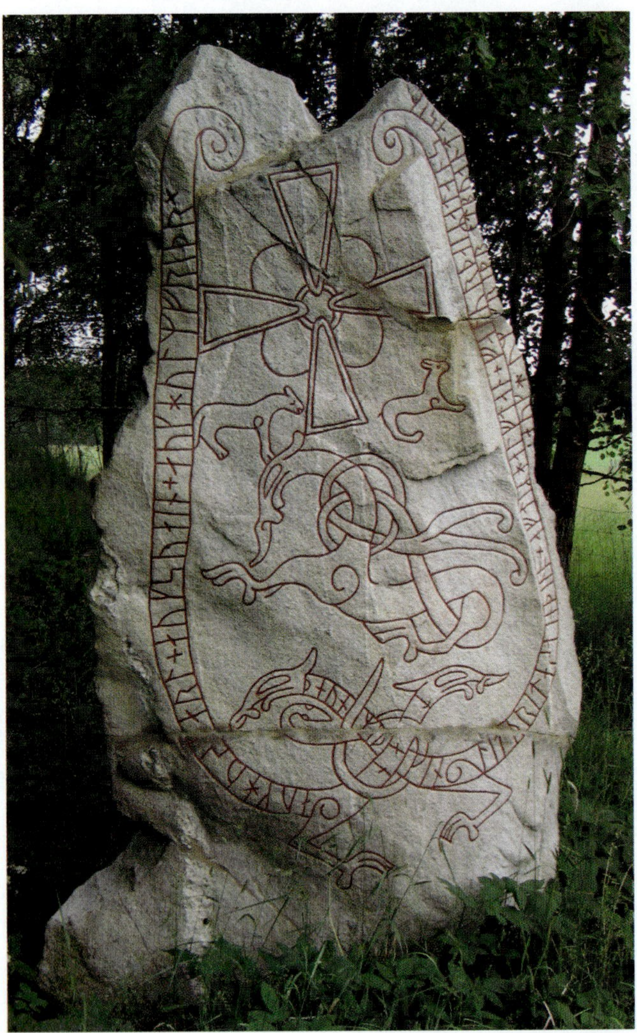

**LINGSBERG RUNESTONE.** This is one of two commemorative runestones erected at Lingsberg, Sweden, at the beginning of the eleventh century. The runic inscription records that a woman named Holmfríðr had it placed here in memory of her husband, Halfdan, whose father had been a Viking raider in England. Runic alphabets were in use among Germanic-speaking peoples of the North prior to the adoption of the Latin alphabet. Some runic letters survive in Anglo-Saxon and Old Norse, including the *edh*, the letter ð in the name of Holmfríðr, which is pronounced *th* as in "the."

**EUROPE, c. 1100.** This map shows the patchwork of political power in western Europe after the millennium, although it cannot accurately illustrate the degree of fragmentation within these major territories, especially those of the Holy Roman Empire. ▪ ***What factors account for the close relationship between Italy and the German principalities?*** ▪ ***How are they related to the northwestern regions of the Continent and the British Isles?*** ▪ ***Which geopolitical entities would you expect to emerge as dominant in the following centuries?***

## The Heirs of Charlemagne

The most powerful monarchs on the Continent were the Saxon kings of eastern Francia (modern Germany). Like the Anglo-Saxon kings of England, they modeled themselves on Charlemagne, but they drew on different aspects of his rule. While England became an effective administrative monarchy, with centralized financial and judicial systems, royal power on the Continent rested on the profits of successful conquest. So just as the Carolingians had built their power on the conquest of Saxony in the eighth century, the Saxon kings now built theirs on the conquests of Slavic lands to the east. They also nurtured their image as guardians of Christendom: in 955, King Otto I of Saxony defeated the pagan Magyars while carrying a sacred lance that had belonged to Charlemagne.

**EMPEROR OTTO THE GREAT.** In this opening from a deluxe set of Gospels he commissioned for himself, Otto is shown seated on a throne and vested with the regalia of imperial and royal authority, surrounded by clerical and secular counselors, and receiving tribute from a procession of women representing the four regions of his domain: Slavinia, Germania, Gallia, and Roma. Compare this image to that of Emperor Justinian on page 210 (Chapter 7). ▪ ***In what ways is Otto making use of similar iconography?*** ▪ ***What claims to power does he make thereby?***

This victory established Otto as a dominant power and as Charlemagne's worthy successor. In 962, accordingly, he went to Rome to be crowned emperor by Pope John XII, who hoped Otto would help him defeat his enemies. But Otto turned the tables on the pope, deposing him for his scandalous lifestyle and selecting a new pope to replace him. Otto thereby laid the foundation for his successors' claims to imperial autonomy. He also advertised his inheritance of Charlemagne's power through his patronage of arts and learning. Under Otto's influence, the Saxon court became a refuge for men and women of talent. The first known female playwright, Hrotsvitha of Gandersheim (c. 935–c. 1002), was raised there, and grew up hearing the works of classical authors read aloud. When she entered a royal convent, she wrote plays blending Roman comedy with the stories of early Christian martyrs for the entertainment and instruction of her fellow nuns. Otto also presided over the establishment of cathedral schools and helped the bishops of his domain turn their own courts into cultural centers.

However, Otto could not control either the papacy or the independent towns of northern Italy unless he maintained a permanent presence there. And if he remained in Italy too long, his authority in Saxony broke down. Balancing local realities with imperial ambitions thus presented a dilemma that neither he nor his succesors were able to solve. The result was a gradually increasing rift between local elites and the king in his guise as Holy Roman Emperor. This alienation would accelerate in the eleventh century, when the imperial crown passed to a new dynasty, the Salians, centered not in Saxony but in neighboring Franconia. By the 1070s, when the Salian emperor Henry IV attempted to assert control over Saxony, he touched off a war that was to have momentous repercussions (see below).

Aspects of Charlemagne's legacy also survived in the Mediterranean world. In Catalonia, counts descended from Carolingian appointees continued to administer justice in public courts of law throughout the tenth century and to draw revenues from tolls and trade. The city of Barcelona grew rapidly as both a long-distance and a regional market under the protection of these counts. In Aquitaine also, the counts of Poitiers and Toulouse continued to rest their authority on Carolingian foundations.

In Charlemagne's own Frankish kingdom, however, Carolingian rule collapsed under the combined weight of Viking raids, economic disintegration, and the growing power of local lords. In some areas, a few Carolingian institutions—such as public courts and a centrally minted coinage—survived, but were used to build up new, autonomous principalities such as Anjou and Flanders. The Norse-Frankish rulers of Normandy also used these techniques effectively. In the Franks' traditional heartland, however, even this modicum of Carolingian authority disappeared. The Franks still had a king, but this king was no longer a descendant of Charlemagne. Moreover, his domain had been reduced to the tiny region around Paris: this was the remnant that the local count, Hugh Capet, had managed to defend against the Vikings in 987, thus earning him the title King of the Franks. Marooned on this Ile de France (literally, "island of France"), the Capetian kings clung to the fiction that they were the heirs of Charlemagne's greatness. It would be another two hundred years before one of them made this fiction a political reality.

## AN AGRICULTURAL REVOLUTION

Like all economies prior to the nineteenth century, the medieval economy rested on agriculture. Agricultural innovation tends to occur slowly, yet it is still appropriate to call the profound changes that took place in this period revolutionary. Indeed, it is arguable that this agricultural revolution was more important than that of the modern era (see Chapter 19).

### New Technologies

The driving force behind the agricultural boom of the Middle Ages was technological. The heavy-wheeled plow, fitted with an iron-tipped coulter and dragged by a team of oxen or horses, could cut and turn the rich soil of northern Europe far more effectively than traditional Mediterranean plows. Related improvements in collars and harnesses enhanced the efficiency of plow oxen and even made it possible for horses to pull heavy loads without choking themselves. The development of iron horseshoes (around 900) and the tandem harnessing of paired teams (around 1050) also made the use of horses more effective, not only in the field but for the transport of agricultural surpluses to new markets.

Labor-saving devices further increased productivity. Since most work was done by individuals using hand tools, the more widespread use of iron for hoes, forks, shovels, and scythes made work faster and easier. The wheelbarrow was a crucial invention, as was the harrow, a tool drawn over the field after plowing to level the earth and mix in the seed. Watermills represented another major innovation. The Romans had relied mainly on human- and animal-powered wheels to grind grain into flour, even though they had known about the use of running water as a power source. But the need for greater efficiency and

**LIGHT PLOW AND HEAVY PLOW.** Compare these two contemporary depictions of plowing: the one at left is taken from a Greek manuscript copied in Byzantium and shows the light plow in use throughout the Mediterranean and Near East since antiquity; the other shows the heavy wheeled plow adapted to northern Europe. Note that the peasant using the light plow has to press his foot on it to give it added weight. Another major innovation of the heavy European plow was the long moldboard, which turned over the ground after the plowshare cut into it. The padded horse collar allowed horses to throw their full weight into pulling.

the lack of slave labor led medieval engineers—probably monks—to experiment with various ways of harnessing water power. Local lords followed suit, recognizing the mill as a source of economic and political power to which they could control access through the imposition of tolls. Mills were also adapted to a variety of purposes beyond the grinding of grain: they drove saws for lumber, processed cloth, pressed olive oil, provided power for iron forges, and crushed pulp for manufacturing paper. The importance of mills cannot be overstated: they would remain the world's only source of mechanical power for manufacturing until the invention of the steam engine powered the Industrial Revolution (see Chapter 19).

## New Conditions for Growth

Although many of these technologies had been invented in the eighth century, it was only in the eleventh that they became sufficiently widespread as to have a decisive impact. Climate change certainly played a role in this. Starting in the eighth or ninth century, average temperatures in Europe gradually rose by about 1° or 2°C (3.6°F)—the same increment that has led to global warming today. Eventually, these higher temperatures made it possible to raise crops as far north as Greenland and to produce wine in southern England. Moreover, the warming climate benefited northern Europe by drying the soil and lengthening the growing season, while hotter summers and diminishing rainfall hurt Mediterranean agriculture in equal measure.

These technologies also took hold after the settlement of Viking and Magyar peoples decreased the threat of invasion and the consequent disruption of planting cycles and damage to crops. Left in relative peace, monasteries could develop and implement the tools described above, which were then copied by local lords who saw the benefits of managing their own lands more efficiently, rather than raiding others'. Indeed, it became clear to entrepreneurial peasants, too, that investment in agricultural improvements would yield surpluses and result in profits. For productivity was also linked to increased population, fundamental changes in patterns of settlement, and the organization of the peasant work force.

## Harnessing People

During the early Middle Ages, most farmers lived on individual plots of land worked by themselves and their families. Starting in the ninth century, however, many of these individual holdings merged into large, common fields that were farmed collectively by the inhabitants of entire villages. The resulting complex is sometimes called a *manor* (from the Latin verb meaning "to dwell").

In many cases, the impetus for the consolidation of manors came from the peasants themselves. Large fields could be farmed more efficiently than small fields. Investment costs were lower and could be shared equally: a single plow and a dozen oxen might suffice for an entire village, obviating the need for every farmer to maintain his own plow and team. Common fields were potentially more productive, too, allowing villagers to experiment with new crops and to support larger numbers of animals on common pastures. In time, prosperous peasants might be able to establish a parish church, a communal oven, a blacksmith, a mill, and a tavern. They could also converse, socialize, and assist their neighbors. In a difficult and demanding natural environment, these were important considerations.

In other cases, a manor could be created or co-opted by a local lord or a monastery acting as a lord. Manors were attractive because their greater productivity meant that lords could take a larger share of the peasants' surplus; it was also easier to control and exploit peasants who lived together in villages and who were bound to one another by ties of kinship and dependence. Over time, some lords were therefore able to reduce formerly free peasants to the status of serfs who could not leave the land without permission. Like slaves, serfs inherited their servile status; but unlike slaves, they were not supposed to be sold apart from the lands they worked. From a material perspective, there may have been little difference between a serf and a free peasant—indeed, some serfs may have been better off. But as we have seen, social mobility is often tied to geographical mobility; and the inability of serfs to move freely would prevent them from achieving the liberties of those who could.

## The Conquest of the Land

The manor's organization of labor opened up more land for cultivation and made that cultivation more efficient. For centuries, farmers had known that if they sowed the same crop in the same field year after year, they would eventually exhaust the soil. The traditional solution was to divide one's land, planting half in the fall to harvest in the spring, and leaving the other half to lie fallow. In the dry, thin soils of the Mediterranean, this remained the most common cropping pattern throughout the Middle Ages. In the more fertile soils of northern Europe, however, farmers slowly discovered that a three-field crop-rotation system could produce a sustainable increase in overall production. One-third of the land would lie fallow or be used as pasture, so that manure would fertilize the soil; one-third would be planted with winter wheat or rye, sown in the fall and harvested in the early summer; and one-third would be planted in the spring with another crop to be harvested in the fall. These fields were then rotated over a three-year cycle.

This system increased the amount of land under cultivation from 50 to 67 percent, while the two separate growing seasons provided some insurance against loss due to natural disasters or inclement weather. The system also produced higher yields per acre, particularly if legumes or fodder crops like oats were a regular part of the crop-rotation pattern and replaced the nitrogen that wheat and rye leach out of the soil. Both humans and animals could eat oats, and legumes provided a source of protein to balance the intake of carbohydrates from bread and beer, the two main staples of the peasant diet in northern and central Europe. Additional fodder supported more and healthier animals, increasing the efficiency of plow beasts, diversifying the economy of the manor, and providing an additional source of protein through meat and milk. The new crop-rotation system also helped spread labor more evenly over the course of the year.

## THE GROWTH OF TOWNS AND TRADE

As we observed in Chapter 7, the urban infrastructure of the western Roman Empire was weakened in the course of the fifth and sixth centuries. A few Roman cities continued to thrive under the lordship of bishops, but many—including Rome itself—began to crumble as their depleted

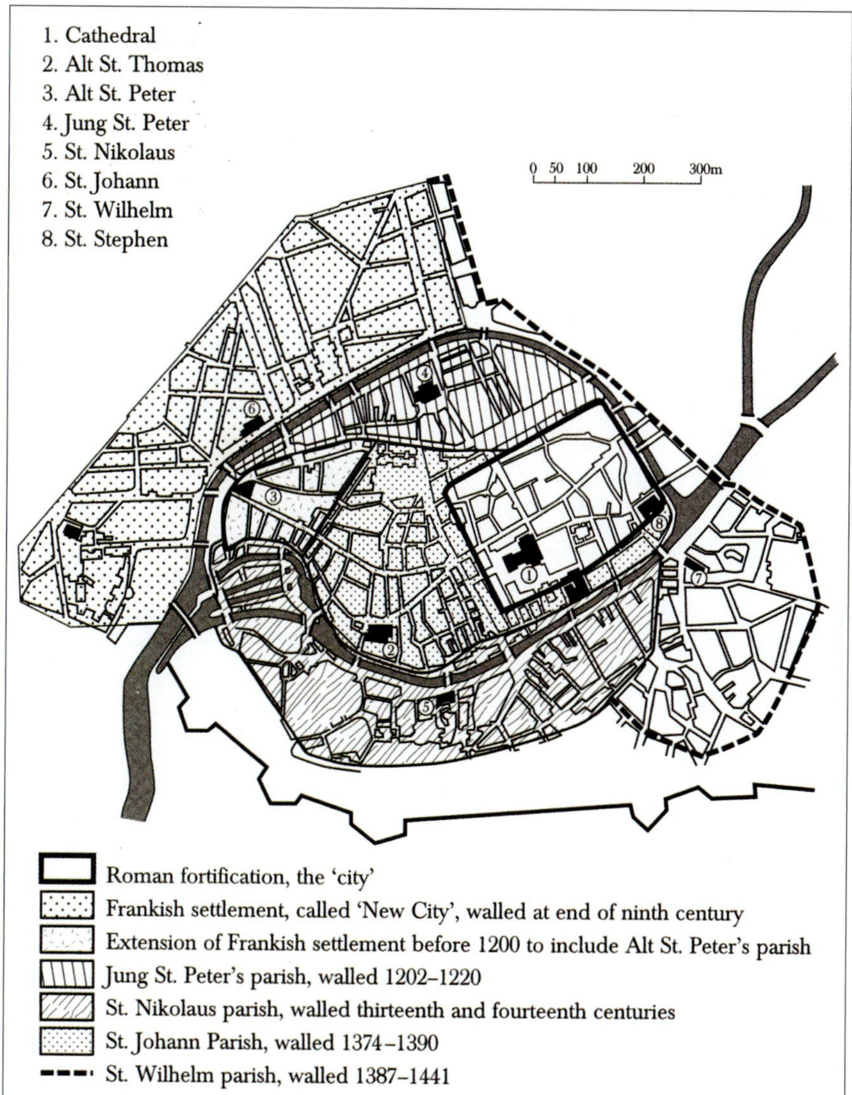


**THE METAMORPHOSIS OF A MEDIEVAL CITY.** The city of Strasbourg, on the long-disputed border between modern Germany and France, exemplifies the multilayered dynamics of urban change throughout the Middle Ages. It began as a Roman settlement, which became the nucleus for an episcopal see—hence the cathedral (1) located in the ancient precinct. It was fortified with new walls at the end of the ninth century, as the Carolingian Empire was collapsing and the Vikings were on the move. It then responded to the renewed prosperity of the eleventh and twelfth centuries, far outgrowing its original bounds, and continued to expand for several centuries thereafter. ▪ ***Note the scale of the map. What can you conclude from this about the density of settlement in a medieval city?***

populations could no longer maintain public buildings, services, and defensive walls. In most areas, monasteries replaced cities as the nuclei of civilization in northwestern Europe. Then, under Charlemagne and his imitators, towns came to be planted by royal initiative, as centers for markets and administration. In Anglo-Saxon England, too, King Alfred and his successors established new towns in strategic locations while at the same time reviving older Roman cities. They also issued a reliable and well-regulated currency that encouraged commerce.

## Fostering Commerce

Although many towns were devastated by the Viking raids of the tenth century, the agricultural revolution helped to revitalize them. The rapid urbanization of Europe in the eleventh and twelfth centuries was also fostered by the initiatives of lords who saw the economic advantages to be gained from providing safe havens for travelers and trade. This was especially true in the principalities of the

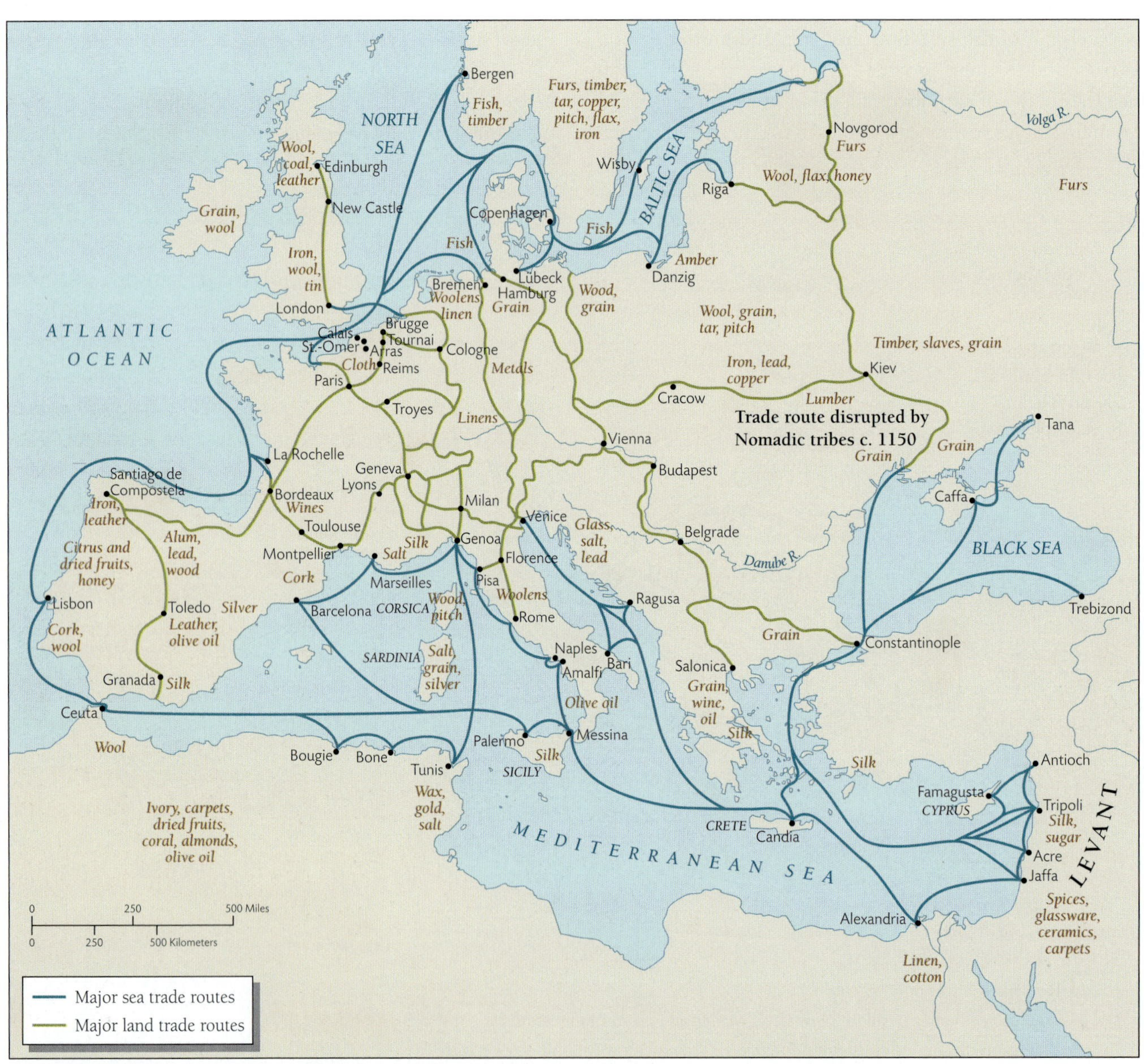


**MEDIEVAL TRADE ROUTES.** ▪ *What does this map reveal about the relationship between waterways and overland routes during the eleventh and twelfth centuries?* ▪ *Which regions appear to be most extensively interconnected, and why?* ▪ *How does the trade in certain specialized goods create certain commercial patterns?*

Rhineland, the Low Countries, and the independent counties of Flanders and Champagne. Towns grew up around monasteries, too, which provided protection and encouraged innovation. In southwestern Europe, towns also prospered from their status as ports or their location along the overland routes connecting the Mediterranean with the Atlantic. In Italy, which had been decimated by five centuries of warfare and invasion, the growth of towns gave rise to especially dramatic changes.

Initially, the renewed prosperity of Italy depended on the Byzantine emperors' suppression of piracy in the eastern Mediterranean. Hence, the most successful cities around the turn of the millennium were situated in the Byzantine-controlled areas of the peninsula: Venice in the north and Amalfi, Naples, and Palermo in the south. These were the trading posts that brought silks, spices, and other luxuries from the East into western Europe. In the eleventh century, however, Norman invasions of southern Italy disrupted this trade and Turkish invasions of Asia Minor turned Byzantine attentions to the empire's eastern frontier. This opened new opportunities to the northern ports of Genoa and Pisa, whose merchant navies took over the task of policing the eastern Mediterranean.

From Italy, exotic goods flowed northward to the towns of Flanders and to the organized system of fairs (international markets convened at certain times of the year) that enriched the county of Champagne. Flemish towns, in turn, kept up a brisk trade with England, processing English wool into the cloth which, alongside wheat and wine, was the staple commodity of medieval Europe. Eventually, merchants would succeed in opening up a direct route by sea between Italy and the Atlantic ports of northern Europe, after which it became practical to import raw wool directly from England to towns like Florence, which began producing its cloth.

It would be misleading, however, to overemphasize the role of long-distance trade in the urbanization of medieval Europe. Some towns that were dependant on such commerce, like Venice and Genoa, attracted populations aproaching 100,000 by 1300. But others that grew to be as large, including Paris and London, drew primarily on the wealth of their surrounding hinterlands for food, raw materials, and the bulk of their population. Towns large and small existed in a symbiotic relationship with the countryside, providing markets for the food surplus of outlying farms and transforming raw materials into marketable goods through manufacturing.

## *"Town Air Makes You Free"*

To modern eyes, most premodern towns would still have seemed half rural. (Indeed, New York City would have seemed so until the end of the nineteenth century.) Streets were often unpaved, houses had gardens for raising vegetables, and animals were everywhere: in the early twelfth

**VIEW OF PARIS, c. 1480.** Although this cityscape dates from the later Middle Ages, many of the buildings pictured here would have been constructed in the boom of the late twelfth century, when the king of France, Philip Augustus, enlarged the city walls and encouraged the paving of streets. The cathedral of Notre Dame is prominent in the center of this image.

century, the heir to the throne of France was killed when his horse tripped over a pig running loose in the streets of Paris. Sanitary conditions were poor, and the air reeked of excrement, both animal and human. (Even in 1900, this was also true of New York, where 150,000 horses produced 45,000 tons of manure each month.) Under these conditions, disease could spead rapidly. Fire was another omnipresent danger, because wooden and thatched buldings were clustered close together.

But these inconveniences were far outweighed by the advantages of urban life, not least of which was the fact that towns provided a means of escape from the strictures of rural life. As a German adage puts it, "Town air makes you free" (*Stadtluft macht Frei*). This is because the citizens of most medieval towns were not subject to the arbitrary jurisdiction of a lord—or if they were, the lord realized that rewarding initiative with further freedoms fostered still more initiative and produced more wealth. Many Catalonian and Flemish towns accordingly received charters of liberty from the counts of these regions, and were given the right to govern themselves. Others seized that right: in 1127, the people of Arras, on the Franco-Flemish border, declared that they were no longer the serfs of the local monastery that had nurtured the growth of their town in the first place. They banded together to form a commune, swearing to maintain solidarity with one another and setting up their own form of representative government. The monastery was forced to free them, and then free to tax them. The arrangement was mutually beneficial: by the end of the century, Arras was the wealthiest and most densely populated town in northern Europe.

**CHRISTIAN BANKERS AND THEIR CLIENTS.** As long-distance trade expanded in the Middle Ages, merchants developed new methods of financing their ventures. Many of these practices conflicted with the official policy of the medieval Church, which decried these new investments as usury. This Italian manuscript depicts the seven vices associated with moneylending, but also makes it clear that the people involved in this practice are Christians. (Compare their attire to that of the Jews pictured on page 287 in Chapter 9.)

Urban areas further expanded through the constant immigration of free peasants and escaped serfs in search of a better life. For once a town had established its independence, newcomers could claim the status of citizens after a year and a day; thereafter, the only authority to which they were subject was that of the town's officials. For this reason, some powerful lords and rulers resisted the efforts of towns to claim independence. Almost inevitably, though, they paid a high price for this. In Rome, the pope's claim to secular authority over the city led to frequent uprisings. In the French city of Laon, the bishop who asserted his lordship over a newly formed commune was murdered in 1112. In 1127, the count of Flanders, Charles the Good (r. 1119–27), was assassinated by a family of powerful officials who resented his claims that they were, in fact, his serfs.

## Portable Wealth: Money and Credit

The growth of towns and trade depends not only on surplus goods, initiative, and mobility. It also depends on money: a reliable supply of cash and the availability of credit. It is no accident that the earliest participants in the commercial revolution of the Middle Ages were cities located in regions whose rulers minted and regulated a strong currency: Byzantium, Al-Andalus, and the Christian kingdoms of Spain; the old Roman region of Provence (southern France); Anglo-Saxon England; and Flanders. Yet precisely because there were so many currencies in circulation, the economy also depended on moneychangers and bankers who could extend credit to merchants, thus obviating the need to travel roads and waterways with bags full of cash.

Most of the sophisticated financial mechanisms for extending credit and making investments had long been in place throughout the Islamic world and Byzantium, but in western Europe much of this crucial activity was carried forward by Jewish bankers situated within the network of close-knit Jewish communites that connected cities like Constantinople, Baghdad, and Córdoba to the burgeoning cities of the north. In many regions, Jews had a virtual monopoly on these activities, because Christians were technically forbidden to lend money at interest or to make a profit from investments. This practice was called *usury* (from the

Latin word for "interest"), and Christian theologians cited various passages from the Old and New Testaments which seemed to condemn it. But in practice, the western Church turned a blind eye to such practices. Indeed, many prominent churchmen, including bishops, made fortunes lending money, as did many laymen, especially in towns like Arras and Florence.

Still, the moral stigma attaching to this necessary practice meant that Jews were often the ones targeted at times of crisis, just as they were the people to whom rulers would turn most readily when they needed funds—helping to explain why many kings, princes, and bishops protected the Jewish communities in their realms and often extended special privileges to them in exchange for money. The unfortunate result of this Christian hypocrisy was the circulation of conspiracy theories harmful to Jews, who were perceived as exercising control over Christians through secret channels of communication and a stranglehold on finance. Jewish communities' reliance on the protection of powerful men also made them vulnerable when those men withdrew their support or were incapable of controlling the violence unleashed by their own policies.

## VIOLENCE AND LORDSHIP

The new wealth of western Europe fostered social mobility, yet it also created a more stratified society. In the Carolingian period, the nobility had comprised a relatively small number of ancient families who counted one another as equals and married among themselves. During the tenth and eleventh centuries, however, new families began to emerge as territorial lords, rivaling and sometimes surpassing the old aristocracy in power and wealth. Some of these new families were descended from lesser officeholders in the Carolingian administration, men who had established independent powers after the empire collapsed, and who used their public offices for private gain. Others, successful interlopers who seized control of undefended manors, sustained war-bands of treasure-hungry young men.

### *Castles and Knights*

The predatory lords who emerged in this period protected their territories, their families, and their followers by building strongholds: castles, from the Latin word *castellum*, "little fortress." These structures, little known in Europe before the Viking invasions, came to dominate the landscape in the eleventh and twelfth centuries. The castle was both defensive and offensive. It rendered its owner more secure from arson and attack—though it was vulnerable to siege—and it enabled him to dominate the surrounding countryside. Indeed, castles often formed the nucleus of a new town by providing protection for the peasants and merchants who clustered their dwellings close to its walls. In case of attack, these outliers could move inside.

Although most early castles were modest structures built of wood, situated on earthwork mounds surrounded by a ditch or moat, stone walls and keeps (fortified towers) soon replaced wooded palisades as the level of competitive violence increased. In Italy, rival families even built castles and towers in the middle of towns. Eventually, some castellans ("castle-holders") acquired enough power and booty to challenge more established lords, laying claim not only to property and influence but to rank. These new lords didn't descend from Roman senators or Carolingian counts; instead, they boasted of lineages reaching back to successful warlords like Rollo the Viking, whom the Normans claimed to be their first duke (from the Latin word *dux*, "leader").

In addition to castle-holding, both the older aristocracy and these self-made lords needed the help of warriors to enforce their claims to power. Essentially, each lord maintained a private army of men heavily equipped with the new weaponry and armor that the widespread availability of iron—and new techniques for smelting it—made possible. These men fought on horseback, and were therefore called "horsemen": in French, *chevaliers*, and in English, *knights*. Knighthood was a career that embraced men of widely varying status. Some eleventh-century knights were the younger sons of lords who sought to increase their chances of winning wealth by attaching themselves to the households of greater lords. Others were youths recruited from the peasantry, mounted and armed. All that bound them together was their function, which was the violent prosecution of their lord's interests. Gradually, though, knights also came to regard themselves as belonging to a special military caste with its own rules of conduct. The beginnings of this process are discernible in the *Song of Roland*, and further developments in the twelfth and thirteenth centiries would transform the meaning of chivalry from "horsemanship" to something very different (see Chapter 9).

### *Kings, Lords, and Vassals*

Despite the emergence of self-governing cities and predatory lordships, Europe remained a continent of kingdoms. For example, the Capetian rulers of Paris kept alive the pretence that everyone dwelling in the lands once ruled

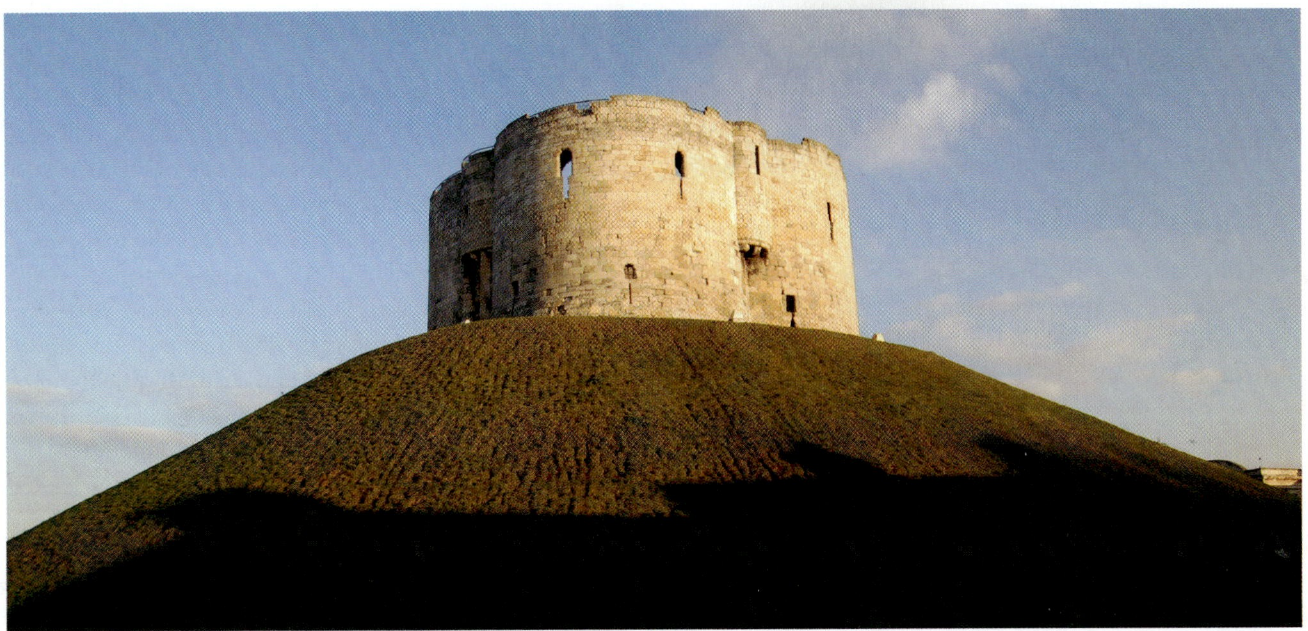

**YORK CASTLE (ENGLAND).** This fortification exemplifies some of the major phases of medieval castle-building. The large mound is the remains of an earthwork erected on the orders of William the Conqueror in 1068, when it would have been crowned by a wooden palisade: this most basic type of construction is called a motte-and-bailey castle. York's castle remained a wooden tower until it was destroyed by fire and rebuilt in stone after 1245. It is now known as Clifford's Tower after a rebel leader called Sir Roger Clifford, who was held there prior to his execution in 1322.

by more powerful Frankish kings still owed allegiance to them, while the Ottonians claimed to be kings in northern Italy as well as in their own Saxon domain. In practice, however, neither the Ottonians nor the Capetians were able to control the territories they claimed to rule. Effective political and military power lay in the hands of dukes, counts, castellans, and knights, all of whom channeled the increasing wealth of the countryside into their own hands. From their castles, these lords (*domini*) constructed dominions: lordships within which they exercised not only property rights but also the rights to mint money, judge legal cases, raise troops, wage war, collect taxes, and impose tolls.

## *The Problem of Feudalism*

This highly diffused distribution of power is conventionally known as "feudalism." This is an unsatisfactory term, for several reasons. First and foremost, it is a modern invention not used in the period of history we are discussing. It is also confusing, because it has been used by different people to mean many different things. For example, scholars influenced by the work of Karl Marx (1818–1883, see Chapter 20) use "feudalism" to describe an economic system, a "mode of production" in which wealth is entirely agricultural and cities have not yet formed; as we have seen, this does not reflect the historical reality of the eleventh and twelfth centuries. For other scholars, "feudalism" is an aristocratic social order in which propertied men are bound together by kinship and shared interests, supported by the labor of serfs attached to manors; again, this does not explain the varieties of power wielded in this period. Legal historians, meanwhile, speak of "feudalism" as a system of landholding in which lesser men hold land from greater men in return for services of various kinds; but it was not always the greater man who held the most land. Meanwhile, military historians use "feudalism" to refer to a system whereby great lords and kings grant land in order to raise troops.

Because all of these definitions are more or less anachronistic, many recent historians of the Middle Ages have abandoned the use of the term altogether. If, however, we look for a common denominator, we can say that "feudalism" entails the abuse of official privileges for personal gain: making use of public resources or institutions for private purposes. In this case, there is general agreement that it took shape in Frankish lands after the Carolingian Empire had disintegrated. From there, its language and customs spread to other areas of Europe, changing as they were adapted to different circumstances. As more powerful territorial monarchies emerged in the twelfth and thirteenth centuries, these customs developed into an ideology that justified a new hierarchy, by which kings were supposed to be able to subordinate other powerful men. In this sense, "feudalism" legitimated royal power and helped to lay the groundwork for the emergence of European nation-states.

So although the people of the time would never have heard the term "feudalism," they would have understood the word at its root: *feudum*, usually translated as "fief" (*FEEF*). A fief is a gift or grant that creates a kind of contractual relationship between the giver and receiver. This gift could be land, but it could also be the revenues from a toll or a mill, or an annual sum of money. In return, the recipient owed the giver loyalty or services of some kind. In many cases, the gift implied that the recipient was subordinate to the giver and had in fact become the giver's *vassal*, from a Celtic word meaning "boy." This relationship was dramatized in an act of *homage*, a powerful ceremony that made the vassal "the man" (in French, *homme*) of his lord. Typically, the vassal would kneel and place his hands together in a position of prayer, and the lord would cover the clasped hands with his own. He would then raise up his new "man" and exchange a kiss with him. The symbolic importance of these gestures is clear: the lord (*dominus*) was literally the dominating figure, who could protect and raise up his man—but could also discipline him. The role of the vassal, meanwhile, was to support the lord and do nothing to incur his displeasure.

In a violent world where no central authority existed, these personal relationships were esssential to creating and maintaining order. At the same time, however, these relationships were not understood in the same ways all over Europe. Many castellans and knights held their lands freely, owing no service whatsoever to the count or duke within whose territories their lands lay. Nor were these relationships neatly hierarchical. Counts sometimes held lands from knights, knights frequently held lands from each other, and many landholders held fiefs from a number of different lords. "Feudalism" therefore created no "feudal pyramids," in which knights held fiefs from counts, and counts held fiefs from kings, all in an orderly fashion. Sometimes, kings would insist that the world *should* be structured this way, but they were seldom able to ensure or enforce this neat hierarchy.

## A New Feudal Monarchy: England

The first place where we can begin to observe the efforts of a particular line of kings to establish a monarchy that operated along these lines is England. In 1066, Duke William of Normandy claimed that he was the rightful successor of the English king, Edward, who had just died. But the English elected a new king, Harold, ignoring William's claim. So William crossed the English Channel to take the kingdom by force, defeating Harold at the Battle of Hastings (see ***Interpreting Visual Evidence*** on page 254). Now, however, William had to subjugate all of the other English chieftains who held power, many of whom also aspired to be king. He accomplished this, first, by asserting that he was king by imperial conquest as well as by succession, and that all the land of England thereby belonged to him. Then William rewarded his Norman followers with fiefs: extensive grants of land taken from their English holders, which the Norman lords were allowed to exploit and subdue; in return, William received their loyalty and a share of their revenues.

The Normans were already accustomed to holding land in return for service in Normandy. But in England, their subordination to the king was enforced by the effective machinery of the English state and by longstanding English customs that had the force of law. As king of England, therefore, William was able to exercise a variety of public powers that he could not have enjoyed in Normandy. For in England, unlike on the Continent, only the king could coin money and only the king's money was allowed to circulate. As kings of England, William and his successors also inherited the right to collect a national land tax, the right to supervise justice in royal courts, and the right to raise an army. They also retained the Anglo-Saxon officers of local government, known as sheriffs, to help them administer and enforce their rights. William was thereby able to insist that all the people of England owed ultimate loyalty to the king, even if they did not hold a scrap of land directly from him. William's kingship thus represented a powerful fusion of Carolingian-style traditions of public power with the new feudal relationships that had grown up in the tenth and eleventh centuries. It was a feudal monarchy.

## The Struggle for Imperial Power

We can contrast the wide-ranging powers of the new Anglo-Norman kings with those of Germany. No German king could claim to rule more than a single principality, and his imperial authority over a host of other rulers was only maintained through a close alliance with the Church. Indeed, the emperor relied heavily on ecclesiastical leaders: his chief administrators were archbishops and bishops whom the emperor himself had appointed and installed in their sacred offices, just as Charlemagne had done. Even the pope was frequently an imperial appointee. The fact that leading churchmen were often members of the imperial family also helped to counter the power of regional rulers.

# Interpreting Visual Evidence

## *The Graphic History of the Bayeux Tapestry*

One of the most famous historical documents of all time is not a document at all: it is an embroidered strip of linen 231 feet long (originally much longer) and 20 inches wide. It is also not an actual tapestry, as its name misleadingly implies, but an elaborate exercise in needlepoint. It tells the story of the Norman Conquest of England and the events leading up to it. The circumstances of its making remain mysterious, but it was certainly commissioned by someone close to William the Conqueror (1027–1087), the Norman duke who claimed the throne of England in 1066. Indeed, its purpose was to demonstrate the truth of William's claim, and to justify his invasion of England when Harold Godwinson (c. 1022–1066), was crowned king of England in his place (image B). One likely patron is Queen Edith of England, the widow of the late King Edward (r. 1042–66) and sister of Harold, who became a friend and advisor to William. Edith was noted for her skill in embroidery as well as for her political acumen, and she would have been able to oversee the making of this visual history by the women of her household. Two of its evocative scenes, with translations of accompanying Latin texts, are reproduced here.

**A. Here Harold Sails the Sea.** In this scene from the first portion of the Tapestry, Harold has been sent on an embassy by King Edward. He feasts with friends in a hall on the English coast before crossing the Channel.

**B. Here is Seated Harold, King of the English.** Although Harold may have promised to relinquish his claim to the English throne in William's favor, the central scene of the tapestry is his coronation. Stigant, the archbishop of Canterbury, stands on his right. Outside the cathedral, the people of London look on curiously. Some appear to be surprised or alarmed.

### *Questions for Analysis*

1. Like a graphic novel or a comic strip, the Bayeux Tapestry tells its story through images; words (in very simple Latin) play a minor role. What do the Tapestry's artists choose to express exclusively through visualization? When do they choose to state something verbally? What might be the motivation behind these choices? What is left out of the story, or left ambiguous? What might be the reason(s) for this?
2. In addition to being a source for political and military historians, the Bayeux Tapestry provides us with fascinating glimpses into the daily life and material culture of the Middle Ages. What, for example, can you conclude about the necessary preparations for a voyage by sea? about the history of clothing, or weaponry, or animals?
3. If Queen Edith is responsible for making the Tapestry, it would constitute one of the few surviving historical accounts by a woman prior to the twentieth century. Would the fact of the creator's gender change your perception of this artifact, or of these particular scenes? Why or why not?

But in the latter half of the eleventh century, this close cooperation between sacred and secular authority was fractured, and so was the ultimate power of the German monarch. In 1056, the six-year-old Henry IV (1050–1106) succeeded his father as king and emperor; and as we have frequently noted, political competition among the advisors of underage rulers often escalates into larger conflicts. In this case, the German princes of various regions—led by disenfranchised Saxon nobility—tried to gain control of the royal government at the expense of Henry's regents; when Henry began to rule in his own right, in 1073, these hostilities escalated into a civil war. At the same time, the newly elected pope, Gregory VII (r. 1073–85), began to insist that no laymen—not even royal ones—should have any influence within the Church; this became part of a movement toward reform that will be discussed further below.

King Henry, of course, resisted any initiative that would prohibit him from selecting his own bishops and abbots—the key players in the administration of his realm. So Pope Gregory allied himself with the rebellious Saxon nobility and together they moved to depose Henry. In order to save his crown, Henry was therefore forced to acknowledge the pope's superiority by begging forgiveness. Crossing the Alps into Italy in 1077, in the depths of winter, he found Gregory installed at the castle of Canossa under the protection of one of Europe's most powerful rulers, Matilda of Tuscany. Encouraged by Matilda, who interceded on his behalf, Henry performed an elaborate ritual of penance, standing for three successive days outside the gates of the castle, barefoot, stripped of his imperial trappings, and clad in the sackcloth of a supplicant.

This performance of subjection and servitude forestalled Henry's deposition, but it did not resolve his dispute with the nobility of the Holy Roman Empire. And it also symbolically reversed the relationship between secular power and religious power. Since the time of Constantine, popes had been dependant on the rulers who protected them. Now an emperor had been bested by the pope. For the other kings and lords of Europe, Henry's humiliation was a chilling example of what could happen when a king let himself be made a vassal.

**MATILDA OF TUSCANY MEDIATES BETWEEN EMPEROR AND POPE.** Matilda was one of the most powerful rulers in eleventh-century Europe, controlling many strategic territories in northern Italy. Fluent in German as well as Latin and Italian, she was a key figure in the struggle between the emperor and the pope and a supporter of the reforming movement within the Church. The Latin inscription accompanying this manuscript miniature reads: "The King entreats the Abbot [i.e., the pope] and even humbles himself before Matilda." ▪ ***How does this image represent the relationships among these figures?*** ▪ ***Which appears to be the most powerful, and why?***

## RELIGIOUS REFORM AND PAPAL POWER

The increased power of the papacy in the eleventh century was a result of the processes we have been surveying in this chapter, and a development that would have been hard to foresee at the time of the Charlemagne's death. In the wake of the Viking invasions and the redistribution of power within the former Carolingian Empire, no ruler could maintain Charlemagne's hold on the Church. Many parish churches had been abandoned or destroyed, while those that survived were often regarded as the personal property of some local family, whose responsibility for protecting parishioners could become an excuse to oppress them. Bishoprics, too, were co-opted by families who regarded Church lands and offices as their private property. Even monasteries underwent a process of privatization, becoming safe havens for aristocratic younger sons and daughters with little inclination for religious life. The power of the Latin Church and the power of kings—closely allied for centuries—rapidly became uncoupled. Meanwhile, the holders of papal office were its worst abusers. Most were incompetent or corrupt, the sons or tools of powerful Roman families. Some, like John XII, who was deposed by Otto the Great, were notoriously debauched. Many fathered sons who themselves succeeded to high ecclesiastical office, including that of pope. As the guardian of the tombs of Peter and Paul, the bishop of Rome had long occupied a privileged position. By the tenth century, however, the papacy's credibility had been severely compromised.

## The Monastic Reform Movement

The first successful attempts to restore the spiritual authority of the Latin Church can be traced to the founding of a new kind of monastery in Burgundy (now southeastern France). In 910, a Benedictine abbey called Cluny freed itself from any obligation to local families by placing itself under the direct protection of the papacy. And although it had a wealthy benefactor, that benefactor relinquished any control over Cluny's property; instead, he and his family and descendants were granted special spiritual privileges in exchange for their support, thus guaranteeing their eternal reward in Heaven.

This arrangement would set a new precedent for the relationship between monasteries and powerful families for centuries to come, as Cluny began to sponsor other monasteries on the same model. Indeed, the foundation of daughter houses was another innovation: prior to this, all Benedictine monasteries had been independent of one another, united only by their observance of Benedict's *Rule*. Now Cluny established a network of Cluniac clones across Europe, all of which remained subordinate to the mother house. By 1049, there were sixty-seven such Cluniac priories (as the daughter monasteries were called), each one performing the same elaborate round of prayer and worship for which Cluny became famous, and each one entirely free from the control of local lords.

Cluniac influence was strongest in the former Frankish territories and in Italy, where the virtual absence of effective kingship allowed monastic reforms to thrive unchecked. In Germany and Anglo-Saxon England, by contrast, monastic reform emerged as an essential responsibility of Christian kings whose role model was the pious Charlemagne. These kings, too, followed Cluniac example by insisting on the strict observance of poverty, chastity, and obedience within the monastery, and on the performance of liturgical prayer. Yet because these kings were the guarantors of the monasteries' freedom from outside interference, it was they who appointed the abbots, just as they also appointed the bishops of their kingdoms. As a result of this trend, and the concurrent Norman conquest of England, future kings of England would have more direct control over Church lands than other European rulers.

Despite the differences in sponsorship, these parallel reforming movements made monasticism the dominant spiritual model for Latin Christianity. The peaceful, orderly round of daily worship in monasteries and convents was regarded as mirroring the perfect harmony of Heaven, and monastic prayers were considered uniquely effective because of nuns' and monks' holy way of life. Monasteries also had an important influence on the piety of ordinary

**THE ABBEY CHURCH AT CLUNY.** Its extraordinary wealth and power made Cluny a major target during the French Wars of Religion and again during the French Revolution, when locals who had been subjected to its lordship for centuries razed most of the buildings to the ground. This artist's reconstruction shows the vast abbey church as it might have looked by the twelfth century, after several extensive building campaigns. In its day, Cluny was one of the largest structures in Europe, and a quintessential example of the architectural style known as Romanesque.

# Analyzing Primary Sources

## *A Miraculous Reliquary*

*Although pilgrimages had been a part of Christian religious practice for centuries, they became much more central elements of popular piety from the tenth century on. Pilgrims brought money and spiritual prestige to the monasteries that housed miracle-working relics, and competition among monastic houses sometimes led one house to steal the relics of another. But some critics worried that these newly popular shrines were encouraging idolatry. Bernard of Angers (c. 960–1028) was one such critic. His account of a visit to the shrines of several saints, including that of Sainte Foy ("Saint Faith") at Conques, reveals the negative impression that ornate reliquaries made on him—and the power of wonder-working relics to correct that impression.*

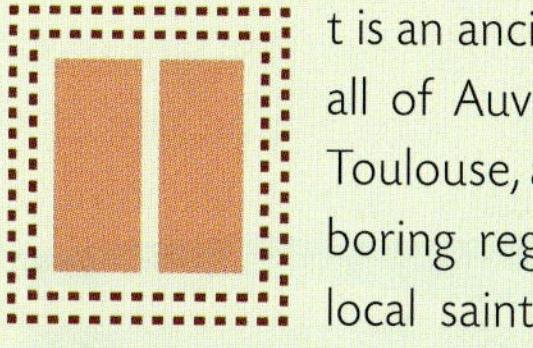t is an ancient custom in all of Auvergne, Rodez, Toulouse, and the neighboring regions that the local saint has a statue of gold, silver, or some other metal . . . [that] serves as a reliquary for the head of the saint or for a part of his body. The learned might see in this a superstition and a vestige of the cult of demons, and I myself . . . had the same impression the first time I saw the statue of Saint Gerard . . . resplendent with gold and stones, with an expression so human that the simple people . . . pretend that it winks at pilgrims whose prayers it answers. I admit to my shame that turning to my friend Bernerius and laughing I whispered to him in Latin, "What do you think of the idol? Wouldn't Jupiter or Mars be happy with it?" . . .

Three days later we arrived at [the shrine of] St. Faith. . . . We approached [the reliquary] but the crowd was such that we could not prostrate ourselves like so many others already lying on the floor. Unhappy, I remained standing, fixing my view on the image and murmuring this prayer, "St. Faith, you whose relics rest in this sham, come to my assistance on the day of judgment." And this time I looked at my companion . . . because I found it outrageous that all of these rational beings should be praying to a mute and inanimate object. . . .

Later I greatly regretted to have acted so stupidly toward the saint of God. This was because among other miracles [that] Don Adalgerius, at that time dean and later . . . abbot [of Conques], told me [was] a remarkable account of a cleric named Oldaric. One day when the venerable image had to be taken to another place, . . . he restrained the crowd from bringing offerings and he insulted and belittled the image of the saint. . . . The next night, a lady of imposing severity appeared to him: "You," she said, "how dare you insult my image?" Having said this, she flogged her enemy with a staff. . . . He survived only long enough to tell the vision in the morning.

The Reliquary of Saint Faith, Early Tenth Century.

Thus there is no place left for arguing whether the effigy of St. Faith ought to be venerated since it is clear that he who reproached the holy martyr nevertheless retracted his reproach. Nor is it a spurious idol where nefarious rites of sacrifice or of divination are conducted, but rather a pious memorial of a holy virgin, before which great numbers of faithful people decently and eloquently implore her efficacious intercession for their sins.

Source: Bernard of Angers, "The Book of the Miracles of St. Faith," in Patrick J. Geary, ed. and trans., *Readings in Medieval History*, 3rd ed. (Peterborough, Ont., Canada: 2003), pp. 333–34 (slightly modified).

### *Questions for Analysis*

1. Why does Bernard initially object to the display of relics in ornate reliquaries? Why would he consider this practice blasphemous? How does he become reconciled to it?
2. Can you think of present-day practices that resemble the medieval fascination with collecting, displaying, and venerating relics? What do such practices reveal about any society?

people, because many monastic communities maintained parishes that ministered directly to the laity. The spiritual practices that had been unique to monks and nuns in earlier centuries therefore came to influence daily life outside the cloister.

One potent example of this new popular spirituality is the growing devotion to relics. Monasteries were often the repositories of cherished objects associated with saints, such as fragments of bone or pieces of cloth cut from the garments of some holy person. These souvenirs were believed to possess special protective and curative powers. Hence, a relic was usually buried beneath the altar of a monastery's church during the ceremony of its consecration, in order to render the church building sacrosanct. Relics were also collected and displayed in elaborate reliquaries made of precious metals and studded with jewels, casings that reflected and augmented the value of the holy objects contained within them. Indeed, relics were so valuable that monasteries competed with one another for their acquistion and even plotted the "holy theft" of a particularly prized treasure. For instance, the relics of Nicholas, a fourth-century bishop of Myra (in Turkey), were stolen from the saint's tomb during the eleventh century and brought to Bari in southeastern Italy, where Benedictine monks built a magnificient church to house them and attract pilgrims.

The possession and display of relics thus became a way for monasteries to garner attention and generate revenue, since those who sought cures or favors at the shrine of a saint would often make a donation to the monastery in the saint's honor. If a saint was especially famous for a particular type of miracle, pilgrims might travel thousands of miles to visit a shrine. Saint Nicholas was famous for increasing the wealth of his suppliants, and for bestowing gifts—hence his later incarnation as Santa Claus. The relics of Sainte Foy ("Saint Faith") of Conques (southern France) were renowned for their power to rectify injustices, restore order, and heal the maladies that afflicted the poor. Those of the apostle James at Compostela (northern Spain) became the chief destination on a major pilgrimage route, rivaling even the holy sites of Rome and Jerusalem. Pilgrimage was another of the important ways in which the new patterns of Christian piety that developed in monasteries began to spread to the laity.

## The Reform of the Papacy

By the eleventh century, the movement toward reform and spiritual renewal in the monasteries of Europe began to embrace the sees of bishops. This was a major change: bishops and the priests who served in their dioceses were secular clergy, living in the world (*saeculum* in Latin); it had long been expected that they would share some of the worldly preoccupations and lifestyles of their parishioners. But as the values and priorities of monasticism began to spread outward, abbots were more often appointed to episcopal office. Meanwhile, nonmonastic bishops were forced to adopt stricter standards of personal conduct. Bishops also began to rebuild and expand their cathedral churches to make them more suitable reflections of divine majesty, in accordance with Cluniac example.

As their influence grew, the monasteries under the sway of Cluny began to lobby for even larger reforms, amounting to a fundamental dismantling of customs that reached back to the organization of the Church under Constantine, seven centuries earlier. They centered their attacks on simony (*SIGH-mony*), a term describing any use of ecclesiastical office for personal gain, including the purchase or sale of a bishopric or a priests's living (i.e., house, goods, and annual salary). In other words, the reform movement targeted the very structure of the Church as a network of independent lordships held by powerful men in trust for their families.

Even more radical was the reformers' demand that secular clergy share the lifestyles of monks, taking vows not only of personal poverty but of celibacy. Although some early councils of the Church had attempted to regulate the marriage of bishops and priests, none had been successful. And for good reason: the task of ministering to the laity was very different from the monk's task of perpetual prayer and communal life. For a thousand years, it had been conceded that the demands of priestly celibacy were unreasonable, and would deprive a priest's parishioners of an additional resource and ministry: that of his wife. In the year 1000, therefore, the vast majority of parish priests all across Europe were married, and in the Eastern Orthodox Church they would remain so. Married bishops were rarer, but not unknown. In Brittany, the archbishop of Dol and his wife publicly celebrated the marriages of their daughters, endowing them with lands belonging to the bishopric; in Milan, the archbishops flatly rejected reformers' calls for celibacy, declaring that their patron saint, Ambrose (Chapter 6), had been married, too.

In Rome, the papacy remained resolutely unreformed until 1046, when the German emperor Henry III deposed three rival Roman nobles who claimed to be pope and appointed in their place his own relative, a monk who adopted the name Leo IX (r. 1049–54). Leo and his supporters took control of the papal court and began to promulgate decrees against simony and clerical marriage. They then took steps to enforce these decrees by traveling throughout the Continent, disciplining and removing from office clerics deemed guilty of simony or obstinently determined not to "put away" their wives—whom the reformers insisted on calling "concubines" as a way of discrediting these respectable relationships.

Implicit in Leo's reforming efforts was a new vision of the Church as a type of feudal monarchy, with the pope at the apex of a spiritual pyramid: an ideal difficult for any secular ruler to realize and one that would severely limit the power of other ecclesiastical officeholders. Not surprisingly, therefore, Leo and his successors met with considerable opposition within the Church itself, and they could only enforce their claims in regions where they had the support of secular rulers. Among these was the pious emperor Henry III, whose protection insulated papal reformers from the Roman nobility, who would otherwise have deposed or assassinated them.

But when Henry III died in 1056, the regents of his child heir Henry IV (whose reign we discussed above) were neither able nor willing to stand behind the reforming movement. In 1058, the Roman aristocracy seized this opportunity to install one of their own number on the papal throne. By this time, however, the reform movement had gathered momentum; a year later, a new pope had been installed and was determined to counter any interference from either the German or Italian nobility. To this end, Nicholas II (r. 1059–61) created a new legislative body, the College of Cardinals (from the Latin for "collection" of "hinges"). Hitherto, local bishops around Rome had served the papacy as advisors and assistants, but now the College became the pivotal force for the creation of papal policy. It also ensured the continuity of the papal office by overseeing the selection of new popes, a role it still plays today.

Needless to say, this novel arrangement infuriated the advisors of the young Henry IV, since it removed the emperor's prerogative to oversee the process of elections himself. And it set the stage for the confrontations that were to follow.

## *The Investiture Conflict*

A few years after Henry IV began to rule in his own right, the new College of Cardinals selected as pope a zealous reformer called Hildebrand, a Cluniac monk of Tuscan origins who had been a protégé of Leo IX. He took the name Gregory VII. Initially, pope and emperor treated one another with deference. Henry IV's position in Germany had been weakened by his wars with the Saxon nobility, and he needed papal backing to restore his authority. In his letters to the new pope, he therefore blamed the advisers of his youth for the troubles that had arisen between his own court and that of Rome, and he promised to make amends. Gregory, in turn, spoke of pope and emperor as the two eyes of a single, Christian body. On the surface, it appeared that the harmonious relations that had existed under Henry's father might be restored.

Two year later, however, relations between papacy and empire were riven by a conflict that would permanently alter the relationship between spiritual and temporal leaders in western Europe. Superficially, the issue that divided Gregory and Henry was that of investiture, the right to appoint bishops and to equip them with the trappings of office. Since the time of the Carolingians, this had been the prerogative of the emperor. But to Gregory, this practice smacked of simony, since a lay lord would obviously choose bishops who would be politically useful to him, regardless of their spiritual qualifications.

The issue, however, was not the political power of bishops; it was the control of that power. For paradoxically, the papal reform movement as it developed under Gregory was predicated on liberating the Church from powerful worldly influences in order that the Church itself might become more worldly and powerful. This was the principle that lay behind the discouraging of clerical marriage, too: Church offices and Church property had to be protected by the Church for the Church. Allowing priests to marry might encourage the handing down of offices to sons, just as allowing rulers to appoint bishops encouraged these bishops to act as the rulers' agents. These practices tainted the austere authority that the pope was trying to cultivate, and it also threatened to alienate property and power that the papacy wanted to harness for its own purposes.

Gregory therefore took the reform movement to a new level, insisting that adherance to these principles was not just a matter of policy but a matter of religious dogma, defined as "a truth necessary for salvation." When Henry IV refused to accept this and proceeded to invest the new archbishop of Milan, Gregory reminded him that, as the succesor of Saint Peter and the representative of Christ on earth, he had the power to save or damn all souls. To drive the point home, Gregory excommunicated a number of Henry's advisors, including several of the bishops who had participated in the investiture at Milan. Henry thereupon renounced his obedience to Gregory, calling on him to resign. Gregory responded by excommunicating Henry, along with a large number of his supporters.

In itself, the excommunication of a king was not terribly unusual. Gregory, however, went much further by equating excommunication with deposition, declaring that since Henry was no longer a faithful son of the Church, he was no longer the king of Germany and his subjects had a sacred duty to rebel against him. It was this that occasioned Henry's humiliating stand before the castle at Canossa in

January of 1077. But the story does not end there, because Henry used his restored powers to crush his Saxon opponents and eventually to drive Gregory himself from Rome. In 1085, the aged pope died in exile in southern Italy. By then, however, he had established the principles on which papal governance would be based for the remainder of the Middle Ages.

In 1122, the conflict over investiture was ultimately resolved through compromise at the Concordat of Worms (*VOHRMS*) in Germany. Its terms declared that the emperor was forbidden to invest prelates with the *religious* symbols of their office but was allowed to invest them with the symbols of their rights as *temporal* rulers, in his capacity as their overlord. In practice, then, the rulers of Europe retained a great deal of influence over ecclesiastical appointments. But they also had to acknowledge that bishops were now part of a clerical hierarchy headed by the pope, loyal to the Church in Rome and not to the ruler of the region in which they lived.

## CRUSADING CAUSES AND OUTCOMES

Gregory VII's equation of excommunication with deposition had given the pope a powerful new weapon to use against wayward rulers. Indeed, according to a series of pronouncements issued in his name, Gregory insisted that the pope has the power to judge all men but cannot himself be judged by any earthly authority. Moreover, he has the power to free any man from his obligations to his lord because every Christian owes ultimate loyalty to the pope, the arbiter of eternal life or death. These were big claims. How could they be realized? Gregory's immediate successors would soon be driven to great lengths in their efforts to establish the credibility of the newly reformed and powerful papacy. In the end, it took the appeal of a Byzantine emperor and the preaching of a crusade against Islam to unite western Christendom under the banner of the papacy.

### *The Expansion and Limitations of Byzantium*

As western Europe expanded and changed, the eastern Roman Empire was undergoing its own series of transformations. The decline of the Abbasid caliphate in Baghdad had relieved some of the pressures on the eastern Roman Empire in the course of the ninth century. Yet at the same time, Byzantium was facing some new threats. In the mid-ninth century, a Muslim fleet captured the Byzantine islands of Sicily and Crete; the migration of pagan Slavs into the Balkans was rapidly undermining Byzantine control of that region; and a formidable enemy had emerged in the north, as the Vikings known as the Rus' established themselves along the river systems that fed into the Black and Caspian Seas. The Rus's most important trading partner was the Abbasid caliphate, with which they exchanged slaves, honey, wax, and furs for silver, Indian spices, and Chinese silks. But the Rus' knew their way to Constantinople, too. In 860, while the Byzantine emperor and his army were busy on the eastern frontier, a fleet of Russian Vikings sailed into the Black Sea and sacked the capital.

A century later, Byzantium had succeeded in making these newer enemies their allies. Greek-speaking missionaries began the process by converting the Balkan Slavs to Orthodox Christianity, devising for them a written language known as Old Church Slavonic and creating the Cyrillic alphabet still used today in Bulgaria, Serbia, and Russia. As usual, military domination went hand in glove with conversion. The Byzantines also established a military and commercial alliance with the Rus' kingdom centered around Kiev, decisively orienting the Rus' toward Constantinople and away from western Europe; in 911, about 700 Rus' served with the Byzantine fleet in an attack on Muslim Crete. In 945, a commercial treaty was established. In 957, a Kievan Christian princess named Olga was lavishly entertained on a state visit to Constantinople. And in 989, the emperor Basil II turned to Vladimir, prince of Kiev, for the troops he needed to win a civil war against an imperial rival. In return for Vladimir's help, Basil married him to his sister Anna; and Vladimir, along with his people, accepted baptism into the Orthodox church. Russia has remained strongly Orthodox to this day, despite Soviet efforts to dismantle the Russian Orthodox Church in the twentieth century.

In the tenth century, the Byzantines also launched a series of successful campaigns against the Abbasids along their eastern and southeastern frontiers, reconquering territories that had been lost since the seventh century. Most of the peoples of this region had remained Christian through three centuries of Islamic rule, although the Armenians and the Syrians in particular had their own distinctive Christian traditions that were at odds, both doctrinally and linguistically, with the Greek-speaking church at Constantinople. Reincorporating these "heretics" into the empire thus strained the limits of Byzantine orthodoxy to a considerable degree, and it also created a center of power that lay outside the imperial capital at Constantinople. Accordingly, rivalries divided the eastern nobility and the imperial court, eventually erupting into warfare after one aristocratic family attempted a coup.

Meanwhile, projects of reconquest and expansion were overextending the Byzantine military and its treasury. In an effort to raise cash, some emperors in the mid-eleventh century began to debase the gold coinage that had kept the empire competitive with the Muslim caliphates, thus undermining Byzantine commerce at the very moment when Venice, Genoa, and Pisa were consolidating their control in the eastern Mediterranean and taking over the lucrative trade between Islamic North Africa (including Egypt) and western Europe.

The failing economy, the ongoing civil war, the weakened condition of the army, and unrest in the Balkans proved fatal to Byzantine sovereignty when the empire was confronted with yet another threat. The Seljuqs, a powerful dynasty of Sunni Muslims who were building their own empire based in Persia, began to move westward in the latter part of the eleventh century. In 1071, they captured Armenia and moved swiftly into the Byzantine heartland of Anatolia (Turkey), where they destroyed a Byzantine army sent to deflect them. At a blow, the wealthiest and most productive part of the empire fell into Muslim hands—and not those of the Abbasids with whom the Byzantines had contended for centuries. In the same year, the Seljuqs captured Jerusalem, which had been part of a Shi'ite caliphate based in Egypt, ruled by the Fatimids. By 1081, when the eastern nobility of Byantium finally emerged trimphant in its ongoing bid for the imperial throne, the new emperor Alexius Comnenus (r. 1081–1118) found himself at the head of a crippled state.

**THE BYZANTINE EMPIRE, c. 1025.** ▪ *According to the map, what political challenges faced the Byzantine Empire in the eleventh century?* ▪ *How was the long-standing influence of Muslims in the Near East likely to affect the character of Byzantine culture?* ▪ *How did the domain of Kievan Russia potentially create additional economic and military pressure on Byzantium, directly as well as indirectly?*

## The Call for a Crusade

Alexius was an able emperor. In the first decade of his rule he managed to shore up the failing economy and secure his hold over the Balkans, and was beginning to plan a campaign against the Seljuqs. But with what forces? The Byzantine army barely existed, having been decimated in Greece by a far superior cavalry of Norman knights in 1085. For by this time, the Normans had established independent principalities in southern Italy and Sicily (which had previously fallen to the Arabs in 965), taking advantage of the perpetual power vacuum in those regions and showcasing the effective tactics of chivalry. As it happened, this encounter between the Byzantine emperor and western Europe's best warriors was historically decisive. It convinced Alexius that such heavily armed horsemen would be successful if pitted against the lightly armored Seljuqs.

It was in the hopes of recruiting a mercenary force, therefore, that Alexius approached Pope Urban II (r. 1088–99). This was a move that played into the hands of the papacy. Urban was trying hard to realize some of the powerful claims that his recent predecessors had made on behalf of papal authority, and this seemed like a golden opportunity. By coming to the aid of Byzantium, he would show the restive princes of western Europe that the papacy was a force to be reckoned with. At the same time, he hoped to show that western military and spiritual might was greater than that of the weakened East, thereby healing the schism between Orthodox and Latin Christianities and realizing the centuries-old dream of a universal Christian Church based in Rome, with the pope at its head. In addition, Urban would show support for another reforming effort that had gained momentum in recent years: a peace movement that was attempting to quell the endemic violence unleashed by competitive bands of knights and their rapacious lords. A new ethos of chivalry was gradually taking hold, but not fast enough. What better way to defuse the situation than to ship those violent energies overseas, deploying them against a common enemy?

So Alexius received a favorable reply, but he got far more than he had asked for—or wanted. He had needed a modest contingent of a few thousand troops, to help him reconquer Anatolia. What he got was a vast army of 100,000 men, charged by Urban II to retake the holy city of Jerusalem for Christendom. For Urban decided to interpret Alexius' request loosely. Speaking before an assembled crowd at an ecclesiastical council at Clermont (central France) in 1095, he announced that he fully supported the peace movement. He said, furthermore, that any knights who wished to fight, pillage, and wreak havoc could do so for a just and Christian cause by liberating the Holy Land from its Muslim captors. At home, they were riffraff and marauders, destined for hellfire and damnation; abroad, they would be crusaders, which meant that anyone fighting or dying in the service of Christ would win absolution for his sins. By taking up the cross (*crux*, hence "crusade"), a warrior stood to win glory, booty, and salvation.

It was an irresistable opportunity for many pious, ambitious, or opportunistic men, and the ultimate response to Urban's call exceeded all expectations. Indeed, his message was amplified by other preachers, including a zealous priest called Peter the Hermit, who alleged that he had been prevented by the Seljuqs from visiting the Holy Land. Within a year, tens of thousands of warriors and a large number of women and children from all over western Europe were on the march toward Constantinople, where they intended to gather before departing for Jerusalem. As with any large enterprise, the participants' motives must have varied. A few might have hoped to win principalities for themselves in the wild East. Others were drawn by the prospect of adventure. Many were the dependents of greater men, who had no choice but to accompany their lords; some hoped to free themselves from dependence by fighting. Most probably had no idea how long the journey would be or knew anything about the places for which they were destined.

But the dominant motive for joining this First Crusade was religious. Except for a few of the greatest lords—mostly Normans from southern Italy—the prospect of winning

**ROLAND AS A CRUSADING KNIGHT.** The association between knighthood and crusading helped to raise the social status of knights and contributed to the refinement of a chivalric ethos. Here, a crusading knight, dressed head to foot in expensive chain mail, is shown kneeling in homage to his lord, God.

**THE ROUTES OF THE CRUSADERS, 1096–1204.** Compare the routes followed by participants in the first three Crusades. ▪ ***What were the three main routes followed by crusaders?*** ▪ ***What geographical and political factors appear to be determining these trajectories?*** ▪ ***Why was the Fourth Crusade so different?***

new lands in the East was both unlikely and undesired. Indeed, one of the greatest challenges facing the Christian kingdom that was established in Jerusalem after 1099 was the fact that crusaders so rarely wanted to stay. After fulfilling their vows, the vast majority went home. So why did they go in the first place? The risks of dying on such a journey were high; the costs of embarking were enormous. Crusading knights needed a minimum of two years' revenues in hand to finance the journey. To raise such sums, most were forced to mortgage lands and borrow heavily from family, friends, monasteries, and merchants. They then had to find some way to pay back these loans if and when they returned home. By any rational assessment, the Crusade was a fool's errand.

Hence the importance of reckoning with the reality of the crusaders' piety, and even their desire to emulate heroes like Roland. Crusading was the ultimate pilgrimage, the holy places of Jerusalem the ultimate Christian shrines. If one could receive special blessings by traveling to Compostela, Conques, or Bari, how much more blessed would one be if one fought through to the Holy Land! Urban II made this point explicit at Clermont, promising that crusaders would be freed from all penances imposed by the Church. Some zealous preachers went even further, promising that crusaders would be entirely freed from otherworldly punishments for all sins committed up to that point in their lives, and that the souls of those who died on crusade would go straight to Heaven.

# Competing Viewpoints

## *Preaching the First Crusade: Two Accounts*

*We owe the following account of Urban II's call for a crusade to Fulcher of Chartres, a priest who was present at the Council of Clermont in 1095 and who later served as a chaplain to the first Norman king of Jerusalem, Baldwin. It forms part of Fulcher's contemporary chronicle of the First Crusade. The second account of the motives behind the crusade come from a biography of the Byzantine emperor Alexius Comnenus, written by his daughter Anna (1083–1153), who also lived through these events.*

### Pope Urban II's Call at Clermont, November 1195

Most beloved brethren: Urged by necessity, I, Urban, by the permission of God chief bishop and prelate over the whole world, have come into these parts as an ambassador with a divine admonition to you, the servants of God. . . .

Although, O sons of God, you have promised more firmly than ever to keep the peace among yourselves and to preserve the rights of the Church, there remains still an important work for you to do. Freshly quickened by the divine correction, you must apply the strength of your righteousness to another matter which concerns you as well as God. For your brethren who live in the east are in urgent need of your help, and you must hasten to give them the aid which has often been promised them. For, as most of you have heard, the Turks and Arabs have attacked them and have conquered the territory of Romania [the Byzantine Empire] as far west as the shore of the Mediterranean and the Hellespont. . . . They have occupied more and more of the lands of those Christians, and have overcome them in seven battles. They have killed and captured many, and have destroyed the churches and devastated the empire.

If you permit them to continue thus for a while with impunity, the faithful of God will be much more widely attacked by them. On this account I, or rather the Lord, beseech you as Christ's heralds to publish this everywhere and to persuade all people of whatever rank, footsoldiers and knights, poor and rich, to carry aid promptly to those Christians and to destroy that vile race from the lands of our friends. I say this to those who are present, but it is meant also for those who are absent. Moreover, Christ commands it.

All who die by the way, whether by land or by sea, or in battle against the pagans, shall have immediate remission of sins. This I grant them through the power of God with which I am invested. O what a disgrace, if such a despised and base race, which worships demons, should conquer a people which has the faith of omnipotent God and is made glorious with the name of Christ! With what reproaches will the Lord overwhelm us if you do not aid those who, with us, profess the Christian religion!

Let those who have been accustomed to wage unjust private warfare against the faithful now go against the infidels and end with victory this war which should have been begun long ago. Let those who for a long time have been robbers now become knights. Let those who have been fighting against their brothers and relatives now fight in a proper way against the barbarians. Let those who have been serving as mercenaries for small pay now obtain the eternal reward. Let those who have been wearing themselves out in both body

Crusade preaching also emphasized the vengeance that Christ's soldiers should exact on his enemies in the East. But to some crusaders, it seemed absurd to wait until they arrived in Jerusalem to undertake this aspect of their mission. Muslims might hold Jesus's property at Jerusalem, but Christian theology held Jews responsible for the death of Jesus himself. Assaults against Jewish communities therefore began in the spring of 1096 and quickly spread eastward with the crusaders. Hundreds of Jews were killed in the German towns of Mainz, Worms, Speyer, and Cologne, and hundreds more were forcibly baptized as the price for escaping death at the hands of

and soul now work for a double honor. Behold! On this side will be the sorrowful and poor, on that, the rich; on this side, the enemies of the Lord, on that, his friends. Let those who go not put off the journey, but rent their lands and collect money for their expenses; and as soon as winter is over and spring comes, let them eagerly set out on the way with God as their guide.

Source: S. J. Allen and Emilie Amt, eds., *The Crusades: A Reader* (Peterborough, Ont., Canada: 2003), pp. 39–40.

## Anna Comnena Describes the Beginnings of the First Crusade

[Alexius] had no time to relax before he heard a rumour that countless Frankish armies were approaching. He dreaded their arrival, knowing as he did their uncontrollable passion, their erratic character and their irresolution, not to mention . . . their greed for money. . . . So far from despairing, however, he made every effort to prepare for war if need arose. What actually happened was more far-reaching and terrible than rumour suggested, for the whole of the West and all the barbarians who lived between the Adriatic and the Straits of Gibraltar migrated in a body to Asia, marching across Europe country by country with all their households. The reason for this mass-movement is to be found more or less in the following events. A certain Kelt, called Peter [the Hermit] . . . left to worship at the Holy Sepulchre and after suffering much ill-treatment at the hands of the Turks and Saracens who were plundering the whole of Asia, he returned home with difficulty. Unable to admit defeat, . . . he worked out a clever scheme. He decided to preach in all the Latin countries. A divine voice, he said, commanded him to proclaim to all the counts in France that all should depart from their homes, set out to worship at the Holy Shrine, and . . . strive to liberate Jerusalem. . . . Surprisingly, he was successful. . . . Full of enthusiasm and ardour they thronged every highway, and with these warriors came a host of civilians, outnumbering the sand of the sea shore or the stars of heaven, carrying palms and bearing crosses on their shoulders. There were women and children, too, who had left their own countries. . . .

The upheaval that ensued as men *and* women took to the road was unprecedented within living memory. The simpler folk were in very truth led on by a desire to worship at Our Lord's tomb and visit the holy places, but the more villainous characters . . . had an ulterior purpose, for they hoped on their journey to seize the capital [Jerusalem] itself, looking upon its capture as a natural consequence of the expedition. . . .

Source: Excerpted from Anna Comnena, *The Alexiad*, trans. E. R. A. Sewter (New York: 1969), pp. 308–11.

### *Questions for Analysis*

1. Given Urban II's explanation of the problems confronting the Byzantine Empire, how do you account for the fact that the Crusades were directed toward the Holy Land, and not to the relief of Byzantium?
2. How does Anna Comnena represent the motives of Peter the Hermit and the crusaders? What distinctions does she make among the various participants?
3. Are there points of comparison between these two accounts? On what do they agree? How would you explain the differences between them?

crusading knights. Many individual churchmen attempted to prevent these attacks, among them the bishops in whose dioceses Jews lived. But the Church's own negative propaganda thwarted these efforts, and pogroms against Europe's Jews would remain a regular and predictable feature of Christian crusading.

## *The Christian Conquest of Jerusalem*

Surprised by the nature and scale of the response to his appeal, Emperor Alexius did his best to move the crusaders quickly through Constantinople and into Asia Minor. Differences in outlook between the western crusaders and the Byzantine emperor quickly became apparent, however. Alexius had little interest in an expedition to Jerusalem, and insisted that the crusaders promise to restore any territory they captured to him. From Alexius's standpoint, the crusader army was a threat, not least because it was headed by several of the Norman knights who had attempted to infiltrate his empire only ten years earlier. To the crusaders—whose mission had been shaped by Urban's policies (not those of Alexius)—this policy seemed like treachery. The crusaders, furthermore, did not understand the Byzantine emperor's willingness to make alliances with some Muslim rulers (the Shi'ite Fatimids of Egypt and the Abassids of Baghdad) against other Muslim rulers (the Sunni Seljuqs), and they ignorantly concluded that the Byzantines were working to undermine the crusading effort, perhaps even supporting the Muslims against them. Such suspicions contributed to a growing western conviction that the Byzantine Empire was itself an obstacle to the successful recovery of Jerusalem.

Viewed from the perspective of Alexius, the Crusade was a disaster. But from that of the papacy and the crusaders themselves, it was a triumph. In 1098, crusaders captured the old Hellenistic city of Antioch and with it most of the Syrian coast. At the end of 1099, they took Jerusalem, indiscriminately slaughtering its Muslim, Jewish, and Christian inhabitants. Their quick success stemmed mainly from the fact that their Muslim opponents were at that moment divided amongst themselves: the Fatimids had in fact recaptured Jerusalem just months before the crusaders arrived, and the defeated Seljuqs were at war with one other. But western military tactics, in particular the dominance of heavily armored knights, also played an important role in the crusaders' success. Equally critical was the naval support offered by Genoa and Pisa, whose merchant adventurers hoped to control the Indian spice trade that passed through the Red Sea and on to Alexandria in Egypt. The Crusade thereby contributed to the further decline of Byzantine commerce and decisively altered the balance of power between Byzantium and western Europe.

## The Consequences of the Crusades

For Byzantium, the consequences of the crusading movement were clearly tragic. On the Islamic world, by contrast, the impact was much more modest. The crusader kingdoms were never more than a sparsely settled cluster of colonies along the coastline of Syria and Palestine. Because the crusaders did not control the Red Sea, the main routes of Islamic commerce with India and the Far East were unaffected by the change in Jerusalem's religious allegiance. In any case, the crusaders did not *want* to interfere with the overland caravan routes that wound through their new territories. Trade between Islam and the West therefore continued despite periodic interruptions. The greatest economic gains went to the Italian maritime republics of Venice and Genoa, and Islamic merchants came to depend on western markets for their goods. Both sides also gained in military terms: Westerners learned new techniques of fortification, and Muslims learned new methods of siege warfare and new respect for the uses of heavy cavalry.

Of course, the most long-lasting consequence of the Crusades has also proved the most deadly in the long run: the development of both Christian and Islamic doctrines of holy war, the ideologies of crusade and *jihad* that continue to be so destructive in the twenty-first century. For Muslims, the Christian occupation of Jerusalem was a religious matter entirely, not a political or economic loss, and it was for pious reasons that they planned its recovery. By 1144, most of the crusader principalities in Syria had been recaptured. When Christian warriors came east in the Second Crusade to recoup the losses, they suffered crushing defeats. Not long afterward, Syria and Egypt were united under the great Muslim leader Salah ad-Din (Saladin), who decisively recaptured Jerusalem in 1187. Further Crusades were launched in response, none of them successful and all of them putting renewed pressure on Byzantium. The worst blow came in 1204, when Venetian ships contracted to transport a crusader army to the Holy Land were diverted to Constantinople, instead. The result was an enormous commercial gain for Venice and the effective destruction of the Byzantine Empire, which for the next sixty years was divided into Latin-ruled and Greek-ruled provinces.

Thereafter, crusading efforts were modest and aimed mainly at Egypt and, in 1270, North Africa. The strategic goal of these ventures was to cut the economic lifelines that supported Muslims in the Holy Land, but the only people who stood to gain from this were merchants who still dreamed of controlling the Far Eastern trade that ran through Egypt as well as the sub-Saharan gold trade that ran through Tunis. The only Latin kingdom that survived throughout these centuries was Acre (Akko in northern Israel), and its fall in 1291 marked the end of any viable western European presence in the region—until the short-lived conquests of Napolean at the end of the eighteenth century (see Chapter 18).

The impact of the Crusades on western Europe is more difficult to assess. From one standpoint, the Crusades represent the limits of western Europe's expansion during

# Analyzing Primary Sources

## *An Arab Aristocrat Encounters the Crusaders*

*Usama ibn Munqidh (1095–1188) was an Arab Muslim from Syria, whose family maintained a prominent place in the local administration even after the conquests of the Seljuqs and the Christian crusaders. He traveled widely and worked in various Islamic cities as a diplomat and scholar. He ended his life in the service of Salah ad-Din (Saladin), the great Muslim leader who reconquered Jerusalem the year before Usama's death. The following excerpt is from Usama's memoir, which he called* The Book of Contemplation. *The Templars mentioned in the account are the Christian military order of the Knights of the Temple, who dedicated themselves to protecting pilgrims in Jerusalem and guarding the holy sites. Their headquarters were in the main mosque of the city, which stood on the Temple Mount.*

Anyone who is recently arrived from the Frankish lands is rougher in character than those who have become acclimated and have frequented the company of Muslims. Here is an instance of their rough character (may God abominate them!):

Whenever I went to visit the holy sites in Jerusalem, I would go in and make my way up to the al-Aqsa Mosque, beside which stood a small mosque that the Franks had converted into a church. When I went into the al-Aqsa Mosque—where the Templars, who are my friends, were—they would clear out that little mosque so that I could pray in it. One day, I went into the little mosque, recited the opening formula 'God is great!' and stood up in prayer. At this, one of the Franks rushed at me and grabbed me and turned my face towards the east, saying, 'Pray like *this*!'

A group of Templars hurried towards him, took hold of the Frank and took him away from me. I then returned to my prayers. The Frank, that very same one, took advantage of their inattention and returned, rushing upon me and turning my face to the east, saying, 'Pray like *this*!'

So the Templars came in again, grabbed him and threw him out. They apologized to me, saying, 'This man is a stranger, just arrived from the Frankish lands sometime in the past few days. He has never before seen anyone who did not pray towards the east.'

'I think I've prayed quite enough,' I said and left. I used to marvel at that devil, the change of his expression, the way he trembled and what he must have made of seeing someone praying towards Mecca.

Source: Usama ibn Munqidh, *The Book of Contemplation: Islam and the Crusades*, trans. Paul M. Cobb (New York: 2008), p. 147.

### *Questions for Analysis*

1. What does Usama's account reveal about the variety of relationships among Christians and Muslims in the crusader kingdom of Jerusalem?
2. Who is the true outsider in this scenario? What does Usama's treatment by the Templars suggest about the policy of Christian leaders toward the city's Muslim residents?

this otherwise extraordinary period of growth. Trade with the Islamic world, and beyond it with India and the Far East, brought enormous prosperity to some Italian maritime powers, but these trading links had existed before the Crusades and continued after they ended. It is undeniable, though, that crusading continued to dictate the terms of western Europeans' attitudes toward the wider world and even toward one another, as we shall see in the following chapters. It fostered a new political and religious ethos that would inform the "reconquest" of the Iberian peninsula by the Christian rulers of Spain and lead to the massacre or forced conversion of Muslims and Jews. Crusading was also the rhetoric underlying English wars against the Welsh and the Scots, and the language that justified the massacre and dispossession of "heretics" in southern France by northern French imperialists. It motivated voyages of discovery from the fifteenth century onward and the subsequent conquest of the Americas and the colonization of Asia, Africa, and Australia (Chapter 11). And it has continued to exacerbate Western relations with Islam to this day.

## THE CULTURE OF THE MUSLIM WEST

It would be misleading to assert that all the consequences of the Crusades were negative. The positive outcomes were hugely important, too. Increased intellectual and cultural contact between the Latin West and the Islamic world had an enormous impact on European learning, literature, music, and art. The study and practical applications of mathematics were revolutionized when Europeans adopted Arabic numerals and the concept of zero—first promoted in western Europe, not surprisingly, by the son of a Pisan merchant who grew up in Algeria, Leonardo Fibonacci (c. 1170–c. 1250).

Even Christian theology was transformed by contact with Islam. For one thing, Muslim scholars were the ones who had inherited, preserved, and developed not only Hellenistic medicine and science but the philosophy of Aristotle, which would form the basis of a new Christian philosophy in the twelfth and thirteenth centuries (see Chapter 9). For another, Europeans had been almost entirely ignorant of Muslim beliefs prior to the Crusades, assuming that Muslims were pagans who worshiped a god called Mahomet or Mahoun. By 1143, a scholar called Robert of Ketton (c. 1100–c. 1160), originally from a small town in England, had completed a Latin translation of the Qu'ran, working in Spain with the encouragement of the abbot of Cluny. In the 1130s, he and a friend, Hermann of Carinthia (in Slovenia), traveled to Byzantium and the crusader kingdoms, where they became students of Arabic. They exemplify the world of possibilities that had been opened up to northwestern Europeans as a result of the processes we have been studying in this chapter.

**ARISTOTLE TEACHING ARAB ASTRONOMERS.** In this Arabic manuscript from the thirteenth century, Aristotle is represented as a contemporary of the astronomers he is instructing. ▪ ***What does this suggest about Muslims' attitude toward Greek philosophy?***

### *Muslim Philosophy, Science, and Medicine*

The scholars of Byzantium took a conservative approach to Greek philosophy, in every sense of the word (Chapter 7). The dialogues of Plato and some works of Aristotle were copied and studied, but the latter's ideas were so hard to reconcile with Orthodox theology that Emperor Alexius Comnenus eventually banned the teaching of Aristotelian logic. Ironically, then, the cultures that provided the most direct access to Greek learning were Arabic-speaking, and it was through Arabic translations that western European intellectuals became acquainted with these ideas, thanks to the labor of Arabists like Robert and Hermann.

Even before the rise of Islam, a number of Greek philosophical texts had been translated into Syriac, a Semitic language closely related to Arabic. Arabic translations soon followed, many sponsored by the Abbasid court at Baghdad, which established a special school for this purpose known as the House of Wisdom. By the end of the tenth century, Arabic translations of Plato, Aristotle, Plotinus, and other Greek authors were widely available and intensively studied throughout the Muslim world. Even in the remote Persian city of Bukhara, the great Muslim philosopher and physician Avicenna (Ibn Sīnq̄, 980–1037) was able to read all of Aristotle's works before he reached the age of eighteen.

Like their counterparts in Byzantium, Muslim philosophers strove to reconcile Greek and Hellenistic philosophical traditions with each other and with the tenets of Islamic theology. Reconciling Aristotelianism and Neoplatonism was the easier task. Many of the translations and commentaries of Aristotle from which Muslim philosophers worked had already been filtered through the philosophical traditions of Alexandria and Rome. Moreover, Aristotle and the Neoplatonists also shared a number of common assumptions, including the eternity of the world and the capacity of the human mind to understand the rational principles that govern the world's workings. Both traditions also stressed the freedom of individual humans to choose between good and evil.

Reconciling Greek philosophy with Islamic theology was more difficult. Like Judaism and Christianity, Islam holds that a single omnipotent God created the world as an act of pure will, and that the world will continue to exist only so long as God wills it. This runs counter to the classical views of the world as eternal. Moreover, both Christian and Islamic theology rests on the immortality of the individual human soul, another doctrine flatly in conflict with Aristotelian and Neoplatonic thought. There were also conflicts over the concept of free will, and again Muslims and Christians had more in common with one another on this head than with ancient Greek tradition. Although medieval theologians strongly emphasized the individual responsibility of believers to choose between good and evil, virtually all Muslims—like most Christians—believed that nothing good could occur unless God actively willed it.

Islamic philosophers adopted an array of different intellectual tactics to deal with these challenges, and in doing so laid the groundwork for the Christian theologians who relied on them. The most influential of these was Averroès (*ah-VER-oh-ayz;* Ibn Rushd, 1126–1198), an amazingly gifted scholar born in the Almoravid capital of Córdoba and active as a judge and physician in Seville. Averroès single-handedly advanced the study of Aristotelian logic by publishing a series of careful commentaries that sought to purge the Greek philosopher's works of all later (and confusing) Neoplatonic influences and thus to allow for their proper analysis and interpretation. Soon translated from Arabic into Latin, these commentaries influenced the way all subsequent Christian scholars read and understood Aristotle, and they earned Averroès the admiration of poets and artists as well as scholars. His prestige was so great that Christian intellectuals called him simply "The Commentator," as if there were no others. Sadly, his learning did not impress the new Muslim dynasty that came to power in his lifetime, the Almohads, who demanded that all philosophical inquiry be subordinated to orthodox Muslim belief. After burning several of Averroès' works, they exiled him to Morocco, where he died in 1198. Thereafter, Islamic philosophy may have had more impact on Europe than in some Islamic kingdoms.

Many Muslim philosophers were also distinguished physicians and scientists. The study of philosophy could bring a man renown (or censure) but few tangible rewards, whereas successful physicians and astrologers might rise to positions of wealth and power. Both astrology and medicine were applied sciences that relied on careful, accurate observation of natural phenomena. Muslim observations of the heavens were so accurate, indeed, that some astronomers corroborated the findings of Hellenistic scientists (see Chapter 4) that the earth must rotate on its axis and revolve around the sun. But because these theories conflicted with the (mistaken) assumptions of Aristotle, that the earth remained stationary with the sun and planets revolving around it, they were not generally accepted in the Islamic world or in Europe. Yet they may have influenced Nicolaus Copernicus (1473–1543), who is usually credited as the first to suggest that the earth orbited the sun (see Chapter 16).

**THE INFLUENCE OF AVERROÈS.** This portrait of the Muslim polymath Averroès is featured in a fourteenth-century fresco celebrating the achievements of the Christian theologian Thomas Aquinas (c. 1225–1274). ▪ ***What does his inclusion in this context indicate about the relationship between Muslim and Christian intellectual traditions?***

Islamic accomplishments in medicine were equally remarkable. Avicenna discovered the contagious nature of tuberculosis, described pleurisy and several varieties of nervous ailments, and noted that diseases could spread through contaminated water and soil. His *Canon of Medicine* would remain an authoritative textbook in the Islamic world and in western Europe until the seventeenth century. Later Islamic physicians would learn the value of cauterization and of styptic agents, diagnose cancer of the stomach, prescribe antidotes in cases of poisoning, and make notable progress in treating eye diseases. They recognized the infectious character of bubonic plague, pointing out that it could be transmitted by clothing. Muslim physicians were also pioneers in organizing hospitals and licensing medical practitioners. At least thirty-four great hospitals were located in the principal cities of Persia, Syria, and Egypt, each with separate wards for particular illnesses, a dispensary for giving out medicine, and a library. Chief physicians and surgeons lectured to students and graduates, examined them, and issued licenses to practice medicine. Even the owners of leeches (used for bloodletting, a standard medical practice of the day) had to submit their medicinal worms for inspection at regular intervals.

**IVORY PYXIS FROM AL-ANDALUS.** Fashioned in the tenth century, this little round box is made from a segment of elephant tusk and would have had a matching lid (now lost). Such boxes usually held spices or incense. Its decorative motifs are echoed in Islamic architecture on a larger scale, reminding us that medieval Islam did not prohibit the representation of natural and fanciful figures, as is often supposed.

Islamic scientists made important advances in optics and chemistry, as well as mathematics. Using what Westerners know as Arabic numerals—which Muslim scholars actually adopted from the Hindus—mathematicians developed a decimal arithmetic based on place values and hinged on the concept of the zero. Their work enabled fundamental advances in entirely new areas, both of which bear Arabic names: algebra and algorithms. Building on Greek geometry and their own astronomical observations, they also made great progress in spherical trigonometry. Muslim mathematicians thus brought together and pushed forward all the areas of mathematical knowledge that would later be adopted and developed in western Europe from the sixteenth century on. And they made an indispensible contribution to the burgeoning European economy, since the sophisticated accounting systems that supported commerce would have been impossible if merchants and bankers had continued to use the clumsy system of Roman numerals (try balancing your checking account in Roman numerals!). Thanks to Arabic mathematics, western Europeans could now add, subtract, divide, and multiply quickly and accurately, with or without the help of another Muslim invention, the abacus.

## *Islamic Literature and Art*

Poetry was integral to Muslim culture. It was a highly developed art form long before the emergence of Islam, and then it became even more important to the development and dissemination of Muslim identity because it was the form in which Muhammad framed the Qu'ran (Chapter 7).

Like medicine and astronomy, poetry was also a route to advancement. Not all poetry was composed in Arabic; particularly around the Abbasid court, poets writing in Persian enjoyed great renown. The best known of these is Umar Khayyam (d. 1123), whose *Rubaiyat* was turned into a popular English verse cycle by the Victorian poet Edward Fitzgerald (1809–1883). Although Fitzgerald's translation distorts much, the lush sensuality of Umar's poetic imagery ("a jug of wine, a loaf of bread—and thou") faithfully reflects themes that were common to much Muslim poetry. One poet wrote of his lover, "such was my kissing, such my sucking of his mouth / that he was almost made toothless." As these lines suggest, much of this poetry was addressed by men to other men, a fact that occasioned no concern

# Analyzing Primary Sources

## *A Hebrew Poem from Muslim Spain*

*In the courts of tenth- and eleventh-century Muslim Spain, Jewish poets began to write a new style of Hebrew verse closely modeled on contemporary Arabic examples. Samuel the Nagid was perhaps the most remarkable of this group of poets. He became the military leader of the Muslim kingdom of Granada as well as the head of the Jewish community there. In addition to his three volumes of poetry, he also wrote treatises on Hebrew grammar and religious law.*

Your debt to God is righteously to live,
And His to you, your recompense to give.
Do not wear out your days in serving God;
Some time devote to Him, some to yourself.
To Him give half your day, to work the rest;
But give the jug no rest throughout the night.
Put out your lamps! Use crystal cups for light.
Away with singers! Bottles are better than lutes.
No song, nor wine, nor friend beneath the sward–
These three, O fools, are all of life's reward.

Source: Raymond P. Scheindlin, ed. and trans., *Wine, Women, and Death: Medieval Hebrew Poems on the Good Life* (Philadelphia, PA: 1986), p. 47.

### Questions for Analysis

1. What values does this poem express? What is its perspective on the relationship between devotion to God, duty, and pleasure?
2. What does the career of Samuel the Nagid–poet, general, scholar–suggest about Jewish identity in this place and time? What does it suggest about the relations between Jewish and Muslim communities in medieval Spain?

within the elite circles in which it was composed and performed. When similar sentiments were adopted by poets in Europe, they tended to be addressed by men to women (see Chapter 9).

Jews also participated in this elite literary world, especially in Al-Andalus, where they wrote similarly sensuous, playful lyrics in both Hebrew and Arabic, praising wine, sexual intimacy, and their own songs. Muslim Spain also saw a great flowering of Jewish intellectual life, which paralleled and intersected with that of the Muslim society around them. The greatest Jewish scholar of the period was Moses Maimonides (*my-MAHN-eh-dees*, c. 1137–1204), whose systematic exposition of Jewish law in the *Mishneh Torah* earned him the title "the second Moses." Like Averroës, Maimonides may have been driven into exile by the Almohads; he traveled first to North Africa and then to Egypt, where he became famous as a teacher, jurist, and physician. Like Averroës, too, he exercised great influence on Christian theologians.

Perhaps the most distinctive of Islamic arts are architectural and decorative, the arts that created the spaces in which poets and scientists interacted with their patrons. Many characteristic elements of Muslim architecture (the dome, the column, and the arch) were adapted from Byzantine models, but were then combined with the intricate tracery and ambitious scale of Persian buildings to form a new architectural vocabulary. Building styles were further inflected by the many different cultures that embraced Islam, from Spain to Egypt to India and beyond. Muslim artistry was also expressed in the magnificent gardens and fountains that adorned palaces, and in the more portable magnificence of gorgeous carpets, tooled leather, brocaded silks and tapestries, inlaid metalwork, enameled glassware, and painted pottery—all decorated with Arabic script, interlacing geometric designs, plants, fruits, flowers, and fantastic animal figures (another Persian influence). These complex designs can often seem strikingly modern, precisely because they anticipate the abstract forms that were considered new in the twentieth century. Indeed, they were the product of a culture that increasingly frowned upon the realistic depiction of natural forms.

## *Islamic Culture and Christian Europe*

Prior to the contacts facilitated by the Crusades, the cultural, economic, intellectual, and political achievements of Islamic civilization had completely overshadowed those of Latin Christian Europe. Even thereafter, the new Europe that emerged in the twelfth century would rely heavily on what it had learned from the Islamic world. This is reflected in the large number of Arabic and Persian words that passed into the languages of northwestern Europe. Essential words for commerce and trade include *traffic, tariff, alcohol, muslin, orange, lemon, alfalfa, saffron, sugar, syrup,* and *musk,* to name just a few. The word *admiral* also comes from Arabic (from the title *emir*), as do words that tell the story of Europe's reliance on Islamic science and technology: *alchemy, algebra, algorithm, alkali, almanac, amalgam, cipher, soda, magazine,* and *zero*—not to mention the names of stars, such as Aldebaran and Betelgeuse.

The Islamic world also had an enormous influence on the imagination and the self-perception of Christian Europe. Byzantine civilization was at once too closely linked to Christian Europe and, from the eleventh century on, too weak to compel western Europeans to take much account of it. Western Christians tended to look down on the Byzantine Greeks, but they respected and feared Muslims. And they were right to do so, for Islamic civilization at its zenith (to use another Arabic word) was surely one of the world's greatest. It brought Arabs, Persians, Turks, Egyptians, Africans, Indians, and Asians together in a common cultural and religious system, creating a diverse society and a splendid legacy of original discoveries and accomplishments that continue to shape the world today. And in the twelfth century, the expanding world of medieval Europe reaped the benefits of its interactions with this rich culture.

# CONCLUSION

In the year 1000, Europe was the least powerful, least prosperous, and least sophisticated of the three civilizations that had emerged out of the Roman world. A hundred years later, it was a force to be reckoned with. This metamorphosis rested on economic foundations: increasingly efficient agriculture, a growing population, and expanding trade. These changes produced a dynamic, expansionist, self-confident, and mobile society in which individuals cast off old roles and took on new ones with bewildering speed.

## After You Read This Chapter

Visit StudySpace for quizzes, additional review materials, and multi-media documents. **wwnorton.com/studyspace**

### REVIEWING THE OBJECTIVES

- The fragmentation of power in the ninth and tenth centuries created a world very different from that of Charlemagne. Describe some of the key changes. What were their causes?
- The agricultural revolution of the Middle Ages had far-reaching economic, social, and political consequences. What were they?
- The reforming movement with the Church changed the relationship between the papacy and the secular rulers of Christendom. Explain why.
- The motives behind the Crusades were political as well as religious. Why was this the case?
- The Crusades had profound effects on western Europe, Byzantium, and Islam, as well as on the relationships among different groups within these societies. In what ways were these three civilizations transformed?

No less important, however, were the political and military changes that began to alter the map of Europe in these centuries. By 1100, the heavily armored, mounted knight had emerged as the most formidable military weapon of the day, and new conceptions of power—both spiritual and temporal—were being articulated and contested within Europe, and on crusade.

But it was not yet possible either for kings or popes to control the energies of the workers, town-dwellers, merchants, knights, and scholars whose endeavors were transforming their world. A new approach to political organization was needed. Up to this point, the civilizations of the West had rested on two basic types of government: city-states and empires. City-states were more capable of mobilizing the loyalty of their citizens; as a result, they could sometimes win extraordinary victories against more-powerful imperial rivals, as the Greeks did against the Persians. But city-states were frequently divided by internal economic and social rivalries; and in the long run, they were not strong enough to defend themselves against foreign conquerors. Empires, by contrast, could win battles and maintain powerful administrative bureaucracies, but they were generally too far-flung to inspire deep loyalties among their subjects.

Where, then, do the monarchies of medieval Europe fit into this picture? How would the struggle for the control of western Europe's expanding resources be carried forward in the wake of the Crusades? And what cultural, spiritual, social, and intellectual innovations would result? These are the questions we address in Chapter 9.

## PEOPLE, IDEAS, AND EVENTS IN CONTEXT

- How was Europe affected by **VIKING** raids and settlements? Which territorial rulers imitated **CAROLINGIAN** models in the wake of these upheavals?
- What new technologies drove the **AGRICULTURAL REVOLUTION** of the Middle Ages? Why did the organization of labor on **MANORS** sometimes lead to **SERFDOM**?
- What conditions led to the growth of medieval **TOWNS** and why did the formation of urban **COMMUNES** foster new types of liberty? How were **MONEY AND CREDIT** essential to medieval commerce?
- Why is **"FEUDALISM"** a problematic concept? How did the ceremony of **HOMAGE** symbolize the relationship between a **VASSAL** and his **LORD**?
- What were the causes of the **INVESTITURE CONFLICT**?
- Why did **EMPEROR ALEXIUS** ask **POPE URBAN II** for assistance? Why did the pope use this as a pretext for urging the **FIRST CRUSADE**?
- How and why did **MUSLIM LEARNING AND CULTURE** exercise a profound influence on western Europeans?

## CONSEQUENCES

- In what ways does the Investiture Conflict reflect the unique historical circumstances of the late eleventh century, and in what ways can it be viewed as an extension of longer-term phenomena?
- Based on what we have learned about the relationship between political power and religious power in previous chapters, would you say that the clash between the papacy and the Holy Roman Empire was inevitable?
- Given the many negative aspects of the crusading movement—and its eventual failure—how might you explain the continuing appeal of crusading rhetoric down to the present day?

# Before You Read This Chapter

## STORY LINES

- The power of Europe's new monarchies and of the papacy depended on new methods of oversight, administration, and documentation.
- Schools and universities were therefore crucial to the development of these institutions, and they also provided ambitious men with unprecedented intellectual, social, and political opportunities.
- The Church's presence in the daily lives of the laity produced vibrant forms of spirituality yet placed strict limitations on women, religious dissidents, and non-Christians.
- Meanwhile, Europe's princely courts, wealthy towns, universities, and cathedrals fostered new forms of entertainment, art, and architecture.

## CHRONOLOGY

| | |
|---|---|
| 1079–1142 | Lifetime of Peter Abelard |
| c. 1090–c. 1164 | Lifetime of Heloise |
| 1098 | Cistercian order established |
| 1098–1179 | Lifetime of Hildegard of Bingen |
| 1099 | First Crusade ends |
| 1122–1204 | Lifetime of Eleanor of Aquitaine |
| c. 1140 | Gratian's *Concordance of Discordant Canons* |
| 1152–1190 | Reign of Frederick II Barbarossa |
| 1180–1223 | Reign of Philip II Augustus |
| 1192–1194 | Alfonso II of Aragon compiles the *Liber feudorum maior* |
| 1194–1250 | Lifetime of Frederick II the Great |
| 1198–1216 | Reign of Pope Innocent III |
| 1215 | Magna Carta and the canons of the Fourth Lateran Council are formulated |
| 1209 | Franciscan order established |
| 1216 | Dominican order established |

# The Consolidation of Europe, 1100–1300

## CORE OBJECTIVES

- **IDENTIFY** the differences among Europe's emerging monarchies.
- **UNDERSTAND** the connections between new religious movements and the power of the papacy.
- **DEFINE** scholasticism and trace its development.
- **EXPLAIN** the changing meaning of *chivalry*.
- **DESCRIBE** the cultural trends of the High Middle Ages.

At the turn of the twelfth century, the eldest son of a nobleman did something unusual; he traded lordship for scholarship. His name was Peter Abelard. In his own estimation, he was the smartest man in the world, and the best looking. He was certainly one of the most ambitious. After leaving his father's lands in Brittany and besting all the established teachers in Paris, he was appointed to the position of master in the cathedral school, one of the highest academic posts then available. There he met Heloise, the niece of a priest called Fulbert. Heloise had received an excellent education in a nearby convent, but the normal path of intellectual advancement—Abelard's school—was closed to her. So Fulbert arranged for her to become Abelard's private pupil. But she soon became more than that: his intellectual partner, his lover, and his wife. This last step was particularly problematic, because marriage was no longer an option for clerics, and would therefore ruin Abelard's chances of a brilliant career in the Church. So it remained a secret, as did Heloise's subsequent pregnancy and the birth of their son. But Fulbert eventually found out, and took revenge on Abelard, sending some local thugs to castrate him. Heloise and Abelard lived out the remainder of their lives in isolation from one another, and most of what we know about their relationship comes from letters they exchanged years later, when Heloise was the leader of a new religious community and Abelard was laying the intellectual foundations of the first university.

The developments of the twelfth and thirteenth centuries altered Europe in profound and lasting ways. This period witnessed the emergence of large-scale territorial monarchies and the papacy as dominant forces, while cathedral schools and universities turned out larger and larger cohorts of the professional men needed to run the bureaucracies that supported secular and religious authority. New opportunities for social advancement and new spiritual practices transformed daily life. In the wake of the Crusades, both ancient texts and novel ideas generated the intellectual revolution in which Abelard and Heloise participated. New artistic and technological influences were galvanizing forces, too, financed by prelates and kings, princely courts and wealthy towns engaged in an integrated and far-reaching economy. Moreover, new literary forms took shape as the spoken vernaculars of Europe came to challenge Latin, becoming languages of learning, devotion, and entertainment. By 1300, the political institutions and cultural identities that still define Europe today had been formed.

**ABELARD AND HELOISE.** This image from a thirteenth century manuscript shows Abelard in a scholar's gown and cap and Heloise wearing a nun's habit; their gestures indicate that they are engaged in heated debate. The story of their fervent attraction and doomed marriage was already famous during their lifetimes, and by the time this manuscript was copied, theirs had become the ultimate example of star-crossed love.

## THE MAKING OF MEDIEVAL MONARCHIES

As we learned in Chapter 8, traditional forms of kingship were challenged by the developments of the tenth and eleventh centuries. Independent towns and lords often refused to acknowledge royal authority, and kings could no longer rely on close-knit kin groups or the broad imperial powers wielded by a ruler like Charlemagne. How, then, did some European rulers build the foundations of states that still exist today? For crucially, the *idea* of a national state, an idea forged in the twelfth and thirteenth centuries, would endure to become the basis on which the political system of the modern world is still constructed.

Not all attempts were equally successful. For example, the France that emerged in the twelfth century would almost collapse two hundred years later (see Chapter 10). Other monarchies would not be consolidated until the nineteenth century (Germany is the best example) and, even then, *political* unification could not hide the continued fact of cultural and linguistic disintegration (as evident in Italy, Belgium, and Switzerland to this day). Yet it became so vital for modern European states to trace their origins to the medieval past that those states without a medieval pedigree would eventually be obliged to invent one.

### *England: From Conquest to Consolidation*

The conquest of England in 1066 allowed the first Norman king, William, to experiment with a new type of kingship. In theory, he commanded the allegiance of every person dwelling in his kingdom, over and above the allegience owed to kin, a local lord, or even the Church. In practice, however, William needed to impose his will on his new subjects, and this often took the form of violence. Yet it was also expressed through the highly effective adminstrative structures of his Anglo-Saxon predecessors, which he adapted to his own needs. This process was carried forward by his energetic son Henry I (r. 1100–35), whose approach to kingship was unusual in its focus on effective governance rather than warfare. Henry strengthened the Anglo-Norman system of local administration and instituted a system of traveling judges to administer royal justice in the countryside. His biggest innovation was the introduction of a method of financial accounting carried out by an office known as the Exchequer, so called because clerks moved counters around on a checkered cloth to calculate receipts and expenditures.

Henry's hands-on approach to royal lordship was both new and unpopular. Then, as now, those opposed to "big government" could react to it violently, and after Henry's death those reactions provoked a civil war that lasted throughout the reign of his cousin and successor, Stephen (r. 1135–54)—until the people of England began to long for a king who would bring back the good old days under Henry. They found such a king in Henry's grandson Henry of Anjou (b. 1133, r. 1154–89), who at the age of twenty-one was already the duke of Normandy and the lord of two other independent counties, Anjou and Maine. He also controlled the Aquitaine, thanks to his recent alliance with its powerful and brilliant ruler, Eleanor (1122–1204), who had annulled her first marriage to the French king Louis VII in order to marry Henry. As a result, England found itself integrated into the political and cultural world of the Continent in unprecedented ways.

Henry II restored his grandfather's royal administration and began, steadily, to extend its reach. He ordered juries (from the Latin *jus*, meaning both "law" and "oath") of reliable local men to report every major crime that occurred in their districts, and also empowered them to investigate civil cases. These innovations are the origin of our modern legal system. Henry II also made it easier for common people to seek justice in the royal courts. All of these measures brought an unprecedented number of average people into the exercise of government and thus increased their sense of loyalty to the king and their personal investment in his rulership.

But these innovations also brought Henry into conflict with the Church, because the extension of royal justice impinged on that of ecclesiastical courts: tribunals overseen by bishops that claimed the exclusive right to try and sentence clergy accused of committing crimes—even in the case of capital crimes like murder. Henry, by contrast, declared that clerics convicted of serious crimes in church courts should lose their clerical status and be handed over to the royal court for sentencing. Opposition to his policy came from an unexpected quarter: Thomas Becket, a long-time friend and supporter of Henry's, who was now the archbishop of Canterbury.

Thomas was a self-made man, the son of immigrants who had benefited from the social mobility of town life (he grew up in London) to obtain an education and thereby rise through the ranks of the Church. He saw the advantages to be gained from maintaining the independence of ecclesiastical procedures, and feared that Henry's real goal was to undermine the rights of the Church. Henry responded by exiling Thomas from England for several years. When Thomas returned in 1170, he was assassinated in his own cathedral by four of Henry's knights. Thomas was quickly proclaimed a martyr and a saint, and his tomb at Canterbury became one of the most important pilgrimage sites of the Middle Ages. Henry, for his part, was compelled to appear as a barefoot pentitent at this tomb and ask the saint's forgiveness for his sins.

**THE MURDER OF THOMAS BECKET.** In this illumination from a thirteenth-century prayer book, one of the knights has struck the archbishop so violently that he has broken his sword. How might a contemporary viewer have interpreted this?

**ENGLAND AND FRANCE, 1180–1223.** ▪ *What would have been its effects on the political orientation of England?* ▪ *What areas did Henry II's empire control in 1180?* ▪ *What advantages would the king of France have when challenging English control over continental territories even though his own power was confined to the "island" (Ile) of France around Paris?*

In the long run, Henry II did not win the right to sentence clerics in royal courts, but he did retain the right to nominate clerics to high office and thereby to exercise a large measure of control over those courts' personnel. The most concrete proof of Henry II's success is that his government continued to work efficiently even after his death, to the extent that his swashbuckling son Richard "the Lionheart" (r. 1189–99) could rule his father's empire for ten years *in absentia*, spending only about six months in England during all that time.

## *The Meaning of Magna Carta*

When Richard was killed by a crossbow bolt while besieging a castle, he was succeeded by his brother John (r. 1199–1216), an efficient administrator but a far less enthusiastic warrior. By 1204, John had been forced to cede nearly all of his father's Continental possessions to the powerful young king of France, Philip; only the Aquitaine, the inheritance of his mother Eleanor, remained. This was politically disastrous for John, not only because it depleted his resources but because it angered the most powerful lords of England, nearly all of whom were of Norman descent and who thus lost their ancestral lands when John lost Normandy. John's response was to attempt a recovery of lost territories by raising taxes to equip an army, thereby angering the nobility further. In 1215 they forced John to set his seal to Magna Carta, a "great charter" that defined the barons' rights while limiting those of the king.

Magna Carta established some important general principles that would continue to shape the laws of England and, eventually, her North American and Australian colonies. The king could levy no taxes without the consent of the kingdom at large, no free man could be punished until he had been judged guilty by a jury of his peers in accordance with the law, no one could be arrested and imprisoned without a warrant, and no unqualified or ignorant person could hold public office. The charter also provided for the establishment of a representative body of barons, which later came to represent the common people of England, too: Parliament (a word derived from the French "talking together"). Above all, Magna Carta expressed the extraordinary idea that a king is bound by the law.

We have frequently noted the achievements of the various powerful lawgivers whose contributions have been essential to Western civilizations, starting with Hammurabi (Chapter 1). But for the most part, those lawgivers held themselves to be above the law. Although medieval monarchs—in England and elsewhere—attempted to behave as though this were true for them as well, they would ultimately be forced to concede the rule of law itself.

Magna Carta contributed to the slow process that transformed the inhabitants of England into Englishmen, people with a shared identity and shared values. It also normalized the idea that strong, centralized government was a good thing. When the barons of England revolted again in the reign of John's son, Henry III (r. 1216–72), they did so because Henry's rule was not effective enough. Henry III's son Edward (r. 1272–1307) accordingly made Parliament into a legislative body that could help run the kingdom and authorize new expenditures. Since Magna Carta had demanded that no taxation be imposed without the common consent of the realm, Edward convened Parliament to explain why such taxation was necessary and to secure such consent. Edward also used meetings of Parliament to take advice about pressing concerns, to hear judicial cases involving great men, to review local administration, to hear complaints from the countryside, and to promulgate new laws. Gradually, England was changing from a feudal monarchy into a constitutional monarchy dependent on representative government, as it remains to this day.

## *The Emergence of France*

Compared to the Anglo-Saxon and Anglo-Norman kings of England, the king of the Franks presided over a miniscule kingdom over which he exercised little control. Since the reign of Hugh Capet (987–96), the kings who succeeded him had trouble making good on any claim to lordship over territories beyind the immediate hinterland of Paris. Most of the Carolingian institutions of governance had collapsed and been further weakened by Viking raids or by ongoing pressure from the Viking state of Normandy. When the empire of Henry II was at its height, therefore, the kingdom of Louis VII (r. 1137–80)—who had lost both his wife Eleanor and her lands to that same Henry—was tiny and insignificant.

But in many ways the Capetian dynasty was fortunate. Against all biological odds, they managed to produce an unbroken line of able male heirs for over 300 years (from 987 to 1328), without interruption—men who were also long lived. On average, each Capetian king ruled for thirty years, which contributed greatly to political stability. And this kingdom, though small, was a rich center of agriculture and trade, which provided a steadily increasing source of income. The prestige of the Capetians was also enhanced by their patronage of the new University of Paris founded by Abelard, which became the intellectual capital of Europe.

Beyond all this, the Capetians proved to be shrewd and wily, carefully husbanding their strengths while more powerful enemies overreached themselves.

The epitome of these strengths was Philip II (r. 1180–1223), a man who styled himself "Augustus" and who was the first to use the title "king of France": king of a soveriegn state (rather than "king of the Franks," a loose agglomeration of people). Philip came to the throne at the age of eighteen, having witnessed the struggles of his father Louis VII against the superior strength of Henry II. He understood that he could not win a direct military confrontation with either Henry or his son Richard. John, however—known to his detractors as "Soft Sword"—was another matter. Philip declared that John owed him homage and allegiance in return for Normandy and its adjacent territories, and then took advantage of his position as John's overlord to undermine John's control over these lands. When John objected, Philip declared all John's lands to be forfeit to the French crown and backed this declaration with armies that won decisive victories in 1204 and 1214.

With Normandy and the other Angevin territories of northern France added to his domain, Philip now had the resources to build an effective system of local administration. He wisely chose to maintain the bureaucratic structures put in place there by generations of Anglo-Norman rule, but he also appointed royal overseers, known as bailiffs, who had full judicial, administrative, and military authority. Philip drew these men from among the needy knights and lesser nobility of his own domain and rotated them frequently from region to region. This ensured their loyalty to Philip, and also prevented them from developing personal ties to the regions they governed.

Philip's administrative pattern, which recognized regional diversity while promoting centralized royal control, would continue to characterize French government down to the time of the French Revolution (see Chapter 18). Philip's son, Louis VIII (r. 1223–26), would extend it to the newly conquered territories of the southeast. His son, Louis IX (r. 1226–70), would deepen and legitimize it by his devotion to justice at home and crusading abroad. Even in his lifetime Louis IX would be celebrated as the paragon of good kingship, and soon after his death he would be canonized as Saint Louis. His successors would draw on that legacy for centuries to come.

Although Philip Augustus and his heirs experimented with representative assemblies similar to the English Parliament, the French Parlement (later known as the Estates General) never played a comparable role in French government. There are many reasons for this, but the most fundamental was the French nobility's successful claim to exemption from taxation, something that would remain a political problem until the French Revolution of 1789. Other significant points of comparison between England and France continue to mark the intertwined history of these two states. England, a far smaller country, was much more tightly unified at a much earlier date. English nobles could and did rebel against their kings, but could rarely draw sustained support from regional resentments. In France, however, regional separatism remained (and still remains) a significant force, to the extent that ambitious insurgents have long capitalized on regional animosity toward the French government when making bids for power.

England and France were also governed in different ways. English kings could rely on local men to do much of the work of local government without pay. This made English administration inexpensive, and it also meant that royal policies had to be popular in order to be implemented. French kings, by contrast, ruled through salaried officers who had little connection to local society. They had less need to summon representative assemblies and, as a result, lacked effective mechanisms for mobilizing public support. In the eigtheenth century, these features would be the undoing of the French monarchy.

## German Kingship and the Holy Roman Empire

We have seen (in Chapter 8) that the struggles between the German emperor Henry IV and the papacy ultimately led to the weakening of imperial authority. But in the middle of the twelfth century, a newly elected emperor made an ambitious attempt to restore the power of the German monarchy and to free it from papal control. This was Frederick Barbarossa ("Red Beard," r. 1152–90), who coined the term "Holy Roman Empire" to describe his realm, thereby asserting that its holiness derived from the blessing of God and did not necessarily depend on the intervention of the pope.

Frederick forged a close alliance with other German princes by supporting their efforts to control their own territories, in exchange for their support of his efforts to reassert imperial control over the wealthy cities of northern Italy. This strategy worked, but it sparked a series of destructive wars. Led by Milan and sanctioned by the pope, the cities of northern Italy formed an alliance, the Lombard League, which put up a staunch resistance to Frederick's rule and finally forced him to guarantee their political independence in return for large cash payments. Meanwhile, Frederick attempted to bypass the power of the papacy by supporting a series of papal pretenders, or "antipopes." This move was successfully countered by the reigning pope, Alexander III

**THE HOLY ROMAN EMPIRE, c. 1200.** ▪ *How would the borders of the Holy Roman Empire have been defined during the Middle Ages?* ▪ *Why were the German states not able to unify during this period?* ▪ *Why would the prospect of a single heir to the Holy Roman Empire and to the Kingdom of the Two Sicilies have been a threat to the papacy?*

(r. 1159–81), who drove a shrewd bargain with Frederick: if Frederick would concede the sovereignty of the pope's rule within Rome and its adjacent territories—lands that came to be known as the Papal States—then Alexander would concede the emperor's sovereignty within his domains and even his overlordship of the Church within those domains. Frederick eventually agreed, thereby gaining the pope's support for his rule in northern Italy.

Frederick also secured the German princes' support for the acceptance of his son as Frederick's heir. When Frederick left for the Holy Land in 1189—joining Richard the Lionheart of England and Philip Augustus of France on the (failed) crusade to reconquer Jerusalem—he left his realm in a powerful position. Although he died soon after, his careful planning bore fruit in the reign of his son, Henry VI, who succeeded to his father's throne without opposition and enjoyed a huge income from the north Italian towns; he ultimately became the king of Sicily, too. This strengthened the empire's position even further, for now the Papal States were surrounded by the lands of a single powerful ruler. Fortunately for the papacy, however, Henry VI died in 1197 at the age of thirty-two, leaving a three-year-old son, the future Frederick II, as his heir apparent.

Frederick II, often called "the Great," is one of the most fascinating of all medieval rulers. Having grown up in Sicily, he spoke Arabic and Italian as well as Latin, German, and French. He was both a patron of learning and a scholar in his own right, the author of an important treatise on falconry that is still considered a model of scientific investigation. He maintained a menagerie of exotic animals, a troop of Muslim archers, and a harem of veiled and secluded women, all of whom traveled with him on his journeys. But despite this appearance of exoticism, he was a conventional king who sought to pursue his grandfather's policies, supporting the territorial princes in Germany while enforcing imperial rights in Italy.

Much had changed, however, as a result of the two decades' civil war that followed his own father's death. In Germany, the princes had become so entirely autonomous that there was little Frederick could do except to recognize their privileges in exchange for their loyalty. In Italy, the cities of the Lombard League had long since ceased to pay their taxes; meanwhile, the powerful administrative structure of Sicily had fallen into chaos.

Frederick tackled all these problems and eventually restored control over the disparate territories of his empire. In 1237, however, he made the mistake of asserting a right to rule the northern Italian cities directly, bypassing their own independent governments. The result was another Lombard League and another lengthy war, which continued until Frederick's death in 1250. The papacy took every advantage of this situation, even excommunicating Frederick and, after his death, denying the rights of his heirs. When Frederick's last legitimate son died in 1254, the prospect of effective imperial rule died with him. For the next five hundred years, until the founding of the modern German state in 1871, political power in the lands of the Holy Roman Empire would be divided among several hundred territorial princes.

**ON THE ART OF HUNTING WITH BIRDS.** This beautifully illuminated manuscript of Frederick II's famous treatise on falconry was commissioned by his son, Manfred, shortly after his father's death in 1250. It is now in the Vatican Library, Rome.

## *The "Reconquest" of Iberia*

Although the Christian kingdoms clustered to the north and east of the Iberian peninsula were even more distinct from one another than were the principalities of Germany, a unified kingdom of Spain would emerge as the most powerful monarchy in Europe and the wider Atlantic world by the end of the Middle Ages (a process we will continue to trace in future chapters). The key to this extraordinary development lay in the successful alliances forged among the peninsula's Christian rulers and their eventual defeat of Iberia's Muslim kingdoms. This process is somewhat misleadingly termed "the Reconquista," or the "reconquest" of Christian lands. In reality, the Roman province of Hispania had been only nominally Christian when the Visigoths settled there in the fifth century (see Chapter 6), and the Visigoths themselves had barely converted to Latin Christianity before the Muslims arrived in 711 (Chapter 7). That said, conceptualizing this struggle as a holy war to "reconquer" Christian territory allowed Christian propagandists to cast it as another Crusade, and on those grounds to earn support for their efforts.

By the middle of the twelfth century, there were four major Christian kingdoms in Iberia. In the far north and northwest were the states of Navarre, which straddled the Pyrenees, and León-Castile, governed as a united kingdom after 1037. Beyond their borders lay a broad swathe of Muslim territory and, beyond it, the Crown of Aragon,

**THE "RECONQUEST" OF IBERIA, 900–1250.** ▪ *What were the boundaries of the Christian kingdoms in 900? 1150? 1250?* ▪ *What geographical factors might have helped to sustain these small kingdoms?* ▪ *Why might Castile have become the largest of the Christian kingdoms over time?* ▪ *How could Aragon and Catalonia have maintained important positions as wealthy and significant powers?*

**LOARRE CASTLE, ARAGON.** No single photograph can capture the size or setting of this massive castle complex in the foothills of the Pyrenees. Initially fortified in the eleventh century as a base for Christian expansion into Muslim territory, it was further enlarged in the twelfth century. The encircling wall and towers were added in the thirteenth and fourteenth centuries.

formed in 1137 when the count of Barcelona, who ruled the independent principality of Catalonia, married the queen of Aragon. Then there was the new kingdom of Portugal, which had been the first territory gained by Christian conquests in the ninth century and which won independence from León-Castile in 1139.

Like their counterparts elsewhere in Europe, the kings of Iberia struggled to control the power of great lords. Centuries of warfare between Muslims and Christians and among competing Christian clans had left the landscape sown with enormous castles, and even those that were nominally controlled by kings were in fact the property of castellans who used them as power bases. A ruler seeking to establish sovereignty thus had to use a combination of force and cunning to bring these rival powers to heel. In Iberia, kings came to deploy a combination of tactics that we have already seen at work in England: conquest and the development of effective administrative structures that made royal power a fact of everyday life. This is best exemplified by King Alfonso II of Aragon (r. 1162–96), who was also the count of Barcelona and the first to rule the united Crown of Aragon. Alfonso used documentation as the ultimate tool of power, presiding over the compilation of a richly illuminated "big book of fiefs" (*Liber feudorum maior*) between 1192 and 1194 (see ***Interpreting Visual Evidence***). This book recounted property transactions and family lineages dating back centuries, citing documents in the royal archives. Alfonso thereby grounded his authority on his command of history and written records.

Throughout the remainder of the twelfth century and into the thirteenth, Christian influence continued to spread southward in Iberia, until all that remained of Muslim dominion was the small kingdom centered on Granada in the extreme southwest. Castile became by far the largest kingdom in area, but it was rivaled in wealth and consequence by the more urbanized and commercially connected Aragon. Indeed, wars between Castile and Aragon would keep either kingdom from achieving supremacy for the next two hundred years, until the marriage of Ferdinand of Aragon and Isabella of Castile joined the two in a unified Spanish monarchy which also included Navarre (see Chapter 10). In 1492, their united army captured Granada while an Italian adventurer named Christopher Columbus set sail under their flag; the first event completed the "reconquest," while the second began Spain's successful conquest of a new and hitherto undreamed-of world (see Chapter 11).

## THE DOMINION OF THE CHURCH

Like their secular counterparts, the popes of this era were committed to establishing their authority, and did so by building up bureaucratic structures that increased the visibility of papal power and its effects on the daily lives of all Christians in western Europe. Specially commissioned papal legates ("legal representatives") began to be sent out from Rome to convey and enforce papal commands, many of which arose from the hundreds (and eventually thousands) of legal cases that poured into Rome. For like the kings of England, France, and Aragon, the pope sought to establish a reputation for justice.

### *The Codification of Canon Law*

The growing number of cases heard in the papal court both encouraged and required the development of a systematic body of law by which such cases could be judged. The

# Interpreting Visual Evidence

## *Picturing Legal Transactions*

Between the years 1192 and 1194, King Alfonso II of Aragon (*r.* 1162–1196) and his court scribes compiled a remarkable book. The codex known today as "the big book of fiefs" (*Liber feudorum maior*) may have been made to assist Alfonso and his descendants in legitimizing their authority over the many areas they controlled, but it was also a way of expressing that authority: its very existence represented a new claim to royal power. In its original form, it consisted of 888 parchment folios (1776 pages) on which 903 separate documents were copied.

This "big book" represents a new trend in Europe. In most places, claims to property were made on the basis of custom and memory, not on documentation. When property changed hands, the chief witnesses were people, and when questions arose it was these people (or their heirs) whose testimony proved ownership. In Catalonia, the habit of documenting things had a long history, and it was not unusual for individual families to keep archives of documents. At the same time, however, documentation was never sufficient on its own: verbal exchanges of agreement and the public performance of transactions constituted legally binding ceremonies meaningful to the entire community, and the validity of these actions was not dependant on the making of a written record.

With all this in mind, it is striking that 79 of the documents copied into the book are accompanied by images that convey important messages about documentation and its limitations.

On the book's opening frontispiece (image A), King Alfonso consults with his chief archivist, Ramón de Caldes. Ramón discusses one of the charters taken from a large pile at his elbow, while a scribe makes copies behind him—perhaps to aid in the compilation of the "big book." The king is backed by men who look on approvingly.

One of the charters copied into the "big book" is accompanied by the second image (B). It records that the viscount of Nîmes betrothed his daughter, Ermengarde of Carcassone, to the count of Roussillon. Ermengarde, her flowing hair uncovered as a sign of her maidenhood, stands between her bearded father and her seated mother, Cecilia of Provence.

### *Questions for Analysis*

1. Why would a book designed to document property transactions contain images too? What functions could they have served?
2. Why would the artist of the "big book" have depicted the king consulting his archivist in the very first image? How does he depict the relationship between them? Why does he include a group of men as witnesses to their discussion?
2. Women figure prominently in many of the book's images, including the one below. On what basis could you argue that their active presence is crucial to the transactions being described?

A. King Alfonso and Ramón de Caldes.

B. Betrothal of Ermengarde to the Count of Roussillon.

crucial step in this development was the codification of papal decrees and decisions of Church councils reaching back to the second century. These formed a body of legal precedents known as canons, from the Greek word meaning "rules" or "supports." The problem, though, was that these precedents often contradicted one another, and so any usable compilation had to determine which was most authoritative.

The resulting *Concordance of Discordant Canons*, first redacted around 1139 and later known as the *Decretum*, is attributed to a jurist known only as Gratian, who was active in the study and teaching of law in Bologna. Significantly, Gratian's codification was influenced by the *Corpus Juris Civilis* codified under Justinian (see Chapter 7). This is because another outcome of the Crusades, and of western Europe's increased contact with Byzantium, was the rediscovery of Roman law and the tradition of legal commentary associated with the great jurists of the later Roman Empire (Chapter 5). The *Decretum* was also made possible by the new intellectual trends that were simultaneously giving rise to the universities of Europe (see below).

The *Decretum* claimed ecclesiastical jurisdiction for all sorts of cases, including such matters as marriage, inheritance, and bequests. Although these cases were supposed to be heard in local ecclesiastical courts overseen by bishops, popes increasingly insisted that they alone could issue dispensations exempting certain petitioners from established precedents—such as the annulment of Eleanor's marriage to Louis VII—and moreover that the papal court should function as a final court of appeals in all cases touching the Church.

Thinking back to the dispute between Henry II of England and Archbishop Thomas Becket, we can better understand what was at stake: both secular and ecclesiastical rulers now defined their power in terms of law, and they had to defend their rights of jursidiction against encroachment by others. And just as kings had to become more skillful administrators, so the popes of this era were almost invariably trained as canon lawyers, a real departure from the monastic origins of the reforming movement.

## The Reign of Innocent III

One examplar of this new breed of popes was Alexander III, who dealt so skillfully with Frederick Barbarossa. Another was Innocent III (r. 1198–1216), a highly successful administrator trained in canon law, whose chief goal was to unify all Christendom under papal hegemony. But unlike Gregory VII (Chapter 8), Innocent never questioned the right of kings and princes to rule in their own secular spheres. Instead, he saw the pope's role as regulatory and disciplinary, which meant that when rulers sinned they should be reprimanded or excommunicated by the pope—who could thereby call into question the legitimacy of their rule. Innocent was even more insistent than his predecessors on the obligation of every Christian to obey the pope as Jesus Christ's representative on earth.

Innocent sought to achieve this goal in many different ways. He made the papacy financially and politically independent by expanding and consolidating papal territories in central Italy. (Vatican City is now the last surviving remnant of these territories and continues to function as an independent state within Rome and Italy.) Innocent displayed his power as kingmaker and -breaker by brokering the selection of the Holy Roman Emperor, and he also disciplined both Philip Augustus of France (for marital misconduct) and John of England, who at one point was compelled to grant England itself to the papacy, as a fief. Innocent also claimed, with varying degrees of success, a comparable lordship over Aragon, Sicily, and Hungary. Further, he levied the first income tax on the clergy, in order to support a Fourth Crusade to the Holy Land.

But the crowning achievement of Innocent's pontificate was the ratification of his agenda at a representative assembly of the entire western Church, the Fourth Lateran Council of 1215 (so called because it was held in the Roman palace of St. John Lateran). This council defined the central dogmas of the Christian faith, and made one of them the acknowledgment of papal supremacy. Since a dogma is defined as "a truth necessary for salvation," this meant that all Christians had to acknowledge the pope's ultimate power; those unwilling to do so (including the Christians of Byzantium) were, by definition, heretics—and as heretics, they could be prosecuted and punished.

In a further effort to achieve unity and uniformity within Christendom, the Fourth Lateran Council took an unprecedented interest in the religious education and habits of every Christian. It responded to the urbanization of Europe by establishing free primary schools (for boys) in all the major cities, requiring bishops to recruit effective preachers, and outlawing all kinds of misbehavior on the part of the clergy. It also sought to increase the distance between Christians and their Muslim and Jewish neighbors by discouraging social relationships, economic exchanges, and intermarriage. Perhaps most disturbingly, Innocent's Council mandated that "infidels" be visibly distinguished from Christians by the wearing of distinctive clothing, the origins of the infamous "Jewish badge" (see Chapter 26).

**THE JEWISH BADGE.** The distinctive apparel that marked Jews as different from their Christian neighbors varied from region to region. In some places it was a pointed hat like the one worn by the Old Testament Jews in this manuscript illumination from a fourteenth-century French vernacular Bible. This hat would later become associated with witchcraft or idiocy, as in the dunce's cap or the witch's peak. In other regions, Jews wore a distinctive patch on their clothing, often colored yellow to make it more visible.

## The Legacy of Innocent III

Innocent's reign achieved the height of papal power, but it also sowed some seeds of future dissent. The popes of the thirteenth century continued to centralize the government of the Church, but they also became involved in protracted political struggles that compromised the papacy's credibility. Innocent had succeeded in seeking new sources of income, but his successors who used the same techniques were perceived as grasping and acquisitive. Moreover, because the Papal States bordered on the kingdom of Sicily, Innocent's successors quickly came into conflict with Frederick II, who became an inveterate opponent of papal monarchy. Instead of merely excommunicating him and calling for his deposition, as Innocent might have done, they called a crusade against him—a cynical admission of crusading's overtly political motives. To implement this crusade they became preoccupied with raising funds and with finding a military champion to advance their cause. They found him in the youngest brother of the French king Louis IX, Charles of Anjou, who saw this as a way of acquiring the kingdom of Sicily for himself. But Charles made matters worse by antagonizing his own subjects, who offered their allegiance to the king of Aragon. The reigning pope then made Aragon the target of another crusade, which resulted in the death of the new French king, Philip III (r. 1270–85). In the wake of this debacle, Philip's son, Philip IV, resolved to punish the papacy for misusing its powers.

## The Limits of Papal Power

In 1300, Pope Boniface VIII (r. 1294–1303) celebrated a papal jubilee in Rome and offered a full crusader's indulgence to every pilgrim: the promise of absolution from all sins. It was a tacit recognition that Rome, not Jerusalem, was henceforth the center of the Christian world. But just nine years later, Rome had become obsolete and the new capital of Christendom was in France: Philip IV had challenged Boniface to a political duel, and won. When Boniface protested against Philip's plan to arraign a French bishop on a charge of treason against the French crown—thus violating the bishop's ecclesiastical immunity—Philip in turn accused Boniface of heresy, and sent a troop of knights to arrest him. At the papal residence of Anagni in 1303, Boniface (then in his seventies) was so mistreated by Philip's thugs that he died a month later. Philip then pressed his advantage. He forced the new pope, Clement V, to thank him publically for his zealous defence of the faith and then, in 1309, he moved the entire papal court from Rome to Avignon (*ah-vee-NYON*), a city near the southeastern border of his own realm. It would remain there until 1378 (see Chapter 10).

The papacy's capitulation to royal power illustrates the enormous gap that had opened up between rhetoric and reality in the centuries since the Investiture Conflict (Chapter 8). Although Boniface continued to claim that kings ruled only through the "will and sufferance" of the Church, in fact the Church now exercised its authority only through the will and sufferance of kings. The growth of strong territorial monarchies, combined with the increasing sophistication of royal justice, taxation, and propaganda, had shifted the balance of power decisively. Paradoxically, Europeans were more zealously devout than they had ever been, but they looked increasingly to secular rulers to spearhead campaigns of moral and spiritual improvement. This trend would continue into the seventeenth century, and would only be halted after a century of religious wars

# Analyzing Primary Sources

## *The Canons of the Fourth Lateran Council*

*In 1215, Innocent III presided over an ecumenical assembly of Church leaders in the papal palace and church of Saint John Lateran in Rome. The resulting canons both reaffirmed older legislation and introduced a number of new laws that responded to widespread social, economic, and cultural changes. Published in the same year as Magna Carta (see above), they too became a standard set of principles and continued to be applied within the Church until they were modified by the Council of Trent in the sixteenth century.*

### *Canon 1*

. . . There is one Universal Church of the faithful, outside of which there is absolutely no salvation. In which there is the same priest and sacrifice, Jesus Christ, whose body and blood are truly contained in the sacrament of the altar under the forms of bread and wine; the bread being changed *(transsubstantiatio)* by divine power into the body, and the wine into the blood, so that to realize the mystery of unity we may receive of Him what He has received of us. And this sacrament no one can effect except the priest who has been duly ordained in accordance with the keys of the Church, which Jesus Christ Himself gave to the Apostles and their successors. . . .

• • •

### *Canon 3*

We excommunicate and anathematize every heresy that rises against the holy, orthodox, and Catholic faith . . . condemning all heretics under whatever names they may be known, for while they have different faces they are nevertheless bound to each other by their tails, since in all of them vanity is a common element. Those condemned, being handed over to the secular rulers of their bailiffs, let them be abandoned, to be punished with due justice, clerics being first degraded from their orders.

• • •

### *Canon 9*

Since in many places within the same city and diocese there are people of different languages having one faith but various rites and customs, we strictly command that the bishops of these cities and dioceses provide suitable men who will, according to the different rites and languages, celebrate the divine offices for them, administer the sacraments of the Church and instruct them by word and example.

### *Canon 10*

. . . It often happens that bishops, on account of their manifold duties or bodily infirmities, or because of hostile invasions or other reasons, to say nothing of lack of learning, which must be absolutely condemned in them and is not to be tolerated in the future, are themselves unable to minister the word of God to the people, especially in large and widespread dioceses. Wherefore we decree that bishops provide suitable men, powerful in work and word, to exercise with fruitful result the office of preaching; who in place of the bishops, since these cannot do it, diligently visiting the people committed to them, may instruct them by word and example. . . .

### *Canon 11*

Since there are some who, on account of the lack of necessary means, are unable to acquire an education or to meet opportunities for perfecting themselves, the Third Lateran Council in a salutary decree provided that in every cathedral church a suitable benefice be assigned to a master who shall instruct *gratis* the clerics of that church and other poor students, . . . we, confirming the aforesaid decree, add that, not only in every cathedral church but also in other churches where means are sufficient, a competent master be appointed . . . who shall instruct *gratis* and to the best of his ability the clerics of those and other churches in the art of grammar and in other branches of knowledge.

• • •

### *Canons 14–16*

That the morals and general conduct of clerics may be better, let all strive to live chastely and virtuously, particularly those in sacred orders, guarding against every vice of desire . . .

. . . All clerics shall carefully abstain from drunkenness. . . .

We forbid hunting and fowling to all clerics; wherefore, let them not presume to keep dogs and birds for these purposes. . . .

Clerics shall not hold secular offices or engage in secular and, above all, dishonest pursuits. They shall not attend the performances of mimics and buffoons, or theatrical representations. They shall not visit taverns except in case of necessity, namely, when on a journey.

They are forbidden to play games of chance or be present at them. They must have a becoming crown and tonsure and apply themselves diligently to the study of the divine offices and other useful subjects. Their garments must be worn clasped at the top and neither too short nor too long. They are not to use red or green garments or curiously sewed-together gloves, or beak-shaped shoes . . .

• • •

### *Canon 68*

In some provinces a difference in dress distinguishes the Jews or Saracens from the Christians, but in certain others such a confusion has grown up that they cannot be distinguished by any difference. Thus it happens at times that through error Christians have relations with the women of Jews or Saracens, and Jews and Saracens with Christian women. Therefore, that they may not, under pretext of error of this sort, excuse themselves in the future for the excesses of such prohibited intercourse, we decree that such Jews and Saracens of both sexes in every Christian province and at all times shall be marked off in the eyes of the public from other peoples through the character of their dress. . . .

Moreover, during the last three days before Easter and especially on Good Friday, they shall not go forth in public at all, for the reason that some of them on these very days, as we hear, do not blush to go forth better dressed and are not afraid to mock the Christians who maintain the memory of the most holy Passion by wearing signs of mourning. . . .

Source: Excerpted from H. J. Schroeder, *Disciplinary Decrees of the General Councils: Text, Translation and Commentary* (St. Louis, MO: 1937), pp. 236–96.

### *Questions for Analysis*

1. Based on this selection of canons, how would you characterize the main concerns of the Fourth Lateran Council? What is it attempting to regulate, and why? What changing historical circumstances do the canons reflect?
2. In what ways do the canons distinguish between clergy and laity? How does legislation work to maintain those distinctions?
3. Why do the canons place so much emphasis on clothing and appearance? Why would it be important for both clerics and "infidels" (Jews and Muslims) to dress in distinctive ways?

brought on by the Protestant Reformation, when the distinction between religious and political athority would be asserted as a fundamental principle (see Chapter 14).

## SPIRITUAL AWAKENINGS AND CHALLENGES

The Investiture Conflict had engaged both clergy and laity in debates over the essential meaning of Jesus Christ's life and teachings. In many regions of western Europe, the papacy's claim to jurisdictional supremacy over the whole Church was supported, but in others there was marked resistance to its encroachment on centuries-old practices and social networks. After all, bishops had been members of the aristocracy since the time of Constantine, and it was customary for bishoprics to be controlled by certain families. Meanwhile, priests had been married men since the etablishment of the first Christian churches, and the wives of priests were not only their husbands' companions and partners, they were also ministers to the communities in which they lived. When the papacy preached against "simony," or "fornicating priests" and their "concubines," it was delegitimizing relationships that had been essential to local communities for generations. No wonder, then, that nothing else was talked about "even in the women's spinning rooms and the artisans' workshops," as one contemporary reported.

On the one hand, therefore, the reforms of Pope Gregory VII and his successors gave the common people an important role to play, by urging them to reject certain practices and sanctioning retaliation against offenders. Combined with the fervor that had been whipped up by the Crusades, the result was more-widespread interest in spiritual matters and increased participation in religious life—as well as increased violence. On the other hand, however, the reforming movement severely limited the ways in which the laity were allowed to express their spirituality or to participate meaningfully in the life of the Church.

## The New Monasticism

One of the first manifestations of the new piety was the growth and diversification of monastic movements. As we saw in Chapter 8, the abbey of Cluny had revived the observance of Benedict's *Rule* in the course of the tenth century and, at the same time, had kept Cluny and its daughter houses independent of local lords. As a result, these monasteries became lordships in their own right, acquiring extensive lands and enormous wealth. Those seeking to reject worldliness, therefore, had to look elsewhere for a lifestyle that would foster intense self-examination and meditative striving toward God. The result, beginning in the late eleventh century, was the founding of new orders such as the Carthusians, whose name derives from the Chartreuse foothills of the French Alps, and whose rule requires monks to live in separate cells and to observe a life of strict asceticism.

Another new order, and one that became more widespread, was that founded at the monastery of Cîteaux in 1098. Cistercian monks followed Benedict's *Rule*, but in the purest and most austere way possible, and they founded new monasteries in wildernesses and remote areas, far from worldly temptations. They also shunned all unnecessary decoration and elaborate liturgical rites. Instead, they practiced contemplation and private prayer, and they committed themselves to hard manual labor. Under the charismatic leadership of Bernard of Clairvaux (1090–1153), a spellbinding preacher and one of the most influential personalities of his age, the Cistercian order grew exponentially, from 5 houses in 1115 to 343 by 1153. This astonishing increase meant that many more men and women were becoming professional religious, but it also meant that still more pious people were donating funds and lands to support monasteries and thereby participating indirectly in their life of devotion.

Another manifestation of popular devotion was a new focus on the sacrament of the Mass, the liturgical reenactment of Christ's last meal with his disciples. This celebration, the Eucharist, had always been an important part of Christian religious and social practice (Chapter 6), but only in the twelfth century did it become the central act of worship in the western Church. Bernard of Clairvaux was instrumental in making it so, by developing and preaching the doctrine of transubstantiation. According to this doctrine,

**THE MYSTERY OF THE MASS.** In this manuscript illumination, the visionary Hildegard of Bingen (see below) illustrates the doctrine of transubstantiation. In the lower register, the bread and wine of the Mass have been placed on the altar and are being transformed into the body and blood of the crucified Christ, depicted in the upper register. Paired scenes from Christ's life (his birth and death, his ministry and resurrection) emphasize the fact that earthly substances—bread and wine—participate in a divine cycle of regeneration. Note that Hildegard does not imagine the mediating figure as a priest, but as the (female) Church, represented as a crowned queen and associated with the Virgin Mary. ▪ ***What might be the significance of this choice?***

every Mass is a miraculous event, because the priest's blessing transforms the bread and wine on the altar into the body and blood of Christ. Hence the term *transubstantiation*, since earthly substances thereby become the substance of Christ's divine body.

Popular reverence for the Eucharist became so great that the Church initiated the practice of elevating the consecrated bread, known as the Host, so that the whole congregation could see it. Not incidentally, this new theology of the Eucharist further enhanced the prestige of the priesthood by seeming to endow it with wonder-working powers. In later centuries, the Latin words spoken at the consecration of the Host, *Hoc est corpus meum* ("This is my body"), were understood as a magical formula: *Hocus pocus*.

## Holy Women, Human and Divine

Popular devotion to the worship of Christ in the Eucharist was matched by another new and hugely influential religious practice: the veneration of Jesus's mother, Mary. In this development, too, Bernard of Clairvaux played an important role, traveling around Europe to promote a theology that made Mary central to Christianity, the most important saint and the very embodiment of the Church. Eventually, orthodox Catholic teaching would hold that Mary had not only given birth to Jesus while still a virgin, but that she remained a virgin even after Jesus' birth—and, more radically, that she herself had been conceived without sin. This made Mary the exact opposite of Eve, the woman whose disobedience had (according to Judeo-Christian tradition) brought sin into the world for the first time; for through God's grace, Mary had given birth to Christ, a second Adam, whose obedient sacrifice of himself atoned for that original sin. New doctrines also raised Mary from the position of God's humble handmaid to that of heaven's queen, with the power to intercede on behalf of all, even the worst sinners. Her soaring reputation as a miracle worker and advocate is amply testified by the thousands of devotional images created during this period, the many stories and hymns celebrating her virtues and miracles, and the fact that practically all the magnificent new cathedrals of the age were dedicated to "Our Lady" (hence the many churches of Notre Dame in France, the Frauenkirchen of Germany, and so on).

The burgeoning cult of the Blessed Virgin had two contradictory effects. On the one hand, it elevated a female figure to a prominent place in the official Church for the first time, and it thereby celebrated virtues associated with femininity: motherhood, healing, nourishment, mercy, kindness. On the other hand, it made Mary an unobtainable, paradoxical model of female perfection: she alone could be both virgin and parent, Christ's mother and bride, God's maidservant and queenly consort. No real woman could begin to emulate her, and thus real women were increasingly compared to Eve and perceived as weak, deceitful, and disobediant. Moroever, the veneration of a single, idealized woman coincided exactly with the suppression of most real women's access to positions of power within the Church; as the cult of the Blessed Virgin grew, so the opportunities for aspiring holy women shrank.

This did not go unremarked at the time. As we noted above, the career of Heloise (c. 1090–1164) exemplifies both the avenues of advancement for women and also the successful blocking of those avenues by new constraints on women's activities. Heloise's exact contemporary, Hildegard of Bingen (1098–1179), was also creative in her efforts to make a place for herself and her female followers, and more outspoken than Heloise in her criticism of attempts to thwart them. Like Heloise, she was an abbess and a highly

**VIRGIN AND CHILD.** This exquisite ivory sculpture (just over seven inches high) was carved in Paris in the mid- to late thirteenth century, as an aid to private devotion and prayer. The mother of Jesus, Mary, was also regarded as the mother of all humanity, the *alma mater* ("nourishing mother") who could be relied on to protect and heal those who asked for her help.

original thinker. But she was not, like Heloise, a scholar; she was a mystic who claimed to receive regular revelations from God.

Hildegard expressed these visions in her own version of Latin and in an alphabet she devised for the purpose, writings that were later transcribed and illustrated under her close supervision. She also composed hymns and ambitious musical dramas for her nuns—music now widely available on CD and MP3—and prepared treatises on subjects as diverse as cosmology, pharmacology, and medicine. Her advice was frequently sought by religious and secular authorities, including Bernard of Clairvaux and Frederick Barbarossa, and she even received a special papal dispensation that allowed her to preach publicly.

Despite all this, Hildegard had to fight constantly for her rights and those of her nuns during her lifetime, and after her death she was never officially recognized as a saint. Indeed, she was one of the first candidates for whom a new canonization process was instituted in the papal curia, as a way of controlling the popular veneration of charismatic figures whom the Church considered threatening. So while many high-ranking clergy of her own day recognized her holiness, the papal courts of subsequent centuries would not acknowledge it. The standards of acceptable female behavior had become too narrow to contain her.

**HILDEGARD OF BINGEN'S DIVINE INSPIRATION.** This portrait of Hildegard and her male secretary, Volmar, appears in her book *Scivias* ("Know the Ways"). It shows Hildegard as the recipient of a divine vision (represented by tongues of heavenly fire) which she transcribes onto a wax tablet using a stylus, a common method for creating the first draft of a written work. Volmar is placed outside the frame in which her vision occurs, but he is prepared to copy it onto parchment. ▪ ***What does this image tell us about medieval ideas of authorship and authority?*** ▪ ***What does it suggest about the relationship and status of the two figures?***

## Heresy or Piety?

Traditionally, Christianity has been successfully transmitted to many different civilizations because it is relatively open-ended and absorbent of new influences. In this area, however, the Church began to lose its capacity to respond quickly or inclusively to new challenges, preferring instead to crack down on "heresies" that undermined its power. This trend would eventually lead to a reforming movement so intense that it could not be contained within the Church: the Protestant Reformation (see Chapter 13). For the more the Church claimed the right to control every aspect of belief and practice, the more it made itself vulnerable to those who challenged its enforcment of orthodoxy. This resulted in large-scale movements of popular opposition to centralized authority, and also to counterinitiatives aimed at harnessing popular piety to that same authority.

The best way to understand this is through Innocent III's very different responses to rather similar popular movements. On the one hand, the pope resolved to crush all disobedience of papal authority; on the other, he wanted to support idealistic groups that could be made to acknowledge papal authority, so as not to frustrate all dynamic spirituality. For example, Innocent labelled as heretical a religious movement that began in southern France, that of the Cathars (from the Greek word for "purity"). He accused Cathars of beliefs that resemble Zoroastrianism (Chapter 2) and Manichaeism (Chapter 6), alleging that they held all material creation to be evil, and even that they believed the power of God to be opposed by that of a malevolent deity associated with Satan or the fallen angel Lucifer. Whatever the truth of these allegations, the fact that many Cathar leaders were women made the movement heretical by definition.

More typical of twelfth-century religious dissent was Waldensianism, so called because it is said to have originated with the teachings of a merchant called Waldes. Waldensians were lay people who wished to imitate the life of Christ to the fullest. They were active in the vernacular translation and study of the Gospels and dedicated to lives of poverty and preaching. None of this contradicted any contemporary doctrines, and for a while the Church did not interfere with Waldensians' ministry. But when they began to preach without authorization they were condemned as heretics. In response, they began to articulate a more radical opposition to the established hierarchy. Many of their leaders, too, were women.

Innocent eventually took steps to eradicate the Cathars, who were also known as Albigensians, by authorizing the violent seizure of their lands and property. This "Albigensian Crusade" was really a war of conquest that expanded the French monarchy into southern lands formerly held by independent counts. Innocent also began the process of instituting inquisitorial procedures that would enable the legal prosecution, torture, and execution of convicted heretics like the Waldensians.

At the same time, however, Innocent embraced two other popular movements and turned them into two new religious orders, the Dominicans and the Franciscans. Like the Waldensians, the friars ("brothers") of these orders imitated the life of Jesus and his apostles by wandering through the countryside and establishing missions in Europe's growing towns, preaching and offering spiritual and material assistance to the poor. They also embraced poverty and begged for a living, hence their categorization as *mendicants*, from the Latin verb *mendicare*, "to beg." In the end, the only thing that separated them from the Waldensians was their willingness to subject themselves to papal authority.

The Dominican order, formally known as the Order of Preachers, was founded by the zealous Dominic of Osma (1170–1221), a Castilian theologian and diplomat. Approved in 1216, it was particularly dedicated to the prosecution of heretics and to the conversion of Jews and Muslims. At first, the Dominicans hoped to achieve these ends by preaching and public debate, and to further these goals many of its members pursued academic careers in the nascent universities and thus contributed to the development of philosophy and theology; indeed, the most influential intellectual of the Middle Ages, Thomas Aquinas (1225–1274), was a Dominican (see below). But the Dominicans soon became associated with the use of other persuasive techniques through the administration of the Inquistition, which became formalized in the thirteenth century. (It is now called the Congregation for the Doctrine of the Faith, and is still staffed by members of the order.)

The Franciscans, formally known as the Order of the Friars Minor ("Little Brothers"), were quite different from the Dominicans, commited less to doctrine and discipline than to the welfare of the poor and the cultivation of personal spirituality. Whereas Dominic and his earliest followers were ordained priests entitled to preach, the founder of the Franciscans was the ne'er-do-well son of an Italian merchant, Francis of Assisi (1182–1226), who eventually rebelled against the materialistic values of his father. Stripping himself (literally) of all his worldly possessions, he put on the tattered garb of a beggar and began to preach salvation in town squares and to minister to outcasts in the darkest corners of Italian cities. Unlike Dominic, Francis did all of this without official approval, thereby risking papal censure. Indeed, a future pope might have rejected Francis as a heretic, but when he showed himself willing to profess obedience in 1209, Innocent granted Francis and his followers permission to preach.

Although the rapid growth of the Franciscan order would eventually necessitate more administrative stability and doctrinal training for all its members, many Franciscans continued to engage in revivalistic outdoor preaching and to offer a model for apostolic living. This was not, however, an approved religious lifestyle for women. Francis's most important female follower, Clare of Assissi (1194–1253), wanted to found an order for women along the same lines, but members of the Order of Poor Ladies (also known as the Poor Clares) were not allowed to work directly among the poor, as men did, but instead lived in cloistered convents supported by charitable donations. Their counterparts in northern Europe were the Beguines, communities of lay women who lived in loosely organized communal quarters and ministered to the poor. Their relationship with Church officials was often strained, because the Beguines embraced many of the precepts and practices associated with the Waldensians, including the unauthorized translation and study of the Bible. The fact that they were women made them even more suspect.

## Christians against Jews

Although violence and exploitative taxation continued to reduce the size and strength of Europe's Jewish communities, the Church's official position held that Jews posed a serious threat to Christians. It never explicitly endorsed the wilder claims made by popular rabble-rousers, but it did little to combat such attitudes either. As a result, many ordinary

# Competing Viewpoints

## Two Conversion Experiences

*Both Peter Waldo (or Waldes), later branded as a heretic, and Francis of Assisi, later canonized as a saint, were moved to take up a life of preaching and poverty after undergoing a process of conversion. These experiences exhibit some striking similarities, despite the different fates of these two men. The first account is that of an anonymous chronicler in Peter's home town of Lyons; the second is by Francis's contemporary and hagiographer, Thomas of Celano (c. 1200–c. 1260/70).*

### The Conversion of Peter Waldo

At about this time, in 1173, there was a citizen of Lyons named Peter Waldo, who had made a great deal of money by the evil means of usury. One Sunday he lingered by a crowd that had gathered round a traveling storyteller, and was much struck by his words. He took him home with him, and listened carefully to his story of how St. Alexis had died a holy death in his father's house. Next morning Waldo hastened to the schools of theology to seek advice about his soul. When he had been told of the many ways of coming to God he asked the master whether any of them was more sure and reliable than the rest. The master quoted to him the words of the Lord, "If thou wilt be perfect go sell what thou hast and give it to the poor and thou shalt have treasure in heaven. And come follow me."

Waldo returned to his wife and gave her the choice between having all his movable wealth or his property in land. . . . She was very upset at having to do this and chose the property. From his movable wealth he returned what he had acquired wrongly, conferred a large portion on his two daughters, whom he placed in the order of Fontevrault without his wife's knowledge, and gave a still larger amount to the poor.

At this time a terrible famine was raging through Gaul and Germany. . . . Waldo generously distributed bread, soup and meat to anyone who came to him. On the [Feast of the] Assumption of the Virgin [August 15] he scattered money among the poor in the streets saying, "You cannot serve two masters, God and Mammon." The people around thought he had gone out of his senses. Then he stood up on a piece of high ground and said, "Friends and fellow-citizens, I am not mad as you think. . . . I know that many of you disapprove of my having acted so publicly. I have done so both for my own sake and for yours: for my sake, because anybody who sees me with money in future will be able to say that I am mad; for your sake, so that you may learn to place your hopes in God and not in wealth." . . .

1177 Waldo, the citizen of Lyons whom we have already mentioned, who had vowed to God that he would possess neither gold nor silver, and take no thought for the morrow, began to make converts to his opinions. Following his example they gave all they had to the poor, and willingly devoted themselves to poverty. Gradually, both in public and in private they began to inveigh against both their own sins and those of others. . . .

1178 Pope Alexander III held a council at the Lateran palace. . . . The council condemned heresy and all those who fostered and defended heretics. The pope embraced Waldo, and applauded the vows of voluntary poverty which he had taken, but forbade him and his companion to assume the office of preaching except at the request of the priests. They obeyed this instruction for a time, but later they disobeyed, and affronted many, bringing ruin on themselves.

Source: Excerpted from *Chronicon universale anonymi Laudunensis*, ed. and trans. Robert I. Moore, *The Birth of Popular Heresy* (London: 1975), pp. 111–13 (slightly modified).

### The Conversion of Francis of Assisi

There was a man by the name of Francis, who from his earliest years was brought up by his parents proud of spirit, in accordance with the vanity of the world. . . .These are the wretched circumstances among which the man whom we venerate today as a saint, for he is truly a saint, lived in his youth; and almost up to the twenty-fifth year of his age, . . . he outdid all his contemporaries in vanities and he came to be a promoter of evil and was

more abundantly zealous for all kinds of foolishness. . . . And while, not knowing how to restrain himself, he was . . . worn down by a long illness, [he] began to think of things other than he was used to thinking upon. When he had recovered somewhat and had begun to walk about the house with the support of a cane to speed the recovery of his health, he went outside one day and began to look about at the surrounding landscape with great interest. But the beauty of the fields, the pleasantness of the vineyards, and whatever else was beautiful to look upon, could stir in him no delight. He wondered therefore at the sudden change that had come over him. . . . From that day on, therefore, he began to despise himself. . . .

Now since there was a certain man in the city of Assisi whom he loved more than any other because he was of the same age as the other, and since the great familiarity of their mutual affection led him to share his secrets with him; he often took him to remote places, places well-suited for counsel, telling him that he had found a certain precious and great treasure. This one rejoiced and, concerned about what he heard, he willingly accompanied Francis whenever he was asked. There was a certain grotto near the city where they frequently went and talked about this treasure. The man of God, who was already holy by reason of his holy purpose, would enter the grotto, while his companion would wait for him outside; and filled with a new and singular spirit, he would pray to his Father in secret. . . .

One day, however, when he had begged for the mercy of God most earnestly, it was shown to him by God what he was to do. . . . He rose up, therefore, fortified himself with the sign of the cross, got his horse ready and mounted it, and taking with him some fine cloth to sell, he hastened to the city called Foligno. There, as usual, he sold everything he had with him . . . and, free of all luggage, he started back, wondering with a religious mind what he should do with the money. . . . When, therefore, he neared the city of Assisi, he discovered a certain church . . . built of old in honor of St. Damian but which was now threatening to collapse because it was so old. . . . And when he found there a certain poor priest, he kissed his sacred hands with great faith, and offered him the money he had with him, . . . begging the priest to suffer him to remain with him for the sake of the Lord. . . .

When those who knew him . . . compared what he was now with what he had been . . . they began to revile him miserably. Shouting out that he was mad and demented, they threw the mud of the streets and stones at him. . . . Now . . . the report of these things finally came to his father . . . [who] shut him up mercilessly in a dark place for several days . . . It happened, however, when Francis' father had left home for a while on business and the man of God remained bound in the basement of the house, his mother, who was alone with him and did not approve of what her husband had done, spoke kindly to her son. . . . and loosening his chains, she let him go free. . . .

He [the father] then brought his son before the bishop of the city, so that, renouncing all his possessions into his hands, he might give up everything he had. . . . Indeed, he [Francis] did not wait for any words nor did he speak any, but immediately putting off his clothes and casting them aside, he gave them back to his father. Moreover, not even retaining his trousers, he stripped himself completely naked before all. The bishop, however, sensing his disposition and admiring greatly his fervor and constancy, arose and drew him within his arms and covered him with the mantle he was wearing. . . .

Source: Excerpted from Thomas of Celano, "The First Life of Saint Francis" in *Saint Francis of Assisi: Writings and Biographies*, ed. Marion A. Habiq (Chicago: 1973), pp. 229–41.

### *Questions for Analysis*

1. How do the conversions of Peter and Francis reflect the social and economic changes of the twelfth century? What new sources of tension and temptation are evident?
2. How do these two accounts describe these new converts' relationship(s) with their families, communities, and Church authorities? What are the similarities and differences, and why would these be important factors in determining the sanctity of either?
3. The story of Peter's conversion is written by an anonymous chronicler of Lyons, that of Francis by his follower and official biographer. How do these different perspectives shape these two accounts? Which is the more reliable, and why?

Christians came to believe that their Jewish neighbors were agents of evil who routinely crucified Christian children, consumed Christian blood, profaned the body of Christ in the Eucharist, and spread disease in Christian communities by poisoning wells. Fanciful stories of Jewish wealth added an economic element to the development of anti-Semitism, as did the fact that the Jews' social and cultural networks facilitated rapid communication and efficient exchange. From these, conspiracy theorists inferred the existence of organized Jewish plots to undermine Christian society, which were regularly cited as justifications for pogroms, mass executions, and other atrocities.

The precarious position of Europe's Jews worsened throughout the thirteenth century as both secular and ecclesiastical authorities devised more systematic mechanisms for controlling and policing undesirable segments of society: not only heretics but the indigent poor, prostitutes, "sodomites," and lepers. The canons of the Fourth Lateran Council had mandated that Jews be exposed and marginalized through the wearing of the Jewish badge, and this made them easier targets in times of unrest. At the same time, the protections which Europe's rulers had once extended to their Jewish subjects were gradually withdrawn. In Iberia, the "Reconquista" had absorbed many of the Muslim kingdoms in which Jews had enjoyed a measure of tolerance, and they were not easily accommodated within the emerging monarchies of Christian Spain. Starting in the 1280s, rulers elsewhere in Europe began to expel their Jewish subjects from their kingdoms altogether, in most cases because they could no longer pretend to repay the enormous sums they had extorted from Jewish moneylenders: this was the case in the kingdoms of Sicily (1288), England (1290), and France (1306). Further expulsions followed during the fourteenth century in the Rhineland, and in 1492 from Spain. By 1500, only northern Italy and various eastern European regions (encompassed today by Poland, Belorus, and Ukraine) were home to sizable Jewish communities. They would survive there until the more efficient persecutions of the Nazi Holocaust eradicated them (see Chapter 26).

**THE BURNING OF JEWS.** This manuscript account, written in the German vernacular, records an incident in which Jews were accused of poisoning the wells in a Christian town—and shows the punishment meted out to them. The wooden enclosure may represent the walls of the Jewish ghetto. As in the image on page 287, the Jews are identified by their distinctive conical hats.

## THE INTELLECTUAL REVOLUTION

The Fourth Lateran Council responded to the growing population and urbanization of Europe by mandating the education of the laity and by insisting on more rigorous training for all clergy. But even before 1215, a number of factors were working together to transform the intellectual landscape of Europe and to open up new opportunities for advancement through education. The growth of towns led to the growth of schools in those towns, for the most part founded by local bishops or monasteries. The Crusades became conduits for the transmission of Muslim learning and, through Muslim mediation, the precepts of ancient Greek philosophy. The infusion of these new ideas created an extraordinary new forum for intellectual endeavor: the university. In much the same way that ease of travel and communication had fostered a scientific revolution in the cities of the Hellenistic world (Chaper 4), so the conditions which gave rise to the university mark the beginning of a revolution in the intellectual history of Europe.

## *Access to Education*

Around 800, Charlemagne had ordered that primary schools be established in every city and monastery of his realm. It is unlikely that this command was carried out, but many schools were certainly founded during this period and primary education continued to be an important mission of some monasteries and cathedral schools. But it was not until the economic revival of the late eleventh century that educational opportunities were more widely available. By 1179, Pope Alexander III decreed that all cathedrals should set aside income for at least one schoolteacher, whose task would be to accept all comers, rich or poor, without fee. He predicted, correctly, that this measure would increase the number of well-trained clerics and administrators, supplying the growing bureaucracy of the Church. The recently martyred Thomas Becket had been an early beneficiary of such schooling.

At first, cathedral schools existed almost exclusively for the training of parish priests, but their curriculum was soon broadened as the growth of both ecclesiastical and secular governments escalated demand for trained men with more sophisticated skills. The most fundamental elements of this curriculum were known as the *trivium*, "the three ways": grammar, logic, and rhetoric. This meant a thorough grounding in Latin through the study of classical Roman authors, such as Cicero and Virgil (Chapter 5), and training in the formulation and expression of sound arguments. Students who mastered the trivium were fit to perform basic clerical tasks, but those who wanted to achieve the reputation and advantages of scholars had to master the remaining branches of learning. These were arithmetic, geometry, astronomy, and music: the *quadrivium* or "four ways." Together, these seven liberal arts—so called because they liberated those who acquired them from menial labor—were the prerequisites for advanced study in philosophy, theology, law, and medicine.

Until about 1200, most students in urban schools would have belonged to the minor orders of the clergy. This means that they took vows of obedience and were immune from prosecution by secular authorities, but were not required to remain celibate, unlike priests and bishops (who were in major orders). Even those who hoped to become

**TWO CONCEPTIONS OF ELEMENTARY EDUCATION.** In the lefthand illumination from a fourteenth-century manuscript, a master of grammar points to the day's lesson in a book while simultaneously keeping order with a cudgel. On the right, a later woodcut represents education as more benign: Lady Wisdom shows an eager schoolboy how to learn his letters while unlocking the door of knowledge, a multi-tiered tower where scholarly men representing the different branches of learning smile out at him.

lawyers or bureaucrats usually found it advantageous to "take orders" in case powerful ecclesiastical offices became open to them: Heloise tried to discourage Abelard from marrying her for this very reason, because it would destroy his chances of being appointed a bishop or papal legate. Abelard, a nobleman's son, is by no means typical of the men who rose to prominence in this era through education. His contemporary and rival, Suger, was an orphan of obscure origins who became abbot of the royal monastery of Saint-Denis and de facto chancellor of France.

By the thirteenth century, however, most boys who entered schools were not members of the clergy and never intended to be. Some were children of wealthy families, who regarded Latin literacy as a badge of status and a practical necessity. Others were future notaries, estate managers, and merchants who needed to be literate and numerate in order to succeed in these careers. Many alternative schools were eventually established to cater to these vocational students, and would become largely independent of ecclesiastical control. In many cases, Latin ceased to be the language of instruction in these schools and was replaced by the vernacular language of the region.

Formal schooling remained restricted to males. Yet many girls and women became highly educated, especially those reared in convents or princely courts. Heloise had an unusual degree of access to the educational milieu of Paris, but the fact remains that she had clearly received excellent preparatory training in the convent at Argentueil before she began her studies with Abelard. Most laywomen were taught at home, sometimes by private tutors but more often by other women. In fact, lay women were more likely to be literate than lay men, and it is for this reason that women were often the patrons of poets and the primary readers and owners of books. Significantly, the effigy that Eleanor of Aquitaine commissioned for her own tomb shows her lying awake till Judgment Day, reading, flanked by her sleeping husband and son.

**THE TOMB OF ELEANOR OF AQUITAINE.** Eleanor probably commissioned the effigies for the tombs representing herself, her husband Henry II, and her son Richard the Lionheart, both of whom died years before she did. She was eventually buried alongside them in the vault of the convent of Fontevrault in Anjou, where she spent the last years of her life.

## The Development of Scholasticism

The educational revolution that began in the eleventh century led to the development of new critical methods for framing and resolving complex theological and philosophical problems. These methods are collectively known as *scholasticism*, meaning that they had their orgins in the pedagogy of medieval schools. Scholastic methods are highly systematic and highly respectful of authority, but they also rely on rigorous questioning and argumentation. They therefore place great emphasis on evidence derived from reason. Indeed, scholasticism can be defined as the theory and practice of reconciling various forms of knowledge through logical debate, often called *dialectic*.

The earliest practitioner of the scholastic method is often considered to be Anselm of Canterbury (1033–1109), the son of a noble family from northern Italy who became prior of the Benedictine monastery of Bec in Normandy and, thereafter, archbishop of Canterbury. The central premise of Anselm's teaching was that the human mind can reconcile wisdom gained through education and experience with divine revelation—so long as one has faith in God and careful scholastic training. As he put it, "I believe in order to understand," so that belief can be enriched and strengthened by understanding.

Building on the writings of Augustine and Boethius (Chapter 6), and so (indirectly) on the teachings of Socrates (Chapter 3), Anselm developed various rational proofs for the underlying truths of Christian doctrine. The most famous of these is his proof for the existence of God, known as the ontological proof ("proof from the fact of existence") because it reasons that human beings could not have ideas of goodness or

# Analyzing Primary Sources

## *Peter Abelard Critiques Theological Contradictions*

*In 1120, Abelard published the* Sic et Non, *"So and Not So," a pioneering work of dialectic theology and a model for the development of later scholastic methods. In it, he arranged passages from Scripture as well as writings of the Church Fathers that had bearing on important doctrinal issues and that appeared to offer contradictory views. His eventual aim, as the prologue to this work indicates, was to reconcile these differences through the use of critical analysis.*

here are many seeming contradictions and even obscurities in the innumerable writings of the church fathers. Our respect for their authority should not stand in the way of an effort on our part to come at the truth. The obscurity and contradictions in ancient writings may be explained upon many grounds, and may be discussed without impugning the good faith and insight of the fathers. A writer may use different terms to mean the same thing, in order to avoid a monotonous repetition of the same word. Common, vague words may be employed in order that the common people may understand; and sometimes a writer sacrifices perfect accuracy in the interest of a clear general statement. Poetical, figurative language is often obscure and vague. . . .

Doubtless the fathers might err; even Peter, the prince of the apostles, fell into error; what wonder that the saints do not always show themselves inspired? The fathers did not themselves believe that they, or their companions, were always right. Augustine found himself mistaken in some cases and did not hesitate to retract his errors. He warns his admirers not to look upon his letters as they would upon the Scriptures, but to accept only those things which, upon examination, they find to be true.

All writings belonging to this class are to be read with full freedom to criticise, and with no obligation to accept unquestioningly; otherwise the way would be blocked to all discussion, and posterity be deprived of the excellent intellectual exercise of debating difficult questions of language and presentation. But an explicit exception must be made in the case of the Old and New Testaments. In the Scriptures, when anything strikes us as absurd, we may not say that the writer erred, but that the scribe made a blunder in copying the manuscripts, or that there is an error in interpretation, or that the passage is not understood. The fathers make a very careful distinction between the Scriptures and later works. They advocate a discriminating, not to say suspicious, use of the writings of their own contemporaries.

In view of these considerations, I have ventured to bring together various dicta of the holy fathers, as they came to mind, and to formulate certain questions which were suggested by the seeming contradictions in the statements. These questions ought to serve to excite tender readers to a zealous inquiry into truth and so sharpen their wits. The master key of knowledge is, indeed, a persistent and frequent questioning. Aristotle, the most clear-sighted of all the philosophers, was desirous above all things else to arouse this questioning spirit, for in his *Categories* he exhorts a student as follows: "It may well be difficult to reach a positive conclusion in these matters unless they be frequently discussed. It is by no means fruitless to be doubtful on particular points." By doubting we come to examine, and by examining we reach the truth.

Source: Peter Abelard, prologue to the *Sic et Non*, trans. James Harvey Robinson in *Readings in European History*, 2 vols. (Boston, MA: 1904), vol. 1, pp. 450–51.

### *Questions for Analysis*

1. On what grounds can religious authorities be challenged, according to Abelard? What distinctions does he make between criticism of the Scriptures and of other authorities, and why?

2. Abelard did not attempt, in this work, to resolve the contradictions among his sources. Based on what you have learned, why would his project have seemed threatening to the authority of the Church?

truth or justice unless some higher being had instilled these ideas in us. He further reasoned that God, as the essence of all ideals, must be "that than which nothing greater can be conceived" and as such must exist, or else God could not be the greatest thing conceivable.

Anselm's writings were influential, but the philosopher who popularized the scholastic method was Abelard. It was largely thanks to him that Paris became the intellectual capital of Europe. As a cathedral town and seat of the French monarchy it already boasted a number of schools, but it was only after Abelard was appointed to the schoolmaster's chair at Notre-Dame that Paris became a magnet for ambitious young men, many of whom were attracted to Abelard's unorthodox teaching style. We can glimpse it through the audacious treatise called the *Sic et Non* ("Yes and No" or "So and Not So"). In this book, Abelard gathered a collection of seemingly contradictory statements from the Church Fathers, organized around 150 key theological problems. Like his contemporary Gratian, the codifier of canon law, his ultimate ambition was to show that these divergent authorities could be reconciled—in this case, through the skillful use of dialectic.

Yet Abelard did not propose any solutions in the *Sic et Non*, and the work therefore caused grave concern. More inflammatory still were Abelard's meditations on the doctrine of the Trinity, which circulated in a book of lectures that was denounced and burned in 1121. Twenty years later, Bernard of Clairvaux had Abelard brought up on another charge of heresy at the Council of Soissons, where he was condemned a second time. Bernard's own mystic spirituality stood in direct opposition to Abelard's tireless quest for reasoned understanding. Abelard, for his part, found no solace in the monastic life beloved of Bernard: teaching was the activity that nurtured his faith. Luckily, teaching also expanded his fame and allowed him to train many pupils who eventually vindicated his teachings. After Abelard's death, his student Peter Lombard would ask the same fundamental questions that his master had done, but he took care to resolve the tensions which the *Sic et Non* had left open-ended. His great work, known as the *Sentences*, became the standard theological textbook of the medieval university, on which all aspirants to the doctorate were required to comment.

## The Nature of the University

The emergence of the university—a unique public forum for advanced study, the questioning of received ideas, and the resolution of critical problems—was the natural extension of Abelard's teachings. His reputation and that of his students attracted many other intellectuals to Paris, and together they began to offer more varied and advanced instruction than anything obtainable in the average cathedral school. By 1200 this loose association of teachers formed themselves into a *universitas* ("corporation" in Latin), and the resulting faculty began to collaborate in the higher academic study of the liberal arts, with a special emphasis on theology. At about the same time, the students of law based in Bologna came together in a *universitas* whose speciality was law.

Paris and Bologna provided the two basic models on which all medieval universities were based. In southern Europe, the universities of Montpellier, Salamanca, and Naples were patterned after Bologna, where the students themselves constituted the corporation. They hired the teachers, paid their salaries, and fined or discharged them for neglect of duty or poor instruction. The universities of northern Europe, including Oxford and Cambridge, were guilds of teachers who governed themselves and established fees for tuition and rules of conduct. They eventually embraced four faculties—liberal arts, theology, law, and medicine—each headed by a dean. By the end of the thirteenth century, the northern universities also expanded to include separate, semi-autonomous colleges, which usually provided housing for poorer students and were often endowed by a private benefactor. Over time, these colleges became centers of instruction as well as residences. The universities of Oxford and Cambridge still retain this pattern of organization, copied from Paris: the colleges of which they are composed are semi-independent educational units.

Most of the academic degrees granted in our modern universities derive from those awarded in the Middle Ages, even though the actual courses of study are very different. No university curriculum included history or vernacular languages, or anything like the social sciences prior to the nineteenth century. The medieval student was assumed to know Latin grammar thoroughly before entrance into a university; he had learned it in the primary (or "grammar") schools discussed above. On admission, he was required to spend about four years studying the basic liberal arts, which meant doing advanced work in Latin grammar and rhetoric, and mastering the rules of logic. If he passed his examinations, he received the preliminary degree of bachelor of arts (the prototype of our BA). But to ensure himself a place in professional life he had to devote additional years to the pursuit of an advanced degree, the master of arts (MA) or doctor of laws, medicine, or theology. This was accomplished by reading and commenting on standard texts such as Peter Lombard's *Sentences* (theology), Gratian's *Decretum* (law), or Aristotle's *Physics* (medicine). The requirements for the degree of doctor of philosophy (PhD) included more

**THE SPREAD OF UNIVERSITIES.** This map shows the geographical distribution of Europe's major universities and indicates the dates of their foundation. ▪ ***Where were the first universities founded and why?*** ▪ Notice the number and location of the universities founded in the fourteenth and fifteenth centuries. ▪ ***What pattern do you see in these later foundations?*** ▪ ***What might explain this?***

specialized training, and those for the doctorate in theology were particularly arduous: by the end of the Middle Ages, the course for the doctorate in theology at Paris had been extended to twelve or thirteen years, over and above the eight years required to earn the MA. University degrees of all grades were recognized as standards of attainment and became pathways to a variety of careers.

Student life in medieval universities was rowdy. Many students began their studies between the ages of twelve and fifteen, and so were working through all the challenges and pleasures of adolescence as they worked toward their degrees; this helps to explain the many injunctions against drunkenness, gambling, and other pursuits included among the canons of the Fourth Lateran Council. Moreover, university students generally believed that they constituted an independent and privileged community, apart from the local communities in which they lived. This often led to riots or even pitched battles between "town" and "gown."

That said, the time devoted to actual study was very intensive. Because books were prohibitively expensive, the primary mode of instruction was the lecture (Latin for "reading") in which a master would read an authoritative work aloud to his students and comment on it while the students took notes. As students advanced in their disciplines, they were expected to develop their own skills of analysis and interpretation in formal, public disputations. Advanced disputations could become extremely complex and abstract; sometimes they might last for days. Often they sparked public debates of great magnitude. The Ninty-five Theses posted by Martin Luther in 1517 were actually a set of debating points organized along these lines (see Chapter 13).

### *Classical Thought and Christian Theology*

The intellectual revolution of the Middle Ages was further advanced by renewed access to classical philosophy and Muslim science, epitomized by the works of Avicenna and Averroès (Chapter 8). Many Greek texts were available in Latin translation after the middle of the twelfth century, and by the middle of the thirteenth nearly all of Aristotle's surviving works and much Arabic scientific knowledge was accessible to western Europeans, in many cases for the first time. (Plato's works were still largely unknown, however, as were the works of the classical Greek poets and dramatists; these remained the cultural preserve of Byzantium and would not be widely available elsewhere until the sixteenth century; see Chapter 12).

Having acquired access to Greek and Arabic science and philosophy, the scholars of western Christendom were now faced with the task of reconciling these "new" ideas with a thousand years of doctrinal developments. In some ways, their task was similar to that of the first generation of Church Fathers in the fourth and fifth centuries (Chapter 6): they had to find a way to preseve the truth of Christian teachings while incorporating ideas and methods of inquiry that might at first seem to challenge those teachings. This was relatively straightforward in the case of the natural sciences, because they seldom conflicted with the principles of Christianity in obvious ways; and because scholasticism had already established the principles for reconciling reason and observation with faith. But many other aspects of Greek and Arabic learning were not readily compatible with Christian faith, and therefore had to be filtered through the dialectical methods pioneered by Abelard and his pupils.

By far the greatest accomplishments in this endeavor were made by Thomas Aquinas (1225–1274), who became the leading theologian at the University of Paris. As a member of the Dominican order, Thomas was committed to the defense of faith through reason. He also believed that the study of the physical world was a legitimate way of gaining knowledge of the divine, because God had created both the world and the many ways of knowing it. Imbued with a deep confidence in the value of human reason and human experience, Thomas worked quietly and steadily on his two great summaries of theology, the *Summa contra Gentiles* (a summary of the arguments for refuting non-Christian religions) and the compendious *Summa Theologiae*. The theology of the modern Roman Catholic Church still rests on Thomistic methods, doctrines, and principles.

## COURTS, CITIES, AND CATHEDRALS

In the eleventh century, it was still possible to describe European society as divided among "those who worked, those who prayed, and those who fought." By 1200, such a description no longer bore much relationship to reality. New elites had emerged in the burgeoning cities of western Europe. The wealthiest members of society were merchants and bankers, and aristocrats either had to best them (by engaging in trade themselves) or join them through strategic intermarriage. The aristocracy still fought, but so did upwardly mobile knights, urban crossbowmen, longbowmen, citizen militias, and peasant levies. Meanwhile, such lines as existed between town and countryside were easily crossed. Rural people moved to towns and townspeople moved back to the countryside with regularity and ease. And the pupils of the new schools made up a growing professional class that further defied neat categorization. We have noted that careers in the Church or royal bureaucracies were particularly open to self-made, educated men. But medieval courts and cities also provided opportunities for advancement.

## *From* Chevalerie *to Chivalry*

The ennoblement of chivalry and the emergence of medieval court culture were connected to the growing wealth of Europe, the competition among monarchies, and contemporary developments in military technology. In 1100, a knight could get by with a woolen tunic and leather corselet, a couple of horses, a groom, and a sword. A hundred years later, a knight needed full-body armor made of iron, a visored helmet, a broadsword, a spear, a shield, and warhorses capable of carrying all this gear. By 1250, a knight also had to keep up appearances at tournaments, which meant maintaining a string of horses, sumptuous silk clothing for himself and caparisons for his steeds, and a retinue of liveried squires and servants. As the costs of a warrior's equipment rose, the number of men who could personally afford it declined dramatically, which made knightly display something increasingly prized by the nobility and upstart merchants alike. Knights who did not inherit or gain sufficient property to support themsleves had to seek wealthy brides or the protection of a lord who could afford to equip them.

There were still other factors contributing to the prestige of knighthood. As part of a larger effort to control the violent competition for land and wealth, both secular and ecclesiastical rulers had begun to promote a new set of values that would come to redefine chivalry: bravery, loyalty, generosity, and civility. This new chivalry appealed to knights because it distinguished them from all the other "new men" who were emerging as powerful in this period, especially merchants and clerics. It also appealed to the nobility, whose status in this socially mobile world no longer depended on descent from high-born ancestors; families who *did* have such ancestors did not necessarily have the wealth to maintain a noble lifestyle, while many families who lived as "nobility" did not have prestigious ancestors.

What, then, was "nobility"? Was high status a matter of birth or was it the result of individual achievement? The amalgamation between knighthood and nobility offered something to all sides. To the older aristocracy, it was a visible sign of good breeding. To professional warriors, and to the merchants and bureaucrats who later adopted its language and customs, chivalry offered a way of legitimizing social positions attained through bravery or skill. As a result, mounted combat—whether on the battlefield, in tournaments, or in the hunt—would remain the defining pastime of European gentlemen until the end of the First World War.

**MAKING A KNIGHTLY APPEARANCE.** The costs of maintaining a chivalric lifestyle mounted steeply in the twelfth and thirteenth centuries, not only because a knight needed the most up-to-date equipment but because he was expected to cut a gallant figure at tournaments and to dazzle female spectators. This image is one of many sumptuous full-page illuminations in the Manesse Codex, made in Zurich in the early fourteenth century and preserving the compositions of courtly poets.

## *The Culture of the Court*

Closely linked to this new ideology of chivalry was a new emphasis on *courtoisie*, "courtliness," the refined behavior appropriate to a court. This stemmed in part from practical necessity. Those great lords who could support a knightly retinue would have households full of randy young men whose appetites had to be controlled. Hence, the emerging code of chivalry encouraged its adherants to view noble women as objects of veneration who could only be wooed and won by politesse, poetry, and valiant deeds; they had to be courted. Non-noble women, though, were fair game and could be taken by force if they did not yield willingly to the desires of a knight.

Whole new genres of poetry, song, and storytelling emerged in the twelfth century to celebrate the allied cultures of chivalry and courtliness. These genres stand in marked contrast to the older entertainments of Europe's warrior class, the heroic epics that are often the earliest literary artifacts of various vernacular languages: the Anglo-Saxon *Beowulf*, the *Song of Roland*, the Norse sagas, the German *Song of the Nibelungs*, and the Spanish *Poem of the Cid*. These epics portray a virile, violent society. Gore flows freely; skulls are cleaved; manly valor, honor, and loyalty are the major themes. If women are mentioned, it is often as prizes to be won in battle. The courtly entertainments introduced in the twelfth century are very different in style, subject matter, and authorship. Many of them were addressed to, and commissioned by, women. In some cases, they were even composed by women, or were composed in close collaboration with a female patron. A example of the former is the collections of *lais* (versified stories) of Marie de France, who was active during the reigns of Henry II and Eleanor of Aquitaine, and who may have been an abbess as well as a member of the Anglo-Norman aristocracy. An example of the latter is one of the Arthurian tales composed by Marie's contemporary, Chrétien de Troyes (*kray-TYAN duh TWAH*, fl. 1165–90), who spent some time working under the patronage of Eleanor's daughter (by her first husband, Louis VII), Marie of Champagne.

Romances were engaging tales of love and adventure, often focusing on the exploits of King Arthur and his knights or some other heroic figure of the past, like Alexander the Great. But they were also attuned to the interests and concerns of women: threats to women's independence, enforced or unhappy marriages, disputed inheritances, fashion, fantasies of power. The heroine of one anonymous romance is a woman who dresses as a knight and travels the world performing valiant deeds. Other heroines accompany their husbands on quests, or defend their castles against attack, or have supernatural powers. Following in Chrétien's footsteps, the German poets Wolfram von Eschenbach and Gottfried von Strassburg vied to produce romances that retained the scope and complexity of heroic epics while featuring women in strong, central roles: Wolfram's *Parzival*, the story of the search for the Holy Grail, and Gottfried's *Tristan*, which retold the Celtic story of the adulterous love between Tristan and Isolde. Both inspired the operatic reconceptions of Richard Wagner (1813–1883).

The poetic tradition initiated by the southern French troubadours and northern French trouvères (terms deriving from the verbs *trobar/trouver*: "to discover, to invent") also contributed to the culture of chivalry and inspired the work of German *minnesänger* ("love singers"). Much troubadour poetry displays sensitivity to feminine beauty and the natural world, and pays eloquent tribute to the political and sexual power of women. Take, for example, a lyric of Bernart de Ventadorn (c. 1135–1195), one of Eleanor's protégés:

> When leaves and grass are lush with renewed growth
> The beauty of my Lady blossoms forth . . .
> I am her slave, her vassal, she my lord;
> I pay her homage, hope to have a word
> Of kindness, or of love, exchanged for mine
> But she is cruel: she will not make a sign.

Other troubadour songs celebrated old-fashioned warlike virtues, as in the verses of Bernart's contemporary, Bertran de Born (c. 1140–1214), a friend of Eleanor's son Richard the Lionheart:

> It pleases me to hear the mirth and song
> Of birds, filling the wood the whole day long.
> But more it pleases me to see the fields
> All planted thick with tents, to see the shields
> And swords of my companions ranged for war,
> To hear the screams, to see the blood and gore.

To what extent do the entertainments of the court reflect real changes in noble women's status? Certainly, there were women throughout this period who wielded tremendous power, particularly in Scandinavia and parts of southern Europe, where women could inherit property, rule in their own right, and were treated as lords in fact and in name (as in Bernart's song). Queen Urraca ruled the combined kingdom of León-Castile from 1109 until 1126. Ermengarde of Narbonne (c. 1127–1197) ruled her strategically placed county from early adolescence to the time of her death. Eleanor remained sole ruler of Aquitaine throughout her long life, and she played a crucial role in the government of England at various times. The strong-willed Blanche of Castile (1188–1252), Eleanor's granddaughter, ruled France during the minority of her son Louis IX and again when he went on crusade.

Queens are not, of course, typical, but their activities in this period reflect some of the opportunities open to other well-born women—and the freedoms that set most

# Analyzing Primary Sources

## *Illicit Love and the Code of Chivalry*

*Little is known about Marie de France, author of a series of popular verse tales that are among the earliest chivalric romances, but she may have been a nun or abbess living in the Anglo-Norman realm of Henry II and Eleanor of Aquitaine. The following excerpt is from her* Lais, *adapted from stories told in the Franco-Celtic county of Brittany (Abelard's home).*

he Bretons, who lived in Brittany, were fine and noble people. In days gone by these valiant, courtly and noble men composed lays for posterity and thus preserved them from oblivion.... One of them, which I have heard recited, should not be forgotten. It concerns Equitan, a most courtly man, lord of Nantes, justiciary and king.

Equitan enjoyed a fine reputation and was greatly loved in his land. He adored pleasure and amorous dalliance: for this reason he upheld the principles of chivalry. Those who lack a full comprehension and understanding of love show no thought for their lives. Such is the nature of love that no one under its sway can retain command over reason. Equitan had a seneschal, a good knight, brave and loyal, who took care of his entire territory, governing it and administering its justice. Never, except in time of war, would the king have forsaken his hunting, his pleasures or his river sports, whatever the need might have been.

As his wedded wife the seneschal had a woman who was to bring great misfortune to the land. She was a lady of fine breeding and extremely beautiful with a noble body and good bearing. Nature had spared no pains when fashioning her: her eyes sparkled, her face and mouth were beautiful and her nose was well set. She had no equal in the kingdom, and the king, having often heard her praised, frequently sent her greetings and gifts.... He went hunting in her region on his own and on returning from his sport took lodging for the night in the place where the seneschal dwelt, in the very castle where the lady was to be found. He had ample occasion to speak with her, to express his feelings and display his fine qualities. He found her most courtly and wise, beautiful in body and countenance....

That night he neither slept nor rested, but spent his time reproaching and reprimanding himself. "Alas," he said, "what destiny brought me to this region? Because of this lady I have seen, my heart has been overwhelmed by a pain so great that my whole body trembles. I think I have no option but to love her. Yet, if I did love her, I should be acting wrongly, as she is the seneschal's wife. I ought to keep faith with him and love him, just as I want him to do with me...."

Source: From "Equitan," in *The Lais of Marie de France*, trans. Glyn S. Burgess and Keith Busby (Harmondsworth: 1985), pp. 56–57.

### *Questions for Analysis*

1. Despite the king's initial misgivings, he and the seneschal's wife eventually have an affair and plot to murder her husband, only to be caught in their own trap. Given this outcome, how would you interpret Marie's remarks about courtliness and "the code of chivalry"? What are the tenets of this code, according to the king?
2. What social tensions does this story reflect, and how might it shed light on historical realities? What moral might contemporary readers draw from it?

western European women apart from their counterparts in the Byzantine and Muslim worlds. A striking symbol of this is the figure of the queen in the game of chess. In the Muslim courts where the game originated, the equivalent of the queen was a male figure, the king's chief minister, who could move only diagonally, and only one square at a time. In twelfth-century Europe, however, this piece became the queen. Eventually, she was the only figure powerful enough to move all over the board.

## *Urban Opportunities and Inequalities*

In 1174, a cleric called William FitzStephen wrote a biography of his former employer, Thomas Becket, who had recently been canonized. In it, William went out of his way to extoll the urban culture of London that had produced this saintly man and other "men of superior quality," as well as all the splendid sights and pastimes to be had there: feasting, churchgoing, ice-skating, bear-baiting, plays, sports—and of course the pleasures of money-making. Towns were crucibles of activity, and as such became cultural powerhouses as well as economic ones. They were also launching pads for the careers of ambitious men.

As we noted in Chapter 8, many of the towns that emerged in the twelfth century were governed by associations of citizens who undertook a wide variety of civic responsibilities. But urban governance was also apt to fall into the hands of oligarchs, a trend that became increasingly marked during the thirteenth century when the enormous wealth generated by some forms of commerce led to marked social inequalities, much as in the Greek poleis of the fifth century B.C.E. (Chapter 3). In Italy, some cities even sought to control the resulting violence by turning to an outsider who would rule as a dictator for a (supposedly) limited term. Others cities adopted the model of Venice and became formal oligarchies, casting off all pretence to democracy. Some cities remained republics in principle, like Florence, but became increasingly oligarchical in practice. Aristocratic families lived in fortified towers surrounded by the houses of their supporters, and their rivalries often produced a violent culture of vendetta.

But even in places where town governance was controlled by a powerful few, there were many meaningful opportunities for collective activity. Urban manufacturing was regulated by professional associations known as guilds or (in some regions) confraternities. Guilds promoted the interests of their members by trying to preserve monopolies and limit competition. To these ends, terms of employment and membership were strictly regulated. If an apprentice or a journeyman worker (from the French *journée*, meaning "day" and, by extension, "day's work") wished to become a master, he had to produce a "masterpiece" to be judged by the masters of the guild. If the market was considered too weak to support additional master craftsmen, even a masterpiece would not secure a craftsman the coveted right to set up his own shop and thus earn enough to marry. Most guilds were closed to Jews and Muslims and they also restricted the opportunities available to women, who had little influence over the terms and conditions under which they worked.

Guilds and confraternities were therefore instruments of economic control, but they were also important social, political, and cultural institutions. Most combined the functions of religious association, drinking club, and benevolent society, looking after members and their families in hard times, supporting the dependents of members who died, and helping to finance funerals. Guilds also empowered their members in much the same way that unions do today, providing them with political representation and raising their social status. In Arras, there was even a guild of professional entertainers, the confraternity of jongleurs, which became the most powerful organization in the town during the thirteenth century.

## *The Varieties of Vernacular Entertainment*

Like courts, towns fostered new kinds of vernacular entertainment in the twelfth and thirteenth centuries. Even the genres of Latin poetry, song, and drama produced in this period can be considered "vernacular" because they made use of vernacular elements (like rhyme, not a feature of classical Latin poetry), dealt with current events, and were popular with a wide audience. In one of Heloise's letters to Abelard, she recalls that he was so renowned for the beauty of his love songs that "every street and tavern resounded with my name." It's possible that some of Abelard's songs were sung in French, but more probable that they used the edgy, colloquial Latin popular among the student singer-songwriters known as "goliards," which means something like "daredevils." Goliards composed parodies of the liturgy and the Gospels. Their lyrics celebrated the carefree life of the open road, the pleasures of drinking and dice, the joys of love, and the agonies of poverty.

Perhaps the genre most representative of urban culture is the fabliau, a "fable" or short story with a salacious, irreverant, or satirical twist. Fabliaux drew attention to the absurdities of urban life and lampooned the different types of people who were striving to reinvent themselves in the permissive world of the town: the oafish peasant, the effete aristocrat, the corrupt priest, the sex-starved housewife, the wily student, the greedy merchant, the con man. Gender-bending and reversals of fortune are common themes. In one fabliau, a young noble woman is forced by her impoverished father to marry a buffoonish shopkeeper who thereby gains a knighthood. To shame him, she herself dresses as a knight and beats her husband in a jousting match. In another, a priest tricks a poor peasant out of his cow by promising that God will reward him by doubling his "investment" in the work of the Church. When the cow breaks out of the priest's pasture and runs for home, she brings the priest's cow, too, and the peasant is delighted by the fulfillment of the promised miracle. The earliest of these fabliaux come from Arras, the prosperous banking center and entertainment capital of Europe in the thirteenth century. Thanks to Arras's close contacts with England, southern France, and Italy, many of the entertainments developed there traveled far abroad.

It was through these channels that the accomplishments of poets active in French-speaking lands came to inspire the work of Dante Alighieri (1265–1321) of Florence. Dante composed a series of semi-autobiographical songs in what he called the "sweet new style" of poetry in his native tongue, Italian, which was now so different from the Latin of Roman Italy that it had become a language in its own right. Yet as a scholar and devotee of classical Latin verse, Dante also strove to make his own vernacular an instrument for serious political and social critique. His great work, known in his own day as the *Comedy* (called by later admirers the *Divine Comedy*) was composed during the years he spent in exile from his beloved city, after the political party he supported was ousted from power in 1301.

The *Comedy* describes the poet's imaginary journey through Hell, Purgatory, and paradise, a journey beginning in a "dark wood," a metaphor for the personal and political crises that threatened his faith. Dante is led out of this forest and through the first two realms by the Roman poet Virgil, who represents the best of classical culture; but Dante can only be guided toward knowledge of the divine by his deceased beloved, Beatrice, who symbolizes Christian wisdom. In the course of this visionary pilgrimage, Dante meets the souls of many historical personages and contemporaries who explain why they met their several fates: this is his ingenious way of commenting on current events and passing judgment on his enemies. In many ways, this monumental poem represents the fusion of classical and Christian cultures, Latin learning and vernacular artistry.

## The Medieval Cathedral

The cathedrals constructed in Europe's major cities during this period exemplify the ways in which the cultural communities of the court, the schools, and the town came together. For although any cathedral-building campaign would have been spearheaded by a bishop looking to glorify his episcopal see, it could not be completed without the support of the nobility, the resources of the wealthy, the

**ROMANESQUE AND GOTHIC.** Some distinguishing features of the Romanesque and Gothic styles are exhibited in these two churches, both dedicated to the Virgin Mary and built within a century of one another. On the left is the west front of the Church of Notre-Dame-la-Grande in Poitiers, the ancestral domain of Eleanor of Aquitaine. Constructed between 1135 and 1145, it featured rounded arches, strong stone walls, massive supporting pillars, and small windows. On the right is the cathedral of Notre-Dame at Reims in Champagne, built between 1220 and 1299. The emphasis on stolid, horizontal registers is here replaced by soaring, vertical lines. The gabled portals, pointed arches, and bristling pinnacles all accentuate the height of this structure, while the multitude of stained-glass windows—chiefly the enormous rose window—flood the vast interior with colored light.

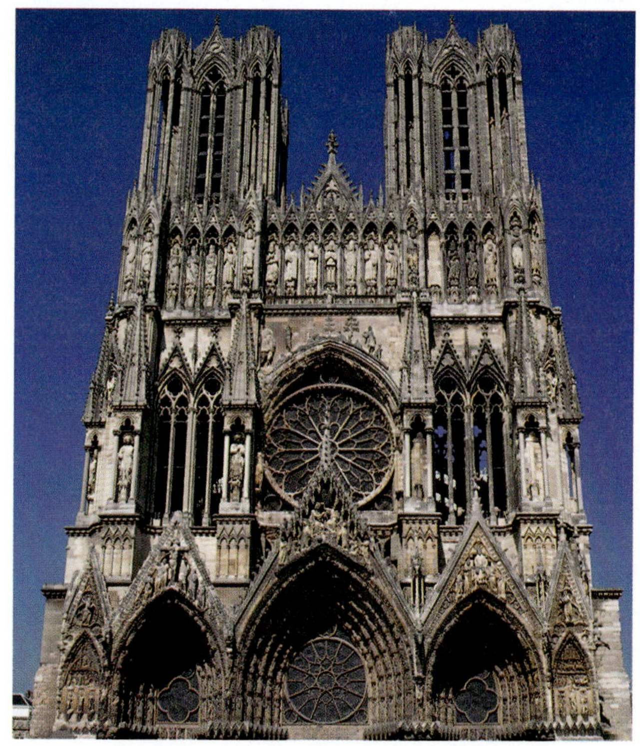

learning of trained theologians, and the talents of urban craftsmen. And cathedrals were not merely edifices: they were theaters for the performance of liturgy, music, drama, preaching.

Cathedrals were not, in themselves, new: the seat of a bishop had long been known as his *cathedra*, his throne, and the church that housed it was the principal church of the diocese. But the size, splendor, and importance of cathedrals increased exponentially in the twelfth and thirteenth centuries alongside the growing power of the Church, the population of cities, and the wealth and knowledge necessary for their construction. Indeed, the cathedrals of this period are readily distinguishable from their predecessors by their architectural style, which came to be called "Gothic," while the style of earlier buildings is known as "Romanesque." As the term suggests, Romanesque buildings use the basic elements of public architecture under the Roman Empire: the rounded arch, massive stone walls, and sturdy supporting columns. These features convey regularity and stability, and they also made churches places of refuge that could be fortified and defended in troubled times. By contrast, the structural elements of Gothic architecture are the pointed arch, groined and ribbed vaulting, and the flying buttress, an external support that strengthened the much thinner stone walls and enormous stained-glass windows whose light illuminated elaborate decorative programs that made the cathedral a microcosm of the medieval world and an encyclopedia of medieval knowledge.

These were not buildings that could be defended and, it was thought, would never have to be: they were manifestations of urban pride, expressions of practical and intellectual genius, and symbols of a triumphant and confident Church. Their proud builders would have been dismayed to learn that the modern term "Gothic" was actually intended to be derogatory, the name for art forms that Renaissance artists—who favored Roman models—considered barbaric (see Chapter 12). They would have been still more shocked to learn that cathedrals were among the first monuments targeted for destruction during the Reformation, the revolutions of the eighteenth and nineteenth centuries, and the wars of the twentieth. One of the prime examples of Gothic architecture, the cathedral dedicated to the Virgin Mary at Reims (shown on page 307), was largely destroyed during World War I; what the visitor sees today is a reconstruction.

## CONCLUSION

A century ago, the American medievalist Charles Homer Haskins described the intellectual, religious, and cultural changes of the High Middle Ages as "the Renaissance of the twelfth century" and the beginning of northwestern Europe's enduring cultural prestige. A generation later, his student Joseph Strayer located "the medieval origins of

## After You Read This Chapter

Visit StudySpace for quizzes, additional review materials, and multi-media documents. **wwnorton.com/studyspace**

### REVIEWING THE OBJECTIVES

- The emerging monarchies of Europe shared certain features but differed from one another in significant ways. What were the major similarities and differences of kingship in England, France, and Iberia?
- The growth of papal power made religion an important part of daily life for all Christians in unprecedented ways, but it also limited lay spirituality and the rights of non-Christians. How?
- Scholasticism was the method of teaching and learning fostered by medieval schools but it was also a method of debating and resolving problems. How did scholasticism assist in the reconciliation of classical and Christian thought?
- The meaning of chivalry changed in the twelfth century. Why?
- The new literary genres and art forms of the High Middle Ages were fostered by courts, universities, and towns. What are some good examples?

the modern state" in this same period, and with them the modern ideas of national sovereignty and national identity. In recent decades, the British medievalists R. I. Moore and Robert Bartlett have also argued that this era marks the beginning of the modern world, but not necessarily in positive ways. Moore sees the growth of strong institutions like the Church and the state as leading to "the formation of a persecuting society" in which governmental bureaucracies are used to identify, control, and punish groups of people deemed threatening to those in power. Bartlett also views this era as the key phase in a brutal process of "conquest and colonization" visible in the eastern expansion of the Holy Roman Empire, the Norman Conquest of England, the growth of papal power, the Crusades, and other movements. Most recently, a former pupil of Strayer's, Thomas Bisson, has argued that the twelfth century was a period of crisis, a crucible out of which new institutions of government emerged to check the personal ambitions of kings and the violence of rapacious lords.

Common to all of these paradigms is a recognition that the expansion of European power and influence that began around the year 1000 continued into the twelfth century and was consolidated in the thirteenth. By 1300, Europe had taken on the geographic, political, linguistic, and cultural characteristics that continue to define it today. Whether or not a direct line runs between the developments of this period and the world in which we live, many European nations look to these centuries for their origins and for the monuments of their cultural heritage. Magna Carta is still cited as a foundational document of English law and the English constitutional monarchy, while the territories united under the rule of the French kings still form the nation of France. The doctrines crystalized in medieval canon law and scholastic theology have become the core doctrines of the Roman Catholic Church, and devotion to the Virgin Mary is still central to the piety of millions. The religious orders that emerged to educate and govern a burgeoning medieval population continue their ministries. The daughter houses of medieval monastic orders continue to proliferate in lands unknown to medieval people: Japan, China, Australia, New Zealand, the Americas. Students still pursue the degrees first granted in medieval universities, and those who earn them wear the caps and gowns of medieval scholars. Meanwhile, poets still aspire to the eloquence of Dante, singers record the music of Hildegard, and Hollywood films are based on chivalric romances and the tragic love of Abelard and Heloise. It is difficult to tell where the Middle Ages end and the modern world begins.

## PEOPLE, IDEAS, AND EVENTS IN CONTEXT

- What was **MAGNA CARTA** and why was it made? How did **PHILIP AUGUSTUS** consolidate royal authority in France, and why were the German emperors unable to do so?
- What were the main achievements of **INNOCENT III**? Why did the imperial power of **FREDERICK THE GREAT** weaken the papacy?
- How do the **CULT OF THE VIRGIN** and the careers of **HILDEGARD OF BINGEN** and **HELOISE** exemplify the ideals and realities of women's roles in the Church?
- Why were **ABELARD**'s teachings condemned by the Church? In what sense can he be considered the founder of the **UNIVERSITY OF PARIS**?
- How did noble women like **ELEANOR OF AQUITAINE** contribute to the emergence of a new vernacular culture? What types of entertainment are characteristic of medieval cities?

## CONSEQUENCES

- The growth of towns, monarchies, and the Church increased the degree of control that those in power could exercise; but they also increased access to education and new forms of social mobility. Is this a paradox, or are these two phenomena related?
- The U.S. Constitution is based on the legal principles and institutions that emerged in medieval England, but it also drew on Roman models. Which do you consider to be more influential, and why?
- Some historians have argued that the extent and methods of persecution discernible in the High Middle Ages are unprecedented in the history of Western civilizations. How would you support or refute this thesis? For example, does the persecution of Jews in medieval Europe differ from their treatment under the neo-Assyrians and Chaldeans, or under the Roman Empire? Why or why not?

# Before You Read This Chapter

## STORY LINES

- The Black Death altered the landscape, economy, and societies of Europe in profound ways.
- The competing territorial claims of Europe's sovereign powers led to warfare on a large scale, as well as to the emergence of national monarchies that could draw on the loyalty and support of their populations.
- The failure of the papacy to make internal reforms led to the decline of papal power and credibility; at the same time, popular piety flourished, and a number of popular religious movements sought more radical reforms of the Church.
- The new opportunities and challenges of this era are dynamically reflected in its artistic, intellectual, and scientific achievements.

## CHRONOLOGY

| | |
|---|---|
| 1240 | Mongol Khanate established at Kiev |
| 1309 | "Babylonian Captivity" of the papacy in Avignon begins |
| 1315–1322 | The Great Famine ravages Europe |
| c. 1330–1384 | Lifetime of John Wyclif |
| 1337 | Edward III of England claims the French throne |
| 1347–1350 | Spread of the Black Death |
| 1377 | The papacy restored to Rome |
| 1378 | The Great Schism begins |
| 1417–1420 | Council of Constance is convened; Jan Hus burned at the stake |
| 1429–1431 | Career of Joan of Arc |
| 1431–1449 | Council of Basel fails to curtail papal power |
| 1453 | The Hundred Years' War ends; fall of Constantinople |
| 1454 | Gutenburg's Bible printed at Mainz |
| 1462–1505 | Reign of Ivan the Great in Muscovy |
| 1492 | Christian armies of Spain conquer Granada; expulsion of Jews |

# Crisis, Unrest, and Opportunity, 1300–1500

## CORE OBJECTIVES

- **EXPLAIN** the economic and social effects of the Black Death.
- **DEFINE** the concept of national monarchy and summarize its implications.
- **IDENTIFY** the factors leading to the rise of Muscovy.
- **UNDERSTAND** the significance of the conciliar movement and its defeat by the papacy.
- **DESCRIBE** the spiritual, cultural, and technological innovations of the later Middle Ages.

In June of 1381, thousands of laborers from the English countryside rose up in rebellion. Most were peasants or village craftsmen, yet the revolt was carefully coordinated. Plans were spread in coded messages circulated by word of mouth and by the followers of a renegade Oxford professor, John Wyclif, who had called for the redistribution of Church property and taught that common people should be able to read the Bible in their own language. The rebellion's immediate cause had been a series of exorbitant taxes levied by Parliament for the support of an ongoing war with France, but its more fundamental cause was an epidemic that had occurred thirty years earlier. The Black Death had reduced the entire population of Europe by 30 to 50 percent, and had drastically altered the world of the survivors. In this new world, workers were valuable and could rebel against those who paid them poorly or treated them like slaves. In that fateful summer of 1381, the workers of England even vowed to kill all the representatives of both the Church and the government—to kill (as they put it) all the lawyers—and to destroy all the documents that had been used to keep them down. It was a revolution, and it partly succeeded. Although the leaders were eventually captured and executed, the rebellion had made the strength of the common people known to all.

The fourteenth and fifteenth centuries are often seen as a time of crisis. And certainly, this was an age of adversity in Europe. Famine and plague cut fearful swaths through the population; war was a brutally recurrent fact of life; and the papacy spent seventy years in continuous exile from Italy, only to see its prestige decline further after its return to Rome. But this period was also a time of opportunity. The exhausted land of Europe recovered from centuries of overfarming while workers gained the economic edge and, eventually, social and political power. Meanwhile, the people of Europe's various monarchies came to identify themselves as members of a new political entity, the nation-state; popular and intellectual movements sought to reform the Church; and a host of artistic and scientific innovations contributed to all of these phenomena. It was a period of intense creativity that would redefine European civilization.

**THE PLAGUE CLAIMS A VICTIM.** A priest gives last rites to a bedridden plague victim, as a smiling devil pierces him with a spear and Christ looks mercifully down from Heaven. ▪ ***What are the possible meanings of this image?*** ▪ ***What does it reveal about contemporary attitudes toward death?***

## THE BLACK DEATH AND ITS CONSEQUENCES

By 1300, the European economy was reaching its limits. Between 1000 and 1300, the population had tripled and the continent had become a sea of grain fields that stretched, almost unbroken, from Ireland to Ukraine. Forests were cleared, marshes drained, and pastureland reduced—but still, Europe was barely able to feed itself. At the same time, the warming trend that had begun in the late eighth century (Chapter 8) reversed itself. For even a reduction of one or two degrees centrigrade is enough to cause substantial changes in rainfall patterns, shorten growing seasons, and lessen agricultural productivity.

The new vulnerability of the European economy and ecosystem was dramatically revealed in the great famine that lasted from 1315 to 1322. In these years, adverse weather conditions were nearly continuous, and the result was starvation on a very large scale. Weakened by malnutrition, people and domestic animals also fell victim to epidemic diseases. Approximately 10 to 15 percent of the population north of the Alps perished. In the decades following, cold winters and floods threatened southern Europe, too, and in 1343 a tsunami destroyed ports in southern Italy. Earthquakes and comets seemed like further terrifying portents of disaster.

### *Tracking the Black Death*

The Black Death is the name given to a deadly plague that spread from Mongolia to China, northern India, and the Middle East during the 1330s and 1340s. By 1346, the disease had reached the Black Sea. From there, in 1347, Genoese ships inadvertantly brought it to Sicily and northern Italy. From Italy it spread westward along trade routes, first striking seaports, then moving inland. It moved with astonishing rapidity, advancing about two miles per day during both summer and winter. By 1350 it had reached Scandinavia and northern Russia, then spread southward until it linked up with the earlier waves of infection that had brought it from Central Asia to the Black Sea. It continued to erupt in local epidemics for the next 300 years; some localities could expect a renewed outbreak every decade. The last Europe-wide instance occurred between 1661 and

**THE PROGRESS OF THE BLACK DEATH, FOURTEENTH CENTURY.** ▪ *What trajectories did the Black Death follow once it was introduced into Europe?* ▪ *How might the growth of towns, trade, and travel have contributed to the spread of the Black Death?* ▪ *Would such a rapid advance have been likely during the early Middle Ages or even in the ancient world?*

1669, although there were sporadic outbreaks in Poland and Russia until the end of the eighteenth century.

The scale of mortality caused by the Black Death is almost unimaginable. At least a third, and probably half, of Europe's people died between 1347 and 1350. By the following century, the combined effects of plague, famine, and warfare had reduced the total population by at least 50 percent, perhaps by as much as two thirds. This massive mortality also had dramatic effects on the landscape. In Germany, more than 40,000 villages disappeared. And even when villages survived, the shortage of workers forced changes in agricultural practice. Around Paris, more than half the farmland cultivated in 1348 had become pasture by 1450. Elsewhere, abandoned fields reverted to woodland,

# Competing Viewpoints

## *Responses to the Black Death*

*Many chroniclers, intellectuals, and private individuals have left accounts of the plague and its effects, and many attempted to understand why it had occurred, how it spread, and how communities should respond to it.*

### The Spread of the Plague According to Gabriele D'Mussis (d. 1356), a Lawyer in Piacenza (Northern Italy)

Oh God! See how the heathen Tartar races, pouring together from all sides, suddenly invested the city of Caffa [near Constantinople] and besieged the trapped Christians there for almost three years.... But behold, [in 1346] the whole army was affected by a disease which overran the Tartars and killed thousands upon thousands every day. It was as though arrows were raining down from heaven to strike and crush the Tartars' arrogance. All medical advice and attention was useless; the Tartars died as soon as the signs of disease appeared on their bodies: swellings in the armpit or groin caused by coagulating humours, followed by a putrid fever.

The dying Tartars, stunned and stupefied by the immensity of the disaster brought about by the disease, and realising that they had no hope of escape, lost interest in the siege. But they ordered corpses to be placed in catapults and lobbed into the city in the hope that the intolerable stench would kill everyone inside. What seemed like mountains of dead were thrown into the city, and the Christians could not hide or flee or escape from them, although they dumped as many of the bodies as they could in the sea. And soon the rotting corpses tainted the air and poisoned the water supply.... Moreover one infected man could carry the poison to others, and infect people and places with the disease by look alone. No one knew, or could discover, a means of defence.

Thus almost everyone who had been in the East ... fell victim ... through the bitter events of 1346 to 1348—the Chinese, Indians, Persians, Medes, Kurds, Armenians, Cilicians, Georgians, Mesopotamians, Nubians, Ethiopians, Turks, Egyptians, Arabs, Saracens and Greeks....

* * *

As it happened, among those who escaped from Caffa by boat were a few sailors who had been infected with the poisonous disease. Some boats were bound for Genoa, others went to Venice and to other Christian areas. When the sailors reached these places and mixed with the people there, it was as if they had brought evil spirits with them....

* * *

Scarcely one in seven of the Genoese survived. In Venice, where an inquiry was held into the mortality, it was found that more than 70 percent of the people had died.... The rest of Italy, Sicily and Apulia and the neighbouring regions maintain that they have been virtually emptied of inhabitants.... The Roman Curia at Avignon, the provinces on both sides of the Rhône, Spain, France, and the Empire cry up their griefs....

* * *

Everyone has a responsibility to keep some record of the disease and the

increasing the forested areas in parts of Europe by as much as one third.

Immediate reactions to the Black Death ran the gamut from panic to resignation. Observers quickly realized that the plague was contagious, but precisely how it spread remained enigmatic. Some believed that it was caused by breathing "bad air" and so urged people to flee from stricken areas, which caused the disease to spread even faster. Others looked for scapegoats, and revived old conspiracy theories that implicated Jews in the poisoning of wells. Scores of Jewish communities were attacked and thousands of their inhabitants massacred in the Rhineland,

deaths, and because I am myself from Piacenza I have been urged to write more about what happened there in 1348. . . .

I don't know where to begin. Cries and laments arise on all sides. Day after day one sees the Cross and the Host being carried about the city, and countless dead being buried. . . . The living made preparations for their [own] burial, and because there was not enough room for individual graves, pits had to be dug in colonnades and piazzas, where nobody had ever been buried before. It often happened that man and wife, father and son, mother and daughter, and soon the whole household and many neighbours, were buried together in one place. . . .

## A Letter From the Town Council of Cologne to the Town Council of Strasbourg (Germany), 12 January 1349

Very dear friends, all sorts of rumours are now flying about against Judaism and the Jews prompted by this unexpected and unparalleled mortality of Christians. . . . Throughout our city, as in yours, many-winged Fame clamours that this mortality was initially caused, and is still being spread, by the poisoning of springs and wells, and that the Jews must have dropped poisonous substances into them. When it came to our knowledge that serious charges had been made against the Jews in several small towns and villages on the basis of this mortality, we sent numerous letters to you and to other cities and towns to uncover the truth behind these rumours, and set a thorough investigation in train. . . .

If a massacre of the Jews were to be allowed in the major cities (something which we are determined to prevent in our city, if we can, as long as the Jews are found to be innocent of these or similar actions) it could lead to the sort of outrages and disturbances which would whip up a popular revolt among the common people—and such revolts have in the past brought cities to misery and desolation. In any case we are still of the opinion that this mortality and its attendant circumstances are caused by divine vengeance and nothing else. Accordingly we intend to forbid any harassment of the Jews in our city because of these flying rumours, but to defend them faithfully and keep them safe, as our predecessors did—and we are convinced that you ought to do the same. . . .

Source: From Rosemary Horrox, ed. and trans. *The Black Death* (Manchester: 1994), pp. 16–21, 219–20.

### *Questions for Analysis*

1. How does Gabriele d'Mussis initially explain the causes of the plague? How and why does his understanding of it change as he traces its movements from East to West?
2. Why does the Council of Cologne wish to quell violence against the Jews? How does this reasoning complement or challenge what we have learned so far about the treatment of Jews in medieval Europe?
3. In your view, do these two perspectives display a rational approach to the horrors of the Black Death? Why or why not?

southern France, and Christian Spain. (No such attacks on Jews are known to have occurred in Muslim areas of Spain or elsewhere in the Muslim world.) The papacy and some local authorities tried to halt these attacks, but these admonitions came too late. Another response to the plague was the Flagellant movement, so called because of the whips (*flagella* in Latin) with which traveling bands of penitents lashed themselves in order to appease the wrath of God. But the unruly and sometimes hysterical mobs that gathered around the flagellants aroused the concern of both ecclesiastical and secular authorities, and the movement was suppressed by papal order.

What caused the Black Death? Most evidence points to the deadly microbe *Yersinia pestis*, which causes bubonic plague and its even deadlier cousins, pneumonic and septicemic plague. In its bubonic form, this microbe is carried by fleas that travel on the backs of rats; humans catch it only if they are bitten by an infected flea or rat. Bubonic plague attacks the lymphatic system, producing enormous swellings (buboes) of the lymph nodes in the groin, neck, and armpits. Pneumonic plague results when *Y. pestis* infects the lungs, allowing the contagion to spread in the same ways as the common cold. Septicemic plague occurs when an infected flea introduces the microbe directly into the human bloodstream, causing death within hours, often before any symptoms of the disease can manifest themselves. One of the things that made the Black Death so frightening, therefore, is that it manifested itself in different ways. Those afflicted by the hideous bubonic plague might actually recover, while others—seemingly untouched—might die suddenly and mysteriously.

## The Impact on the Countryside

The economic and social consequences of the plague were profound. Crops rotted in the fields, manufacturing ceased, and trade was disrupted. Basic commodities became scarcer and prices rose, prompting ineffectual efforts to control prices and to force surviving laborers to work. But these were short-term effects. In the decades following, the new demographic reality permanently altered established social and economic patterns.

First and foremost, the drastic decrease in population meant a relative abundance of food. The price of grain eventually fell, which made it more affordable. At the same time, the scarcity of workers made peasant labor valuable: wages rose and work became easily obtainable. With wages high and food prices low, ordinary people could now afford more bread, and could also spend their surplus cash on dairy products, meat, fish, fruits, and wine. As a result, the people of Europe in the later Middle Ages were better nourished than they had ever been—better than many are today. A recent study of fifteenth-century rubbish dumps has concluded that the people of Glasgow (Scotland) ate a healthier diet in 1405 than they did in 2005.

A healthier ecological balance was also reestablished in the wake of the plague. With the lessened demand for fuel, forests that had almost disappeared by 1300 began to recover and expand. Meanwhile, the declining demand for grain allowed many farmers to expand their livestock herds. By turning arable land into pasture land, farmers reduced the need to hire workers and thus increased their profits while improving the fertility of the soil through manuring. Some farmers were even able to enlarge their holdings because so much land had been abandoned.

Most of these innovations were made by small farmers, because great lords—individuals, as well as monasteries—were slower to adjust to the changing circumstances. Some landholders responded to the shortage of workers and the rising costs of wages by forcing their tenants to perform additional unpaid labor. In eastern Europe, many free peasants became serfs for the first time. In Castile, Poland, and Germany, too, lords succeeded in imposing new forms of servitude. In other parts of Iberia and in Italy, actual slavery—which had nearly been eradicated during the economic boom of the twelfth and thirteenth centuries—became common for the first time in centuries.

In France, by contrast, peasants remained relatively free, although many were forced to pay a variety of fees and taxes to their lords and to the king. In England, where peasant bondage had been more common than in France, serfdom ultimately disappeared altogether. In the new world of geographical mobility and economic opportunity, English serfs were able to vote with their feet, either by moving to town or to the lands of a lord who offered more favorable terms: lower rents, more animals, fewer work requirements, and greater personal freedoms.

## The Urban Impact

Towns were especially sensitive to the changing economic and social climate. Some had already shrunk in size as a result of the Great Famine. Others, overcrowded and unsanitary, were particularly vulnerable to plague. Thereafter, they were vulnerable to the effects of violence. In Florence, the population rebounded quickly after the Black Death only to be depleted again by civil unrest: by 1427, it had dropped from around 300,000 to about 100,000. In Toulouse (southern France), the population remained fairly stable until 1430, when it was reduced by over 75 percent by the Hundred Years' War (see below). In London and Paris, however, large-scale immigration from the countryside reversed the short-term declines of the plague. Many of these new workers were women, whose economic opportunities were greatly enhanced by urban labor shortages.

Although the overall population declined, a far larger percentage of all people were living in towns by 1500: approximately 20 precent, as opposed to 10 or 15 percent prior to the Black Death. Fueling this urban growth was the increasing specialization of the late-medieval economy. With farmers under less pressure to produce grain in bulk, land could be devoted to livestock, dairy farming, and the production of a more diverse array of fruits and vegetables; and these could now be exchanged efficiently on the open market. Towns with links to extant trading networks benefited accordingly. In northern Germany, a group of cities even formed a coalition to build a new network, the Hanseatic League, whose members controlled commerce from Britain and Scandinavia to the Baltic. In northern Italy, the increased demand for luxury goods—which even some peasants and urban laborers could now afford—brought new wealth to the spice- and silk-trading city of Venice and also to the fine-cloth manufacturers of Milan and the jewelers of Florence. Milan's armaments industry also prospered, supplying its warring neighbors and the armies of Europe.

Not all the urban areas of Europe fared well. The Franco-Flemish cities that had played such a large role in the economic and cultural life of the High Middle Ages suffered a serious economic depression and the ravages of various wars. But on the whole, Europe profited from the plague, and was poised to extend its commercial networks into Africa, Asia, and ultimately, in the fifteenth century, the Americas (see Chapter 11).

The economic boom also stimulated the development of business practices and accounting techniques. New forms of partnership and the development of insurance contracts helped to minimize the risks associated with long-distance trading. Double-entry bookkeeping, widely used in Italy by the mid-fourteenth century, gave merchants a much clearer picture of their profits and losses than had been possible before. The Medici family of Florence established branches of their bank in each of the major cities of Europe and were careful that the failure of one would no longer bankrupt the entire firm, as previous branch-banking arrangements had done. Banks also experimented with advanced credit techniques borrowed from Muslim and Jewish financiers, allowing their clients to transfer funds between branches without any real money changing hands. Such transfers were carried out by written orders, the ancestors of the modern check.

***THE BANKER AND HIS WIFE* BY QUENTIN MASSYS (1466–1530).** This painting exemplifies the realistic art of the later Middle Ages: the wealthy banker and his wife display all the fashionable trappings and gadgets of the era, including an illuminated prayer book and a mirror. ***What does this image convey about the values and lifestyle of the merchant class?***

## SOCIAL MOBILITY AND SOCIAL INEQUALITY

The consequences of the Black Death were ultimately beneficial for many of those who survived it. But European society did not adjust easily to the new world created by the plague. It seemed to many like a world turned upside down, so rapidly had changes occurred.

### *Revolts and Rebellions*

Between 1350 and 1425, hundreds of popular rebellions challenged the status quo in many regions of Europe. In 1358, for example, peasants in northeastern France rose up violently against their lords, destroying property, burning buildings and crops, and even murdering or raping targeted individuals. This incident is known as the Jacquerie Rebellion because all French peasants were caricatured by the aristocracy as "Jacques" ("Jack"). In England, as we have already noted, a very different uprising occurred in June of 1381, much more organized and involving a much wider segment of society. Thousands of people marched on London, targeting the bureaucracies of the royal government and the Church, capturing and killing the archbishop of Canterbury, and meeting personally with the fourteen-year-old king, Richard II, to demand an end to serfdom and taxation, and the redistribution of property. It ended with the arrest and execution of the ringleaders. In Florence, workers in the cloth industry—known as the Ciompi (*chee-OM-pee*)—protested high unemployment and mistreatment by the manufacturers who also ran the Florentine government.

They seized control of the city, demanding relief from taxes, full employment, and political representation. They maintained power for a remarkable six weeks before their reforms were revoked.

The local circumstances that lay behind each of these revolts are unique, but these and hundreds of other rebellions exhibit certain common features. First of all, these uprisings were not bread riots spurred by destitution. Those who took part in them had actually been empowered by the new economic conditions and wanted to leverage their position in order to enact even larger changes. Some rebellions, like the English Peasants' Revolt, were touched off by resistance to new and higher taxes. Others, like the Jacquerie and the revolt of the Ciompi, took place at moments when unpopular governments were weakened by factionalism and military defeat. The English revolt was also fueled by the widespread perception of corruption within the Church and the royal administration.

**A HUNTING PARTY.** This fifteenth-century illustration shows an elaborately dressed group of noble men and women setting out with falcons, accompanied by their servants and their dogs. Hunting was an activity restricted to the aristocracy, and an occasion for conspicuous consumption and display.

Behind this social and political unrest, therefore, lies not poverty and hunger but the growing prosperity and self-confidence that village communities and urban workers felt in the changed economic circumstances that arose from the plague. For the most part, the rebels' hopes that they could fundamentally alter the conditions of their lives were frustrated. Kings, aristocrats, and urban oligarchs sometimes lost their nerve in the middle of an uprising, but they were almost always successful, after a time, in reasserting dominance. Yet this tradition of popular rebellion, established during the the later Middle Ages, would remain an important feature of Western civilizations and would culminate in the French Revolution (Chapter 18). It continues to this day.

## *Aristocratic Life in the Later Middle Ages*

The urban elites and rural aristocracies of Europe did not adapt easily to the new world created by the plague. Yet the later Middle Ages was a hardly a period of crisis for those in power. Quite the contrary: the great noble families of Europe were far wealthier than their ancestors had been. Nor did the plague undermine the dominant position they had established in European society. It did, however, make their world substantially more complex and uncertain, at a time when the costs of maintaining a fashionable lifestyle were escalating rapidly.

Across Europe, most noble families continued to derive much of their revenue from vast landholdings. But many lords also tried to increase their sources of income through investment in trading ventures. In Catalonia, Italy, Germany, and England, this became common practice. In France and Castile, however, direct involvement in commerce was regarded as socially demeaning and was, therefore, avoided by established families. Commerce could still be a route to ennoblement in these kingdoms, but once aristocratic rank was achieved one was expected to abandon these employments and adopt an appropriate way of life: living in a rural castle or urban palace surrounded by a lavish household, embracing the values and conventions of chivalry (including hunting and a family coat of arms), and serving the prince at court and in war.

Nobility became, as a result, even more difficult to define than it had been during the twelfth and thirteenth centuries. In countries where nobility entailed clearly defined legal privileges—such as the right to be tried only in special courts—proven descent from noble ancestors might be sufficient to qualify a family as noble in the eyes of the law. Legal nobility of this sort was, however, a somewhat less exclusive distinction than one might expect. In fifteenth-century Castile and Navarre, 10 to 15 percent of the total population had claims to be recognized as noble on these terms. In Poland, Hungary, and Scotland, the legally privileged nobility was closer to 5 percent; whereas in England and France, fewer than 2 percent could plausibly claim the legal privileges of noble status.

Fundamentally, however, nobility was a marker of social rank, expressed and epitomized by an individual's lifestyle. Hereditary land ownership, political influence, deference from social inferiors, courtly manners, and the ostentatious display of wealth: these combined to constitute a family's honor and hence to mark it as noble. But in practice, the lines of social distinction between noble and non-noble families remained fuzzy. Even on the battlefield, the supremacy of the mounted noble knight was being threatened by the growing importance of professional soldiers, archers, and artillery experts. There were even hints of a more radical critique of claims to innate superiority. As the English rebels put it in 1381: "When Adam dug and Eve spun, Who then was a gentleman?" In other words, they recognized that all human beings are equal and that social distinctions are entirely artificial.

Precisely because nobility was contested during the later Middle Ages, those who claimed the status took elaborate measures to assert its exclusivity. This accounts, in part, for the extraordinary number, variety, and richness of the artifacts and artworks that survive from this period. Aristocrats vied with one another in hosting lavish banquets. They dressed in rich and extravagant clothing: close-fitting doublets and hose with long pointed shoes for men, multilayered silk dresses with ornately festooned headdresses for women. They maintained enormous households: in France around 1400, the duke of Berry had 400 matched pairs of hunting dogs and 1,000 servants. They took part in elaborately ritualized tournaments and pageants, in which the participants pretended to be the heroes of chivalric romances. Aristocrats also emphasized their tastes and refinement by supporting authors and artists, and sometimes by becoming accomplished poets themselves. Nobility existed only if it was recognized; and to be recognized, noble status had to be constantly reasserted and displayed.

Rulers contributed to this process of noble self-assertion; indeed, they were among its principal supporters and patrons. Kings and princes across Europe competed in founding chivalric orders such as the Knights of the Garter in England and the Order of the Star in France. These orders honored men who had demonstrated the idealized virtues of knighthood, virtues celebrated as characteristic of the nobility as a whole. By exalting the nobility as a class, then, chivalric orders helped cement the links that bound the nobility to their kings and princes. So too did the gifts, pensions, offices, and marriage prospects that kings and princes could bestow on their noble followers. Given the decline in the agricultural revenues of noble estates, such rewards of princely service were critically important to maintaining noble fortunes. Indeed, the alliance that was forged in the fifteenth century between kings and their noble supporters would become one of the most characteristic features of "old regime" (in

**A NOBLE BANQUET.** Uncle of the mad king Charles VI, the duke of Berry left politics to his brothers, the dukes of Burgundy and Anjou. In return, he received enormous subsidies from the royal government, which he spent on sumptuous buildings, festivals, and artworks, including the famous Book of Hours (prayer book) that includes this image. Here, the duke (seated at right, in blue) gives a New Year's Day banquet for his household, who exchange gifts while his hunting dogs dine on scraps from the table. In the background, knights confront one another in a battle—or a tournament.

French, *ancien régime*) Europe. In France, this alliance lasted until the French Revolution of 1789. In Germany, Austria, and Russia it would last until the outbreak of World War I. In England, it persisted in some respects until World War II.

## WARFARE AND NATION-BUILDING

The partnership between royalty and nobility was partly a response to the new social and economic world created by the plague. But it was also a product of the unprecedented prevalence and scale of warfare. Beginning in the fourteenth century and continuing into the twentieth, Europeans were almost constantly at war. To fight these wars, governments claimed new powers to tax their subjects and to control their subjects' lives. Armies became larger, military technology deadlier. Wars became more destructive, society more militarized. As a result of these developments, the most successful European states—the monarchies of Portugal, Spain, and France—were aggressively expansionist. By 1600, their impact would be global (see Chapter 11).

### *England, France, and the Hundred Years' War*

The Hundred Years' War was the largest, longest, and most wide-ranging military conflict since Rome's wars with Carthage in the third and second centuries B.C.E. (Chapter 5). England and France were its principal antagonists, but almost all of the major European powers became involved in it at some stage. Active hostilities lasted from 1337 until 1453, interrrupted by truces of varying lengths. The roots of the conflict, however, reached back into the 1290s, when King Edward I of England attempted to conquer the neighboring kingdom of Scotland, thereby provoking the Scots to ally with France. And the threat of war continued until 1558, when Calais, the last English toehold on the Continent, passed into French hands.

The war had several causes. The most fundamental source of conflict, and the most difficult to resolve, was the fact that the kings of England held the duchy of Gascony as vassals of the French king; this was part of Eleanor of Aquitaine's domains, added to the Anglo-Norman Empire in 1154 (Chapter 9). In the twelfth and thirteenth centuries, when the French kings had not yet absorbed this region, this fact had seemed less of an anomaly. But as Europe's territorial monarchies began to claim sovereignty based on the free exercise of power within the "natural" boundaries of their domains, the English presence in "French" Gascony became more and more problematic. That England also had close commercial links, through the wool trade, with Flanders—which consistently resisted French imperialism—added fuel to the fire. So did the French alliance with the Scots, who had been resolutely resisting English imperialism.

Complicating this volatile situation was the disputed succession of the French crown. In 1328, the last of King Philip IV's three sons died without leaving a son to succeed him: the Capetian dynasty, founded by the Frankish warlord Hugh Capet in 987 (Chapter 8), had finally exhausted itself. A new dynasty, the Valois, came to the throne—but only by insisting that women could neither inherit royal power nor pass it on. For otherwise, the heir to France was Edward III of England, whose mother, Isabella, was Philip IV's only daughter. When his claim was initially passed over, Edward was only fifteen and in no position to protest. In 1337, however, when the disputes over Gascony and Scotland erupted into war, Edward raised the stakes by claiming to be the rightful king of France, a claim that subsequent English kings would maintain until the eighteenth century.

The hostilities that make up the Hundred Years' War can be divided into three main phases (see the maps on page 321). In the first phase, from 1337 until 1360, the English won a series of startling military victories, most famously at Crécy (1346), Calais (1347), and Poitiers (1356). Although France was richer and more populous than England by a factor of at least three to one, the English government was more effective in mobilizing the entire population, for reasons that were discussed in Chapter 9. King Edward was therefore able to levy and maintain a professional army of seasoned and well-disciplined soldiers, cavalry, and longbowmen. The huge but poorly led armies assembled by the French proved no match for the tactical superiority of these smaller English forces. English armies pillaged the French countryside at will, while civil wars broke out between individual French lords. Meanwhile, mercenary bands of soldiers roamed the countryside, attacking and looting peasant villages and holding towns to ransom just at the time when they were struggling to recover from the Black Death. In 1358, popular frustration boiled over in the savage rebellion of the Jacquerie (discussed above).

In 1360, Edward III agreed to renounce his claim to the French throne in return for full sovereignty over a greatly enlarged duchy of Gascony and the promise of a huge ransom for the king of France, whom he held captive. But the terms of the treaty were never honored. The French king continued to treat the English king as his vassal, and the king of England never ceased to claim the throne of France. Nor did the treaty resolve the underlying issues that had

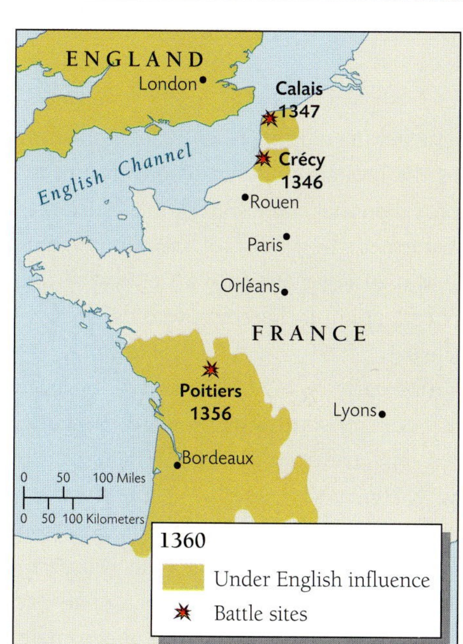

**THE PROGRESS OF THE HUNDRED YEARS' WAR.** Here we see three snapshots of the political geography of France during the Hundred Years' War. ▪ *In what areas of France did England make its greatest territorial gains before 1360?* ▪ *How and why did this change in the period leading up to 1429?* ▪ *What geographic and strategic advantages did the French monarchy enjoy after 1429 that might help explain its success in recapturing the French kingdom from the English?*

led to the war itself. Instead, a proxy war developed during the 1360s and 1370s, in which English and French troops organized into "Free Companies" hired themselves out in the service of warring factions in Castile and competing city-states in northern Italy. By 1376, when hostilties resumed between England and France, the Hundred Years' War had become a Europe-wide phenomenon.

In this second phase of the war, the tide quickly shifted in favor of France. In England, the aging Edward III was succeeded by his nine-year-old grandson, Richard II (r. 1377–99). Meanwhile, the new king of France, Charles V (r. 1364–80), imposed a series of new national taxes on the common people, restored order by disbanding the Free Companies, and hired the leader of one of these bands as the commander of his army. He thereby created a professional military that could match the English in discipline and tactics. By 1380, English territories in France had been reduced to a core area around the southwestern city of Bordeaux and the port of Calais in the extreme northeast.

Unlike his grandfather Edward III, Richard II had no interest in the French war. And although the war had been extremely popular in England, it ceased to be so during Richard's minority, when its conduct was mismanaged by his advisors. Indeed, this was one of the issues that had triggered the Peasants' Revolt in 1381. However, the nobility stood to gain from the war's continuation, and Richard's

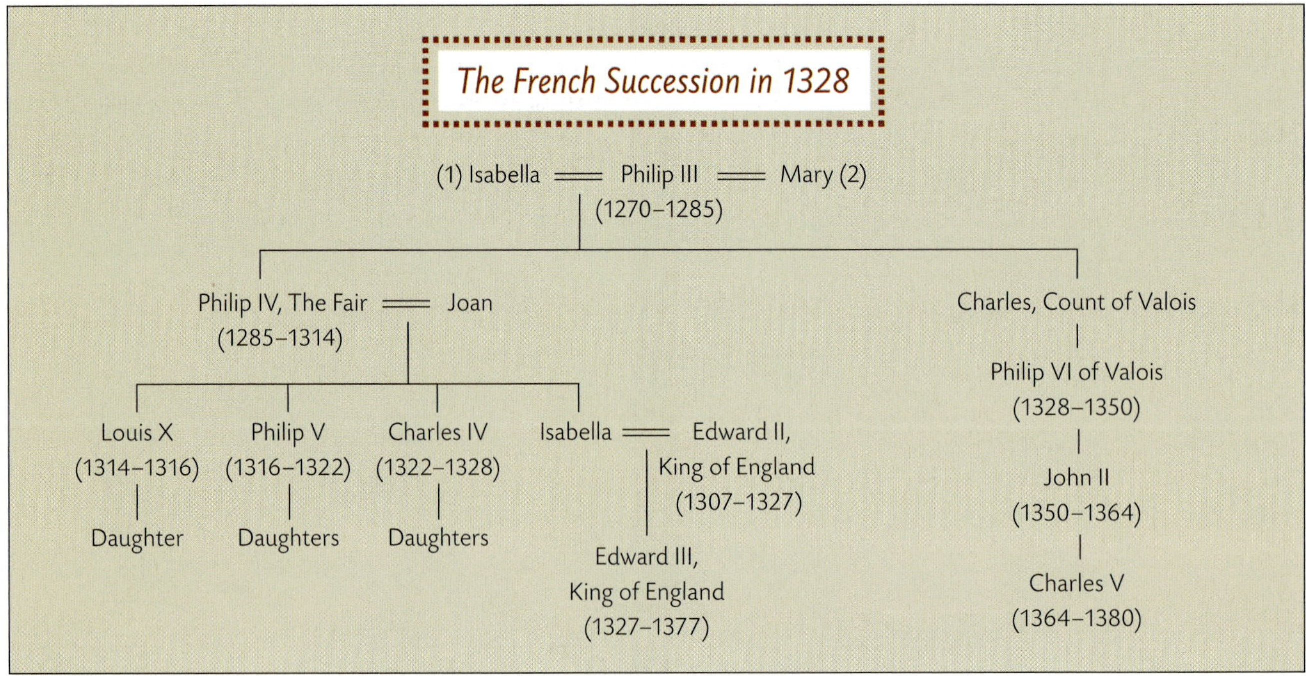


failure to press his claims to the French throne turned the barons against him. When Richard attempted to confiscate the inheritance of his cousin, Henry of Lancaster, Henry's supporters used this as pretext for rebellion. In 1399, Richard was deposed and eventually murdered. Henry seized the throne.

As a usurper, Henry IV (r. 1399–1413) struggled to maintain his authority in the face of repeated rebellions and challenges. Frequently ill, he was in no position to pursue the French war. When his son Henry V succeeded him in 1413, however, the new king immediately began to prepare for renewed war with France. A brilliant diplomat, Henry sealed alliances with both the emperor in Germany and the powerful duke of Burgundy, who was in control of the French royal government, then foundering due to the insanity of the French king, Charles VI (r. 1380–1422). When Henry V invaded France in 1415, he therefore faced only a partial army representing the anti-Burgundian faction within the royal court; the duke of Burgundy and his forces stayed home. Then, at Agincourt, Henry managed to win a crushing victory over a vastly larger, but badly disciplined French force. By 1420, he had conquered most of northern France and had forced the aged and infirm King Charles VI to give him his daughter Catherine's hand in marriage and to recognize him as heir to the throne of France—thus dispossessing the heir apparent, known as the Dauphin ("the dolphin"), the future King Charles VII.

Unlike his great-grandfather Edward III, who used his claim to the French throne largely as a bargaining chip to secure sovereignty over Gascony, Henry V honestly believed himself to be the rightful king of France. And his astonishing success in capturing the French kingdom seemed to put the stamp of divine approval on that claim. But Henry's successes in France also transformed the nature of the war, turning it from a profitable war of conquest into an extended and expensive military occupation. It thereby sowed the seeds of eventual English defeat.

Henry himself died early in 1422, still actively engaged in extending English control southward, toward the Loire. King Charles VI died only a few months later. The new king of England and France, Henry VI (r. 1422–61), was an infant, but the English armies under the command of his advisors continued to press southward. Meanwhile, the Dauphin's confidence in his right to the throne had been shattered by his own mother's declaration that he was illegitimate. Although it seemed unlikely that English forces would ever succeed in dislodging him from territories south of the Loire, it might have happened that England would once again rule an empire comprising much of northern France, as it had for a century and a half after the Norman Conquest.

But this scenario fails to reckon with Joan of Arc. In 1429, a peasant girl from Lorraine (a territory only nominally part of France) made her way to the Dauphin's court and announced that an angel had told her that he, Charles, was the rightful king, and that she, Joan, should drive the English out of France. The fact that she even got a hearing underscores the hopelessness of the Dauphin's position, as does the extraordinary fact that he gave her a contingent of troops. With this force, Joan liberated the strategic city of Orléans, then under siege, after which a series of victories

# Analyzing Primary Sources

## *The Condemnation of Joan of Arc by the University of Paris, 1431*

*After Joan's capture by the Burgundians, she was handed over to the English and tried for heresy at an ecclesiastical court set up in Rouen. It was on this occasion that the theology faculty of Paris pronounced the following verdict on her actions.*

ou, Joan, have said that, since the age of thirteen, you have experienced revelations and the appearance of angels, of St. Catherine and St. Margaret, and that you have very often seen them with your bodily eyes, and that they have spoken to you. As for the first point, the clerks of the University of Paris have considered the manner of the said revelations and appearances . . . Having considered all . . . they have declared that all the things mentioned above are lies, falsenesses, misleading and pernicious things and that such revelations are superstitions, proceeding from wicked and diabolical spirits.

Item: You have said that your king had a sign by which he knew that you were sent by God, for St. Michael, accompanied by several angels, some of which having wings, the others crowns, with St. Catherine and St. Margaret, came to you at the chateau of Chinon. All the company ascended through the floors of the castle until they came to the room of your king, before whom the angel bearing the crown bowed. . . . As for this matter, the clerks say that it is not in the least probable, but it is rather a presumptuous lie, misleading and pernicious, a false statement, derogatory of the dignity of the Church and of the angels. . . .

Item: you have said that, at God's command, you have continually worn men's clothes, and that you have put on a short robe, doublet, shoes attached by points, also that you have had short hair, cut around above the ears, without retaining anything on your person which shows that you are a woman, and that several times you have received the body of Our Lord dressed in this fashion, despite having been admonished to give it up several times, the which you would not do. You have said that you would rather die than abandon the said clothing, if it were not at God's command, and that if you were wearing those clothes and were with the king, and those of your party, it would be one of the greatest benefits for the kingdom of France. You have also said that not for anything would you swear an oath not to wear the said clothing and carry arms any longer. And all these things you say you have done for the good and at the command of God. As for these things, the clerics say that you blaspheme God and hold him in contempt in his sacraments; you transgress Divine Law, Holy Scripture, and canon law. You err in the faith. You boast in vanity. You are suspected of idolatry and you have condemned yourself in not wishing to wear clothing suitable to your sex, but you follow the custom of Gentiles and Saracens.

Source: Carolyne Larrington, ed. and trans., *Women and Writing in Medieval Europe* (New York: 1995), pp. 183–84.

### *Questions for Analysis*

1. Paris was in the hands of the English when this condemnation was issued. Is there any evidence that its authors were coerced into making this pronouncement?
2. On what grounds was Joan condemned for heresy?
3. In what ways does Joan's behavior highlight larger trends in late medieval spirituality and popular piety?

culminated in Charles's coronation in the cathedral of Reims, the traditional site for the crowning of French kings. But despite her victories, Joan was an embarrassment whose very charisma made her dangerous: a peasant leading aristocrats, a woman leading men, and a commoner who claimed to have been commissioned by God. When, a few months later, the Burgundians captured her in battle and handed her over to the English, King Charles VII did nothing to save her. Accused of witchcraft, condemned by the theologians of Paris, and tried for heresy by an English ecclesiastical court, Joan was burned to death in the market square at Rouen in 1431. She was nineteen years old.

The French forces whom Joan had inspired, however, continued on the offensive. In 1435, the Duke of Burgundy

**JOAN OF ARC.** A contemporary sketch of Joan was drawn in the margin of this register documenting official proceedings at the Parlement of Paris in 1429.

withdrew from his alliance with England; and when the young English king, Henry VI, proved first incompetent and then insane, a series of French military victories brought hostilities to an end with the capture of Bordeaux in 1453. English kings would threaten to renew the war for another century, and Anglo-French hostility would last until the defeat of Napoleon in 1815. But after 1453, English control over French territory would be limited to the port of Calais, which fell in 1558.

## The Effects of the Hundred Years' War

The Hundred Years' War challenged the very existence of France. The disintegration of that kingdom, first during the 1350s and 1360s, and again between 1415 and 1435, glaringly revealed the fragility of the bonds that tied the king to the nobility, and Paris to the outlying regions. Nonetheless, the king's power was actually increased by the war's end, laying the foundations on which the power of early modern France would be built.

The Hundred Years' War also had dramatic effects on the English monarchy. When English armies in France were successful, the king rode a wave of popularity that fueled an emerging sense of English identity. When the war turned against the English, however, defeats abroad undermined support for the monarch at home. Of the nine English kings who ruled England between 1307 and 1485, five were deposed and murdered by factions. This was a consequence of England's peculiar form of kingship, whose strength depended on the king's ability to mobilize popular support through Parliament while maintaining the support of his nobility through successful wars. Failure to maintain this balance was even more destablizing in England than it would have been elsewhere, precisely because royal power was so centralized. In France, the nobility could endure the insanity of Charles VI because his government was not powerful enough to threaten them. In England, neither the nobility nor the nation could afford the incompetent kingship of Henry VI. The result was an aristocratic rebellion against the king that led to a full-blown civil war: the Wars of the Roses, so called—by the novelist Sir Walter Scott (1771–1832)—because of the emblems of the two competing noble families descended from Edward III, Lancaster and York. It ended only when a Lancastrian claimant, Henry Tudor (r. 1485–1509), resolved the dynastic feud by marrying Elizabeth of York, ruling as Henry VII and establishing a new Tudor dynasty whose symbol was a rose with both white and red petals. His son was Henry VIII (see Chapter 13).

Despite England's ultimate defeat, the Hundred Years' War strengthened a characteristically English equation between national identity and the power of the state. Mounting anti-French sentiment also contributed to the triumph of the English vernacular over French for the first time since the Norman Conquest. And having lost its continental possessions, England became, for the first time, a self-contained island nation that looked to the sea for defense and opportunity. This would later prove to be an advantage in many ways.

## Conflict in the Holy Roman Empire and Italy

The endemic warfare that begins to characterize the history of Europe in the later Middle Ages was usually even more destructive than it proved to be in the struggle between England and France. In the lands of the Holy Roman Empire, armed conflict among territorial princes, and between these princes and the German emperors, weakened all the principal combatants significantly. Periodically, a powerful emperor would emerge to play a major role, but the dominant trend was toward the continuing dissolution of power, with German princes dividing their territories among their heirs while free cities and local lords strove to shake off the princes' rule. Between 1350 and 1450, near anarchy prevailed in many regions. In the eastern empire, however, the rulers of Bavaria, Austria, and Brandenburg-Prussia were able to strengthen their authority by supporting the efforts of the nobility to subject their peasants to serfdom and by conquering and colonizing new territories on their eastern frontiers.

In northern and central Italy, the last half of the fourteenth century was also marked by incessant conflict. With the papacy based in Avignon from 1309 until 1377, the Papal States collapsed and Rome itself was riven by factional violence. Warfare among northern city-states added to the violence caused by urban rebellions in the wake of the plague. By around 1400, however, Venice, Milan, and Florence had succeeded in stabilizing their differing forms of government. Venice was now ruled by an oligarchy of merchants; Milan by a family of despots; and Florence was ruled as a republic but dominated by the influence of a few wealthy clans, especially the Medici banking family. Having settled their internal problems, these three cities then began to expand their territories by subordinating other cities to their rule. By 1454, almost all the towns of northern Italy were allied with one of these powers. An exception was the port of Genoa, which remained prosperous and independent as a shipping and trading hub. The papacy, meanwhile, reasserted its control over central Italy when it was restored to Rome in 1377, while the southern kingdom of Naples persisted as a separate entity, but plagued by constant local warfare and poor government.

For about forty years, a treaty negotiated in 1454 brought peace among this cluster of Italian powers, while frequently shifting alliances checked the ambitions of any one state for further expansion. In 1494, however, a large-scale invasion of Italy by the French destroyed the diplomatic and military balance. Moreover, it revealed that none of these small-scale Italian states could oppose the powerful national monarchies that had developed north of the Alps—or the new kingdom of Spain.

## *The Emergence of Spain*

The kingdoms of the Iberian peninsula were also in constant conflict during the fourteenth and fifteenth centuries. In Castile, civil war and incompetent governance allowed the Castilian nobility to gain greater control over the peasantry and greater independence from the crown. In Aragon, the crown preserved its authority and benefitted from the extended commercial influence of Catalonia. But after 1458, Aragon was enmeshed in a civil war over a disputed succession, a war in which both France and Castile became involved.

The solution would ultimately lie in the blending of powerful families. In 1469, Prince Ferdinand of Aragon was recognized as the undisputed heir to that throne and, in the same year, secured this position by marrying Isabella, the heiress to Castile. Isabella became a queen in 1474, Ferdinand a king in 1479, and although Castile and Aragon continued to be ruled as separate kingdoms until 1714 (even now, tensions between the two former kingdoms continue), the marriage of Ferdinand and Isabella enabled the pursuit of several ambitious policies. Their union allowed them to spend their extraordinary resources on the creation of Europe's most powerful army, which was initially employed to conquer Granada, the last remaining Muslim principality in Spain. Granada fell in 1492, and a decade later Spanish armies intervened in Italy, eventually turning all of Italy into a Spanish protectorate.

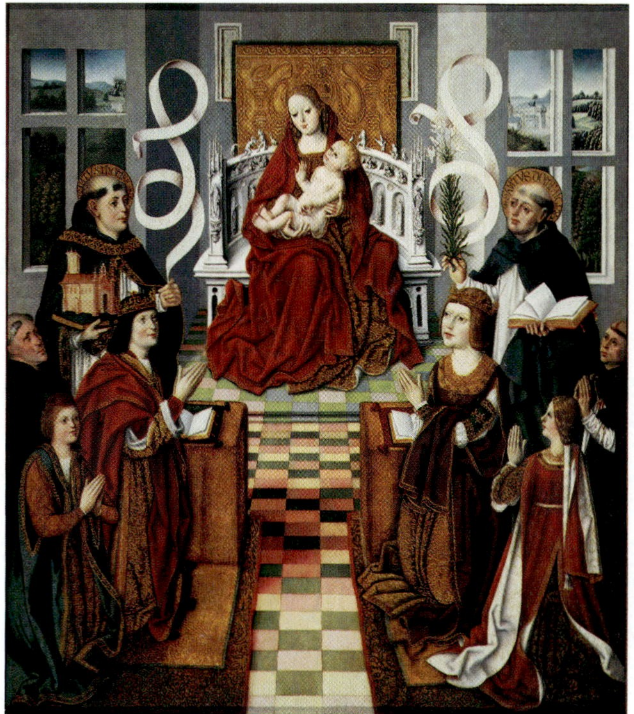

**FERDINAND AND ISABELLA HONORING THE VIRGIN.** In this contemporary Spanish painting, the royal couple are shown with two of their children and two household chaplains, and in the company of the Blessed Virgin, the Christ Child, and saints from the Dominican order (the Dominicans were instrumental in conducting the affairs of the Spanish Inquisition). ▪ ***How clear is the distinction between these holy figures and the royal family?*** ▪ ***What message is conveyed by their proximity?***

The conquest of Granada was a turning point for the emerging Spanish monarchy. Both Castile and Aragon had been shaped for centuries by their involvement in the "reconquest" of Iberia, and the victory of 1492 earned Ferdinand and Isabella the title of Europe's "Most Catholic" monarchs. It also associated Castile, in particular, with the crusading ethos, which now sought outlets elsewhere. Only a few months after the conquest of Granada, Queen Isabella granted three ships to a Genoese adventurer who promised to reach India by sailing westward across the Atlantic Ocean. He failed, of course; but by landing in two new continents, which he claimed for Spain, Columbus extended the Castilian crusading tradition to the New World, with enduring consequences (see Chapter 11).

The year 1492 also saw the expulsion of the entire Jewish community from Spain, the culmination of a process of Jewish exclusion from Christian Europe that had accelerated in the late thirteenth century (Chapter 9). The Spanish expulsion stands out, however, for the total number of Jews involved (at least 100,000 and possibly as many as 200,000) and because of the rich cultural legacy fostered by the Jews of this region over a period of a thousand years. The Catholic monarchs' motives for ordering this expulsion are still debated. Tens of thousands of Spanish Jews had converted to Christianity between 1391 and 1420, many as a result of coercion but some from sincere religious conviction. And for a generation or so it seemed possible that these converts, known as *conversos*, might successfully assimilate into Christian society. But the internal and external conflicts that led to the union of Ferdinand and Isabella made the *conversos* targets of discriminatory legislation and may also have fueled popular suspicions that they remained Jews in secret. To make "proper" Christians out of the *conversos*, the "Most Catholic" monarchs may have concluded that they needed to remove the "bad influence" posed by the continuing presence of a Jewish community in Spain.

The expulsion of Jews thus enabled the creation of a new and explicitly Christian identity for the hybrid Spanish nation, transcending the many rival regional identities there. Like other contemporary monarchs, Ferdinand and Isabella may have sought to strengthen their emerging nation-state by constructing an exclusively Christian identity for its people, and by attaching that new identity to the crown.

### *The Growth of National Monarchies*

In France, England, and Spain, as well as in smaller kingdoms like Scotland and Portugal, the later Middle Ages thus saw the emergence of European states more powerful and cohesive than any that had existed before. The basic political patterns established in the formative twelfth and thirteenth centuries had made this possible, yet the active construction of a sense of national identity in these territories, and the fusion of that identity with kingship, were new phenomena. Forged by war and fueled by the growing cultural importance of vernacular languages, this fusion produced a new type of political organization: the national monarchy.

The advantages of these national monarchies when compared to older forms of political organization—such as the empire and the city-state—is most clearly visible in Italy. Until the end of the fifteenth century, the Italian city-states had appeared to be well governed and powerful, and Venice even had a maritime empire of its own. But when the armies of France and Spain invaded the Italian peninsula, neither the militias of the city-states nor the far-flung resources of Venice were a match for them. Germany and the Low Countries would suffer the same fate only a few generations later, and would remain battlegrounds for competing armies until the early nineteenth century. But the new national monarchies brought significant disadvantages, too. They guaranteed the continued prevalence of warfare in Europe, and they eventually transported their rivalry to every corner of the globe in the late nineteenth and early twentieth centuries.

## THE RISE OF MUSCOVY, "THE THIRD ROME"

The fourteenth and fifteenth centuries also witnessed the consolidation of a state that would become the dominant power in eastern Europe and, in the twentieth century, one of the great powers of the world. Yet Russia developed very differently from the national monarchies of western Europe. It was, instead, the largest multiethnic empire in the pre-modern world. And by 1500, it claimed to be the rightful successor to the Rome of the Caesars, as well as to that of Constantine.

### *Kievan Rus' and the Mongol Khanate*

As we saw in Chapter 8, the Viking people known as Rus' had played a key role in establishing a principality at Kiev (now in Ukraine), which maintained diplomatic and trading relations with both western Europe and Byzantium throughout the tenth and eleventh centuries. That dynamic changed with the arrival of the Mongols (whose movements will be discussed more fully in Chapter 11). Commanded by a grandson of the great Chingiz (Genghis) Khan, the Mongols overran Kiev in 1240. Two years later, they created their own state on the lower Volga River, known as the Khanate of the Golden Horde, and from this base they wielded power for 150 years.

Initially, the Mongols ruled their Russian territories directly, installing their own administrative officials and requiring Russian princes to subject themselves to the Great Khan himself, by traveling to Mongolia. Around 1300, however, the Mongols began to tolerate the existence of several semi-independent principalities from which they demanded regular tribute. Kiev never recovered its dominant position, but one of the newer principalities would enable the construction of a Russian state: Muscovy, the duchy centered on Moscow.

## The Rise of Muscovy

In the early fourteenth century, Moscow was the tribute-collecting center for the Mongol Khanate. This did not always protect it from attack, but Mongol support did help Moscow's dukes to absorb neighboring territories. And because Moscow was far from the Mongol base on the lower Volga, its dukes could further consolidate their strength without attracting too much attention from the khans. This location was also advantageous for forging commercial contacts with the Baltic and Black Sea regions.

Yet Moscow's ties with western Europe remained undeveloped—not because it was under the thumb of the Mongols, but because it was loyal to the Orthodox Church of Byzantium. Relations between eastern and western Christians had deteriorated steadily during the Crusades and were openly hostile after Constantinople was captured and sacked by crusaders in 1204, a calamity from which it never recovered. Then, during the fourteenth and fiteenth centuries, Moscow's sensitivity to threats from European Christianity was escalated by the growing strength of a Catholic kingdom on its borders.

## The Expansion of Poland

In the thirteenth century, the small kingdom of Poland had struggled to defend itself from neighboring German princes and from absorption into the Holy Roman Empire. But when the empire's strength waned after the death of Frederick the Great (Chapter 9), Poland's situation grew more secure. In 1386, its reigning queen, Jadwiga, enabled its dramatic expansion when she married Jagiello, the duke of neighboring Lithuania, thus doubling the size of her kingdom. Lithuania had begun to carve out an extensive territory stretching from the Baltic to modern-day Belarus and Ukraine, and this expansionist momentum increased after its union with Poland. In 1410, at the Battle of Tannenberg, combined Polish and Lithuanian forces defeated the Teutonic Knights, a military order that controlled a crucial region lying between the allied kingdoms. Thereafter, Poland-Lithuania began to push eastward toward Muscovy.

Although many of Lithuania's aristocratic families were Orthodox Christians, the established church in Lithuania was loyal to Rome, as it was in Poland. Thus when the inhabitants of the region around Moscow began to feel threatened by Poland-Lithuania, one way of constructing a shared Muscovite identity was to direct shared hostility toward Latin Christendom.

## The Russian Church and the Third Rome

Muscovy's alienation from western Europe increased as Byzantium grew weaker and the responsibility for defending Orthodox Christianity devolved onto the Russian Church. Muscovites prided themselves on their descent from the Rus' who had been converted by Byzantine missionaries in the tenth century (Chapter 8), and they saw themselves as the natural champions of Constantinople, which was now surrounded by the Muslim empire of the Ottoman Turks (to be discussed further in Chapter 11). But when the patriarch of Constantinople agreed to submit to the authority of Rome in 1438, in the desperate hope that the papacy would rally military support for the besieged city, Russian clergy refused to follow suit. After Constantinople fell to the Turks in 1453—predictably, without any help from Latin Christendom—the Russian Church therefore emerged as the only surviving proponent of Orthodox Christianity, while the Muscovite state declared itself the divinely appointed successor to Rome. To drive the point home, Muscovite dukes began to take the title of *tsar*, "caesar." In their eyes, Moscow had become the last and greatest heir of the Roman Empire. "Two Romes have fallen," said a Muscovite chonicler, "the third is still standing, and a fourth there shall not be."

## The Reign of Ivan the Great (1462–1505)

Along with the imperial title, the Muscovite rulers borrowed the Byzantine ideology of the ruler's divine election,

**THE EXPANSION OF MUSCOVITE RUSSIA TO 1505.** The grand duchy of Moscow was the heart of what would soon become the Russian Empire. ▪ ***With what other empires and polities did the Muscovites have to compete during this period of expansion?*** ▪ ***How did the relative isolation of Moscow, compared with early Kiev, allow for the growth of Muscovite power on the one hand and Moscow's distinctively non-Western culture on the other?*** ▪ ***How might the natural direction of the expansion of Muscovite power until 1505 help to encourage attitudes often at odds with those of western European civilization?***

and this undergirded the sacred position later ascribed to the tsars. But ideology alone could not have built the Russian Empire. Behind its growth lay the steadily growing power of Moscow's rulers, who achieved effective independence from the Mongols when a rebellious Mongol warlord named Timur the Lame (Tamburlane) destroyed the Khanate of the Golden Horde at the end of the fourteenth century. This allowed the Muscovite grand duke, Ivan III, known as Ivan the Great, to fill the power vacuum and carry forward his own imperial agenda.

Ivan launched a series of conquests that annexed all the independent Russian principalities lying between Moscow and the border of Poland-Lithuania. After invading Lithuania in 1492 and 1501, Ivan even succeeded in bringing parts of that domain (portions of modern Belarus and Ukraine) under his control. Meanwhile, he married the

**IVAN THE GREAT.** This modern tribute to Ivan III prominently displays the two-headed eagle of imperial Rome. ***What is the significance of this symbolic choice?***

niece of the last Byzantine emperor, giving substance to the claim that Muscovy was a new New Rome. He also rebuilt his fortified Moscow residence, known as the Kremlin, in magnificant Italianate style. He would later adopt, as his imperial insignia, the double-headed eagle of Rome and its legions. By the time of his death in 1505, Muscovy was firmly established as a dominant power and the power of the tsar was revealed as more absolute than that of any European monarch.

## THE TRIALS OF THE ROMAN CHURCH

The later Middle Ages changed the Roman Church in ways that would prove definitive. Like other large landowners, monasteries suffered from the economic changes brought about by the Black Death, as did bishops, who confronted the same dilemmas as the secular nobility. But no ecclesiastical institution suffered more severe trials than the papacy, which endured almost seventy years of exile from Rome followed by a debilitating forty-year schism. It then faced a protracted battle with reformers who sought to reduce the pope's role in Church governance. Even though the papacy won this battle in the short term, the renewed abuse of papal power would, in the long run, bring about the permanent schism caused by the Reformation of the sixteenth century (Chapter 13).

### *The "Babylonian Captivity" of the Papacy*

As we saw in Chapter 9, Boniface VIII's humiliation at the hands of the French king Philip IV was followed by the wholesale subjugation of papal authority to the French crown. This period is often called the "Babylonian Captivity" of the papacy, recalling the Jews' exile in Babylon during the sixth century B.C.E. (see Chapter 2). From 1309 until 1378, the papal court resided at Avignon, a small city in southern France. It had not intended to remain there and, after Philip's death in 1314, it probably could have left. But Avignon soon proved to have a number of advantages over Rome. It was closer to the major centers of power, it was far removed from the tumultuous politics of Rome and the Papal States, and it was safe from the aggressive attentions of the German emperors. And as the papal bureaucracy grew in size, it became more difficult to move. In time, Avignon began to feel like home; in fact it *was* home for all of the popes elected there, who were natives of the region, as were nearly all the cardinals whom they appointed. This helped to cement their loyalty to the French king.

The papacy never abandoned its claims to the overlordship of Rome and the Papal States, but making good on these claims took decades of planning and a great deal of money. The Avignon popes accordingly imposed new taxes and obligations on the dioceses of France, England, Germany, and Spain. Judicial cases from ecclesiastical courts also brought large revenues into the papal coffers. Most controversially, the Avignon popes claimed the right to appoint bishops and priests to vacant offices, bypassing the electoral rights of individual dioceses and collecting huge fees from successful appointees.

By these and other measures, the Avignon popes strengthened their administrative control over the Church but weakened their moral authority. Stories of the court's unseemly luxury circulated widely, especially during the

**THE PAPAL PALACE AT AVIGNON.** This great palace was begun in 1339, and symbolizes the apparent permanence of the papal residence in Avignon.

reign of the notoriously corrupt Clement VI (r. 1342–52), whose rule coincided with the Black Death. Clement openly sold spiritual benefits for money, boasted that he would appoint a jackass to a bishopric if he thought it would turn a profit, and defended his sexual transgressions by insisting that they were therapeutic. After his death, in the decades that were transforming European society in so many other ways, calls for the papacy's return to Rome grew more insistent. The most successful of these was the letter-writing campaign of the nun and mystic Catherine of Siena (1347–1380), whose teasing but pious missives to Gregory XI (r. 1370–78) ultimately persuaded him to make the move.

## The Great Schism and the Conciliar Movement

The papacy's restoration was short-lived. A year after Gregory's return to Rome, he died. His cardinals—many of them Frenchmen—struggled to interpret the wishes of the volatile Romans, whose habit of expressing themselves through violence was unsettling to outsiders. Later, the cardinals would claim to have capitulated to the Roman mob when they elected an Italian candidate, Urban VI. When Urban fell out with them soon afterward, the cardinals fled the city and, from a safe distance, declared his selection invalid because it had been made under duress. They then elected a new pope, a Frenchman who took the name Clement VII. Urban retaliated by naming a new, entirely Italian, College of Cardinals and by refusing Clement access to the city. The French pope and his cardinals withdrew ignominiously to Avignon, while the Italian pope remained in Rome. The resulting rift is known as the Great Western Schism. For between 1378 and 1417, the Latin Church was divided between two (and, ultimately, three) competing papacies, each claiming to be legitimate and each denouncing the heresy of the others.

Not surprisingly, Europe's religious allegiances fractured along the political lines drawn by the ongoing Hundred Years' War: France and her allies Scotland, Castile, Aragon, and Naples recognized the pope in Avignon; while England, Germany, northern Italy, Scandinavia, Bohemia, Poland, and Hungary recognized the Roman pope. Nor was there any obvious way to end this embarrassing state of affairs. The two rival Colleges of Cardinals continued to elect successors every time a pope died, perpetuating the problem. Finally, in 1409, some cardinals from both camps met at Pisa, where they ceremoniously declared the deposition of both popes and named a new one from among their number. But neither of the popes reigning in Rome and Avignon accepted that decision, so there were now three rival popes excommunicating each other, instead of only two.

This debacle was ultimately addressed between 1417 and 1420 at the Council of Constance, the largest and longest ecclesiastical gathering since the Council of Nicea, over a thousand years before (Chapter 6). Its chief mission was to remove all rival claimants for papal office before agreeing on the election of a new pope: an Italian who took the name Martin V. But many of the council's delegates had even more far-reaching plans for the reform of the Church, ambitions that stemmed from the legal doctrine that gave the council power to depose and elect popes in the first place. This doctrine, known as conciliarism, holds that supreme authority within the Church rests not with the pope, but with a representative general council—and not just the council convened at Constance, but any future council. The delegates at Constance thus decreed that general councils should meet

**THE GREAT SCHISM, 1378–1417.** During the Great Schism, the various territories of Europe were divided in their allegiances. ▪ ***According to the map key, who were they choosing between?*** ▪ ***What common interests would have united the supporters of the Avignon pope, or the Roman pope?*** ▪ ***Why would areas like Portugal and Austria waver in their support?***

regularly to oversee the governance of the Church and to act as a check on the unbridled use of papal power.

Had conciliarism triumphed, the Reformation of the following century might not have occurred. But, predictably, Martin V and his successors did everything they could to undermine this doctrine, precisely because it limited their power. So when the next general council met at Siena in 1423, Pope Martin duly sent representatives—who then turned around and went back to Rome. (The Council of Constance had specified that councils must meet frequently, but had not specified how long those meetings should last.) The following year, the delegates to a general council at Basel took steps to ensure that the pope could not dismiss it, after which a lengthy struggle for power ensued between the advocates of papal monarchy and the conciliarists. Twenty-five years later, in 1449, the Council of Basel dissolved itself, bringing to an end a radical experiment in conciliar government—and dashing the hopes of those who thought

# Competing Viewpoints

## Council or Pope?

*The Great Schism spurred a fundamental and far-reaching debate about the nature of authority within the Church. Arguments for papal supremacy rested on traditional claims that the popes were the successors of Saint Peter, to whom Jesus Christ had delegated his own authority. Arguments for the supremacy of a general council had been advanced by many intellectuals throughout the fourteenth century, but it was only in the circumstances of the schism that these arguments found a wide audience. The following documents trace the history of the controversy, from the declaration of conciliar supremacy at the Council of Constance (*Haec Sancta*), to the council's efforts to guarantee regular meetings of general councils thereafter (*Frequens*), to the papal condemnation of appeals to the authority of general councils issued in 1460 (*Execrabilis*).*

### *Haec Sancta Synodus* (1415)

This holy synod of Constance . . . declares that being lawfully assembled in the Holy Spirit, constituting a general council and representing the Catholic Church Militant, it has its power directly from Christ, and that all persons of whatever rank or dignity, even a Pope, are bound to obey it in matters relating to faith and the end of the Schism and the general reformation of the church of God in head and members.

Further, it declares that any person of whatever position, rank, or dignity, even a Pope, who contumaciously refuses to obey the mandates, statutes, ordinances, or regulations enacted or to be enacted by this holy synod, or by any other general council lawfully assembled, relating to the matters aforesaid or to other matters involved with them, shall, unless he repents, be . . . duly punished. . . .

Source: R. L. Loomis, ed. and trans., *The Council of Constance* (New York: 1961), p. 229

### *Frequens* (1417)

The frequent holding of general councils is the best method of cultivating the field of the Lord, for they root out the briars, thorns, and thistles of heresies, errors, and schisms, correct abuses, make crooked things straight, and prepare the Lord's vineyard for fruitfulness and rich fertility. Neglect of general councils sows the seeds of these evils and encourages their growth. This truth is borne in upon us as we recall times past and survey the present.

Therefore by perpetual edict we . . . ordain that henceforth general councils shall be held as follows: the first within the five years immediately following the end of the present council, the second within seven years from the end of the council next after this, and subsequently every ten years forever. . . . Thus there will always be a certain continuity. Either

it would lead to an internal reformation thorough enough to keep the Roman Church intact.

## *The Growth of National Churches*

The papacy's victory over the conciliarists was a costly one in the short term, as well as in the long term. To win the support of Europe's kings and princes, various popes negotiated a series of treaties, known as "concordats," which granted these rulers extensive authority over churches within their domains. The popes thus secured their own theoretical supremacy by surrendering their real power. For under the terms of these concordats, kings now received many of the revenues that had previously gone to the papacy. They also acquired new powers to appoint candidates to church offices. It was a reversal of the hard-won reforms of the eleventh and twelfth centuries.

With both papal authority and spiritual prestige in decline, kings and princes became the primary figures to whom both clergy and laity looked for religious and moral guidance. Many secular rulers responded to such expec-

a council will be in session or one will be expected at the end of a fixed period. . . .

Source: R. L. Loomis, ed. and trans., *The Council of Constance* (New York: 1961), pp. 246–47

## *Execrabilis* (1460)

An execrable abuse, unheard of in earlier times, has sprung up in our period. Some men, imbued with a spirit of rebellion and moved not by a desire for sound decisions but rather by a desire to escape the punishment for sin, suppose that they can appeal from the Pope, Vicar of Jesus Christ—from the Pope, to whom in the person of blessed Peter it was said, "Feed my sheep" and "whatever you bind on earth will be bound in heaven"—from this Pope to a future council. How harmful this is to the Christian republic, as well as how contrary to canon law, anyone who is not ignorant of the law can understand. For . . . who would not consider it ridiculous to appeal to something which does not now exist anywhere nor does anyone know when it will exist? The poor are heavily oppressed by the powerful, offenses remain unpunished, rebellion against the Holy See is encouraged, license for sin is granted, and all ecclesiastical discipline and hierarchical ranking of the Church are turned upside down.

Wishing therefore to expel this deadly poison from the Church of Christ, and concerned with the salvation of the sheep committed to us . . . with the counsel and assent of our venerable brothers, the Cardinals of the Holy Roman Church, together with the counsel and assent of all those prelates who have been trained in canon and civil law who follow our Court, and with our own certain knowledge, we condemn appeals of this kind, reject them as erroneous and abominable, and declare them to be completely null and void. And we lay down that from now on, no one should dare . . . to make such an appeal from our decisions, be they legal or theological, or from any commands at all from us or our successors. . . .

Source: Reprinted by permission of the publisher from *Defensorum Obedientiae Apostolicae Et Alia Documenta* by Gabriel Biel, edited and translated by Heiko A. Oberman, Daniel E. Zerfoss, and William J. Courtenay, pp. 224–27, Cambridge, Mass.: The Belknap Press of Harvard University Press, Copyright © 1968 by the President and Fellows of Harvard College.

### *Questions for Analysis*

1. On what grounds does *Haec Sancta* establish the authority of a council? Why would this be considered a threat to papal power?
2. Why was it considered necessary for councils to meet regularly (*Frequens*)? What might have been the logical consequences of such regular meetings?
3. On what grounds does *Execrabilis* condemn the appeals to future councils that have no specified meeting date? Why would it not have condemned the conciliar movement altogether?

tations aggressively, closing scandal-ridden monasteries, suppressing alleged heretics, regulating prostitution, and prohibiting the lower classes from dressing as if they were nobles. By these and other such measures, rulers could present themselves as champions of moral reform while also strengthening their political power. The result was an increasingly close link between national monarchies and national churches, a link that would become even stronger after the Reformation (see Chapter 13).

Having given away so many sources of revenue, the popes of the late fifteenth century became even more dependent on their own territories in central Italy. But to tighten their hold on the Papal States they had to rule like other Italian princes: leading armies, jockeying for alliances, and undermining their oppponents by every possible means—including covert operations, murder, and assassination. Judged by the secular standards of the day, these efforts paid off: the Papal States became one of the better-governed and wealthier principalities in Italy. But such methods did nothing to increase the popes' reputation for piety, and disillusionment with the papacy as a force for the advancement of spirituality became even more widespread.

## THE PURSUIT OF HOLINESS

Despite the travails of the institutional Church, religious devotion among the laity was more widespread and intense during the later Middle Ages than it had ever been. The fundamental theme of preachers in this era, that salvation lay open to any Christian who strove for it, bore fruit in the multiplying variety of paths that could lead to God. Some of these paths led believers in directions the Church declared heretical. But for the vast majority of Christians, extreme forms of dissent held no appeal. The local parish church, and especially the sacraments performed by the parish priest, became the center of religious life. To understand late medieval Christianity, we therefore need to start in the parish.

### *Sacrament and Ritual*

Innocent III's insistence that all Christians should have direct access to sound religious instruction (Chapter 9) ensured that nearly all of Europe was covered by a network of local parish churches by the time of the Black Death. In these churches, parish priests administered the sacraments ("holy rites") that conveyed the grace of God to individual Christians and that marked significant moments in the lifecycle of every person. Late medieval piety revolved around these sacraments, of which there were seven: baptism, confirmation, confession (or penance), marriage, extreme unction, ordination, and communion. Baptism, a ceremony of initiation administered in the early centuries of Christianity to adults (Chapter 6), became in the course of the Middle Ages a sacrament administered to infants as soon as possible after birth. Confirmation of adolescents therefore "confirmed" the promises made on a child's behalf at baptism by parents and godparents. Periodic confession of sins to a priest guaranteed forgiveness by God, for if a sinner did not perform appropriate acts of penance to atone for sins, penance would have to be completed in Purgatory, the netherworld between Heaven and Hell. Marriage was a relatively new sacrament, increasingly emphasized in the later Middle Ages but very seldom practiced; for in order to be valid, marriage in this period required only that solemn promises be exchanged by a man and a woman, and in many cases the fact of cohabitation was taken to be proof of marriage. Extreme unction (or last rites) was administered to a dying person. It ensured the final absolution of all sins and so was essential to the assurance of salvation.

Like baptism, extreme unction could, in an emergency, be administered by any Christian believer. The other sacraments, however, could be administered only by a properly ordained priest—or, in the case of confirmation and ordination, by a bishop. Ordination was therefore the only sacrament reserved for the small percentage of Christians who became priests, and it conveyed to the priest his special authority to share God's grace through the sacraments: a power that could never be lost, even by a priest who led an immoral life.

This sacramental system was the foundation on which the practices of late medieval popular piety rested. Pilgrimages, for example, were a form of penance, and could lessen one's time in Purgatory. Crusading was a kind of extreme pilgrimage that promised the complete fulfillment of all

**THE REAL PRESENCE OF CHRIST.** This painting, executed in the mid-fifteenth century, refers to a popular legend underscoring the truth of transubstantiation. According to this legend, Pope Gregory the Great (c. 540–604) was celebrating Mass in his private chapel when he had a vision of the crucified Christ, whose body and blood were rendered visible when he consecrated the bread and wine on the altar. Here, Christ displays his wounds to the astonished onlookers. The instruments of Christ's passion—the people and implements that tortured and killed him—are also displayed.

penances the crusader might owe for all the sins of his (or her) life. Many other pious acts—saying the prayers of the rosary, for example, or giving alms to the poor—could also serve as penance for one's sins while constituting good works that would help the believer in his or her journey toward salvation.

But the sacrament that was most central to the religious lives of medieval Christians was the communion ceremony of the Mass (or the Eucharist). As we noted in Chapter 9, the ritual power of the Mass was greatly enhanced in the twelfth century, when the Church began promoting the doctrine of transubstantiation. Christians attending Mass understood that when the priest spoke the ritual words "This is my body" and "This is my blood," the substances of bread and wine held in the priest's hands were miraculously transformed into the body and blood of Jesus Christ. To consume one or both of these substances was to ingest holiness; and so powerful was this idea that many Christians only received the sacramental bread once a year, at Easter.

But to share in the miracle of the Eucharist one did not have to consume it: one had only to witness the elevation of the Host. So daily attendance at Mass merely to view the Host became a common form of devotion, as did the practice of displaying a consecrated wafer in a special reliquary called a monstrance ("show case"), which could be set up on a special altar or carried through the streets on feast days. Believers sometimes attributed astonishing properties to the eucharistic Host, feeding it to sick animals or rushing from church to church to see the consecrated bread as many times as possible in a day. Some of these practices were criticized by reformers as superstitious or even heretical. But by and large, these expressions of devotion were encouraged, and efforts to stop them were also met with staunch opposition from faithful laymen and laywomen.

## Spirituality and the Social Order

The spiritual and social lives of medieval Christians were inextricably intertwined; indeed, any distinction between the two would have made little sense to the people of this era. The parish church stood literally at the center of their lives. Churchyards were communal meeting places, sometimes even the sites of markets, and church buildings were a refuge from attack and a gathering place for parish business. The church's holidays marked the passage of the year, and the church's bells marked the hours of the day. The church was holy, but it was also essential to daily life.

Yet some medieval Christians—many regarded today as saints—were not satisfied with these conventional practices and developed forms of piety that were distinctly controversial during their lifetimes. Indeed, the distinction between the superhuman powers of a saint and those of a witch could be difficult to discern. As Joan of Arc's predicament reveals, medieval women found it particularly challenging to find outlets for their piety that would not earn them the condemnation of the Church. Many women therefore internalized those practices or confined them to the domestic sphere—sometimes to the inconvenience of their families and communities. For example, the young Catherine of Siena refused to help with the housework or to support her working-class family, and instead took over one of the house's two rooms for her own private prayers, confining her parents and a dozen siblings to the remaining room. Julianna of Norwich (1342–1416) withdrew from the world into a small cell built next to her local church, where she spent the rest of her life in prayer and contemplation. Her younger contemporary, the housewife Margery Kempe (c. 1372–c. 1439), resented the fact that she had a husband, several children, and a household to support, and thus could not take such a step. In later life, she renounced her wifely duties and devoted her life to performing acts of histrionic piety which alienated most of those who came into contact with her. For example, she was so moved by the contemplation of Jesus' sufferings on the cross that she would cry hysterically for hours, disrupting the Mass. When on pilgrimage in Rome, she cried at the sight of babies that reminded her of the infant Jesus, or young men whom she thought resembled him.

The extraordinary piety of such individuals could be inspiring, but it could also threaten the Church's control over religious life and the links that bound individuals to their communities. It could, therefore, be dangerous. Some believers who sought to achieve a mystical union with God through rigorous prayer, penance, and personal sacrifice were ultimately condemned for heresy because they did not subordinate their mystical quests to the authority of the Church, and indeed declared that it was not necessary to obey God's Church on earth. Even less radical figures might find themselves treading on dangerous ground, especially if they published their experiences and ideas in the vernacular. The preacher Master Eckhart (c. 1260–1327), a German Dominican, taught that there was a "spark" deep within every human soul, and it was in this spark that God lived. Through prayer and self-renunciation, any person could therefore retreat into the inner recesses of her being and access divinity. This conveyed the message that a layperson might attain salvation through her own efforts, without the intervention of a priest. As a result, many of Eckhart's teachings were condemned as heretical. More safely orthodox was the practical mysticism preached by Thomas à Kempis, whose *Imitation of Christ* (c. 1427) taught readers how to appreciate aspects of the divine in their everyday lives. Originally written in Latin, the *Imitation* was quickly translated into many vernacular languages and is now more widely read than any other Christian book except the Bible.

## Lollards and Hussites

For the most part, the threat of heretical movements was less dangerous to the Church than the corruption of the papacy. But in England and Bohemia, some popular movements did pose serious challenges. The key figure in both cases was John Wyclif (c. 1330–1384), an Oxford theologian and powerful critic of the Church. A survivor of the Black Death, Wyclif lived at a time when the authority and integrity of the papacy were at a particularly low ebb. Indeed, he concluded that the empty sacraments of a corrupt Church could not save anyone. He therefore urged the English king to confiscate ecclesiastical wealth and to replace corrupt priests and bishops with men who would live according to apostolic standards of poverty and piety. Some of Wyclif's followers, known to their detractors as Lollards (from a word meaning "mumblers" or "beggars"), went even further, dismissing the sacraments as fraudulent attempts to extort money from the faithful. Lollard preachers also advocated for direct access to the Scriptures, and promoted an English translation of the Bible attributed to Wyclif himself.

Wylclif's teachings played an important role in the Peasants' Revolt of 1381, and Lollardy gained numerous adherents in the decades after his death. The movement was even supported by a number of aristocratic families; certainly the idea of the dissolving the Church's wealth would have been attractive to many of those who stood to gain from it. But after a failed Lollard uprising in 1414, both the movement and its supporters went underground in England.

In Bohemia and eastern Europe, however, Wyclif's ideas lived on and struck even deeper roots. They were adopted by Jan Hus (c. 1373–1415), a charismatic teacher at the royal university in Prague. In contrast to the Lollards, who had scornfully dismissed the Mass and thereby lost much popular support, Hus emphasized the centrality of the Eucharist to Christian piety. Indeed, he demanded that the laity be allowed to receive not only the consecrated bread but also the consecrated wine, which was usually reserved solely for priests. This demand became a rallying cry for the Hussite movement. Influential nobles also supported Hus, partly in the hope that the reforms he demanded might restore revenues they had lost to the Church over the previous century. Accordingly, most of Bohemia was behind him when Hus traveled to the Council of Constance to publish his views and to urge the assembled delegates to undertake sweeping reforms.

But rather than giving him a hearing, the other delegates to the council convicted Hus of heresy and had him burned at the stake. Back home, Hus's supporters raised the banner of open revolt, and the aristocracy took advantage of the situation to seize Church property. Between 1420 and 1424, armed bands of fervent Hussites resoundingly

Základ Přt Mistra Jana Husa Swaté
paměti/zknih geho wybraný.
Wjce slussj poslauchati Boha nežli lidj.
Zákon Krystů dostatečný gest k zprawowánj Cýrkwe
rytěřugjcý/bezpřičjněnj a přimjssenj zákonů lidských.

Po Sm letech Bohu a mně odpowjdati budete.

Hęc pictura refert faciem venerabilis Hussi,
Quem genuit gremio terra Bohema suo.

Čechowé náſſi neyvkrutněgſſj nepřátelé/wydali nás gi-
ným nepřátelům wmoc a vwězenj.
To psal wlistu zwězenj.
Ppp iij.

**THE TEACHINGS OF JAN HUS.** An eloquent religious reformer, Jan Hus was burned at the stake in 1415 after having been found guilty of heresy at the Council of Constance. This lavishly illustrated booklet of his teachings was published over a century later in his native Bohemia, and includes texts in the Czech vernacular and in Latin. ▪ ***What does its later publication suggest about the uses to which Hus's image and theology were put during the Protestant Reformation?***

defeated several armies, as priests, artisans, and peasants rallied to pursue Hus's goals of religious reform and social justice. These victories increased popular fervor, but they also made these radical reformers increasingly volatile. In 1434, accordingly, a more conservative arm of the Hussite movement was able to negotiate a settlement with the Bohemian church. By the terms of this settlement, Bohemians could receive both the bread and wine of the Mass, which thus placed them beyond the pale of Latin orthodoxy and effectively separated the Bohemian national church from the Church of Rome.

Lollardy and Hussitism exhibit a number of striking similarities. Both began in the university and then spread to the countryside. Both called for the clergy to live in simplicity and poverty, and both attracted noble support, especially in their early days. Both movements were also strongly nationalistic, employing their own vernacular languages (English and Czech) and identifying themselves with the English or Czech people in opposition to a "foreign" Church. They also relied on vernacular preaching and social activism. In all these respects, they established patterns that would emerge again in the vastly larger currents of the Protestant Reformation (Chapter 13).

## MEDIEVAL CREATIVITY AND INNOVATION

Many of the extraordinary achievements of the later Middle Ages have often been ascribed to the Renaissance, the name given to an intellectual and artistic movement that began concurrently in Italy, in the fourteenth and fifteenth centuries. We will discuss the causes and outcomes of this movement more fully in Chapter 12. For now, we focus on parallel developments closely tied to the trends discussed above.

### *Knowledge of the World and of God*

In the thirteenth century, Thomas Aquinas had constructed a theological view of the world as rational, organized, and comprehensible to the inquiring human mind (Chapter 9). Confidence in this picture began to wane in the fourteenth century, even before the Black Death posed a new challenge to it. Philosophers such as the English Franciscan William of Ockham (d. 1349) denied that human reason could prove fundamental theological truths such as the existence of God. Instead, he argued that human knowledge of God, and hence salvation, depends entirely on what God himself has chosen to reveal through scripture. Humans can investigate the natural world, but there is no necessary connection between the observable regularities of nature and the unknowable essence of divinity.

This philosophical position, known as nominalism, has its roots in the philosophy of Plato (Chapter 4) and has had an enormous impact on modern thought. The nominalists' distinction between the rational comprehensibility of the natural world and the incomprehensibility of God encourages investigation of the natural world without reference to supernatural explanations: one of the most important foundations of the modern scientific method (see Chapter 16). Nominalism also encourages empirical observation by positing that knowledge of the world should rest on sensory experience rather than abstraction. Late medieval philosophy is thus fundamental to modern science.

### *Capturing Reality in Writing*

The entertainments of the later Middle Ages also exhibit an intense interest in the the world as it is. Such naturalism was not new, but later medieval authors were able to reach a far larger and more diverse audience than their predecessors. For increasingly, the most innovative and ambitious ideas were expressed in the vernacular languages of Europe. Behind this phenomenon lay three interrelated developments: the growing identification between vernacular language and nationalism, the increasing accessibility of lay education, and the emergence of a substantial reading public for vernacular literature. We can see these influences at work in three of the major authors of this period: Giovanni Boccaccio, Geoffrey Chaucer, and Christine de Pisan.

Boccaccio (*bohk-KAHT-chee-oh*, 1313–1375) is best known for the *Decameron*, a collection of prose tales about sex, adventure, and trickery which he represents as being told over a period of ten days by a sophisticated party of ten young women and men temporarily residing in a country villa outside Florence to escape the Black Death. Boccaccio borrowed the outlines of many of these tales from earlier sources, especially the fabliaux discussed in Chapter 9, but he couched them in a freely colloquial style, in an attempt to capture the relationships and foibles of real human beings. His men and women are flesh-and-blood creatures with minds and bodies, who interact comfortably and naturally. Indeed, Boccaccio's treatment of sexual relations is often graphic.

Similar in many ways to Boccaccio, whose influence on him was profound, is the English poet Geoffrey Chaucer (c. 1340–1400). Chaucer was among the first generation of

English authors whose compositions can be understood by modern readers with relatively little effort. For by the fourteenth century, the Anglo-Saxon language of England's pre-Conquest inhabitants had mixed with the French spoken by their Norman conquerors, to create the language which is the ancestor of our own. Chaucer's masterpiece is the *Canterbury Tales*. Like the *Decameron*, this is a collection of stories held together by a framing narrative: in this case, the stories are told by an array of people traveling together on a pilgrimage from London to the shrine of Saint Thomas Becket at Canterbury. But there are also significant differences between the *Decameron* and the *Canterbury Tales*. Chaucer's stories are in verse, for the most part, and they are recounted by people of all different classes—from a high-minded knight to a poor university student to a lusty widow. Each character tells a story that is particularly illustrative of his or her own occupation and outlook on the world, forming a kaleidoscopic human comedy.

The later Middle Ages also saw the emergence of professional authors who made their living with their pens. Significantly, one of the first was a woman, Christine de Pisan (c. 1365–c. 1434). Although born in northern Italy, Christine spent her adult life in France, where her husband was a member of the king's household. When he died, the widowed Christine wrote to support herself and her children. She mastered a wide variety of literary genres, including treatises on chivalry and warfare that she dedicated to her patron, Charles VI of France. She also wrote for a larger and more popular audience. Her imaginative *Book of the City of Ladies* is an extended defense of the character, capacities, and history of women, designed to refute their male detractors. Christine also took part in a vigorous pamphlet campaign that refuted misogynistic claims made by male authors like Boccaccio. This debate was ongoing for several hundred years, and became so famous that it was given a name: the *querelle des femmes*, "the debate over women." Remarkably, Christine also wrote a song in praise of Joan of Arc. Sadly, she probably lived long enough to learn that this other extraordinary woman had been put to death for behaving in a way that was considered unwomanly.

## Visualizing Reality

Just as naturalism was a dominant trait of late medieval literature, so it was of later medieval art. Whereas earlier medieval art had emphasized abstract design, the sculptors of the thirteenth century were already paying close attention to the way plants, animals, and human beings really looked. Carvings of leaves and flowers were now being made from direct observation and are clearly recognizable to modern botanists as distinct species. Statues of humans also became more realistic in their portrayals of facial expressions and bodily proportions. According to a story in circulation around 1290, a sculptor working on a likeness of the German emperor allegedly made a hurried return trip to study his subject's face a second time, because he'd heard that a new wrinkle had appeared on the emperor's brow.

In the fourteenth and fifteenth centuries, the trend toward naturalism in sculpture was extended to manuscript illumination and painting. The latter was, to a large extent, a new art. As we saw in Chapter 1, walls paintings are one of the oldest forms of artistic expression in human history, and throughout antiquity and the Middle Ages artists had decorated the walls of public and private buildings with frescoes (paintings executed on "fresh"—wet—plaster). But in addition to frescoes, Italian artists in the thirteenth century began to

**CHRISTINE DE PISAN.** One of the most prolific authors of the fifteenth century, Christine used her influence to uphold the dignity of women and to celebrate their history and achievements. Here she is seen describing the prowess of an Amazon warrior who could defeat men effortlessly in armed combat.

# Analyzing Primary Sources

## *Why a Woman Can Write about Warfare*

*Christine de Pisan (c. 1365–c. 1434) was one of the West's first professional writers, best known today for her* Book of the City of Ladies *and* The Treasure of the City of Ladies, *works which aimed to provide women with an honorable and rich history, and to combat generations of institutionalized misogyny. But in her own time, she was probably best known for the work excerpted here,* The Book of the Deeds of Arms and of Chivalry, *a manual of military strategy and conduct written at the height of the Hundred Years' War, in 1410.*

As boldness is essential for great undertakings, and without it nothing should be risked, I think it is proper in this present work to set forth my unworthiness to treat such exalted matter. I should not have dared even to think about it, but although boldness is blameworthy when it is foolhardy, I should state that I have not been inspired by arrogance or foolish presumption, but rather by true affection and a genuine desire for the welfare of noble men engaging in the profession of arms. I am encouraged, in the light of my other writings, to undertake to speak in this book of the most honorable office of arms and chivalry. . . . So to this end I have gathered together facts and subject matter from various books to produce this present volume. But inasmuch as it is fitting for this matter to be discussed factually, diligently, and sensibly . . . and also in consideration of the fact that military and lay experts in the aforesaid art of chivalry are not usually clerks or writers who are expert in language, I intend to treat the matter in the plainest possible language. . . .

As this is unusual for women, who generally are occupied in weaving, spinning, and household duties, I humbly invoke . . . the wise lady Minerva [Athena], born in the land of Greece, whom the ancients esteemed highly for her great wisdom. Likewise the poet Boccaccio praises her in his *Book of Famous Women*, as do other writers praise her art and manner of making trappings of iron and steel, so let it not be held against me if I, as a woman, take it upon myself to treat of military matters. . . .

O Minerva! goddess of arms and of chivalry, who, by understanding beyond that of other women, did find and initiate among the other noble arts and sciences the custom of forging iron and steel armaments and harness both proper and suitable for covering and protecting men's bodies against arrows slung in battle—helmets, shields, and protective covering having come first from you—you instituted and gave directions for drawing up a battle order, how to begin an assault and to engage in proper combat. . . . In the aforementioned country of Greece, you provided the usage of this office, and insofar as it may please you to be favorably disposed, and I in no way appear to be against the nation from which you came, the country beyond the Alps that is now called Apulia and Calabria in Italy, where you were born, let me say that like you I am an Italian woman.

Source: From *The Book of the Deeds of Arms and of Chivalry*, trans. Sumner Willard and ed. Charity Cannon Willard (University Park, PA: 1999), pp. 11–13.

### *Questions for Analysis*

1. Christine very cleverly deflects potential criticism for her "boldness" in writing about warfare. What tactics does she use?
2. The Greco-Roman goddess Athena (Minerva) was the goddess of wisdom, weaving, and warfare. Why does Christine invoke her aid? What parallels does she draw between her own attributes and those of Minerva?

adapt the techniques used by icon painters in Byzantium, painting free-standing pictures on pieces of wood or canvas using tempera (pigments mixed with water and natural gums). Around 1400, painting in oils was introduced in the Low Countries, and these techniques soon spread southward to Italy and beyond.

This diversification of artistic media created new aesthetic and commercial opportunities. Artists were now able to paint and sell portable altarpieces, devotional images, and portraits. And so long as they could afford the necessary materials, they did not have to wait for a specific commission from a patron. This meant that they had more freedom to choose their subject matter and to put an individual stamp on their work—one of the reasons why we know the names of so many late-medieval artists. One of these, Giotto di Bondone of Florence (c. 1267–1337), painted both walls and portable wooden panels. Giotto (*gee-AHT-toh*) was preeminently an imitator of nature. Not only do his human beings and animals look lifelike, they seem to do natural things. When Christ enters Jerusalem on Palm Sunday, boys climb trees to get a better view; when Saint Francis is laid out in death, someone checks to see whether he has really received the marks of Christ's wounds, the *stigmata*; and when the Virgin's parents, Joachim and Anna, meet after a long separation, they embrace and kiss one another tenderly. Although many of the artists who came after Giotto moved away from naturalism, this style became the norm by 1400. It is for this reason that he is often regarded as the first painter of the Renaissance, a movement that is really an outgrowth of the later Middle Ages (see Chapter 12).

In northern Europe, manuscript illumination remained the dominant artistic medium, and during this period many breathtaking books were created for wealthy patrons like the duke of Berry (noted above). But oil painting also caught on, especially in Flanders, where artists found a market for their works among the nobility and wealthy merchants. Practitioners like Rogier van der Weyden (c. 1400–1464) excelled at communicating both deep piety and the minute details of everyday experience (see ***Interpreting Visual Evidence***). Just as contemporary spirituality saw divinity in material objects, so a Flemish painter could portray the Virgin and Child against a background vista of contemporary life, with people going about their business or a man urinating against a wall. This was not blasphemous; quite the contrary. It conveyed the message that the events of the Bible are constantly present, here and now: Christ is contemporary, not some distant figure whose life and experiences are irrelevant to us.

***THE MEETING OF JOACHIM AND ANNA*** **BY GIOTTO.** According to legend, Anna and Joachim were an aged and infertile couple who were able to conceive their only child, Mary, through divine intervention. Since Mary was supposed to have been conceived without the taint of sin, theologians taught that she had been miraculously engendered without sexual contact. Hence, this painting may portray the moment of her conception—but it also portrays the affection of husband and wife. ▪ ***What values does it convey to the viewer?***

The same immediacy is also evident in medieval drama. Plays were often devotional exercises that involved the efforts of an entire community. In the English city of York, for example, an annual series of pageants reenacted the entire history of human salvation from the Creation to the Last Judgment in a single summer day, beginning at dawn and ending late at night. Each pageant was produced by a particular craft guild and showcased that guild's special talents: "The Last Supper" was performed by the bakers, whose bread was a key element in their reenactment of the first Eucharist, while "The Crucifixion" was performed by the nail-makers, whose wares were thereby put on prominent display. In Italy, confraternities competed with one another to honor the saints with songs and processions. In Spain and Catalonia, there were elaborate dramas celebrating the life and miracles of the Virgin, one of which is still performed every year in the Basque town of Elche: it is the oldest European play in continuous production. Elsewhere on the Continent there were civic spectacles performed over a period of several days. But not all plays were pious. Some honored visiting kings and princes. Others celebrated the flouting of social conventions, featuring cross-dressing and the reversal of hierarchies.

## Technological Advances

In the later Middle Ages, as in other places and times, warfare was the engine driving the development of many new technologies. Although explosive powder had been invented in China, it was first put to devastating use in the guns of the Hundred Years' War. The earliest cannons were as dangerous to those who fired them as to those who were targeted, but by the middle of the fifteenth century they were reliable enough to revolutionize the nature of warfare. In 1453, heavy artillery played a leading role in

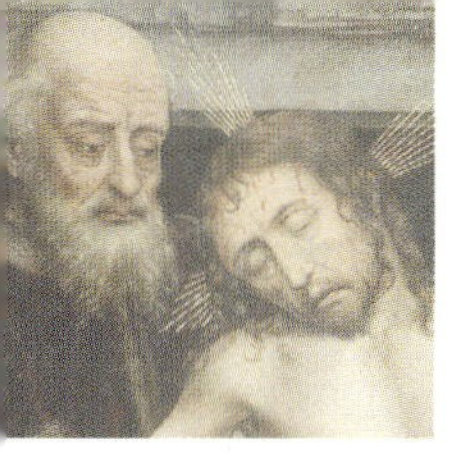

# Interpreting Visual Evidence

## *Realizing Devotion*

These two paintings by the Flemish artist Rogier van der Weyden (*FAN-der-VIE-den*, c. 1400–1464) capture some of the most compelling characteristics of late medieval art, particularly the trend toward realistic representations of holy figures and sacred stories. On the left (image A), the artist depicts himself as the evangelist Luke, regarded in Christian tradition as a painter of portraits; he sketches the Virgin nursing the infant Jesus in a town house overlooking a Flemish city. On the right (image B), van der Weyden imagines the entombment of the dead Christ by his followers, including the Virgin (left), Mary Magdalene (kneeling), and the disciple John (right). Here, he makes use of a motif that became increasingly prominent in the later Middle Ages: Christ as the Man of Sorrows, displaying his wounds and inviting the viewer to share in his suffering. In both paintings, van der Weyden emphasizes the humanity of his subjects rather than their iconic status (see Chapter 7), and he places them in the urban and rural landscapes of his own world.

### *Questions for Analysis*

1. How are these paintings different from the sacred images of the earlier Middle Ages (see, for example, pages 213 and 290)? What messages does the artist convey by setting these events in his own immediate present?
2. In what ways do these paintings reflect broad changes in popular piety and medieval devotional practices? Why, for example, would the artist display the dead and wounded body of Christ—rather than depicting him as resurrected and triumphant, or as an all-seeing creator and judge?
3. In general, how would you use these images as evidence of the worldview of the fifteenth century? What do they tell us about people's attitudes, emotions, and values?

A. Saint Luke drawing the portrait of the Virgin.

B. The Deposition.

the outcomes of two crucial conflicts: the Ottoman Turks breached the defenses of Constantinople (see Chapter 11) and the French captured the city of Bordeaux, thereby ending the Hundred Years' War. Thereafter, cannons made it more difficult for rebellious aristocrats to hole up in their stone castles, and so consequently aided in the consolidation of national monarchies. Cannons placed aboard ships made Europe's developing navies more effective. A handheld firearm, the pistol, was also invented in the fourteenth century, and around 1500 the musket ended forever the military dominance of heavily armored cavalry, giving the advantage to foot soldiers.

Other late medieval technologies were more life enhancing. Eyeglasses, first invented in the 1280s, were perfected in the fourteenth century, extending the careers of those who made a living by reading and writing. The use of the magnetic compass helped ships sail farther away from land. Subsequently, numerous improvements in shipbuilding, mapmaking, and navigational devices enabled Europeans to venture out into the Atlantic. We will discuss the implications of these developments in Chapter 11.

Among the many implements of modern daily life invented in this era, the most familiar are clocks and printed books. Mechanical clocks came into use shortly before 1300 and proliferated immediately thereafter. They were too large and expensive for private purchase, but towns vied with one another to install them in prominent public buildings, thus advertising municipal wealth and good governance. Mechanical timekeeping had two profound effects. One was the further stimulation of interest in complex machinery of all sorts, an interest already awakened by the widespread use of mills in the eleventh and twelfth centuries (Chapter 8). More significant was the way that clocks regulated daily life. Until the advent of clocks, time was flexible. Days had been theoretically divided into hours and hours into minutes and minutes into seconds since the time of the Sumerians (Chapter 1), but there had never been a way of mapping these temporal measurements onto an actual day. Clocks relentlessly divided time into exact units and thus gave rise to new expectations about labor and productivity. People were expected to start and end work "on time," and many came to believe that "time is money." This emphasis on timekeeping brought new efficiencies but also created new tensions and obsessions.

The development of printing was even more momentous. A major stimulus for this was the more widespread availability of paper. Parchment, Europe's chief writing material since the seventh century, was extremely expensive

**A FIFTEENTH-CENTURY SIEGE WITH CANNON.** Cannons were an essential element in siege warfare during the Hundred Years' War and thereafter.

**THE SPREAD OF PRINTING.** This map shows how quickly the technology of printing spread throughout Europe between 1470 and 1500. ▪ ***In what regions were printing presses most heavily concentrated? ▪ What factors would have led to their proliferation in the Low Countries, northern Italy, and Germany—as compared to France, Spain, and England? ▪ Why would so many have been located along waterways?***

**DEVIL WITH EYEGLASSES.** Spectacles were most commonly worn by those who made a living by reading and writing, notably bureaucrats and lawyers. In this conceptualization of Hell, the devil charged with keeping track of human sin wears eyeglasses. ▪ ***What might this image reveal about popular attitudes toward record-keeping and the growing legal and administrative bureaucracies of the later Middle Ages?***

to manufacture and even required special training on the part of scribes—one reason why writing remained a specialized skill for much of the Middle Ages, while the ability to read was common. Paper, made from rags turned into pulp by mills, was both cheaper and far easier to use. Accordingly, reading and writing also became cheaper and easier. Increased literacy led to a growing demand for books, which in turn led to experimentation with different methods of book production. A breakthrough came around 1450, when it was discovered that movable type (cast-iron letter forms and punctuation marks) could be slotted into frames to form lines of words, and whole pages could thus be reproduced by coating those frames with ink and pressing them onto paper or parchment, after which the type could be reused. The most famous early result of this technique is the Bible completed in the workshop of Johann Gutenberg in Mainz, around 1454.

By saving labor and time, the printing press made the cost of printed books about one fifth as expensive as hand-copied books and made book culture a more basic part of daily life. Printing thereby facilitated the more rapid exchange of information and ideas, and also made it more difficult for those in power to suppress these ideas effectively. Martin Luther could create an immediate and far-flung network of support by employing this new communication technology (Chapter 13); had printing not been available, he might have died ignominously, as Hus had done a century before. The spread of books also standardized national languages. Regional dialects were often so diverse that

# After You Read This Chapter

Visit StudySpace for quizzes, additional review materials, and multi-media documents. **wwnorton.com/studyspace**

## REVIEWING THE OBJECTIVES

- The Black Death had short-term and long-term effects on the economy and societies of Europe. What were some of the most important changes?
- The melding of strong kingship with the promotion of national identity was a new development in the later Middle Ages. What circumstances made this possible? Why is this development significant?
- Several key factors enabled the growth of a Russian state centered on Muscovy. What were they?
- The conciliar movement sought to limit the power of the papacy. How? Why was this movement unsuccessful?
- In what ways do the spiritual, cultural, and technological innovations of the later Middle Ages reflect the political, social, and economic changes brought about by the Black Death?

people living within the same state could not understand each other. Now, each European country began to develop its own linguistic standards, which could be disseminated more uniformly through the imposition of these standards. For example, the "king's English," the dialect of London, could be promulgated throughout the realm, allowing the government to operate more efficiently.

## CONCLUSION

The later Middle Ages constitute a period of tremendous creativity and revolutionary change. The effects of the Black Death were catastrophic, but the resulting labor shortages encouraged experimentation and opened up new opportunities. Europe's economy diversified and expanded. Increasing wealth and access to education produced new inventions, ideas, and forms of art. Between 1300 and 1500, hundreds and perhaps thousands of new schools were established, and scores of new universities emerged. Medieval intellectuals came to see the natural world as operating according to its own laws, which were empirically verifiable and which did not necessarily reflect the mind of God: an essential step toward the emergence of a scientific worldview. Women were still excluded from formal schooling, but nevertheless became active—and perhaps dominant—participants in literate culture and in the religious life of their communities. Average men and women also became more active in cultivating their own individual spiritualities, at a time when the institutional Church provided little inspiring leadership. Meanwhile, incessant warfare enabled more powerful governments to harvest a larger percentage of their subjects' wealth through taxation, which they proceeded to invest in ships, guns, and the standing armies made possible by new technologies and more effective administration.

In short, the generations who survived the calamaties of famine, plague, and warfare seized the opportunities their new world presented to them. By 1500, most Europeans lived more secure lives than their ancestors had, and they stood on the verge of an extraordinary period of expansion and conquest that enabled them to dominate the globe.

### PEOPLE, IDEAS, AND EVENTS IN CONTEXT

- Compare and contrast the **BLACK DEATH'S** effects on rural and urban areas.
- In what ways do the rebellions of the later fourteenth and fifteenth centuries reflect the changes brought about by the plague? How did the nobility of Europe respond to this changing world?
- What were the main causes and consequences of the **HUNDRED YEARS' WAR?** How did **FERDINAND AND ISABELLA** begin to construct a national monarchy in Spain?
- On what grounds did **MUSCOVY** claim to be "the third Rome"? What is the significance of **IVAN THE GREAT'S** use of the title ***TSAR?***
- How did the **COUNCIL OF CONSTANCE** respond to the crisis of the **GREAT SCHISM?**
- How did the teachings of **JOHN WYCLIF** and **JAN HUS** critique religious trends?
- What were the major artistic and technological innovations of the later Middle Ages?

### CONSEQUENCES

- In 2000, a group of historians was asked to identify the most significant historical figure of the past millennium; but rather than choosing a person (e.g., Martin Luther, Napoleon, Adolf Hitler) they chose the microbe *Yersinia pestis*. Do you agree with this assessment? Why or why not?
- In your view, which was more crucial to the formation of the modern state: the political and legal developments we surveyed in Chapter 9 or the emergence of national identities in the later Middle Ages? Why?
- Was the conciliar movement doomed to failure, given what we have learned about the history of the Roman Church? How far back does one need to go, in order to trace the development of disputes over ecclestiastical governance?

# Before You Read This Chapter

## STORY LINES

- The consolidation of the Mongol Empire briefly opened new channels of communication and commerce between Europe and the Far East, spurring exploration by Europeans in subsequent centuries.
- Muslim caliphates were weakened by the Mongols but were more directly challenged by the Ottoman Turks, who eventually established themselves as leaders of the Islamic world and the new rulers of the former Byzantine Empire.
- Europeans' hunger for spices and gold led to the establishment of colonies in the Mediterranean and Atlantic, and spurred trading ventures to Africa and the Indies. Advances in technology made longer voyages possible, while developments in weaponry facilitated conquest.
- As the Portuguese came to control African and Asian routes, the Spanish sought to discover a westward route to the Indies—with unforeseen and far-reaching consequences.

## CHRONOLOGY

| | |
|---|---|
| 1206–1260 | Expansion of the Mongol Empire |
| 1271–1295 | Travels of Marco Polo |
| 1345–1389 | Rise of the Ottoman Turks |
| 1352 | Publication of the *Book of Marvels* by Jehan de Mandeville |
| 1420–1440 | Colonization of the Canary Islands and the Azores |
| 1453 | Turks conquer Constantinople |
| 1488 | Bartolomeu Dias rounds the Cape of Good Hope |
| 1492 | Columbus lands on Hispaniola |
| 1497–1498 | Vasco da Gama reaches India |
| 1511–1515 | The Portuguese venture into Indonesia |
| 1513 | Balboa reaches the Pacific Ocean |
| 1519–1522 | Magellan's fleet circumnavigates the globe |
| 1521 | Cortés conquers the Aztecs |
| 1533 | Pizarro conquers the Incas |
| 1571 | Ottoman expansion is halted at the Battle of Lepanto |

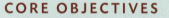

## CORE OBJECTIVES

- **DESCRIBE** the effects of the Mongol conquests.
- **EXPLAIN** the consequences of the Ottoman Empire's dependence on slave labor.
- **IDENTIFY** the factors that drove exploration and colonialism in the fourteenth and fifteenth centuries.
- **DEFINE** the essential difference between modern slavery and that of all previous civilizations.
- **UNDERSTAND** the far-reaching impact of the New World conquests.

# Commerce, Conquest, and Colonization, 1300–1600

When Christopher Columbus set sail from Genoa in 1492, he carried with him two influential travel narratives. One was largely factual and one was fantastic, but it is doubtful that Columbus could tell the difference between them. The first was the *Book of Marvels*, attributed to Jehan de Mandeville, an English adventurer (writing in French) who claimed to have traveled beyond the boundaries of the known world. The second was Marco Polo's account of his journeys in the Far East and of his sojourn at the court of the Great Khan in China. Both of these books shaped the Genoese mariner's expectations of what he would find when he embarked on his travels, and they also shaped his descriptions of the places and peoples he encountered. As a result, it is difficult to separate fiction from fact when we read his accounts—or those of many other European explorers. What we can now for certain is that the civilizations of the New World and those of the Old had a profound impact on one another.

In 1352, when Mandeville's *Book of Marvels* began to circulate, Europe had become a politically consolidated and culturally unified region. It had also reached its geographical limits;

there was, it seemed, no more room for expansion. With the completed conquest of Muslim territory in 1492, Ferdinand and Isabella eradicated an Islamic presence in western Europe that dated to the seventh century. Yet there was no longer any viable prospect of Latin Christendom's dominion in the Holy Land, North Africa, or any of the other Muslim territories that had been targeted by crusaders. The growing power of the Ottoman Turks was forging a new empire that would soon come to encompass all these regions, as well as the lands of the eastern Roman Empire in Byzantium. Meanwhile, German princes' drive to conquer territories in eastern Europe was slowed by the rise of Poland-Lithuania and the emergence of Muscovy as a contender for power on Europe's northeastern frontier; and their efforts would be halted altogether by the arrival of the Mongols and the eventual absorption of eastern Europe into the Ottoman Empire. Europe was also reaching its ecological limits. Indeed, the pressure on its natural resources was eased only by the dramatic population losses that had resulted from the combined effects of famine, plague, and war in the fourteenth and fifteenth centuries.

But despite these checks—or because of them—Europeans did not turn inward. As land-based conquests became less viable, new maritime empires coalesced around chains of colonies that extended from the Black Sea to Canary Islands. Trade routes were opened through the Strait of Gibraltar, resulting in greater economic integration between the Mediterranean and Atlantic economies and increasing Europe's demand for Asian spices and African gold. By the late fifteenth century, Mediterranean mariners and colonists were reaching farther into the Atlantic and pushing down the west coast of Africa. In 1498, one such expedition would make its way to India.

This fifteenth-century expansion of the Mediterranean world into the Atlantic was the essential preliminary to Columbus's voyages, and to the eventual conquests of the Americas. Because these events seem so familiar, we can easily underestimate both their improbability and their significance for the Western civilizations we have been studying, and for the "new world" they encountered. For the indigenous peoples and empires of the Americas, the results were cataclysmic. Within a hundred years of Europeans' arrival, between 50 and 90 percent of the native population had perished from disease, massacre, and enslavement. Moreover, Europeans' capacity to further their imperial ambitions wherever ships could sail and guns could penetrate profoundly destabilized Europe and its neighbors, sharpening the divisions among competing kingdoms and empires. The effects of this process, which reached its apogee in the nineteenth century, are still being felt today.

## MONGOLS, EUROPEANS, AND THE FAR EAST

Trade between the Mediterranean world and the Far East dates back to antiquity, but it was not until the late thirteenth century that Europeans began to establish direct trading connections with India, China, and the so-called Spice Islands of the Indonesian archipelago. For Europeans, these connections would prove profoundly important, as much for their impact on the European imagination as for their economic significance. For the peoples of Asia, however, the appearance of European traders on the fabled Silk Road between Central Asia and China was merely a curiosity. The really consequential event was the rise of the Mongol Empire that made such connections possible.

**THE HEAD OF TIMUR THE LAME.** This bust of the Mongol leader known in the West as Tamerlane is based on a forensic reconstruction of his exhumed skull.

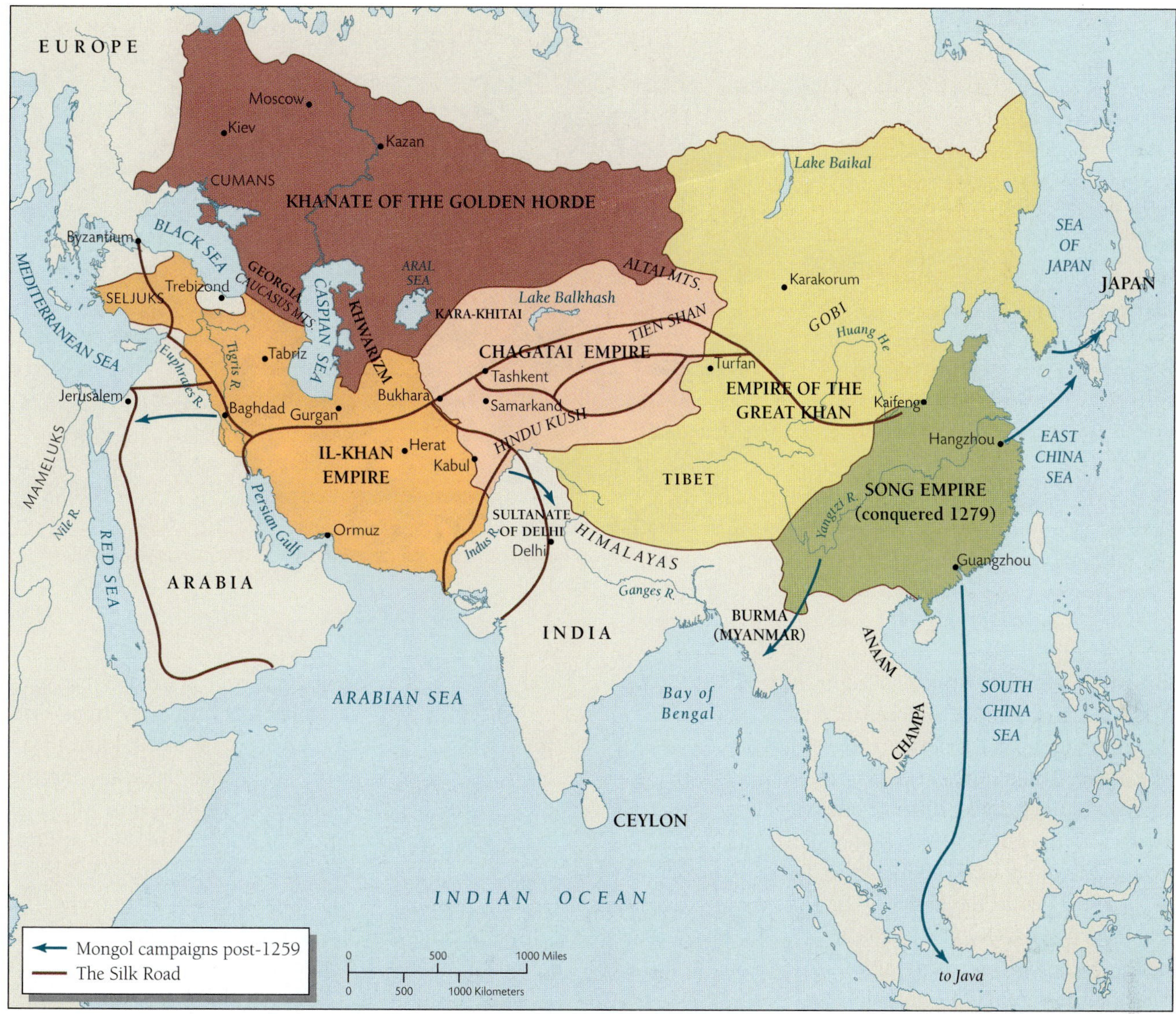


**THE MONGOL SUCCESSOR STATES.** Like Alexander's, Chingiz Khan's empire was swiftly assembled and encompassed vast portions of Europe and Asia. ▪ ***How many separate Mongol empires were there after 1259, and how far did they stretch geographically?*** ▪ ***How might the Mongol occupation of the Muslim world have aided the expansion of European trade?*** ▪ ***At the same time, why would it have complicated the efforts of Crusader armies in the Holy Land?***

## The Expansion of the Mongol Empire

The Mongols were one of many nomadic peoples inhabiting the steppes of Central Asia. Although closely connected with the Turkish populations with whom they frequently intermarried, the Mongols spoke their own distinctive language and had their own homeland, to the north of the Gobi Desert in present-day Mongolia. Sheep provided them with shelter (sheepskin tents), woolen clothing, milk, and meat. Like many nomadic peoples, the Mongols were highly accomplished horsemen and raiders. Indeed, it was in part to control their raiding ventures that the Chinese had built the fortified Great Wall, many centuries before. Primarily, though, China defended itself by attempting to ensure that the Mongols remained internally divided, with their energies turned against each other.

In the late twelfth century, however, a Mongol chief named Temüjin began to unite the various tribes under his rule. He did so by incorporating the warriors of each defeated tribe into his own army, thus building up a large military force. In 1206 his supremacy was formally acknowledged by all the Mongols, and he took the title Chingiz (Genghis) Khan, or "universal ruler." He now directed his enormous army against his neighbors, taking advantage of the fact

**THE BATTLE OF LEIGNITZ, 1241.** This image from a fourteenth-century chronicle shows heavily armored knights from Poland and Germany confronting the swift-moving mounted archers of the Mongol cavalry. Mongol warriors often had the advantage over Europeans because their smaller, faster horses carried lighter loads, and because the warriors themselves could shoot down their opponents at long range. ▪ ***Which army appears to be gaining the upper hand here?***

that China was at this time divided into three hostile states. In 1209, Chingiz Khan launched an attack on one of these, the Chin Empire of the north, and in 1211 managed to raid its interior. These initial attacks were probably looting expeditions rather than deliberate attempts at conquest, but by the 1230s a full-scale invasion of northern and western China was under way, culminating in 1234 wih the fall of these regions to the Mongols. In 1279, Chingiz Khan's grandson Qubilai (Kublai) Khan completed the conquest of southern China, thus reuniting China for the first time in centuries, and under Mongol rule.

At the same time, Chingiz Khan was also turning his forces westward, conquering much of Central Asia and incorporating the important commercial cities of Tashkent, Samarkand, and Bukhara into his empire. When he died in 1227, his son and successor, Ögedei (*EHRG-uh-day*), not only completed the conquest of the China, he laid plans for a massive invasion of the West. Between 1237 and 1240, the Mongol horde (so called from the Turkish word *ordu*, meaning "tent" or "encampment") conquered southern Russia and then launched a two-pronged assault that pushed them farther west. The smaller of the two Mongol armies swept through Poland toward eastern Germany; the larger army went southwest toward Hungary. In April of 1241, the smaller Mongol force met a hastily assembled army of Germans and Poles at the battle of Liegnitz, where the two sides fought to a bloody standstill. Two days later, the larger Mongol army annihilated the Hungarian army at the River Sajo.

It is possible that the Mongol armies could have moved even farther west after this important victory, but when the Great Khan Ögedei died in December of that same year, 1241, the leaderless Mongol forces withdrew from eastern Europe. It took five years for a new great khan to establish himself, only to die a few years later, leaving the Mongols without a leader for another three years. Although Mongol conquests continued in Persia, the Middle East, and China, attacks on Europe never resumed. By 1300, the period of Mongol expansion had come to an end. Yet the descendants of Chingiz Khan continued to rule this enormous empire—the largest land empire in the history of the world—for another half-century. Later, under the leadership of Timur the Lame (known as Tamerlane to Europeans) it looked briefly as if the Mongol Empire might be reunited. But Timur died in 1405 on his way to invade China; thereafter the various parts of the Mongol Empire fell into the hands of local rulers, including (in Asia Minor) the Ottoman Turks. Mongol influence continued, however, in the Mughal Empire of India, whose rulers were descended from the followers of Chingiz Khan.

The Mongols owed their success to the size, speed, and training of their mounted armies; to the intimidating savagery with which they treated those who resisted them; and to their ability to adapt the administrative traditions of their subjects to their own purposes. They were also highly tolerant of the religious beliefs of others—a distinct advantage in controlling an empire that comprised an array of Buddhist, Christian, and Muslim sects. And for the most part, Mongol governance was directed at securing the steady payment of tribute from the empire's subjects, which meant that local rulers could retain much of their power. Except in China, where the Mongol Yuan Dynasty maintained a complex administrative bureaucracy, Mongol rule was highly decentralized.

## A Bridge to the East

The Mongols had a keen eye for the commercial advantages of their empire. They began to control the caravan routes that led from China through Central Asia to the Black Sea. They also encouraged commercial contacts with European traders, especially through the Persian city of Tabriz, from which both land and sea routes led on to China. Until the Mongol conquests, the Silk Road to China had been closed to most Western merchants and travelers. But almost as soon as the Mongol Empire was established, we find Europeans venturing on these routes. The first such travelers were Franciscan missionaries like William of Rubruck, sent by King Louis IX of France in 1253 as his ambassador to the Mongol court. But Western merchants quickly followed. The most famous of these were three Venetians: the brothers Niccolò and Matteo Polo, and Niccolò's son, Marco. Marco Polo's account of his travels, which began when he was seventeen, includes details of his twenty-year sojourn in the service of Qubilai Khan and of his journey home through the Spice Islands, India, and Persia. The book had an enormous effect on the imagination of his contemporaries: for the next two centuries, most of what Europeans knew about the Far East they learned from Marco Polo's *Travels*. Christopher Columbus's copy of this book still survives.

European connections with the western ends of the Silk Road would continue until the mid-fourteenth century. The Genoese were especially active in this trade, not least because their rivals, the Venetians, already dominated the Mediterranean trade with Alexandria and Beirut, through

**VENETIAN AMBASSADORS TO THE GREAT KHAN.** Around 1270, the Venetian merchants Niccolò and Matteo Polo returned to Europe after their first prolonged journey through the empire of the Great Khan, bearing with them an official letter to the Roman pope. This image shows them at the moment of their arrival at the Great Khan's court, to which they have allegedly carried a Christian cross and a Bible. It comes from a manuscript copy of Jehan de Mandeville's *Book of Marvels*, which offered readers an alternative vision of the lands and peoples also described by Niccolò's famous son, Marco, who accompanied his father and uncle when they made their second journey to the Great Khan's court several years later. ▪ ***Why might many such visual references to the Polo family's adventures have been included in Mandeville's more fanciful travel narrative?***

# Competing Viewpoints

## Two Travel Accounts

*Two of the books that influenced Columbus and his contemporaries were travel narratives describing the exotic worlds that lay beyond Europe: worlds that may or may not have existed as they are described. The first excerpt below is taken from the account published by Marco Polo of Venice in the early fourteenth century. The young Marco traveled overland from Constantinople to the court of Qubilai Khan in the early 1270s, together with his father and uncle. He became a gifted linguist, and remained at the Mongol court until the early 1290s, when he returned to Europe after a journey through Southeast Asia, Indonesia, and the Indian Ocean. The second excerpt is from the* Book of Marvels *attributed to Jehan de Mandeville, an almost entirely fictional account of wonders that also became a source for European ideas about South and East Asia. This particular passage concerns a legendary Christian figure called Prester ("Priest") John, who is alleged to have traveled to the East and become a great ruler.*

### Marco Polo's Description of Java

Departing from Ziamba, and steering between south and south-east, fifteen hundred miles, you reach an island of very great size, named Java. According to the reports of some well-informed navigators, it is the greatest in the world, and has a compass above three thousand miles. It is under the dominion of one king only, nor do the inhabitants pay tribute to any other power. They are worshipers of idols.

The country abounds with rich commodities. Pepper, nutmegs, spikenard, galangal, cubebs, cloves and all the other valuable spices and drugs, are the produce of the island; which occasion it to be visited by many ships laden with merchandise, that yields to the owners considerable profit.

The quantity of gold collected there exceeds all calculation and belief. From thence it is that . . . merchants . . . have imported, and to this day import, that metal to a great amount, and from thence also is obtained the greatest part of the spices that are distributed throughout the world. That the Great Khan [Qubilai] has not brought the island under subjection to him, must be attributed to the length of the voyage and the dangers of the navigation.

Source: *The Travels of Marco Polo,* rev and ed. Manuel Komroff (New York: 1926), pp. 267–68.

### Mandeville's Description of Prester John

This emperor Prester John has great lands and has many noble cities and good towns in his realm and many great, large islands. For all the country of India is separated into islands by the great floods that come from Paradise, that divide the land into many parts. And also in the sea he has many islands. . . .

This Prester John has under him many kings and many islands and many varied people of various conditions. And this land is full good and rich, but not so rich as is the land of the Great Khan. For the merchants do not come there so commonly to buy merchandise as they do in the land of the Great Khan, for it is too far to travel to. . . .

[Mandeville then goes on to describe the difficulties of reaching Prester John's lands by sea.]

This emperor Prester John always takes as his wife the daughter of the Great Khan, and the Great Khan in the same way takes to wife the daughter of Prester John. For these two are the greatest lords under the heavens.

In the land of Prester John there are many diverse things, and many precious stones so great and so large that men make them into vessels such as platters, dishes, and cups. And there are many other marvels there that it would be too cumbrous and too long to put into the writing of books. But of the principal islands and of his estate and of his law I shall tell you some part.

This emperor Prester John is Christian and a great part of his country is Christian also, although they do not hold to all the articles of our faith as we do. . . .

And he has under him 72 provinces, and in every province there is a king. And these kings have kings under them, and all are tributaries to Prester John.

And he has in his lordships many great marvels. For in his country is the sea that men call the Gravelly Sea, that is all gravel and sand without any drop of water. And it ebbs and flows in great waves as other seas do, and it is never still. . . . And a three-day journey from that sea there are great mountains out of which flows a great flood that comes out of Paradise. And it is full of precious stones without any drop of water. . . .

He dwells usually in the city of Susa [in Persia]. And there is his principal palace, which is so rich and so noble that no one will believe the report unless he has seen it. And above the chief tower of the palace there are two round pommels of gold and in each of them are two great, large rubies that shine full brightly upon the night. And the principal gates of his palace are of a precious stone that men call sardonyxes [a type of onyx], and the frames and the bars are made of ivory. And the windows of the halls and chambers are of crystal. And the tables upon which men eat, some are made of emeralds, some of amethyst, and some of gold full of precious stones. And the legs that hold up the tables are made of the same precious stones. . . .

Source: *Mandeville's Travels,* ed. M. C. Seymour (Oxford: 1967), pp. 195–99 (language modernized from Middle English by R. C. Stacey).

### *Questions for Analysis*

1. What does Marco Polo want his readers to know about Java, and why? What does this suggest about the interests of these intended readers?
2. What does Mandeville want his readers to know about Prester John and his domains? Why are these details so important?
3. Which of these accounts seems more trustworthy, and why? Even if we cannot accept one or both at face value, what insight do they give us into the expectations of Columbus and the other Europeans adventurers who relied on these accounts?

which the bulk of Europe's Far Eastern luxury goods continued to pass. But the Mongols of Persia became progressively more hostile to Westerners, and the Genoese finally abandoned Tabriz after attacks had made their position there untenable. Then, in 1346, the Mongols of the Golden Horde besieged the Genoese colony at Caffa on the Black Sea, a siege memorable chiefly because it became a conduit for the Black Death, which was passed from the Mongol army to the Genoese defenders, who returned with it to western Europe (see Chapter 10).

The window of opportunity that made Marco Polo's travels possible was thus relatively small. By the middle of the fourteenth century, hostilities between the various parts of the Mongol Empire were already making travel along the Silk Road perilous. After 1368, when the last Mongol dynasty was overthrown, most Westerners were excluded from China and Mongols were restricted to cavalry service in the imperial armies of the new Ming Dynasty. The overland trade routes from China to the Black Sea continued to operate, but Europeans had no direct access to them. Yet the new, more integrated world that Mongol rule had created continued to exercise a lasting effect on Europe, despite the relatively short time during which Europeans themselves were able to participate directly in it. European memories of the Far East would be preserved, and the dream of reestablishing close connections between Europe and China would survive to influence a new round of European commercial and imperial expansion from the late fifteenth century onward.

## THE RISE OF THE OTTOMAN EMPIRE

Like the Mongols, the Turks were initially a nomadic people whose economy depended on raiding. They were already established in northwestern Anatolia when the Mongols arrived there, and were being converted to Islam. But unlike the established Muslim powers in the region, whom the Mongols weakened and ultimately destroyed, the Turks were the principal beneficiaries of the Mongol conquest. For when the Mongols toppled the Seljuk sultanate and the Abbasid caliphate of Baghdad, they eliminated the two traditional authorities that had previously kept Turkish border chieftains like the Ottomans in check. Now they were free to raid, unhindered, along the soft frontiers of Byzantium. At the same time, they remained far enough from the centers of Mongol authority to avoid being destroyed themselves.

## *The Conquest of Constantinople*

By the end of the thirteenth century, members of the Ottoman dynasty had established themselves as leaders among the Turks of the Anatolian frontier. By the mid-fourteenth century, they had solidified their preeminence by capturing a number of important cities. These successes brought the Ottomans to the attention of the Byzantine emperor, who hired a contingent of them as mercenaries in 1345. They were extraordinarily successful—so much so that the eastern Roman Empire could not control their movements. By 1370, they had extended their control all the way to the Danube. In 1389, Ottoman forces defeated a powerful coalition of Serbian forces at the battle of Kosovo, enabling them to extend control over Greece, Bulgaria, and the Balkans.

In 1396, the Ottoman army attacked Constantinople, but withdrew to repel a Western crusading force that had been sent against them. In 1402 they attacked Constantinople again, but were once more were forced to withdraw, this time to confront a Mongolian invasion of Anatolia. Led by Timur the Lame, the Mongol army captured the Ottoman sultan and destroyed his army; for the next decade it appeared that Ottoman hegemony over Anatolia might have ended. By 1413, however, Timur was dead, a new sultan had emerged, and the Ottomans were able to resume their conquests.

Ottoman pressure on Constantinople continued during the 1420s and 1430s, producing a steady stream of Byzantine refugees who brought with them to Italy the surviving masterworks of classical Greek literature (see Chapter 12). But it was not until 1451 that a new sultan, Mehmet II, turned his full attention to the conquest of the imperial city. In 1453, after a brilliantly executed siege, Mehmet succeeded in breaching the city walls. The Byzantine emperor was killed in the assault, the city itself was thoroughly plundered, and its remaining population was sold into slavery. The Ottomans then settled down to rule their new capital in a style reminiscent of their Byzantine predecessors.

The Ottoman conquest of Constantinople administered an enormous psychological shock to many European rulers and intellectuals, but its economic impact was minor. Ottoman control over the former Byzantine Empire reduced European access to the Black Sea, but the bulk of the Far Eastern luxury trade with Europe had never passed through the Black Sea ports in the first place. Europeans got most of their spices and silks through Venice, which imported them from Alexandria and Beirut, and these two cities did not fall to the Ottomans until the 1520s. So the Ottoman Empire was not necessarily the force that propelled Portuguese efforts to locate a sea route to India and the Spice Islands. If anything, it was Portuguese access to India, and European attempts to exclude Muslims from

**SULTAN MEHMET II, "THE CONQUEROR" (r. 1451–81).** This portrait, executed by the Ottoman artist Siblizade Ahmed, exhibits features characteristic of both Central Asia and Europe. The sultan's pose—his aesthetic appreciation of the rose, his elegant handkerchief—are indicative of the former, as is the fact that he wears the white turban of a scholar and the thumb ring of an archer. But the subdued coloring and three-quarter profile may reflect the influence of Italian portraits. ▪ ***What did the artist achieve through this blending of styles and symbols?*** ▪ ***What messages does this portrait convey?***

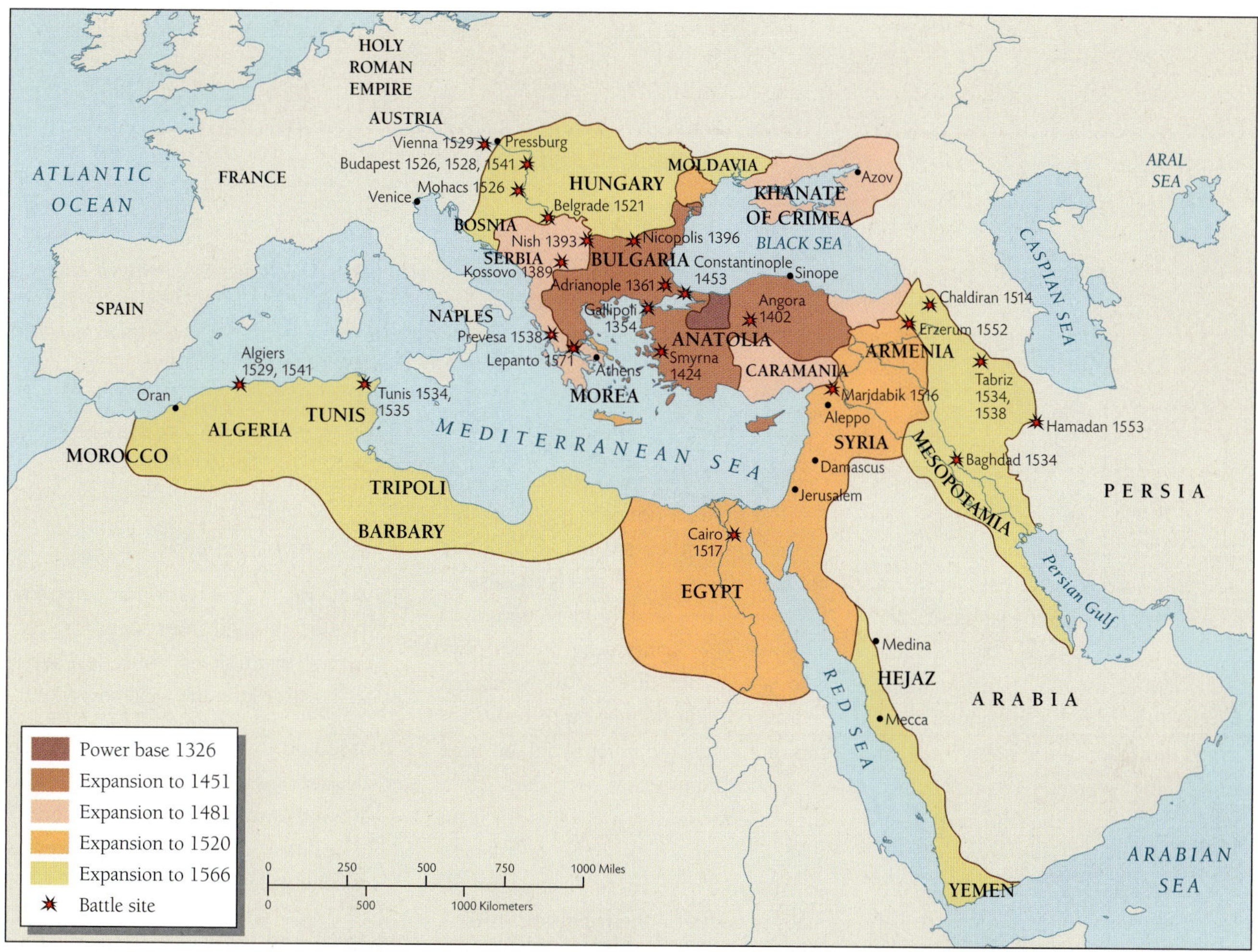


**THE GROWTH OF THE OTTOMAN EMPIRE.** Consider the patterns of Ottoman expansion revealed in this map. ▪ ***Where is Constantinople, and how might the capture of Constantinople in 1453 have facilitated further conquests?*** ▪ ***Compare the extent of the Ottoman Empire in 1566 with that of the Byzantine Empire under Justinian (see the map on page 208). How would you account for their similarities?*** ▪ ***How might you explain the fact that the Ottoman Empire did not continue its rapid expansion after 1566?***

the Indian spice trade, that helped spur the Ottoman conquests of Syria, Egypt, and Hungary during the 1520s and 1530s. To be sure, these conquests had other motives, too, including control of Egyptian grain exports. And by eliminating the merchants who had traditionally dominated the overland spice trade through Beirut and Alexandria, the Ottomans also hoped to redirect this trade through Constantinople, and so up the Danube into western Europe.

But if the practical effects of the Ottoman conquest were modest where western Europe was concerned, the effects on the Turks themselves were transformative. Vast new wealth poured into Anatolia, which the Ottomans increased by carefully tending to the industrial and commercial interests of their new capital city Constantinople, which they also called Istanbul—the Turkish pronunciation of the Greek phrase "in the city." Trade routes were redirected to feed the capital, and the Ottomans became a naval power in the eastern Mediterranean and the Black Sea. As a result, Constantinople's population grew from fewer than 100,000 in 1453 to more than 500,000 in 1600, making it the largest city in the world outside of China.

## *War, Slavery, and Social Advancement*

Despite the Ottomans' careful attention to commerce, their empire continued to rest on the spoils of conquest until the end of the sixteenth century. In order to manage this continual expansion, the size of the Ottoman army and administration grew exponentially, drawing more and more manpower from the empire. And because the Ottoman army and administration were largely composed of slaves,

# Analyzing Primary Sources

## Ottoman Janissaries

*The following account is from a memoir written by Konstantin Mihailovic, a Serbian Christian who was captured as a youth by the army of Sultan Mehmet II. For eight years, he served in the Ottoman janissary ("gate-keeper") corps. In 1463, the fortress he was defending for the Sultan was captured by the Hungarians, after which he recorded his experiences for a Christian audience.*

Whenever the Turks invade foreign lands and capture their people, an imperial scribe follows immediately behind them, and whatever boys there are, he takes them all into the janissaries and gives five gold pieces for each one and sends them across the sea [to Anatolia]. There are about two thousand of these boys. If, however, the number of them from enemy peoples does not suffice, then he takes from the Christians in every village in his land who have boys, having established what is the most every village can give so that the quota will always be full. And the boys whom he takes in his own land are called *cilik*. Each one of them can leave his property to whomever he wants after his death. And those whom he takes among the enemies are called *pendik*. These latter after their deaths can leave nothing; rather, it goes to the emperor, except that if someone comports himself well and is so deserving that he be freed, he may leave it to whomever he wants. And on the boys who are across the sea the emperor spends nothing; rather, those to whom they are entrusted must maintain them and send them where he orders. Then they take those who are suited for it on ships and there they study and train to skirmish in battle. There the emperor already provides for them and gives them a wage. From there he chooses for his own court those who are trained and then raises their wages.

Source: Konstantin Mihailovic, *Memoirs of a Janissary* (Michigan Slavic Translations 3), trans. Benjamin Stolz (Ann Arbor, MI: 1975), pp. 157–59.

### Questions for Analysis

**1.** Why might the Ottoman emperor have established this system for "recruiting" and training janissaries? What are its strengths and weaknesses?

**2.** Based on your knowledge of Western civilizations, how unusual would you deem this method of raising troops? How does it compare to the strategies of other rulers we have studied?

the demand for more soldiers and administrators could best be met through further conquests that would capture yet more slaves. Further conquests, however, required a still larger army and an even more extensive bureaucracy; and so the cycle continued. It mirrors, in many respects, the dilemma of the Roman Empire (Chapter 5). Indeed, another way in which the Ottoman Empire resembled that of Rome was in this insatiable demand for slaves.

Not only were slaves were the backbone of the Ottoman army administration, they were also critical to the lives of the Turkish upper class. One of the important measures of status in Ottoman society was the number of slaves in one's household. After 1453, new wealth permitted some elites to maintain households in the thousands. In the sixteenth century, the sultan alone possessed more than 20,000 slave attendants, not including his bodyguard and elite infantry units, both of which were also composed of slaves.

Where did all of these slaves come from? Many were captured in war. Many others were taken on raiding forays into Poland and Ukraine and sold to Crimean slave merchants, who shipped their captives to the slave markets of Constantinople. But slaves were also recruited (some willingly, some by coercion) from rural areas of the Ottoman Empire itself. Because the vast majority of slaves were household servants and administrators rather than laborers, some people willingly accepted enslavement, believing that they would be better off as slaves in Constantinople than as impoverished peasants in the countryside. In the Balkans especially, many people were enslaved as children, handed over by their families to pay the "child tax" the Ottomans imposed on rural areas too poor to pay a monetary tribute. Although unquestionably a wrenching experience for families, this practice did open up opportunities for social advancement. Special academies were created at

Constantinople to train the most able of the enslaved male children to act as administrators and soldiers, and some rose to become powerful figures in the Ottoman Empire. Slavery, indeed, carried relatively little social stigma. Even the sultan himself was most often the son of an enslaved woman.

Because Muslims were not permitted to enslave other Muslims, the vast majority of Ottoman slaves were Christian—although many eventually converted to Islam. And because so many of the elite positions within Ottoman government were held by these slaves, the paradoxical result was that Muslims, including the Turks themselves, were effectively excluded from the main avenues of social and political influence in the Ottoman Empire. Nor was Ottoman society dominated by a powerful hereditary nobility like those of contemporary European society. Avenues to power were therefore remarkably open to men of ability and talent, most of them non-Muslim slaves. Nor was this power limited to the government and the army. Commerce and business also remained largely in the hands of non-Muslims, most frequently Greeks, Syrians, and Jews. Jews in particular found in the Ottoman Empire a welcome refuge from the persecutions and expulsions that had characterized Jewish life in late-medieval Europe. After their expulsion from Spain in 1492, more than 100,000 Spanish (Sephardic) Jews ultimately immigrated to the territories of the Ottoman Empire.

## *Religious Conflicts*

The Ottoman sultans were Sunni Muslims who lent staunch support to the religious and legal pronouncements of the Islamic schools in their realm. When Ottomans captured the cities of Medina and Mecca in 1516, they also became the defenders of the two principal holy sites of Islam. Soon after, they captured Jerusalem and Cairo too, putting an end to the Mamluk sultanate of Egypt and becoming the keepers of the Holy Land. In 1538, accordingly, the Ottoman ruler formally adopted the title of caliph, thereby declaring himself to be the legitimate successor of the Prophet Muhammad.

In keeping with Sunni traditions, the Ottomans were tolerant of non-Muslims, especially during the fifteenth and sixteenth centuries. They organized the major religious groups of their empire into legally recognized units and permitted them considerable rights of self-government. After 1453, however, when they gained control of Constantinople, the Ottomans were especially careful to protect and promote the authority of the Greek Orthodox patriarch of Constantinople over the Orthodox Christians of their empire. As a result, the Ottomans enjoyed staunch support from their Orthodox Christian subjects during their wars with the Christians of western Europe. The Ottomans' principal religious conflicts were therefore not with their own subjects, but with the Shi'ite Muslim dynasty that ruled neighboring Persia. Time and again during the sixteenth century, Ottoman expeditions into western Europe had to be abandoned when hostilities erupted with the Persians.

**OTTOMAN ORTHODOXY.** This genealogical chart is designed to show the descent of Sultan Mehmet III (1595–1603) from his own illustrious ancestors—both warriors and scholars—as well as from Muhammad, whose central image is piously veiled. ▪ ***Why was it desirable for the Ottoman sultans to proclaim themselves caliphs, too, and therefore heirs to Muhammad?*** ▪ ***How might this have increased the hostility between the Sunni Turks and the Shi'ite Muslims of neighboring Persia?***

## The Ottomans and Europe

For a variety of reasons, the contest between the Ottoman Empire and the rulers of western Europe never lived up to the rhetoric of holy war that both sides employed in their propaganda. In Europe, especially, there were internal divisions that frustrated any attempts to mount a unified campaign. By the sixteenth century, as we shall see (Chapters 13 and 14), Catholic and Protestant sects were turning that same crusading rhetoric against one another. But even before that, Christian military initiatives were ineffectual. In 1396, a Western crusader army was annihilated by the Ottomans at the battle of Nicopolis, and Ottoman armies besieged Vienna several times during the following two centuries.

But apart from these few dramatic events, conflicts between the Ottomans and the rulers of western Europe were fought out mainly through pirate raids and naval battles in the Mediterranean. The result was a steady escalation in the scale and cost of navies. In 1571, when a combined Habsburg and Venetian force defeated the Ottoman fleet at Lepanto, more than 400 ships took part, with both sides deploying naval forces ten times larger than they had possessed half a century before. Although undeniably a victory for the Habsburgs and their Venetian allies, the battle of Lepanto was far less decisive than is often suggested. The Ottoman navy was speedily rebuilt; and by no means did Lepanto put an end to Ottoman influence over the eastern Mediterranean Sea.

**THE BATTLE OF LEPANTO, 1571.** This oil painting by the Venetian artist Paolo Veronese (1528–1588) celebrates the victory of a Christian navy over the forces of the Ottoman Empire. Over 400 ships took part in the massive engagement. In the lower register of his canvas, Veronese strives to capture the tumult and confusion. In the upper register, warlike saints and angels gather to support the efforts of the Spanish and Venetian mariners.

In any case, both Ottoman and Habsburg interests soon shifted away from their conflict with each other. The Ottomans embarked on a long and costly war with Persia, while the Spanish Habsburgs turned their attention toward their new empire in the Atlantic. By the mid-seventeenth century, when a new round of Ottoman-European conflicts began, the strength of the Ottoman Empire had been sapped by a series of indolent sultans and by the tensions that arose within the empire itself as it ceased to expand. Although the empire would last until 1918 (see Chapter 24), it was in no position to rival the global hegemony that European powers were beginning to achieve.

# MEDITERRANEAN COLONIALISM

During the fifteenth century, Europeans focused their commercial ambitions more and more on the western Mediterranean and Atlantic. As we noted above, however, this reorientation can only partially be attributed to the rising power of the Ottoman Empire. It was more significantly the product of two related developments: the growing importance of the African gold trade and the growth of European colonial empires in the western Mediterranean.

## The Search for African Gold

The European trade in African gold was not new. It had been going on for centuries, facilitated by Muslim middlemen whose caravans brought it from the Niger River to the North African ports of Algiers and Tunis. In the thirteenth century, Catalan and Genoese merchants established trading colonies in Tunis to expedite this process, exchanging woolen cloth from northern Europe for North African grain and sub-Saharan gold.

But the medieval demand for gold was greatly accelerated during the fourteenth century, when a silver shortage began to affect the entire European economy. Silver production—which enabled the circulation of coinage in

Europe—fell markedly during the 1340s and remained at a low level thereafter, as Europeans reached the limits of their technological capacity to extract silver ore from deep mines. This shortfall was compounded during the fifteenth century by a serious cash-flow problem: more European silver was moving east in the spice trade than could be now be replenished from extant sources. Gold therefore represented an obvious alternative currency for large transactions, and in the thirteenth century some European rulers began minting gold coins. But Europe itself had few natural gold reserves. To maintain and expand these gold coinages, new and larger supplies of gold were needed. The most obvious source was Africa.

## *Mediterranean Empires: Catalonia, Venice, and Genoa*

European interest in the African gold trade coincided with the creation of entrepreneurial empires in the Mediterranean. During the thirteenth century, the Catalans conquered and colonized a series of western Mediterranean islands, including Majorca, Ibiza, Minorca, Sicily, and Sardinia. Except in Sicily, the pattern of Catalan exploitation was largely the same on all these islands: expulsion or extermination of the existing population, usually Muslim; the extension of economic concessions to attract new settlers; and a heavy reliance on slave labor to produce foodstuffs and raw materials for export.

**SPANISH GALLEON.** The larger, full-bottomed ships that came into use during the fifteenth century would become engines of imperial conquest and the vessels that brought the riches of those conquests back to Europe. This wooden model was made for the Museo Storico Navale di Venezia (Naval History Museum) in Venice.

These new colonial efforts were mainly carried out by private individuals operating under royal charters. They therefore contrast strongly with older patterns of Venetian colonization, which had long been directed by the city's rulers and which were focused mainly on the eastern Mediterranean, where the Venetians dominated the trade in spices and silks. The Genoese, to take yet another case, also had extensive interests in the western Mediterranean, where they traded bulk goods such as cloth, hides, grain, timber, and sugar. But Genoese colonies tended to be more informal than either Venetian or Catalan colonies, constituting family networks rather than an extension of state sovereignty. The Genoese were also more closely integrated with the societies of North Africa, Spain, and the Black Sea than were their Venetian or Catalan counterparts.

Genoese colonists pioneered the production of sugar and sweet wines in the western Mediterranean and later in the Atlantic islands off the west coast of Africa, particularly Madeira. They also moved away from reliance on the oared galleys favored by the Venetians toward larger, fuller-bodied sailing ships that could carry greater volumes of cargo. With further modifications to accommodate the rougher sailing conditions of the Atlantic Ocean, these were the ships that would carry sixteenth-century Europeans around the globe.

## *From the Mediterranean to the Atlantic*

For centuries, European maritime commerce had been divided between a Mediterranean and a northeastern Atlantic world. Starting around 1270, however, Italian merchants began to sail through the Strait of Gibraltar and on up to the wool-producing regions of England and the Netherlands. This was a step toward the extension of Mediterranean patterns of commerce and colonization into the Atlantic Ocean. Another step was the discovery (or possibly the rediscovery) of the Atlantic island chains known as the Canaries and the Azores, which Genoese sailors reached in the fourteenth century. Efforts to colonize the Canary Islands, and to convert and enslave their inhabitants, began almost immediately. But an effective conquest of the Canary Islands did not really begin until the fifteenth century, when it was undertaken by Portugal and completed by

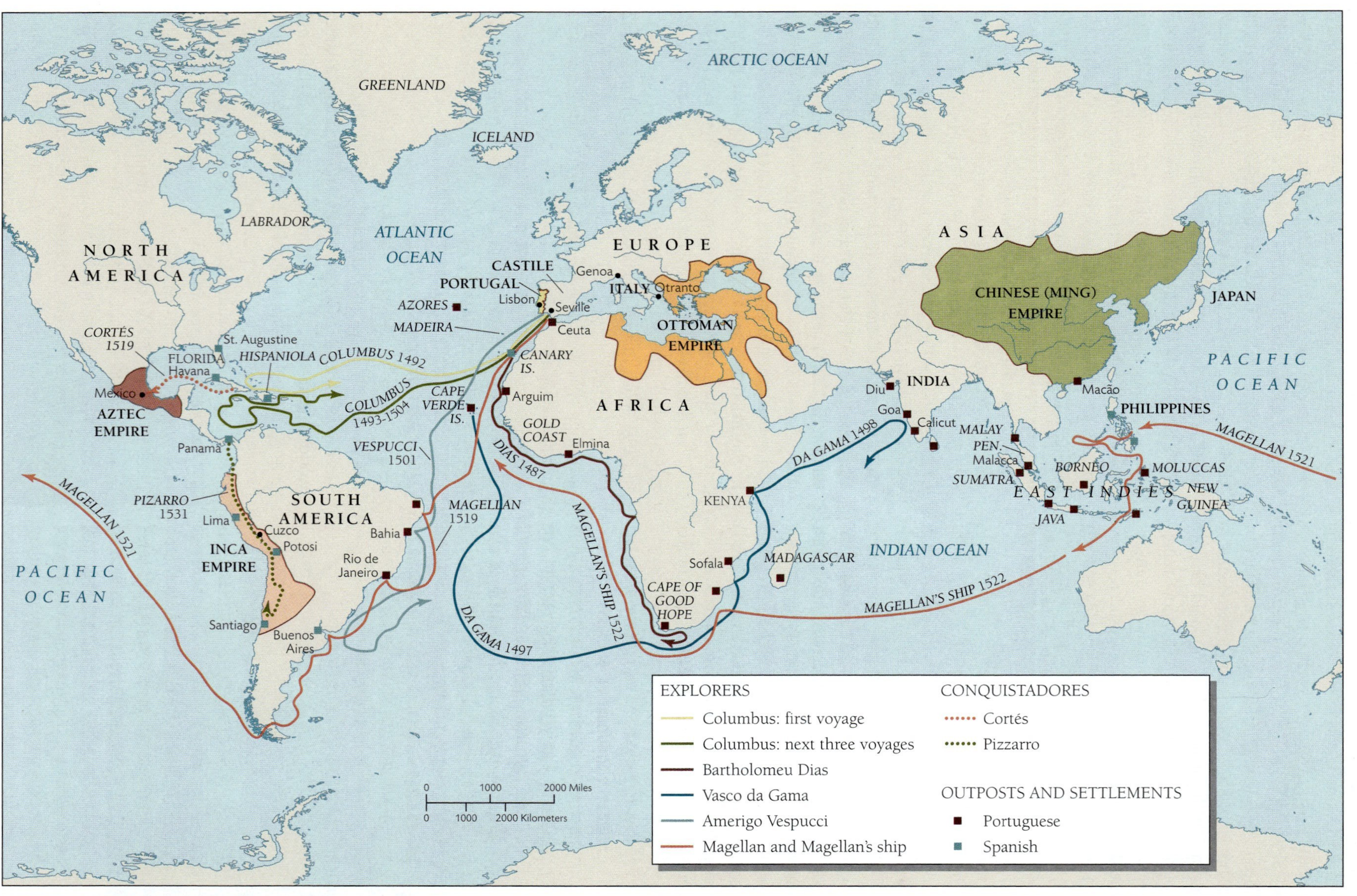


**OVERSEAS EXPLORATION IN THE FIFTEENTH AND SIXTEENTH CENTURIES.** ▪ *What were the major routes taken by European explorers of the fifteenth and sixteenth centuries?* ▪ *What was the explorers' main goal?* ▪ *How might the establishment of outposts in Africa, America, and the East Indies have radically altered the balance of power in the Old World, and why?*

Castile. The Canaries, in turn, became the base from which further Portuguese voyages down the west coast of Africa proceeded. They were also the jumping-off point from which Christopher Columbus would sail westward across the Atlantic Ocean in the hope of reaching Asia.

## *Naval Technology and Navigation*

The new European empires of the fifteenth and sixteenth centuries rested on a mastery of the oceans. The Portuguese caravel—the workhorse ship of the fifteenth-century voyages to Africa—was based on ship and sail designs that had been in use among Portuguese fishermen since the thirteenth century. Starting in the 1440s, however, Portuguese shipwrights began building larger caravels of about 50 tons displacement with two masts, each carrying a triangular (lateen) sail. Columbus's *Niña* was of this design, having been refitted with two square sails in the Canary Islands to enable it to sail more efficiently before the wind during the Atlantic crossing. Such ships required much smaller crews than did the multi-oared galleys that were still commonly used in the Mediterranean. By the end of the fifteenth century, even larger caravels of around 200 tons were being constructed, with a third mast and a combination of square and lateen sails.

Europeans were also making significant advances in navigation during the fifteenth and sixteenth centuries. Quadrants, which could calculate latitude in the Northern Hemisphere by the height of the North Star above the horizon, were in widespread use by the 1450s. As sailors approached the equator, however, the quadrant became less and less useful, and navigators instead made use of astrolabes, which reckoned latitude by the height of the sun. Like quadrants, astrolabes had been known in western Europe for centuries. But it was not until the 1480s that the astrolabe became a really useful instrument for seaborne navigation, with the preparation of standard tables sponsored by the Portuguese crown. Compasses, too, were coming into more widespread use during the fifteenth century. Longitude, however, remained impossible to calculate accurately until the eighteenth century, when the invention

**PORTOLAN CHART.** Maritime maps like this one were crucial navigational aids, and came to be widely used outside the Mediterranean in the fifteenth century. This chart, made by Vesconte Maggiolo in 1541, shows the Mediterranean and Atlantic coastlines of Europe and North Africa.

of the marine chronometer finally made it possible to keep accurate time at sea. In the sixteenth century, Europeans sailing east or west across the oceans generally had to rely on their skill at dead reckoning to determine where they were on the globe.

European sailors also benefited from a new interest in maps and navigational charts. Especially important to Atlantic sailors were books known as *rutters* or *routiers*. These contained detailed sailing instructions and descriptions of the coastal landmarks a pilot could expect to encounter en route to a variety of destinations. Mediterranean sailors had used similar books since at least the fourteenth century. Known as *portolani*, or portolan charts, they mapped the ports along the coastlines, tracked prevailing winds and tides, and warned of reefs and shallow harbors. In the fifteenth century, these map-making techniques were extended to the Atlantic Ocean; by the end of the sixteenth century, the accumulated knowledge contained in rutters spanned the globe.

## Portugal, Africa, and the Sea Route to India

It was among the Portuguese that two critical interests—the African gold trade and Atlantic colonization—first came together. In 1415, a Portuguese expedition captured the North African port of Ceuta. During the 1420s, the Portuguese colonized both the island of Madeira and the Canary Islands. During the 1430s, they extended these colonization efforts to the Azores. By the 1440s, they had reached the Cape Verde Islands. In 1444, Portuguese explorers first landed on the African mainland in the area between the Senegal and the Gambia river mouths, where they began to collect cargoes of gold and slaves for export back to Portugal. By the 1470s, Portuguese sailors had rounded the West African "bulge" and were exploring the Gulf of Guinea.

In 1483, they reached the mouth of the Congo River. In 1488, the Portuguese captain Bartholomeu Dias was accidentally blown around the southern tip of Africa by a gale, after which he named the point "Cape of Storms." But the king of Portugal, João II (r. 1481–95), took a more optimistic view of Dias's achievement: he renamed it the Cape of Good Hope and began planning a naval expedition to India. In 1497–98, accordingly, Vasco da Gama rounded the cape, and then, with the help of a Muslim navigator named Ibn Majid, crossed the Indian Ocean to Calicut, on the southwestern coast of India, opening up for the first time a sea route between Europe and the Far Eastern spice trade. Although da Gama lost half his fleet and one-third of his men on his two-year voyage, his cargo of spices was so valuable that his losses were deemed insignificant. His heroism became legendary, and his story became the basis for the Portuguese national epic, the *Lusiads*.

Now masters of the quickest route to riches in the world, the Portuguese swiftly capitalized on da Gama's accomplishment. After 1500, Portuguese trading fleets sailed regularly to India. In 1509, the Portuguese defeated an Ottoman fleet and then blockaded the mouth of the Red Sea, attempting to cut off one of the traditional routes by which spices had traveled to Alexandria and Beirut. By 1510, Portuguese military forces had established a series of forts along the western Indian coastline, including their headquarters at Goa. In 1511 Portuguese ships seized Malacca, a center of the spice trade on the Malay peninsula. By 1515, they had reached the Spice Islands and the coast of China. So completely did the Portuguese now dominate the spice trade that by the 1520s even the Venetians were forced to buy their pepper in the Portuguese capital of Lisbon.

## Artillery and Empire

Larger, more maneuverable ships and improved navigational aids made it possible for the Portuguese and other European mariners to reach Africa, Asia, and the Americas by sea. But fundamentally, these sixteenth-century European commercial empires were a military achievement. As such, they reflected what Europeans had learned in their wars against each other during the fourteenth and fifteenth centuries. Perhaps the most critical military advance was the increasing sophistication of artillery, a development made possible not only by gunpowder, but also by improved metallurgical

**A TURKISH BRASS CANNON OF THE FIFTEENTH CENTURY.** This eighteen-ton gun fired iron projectiles twenty-five inches in diameter.

techniques for casting cannon barrels. By the middle of the fifteenth century, as we observed in Chapter 10, the use of artillery pieces had rendered the stone walls of medieval castles and towns obsolete, a fact brought home in 1453 by the successful French siege of Bordeaux (which ended the Hundred Years' War), and by the Ottoman siege of Constantinople (which ended the Byzantine Empire).

Indeed, the new ship designs (first caravels, and later the larger galleons) were important in part because their larger size made it possible to mount more effective artillery pieces on them. European vessels were now conceived as floating artillery platforms, with scores of guns mounted in fixed positions along their sides and swivel guns mounted fore and aft. These guns were vastly expensive, as were the ships that carried them; but for those rulers who could afford them, such ships made it possible to project military power around the world. Even though Vasco da Gama had been able to sail into the Indian Ocean in 1498, the Portuguese did not gain control of that ocean until 1509, when they defeated a combined Ottoman and Indian naval force at the battle of Div. Portuguese trading outposts in Africa and Asia were also fortifications, built not so much to guard against the attacks of native peoples as to ward off assaults from other Europeans. Without this essential military component, the European maritime empires of the sixteenth century could not have existed.

**PRINCE HENRY THE NAVIGATOR.** This image shows a detail from a larger group portrait of the Portuguese royal family.

## *Prince Henry the Navigator*

Because we know that Portuguese expeditions down the African coast ultimately opened up a sea route to India and the Far East, it is tempting to presume that this was their goal from the beginning. The traditional narrative of these events presents exploration as their mission, India as their goal, and Prince Henry the Navigator (1394–1460) as the guiding genius behind them. But it was only a generation after Henry's death, in the 1480s, that India became the target toward which these voyages were directed. Before this time, Portuguese involvement in Africa was driven instead by much more traditional goals: crusading ambitions against the Muslims of North Africa; the desire to establish direct links with the sources of African gold production south of the Sahara Desert; the desire to colonize the Atlantic islands; the burgeoning market for slaves in Europe and in the Ottoman Empire; and the hope that somewhere in Africa they might find the kingdom of the legendary Prester John, the mythical Christian king whom Europeans believed would be their ally against the Muslims if only they could locate him (see page 352). In the twelfth and thirteenth centuries, they had sought him in Asia. But from the 1340s on, he was believed to reside in Ethiopia, an expansive term that to most Europeans seems to have meant "somewhere in Africa."

Still, Prince Henry (whose nickname, "the Navigator," was assigned to him in the seventeenth century) remains a central figure in the history of Portuguese exploration, even though the stories about his school for navigators and cartographers, as well as his role in designing improved ships and navigational instruments, are probably exaggerated. He personally directed eight of the thirty-five Portuguese voyages to Africa that occurred during his lifetime, and he played an important part in organizing the Portuguese colonization of Madeira, the Canary Islands, and the Azores. He also pioneered the Portuguese slave trade, first on the Canaries (whose population was almost entirely eradicated) and then along the Senegambian coast of western Africa. His main motivation was to outflank the cross-Saharan African gold trade by intercepting this trade at its source. To this end, he built a series of forts along the African coastline, most famously at Arguim, to which he hoped to divert the trans-Saharan gold caravans. This was also his reason for colonizing the Canary Islands, which he saw as a staging ground for expeditions into the African interior. He was therefore a man of his time, rather than a visionary: a crusader against Islam, a prince in search of an empire, a lord seeking resources to support his followers, and an aspiring merchant who hoped to make a killing in the gold trade but instead found his main profits in slaving.

## *Atlantic Colonization and Slave Networks*

Although slavery had effectively disappeared in much of northwestern Europe by the early twelfth century, slavery continued in Iberia, Italy, and elsewhere in the Mediterranean world. It existed, however, on a small scale; there were no slave-powered factories or large-scale agricultural systems in this period. The major slave markets and slave economies, as we have noted, were in the Ottoman Empire. And, as had been the case since antiquity, no aspect of this slave trade was racially based. Most slaves of this era were European Christians, predominantly Poles, Ukrainians, Greeks, and Bulgarians; in previous eras, they had been Germanic and Celtic peoples.

What was new about slavery in the fifteenth century, then, was its racialization—an aspect of modern slavery that has made an indelible impact on our own society. To Europeans, African slaves were visible in ways that other slaves were not, and it became convenient for those who dealt in them to justify the mass deportation of entire populations by claiming their racial inferiority and their "natural" fitness for a life of bondage. This nefarious practice, too, has had long-lasting and tragic consequences that still afflict the civilizations of our own world.

From as early as the mid-fifteenth century, Lisbon began to emerge as a significant market for enslaved Africans. Something on the order of 15,000 to 20,000 Africans were sold there within a twenty-year period during Prince Henry's lifetime. In the following half century, the numbers amounted to perhaps 150,000 by 1505. For the most part, the purchasers of these slaves regarded them as status symbols; it became fashionable to have African footmen, page boys, and ladies' maids. Still, in the Atlantic colonies—Madeira, the Canaries, and the Azores—land was worked mainly by European settlers and sharecroppers. Slave labor, if it was employed at all, was generally used only in sugar mills. On Madeira and the Canaries, where sugar became the predominant cash crop during the last quarter of the fifteenth century, some slaves were therefore introduced. But even sugar production did not lead to the widespread introduction of slavery on these islands.

However, a new kind of slave-based sugar plantation began to emerge in Portugal's Atlantic colonies in the 1460s, starting on the Cape Verde Islands and then extending southward into the Gulf of Guinea. These islands were not populated when the Portuguese began to settle them, and their climate generally discouraged most Europeans from living there. They were ideally located, however, along the routes of slave traders venturing outward from the nearby West African coast. It was this plantation model that would be exported to Brazil by the Portuguese and to the Caribbean islands of the Americas by their Spanish conquerors, with incalculable consequences for the peoples of Africa, the Americas, and Europe.

# NEW WORLD ENCOUNTERS

When King Ferdinand and Queen Isabella of Spain decided to underwrite a voyage of exploration, they were hoping to steal some thunder from the successful Portuguese ventures of the past half century. For it was clear that tiny Portugal would soon dominate the sea-lanes if rival entrepreneurs

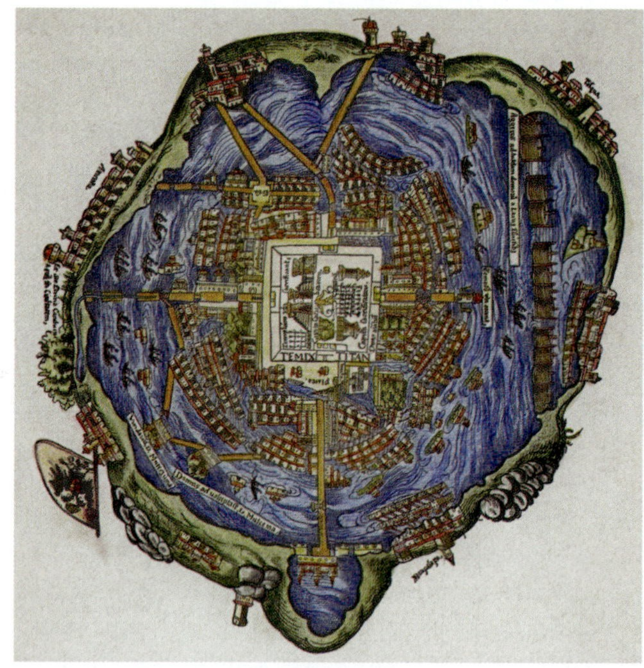

**THE AZTEC CITY OF TENOCHTITLAN.** The Spanish conquistador Bernal Díaz del Castillo (1492–1585) took part in the conquest of the Aztec Empire and later wrote a historical account of his adventures. His admiring description of the Aztec capital at Tenochtitlan records that the Spaniards were amazed to see such a huge city built in the midst of vast lake, with gigantic buildings arranged in a meticulous urban plan around a central square, and broad causeways linking the city to the mainland. This hand-colored woodcut was included in an early edition of Hernando Cortés's letters to Emperor Charles V, printed at Nuremberg (Germany) in 1524.

# Interpreting Visual Evidence

## *America as an Object of Desire*

Under the influence of Mandeville's *Book of Marvels* and a host of other popular narratives, Columbus and his fellow voyagers were prepared to find the New World full of cannibals. They also assumed that the indigenous peoples' custom of wearing little or no clothing—not to mention their "savagery"—would render their women sexually available. In the letters he sent back to Europe, Columbus recounts one notable encounter with a "cannibal girl" whom he had taken captive in his tent. Her naked body aroused his desire, but she resisted his advances so fiercely that he had to tie her up—which of course made it easier for him to "subdue" her. In the end, he cheerfully reports, the girl's sexual performance was so satisfying that she might have been trained, as he put it, in a "school for whores."

The Flemish artist Jan van der Straet (1523–1605) would have heard many such reports of the encounters between (mostly male) Europeans and the peoples of the New World. This engraving, based on one of his drawings, is among the thousands of mass-produced images that circulated widely in Europe, thanks to the invention of printing. It imagines the first encounter between a male "Americus" (like Columbus, or Amerigo Vespucci himself) and the New World, "America," depicted as a voluptuous, available woman. The Latin caption reads: "America rises to meet Americus; and whenever he calls her, she will always be aroused."

AMERICA.
Americen Americus retexit, & Semel vocauit inde ſemper excitam.


### *Questions for Analysis*

1. Study the details of this image carefully. What does each symbolize, and how do they work together as an allegory of conquest and colonization?
2. On what stereotypes of indigenous peoples does this image draw? Notice, for example, the cannibalistic campfire of the group in the background, or the posture of "America."
3. The New World itself—America—is imagined as female in this image. Why is this? What messages might this—and the suggestive caption—have conveyed to a European viewer?

did not attempt to find alternate routes. Hence the bold—and ill-informed—decision to reach Asia by sailing west. Like his contemporaries, Christoffa Corombo (1451–1506) of Genoa understood that the world was a sphere, but like them he also thought it was much smaller than it actually is. (As we saw in Chapter 4, the accurate calculation of the globe's circumference made in ancient Alexandria had been suppressed centuries later by the Roman geographer Ptolemy.) Furthermore, it had been accepted since antiquity that there were only three continents: Europe, Asia, and Africa.

What made the scheme seem plausible to Ferdinand and Isabella was, first, the discovery and colonization of the Canary Islands and the Azores, which had reinforced the

# Analyzing Primary Sources

## *A Spanish Critique of New World Conquest*

*Not all Europeans approved of European imperialism or its "civilizing" effects on the peoples of the New World. One of the most influential contemporary critics was Bartolomé de las Casas (1474–1566), who left his home city of Seville at the age of eighteen, joined the Dominican order, and eventually became bishop of Chiapas (Mexico). Although he was a product of his times—he owned many slaves—he was also prescient in discerning the devastating effects of European settlement in the West Indies and Central America, and he particularly deplored the exploitation and extermination of indigenous populations. The following excerpt is from one of the many eloquent manifestos he published in an attempt to gain the sympathies of the Spanish crown and to reach a wide readership. It was printed in 1542.*

God made all the peoples of this area, many and varied as they are, as open and as innocent as can be imagined. The simplest people in the world—unassuming, long-suffering, unassertive, and submissive—they are without malice or guile, and are utterly faithful and obedient both to their own native lords and to the Spaniards in whose service they now find themselves. . . . They are innocent and pure in mind and have a lively intelligence, all of which makes them particularly receptive to learning and understanding the truths of our Catholic faith and to being instructed in virtue; indeed, God has invested them with fewer impediments in this regard than any other people on earth. . . .

It was upon these gentle lambs . . . that from the very first day they clapped eyes on them the Spanish fell like ravening wolves upon the fold, or like tigers and savage lions who have not eaten meat for days. The pattern established at the outset has remained unchanged to this day, and the Spaniards still do nothing save tear the natives to shreds, murder them and inflict upon them untold misery, suffering and distress, tormenting, harrying and persecuting them mercilessly. . . .

When the Spanish first journeyed there, the indigenous population of the island of Hispaniola stood at some three million; today only two hundred survive. The island of Cuba, which extends for a distance almost as great as that separating Valladolid from Rome, is now to all intents and purposes uninhabited; and two other large, beautiful and fertile islands, Puerto Rico and Jamaica, have been similarly devastated. Not a living soul remains today on any of the islands

hypothesis that the Atlantic was dotted with islands all the way to Japan; and second, the Genoese mariner's egregious miscalculation of the earth's size, which convinced him that he could reach Japan and China in about a month's clear sailing after leaving the Canary Islands. The man we know as Christopher Columbus never realized his mistake. When he reached the Bahamas and the island of Hispaniola in 1492 after only a month's sailing, he returned to Spain to report that he had reached the outer islands of Asia.

## Discoveries

Of course, Columbus was not the first European to set foot on the American continents. As we noted in Chapter 8, Viking sailors briefly settled present-day Newfoundland, Labrador, and perhaps even portions of New England around the year 1000. But knowledge of these Viking landings had been forgotten or ignored outside of Iceland for hundreds of years. Moreover, the tiny Scandinavian colonies on Greenland had been abandoned by the fifteenth century, when the cooling of the climate (Chapter 10) destroyed the fragile ecosystems that had barely sustained the lives of Norse settlers there.

Although Columbus brought back no Asian spices to prove that he had found an alternate route on his voyages, he did return with some small samples of gold and a few indigenous people—whose existence gave promise of entire tribes that might be "saved" (by conversion to Christianity) and enslaved by Europeans. This provided sufficient incentive for the Spanish monarchs to finance three more expeditions by Columbus, and many more by others. Soon the of the Bahamas . . . even though every single one of the sixty or so islands in the group . . . is more fertile and more beautiful than the Royal Gardens in Seville and the climate is as healthy as anywhere on earth. The native population, which once numbered some five hundred thousand, was wiped out by forcible expatriation to the island of Hispaniola, a policy adopted by the Spaniards in an endeavour to make up losses among the indigenous population of that island. . . .

At a conservative estimate, the despotic and diabolical behaviour of the Christians has, over the last forty years, led to the unjust and totally unwarranted deaths of more than twelve million souls, women and children among them. . . .

The reason the Christians have murdered on such a vast scale and killed anyone and everyone in their way is purely and simply greed. . . . The Spaniards have shown not the slightest consideration for these people, treating them (and I speak from first-hand experience, having been there from the outset) not as brute animals–indeed, I would to God they had done and had shown them the consideration they afford their animals–so much as piles of dung in the middle of the road. They have had as little concern for their souls as for their bodies, all the millions that have perished having gone to their deaths with no knowledge of God and without the benefit of the Sacraments. One fact in all this is widely known and beyond dispute, for even the tyrannical murderers themselves acknowledge the truth of it: the indigenous peoples never did the Europeans any harm whatever. . . .

Source: Bartolomé de la Casas, *A Short Account of the Destruction of the Indies*, trans. Nigel Griffin (Harmondsworth: 1992), pp. 9–12.

### *Questions for Analysis*

1. Given his perspective on the behavior of his countrymen, how might Bartolomé de las Casas have justified his own presence in New Spain (Mexico)? What do you think he may have hoped to achieve by publishing this account?
2. What comparisons does the author make between New Spain (Mexico) and the Old, and between indigenous peoples and Europeans? What is he trying to convey?
3. Compare this account with the contemporary engraving on page 365. What new light does this excerpt throw on that visual allegory? How might a reader-viewer of the time have reconciled these two very different pictures of European imperialism?

mainlands of two hitherto unknown continents were identified, as were clusters of new islands. Gradually, Europeans reached the conclusion that what they had encounterd was an entirely "New World," and one that had—shockingly—never been foretold either by the teachings of Christianity or the wisdom of the ancients. Awareness of this fact was most widely publicized by the Italian explorer and geographer Amerigo Vespucci (1454–1512), whose name was soon adapted as a descriptor for the new continents (see ***Interpreting Visual Evidence*** on page 365).

At first, the realization that this world was not, in fact, an outpost of Asia came as a disappointment to the Spanish: two major land masses and two vast oceans disrupted their plans to beat the Portuguese to the Spice Islands. But this sense of frustration began to lift in 1513, when Vasco Núñez de Balboa first viewed the Pacific Ocean from the Isthmus of Panama. Thereafter, Ferdinand and Isabella's grandson, the Holy Roman Emperor Charles V, renewed their dream when he accepted Ferdinand Magellan's proposal to see whether a route to Asia could be found by sailing around South America. But Magellan's voyage of 1519 demonstrated beyond question that the globe was simply too large for any such plan to be feasible. Of the five ships that left Spain under his command, only one returned, three years later, having been forced to circumnavigate the globe. Out of a crew of 265 sailors, only eighteen survived. Most had died of scurvy or starvation; Magellan himself had been killed in a skirmish with native peoples in the Philippines.

This fiasco ended all hope of discovering an easy southwest passage to Asia—although the deadly dream of a northwest passage survived, and motivated many European explorers of North America into the twentieth century. It has been revived today: in our age of global warming, the retreat of Arctic pack ice has led to the opening of new shipping lanes, and in 2008 the first commercial voyage successfully traversed the Arctic Ocean.

## The Spanish Conquest of America

Although the discovery of two continents was initially construed as a setback, it quickly became clear that this New World had great wealth of its own. From the start, Columbus's gold samples, in themselves rather paltry, had nurtured hopes that gold might lie piled in ingots somewhere in these vast new lands, ready to enrich any European adventurer who discovered them. Rumor fed rumor, until a few freelance Spanish soldiers really did strike it rich beyond their most avaricious imaginings. Between 1519 and 1521, the *conquistador* (Spanish for "conqueror") Hernánd Cortés, with a force of only 600 men, overthrew the Aztec Empire of Mexico and plundered its rulers' fabulous wealth. Then in 1533, another conquistador, Francisco Pizarro, toppled the highly centralized South American empire of the Incas and seized its great stores of gold and silver. His force numbered only 180. Despite the vast populations, sophistication, and enormous resources of these two extraordinary empires—the Aztec capital of Tenochtitlan (*ten-och-tit-LAN*, now Mexico City) rivaled any European city in size and amazed its conquerors by the height and grandeur of its buildings—Cortés and Pizarro had the advantage. They had cannons, firearms, steel swords, armor, and horses, all unknown to the native peoples of the Americas. They were also aided by the indigenous peoples' extreme susceptibility to infectious European diseases, which had already weakened these populations as a result of their earlier contacts with explorers and settlers following in the wake of Columbus. Those who survived were promised liberation from the oppressive regimes of the Aztecs and Incas—little knowing how much worse their new oppressors would be.

## The Profits of Empire

Cortés and Pizarro captured hoards of gold and silver that had been accumulated for centuries by the native civilizations of Mexico and Peru. Almost immediately, however, a search for the sources of these precious metals was launched by conquistadors. The first gold deposits were

**SPANISH CONQUISTADORS IN MEXICO.** This sixteenth-century drawing of conquistadors slaughtering the Aztec aristocracy emphasizes the advantages that plate armor and steel swords gave to the Spanish soldiers.

# Analyzing Primary Sources

## *Enslaved Native Laborers at Potosí*

*Since the Spanish crown received one-fifth of all revenues from the mines of New Spain, as well as maintaining a monopoly over the mercury used to refine the silver ore into silver, it had an important stake in ensuring the mines' productivity. To this end, the crown granted colonial mine owners the right to conscript native peoples and gave them considerable freedom when it came to the treatment of the workers. This account, dated to about 1620, describes the conditions endured by these native laborers.*

According to His Majesty's warrant, the mine owners on this massive range [at Potosí] have a right to the conscripted labor of 13,300 Indians in the working and exploitation of the mines, both those [mines] which have been discovered, those now discovered, and those which shall be discovered. It is the duty of the *Corregidor* [municipal governor] of Potosí to have them rounded up and to see that they come in from all the provinces between Cuzco . . . and as far as the frontiers of Tarija and Tomina. . . .

The conscripted Indians go up every Monday morning to the . . . foot of the range; the *Corregidor* arrives with all the provincial captains or chiefs who have charge of the Indians assigned him for his miner or smelter; that keeps him busy till 1 P.M., by which time the Indians are already turned over to these mine and smelter owners.

After each has eaten his ration, they climb up the hill, each to his mine, and go in, staying there from that hour until Saturday evening without coming out of the mine; their wives bring them food, but they stay constantly underground, excavating and carrying out the ore from which they get the silver. They all have tallow candles, lighted day and night; that is the light they work with, for as they are underground, they have need for it all the time. . . .

These Indians have different functions in the handling of the silver ore; some break it up with bar or pick, and dig down in, following the vein in the mine; others bring it up; others up above keep separating the good and the poor in piles; others are occupied in taking it down from the range to the mills on herds of llamas; every day they bring up more than 8,000 of these native beasts of burden for this task. These teamsters who carry the metal are not conscripted, but are hired.

Source: Antonio Vázquez de Espinosa, *Compendium and Description of the West Indies*, trans. Charles Upson Clark (Washington, DC: 1968), p. 62.

### *Questions for Analysis*

1. From the tone of this account, what do you think was the narrator's purpose in writing? Who is his intended audience?
2. Reconstruct the conditions in which these laborers worked. What would you estimate to be the human costs of this week's labor? Why, for example, would a fresh workforce be needed every Monday?

discovered in Hispaniola, where surface mines were speedily established using native laborers, who died in appalling numbers from disease, brutality, and overwork. Of the approximately 1 million native people who had welcomed Columbus in 1492, only 100,000 survived by 1510; 90 percent of the population had died within a generation. By 1538, there were fewer than 500.

With the loss of so many workers, the mines of Hispaniola became uneconomical to operate, and the European colonists turned instead to cattle raising and sugar production. Modeling their sugarcane plantations on those of the Cape Verde Islands and St. Thomas (São Tomé) in the Gulf of Guinea, colonists began to import thousands of African slaves to labor in the new industry. Sugar production was, by its nature, a capital-intensive undertaking. The need to import slave labor added further to its costs, guaranteeing that control over the new industry would fall into the hands of a few extremely wealthy planters and financiers.

Despite the importance of sugar production in the Caribbean and of cattle ranching on the Mexican mainland—which had a devastating effect on the fragile ecosystem of Central America—it was mining that shaped the Spanish colonies of Central and South America most fundamentally. Gold was the lure that had initially drawn the Spanish to the New World, but silver became their most lucrative export. Between 1543 and 1548, vast silver deposits were discovered north of Mexico City and at Potosí in Bolivia. But even before these discoveries, the Spanish crown had taken steps to assume direct control over its new colonies. It was therefore to the Spanish crown that the profits from these astonishingly productive mines accrued. Potosí quickly became the most important mining town in the world. By 1570, it numbered 120,000 inhabitants, despite being located at an altitude of 15,000 feet, where the temperature never climbs above 59° F. As in Hispaniola, enslaved native laborers died by the tens of thousands in these mines and in the disease-infested boom towns that surrounded them (see page 369).

New mining techniques made it possible to produce even greater quantities of silver, though at the cost of even greater mortality among the native laborers. Between 1571 and 1586, silver production at Potosí quadrupled, reaching a peak in the 1590s, when 10 million ounces of silver per year were arriving in Spain from the Americas. In the 1540s, by contrast, the corresponding figure was only 1.5 million ounces. In the peak years of domestic European silver production, by contrast, only about 3 million ounces of silver per year were produced between 1525 and 1535, and this figure dropped steadily from about 1550 on. Europe's silver shortage therefore came to an end during the sixteenth century, but the silver that now circulated there came almost entirely from the New World.

This massive infusion of silver into the European economy accelerated an inflation that had already begun in the late fifteenth century. Initially, it was driven by the renewed growth of the European population, an expanding economy, and a relatively fixed supply of food. From the 1540s on, however, inflation was largely the product of the greatly increased supply of coinage that was now entering the European economy. The result was a rapid rise in prices. Although the effects of this were felt throughout Europe, Spain was particularly hard hit. Prices doubled between 1500 and 1560, and they doubled again between 1560 and 1600. These price spikes in turn undermined the competitiveness of Spanish industries. Then, when the flow of New World silver slowed dramatically during the 1620s and 1630s, the Spanish economy collapsed.

After 1600, when smaller quantities of New World silver were entering the European economy, prices rose more

## After You Read This Chapter

Visit StudySpace for quizzes, additional review materials, and multi-media documents. **wwnorton.com/studyspace**

### REVIEWING THE OBJECTIVES

- The conquests of the Mongols had a significant impact on Europe. What were some key effects?
- The Ottomans' dependence on slavery had a number of notable consequences. What were they?
- Colonialism and overseas exploration were driven by an array of factors. Identify some of the main economic and technological changes that occurred during the fourteenth and fifteenth centuries.
- In what ways did the practice of slavery and its justification change in the fifteenth century?
- The "discovery" of the New World had profound effects on the Old World, as well as on the indigenous peoples of the Americas. Describe some of these effects.

slowly. But the price of grain still ballooned to five or six times the level of the previous century by 1650, producing social dislocation and widespread misery for many of Europe's poorest inhabitants (see Chapter 14). In England, for example, the period between about 1590 and 1610 was the most desperate the country had experienced since the Great Famine, nearly three hundred years before. As the population rose and wages fell, living standards declined dramatically. Indeed, if we compute living standards by dividing the price of an average basket of food by the average daily wage of a common laborer, then standards of living were lower in England at the beginning of the modern era than they had been at any time during the Middle Ages. It is no wonder, then, that so many Europeans found emigration to the Americas a tempting prospect.

## CONCLUSION

By 1600, commerce, colonization and overseas conquest had profoundly changed both Europe and the wider world. Even though Europeans had little direct contact with China after the fall of the Mongol Empire, the economy of Europe became more closely tied to that of Asia through the trade routes maintained by the Ottoman Empire. At the same time, the emergence of Portugal and Spain as Europe's leading long-distance traders was moving the center of economic gravity away from the Mediterranean toward the Atlantic. Displaced by Ottoman Constantinople from its role as the principal conduit for the spice trade, Venice gradually declined, while the Genoese moved increasingly into the world of finance, backing the commercial ventures of other powers, particularly Spain, whose Atlantic ports bustled with vessels and shone with wealth. By the mid-seventeenth century, however, both Spain and Portugal had become the victims of their own success. They would retain their American colonies until the nineteenth century, but it would be the Dutch, the French, and especially the English who would establish the most successful European empires in North America, Asia, Africa, and Australia. Meanwhile, these and other developments were moving Italy to the center of European affairs for the first time since the fragmentation of the Roman Empire. How this happened is the subject of Chapter 12.

### PEOPLE, IDEAS, AND EVENTS IN CONTEXT

- What circumstances enabled **MARCO POLO**'s travels in the East? Why was the period of commercial contact between the **MONGOL EMPIRE** and Europe so brief?
- What forces drove the **OTTOMAN EMPIRE** to expand its reach? Why was the Ottoman caliph more tolerant of Jews and Christians than of dissent within Islam?
- What set the **GENOESE** entrepreneurs apart from other colonial powers in the Mediterranean?
- How does **PRINCE HENRY THE NAVIGATOR** exemplify the motives for pursuing overseas expansion, as well as the mythology that has grown up around these early efforts?
- What were the expectations that launched **COLUMBUS**'s voyage? Why were **FERDINAND AND ISABELLA** of Spain motivated to finance it?
- What advantages did the Spanish **CONQUISTADORS** have over the native peoples of the **AMERICAS**? What were the immediate effects of European conquest on the Americas?

### CONSEQUENCES

- How do the patterns of conquest and colonization discussed in this chapter compare to those of earlier periods, particularly those of antiquity? How many of these developments were new?
- In what ways did the slave trade of the Atlantic world differ from the slave economies of antiquity? How might Europeans have used Greek and Roman justifications of slavery in defense of these new ventures? (See Chapters 4 and 5.)
- How important a role does technology play in the developments we have surveyed in this chapter? In your view, which technological innovation was of the greatest historical significance?

# Before You Read This Chapter

## STORY LINES

- The intellectual and artistic phenomenon known as the Renaissance is contemporaneous with both the later Middle Ages (Chapter 10) and the beginnings of Europe's commercial and colonial expansion (Chapter 11).
- It began in Italy, where the absence of centralized political power created nostalgia for an era when Rome and its empire had ruled the world. At the same time, the competition among small city-states suggested that models for their governance might be found in ancient Greece.
- Knowledge of the classics and of the Greek language was facilitated at this time by the flight of Greek-speaking intellectuals from Constantinople to Italy, as the Ottoman Turks absorbed the lands of the Byzantine Empire.
- In time, the literary, artistic, and philosophical achievements of Renaissance Italy came to influence all of Europe.

## CHRONOLOGY

| | |
|---|---|
| 1304–1374 | Lifetime of Petrarch |
| 1377 | The papacy returns to Rome |
| 1378–1417 | The Great Schism |
| 1434 | The Medici family rules Florence |
| 1440 | Lorenzo Valla debunks the "Donation of Constantine" |
| 1453 | The fall of Constantinople prompts a disapora of Greek scholars |
| 1455 | Invention of the printing press |
| 1492 | Columbus's first voyage |
| 1498 | Leonardo da Vinci's *The Last Supper* |
| 1511 | Raphael's *The School of Athens* |
| 1512 | Michelangelo completes the Sistine ceiling |
| 1513 | Niccolò Machiavelli's *The Prince* |
| 1514 | Albrecht Dürer's *Saint Jerome* |
| 1516 | Thomas More publishes *Utopia* |
| 1522 | Erasmus completes his new translation of the Bible |
| 1528 | Castiglione's *Book of the Courtier* |

# Renaissance Ideals and Realities, c. 1350–1550

## CORE OBJECTIVES

- **DEFINE** the movement known as the Renaissance.
- **EXPLAIN** why the Renaissance began in Italy.
- **IDENTIFY** the principle characteristics of Renaissance art.
- **UNDERSTAND** the relationship between Renaissance ideals and political realities.
- **DESCRIBE** the ways in which the Renaissance of northern Europe differed from that of Italy.

Rummaging through the books in a remote monastic library, an Italian bureaucrat attached to the papal curia at Avignon was surprised to find a manuscript of Cicero's letters—letters that no living person had known to exist. They had probably been copied in the time of Charlemagne, and had then been forgotten for hundreds of years. How many other works of this great Roman orator had met the same fate? he wondered. And how many more books might still remain to be discovered? Clearly, thought Francesco Petrarca (1304–1374), he was living in an age of ignorance. A great gulf seemed to open up between his own time and that of the ancients: a middle age that separated him from those well-loved models.

For centuries, Christian intellectuals had regarded "the dark ages" as the time between Adam's expulsion from Eden and the birth of Christ. But now, Petrarca redefined that concept and applied it to his own era. According to him, the Middle Ages was not the pagan past but the time that separated him from direct communion with the classics. Yet this did not stop him from trying to bridge the gap. "I would have written to you long ago," he said in a Latin letter to the Greek poet Homer (dead for over two thousand years), "had it not been for the fact that we lack a common language."

Petrarca (known to English-speakers as Petrarch) would later become famous in his own day as an Italian poet, a Latin stylist, and a tireless advocate for the resuscitation of the classical past. And the values that he and his contemporaries began to espouse would give rise to a new intellectual and artistic movement in Italy, a movement strongly critical of the present and admiring of a past that had disappeared with the fragmentation of Rome's empire and the end of Italy's greatness. We know this movement as the Renaissance, the French word for "rebirth" that was applied to it in the eighteenth century. It has since become shorthand for the epoch following the Middle Ages, but it is really a parallel phenomenon—as the overlapping chronologies of this chapter and the two previous chapters show. Talking about the Renaissance is therefore a way of talking about some significant changes in education and outlook that transformed the culture of Italy from the late fourteenth to the early sixteenth centuries, and which eventually influenced the rest of Europe in important ways.

These changes were fueled by the intensified warfare, political competition, and commercial expansion of this era. They began in Italy because the intellectuals of its warring city-states desperately sought for new models of governance in the older civilizations of Greece and Rome, and because they were the first to receive the intellectuals of Constantinople after the conquests of the Ottoman Turks spurred a diaspora of Greek-speaking refugees. They resulted in new—or renewed—approaches to education, scholarship, civic engagement, history, literature, and art. And they soon spread beyond Italy, influencing the intellectual and artistic endeavors of other Europeans.

## MEDIEVAL OR RENAISSANCE?

The term *renaissance* has usually been taken literally, as though the cultural accomplishments of antiquity had ceased to be appreciated and imitated, and therefore needed to be "reborn." Yet we have been tracing the enduring influence of classical civilization throughout the Middle Ages for many chapters, and we have constantly noted the reverence accorded to Aristotle, Virgil, Cicero, and a host of other figures, as well as the persistence of Roman law and Roman institutions. It is also misleading to characterize the Renaissance as rejecting the fervent Christianity of the Middle Ages, and as a return to the pagan past: however much the scholars and artists of this age loved the classics, none saw classicism as superseding Christianity. Indeed, all discussions of "the Renaissance" must be qualified by the fact that there was no single set of Renaissance ideals, and that these ideals were constantly reshaped and determined by political, social, and economic realities.

### *Renaissance Classicism*

Renaissance thinkers and artists were enormously diverse in their attitudes, achievements, and approaches. That said, one can certainly find distinguishing traits that make the concept of a "Renaissance" meaningful. With respect to knowledge of the classics, for example, there was a significant quantitative difference between the learning of the Middle Ages and that of the Renaissance. Medieval scholars knew many Roman authors—especially Virgil, Ovid, and Cicero—but the discovery of "new" works by Livy, Tacitus, and Lucretius expanded the classical canon considerably. Equally if not more important was the recovery of Greek literature, whose study had hitherto thrived only in Byzantium. In the twelfth and thirteenth centuries, as we have seen (Chapters 8 and 9), Greek scientific and philosophical works became available to western Europeans thanks to increased contact with Islam; but no Greek poems or plays were available in Latin translations, and neither were the major dialogues of Plato. Nor could more than a handful of western Europeans read the language of classical Greece. But as the Ottomon Turks put increasing pressure on the shrinking borders of the Byzantine Empire (Chapter 11), more and more Greek-speaking intellectuals fled to Italy, bringing their books and their knowledge with them.

Renaissance thinkers not only knew many more classical texts, they used them in new ways. Medieval intellectuals had long regarded ancient sources as complementing and confirming their own assumptions. By contrast, the new reading methods of the Renaissance fostered an increased awareness of the conceptual gap that separated the contemporary world from that of antiquity. At the same time, the structural similarities between ancient Greek poleis and the city-states of Italy encouraged political theorists to use these ancient forms of government as models. This firm determination to learn from antiquity was even more pronounced in the realms of architecture and art, areas in which classical models contributed most strikingly to the creation of a distinctive Renaissance style.

Finally, although Renaissance culture was by no means pagan, it was more overtly materialistic and more commer-

# Analyzing Primary Sources

## *Some Renaissance Attitudes toward Women*

*Italian society in the fourteenth and fifteenth centuries was characterized by marriage patterns in which men in their late twenties or thirties customarily married women in their mid- to late teens. This demographic fact probably contributed to the widely shared belief that wives were essentially children, who could not be trusted with important matters and who were best trained by being beaten. Renaissance humanism did little to change such attitudes. In some cases, it even reinforced them.*

After my wife had been settled in my house a few days, and after her first pangs of longing for her mother and family had begun to fade, I took her by the hand and showed her around the whole house. I explained that the loft was the place for grain and that the stores of wine and wood were kept in the cellar. I showed her where things needed for the table were kept, and so on, through the whole house. At the end there were no household goods of which my wife had not learned both the place and the purpose. . . .

Only my books and records and those of my ancestors did I determine to keep well sealed. . . . These my wife not only could not read, she could not even lay hands on them. I kept my records at all times . . . locked up and arranged in order in my study, almost like sacred and religious objects. I never gave my wife permission to enter that place, with me or alone. . . .

[Husbands] who take counsel with their wives . . . are madmen if they think true prudence or good counsel lies in the female brain. . . . For this very reason I have always tried carefully not to let any secret of mine be known to a woman. I did not doubt that my wife was most loving, and more discreet and modest in her ways than any, but I still considered it safer to have her unable, and not merely unwilling, to harm me. . . . Furthermore, I made it a rule never to speak with her of anything but household matters or questions of conduct, or of the children.

Source: Leon Battista Alberti, "On the Family," in *The Family in Renaissance Florence*, trans. and ed. Renée N. Watkins. (Columbia, S.C.: 1969), pp. 208–13, as abridged in Julie O'Faolain and Lauro Martines, eds., *Not in God's Image: Women in History from the Greeks to the Victorians* (New York: 1973), pp. 187–88.

### *Questions for Analysis*

1. For what reasons did Alberti argue that a wife should have no access to books or records?
2. Would you have expected humanism to make attitudes to women more liberal and "modern"? How do views like Alberti's challenge such assumptions?

cialized. For one thing, the competition among and within Italian city-states fostered a culture of display and conspicuous consumption. The relative weakness of the Church in Italy also contributed to the growth of secular power and a more worldly outlook. Italian bishoprics were small and relatively powerless compared to those north of the Alps, and Italian universities were much more independent of ecclesiastical supervision than those elsewhere. Even the papacy—restored to Rome only after Petrarca's death—was severely limited, not the least because the papacy's role as a political rival in central Italy compromised its moral authority. All these factors fostered the emergence of new aesthetics, ideals, and aspirations.

## Renaissance Humanism

The most basic of Renaissance intellectual ideals is summarized in the term *humanism*. This was a program of study that aimed to replace the scholastic emphasis on logic and metaphysics with the study of language, literature, rhetoric, history, and ethics. The humanists always preferred ancient literature to the writings of more recent authors. Although some wrote in both Latin and the vernacular, most humanists regarded vernacular literature as a lesser diversion for the uneducated; serious scholarship and praiseworthy poetry could be written only in Latin or Greek. Latin,

# Competing Viewpoints

## *The Humanists' Educational Program*

*These three selections illustrate the confidence placed by humanists in their elite educational program, and their conviction that it would be of supreme value to the state as well as to the individual students who pursued it. Not everyone agreed with the humanists' claims, however, and a good deal of self-promotion lies behind them.*

### Vergerius on Liberal Studies

We call those studies *liberal* which are worthy of a free man; those studies by which we attain and practice virtue and wisdom; that education which calls forth, trains, and develops those highest gifts of body and of mind which ennoble men, and which are rightly judged to rank next in dignity to virtue only. . . . It is, then, of the highest importance that even from infancy this aim, this effort, should constantly be kept alive in growing minds. For . . . we shall not have attained wisdom in our later years unless in our earliest we have sincerely entered on its search. [P. P. Vergerius (1370–1444), *"Concerning Excellent Traits."*]

### Alberti on the Importance of Literature

Letters are indeed so important that without them one would be considered nothing but a rustic, no matter how much a gentlemen [he may be by birth]. I'd much rather see a young nobleman with a book than with a falcon in his hand. . . .

Be diligent, then, you young people, in your studies. Do all you can to learn about the events of the past that are worthy of memory. Try to understand all the useful things that have been passed on to you. Feed your minds on good maxims. Learn the delights of embellishing your souls with good morals. Strive to be kind and considerate [of others] when conducting civil business. Get to know those things human and divine that have been put at your disposal in books for good reason. Nowhere [else] will you find . . . the elegance of a verse of Homer, or Virgil, or of some other excellent poet. You will find no field so delightful or flowering as in one of the orations of Demosthenes, Cicero, Livy, Xenophon, and other such pleasant and perfect orators. No effort is more fully compensated . . . as the constant reading and rereading of good things. From such reading you will rise rich in good maxims and good arguments, strong in your ability to persuade others and get them to listen to you; among the citizens you will willingly be heard, admired, praised, and loved. [Leon Battista Alberti (1404–1472), *"On the Family."*]

moreover, had to be the classical Latin of Cicero and Virgil, not the evolving, changing Latin of the universities and the Church.

Renaissance humanists therefore condemned the living Latin of their scholastic contemporaries as a barbarous departure from ancient (and therefore "correct") standards of Latin style. Despite their belief that they were thereby reviving the study of the classics, the humanists actually contributed to Latin's demise. By insisting on ancient standards of grammar, syntax, and diction, they turned Latin into a fossilized language that ceased to have any direct relevance to daily life. They also contributed, ironically and unwittingly, to the ultimate triumph of the various European vernaculars as languages of intellectual and cultural life, and to the death of Latin as a common European language.

## Bruni on the Humanist Curriculum

The foundations of all true learning must be laid in the sound and thorough knowledge of Latin: which implies study marked by a broad spirit, accurate scholarship, and careful attention to details. Unless this solid basis be secured it is useless to attempt to rear an enduring edifice. Without it the great monuments of literature are unintelligible, and the art of composition impossible. To attain this essential knowledge we must never relax our careful attention to the grammar of the language, but perpetually confirm and extend our acquaintance with it until it is thoroughly our own. . . .

But the wider question now confronts us, that of the subject matter of our studies, that which I have already called the realities of fact and principle, as distinct from literary form. . . . First among such studies I place History: a subject which must not on any account be neglected by one who aspires to true cultivation. . . . For the careful study of the past enlarges our foresight in contemporary affairs and affords to citizens and to monarchs lessons . . . in the ordering of public policy. From History, also, we draw our store of examples of moral precepts. . . .

The great Orators of antiquity must by all means be included. Nowhere do we find the virtues more warmly extolled, the vices so fiercely decried. From them we may learn, also, how to express consolation, encouragement, dissuasion or advice. . . .

Familiarity with the great poets of antiquity is essential to any claim to true education. For in their writings we find deep speculations upon Nature, and upon the Causes and Origins of things, which must carry weight with us both from their antiquity and from their authorship. . . .

Proficiency in literary form, not accompanied by broad acquaintance with facts and truths, is a barren attainment; whilst information, however vast, which lacks all grace of expression would seem to be put under a bushel or partly thrown away. . . . Where, however, this double capacity exists—breadth of learning and grace of style—we allow the highest title to distinction and to abiding fame. . . . [Leonardo Bruni (1369–1444), *"Concerning the Study of Literature."*]

Sources: Vergerius and Bruni: William Harrison Woodward, ed., *Vittorino da Feltre and Other Humanist Educators* (London: 1897), pp. 96–110, 124–29, 132–33. Alberti: Eric Cochrane and Julius Kirshner, eds., *University of Chicago Readings in Western Civilization*. Vol. 5: *The Renaissance* (Chicago: 1986), pp. 81–82.

### *Questions for Analysis*

1. What is the purpose of education, according to these authorities? What elements do their programs share? What are their potential areas of contention?
2. Why did humanists such as Leonardo Bruni consider the study of history essential to education?

Humanists were also convinced that their own educational program—which placed the study of Latin language and literature at the core of the curriculum and then encouraged the study of Greek—was the best way to produce virtuous citizens and able public officials. And because women were excluded from Italian political life, the education of women was therefore of little concern to most humanists, although some aristocratic women did acquire humanist training. Here again there are paradoxes: for as more and more Italian city-states fell into the hands of autocratic rulers, the humanist educational curriculum lost its immediate connection to the republican ideals of Italian political life. Nevertheless, humanists never lost their conviction that the study of the "humanities" (as the humanist curriculum came to be known) was the best way to produce political leaders.

## THE RENAISSANCE OF ITALY

Although the Renassiance eventually became a Europe-wide intellectual and artistic movement, it developed first and most distinctively in Italy. Understanding why this happened is important not only to explaining the origins of this movement, but also to understanding its essential characteristics.

The most fundamental reason was that, after the Black Death, northern Italy became the most urbanized region of Europe. Moreover, Italian aristocrats customarily lived in urban centers rather than in rural castles, and consequently became more fully involved in urban public affairs than their counterparts north of the Alps. Elsewhere in Europe, most aristocrats lived on the income from their landed estates, while rich town dwellers gained their living from trade; but in Italy, many town-dwelling aristocrats engaged in banking or mercantile enterprises while many rich mercantile families imitated the manners of the aristocracy. The noted Florentine family the Medici, for example, were originally physicians and apothecaries (as their name suggests). But they eventually made a fortune in banking and commerce, and were able to assimiliate into the aristocracy.

The results of these developments are tied to the history of the new humanist education mentioned above. Not only was there great demand for the skills of reading and accounting necessary to become a successful merchant, but the richest and most prominent families sought above all to find teachers who would impart to their sons the knowledge and skills necessary to cutting a figure in society and speaking with authority in public affairs. Consequently, Italy produced a large number of lay educators, many of whom not only taught students but also demonstrated their learning by producing political and ethical treatises and works of literature. Italian schools and tutors accordingly turned out the best-educated urban elites in all of Europe, men who became wealthy, knowledgeable patrons ready to invest in the cultivation of new ideas and new forms of literary and artistic expression.

A second reason why late-medieval Italy was the birthplace of an intellectual and artistic renaissance has to do with its vexed political situation. Unlike France, England, Spain, and the kingdoms of Scandinavia and eastern Europe, Italy had no unifying political institutions. Italians therefore looked to the classical past for their time of glory, dreaming of a day when Rome would be, again, the center of the world. They boasted that ancient Roman monuments were omnipresent in their landscape, and that classical Latin literature referred to cities and sites they recognized as their own.

Italians were particularly intent on reappropriating their classical heritage because they were seeking to establish an independent cultural identity that could help them oppose the intellectual and political supremacy of France. The removal of the papacy to Avignon for most of the fourteenth century and the subsequent Great Schism (Chapter 10) had heightened antagonism between the city-states of Italy and the burgeoning nation-states and empires of the Continent. This coincided with a rejection of the scholasticism taught in northern Europe's universities, and the embrace of the intellectual alternatives offered by new readings of classical sources. As Roman literature and learning took hold in the imaginations of Italy's intellectuals, so too did Roman art and architecture, for Roman models could help Italians create an artistic alternative to French Gothic, just as Roman learning offered an intellectual alternative to the scholasticism of Paris.

Finally, the Italian Renaissance could not have occurred without the underpinning of Italian wealth gained through the increasing commercial ventures described in Chapter 11. This meant that talented men seeking employment and patronage were more likely to stay at home than

**POPE JULIUS II (r. 1503–15).** This portrait of one of the most powerful popes of the Renaissance—it was he who commissioned Michelangelo's paintings in the Sistine Chapel—was executed by Raffaello Sanzio da Urbino, known as Raphael (1483–1520). The acorns atop the posts of the throne are visual puns on the pope's family name, della Rovere ("of the oak"). ▪ ***What impression of the pope's personality does this portrait convey?***

to seek opportunities abroad. Intensive investment in culture also arose from an intensification of urban pride and the concentration of individual and family wealth in urban areas. Cities themselves became the primary patrons of art and learning in the fourteenth century. During the fifteenth century, however, when most city-states succumbed to the hereditary rule of powerful dynasties, patronage was monopolized by the princely aristocracy. Among these great princes were the popes in Rome, who controlled the Papal States, employed the greatest artists of the day, and for a few decades made Rome the artistic capital of Europe.

## LITERARY AND INTELLECTUAL ACTIVITY

We have already encountered the man who strove to leave behind "the middle age" of his own time, and who is therefore considered the founder of the Renaissance movement: Francesco Petrarca (1304–1374). Petrarch was an ordained priest, but he believed that the scholastic theology taught in universities was entirely misguided, because it concentrated on abstract speculation rather than the achievement of virtue and ethical conduct. Instead, he felt that the truly Christian writer must cultivate literary eloquence, and so inspire others to do good through the pursuit of beauty and truth. For him, the best models of eloquence were to be found in the classical texts of Latin literature, which were doubly valuable because they were also filled with ethical wisdom. Petrarch dedicated himself, therefore, to rediscovering such texts and to writing his own poems and moral treatises in a Latin style modeled on classical authors. But Petrarch was also a prolific vernacular poet. His Italian sonnets—which spawned a new literary genre—were written in praise of his semi-fictional beloved, Laura, in the chivalrous style of the troubadours. They were widely admired and imitated, inspiring poets in other European vernaculars. William Shakespeare (1564–1616) would later adopt the form.

Petrarch's ultimate ideal for human conduct was a solitary life of contemplation and asceticism. But subsequent Italian thinkers and scholars, located mainly in Florence, developed a different vision of life's true purpose. For them, the goal of classical education was civic. Humanists such as Leonardo Bruni (c. 1370–1444) and Leon Battista Alberti (1404–1472) agreed with Petrarch on the importance of eloquence and the value of classical literature, but they also taught that man's nature equipped him for action, for usefulness to his family and society, and for serving the state—ideally a city-state after the Florentine model. In their view, ambition and the quest for glory were noble impulses that ought to be encouraged and channeled toward these ends. They also refused to condemn the accumulation of material possessions, arguing that the history of human progress is inseparable from the human dominion of the earth and its resources.

Many of the humanists' civic ideals are expressed Alberti's treatise *On the Family* (1443), in which he argued that the nuclear family was the fundamental unit of the city-state and should be governed in such a way as to further the city-state's political, social, and economic goals. Alberti accordingly argued that the family should mirror the city-state's own organization, and he thus consigned women—who, in reality, governed the household—to child-bearing, child-rearing, and subservience to men (see ***Analyzing Primary Sources*** on page 375). He asserted, furthermore, that women should play no role whatsoever in the public sphere. Although such dismissals of women's abilities were fiercely resisted by actual women, the humanism of the Renaissance was characterized by a pervasive denigration of them—a denigration often mirrored in the works of classical literature that these humanists so much admired.

### *The Emergence of Textual Scholarship*

The humanists of Florence also went far beyond Petrarch in their knowledge of classical (especially Greek) literature and philosophy. In this they were aided by a number of Byzantine scholars who had migrated to Italy in the first half of the fifteenth century and who gave instruction in the language. There were also attempts on the part of Italians to acquire Greek masterpieces for themselves, which often involved journeys back to Constantinople. In 1423, for example, one adventurous scholar managed to bring back 238 manuscript books, among them rare works of Sophocles, Euripides, and Thucydides, all of which were quickly paraphrased in Latin and thus made accessible to western Europeans for the first time. By 1500, most of the Greek classics, including the writings of Plato, the dramatists, and the historians, had been translated and were more widely available than they had ever been, even in their own day.

This influx of new texts spurred a new interest in textual criticism. A pioneer in this activity was Lorenzo Valla (1407–1457). Born in Rome and active primarily as a secretary to the king of Naples and Sicily, Valla had no allegiance to the republican ideals of the Florentine humanists. Instead, he turned his skills to the painstaking analysis of Greek and Latin texts in order to show how the thorough study of language could discredit old assumptions about these texts' meanings and even unmask some texts as forgeries. For example, propagandists argued that the papacy's claim to secular power in Europe derived from rights granted to the bishop of Rome by the emperor Constantine in the fourth century, enshrined in the so-called Donation of Constantine. By analyzing the language of this spurious document, Valla proved that it could not have been written in the time of Constantine because it contained more recent Latin usages and vocabulary. He concluded that it had in fact been the work of a papal supporter active many centuries after Constantine's death. This demonstration not only discredited the more traditional methods of scholasticism, it introduced the concept of anachronism into all subsequent textual study and historical thought. Indeed, Valla even applied his expert knowledge of Greek to elucidating the meaning of Saint Paul's letters, which he believed had been obscured by Jerome's Latin translation (Chapter 6). This work was to prove an important link between Italian Renaissance scholarship and the subsequent Christian humanism of the north, which in turn fed into the Reformation (see Chapter 13).

**PICO DELLA MIRANDOLA.** When this young nobleman arrived in Florence at the age of nineteen, he was said to have been "of beauteous feature and shape." This contemporary portrait has often been attributed to Botticelli.

## *Renaissance Neoplatonism*

In the wake of these discoveries, Italian thought became dominated by a new interest in the philosophy of Plato (Chapter 4) and in the Neoplatonism of Plotinus (Chapter 6). So many intellectuals were engaged in the study of Plato that scholars used to believe that there was even a "Platonic Academy" in Florence; but in reality, the work of intellectuals like Marsilio Ficino (1433–1499) and Giovanni Pico della Mirandola (1463–1494) was informally fostered by the patronage of the wealthy Cosimo de' Medici. From the standpoint of posterity, Ficino's greatest achievement was his translation of Plato's works into Latin, which made them widely available to Europeans for the first time. Ficino himself regarded his *Hermetic Corpus*, a collection of passages drawn from ancient mystical writings, to be his greatest contribution to learning. It contained, among other texts, portions of the Hebrew Kabbalah.

Ficino's Platonic philosophy moved away from the ethics of civic humanism. He taught that the individual should look primarily to the salvation of the immortal soul from its "always miserable" mortal body: a very Platonic idea. His disciple Pico likewise rejected the mundanity of public affairs and shared his teacher's penchant for extracting and combining snippets taken out of context from ancient mystical tracts. But he also argued that man has the capacity to achieve union with God through the exercise of his unique talents, a glory that can be attained in life as well as in death.

## *The Influence of Machiavelli*

The greatness of these humanist scholars lay not in their originality but in their efforts to popularize aspects of ancient thought. But none of them was so influential as the era's greatest philosphical pragmatist, the Florentine Niccolò Machiavelli (1469–1527). Machiavelli's political writings both reflect the unstable condition of Italy and strive to address it. Since the end of the fifteenth century, Italy had become the arena of bloody international struggles. Both France and Spain had invaded the peninsula and were competing for the allegiance of the Italian city-states, which in turn were torn by internal dissension.

In 1498, Machiavelli became a prominent official in the government of the Florentine Republic, set up four years earlier when the French invasion had led to the expulsion of the Medici. His duties largely involved diplomatic missions to other Italian city-states. While in Rome, he became fascinated with the attempt of Cesare Borgia, son of Pope Alexander VI, to create his own principality in central Italy.

# Analyzing Primary Sources

## *Machiavelli's Patriotism*

*These passages are from the concluding chapter to Machiavelli's treatise* The Prince. *Like the book itself, they are addressed to Lorenzo de' Medici, head of Florence's most powerful family. In it, Machiavelli laments Italy's "barbarian occupation" by foreign powers, by which he means the invading armies of France, Spain, and the Holy Roman Empire. He may also be alluding to the many companies of foreign mercenaries that fought for Italy's various city-states.*

Reflecting on the matters set forth above and considering within myself whether the times were propitious in Italy at present to honor a new prince and whether there is at hand the matter suitable for a prudent and virtuous leader to mold in a new form, giving honor to himself and benefit to the citizens of the country, I have arrived at the opinion that all circumstances now favor such a prince, and I cannot think of a time more propitious for him than the present. If, as I said, it was necessary in order to make apparent the virtue of Moses, that the people of Israel should be enslaved in Egypt, and that the Persians should be oppressed by the Medes to provide an opportunity to illustrate the greatness and the spirit of Cyrus, and that the Athenians should be scattered in order to show the excellence of Theseus, thus at the present time, in order to reveal the valor of an Italian spirit, it was essential that Italy should fall to her present low estate, more enslaved than the Hebrews, more servile than the Persians, more disunited than the Athenians, leaderless and lawless, beaten, despoiled, lacerated, overrun and crushed under every kind of misfortune. . . . So Italy now, left almost lifeless, awaits the coming of one who will heal her wounds, putting an end to the sacking and looting in Lombardy and the spoliation and extortions in the Realm of Naples and Tuscany, and cleanse her sores that have been so long festering. Behold how she prays God to send her some one to redeem her from the cruelty and insolence of the barbarians. See how she is ready and willing to follow any banner so long as there be someone to take it up. Nor has she at present any hope of finding her redeemer save only in your illustrious house [the Medici] which has been so highly exalted both by its own merits and by fortune and which has been favored by God and the church, of which it is now ruler. . . .

This opportunity, therefore, should not be allowed to pass, and Italy, after such a long wait, must be allowed to behold her redeemer. I cannot describe the joy with which he will be received in all these provinces which have suffered so much from the foreign deluge, nor with what thirst for vengeance, nor with what firm devotion, what solemn delight, what tears! What gates could be closed to him, what people could deny him obedience, what envy could withstand him, what Italian could withhold allegiance from him? THIS BARBARIAN OCCUPATION STINKS IN THE NOSTRILS OF ALL OF US. Let your illustrious house then take up this cause with the spirit and the hope with which one undertakes a truly just enterprise. . . .

Source: Niccolò Machiavelli, *The Prince,* trans. and ed. Thomas G. Bergin (Arlington Heights, IL: 1947), pp. 75–76, 78.

### *Questions for Analysis*

1. Why does Machiavelli argue that Italy needed the type of ruler he described in *The Prince*?
2. According to Machiavelli, what was wrong with the Italy of his own day? What does "patriotism" mean for him?
3. How does Machiavelli use historical precedents and parallels to make his argument?

He noted with approval Cesare's ruthlessness and his complete subordination of personal ethics to political ends. In 1512, when the Medici returned to overthrow the republic of Florence, Machiavelli was deprived of his position. Disappointed and embittered, he retired to the country and devoted his energies to the articulation of a new political philosophy that he hoped would earn him a powerful job.

Machiavelli remains a controversial figure. Some modern scholars, like many of his own contemporary readers, see him as disdainful of conventional morality, interested solely in the acquisition and exercise of power as an end in itself. Others see him as an Italian patriot, who viewed princely tyranny as the only way to liberate Italy from its foreign conquerors. Still others see him as influenced by

**THE STATES OF ITALY, c. 1494.** This map shows the divisions of Italy on the eve of the French invasion in 1494. Contemporary observers often described Italy as being divided among five great powers: Milan, Venice, Florence, the Papal States, and the Kingdom of the Two Sicilies (based in Naples). ▪ ***Which of these powers would have been most capable of expanding their territories?*** ▪ ***Which neighboring states would have been most threatened by such attempts at expansion?*** ▪ ***Why would Florence and the Papal States so often find themselves in conflict with each other?***

Saint Augustine, who understood that in a fallen world populated by sinful people, a ruler's good intentions do not guarantee that his policies will have good results. Accordingly, Machiavelli insisted that a prince's actions must be judged by their consequences and not by their intrinsic moral quality. He argued that "the necessity of preserving the state will often compel a prince to take actions which are opposed to loyalty, charity, humanity, and religion. . . . So far as he is able, a prince should stick to the path of good but, if the necessity arises, he should know how to follow evil."

On the surface, Machiavelli's two great works of political analysis appear to contradict each other. In his *Discourses on Livy*, which drew on the works of that Roman historian, he praised the ancient Roman Republic as a model for his own contemporaries, lauding constitutional government, equality among citizens, and the subordination of religion to the service of the state. There is little doubt, in fact, that Machiavelli was a committed believer in the free city-state as the ideal form of human government. But Machiavelli also wrote *The Prince*, "a handbook for tyrants" in the eyes of his critics, and he dedicated this work to Lorenzo, son of Piero de' Medici, whose family had overthrown the Florentine republic that Machiavelli himself had served.

Because *The Prince* has been so much more widely read than the *Discourses*, interpretations of Machiavelli's political thought have often mistaken the former as an endorsement of power for its own sake. Machiavelli's real position was quite different. In the political chaos of early-sixteenth-century Italy, Machiavelli saw the likes of Cesare Borgia as the only hope for revitalizing the spirit of independence among his contemporaries, and so making Italy fit, eventually, for self-governance. However dark his vision of human nature, Machiavelli never ceased to hope that his Italian contemporaries would rise up, expel their French and Spanish conquerors, and restore ancient traditions of liberty and equality. He regarded a period of despotism as a necessary step toward that end, not as a permanent and desirable form of government.

## The Ideal of the Courtier

Far more congenial to contemporary tastes than the shockingly frank political theories of Machiavelli were the guidelines for proper aristocratic conduct offered in *The Book of the Courtier* (1528), by the diplomat and nobleman Baldassare Castiglione. This forerunner of modern handbooks of etiquette stands in sharp contrast to earlier treatises on civic humanism. Whereas Bruni and Alberti taught the sober virtues of strenuous service on behalf of the city-state, Castiglione taught how to attain the elegant and

**THE IMPACT OF PERSPECTIVE.** Masaccio's painting *The Trinity with the Virgin* illustrates the startling sense of depth made possible by observing the rules of perspective.

seemingly effortless skills necessary for advancement in Italy's princely courts. More than anyone else, Castiglione developed and popularized a set of talents now associated with the "Renaissance man": one accomplished in many different pursuits, witty, canny, and stylish. Castiglione also eschewed the misogyny of the humanists by stressing the ways in which court ladies could rise to influence and prominence through the graceful exercise of their womanly powers. Widely read throughout Europe, Castiglione's *Courtier* set the standard for polite behavior into the nineteenth century.

The literature of Renaissance Italy was not entirely devoted to the philosophy of political advancement. Machiavelli himself wrote delightful short stories and an engagingly bawdy play, the *Mandragola*; the great artist Michelangelo (see below) wrote many masterful sonnets; and Ludovico Ariosto (1474–1533), the most eminent of sixteenth-century Italian poets, wrote a lengthy verse narrative called *Orlando Furioso* (The Madness of Roland), a retelling of the heroic exploits celebrated in the French *Song of Roland* (Chapter 8). Yet this work differs radically from previous chivalric epics, not least because it is totally devoid of heroic idealism. Ariosto wrote to make readers laugh and to charm them with descriptions of natural beauties and the passions of lovers. His work embodies the disillusionment of the later Renaissance, and the tendency to seek consolation in the pursuit of pleasure and aesthetic delight.

## RENAISSANCE ARTS

Without question, the most enduring legacy of the Italian Renaissance has been the contributions of its artists, particularly those who embraced new techniques and approaches to painting. We have already noted (Chapter 10) the creative and economic opportunities afforded by this medium, which freed artists from having to work on site and on commission: paintings executed on wooden panels are portable—unlike wall paintings—and can be displayed in different settings, reach different markets, and be more widely distributed. To these benefits, the artists of Italy added an important technical ingredient: mastery of a vanishing (one-point) perspective that gave to painting an illusion of three dimensional space. Fifteenth-century artists also experimented with effects of light and shade, and studied intently the anatomy and proportions of the human body.

Meanwhile, increasing private wealth and the growth of lay patronage opened up new markets and created a huge demand for a diverse array of visual narratives: not only religious images, which were as important as ever, but the depiction of classical subjects. Portraiture also came into its own, as princes and merchants alike sought to glorify themeselves and their families. The use of oil paints, a medium that had been pioneered in Flanders, further revolutionized fifteenth-century painting styles. Because oil does not dry as quickly as water-based pigments, a painter can work more slowly, taking time with the more difficult parts of a picture and making corrections as he or she goes along.

### *Painting in Florence*

In the fifteenth century, the majority of the great painters were Florentines. First among them was the precocious Masaccio (1401–1428) who, although he died at the age of only twenty-seven, inspired the work of artists for the next century. Masaccio's greatness as a painter rested on his

# Interpreting Visual Evidence

## *The Blending of Classical and Christian*

The paintings known today as *The Birth of Venus* (image A) and *The Madonna of the Pomegranate* (image B) were both executed by Boticelli in Florence between the years 1485–87. Separately and together, they exhibit the artist's signature devotion to blending classical and Christian motifs by using ideas associated with the pagan past to illuminate sacred stories. For example, Neoplatonic philosophers like Ficino taught that all pagan myths prefigure Christian truths—including the story that Aphrodite, goddess of love, was miraculously engendered from the foam of the sea by the god of Time. This also helps to

A. *The Birth of Venus.*

successful employment of one-point perspective and his use of dramatic lighting effects. Both are evident in his painting of the Trinity, where the body of the crucified Christ appears to be thrust forward by the impassive figure of God the Father, while the Virgin's gaze directly engages the viewer.

Masaccio's best-known successor was Sandro Botticelli (1445–1510), who was equally drawn to classical and Christian subjects. Botticelli excels in depicting graceful motion and the sensuous pleasures of nature. He is most famous today for paintings that evoke classical mythology without any overtly Christian frame of reference.

explain the visual reference to a pomegranate in the painting of the Virgin holding the infant Jesus. In Greek mythology, the pomegranate was the fruit whose seeds were eaten by Persephone, daughter of the goddess of fertility, when she was sent to the Underworld to become the bride of Hades. Because she had eaten six of these seeds, Persephone was allowed to return to her mother Demeter for only part of the year; in the winter months, consequently, the Earth becomes less fertile, because Demeter is in mourning for her child.

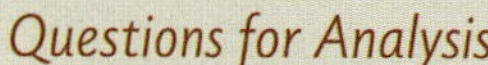

### Questions for Analysis

1. Scholars have recently argued that *The Birth of Venus* is an allegory of Christian love that also prefigures the Blessed Virgin's immaculate conception and sinless nature. How would you go about proving this? What elements in this painting and in the myth of Aphrodite's birth lend themselves to that interpretation?
2. In what ways can the cyclical story of Jesus' death and resurrection, which Christians celebrate each year, be linked to the Greek myth invoked by *The Madonna of the Pomegranate*?
3. Like many artists, Botticelli used the same models for an array of different pictures. Do you recognize the resemblance between the Virgin and Venus? How does the depiction of the same young woman in these two different contexts underscore the relationship between pagan mythology and Christian sacred history?

B. *The Madonna of the Pomegranate.*

For centuries, these were misunderstood as expressions of Renaissance "paganism," but they have more recently been unmasked as Christian allegories whose ancient deities represent aspects of later Christian ideas (see ***Interpreting Visual Evidence***).

The most technically adventurous and versitile artist of this period was Leonardo da Vinci (1452–1519). Leonardo personifies our ideal of the Renaissance man: he was a painter, architect, musician, mathematician, engineer, and inventor. The illegitimate son of a notary, Leonardo set up

***THE VIRGIN OF THE ROCKS.*** This painting reveals Leonardo's interest in the variety of human faces and facial expressions, and in natural settings.

an artist's shop in Florence by the time he was twenty-five and gained the patronage of the Medici ruler, Lorenzo the Magnificent. But Leonardo had a weakness: he worked slowly, and he had difficulty finishing anything. This naturally displeased Lorenzo and other Florentine patrons, who regarded artists as craftsmen who worked on commission, and on their patrons' time—not their own. Leonardo, however, strongly objected to this view; he considered himself to be an inspired, independent innovator. He therefore left Florence in 1482 and went to work for the court of the Sforza dictators in Milan, where he was given freer rein in structuring his time and work (see page 390). He remained there until the French invasion of 1499; he then wandered about, finally accepting the patronage of the French king, Francis I, under whose auspices he lived and worked until his death.

Leonardo's approach to painting was that it should be the most accurate possible imitation of nature. He based his work on his own detailed observations of a blade of grass, the wing of a bird, a waterfall. He obtained human corpses for dissection and reconstructed in drawing the minutest features of anatomy, carrying this knowledge over to his paintings.

Indeed, Leonardo was convinced of the essential divinity in all living things. It is not surprising, therefore, that he was a vegetarian and that he went to the marketplace to buy caged birds, which he released to their native habitat. *The Virgin of the Rocks* typifies not only his marvelous technical skill but also his passion for science and his belief in the universe as a well-ordered place. The figures are arranged geometrically, with every stone and plant depicted in accurate detail. *The Last Supper*, painted on the refectory walls of a monastery in Milan (and now in an advanced state of decay) is a study of human psychology. A serene Christ, resigned to his terrible fate, has just announced to his disciples that one of them will betray him. The artist succeeds in portraying the mingled emotions of surprise, horror, and guilt on the faces of the disciples as they gradually perceive the meaning of their master's statement. He also implicates the painting's viewers in this dramatic scene, since they too dine alongside Christ, in the very same room.

## *The Venetian and Roman Schools*

The innovations of Florentine artists were widely imitated. By the end of the fifteenth century, they had influenced a group of painters active in the wealthy city of Venice, among them Tiziano Vecelli, better known as Titian (c. 1490–1576).

***THE LAST SUPPER.*** This fresco on the refectory wall of the monastery of Santa Marie della Grazie in Milan is a testament to both the powers and limitations of Leonardo's artistry. It skillfully employs the techniques of one-point perspective to create the illusion that Jesus and his disciples are actually dining at the monastery's head table; but because Leonardo had not mastered the techniques of fresco painting, he applied tempera pigments to a dry wall which had been coated with a sealing agent. As a result, the painting's colors began to fade just years after its completion. By the middle of the sixteenth century, it had seriously deteriorated. Large portions of it are now invisible.

***DOGE FRANCESCO VENIER* (1555).** Titian served as the official painter of the Venetian Republic for sixty years. This superb portrait of Venice's ruler shows the artist's mastery of light and color while also displaying the mastery and wealth of his patron.

Many of Titian's paintings evoke the luxurious, pleasure-loving life of this thriving commercial center. For although they copied Florentine techniques, most Venetian painters showed little of that city's concerns for philosophical issues and religious allegory. Their aim was to appeal to the senses by painting idyllic landscapes and sumptuous portraits of the rich and powerful. In the subordination of form and meaning to color and elegance they may have mirrored the tastes of the men for whom they worked.

Rome, too, became a major artistic center in this era, and a place where the Florentine school exerted a more potent influence. Among its eminent painters was Raffaello Sanzio (1483–1520) or Raphael, a native of Urbino. Although Raphael was influenced by Leonardo, he cultivated a more spiritual and philosophical approach to his subjects, suggestive of Boticelli. As we noted in Chapter 4, his fresco *The School of Athens* depicts both the harmony and the differences of Platonic and Aristotelian thought (see page 114). It also includes a number of Raphael's contemporaries as models. The image of Plato is actually a portrait of Leonardo, while the architect Donato Bramante (c. 1444–1514) stands in for the geometer Euclid, and Michelangelo for the philosopher Heraclitus.

Michelangelo Buonarroti (1475–1564), who spent many decades in Rome, was actually a native of Florence. If Leonardo was a naturalist, Michelangelo was an idealist, despite the harsh political and material realities of the conditions in which he worked. He was also a polymath: painter, sculptor, architect, poet—and he expressed himself in all these forms with a similar power. At the center of all of his work—as at the center of Renaissance humanism—is the male figure, the embodied male mind.

Michelangelo's greatest achievements in painting appear in a single location, the Sistine Chapel of the Vatican palace, yet they are products of two different periods in the artist's life and consequently exemplify two different artistic styles and outlooks on the human condition. More famous are the extraordinary frescoes painted on the ceiling from 1508 to 1512, depicting scenes from the book of Genesis. All the panels in this series, including *The Creation of Adam*, exemplify the young artist's commitment to classical artistic principles. Correspondingly, all affirm the sublimity of the Creation and the heroic qualities of humankind. But a quarter of a century later, when Michelangelo returned to work in the Sistine Chapel, both his style and mood had changed dramatically. In the enormous *Last Judgment*, a fresco done for the Chapel's altar wall in 1536, Michelangelo repudiated classical restraint and substituted a style that emphasized tension and distortion to communicate the older man's

**SELF-PORTRAIT OF THE ARTIST AS AN OLD MAN: DETAIL FROM *THE LAST JUDGMENT*.** When Michelangelo returned to the Sistine Chapel to paint this fresco on the wall behind the main altar, he emphasized different aspects of humanity: not the youthful heroism of the new-born Adam, but the grotesque weakness of the aging body. Here, St. Bartholomew holds his own flayed skin (tradition held that he had been skinned alive) – but the face is that of Michelangelo himself.

pessimistic conception of humanity as wracked with fear, guilt, and frailty. He included himself in it: but unlike Raphael's, his self-portrait is a doomed soul whose flayed skin is all that remains of worldly ambition.

## Renaissance Sculpture

Sculpture was not a new medium for artists, the way that oil painting was, but it too was an important area of Renaissance innovation. Statues were not only incorporated into columns or doorways or as effigies on tombs; for the first time since late antiquity they became figures "in the round." By freeing sculpture from its bondage to architecture, the Renaissance reestablished it as a separate, secular art form.

The first great master of Renaissance sculpture was Donatello (c. 1386–1466). His bronze statue of David, triumphant over the head of the slain Goliath, is the first free-standing nude of the period. Yet this David is clearly an agile adolescent rather than a muscular Greek athlete—like that of Michelangelo—whose *David*, executed in 1501, was a public expression of Florentine ideals, not merely graceful but heroic. Michelangelo regarded sculpture as the most exalted of the arts because it allowed the artist to imitate God most fully in recreating human forms. Furthermore, in Michelangelo's view, the most God-like sculptor disdained slavish naturalism: anyone can make a plaster cast of a human figure, but only an inspired creative genius can endow his sculpted figures with a sense of life. Accordingly, Michelangelo's sculpture subordinated reality to the force of his imagination and sought to express his ideals in ever more astonishing forms. He also insisted on working in marble—the "noblest" sculptural material—and created a figure twice as large as life. By sculpting a serenely confident young man at the peak of physical fitness, Michelangelo celebrated the Florentine republic's own determination in resisting tyrants and upholding ideals of civic justice.

Yet the serenity seen in *David* is no longer prominent in the works of Michelangelo's later life, when, as in his painting, he began to explore the use of anatomical distortion

**SELF-PORTRAIT OF THE ARTIST AS A YOUNG MAN: DETAIL FROM *THE SCHOOL OF ATHENS*.** We have already analyzed aspects of Raphael's famous group portrait of the Greek philosophers, with Plato and Aristotle at their center: see page 114 of Chapter 4. In addition to featuring his own contemporaries as models—including the artists Leonardo and Michelangelo and the architect Bramante—Raphael put himself in the picture, too. ▪ ***What messages does this choice convey?***

***THE CREATION OF ADAM.*** This is one of a series of frescoes painted on the ceiling of the Sistine Chapel of the Vatican palace in Rome, executed by Michelangelo over a period of many years and in circumstances of extreme physical hardship. It has since become an iconic image. ▪ ***How might it be said to capture Renaissance ideals?***

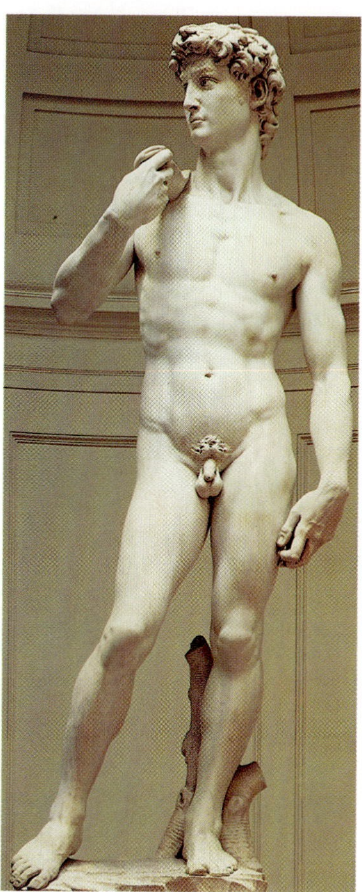

**THE POWER AND VULNERABILITY OF THE MALE BODY.** Donatello's *David* (left) was the first free-standing nude executed since antiquity. It shows the Hebrew leader as an adolescent youth, and is a little over 5 feet tall. The *David* by Michelangelo (center) stands thirteen feet high, and was placed prominently in front of Florence's city hall to proclaim the city's power and humanistic values. Michelangelo's *Descent from the Cross* (right), which shows Christ's broken body in the arms of the elderly Nicodemus, was made by the sculptor for his own tomb. (The gospels describe Nicodemus as a Pharisee who became a follower of Jesus and who was present at his death.) ▪ ***Why would Michelangelo choose this figure to represent himself?*** ▪ ***How does his representation of David—and the context in which this figure was displayed—compare to that of Donatello?***

to create effects of emotional intensity. While his statues remained awesome in scale, they also communicate rage, depression, and sorrow. The culmination of this trend is his unfinished but intensely moving *Descent from the Cross*, a depiction of an old man (the sculptor himself) grieving over the distorted, slumping body of the dead Christ.

## Renaissance Architecture

To a much greater extent than either sculpture or painting, Renaissance architecture had its roots in the past. The Gothic style pioneered in northern France (Chapter 9) had seldom found a friendly reception in Italy; most of the buildings constructed there during the Middle Ages were Romanesque in style, and the great architects of the Renaissance generally adopted their building plans from these structures—some of which they believed (mistakenly) to be ancient rather than medieval. They also copied decorative devices from the authentic ruins of ancient Rome.

Renaissance buildings also emphasize geometrical proportion. Italian architects of this era, under the influence of Neoplatonism, concluded that certain mathematical ratios reflect the harmony of the universe. For example, the proportions of the human body serve as the basis for the proportions of the quintessential Renaissance building: St. Peter's Basilica in Rome. Designed by some of the most celebrated architects of the time, including Bramante and Michelangelo, it is still one of the largest buildings in the world. Yet it seems smaller than a Gothic cathedral because

# Analyzing Primary Sources

## *Leonardo da Vinci Applies for a Job*

*Few sources illuminate the tensions between Renaissance ideals and realities better than the résumé of accomplishments submitted by Leonardo da Vinci to a prospective employer, Ludovico Sforza of Milan. In the following letter, Leonardo explains why he deserves to be appointed chief architect and military engineer in the duke's household administration. He got the job, and moved to Milan in 1481.*

**1.** I have the kind of bridges that are extremely light and strong, made to be carried with great ease, and with them you may pursue, and, at any time, flee from the enemy; . . . and also methods of burning and destroying those of the enemy.

**2.** I know how, when a place is under attack, to eliminate the water from the trenches, and make endless variety of bridges . . . and other machines. . . .

**3.** . . . I have methods for destroying every rock or other fortress, even if it were built on rock, etc.

**4.** I also have other kinds of mortars [bombs] that are most convenient and easy to carry. . . .

**5.** And if it should be a sea battle, I have many kinds of machines that are most efficient for offense and defense. . . .

**6.** I also have means that are noiseless to reach a designated area by secret and tortuous mines. . . .

**7.** I will make covered chariots, safe and unattackable, which can penetrate the enemy with their artillery. . . .

**8.** In case of need I will make big guns, mortars, and light ordnance of fine and useful forms that are out of the ordinary.

**9.** If the operation of bombardment should fail, I would contrive catapults, mangonels, trabocchi [trebuchets], and other machines of marvelous efficacy and unusualness. In short, I can, according to each case in question, contrive various and endless means of offense and defense.

**10.** In time of peace I believe I can give perfect satisfaction that is equal to any other in the field of architecture and the construction of buildings. . . . I can execute sculpture in marble, bronze, or clay, and also in painting I do the best that can be done, and as well as any other, whoever he may be.

Having now, most illustrious Lord, sufficiently seen the specimens of all those who consider themselves master craftsmen of instruments of war, and that the invention and operation of such instruments are no different from those in common use, I shall now endeavor . . . to explain myself to your Excellency by revealing to your Lordship my secrets. . . .

Source: Excerpted from Leonardo da Vinci, *The Notebooks*, in *The Italian Renaissance Reader*, eds. Julia Conaway and Mark Mosa (Harmondsworth: 1987), pp. 195–196.

### *Questions for Analysis*

**1.** Based on the qualifications highlighted by Leonardo in this letter, what can you conclude about the political situation in Milan and the priorities of its duke? What can you conclude about the state of military technologies in this period and the conduct of warfare?

**2.** What do you make of the fact that Leonardo mentions his artistic endeavors only at the end of the letter? Does this fact alter your opinion or impression of him? Why or why not?

it is built to human scale. The same artful proportions are evident in smaller-scale buildings, too, as in the aristocratic country houses designed by the northern Italian architect Andrea Palladio (1508–1580), who created secular miniatures of ancient temples (such as the Roman Pantheon) to glorify the aristocrats who dwelled within them.

## *The Waning of the Renaissance*

The intensive intellectual and artistic activity that characterizes the Renaissance began to wane toward the end of the fifteenth century. The causes of this decline are varied. The French invasion of 1494 and the incessant warfare that

**ST. PETER'S BASILICA, ROME.** This eighteenth-century painting shows the massive interior of the Renaissance building. But were it not for the perspective provided by the tiny human figures, the human eye would be fooled into thinking this a much smaller space.

ensued were among the major factors. The French king, Charles VIII, viewed Italy as an attractive target for his expansive dynastic ambitions, and he led an army of 30,000 well-trained troops across the Alps to press his claims to the Duchy of Milan and the Kingdom of the Two Sicilies. Florence swiftly capitulated; within less than a year the French had swept down the peninsula and conquered Naples. By so doing, however, they aroused the suspicions of the rulers of Spain, who also claimed the territory of Sicily. An alliance among Spain, the Papal States, the Holy Roman Empire, Milan, and Venice finally forced Charles to withdraw from Italy.

But the respite was brief. Charles's successor, Louis XII, launched a second invasion, and from 1499 until 1529 warfare in Italy was virtually uninterrupted. Alliances and counteralliances followed each other in bewildering succession, but they managed only to prolong the hostilities. The worst disaster came in 1527, when rampaging troops under the command of the Spanish ruler and Holy Roman emperor, Charles V, sacked the city of Rome, causing enormous destruction. Only in 1529 did Charles finally manage to gain control over most of the Italian peninsula, putting an end to the fighting for a time. Once triumphant, he retained two of the largest portions of Italy for Spain—the Duchy of Milan and the Kingdom of the Two Sicilies—and installed favored princes as the rulers of almost all the other Italian political entities except for Venice and the Papal States. These protégés of the Spanish crown continued to preside over their own courts, to patronize the arts, and to adorn their cities with luxurious buildings; but they were puppets of a foreign power and unable to inspire their retinues with a sense of vigorous cultural independence.

To these political disasters was added a waning of Italian prosperity. Italy's virtual monopoly of trade with Asia in the fifteenth century had been one of the chief economic underpinnings for Renaissance patronage, but the gradual shifting of trade routes from the Mediterranean to the Atlantic region (Chapter 11), slowly cost Italy its supremacy as the center of European trade. Warfare also contributed to Italy's economic hardships, as did Spanish financial exactions in Milan and Naples. As Italian wealth diminished, there was less and less of a surplus to support artistic endeavors. But by this time, Renaissance ideas and techniques were spreading from Italy to the rest of Europe; so even as Italy's political and economic power waned, its cultural and intellectual cachet lent it more prominence than it had enjoyed for centuries.

## THE RENAISSANCE NORTH OF THE ALPS

Contacts between Italy and northern Europe continued throughout the fourteenth and fifteenth centuries. Italian merchants and financiers were familiar figures at northern courts; students from all over Europe studied at Italian universities such as Bologna or Padua; poets (including Geoffrey Chaucer, Chapter 10) and their works traveled to and from Italy; and northern soldiers were frequent participants in Italian wars. Only at the end of the fifteenth century, however, did the new currents of Italian Renaissance learning begin to be exported to Spain and northern Europe.

A variety of explanations have been offered for this delay. Northern European intellectual life in the later Middle Ages was dominated by universities such as Paris, Oxford, and Charles University in Prague, whose curricula focused on the study of philosophical logic and Christian theology. This approach left little room for the study of classical literature. In Italy, by contrast, universities were more often professional schools for law and medicine, and universities themselves exercised much less influence over intellectual life. As a result, a more secular, urban-oriented educational tradition took shape in Italy, within which Renaissance humanism was able to develop. Even in the sixteenth century, northern scholars influenced by Italian Renaissance ideals usually worked outside the university system under the patronage of kings and princes.

Before the sixteenth century, northern rulers were also less interested in patronizing artists and intellectuals than were the city-states and princes of Italy. In Italy, as we may have seen, such patronage was an important arena for competition between political rivals. In northern Europe, however, political units were larger and political rivals were fewer. It was therefore less necessary to use art for political purposes in a kingdom than it was in a city-state. In Florence, a statue erected in a central square would be seen by nearly all the city's residents. In Paris, such a statue would be seen by only a tiny minority of the French king's subjects. But in the sixteenth century, as northern nobles began to spend more time in residence at the royal court, could kings be reasonably certain that their patronage of artists and intellectuals would be noticed by those whom they were trying to impress.

**THE VILLA ROTUNDA.** This country house, designed by Andrea Palladio (1508–1580), mimics the design of Rome's ancient Pantheon, the temple dedicated to "all the gods." But it is a human dwelling, built to human scale.

## *Christian Humanism and the Career of Erasmus*

The northern Renaissance was the product of the grafting of certain Italian Renaissance ideals onto preexisting northern traditions. This can be seen very clearly in the case of the most prominent northern Renaissance intellectual movement, Christian humanism. Although they shared the Italian humanists' rejection of scholasticism, northern Christian humanists more often sought ethical guidance from biblical and religious precepts rather than from Cicero or Virgil. Like their Italian counterparts, they sought wisdom from antiquity; but the antiquity they had in mind was Christian rather than classical—the antiquity, that is, of the New Testament and the early Church. Similarly, northern Renaissance artists were inspired by the accomplishments of Italian masters to learn classical techniques. But northern artists depicted classical subject matter far less frequently than did Italians, and almost never portrayed completely nude human figures.

Any discussion of the northern Renaissance must begin with the career of Desiderius Erasmus (c. 1469–1536). The illegitimate son of a priest, Erasmus was born near Rotterdam in the Netherlands. Later, as a result of his wide travels, he became a virtual citizen of all northern Europe. Forced into a monastery against his will when he was a teenager, the young Erasmus found little formal instruction there but plenty of freedom to read what he liked. He devoured all the classics he could get his hands on and the writings of the Church Fathers (Chapter 6). When he was about thirty years old, he obtained permission to leave the monastery and enroll in the University of Paris, where he completed the requirements for the degree of bachelor of divinity.

But Erasmus subsequently rebelled against what he considered the arid learning of Parisian scholasticism. Nor did he ever serve actively as a priest. Instead he made his living from teaching, writing, and the proceeds of various ecclesiastical offices that required no pastoral duties. Ever on the lookout for new patrons, he traveled often to England, stayed once for three years in Italy, and resided in several different cities in Germany and the Netherlands before settling finally, toward the end of his life, in Basel (Switzerland). By means of a voluminous correspondence that he kept up with learned friends, Erasmus became the leader of a humanist coterie. And through the popularity of his numerous publications, he became the arbiter of northern European cultural tastes during his lifetime.

Erasmus's many-sided intellectual activity may be assessed from two different points of view: the literary and the doctrinal. As a Latin prose stylist, Erasmus was unequaled since the days of Cicero. Extraordinarily eloquent and witty, he reveled in tailoring his mode of discourse to fit his subject, creating dazzling verbal effects and coining puns that took on added meaning if the reader knew Greek as well as Latin. Above all, Erasmus excelled in the deft use of irony, poking fun at all and sundry, including himself. For example, in his *Colloquies* (from the Latin for "discussions") he

***ERASMUS* BY HANS HOLBEIN THE YOUNGER.** This is generally regarded as the most evocative portrait of the preeminent Christian humanist.

had a fictional character lament the evil signs of the times: "kings make war, priests strive to line their pockets, theologians invent syllogisms, monks roam outside their cloisters, the commons riot, and Erasmus writes colloquies."

But although Erasmus's urbane Latin style and humor earned him a wide audience on those grounds alone, he intended everything he wrote to promote what he called the "philosophy of Christ." Erasmus believed that the society of his day was caught up in corruption and immorality because people had lost sight of the simple teachings of the Gospels. Accordingly, he offered his contemporaries three different kinds of publication: clever satires meant to show people the error of their ways, serious moral treatises meant to offer guidance toward proper Christian behavior, and scholarly editions of basic Christian texts.

In the first category belong the works of Erasmus that are still widely read today: *The Praise of Folly* (1509), in which he ridiculed scholastic pedantry and dogmatism as well as ignorance and gullibility; and the *Colloquies* (1518), in which he held up contemporary religious practices for examination in a more serious but still pervasively ironic tone. In such works, Erasmus let fictional characters do the talking; hence his own views can be determined only by inference. But in his second mode Erasmus did not hesitate to speak clearly in his own voice. The most prominent treatises in this second genre are the quietly eloquent *Handbook of the Christian Knight* (1503), which urged the laity to pursue lives of serene inward piety, and the *Complaint of Peace* (1517), which pleaded movingly for Christian pacifism. Erasmus's pacifism was one of his most deeply held values, and he returned to it again and again in his published works.

Despite the success of his writings, Erasmus considered textual scholarship his greatest achievement. Revering the authority of Augustine, Jerome, and Ambrose, he brought out reliable editions of all their works. He also used his extraordinary command of Latin and Greek to produce a more accurate edition of the New Testament. After reading Lorenzo Valla's *Notes on the New Testament* in 1504, Erasmus became convinced that nothing was more imperative than divesting the New Testament of the myriad errors in transcription and translation that had piled up in the course of preceding centuries—for no one could be a good Christian without being certain of exactly what Christ's message really was. Hence he spent ten years studying and comparing all the early Greek biblical manuscripts he could find in order to establish an authoritative text. When it finally appeared in 1516, Erasmus's Greek New Testament, published together with explanatory notes and his own new Latin translation, became one of the most important landmarks of biblical scholarship of all time. In the hands of Martin Luther, it would play a critical role in the early stages of the Reformation (see Chapter 13).

## The Influence of Erasmus

One of Erasmus's closest friends, and a close second to him in distinction among Christian humanists, was the Englishman Sir Thomas More (1478–1535). Following a successful career as a lawyer and as speaker of the House of Commons, More was appointed lord chancellor of England in 1529. He was not long in this position, however, before he opposed the king's design to establish a national church under royal control, thus denying the supremacy of the pope (see Chapter 13). In 1534, when More refused to take an oath acknowledging Henry as head of the Church of England, he was thrown into the Tower of London and executed a year later. He is now revered as a Catholic martyr.

Much earlier, however, in 1516, More published the work for which he is best remembered, *Utopia* (Noplace). Purporting to describe an ideal community on an imaginary island, the book is really an Erasmian critique of the glaring abuses of the era—poverty undeserved and wealth unearned, drastic punishments, religious persecution, and the senseless slaughter of war. The inhabitants of Utopia hold all their goods in common, work only six hours a day so that all may have leisure for intellectual pursuits, and practice the natural virtues of wisdom, moderation, fortitude, and justice. Iron is the precious metal "because it is useful," war and monasticism do not exist, and toleration is granted to all who recognize the existence of God and the immortality of the soul. Although More advanced no explicit arguments in his *Utopia* in favor of Christianity, he probably meant to imply that if the Utopians could manage their society so well without the benefit of Christian revelation, Europeans who knew the Gospels ought to be able to do even better.

Erasmus and More head a long list of energetic and eloquent Christian humanists who made signal contributions to the collective enterprise of revolutionizing the study of early Christianity, and their achievements had a direct influence on Martin Luther and other Protestant reformers. Yet very few of them were willing to join Luther in rejecting the fundamental principles on which the power of the Church was based. Most tried to remain within its fold while still espousing an ideal of inward piety and scholarly inquiry. But as the leaders of the Church grew less and less tolerant of dissent, even mild criticism came to seem like heresy. Erasmus himself died early enough to escape persecution, but several of his less fortunate followers lived on to suffer as victims of the Inquisition.

***SIR THOMAS MORE* BY HANS HOLBEIN THE YOUNGER.** Holbein's skill in rendering the gravity and interiority of his subject is matched by his masterful representation of the sumptuous chain of office, furred mantle, and velvet sleeves that indicate the political and professional status of Henry VIII's chancellor.

## The Literature of the Northern Renaissance

Although Christian humanism would be severely challenged by the Reformation, the artistic Renaissance in the North continued throughout the sixteenth century. Poets in France and England vied with one another to adapt the elegant lyric forms pioneered by Petrarch, particularly the sonnet. The English poet Edmund Spenser (c. 1552–1599) also drew on the literary innovation of Ariosto's *Orlando Furioso*: his *Faerie Queene* is a similarly long chivalric romance that revels in sensuous imagery. Meanwhile, the more satirical side of Renaissance humanism was embraced by the French writer François Rabelais (*RA-beh-lay*, c. 1494–1553). Like Erasmus, whom he greatly admired, Rabelais began his career in the Church, but soon left the cloister to study medicine. A practicing physician, Rabelais interspersed his professional activities with literary endeavors, the most enduring of which is *Gargantua and Pantagruel*, a series of "chronicles" describing the lives and times of giants whose fabulous size and gross appetites serve as vehicles for much lusty humor. Like Erasmus, too, Rabelais satirized religious ceremonialism, scholasticism, superstition, and bigotry. But unlike Erasmus, who wrote in a highly cultivated classical Latin style comprehensible only to learned readers, Rabelais chose to address a far wider audience by writing in extremely crude French, and by glorifying every human impulse as natural and healthy.

## Northern Architecture and Art

Although many architects in northern Europe continued to build in the flamboyant Gothic style of the later Middle Ages, the classical values of Italian architects can be seen in some of the splendid new castles constructed in France's Loire valley—châteaux too elegant to be defensible—and in the royal palace (now museum) of the Louvre in Paris, which replaced an old twelfth-century fortress. The influence of Renaissance ideals are also visible

**THE CHÂTEAU OF CHAMBORD.** Built in the early sixteenth century by an Italian architect in the service of King Francis I of France, this magnificent palace in the Loire Valley combines Gothic and Renaissance architectural features.

in the work of the foremost artist of this era, the German Albrecht Dürer (1471–1528). Dürer (*DIRR-er*) was the first northerner to master the techniques of proportion and perspective, and he also shared with contemporary Italians a fascination with nature and the human body. But Dürer never really embraced classical allegory, drawing inspiration instead from more traditional Christian legends and from the self-effacing Christian humanism of Erasmus. Thus Dürer's serenely radiant engraving of Saint Jerome expresses the scholarly absorption that Erasmus may have enjoyed while working quietly in his study.

Indeed, Dürer aspired to immortalize Erasmus in a major portrait, but circumstances prevented him from doing this because the paths of the two men crossed only once; and after Dürer started sketching his hero on that occasion, his work was interrupted by Erasmus's press of business. Instead, the accomplishment of capturing Erasmus's pensive spirit in oils was left to another great northern artist, the German Hans Holbein the Younger (1497–1543, see page 393). As good fortune would have it, during a stay in England, Holbein also painted an extraordinarily acute portrait of Erasmus's friend and kindred spirit Sir Thomas More, which enables us to see clearly why a contemporary called More "a man of . . . sad gravity; a man for all seasons" (see page 394). These two portraits in and of themselves point to a major difference between medieval and Renaissance culture. Whereas the Middle Ages produced

***SAINT JEROME IN HIS STUDY* BY DÜRER.** Jerome, the biblical translator of the fourth century (Chapter 6), was a hero to both Dürer and Erasmus: the paragon of inspired Christian scholarship. Note how the scene exudes contentment, even down to the sleeping lion, which seems more like an overgrown tabby cat than a symbol of Christ.

no convincing naturalistic likenesses of any leading intellectual figures, Renaissance culture's greater commitment to human individuality created the environment in which Holbein was able to make Erasmus and More come to life.

## Renaissance Music

Music in western Europe in the fifteenth and sixteenth centuries reached such a high point of development that it constitutes, together with painting and sculpture, one of the most brilliant aspects of Renaissance endeavor. The musical theory of the Renaissance was driven largely by the humanist-inspired (but largely fruitless) effort to recover and imitate classical musical forms and modes. Musical practice, however, showed much more continuity with medieval musical traditions, with an added emphasis on heightened expression and emotional intensity. New musical instruments were developed to add nuance and texture to existing musical forms: the lute, the viol, the violin, and a variety of woodwind and keyboard instruments including the harpsichord. New musical genres also emerged, among them the opera. Most composers of this period were men trained in the service of the Church, but they rarely made sharp distinctions between sacred and secular music. Music was coming into its own as a serious independent art.

During the early fourteenth century, a musical movement called *ars nova* (Latin for "new art") was already flourishing in France, and it naturally spread to Italy during the lifetime of Petrarch. Its outstanding composers were Guillaume de Machaut (c. 1300–1377) and Francesco Landini (c. 1325–1397). The madrigals, ballads, and other songs composed by these musicians testify to a rich medieval tradition of secular music, but the greatest achievement of the period was a highly complicated yet delicate contrapuntal style adapted for the liturgy of the Church. Machaut, indeed, was the first-known composer to provide a polyphonic (harmonized) version of the major sections of the Mass.

In the fifteenth century, the dissemination of this new musical aesthetic combined with a host of French, Flemish, and Italian elements in the multicultural courts of Europe, particularly that of Burgundy. By the beginning of the sixteenth century, Franco-Flemish composers came to dominate many important courts and cathedrals, creating a variety of new genres and styles that bear a close affinity to Renaissance art and poetry. The Flemish composer Roland de Lassus (1532–1594) and the Italian Giovanni Pierluigi da Palestrina (c. 1525–1594) were recognized as masters by their peers, and Palestrina was especially influential because his highly intricate choral music was written under the patronage of the papacy in Rome. Music also flourished in sixteenth-century England, where the Italian madrigal was adapted and enlivened, and where William Byrd (1543–1623) rivaled the great Flemish and Italian composers of the day. Throughout Europe, the general level

# After You Read This Chapter

Visit StudySpace for quizzes, additional review materials, and multi-media documents. **wwnorton.com/studyspace**

### REVIEWING THE OBJECTIVES

- The Renaissance was an intellectual and cultural movement that coincided with the later Middle Ages but fostered a new outlook on the world. Explain the ways in which this outlook differed.
- The Renaissance began in Italy. Why?
- What was the relationship between Renaissance ideals and Italy's political realities?
- What were the principal features of Renaissance art?
- How were Renaissance ideas adapted in northern Europe?

of musical proficiency was very high: the singing of part-songs was a popular pastime in homes and at informal social gatherings, and the ability to read a part at sight was expected of the educated elite.

## CONCLUSION

The ideals of the Renaissance often stand in sharp contrast to the harsh realities alongside which they coexisted, and in which they were rooted. They arose from the calamitous events of the fourteenth century, which had a particularly devastating effect on Italy. Ravaged by the Black Death, abandoned by the papacy, reduced to the status of pawn in other powers' rivalries, Italy was exposed as a mere shadow of what it had been under the Roman Empire. It was therefore to the precedents and glories of the past that Italian intellectuals, artists, and statesmen looked for inspirations, in order to restore its prominence. But to which aspects of the past? Some humanists may have wanted to revive the principles of the Roman Republic, but many of them worked for ambitious despots who modeled themselves on Rome's dictators or on the tyrants of ancient Greece. Artists could thrive in the atmosphere of competition and one-upmanship that characterized Italy's warring principalities and city-states, but they could also find themselves reduced to the status of servants in the households of the wealthy and powerful—or forced to subordinate their artistry to the demands of warfare and espionage. Access to a widening array of classical texts, in Greek as well as Latin, widened the horizons of Renaissance readers; yet women were largely barred from the humanist education that led men to boast of their proximity to God. New critical tools enabled the study of classical texts, but the insistence on a return to the "pure" language of the Roman Empire eventually succeeded in bringing about the death of Latin as a living medium of communication.

Although the Renaissance began in northern Italy, where it filled a cultural and political vacuum, it did not remain confined there. By the end of the fifteenth century, humanist approaches to education and textual criticism had begun to influence intellectual endeavors all over Europe. The techniques of Renaissance artists melded with the artistry of the later Middle Ages in striking ways, while opportunities for patronage expanded along with the demand for artworks and the prestige they lent to their owners. And the theories that undergirded Renaissance politics—civic and princely—were being used to legitimize many different kinds of power, including that of the papacy. All of these trends would be carried forward into the sixteenth century, and would have a role to play in the upheaval that shattered Europe's fragile religious unity and tenuous balance of power. It is to this upheaval, the Reformation, that we turn in Chapter 13.

### PEOPLE, IDEAS, AND EVENTS IN CONTEXT

- Why was the ancient past so important to the intellectuals and artists of the **RENAISSANCE**? What was **HUMANISM**, and how did it influence education during this era?
- What were the political and economic underpinnings of the Renaissance? How do the **MEDICI** of Florence and the papacy exemplify new trends in patronage?
- What were some major scholarly achievements of the Renaissance? How did **LORENZO VALLA** and **NICCOLÒ MACHIAVELLI** advance new intellectual and political ideas?
- How do the works of **BOTICELLI**, **LEONARDO**, **RAPHAEL**, and **MICHELANGELO** capture Renaissance ideals? Which is the most paradigmatic Renaissance artist, in your opinion, and why?
- How did Christian humanists like **DESIDERIUS ERASMUS** and **THOMAS MORE** apply Renaissance ideas in new ways? How were these ideas expressed in art?

### CONSEQUENCES

- The Renaissance is often described as being the antithesis of the Middle Ages, yet it was actually a simultaneous movement. Can you think of other eras when two or more divergent outlooks have coexisted?
- To what extent do the ideals of the Renaissance anticipate those we associate with modernity? To what extent are they more faithful to either the Christian or the classical past?
- Phrases like "Renaissance man" and "a Renaissance education" are still part of our common vocabulary. Given what you have learned in this chapter, how has your understanding of such phrases changed? How would you explain their true meaning to others?

# Before You Read This Chapter

## STORY LINES

- The movement catalyzed by Martin Luther's challenge to the Church grew out of much earlier attempts at reform, but it was also a response to more recent religious and political developments.
- Within a decade after Luther's break with Rome, religious dissent was widespread and a number of different Protestant faiths were taking hold in various regions of Europe.
- Protestantism not only transformed the political landscape of Europe, it changed the basic structures of the family and attitudes toward marriage and sexuality which still shape our lives today.
- These changes also affected the structures and doctrine of the Roman Catholic ("universal") Church, which reemerged as an institution different in many ways from the medieval Church, and more similar to that of today.

## CHRONOLOGY

| | |
|---|---|
| 1517 | Luther posts Ninety-five Theses |
| 1520s | Lutheranism becomes the official religion of Scandinavian countries |
| 1521 | Luther is excommunicated at the Diet of Worms |
| 1525 | Swabian peasants' revolt |
| 1529 | Luther breaks with Zwingli |
| 1534 | Henry VIII establishes the Church of England |
| 1534 | Ignatius Loyola founds the Society of Jesus (the Jesuits) |
| 1541 | Geneva adopts a theocratic government based on Calvinism |
| 1545–1563 | Council of Trent is convened |
| 1553–1558 | Mary Tudor attempts to restore the Catholic faith in England |
| 1559 | Elizabeth reestablishes Protestantism in England |
| 1564 | Index of prohibited books is published for the first time |

## CORE OBJECTIVES

- **DEFINE** the main premises of Lutheranism.
- **EXPLAIN** why Switzerland emerged as an important Protestant center.
- **IDENTIFY** the ways in which family structures and values changed during the Reformation.
- **UNDERSTAND** the reasons behind England's unusual brand of Protestantism.
- **DESCRIBE** the Catholic Church's response to the challenge of Protestantism.

# The Age of Dissent and Division, 1500–1600

In the year 1500, Europe's future seemed bright. After two centuries of economic, social, and political turmoil, its economy was expanding, its cities were growing, and the monarchs of France, England, Spain, Scotland, and Poland were all securely established on their thrones. The population was increasing, and governments at every level were extending and deepening their control over people's lives. Europeans had also embarked on a new period of colonial expansion. And although the papacy pursued its territorial wars in Italy, the Church itself had weathered the storms of the Avignon captivity and the Great Schism. Heresies had been suppressed or contained. In the struggle over conciliarism, the papacy had won the support of all major European rulers, which effectively relegated the conciliarists to academic isolation at the University of Paris. Meanwhile, at the local level, the devotion of ordinary Christians was strong and the parish a crucial site of community identity. To be sure, there were some problems. The educational standards of parish clergy were higher than they had ever been, but reformers noted that too many priests were ignorant or neglectful of their spiritual duties. Monasticism, by and large, seemed to have lost its spiritual fire. Religious enthusiasm sometimes led to superstition. Yet on the whole, the Church's problems were manageable.

No one could have predicted that Europe's religious and political coherence would be irreparably shattered in the course of a generation, or that the next century would witness an appallingly destructive series of wars. Nor could anyone have foreseen that the catalyst for these extraordinary events would be a university professor. For it was Martin Luther (1483–1546), a German monk and teacher of theology, who set off the chain reaction we know as the Reformation. Initially intended as a call for another phase in the Church's long history of internal reforms, Luther's teachings would instead launch a religious revolution that would splinter western Christendom into a variety of Protestant ("dissenting") faiths, while prompting the Church of Rome to re-affirm its status as the only true Catholic ("universal) faith through a parallel revolution. At the same time, these movements deepened existing divisions among peoples, rulers, and states while opening up new divisions and points of contention. The result was a profound transformation of the religious, social, and political landscape that affected the lives of everyone in Europe—and everyone in the new European colonies, then and now.

## MARTIN LUTHER'S CHALLENGE

To explain the impact of Martin Luther's ideas, we must answer three central questions:

1. Why did Luther's theology lead him to break with Rome?
2. Why did large numbers of people rally to his cause?
3. Why did so many German princes and towns impose the new religion within their territories?

As we shall see, those who followed Luther found his message appealing for different reasons. Many peasants hoped that the new religion would free them from the exactions of their lords; towns and princes thought it would allow them to consolidate their political independence; nationalists thought it would liberate Germany from the demands of foreign popes bent on feathering their own nest in central Italy.

But what Luther's followers shared was a conviction that their new understanding of Christianity would lead them to Heaven, whereas the traditional religion of Rome would not. For this reason, *reformation* is a misleading term for the movement they initiated. Although Luther himself began as a reformer seeking to change the Church from within, he quickly developed into an uncompromising opponent of its principles and practices. Many of his followers were even more radical. The movement that began with Luther therefore went beyond "reformation." It was a frontal assault on religious, political, and social instututions that had been in place for a thousand years.

### *Luther's Quest for Justice*

Although Martin Luther became an inspiration to millions, he was a terrible disappointment to his father. The elder Luther was a Thuringian peasant who had prospered by leasing some mines. Eager to see his clever son rise still further, he sent young Luther to the University of Erfurt to study law. In 1505, however, Martin shattered his hopes by becoming a monk of the Augustinian order. In some sense, though, Luther was a chip off the old block. Throughout his life, he lived simply and expressed himself in the vigorous, earthy vernacular of the German peasantry.

Luther arrived at his new understanding of religious truth by a dramatic conversion experience. As a monk, he zealously pursued all the traditional means for achieving his own salvation. Not only did he fast and pray continu-

**MARTIN LUTHER.** This late portrait is by Lucas Cranach the Elder (1472–1553), court painter to the electors of Brandenburg and a friend of Luther.

ously but he confessed so often that his exhausted confessor would sometimes jokingly suggest that if he really wanted to do penance he should go out and do something dramatic like committing adultery. Yet, try as he might, Luther could find no spiritual peace because he feared that he could never perform enough good deeds to deserve so great a gift as salvation. But in 1513 he hit upon an insight that changed the course of his life.

Luther's insight was a new understanding of God's justice. For years, he had worried that it seemed unfair for God to issue commandments that he knew human beings could not observe, and then to punish them with eternal damnation. But after becoming a professor of theology at the University of Wittenberg, Luther's further study of the Bible revealed to him that God's justice had nothing to do with his power to punish, but rather with his mercy in saving sinful mortals through faith. As Luther later wrote, "At last, by the mercy of God, I began to understand the justice of God as that by which God makes *us* just, in his mercy and through faith . . . and at this I felt as though I had been born again, and had gone through open gates into paradise." Since this revelation came to Luther in the tower room of his monastery, it is often termed his "tower experience."

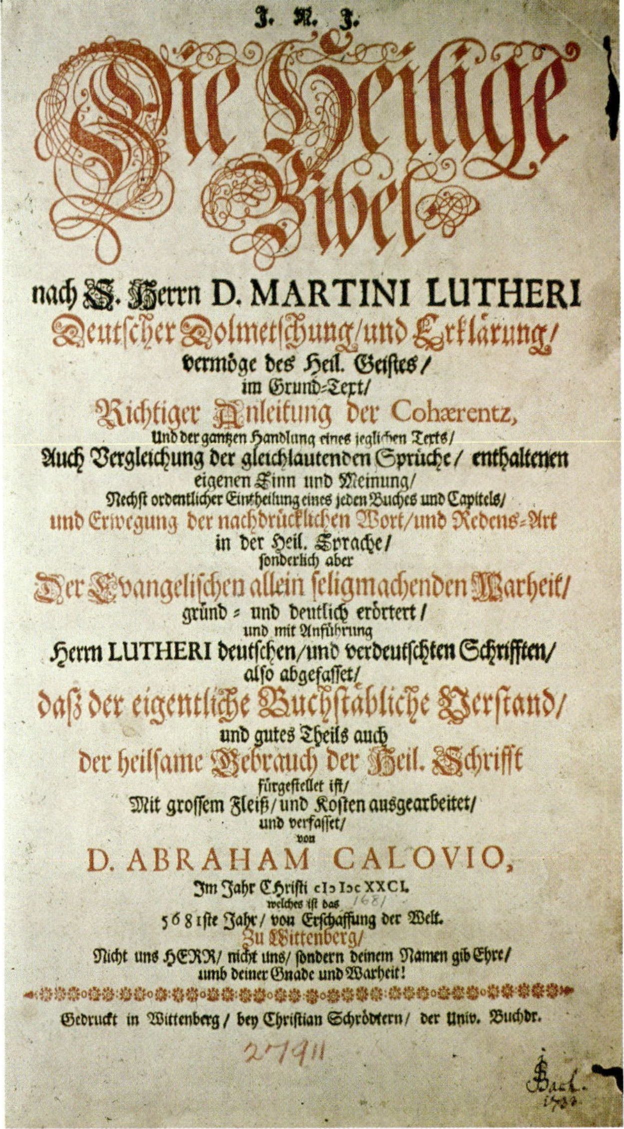

J. N. J.

Die Heilige Bibel

nach S. Herrn D. MARTINI LUTHERI
Deutscher Dolmetschung/und Erklärung/
vermöge des Heil. Geistes/
im Grund-Text/
Richtiger Anleitung der Cohærentz,
Und der gantzen Handlung eines jeglichen Texts/
Auch Vergleichung der gleichlautenden Sprüche/ enthaltenen
eigenen Sinn und Meinung/
Nechst ordentlicher Eintheilung eines jeden Buches und Capitels/
und Erwegung der nachdrücklichen Wort/und Redens-Art
in der Heil. Sprache/
sonderlich aber
Der Evangelischen allein seligmachenden Warheit/
gründ- und deutlich erörtert/
und mit Anführung
Herrn LUTHERI deutschen/und verdeutschten Schrifften/
also abgefasset/
daß der eigentliche Buchstäbliche Verstand/
und gutes Theils auch
der heilsame Gebrauch der Heil. Schrifft
fürgestellet ist/
Mit grossem Fleiß/und Kosten ausgearbeitet/
und verfasset/
von
D. ABRAHAM CALOVIO,
Im Jahr Christi cIↃIↃcXXCI.
welches ist das 1681
5681ste Jahr/ von Erschaffung der Welt.
Zu Wittenberg/
Nicht uns HERR/ nicht uns/ sondern deinem Namen gib Ehre/
umb deiner Gnade und Warheit!

Gedruckt in Wittenberg/ bey Christian Schrödtern/ der Univ. Buchdr.

27911

**LUTHER'S TRANSLATION OF THE BIBLE.** The printing press was instrumental to the rapid dissemination of Luther's messages, as well as those of his supporters and challengers. Also essential was the fact that Luther addressed his audience in plain language, in their native German, and that pamphlets and vernacular Bibles like this one could be rapidly and cheaply mass produced.

After that, everything seemed to fall into place. Lecturing at Wittenberg in the years immediately following, Luther pondered a passage in Saint Paul's Letter to the Romans—"[T]he just shall live by faith" (1:17)—until he reached his central doctrine of "justification by faith alone." Luther concluded that God's justice does not demand endless good works and religious rituals for salvation, because humans can never be saved by their own efforts. Rather, humans are saved by God's grace alone, which God offers as an utterly undeserved gift to those whom he has predestined for salvation. Because this grace comes to humans through the gift of faith, men and women are "justified" (i.e., made worthy of salvation) by faith alone. Those whom God has justified through faith will manifest that fact by performing works of piety and charity, but such works are not what saves them. Piety and charity are merely visible signs of each believer's invisible spiritual state, which is known to God alone.

The essence of this doctrine was not original to Luther. It had been central to the thought of Augustine (see Chapter 6), the patron saint of Luther's own monastic order. During the twelfth and thirteenth centuries, however, theologians such as Peter Lombard and Thomas Aquinas (Chapter 9) had developed a very different understanding of salvation. They emphasized the role that the Church itself (through its sacraments) and the individual believer (through acts of piety and charity) could play in the process of salvation. None of these theologians claimed that a human being could earn his or her way to Heaven by good works alone, but the late medieval Church unwittingly encouraged this misunderstanding by presenting the process of salvation in increasingly quantitative terms—declaring, for example, that by performing a specific action (such as a pilgrimage or a pious donation), a believer could reduce the penance she or he owed to God by a specific number of days.

From the fourteenth century on, popes claimed to dispense such special grace from the so-called Treasury of Merits, a storehouse of surplus good works piled up by Christ and the saints in Heaven. By the late fifteenth century, popes also began to teach that the dead could receive this grace, too, to speed their way through Purgatory. In both cases, grace was withdrawn from this "Treasury" through indulgences: special remissions of penitential obligations. When indulgences were first conceived, in the eleventh and twelfth centuries, they could be earned only by demanding spiritual exercises, such as joining a crusade (see Chapter 8). By the end of the fifteenth century, however, indulgences were for sale.

To many, this looked like simony: the sin of exchanging God's grace for cash. It had been a practice loudly condemned by Wyclif and his followers (Chapter 10), and it was even more widely criticized by reformers like Erasmus (Chapter 12). But Luther's objections to indulgences had much more radical consequences, because they rested on a set of theological presuppositions that, taken to their logical conclusion, resulted in dismantling much of contemporary religious practice, not to mention the authority and sanctity of the Church. Luther himself does not appear to have realized this at first. But as the implications of his ideas became clear, he did not withdraw from them. Instead, he pressed on.

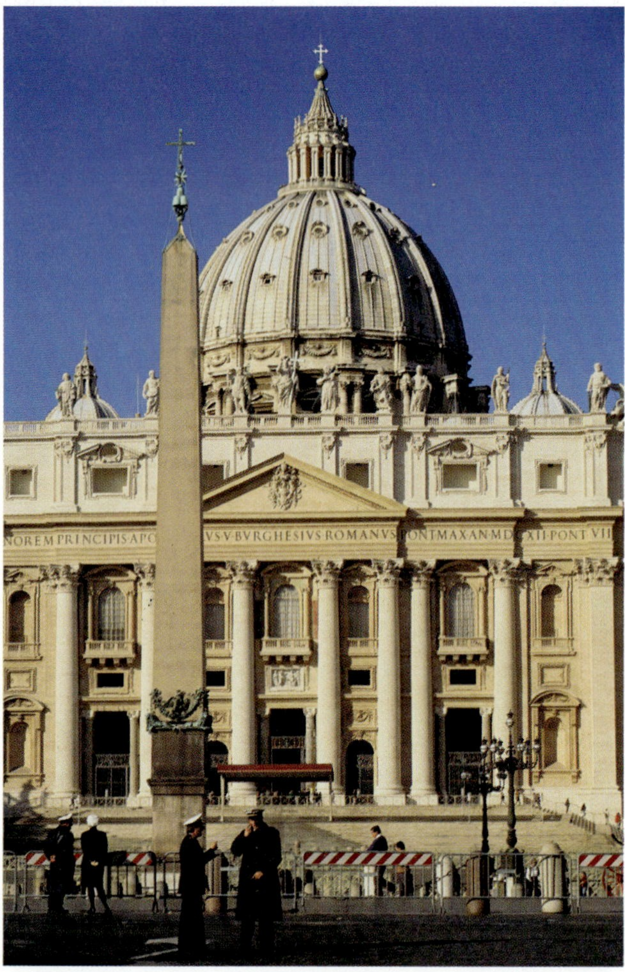


**SAINT PETER'S BASILICA, ROME.** The construction of a new papal palace and monumental church was begun in 1506. This enormous complex replaced a modest, dilapidated Romanesque basilica that had replaced an even older church built on the site of the apostle Peter's tomb. ▪ ***How might this building project have been interpreted in different ways, depending on one's attitude toward the papacy?***

## *The Scandal of Indulgences*

Luther developed his ideas as a university professor. But in 1517 he was provoked, by a scandalous abuse of spiritual power, into attacking actual practice more publicly. The worldly bishop Albert of Hohenzollern, youngest brother of the elector of Brandenburg, had sunk himself into debt, and in 1513 he paid a large sum for papal permission to hold the bishoprics of Magdeburg and Halberstadt concurrently—even though, at twenty-three, he was not old enough to be a bishop at all. Moreover, when the prestigious and lucrative archbishopric of Mainz fell vacant in the next year, Albert bought that, too. Obtaining the necessary funds by taking out loans from a German banking firm, he then struck a bargain with Pope Leo X (r. 1513–21): Leo would authorize the sale of indulgences in Albert's ecclesiastical territories with the understanding that half of the income would go to Rome for the building of St. Peter's Basilica, the other half going to Albert.

Luther did not know the sordid details of Albert's bargain, but he did know that a Dominican friar named Tetzel was soon hawking indulgences throughout much of the region, and that Tetzel was deliberately giving people the impression that an indulgence was an automatic ticket to Heaven for oneself or one's loved ones in Purgatory. For Luther, this was doubly offensive: not only was Tetzel violating Luther's conviction that people are saved by faith, not the purchase of grace, he was also misleading people into thinking that if they purchased an indulgence, they no longer needed to confess their sins to a priest. Tetzel was thus putting innocent souls at risk. So on the eve of the feast of All Souls—Hallowe'en night—in 1517, Luther published a list of Ninety-five Theses that he was prepared to debate, all aimed at dismantling the doctrine of indulgences. According to tradition, he nailed this document to the door of the church—and whether or not he did so in fact, the metaphor is clear.

Luther wrote up these points for debate in Latin, not German, and meant them only for academic discussion within the University of Wittenberg. But when some unknown person translated and published them, the hitherto obscure academic suddenly gained widespread notoriety.

**POPE LEO X.** Raphael's unflinching portrait shows the pope with his nephews: Giulio de' Medici (who would succeed him as pope) and Cardinal de Rossi.

Tetzel and his allies now demanded that Luther withdraw his theses. Rather than backing down, however, Luther became even bolder in his attacks. In 1519, at a public disputation held before throngs in Leipzig, Luther defiantly maintained that the pope and all clerics were merely fallible men, and that the highest authority for an individual's conscience was the truth of Scripture. Pope Leo X responded by charging Luther with heresy; after that Luther had no alternative but to break with the Church entirely.

Luther's year of greatest activity came in 1520 when, in the midst of the crisis caused by his defiance, he composed a series of pamphlets setting forth his three primary premises: justification by faith, the authority of Scripture, and "the priesthood of all believers." We have already examined the meaning of the first premise. By the second he simply meant that the reading of Scripture took precedence over Church traditions—including the teachings of all theologians—and that beliefs (such as Purgatory) or practices (such as prayers to the saints) not explicitly grounded in Scripture could be rejected as human inventions. Luther also declared that Christian believers were spiritually equal before God, which meant denying that priests, monks, and nuns had any special qualities by virtue of their vocations: hence "the priesthood of all believers."

From these premises a host of practical consequences followed. Because works could not lead to salvation, Luther declared fasts, pilgrimages, and the veneration of relics to be spiritually valueless. He also called for the dissolution of all monasteries and convents. He advocated a demystification of religious rites, proposing the substitution of German and other vernaculars for Latin and calling for a reduction in the number of sacraments from seven to two. In his view, the only true sacraments were baptism and the Eucharist, both of which had been instituted by Christ. (Later, he included penance.) Although Luther continued to believe that Christ was really present in the consecrated bread and wine of the Lord's Supper, he insisted that it was only through the faith of each individual believer that this sacrament could lead anyone to God; it was not a magic trick performed by a priest. To further emphasize that those who served the Church had no supernatural authority, he insisted on calling them "ministers" or "pastors" rather than priests. He also proposed to abolish the entire ecclesiastical hierarchy from popes to bishops on down. Finally, on the principle that no spiritual distinction existed between clergy and laity, Luther argued that ministers could and should marry. In 1525 he himself took a wife, Katharina von Bora, one of a dozen nuns he had helped to escape from a Cistercian convent.

## *The Break with Rome*

Widely disseminated by means of the printing press, Luther's polemical pamphlets of 1520 electrified much of Germany, gaining him passionate popular support and touching off a national religious revolt against the papacy. In highly colloquial German, Luther declared that "if the pope's court were reduced ninety-nine percent it would still be large enough to give decisions on matters of faith"; that "the cardinals have sucked Italy dry and now turn to Germany"; and that, given Rome's corruption, "the reign of Antichrist could not be worse." As word of Luther's defiance spread, his pamphlets became a publishing sensation. Whereas the average press run of a printed book before 1520 had been 1,000 copies, the first run of *To the Christian Nobility* (1520) was 4,000—and it sold out in a few days. Many thousands of copies quickly followed. Even more popular were woodcut illustrations mocking the papacy and exalting Luther. These sold in the tens of thousands and could be readily understood even by the illiterate. (**See *Interpreting Visual Evidence*.**)

# Interpreting Visual Evidence

## *Decoding Printed Propaganda*

The printing press has been credited with helping to spread the teachings of Martin Luther and so to securing the success of the Protestant Reformation. But even before Luther's critiques were published, reformers were using the new technology to disseminate images that attacked the corruption of the Church. After Luther rose to prominence, both his supporters and detractors vied with one another in disseminating propaganda that appealed, visually, to a lay audience and that could be understood even by those who were unable to read.

The first pair of images below is really a single printed artifact datable to around 1500: an early example of a "pop-up" card. It shows Pope Alexander VI (r. 1492–1503) as stately pontiff (image A) whose true identity is concealed by a flap. When the flap is raised (image B), he is revealed as a devil. The Latin texts read: "Alexander VI, *pontifex maximus*" (image A) and "I am the pope" (image B). The other two images represent two sides of the debate as it had developed by 1530, and both do so with reference to the same image: the seven-headed beast mentioned in the

A. Alexander as pontiff.

B. Alexander as a devil.

Bible's Book of Revelation. On the left (image C), a Lutheran engraving shows the papacy as the beast, with seven heads representing seven orders of Catholic clergy. The sign on the cross (referring to the sign hung over the head of the crucified Christ) reads, in German: "For money, a sack full of indulgences." (The Latin words on either side say "Reign of the Devil.") On the right (image D), a Catholic engraving produced in Germany shows Luther as Revelation's beast, with its seven heads labeled: "Doctor–Martin–Luther–Heretic–Hypocrite–Fanatic–Barabbas," the last alluding to the thief who should have been executed instead of Jesus, according to the Gospels.

## *Questions for Analysis*

1. Given that this attack on Pope Alexander VI precedes Martin Luther's critique of the Church by nearly two decades, what can you conclude about its intended audience? To what extent can it be read as a barometer of popular disapproval? What might have been the reason(s) for the use of the concealing flap?
2. What do you make of the fact that both Catholic and Protestant propagandists were using the same imagery? What do you make of the key differences—for example, the fact that the seven-headed beast representing the papacy sprouts out of an altar in which a Eucharistic chalice is displayed, while the seven-headed Martin Luther is reading a book?
3. All of these printed images also make use of words. What are some of the different relationships between these two media? Would the message of each image be clear without the use of texts? Why or why not?

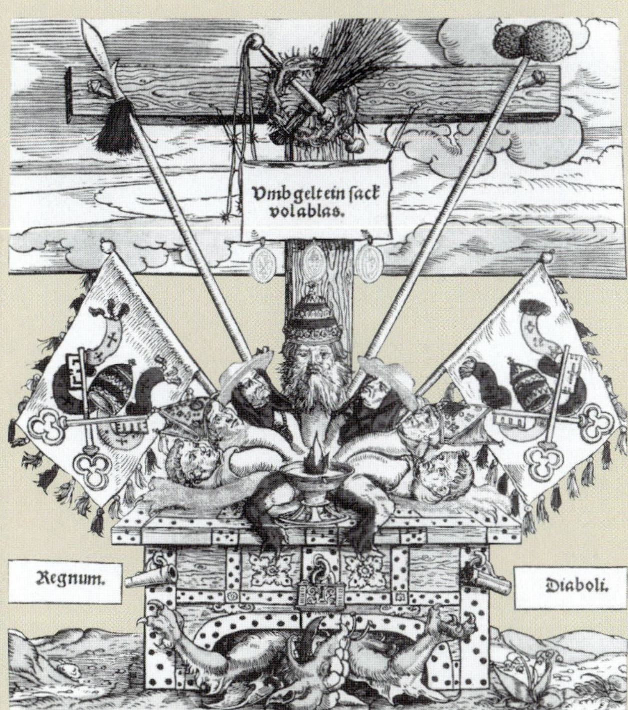

C. The seven-headed papal beast.

D. The seven-headed Martin Luther.

Luther's denunciations reflected widespread public dissatisfaction with the conduct and corruption of the papacy. Pope Alexander VI (r. 1492–1503) had bribed cardinals to gain his office, and had then used the money raised from the papal jubilee of 1500 to support the military campaigns of his illegitimate son. He was also suspected of incest with his own daughter, Lucrezia Borgia. Julius II (r. 1503–13) devoted his reign to enlarging the Papal States in a series of wars; a contemporary remarked of him that he would have gained great glory—if only he had been a secular prince. Leo X (r. 1513–21), Luther's opponent, was a member of the Medici family of Florence. Although not spectacularly immoral, he was a self-indulgent aesthete who, in the words of a modern Catholic historian, "would not have been deemed fit to be a doorkeeper in the house of the Lord had he lived in the days of the apostles." In *The Praise of Folly*, first published in 1511 and frequently reprinted (see Chapter 12), Erasmus declared that if the popes of his day were ever forced to lead Christlike lives, as their office demanded, they would be incapable of it. In *Julius Excluded*, published anonymously in 1517, he went even further, imagining a conversation at the gates of Heaven between Saint Peter and Julius II, in which Peter refuses to admit the pope because he cannot believe that this armored, vainglorious figure could possibly be his own earthly representative.

In Germany, resentment of the papacy ran especially high because there were no special agreements (concordats) limiting papal authority in its principalities, as there were in Spain, France, and England (see Chapter 10). As a result, German princes complained that papal taxes were so high that the country was drained of its wealth. And yet Germans had almost no influence over papal policy. Frenchmen, Spaniards, and Italians dominated the College of Cardinals and the papal bureaucracy, and the popes were now invariably Italian, as they would continue to be until 1978 and the election of John Paul II. As a result, graduates from the rapidly growing German universities almost never found employment in Rome. Instead, many joined the throngs of Luther's supporters to become leaders of the new religious movement.

## The Condemnation at Worms

In the year 1520, Pope Leo X issued a papal edict condemning Luther's publications as heretical, and threatening him with excommunication if he did not recant. This edict was of the most solemn kind, known as a *bulla* or "bull," from the lead seal it bore. Luther's reponse was flagrantly defiant: rather than acquiescing to the pope's demand, he staged a public burning of the document. Thereafter, his heresy confirmed, he was formally given over for punishment to his lay overlord, the elector Frederick "the Wise" of Saxony. Frederick, however, proved a supporter of Luther and a critic of the papacy. Rather than burning Luther at the stake for heresy, Frederick declared that Luther had not yet received a fair hearing. Early in 1521, he therefore brought him to the city of Worms to be examined by a select representative assembly known as a "diet."

At Worms, the diet's presiding officer was the newly elected Holy Roman emperor, Charles V. As a member of the Habsburg family, he had been born and bred in his ancestral holding of Flanders, then part of the Netherlands. By 1521, however, through the unpredictable workings of dynastic inheritance, marriage, election, and luck, he had become not only the ruler of the Netherlands, but also king of Germany and Holy Roman emperor, duke of Austria,

**THE EMPEROR CHARLES V.** This portrait by the Venetian painter Titian depicts Europe's most powerful ruler sitting quietly in a chair, dressed in simple clothing of the kind worn by judges or bureaucrats. ▪ ***Why might Charles have chosen to represent himself in this way—rather than in the regalia of his many royal, imperial, and princely offices?***

**THE EUROPEAN EMPIRE OF CHARLES V, c. 1550.** Charles V ruled a vast variety of widely dispersed territories in Europe and the New World, and as Holy Roman Emperor he was also the titular ruler of Germany. ▪ ***What were the main countries and kingdoms under his control?*** ▪ ***Which regions would have been most threatened by Charles's extraordinary power, and where might the rulers of these regions turn for allies?*** ▪ ***How might the expansion of the Ottoman Empire have complicated political and religious struggles within Christian Europe?***

duke of Milan, and ruler of the Franche-Comté. And as the grandson of Ferdinand and Isabella on his mother's side, he was also king of Spain; king of Naples, Sicily, and Sardinia; and ruler of all the Spanish possessions in the New World. Governing such an extraordinary combination of territories posed enormous challenges. Charles's empire had no capital and no centralized administrative institutions; it shared no common language, no common culture, and no geographically contiguous borders. It thus stood completely apart from the growing nationalism of late medieval political life.

Charles recognized the diversity of his empire and tried wherever possible to rule it through local officials and institutions. But he could not tolerate threats to the two fundamental forces that held his empire together: himself

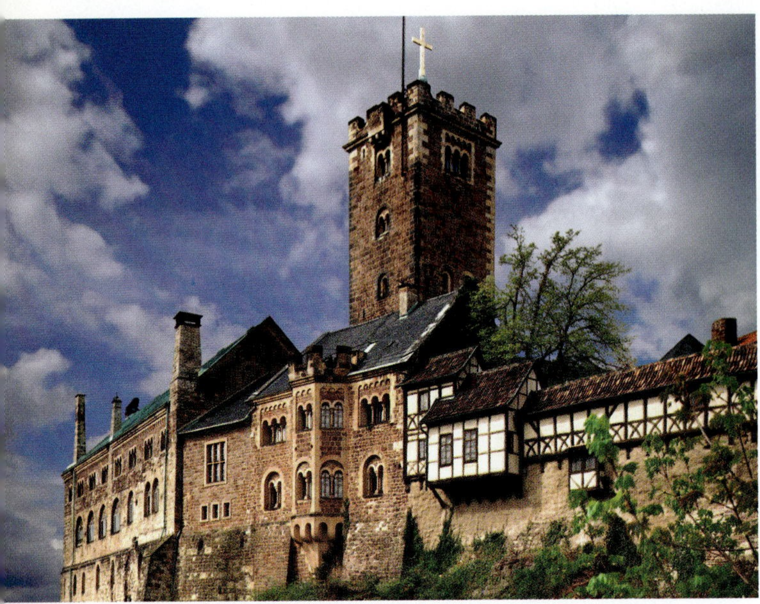

**THE WARTBURG, EISENACH (GERMANY).** This medieval stronghold became the refuge of Martin Luther after his condemnation at the Diet of Worms in 1520. His room in the castle has since been preserved.

as emperor and Catholicism (as the religion of Rome was coming to be called). Beyond such political calculations, however, Charles was also a faithful and committed servant of the Church, and deeply disturbed by the prospect of heresy within his empire. There was therefore little doubt that the Diet of Worms would condemn Martin Luther for heresy. And when Luther refused to back down, thereby endangering his life, his lord Frederick the Wise once more intervened, this time arranging for Luther to be "kidnapped" and hidden for a year at the elector's castle of the Wartburg, where he was kept out of harm's way.

Thereafter, Luther was never again in mortal danger. Although the Diet of Worms proclaimed him an outlaw, this edict was never enforced. Instead, Charles V left Germany in order to conduct a war with France, and in 1522 Luther returned in triumph to Wittenberg, to find that the changes he had called for had already been put into practice by his university supporters. When several German princes formally converted to Lutheranism, they brought their territories with them. In a little over a decade, a new form of Christianity had been established.

## *The German Princes and the Lutheran Church*

At this point, the last of our three major questions must be addressed: Why did some German princes, secure in their own powers, nonetheless establish Lutheran religious practices within their territories? This is a crucial development, because popular support for Luther would not have been enough to ensure the success of his teachings had they not been embraced by a number of powerful princes and free cities. Indeed, it was only in those territories where rulers formally established Luthernism that the new religion prevailed. Elsewhere in Germany, Luther's sympathizers were forced to flee, face death, or conform to Catholicism.

The power of individual rulers to determine the religion of their territories reflects developments we noted in Chapter 10. Rulers had long sought to control appointments to Church offices in their own realms, to restrict the flow of money to Rome, and to limit the independence of ecclesiastical courts. The most powerful rulers in western Europe—primarily the kings of France and Spain—had already taken advantage of the continuing struggles between the papacy and the conciliarists to extract such concessions from the embattled popes during the fifteenth century (Chapter 10). But in Germany, as noted above, neither the emperor nor the princes were strong enough to secure special treatment.

This changed as a result of Luther's initiatives. As early as 1520, the Pope's fiery challenger had recognized that he could never hope to institute new religious practices without the strong arms of princes, so he explicitly encouraged them to confiscate the wealth of the Church as an incentive. At first the princes bided their time, but when they realized that Luther had enormous public support and that Charles V would not act swiftly to defend the Catholic faith, several moved to introduce Lutheranism into their territories. Personal piety surely played a role in individual cases, but political and economic considerations were generally more decisive. Protestant princes could consolidate authority by naming their own pastors, cutting off fees to Rome, and curtailing the jurisdiction of Church courts. They could also guarantee that the political and religious boundaries of their territories would now coincide. No longer would a rival ecclesiastical prince (such as a bishop or archbishop) be able to use his spiritual position to undermine a neighboring secular prince's sovereignty.

Similar considerations also moved a number of free cities (independent of territorial princes) to adopt Lutheranism. Town councils and guild masters could thus establish themselves as the supreme governing authorities within their towns, cutting out local bishops or powerful monasteries. Given the added fact that under Lutheranism monasteries and convents could be shut down and their lands appropriated by the newly sovereign secular authorities, the practical advantages of the new faith were overwhelming, quite apart from any considerations of religious zeal.

**CONFESSIONAL DIFFERENCES, c. 1560.** The religious affiliations (confessions) of Europe's territories had become very complicated by the year 1560, roughly a generation after the adoption of Lutheranism in some areas. ▪ ***What major countries and kingdoms had embraced Protestantism by 1560?*** ▪ ***To what extent do these divisions conform to political boundaries, and to what extent would they have complicated the political situation?*** ▪ ***Why might Lutheranism have spread north into Scandinavia, but not south into Bavaria or west across the Rhine?***

Once safely ensconced in Wittenberg under princely protection, Luther began to express ever more vehemently his own political and social views, which tended toward the strong support of the new political order. In a treatise of 1523, *On Temporal Authority*, he insisted that "godly" (Protestant) rulers must be obeyed in all things and that even "ungodly" ones should never be actively resisted since tyranny "is not to be resisted but endured." In 1525, when peasants throughout Germany rebelled against their landlords, Luther therefore responded with intense hostility. In his vituperative pamphlet of 1525, *Against the Thievish, Murderous Hordes of Peasants*, he urged readers to hunt the rebels down as though they were mad dogs: to "strike, strangle, stab secretly or in public, and remember that nothing can be more poisonous than a man in rebellion." After the ruthless suppression of this revolt, which may have cost as many as 100,000 lives, the firm alliance of Lutheranism with state power helped preserve and sanction the existing social order.

As for Luther himself, he concentrated in his last years on debating with younger, more radical religious reformers and offering spiritual counsel to all who sought it. Never tiring in his amazingly prolific literary activity, he wrote an average of one treatise every two weeks for twenty-five years.

## THE SPREAD OF PROTESTANTISM

Originating as a term applied to Lutherans who "protested" against the German Imperial Diet of 1529, the word *Protestant* was soon applied to a much wider range of dissenting Christianities. Lutheranism itself struck lasting roots only in northern Germany and Scandinavia, where it became the state religion of Denmark, Norway, and Sweden as early as the 1520s. Early Lutheran successes in southern Germany, Poland, and Hungary were eventually rolled back. Elsewhere in Europe, meanwhile, competing forms of Protestantism soon emerged from the seeds that Luther had sown. By the 1550s, Protestantism had become a truly international movement, but an increasingly diverse and divisive one.

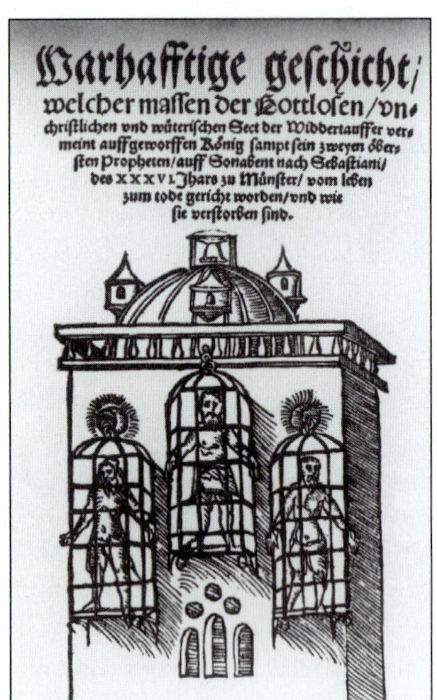

**THE ANABAPTISTS' CAGES, THEN AND NOW.** After the three Anabaptist leaders of Münster were executed in 1535, their corpses were prominently displayed in cages hung from a tower of the marketplace church. As can be seen from the photo on the right, the bones are gone but the iron cages remain. ▪ ***What would be the purpose of keeping these cages on display?***

### *Protestantism in Switzerland*

In the early sixteenth century, Switzerland was ruled neither by kings nor by territorial princes; instead, prosperous Swiss cities were either independent or on the verge of becoming so. Hence, when the leading citizens of a Swiss municipality decided to adopt Protestant reforms, no one could stop them. Although religious arrangements varied from city to city, three main forms of Protestantism emerged in Switzerland between 1520 to 1550: Zwinglianism, Anabaptism, and Calvinism.

Zwinglianism, founded by Ulrich Zwingli (*TSVING-lee,* 1484–1531) in Zürich, was the most theologically moderate form of the three. Although Zwingli began his career as a Catholic priest, his humanist-inspired study of the Bible convinced him that Catholic theology and practice conflicted with the Gospels. His biblical studies eventually led him also to condemn religious images and hierarchical authority within the Church. But he did not speak out publicly until Luther set the precedent. In 1522, Zwingli began attacking the authority of the Catholic Church in Zürich. Soon all Zürich and much of northern Switzerland had accepted his religious leadership.

Zwingli's reforms closely resembled those of the Lutherans in Germany. Zwingli differed from Luther, however, as to the theology of the Eucharist: whereas Luther believed in the real presence of Christ's body in the sacrament, for Zwingli the Eucharist conferred no grace at all; it was simply a reminder and communal celebration of Christ's historical sacrifice on the cross. This fundamental disagreement prevented Lutherans and Zwinglians from uniting in a common Protestant front. Fighting independently, Zwingli fell in battle against Catholic forces in 1531. Soon thereafter, his movement was absorbed by the more systematic Protestantism of John Calvin (see below).

Before Calvinism prevailed, however, an even more radical form of Protestantism arose in Switzerland and Germany. The first Anabaptists were members of Zwingli's circle in Zürich, but they broke with him around 1525 on the issue of infant baptism. Because Anabaptists were convinced that the sacrament of baptism was only effective if administered to willing adults who understood its significance, they required followers who had been baptized as infants to be baptized again as adults (the term *Anabaptism* means "rebaptism"). This doctrine reflected the Anabaptists' fundamental belief that the true church was a small community of believers whose members had to make a deliberate, inspired decision to join it. No other Protestant groups were prepared to go so far in rejecting the medieval Christian view of the Church as a single vast body to which all members of society belonged from birth. In an age when almost everyone assumed that church and state were inextricably connected, Anabaptism was bound to be anathema to the established powers, both Protestant and Catholic. Yet in its first few years the movement did gain numerous adherents in Switzerland and Germany, above all because it appealed to sincere religious piety in calling for pacifism, strict personal morality, and extreme simplicity of worship.

This changed when a group of Anabaptist extremists managed to gain control of the German city of Münster in 1534. These zealots combined sectarianism with millenarianism, the belief that God intends to institute a completely new order of justice and spirituality throughout the world before the end of time. Determined to help God bring about this goal, the extremists attempted to turn Münster into a new Jerusalem. A former tailor named John of Leyden assumed the title "King of the New Temple" and proclaimed himself the successor of the Hebrew king David. Under his leadership, Anabaptist religious practices were made obligatory, private property was abolished, and even polygamy was permitted on the grounds of Old Testament precedents. Such practices were deeply shocking to Protestants and Catholics alike. Accordingly, Münster was besieged and captured by Catholic forces little more than a year after the Anabaptist takeover; and the new "David," together with two of his lieutenants, was put to death by torture.

Thereafter, Anabaptists throughout Europe were ruthlessly persecuted on all sides. The few who survived banded together in the Mennonite sect, named for its founder, the Dutchman Menno Simons (c. 1496–1561). This sect, dedicated to pacifism and the simple "religion of the heart" of original Anabaptism, has continued to exist to the present day and is particularly strong in the central United States.

## John Calvin's Reformed Theology

A year after the events in Münster, a twenty-six-year-old Frenchman named John Calvin (1509–1564), published the first version of his *Institutes of the Christian Religion*, the most influential formulation of Protestant theology ever written. Born in Noyon in northern France, Calvin had originally trained for the law, but by 1533 was studying the Greek and Latin classics while living off the income from a priestly benefice. As he later wrote, although he was "obstinately devoted to the superstitions of popery," he experienced a miraculous conversion. He became a Protestant theologian and propagandist, and evenually fled to the Swiss city of Basel to escape persecution.

Although some aspects of Calvin's early career resemble those of Luther, the two men were very different. Luther was an emotionally volatile personality and a lover of controversy. He responded to theological problems as they arose or as the impulse struck him; he never attempted to systematize his beliefs. Calvin, however, was a coolly analytical legalist, who resolved in his *Institutes* to set forth all the principles of Protestantism comprehensively, logically, and systematically. As a result, after several revisions and enlargements (the definitive edition appeared in 1559), Calvin's *Institutes* became the Protestant equivalent of Thomas Aquinas's *Summa Theologiae* (Chapter 9).

Calvin's austere theology started with the omnipotence of God and worked downward. For Calvin, the entire universe depends utterly on the will of the Almighty, who created all things for his greater glory. Because of man's original fall from grace, all human beings are sinners by nature, bound to an evil inheritance they cannot escape. Nevertheless, God (for reasons of his own) has predestined some for eternal salvation and damned all the rest to the torments of Hell. Nothing that human beings may do can alter their fate; all souls are stamped with God's blessing or curse before they are born. Nevertheless, Christians cannot be indifferent to their conduct on earth. If they are among the elect, God will implant in them the desire to live according to his laws. Upright conduct is thus a sign, though not an infallible one, that an individual has been chosen to sit at the throne of glory. Membership in the reformed church (as Calvinist churches are more properly known) is another presumptive sign of election to salvation. But most of all, Calvin urged Christians to conceive of themselves as chosen instruments of God, charged to work actively to fulfill God's purposes on earth. Because sin offends God, Christians should do all they can to prevent it, not because their actions will lead to anyone's salvation (they will not), but simply because God's glory is diminished if sin is allowed to flourish unchecked by the efforts of those whom he has chosen for salvation.

Calvin always acknowledged a great theological debt to Luther, but his religious teachings diverged from those of the Wittenberg reformer in several essentials. First of all, Luther's attitude toward proper Christian conduct in the world was much more passive than Calvin's. For Luther, a Christian should endure the trials of this life through

**JOHN CALVIN.** This recently discovered portrait by an anonymous artist shows the Protestant reformer as a serene and authoritative figure. It places the grotesque caricature of Calvin (right) in perspective.

**CALVIN AS SEEN BY HIS ENEMIES.** In this image, which circulated among Calvin's Catholic detractors, the reformer's facial features are a disturbing composite of fish, toad, and chicken.

suffering, whereas for Calvin the world was to be mastered in unceasing labor for God's sake. Calvin's religion was also more legalistic than Luther's. Luther, for example, insisted that his followers attend church on Sunday, but he did not demand that during the remainder of the day they refrain from all pleasure or work. Calvin, however, issued stern strictures against worldliness of any sort on the Sabbath and forbade all sorts of minor self-indulgences, even on non-Sabbath days.

The two men also differed on fundamental matters of church governance and worship. Although Luther broke with the Catholic system of hierarchical church government, Lutheran district superintendents exercised some of the same powers as bishops, including supervision of parish clergy. Luther also retained many features of traditional worship, including altars, music, and ritual. Calvin, however, rejected everything that smacked to him of "popery." Thus he argued for the elimination of all traces of hierarchy within the church. Instead, each congregation should elect its own ministers, and assemblies of ministers and "elders" (laymen responsible for maintaining proper religious conduct among the faithful) were to govern the reformed church as a whole. Calvin also insisted on the utmost simplicity in worship, prohibiting (among much else) vestments, processions, instrumental music, and religious images of any sort, including stained-glass windows. He also dispensed with all remaining vestiges of Catholic sacramental theology by making the sermon, rather than the Eucharist, the centerpiece of reformed worship.

## Calvinism in Geneva

Consistent with his theological convictions, Calvin was intent on putting his religious teachings into practice. Sensing an opportunity in the French-speaking Swiss city of Geneva—then in the throes of political and religious upheaval—he moved there late in 1536 and immediately began preaching and organizing. In 1538, his activities caused him to be expelled by the city council, but in 1541 he returned and brought the city under his sway.

Under Calvin's guidance, Geneva's government became a theocracy. Supreme authority was vested in a "Consistory" composed of twelve lay elders and between ten and twenty pastors, whose weekly meetings Calvin dominated. Aside from passing legislation proposed to it by a congregation of ministers, the Consistory's main function was to supervise morality, both public and private. To this end, Geneva was divided into districts, and a committee of the Consistory visited every household, without prior warning, to check on the behavior of its members. Dancing, card playing, attending the theater, and working or playing on the Sabbath—all were outlawed as works of the devil. Innkeepers were forbidden to allow anyone to consume food or drink without first saying grace, or to permit any patron to stay up after nine o'clock. Murder, treason, adultery, witchcraft, blasphemy, and heresy were all capital crimes. Even penalties for lesser crimes were severe. During the first four years after Calvin gained control in Geneva, there were no fewer than fifty-eight executions in this city with a total population of only 16,000.

As objectionable as such punishments may seem today, Calvin's Geneva was a beacon of light to thousands of Protestants throughout Europe in the mid-sixteenth century. Calvin's disciple John Knox, who brought the reformed religion to Scotland, declared Geneva "the most perfect school of Christ that ever was on earth since the days of the Apostles." Converts such as Knox flocked to Geneva for refuge or instruction and then returned home to become ardent proselytizers for the new religion. Geneva thus became the center of an international movement dedicated to spreading reformed religion to France and the rest of Europe through organized missionary activity and propaganda.

These efforts were remarkably successful. By the end of the sixteenth century, Calvinists were a majority in Scotland (where they were known as Presbyterians) and Holland (where they founded the Dutch Reformed Church). They were also influential in England; although the Church of England adopted reformed theology but not reformed worship (Calvinists there who sought further reforms in worship were known as Puritans). There were also substantial Calvinist minorities in France (where they were called Huguenots), Germany, Hungary, Lithuania, and Poland. God's kingdom on Earth had not yet been fully realized: on his deathbed in 1564, Calvin pronounced the Genevans to still be "a perverse and unhappy nation." But an extraordinary revolution had taken place in the religious life and practices of Europe, and they would soon spread to the New World.

## THE DOMESTICATION OF REFORM

Protestantism was a revolutionary movement whose radical claims for the spiritual equality of all true Christian believers had the potential to undermine the political, social, and even gender hierarchies on which European society rested. Luther himself did not anticipate that his ideas might have such implications, and he was genuinely shocked when the rebellious German peasants and the radical Anabaptists at Münster interpreted his teachings in this way. And Luther was by no means the only staunchly conservative Protestant. None of the prominent early Protestants were social or political radicals. Most Protestant reformers depended on the support of existing social and political leaders: territorial princes, of course, but also the ruling elites of towns. As a result, the Reformation movement was speedily "domesticated," in two senses. Its revolutionary potential was muffled—Luther himself rarely spoke about "the priesthood of all believers" after 1525—and there was an increasing emphasis on the patriarchal family as the central institution of reformed life.

### *Reform and Discipline*

As we have seen, injunctions to lead a more disciplined and godly life had been a frequent message of fifteenth-century religious reform movements. Many of these efforts were actively promoted by princes and town councils, most famously perhaps in Florence, where the Dominican preacher Girolamo Savonarola led the city on an extraordinary but short-lived campaign of puritanism and moral reform between 1494 and 1498. But there are many other examples of rulers legislating against sin. When Desiderius Erasmus called on secular authorities to think of themselves as abbots and of their territories as giant monasteries, he was sounding an already-famliar theme.

Protestant rulers, however, took the need to enforce godly discipline with particular seriousness, because the depravity of human nature was a fundamental tenet of Protestant belief. Like Saint Augustine at the end of the fourth century (Chapter 6), Protestants believed that people would inevitably turn out bad unless they were compelled to be good. It was, therefore, the responsibility of secular and religious leaders to control and punish the behavior of their people, because otherwise their evil deeds would anger God and destroy human society.

Protestant godliness began with the discipline of children. Luther himself wrote two catechisms (instructional tracts) designed to teach children the tenets of their faith and the obligations—toward parents, masters, and rulers—that God imposed on them. Luther also insisted that all children, boys and girls alike, should be taught to read the Bible in their own languages. Schooling thus became a characteristically Protestant preoccupation and rallying cry. Even the Protestant family was designated a "school of godliness," in which fathers were expected to instruct and discipline their wives, their children, and their household servants.

But family life in the early sixteenth century still left much to be desired in the eyes of Protestant reformers. Drunkenness, domestic violence, illicit sexual relations, lewd dancing, and the blasphemous swearing of oaths were frequent topics of reforming discourse. Various methods of discipline were attempted, including private counseling, public confessions of wrongdoing, public penances and shamings, exclusion from church services, and even imprisonment. All these efforts met with varying, but generally modest, success. To create godly Protestant families, and to enforce godly discipline on entire communities, was going to require the active cooperation of godly authorities.

## Protestantism, Government, and the Family

The domestication of the Reformation in this sense took place principally in the free towns of Germany and Switzerland—and from there spread westward to the New World. Protestant attacks on monasticism and clerical celibacy found a receptive audience among townsmen who resented the immunity of monastic houses from taxation and regarded clerical celibacy as a subterfuge for the seduction of their own wives and daughters. Protestant emphasis on the depravity of the human will and the consequent need for that will to be disciplined by authority also resonated powerfully with guilds and town governments, which were anxious to maintain and increase the control exercised by urban elites (mainly merchants and master craftsmen) over the apprentices and journeymen who made up the majority of the male population. By eliminating the competing jurisdictional authority of the Catholic Church, Protestantism allowed town governments to consolidate all authority within the city into their own hands.

Meanwhile, Protestantism reinforced the control of individual men over their own households by emphasizing the family as the basic unit of religious education. An all-powerful father figure was expected to assume responsibility for instructing and disciplining his household according to the precepts of reformed religion. At the same time, Protestantism introduced a new religious ideal for women. No longer was the celibate nun the exemplar of female holiness; in her place now stood the married and obedient Protestant "goodwife." As one Lutheran prince wrote in 1527: "Those who bear children please God better than all the monks and nuns singing and praying." To this extent, Protestantism resolved the tensions between piety and sexuality that had long characterized Christian teachings, by declaring the holiness of marital sex.

But this did not promote a new view of women's spiritual potential, nor did it elevate their social and political status; quite the contrary. Luther regarded women as more sexually driven than men and less capable of controlling their sexual desires—despite the fact that Luther confessed himself incapable of celibacy. His opposition to convents allegedly rested on his belief that it was impossible for women to remain chaste, so that sequestering them simply made illicit behavior inevitable. To prevent sin, it was necessary that all women should be married, preferably at a young age, and so placed under the governance of a godly husband.

For the most part, Protestant town governments were happy to cooperate in shutting down convents. The convent's property went to the town, after all. But conflicts did arise between Protestant reformers and town fathers over marriage and sexuality, especially over the reformers' insistence that both men and women should marry young as a restraint on lust. In many German towns, men were traditionally expected to delay marriage until they had achieved the status of a master craftsman—a requirement that had become increasingly difficult to enforce as guilds sought to restrict the number of journeymen permitted to become masters. In theory, then, apprentices and journeymen were not supposed to marry. Instead, they were expected to frequent brothels and taverns, a legally sanctioned outlet for extramarital sexuality long viewed as necessary to men's physical well-being, but that Protestant reformers found morally abhorrent and demanded be abolished.

Towns responded in a variety of ways to these opposing pressures. Some instituted special committees to police public morals, of the sort we have noted in Calvin's Geneva. Some abandoned Protestantism altogether. Others, like Augsburg, flip-flopped back and forth between Protestantism and Catholicism for several decades. Yet regardless of a town's final choice of religious allegiance, by the end of the sixteenth century a revolution had taken place with respect to town governments' attitudes toward public morality. In their competition with each other, neither Catholics nor Protestants wished to be seen as soft on sin. The result, by 1600, was the widespread abolition of publicly licensed brothels, the outlawing of prostitution, and far stricter governmental supervision of many other aspects of private life than had ever been the case in any Western civilization.

## The Control of Marriage

Protestantism also increased parents' control over their children's choice of marital partners. The medieval Church defined marriage as a sacrament that did not require the involvement of a priest. The mutual free consent of two individuals, even if given without witnesses or parental approval, was enough to constitute a legally valid marriage in

# Competing Viewpoints

## *Marriage and Celibacy: Two Views*

*These two selections illustrate the strongly contrasting views on the spiritual value of marriage versus celibacy that came to be embraced by Protestant and Catholic religious authorities. The first selection is part of Martin Luther's more general attack on monasticism, which emphasizes his contention that marriage is the natural and divinely intended state for all human beings. The second selection, from the decrees of the Council of Trent (1545–63), restates traditional Catholic teaching on the holiness of marriage but also emphasizes the spiritual superiority of virginity to marriage as well as the necessity of clerical celibacy.*

### Luther's Views on Celibacy

Listen! In all my days I have not heard the confession of a nun, but in the light of Scripture I shall hit upon how matters fare with her and know I shall not be lying. If a girl is not sustained by great and exceptional grace, she can live without a man as little as she can without eating, drinking, sleeping, and other natural necessities. Nor, on the other hand, can a man dispense with a wife. The reason for this is that procreating children is an urge planted as deeply in human nature as eating and drinking. That is why God has given and put into the body the organs, arteries, fluxes, and everything that serves it. Therefore what is he doing who would check this process and keep nature from running its desired and intended course? He is attempting to keep nature from being nature, fire from burning, water from wetting, and a man from eating, drinking, and sleeping.

Source: E. M. Plass, ed., *What Luther Says,* vol. 2 (St. Louis, MO: 1959), pp. 888–89.

### Canons on the Sacrament of Matrimony (1563)

Canon 1. If anyone says that matrimony is not truly and properly one of the seven sacraments . . . instituted by Christ the Lord, but has been devised by men in the Church and does not confer grace, let him be anathema [cursed].

Canon 9. If anyone says that clerics constituted in sacred orders or regulars [monks and nuns] who have made solemn profession of chastity can contract marriage . . . and that all who feel that they have not the gift of chastity, even though they have made such a vow, can contract marriage, let him be anathema, since God does not refuse that gift to those who ask for it rightly, neither does *he suffer us to be tempted above that which we are able.*

Canon 10: If anyone says that the married state excels the state of virginity or celibacy, and that it is better and happier to be united in matrimony than to remain in virginity or celibacy, let him be anathema.

Source: H. J. Schroeder, *Canons and Decrees of the Council of Trent* (St. Louis, MO: 1941), pp. 181–82.

### *Questions for Analysis*

1. On what grounds does Luther attack the practice of celibacy? Do you agree with his basic premise?
2. How do the later canons of the Catholic Church respond to Protestant views like Luther's? What appears to be at stake in this defense of marriage and celibacy?

the eyes of the Church. Opposition to this doctrine came from many quarters, especially from families who stood to lose from this *laissez faire* doctrine. Because marriage involved rights of inheritance to property, it was regarded as too important a matter to be left to the choice of adolescents. Instead, parents wanted the power to prevent unsuitable matches and, in some cases, to force their children to accept the marriage arrangements their families might negotiate on their behalf. Protestantism offered an opportunity to achieve such control. Luther had declared marriage to be a purely secular matter, not a sacrament at all, and one that could be regulated however the governing authorities thought best. Calvin largely followed suit, although Calvinist theocracy drew less of a distinction than did Lutheranism between the powers of church and state.

Even Catholicism was eventually forced to give way. Although it never abandoned its insistence that both members of the couple must freely consent to their marriage, by the end of the sixteenth century the Catholic Church required formal public notice of intent to marry and insisted on the presence of a priest at the actual wedding ceremony. Both were efforts to prevent elopements, allowing families time to intervene before an unsuitable marriage was concluded. Individual Catholic countries sometimes went even further in trying to assert parental control over their children's choice of marital partners. In France, for example, although couples might still marry without parental consent, those who did so now forfeited all of their rights to inherit their families' property. In somewhat different ways, both Protestantism and Catholicism thus moved to strengthen the control that parents could exercise over their children—and, in the case of Protestantism, that husbands could exercise over their wives.

## THE REFORMATION OF ENGLAND

In England, the Reformation took a rather different course than it did in continental Europe. Although a tradition of popular reform survived into the sixteenth century, the number of dissidents was too small and their influence too limited for Lollardy to play a significant role in paving the way for the ultimate triumph of Protestantism in England (see Chapter 10). Nor was England particularly oppressed by the papal exactions and abuses that roiled Germany. When the sixteenth century began, English monarchs already exercised close control over Church appointments within their kingdom; they also received the lion's share of the papal taxation collected from England. Nor did ecclesiastical courts inspire any particular resentments. On the contrary, they would continue to function in Protestant England until the eighteenth century. Why, then, did sixteenth-century England become a Protestant country at all?

### *"The King's Great Matter"*

By 1527, King Henry VIII of England had been married for eighteen years to Ferdinand and Isabella's daughter, Catherine of Aragon. Yet all the offspring of this union had died in infancy, with the exception of a daughter, Mary. Because Henry needed a male heir to preserve the peaceful succession to the throne and because Catherine was now past childbearing age, Henry had political reasons to propose a change of wife. He also had more personal motives, having become infatuated with a lady-in-waiting named Anne Boleyn.

Henry therefore appealed to Rome to annul his marriage to Catherine, arguing that because she had previously been married to his older brother Arthur (who had died in adolescence), Henry's marriage to Catherine had

**HENRY VIII OF ENGLAND.** Hans Holbein the Younger executed several portraits of the English king. This one represents him in middle age, confident of his powers.

# Analyzing Primary Sources

## *The Six Articles of the English Church*

*Although Henry VIII withdrew the Church of England from obedience to the papacy, he continued to reject most Protestant theology. Some of his advisers, most notably Thomas Cromwell, were committed Protestants; and the king allowed his son and heir, Edward VI, to be raised as a Protestant. But even after several years of rapid (and mostly Protestant) change in the English church, Henry reasserted a set of traditional Catholic doctrines in the Six Articles of 1539. These would remain binding on the Church of England until the king's death in 1547.*

First, that in the most blessed sacrament of the altar, by the strength and efficacy of Christ's mighty word, it being spoken by the priest, is present really, under the form of bread and wine, the natural body and blood of our Savior Jesus Christ, conceived of the Virgin Mary, and that after the consecration there remains no substance of bread or wine, nor any other substance but the substance of Christ, God and man;

Secondly, that communion in both kinds is not necessary for salvation, by the law of God, to all persons, and that it is to be believed and not doubted . . . that in the flesh, under the form of bread, is the very blood, and with the blood, under the form of wine, is the very flesh, as well apart as though they were both together;

Thirdly, that priests, after the order of priesthood received as afore, may not marry by the law of God;

Fourthly, that vows of chastity or widowhood by man or woman made to God advisedly ought to be observed by the law of God. . . .

Fifthly, that it is right and necessary that private masses be continued and admitted in this the king's English Church and congregation . . . whereby good Christian people . . . do receive both godly and goodly consolations and benefits; and it is agreeable also to God's law;

Sixthly, that oral, private confession is expedient and necessary to be retained and continued, used and frequented in the church of God.

Source: *Statutes of the Realm*, vol. 3 (London: 1810–28), p. 739 (modernized).

### *Questions for Analysis*

1. Three of these six articles focus on the sacrament of the Mass. Given what you have learned in this chapter, why would Henry have been so concerned about this sacrament? What does this reveal about his values and those of his contemporaries?

2. Given Henry's insistence on these articles, why might he have allowed his son to be raised a Protestant? What does this suggest about the political situation in England?

been invalid from the beginning. As Henry's representatives pointed out, the Bible pronounced it "an unclean thing" for a man to take his brother's wife and cursed such a marriage with childlessness (Leviticus 20:31). Even a papal dispensation (which Henry and Catherine had long before obtained for their marriage) could not exempt them from such a clear prohibition, as the marriage's childlessness proved.

Henry's suit put Pope Clement VII (r. 1523–34) in a quandary. Henry was firmly convinced that this Scriptural curse had blighted his chances of perpetuating his lineage; and both Henry and Clement knew that popes in the past had granted annulments to reigning monarchs on far weaker grounds than the ones Henry was alleging. If, however, the pope granted Henry's annulment, he would cast doubt on the validity of all papal dispensations. More seriously, however, he would provoke the wrath of the emperor Charles V, Catherine of Aragon's nephew, whose armies were in firm command of Rome and who at that moment held the pope himself in captivity. Clement was trapped; all he could do was procrastinate and hope that the matter would resolve itself. For two years, he allowed the suit to proceed in England without ever reaching a verdict. Then, suddenly, he transferred the case to Rome, where the legal process began all over again.

Exasperated by these delays, Henry began to increase the pressure on the pope. In 1531 he compelled an assembly of English clergy to declare him "protector and only supreme head" of the Church in England. In 1532 he encouraged

Parliament to produce an inflammatory list of grievances against the English clergy, and used this threat to force them to concede his right as king to approve or disapprove all Church legislation. In January 1533, Henry married Anne Boleyn (already pregnant) even though his marriage to Queen Catherine had still not been annulled. The new archbishop of Canterbury, Thomas Cranmer, provided the required annulment in May, acting on his own authority.

In September, Princess Elizabeth was born; her father, disappointed again in his hopes for a son, refused to attend her christening. Nevertheless, Parliament settled the succession to the throne on the children of Henry and Anne, redirected all papal revenues from England into the king's hands, prohibited appeals to the papal court, and formally declared "the King's highness to be Supreme Head of the Church of England." In 1536, Henry executed his former tutor and chancellor Sir Thomas More (Chapter 12) for his refusal to endorse this declaration of supremacy, and took the first steps toward dissolving England's monasteries. By the end of 1539, the monasteries and convents were gone and their lands and wealth confiscated by the king, who distributed them to his supporters.

These measures broke the bonds that linked the English Church to Rome, but they did not make England a Protestant country. Although certain traditional practices (such as pilgrimages and the veneration of relics) were prohibited, the English Church remained overwhelmingly Catholic in organization, doctrine, ritual, and language. The Six Articles promulgated by Parliament in 1539 at Henry VIII's behest left no room for doubt as to official orthodoxy: oral confession to priests, masses for the dead, and clerical celibacy were all confirmed; the Latin Mass continued; and Catholic Eucharistic doctrine was not only confirmed but its denial made punishable by death. To most English people, only the disappearance of the monasteries and the king's own continuing matrimonial adventures (he married six wives in all) were evidence that their Church was no longer in communion with Rome.

## The Reign of Edward VI

For truly committed Protestants, and especially those who had visited Calvin's Geneva, the changes Henry VIII enforced on the English Church did not go nearly far enough. In 1547, the accession of the nine-year-old king Edward VI (Henry's son by his third wife, Jane Seymour) gave them their opportunity to finish the task of reform. Encouraged by the apparent sympathies of the young king, Edward's government moved quickly to reform the creeds and ceremonies of the English Church. Priests were permitted to marry; English services replaced Latin ones; the veneration of images was discouraged, and the images themselves defaced or destroyed; prayers for the dead were discouraged, and endowments for such prayers were confiscated; and new articles of belief were drawn up, repudiating all sacraments except baptism and communion and affirming the Protestant doctrine of justification by faith alone. Most important, a new prayer book was published to define precisely how the new English-language services of the church were to be conducted. Much remained unsettled with respect to both doctrine and worship; but by 1553, when the youthful Edward died, the English Church appeared to have become a distinctly Protestant institution.

## Mary Tudor and the Restoration of Catholicism

Edward's successor, however, was his pious and much older half-sister Mary (r. 1553–58), granddaughter of "the most Catholic monarchs" of Spain, Ferdinand and Isabella (see Chapter 11). Mary speedily reversed her brother's religious policies, restoring the Latin Mass and requiring married priests to give up their wives. She even prevailed on Parliament to vote a return to papal allegiance. Hundreds of Protestant leaders fled abroad, many to Geneva; others, including Archbishop Thomas Cranmer, were burned at the stake for refusing to abjure their Protestantism. News of the martyrdoms spread like wildfire through Protestant Europe. In England, however, Mary's policies sparked relatively little resistance. After two decades of religious upheaval, most English men and women were probably hoping that Mary's reign would bring some stability to their lives.

This, however, Mary could not do. The executions she ordered were insufficient to wipe out religious resistance—instead, Protestant propaganda about "Bloody Mary" caused widespread unease, even among those who welcomed the return of traditional religious forms. Nor could Mary do anything to restore monasticism: too many leading families had profited from Henry VIII's dissolution of the monasteries for this to be reversed. Mary's marriage to her cousin Philip, Charles V's son and heir to the Spanish throne, was another miscalculation. Although the marriage treaty stipulated that in the event of Mary's death Philip could not succeed her, some of her English subjects never trusted him. When the queen allowed herself to be drawn by Philip into a war with France on Spain's behalf—in which England lost Calais, its last foothold on the European continent—many English people became highly disaffected. Ultimately, how-

**QUEEN MARY AND QUEEN ELIZABETH.** The two daughters of Henry VIII were the first two queens regnant of England: the first women to rule in their own right. Despite the similar challenges they faced, they had strikingly different fates and have been treated very differently in popular histories. ▪ ***How do these two portraits suggest differences in their personalities and their self-representation as rulers?***

ever, what doomed Mary's policies was simply the accident of biology: Mary was unable to conceive an heir, and when she died after only five years of rule, her throne passed to her Protestant sister, Elizabeth.

## The Elizabethan Compromise

The daughter of Henry VIII and Anne Boleyn, Elizabeth (r. 1558–1603) was predisposed in favor of Protestantism by the circumstances of her parents' marriage as well as by her upbringing. But Elizabeth was no zealot, and wisely recognized that supporting radical Protestantism in England might provoke bitter sectarian strife. Accordingly, she presided over what is often known as "the Elizabethan settlement." By a new Act of Supremacy (1559), Elizabeth repealed Mary's Catholic legislation, prohibiting foreign religious powers (i.e., the pope) from exercising any authority within England, and declaring herself "supreme governor" of the English church—a more Protestant title than Henry VIII's "supreme head," insofar as most Protestants believed that Christ alone was the head of the Church. She also adopted many of the Protestant liturgical reforms instituted by her brother, Edward, including a revised version of the prayer book. But she retained vestiges of Catholic practice too, including bishops, church courts, and vestments for the clergy. On most doctrinal matters, including predestination and free will, Elizabeth's Thirty-nine Articles of Faith (approved in 1562) struck a decidedly Protestant, even Calvinist, tone. But the prayer book was more moderate, and on the critical issue of the Eucharist was deliberately ambiguous. By combining Catholic and Protestant interpretations ("This is my body. . . . Do this in remembrance of me") into a single declaration, the prayer book permitted an enormous latitude for competing interpretations of the service by priests and parishioners alike.

Yet religious tensions persisted in Elizabethan England, not only between Protestants and Catholics but also between moderate and more extreme Protestants. The queen's artful fudging of these competing Christianities was by no means a recipe for success. Rather, what preserved "the Elizabethan settlement," and ultimately made England a Protestant country, was the extraordinary length of Queen Elizabeth's reign combined with the fact that for much of that time Protestant England was at war with Catholic Spain. Under Elizabeth, Protestantism and English nationalism gradually fused together into a potent conviction that God himself had chosen England for greatness. After 1588, when English naval forces won an improbable victory over a Spanish Armada (Chapter 11), Protestantism and Englishness became nearly indistinguishable to most of Queen Elizabeth's subjects. Laws against Catholic practices became increasingly severe, and although an English Catholic tradition did survive, its adherents were a persecuted minority. Significant, too, was the situation in Ireland, where the vast majority of the population remained Catholic despite the government's efforts to impose Protestantism on them. By 1603, Irishness was as firmly identified with Catholicism as was Englishness with Protestantism; but it was the Protestants who were in power in both countries.

## THE REBIRTH OF THE CATHOLIC CHURCH

So far, our emphasis on the spread of Protestantism has cast the spotlight on dissident reformers such as Luther and Calvin. But there was also a powerful internal reform movement within the Church during the sixteenth century, which resulted in the birth (or rebirth) of a Catholic ("universal") faith. For some, this movement is the "Catholic Reformation"; for others, it is the "Counter-Reformation." Those who prefer the former term emphasize that the Church continued significant reforming movements that can be traced back to the eleventh century (Chapter 8) and which gained new momentum in the wake of the Great Schism (Chapter 10). Others, however, insist that most Catholic reformers of this period were inspired primarily by the urgent need to resist Protestantism and to strengthen the power of the Roman Church in opposition to it.

### *Catholic Reforms*

Even before Luther's challenge to the Church, as we have seen, there was a movement for moral and institutional reform within some religious orders. But while these efforts received strong support from several secular rulers, the papacy showed little interest in them. In Spain, reforming activities directed by Cardinal Francisco Ximenes de Cisneros (1436–1517) led to the imposition of strict rules of behavior and the elimination of abuses prevalent among the clergy. Ximenes (*he-MEN-ez*) also helped to regenerate the spiritual life of the Spanish Church. In Italy, earnest clerics labored to make the Italian Church more worthy of its calling. Reforming existing monastic orders was a difficult task, not least because the papal court set such a poor example; but Italian reformers did manage to establish several new orders dedicated to high ideals of piety and social service. In northern Europe, Christian humanists such as Erasmus and Thomas More played a role in this Catholic reform movement, not only by criticizing abuses and editing sacred texts but also by encouraging the laity to lead lives of sincere religious piety (Chapter 12).

As a response to the challenges posed by Protestantism, however, these internal reforms proved entirely inadequate. Starting in the 1530s, therefore, a more aggressive phase of reform under a new style of vigorous papal leadership began to gather momentum. The leading Counter-Reformation popes—Paul III (r. 1534–49), Paul IV (r. 1555–59), Pius V (r. 1566–72), and Sixtus V (r. 1585–90)—were the most zealous reformers of the Church since the twelfth century. All led upright lives; some, indeed, were so grimly ascetic that contemporaries longed for the bad old days. As a Spanish councilor wrote of Pius V in 1567, "We should like it even better if the present Holy Father were no longer with us, however great, inexpressible, unparalleled, and extraordinary His Holiness may be." In confronting Protestantism,

**THE COUNCIL OF TRENT.** This fresco depicts the General Council of the Catholic Church, which met at intervals for nearly twenty years between 1545 and 1563 in the city of Trent (in modern-day Italy) in order to enact significant internal reforms.

however, an excessively holy pope was vastly preferable to a self-indulgent one. And these Counter-Reformation popes were not merely holy men. They were also accomplished administrators who reorganized papal finances and filled ecclesiastical offices with bishops and abbots no less renowned for austerity and holiness than were the popes themselves.

Papal reform efforts intensified at the Council of Trent, a General Council of the entire Church convoked by Paul III in 1545, which met at intervals thereafter until 1563. The decisions taken at Trent (a provincial capital of the Holy Roman Empire, located in modern-day Italy) provided the foundations on which a new Catholic Church would be erected. Although the council began by debating some form of compromise with Protestantism, it ended by reaffirming all of the Catholic tenets challenged by Protestant critics. "Good works" were affirmed as necessary for salvation, and all seven sacraments were declared indispensable means of grace, without which salvation was impossible. Transubstantiation, Purgatory, the invocation of saints, and the rule of celibacy for the clergy were all confirmed as dogmas—essential elements—of the Catholic faith. The Bible (in its imperfect Vulgate form) and the traditions of apostolic teaching were held to be of equal authority as sources of Christian truth. Papal supremacy over every bishop and priest was expressly maintained, and the supremacy of the pope over any Church council was taken for granted outright, signalling a final defeat of the still-active conciliar movement (Chapter 10). The Council of Trent even reaffirmed the doctrine of indulgences that had touched off the Lutheran revolt, although it condemned the worst abuses connected with their sale.

The legislation of Trent was not confined to matters of doctrine. To improve pastoral care of the laity, bishops and priests were forbidden to hold more than one spiritual office. To address the problem of an ignorant priesthood, a theological seminary was to be established in every diocese. The council also suppressed a variety of local religious practices and saints' cults, replacing them with new cults authorized and approved by Rome. To prevent heretical ideas from corrupting the faithful, the council further decided to censor or suppress dangerous books. In 1564, a specially appointed commission published the first Index, an official list of writings that ought not to be read by faithful Catholics. All of Erasmus's works were immediately placed on the Index, even though he had been a chosen champion of the Church against Martin Luther only forty years before. A permanent agency known as the Congregation of the Index was later set up to revise the list, which was maintained until the Index was abolished in 1966 after the Second Vatican Council. It was to become symbolic of the doctrinal intolerance that characterized sixteenth-century Christianity, both in its Catholic and Protestant varieties.

***THE INSPIRATION OF SAINT JEROME* BY GUIDO RENI.** The Council of Trent declared Saint Jerome's Latin translation of the Bible, the Vulgate, to be the official version of the Catholic Church, and in 1592 Pope Clement VIII chose one edition to be authoritative above all others. Since biblical scholars had known since the early sixteenth century that Saint Jerome's translation contained numerous mistakes, Catholic defenders of the Vulgate insisted that even his mistakes had been divinely inspired. ▪ ***How does Guido Reni's painting of 1635 attempt to make this point?***

## *Ignatius Loyola and the Society of Jesus*

In addition to the independent activities of popes and the legislation of the Council of Trent, a third main force propelling the Counter-Reformation was the foundation of the Society of Jesus (commonly known as the Jesuits) by Ignatius Loyola (1491–1556). In the midst of a career as a mercenary, this young Spanish nobleman was wounded in battle in 1521, the same year in which Luther defied authority at the Diet of Worms. While recuperating, he turned from the reading of chivalric romances to a romantic vernacular retelling of the life of Jesus—and on the strength

# Analyzing Primary Sources

## The Demands of Obedience

*The necessity of obedience in the spiritual formation of monks and nuns can be traced back to the* Rule of Saint Benedict *in the early sixth century, and beyond. In keeping with the mission of its founder, Ignatius of Loyola (1491–1556) the Society of Jesus brought a new militancy to this old ideal.*

### *Rules for Thinking with the Church*

**1.** Always to be ready to obey with mind and heart, setting aside all judgment of one's own, the true spouse of Jesus Christ, our holy mother, our infallible and orthodox mistress, the Catholic Church, whose authority is exercised over us by the hierarchy.

**2.** To commend the confession of sins to a priest as it is practised in the Church; the reception of the Holy Eucharist once a year, or better still every week, or at least every month, with the necessary preparation. . . .

**4.** To have a great esteem for the religious orders, and to give the preference to celibacy or virginity over the married state. . . .

**6.** To praise relics, the veneration and invocation of Saints: also the stations, and pious pilgrimages, indulgences, jubilees, the custom of lighting candles in the churches, and other such aids to piety and devotion. . . .

**9.** To uphold especially all the precepts of the Church, and not censure them in any manner; but, on the contrary, to defend them promptly, with reasons drawn from all sources, against those who criticize them.

**10.** To be eager to commend the decrees, mandates, traditions, rites, and customs of the Fathers in the Faith or our superiors. . . .

**11.** That we may be altogether of the same mind and in conformity with the Church herself, if she shall have defined anything to be black which to our eyes appears to be white, we ought in like manner to pronounce it to be black. For we must undoubtingly believe, that the Spirit of our Lord Jesus Christ, and the Spirit of the Orthodox Church His Spouse, by which Spirit we are governed and directed to salvation, is the same. . . .

### *From the Constitutions of the Jesuit Order*

Let us with the utmost pains strain every nerve of our strength to exhibit this virtue of obedience, firstly to the Highest Pontiff, then to the Superiors of the Society; so that in all things . . . we may be most ready to obey his voice, just as if it issued from Christ our Lord . . . leaving any work, even a letter, that we have begun and have not yet finished; by directing to this goal all our strength and intention in the Lord, that holy obedience may be made perfect in us in every respect, in performance, in will, in intellect; by submitting to whatever may be enjoined on us with great readiness, with spiritual joy and perseverance; by persuading ourselves that all things [commanded] are just; by rejecting with a kind of blind obedience all opposing opinion or judgment of our own. . . .

Source: Henry Bettenson, ed., *Documents of the Christian Church,* 2nd ed. (Oxford: 1967), pp. 259–61.

### *Questions for Analysis*

**1.** How might Loyola's career as a soldier have inspired the language used in his "Rules for Thinking with the Church"?

**2.** In what ways do these Jesuit principles respond directly to the challenges of Protestant reformers?

of this decided to become a spiritual soldier of Christ. For ten months he lived as a hermit in a cave near the town of Manresa, where he experienced ecstatic visions and worked out the principles of his subsequent guidebook, the *Spiritual Exercises*. This manual, completed in 1535 and first published in 1541, offered practical advice on how to master one's will and serve God through a systematic program of meditations on sin and the life of Christ. It eventually became a basic handbook for all Jesuits and has been widely studied by Catholic laypeople as well. Indeed, Loyola's *Spiritual Exercises* ranks alongside Calvin's *Institutes* as the most influential religious text of the sixteenth century.

The Jesuit order originated as a small group of six disciples who gathered around Loyola during his belated career as a student in Paris. They vowed to serve God in poverty, chastity, and missionary work, and were formally constituted by Pope Paul III in 1540; by the time of Loyola's death, the Society of Jesus already numbered some 1,500 members. And it was by far the most militant of the religious orders fostered by the Catholic reform movements of the sixteenth century—not merely a monastic society but a company of soldiers sworn to defend the faith. Their weapons were not bullets and swords but eloquence, persuasion, and instruction in correct doctrines; yet the Society also became accomplished in more worldly methods of exerting influence. Its organization was patterned after that of a military unit, whose commander in chief enforced iron discipline on all members. Individuality was suppressed, and a soldierlike obedience was required from the rank and file. Indeed, the Jesuit general, sometimes known as the "black pope" (from the color of the order's habit), was elected for life and answered only to the pope in Rome, to whom all senior Jesuits took a special vow of strict obedience. As a result of this vow, all Jesuits were held to be at the pope's disposal at all times.

The activities of the Jesuits consisted primarily of proselytizing and establishing schools. As missionaries, the early Jesuits preached to non-Christians in India, China, and Spanish America. One of Loyola's closest associates, Francis Xavier (1506–1552), baptized thousands of native people and traveled thousands of miles in South and East Asia. Yet although Loyola had not at first conceived of his society as a batallion of "shock troops" in the fight against Protestantism, that is what it primarily became. Through preaching and diplomacy—sometimes at the risk of their lives—Jesuits in the second half of the sixteenth century fanned out across Europe in direct confrontation with Calvinists. In many places, the Jesuits were instrumental in keeping rulers and their subjects loyal to Catholicism; in others they met martyrdom; and in some others, notably Poland and parts of Germany and France, they succeeded in regaining territory previously lost to Protestantism. Wherever they were allowed to settle, they set up schools and colleges, on the grounds that only a vigorous Catholicism nurtured by widespread literacy and education could combat Protestantism.

## *A New Catholic Christianity*

The greatest achievement of these reform movements was the revitalization of the Church. Had it not been for such determined efforts, Catholicism would not have swept over the globe during the seventeenth and eighteenth centuries or reemerged in Europe as a vigorous spiritual force. There were some other consequences, as well. One was the advancement of lay literacy in Catholic countries. Another was the growth of intense concern for acts of charity; because Catholicism continued to emphasize good works as well as faith, charitable activities took on an extremely important role.

There was also a renewed emphasis on the role of religious women. Reformed Catholicism did not exalt marriage as a route to holiness to the same degree as did Protestantism, but it did encourage the piety of a female religious elite. For example, it embraced the mysticism of Saint Teresa of Avila (1515–1582) and established new orders of nuns, such as the Ursulines and the Sisters of Charity. Both Protestants and Catholics continued to exclude women from the priesthood or ministry, but Catholic women could pursue religious lives with at least some degree of independence, and the convent continued to be a route toward spiritual and even political advancement in Catholic countries.

The Reformed Catholic Church did not, however, perpetuate the tolerant Christianity of Erasmus. Instead,

**THERESA OF AVILA.** Theresa of Avila (1515–1582) was one of many female religious figures who played an important role in the Reformed Catholic Church. She was canonized in 1622. This image is dated 1576. The Latin wording on the scroll unfurled above Theresa's head reads: "I will sing forever of the mercy of the Holy Lord."

Christian humanists lost favor with the papacy, and even scientists such as Galileo were regarded with suspicion (see Chapter 16). Yet contemporary Protestantism was just as intolerant, and even more hostile to the cause of rational thought. Indeed, because Catholic theologians turned for guidance to the scholasticism of Thomas Aquinas, they tended to be much more committed to the dignity of human reason than were their Protestant counterparts, who emphasized the literal interpretation of the Bible and the importance of unquestioning faith. It is no coincidence that René Descartes, one of the pioneers of rational philosophy ("I think, therefore I am"), was educated by Jesuits.

It would be wrong, therefore, to claim that the Protestantism of this era was more forward-looking or progressive than Catholicism. Both were, in fact, products of their time. Each variety of Protestantism responded to specific historical conditions and the needs of specific peoples in specific places, while carrying forward certain aspects of the Christian tradition considered valuable by those communities. The Catholic Church also responded to new spiritual, political, and social realities—to such an extent that it must be regarded as distinct from either the early Church of the later Roman Empire or even the oft-reformed Church of the Middle Ages. That is why the phrase "Roman Catholic Church" has not been used in this book prior to this chapter, because the Roman Catholic Church as we know it emerged for the first time in the sixteenth century. Like Protestantism, it is a more modern phenomenon.

## CONCLUSION

The Reformation grew out of complex historical processes that we have been tracing in the last few chapters. Foremost among these was the increasing power of Europe's sovereign states (Chapter 10). As we have seen, those German princes who embraced Protestantism were moved to do so by the desire for sovereignty. The kings of Denmark, Sweden, and England followed suit for many of the same reasons. Since Protestant leaders preached absolute obedience to godly rulers, and since the state in Protestant countries assumed direct control of its churches, Protestantism bolstered state power. Yet the power of the state had been growing for a long time prior to this, especially in such countries as France and Spain, where Catholic kings already exercised most of the same rights that were seized by Lutheran German princes and by Henry VIII of England in the course of their own reformations. Those rulers who

## After You Read This Chapter

Visit StudySpace for quizzes, additional review materials, and multi-media documents. **wwnorton.com/studyspace**

### REVIEWING THE OBJECTIVES

- The main premises of Luther's theology had religious, political, and social implications. What were they?
- Switzerland fostered a number of different Protestant movements. Why was this the case?
- The Reformation had a profound effect on the basic structures of family life and on attitudes toward marriage and morality. Describe these changes.
- The Church of England was established in response to a specific political situation. What was this?
- How did the Catholic Church respond to the challenge of Protestantism?

aligned themselves with Catholicism, then, had the same need to bolster their sovereignty and authority.

Ideas of national identity, too, were already influential and thus available for manipulation by Protestants and Catholics alike. These new religions, in turn, became new sources of identity and disunity. Until the sixteenth century, for example, the peoples in the different regions of Germany spoke such different dialects that they had difficulty understanding each other. But Luther's Bible gained such currency that it eventually became the linguistic standard for all these disparate regions, which eventually began to conceive of themselves as part of a single nation. Yet religion alone could not achieve the political unification of Germany, which did not occur for another three hundred years (see Chapter 21); indeed, it contributed to existing divisions by cementing the opposition of Catholic princes and peoples. Elsewhere in Europe—as in Holland, where Protestants fought successfully against a foreign, Catholic overlord—religion created a shared identity where politics could not. In England, where it is arguable that a sense of nationalism had already been fostered before the Reformation, membership in the Church of England became a new, but not uncontested, attribute of "Englishness."

Ideals characteristic of the Renaissance (Chapter 12) also contributed something to the Reformation and the Catholic responses to it. The criticisms of Christian humanists helped to prepare Europe for the challenges of Lutheranism, and close textual study of the Bible led to the publication of the newer, more accurate editions used by Protestant reformers. For example, Erasmus's improved edition of the Latin New Testament enabled Luther to reach some crucial conclusions concerning the meaning of penance and became the foundation for Luther's own translation of the Bible. Yet Erasmus was no supporter of Lutheran principles and most other Christian humanists followed suit, shunning Protestantism as soon as it became clear to them what Luther was actually teaching. Indeed, in certain basic respects Protestant principles were completely at odds with the principles, politics, and beliefs of most Renaissance humanists, who were staunch supporters of the Catholic Church.

In the New World and Asia, both Protestantism and Catholicism became forces of imperialism and new catalysts for competition. The race to secure colonies and resources now became a race for converts, too, as missionaries of both faiths fanned out over the globe. In the process, the confessional divisions of Europe were mapped onto these regions, often with violent results. Over the course of the ensuing century, newly sovereign nation-states would struggle for hegemony at home and abroad, setting off a series of religious wars that would cause as much destruction as any plague.

## PEOPLE, IDEAS, AND EVENTS IN CONTEXT

- How did **MARTIN LUTHER**'s attack on **INDULGENCES** tap into more widespread criticism of the papacy? What role did the printing press and the German vernacular play in the dissemination of his ideas?
- Why did many German principalities and cities rally to Luther's cause? Why did his condemnation at the **DIET OF WORMS** not lead to his execution on charges of heresy?
- How did the Protestant teachings of **ULRICH ZWINGLI**, **JOHN CALVIN**, and the **ANABAPTISTS** differ from one another and from those of Luther?
- What factors made some of Europe's territories more receptive to **PROTESTANTISM** than others? Why, for example, did Switzerland, the Netherlands, and the countries of Scandinavia embrace it?
- How did the **REFORMATION** alter the status and lives of women in Europe? Why did it strengthen male authority in the family?
- Why did **HENRY VIII** break with Rome? How did the **CHURCH OF ENGLAND** differ from other Protestant churches in Europe?
- What decisions were made at the **COUNCIL OF TRENT**? What were the founding principles of **IGNATIUS LOYOLA**'s **SOCIETY OF JESUS**, and what was its role in the **COUNTER-REFORMATION** of the **CATHOLIC CHURCH**?

## CONSEQUENCES

- Our study of Western civilizations has shown that reforming movements are nothing new: Christianity has been continuously reformed throughout its long history. What made this Reformation so different?
- Was a Protestant break with the Catholic Church inevitable? Why or why not?
- The political, social, and religious structures put in place during the Reformation continue to shape our lives in such profound ways that we scarcely notice them—or we assume them to be inevitable and natural. In your view, what is the most far-reaching consequence of this age of dissent and division, and why? In what ways has it formed your own values and assumptions?

# Before You Read This Chapter

## STORY LINES

- The religious differences that began to divide Europe during Martin Luther's lifetime soon erupted into prolonged, widespread warfare. At the same time, deeply entrenched political convictions contributed to the length, ferocity, and extent of these wars.
- Social and economic tensions also played a role in the violence of this period, and these manifested themselves in new forms of intolerance and persecution. For the first time, accusations of witchcraft were supported by intellectual arguments and sanctioned by the state.
- States themselves were becoming more powerful, as other sources of authority seemed less secure. Political philosophers and politicians worked to bolster this power and to define the sovereignty of the state.
- For all its violence—or perhaps, because of it—this period was an extremely fertile one for the arts, fostering the genius of French intellectuals, English poets and playwrights, and artists in Spain, Italy, and the Netherlands.

## CHRONOLOGY

| | |
|---|---|
| 1540–1555 | Regional wars in Germany |
| 1547–1616 | Lifetime of Miguel de Cervantes |
| 1562–1598 | French wars of religion |
| 1564–1616 | Lifetime of William Shakespeare |
| 1566–1609 | Dutch wars with Spain |
| 1572–1580 | Montaigne composes his *Essays* |
| 1576 | Jean Bodin publishes *Six Books of the Commonwealth* |
| 1603 | Reign of King James VI of Scotland begins in England |
| 1618–1648 | Thirty Years' War |
| 1625–1649 | Reign of King Charles I of England |
| 1642–1649 | English Civil War |
| 1643–1715 | Reign of Louis XIV of France |
| 1649 | King Charles is executed by act of Parliament |
| 1651 | Hobbes publishes *Leviathan* |
| 1660 | Restoration of the monarchy in England |
| 1670 | Publication of Pascal's *Pensées* |

# Religion, Warfare, and Sovereignty: 1540–1660

## CORE OBJECTIVES

- **UNDERSTAND** the ways in which early modern religious and political conflicts were intertwined.
- **TRACE** the main phases of religious warfare on the Continent.
- **IDENTIFY** the causes for Spain's decline and France's rise to power.
- **EXPLAIN** the origins and significance of the English Civil War.
- **DESCRIBE** some of the ways that intellectuals and artists responded to the challenges of this era.

In the early spring of 1592, a new play was mounted at the Rose Theatre, one of the enclosed places of entertainment recently constructed in London's suburbs. It was the prequel to two vastly popular plays that had already chronicled the dynastic wars that divided England in the fifteenth century, when English losses in the Hundred Years' War gave way to civil wars at home. The play, *The First Part of Henry VI*, was intended to explore the origins of those wars during the reign of the child-king who had suceeded the heroic Henry V, and it completed a trilogy that launched an ambitious young playwright called Will Shakespeare. Civil strife was a hot topic in the sixteenth century. Shakspeare's England was much more peaceful and unified than almost any other country in Europe, but that unity was fragile. It had been shattered numerous times because of ongoing religious divisions, and it was only now being maintained by a growing sense of national identity. Shakespeare's early plays promoted that identity by celebrating the superiority of the average Englishman over his European neighbors, who were often represented as either ridiculous or villainous. So in this new play the most interesting and ultimately dangerous character is the French heroine Joan of Arc, whose fervent Catholic faith turns out to be a mask for witchcraft. In Shakespeare's version of her legend, Joan actually attempts to be released from the tortures of the stake by claiming to be pregnant, and dies calling on her demon familiars to rescue her from the flames.

Shakespeare's plays, like many other products of contemporary popular culture, reveal the profound tensions that fractured the kingdoms and communities of Europe in the century after the Reformation. Martin Luther's call for universal access to the Bible had not resulted in a unified interpretation of the Christian faith; nor did his dream of a "priesthood of all believers" topple the clerical hierarchy of the Roman Church. Instead, Europe's religious divisions multiplied, often crystallizing along political lines. By the time of Luther's death in 1546, a clear pattern had already emerged. With only rare exceptions, Protestantism triumphed in areas where those in power stood to gain by rejecting the Church's hold over them; meanwhile, Catholicism prevailed in territories whose rulers had forged close political alliances with Rome. In both cases, Protestants and Catholics clung to the same belief in the mutual interdependence of religion and politics, an old certainty that had also undergirded the civilization of ancient Rome (Chapter 5) and most other Western civilizations before it.

Because many Europeans continued to believe that the proper role of the state was to enforce "true religion" on those subject to its authority, most sixteenth-century rulers were convinced that religious pluralism could bring only chaos and disloyalty. Ironically, then, Catholics and Protestants were united in one conviction: that western Europe had to return to a single religious faith enforced by properly constituted political authorities. What they could not agree on was *which* faith—and which authorities. The result was a brutal series of wars whose reverberations continue to be felt in many regions of Europe and in her former colonies. Vastly expensive and destructive, these wars affected everyone in Europe, from peasants to princes. Yet it would be misleading to suggest that they were caused by religious differences alone. Regional tensions, dynastic politics, and nascent nationalist tendencies were also potent contributors to the violence into which Europe was plunged and were therefore staple elements of Shakespeare's dramatic histories. Together, these forces of division and disorder brought into question the very survival of the political order that had emerged in the twelfth and thirteenth centuries (Chapter 9). Faced with the prospect of political collapse, those who still held power a century later were forced to embrace, gradually and grudgingly, a notion that had seemed impossible: religious tolerance was the only way to preserve political, social, and economic order.

## SOURCES OF TENSION AND UNREST

The troubles that engulfed Europe during the long, traumatic century between 1540 and 1660 caught contemporaries unaware. Most of Europe had enjoyed steady economic growth since the midle of the fifteenth century, and the colonization of the Americas seemed certain to be the basis of greater prosperity to come. Political trends too seemed auspicious, because most western European governments were becoming more efficient and and effective. By the middle of the sixteenth century, however, there were warning signs.

### *The Price Revolution*

The first of these warning signs was economic: an unprecedented inflation in prices that had begun in the latter half of the sixteenth century. Nothing like it had ever happened before, at least not on this scale, even during the Roman Empire's turbulent third century (Chapter 6). In Flanders, the cost of wheat tripled between 1550 and 1600, grain prices in Paris quadrupled, and the overall cost of living in England more than doubled. The twentieth century would see much more dizzying inflations than this, but in the sixteenth century the skyrocketing of prices was a terrifying novelty, what most historians describe as the "price revolution."

Two developments in particular underlay the soaring prices. The first was demographic. Starting in the later fifteenth century, Europe's population began to grow again after the plague-induced decline of the fourteenth century (Chapter 10); roughly estimated, Europe had about 50 million people around 1450, and 90 million around 1600. Because Europe's food supply remained more or less constant, owing to the lack of any noteworthy breakthroughs in agricultural technology analogous to those of the eleventh century (Chapter 8), food prices were driven sharply higher by greater demand. At the same time, wages stagnated or even declined. As a result, workers around 1600 were paying a higher percentage of their wages to buy food, even though basic nutritional levels were declining.

Population trends explain much, but since Europe's population did not increase nearly so rapidly in the second half of the sixteenth century as did prices, other explanations for the great inflation are necessary. Foremost among these is the enormous influx of bullion from Spanish America. From 1556 to 1560, roughly 10 million ducats' worth of silver passed through the Spanish entry port of

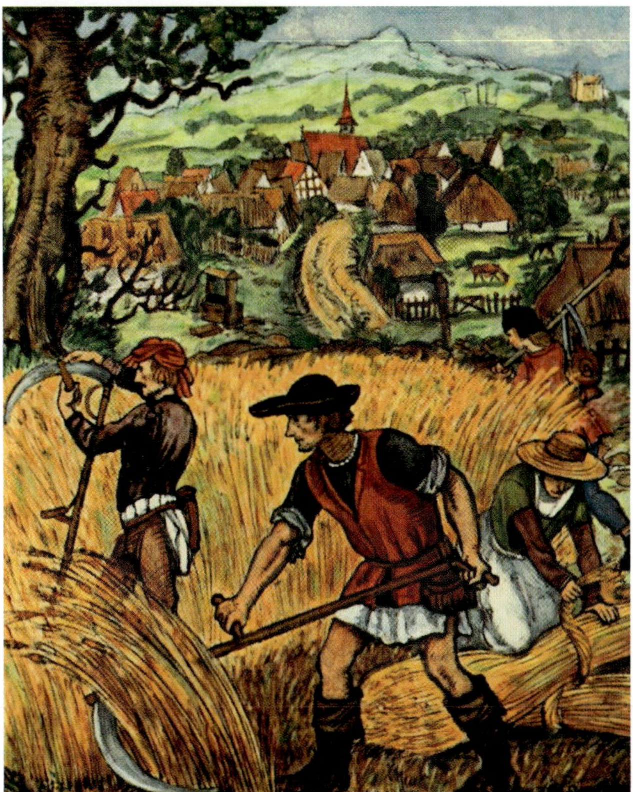

**PEASANTS HARVESTING WHEAT, SIXTEENTH CENTURY.** The inflation that swept through Europe in the late sixteenth century affected poorer workers most acutely, as the abundant labor supply dampened wages while at the same time the cost of food rose because of poor harvests.

Seville. Between 1576 and 1580 that figure doubled, and between 1591 and 1595 it more than quadrupled. Most of this silver was used by the Spanish crown to pay its foreign creditors and its armies abroad; as a result, this bullion quickly circulated throughout Europe, where much of it was minted into coins. This dramatic increase in the volume of money in circulation fueled the spiral of rising prices. "I learned a proverb here," said a French traveler in Spain in 1603: "everything costs a lot, except silver."

Aggressive entrepreneurs and large-scale farmers profited most from the changed economic circumstances, while the masses of laboring people were hurt the most. Landlords benefited from the rising prices of agricultural produce, and merchants from the increasing demand for luxury goods. But laborers were caught in a squeeze because wages rose far more slowly than prices, owing to the presence of a more than adequate labor supply. Moreover, because the cost of food staples rose at a sharper rate than the cost of most other items of consumption, poor people had to spend an ever-greater percentage of their paltry incomes on necessities. When disasters such as wars or bad harvests drove grain prices out of reach, some of the poor starved to death. The picture that emerges is one of the rich getting richer and the poor getting poorer—splendid feasts enjoyed amid the most appalling misery.

The price revolution also placed new pressures on the sovereign states of Europe. Since inflation depressed the real value of money, fixed incomes from taxes and tolls yielded less and less income. Thus, merely to keep their revenues constant, governments were forced to raise taxes. But to compound this problem, most states still needed more real income because they were engaging in more wars; and warfare was becoming increasingly expensive. The only recourse, then, was to raise taxes precipitously, which aroused great resentment. Hence governments faced continuous threats of defiance and even armed resistance. Although prices rose less rapidly after 1600, as population growth slowed and the flood of silver from America began to slow down, the period from 1600 to 1660 was one of economic stagnation rather than growth. A few areas—notably Holland—bucked the trend, and the rich were usually able to hold their own, but the poor as a group made no advances because the relationship of prices to wages remained fixed, to their disadvantage. Indeed, the lot of the poor in many places deteriorated further because the mid-seventeenth century saw particularly destructive wars in which helpless civilians were plundered by rapacious tax collectors or looting soldiers, or sometimes both. The Black Death also returned, wreaking havoc in London and elsewhere during the 1660s.

## *Political and Religious Instability*

Compounding these economic problems were the disunities inherent in major European monarchies. Most had grown during the later Middle Ages by absorbing or colonizing smaller, traditionally autonomous, territories—sometimes by conquest, but more often through marriage alliances or inheritance arrangements among ruling families (a policy known as "dynasticism"). At first, some degree of provincial autonomy was usually preserved in these newly absorbed territories. But in the period we are now examining, governments began making ever-greater financial claims on all their subjects while trying to enforce religious uniformity. As a result, rulers often rode roughshod over the rights of these traditionally autonomous provinces.

At the same time, claims to the sovereignty—the unity, autonomy, and authority—of these states were increasingly made on the basis of religious uniformity. Rulers on both sides felt that religious minorities, if allowed to flourish in their realms, would inevitably engage in sedition; nor were they always wrong, since militant Calvinists and Jesuits were indeed dedicated to subverting constituted powers in areas where their parties had not yet triumphed. Thus states tried to extirpate all potential religious resistance but, in the process, sometimes provoked civil wars in which each side tended to assume there could be no victory until the other was exterminated. And of course, civil wars could become international in scope if foreign powers chose to aid their embattled religious allies elsewhere.

Regionalism, economic grievances, and religious animosities were thus compounded into a volatile and destructive mixture. Nor was that all, since most governments seeking money and/or religious uniformity tried to rule with a firmer hand than before and thus increasingly provoked armed resistance from subjects seeking to preserve traditional liberties. As a result, the long century between 1540 and 1660 was one of the most turbulent in all of European history.

## A CENTURY OF RELIGIOUS WARS

The greatest single cause of warfare during this period was religious conflict. These "wars of religion" are usually divided into four phases:

1. a series of regional wars in Germany from the 1540s to 1555
2. the French wars of religion from 1562 until 1598
3. the simultaneous revolts of the (Protestant) Dutch against the (Catholic) Spanish Habsburg Empire between 1566 and 1609
4. the Thirty Years' War that devasted German-speaking lands again, between 1618 and 1648.

### *Regional Warfare in Germany*

Wars between Catholics and Protestant rulers in Germany began in the 1540s, less than a generation after Lutheranism first took hold there. The Holy Roman emperor, Charles V (Chapter 13), was also king of Spain and a devout supporter of the Church. His goal was therefore to reestablish Catholic unity in Germany by launching a military campaign against several German princes who had instituted Lutheran worship in their territories. But despite several notable victories, Charles's efforts to defeat the Protestant princes failed. In part, this was because he was also involved in wars against France, but primarily it was because the Catholic princes of Germany worked against him, fearing that any suppression of Protestant princes might also suppress their own independence. As a result, the Catholic princes' support for the foreign-born Charles was only lukewarm; at times, they even joined with Protestants in battle against the emperor.

This regional warfare sputtered on and off until a compromise settlement was reached via the Peace of Augsburg in 1555. Its governing principle was *cuius regio, eius religio*: "as the ruler, so the religion." This meant that in those principalities where Lutherans ruled, Lutheranism would be the sole state religion; but where Catholic princes ruled, the people of their territories would also be Catholic. For better and for worse, the Peace of Augsburg was a historical

***THE EMPEROR CHARLES V* BY TITIAN.** Charles V's attempts to enforce Catholicism in his German territories failed. In 1555, the Peace of Augsburg recognized the existence of both Protestant and Catholic territories, with the faith of each determined by the religion of the ruler. ▪ ***How does this portrait of Charles compare to that on page 406 (Chapter 13)?*** ▪ ***How might changing historical circumstances account for these different representations of the same ruler?***

milestone. For the first time since Luther had been excommunicated, on the one hand, Catholic rulers were forced to acknowledge the legality of Protestantism. But on the other hand, the peace set a dangerous precedent because it established the principle that no sovereign state could tolerate religious diversity. Moreover, it excluded Calvinism entirely, and thus spurred German Calvinists to become aggressive opponents of the status quo.

## *The French Wars of Religion*

From the 1560s on, Europe's religious wars became far more brutal, partly because the combatants had become more intransigent (with Calvinists and Jesuits taking the lead on their respective sides), and partly because these later wars were aggravated by regional, political, and dynastic animosities. For example, Calvin's Geneva bordered on France; and because Calvin himself was a Frenchman, Calvinist missionaries made considerable headway there after 1541, when he took power. But their concentration in the southern part of the country reflected long-standing hosilities that reached back to the ravages of northern French "crusaders" against Albigensian "heretics" during the thirteenth century (Chapter 9). Also assisting the Calvinist cause was the conversion of many aristocratic Frenchwomen, who in turn won over their husbands, many of whom maintained large private armies. The foremost example of these was Jeanne d'Albret, queen of Navarre, who converted her husband, the prominent aristocrat Antoine de Bourbon, and her brother-in-law, the prince of Condé.

Within two decades, Calvinists—known in France as Huguenots (*YOO-guh-nohs*), for reasons that remain obscure—made up between 10 and 20 percent of France's population. Although they lived uneasily alongside their Catholic neighbors, there was no open warfare until 1562, when the reigning king died unexpectedly, leaving a young child as his heir. This spurred a struggle between two factions within the regency government which formed along religious lines: the Huguenots, led by the prince of Condé, and the Catholics, led by the duke of Guise. And since both Catholics and Protestants believed that a kingdom could have only one *roi, foi,* and *loi* ( "king," "faith," and "law"), this political struggle turned into a religious war. Soon all France was aflame. Rampaging mobs, often incited by members of the clergy, used this opportunity to settle local scores. Although the Huguenots were not numerous enough to gain a victory, they were too strong to be defeated, especially in their stronghold of southern France. Hence warfare dragged on for a decade until a truce was arranged in 1572. This truce required the young Huguenot leader, Prince Henry of Navarre, to marry the Catholic sister of the reigning French king.

But this compromise was defeated by the powerful dowager queen of France, Catherine de' Medici, scion of the Florentine family that was closely aligned with the papacy (Chapter 13). Instead of honoring the truce, she plotted with members of the Catholic faction to kill all the Huguenot leaders while they were assembled in Paris for her daugher's wedding to Henry of Navarre. In the early morning of St. Bartholomew's Day (August 24), most of these leaders were murdered in their beds, while thousands of other Protestants were slaughtered in the streets or drowned in the Seine by Catholic mobs. When word of the Parisian massacre spread to the provinces, some 10,000 more Huguenots were killed. Henry of Navarre escaped, along with his new bride; but now the conflict entered a new and even more bitter phase.

**HENRY IV OF FRANCE.** The rule of Henry of Navarre (r. 1589–1610) initiated the Bourbon dynasty that would rule France until 1792, and ended the bitter civil war between Catholic and Huguenot factions.

Catherine's death in 1589 enabled Henry of Navarre to be crowned king as Henry IV, but peace was not restored until he renounced his Protestant faith in order to placate France's Catholic majority. In 1598, however, he offered limited religious freedom to the Huguenots by issuing the Edict of Nantes. This edict recognized Catholicism as the official religion of the kingdom, but allowed Huguenot aristocrats to hold Protestant services privately in their homes, while other Huguenots were allowed to worship in certain specified places at certain times. The Huguenot party was also permitted to fortify some towns, especially in the south and west, for their own military defense. Huguenots were further guaranteed the right to hold public office and to enter universities and hospitals.

The Edict of Nantes did not guarantee absolute freedom of worship, but it was still a major stride in the direction of tolerance. Unfortunately, however, the effect was to divide the kingdom into separate religious enclaves. In southern and western France, Huguenots came to have their own law courts, staffed by their own judges. They also received substantial powers of self-government, because it was presumed on all sides that the members of one religious group could not be ruled equitably by the adherents of a competing religion. Because of its regional character, the edict also represented a concession to the long-standing traditions of provincial autonomy within the kingdom of France. In some ways, indeed, Huguenot areas became a confederacy within the state, thus raising the fear that the kingdom might once again crumble into its constituent parts, as had happened during the Hundred Years' War. On its own terms, however, the Edict of Nantes was a success. France began to recover from decades of devastation, and peace was maintained even after Henry IV was assassinated by a Catholic in 1610.

## The Revolt of the Netherlands

Bitter warfare also broke out between Catholics and Protestants in the Low Countries, where regional resentments exacerbated religious animosities. For almost a century, the territories comprising much of the modern-day Netherlands and Belgium had been ruled by the Habsburg family of Holy Roman emperors, who also ruled Spain. The southern Netherlands in particular had prospered greatly from this, through trade and manufacture: their inhabitants generated the greatest per capita wealth of all Europe, and their metropolis of Antwerp was northern Europe's leading commercial and financial center. Moreover, the half-century rule of Charles V had been successful here. Charles had been born in the Flemish city of Ghent, and had a strong rapport with his subjects, whom he allowed a large measure of self-government.

But a year after the Peace of Augsburg in 1555, Charles V retired to a monastery and ceded all of his vast territories outside of the Holy Roman Empire and Hungary to his son Philip II (r. 1556–98). Unlike Charles, Philip had been born in Spain and, thinking of himself as a Spaniard, made Spain his residence and the focus of his policy. He viewed the Netherlands primarily as a source of income necessary for pursuing Spanish imperial conquests in the New World. The better to exploit the region's wealth, Philip therefore tried to tighten control over the Netherlands. This aroused the resentment of the region's fiercely independent cities and of the local magnates who had dominated the government under Charles V. A religious storm was also brewing. French Calvinists were beginning to

**THE NETHERLANDS AFTER 1609.** ▪ *What were the two main divisions of the Netherlands?* ▪ *Which was Protestant, and which was Catholic?* ▪ *How could William the Silent and his allies use the geography of the northern Netherlands against the Spanish?* ▪ *Why were the southern provinces of the Netherlands wealthier than the northern ones?*

**PROTESTANTS RANSACKING A CATHOLIC CHURCH IN THE NETHERLANDS.** Protestant destruction of religious images provoked a stern response from Phillip II. ▪ ***Why would Protestants have smashed statuary and other devotional artifacts?***

stream into the southern Netherlands, intent on making converts. Within decades, there were more Calvinists in Antwerp than in Geneva. To Philip, an ardent supporter of the Catholic Church, this was intolerable. As he declared to the pope, "Rather than suffer the slightest harm to the true religion and service of God, I would lose all my states and even my life a hundred times over, because I am not and will not be the ruler of heretics."

Worried by the growing tensions, a group of Catholic aristocrats appealed to Philip to allow toleration for Calvinists within the Netherlands. They were led by William of Orange, known as "William the Silent" because he was so successful at hiding his religious and political leanings. But before Philip could respond, radical Protestant mobs began ransacking Catholic churches throughout the country, desecrating altars, smashing statuary, and shattering stained-glass windows. Local troops brought the situation under control, but Philip nonetheless decided to dispatch an army of 10,000 Spanish soliders, led by the duke of Alva, to wipe out Protestantism in the Netherlands. Alva's rule as governor quickly became a reign of terror. Operating under martial law, his "Council of Blood" examined some 12,000 people on charges of heresy or sedition, of whom 9,000 were convicted and thousands executed. William fled the country, and all hope for peace in the Netherlands seemed lost.

Yet the tide turned quickly. The exiled William converted openly to Protestantism and sought help from religious allies in France, Germany, and England; meanwhile, organized bands of Protestant privateers harassed Spanish shipping on the Netherlandish coast. Alva's tyranny also advanced William's cause, especially when the hated Spanish governor attempted to levy a devastating sales tax. In 1572, William was able to seize the northern Netherlands, even though the north until then had been predominantly Catholic. Thereafter, geography played a major role in determining the outcome of the conflict. Spanish armies repeatedly attempted to win back the north, but they were stopped by a combination of impassable rivers and dikes that could be opened to flood out the invaders. Although William was assassinated by a Catholic in 1584, his son continued to lead the resistance until the Spanish crown finally agreed to recognize the independence of a northern Dutch Republic in 1609. Meanwhile, the pressures of war and persecution had made the whole north Calvinist, whereas the south—which remained under Spanish control—returned to Catholicism.

## England and the Spanish Armada

Religious strife could spark civil war, as in France, or political rebellion, as in the Netherlands. But it could also provoke warfare between sovereign states, as in the struggle between England and Spain. As we noted in Chapter 13, the Catholic queen Mary of England (r. 1553–58), herself the granddaughter of Ferdinand and Isabella of Spain, had married her cousin Philip II of Spain in 1554. After her death, Philip appears to have extended a marriage proposal to her half-sister, the Protestant queen Elizabeth (r. 1558–1603), and to have been rejected. Adding to the animosity created by religious differences and dynastic politics was the fact that English economic interests were directly opposed to those of Spain. English seafarers and traders were steadily making inroads into Spanish naval and commercial networks and were also engaged in lucrative trade with the Spanish Netherlands. But the greatest source of antagonism lay in the Atlantic, where English privateers, with the tacit consent of Queen Elizabeth, began attacking Spanish treasure ships. Taking as an excuse the Spanish oppression of Protestants in the Netherlands, English sea captains such as Sir Francis Drake and Sir John Hawkins plundered Spanish vessels on the high seas. In a particularly dramatic exploit lasting from 1577 to 1580, prevailing winds and lust for treasure propelled Drake all the way around the world, to return with stolen Spanish treasure worth twice as much as Queen Elizabeth's annual revenue.

All this would have been sufficient provocation for Spain to retaliate against England, but Philip resolved to invade the island only after the English openly allied with Dutch rebels in 1585. Even then, Philip moved slowly. Finally, in 1588 he dispatched an enormous fleet, confidently called the "Invincible Armada," to invade insolent England. After an initial standoff in the English Channel, however, the smaller English warships, more agile and armed with longer-range guns, outmaneuvered the Spanish fleet, while English fireships set some Spanish galleons ablaze and forced the rest to break formation. A fierce "Protestant wind" did the rest. After a disastrous circumnavigation of the British Isles and Ireland, the shattered Spanish flotilla limped home with almost half its ships lost. Elizabeth quickly took credit for her country's miraculous escape. Although the war with Spain dragged on until 1604, the fighting was just lively enough to foster feelings of English nationalism and Protestant fervor.

**THE "ARMADA PORTRAIT" OF ELIZABETH.** This is one of several portraits that commemorated the defeat of the Spanish Armada in 1588. Through the window on the left (the queen's right hand), an English flotilla sails serenely on sunny seas; on the right, Spanish ships are wrecked by a "Protestant wind." Elizabeth's right hand rests protectively—and commandingly—on the globe. ▪ ***How would you "read" this image?***

## *The Thirty Years' War*

With the promulgation of the French Edict of Nantes in 1598, the peace between England and Spain of 1604, and the truce between Spain and the Dutch republic of 1609, religious warfare in northwestern Europe came briefly to an end. But in 1618 a major new war broke out in Germany. Because this struggle raged more or less incessantly until 1648, it is known as the Thirty Years' War, and it eventually encompassed Spain and France as well, becoming an international struggle in which the initial religious provocations were all but forgotten.

After the Peace of Augsburg in 1555, the balance of powers between Protestant and Catholic territories within the Holy Roman Empire had remained laregly undisturbed. In 1618, however, the Catholic Habsburg prince who ruled Poland, Austria, and Hungary was elected king of Protestant Bohemia, prompting a rebellion among the Bohemian aristocracy. When this same prince, Ferdinand, became Holy Roman Emperor a year later, German Catholic forces were sent to crush the rebellion. Within a decade, then, a German imperial Catholic league seemed close to extirpating Protestantism throughout Germany. But this threatened the political autonomy of all German princes, Catholic and Protestant alike. So when the Lutheran king of Sweden, Gustavus Adolphus, championed the Protestant cause in 1630, he was welcomed by several German Catholic princes, too.

To make matters still more complicated, the Swedish king's Protestant army was secretly subsidized by Catholic France, whose policy was then dictated by Cardinal Richelieu (*RIH-shlyuh*, 1585–1642). Sweden had French support because Richelieu was determined to prevent France from being surrounded by a strong Habsburg alliance on the north, east, and south. Something of a military genius, Gustavus Adolphus began routing the Habsburgs. But when Gustavus died in battle in 1632, Cardinal Richelieu found himself having to conduct the war himself; in 1635, France openly declared

# Analyzing Primary Sources

## *The Devastation of the Thirty Years' War*

*The author of the following excerpt, Hans Jakob Christoph von Grimmelshausen (1621–1676), barely survived the horrors of the Thirty Years' War. His parents were killed, probably when he was thirteen years old, and he himself was kidnapped the following year and forced into the army. By age fifteen, he was a soldier. His darkly satiric masterpiece,* Simplicissimus (The Simpleton), *drew heavily on these experiences. Although technically a fictional memoir, it portrays with brutal accuracy the terrible realities of this era.*

Although it was not my intention to take the peaceloving reader with these troopers to my dad's house and farm, seeing that matters will go ill therein, yet the course of my history demands that I should leave to kind posterity an account of what manner of cruelties were now and again practised in this our German war: yes, and moreover testify by my own example that such evils must often have been sent to us by the goodness of Almighty God for our profit. For, gentle reader, who would ever have taught me that there was a God in Heaven if these soldiers had not destroyed my dad's house, and by such a deed driven me out among folk who gave me all fitting instruction thereupon? . . .

The first thing these troopers did was, that they stabled their horses: thereafter each fell to his appointed task: which task was neither more nor less than ruin and destruction. For though some began to slaughter and to boil and to roast so that it looked as if there should be a merry banquet forward, yet others there were who did but storm through the house above and below stairs. Others stowed together great parcels of cloth and apparel and all manner of household stuff, as if they would set up a frippery market. All that they had no mind to take with them they cut in pieces. Some thrust their swords through the hay and straw as if they had not enough sheep and swine to slaughter: and some shook the feathers out of the beds and in their stead stuffed in bacon and other dried meat and provisions as if such were better and softer to sleep upon. Others broke the stove and the windows as if they had a never-ending summer to promise. Houseware of copper and tin they beat flat, and packed such vessels, all bent and spoiled, in with the rest. Bedsteads, tables, chairs, and benches they burned, though there lay many cords of dry wood in the yard. Pots and pipkins must all go to pieces, either because they would eat none but roast flesh, or because their purpose was to make there but a single meal.

Our maid was so handled in the stable that she could not come out, which is a shame to tell of. Our man they laid bound upon the ground, thrust a gag into his mouth, and poured a pailful of filthy water into his body: and by this, which they called a Swedish draught, they forced him to lead a party of them to another place where they captured men and beasts, and brought them back to our farm, in which company were my dad, my mother, and our Ursula.

And now they began: first to take the flints out of their pistols and in place of them to jam the peasants' thumbs in and so to torture the poor rogues as if they had been about the burning of witches: for one of them they had taken they thrust into the baking oven and there lit a fire under him, although he had as yet confessed no crime: as for another, they put a cord round his head and so twisted it tight with a piece of wood that the blood gushed from his mouth and nose and ears. In a word each had his own device to torture the peasants, and each peasant his several tortures.

Source: Hans Jakob Christoph von Grimmelshausen, *Simplicissimus*, trans. S. Goodrich (New York: 1995), pp. 1–3, 8–10, 32–35.

### *Questions for Analysis*

1. The first-person narrator here recounts the atrocities committed "in this our German war," in which both perpetrators and victims are German. How believable is this description? What lends it credibility?

2. Why might Grimmelshausen have chosen to publish his account as a satirical fiction, rather than as a straightforward historical narrative or autobiography? How would this choice affect a reader's response to scenes such as this?

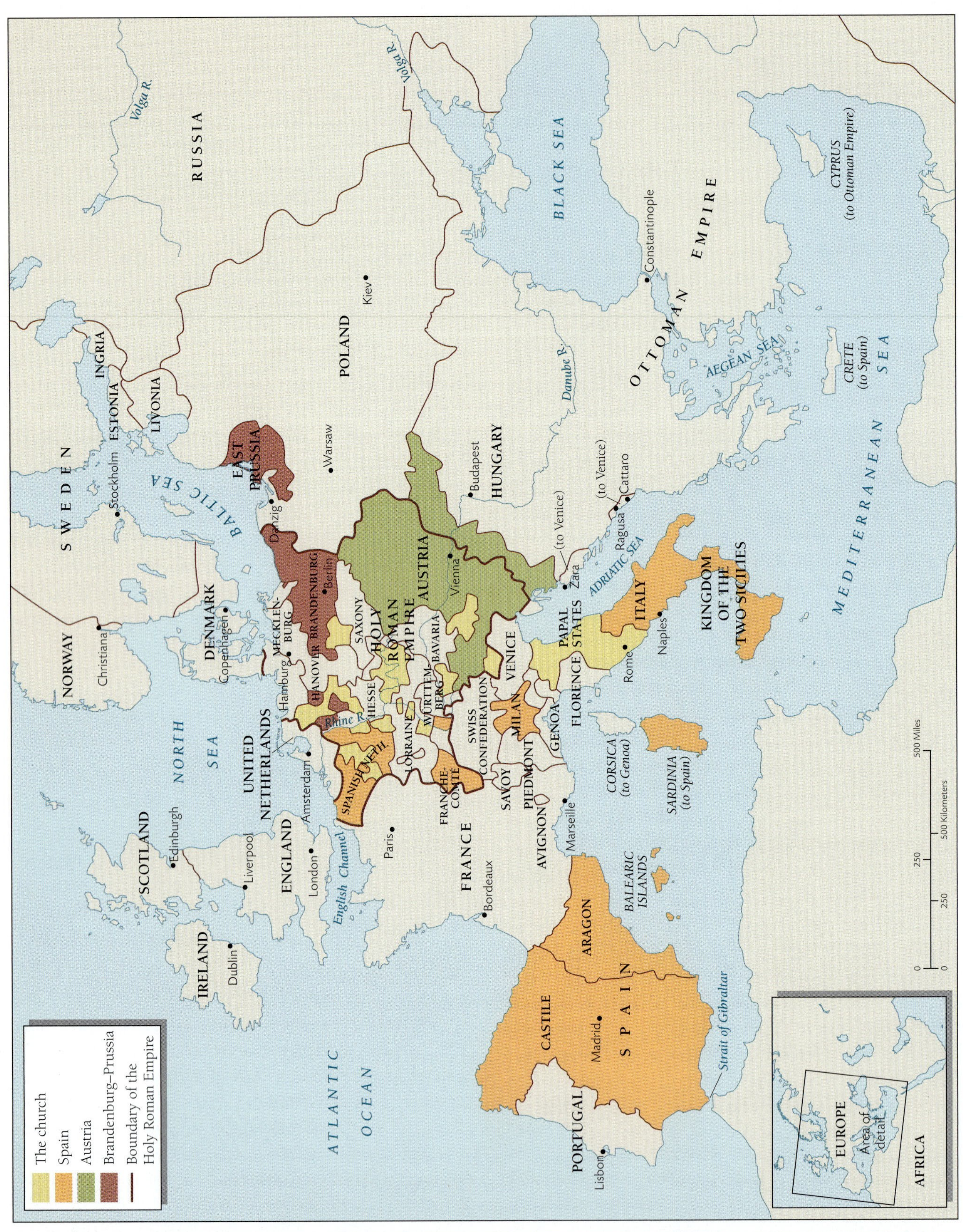


**EUROPE AT THE END OF THE THIRTY YEARS' WAR.** This map shows the fragile political checkerboard that resulted from Peace of Westphalia in 1648. ▪ ***When you compare this map to the map on page 407 in Chapter 13, what are the most significant territorial changes between 1550 and 1648?*** ▪ ***Which regions would have been weakened or endangered by this arrangement?*** ▪ ***Which would be in a strong position to dominate Europe?***

itself for Sweden and against Austria and Spain. In the middle lay Germany, a helpless battleground.

Germany suffered more from warfare in the terrible years between 1618 and 1648 than than at any time until the twentieth century. Several German cities were besieged and sacked nine or ten times over, and soldiers from all nations, who often had to sustain themselves by plunder, gave no quarter to defenseless civilians. With plague and disease adding to the toll of outright butchery, some parts of Germany lost more than half their populations. Most horrifying was the loss of life in the final four years of the war, when the carnage continued unabated even after peace negotiators arrived at broad areas of agreement.

The eventual adoption of the Peace of Westphalia in 1648 was a watershed in European history. It marked the emergence of France as the predominant power on the Continent, a position it would hold for the next two centuries. The greatest losers in the conflict (aside from the millions of German victims) were the Austrian Habsburgs, who were forced to surrender all the territory they had gained and to abandon their hopes of using the office of Holy Roman Emperor to dominate central Europe. Spain became increasingly relegated to the margins of Europe, and Germany remained a volatile checkerboard of Protestant and Catholic principalities.

## DIVERGENT POLITICAL PATHS: SPAIN AND FRANCE

The long century of war between 1540 and 1648 decisively altered the balance of power among the major kingdoms of western Europe. Germany emerged from the Thirty Years' War a devastated and exhausted land. Spain, too, was crippled by its unremitting military exertions. The French monarchy, by contrast, steadily increased its power. By 1660, France had become the most powerful country on the European mainland. In England, meanwhile, a bloody civil war had broken out between the king and his critics in Parliament, culminating in an unprecedented event: the legal execution of a reigning monarch by his own parliamentary government.

### *The Decline of Spain*

The story of Spain's fall from grandeur unfolds almost as relentlessly as a Greek tragedy. In 1600, the Spanish Empire—comprising all of the Iberian Peninsula (including Portugal, which had been annexed by Phillip II in 1580), half of Italy, half of the Netherlands, all of Central and South America, and the Philippine Islands in the Pacific Ocean—was the mightiest power not just in Europe but in the world. Yet only a half century later, this empire was beginning to fall apart.

Spain's greatest underlying weakness was economic. At first this may seem odd considering that in 1600, as in the three or four previous decades, huge amounts of American silver were being unloaded at the harbor of Seville. Yet as contemporaries themselves recognized, the New World that Spain had conquered was now conquering Spain. Lacking both agricultural and mineral resources of its own, Spain desperately needed to develop industries and a balanced trading pattern, as some of its Atlantic rivals were doing. But the Spanish nobility prized honor and chivalric ideals over practical business affairs. They used imperial silver to buy manufactured goods from other parts of Europe and, as a result, had no incentive to develop industries and exports of their own. When the river of silver began to abate, Spain was plunged into debt.

Meanwhile, the crown's commitment to supporting the Catholic Church and maintaining Spain's international dominance meant the continuance of costly wars. Even in the relatively peaceful year of 1608, about 4 million ducats—out of a total revenue of 7 million—were spent on military ventures. Spain's involvement in the Thirty Years' War was the last straw. In 1643, French troops inflicted a stunning defeat on the famed Spanish infantry at Rocroi in nothern France, the first time that a Spanish army had been overcome in battle since the reign of Ferdinand and Isabella (Chapter 11).

By then, two of Spain's Iberian territories were in open revolt. The governing power of Spain lay entirely in Castile, which had emerged as the dominant power after the marriage of Isabella to Ferdinand of Aragon in 1469. Castile became even more dominant when it took over Portugal in 1580. In the absence of any great financial hardships, semi-autonomous Catalonia (historically, an independent part of Aragon) also endured Castilian hegemony. But in 1640, when the strains of warfare induced Castile to limit Catalan liberties and to raise more money and men for combat, Catalonia revolted and drove out its Castilian governors. When the Portuguese learned of the Catalan uprising, they revolted as well, followed by southern Italians who rose up against Castilian viceroys in Naples and Sicily in 1647. It was only by chance that Spain's greatest external enemies, France and England, could not act in time to take advantage of its plight. This gave the Castilian government time to put down the Italian revolts; by 1652 it had also brought Catalonia to heel. But Portugal retained its independence, and Spain's isolation after the Peace of Westphalia further increased.

**THE BATTLE OF ROCROI, 1643.** Spain's defeat by the French at Rocroi was the first time the Spanish army had lost a land battle since the reign of Ferdinand and Isabella (Chapter 11), and was yet another contributing factor to the decline of Spanish power during the Thirty Years' War. This painting shows the victorious French general, the duke d'Enghien, surveying the battlefield from afar.

## *The Growth of France*

A comparison of the fortunes of Spain and France in the first half of the seventeenth century shows some striking similarities between the two countries. Both were of almost identical territorial extent, and both had been created by the same process of accretion and conquest over the course of the previous centuries (Chapters 9 and 10). Just as the Castilian crown had gained Aragon, Catalonia, Granada, and then Portugal, so the kingdom of France had grown by adding such diverse territories as Languedoc, Provence, Burgundy, and Brittany. Since the inhabitants of all these territories cherished traditions of local independence, and since French and Spanish monarchs were determined to govern their provinces ever more firmly—especially when costs of the Thirty Years' War made ruthless tax collecting an urgent necessity—a direct confrontation between the central government and the provinces became inevitable in both cases.

The fact that France emerged powerfully from this while Spain did not can be attributed in part to France's greater natural resources and the greater prestige of the French monarchy. Most subjects of the French king, including those from the outlying provinces, were loyal to him. Certainly they had excellent reason to be so during the reign of Henry IV. Having established religious peace by the Edict of Nantes, the affable Henry declared that there should be a chicken in every French family's pot each Sunday, and therefore set out to restore the prosperity of a country devastated by civil war. And France had enormous economic resiliency, owing primarily to its extremely rich and varied agricultural productivity. Unlike Spain, which had to import food, France was able to feed itself; and Henry's finance minister, the duke of Sully, quickly ensured that it did just that. Among other things, Sully distributed free copies of a guide to recommended farming techniques and financed the rebuilding or construction of roads, bridges, and canals to facilitate the flow of goods. Henry IV, meanwhile, ordered the construction of royal factories to manufacture luxury goods such as crystal, glass, and tapestries while supporting the growth of silk, linen, and woolen cloth industries in many different parts of the country. Henry's patronage also allowed the explorer Samuel de Champlain to claim parts of Canada as France's first foothold in the New World.

# Analyzing Primary Sources

## *Cardinal Richelieu on the Common People of France*

*Armand Jean du Plessis, duke of Richelieu and cardinal of the Roman Catholic Church, was the effective ruler of France from 1624 until his death in 1642. His* Political Testament *was assembled after his death from historical sketches and memoranda of advice which he prepared for King Louis XIII, the ineffectual monarch whom he ostensibly served. This book was eventually published in 1688, during the reign of Louis XIV.*

All students of politics agree that when the common people are too well off it is impossible to keep them peaceable. The explanation for this is that they are less well informed than the members of the other orders in the state, who are much more cultivated and enlightened, and so if not preoccupied with the search for the necessities of existence, find it difficult to remain within the limits imposed by both common sense and the law.

It would not be sound to relieve them of all taxation and similar charges, since in such a case they would lose the mark of their subjection and consequently the awareness of their station. Thus being free from paying tribute, they would consider themselves exempted from obedience. One should compare them with mules, which being accustomed to work, suffer more when long idle than when kept busy. But just as this work should be reasonable, with the burdens placed upon these animals proportionate to their strength, so it is likewise with the burdens placed upon the people. If they are not moderate, even when put to good public use, they are certainly unjust. I realize that when a king undertakes a program of public works it is correct to say that what the people gain from it is returned by paying the *taille* [a heavy tax imposed on the peasantry]. In the same fashion it can be maintained that what a king takes from the people returns to them, and that they advance it to him only to draw upon it for the enjoyment of their leisure and their investments, which would be impossible if they did not contribute to the support of the state.

Source: *The Political Testament of Cardinal Richelieu*, trans. Henry Bertram Hill (Madison, WI: 1961), pp. 31–32.

### *Questions for Analysis*

1. According to Cardinal Richelieu, why should the state work to subjugate the common people? What assumptions about the nature and status of "common people" underlie this argument?
2. What theory of "the state" emerges from this argument? What is the relationship between the king and the state, and between the king and the people, according to Richelieu?

## Cardinal Richelieu

Henry IV's reign can be counted as one of the most benevolent and effective in France's history. Far less benevolent was that of Henry's de facto successor, Cardinal Richelieu. The real king of France, Henry's son Louis XIII (r. 1610–43), came to the throne at the age of nine. But his reign was dominated by Richelieu, his chief minister of state. It was Richelieu who centralized royal power at home and expanded French influence abroad. For example, when Huguenots rebelled against certain restrictions that been placed on them by the Edict of Nantes, Richelieu amended the edict to revoke their political and military rights altogether. He then moved to gain more income for the crown by ending the semi-autonomy of Burgundy, the Dauphiné, and Provence so that he could introduce direct royal taxation in all three areas. Later, to make sure taxes were efficiently collected, Richelieu instituted a new system of local government by royal officials who were expressly commissioned to put down provincial resistance. By these and other methods Richelieu made the French monarchy more powerful than any in Europe and managed to double the crown's income during his rule. He also engaged in ambitious foreign wars against the Habsburgs of Austria and Spain, as we have seen. Yet increased centralization and France's costly involvement in the Thirty Years' War would lead to increased internal pressures in the years after Richelieu's death.

## *The Fronde*

An immediate reaction to French governmental control was the series of uncoordinated revolts known collectively the *Fronde* (from the French word for "slingshot") which occured in 1643. Louis XIII had just been succeeded by the five-year-old Louis XIV, whose regents were his mother, Anne of Austria, and her paramour, Cardinal Mazarin. Both were foreigners—Anne was a Habsburg and Mazarin was an Italian adventurer named Giulio Mazarini—and many of their subjects, including some extremely powerful nobles, hated them. Popular resentments were greater still because the costs of the ongoing Thirty Years' War were now combined with several consecutive years of bad harvests. So when cliques of nobles expressed their disgust for Mazarin, they found much popular support throughout the country.

France did not, however, come close to falling apart. Neither the aristocratic leaders of the Fronde nor the commoners who joined them in revolt claimed to be resisting the young king; their targets were the alleged corruption and mismanagement of Mazarin. Some of the rebels, it is true, insisted that part of Mazarin's fault lay in his pursuit of Richelieu's centralizing, antiprovincial policy. But most were aristocrats who wanted to become part of this centralizing process. Thus when Louis XIV began to rule in his own right in 1651, and pretexts for revolt against corrupt ministers no longer existed, the opposition was soon silenced. Yet Louis XIV remembered the turbulence of the Fronde for the rest of his life, and resolved never to let his aristocracy or his provinces get out of hand. Pursuing this policy, he became the most effective absolute monarch in Europe (see Chapter 15).

# MONARCHY AND CIVIL WAR IN ENGLAND

The power of Louis XIV in France stands in stark contrast to the challenges faced by his older contemporary, King Charles I of England. Of all the revolts that shook mid-seventeenth-century Europe, the most radical in its consequences was the English Civil War. The causes of this conflict were similar to those that sparked rebellions in Spain and France: hostilities between the component parts of a composite kingdom; religious animosities between Catholics and Protestants and within the ruling (Protestant) camp; struggles for power among competing factions of aristocrats at court; and a fiscal system that could not keep pace with the increasing costs of government, much less those of war. But in England, these conflicts led to the unprecedented deposition and execution of the king (1649), an eleven-year "interregnum" during which England was ruled as a parliamentary republic (1649–60), and ultimately to the restoration of the monarchy under conditions designed to safeguard Parliament's place in government up to the present day.

## *The Origins of the English Civil War*

The chain of events leading to war between royalist and Parliamentary forces in 1642 can be traced to the last decades of Queen Elizabeth's reign. During the 1590s, the expenses of war with Spain, together with a rebellion in Ireland, widespread crop failures, and the inadequacies of the antiquated English taxation system, drove the queen's government deeply into debt. Factional disputes around the court also became more bitter as courtiers, anticipating the aging queen's death, jockeyed for position under her presumed successor, the Scottish king James Stuart (James VI). Only on her deathbed, however, did the queen finally confirm that her throne should go to her Scottish cousin. As a result, neither James nor his new English subjects knew very much about each other when he took the throne at the end of 1603, ruling England as James I.

The relationship did not begin well. James's English subjects looked down on the Scots whom he brought with him to London. Although English courtiers were pleased to accept their new king's generosity to themselves, they resented the grants he made to his Scottish supporters, whom they blamed, quite unreasonably, for the crown's indebtedness. James, meanwhile, saw that to resolve his debts he had to have more revenue. But rather than bargain with parliamentary representatives for increased taxation, he chose to lecture them on the prerogatives of kingship, comparing kings to gods on earth: "As it is atheism and blasphemy to dispute what God can do, so it is presumption and high contempt in a subject to dispute what a king can do." When this approach failed, James raised what revenues he could without parliamentary approval, imposing new tolls on trade and selling trading monopolies to favored courtiers. These measures aroused further resentments against the king and so made voluntary grants of taxation from Parliament even less likely.

James was more adept with respect to religious policy. Scotland had been a firmly Calvinist country since the 1560s. England, too, was a Protestant country, but of a very different kind, since the Church of England retained many of the rituals, hierarchies, and doctrines of the medieval Church (Chapter 13). A significant number of English

Protestants wanted to bring their church more firmly into line with Calvinist principles, but others resisted such efforts and labeled their Calvinist opponents "Puritans." As king, James was compelled to mediate these conflicts. By and large, he did so successfully. In Scotland, he convinced the reformed (Calvinist) church to retain its bishops, and in England, he encouraged Calvinist doctrine while resisting any alterations to the religious tenets articulated in the English Prayer Book and the Thirty-Nine Articles of the Faith. Only in Ireland, which remained overwhelmingly Catholic, did James stir up future trouble. By encouraging the "plantation" of more than 8,000 Scottish Calvinists in the northern province of Ulster, he undermined the property rights of Irish Catholics and created religious animosities that have lasted to the present day.

## The Reign of Charles Stuart

This state of affairs became volatile in 1625, when James was succeeded by his surviving son, Charles. Charles almost immediately launched a new war with Spain, exacerbating his financial problems. He then alarmed his Protestant subjects by marrying Henrietta Maria, the Catholic daughter of France's Louis XIII. The situation became truly dangerous, however, when Charles and his archbishop of Canterbury, William Laud, began to favor the most anti-Calvinist elements in the English church, thus threatening the forthrightly Calvinist church in Scotland. The Scots rebelled, and in 1640 a Scottish army marched south into England to demand the withdrawal of Charles's "Catholicizing" reforms.

To meet the Scottish threat, Charles was forced to summon the English Parliament, something he (like his father) had avoided doing. Relations between the king and Parliament had broken down severely in the late 1620s, when Charles responded to Parliament's refusal to grant him additional funds by demanding forced loans from his subjects—and punishing those who refused by forcing them to lodge soldiers in their homes, or throwing them into prison without trial. In response, Parliament had forced the king to accept the Petition of Right in 1628, which declared all taxes not voted by Parliament illegal, condemned the quartering of soldiers in private houses, and prohibited arbitrary imprisonment and martial law in time of peace. Angered rather than chastened by the Petition of Right, Charles resolved to rule without Parliament, funding his government during the 1630s with a variety of levies and fines imposed without parliamentary consent.

When the Scottish invasion forced Charles to summon a new Parliament, therefore, its representatives were determined to impose a series of radical reforms on the king's government before they would even consider granting him funds to raise an army against the Scots. Charles initially cooperated with these reforms, even allowing Parliament to execute his chief minister. But it soon became clear that parliamentary leaders had no intention of fighting the Scots, but actually shared with them a common Calvinist outlook. In 1642, Charles attempted to break this stalemate by marching his guards into the House of Commons and attempting to arrest its leaders. When he failed in this, he withdrew from London to raise his own army. Parliament responded by summoning its own force and voting the taxation to pay for it. By the end of 1642, open warfare had erupted between the

**CHARLES I.** King Charles of England was a connoisseur of the arts and a patron of artists. He was adept at using portraiture to convey the magnificence of his tastes and the grandeur of his conception of kingship. ▪ ***How does this portrait by Anthony Van Dyck compare to the engravings of the "martyred" king on page 444 in* Interpreting Visual Evidence?**

# Competing Viewpoints

## *Debating the English Civil War*

*The English Civil War raised fundamental questions about political rights and responsibilities. Many of these are addressed in the two excerpts below. The first comes from a lengthy debate held within the General Council of Cromwell's army in October of 1647. The second is taken from the speech given by King Charles, moments before his execution in 1649.*

### The Army Debates, 1647

*Colonel Rainsborough*: Really, I think that the poorest man that is in England has a life to live as the greatest man, and therefore truly, sir, I think it's clear, that every man that is to live under a government ought first by his own consent to put himself under that government, and I do think that the poorest man in England is not at all bound in a strict sense to that government that he has not had a voice to put himself under . . . insomuch that I should doubt whether I was an Englishman or not, that should doubt of these things.

*General Ireton*: Give me leave to tell you, that if you make this the rule, I think you must fly for refuge to an absolute natural right, and you must deny all civil right, and I am sure it will come to that in the consequence. . . . For my part, I think it is no right at all. I think that no person has a right to an interest or share in the disposing of the affairs of the kingdom, and in determining or choosing those that shall determine what laws we shall be ruled by here, no person has a right to this that has not a permanent fixed interest in this kingdom, and those persons together are properly the represented of this kingdom who, taken together, and consequently are to make up the representers of this kingdom. . . .

We talk of birthright. Truly, birthright there is. . . . [M]en may justly have by birthright, by their very being born in England, that we should not seclude them out of England. That we should not refuse to give them air and place and ground, and the freedom of the highways and other things, to live amongst us, not any man that is born here, though he in birth or by his birth there come nothing at all that is part of the permanent interest of this kingdom to him. That I think is due to a man by birth. But that by a man's being born here he shall have a share in that power that shall dispose of the lands here, and of all things here, I do not think it is a sufficient ground.

Source: *Divine Right and Democracy: An Anthology of Political Writing in Stuart England*, ed. David Wootton (New York: 1986), pp. 286–87 (language modernized).

English king and the English government—something inconceivable in France, where the king and the government were inseparable.

Arrayed on the king's side were most of England's aristocrats and largest landowners, who were almost all loyal to the established Church of England, despite their opposition to some of Charles's own religious innovations. The parliamentary forces were made up of smaller landholders, tradesmen, and artisans, many of whom were Puritan sympathizers. The king's royalist supporters were commonly known by the aristocratic name of Cavaliers. Their opponents, who cut their hair short in contempt for the fashionable custom of wearing curls, were derisively called Roundheads. At first the Cavaliers, having obvious advantages of military experience, won most of the victories. In 1644, however, the parliamentary army was effectively reorganized, and afterward the fortunes of battle shifted. The royalist forces were badly beaten, and in 1646 the king was compelled to surrender. Soon thereafter, the episcopal hierarchy was abolished and a Calvinist-style church was mandated throughout England and Wales.

The struggle might have ended here had not a quarrel developed within the parliamentary party. The majority of its members were ready to restore Charles to the throne as a limited monarch, under an arrangement whereby a uniformly Calvinist faith would be imposed on both Scotland and England as the state religion. But a radical minority of Puritans, commonly known as Independents, distrusted

## Charles I on the Scaffold, 1649

I think it is my duty, to God first, and to my country, for to clear myself both as an honest man, a good king, and a good Christian.

I shall begin first with my innocence. In truth I think it not very needful for me to insist long upon this, for all the world knows that I never did begin a war with the two Houses of Parliament, and I call God to witness, to whom I must shortly make an account, that I never did intend to incroach upon their privileges. . . .

As for the people—truly I desire their liberty and freedom as much as anybody whatsoever. But I must tell you that their liberty and freedom consists in having of government those laws by which their lives and goods may be most their own. It is not for having share in government. That is nothing pertaining to them. A subject and a sovereign are clean different things, and therefore, until they do that—I mean that you do put the people in that liberty as I say—certainly they will never enjoy themselves.

Sirs, it was for this that now I am come here. If I would have given way to an arbitrary way, for to have all laws changed according to the power of the sword, I needed not to have come here. And therefore I tell you (and I pray God it be not laid to your charge) that I am the martyr of the people.

Source: Brian Tierney, Donald Kagan, and L. Pearce Williams, eds., *Great Issues in Western Civilization* (New York: 1967), pp. 46–47.

### *Questions for Analysis*

1. What fundamental issues are at stake in both of these excerpts? How do the debaters within the parliamentary army (first excerpt) define "natural" and "civil" rights?
2. How does Charles defend his position? What is his theory of kingship, and how does it compare to that of Cardinal Richelieu (page 439)? How does it conflict with the ideas expressed in the army's debate?
3. It is interesting that none of the participants in these debates seems to have recognized the implications their arguments might have for the political rights of women. Why would that have been the case?

Charles and insisted on religious toleration for themselves and all other Protestants. Their leader was Oliver Cromwell (1599–1658), who had risen to command the Roundhead army, which he had reconstituted as "the New Model Army." Ultimately, he became the new leader of Parliament, too.

## *The Fall of Charles Stuart and the Commonwealth*

Taking advantage of the dissension within the ranks of his opponents, Charles renewed the war in 1648 but, after a brief campaign, was forced to surrender. Cromwell was now resolved to end the life of "that man of blood" and, ejecting all the moderates from Parliament by force, he obliged this "Rump" (remaining) Parliament to put the king on trial and eventually to condemn him to death for treason against his own subjects. Charles Stuart was publicly beheaded on 30 January 1649: the first time in history that a reigning king had been legally deposed and executed by his own government. Europeans reacted to his death with horror, astonishment, or rejoicing, depending on their own political convictions (see ***Interpreting Visual Evidence*** on page 444).

A short time later, Parliament's hereditary House of Lords was abolished and England was declared a Commonwealth, an English translation of the Latin *res publica*. But founding a republic was far easier than maintaining

# Interpreting Visual Evidence

## *The Execution of a King*

This allegorical engraving (image A) accompanied a pamphlet called *Eikon Basilike* ("The Kingly Image"), which began to circulate in Britain just weeks after the execution of King Charles I. It purported to be an autobiographical account of the king's last days and a justification of his royal policies. It was intended to arouse widespread sympathy for the king and his exiled heir, Charles II, and it succeeded admirably: the cult of Charles "King and Martyr" became increasingly popular. Here, the Latin inscription on the shaft of light suggests that Charles' piety will beam "brighter through the shadows," while the scrolls at the left proclaim that "virtue grows beneath weight" and "unmoved, triumphant." Charles' earthly crown (on the floor at his side) is "splendid and heavy," while the crown of thorns he grasps is "bitter and light" and the heavenly crown is "blessed and eternal." Even people who could not read these and other Latin mottoes would have known that Charles' last words were: "I shall go from a corruptible to an incorruptible Crown, where no disturbance can be."

At the same time, broadsides showing the moment of execution (image B) circulated in various European countries with explanatory captions. This one was

A. King Charles I as a martyr.

one. Technically, the Rump Parliament continued as the legislative body; but Cromwell, with the army at his command, possessed the real power and soon became exasperated by the legislators' attempts to enrich themselves by confiscating their opponents' property. In 1653, he marched a detachment of troops into the Rump Parliament. The Commonwealth thus ceased to exist and was soon replaced by the "Protectorate," a thinly disguised autocracy established under a constitution drafted by officers of the army. Called the Instrument of Government, this text is the nearest approximation to a written constitution England has ever had. Extensive powers were given to Cromwell as Lord Protector for life, and his office was made hereditary. At first, a new Parliament exercised limited authority to make laws and levy taxes, but in 1655 Cromwell abruptly dismissed its members. Thereafter the government became a virtual dictatorship, with Cromwell wielding a sovereignty more absolute than any previous English monarch ever dreamed of claiming. Many intellectuals noted the similiarities between these events and those that had given rise to the Principate of Augustus after the death of Julius Caesar (Chapter 5).

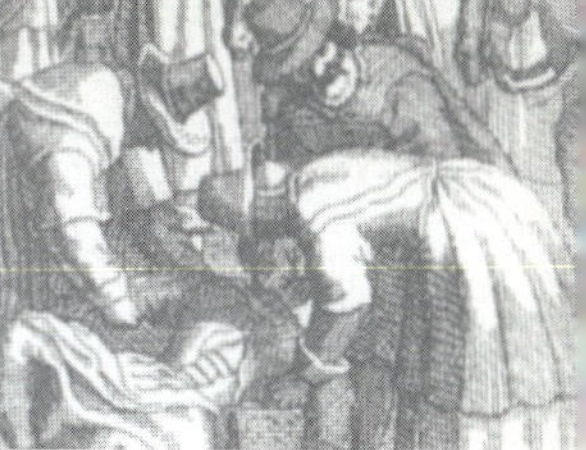

printed in Germany, and there are almost identical versions surviving from the Netherlands. It shows members of the crowd fainting and turning away at the sight of blood spurting from the king's neck, while the executioner holds up the severed head.

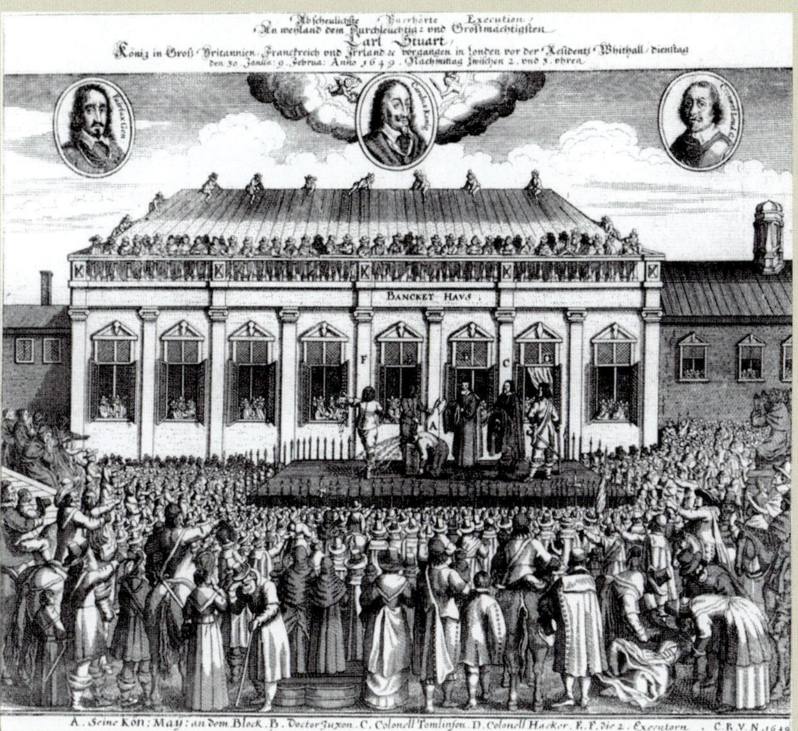

B. The execution of Charles I.

*Questions for Analysis*

1. How would you interpret the message of the first image? How might it have been read differently by Catholics and by Protestants, within Britain and in Europe?
2. What would have been the political motives underlying the publication and display of these images? For example, would you expect the depiction of the king's execution to be intended as supportive of monarchy, or as antiroyalist? Why?
3. Given what you have learned about political and religious divisions in Europe at the time of the king's execution, where do you think the first image would have found the most sympathetic audiences? Why might it be significant that the second circulated more in Germany and the Netherlands, rather than in France or Spain?

## The Restoration of the Monarchy

Given the choice between a Puritan military dictatorship and the old royalist regime, most of England opted for the latter. Years of unpopular Calvinist austerities—such as the prohibition of any public recreation on Sundays and the closing of London's theaters—had made most people long for the milder Church of England, and for monarchy. So not long after Cromwell's death in 1658, one of his generals seized power and called for the election of a new Parliament, which met in the spring of 1660. Almost overnight, England was a monarchy again and Charles I's exiled son, Charles II, was proclaimed its king and recalled from the court of his cousin, Louis XIV.

Charles II (r. 1660–85) restored bishops to the Church of England but he did not return to the provocative religious policies of his father. Quipping that he did not wish to "resume his travels," Charles agreed to respect Parliament and to observe the Petition of Right that had so enraged his father. He also accepted all the legislation passed by Parliament immediately before the outbreak of civil war

**OLIVER CROMWELL AS PROTECTOR OF THE COMMONWEALTH.** This coin, minted in 1658, shows the Lord Protector wreathed with laurel garlands like a classical hero or a Roman consul, but it also proclaims him to be "by the Grace of God Protector of the Commonwealth." ▪ ***What mixed messages does this coin convey?***

in 1642, including the requirement that Parliament be summoned at least once every three years. England thus emerged from its civil war as a limited monarchy, in which power was exercised by "the king in Parliament." It remains a constitutional monarchy to this day.

## THE PROBLEM OF DOUBT AND THE QUEST FOR CERTAINTY

Between 1540 and 1660, Europeans were forced to confront a world in which all that they had once taken for granted was suddenly cast into doubt. Vast new continents had been discovered in the Americas, populated by millions of people whose very existence compelled Europeans to rethink some of their most basic ideas about humanity and human nature. Equally disorienting, the religious uniformity of medieval Europe, although never absolute, had been shattered to an unprecedented extent by the Reformation and the religious wars that arose from it. In 1540, it was still possible to imagine that these religious divisions might be temporary. By 1660, it was clear they would be permanent. No longer, therefore, could Europeans regard revealed religious faith as an adequate foundation for universal philosophical conclusions, for even Christians now disagreed about the fundamental truths of the faith. Political allegiances were similarly under threat, as intellectuals and common people alike began to assert a right to resist princes with whom they disagreed on matters of religion. Even morality and custom were beginning to seem arbitrary and detached from the natural ordering of the world.

Europeans responded to this pervasive climate of doubt in a variety of ways, ranging from radical skepticism to authoritarian assertions of ecclesiastical control and political absolutism. What united their responses, however, was a sometimes desperate search for new foundations on which to construct some measure of certainty in the face of intellectual, religious, and political challenges.

### *Witchcraft and the Power of the State*

Adding to Europeans' fears was the conviction of many that witchcraft was a new and increasing threat to their world. Although the belief that certain individuals could heal or harm through the practice of magic had always been widespread, it was not until the late fifteenth century that authorities began to insist that such powers could derive only from some kind of satanic bargain. Once this belief became widely accepted, judicial officers became much more active in seeking out suspected witches for prosecution. In 1484, Pope Innocent VIII had ordered papal inquisitors to use all means at their disposal to detect and eliminate witchcraft, even condoning the torture of suspected witches. Predictably, torture increased the number of accused witches who "confessed" to their alleged crimes; and as more accused witches "confessed," more and more witches were "discovered," tried, and executed—even in realms like England and Scotland where torture was not legal and where the Inquisition of the Roman Catholic Church did not operate.

In considering the rash of witchcraft persecutions that swept early modern Europe, then, we need to keep two facts in mind. First of all, witchcraft trials were by no means limited to Catholic countries. Protestant reformers believed in the insidious powers of Satan just as much as Catholics did, if not more so. Both Luther and Calvin urged that accused witches be tried more peremptorily and sentenced with less leniency than ordinary criminals, a recommendation that their followers heeded. Second, it was only when religious authorities' efforts to detect witchcraft were backed by the coercive powers of secular governments that the fear of witches could translate into imprisonment and execution. It was therefore through this fundamental agreement between Catholics and Protestants, and with the complicity of secular states, that this witch craze could claim tens of thousands of victims, of whom the vast majority were women.

The final death toll will never be known, but in the 1620s there were, on average, 100 burnings a year in the German cities of Würzburg and Bamberg; around the same time, it was said that the town square of Wolfenbüttel "looked like a little forest, so crowded were the stakes." When accusations of witchcraft diminished in Europe, they became endemic in some European colonies, as at the English settlement of Salem, Massachusetts.

This witch mania reflects the fears that early modern Europeans held about the adequacy of traditional remedies (such as prayers, relics, and holy water) to combat the evils of their world, another consequence of religious dissent and uncertainty. It also reflects their growing conviction that only the state had the power to protect them. One of the most striking features of the mania for hunting down witches is the extent to which these prosecutions, in both Catholic and Protestant countries, were state-sponsored processes, carried out by secular authorities claiming to act as the protectors of society against the spiritual and temporal evils that assailed it. Even in Catholic countries, where witchcraft prosecutions were sometimes begun in Church courts, these cases would be transferred to the state's courts for final judgment and punishment, because Church courts were forbidden to impose capital penalties. In most Protestant countries, where ecclesiastical courts had been abolished (only England retained them), the entire process of detecting, prosecuting, and punishing suspected witches was carried out under the supervision of the state. In both Catholic and Protestant countries, the result of these witchcraft trials was thus a considerable increase in the scope of the state's powers to regulate the lives of its subjects.

**ALLEGED "WITCHES" WORSHIPING THE DEVIL IN THE FORM OF A GOAT.** This is one of the earliest visual conceptions, dating from around 1460, of witchcraft's reliance on satanic support. In the background, other witches ride bareback on flying demons.

## *The Search for a Source of Authority*

The crisis of Europe's "iron century"—the name given to the sixteenth century by some contemporary intellectuals—was fundamentally a crisis of authority, with far-reaching implications. Attempts to reestablish some foundation for a new authority therefore took many forms. For the French nobleman Michel de Montaigne (1533–1592), who wrote during the height of the French wars of religion, the result was a searching skepticism about the possibilities of any certain knowledge whatsoever. The son of a Catholic father and a Huguenot mother of Jewish ancestry, the well-to-do Montaigne retired from a legal career at the age of thirty-eight to devote himself to a life of reflection. The *Essays* that resulted were a new literary form originally conceived as "experiments" (the French *essai* means "attempt"). Because they are beautifully composed as well as searchingly reflective, Montaigne's *Essays* are among the most enduring classics of European literature and thought.

Although the range of subjects covered by the *Essays* is wide, two main themes are dominant. One is constant questioning. Making his motto *Que sais-je?* ("What do I know?"), Montaigne decided that he knew very little for certain. According to him, "it is folly to measure truth and error by our own capacities" because our capacities are severely limited. As he maintained in one of his most famous essays, "On Cannibals," what may seem indisputably true and moral to one nation may seem absolutely false to another because "everyone gives the title of barbarism to everything that is not of his usage." From this Montaigne's second main principle followed: the need for moderation. Because all people think they know the perfect religion and the perfect government, yet few agree on what that perfection might be, Montaigne concluded that no religion or government is really perfect, and consequently no belief is worth fighting or dying for. Instead, people should accept the teachings of religion on faith, and obey the governments

# Analyzing Primary Sources

## *Montaigne on Skepticism and Faith*

*The* Essays *of Michel de Montaigne (1533–1592) reflect the sincerity of his own attempts to grapple with the contradictions of his time, even if he could not resolve those contradictions. Here, he discusses the relationship between human knowledge and the teachings of religious authorities.*

Perhaps it is not without reason that we attribute facility in belief and conviction to simplicity and ignorance, for . . . the more a mind is empty and without counterpoise, the more easily it gives beneath the weight of the first persuasive argument. That is why children, common people, women, and sick people are most subject to being led by the ears. But then, on the other hand, it is foolish presumption to go around disdaining and condemning as false whatever does not seem likely to us; which is an ordinary vice in those who think they have more than common ability. I used to do so once. . . . But reason has taught me that to condemn a thing thus, dogmatically, as false and impossible, is to assume the advantage of knowing the bounds and limits of God's will and of the power of our mother Nature, and that there is no more notable folly in the world than to reduce these things to the measure of our capacity and competence. . . .

It is a dangerous and fateful presumption, besides the absurd temerity that it implies, to disdain what we do not comprehend. For after you have established, according to your fine understanding, the limits of truth and falsehood, and it turns out that you must necessarily believe things even stranger than those you deny, you are obliged from then on to abandon these limits. Now what seems to me to bring as much disorder into our consciences as anything, in these religious troubles that we are in, is this partial surrender of their beliefs by Catholics. It seems to them that they are being very moderate and understanding when they yield to their opponents some of the articles in dispute. But, besides the fact that they do not see what an advantage it is to a man charging you for you to begin to give ground and withdraw, and how much that encourages him to pursue his point, those articles which they select as the most trivial are sometimes very important. We must either submit completely to the authority of our ecclesiastical government, or do without it completely. It is not for us to decide what portion of obedience we owe it.

Source: *Montaigne: Selections from the Essays,* trans. and ed. Donald M. Frame (Arlington Heights, IL: 1971), pp. 34–38.

### *Questions for Analysis*

1. Why does Montaigne say that human understanding is limited? How do his assumptions compare to those of Richelieu (page 439)?
2. What does Montaigne mean by the "partial surrender" of belief? If a Catholic should place his faith in the Church, what then is the purpose of human intellect?

constituted to rule over them, without resorting to fanaticism in either sphere.

Although Montaigne's writings seem modern in many ways—that is, familiar—he was very much a man of his time, and also the product of a long philosophical tradition reaching back to antiquity (Chapters 3 and 4). At heart, he was a Stoic: in a world governed by unpredictable fortune, he believed that the best human strategy was to face the good and the bad with steadfastness and dignity. And indeed, the wide circulation of Montaigne's *Essays* actually helped to combat the fanaticism and religious intolerance of his own and subsequent ages.

Another attempt to resolve the problem of doubt was offered by the French philosopher Blaise Pascal (1623–1662). Pascal began his career as a mathematician and scientist. But at age thirty he abandoned science after a profound conversion experience. This led him to embrace an extreme form of puritanical Catholicism known as Jansenism (after its Flemish founder, Cornelius Jansen). From then until his death he worked on a highly ambitious philosophical-religious project meant to establish the truth of Christianity by appealing simultaneously to intellect and emotion.

After his premature death, the results of this effort were published as a series of "Thoughts" (*Pensées*). In this collection of intellectual fragments, Pascal argues that faith alone can resolve the contradictions of the world and that "the heart has its reasons of which reason itself knows nothing." Pascal's *Pensées* express the author's own terror, anguish, and awe in the face of evil and uncertainty, but present that awe as evidence for the existence of God. Pascal's hope was that, on this foundation, some measure of confidence in humanity and its capacity for self-knowledge could be rediscovered, thus avoiding both the dogmatism and the extreme skepticism that were so prominent in seventeenth-century society.

### *Theories of Absolute Government*

Montaigne's contemporary, the French lawyer Jean Bodin (1530–1596), took a more active approach to the problem of uncertain authority. He wanted to resolve the disorders of the day by reestablishing the powers of the state on new and more secure foundations. Like Montaigne, Bodin was particularly troubled by the upheavals caused by the religious wars in France; he had witnessed the St. Bartholomew's Day Massacre of 1572. But he was resolved to offer a practical, political solution to such turbulence. In his monumental *Six Books of the Commonwealth* (1576), he developed a theory of absolute state sovereignty. According to Bodin, the state arises from the needs of collections of families and, once constituted, should brook no opposition to its authority because maintaining order is its paramount duty. For Bodin, sovereignty was "the most high, absolute, and perpetual power over all subjects," which could make and enforce laws without the consent of those governed by the state—precisely what Charles I of England would have argued, and precisely what his Puritan subjects disputed. Although Bodin acknowledged the possibility of government by the aristocracy or even by a democracy, he assumed that the powerful nation-states of his day would have to be ruled by monarchs, and insisted that such monarchs should in no way be limited—whether by legislative and judicial bodies, or even by laws made by their own predecessors. Bodin maintained that every subject must trust in the ruler's "mere and frank good will." Even if the ruler proved a tyrant, Bodin insisted that the subject had no right to resist, for any resistance would open the door "to a licentious anarchy which is worse than the harshest tyranny in the world."

Like Bodin, Thomas Hobbes (1588–1679) was moved by the turmoil of the English Civil War to advance a new political theory in his treatise *Leviathan* (1651). Yet Hobbes's formulation differs from that of Bodin in several respects. Whereas Bodin assumed that absolute sovereign power should be vested in a monarch, Hobbes argued that any form of government capable of protecting its subjects' lives and property might act as sovereign and hence all-powerful. And whereas Bodin defined his state as "the lawful government of families" and hence did not believe that the state could abridge private property rights because families could not exist without property, Hobbes's state existed to rule over atomistic individuals and was thus licensed to trample over both liberty and property if the government's own survival was at stake.

But the most fundamental difference between Bodin and Hobbes lay in the latter's uncompromisingly pessimistic view of human nature. Hobbes posited that the "state of nature" that existed before government was "war of all against all." Because man naturally behaves as "a wolf" toward other men, human life without government is necessarily "solitary, poor, nasty, brutish, and short." To escape such consequences, people must therefore surrender their liberties to a sovereign ruler in exchange for his obligation to keep the peace. Having traded away their liberties, subjects have no right to win them back, and the sovereign may rule as he likes—free to oppress his subjects in any way other than to kill them, an act that would negate the very purpose of his rule, which is to preserve his people's lives.

## THE ART OF BEING HUMAN

Doubt and uncertainty were also primary themes in the profusion of literature and art produced in this era. Moved by the ambiguities and ironies of existence and the horrors of war and persecution, writers and artists sought to find redemptive qualities in human suffering and hardship.

### *The Adventures of Don Quixote*

A timeless example of this artistic response is the satirical novel *Don Quixote*, which its author, Miguel de Cervantes (1547–1616), composed largely in prison. It recounts the adventures of an idealistic Spanish gentleman, Don Quixote of La Mancha, who becomes deranged by his constant reading of chivalric romances. His mind filled with all kinds of fantastic adventures, he sets out at the age of fifty on the slippery road of knight-errantry, imagining windmills to be glowering giants and flocks of sheep to be armies of infidels. In his distorted world view he mistakes inns for castles and serving girls for courtly ladies. His sidekick, Sancho Panza, is his exact opposite: a plain, practical man with his feet on the ground, content with modest bodily pleasures. Yet Cervantes does not suggest that realism is categorically preferable to "quixotic" idealism. Rather, these two men represent different facets of human nature. On the one hand, *Don Quixote* is a devastating satire on the anachronistic chivalric mentality that was already hastening Spain's decline. On the other, it is a sincere celebration of the human capacity for optimism and goodness.

## English Playwrights and Poets

In the late sixteenth century, the emergence of public playhouses made drama an especially effective mass medium for the expression of opinions, the dissemination of ideas, and the articulation of national identies. This was especially so in England during the last two decades of Elizabeth's reign and that of her successor, James. Among the large number of playwrights at work in London during this era, the most noteworthy are Christopher Marlowe (1564–1593), Ben Jonson (c. 1572–1637), and William Shakespeare (1564–1616). Marlowe, who may have been a spy for Elizabeth's government and who was mysteriously murdered in a tavern brawl before he reached the age of thirty, was extremely popular in his own day. In plays such as *Tamburlaine*—about the life of the Mongolian emperor Timur the Lame (Chapter 11)—and *Doctor Faustus*, Marlowe created vibrant heroes who pursue larger-than-life ambitions only to be felled by their own human limitations. In contrast to the heroic tragedies of Marlowe, Ben Jonson wrote dark comedies that expose human vices and foibles. In the particularly bleak *Volpone*, Jonson shows people behaving like deceitful and lustful animals. In the later *Alchemist*, he balances an attack on pseudo-scientific quackery with admiration for resourceful lower-class characters who cleverly take advantage of their supposed betters.

William Shakespeare was born into the family of a tradesman in the provincial town of Stratford-upon-Avon, where he attained a modest education before moving to London around the age of twenty. There he found employment in the theater as an actor and playwright, a "maker of plays." He eventually earned a reputation as a poet, too, but it was his success at the box office that enabled him to retire, rich, to his native Stratford about twenty-five years later. Shakespeare composed or collaborated in the writing of an unknown number of plays, of which some forty survive in whole or in part. They have since become a kind of secular English Bible, and owe their longevity to the author's unrivaled gifts of verbal expression, humor, and psychological insight.

Shakespeare's dramas fall thematically into three groups. Those written during the playwright's early years reflect the political, religious, and social upheavals of the late sixteenth century. As we have already seen, these include many history plays which recount episodes from England's medieval past and the struggles that established the Tudor dynasty of Elizabeth's grandfather, Henry VII. They also include the lyrical tragedy *Romeo and Juliet* and a number of comedies, including *A Midsummer Night's Dream*, *Twelfth Night*, *As You Like It*, and *Much Ado about Nothing*. Most explore fundamental problems of identity, honor and ambition, love and friendship.

The plays from Shakespeare's second period are, like other contemporary artworks, characterized by a troubled searching into the mysteries and meaning of human existence. They showcase the perils of indecisive idealism (*Hamlet*) and the abuse of power (*Measure for Measure*), culminating in the searing tragedies of *Macbeth* and *King Lear*. Those plays composed at the end of his career emphasize the possibilities of reconciliation and peace, even after

***DAVID* BY BERNINI (1598–1680).** Whereas the earlier conceptions of David by the Renaissance sculptors Donatello and Michelangelo were serene and dignified (see page 389), the Baroque sculptor Bernini chose to portray his young hero at the peak of physical exertion. ▪ ***Can you discern the influence of Hellenistic sculpture (Chapter 4, pages 135–136) in this work?*** ▪ ***What are some shared characteristics?***

***VIEW OF TOLEDO* BY EL GRECO.** This is one of many landscape portraits representing the hilltop city that became the artist's home in later life. Its supple "Mannerist" style almost defies historical periodization.

years of misunderstanding and sorrow: *A Winter's Tale*, *Cymbeline*, and finally *The Tempest*, an extended reflection on the paradoxical relationship between the weakness of human nature and the power of the human artist.

Though less versatile than Shakespeare, the Puritan poet John Milton (1608–1674) is considered to be his equal in the grandeur of his artistic vision. The leading publicist of Oliver Cromwell's regime, Milton wrote the official defense of the beheading of Charles I as well as a number of treatises justifying Puritan ideologies. But he loved the Greek and Latin classics at least as much as the Bible. He wrote a pastoral elegy, *Lycidas*, mourning (in classical terms) the loss of a dear friend. And later, when forced into retirement by the accession of Charles II, Milton (now blind) embarked on a classical epic based on Genesis, *Paradise Lost*. Setting out to "justify the ways of God to man," Milton first plays "devil's advocate" by creating the compelling character of Satan, who defies God with boldness and subtlety. Indeed, the eloquence of Satan is never quite counterbalanced by the supposed hero, Adam, who learns to accept the human lot of moral responsibility and suffering.

## The Artistry of Southern Europe

The ironies and tensions inherent in human existence were also explored in the visual arts. In Italy and Spain, many painters of the sixteenth century cultivated a highly dramatic and emotionally compelling style sometimes known as "Mannerism." The most unusual of these artists was El Greco ("the Greek," c. 1541–1614), a pupil of the Venetian master Tintoretto (1518–1594). Born Domenikos Theotokopoulos on the Greek island of Crete, El Greco absorbed some of the stylized elongation characteristic of Byzantine icon painting (Chapter 7) before traveling to Italy. He eventually settled in Spain. Many of his paintings were too strange to be greatly appreciated in his own day and even now appear so *avant garde* as to be almost surreal. His *View of Toledo*, for example, is a transfigured landscape, mysteriously lit from within. Equally amazing are his swirling Biblical scenes and the stunning portraits of gaunt, dignified saints who radiate austerity and spiritual insight.

The dominant artistic style of southern Europe in the seventeenth century was that of the Baroque, a school whose name has become a synonym for elaborate, highly wrought sculpture and architecural details. The Baroque style originated in Rome during the Counter-Reformation and promoted a glorified Catholic worldview. Its most imaginative and influential figure was the architect and sculptor Gianlorenzo Bernini (1598–1680), a frequent employee of the papacy who created a magnificent celebration of papal grandeur in the sweeping colonnades leading up to St. Peter's Basilica. Breaking with the serene Renaissance classicism of Palladio (Chapter 13), Bernini's architecture retained such classical elements as columns and domes

***THE MAIDS OF HONOR (LAS MERINAS)* BY DIEGO VELÁZQUEZ.** The artist himself (at left) is shown working at his easel and gazing out at the viewer—or at the subjects of his double portrait, the Spanish king and queen, depicted in a distant mirror. But the real focus of the painting is the delicate, impish princess in the center, flanked by two young ladies-in-waiting, a dwarf, and another royal child. Courtiers in the background look on.

but combined them in ways meant to express aggressive restlessness and power. Bernini was also one of the first to experiment with church facades built "in depth"—that is, with frontages not conceived as continuous surfaces but instead jutting out at odd angles and thus seeming to invade the open space in front of them. The purpose of these innovations was to pull the viewer into the work of art. This was also the aim of Bernini's sculpture, which drew inspiration from the restless motion and artistic bravado of Hellenistic statuary (Chapter 4).

Although the Baroque movement began in Rome and was originally expressed in three dimensions, characteristics of this style can also be found in painting. Many consider its greatest master to be the Spanish painter Diego Velázquez (1599–1660). Unlike Bernini, however, Velázquez was a court painter in Madrid, not a servant of the Church. And although many of his canvases display a Baroque attention to motion and drama, his most characteristic work is more restrained and conceptually thoughtful. An example is *The Maids of Honor*, completed around 1656 and a masterpiece of self-referentiality. It shows the artist himself at work on a double portrait of the Spanish king and queen, but the scene is dominated by the children and servants of the royal family.

## Dutch Painting in the Golden Age

Southern Europe's main rival for artistic laurels was the Netherlands, where three exemplary but dissimilar painters explored the theme of the greatness and wretchedness of man to the fullest. Peter Bruegel the Elder (*BROY-ghul*, c. 1525–1569) exulted in portraying the busy, elemental life of the peasantry. Most famous in this respect are his rollicking *Peasant Wedding* and *Peasant Wedding Dance* and his spacious *Harvesters*, in which guzzling and snoring field hands are taking a well-deserved break from their heavy labors under the noon sun. Such vistas celebrate the uninterrupted rhythms of life; but late in his career Bruegel became appalled by the intolerance and bloodshed he witnessed during the Calvinist riots and the Spanish repression of the Netherlands, expressing his criticism in an understated yet searing manner. From a distance, *The Massacre of the Innocents* looks like a snug scene of Flemish village life. In fact, however, soldiers are methodically breaking into homes and slaughtering helpless infants, just as Herod's soldiers once did. The artist—alluding to a Gospel message unheeded by warring Catholics and Protestants alike—seems to be saying "as it happened in the time of Christ, so it happens now."

**SELF-PORTRAITS.** Self-portraits became common during the sixteenth and seventeenth centuries, reflecting the intense introspection of the period. Left: Rembrandt painted more than sixty self-portraits; this one, dating from around 1660, captures the artist's creativity, theatricality (note the costume), and honesty of self-examination. Right: Judith Leyster (1609–1660) was a contemporary of Rembrandt who pursued a successful career during her early twenties, before she married. Respected in her own day, she was all but forgotten for centuries thereafter but is once against the object of much attention.

***THE MASSACRE OF THE INNOCENTS* BY BRUEGEL (c. 1525–1569).** This painting shows how effectively art can be used as a means of political and social commentary. Here, Bruegel depicts the suffering of the Netherlands at the hands of the Spanish in his own day, with reference to the Biblical story of Herod's slaughter of Jewish children after the birth of Jesus—thereby collapsing these two historical incidents.

***THE HORRORS OF WAR* BY RUBENS (1577–1640).** In his old age, Rubens took a far more critical view of war than he had done for most of his earlier career. Here, the war-god Mars casts aside his mistress Venus, goddess of love, and threatens humanity with death and destruction.

Vastly different from Bruegel was the Netherlandish painter Peter Paul Rubens (1577–1640). Since the Baroque was an international movement closely linked to the spread of the Counter-Reformation, it should offer no surprise that Baroque style was extremely well represented in just that part of the Netherlands which, after long warfare, had been retained by Spain and reintroduced to the Catholic faith. Indeed, Rubens of Antwerp was a far more typical Baroque artist than Velázquez of Madrid, painting literally thousands of robust canvases that glorified resurgent Catholicism or exalted second-rate aristocrats by portraying them as epic heroes dressed in bearskins. Even when Rubens's intent was not overtly propagandistic, he customarily reveled in the sumptuous extravagance of the Baroque style; he is most famous today for the pink and rounded flesh of his well-nourished nudes. But unlike a host of lesser Baroque artists, Rubens was not lacking in subtlety or depth. Although he celebrated martial valor for most of his career, his late *The Horrors of War* movingly portrays what he himself called "the grief of unfortunate Europe, which, for so many years now, has suffered plunder, outrage, and misery."

In some ways a blend of Bruegel and Rubens, Rembrandt van Rijn (*vahn-REEN*, 1606–1669) defies all attempts at easy characterization. Living across the border from the Spanish Netherlands in the staunchly Calvinistic Dutch Republic, Rembrandt belonged to a society that was too austere to tolerate the unbuckled realism of Brueghel or the fleshy pomposity of Rubens. Yet Rembrandt managed to put both realistic and Baroque traits to new uses. In his early career he gained fame and fortune as a painter of biblical scenes and was also active as a portrait painter who knew how to flatter his subjects—to the great advantage of his purse. But gradually his prosperity waned, and as personal tragedies mounted in his middle and declining years, the painter's art gained in dignity, subtlety, and mystery. His later portraits, including several self-portraits, are highly introspective and suggest that only part of the story is being told. Equally compelling are explicitly philosophical paintings such as *Aristotle Contemplating the Bust of Homer*,

# After You Read This Chapter

Visit StudySpace for quizzes, additional review materials, and multi-media documents. **wwnorton.com/studyspace**

## REVIEWING THE OBJECTIVES

- Religious and political conflicts have always been intertwined, but the combination was especially deadly in the era between 1540 and 1660. Why was this?
- Although the religious warfare of this period seems almost continuous, it took distinctive forms in France, the Netherlands, and Germany. Explain why.
- What factors led to the decline of Spain as Europe's dominant power, and to the rise of France?
- The main causes of the English Civil War can be traced back to the reign of Elizabeth I and her successor, James Stuart of Scotland. What were the main sources of disagreement between the Stuart monarchy and Parliament?
- Intellectuals and artists responded to the challenges of this era in creative ways. Identify some of the major figures and ideas that emerged from this period of crisis.

in which the philosopher seems spellbound by the radiance of the epic poet, and *The Polish Rider*, in which realistic and symbolic elements merge to portray a pensive young man setting out fearlessly into a perilous world. Equally fearless is the frank gaze of Rembrandt's slightly younger contemporary, Judith Leyster (1609–1660), who looks out of her own self-portrait with a refreshingly optimistic and good-humored expression.

## CONCLUSION

Between 1540 and 1660, Europe was racked by a combination of religious war, political rebellion, and economic crisis that undermined confidence in traditional structures of social, religious, and political authority. The result was fear, skepticism, and a search for new foundations on which to rebuild Europe. For artists and intellectuals, the period proved to be one of the most creative epochs in the history of Western civilizations. But for common people, the century was one of extraordinary suffering.

By 1660, after a hundred years of destructive efforts to restore the religious unity of Europe through war, a de facto religious toleration among states was beginning to emerge as the only way to preserve political order. But within states, toleration was still very limited. In territories where religious rivalries ran too deep to be overcome, therefore, rulers began to discover that loyalty to the state could override even religious divisions among their subjects. The end result of this century of crises was thus to strengthen Europeans' reliance on in the state's capacity to heal their wounds and right their wrongs, with religion relegated more and more to the private sphere of individual conscience. In the following centuries, this new confidence in the state as an autonomous moral agent acting in accordance with its own "reasons of state" and for its own purposes, would prove a powerful challenge to the traditions of limited consensual government that had emerged from the Middle Ages.

### PEOPLE, IDEAS, AND EVENTS IN CONTEXT

- What were the main sources of instability in Europe during the sixteenth century? How did the **PRICE REVOLUTION** exacerbate these?
- How did the **EDICT OF NANTES** challenge the doctrine ***CUIUS REGIO, EIUS RELIGIO*** ("as the ruler, so the religion") established by the **PEACE OF AUGSBURG**?
- What were the initial causes of the **THIRTY YEARS' WAR**? Why did Sweden and France become involved in it?
- Describe the political configuration of Europe after the **PEACE OF WESTPHALIA**. Why did Spain's power decline while France emerged as dominant? How did the policies of **CARDINAL RICHELIEU** strengthen the power of the French monarchy?
- What factors led to the **ENGLISH CIVIL WAR** and the execution of **CHARLES I**?
- In what ways did the **WITCH CRAZE** of early modern Europe reveal the religious and social tensions of the sixteenth and seventeenth centuries?
- How did **MONTAIGNE** and **PASCAL** respond to the problem of authority? What were the differences between **JEAN BODIN**'s theory of absolute sovereignty and that of **THOMAS HOBBES**?

### CONSEQUENCES

- The period between 1540 and 1660 is considered to be one of the most turbulent in Europe's history, but it also has deep roots in the more distant past of Western civilizations. How far back would you trace the origins of this "perfect storm"?
- The execution of King Charles I of England was a watershed event, and yet the English monarchy itself survived this crisis. How would you account for this remarkable fact? In what ways did the concept of English kingship have to change in order for this to happen?
- In your view, do the various artistic movements of this era seem especially modern? Or are they better understood as comparable to the movements responding to the Black Death (Chapter 10) or to the artistic innovations characteristic of the Renaissance (Chapter 12)? What elements make a work of art seem "modern"?

# Before You Read This Chapter

## STORY LINES

- After the devastation caused by the crisis of the seventeenth century, European rulers sought stability in the centralization of government authority and by increasing their own power at the expense of other groups and institutions in society, such as the nobility and the church.
- Population growth, increased agricultural productivity, and innovations in business practices created new wealth and new incentives for economic development and colonial expansion to other continents. All of these processes favored European powers with access to Atlantic trade, especially France and Britain, who opened up profitable trading networks to the Americas and the Caribbean.
- Within Europe, only a few European powers continued to pursue expansionist foreign policies. Others sought stability through treaties that aimed at an international balance of powers.

## CHRONOLOGY

| | |
|---|---|
| 1600s | British and French establish colonies in North America and the Caribbean and outposts in Africa and India |
| 1500s–1800s | Europeans engage in African slave trade from Africa to the Caribbean, Brazil, and North America |
| 1643–1715 | Louis XIV of France |
| 1685 | Revocation of the Edict of Nantes |
| 1688 | Glorious Revolution in England |
| 1689–1725 | Peter the Great of Russia's reign |
| 1702–1713 | War of the Spanish Succession |
| 1713 | Treaty of Utrecht |
| 1740–1780 | Maria Theresa of Austria's reign |
| 1740–1786 | Frederick the Great of Prussia's reign |
| 1756–1763 | The Seven Years' War |
| 1762–1796 | Catherine the Great of Russia's reign |
| 1772-1795 | Partition of Poland |
| 1775–1783 | United States Independence |

# Absolutism and Empire, 1660–1789

## CORE OBJECTIVES

- **DEFINE** *absolutism* and understand its central principles as a theory of government.
- **IDENTIFY** the absolutist monarchs who were most successful in imposing their rule in Europe between 1600 and 1800.
- **EXPLAIN** the alternatives to absolutism that emerged, most notably in England.
- **DESCRIBE** the eighteenth-century commercial revolution in Europe.
- **UNDERSTAND** the new economic and cultural linkages between Europe and the Atlantic world that emerged as a result of colonial expansion and the slave trade in the seventeenth and eighteenth centuries.

In the mountainous region of south-central France known as the Auvergne in the 1660s, the marquis of Canillac had a notorious reputation. His noble title gave him the right to collect minor taxes on special occasions, but he insisted that these small privileges be converted into annual tributes. To collect these payments, he housed twelve accomplices in his castle that he called his apostles. Their other nicknames—one was known as Break Everything—gave a more accurate sense of their activities in the local villages. The marquis imprisoned those who resisted and forced their families to buy their freedom. In an earlier age, the marquis might have gotten away with this profitable arrangement. In 1662, however, he ran up against the authority of a king, Louis XIV, who was determined to demonstrate that the power of the central monarch was absolute. The marquis was brought up on charges before a special court of judges from Paris. He was found guilty and forced to pay a large fine. The king confiscated his property and had the marquis's castle destroyed.

Louis XIV's special court in the Auvergne heard nearly a thousand civil cases over four months in 1662. It convicted 692 people, and many of them, like the marquis of Canillac, were noble. The verdicts were an extraordinary example of Louis XIV's ability to project his authority into the remote corners of his realm and to do so in a way that diminished the power of other elites. During his long reign (1643–1715), Louis XIV systematically pursued such a policy on many fronts, asserting his power over the nobility, the clergy, and the provincial courts. Increasingly, these elites were forced to look to the crown to guarantee their interests, and their own power became more closely connected with the sacred aura of the monarchy itself. Louis XIV's model of kingship was so successful that it became known as absolute monarchy. In recognition of the success and influence of Louis XIV's political system, the period from around 1660 (when the English monarchy was restored and Louis XIV began his personal rule in France) to 1789 (when the French Revolution erupted) is traditionally known as the age of absolutism. This is a crucial period in the development of the modern, centralized, bureaucratic state.

*Absolutism* was a political theory that encouraged rulers to claim complete sovereignty within their territories. An absolute monarch could make law, dispense justice, create and direct a bureaucracy, declare war, and levy taxation, without the approval of any other governing body. Assertions of absolute authority were buttressed by claims that rulers governed by divine right, just as fathers ruled over their households. After the chaos of the previous century, many Europeans came to believe that it was only by exalting the sovereignty of absolute rulers that order could be restored to European life.

European monarchs also successfully projected their power abroad during this period. By 1660, the French, Spanish, Portuguese, English, and Dutch had all established important colonies in the Americas and in Asia. These colonies created important trading networks that brought profitable new consumer goods such as sugar, tobacco, and coffee to a wide public in Europe, while also encouraging the spread of slavery to produce these goods. Rivalry among colonial powers to control the trade in slaves and consumer goods was intense. In the eighteenth century, Europe's wars were driven by colonial considerations and imperial conflicts, as global commerce assumed a growing role in the European economy.

Absolutism was not the only political theory used by European governments during this period. England, Scotland, the Dutch Republic, Switzerland, Venice, Sweden, and Poland-Lithuania were all either limited monarchies, or republics. In Russia, an extreme autocracy emerged that gave the tsar a degree of control over his subjects' lives and property far beyond anything imagined by western European absolutists. Even in Russia, however, absolutism was never unlimited in practice. Even the most absolute monarchs could rule effectively only with the consent of their subjects (particularly the nobility). When serious opposition erupted, even absolutists were forced to back down. In 1789, when an outright political revolution occurred, the entire structure of absolutism came crashing to the ground.

## THE APPEAL AND JUSTIFICATION OF ABSOLUTISM

Absolutism's promise of stability, prosperity, and order was an appealing alternative to the disorder of the "iron century" that preceded it. Louis XIV was profoundly disturbed by an aristocratic revolt that occurred while he was still a child. When marauding Parisians entered his bedchamber one night in 1651, Louis saw the intrusion as a horrid affront not only to his own person but to the majesty of the French state he personified. Such experiences convinced him that he must rule assertively and without limitation if France was to survive as a great European state.

Absolutist monarchs sought control of the state's armed forces and its legal system and demanded the right to collect and spend the state's financial resources at will. To achieve these goals, they also needed to create an efficient, centralized bureaucracy that owed its allegiance directly to the monarch. Creating and sustaining such a bureaucracy was expensive but essential to the larger absolutist goal of weakening the special interests that hindered the free exercise of royal power. The nobility and the clergy, with their traditional legal privileges; the political authority of semi-autonomous regions; and representative assemblies such as parliaments, diets, or estates general were all obstacles—in the eyes of absolutists—to strong, centralized monarchical government. The history of abolutism is a history of attempts by aspiring absolutists to bring such institutions to heel.

In most Protestant countries, the power of the church had already been subordinated to the the state when the age of absolutism began. In France, Spain, and Austria, however, where Roman Catholicism remained the state religion, absolutist monarchs now devoted considerable attention to bringing the church and its clergy under royal control. These efforts built on agreements that the French and Spanish monarchies extracted from the papacy during the fifteenth and sixteenth centuries, but they went much further in consolidating the king's authority over the church. In Austria, Joseph II (1741–1790) closed hundreds of monasteries, drastically limited the number of monks and nuns permitted to live in contemplative orders, and ordered that the education of priests be placed under government supervision. Even Charles III, the devout Spanish king who ruled from 1759 to 1788, pressed successfully for a papal concordat granting him control over ecclesiastical appointments and the right to nullify any papal bull affecting Spain.

The most important potential opponents of royal absolutism were not churchmen, however, but nobles. Monarchs dealt with this threat in various ways. Louis XIV deprived the French nobility of political power in the provinces but increased their social prestige by making them live at his lavish court at Versailles. Peter the Great of Russia (1689–1725) forced his nobles into lifelong government service. Later in the century, Catherine II of Russia (1762–1796) struck a bargain whereby in return for vast estates and a variety of privileges (including exemption from taxation) the Russian nobility virtually surrendered the administrative and political power of the state into the empress's hands. In Prussia, the army was staffed by nobles, as was generally the case in Spain, France, and England. But in eighteenth-century Austria, the emperor Joseph II (1765–1790) denied the nobility exemption from taxation and blurred the distinctions between nobles and commoners.

Struggles between monarchs and nobles frequently affected relations between local and central government. In France, the requirement that nobles live at the king's court undermined the provincial institutions that the nobility used to exercise their power. In Spain, the monarchy, based in Castile, battled the independent-minded nobles of Aragon and Catalunya. Prussian rulers asserted control over formerly "free" cities by claiming the right to police and tax their inhabitants. The Habsburg emperors tried, unsuccessfully, to suppress the largely autonomous nobility of Hungary. Rarely, however, was the path of confrontation between crown and nobility successful in the long run. The most effective absolutist monarchies of the eighteenth century continued to trade privileges for allegiance, so that nobles came to see their own interests as tied to those of the crown. For this reason, cooperation more often characterized the relations between kings and nobles during the eighteenth-century "old regime" (*ancien régime*) than did conflict.

## THE ABSOLUTISM OF LOUIS XIV

In Louis XIV's state portrait, it is almost impossible to discern the human being behind the facade of the absolute monarch, dressed in his coronation robes and surrounded by the symbols of his authority. That facade was artfully constructed by Louis, who recognized, more fully than any other early modern ruler, the importance of theater to effective kingship. Louis and his successors deliberately staged theatrical demonstrations of their sovereignty to enhance their position as rulers endowed with godlike powers.

### *Performing Royalty at Versailles*

Louis's most elaborate exhibitions of his sovereignty took place at his palace at Versailles (*vuhr-SY*), the town outside of Paris to which he moved his court. The palace and its grounds became a stage for Louis's performance of his daily rituals and demonstrations of royal power. The main facade of the palace was a third of a mile in length. Inside, tapestries and paintings celebrated French military victories and royal triumphs; mirrors reflected shimmering light throughout the building. In the vast gardens outside, statues of the Greek god Apollo, god of the sun, recalled Louis's claim to be the "Sun King" of France. Noblemen vied to attend him when he arose from bed, ate his meals (usually stone cold after having traveled the distance of several city blocks from kitchen to table), strolled in his gardens (even the way the king walked was choreographed by the royal dancing master), or rode to the hunt. As the home of the Sun King, Louis's court was the epicenter of his gleaming royal resplendence. France's leading nobles were required to reside with him at Versailles for a portion of the year; the splendor of Louis's court was deliberately calculated to blind them to the possibility of disobedience while raising their prestige by associating them with himself. Instead of plotting some minor treason on his estate, a marquis could instead enjoy the pleasure of knowing that on the morrow he would be privileged to engage the king in two or three minutes of conversation as the royal party made its way through the vast palace halls. At the same time, the almost impossibly detailed rules of etiquette at court left these privileged nobles in constant suspense, forever fearful of offending the king by committing some trivial violation of proper manners.

Of course, the nobility did not surrender their social and political power entirely under the absolutist system. The social order defended by the monarchy was still a hierarchical one, and the nobility retained enormous privileges and rights over local peasants within their jurisdiction. The absolutist system may have forced the nobility to depend on the crown to defend their privileges, but it did not seek to undermine their superior place in society. In this sense, the relationship between Louis XIV and the nobility was more of a negotiated settlement than a complete victory of

# Competing Viewpoints

## *Absolutism And Patriarchy*

*These selections show how two political theorists justified royal absolutism by deriving it from the absolute authority of a father over his household. Bishop Jacques-Benigne Bossuet (1627–1704) was a famous French preacher who served as tutor to the son of King Louis XIV of France before becoming bishop of Meaux. Sir Robert Filmer (1588–1653) was an English political theorist. Filmer's works attracted particular attention in the 1680s, when John Locke directed the first of his Two Treatises of Government to refuting Filmer's views on the patriarchal nature of royal authority.*

### Bossuet on the Nature of Monarchical Authority

There are four characteristics or qualities essential to royal authority. First, royal authority is sacred; Secondly, it is paternal; Thirdly, it is absolute; Fourthly, it is subject to reason. . . . All power comes from God. . . . Thus princes act as ministers of God, and his lieutenants on earth. It is through them that he exercises his empire. . . . In this way . . . the royal throne is not the throne of a man, but the throne of God himself. . . .

We have seen that kings hold the place of God, who is the true Father of the human race. We have also seen that the first idea of power that there was among men, is that of paternal power; and that kings were fashioned on the model of fathers. Moreover, all the world agrees that obedience, which is due to public power, is only found . . . in the precept which obliges one to honor his parents. From all this it appears that the name "king" is a father's name, and that goodness is the most natural quality in kings. . . .

Royal authority is absolute. In order to make this term odious and insupportable, many pretend to confuse absolute government and arbitrary government. But nothing is more distinct, as we shall make clear when we speak of justice. . . . The prince need account to no one for what he ordains. . . . Without this absolute authority, he can neither do good nor suppress evil: his power must be such that no one can hope to escape him. . . . [T]he sole defense of individuals against the public power must be their innocence. . . .

One must, then, obey princes as if they were justice itself, without which there is neither order nor justice in affairs. They are gods, and share in some way in divine independence. . . . It follows from this that he who does not want to obey the prince . . . is condemned irremissibly to death as an enemy of public peace and of human society. . . . The prince can correct himself when he knows that he has done badly; but against his authority there can be no remedy. . . .

Source: Jacques-Benigne Bossuet, *Politics Drawn from the Very Words of Holy Scripture*, trans. Patrick Riley (Cambridge: 1990), pp. 46–69 and 81–83.

the king over other powerful elites. Louis XIV understood this, and in a memoir that he prepared for his son on the art of ruling he wrote, "The deference and the respect that we receive from our subjects are not a free gift from them but payment for the justice and the protection that they expect from us. Just as they must honor us, we must protect and defend them." In their own way, absolutists depended on the consent of those they ruled.

## *Administration and Centralization*

Louis defined his responsibilities in absolutist terms: to concentrate royal power so as to produce domestic tranquillity. While coopting the nobility into his own theater of royalty, he also recruited the upper bourgeoisie as royal administrators and especially as intendants, responsible for

## Filmer on the Patriarchal Origins of Royal Authority

The first government in the world was monarchical, in the father of all flesh, Adam being commanded to multiply, and people the earth, and to subdue it, and having dominion given him over all creatures, was thereby the monarch of the whole world; none of his posterity had any right to possess anything, but by his grant or permission, or by succession from him. . . . Adam was the father, king and lord over his family: a son, a subject, and a servant or a slave were one and the same thing at first. . . .

I cannot find any one place or text in the Bible where any power . . . is given to a people either to govern themselves, or to choose themselves governors, or to alter the manner of government at their pleasure. The power of government is settled and fixed by the commandment of "honour thy father"; if there were a higher power than the fatherly, then this commandment could not stand and be observed. . . .

All power on earth is either derived or usurped from the fatherly power, there being no other original to be found of any power whatsoever. For if there should be granted two sorts of power without any subordination of one to the other, they would be in perpetual strife which should be the supreme, for two supremes cannot agree. If the fatherly power be supreme, then the power of the people must be subordinate and depend on it. If the power of the people be supreme, then the fatherly power must submit to it, and cannot be exercised without the licence of the people, which must quite destroy the frame and course of nature. Even the power which God himself exercises over mankind is by right of fatherhood: he is both the king and father of us all. As God has exalted the dignity of earthly kings . . . by saying they are gods, so . . . he has been pleased . . . [t]o humble himself by assuming the title of a king to express his power, and not the title of any popular government.

Source: Robert Filmer, "Observations upon Aristotle's Politiques" (1652), in *Divine Right and Democracy: An Anthology of Political Writing in Stuart England,* ed. David Wootton (Harmondsworth: 1986), pp. 110–118.

### *Questions for Analysis*

1. Bossuet's definition of *absolutism* connected the sacred power of kings with the paternal authority of fathers within the household. What consequences does he draw from defining the relationship between king and subjects in this way?
2. What does Filmer mean when he says, "All power on earth is either derived or usurped from the fatherly power"? How many examples does he give of paternal or monarchical power?
3. Bossuet and Filmer make obedience the basis for order and justice in the world. What alternative political systems did they most fear?

administering the thirty-six *generalités* into which France was divided. Intendants usually served outside the region where they were born and were thus unconnected with the local elites over whom they exercised authority. They held office at the king's pleasure and were clearly his men. Other administrators, often from families newly ennobled as a reward for their service, assisted in directing affairs of state from Versailles. These men were not actors in the theater of Louis the Sun King; rather, they were the hardworking assistants of Louis the royal custodian of his country's welfare.

Louis's administrators devoted much of their time and energy to collecting the taxes necessary to finance the large standing army on which his aggressive foreign policy depended. Absolutism was fundamentally an approach to government by which ambitious monarchs could increase their own power through conquest and display. As such, it

# Interpreting Visual Evidence

## *The Performance and Display of Absolute Power at the Court of Louis XIV*

istorians studying the history of absolutism and the court of Louis XIV in particular have emphasized the Sun King's brilliant use of symbols and display to demonstrate his personal embodiment of sovereignty. Royal portraits, such as that painted by Hyacinthe Rigaud in 1701, vividly illustrate the degree to which Louis's power was based on a studied performance. His pose, with his exposed and shapely calf, was an important indication of power and virility, necessary elements of legitimacy for a hereditary monarch. In the elaborate rituals of court life at Versailles, Louis often placed his own body at the center of attention, performing in one instance as the god Apollo in a ballet before his assembled courtiers. His movements through the countryside, accompanied by a retinue of soldiers, servants, and aristocrats, were another occasion for highly stylized ritual demonstrations of his quasi-divine status. Finally, of course, the construction of his palace at Versailles, with its symmetrical architecture and its sculpted gardens, was a demonstration that his power extended over the natural world as easily as it did over the lives of his subjects.

### *Questions for Analysis*

1. Who was the intended audience for the king's performance of absolute sovereignty?
2. Who were Louis's primary competitors in this contest for eminence through the performance of power?
3. What possible political dangers might lay in wait for a regime that invested so heavily in the sumptuous display of semi-divine authority?

A. Hyacinthe Rigaud's 1701 portrait of Louis XIV.

B. Louis XIV as the Sun King.

C. *The Royal Procession of Louis XIV* by Adam Franz van der Meulen.

D. Louis XIV arrives at the Palace of Versailles.

was enormously expensive. In addition to the *taille*, or land tax, which increased throughout the seventeenth century, Louis's government introduced a *capitation* (a head tax) and pressed successfully for the collection of indirect taxes on salt (the *gabelle*), wine, tobacco, and other goods. Because the nobility was exempt from the *taille*, its burden fell most heavily on the peasantry, whose local revolts Louis easily crushed.

Regional opposition was curtailed, but not eliminated, during Louis's reign. By removing the provincial nobility to Versailles, Louis cut them off from their local sources of power and influence. To restrict the powers of regional parlements, Louis decreed that members of any parlement that refused to approve and enforce his laws would be summarily exiled. The Estates-General, the national French representative assembly last summoned in 1614, did not meet at all during Louis's reign. It would not meet again until 1789.

## Louis XIV's Religious Policies

Both for reasons of state and of personal conscience, Louis was determined to impose religious unity on France, regardless of the economic and social costs.

Although the vast majority of the French population was Roman Catholic, French Catholics were divided between Quietists, Jansenists, Jesuits, and Gallicans. Quietists preached retreat into personal mysticism, emphasizing a direct relationship between God and the individual human heart. Such doctrine, dispensing as it did with the intermediary services of the church, was suspect in the eyes of absolutists wedded to the doctrine of *un roi, une loi, une foi* ("one king, one law, one faith"). Jansenism—a movement named for its founder Cornelius Jansen, a seventeenth-century bishop of Ypres—held to an Augustinian doctrine of predestination that could sound and look surprisingly like a kind of Catholic Calvinism. Louis vigorously persecuted Quietists and Jansenists, offering them a choice between recanting and prison and exile. Instead, he supported the Jesuits in their efforts to create a Counter-Reformation Catholic Church in France. Louis's support for the Jesuits upset the traditional Gallican Catholics of France, however, who desired a French church independent of papal, Jesuit, and Spanish influence. As a result of this dissension among Catholics, the religious aura of Louis's kingship diminished during the course of his reign.

Against the Protestant Huguenots, however, Louis waged unrelenting war. Protestant churches and schools were destroyed, and Protestants were banned from many professions, including medicine and printing. In 1685, Louis revoked the Edict of Nantes, the legal foundation of the toleration Huguenots had enjoyed since 1598. Protestant clerics were exiled, laymen were sent to the galleys as slaves, and their children were forcibly baptized as Catholics. Many families converted, but 200,000 Protestant refugees fled to England, Holland, Germany, and America, bringing with them their professional and artisanal skills. This was an enormous loss to France. Among many other examples, the silk industries of Berlin and London were established by Huguenots fleeing Louis XIV's persecution.

## Colbert and Royal Finance

Louis's drive to unify and centralize France depended on a vast increase in royal revenues engineered by Jean Baptiste Colbert, the king's finance minister from 1664 until his death in 1683. Colbert tightened the process of tax collection and eliminated wherever possible the practice of tax farming (which permitted collection agents to retain for themselves a percentage of the taxes they gathered for the king). When Colbert assumed office, only about 25 percent of the taxes collected throughout the kingdom reached the treasury. By the time he died, that figure had risen to 80 percent. Under Colbert's direction, the state sold public offices, including judgeships and mayoralties, and guilds purchased the right to enforce trade regulations. Colbert also tried to increase the nation's income by controlling and regulating foreign trade. As a confirmed mercantilist (see ***Analyzing Primary Sources*** on page 465), Colbert believed that France's wealth would increase if its imports were reduced and its exports increased. He therefore imposed tariffs on foreign goods imported into France while using state money to promote the domestic manufacture of formerly imported goods, such as silk, lace, tapestries, and glass. He was especially anxious to create domestic industries capable of producing the goods France would need for war. To encourage domestic trade, he improved France's roads, bridges, and waterways.

Despite Colbert's efforts to increase crown revenues, his policies ultimately foundered on the insatiable demands of Louis XIV's wars (see page 469). Colbert himself foresaw this result when he lectured the king in 1680: "Trade is the source of public finance and public finance is the vital nerve of war. . . . I beg your Majesty to permit me only to say to him that in war as in peace he has never consulted the amount of money available in determining his expenditures." Louis, however, paid him no heed. By the end of Louis's reign, his aggressive foreign policy lay in ruins and his country's finances had been shattered by the unsustainable costs of war.

# Analyzing Primary Sources

## *Mercantilism and War*

*Jean-Baptiste Colbert (1619–1683) served as Louis XIV's finance minister from 1664 until his death. He worked assiduously to promote commerce, build up French industry, and increase exports. However much Colbert himself may have seen his economic policies as ends in themselves, to Louis they were always means to the end of waging war. Ultimately, Louis's wars undermined the prosperity that Colbert tried so hard to create. This memorandum, written to Louis in 1670, illustrates clearly the mercantilist presumptions of self-sufficiency on which Colbert operated: every item needed to build up the French navy must ultimately be produced in France, even if it could be acquired at less cost from elsewhere.*

And since Your Majesty has wanted to work diligently at reestablishing his naval forces, and since afore that it has been necessary to make very great expenditures, since all merchandise, munitions and manufactured items formerly came from Holland and the countries of the North, it has been absolutely necessary to be especially concerned with finding within the realm, or with establishing in it, everything which might be necessary for this great plan.

To this end, the manufacture of tar was established in Médoc, Auvergne, Dauphiné, and Provence; iron cannons, in Burgundy, Nivernois, Saintonge and Périgord; large anchors in Dauphiné, Nivernois, Brittany, and Rochefort; sailcloth for the Levant, in Dauphiné; coarse muslin, in Auvergne; all the implements for pilots and others, at Dieppe and La Rochelle; the cutting of wood suitable for vessels, in Burgundy, Dauphiné, Brittany, Normandy, Poitou, Saintonge, Provence, Guyenne, and the Pyrenees; masts, of a sort once unknown in this realm, have been found in Provence, Languedoc, Auvergne, Dauphiné, and in the Pyrenees. Iron, which was obtained from Sweden and Biscay, is currently manufactured in the realm. Fine hemp for ropes, which came from Prussia and from Piedmont, is currently obtained in Burgundy, Mâconnais, Bresse, Dauphiné; and markets for it have since been established in Berry and in Auvergne, which always provides money in these provinces and keeps it within the realm.

In a word, everything serving for the construction of vessels is currently established in the realm, so that Your Majesty can get along without foreigners for the navy and will even, in a short time, be able to supply them and gain their money in this fashion. And it is with this same objective of having everything necessary to provide abundantly for his navy and that of his subjects that he is working at the general reform of all the forests in his realm, which, being as carefully preserved as they are at present, will abundantly produce all the wood necessary for this.

Source: Charles W. Cole, *Colbert and a Century of French Mercantilism,* 2 vols. (New York: 1939), p. 320.

### *Questions for Analysis*

1. Why would Colbert want to manufacture materials for supplying the navy within France rather than buying them from abroad?
2. From this example, does Colbert see the economy as serving any other interest other than that of the state?
3. Was there a necessary connection between mercantilism and war?

## ALTERNATIVES TO ABSOLUTISM

Although absolutism was the dominant model for seventeenth- and eighteenth-century European monarchs, it was by no means the only system by which Europeans governed themselves. A republican oligarchy continued to rule in Venice. In The Netherlands, the territories that had won their independence from Spain during the early seventeenth century combined to form the United Provinces, the only truly new country to take shape in Europe during the early modern era. The Spanish wars created a deep distrust among the Dutch toward monarchs of any stripe. As a result, although Holland dominated the United Provinces, its House of Orange, which had led the wars for independence, never attempted to transform the new country from a republic into a monarchy. Even after 1688, when William of Orange also became King William III of England, the United Provinces remained a republic.

## Limited Monarchy: The Case of England

While the powers of representative assemblies were being undermined across much of Europe, the English Parliament was the longest-surviving such body in Europe. English political theorists had long seen their government as a mixed monarchy, composed of monarchical, noble, and nonnoble elements. During the seventeenth century, these traditions came under threat, first through Charles I's attempts to rule without Parliament and then during Oliver Cromwell's dictatorial Protectorate. The restoration of the monarchy in 1660 resolved the question of whether England would in future be a republic or a monarchy, but the sort of monarchy England would become remained an open question.

### THE REIGN OF CHARLES II

Despite the fact that he was the son of the beheaded and much-hated Charles I, Charles II (1660–1685) was initially welcomed by most English men and women. He declared limited religious toleration for Protestant "dissenters" (Protestants who were not members of the official Church of England). He promised to observe the Magna Carta and the Petition of Right, declaring, with characteristic good humor, that he did not wish to "resume his travels." The unbuttoned moral atmosphere of his court, with its risqué plays, dancing, and sexual licentiousness, reflected a public desire to forget the restraints of the Puritan past. Some critics suggested that Charles, "that known enemy to virginity and chastity," took his role as the father of his country rather too seriously, but in fact he produced no legitimate heir and only a single illegitimate son to vie for the throne.

Having grown up an exile in France, Charles was an admirer of all things French. During the 1670s, however, he began openly to model his kingship on the absolutism of Louis XIV. As a result, the great men of England soon came to be publically divided between Charles's supporters (called by their opponents "Tories," a popular nickname for Irish Catholic bandits) and his opponents (called by their opponents "Whigs," a nickname for Scottish Presbyterian rebels). Both sides feared absolutism, just as both sides feared a return to the bad old days of the 1640s, when resistance to the crown had led to civil war and ultimately to republicanism. What they could not agree on was which possibility frightened them more.

**CHARLES II OF ENGLAND (1660–1685) IN HIS CORONATION ROBES.** This full frontal portrait of the monarch, holding the symbols of his rule, seems to confront the viewer personally with the overwhelming authority of the sovereign's gaze. Compare this classic image of the absolutist monarch with the very different portraits of William and Mary, who ruled after the Glorious Revolution of 1688 (page 467). ▪ ***What had changed between 1660, when Charles II came to the throne, and 1688, when the more popular William and Mary became the rulers of England?***

Religion also remained a divisive issue. Charles was sympathetic to Roman Catholicism, even to the point of a deathbed conversion in 1685. During the 1670s, he briefly suspended civil penalties against Catholics and Protestant dissenters by asserting his right as king to ignore Parliamentary legislation. The resulting public outcry compelled him to retreat, but this controversy, together with rising opposition to Charles's ardently Catholic brother James as the heir to the throne, led to a series of Whig electoral victories between 1679 and 1681. When a group of radical Whigs attempted to exclude James by law from succeeding his brother on the throne, however, Charles stared the opposition down in the so-called Exclusion Crisis. Thereafter, Charles found that his rising revenues from customs duties, combined with a secret subsidy from Louis XIV, enabled him to govern without relying on Parliament for money.

Charles further alarmed Whig politicans by executing several of them on charges of treason and by remodeling local government to make it more amenable to royal control. Charles died in 1685 with his power enhanced, but he left behind a political and religious legacy that was to be the undoing of his less able and adroit successor.

## THE REIGN OF JAMES II

James II was the very opposite of his worldly brother. A zealous Catholic convert, he alienated his Tory supporters, who were close to the established Church of England, by suspending the laws preventing Catholics and Protestant dissenters from holding political office. James flaunted his own Roman Catholicism, openly declaring his wish that his subjects convert and publicly parading papal legates through the streets of London. When, in June 1688, he ordered all Church of England clergymen to read his decree of religious toleration from their pulpits, seven bishops refused and were promptly imprisoned. At their trial, however, they were declared not guilty of sedition, to the enormous satisfaction of the Protestant English populace.

The trial of the bishops was one event that brought matters to a head. The other was the unexpected birth of a son in 1688 to James and his second wife, Mary of Modena. This child, who was to be raised a Catholic, replaced James's much older Protestant daughter Mary Stuart as heir to the thrones of Scotland and England. So unexpected was this birth that there were widespread rumors that the child was not in fact James's son at all but had been smuggled into the royal bedchamber in a warming pan.

With the birth of the "warming-pan baby," events moved swiftly toward a climax. A delegation of Whigs and Tories crossed the channel to Holland to invite Mary Stuart and her Protestant husband, William of Orange, to cross to England with an invading army to preserve Protestantism and English liberties by summoning a new Parliament. As the leader of a continental coalition then at war with France, William also welcomed the opportunity to make England an ally against Louis XIV's expansionist foreign policy.

**WILLIAM AND MARY.** In 1688, William of Orange and his wife, Mary Stuart, became Protestant joint rulers of England, in a bloodless coup that took power from her father, the Catholic James II. Compare this contemporary print with the portraits of Louis XIV (page 462) and Charles II (page 466). ▪ ***What relationship does it seem to depict between the royal couple and their subjects?*** ▪ ***What is the significance of the gathered crowd in the public square in the background?*** ▪ ***How is this different from the spectacle of divine authority projected by Louis XIV or the image of Charles II looking straight at the viewer?***

## THE GLORIOUS REVOLUTION

William and Mary's invasion became a bloodless coup (although James is reputed to have suffered a nosebleed at the moment of crisis). James fled the country, and Parliament declared the throne vacant, clearing the way for William and Mary to succeed him as joint sovereigns. The Bill of Rights, passed by Parliament and accepted by the new king and queen in 1689, reaffirmed English civil liberties, such as trial by jury, habeas corpus (a guarantee that no one could be imprisoned unless charged with a crime), and the right to petition the monarch through Parliament. The Bill of Rights also declared that the monarchy was subject to the law of the land. The Act of Toleration, also passed in 1689, granted Protestant dissenters the right to worship freely, though not to hold political office. And in 1701, the Act of Succession ordained that every future English monarch must be a member of the Church of England. Queen Mary died childless, and the throne passed from William to Mary's Protestant sister Anne (1702–1714) and then to George, elector of the German principality of Hanover and the Protestant great-grandson of James I. In 1707, the formal Act of Union between Scotland and England ensured that the Catholic heirs of King James II would in future have no more right to the throne of Scotland than they did to the throne of England.

The English soon referred to the events of 1688 and 1689 as the "Glorious Revolution," because it firmly established England as a mixed monarchy governed by the "king in Parliament." Although William and Mary and their successors continued to exercise a large measure of executive power, after 1688 no English monarch attempted to govern without Parliament, which has met annually from that time on. Parliament, and especially the House of Commons, also strengthened its control over taxation and expenditure. Protestants in particular celebrated the Glorious Revolution as another sign of God's special favor to England, noting the favorable (Protestant) winds that blew William and Mary so speedily to England and kept King James's fleet from mounting an effective resistance.

Yet 1688 was not all glory. It was a revolution that consolidated the position of large property holders, whose control over local government had been threatened by Charles II and James II. It thus restored the status quo on behalf of a wealthy class of magnates that would soon become even wealthier from government patronage and the profits of war. It also brought misery to the Catholic minority in Scotland and to the Catholic majority in Ireland. After 1690, when King William won a decisive victory over James II's forces at the Battle of the Boyne, power in Ireland would lie firmly in the hands of a "Protestant Ascendancy," whose dominance over Irish society would last until modern times.

JOHN LOCKE.

## JOHN LOCKE AND THE CONTRACT THEORY OF GOVERNMENT

The Glorious Revolution was the product of unique circumstances, but it also reflected antiabsolutist theories of politics that were taking shape in the late seventeenth century in response to the ideas of writers such as Bodin, Hobbes, Filmer, and Bossuet. Chief among these opponents of absolutism was the Englishman John Locke (1632–1704), whose *Two Treatises of Government* were written before the revolution but published for the first time in 1690.

Locke maintained that humans had originally lived in a state of nature characterized by absolute freedom and equality, with no government of any kind. The only law was the law of nature (which Locke equated with the law of reason), by which individuals enforced for themselves their natural rights to life, liberty, and property. Soon, however, humans began to perceive that the inconveniences of the state of nature outweighed its advantages. Accordingly, they agreed first to establish a civil society based on absolute equality and then to set up a government to arbitrate the disputes that might arise within this civil society. But they did not make government's powers absolute. All powers not expressly surrendered to the government were reserved to the people themselves; as a result, governmental authority was both contractual and conditional. If a government exceeded or abused the authority granted to it, society had the right to dissolve it and create another.

Locke condemned absolutism in every form. He denounced absolute monarchy, but he was also critical of claims for the sovereignty of parliaments. Government, he argued, had been instituted to protect life, liberty, and property; no political authority could infringe these natural rights. The law of nature was therefore an automatic and absolute limitation on every branch of government.

In the late eighteenth century, Locke's ideas would resurface as part of the intellectual background of both the American and French revolutions. Between 1690 and 1720, however, they served a far less radical purpose. The landed magnates who replaced James II with William and Mary read Locke as a defense of their conservative revolution. Rather than protecting their liberty and property, James II had threatened both; hence the magnates were entitled to overthrow the tyranny he had established and replace it with a government that would defend their interests by preserving these natural rights. English government after 1689 would be dominated by Parliament; Parliament in turn was controlled by a landed aristocracy who were firm in the defence of their common interests.

During the beginning of the eighteenth century, then, both France and Britain had solved the problem of political dissent and social disorder in their own way. The emergence of a stable constitutional monarchy in England after

1688 contrasted vividly with the absolutist system developed by Louis XIV, but both systems worked well enough to contain the immediate threat to royal authority posed by a powerful class of landed nobles. Domestic stability was no guarantee of international peace, however, and the period from 1661, when Louis XIV assumed personal rule, to his death in 1715, was marked by almost constant warfare.

## WAR AND THE BALANCE OF POWER, 1661–1715

Louis XIV's foreign policy reflected his belief that military victories abroad were necessary to reinforce the glory of his realm and the power that he wielded at home. Louis's wars sought to meet the threat posed by the Habsburg powers in Spain, the Spanish Netherlands, and the Holy Roman Empire and to promote his own dynastic interests. Through a series of campaigns in the Low Countries, Louis expanded his territory, eventually taking Strasbourg (1681), Luxembourg (1684), and Cologne (1688). In response, William of Orange (1672–1702) organized the League of Augsburg, which over time included Holland, England, Spain, Sweden, Bavaria, Saxony, the Rhine Palatinate, and the Austrian Habsburgs. The resulting Nine Years' War extended from Ireland to India to North America (where it was known as King William's War).

The League of Augsburg reflected the emergence of a new diplomatic goal in western and central Europe: the preservation of a balance of power. This goal would animate European diplomacy for the next two hundred years, until the balance of power system collapsed with the outbreak of the First World War. The main proponents of balance of power diplomacy were England, the United Provinces (Holland), Prussia, and Austria. By 1697, the league forced Louis XIV to make peace, because France was exhausted by war and famine. Louis gave back much of his recent gains but kept Strasbourg and the surrounding territory of Alsace. He was nevertheless looking at the real prize: a French claim to succeed to the throne of Spain and so control the Spanish Empire in the Americas, Italy, the Netherlands, and the Philippines.

### *The War of the Spanish Succession*

In the 1690s it became clear that King Charles II of Spain (1665–1700) would soon die without a clear heir, and both Louis XIV of France and Leopold I of Austria (1658–1705) were interested in promoting their own relatives to succeed him. Either solution would have upset the balance of power in Europe, and several schemes to divide the Spanish realm between French and Austrian candidates were discussed. Meanwhile, King Charles II's advisers sought to avoid partition by passing the entire Spanish Empire to a single heir: Louis XIV's grandson, Philip of Anjou. Philip was to renounce any claim to the French throne in becoming king of Spain, but the terms of this will were kept secret. When Charles II died, Philip V (1700–1746) was proclaimed king of Spain, and Louis XIV rushed troops into the Spanish Netherlands, while also sending French merchants into Spanish America and withdrawing his recognition of William of Orange as king of England.

**THE TREATY OF UTRECHT, 1713.** This illustration from a French royal almanac depicts the treaty that ended the War of Spanish Succession and reshaped the balance of power in western Europe in favor of Britain and France.

The resulting war, known as the War of the Spanish Succession, pitted England, the United Provinces, Austria, and Prussia against France, Bavaria, and Spain. Although William of Orange died in 1702, just as the war was beginning, his generals led an extraordinary march deep into the European Continent, inflicting a devastating defeat on the French and their Bavarian allies at Blenheim (1704). Soon after, the English captured Gibraltar, establishing a commercial foothold in the Mediterranean. By 1709, France was on the verge of defeat, but when they met the British at the battle of Malplaquet in present-day Belgium they inflicted twenty-four thousand casualties before retreating from the field. Meanwhile, the costs of the campaign created a chorus of complaints from English and Dutch merchants, who feared the damage that was being done to trade and commerce. Queen Anne of England (Mary's sister and William's successor) gradually grew disillusioned with the war, and her government sent out peace feelers to France.

### *The Treaty of Utrecht*

In 1713 the war finally came to an end with the Treaty of Utrecht. Its terms were reasonably fair to all sides. Philip V, Louis XIV's grandson, remained on the throne of Spain and retained Spain's colonial empire intact. In return, Louis agreed that France and Spain would never be united under the same ruler. Austria gained territories in the Spanish Netherlands and Italy, including Milan and Naples. The Dutch were guaranteed protection of their borders against future invasions by France, but the French retained both Lille and Strasbourg. The biggest winner by far was Great Britain, as the combined kingdoms of England and Scotland were known after 1707. The British kept Gibraltar and Minorca in the Mediterranean and also acquired large chunks of French territory in the New World, including Newfoundland, mainland Nova Scotia, the Hudson Bay, and the Caribbean island of St. Kitts. Even more valuable, however, Britain also extracted from Spain the right to transport and sell African slaves in Spanish America. As a result, the British were now poised to become the principal slave merchants and the dominant colonial and commercial power of the eighteenth-century world.

The Treaty of Utrecht reshaped the balance of power in western Europe in fundamental ways. Spain's collapse was already precipitous; by 1713 it was complete. Spain would remain the "sick man of Europe" for the next two centuries. Holland's decline was more gradual, but by 1713, its greatest days were also over. In the Atlantic world, Britain and France were now the dominant powers. Although they would duel for another half century for control of North America, the balance of colonial power tilted decisively in Britain's favor after Utrecht. Within Europe, the myth of French military supremacy had been shattered. Britain's navy, not France's army, would rule the new imperial and commercial world of the eighteenth century.

## THE REMAKING OF CENTRAL AND EASTERN EUROPE

The decades between 1680 and 1720 were also decisive in reshaping the balance of power in central and eastern Europe. As Ottoman power waned, the Austro-Hungarian Empire of the Habsburgs emerged as the dominant power in central and southeastern Europe. To the north, Brandenburg-Prussia was also a rising power. The most dramatic changes, however, occurred in Russia, which emerged from a long war with Sweden as the dominant power in the Baltic Sea and would soon threaten the combined kingdom of Poland-Lithuania.

**MARIA THERESA OF AUSTRIA AND HER FAMILY.** A formidable and capable ruler who fought to maintain Austria's dominance in central Europe against the claims of Frederick the Great of Prussia, Maria Theresa had sixteen children, including Marie Antoinette, later queen of France as wife of Louis XVI. ▪ ***Why did she emphasize her role as mother in a royal portrait such as this one, rather than her other undeniable political skills?*** ▪ ***How does this compare to the portraits of William and Mary or of Louis XIV elsewhere in this chapter?***

**EUROPE AFTER THE TREATY OF UTRECHT (1713).** ▪ ***What were the major Habsburg Dominions?*** ▪ ***What geographical disadvantage faced the kingdom of Poland as Brandenburg-Prussia grew in influence and ambition?*** ▪ ***How did the balance of power change in Europe as a result of the Treaty of Utrecht?***

## The Habsburg Empire

In 1683, the Ottoman Turks launched their last assault on Vienna. Only the arrival of seventy thousand Polish troops saved the Austrian capital from capture. Thereafter, Ottoman power in southeastern Europe declined rapidly. By 1699, Austria had reconquered most of Hungary from the Ottomans; by 1718, it controlled all of Hungary and also Transylvania and Serbia. In 1722, Austria acquired the territory of Silesia from Poland. With Hungary now a buffer state between Austria and the Ottomans, Vienna emerged as one of the great cultural and political capitals of eighteenth-century Europe, and Austria became one of the arbiters of the European balance of power.

Although the Austrian Habsburgs retained their title as Holy Roman emperors and after 1713 also held lands in the Netherlands and Italy, their real power lay in Austria, Bohemia, Moravia, Galicia, and Hungary. These territories were geographically contiguous, but they were deeply divided by ethnicity, religion, and language. Despite the centralizing efforts of a series of Habsburg rulers, their empire would remain a rather loose confederation of distinct territories.

In Bohemia and Moravia, the Habsburgs encouraged landlords to produce crops for export by forcing peasants to

**PRUSSIANS SWEARING ALLEGIANCE TO THE GREAT ELECTOR AT KÖNIGSBERG, 1663.** The occasion on which the Prussian estates first acknowledged the overlordship of their ruler. This ceremony marked the beginning of the centralization of the Prussian state.

provide three days of unpaid work per week to their lords. In return, the landed elites of these territories permitted the emperors to reduce the political independence of their traditional legislative estates. In Hungary, however, the powerful and independent nobility resisted such compromises. Habsburg efforts to administer Hungary through the army and to impose Catholic religious uniformity also met with stiff resistance. As a result, Hungary would remain a semi-autonomous region within the empire whose support the Austrians could never take for granted.

After 1740, the empress Maria Theresa (1740–1780) and her son Joseph II (1765–1790; from 1765 until 1780 the two were co-rulers) pioneered a new style of "enlightened absolutism" within their empire: centralizing the administration in Vienna, increasing taxation, creating a professional standing army, and tightening their control over the church while creating a statewide system of primary education, relaxing censorship, and instituting a new, more liberal criminal code. But in practice, Habsburg absolutism, whether enlightened or not, was always limited by the diversity of its imperial territories and by the weakness of its local governmental institutions.

## The Rise of Brandenburg-Prussia

After the Ottoman collapse, the main threat to Austria came from the rising power of Brandenburg-Prussia. Like Austria, Prussia was a composite state made up of several geographically divided territories acquired through inheritance by the Hohenzollern family. Their two main holdings were Brandenburg, centered on its capital city, Berlin, and the duchy of East Prussia. Between these two territories lay Pomerania (claimed by Sweden) and an important part of the kingdom of Poland, including the port of Gdansk (Danzig). The Hohenzollerns' aim was to unite their state by acquiring these intervening territories. Over the course of more than a century of steady state building, they finally succeeded in doing so. In the process, Brandenburg-Prussia became a dominant military power and a key player in the balance-of-power diplomacy of the mid-eighteenth century.

The foundations for Prussian expansion were laid by Frederick William, the "Great Elector" (1640–1688). He obtained East Prussia from Poland in exchange for help in a war against Sweden. Behind the Elector's diplomatic triumphs lay his success in building an army and mobilizing the resources to pay for it. He gave the powerful nobles of his territories (known as *Junkers*) the right to enserf their peasants and guaranteed them immunity from taxation. In exchange, they staffed the officer corps of his army and supported his highly autocratic taxation system. Secure in their estates and made increasingly wealthy in the grain trade, the Junkers surrendered management of the Prussian state to the Elector's newly reformed bureaucracy, which set about its main task: increasing the size and strength of the Prussian army.

By supporting Austria in the War of the Spanish Succession, the Great Elector's son, Frederick I (1688–1713) earned the right to call himself king of Prussia from the Austrian emperor. He too was a crafty diplomat, but his main attention was devoted to developing the cultural life of his new royal capital, Berlin. His son, Frederick William I (1713–1740) focused, like his grandfather, on building the army. During his reign, the Prussian army grew from thirty thousand to eighty-three thousand men, becoming the fourth largest army in Europe, after France, Austria, and Russia. To support his army, Frederick William I increased taxes and shunned the luxuries of court life. For him, the theater of absolutism was not the palace but the office, where he personally supervised his army and the growing bureaucracy that sustained it.

A hard, unimaginative man, Frederick William I had little use for his son Frederick, whose passion was not the army but the flute and who admired French culture as much as his father disdained it. It is not surprising that young Frederick rebelled. In 1730, when he was eighteen, he ran away from court with a friend. Apprehended, the companions were returned to the king, who executed his son's friend before Frederick's eyes. The grisly lesson took. Although Frederick never gave up his love of music and literature, he thereafter bound himself to his royal duties, living in accordance with his own image of himself as "first servant of the state" and earning history's title of Frederick the Great.

Frederick William I had made Prussia a strong state. Frederick the Great (1740–1786) raised his country to the status of a major power. As soon as he became king in 1740, Frederick mobilized the army his father had never taken into battle and occupied the Austrian province of Silesia. Prussia had no conceivable claim to Silesia, but the territory was both rich and poorly defended, and so Frederick seized it with French support. The new Habsburg empress, Maria Theresa, counterattacked; but despite the support of both Britain and Hungary, she was unable to recover Silesia. Emboldened, Frederick spent the rest of his reign consolidating his gains in Silesia and extending his control over the Polish territories that lay between Prussia and Brandenburg. Through relentless diplomacy and frequent war, Frederick transformed Prussia by 1786 into a powerful, contiguous territorial kingdom.

To ensure a united domestic front against Prussia's enemies, Frederick was careful to cultivate Junker support for his policies. His father had recruited civil servants according to merit rather than birth, but Frederick relied on the Junker nobility to staff the army and his expanding administration. Remarkably, Frederick's strategy worked. His nobility remained loyal, and Frederick fashioned the most professional and efficient bureaucracy in Europe.

Like his contemporary Joseph II of Austria, Frederick was an enlightened absolutist. He supervised a series of social reforms, prohibited the judicial torture of accused criminals, abolished the bribing of judges, and established a system of elementary schools. Although strongly anti-Semitic, he encouraged religious toleration toward Christians and declared that he would happily build a mosque in Berlin if he could find enough Muslims to fill it. On his own royal estates he abolished capital punishment, curtailed the forced labor services of his peasantry, and granted them long leases on the land they worked. He encouraged scientific forestry and the cultivation of new crops. He cleared new lands in Silesia and brought in thousands of immigrants to cultivate them. When wars ruined their farms, he supplied his peasants with new livestock and tools. But he never attempted to extend these reforms to the estates of the Prussian nobility. To have done so would have alienated the very group on whom Frederick's rule depended.

***THE CITY OF STETTIN UNDER SIEGE BY THE GREAT ELECTOR FREDERICK WILLIAM IN THE WINTER OF 1677–78* (c. 1680).** This painting depicts the growing sophistication and organization of military operations under the Prussian monarchy. Improvements in artillery and siege tactics forced cities to adopt new defensive strategies, especially the zone of battlements and protective walls that became ubiquitous in central Europe during this period. ▪ ***How might these developments have shaped the layout of Europe's growing towns and cities?*** ▪ ***How might this emphasis on the military and its attendant bureaucracy have affected the relationship between the monarchy and the nobility or between the king and his subjects?***

## AUTOCRACY IN RUSSIA

An even more dramatic transformation took place in Russia under Tsar Peter I (1672–1725). Peter's accomplishments alone would have earned him his title of "Great." But his imposing height—he was six feet eight inches tall—as well as his mercurial personality—jesting one moment, raging the next—certainly added to the outsize impression he made on his contemporaries. Peter was not the first tsar to bring his country into contact with western Europe, but his policies were decisive in making Russia a great European power.

### *The Early Years of Peter's Reign*

Since 1613 Russia had been ruled by members of the Romanov Dynasty, who had attempted to restore political stability after the chaotic "time of troubles" that followed the death of the bloodthirsty, half-mad tsar Ivan the Terrible in 1584. The Romanovs faced a severe threat to their rule between 1667 and 1671, when a Cossack leader (the Russian Cossacks were semi-autonomous bands of peasant cavalrymen) named Stenka Razin led a rebellion in southeastern Russia. This uprising found widespread support, not only from oppressed serfs but also from non-Russian tribes in the lower Volga region who longed to cast off the domination of Moscow. Ultimately Tsar Alexis I (1654–1676) and the Russian nobility were able to defeat Razin's zealous but disorganized bands of rebels, slaughtering more than a hundred thousand of them in the process.

Like Louis XIV of France, Peter came to the throne as a young boy, and his minority was marked by political dissension and court intrigue. In 1689, however, at the age of seventeen, he overthrew the regency of his half-sister Sophia and assumed personal control of the state. Determined to make Russia into a great military power, the young tsar traveled to Holland and England during the 1690s to study shipbuilding and to recruit skilled foreign workers to help him build a navy. While he was abroad, however, his elite palace guard (the *streltsy*) rebelled, attempting to restore Sophia to the throne. Peter quickly returned home from Vienna and crushed the rebellion with striking savagery. About twelve hundred suspected conspirators were summarily executed, many of them gibbeted outside the walls of the Kremlin, where their bodies rotted for months as a graphic reminder of the fate awaiting those who dared challenge the tsar's authority.

### *The Transformation of the Tsarist State*

Peter is most famous as the tsar who attempted to westernize Russia by imposing a series of social and cultural reforms on the traditional Russian nobility: ordering noblemen to cut off their long beards and flowing sleeves; publishing a book of manners that forbade spitting on the floor and eating with one's fingers; encouraging polite conversation between the sexes; and requiring noblewomen to appear, together with men, in Western garb at weddings, banquets, and other public occasions. The children of Russian nobles were sent to western European courts for their education. Thousands of western European experts were brought to Russia to staff the new schools and academies Peter built; to design the new buildings he constructed; and to serve in the tsar's army, navy, and administration.

**PETER THE GREAT CUTS THE BEARD OF AN OLD BELIEVER.** This woodcut depicts the Russian emperor's enthusiastic policy of westernization, as he pushed everybody in Russia who was not a peasant to adopt Western styles of clothes and grooming. The Old Believer (a member of a religious sect in Russia) protests that he has paid the beard tax and should therefore be exempt. ▪ ***Why would an individual's choices about personal appearance be so politically significant in Peter's Russia?*** ▪ ***What customs were the target of Peter's reforms?***

These measures were important, but the tsar was not primarily motivated by a desire to modernize or westernize Russia. Peter's policies transformed Russian life in fundamental ways, but his real goal was to make Russia a great military power, not to remake Russian society. His new taxation system (1724), for example, which assessed taxes on individuals rather than on households, rendered many of the traditional divisions of Russian peasant society obsolete. It was created, however, to raise more money for war. His Table of Ranks, imposed in 1722, had a similar impact on the nobility. By insisting that all nobles must work their way up from the (lower) landlord class to the (higher) administrative class and to the (highest) military class, Peter reversed the traditional hierarchy of Russian noble society, which had valued landlords by birth above administrators and soldiers who had risen by merit. But he also created a powerful new incentive to lure his nobility into administrative and military service to the tsar.

As autocrat of all the Russias, Peter the Great was the absolute master of his empire to a degree unmatched elsewhere in Europe. After 1649, Russian peasants were legally the property of their landlords; by 1750, half were serfs and the other half were state peasants who lived on lands owned by the tsar himself. State peasants could be conscripted to serve as soldiers in the tsar's army, workers in his factories (whose productive capacity increased enormously during Peter's reign), or as forced laborers in his building projects. Serfs could also be taxed by the tsar and summoned for military service, as could their lords. All Russians, of whatever rank, were expected to serve the tsar, and all Russia was considered in some sense to belong to him.

To further consolidate his power, Peter replaced the Duma—the nation's rudimentary national assembly—with a hand-picked senate, a group of nine administrators who supervised military and civilian affairs. In religious matters, he took direct control over the Russian Orthodox Church by appointing an imperial official to manage its affairs. To cope with the demands of war, he also fashioned a new, larger, and more efficient administration, for which he recruited both nobles and nonnobles. But rank in the

**THE GROWTH OF RUSSIAN EMPIRE.** ▪ *How did Peter the Great expand the territory controlled by Russia?* ▪ *What neighboring dynasties would have been the most affected by Russian expansion?* ▪ *How did the emergence of a bigger, more powerful Russia affect the European balance of power?*

new bureaucracy did not depend on birth. One of his principal advisers, Alexander Menshikov, began his career as a cook and finished as a prince. This degree of social mobility would have been impossible in any contemporary western European country. Instead, noble status depended on governmental service, with all nobles expected to participate in Peter's army or administration. Peter was not entirely successful in enforcing this requirement, but the administrative machinery he devised furnished Russia with its ruling class for the next two hundred years.

## Peter's Foreign Policy

The goal of Peter's foreign policy was to secure year-round ports for Russia on the Black Sea and the Baltic Sea. In the Black Sea, his enemy was the Ottomans. Here, however, he had little success; although he captured the port of Azov in 1696, he was forced to return it in 1711. Russia would not secure its position in the Black Sea until the end of the eighteenth century. In the north, however, Peter achieved much more. In 1700, he began what would become a twenty-one-year war with Sweden, then the dominant power in the Baltic Sea. By 1703, Peter had secured a foothold on the Gulf of Finland and immediately began to build a new capital city there, which he named St. Petersburg. After 1709, when Russian armies, supported by Prussia, decisively defeated the Swedes at the battle of Poltava, work on Peter's new capital city accelerated. An army of serfs was now conscripted to build the new city, whose centerpiece was a royal palace designed to imitate and rival Louis XIV's Versailles.

The Great Northern War with Sweden ended in 1721 with the Peace of Nystad. This treaty marks a realignment of power in eastern Europe comparable to that effected by the Treaty of Utrecht in the West. Sweden lost its North Sea territories to Hanover and its Baltic German territories to Prussia. Its eastern territories, including the entire Gulf of Finland, Livonia, and Estonia, passed to Russia. Sweden was now a second-rank power in the northern European world. Poland-Lithuania survived but faced the expanding power of Prussia in the West and the expanding power of Russia in the East. It too was a declining power; by the end of the eighteenth century, the kingdom would disappear altogether, its territories swallowed up by its more powerful neighbors. The victors at Nystad were the Prussians and the Russians. These two powers secured their position along the Baltic coast, positioning themselves to take advantage of the lucrative eastern European grain trade with western Europe.

Peter's victory came at enormous cost. Direct taxation increased 500 percent during his reign, and his army in the 1720s numbered more than three hundred thousand men. Peter made Russia a force to be reckoned with on the European scene; but in so doing, he also aroused great resentment, especially among his nobility. Peter's only son and heir, Alexis, became the focus for conspiracies against the tsar, until finally Peter had him arrested and executed in 1718. As a result, when Peter died in 1725, he left no son to succeed him. A series of ineffective tsars followed, mostly creatures of the palace guard, under whom the resentful nobles reversed many of Peter the Great's reforms. In 1762, however, the crown passed to Catherine the Great, a ruler whose ambitions and determination were equal to those of her great predecessor.

## Catherine the Great and the Partition of Poland

Catherine was a German who came to the throne in 1762 on the death of her husband, the weak (and possibly mad) Tsar Peter III, who was deposed and executed in a palace coup

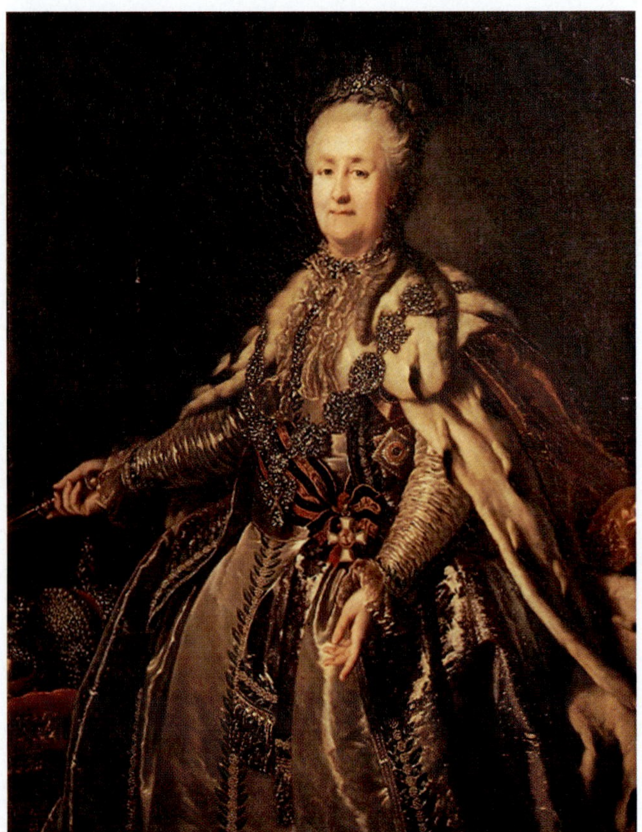

**CATHERINE THE GREAT.**

that Catherine herself may have helped arrange. Although she cultivated an image of herself as an enlightened ruler (she corresponded with French philosophers, wrote plays, and began to compose a history of Russia), Catherine was determined not to lose the support of the nobility who had placed her on the throne. As a result, her efforts at social reform did not extend much beyond the founding of hospitals and orphanages and the creation of an elementary school system for the children of the provincial nobility. Like her contemporary enlightened absolutists Joseph of Austria and Frederick the Great of Prussia, she too summoned a commission, in 1767, to codify and revise Russian law. But few of its radical proposals (which included the abolition of capital punishment, an end to judicial torture, and prohibitions on the selling of serfs) were ever implemented. Any possibility such measures might have been enforced ended in 1773–1775, when a massive peasant revolt led by a Cossack named Emelyan Pugachev briefly threatened Moscow itself. Catherine responded to the uprising by further centralizing her own government and by tightening aristocratic control over the peasantry.

Catherine's greatest achievements were gained through war and diplomacy. In 1769, she renewed Peter the Great's push to secure a warm-water port on the Black Sea. In the resulting war with the Ottoman Turks (which ended in 1774), Russia won control over the northern coast of the Black Sea, secured the independence of Crimea (which Russia would annex in 1783), and obtained safe passage for Russian ships through the Bosporus and into the Mediterranean Sea. In the course of this campaign, Russia also won control over several Ottoman provinces along the Danube River.

Russia's gains in the Balkans alarmed Austria, however, which now found itself with the powerful Russian Empire on its southern doorstep. Prussia too was threatening to become involved in the war as an ally of the Ottomans. Frederick the Great's real interests, however, lay much closer to home. To preserve the peace among Russia, Prussia, and Austria, he proposed instead a partition of Poland. Russia would abandon its Danubian conquests and, in return, would acquire the grain fields of eastern Poland, along with a population of 1 to 2 million Poles. Austria would take Galicia, acquiring 2.5 million Poles. Prussia, meanwhile, would take the coastal regions of Poland, including the port of Gdansk (Danzig), that separated Brandenburg and Pomerania from East Prussia. As a result of this agreement, finalized in 1772, Poland lost about 30 percent of its territory and about half of its population.

Poland was now paying the price for its political conservatism. Alone among the major central European powers, the Polish nobility had successfully opposed any move toward monarchical centralization as a threat to its liberties, among which was the right of every individual noble to veto any measure proposed in the Polish representative assembly, the Diet. To make matters worse, Polish aristocrats were also quite prepared to accept bribes from foreign powers in return for their vote in elections for the Polish king. In 1764, Catherine the Great had intervened in this way to secure the election of one of her former lovers, Stanislaus Poniatowski, as the new king of Poland. In 1772, King Stanislaus reluctantly accepted the partition of his country because he was too weak to resist it. In 1788, however, he took advantage of a new Russo-Turkish war to try to strengthen his control over what remained of his kingdom. In May 1791 a new constitution was adopted that established a much stronger

**DIVIDING THE ROYAL SPOILS.** A contemporary cartoon showing the monarchs of Europe at work carving up a hapless Poland. Note there is little reference here to the people who lived in the Polish territories that were being divided up between Russia, Prussia, and the Habspurg Empire. All three of these realms already contained people who spoke different languages and practiced different religions. The result of such expansion was to increase the linguistic and cultural diversity of these kingdoms. ▪ ***How might this have complicated the internal politics of these monarchies?*** ▪ ***What long-term consequences might one expect from such multiethnic or multireligious societies?***

monarchy than had previously existed. But it was too late. In January 1792 the Russo-Turkish war ended, and Catherine the Great pounced. Together the Russians and Prussians took two more enormous bites out of Poland in 1793, destroying the new constitution in the process. A final swallow by Russia, Austria, and Prussia in 1795 left nothing of Poland or Lithuania at all.

## COMMERCE AND CONSUMPTION

Despite the increased military power of Russia, Prussia, and Austria, the balance of power within Europe was shifting steadily toward the West during the eighteenth century. The North Atlantic economies in particular were growing more rapidly than those anywhere else in Europe. As a result, France and Britain were becoming preponderant powers both in Europe and the wider world.

### *Economic Growth in Eighteenth-Century Europe*

The reasons for this rapid economic and demographic growth in northwestern Europe are complex. In Britain and Holland, new, more intensive agricultural systems produced more food per acre. Combined with improved transportation, the new farming methods resulted in fewer famines and a better-nourished population. New crops, especially maize and potatoes (both introduced to Europe from the Americas), also helped increase the supply of food. Although famines became less common and less widespread, infectious disease continued to kill half of all Europeans before the age of twenty. Even here, however, some progress was being made. Plague was ceasing to be a major killer, as a degree of immunity (perhaps the result of a genetic mutation) began to emerge within the European population. Together with a better diet, improved sanitation may also have played some role in reducing the infection rates from typhoid, cholera, smallpox, and measles.

Northwestern Europe was also becoming increasingly urbanized. Across Europe as a whole the total number of urban dwellers did not change markedly between 1600 and 1800. At both dates, approximately two hundred cities in Europe had a population of over ten thousand. What did change was, first, the fact that these cities were increasingly concentrated in northern and western Europe and, second, the extraordinary growth of the very largest cities. Patterns of trade and commerce had much to do with these shifts. Cities such as Hamburg in Germany, Liverpool in England, Toulon in France, and Cadíz in Spain grew by about 250 percent between 1600 and 1750. Amsterdam, the hub of early modern international commerce, increased from 30,000 in 1530 to 200,000 by 1800. Naples, the busy Mediterranean port, went from a population of 300,000 in 1600 to nearly half a million by the late eighteenth century. Even more spectacular population growth occurred in the administrative capitals of Europe. London grew from 674,000 in 1700 to 860,000 a century later. Paris went from 180,000 people in 1600 to more than 500,000 in 1800. Berlin grew from a population of 6,500 in 1661 to 140,000 in 1783.

The rising prosperity of northwestern Europe depended on developments in trade and manufacturing as well as agriculture. Spurred by improvements in transportation, entrepreneurs began to promote the production of textiles in the countryside. They distributed ("put out") wool and flax to rural workers who would card, spin, and weave it into cloth on a piece-rate basis. The entrepreneur then collected and sold the finished cloth in a market that extended from local towns to international exporters. For country dwellers, this system (sometimes called *protoindustrialization*) provided welcome employment during otherwise slack seasons of the agricultural year. For the merchant-entrepreneurs who administered it, the system allowed them to avoid expensive guild restrictions in the towns and to reduce their levels of capital investment, thus reducing their overall costs of production. Urban cloth workers suffered, but the system led nonetheless to markedly increased employment and to much higher levels of industrial production, not only for textiles but also for iron, metalworking, and even toy and clock making.

The role of cities as manufacturing centers also continued to grow during the eighteenth century. In northern France, many of the million or so men and women employed in the textile trade lived and worked in Amiens, Lille, and Rheims. The rulers of Prussia made it their policy to develop Berlin as a manufacturing center, taking advantage of an influx of French Protestants to establish a silk-weaving industry there and constructing canals to link the city with Breslau and Hamburg. Most urban manufacturing took place in small shops employing from five to twenty journeymen working under a master. But the scale of such enterprise was growing and becoming more specialized, as workshops began to group together to form a single manufacturing district in which several thousand workers might be employed to produce the same product.

Techniques in some crafts remained much as they had been for centuries. In others, however, inventions changed the pattern of work as well as the nature of the product. Knitting frames, simple devices to speed the manufacture of textile goods, made their appearance in Britain and Holland.

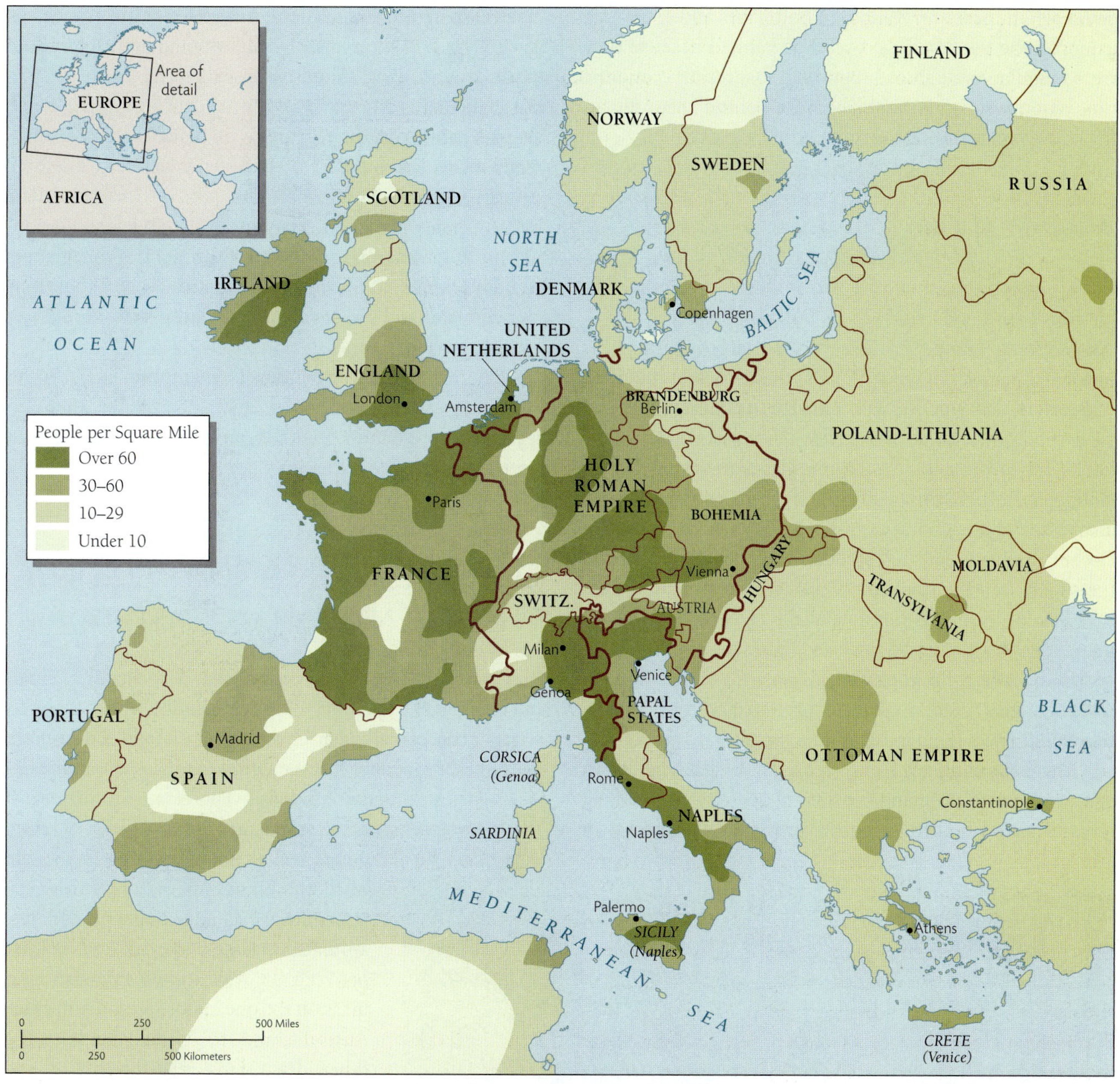


**POPULATION GROWTH c. 1600.** ▪ ***Where did the population grow more rapidly?*** ▪ ***Why were the largest gains in population on the coasts?*** ▪ ***How did urbanization affect patterns of life and trade?***

Wire-drawing machines and slitting mills, the latter enabling nail makers to convert iron bars into rods, spread from Germany into Britain. Techniques for printing colored designs directly on calico cloth were imported from Asia. New and more efficient printing presses appeared, first in Holland and then elsewhere. The Dutch even invented a machine called a "camel," with which the hulls of ships could be raised in the water so that they could be more easily repaired.

Workers did not readily accept innovations of this kind. Labor-saving machines threw people out of work. Artisans, especially those organized into guilds, were by nature conservative, anxious to protect not only their rights but also the secrets of their trade. Often, therefore, governments would intervene to block the widespread use of machines if they threatened to increase unemployment or in some other way to create unrest. States might also intervene to protect the interests of their powerful commercial and financial backers. On behalf of domestic textile manufacturers and importers of Indian goods, both Britain and France outlawed calico printing for a time. Mercantilist doctrines could also impede innovation. In both Paris and Lyons, for example, the use of indigo dyes was banned because they were manufactured abroad. But the pressures for economic innovation were irresistible, because behind them lay an insatiable eighteenth-century appetite for goods.

## *A World of Goods*

In the eighteenth century, for the first time, a mass market for consumer goods emerged in Europe, and especially in northwestern Europe. Houses became larger, particularly in towns; but even more strikingly, the houses of middling ranks were now stocked with hitherto uncommon luxuries such as sugar, tobacco, tea, coffee, chocolate, newspapers, books, pictures, clocks, toys, china, glassware, pewter, silver plate, soap, razors, furniture (including beds with mattresses, chairs, and chests of drawers), shoes, cotton cloth, and spare clothing. Demand for such products consistently outstripped the supply, causing prices for these items to rise faster than the price of foodstuffs throughout the century. But the demand for them continued unabated. Such goods were indulgences, of course, but they were also repositories of value in which families could invest their surplus cash, knowing that they could pawn them in hard times if cash were needed.

The exploding consumer economy of the eighteenth century spurred demand for manufactured goods of all sorts. But it also encouraged the provision of services. In eighteenth-century Britain, the service sector was the fastest-growing part of the economy, outstripping both agriculture and manufacturing. Almost everywhere in urban Europe, the eighteenth century was the golden age of the small shopkeeper. People bought more prepared foods and more ready-made (as opposed to personally tailored) clothing. Advertising became an important part of doing business, helping create demand for new products and shaping popular taste for changing fashions. Even political allegiances could be expressed through consumption when people purchased plates and glasses commemorating favorite rulers or causes.

The result of all these developments was a European economy vastly more complex, more specialized, more integrated, more commercialized, and more productive than anything the world had seen before.

***TOPSY-TURVY WORLD* BY JAN STEEN.** This Dutch painting depicts a household in the throes of the exploding consumer economy that hit Europe in the eighteenth century. Consumer goods ranging from silver and china to clothing and furniture cluttered the houses of ordinary people as never before.

# COLONIZATION AND TRADE IN THE SEVENTEENTH CENTURY

Many of the new consumer goods that propelled the economy of eighteenth-century Europe, including such staples as sugar, tobacco, tea, coffee, chocolate, china, and cotton cloth, were the products of Europe's growing colonial empires in Asia, Africa, and the Americas. The economic history of these empires is part of a broader pattern of accelerating global connection beginning in the late fifteenth century that witnessed an extraordinary exchange of peoples, plants, animals, diseases, goods, and culture between the African and Eurasian land mass on the one hand, and the Americas, Australia, and the Pacific Islands on the other. Historians refer to this as the "Columbian exchange"—a reference to Columbus's voyage in 1492—and many see it as a fundamental turning point in human history and in the history of the earth's ecology. The exchange brought new agricultural products to Europe—such as cane sugar, tobacco, corn, and the potato—and new domesticated animals to the Americas and Australia, transforming agriculture on both sides of the Atlantic and the Pacific Oceans, and reshaping the landscape itself. The transfer of human populations in the form of settlers, merchants, and slaves accelerated the process of cultural change for many peoples, even as other groups saw their cultures wiped out through violence or forced resettlement. The accompanying transfer of disease agents, meanwhile, had devastating effects—some historians suggest that between 50 and 90 percent of the pre-Columbian population of the Americas died from communicable diseases brought from Europe such as smallpox, cholera, influenza, typhoid, and measles.

Europe's growing colonial empires between the fifteenth and eighteenth centuries were thus a part of a series of fundamental changes that transformed people's lives, and their relation to their environment over the long term in many parts of the world. Europe's growing wealth during this period had complex causes, but it is impossible to imagine the prosperity of the eighteenth century without understanding this history of colonialism.

## *Spanish Colonialism*

After the exploits of the conquistadors, the Spanish established colonial governments in Peru and in Mexico, which they controlled from Madrid. In keeping with the doctrines of mercantilism, the Spanish government allowed only Spanish merchants to trade with their American colonies, requiring all colonial exports and imports to pass through a single Spanish port (first Seville, then later the more navigable port of Cadíz), where they were registered at the government-operated customs house. During the sixteenth century, this system worked reasonably well. The Spanish colonial economy was dominated by mining; the lucrative market for silver in East Asia even made it profitable to establish an outpost in Manila, where Spanish merchants exchanged Asian silk for South American bullion. But Spain also took steps to promote farming and ranching in Central and South America and established settlements in Florida and California.

Throughout this empire, a relatively small number of Spaniards had conquered complex and highly populous Native American societies. To rule these new territories, the Spanish replaced existing elites with Spanish administrators and churchmen. By and large, they did not attempt to uproot or eliminate existing native cultures but focused on controlling and exploiting native labor for their own profit, above all in extracting mineral resources. The native peoples of Spanish America already lived, for the most part, in large, well-organized villages and towns. The Spanish collected tribute from these communities and attempted to convert them to Catholicism but did not attempt to change their basic patterns of life.

The result was widespread cultural assimilation between the Spanish colonizers and the native populations, combined with a relatively high degree of intermarriage between them. Out of this reality emerged a complex and distinctive system of racial and social castes, with Spaniards at the top, peoples of mixed descent (combinations of Spanish, African, and Native American) in the middle, and nontribal American Indians at the bottom. In theory, these racial categories corresponded with class distinctions, but in practice race and class did not always coincide, and race itself was often a social fiction. Individuals of mixed descent who prospered economically often found ways to establish their "pure" Spanish ancestry by adopting the social practices that characterized elite (that is, Spanish) status. Spaniards always remained at the top of the social hierarchy, however, even when they fell into poverty.

The wealth of Spain's colonial trade tempted the merchants of other countries to win a share of the treasure for themselves. Probably the boldest challengers were the English, whose leading buccaneer was the sea dog Sir Francis Drake. Three times Drake raided the east and west coasts of Spanish America. In 1587 he attacked the Spanish fleet at its anchorage in Cadíz harbor; and in 1588 he played a key role in defeating the Spanish Armada. His career illustrates the mixture of piracy and patriotism that characterized England's early efforts to break into the colonial trade. Until the 1650s, however, the English could only dent the lucrative Spanish trade in bullion, hides, silks, and slaves.

## *French Colonialism*

French colonial policy matured under Louis XIV's mercantilist finance minister, Jean Baptiste Colbert, who regarded overseas expansion as an integral part of state economic policy. Realizing the profits to be made in responding to Europe's growing demand for sugar, he encouraged the development of sugar-producing colonies in the West Indies, the largest of which was Saint-Domingue (present-day Haiti). Sugar, virtually unknown in Christian Europe during the Middle Ages, became a popular luxury item in the late fifteenth century. It took the slave plantations of the Caribbean to turn sugar into a mass-market product. By 1750, slaves in Saint-Domingue produced 40 percent of the world's sugar and 50 percent of its coffee, exporting more sugar than Jamaica, Cuba, and Brazil combined. France also dominated the interior of the North American continent, where French traders brought furs to the American Indians and missionaries preached Christianity in a vast territory that stretched from Quebec to Louisiana. The financial returns from North America were never large, however. Furs, fish, and tobacco were exported to European markets but never matched the profits from the Caribbean

**ILLINOIS INDIANS TRADING WITH FRENCH SETTLERS.** This engraving from Nicholas De Fer's 1705 map of the Western Hemisphere illustrates the economic interdependence that developed between early French colonies and the native peoples of the surrounding region. ▪ ***How did this differ from relations between Native Americans and English agricultural communities on the Atlantic coast?***

sugar colonies or from the trading posts that the French maintained in India.

Like the Spanish colonies, the French colonies were established and administered as direct crown enterprises. French colonial settlements in North America were conceived mainly as military outposts and trading centers, and they were overwhelmingly populated by men. The elite of French colonial society were military officers and administrators sent from Paris. Below their ranks were fishermen, fur traders, small farmers, and common soldiers who constituted the bulk of French settlers in North America. Because the fishing and the fur trades relied on cooperative relationships with native peoples, a mutual economic interdependence grew up between the French colonies and the peoples of the surrounding region. Intermarriage, especially between French traders and native women, was common. These North American colonies remained dependent on the wages and supplies sent to them from the mother country. Only rarely did they become truly self-sustaining economic enterprises.

The phenomenally successful sugar plantations of the Caribbean had their own social structure, with slaves at the bottom, people of mixed African and European descent forming a middle layer, and wealthy European plantation owners at the top, controlling the lucrative trade with the outside world. Well over half of the sugar and coffee sent to France was resold and sent elsewhere to markets throughout Europe. Because the monarchy controlled the prices that colonial plantation owners could charge French merchants for their goods, traders in Europe who bought the goods for resale abroad could also make vast fortunes. Historians estimate that as many as a million of the twenty-five million inhabitants of France in the eighteenth century lived off the money flowing through this colonial trade, making the slave colonies of the Caribbean a powerful force for economic change in France.

## *English Colonialism*

England's own American colonies had no significant mineral wealth. As a result, English colonists sought profits by establishing agricultural settlements in North America and the Caribbean basin. Their first permanent, though ultimately unsuccessful, colony was founded in 1607 at Jamestown, Virginia. Over the next forty years, eighty thousand English emigrants would sail to more than twenty autonomous settlements in the New World. Many of these early settlers were driven by religious motives. The Pilgrims who landed at Plymouth, Massachusetts, in 1620 were one of many dissident groups, both Protestant and Catholic, that sought to escape the English government's religious intolerance by emigrating to North America. Strikingly, however, English colonists showed little interest in trying to convert Native American peoples to Christianity. Missionizing played a much larger role in Spanish efforts to colonize Central and South America and French efforts to penetrate the North American hinterlands.

These English colonies did not begin as crown enterprises as in the Spanish or French empires. Instead they were private ventures, either proprietary (as in Maryland and Pennsylvania) or joint-stock companies (as in Virginia and the Massachusetts Bay colony). Building on their experience in Ireland, English colonists established planned settlements known as plantations, in which they attempted to replicate as many features of English life as possible. Geography also contributed to the English settlement patterns, as the rivers and bays of the northeast Atlantic coast provided the first locations for colonists. Aside from the Hudson, however, there were no great rivers to lead colonists very far inland, and the English colonies clung to the coast and to each other.

Once they realized the profits to be made in colonial trade, however, the governments of both Oliver Cromwell

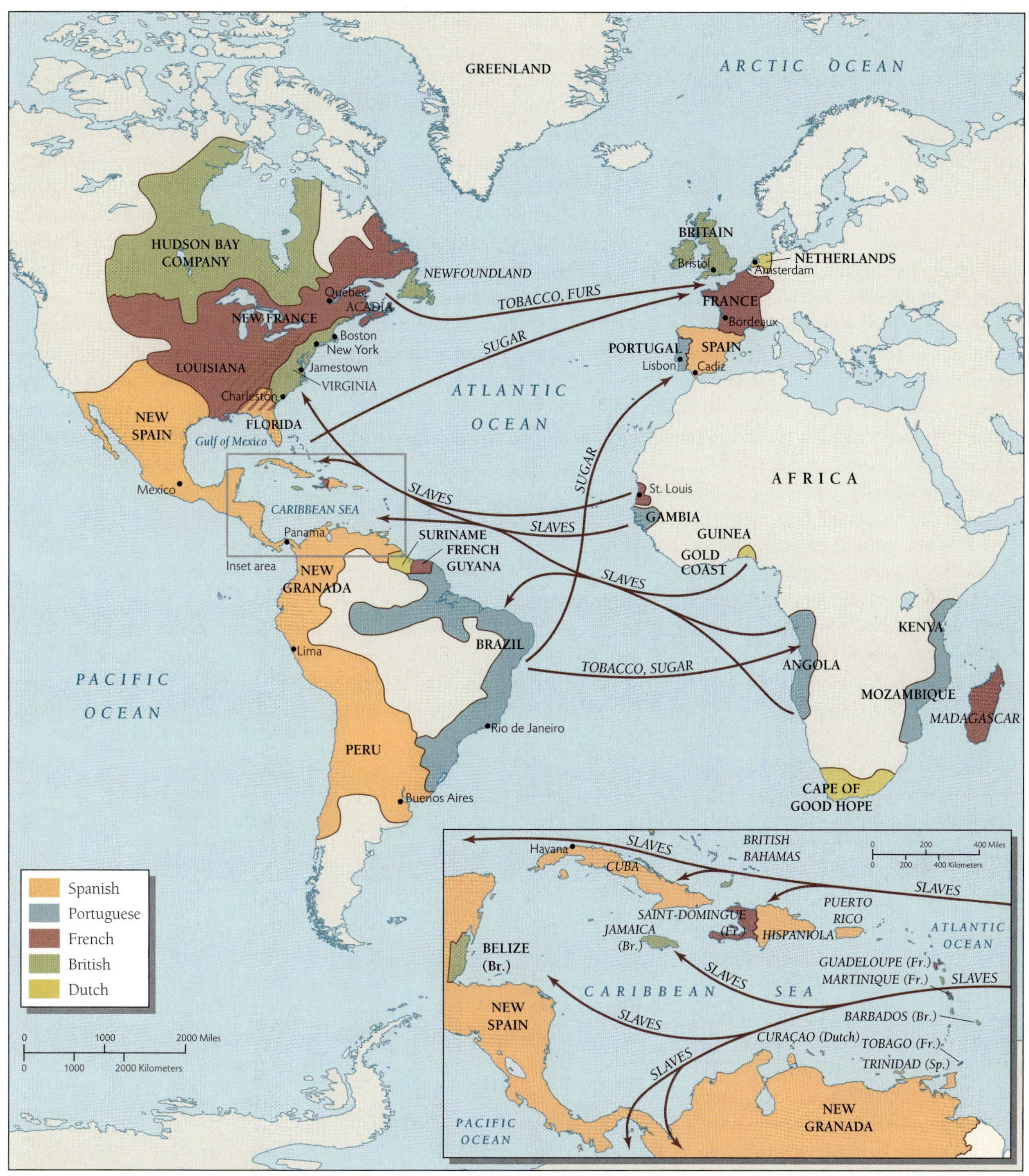


**THE ATLANTIC WORLD.** ▪ *What products did French and British colonies in North America provide to the European market in the eighteenth century?* ▪ *Which colonies were most dependent on slave labor?* ▪ *What products did they produce?* ▪ *Why were European governments so concerned with closely controlling the means by which certain products traveled from the colonies to European ports?*

and Charles II began to intervene in their management. Mercantilist-inspired navigation acts, passed in 1651 and 1660 decreed that exports from English colonies to the mother country be carried in English ships and forbade the direct exporting of "enumerated" products, such as sugar and tobacco, directly from the colonies to foreign ports. The English sugar-producing colonies competed directly with the French, and during the eighteenth century, profits from the tiny islands of Jamaica and Barbados were worth more than all of British imports from China and India combined. Tobacco, which was first brought to Europe by the Spaniards, became profitable as smoking caught on in Europe in the seventeenth century, popularized by English explorers who learned about it from Native Americans in Virginia. Governments at first joined the church in condemning it, but eventually encouraged its production and consumption, realizing the profits to be made from the trade.

The early English colonies in North America relied on fishing and the fur trade for their exports, but they soon grew into agricultural communities populated by small- and medium-scale landholders for whom the key to wealth was control over land. In part this reflected the kinds of people recruited by the private colonial enterprises for settlement in North America. But the focus on agriculture also resulted from the demographic catastrophe that struck the native populations of the Atlantic seaboard during the second half of the sixteenth century. European diseases—brought by Spanish armies and by the French, British, and Portuguese fisherman who frequented the rich fishing banks off the New England coast—had already decimated the native peoples of eastern North America even before the first European colonists set foot there. By the early seventeenth century, a great deal of rich agricultural land had been abandoned simply because there were no longer enough native farmers to till it—one reason that many native groups initially welcomed the new arrivals.

Unlike the Spanish, English colonists along the Atlantic seaboard had neither the need nor the opportunity to control a large native labor force. What they wanted, rather, was complete and exclusive control over native lands. To this end, the English colonists soon set out to eliminate, through expulsion and massacre, the indigenous peoples of their colonies. There were exceptions—in the Quaker colony of Pennsylvania, colonists and Native Americans maintained friendly relations for more than half a century. In the Carolinas, on the other hand, there was widespread enslavement of native peoples, either for sale to the West Indies or, from the 1690s, to work on the rice plantations along the coast. Elsewhere, however, attempts to enslave the native peoples of North American failed. When English planters looked for bond laborers, they either recruited indentured servants from England (most of whom would be freed after a specified period of service) or purchased African captives (who would usually be enslaved for life).

In contrast to the Spanish and French colonies, intermarriage between English colonists and native populations was rare. Instead, a rigid racial division emerged that distinguished all Europeans from all Native Americans and Africans. Intermarriage between natives and Africans was relatively common, but between the English and the native peoples of the colonies an unbridgeable gulf developed.

## *Dutch Colonialism*

Until the 1670s, the Dutch controlled the most prosperous commercial empire of the seventeenth century. Although some Dutch settlements were established, including one at the Cape of Good Hope in modern-day South Africa, Dutch

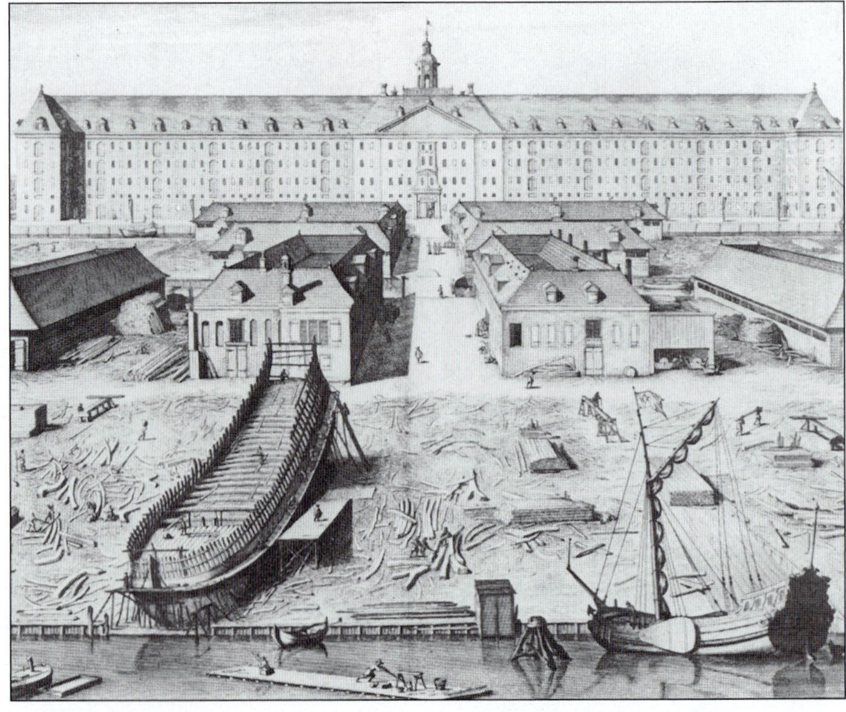

**THE DUTCH EAST INDIA COMPANY WAREHOUSE AND TIMBER WHARF AT AMSTERDAM.** The substantial warehouse, the stockpiles of lumber, and the company ship under construction in the foreground illustrate the degree to which overseas commerce could stimulate the economy of the mother country.

colonialism generally followed the "fort and factory" model established by the Portuguese in Asia. In Southeast Asia, the Dutch East India Company, founded in 1602, seized control of Sumatra, Borneo, and the Moluccas (Spice Islands), driving Portuguese traders from an area they had previously dominated and establishing a Dutch monopoly within Europe over pepper, cinnamon, nutmeg, mace, and cloves. The Dutch also secured an exclusive right to trade with Japan and maintained military and trading outposts in China and India as well. In the Western Hemisphere, however, their achievements were less spectacular. After a series of trade wars with England, in 1667 they formally surrendered their colony of New Amsterdam (subsequently renamed New York), retaining only Surinam (off the northern coast of South America) and Curaçao and Tobago (in the West Indies). Although the Dutch dominated the seventeenth-century slave trade with Africa, they lost this position to the British after 1713.

***THE DEFENSE OF CADÍZ AGAINST THE ENGLISH* BY FRANCISCO ZURBARAN.** The rivalry between European powers that played out over the new colonial possessions further proved the decline of Spain, which lost the island of Jamaica and ships in the harbor of Cadíz to the English in the 1650s.

The Dutch also pioneered new financial mechanisms for investing in colonial enterprises. One of the most important of these was the joint-stock company, of which the Dutch East India Company was among the first. Such companies raised cash by selling shares in their enterprise to investors. Even though the investors might not take any role in managing the company, they were joint owners of the business and therefore entitled to a share in the profits. Initially, the Dutch East India Company intended to pay off its investors ten years after its founding, but the directors soon recognized the impossibility of this plan. By 1612, the company's assets—ships, wharves, warehouses, and cargoes—were scattered around the globe. Moreover, its commercial prospects were continuing to improve. The directors therefore urged investors anxious to realize their profits to sell their shares on the Amsterdam stock exchange to other investors, thereby ensuring the continued operation of their enterprise and, in the process, establishing a method of continuous business financing that would soon spread elsewhere in Europe.

## Colonial Rivalries

The fortunes of these colonial empires changed dramatically in the course of the seventeenth and early eighteenth centuries. Spain proved unable to defend its early monopoly over colonial trade, and in 1650 the Spanish suffered a crippling blow when they were forced to surrender Jamaica and several treasure ships lying off of the Spanish harbor of Cadíz. By 1700, although Spain still possessed a colonial empire, it lay at the mercy of its more dynamic rivals. Portugal, too, found it impossible to prevent foreign penetration of its colonial empire. In 1703, the English signed a treaty with Portugal allowing English merchants to export woolens duty free into Portugal and allowing Portugal to ship its wines duty free into England. Access to Portugal also led British merchants to trade with the Portuguese colony of Brazil, an important sugar producer and the largest of all the American markets for African slaves. In the eighteenth century, English merchants would dominate these Brazilian trade routes.

The 1713 Treaty of Utrecht opened a new era of colonial rivalries. The biggest losers were the Dutch, who gained only a guarantee of their own borders, and the Spanish, who were forced to concede to Britain the right to market slaves in the Spanish colonies. The winners were the British (who acquired large chunks of territory in North America) and to a lesser extent, the French, who retained Quebec and other territories in North America, as well as their foothold in India. The eighteenth century would witness a continuing struggle between Britain and France for control over the expanding commerce that now bound the European economy to the Americas and to Asia.

## THE TRIANGULAR TRADE IN SUGAR AND SLAVES

During the eighteenth century, European colonial trade came to be dominated by trans-Atlantic routes that developed in response to the increased demand for sugar and tobacco and the corresponding market for slaves to produce these goods on American and Caribbean plantations. In this "triangular" trade, naval superiority gave Britain a decisive advantage over its French, Spanish, Portuguese, and Dutch rivals. Typically, a British ship might begin its voyage from New England with a consignment of rum and sail to Africa, where the rum would be exchanged for a cargo of slaves. From the west coast of Africa the ship would then cross the South Atlantic to the sugar colonies of Jamaica or Barbados, where slaves would be traded for molasses. It would then make the final leg of the journey back to New England, where the molasses would be made into rum. A variant triangle might see cheap manufactured goods move from England to Africa, where they would be traded for slaves. Those slaves would then be shipped to Virginia and exchanged for tobacco, which would be shipped to England and processed there for sale throughout Europe.

The cultivation of New World sugar and tobacco depended on slave labor. As European demand for these products increased, so too did the traffic in enslaved Africans. At the height of the Atlantic slave trade in the eighteenth century, seventy-five to ninety thousand Africans were shipped across the Atlantic yearly: at least six million in the eighteenth century, out of a total of over eleven million for the entire history of the trade. About 35 percent went to English and French Caribbean plantations, 5 percent (roughly five hundred thousand) to North America, and the rest to the Portuguese colony of Brazil and to the Spanish colonies in Central and South America. By the 1780s, there were more than five hundred thousand slaves on the largest French plantation island, Saint-Domingue, and at least two hundred thousand on its English counterpart, Jamaica.

Although run as a monopoly by various governments in the sixteenth and early seventeenth centuries, the slave trade in the eighteenth century was open to private entre-

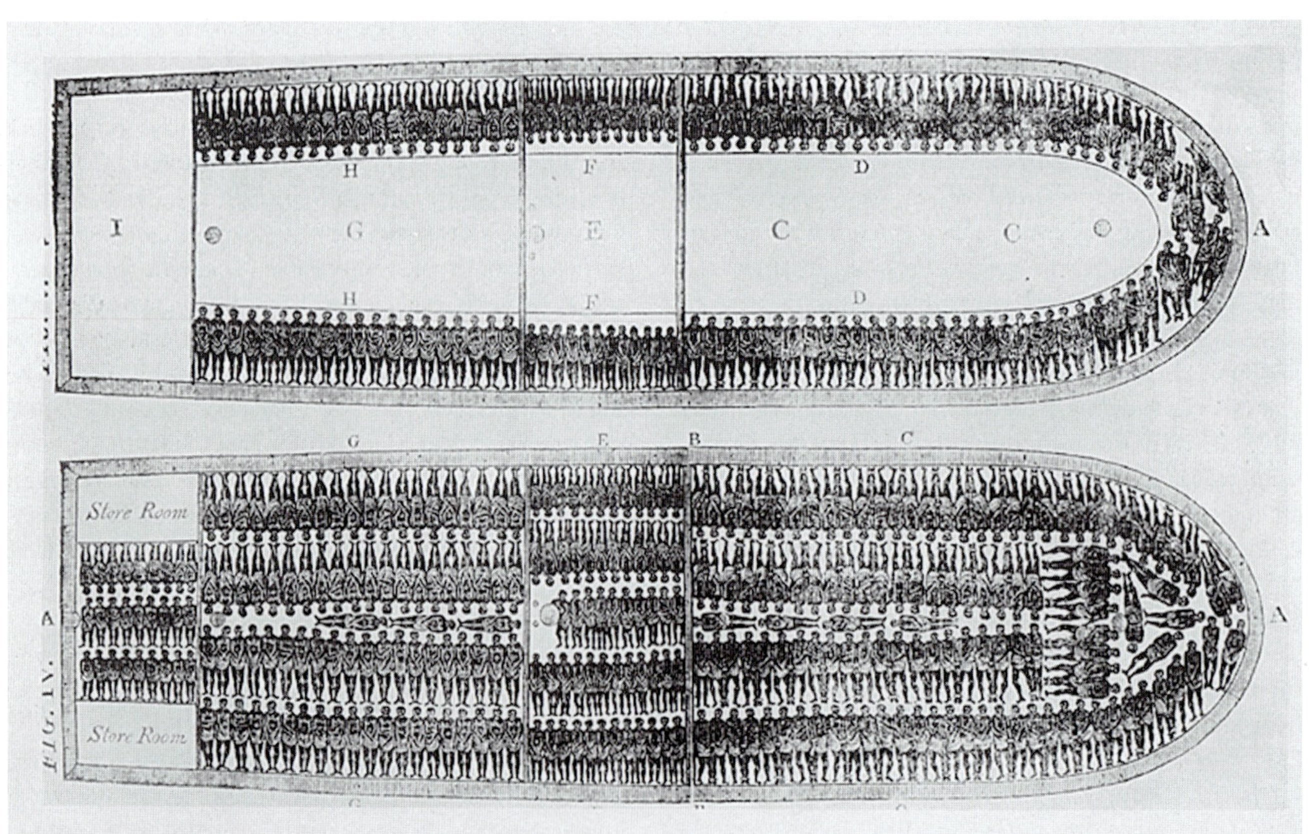


**HOW SLAVES WERE STOWED ABOARD SHIP DURING THE MIDDLE PASSAGE.** Men were "housed" on the right; women on the left; children in the middle. The human cargo was jammed onto platforms six feet wide without sufficient headroom to permit an adult to sit up. This diagram is from evidence gathered by English abolitionists and depicts conditions on the Liverpool slave ship *Brookes*.

preneurs who operated ports on the West African coast. These traders exchanged Indian cloth, metal goods, rum, and firearms with African slave merchants in return for their human cargo, who would then be packed by the hundreds into the holds of slave ships for the gruesome Middle Passage across the Atlantic (so called to distinguish it from the slave ship's voyage from Europe to Africa, and then from the colonies back to Europe). Shackled belowdecks without sanitary facilities, the captive men, women, and children suffered horribly. The mortality rate, however, remained at about 10 or 11 percent, not much higher than the rate for a normal sea voyage of a hundred days or more. Since traders had to invest as much as £10 per slave in their enterprise, they were generally anxious to ensure that their consignment would reach its destination in good enough shape to be sold for a profit.

## The Commercial Rivalry between Britain and France

British dominance of the slave trade gave it decisive advantages in its colonial struggles with France. As one Englishman wrote in 1749, the slave trade had provided "an unexhastible fund of wealth to this nation." But even apart from the slave trade, the value of colonial commerce was increasing dramatically during the eighteenth century. French colonial trade, valued at 25 million livres in 1716, rose to 263 million livres in 1789. In England, during roughly the same period, foreign trade increased in value from £10 million to £40 million, the latter amount more than twice that for France.

The growing value of colonial commerce tied the interests of governments and transoceanic merchants together in an increasingly tight embrace. Merchants engaged in the colonial trade depended on their governments to protect and defend their overseas investments; but governments depended in turn on merchants and their financial backers to build the ships and sustain the trade on which national power depended. In the eighteenth century, even the ability to wage war rested largely (and increasingly) on a government's ability to borrow the necessary funds from wealthy investors and then to pay back those debts, with interest, over time. As it did in commerce, so too in finance, Britain came to enjoy a decisive advantage in this respect over France. The Bank of England, founded in the 1690s, managed the English national debt with great success, providing the funds required for war by selling shares to investors, then repaying those investors at moderate rates of interest. In contrast, chronic governmental indebtedness forced the French crown to borrow at ruinously high rates of interest, provoking a series of fiscal crises that in 1789 finally led to the collapse of the French monarchy.

## War and Empire in the Eighteenth-Century World

After 1713, western Europe remained largely at peace for a generation. In 1740, however, that peace was shattered when Frederick the Great of Prussia took advantage of the accession of a woman, the empress Maria Theresa, to the throne of Austria to seize the Austrian province of Silesia (discussed earlier in this chapter). In the resulting War of the Austrian Succession, France and Spain fought on the side of Prussia, hoping to reverse some of the losses they had suffered in the Treaty of Utrecht. As they had done since the 1690s, Britain and the Dutch Republic sided with Austria. Like those earlier wars, this war quickly spread beyond the frontiers of Europe. In India, the British East India Company lost control over the coastal area of Madras to its French rival; but in North America, British colonists from New England captured the important French fortress of Louisbourg on Cape Breton Island, hoping to put a stop to French interference with their fishing and shipping. When the war finally ended in 1748, Britain recovered Madras and returned Louisbourg to France.

Eight years later, these colonial conflicts reignited when Prussia once again attacked Austria. This time, however, Prussia allied itself with Great Britain. Austria found support from both France and Russia. In Europe, the Seven Years' War (1756–1763) ended in stalemate. In India and North America, however, the war had decisive consequences. In India, mercenary troops employed by the British East India Company joined with native allies to eliminate their French competitors. In North America (where the conflict was known as the French and Indian War), British troops captured both Louisbourg and Quebec and also drove French forces from the Ohio River Valley and the Great Lakes. By the Treaty of Paris in 1763, which brought the Seven Years' War to an end, France formally surrendered both Canada and India to the British. Six years later, the French East India Company was dissolved.

## The American Revolution

Along the Atlantic seaboard, however, the rapidly growing British colonies were beginning to chafe at rule from London. To recover some of the costs of the Seven Years'

War and to pay for the continuing costs of protecting its colonial subjects, the British Parliament imposed a series of new taxes on its American colonies. These taxes were immediately unpopular. Colonists complained that because they had no representatives in Parliament, they were being taxed without their consent—a fundamental violation of their rights as British subjects. They also complained that British restrictions on colonial trade, particularly the requirement that certain goods pass first through British ports before being shipped to the Continent, were strangling American livelihoods and making it impossible to pay even the king's legitimate taxes.

The British government, led since 1760 by the young and inexperienced King George III, responded to these complaints with a badly calculated mixture of vacillation and force. Various taxes were imposed and then withdrawn in the face of colonial resistance. In 1773, however, when East India Company tea was dumped in Boston Harbor by rebellious colonials objecting to the customs duties that had been imposed on it, the British government closed the port of Boston and curtailed the colony's representative institutions. These "Coercive Acts" galvanized the support of the other American colonies for Massachusetts. In 1774, representatives from all the American colonies met at Philadelphia to form the Continental Congress to negotiate with the crown over their grievances. In April 1775, however, local militiamen at Lexington and Concord clashed with regular British troops sent to disarm them. Soon thereafter, the Continental Congress began raising an army, and an outright rebellion erupted against the British government.

On July 4, 1776, the thirteen colonies formally declared their independence from Great Britain. During the first two years of the war, it seemed unlikely that such independence would ever become a reality. In 1778, however, France, anxious to undermine the colonial hegemony Great Britain had established since 1713, joined the war on the side of the Americans. Spain entered the war in support of France, hoping to recover Gibraltar and Florida (the latter lost in 1763 to Britain). In 1780, Britain also declared war on the Dutch Republic for continuing to trade with the rebellious colonies. Now facing a coalition of its colonial rivals, Great Britain saw the war turn against it. In 1781, combined land and sea operations by French and American troops

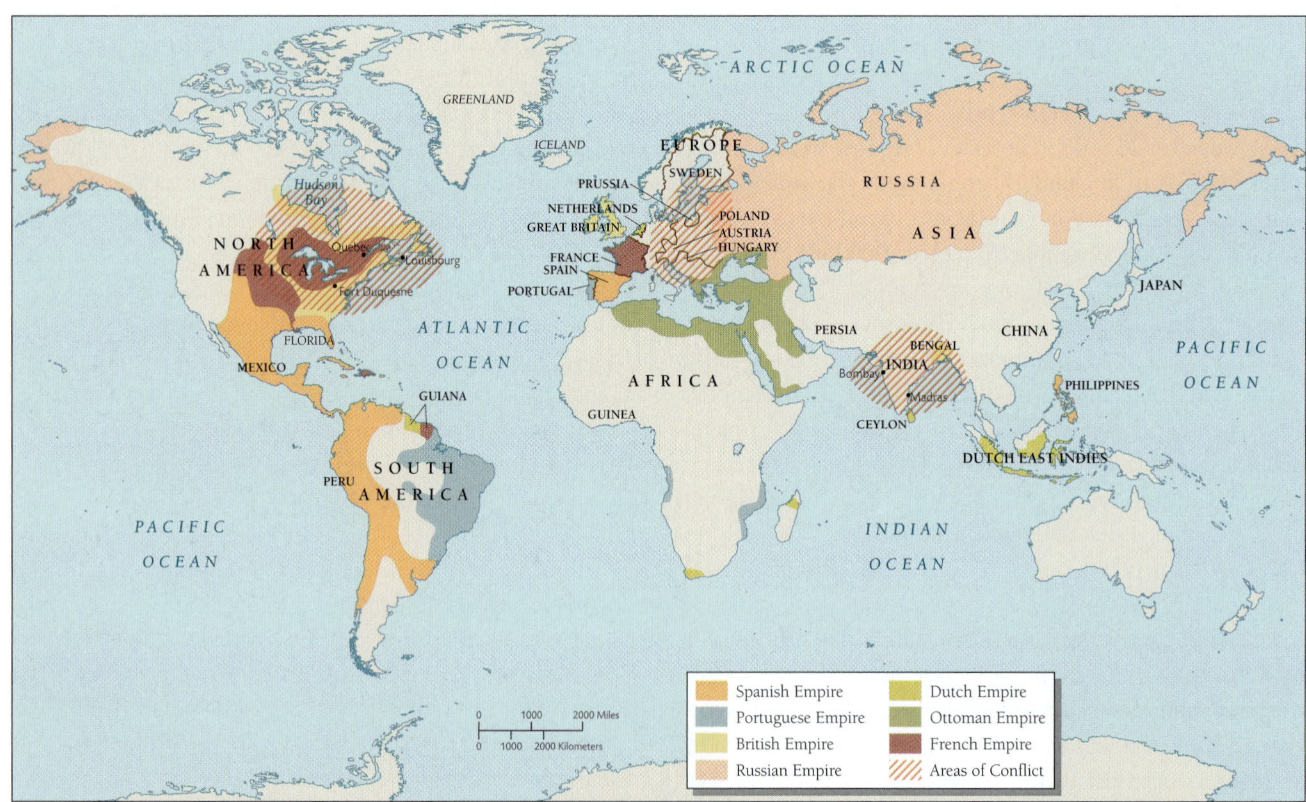


**THE SEVEN YEARS' WAR, 1756–1763.** ▪ *What continents were involved in the Seven Years' War?* ▪ *What was the impact of naval power on the outcome of the war?* ▪ *What were the consequences for the colonies involved in the conflict?*

# Analyzing Primary Sources

## *The American Declaration of Independence*

*The Declaration of Independence, issued from Philadelphia on July 4, 1776, is perhaps the most famous single document of American history. But its familiarity does not lesssen its interest as a piece of political philosophy. The indebtedness of the document's authors to the ideas of John Locke will be obvious from the selections here. But Locke, in turn, drew many of his ideas about the contractual and conditional nature of human government from the conciliarist thinkers of the fifteenth and early sixteenth centuries. The appeal of absolutism notwithstanding, the declaration shows how vigorous the medieval tradition of contractual, limited government remained at the end of the eighteenth century.*

hen in the course of human events, it becomes necessary for one people to dissolve the political bonds which have connected them with another, and to assume among the powers of the earth the separate and equal station to which the Laws of Nature and of Nature's God entitle them, a decent respect to the opinions of mankind requires that they should declare the causes which impel them to the separation. . . . We hold these truths to be self-evident, that all men are created equal, that they are endowed by their Creator with certain unalienable rights, that among these are Life, Liberty and the pursuit of Happiness. . . . That to secure these rights, Governments are instituted among men, deriving their just powers from the consent of the governed. . . . That whenever any form of Government becomes destructive of these ends, it is the Right of the People to alter or to abolish it, and to institute new Government, laying its foundation upon such principles and organizing its power in such form, as to them shall seem most likely to effect their Safety and Happiness. Prudence, indeed, will dictate that Governments long established should not be changed for light and transient causes; and accordingly all experience has shown, that mankind are more disposed to suffer, while evils are sufferable, than to right themselves by abolishing the forms to which they are accustomed. But when a long train of abuses and usurpations, pursuing invariably the same Object, evinces a design to reduce them under absolute despotism, it is their right, it is their duty, to throw off such Government, and to provide new Guards for their future security. . . . Such has been the patient sufferance of these Colonies; and such is now the necessity which constrains them to alter their former Systems of Government. . . .

### *Questions for Analysis*

1. Who are "the people" mentioned in the first sentence of this selection? Are the rights of "the people" the same as individual rights? How did the authors of this declaration come to think of themselves as the representatives of such a body?
2. What is the purpose of government, according to this document? Who gets to decide if the government is doing its job?
3. How would Robert Filmer or Bossuet have viewed such a declaration? How might John Locke have defended it?

forced the surrender of the main British army at Yorktown in Virginia. As the defeated British soldiers surrendered their weapons, their band played a song titled "The World Turned Upside Down."

Negotiations for peace began soon after the defeat at Yorktown but were not concluded until September 1783. The Treaty of Paris left Great Britain in control of Canada and Gibraltar. Spain retained its possessions west of the Mississippi River and recovered Florida. The United States gained its independence; its western border was fixed on the Mississippi River, and it secured valuable fishing rights off the eastern coast of Canada. France gained only the satisfaction of defeating its colonial rival; but even that satisfaction was short lived. Six years later, the massive debts France had incurred in supporting the American Revolution helped bring about another, very different kind of revolution in France that would permanently alter the history of Europe.

## CONCLUSION

Seen in this light, the American War of Independence was the final military conflict in a century-long struggle between Great Britain and France for colonial dominance. But the consequences of Britain's defeat in 1783 were far less significant than might have been expected. Even after American independence, Great Britain would remain the most important trading partner for its former American colonies, while elsewhere around the globe, the commercial dominance Britain had already established would continue to grow. The profits of slavery certainly helped fuel the eighteenth-century British economy; by the end of the century, however, British trade and manufacturing had reached such high levels of productivity that even the abolition of the slave trade (in 1808) and of slavery itself (in 1833) did not impede its continuing growth.

The economic prosperity of late-eighteenth-century Britain was mirrored to some degree throughout northwestern Europe. Improved transportation systems, more reliable food supplies, and growing quantities of consumer goods brought improved standards of living to large numbers of Europeans, even as the overall population of Europe was rising faster after 1750 than it had ever done before. Population growth was especially rapid in the cities, where a new urban

| SEVENTEENTH- AND EIGHTEENTH-CENTURY WARS | |
|---|---|
| Glorious Revolution | 1688–1689 |
| War of the League of Augsburg | 1689–1697 |
| War of the Spanish Succession | 1702–1713 |
| Seven Years' War | 1756–1763 |
| American Revolution | 1775–1783 |
| The Russo-Turkish War | 1787–1792 |

## After You Read This Chapter

Visit StudySpace for quizzes, additional review materials, and multi-media documents. **wwnorton.com/studyspace**

### REVIEWING THE OBJECTIVES

- Absolutist rulers claimed a monopoly of power and authority within their realms. What did they do to achieve this goal?
- Monarchies in both western and eastern Europe adopted the absolutist system, but they faced different challenges. How did the absolutist monarchies in eastern Europe differ from their counterparts in western Europe?
- England developed an alternative to absolutism by the end of the seventeenth century. What was it?
- The commercial revolution of the eighteenth century resulted in major changes in the European economy. What were they?
- Colonial expansion in the Atlantic world and the African slave trade connected Africa and the Americas with Europe in new ways. Who profited most from the Atlantic's new political and economic relationships?

middle class was emerging whose tastes drove the market for goods and whose opinions were reshaping the world of ideas.

But the prosperity of late-eighteenth-century Europe remained very unevenly distributed. In the cities, rich and poor lived separate lives in separate neighborhoods. In the countryside, regions bypassed by the developing commercial economy of the period continued to suffer from hunger and famine, just as they had done in the sixteenth and seventeenth centuries. In eastern Europe the contrasts between rich and poor were even more extreme, as many peasants fell into a new style of serfdom that would last until the end of the nineteenth century. War too remained a fact of European life, bringing death and destruction to hundreds of thousands of people across the continent and around the world—yet another consequence of the worldwide reach of these European colonial empires.

Political change was more gradual. Throughout Europe, the powers of governments steadily increased. Administrators became more numerous, more efficient, and more demanding, partly to meet the mounting costs of war but also because governments were starting to take on a much wider range of responsibilities for the welfare of their subjects. Despite the increasing scope of government, however, the structure and principles of government changed relatively little. Apart from Great Britain and the Dutch Republic, the great powers of eighteenth-century Europe were still governed by rulers who styled themselves as absolutist monarchs in the mold of Louis XIV. By 1789, however, the European world was a vastly different place than it had been a century before, when the Sun King had dominated European politics. The full extent of those differences was about to be revealed.

## PEOPLE, IDEAS, AND EVENTS IN CONTEXT

- What did **LOUIS XIV** of France, **PETER THE GREAT** of Russia, **FREDERICK THE GREAT** of Prussia, and **MARIA THERESA** of Austria have in common? How did they deal with those who resisted their attempts to impose absolutist rule?
- What limits to royal power were recognized in Great Britain as a result of the **GLORIOUS REVOLUTION**?
- What does the **TREATY OF UTRECHT** (1713) tell us about the diminished influence of Spain and the corresponding rise of Britain as a European power?
- How did European monarchies use the economic theory known as **MERCANTILISM** to strengthen the power and wealth of their kingdoms?
- What was the **COLUMBIAN EXCHANGE**? What combination of demographic, cultural, and ecological transformations are contained within this idea?
- How did the **COMMERCIAL REVOLUTION** change social life in Europe?
- What was the **TRIANGULAR TRADE** and how was it related to the growth of commerce in the Atlantic world during this period?
- What debt does the American **DECLARATION OF INDEPENDENCE** owe to the ideas of the English political thinker **JOHN LOCKE**?

## CONSEQUENCES

- Was any European monarch's power ever really *absolute*?
- What do you suppose had more effect on the lives of ordinary Europeans: the rise of absolutist regimes or the commercial revolution of the eighteenth century?
- In a world in which a British merchant's fortune depended on the price of molasses in Boston, the demand for African slaves in Jamaica, and the price of rum in Senegal, could one already speak of *globalization*?

# Rulers of Principal States

## THE CAROLINGIAN DYNASTY

Pepin of Heristal, Mayor of the Palace, 687–714
Charles Martel, Mayor of the Palace, 715–741
Pepin III, Mayor of the Palace, 741–751; King, 751–768
Charlemagne, King, 768–814; Emperor, 800–814
Louis the Pious, Emperor, 814–840

### Middle Kingdoms

Lothair, Emperor, 840–855
Louis (Italy), Emperor, 855–875
Charles (Provence), King, 855–863
Lothair II (Lorraine), King, 855–869

### West Francia

Charles the Bald, King, 840–877; Emperor, 875–877
Louis II, King, 877–879
Louis III, King, 879–882
Carloman, King, 879–884

### East Francia

Ludwig, King, 840–876
Carloman, King, 876–880
Ludwig, King, 876–882
Charles the Fat, Emperor, 876–887

## HOLY ROMAN EMPERORS

### Saxon Dynasty

Otto I, 962–973
Otto II, 973–983
Otto III, 983–1002
Henry II, 1002–1024

### Franconian Dynasty

Conrad II, 1024–1039
Henry III, 1039–1056
Henry IV, 1056–1106
HenryV, 1106–1125
Lothair II (Saxony), 1125–1137

### Hohenstaufen Dynasty

Conrad III, 1138–1152
Frederick I (Barbarossa), 1152–1190
Henry VI, 1190–1197
Philip of Swabia, 1198–1208 } Rivals
Otto IV (Welf), 1198–1215 }
Frederick II, 1220–1250
Conrad IV, 1250–1254

### Interregnum, 1254–1273

### Emperors from Various Dynasties

Rudolf I (Habsburg), 1273–1291
Adolf (Nassau), 1292–1298
Albert I (Habsburg), 1298–1308
Henry VII (Luxemburg), 1308–1313
Ludwig IV (Wittelsbach), 1314–1347
Charles IV (Luxemburg), 1347–1378
Wenceslas (Luxemburg), 1378–1400
Rupert (Wittelsbach), 1400–1410
Sigismund (Luxemburg), 1410–1437

### Habsburg Dynasty

Albert II, 1438–1439
Frederick III, 1440–1493

Maximilian I, 1493–1519
Charles V, 1519–1556
Ferdinand I, 1556–1564
Maximilian II, 1564–1576
Rudolf II, 1576–1612
Matthias, 1612–1619
Ferdinand II, 1619–1637
Ferdinand III, 1637–1657
Leopold I, 1658–1705
Joseph I, 1705–1711
Charles VI, 1711–1740
Charles VII (not a Habsburg), 1742–1745
Francis I, 1745–1765
Joseph II, 1765–1790
Leopold II, 1790–1792
Francis II, 1792–1806

## RULERS OF FRANCE FROM HUGH CAPET

### Capetian Dynasty

Hugh Capet, 987–996
Robert II, 996–1031
Henry I, 1031–1060
Philip I, 1060–1108
Louis VI, 1108–1137
Louis VII, 1137–1180
Philip II (Augustus), 1180–1223
Louis VIII, 1223–1226
Louis IX (St. Louis), 1226–1270
Philip III, 1270–1285
Philip IV, 1285–1314
Louis X, 1314–1316
Philip V, 1316–1322
Charles IV, 1322–1328

### Valois Dynasty

Philip VI, 1328–1350
John, 1350–1364
Charles V, 1364–1380
Charles VI, 1380–1422
Charles VII, 1422–1461
Louis XI, 1461–1483
Charles VIII, 1483–1498
Louis XII, 1498–1515
Francis I, 1515–1547
Henry II, 1547–1559
Francis II, 1559–1560
Charles IX, 1560–1574
Henry III, 1574–1589

### Bourbon Dynasty

Henry IV, 1589–1610
Louis XIII, 1610–1643
Louis XIV, 1643–1715
Louis XV, 1715–1774
Louis XVI, 1774–1792

### After 1792

First Republic, 1792–1799
Napoleon Bonaparte, First Consul, 1799–1804
Napoleon I, Emperor, 1804–1814
Louis XVIII (Bourbon dynasty), 1814–1824
Charles X (Bourbon dynasty), 1824–1830
Louis Philippe, 1830–1848
Second Republic, 1848–1852
Napoleon III, Emperor, 1852–1870
Third Republic, 1870–1940
Pétain regime, 1940–1944
Provisional government, 1944–1946
Fourth Republic, 1946–1958
Fifth Republic, 1958–

## RULERS OF ENGLAND

### Anglo-Saxon Dynasty

Alfred the Great, 871–899
Edward the Elder, 899–924
Ethelstan, 924–939
Edmund I, 939–946
Edred, 946–955
Edwy, 955–959
Edgar, 959–975
Edward the Martyr, 975–978
Ethelred the Unready, 978–1016
Canute, 1016–1035 (Danish Nationality)
Harold I, 1035–1040
Hardicanute, 1040–1042
Edward the Confessor, 1042–1066
Harold II, 1066

### House of Normandy

William I (the Conqueror), 1066–1087
William II, 1087–1100
Henry I, 1100–1135
Stephen, 1135–1154

### House of Plantagenet

Henry II, 1154–1189
Richard I, 1189–1199
John, 1199–1216
Henry III, 1216–1272
Edward I, 1272–1307
Edward II, 1307–1327
Edward III, 1327–1377
Richard II, 1377–1399

### House of Lancaster

Henry IV, 1399–1413
Henry V, 1413–1422
Henry VI, 1422–1461

### House of York

Edward IV, 1461–1483
Edward V, 1483
Richard III, 1483–1485

### House of Tudor

Henry VII, 1485–1509
Henry VIII, 1509–1547
Edward VI, 1547–1553
Mary, 1553–1558
Elizabeth I, 1558–1603

### House of Stuart

James I, 1603–1625
Charles I, 1625–1649

### Commonwealth and Protectorate, 1649–1659

### House of Stuart Restored

Charles II, 1660–1685
James II, 1685–1688
William III and Mary II, 1689–1694
William III alone, 1694–1702
Anne, 1702–1714

### House of Hanover

George I, 1714–1727
George II, 1727–1760
George III, 1760–1820
George IV, 1820–1830
William IV, 1830–1837
Victoria, 1837–1901

### House of Saxe-Coburg-Gotha

Edward VII, 1901–1910
George V, 1910–1917

### House of Windsor

George V, 1917–1936
Edward VIII, 1936
George VI, 1936–1952
Elizabeth II, 1952–

## RULERS OF AUSTRIA AND AUSTRIA-HUNGARY

*Maximilian I (Archduke), 1493–1519
*Charles V, 1519–1556
*Ferdinand I, 1556–1564
*Maximilian II, 1564–1576
*Rudolf II, 1576–1612
*Matthias, 1612–1619
*Ferdinand II, 1619–1637
*Ferdinand III, 1637–1657
*Leopold I, 1658–1705
*Joseph I, 1705–1711
*Charles VI, 1711–1740
Maria Theresa, 1740–1780
*Joseph II, 1780–1790
*Leopold II, 1790–1792
*Francis II, 1792–1835 (Emperor of Austria as Francis I after 1804)
Ferdinand I, 1835–1848
Francis Joseph, 1848–1916 (after 1867 Emperor of Austria and King of Hungary)
Charles I, 1916–1918 (Emperor of Austria and King of Hungary)
Republic of Austria, 1918–1938 (dictatorship after 1934)
Republic restored, under Allied occupation, 1945–1956
Free Republic, 1956–

*also bore title of Holy Roman Emperor

## RULERS OF PRUSSIA AND GERMANY

*Frederick I, 1701–1713
*Frederick William I, 1713–1740
*Frederick II (the Great), 1740–1786
*Frederick William II, 1786–1797
*Frederick William III,1797–1840
*Frederick William IV, 1840–1861
*William I, 1861–1888 (German Emperor after 1871)
Frederick III, 1888
*William II, 1888–1918
Weimar Republic, 1918–1933
Third Reich (Nazi Dictatorship), 1933–1945
Allied occupation, 1945–1952
Division into Federal Republic of Germany in west and German Democratic Republic in east, 1949–1991
Federal Republic of Germany (united), 1991–

*Kings of Prussia

## RULERS OF RUSSIA

Ivan III, 1462–1505
Vasily III, 1505–1533
Ivan IV, 1533–1584
Theodore I, 1534–1598
Boris Godunov, 1598–1605
Theodore II,1605
Vasily IV, 1606–1610
Michael, 1613–1645
Alexius, 1645–1676
Theodore III, 1676–1682
Ivan V and Peter I, 1682–1689
Peter I (the Great), 1689–1725
Catherine I, 1725–1727
Peter II, 1727–1730
Anna, 1730–1740
Ivan VI, 1740–1741
EIlzabeth, 1741–1762
Peter III, 1762
Catherine II (the Great), 1762–1796
Paul, 1796–1801
Alexander I,1801–1825
Nicholas I, 1825–1855
Alexander II,1855–1881
Alexander III, 1881–1894
Nicholas II, 1894–1917
Soviet Republic, 1917–1991
Russian Federation, 1991–

## RULERS OF UNIFIED SPAIN

Ferdinand { and Isabella, 1479–1504
and Philip I, 1504–1506
and Charles I, 1506–1516 }
Charles I (Holy Roman Emperor Charles V), 1516–1556
Philip II, 1556–1598
Philip III, 1598–1621
Philip IV, 1621–1665
Charles II, 1665–1700
Philip V, 1700–1746
Ferdinand VI, 1746–1759
Charles III, 1759–1788
Charles IV, 1788–1808
Ferdinand VII, 1808
Joseph Bonaparte, 1808–1813
Ferdinand VII (restored), 1814–1833
Isabella II, 1833–1868
Republic, 1868–1870
Amadeo, 1870–1873
Republic, 1873–1874
Alfonso XII, 1874–1885
Alfonso XIII, 1886–1931
Republic, 1931–1939
Fascist Dictatorship, 1939–1975
Juan Carlos I, 1975–

## RULERS OF ITALY

Victor Emmanuel II, 1861–1878
Humbert I, 1878–1900
Victor Emmanuel III, 1900–1946
Fascist Dictatorship, 1922-1943 (maintained in northern Italy until 1945)
Humbert II, May 9–June 13, 1946
Republic, 1946–

## PROMINENT POPES

Silvester I, 314–335
Leo I, 440–461
Gelasius I, 492–496
Gregory I, 590–604
Nicholas I, 858–867
Silvester II, 999–1003
Leo IX, 1049–1054
Nicholas II, 1058–1061
Gregory VII, 1073–1085
Urban II, 1088–1099
Paschal II, 1099–1118
Alexander III, 1159–1181
Innocent III, 1198–1216
Gregory IX, 1227–1241
Innocent IV, 1243–1254
Boniface VIII, 1294–1303
John XXII, 1316–1334
Nicholas V, 1447–1455
Pius II, 1458–1464
Alexander VI, 1492–1503
Julius II, 1503–1513
Leo X, 1513–1521
Paul III, 1534–1549
Paul IV, 1555–1559
Sixtus V, 1585–1590
Urban VIII, 1623–1644
Gregory XVI, 1831–1846
Pius IX, 1846–1878
Leo XIII, 1878–1903
Pius X, 1903–1914
Benedict XV, 1914–1922
Pius XI, 1922–1939
Pius XII, 1939–1958
John XXIII, 1958–1963
Paul VI, 1963–1978
John Paul I, 1978
John Paul II, 1978–2005
Benedict XVI 2005–

# Further Readings

## CHAPTER 1

Aldred, Cyril. *The Egyptians*. 3d ed. London, 1998. An indispensable, lively overview of Egyptian culture and history by one of the great masters of Egyptology.

Baines, J., and J. Málek. *Atlas of Ancient Egypt*. Rev. ed. New York, 2000. A reliable, well-illustrated survey, with excellent maps.

Bottéro, Jean. *Everyday Life in Ancient Mesopotamia*. Trans. Antonia Nevill. Baltimore, MD, 2001. A wide-ranging, interdisciplinary account.

Bottéro, Jean. *Religion in Ancient Mesopotamia*. Chicago, 2001. An accessible, engaging survey.

George, Andrew, trans. *The Epic of Gilgamesh: A New Translation. The Babylonian Epic Poem and Other Texts in Akkadian and Sumerian*. New York and London, 1999. The newest and most reliable translation, which carefully distinguishes the chronological "layers" of this famous text; also includes many related texts.

Hodder, Ian. *The Leopard's Tale:Revealing the Mysteries of Çatalhöyük*. London and New York, 2006. The most up-to-date account of this fascinating archaeological site, written for general readers by the director of the excavation.

Hornung, Erik. *History of Ancient Egypt: An Introduction*. Ithaca, NY, 1999. Concise and authoritative.

Kemp, Barry J. *Ancient Egypt: Anatomy of a Civilization*. London, 1989. An imaginative examination of Egyptian social and intellectual history.

Leick, Gwendolyn. *The Babylonians: An Introduction*. London and New York, 2002. A wide-ranging survey of Babylonian civilization across the centuries.

Lichteim, Miriam. *Ancient Egyptian Literature: A Book of Readings*. 3 vols. Berkeley, CA, 1973–1980. A compilation used by students and scholars alike.

McDowell, A. G. *Village Life in Ancient Egypt: Laundry Lists and Love Songs*. Oxford, 1999. A fascinating collection of translated texts recovered from an Egyptian peasant village, dating from 1539 to 1075 B.C.E.

Mertz, Barbara. *Red Land, Black Land: Daily Life in Ancient Egypt*. Rev. ed. New York, 1990. Emphasizes the role of the Nile and the forbidding natural environment of Egypt.

Pollock, Susan. *Ancient Mesopotamia*. Cambridge, 1999. An advanced textbook that draws on theoretical anthropology to interpret Mesopotamian civilization up to 2100 B.C.E.

Redford, Donald B., ed. *The Oxford Encyclopedia of Ancient Egypt*. 3 vols. New York, 2001. An indispensible reference work, intended for both specialists and beginners.

Roaf, Michael. *Cultural Atlas of Mesopotamia and the Ancient Near East*. New York, 1990. An informative, authoritative, and lavishly illustrated guide, with excellent maps.

Robins, Gay. *The Art of Ancient Egypt*. London, 1997. An excellent survey, now the standard account.

Shafer, Byron E., ed. *Religion in Ancient Egypt: Gods, Myths, and Personal Practice*. London, 1991. A scholarly examination of Egyptian belief and ritual, with contributions from leading authorities.

Shaw, Ian, ed. *The Oxford History of Ancient Egypt*. Oxford, 2000. An outstanding collaborative survey of Egyptian history from the Stone Age to c. 300 C.E., with excellent bibliographical essays.

Smail, Daniel Lord. *On Deep History and the Brain*. Berkeley, 2008. A pioneering introduction to the historical uses of neuroscience and evolutionary biology.

Snell, Daniel C., ed. *A Companion to the Ancient Near East*. Oxford, 2005. A topical survey of recent scholarly work, particularly strong on society, economy, and culture.

Wengrow, David. *The Archaeology of Early Egypt: Social Transformations in North-East Africa, 10,000 to 2650 B.C.* Cambridge, 2006. An authoritative account of archeological evidence and its interpretation.

## CHAPTER 2

Aubet, Maria Eugenia. *Phoenicia and the West: Politics, Colonies, and Trade*. Trans. Mary Turton. Cambridge, 1993. An intelligent and thought-provoking examination of Phoenician civilization and its influence.

Boardman, John. *Assyrian and Babylonian Empires and Other States of the Near East from the Eighth to the Sixth Centuries B.C.* New York, 1991. Scholarly and authoritative.

Boardman, John. *Persia and the West*. London, 2000. A great book by a distinguished scholar, with a particular focus on art and architecture as projections of Persian imperial ideologies.

Boyce, Mary. *Textual Sources for the Study of Zoroastrianism*. Totowa, NJ, 1984. An invaluable collection of documents.

Bryce, Trevor. *The Kingdom of the Hittites*. Oxford, 1998. And *Life and Society in the Hittite World*. Oxford, 2002. An extraordinary synthesis, now the standard account of Hittite political, military, and daily life.

Curtis, John. *Ancient Persia*. Cambridge, MA, 1990. Concise, solid, reliable.

Dever, William. *Who Were the Early Israelites and Where Did They Come From?* Grand Rapids, MI, 2003. A balanced, fair-minded account with excellent bibliographical guidance to recent work.

Dickinson, O. T. P. K. *The Aegean Bronze Age*. Cambridge, 1994. An excellent summary of archaeological evidence and scholarly argument concerning Minoan, Mycenaean, and other cultures of the Bronze Age Aegean basin.

Dothan, Trude, and Moshe Dothan. *Peoples of the Sea: The Search for the Philistines*. New York, 1992. The essential starting point for understanding Philistine culture and its links to the Aegean basin.

Drews, Robert. *The End of the Bronze Age: Changes in Warfare and the Catastrophe ca. 1200 B.C.* Princeton, NJ, 1993. A stimulating analysis and survey, with excellent bibliographies.

Finkelstein, Israel, and Nadav Na'aman, eds. *From Nomadism to Monarchy: Archaeological and Historical Aspects of Early Israel*. Jerusalem, 1994. Scholarly articles on the Hebrews' transformation from pastoralists to a sedentary society focused on the worship of Yahweh.

Fitton, J. Lesley. *Minoans: Peoples of the Past* (British Museum Publications). London, 2002. A careful, reliable debunking of myths about the Minoans, written for nonspecialists.

Kamm, Antony. *The Israelites: An Introduction*. New York, 1999. A short, accessible history of the land and people of Israel up to 135 C.E., aimed at students and general readers.

Kuhrt, Amélie. *The Ancient Near East, c. 3000–330 B.C.* 2 vols. London and New York, 1995. An outstanding survey, written for students, that includes Egypt and Israel as well as Mesopotamia, Babylonia, Assyria, and Persia.

Luckenbill, Daniel David, ed. and trans. *Ancient Records of Assyria and Babylonia*. 2 vols. Chicago, 1926–27. Still one of the best and most readily accessible collections of primary sources on Assyrian attitudes and policies in war, religion, and politics.

Metzger, Bruce M., and Michael D. Coogan, eds. *The Oxford Companion to the Bible*. New York, 1993. An outstanding reference work, with contributions by leading authorities.

Niditch, Susan. *Ancient Israelite Religion*. New York, 1997. A short introduction designed for students, emphasizing the diversity of Hebrew religious practices.

Redford, Donald B. *Egypt, Canaan, and Israel in Ancient Times*. Princeton, NJ, 1992. An overview of the interactions between these peoples from about 1200 B.C.E. to the beginning of the Common Era.

Renfrew, Colin. *Archaeology and Language: The Puzzle of Indo-European Origins*. Cambridge, 1987. A masterful but controversial work by one of the most creative archaeologists of the twentieth century.

Saggs, H. W. F. *The Might That Was Assyria*. London, 1984. A lively narrative history of the Assyrian Empire, with analysis of the institutions that underlay its strength.

Sandars, Nancy K. *The Sea Peoples: Warriors of the Ancient Mediterranean*. Rev. ed. London, 1985. An introductory account for students and scholars.

Tubb, Jonathan N., and Rupert L. Chapman. *Archaeology and the Bible*. London, 1990. A good starting point for students that clearly illustrates the difficulties in linking archeological evidence to biblical accounts of early Hebrew history and society.

Wood, Michael. *In Search of the Trojan War*. New York, 1985. Aimed at a general audience, this carefully researched and engagingly written book is an excellent introduction to the late–Bronze Age context of the Trojan War.

## CHAPTER 3

Penguin Classics and the Loeb Classical Library both offer reliable translations of Greek literary, philosophical, and historical texts.

Beard, Mary. *The Parthenon*. Cambridge, MA, 2003. A book that traces the successive stages of this monument's construction, deconstruction, reconstruction, and restoration.

Boardman, John, Jaspar Griffin, and Oswyn Murray, eds. *Greece and the Hellenistic World*. Oxford, 1988. A reprint of the Greek and Hellenistic chapters from *The Oxford History of the Classical World*, originally published in 1986. Excellent, stimulating surveys, accessible to a general audience.

Brunschwig, Jacques, and Geoffrey E. R. Lloyd. *Greek Thought: A Guide to Classical Knowledge*. Translated by Catherine Porter. Cambridge, MA, 2000. An outstanding work of reference.

Buckley, Terry, ed. *Aspects of Greek History, 750–323 B.C.: A Source-Based Approach*. London, 1999. An outstanding collection of source materials.

Cartledge, Paul A. *The Spartans: An Epic History*. New York, 2003. A lively and authoritative history of Sparta from its origins to the Roman conquest.

Dover, Kenneth J. *Greek Homosexuality*. Cambridge, MA, 1978. The standard account of an important subject.

Fantham, Elaine, Helene Foley, Natalie Kampen, Sarah B. Pomeroy, and H. A. Shapiro. *Women in the Classical World: Image and Text*. Oxford, 1994. Wide-ranging analysis drawing on both visual and written sources, covering both the Greek and the Roman periods.

Fornara, Charles W., and Loren J. Samons II. *Athens from Cleisthenes to Pericles*. Berkeley, 1991. An excellent narrative history of Athenian politics during the first half of the fifth century B.C.E.

Freeman, Charles. *The Greek Achievement: The Foundation of the Western World*. New York, 1999. An admiring survey written for a general audience.

Garlan, Yvon. *Slavery in Ancient Greece*. Ithaca, NY, 1988. Now the standard account.

Hanson, Victor Davis. *The Other Greeks: The Family Farm and the Agrarian Roots of Western Civilization*. New York, 1995. Polemical and idiosyncratic, but convincing in its emphasis on smallholding farmers as the backbone of Greek urban society.

Havelock, Eric A. *The Literate Revolution in Greece and Its Cultural Consequences*. Princeton, 1982. A now-classic account of the wide-ranging effects of writing on Greek society.

Jones, Nicholas F. *Ancient Greece: State and Society*. Upper Saddle River, NJ, 1997. A concise survey from the Minoans up to the end of the Classical Period that emphasizes the connections between the social order and politics.

Lefkowitz, Mary, and Maureen Fant. *Women's Life in Greece and Rome: A Source Book in Translation*. 3rd ed. Baltimore, MD, 2005. A remarkably wide-ranging collection, topically arranged, invaluable to students.

Levi, Peter. *Atlas of the Greek World.* New York, 1984. Excellent maps and illustrations supplement an outstanding text.

Morris, Ian, and Barry Powell, eds. *A New Companion to Homer.* Leiden, 1997. A collection of thirty specialized but accessible scholarly articles, encompassing the most recent research on Homer and Dark Age Greece.

Pomeroy, Sarah B., Stanley M. Burstein, Walter Donlan, and Jennifer Tolbert Roberts. *Ancient Greece: A Political, Social, and Cultural History.* Oxford, 1999. An outstanding textbook; clear and lively.

Price, Simon. *Religions of the Ancient Greeks.* Cambridge, 1999. Concise and authoritative, this survey extends from the Archaic Period up to the fifth century C.E.

Seaford, Richard. *Money and the Greek Mind: Homer, Philosophy, Tragedy.* Cambridge, 2004. A provocative study of portable wealth and its far-reaching effects.

Strassler, Robert B., ed. *The Landmark Thucydides.* New York, 1996. Reprints the classic Richard Crawley translation with maps, commentary, notes, and appendices by leading scholars.

Thomas, Carol G., and Craig Conant. *Citadel to City-State: The Transformation of Greece, 1200–700 B.C.E.* Bloomington, IN, 1999. A lucid and accessible study that examines developments at a number of different Dark Age sites.

Thomas, Rosalind. *Oral Tradition and Written Record in Classical Athens.* Cambridge, 1989. A fascinating look at how oral epic, lyric, and drama were transmitted over time.

## CHAPTER 4

Penguin Classics and the Loeb Classical Library both offer reliable translations of scores of literary and historical texts from this period. Particularly important are historical works by Arrian *(Anabasis of Alexander)*, Plutarch *(Life of Alexander)*, and Polybius *(The Histories)*.

Adcock, F. E. *The Greek and Macedonian Art of War.* Berkeley, 1957. Still a valuable introduction to the guiding principles and assumptions of warfare in the fourth century.

Austin, M. M. *The Hellenistic World from Alexander to the Roman Conquest: A Selection of Ancient Sources in Translation.* Cambridge, 1981. A good collection of primary documents.

Bagnall, R. S., and P. Derow. *Greek Historical Documents: The Hellenistic Period.* Chico, CA, 1981. Another useful collection.

Borza, Eugene N. *In the Shadow of Olympus: The Emergence of Macedon.* Princeton, NJ, 1990. The standard account of the rise of Macedon up to the accession of Philip II.

Bosworth, A. B. *Conquest and Empire: The Reign of Alexander the Great.* Cambridge, 1988. A political and military analysis of Alexander's career that strips away the romance, maintaining a clear vision of the ruthlessness and human cost of his conquests.

Bosworth, A. B. *The Legacy of Alexander: Politics, Warfare, and Propaganda under the Successors.* Oxford, 2002. The most recent survey of the half century following Alexander's death and of the people who created the Hellenistic kingdoms of Egypt, Persia, and Macedon.

Burstein, Stanley M., ed. and trans. *The Hellenistic Age from the Battle of Ipsos to the Death of Kleopatra VII.* Cambridge, 1985. An excellent collection, with sources not found elsewhere.

Cartledge, Paul. *Agesilaus and the Crisis of Sparta.* Baltimore, MD, 1987. A thorough but readable analysis of the social and political challenges besetting Sparta in the fourth century B.C.E.

Cartledge, Paul. *Alexander the Great: The Hunt for a New Past.* Woodstock, NY, 2004. A compelling account of Alexander's life, times, and influences.

Green, Peter. *Alexander to Actium: The Historical Evolution of the Hellenistic Age.* Berkeley, CA. 1990. An outstanding, comprehensive, and wide-ranging history of the period.

Green, Peter. *Alexander of Macedon, 356–323 B.C.* Berkeley, CA, 1991. Revised edition of the author's earlier biography; entertainingly written, rich in detail and insight.

———. *The Hellenistic Age: A Short History.* New York, 2007. An authoritative synthesis that carries the history of Greek influence into the fourth century C.E.

Nicholas, G. L. *The Genius of Alexander the Great.* Chapel Hill, NC, 1998. A clear, authoritative, admiring account, distilling a lifetime of research on the subject.

Hansen, Mogens H. *The Athenian Democracy in the Age of Demosthenes.* Oxford, 1991. An examination of the political institutions of Athens in the fourth century B.C.E.

Lloyd, Geoffrey, and Nathan Sivin. *The Way and the Word: Science and Medicine in Early China and Greece.* New Haven, CT, 2002. An extraordinary comparative study.

Ober, Josiah. *Mass and Elite in Democratic Athens: Rhetoric, Ideology, and the Power of the People.* Princeton, NJ, 1989. An excellent study of the ideology of democracy in Athens that borrows from the insights of modern social science.

Pollitt, Jerome J. *Art in the Hellenistic Age.* New York, 1986. The standard account, blending cultural history with art history.

Sherwin-White, Susan, and Amélie Kuhrt. *From Samarkhand to Sardis: A New Approach to the Seleucid Empire.* London, 1993. A stimulating examination of the relationship between rulers and ruled in the vast expanses of the Seleucid Empire.

Shipley, Graham. *The Greek World after Alexander, 323–30 B.C.* New York and London, 2000. A study of the social, intellectual, and artistic changes in the Hellenistic era.

Thomas, Carol G. *Alexander the Great in His World.* Oxford and Malden, MA, 2007. A study of the contexts—familial, political, and social—that shaped Alexander's career.

Tripolitis, Antonia. *Religions of the Hellenistic-Roman Age.* Grand Rapids, MI, 2002. Survey of the variety of religious experience, ritual, and belief in the centuries before the emergence of Christianity.

Tritle, Lawrence A., ed. *The Greek World in the Fourth Century: From the Fall of the Athenian Empire to the Successors of Alexander.* New York, 1997. A wide-ranging collection of scholarly essays.

Worthington, Ian. *Alexander the Great: A Reader.* London and New York, 2002. A collection of influential interpretations of Alexander by modern historians.

## CHAPTER 5

Translations of Roman authors are available in both the Penguin Classics series and in the Loeb Classical Library.

Barker, Graeme, and Tom Rasmussen. *The Etruscans.* Oxford and Malden, MA, 1998. A fine survey, from the Blackwell *Peoples of Europe* series.

Beard, Mary. *Pompeii: The Life of a Roman Town.* A fascinating, cutting-edge study of daily life.

Boardman, John, Jasper Griffin, and Oswyn Murray. *The Oxford History of the Roman World.* Oxford, 1990. Reprint of relevant portions of the excellent *Oxford History of the Classical World* (1986). Stimulating, accessible topical chapters by British specialists.

Cornell, T. J. *The Beginnings of Rome: Italy and Rome from the Bronze Age to the Punic Wars (c. 1000–264 B.C.).* London, 1995. An ambitious survey of the archaeological and historical evidence for early Rome.

Crawford, Michael. *The Roman Republic,* 2d ed. Cambridge, MA, 1993. A lively, fast-paced survey of republican Rome. An excellent place to start.

Fantham, Elaine, Helene Peet Foley, Natalie Boymel Kampen, Sarah B. Pomeroy, and H. Alan Shapiro. *Women in the Classical World.* Oxford, 1994. An expert survey of both Greece and Rome.

Garnsey, Peter, and Richard Saller. *The Roman Empire: Economy, Society, and Culture.* Berkeley, CA, 1987. A straightforward short survey.

Gruen, Erich S. *The Hellenistic World and the Coming of Rome.* 2 vols. Berkeley, CA, 1984. A massive survey, focused on the unpredictable rise of Rome to a position of dominance within the Mediterranean world.

Harris, William V. *War and Imperialism in Republican Rome, 327–70 B.C.* Oxford, 1979. A challenging study arguing that Rome's need for military conquest and expansion was deeply embedded in the fabric of Roman life.

Lancel, Serge. *Carthage: A History.* Trans. Antonia Nevill. Oxford, 1995. An account of Rome's great rival for control of the Mediterranean world.

Lewis, Naphtali, and M. Reinhold. *Roman Civilization: Selected Readings.* 2 vols. New York, 1951–55. The standard collection, especially for political and economic subjects. Vol. 1 covers the republic; vol. 2, the empire.

Millar, Fergus G. B. *The Emperor in the Roman World, 31 B.C.–A.D. 337.* London, 1977. A classic work that showed (among much else) the importance of emperor worship to the religious outlook of the Roman Empire.

———. *The Crowd in Rome in the Late Republic.* Ann Arbor, MI, 1999. A revisionist account that emphasizes the reality of Roman democracy in the late republic, against those who would see the period's politics as entirely under the control of aristocratic families.

Ward, Allen M., Fritz Heichelheim, and Cedric A. Yeo. *A History of the Roman People,* 3d ed. Upper Saddle River, NJ, 1999. An informative, well-organized textbook covering Roman history from its beginnings to the end of the sixth century C.E.

Watkin, David. *The Roman Forum.* London, 2009. A history of the successive buildings and archeological excavations of this central Roman space.

Wells, Colin. *The Roman Empire,* 2d ed. Cambridge, MA, 1992. An easily readable survey from the reign of Augustus to the mid-third century C.E., particularly useful for its treatment of the relationship between the Roman central government and its Italian provinces.

Wiseman, T. P. *Remembering the Roman People.* Oxford, 2009. A collection of studies devoted to popular politics in the late republic.

Woolf, Greg. *Becoming Roman: The Origins of Provincial Civilization in Gaul.* Cambridge, 1998. An exemplary study of how provincial elites made themselves "Roman."

## CHAPTER 6

Augustine. *The City of God.* Trans. Henry Bettenson. Baltimore, MD, 1972.

———. *Confessions.* Trans. Henry M. Chadwick. Oxford, 1991.

———. *On Christian Doctrine.* Trans. D. W. Robertson Jr. New York, 1958.

Boethius. *The Consolation of Philosophy.* Trans. R. Green. Indianapolis, IN, 1962.

Bowersock, G. W., Peter Brown, and Oleg Grabar. *Late Antiquity: A Guide to the Postclassical World.* Cambridge, MA, 1999. An authoritative compilation. The first half is devoted to essays on the cultural features of the period; the second half is organized as an encyclopedia.

Brown, Peter. *Augustine of Hippo.* Berkeley, CA, 1967. A great biography by the great scholar of late antiquity.

———. *The Body and Society: Men, Women and Sexual Renunciation in Early Christianity.* New York, 1988. A revealing study of the fundamental transformations wrought by Christianity in the late antique world.

———. *Power and Persuasion in Late Antiquity: Toward a Christian Empire.* Madison, WI, 1992. An important account of Christianity's effects on the political culture of the later Roman Empire.

———. *The Rise of Western Christendom: Triumph and Diversity, 200–1000,* 2d ed. Oxford, 2002. An evocative picture of Christianity's spread eastward and northward from the Mediterranean world.

Brown, Peter. *The World of Late Antiquity.* New York, 1971. Still the best short survey of the period, with excellent illustrations.

Cameron, Averil. *The Later Roman Empire, A.D. 284–430.* London, 1993. Now the standard account of its period, with an emphasis on imperial politics.

———. *The Mediterranean World in Late Antiquity, A.D. 395–600.* London, 1993. Masterful, with excellent, succinct bibliographical essays.

Cassiodorus. *An Introduction to Divine and Human Readings.* Trans. L. W. Jones. New York, 1946.

Chadwick, Henry M. *Augustine.* Oxford, 1986. A short introduction to Augustine's thought.

———. *Boethius*. Oxford, 1981. An intellectual biography of this important thinker.

Clark, Gillian. *Christianity and Roman Society*. Cambridge, 2004. A short, stimulating survey that places early Christianity firmly in its Roman social context.

Clark, Gillian. *Women in Late Antiquity*. Oxford, 1993. A clear, compact account of an important subject.

Coogan, Michael, ed. *The Oxford History of the Biblical World*. Oxford, 1998. A reliable but rather traditional account of the historical events recounted in the Hebrew Bible and the New Testament.

Ehrman, Bart D. *The New Testament: A Historical Introduction to the Early Christian Writings*, 4th ed. Oxford, 2008. The standard textbook by a leading authority.

Eusebius. *The History of the Church*. Trans. G. A. Williamson. Baltimore, MD, 1965. A contemporary account of Constantine's reign, written by one of his courtier-bishops.

———. *Eusebius' Life of Constantine*. Trans. Averil Cameron and Stuart Hall. Oxford, 1999. An admiring biography that reflects Constantine's own vision of his religious authority.

Hopkins, Keith. *A World Full of Gods: The Strange Triumph of Christianity*. Penguin, 1999. An imaginative study of religious pluralism in the Roman world and the context in which Christianity emerged.

Kulikowski, Michael. *Rome's Gothic Wars: From the Third Century to Alaric*. Cambridge, 2007. An authoritative and critical account.

Lane Fox, Robin. *Pagans and Christians*. New York, 1987. A subtle, perceptive, and highly readable exploration of the pagan world within which Christianity grew up.

Lawrence, Clifford Hugh. *Medieval Monasticism*, 3d ed. London, 2000. Concise, perceptive survey of monasticism from its beginnings to the end of the Middle Ages.

Markus, R. A. *The End of Ancient Christianity*. New York, 1990. An expert synthetic study of Christianity in the western Roman Empire between 350 and 600 C.E.

Pagels, Elaine. *The Gnostic Gospels*. New York, 1979. A pathbreaking study of the noncanonical gospels and the history of their exclusion from the Bible.

Pelikan, Jaroslav. *The Christian Tradition*. Vol. 1, *The Emergence of the Catholic Tradition*. Chicago, 1971. A history of Christian doctrine that is one of the tours-de-force of twentieth-century scholarship.

Potter, David. *The Roman Empire at Bay, A.D. 180–395*. London and New York, 2004. The most up-to-date account of the empire's reorganization and transformation in this era.

Sanders, E. P. *The Historical Figure of Jesus*. London and New York, 1993. A fine study of Jesus in his first-century Jewish context.

Shanks, Hershel, ed. *Christianity and Rabbinic Judaism: A Parallel History of Their Origins and Early Development*. Washington, DC, 1992. Accessible chapters written by top authorities, describing both Jewish and Christian developments from the first to the sixth centuries C.E.

Sherwin-White, A. N. *Roman Society and Roman Law in the New Testament*. Oxford, 1963. A fascinating reading of the New Testament in its historical context.

Wallace-Hadrill, John Michael. *The Barbarian West*, 3d ed. London, 1966. A classic analysis of the hybrid culture of the late Roman West.

Whittaker, C. R. *Frontiers of the Roman Empire: A Social and Economic Study*. Baltimore, MD, 1994. A convincing picture of the frontiers of the Roman Empire as zones of intensive cultural interaction.

Williams, Stephen. *Diocletian and the Roman Recovery*. New York, 1997. Thorough and authoritative.

## CHAPTER 7

Bede. *A History of the English Church and People*. Trans. Leo Sherley-Price. Baltimore, MD., 1955. The fundamental source for early Anglo-Saxon history.

Bloom, Jonathan M. *Paper Before Print: The Impact and History of Paper in the Islamic World*. New Haven, CT, 2001. A fascinating account, with beautiful illustrations.

Boniface. *Letters of Saint Boniface*. Trans. Ephraim Emerton. New York, 1972.

Campbell, James, ed. *The Anglo-Saxons*. Oxford, 1982. An authoritative and splendidly illustrated volume.

Collins, Roger. *Early Medieval Europe, 300–1000*. 2d ed. New York, 1999. Dry and detailed, but a useful textbook nonetheless.

Donner, Fred. *The Early Islamic Conquests*. Princeton, NJ, 1981. A scholarly but readable narrative and analysis.

Einhard and Notker the Stammerer. *Two Lives of Charlemagne*. Trans. Lewis Thorpe. Baltimore, MD, 1969. Lively and entertaining works of contemporary biography.

Fletcher, Richard A. *The Barbarian Conversion: From Paganism to Christianity*. Berkeley, CA, 1999. Slow paced but informative and perceptive.

———. *Moorish Spain*. Berkeley, CA, 1993. The best short survey in English.

Geanakoplos, Deno John, ed. *Byzantium: Church, Society and Civilization Seen through Contemporary Eyes*. Chicago, 1984. An outstanding source book.

Gregory, Timothy E. *A History of Byzantium*. Malden, MA, and Oxford, 2005. The most accessible of the recent textbooks on Byzantium. An excellent place to start.

Herrin, Judith. *The Formation of Christendom*. Princeton, NJ, 1987. A synthetic history of the Christian civilizations of Byzantium and western Europe from 500 to 800, written by a prominent historian.

Hodges, Richard, and David Whitehouse. *Mohammed, Charlemagne and the Origins of Europe*. London, 1983. A critical analysis of the "Pirenne thesis," reexaming the relationship between the Mediterranean world and northern Europe.

Hourani, Albert. *A History of the Arab Peoples*. New York, 1992. A sympathetic and clear survey written for nonspecialists.

Kazhdan, Alexander P., ed. *The Oxford Dictionary of Byzantium*. 3 vols. Oxford, 1991. An authoritative reference work.

Kennedy, Hugh. *The Prophet and the Age of the Caliphates*. 2d ed. Harlow, UK, 2004. A lucid introduction to the political history of the Islamic world from the sixth through the eleventh centuries.

Krautheimer, Richard. *Early Christian and Byzantine Architecture*. 4th ed. New York, 1986. A classic work by one of the greatest Byzantine art historians of the twentieth century.

Mango, Cyril, ed. *The Oxford History of Byzantium.* Oxford and New York, 2002. Full of sharp judgments and attractively illustrated.

McCormick, Michael. *The Origins of the European Economy: Communications and Commerce A.D. 300–900.* Cambridge, 2002. An astonishing reinterpretation of the evidence for the myriad contacts between Christian Europe and Islam.

McKitterick, Rosamond. *Charlemagne: The Formation of a European Identity.* Cambridge, 2008. A history of Charlemagne's career and its lasting impact by an eminent scholar of the Carolingian world.

———, ed. *The Uses of Literacy in Early Medieval Europe.* New York, 1990. A superb collection of essays.

McNamara, Jo Ann, and John E. Halborg, eds. *Sainted Women of the Dark Ages.* Durham, NC, 1992. Translated saints' lives from Merovingian and Carolingian Europe.

Murray, A. C., ed. *From Roman to Merovingian Gaul: A Reader.* Toronto, 2000. An excellent collection of sources.

Pelikan, Jaroslav. *The Christian Tradition.* Vol. II, *The Spirit of Eastern Christendom.* Chicago, 1974. An outstanding synthetic treatment of the doctrines of Byzantine Christianity.

Procopius. *The Secret History.* Trans. G. A. Williamson. Baltimore, MD, 1966. An "unauthorized" account of Justinian's reign, written by the emperor's offical historian.

Reuter, Timothy. *Germany in the Early Middle Ages, 800–1056.* New York, 1991. The best survey in English.

Sawyer, Peter, ed. *The Oxford Illustrated History of the Vikings.* Oxford, 1997. The best one-volume account, lavishly illustrated.

Todd, Malcolm. *The Early Germans.* Oxford, 1992. A reliable survey, particularly strong in its use of archaeological evidence.

Treadgold, Warren. *A History of the Byzantine State and Society.* Stanford, CA, 1997. A massive, encyclopedic narrative of the political, economic, and military history of Byzantium from 284 until 1461.

Wallace-Hadrill, John Michael. *Early Germanic Kingship in England and on the Continent.* Oxford, 1971. A classic analysis of changing ideas about kingship in early medieval Europe, emphasizing the links between Anglo-Saxon and Carolingian cultures.

———. *The Frankish Church.* Oxford, 1983. A masterful account that links the Merovingian and Carolingian churches.

Watt, W. Montgomery. *Islamic Philosophy and Theology,* 2d ed. Edinburgh, UK, 1985. The standard English account.

Wemple, Suzanne Fonay. *Women in Frankish Society: Marriage and the Cloister, 500–900.* Philadelphia, PA, 1981. An influential account of changing attitudes toward marriage among the early Franks.

Whittow, Mark. *The Making of Orthodox Byzantium, 600–1025.* London, 1996. Emphasizes the centrality of orthodoxy in shaping Byzantine history. Particularly good on Byzantine relations with the peoples outside the empire.

Wickham, Chris. *Framing the Middle Ages: Europe and the Mediterranean, 400–800.* Oxford, 2007. An eye-opening history that spans the transitional periods of late antiquity and the early Middle Ages, paying careful attention to regional differences.

Wood, Ian. *The Merovingian Kingdoms, 450–751.* New York, 1994. A detailed study, but difficult for beginners.

## CHAPTER 8

Amt, Emily, ed. *Women's Lives in Medieval Europe: A Sourcebook.* New York, 1993. An excellent collection of primary texts.

*The Song of Roland.* Trans. Robert Harrison. Penguin, 1970. A lively translation.

Arnold, Benjamin. *Princes and Territories in Medieval Germany.* Cambridge and New York, 1991. The best such survey in English.

Blumenthal, Uta-Renate. *The Investiture Controversy.* Philadelphia, 1988. A clear review of a complicated subject.

Burman, Thomas E. *Reading the Qur'ān in Latin Christendom, 1140–1560.* Philadelphia, 2007. A fascinating account of the Qu'ran's reception in medieval Europe.

Dunbabin, Jean. *France in the Making, 843–1180,* 2d ed. Oxford and New York, 2000. An authoritative survey of the disparate territories that came to make up the medieval French kingdom.

Dyer, Christopher. *Making a Living in the Middle Ages: The People of Britain 850–1520.* New Haven, 2002. A splendid new synthesis that combines social, economic, and archaeological evidence.

Fuhrmann, Horst. *Germany in the High Middle Ages, c. 1050–1200.* Cambridge, 1986. A useful, short history of twelfth-century Germany.

Hicks, Carola. *The Bayeux Tapestry: The Life Story of Masterpiece.* London, 2006. An art historian's engrossing account of the making, reception, and interpretation of this amazing artifact.

Jones, P. J. *The Italian City-State: From Commune to Signoria.* Oxford and New York, 1997. A fundamental reinterpretation of the evidence.

Kaeuper, Richard W. *Chivalry and Violence in Medieval Europe.* Oxford and New York, 1999. A darker view of chivalry than Keen's.

Keen, Maurice. *Chivalry.* New Haven, CT, 1984. A comprehensive treatment of chivalry from its origins to the sixteenth century.

Leyser, Henrietta. *Medieval Women: A Social History of Women in England, 440–1500.* New York, 1995. Although limited to one country, this is the best of the recent surveys treating medieval women.

Leyser, Karl. *Rule and Conflict in an Early Medieval Society: Ottonian Saxony.* Oxford, 1979. A concise, challenging account of the dynamics of rule in tenth-century Saxony, paying special attention to the importance of royal women.

Lopez, Robert S., and Irving W. Raymond, eds. *Medieval Trade in the Mediterranean World.* New York, 1990. A pathbreaking collection of source material.

Miller, Maureen C. *Power and the Holy in the Age of the Investiture Conflict. A Brief History with Documents.* Boston, 2005. A stimulating approach to the eleventh-century conflicts over temporal and spiritual power, with many newly translated sources.

Moore, Robert I. *The First European Revolution, c. 970–1215.* Oxford and Cambridge, MA, 2000. A remarkable description of the ways in which European society was fundamentally reshaped during the eleventh and twelfth centuries.

Peters, F. E. *Aristotle and the Arabs.* New York, 1968. Well written and engaging.

Reilly, Bernard F. *The Medieval Spains.* New York, 1993. A succinct account that covers the entire Iberian peninsula from 500 to 1500.

Reynolds, Susan. *Fiefs and Vassals: The Medieval Evidence Reinterpreted.* Oxford and New York, 1994. A detailed revisionist history of "feudalism."

Sheingorn, Pamela, trans. *The Book of Sainte Foy.* Philadelphia, 1995.

Southern, Richard W. *The Making of the Middle Ages.* New Haven, CT, 1992. A classic work, first published in 1951 but still fresh and exciting.

Stillman, Norman A. *The Jews of Arab Lands: A History and Source Book.* Philadelphia, PA, 1979. An essential resource.

Stow, Kenneth R. *Alienated Minority: The Jews of Medieval Latin Europe.* Cambridge, MA, 1992. An excellent survey.

Tierney, Brian. *The Crisis of Church and State, 1050–1300.* Toronto, 1988. An indispensable collection for both teachers and students.

## CHAPTER 9

Abelard and Heloise. *The Letters and Other Writings.* Trans. William Levitan. Indianapolis, 2007. A beautiful and accurate translation of the correspondence and related documents, with a full introduction and notes.

Abulafia, David. *Frederick II: A Medieval Emperor.* London and New York, 1988. A reliable biography that strips away much of the legend that has hitherto surrounded this monarch.

Abulafia, David, ed. *The New Cambridge Medieval History. Volume 5: c. 1198–c. 1300.* Cambridge, 1999. Contributions by more than thirty specialists. Excellent bibliographies.

Baldwin, John W. *The Government of Philip Augustus.* Berkeley and Los Angeles, CA, 1986. A landmark scholarly account.

Bartlett, Robert. *The Making of Europe: Conquest, Colonization and Cultural Change, 950–1350.* Princeton, NJ, 1993. A wide-ranging examination of the economic, social, and religious expansion of Europe, full of stimulating insights.

Bisson, Thomas N. *The Crisis of the Twelfth Century: Power, Lordship, and the Origins of European Government.* Princeton, NJ, 2009. A new interpretation of the evidence.

Boswell, John E. *Christianity, Social Tolerance, and Homosexuality: Gay People in Western Europe from the Beginning of the Christian Era to the Fourteenth Century.* Chicago, 1980. A pioneering account, hotly debated but highly respected.

Camille, Michael. *Gothic Art: Glorious Visions.* New York, 1996. A succinct and beautifully illustrated introduction.

Chrétien de Troyes. *Arthurian Romances.* Trans. W. W. Kibler. New York, 1991.

Clanchy, Michael T. *Abelard: A Medieval Life.* Oxford and Cambridge, MA, 1997. A great biography.

———. *From Memory to Written Record: England, 1066–1307.* Oxford, 1992. A fascinating and hugely influential account of this revolutionary shift.

Cobban, Alan B. *The Medieval Universities.* London, 1975. The best short treatment in English.

Colish, Marcia. *Medieval Foundations of the Western Intellectual Tradition, 400–1400.* New Haven, CT, 1997. An encyclopedic work, best used as a reference.

Dante Alighieri. *The Divine Comedy.* Trans. Mark Musa. 3 vols. Baltimore, MD, 1984–86.

Dronke, Peter. *Women Writers of the Middle Ages.* New York, 1984. A rich literary study.

Fassler, Margot. *Gothic Song: Victorine Seqeunces and Augustinian Reform in Twelfth-Century Paris.* Cambridge, UK, 1993. The emergence of new musical genres and their cultural context.

Gillingham, John. *The Angevin Empire,* 2d ed. Oxford and New York, 2001. The best treatment by far of its subject, brief but full of ideas.

Gottfried von Strassburg. *Tristan.* Trans. A. T. Hatto. Baltimore, MD, 1960.

Hallam, Elizabeth, and Judith Everard. *Capetian France, 987–1328,* 2d ed. New York, 2001. A clear and well-organized account.

Haskins, Charles Homer. *The Renaissance of the Twelfth Century.* Cambridge, MA, 1927. A classic and influential study.

Jordan, William C. *Europe in the High Middle Ages: The Penguin History of Europe.* Vol. III. New York and London, 2003. An outstanding new survey.

Knowles, David. *The Evolution of Medieval Thought,* 2d ed. London, 1988. An authoritative survey, thoroughly revised in the second edition.

Lambert, Malcolm. *Medieval Heresy,* 3d ed. Oxford and Cambridge, 2002. The standard synthesis; deeply learned and fully annotated.

Lawrence, Clifford Hugh. *The Friars: The Impact of the Early Mendicant Movement on Western Society.* London and New York, 1994. The best short introduction to the early history of the Franciscans and the Dominicans.

Leclerq, Jean. *The Love of Learning and the Desire for God,* 3d ed. New York, 1982. A beautiful interpretation of twelfth-century monastic culture and the influence of Bernard of Clairvaux.

Little, Lester. *Religious Poverty and Profit Economy in Medieval Europe.* Ithaca, 1978. A fascinating study of the relationship between religious practice and economic reality.

Marie de France. *Lais.* Trans. Glyn S. Burgess and Keith Busby. Harmondsworth, UK, 1999. A compelling and entertaining prose translation.

Moore, R. I. *The Formation of a Persecuting Society: Authority and Deviance in Western Europe, 950–1250.* 2d ed. Malden, MA, 2007. This new edition responds to some of the debates generated by the publication of the first in 1987.

Morris, Colin. *The Papal Monarchy: The Western Church from 1050 to 1250.* Oxford, 1989. An excellent scholarly survey; part of the Oxford History of the Christian Church series.

Newman, Barbara, ed. *Voice of the Living Light: Hildegard of Bingen and Her World.* Berkeley and Los Angeles, CA, 1998. An introduction to Hildegard's life and work.

Otto, Bishop of Freising. *The Deeds of Frederick Barbarossa.* Trans. C. C. Mierow. New York, 1953. A contemporary chronicle interesting enough to read from start to finish.

Smalley, Beryl. *The Study of the Bible in the Middle Ages,* 3d ed. Oxford, 1983. The standard work, gracefully written and illuminating.

Southern, Richard W. *Western Society and the Church in the Middle Ages.* Baltimore, MD, 1970. An insightful interpretation of the interplay between society and religion by one of the greatest historians of the twentieth century.

Strayer, Joseph R. *On the Medieval Origins of the Modern State*. With new forewords by Charles Tilly and William Chester Jordan. Princeton, 2005. This new edition of Strayer's series of lectures places them in their scholarly context.

Swanson, R. N. *The Twelfth-Century Renaissance*. Manchester, UK, 1999. An updated survey of the intellectual developments of the twelfth century.

Symes, Carol. *A Common Stage: Theater and Public Life in Medieval Arras*. Ithaca, NY, 2007. A study of a vibrant cultural hub.

Wakefield, Walter, and Austin P. Evans, eds. and trans. *Heresies of the High Middle Ages*. New York, 1969, 1991. A comprehensive collection of sources.

Wilhelm, James J., ed. and trans. *Medieval Song: An Anthology of Hymns and Lyrics*. New York, 1971. An excellent collection of sacred and secular poetry that illustrates the connections between them.

Wolfram von Eschenbach. *Parzival*. Trans. H. M. Mustard and C. E. Passage. New York, 1961.

## CHAPTER 10

Allmand, Christopher T., ed. *Society at War: The Experience of England and France During the Hundred Years' War*. Edinburgh, 1973. An outstanding collection of documents.

———. *The Hundred Years' War: England and France at War, c. 1300–c. 1450*. Cambridge and New York, 1988. Still the best analytic account of the war; after a short narrative, the book is organized topically.

Boccaccio, Giovanni. *The Decameron*. Trans. Mark Musa and P. E. Bondanella. New York, 1977.

Bynum, Caroline Walker. *Holy Feast and Holy Fast: The Religious Significance of Food to Medieval Women*. Berkeley and Los Angeles, 1988. One of the most influential and important works of scholarship published in the late twentieth century.

Chaucer, Geoffrey. *The Canterbury Tales*. Trans. Nevill Coghill. New York, 1951. A modern English verse translation, lightly annotated.

Cohn, Samuel K., Jr. *Lust for Liberty: The Politics of Social Revolt in Medieval Europe, 1200–1425. Italy, France, and Flanders*. Cambridge, MA, 2006. An important new study.

Cole, Bruce. *Giotto and Florentine Painting, 1280–1375*. New York, 1976. A clear and stimulating introduction.

Crummey, Robert O. *The Formation of Muscovy, 1304–1613*. New York, 1987. The standard account.

Dobson, R. Barrie. *The Peasants' Revolt of 1381*, 2d ed. London, 1983. A comprehensive source collection, with excellent introductions to the documents.

Dyer, Christopher. *Standards of Living in the Later Middle Ages: Social Change in England, c. 1200–1520*. Cambridge and New York, 1989. Detailed but highly rewarding.

Froissart, Jean. *Chronicles*. Trans. Geoffrey Brereton. Baltimore, MD, 1968. A selection from the most famous contemporary account of the Hundred Years' War to about 1400.

Hobbins, Daniel, ed. and trans. *The Trial of Joan of Arc*. Cambridge, MA, 2007. A new and excellent translation of the transcripts of Joan's trial.

Horrox, Rosemary, ed. *The Black Death*. New York, 1994. A fine collection of documents reflecting the impact of the Black Death, especially in England.

*John Hus at the Council of Constance*. Trans. M. Spinka, New York, 1965. The translation of a Czech chronicle with an expert introduction and appended documents.

Jordan, William Chester. *The Great Famine: Northern Europe in the Early Fourteenth Century*. Princeton, NJ, 1996. An outstanding social and economic study.

Keen, Maurice, ed. *Medieval Warfare: A History*. Oxford and New York, 1999. The most attractive introduction to this important subject. Lively and well illustrated.

Kempe, Margery. *The Book of Margery Kempe*. Trans. Barry Windeatt. New York, 1985. A fascinating personal narrative by an early-fifteenth-century Englishwoman who hoped she might be a saint.

Lerner, Robert E. *The Heresy of the Free Spirit in the Later Middle Ages*, 2d ed. Notre Dame, IN, 1991. A revealing study of a heretical movement that hardly existed at all.

Lewis, Peter S. *Later Medieval France: The Polity*. London, 1968. Still fresh and suggestive after forty years. A masterwork.

*Memoirs of a Renaissance Pope: The Commentaries of Pius II*. Abridged ed. Trans. F. A. Gragg, New York, 1959. Remarkable insights into the mind of a particularly well-educated mid-fifteenth-century pope.

Nicholas, David. *The Transformation of Europe, 1300–1600*. Oxford and New York, 1999. The best textbook presently available.

Oakley, Francis C. *The Western Church in the Later Middle Ages*. Ithaca, NY, 1979. The best book by far on the history of conciliarism, the late medieval papacy, Hussitism, and the efforts at institutional reform during this period. On popular piety, see Swanson.

Shirley, Janet, trans. *A Parisian Journal, 1405–1449*. Oxford, 1968. A marvelous panorama of Parisian life recorded by an eyewitness.

Sumption, Jonathan. *The Hundred Years' War*. Vol. 1: *Trial by Battle*. Vol. 2: *Trial by Fire*. Philadelphia, 1999. The first two volumes of a massive narrative history of the war, carrying the story up to 1369.

Swanson, R. N. *Religion and Devotion in Europe, c. 1215–c. 1515*. Cambridge and New York, 1995. An excellent study of late-medieval popular piety; an excellent complement to Oakley.

Vaughan, Richard. *Valois Burgundy*. London, 1975. A summation of the author's four-volume study of the Burgundian dukes.

Ziegler, Philip. *The Black Death*. New York, 1969. A popular account, but reliable and engrossing.

## CHAPTER 11

Abu-Lughod, Janet L. *Before European Hegemony: The World System A.D. 1250–1350*. Oxford and New York, 1989. A study of the trading links among Europe, the Middle East, India, and China, with special attention to the role of the Mongol Empire; extensive bibliography.

Allsen, Thomas T. *Culture and Conquest in Mongol Eurasia*. Cambridge and New York, 2001. A synthesis of the author's earlier studies, emphasizing Mongol involvement in the cultural and commercial exchanges that linked China, Central Asia, and Europe.

Amitai-Preiss, Reuven, and David O. Morgan, eds. *The Mongol Empire and Its Legacy.* Leiden, 1999. A collection of essays that represents some of the new trends in Mongol studies.

Christian, David. *A History of Russia, Central Asia and Mongolia.* Vol. 1, *Inner Eurasia from Prehistory to the Mongol Empire.* Oxford, 1998. The authoritative English-language work on the subject.

Coles, Paul. *The Ottoman Impact on Europe.* London, 1968. An excellent introductory text, still valuable despite its age.

Fernández-Armesto, Felipe. *Before Columbus: Exploration and Colonisation from the Mediterranean to the Atlantic, 1229–1492.* London, 1987. An indispensible study of the medieval background to the sixteenth-century European colonial empires.

———. *Columbus.* Oxford and New York, 1991. An excellent biography that stresses the millenarian ideas that underlay Columbus's thinking.

Flint, Valerie I. J. *The Imaginative Landscape of Christopher Columbus.* Princeton, NJ, 1992. A short, suggestive analysis of the intellectual influences that shaped Columbus's geographical ideas.

Goffman, Daniel. *The Ottoman Empire and Early Modern Europe.* Cambridge and New York, 2002. A revisionist account that presents the Ottoman Empire as a European state.

*The History and the Life of Chinggis Khan: The Secret History of the Mongols.* Trans. Urgunge Onon. Leiden, 1997. A newer version of *The Secret History*, now the standard English version of this important Mongol source.

Inalcik, Halil. *The Ottoman Empire: The Classical Age, 1300–1600.* London, 1973. The standard history by the dean of Turkish historians.

———, ed. *An Economic and Social History of the Ottoman Empire, 1300–1914.* Cambridge, 1994. An important collection of essays, spanning the full range of Ottoman history.

Jackson, Peter. *The Mongols and the West, 1221–1410.* Harlow, UK, 2005. A well-written survey that emphasizes the interactions among the Mongol, Latin Christian, and Muslim worlds.

Kafadar, Cemal. *Between Two Worlds: The Construction of the Ottoman State.* Berkeley and Los Angeles, 1995. An important study of Ottoman origins in the border regions between Byzantium, the Seljuk Turks, and the Mongols.

Larner, John. *Marco Polo and the Discovery of the World.* New Haven, CT, 1999. A study of the influence of Marco Polo's *Travels* on Europeans.

Morgan, David. *The Mongols.* 2d ed. Oxford, 2007. An accessible introduction to Mongol history and its sources, written by a noted expert on medieval Persia.

Parker, Geoffrey. *The Military Revolution: Military Innovation and the Rise of the West (1500–1800).* 2d ed. Cambridge and New York, 1996. A work of fundamental importance for understanding the global dominance achieved by early modern Europeans.

Phillips, J. R. S. *The Medieval Expansion of Europe.* 2d ed. Oxford, 1998. An outstanding study of the thirteenth- and fourteenth-century background to the fifteenth-century expansion of Europe. Important synthetic treatment of European relations with the Mongols, China, Africa, and North America. The second edition includes a new introduction and a bibliographical essay; the text is the same as in the first edition (1988).

Phillips, William D., Jr., and Carla R. Phillips. *The Worlds of Christopher Columbus.* Cambridge and New York, 1991. The first book to read on Columbus: accessible, engaging, and scholarly. Then read Fernández-Armesto's biography.

Ratchnevsky, Paul. *Genghis Khan: His Life and Legacy.* Trans. Thomas Nivison Haining. Oxford, 1991. An English translation and abridgment of a book first published in German in 1983. The author was one of the greatest Mongol historians of his generation.

Rossabi, M. *Khubilai Khan: His Life and Times.* Berkeley, CA, 1988. The standard English biography.

Russell, Peter. *Prince Henry "The Navigator": A Life.* New Haven, CT, 2000. A masterly biography by a great historian who has spent a lifetime on the subject. The only book one now needs to read on Prince Henry.

Saunders, J. J. *The History of the Mongol Conquests.* London, 1971. Still the standard English-language introduction; somewhat more positive about the Mongols' accomplishments than is Morgan.

Scammell, Geoffrey V. *The First Imperial Age: European Overseas Expansion, 1400–1715.* London, 1989. A useful introductory survey, with a particular focus on English and French colonization.

*The Book of Prophecies, Edited by Christopher Columbus.* Trans. Blair Sullivan, ed. Roberto Rusconi. Berkeley and Los Angeles, 1996. After his third voyage, from which Columbus was returned to Spain in chains, he compiled a book of quotations from various sources selected to emphasize the millenarian implications of his discoveries; a fascinating insight into the mind of the explorer.

*The Four Voyages: Christopher Columbus.* Trans. J. M. Cohen. New York, 1992. Columbus's own self-serving account of his four voyages to the Indies.

*Mandeville's Travels.* Ed. M. C. Seymour. Oxford, 1968. An edition of the *Book of Marvels* based on the Middle English version popular in the fifteenth century.

*The Secret History of the Mongols.* Trans. F. W. Cleaves. Cambridge, MA, 1982.

*The Secret History of the Mongols and Other Pieces.* Trans. Arthur Waley. London, 1963. The later Chinese abridgment of the Mongol original.

*The Travels of Marco Polo,* trans. R. E. Latham. Baltimore, MD, 1958. The most accessible edition of this remarkably interesting work.

## CHAPTER 12

Alberti, Leon Battista. *The Family in Renaissance Florence (Della Famiglia).* Trans. Renée Neu Watkins. Columbia, SC, 1969.

Baxandall, Michael. *Painting and Experience in Fifteenth-Century Italy.* Oxford, 1972. A classic study of the perceptual world of the Renaissance.

Brucker, Gene. *Florence, the Golden Age, 1138–1737.* Berkeley and Los Angeles, CA, 1998. The standard account.

Bruni, Leonardo. *The Humanism of Leonardo Bruni: Selected Texts.* Trans. Gordon Griffiths, James Hankins, and David Thompson. Binghamton, NY, 1987. Excellent translations, with introductions, to the Latin works of a key Renaissance humanist.

Burke, Peter. *The Renaissance.* New York, 1997. A brief introduction by an influential modern historian.

Burkhardt, Jacob. *The Civilization of the Renaissance in Italy.* Many editions. The nineteenth-century work that first crystallized an image of the Italian Renaissance, and with which scholars have been wrestling ever since.

Cassirer, Ernst, et al., eds. *The Renaissance Philosophy of Man.* Chicago, 1948. Important original works by Petrarch, Ficino, and Pico della Mirandola, among others.

Castiglione, Baldassare. *The Book of the Courtier.* Many editions. The translations by C. S. Singleton (New York, 1959) and by George Bull (New York, 1967) are both excellent.

Cellini, Benvenuto. *Autobiography.* Trans. George Bull. Baltimore, MD, 1956. This Florentine goldsmith (1500–1571) is the source for many of the most famous stories about the artists of the Florentine Renaissance.

Cochrane, Eric, and Julius Kirshner, eds. *The Renaissance.* Chicago, 1986. An outstanding collection, from the University of Chicago Readings in Western Civilization series.

Erasmus, Desiderius. *The Praise of Folly.* Trans. J. Wilson. Ann Arbor, MI, 1958.

Fox, Alistair. *Thomas More: History and Providence.* Oxford, 1982. A balanced account of a man too easily idealized.

Grafton, Anthony, and Lisa Jardine. *From Humanism to the Humanities: Education and the Liberal Arts in Fifteenth- and Sixteenth-Century Europe.* London, 1986. An account that presents Renaissance humanism as the elitist cultural program of a self-interested group of pedagogues.

Grendler, Paul, ed. *Encyclopedia of the Renaissance.* New York, 1999. A valuable reference work.

Hale, John R. *The Civilization of Europe in the Renaissance.* New York, 1993. A synthetic volume summarizing the life's work of a major Renaissance historian.

Hankins, James. *Plato in the Italian Renaissance.* Leiden and New York, 1990. A definitive study of the reception and influence of Plato on Renaissance intellectuals.

———, ed. *Renaissance Civic Humanism: Reappraisals and Reflections.* Cambridge and New York, 2000. An excellent collection of scholarly essays reassessing republicanism in the Renaissance.

Jardine, Lisa. *Worldly Goods.* London, 1996. A revisionist account that emphasizes the acquisitive materialism of Italian Renaissance society and culture.

Kanter, Laurence, Hilliard T. Goldfarb, and James Hankins. *Botticelli's Witness: Changing Style in a Changing Florence.* Boston, 1997. This catalog for an exhibition of Botticelli's works, at the Gardner Museum in Boston, offers an excellent introduction to the painter and his world.

King, Margaret L. *Women of the Renaissance.* Chicago, 1991. Deals with women in all walks of life and in a variety of roles.

Kristeller, Paul O. *Eight Philosophers of the Italian Renaissance.* Stanford, 1964. An admirably clear and accurate account that fully appreciates the connections between medieval and Renaissance thought.

———. *Renaissance Thought: The Classic, Scholastic, and Humanistic Strains.* New York, 1961. Very helpful in defining the main trends of Renaissance thought.

Lane, Frederic C. *Venice: A Maritime Republic.* Baltimore, MD, 1973. An authoritative account.

Machiavelli, Niccolò. *The Discourses* and *The Prince.* Many editions. These two books must be read together if one is to understand Machiavelli's political ideas properly.

Martines, Lauro. *Power and Imagination: City-States in Renaissance Italy.* New York, 1979. Insightful account of the connections among politics, society, culture, and art.

More, Thomas. *Utopia.* Many editions.

Murray, Linda. *High Renaissance and Mannerism.* London, 1985. The place to begin a study of fifteenth- and sixteenth-century Italian art.

Olson, Roberta, *Italian Renaissance Sculpture.* New York, 1992. The most accessible introduction to the subject.

Perkins, Leeman L. *Music in the Age of the Renaissance.* New York, 1999. A massive new study that needs to be read in conjunction with Reese.

Rabelais, François. *Gargantua and Pantagruel.* Trans. J. M. Cohen. Baltimore, MD, 1955. A robust modern translation.

Reese, Gustave. *Music in the Renaissance,* rev. ed. New York, 1959. A great book; still authoritative, despite the more recent work by Perkins, which supplements but does not replace it.

Rice, Eugene F., Jr., and Anthony Grafton. *The Foundations of Early Modern Europe, 1460–1559,* 2d ed. New York, 1994. The best textbook account of its period.

Rowland, Ingrid D. *The Culture of the High Renaissance: Ancients and Moderns in Sixteenth-Century Rome.* Cambridge and New York, 2000. Beautifully written examination of the social, intellectual, and economic foundations of the Renaissance in Rome.

## CHAPTER 13

Bainton, Roland. *Erasmus of Christendom.* New York, 1969. Still the best biography in English of the Dutch reformer and intellectual.

———. *Here I Stand: A Life of Martin Luther.* Nashville, TN, 1950. Although old and obviously biased in Luther's favor, this remains an absorbing and dramatic introduction to Luther's life and thought.

Benedict, Philip. *Christ's Churches Purely Reformed: A Social History of Calvinism.* New Haven, CT, 2002. A wide-ranging recent survey of Calvinism in both western and eastern Europe.

Bossy, John. *Christianity in the West, 1400–1700.* Oxford and New York, 1985. A brilliant, challenging picture of the changes that took place in Christian piety and practice as a result of the sixteenth-century reformations.

Bouwsma, William J. *John Calvin: A Sixteenth-Century Portrait.* Oxford and New York, 1988. The best biography of the magisterial reformer.

Collinson, Patrick. *The Religion of Protestants: The Church in English Society, 1559–1625.* Oxford, 1982. A great book by a noted historian of early English Protestantism.

Dixon, C. Scott, ed. *The German Reformation: The Essential Readings*. Oxford, 1999. A collection of important recent articles.

Duffy, Eamon. *The Stripping of the Altars: Traditional Religion in England, c. 1400–c. 1550*. A brilliant study of religious exchange at the parish level.

Hillerbrand, Hans J., ed. *The Protestant Reformation*. New York, 1967. Source selections are particularly good for illuminating the political consequences of Reformation theological ideas.

*John Calvin: Selections from His Writings*, ed. John Dillenberger. Garden City, NY, 1971. A judicious selection, drawn mainly from Calvin's *Institutes*.

Loyola, Ignatius. *Personal Writings*. Trans. by Joseph A. Munitiz and Philip Endean. London and New York, 1996. An excellent collection that includes Loyola's autobiography, his spiritual diary, and some of his letters, as well as his *Spiritual Exercises*.

Luebke, David, ed. *The Counter-Reformation: The Essential Readings*. Oxford, 1999. A collection of nine important recent essays.

MacCulloch, Diarmaid. *Reformation: Europe's House Divided, 1490–1700*. London and New York, 2003. A definitive new survey; the best single-volume history of its subject in a generation.

*Martin Luther: Selections from His Writings*, ed. John Dillenberger. Garden City, NY, 1961. The standard selection, especially good on Luther's theological ideas.

McGrath, Alister E. *Reformation Thought: An Introduction*. Oxford, 1993. A useful explanation, accessible to non-Christians, of the theological ideas of the major Protestant reformers.

Mullett, Michael A. *The Catholic Reformation*. London, 2000. A sympathetic survey of Catholicism from the mid-sixteenth to the eighteenth century that presents the mid-sixteenth-century Council of Trent as a continuation of earlier reform efforts.

Oberman, Heiko A. *Luther: Man between God and the Devil*. Trans. by Eileen Walliser-Schwarzbart. New Haven, CT, 1989. A biography stressing Luther's preoccupations with sin, death, and the devil.

O'Malley, John W. *The First Jesuits*. Cambridge, MA, 1993. A scholarly account of the origins and early years of the Society of Jesus.

———. *Trent and All That: Renaming Catholicism in the Early Modern Era*. Cambridge, MA, 2000. Short, lively, and with a full bibliography.

Pettegree, Andrew, ed. *The Reformation World*. New York, 2000. An exhaustive multi-author work representing the most recent thinking about the Reformation.

Pelikan, Jaroslav. *Reformation of Church and Dogma, 1300–1700*. Vol. 4 of *A History of Christian Dogma*. Chicago, 1984. A masterful synthesis of Reformation theology in its late-medieval context.

Roper, Lyndal. *The Holy Household: Women and Morals in Reformation Augsburg*. Oxford, 1989. A pathbreaking study of Protestantism's effects on a single town, with special attention to its impact on attitudes toward women, the family, and marriage.

Shagan, Ethan H. *Popular Politics and the English Reformation*. Cambridge, 2002. Argues that the English Reformation reflects an ongoing process of negotiation, resistance, and response.

Tracy, James D. *Europe's Reformations, 1450–1650*. 2d ed. Lanham, MD, 2006. An outstanding survey, especially strong on Dutch and Swiss developments, but excellent throughout.

Williams, George H. *The Radical Reformation*. 3d ed. Kirksville, MO, 1992. Originally published in 1962, this is still the best book on Anabaptism and its offshoots.

## CHAPTER 14

Bonney, Richard. *The European Dynastic States, 1494–1660*. Oxford and New York, 1991. An excellent survey of continental Europe during the "long" sixteenth century.

Briggs, Robin. *Early Modern France, 1560–1715*, 2d ed. Oxford and New York, 1997. Updated and authoritative, with new bibliographies.

———. *Witches and Neighbors: The Social and Cultural Context of European Witchcraft*. New York, 1996. An influential recent account of Continental witchcraft.

Cervantes, Miguel de. *Don Quixote*. Trans. Edith Grossman. New York, 2003. A splendid new translation.

Clarke, Stuart. *Thinking with Demons: The Idea of Witchcraft in Early Modern Europe*. Oxford and New York, 1999. By placing demonology into the context of sixteenth- and seventeenth-century intellectual history, Clarke makes sense of it in new and exciting ways.

Cochrane, Eric, Charles M. Gray, and Mark A. Kishlansky. *Early Modern Europe: Crisis of Authority*. Chicago, 1987. An outstanding source collection from the University of Chicago Readings in Western Civilization series.

Held, Julius S., and Donald Posner. *Seventeenth- and Eighteenth-Century Art: Baroque Painting, Sculpture, Architecture*. New York, 1971. The most complete and best-organized introductory review of the subject in English.

Hibbard, Howard. *Bernini*. Baltimore, MD, 1965. The basic study in English of this central figure of Baroque artistic activity.

Hirst, Derek. *England in Conflict, 1603–1660: Kingdom, Community, Commonwealth*. Oxford and New York, 1999. A complete revision of the author's *Authority and Conflict* (1986), this is an up-to-date and balanced account of a period that has been a historical battleground over the past twenty years.

Hobbes, Thomas. *Leviathan*. Ed. Richard Tuck. 2d ed. Cambridge and New York, 1996. The most recent edition, containing the entirety of *Leviathan*, not just the first two parts.

Holt, Mack P. *The French Wars of Religion, 1562–1629*. Cambridge and New York, 1995. A clear account of a confusing time.

Kors, Alan Charles, and Edward Peters. *Witchcraft in Europe, 400–1700: A Documentary History*, 2d ed. Philadelphia, 2000. A superb collection of documents, significantly expanded in the second edition, with up-to-date commentary.

Kingdon, Robert. *Myths about the St. Bartholomew's Day Massacres, 1572–1576*. Cambridge, MA, 1988. A detailed account of this pivotal moment in the history of France.

Levack, Brian P. *The Witch-Hunt in Early Modern Europe*, 2d ed. London and New York, 1995. The best account of the persecution of suspected witches; coverage extends from Europe in 1450 to America in 1750.

Levin, Carole. *The Heart and Stomach of a King: Elizabeth I and the Politics of Sex and Power*. Philadelphia, 1994. A provocative argument for the importance of Elizabeth's gender for understanding her reign.

Limm, Peter, ed. *The Thirty Years' War.* London, 1984. An outstanding short survey, followed by a selection of primary-source documents.

Lynch, John. *Spain, 1516–1598: From Nation-State to World Empire.* Oxford and Cambridge, MA, 1991. The best book in English on Spain at the pinnacle of its sixteenth-century power.

MacCaffrey, Wallace. *Elizabeth I.* New York, 1993. An outstanding traditional biography by an excellent scholar.

Martin, Colin, and Geoffrey Parker. *The Spanish Armada.* London, 1988. Incorporates recent discoveries from undersea archaeology with more traditional historical sources.

Martin, John Rupert. *Baroque.* New York, 1977. A thought-provoking, thematic treatment, less a survey than an essay on the painting, sculpture, and architecture of the period.

Mattingly, Garrett. *The Armada.* Boston, 1959. A great narrative history that reads like a novel; for more recent work, however, see Martin and Parker.

Parker, Geoffrey. *The Dutch Revolt,* 2d ed. Ithaca, NY, 1989. The standard survey in English on the revolt of the Netherlands.

———. *Philip II.* Boston, 1978. A fine biography by an expert in both the Spanish and the Dutch sources.

———, ed. *The Thirty Years' War,* rev. ed. London and New York, 1987. A wide-ranging collection of essays by scholarly experts.

Pascal, Blaise. *Pensées* (French-English edition). Ed. H. F. Stewart. London, 1950.

Quint, David. *Montaigne and the Quality of Mercy: Ethical and Political Themes in the "Essais."* Princeton, NJ, 1999. A fine treatment that presents Montaigne's thought as a response to the French wars of religion.

Roberts, Michael. *Gustavus Adolphus and the Rise of Sweden.* London, 1973. Still the authoritative English-language account.

Russell, Conrad. *The Causes of the English Civil War.* Oxford, 1990. A penetrating and provocative analysis by one of the leading "revisionist" historians of the period.

Tracy, James D. *Holland under Habsburg Rule, 1506–1566: The Formation of a Body Politic.* Berkeley and Los Angeles, CA, 1990. A political history and analysis of the formative years of the Dutch state.

Van Gelderen, Martin. *Political Theory of the Dutch Revolt.* Cambridge, 1995. A fine book on a subject whose importance is too easily overlooked.

## CHAPTER 15

Beik, William. *Louis XIV and Absolutism.* New York, 2000. A helpful short examination of the French king, the theory of absolutism, and the social consequences of absolutist rule. Supplemented by translated documents from the period.

Jones, Colin. *The Great Nation: France From Louis XV to Napoleon.* New York, 2002. An excellent and readable scholarly account that argues that the France of Louis XV in the eighteenth century was even more dominant than the kingdom of Louis XIV in the preceding century.

Kishlansky, Mark A. *A Monarchy Transformed: Britain, 1603–1714.* London, 1996. An excellent survey that takes seriously its claims to be a "British" rather than merely an "English" history.

Klein, Herbert S. *The Atlantic Slave Trade.* Cambridge and New York, 1999. An accessible survey by a leading quantitative historian.

Koch, H. W. *A History of Prussia.* London, 1978. Still the best account of its subject.

Lewis, William Roger, gen. ed. *The Oxford History of the British Empire.* Vol. I: *The Origins of Empire: British Overseas Enterprise to the Close of the Seventeenth Century,* ed. Nicholas Canny. Vol. II: *The Eighteenth Century,* ed. Peter J. Marshall. Oxford and New York, 1998. A definitive, multiauthor account.

Locke, John. *Two Treatises of Government.* Ed. Peter Laslett. Rev. ed. Cambridge and New York, 1963. Laslett has revolutionized our understanding of the historical and ideological context of Locke's political writings.

Miller, John, ed. *Absolutism in Seventeenth-Century Europe.* London, 1990. An excellent, multiauthor survey, organized by country.

Monod, Paul K. *The Power of Kings: Monarchy and Religion in Europe, 1589–1715.* New Haven, Conn. 1999. A study of the seventeenth century's declining confidence in the divinity of kings.

Quataert, Donald. *The Ottoman Empire, 1700–1822.* Cambridge and New York, 2000. Well balanced and intended to be read by students.

Riasanovsky, Nicholas V., and Steinberg, Mark D. *A History of Russia.* 7th ed. Oxford and New York, 2005. Far and away the best single-volume textbook on Russian history: balanced, comprehensive, intelligent, and with full bibliographies.

Saint-Simon, Louis. *Historical Memoirs.* Many editions. The classic source for life at Louis XIV's Versailles.

Thomas, Hugh. *The Slave Trade: The History of the Atlantic Slave Trade, 1440–1870.* London and New York, 1997. A survey notable for its breadth and depth of coverage and for its attractive prose style.

Tracy, James D. *The Rise of Merchant Empires: Long-Distance Trade in the Early Modern World, 1350–1750.* Cambridge and New York, 1990. Important collection of essays by leading authorities.

White, Richard. *It's Your Misfortune and None of My Own: A History of the American West.* Norman, Okla., 1991. An outstanding textbook with excellent introductory chapters on European colonialism in the Americas.

# Glossary

**1973 OPEC oil embargo** Some leaders in the Arab-dominated Organization of the Petroleum Exporting Countries (OPEC) wanted to use oil as a weapon against the West in the Arab-Israeli conflict. After the 1972 Arab-Israeli war, OPEC instituted an oil embargo against Western powers. The embargo increased the price of oil and sparked spiraling inflation and economic troubles in Western nations, triggering in turn a cycle of dangerous recession that lasted nearly a decade. In response, Western governments began viewing the Middle Eastern oil regions as areas of strategic importance.

**Abbasid Caliphate** (750–930) The Abbasid family claimed to be descendants of Muhammad, and in 750 they successfully led a rebellion against the Umayyads, seizing control of Muslim territories in Arabia, Persia, North Africa, and the Near East. The Abbasids modeled their behavior and administration on that of the Persian princes and their rule on that of the Persian Empire, establishing a new capital at Baghdad.

**Peter Abelard** (1079–1142) Highly influential philosopher, theologian, and teacher, often considered the founder of the University of Paris.

**absolutism** Form of government in which one body, usually the monarch, controls the right to make war, tax, judge, and coin money. The term was often used to refer to the state monarchies in seventeenth- and eighteenth-century Europe. In other countries the end of feudalism is often associated with the legal abolition of serfdom, as in Russia in 1861.

**abstract expressionism** The mid-twentieth-century school of art based in New York that included Jackson Pollock, Willem de Kooning, and Franz Kline. It emphasized form, color, gesture, and feeling instead of figurative subjects.

**Academy of Sciences** This French institute of scientific inquiry was founded in 1666 by Louis XIV. France's statesmen exerted control over the academy and sought to share in the rewards of any discoveries its members made.

**Aeneas** Mythical founder of Rome, Aeneas was a refugee from the city of Troy whose adventures were described by the poet Virgil in the *Aeneid,* which mimicked the oral epics of Homer.

**Aetolian and Achaean Leagues** These two alliances among Greek poleis formed during the Hellenistic period in opposition to the Antigonids of Macedonia. Unlike the earlier defensive alliances of the classic period, each league represented a real attempt to form a political federation.

**African National Congress (ANC)** Multiracial organization founded in 1912 whose goal was to end racial discrimination in South Africa.

**Afrikaners** Descendants of the original Dutch settlers of South Africa; formerly referred to as Boers.

**agricultural revolution** Numerous agricultural revolutions have occurred in the history of western civilizations. One of the most significant began in the tenth century C.E., and increased the amount of land under cultivation as well as the productivity of the land. This revolution was made possible through the use of new technology, an increase in global temperatures, and more efficient methods of cultivation.

**AIDS** Acquired Immunodeficiency Syndrome. AIDS first appeared in the 1970s and has developed into a global health catastrophe; it is spreading most quickly in developing nations in Africa and Asia.

**Akhenaten** (r. 1352–1336) Pharaoh whose attempt to promote the worship of the sun god, Aten, ultimately weakened his dynasty's position in Egypt.

**Alexander the Great** (356–323 B.C.E.) The Macedonian king whose conquests of the Persian Empire and Egypt created a new Hellenistic world.

**Tsar Alexander II** (1818–1881) After the Crimean War, Tsar Alexander embarked on a program of reform and modernization, which included the emancipation of the serfs. A radical assassin killed him in 1881.

**Alexius Comnenus** (1057–1118) This Byzantine emperor requested Pope Urban II's help in raising an army to recapture Anatolia from the Seljuq Turks. Instead, Pope Urban II called for knights to go to the Holy Land and liberate it from its Muslim captors, which launched the First Crusade.

**Algerian War** (1954–1962) The war between France and Algerians seeking independence. Led by the National Liberation Front (FLN), guerrillas fought the French army in the mountains and desert of Algeria. The FLN also initiated a campaign of bombing and terrorism in Algerian cities that led French soldiers to torture many Algerians, attracting world attention and international scandal.

**Allied Powers** The First World War coalition of Great Britain, Ireland, Belgium, France, Italy, Russia, Portugal, Greece, Serbia, Montenegro, Albania, and Romania.

**al Qaeda** The radical Islamic organization founded in the late 1980s by former *mujahidin* who had fought against the Soviet Union in Afghanistan. Al Qaeda carried out the 9/11 terrorist attacks and is responsible as well for attacks in Africa, southeast Asia, Europe, and the Middle East.

**Americanization** The fear of many Europeans, since the 1920s, that U.S. cultural products, such as film, television, and music, exerted too much influence. Many of the criticisms centered on America's emphasis on mass production and organization. The fears about Americanization were not limited to culture. They extended to corporations, business techniques, global trade, and marketing.

**Americas** The name given to the two great land masses of the New World, derived from the name of the Italian geographer Amerigo Vespucci. In 1492, Christopher Columbus reached the Bahamas and the island of Hispaniola, which began an era of Spanish conquest in North and South America. Originally, the Spanish sought a route to Asia. Instead they discovered two continents whose wealth they decided to exploit. They were especially interested in gold and silver, which they either stole from indigenous peoples or mined using indigenous peoples as labor. Silver became Spain's most lucrative export from the New World.

**Ambrose** (c. 340–397) One of the early "fathers" of the Church, he helped to define the relationship between the sacred authority of bishops and other Church leaders and the secular authority of worldly rulers. He believed that secular rulers were a part of the Church, and therefore subject to it.

**Amnesty International** Nongovernmental organization formed in 1961 to defend "prisoners of conscience"—those detained for their beliefs, color, sex, ethnic origin, language, or religion.

**Anabaptists** Protestant movement that emerged in Switzerland in 1521; its adherents insisted that only adults could be baptized Christians.

**anarchists** In the nineteenth century, they were a political movement with the aim of establishing small-scale, localized, and self-sufficient democratic communities that could guarantee a maximum of individual sovereignty. Renouncing parties, unions and any form of modern mass organization, the anarchists fell back on the tradition of conspiratorial violence.

**Anti–Corn Law League** This organization successfully lobbied Parliament to repeal Britain's Corn Laws in 1846. The Corn Laws of 1815 had protected British landowners and farmers from foreign competition by establishing high tariffs, which kept bread prices artificially high for British consumers. The League saw these laws as unfair protection of the aristocracy and pushed for their repeal in the name of free trade.

**anti-Semitism** Anti-Semitism refers to hostility toward Jewish people. Religious forms of anti-Semitism have a long history in Europe, but in the nineteenth century anti-Semitism emerged as a potent ideology for mobilizing new constituencies in the era of mass politics. Playing on popular conspiracy theories about alleged Jewish influence in society, anti-Semites effectively rallied large bodies of supporters in France during the Dreyfus Affair, and then again during the rise of National Socialism in Germany after the First World War. The Holocaust would not have been possible without the acquiescence or cooperation of many thousands of people who shared anti-Semitic views.

**apartheid** The racial segregation policy of the Afrikaner-dominated South African government. Legislated in 1948 by the Afrikaner National Party, it existed in South Africa for many years.

**appeasement** The policy pursued by Western governments in the face of German, Italian, and Japanese aggression leading up to the Second World War. The policy, which attempted to accommodate and negotiate peace with the aggressive nations, was based on the belief that another global war like the First World War was unimaginable, a belief that Germany and its allies had been mistreated by the terms of the Treaty of Versailles, and a fear that fascist Germany and its allies protected the West from the spread of Soviet communism.

**Thomas Aquinas** (1225–1274) Dominican friar and theologian whose systematic approach to Christian doctrine was influenced by Aristotle.

**Arab-Israeli conflict** Between the founding of the state of Israel in 1948 and the present, a series of wars has been fought between Israel and neighboring Arab nations: the war of 1948 when Israel defeated attempts by Egypt, Jordon, Iraq, Syria, and Lebanon to prevent the creation of the new state; the 1956 war between Israel and Egypt over the Sinai peninsula; the 1967 war, when Israel gained control of additional land in the Golan Heights, the West Bank, the Gaza strip, and in the Sinai; and the Yom Kippur War of 1973, when Israel once again fought with forces from Egypt and Syria. A particularly difficult issue in all of these conflicts has been the situation of the 950,000 Palestinian refugees made homeless by the first war in 1948, and the movement of Israeli settlers into the occupied territories (outside of Israel's original borders). In the late 1970s, peace talks between Israel and Egypt inspired some hope of peace, but an on-going cycle of violence between Palestinians and the Israeli military have made a final settlement elusive.

**Arab nationalism** During the period of decolonization, secular forms of Arab nationalism, or pan-Arabism, found a wide following in many countries of the Middle East, especially in Egypt, Syria, and Iraq.

**Arianism** A variety of Christianity condemned as a heresy by the Roman Church, it derives from the teaching of a fourth-century priest called Arius, who rejected the idea that Jesus could be the divine equal of God.

**aristocracy** From the Greek word meaning "rule of the best." By 1000 B.C.E., the accumulated wealth of successful traders in Greece had created a new type of social class, which was based on wealth rather than warfare or birth. These men saw their wealth as a reflection of their superior qualities and aspired to emulate the heroes of old.

**Aristotle** (384–322 B.C.E.) A student of Plato, his philosophy was based on the rational analysis of the material world. In contrast to his teacher, he stressed the rigorous investigation of real phenomena, rather than the development of universal ethics. He was, in turn, the teacher of Alexander the Great.

**Asiatic Society** A cultural organization founded in 1784 by British Orientalists who lauded native culture but believed in colonial rule.

**Assyrians** A Semitic-speaking people that moved into northern Mesopotamia around 2400 B.C.E.

**Athens** Athens emerged as the Greek polis with the most markedly democratic form of government through a series of political struggles during the sixth century B.C.E. After its key role in the defeat of two invading Persian forces, Athens became the preeminent naval power of ancient Greece and the exemplar of Greek culture. But it antagonized many other poleis, and became embroiled in a war with Sparta and her allies in 431 B.C.E. Called the Peloponnesian War, this bloody conflict lasted until Athens was defeated in 404 B.C.E.

**atomic bomb** In 1945, the United States dropped atomic bombs on Hiroshima and Nagasaki in Japan, ending the Second World War. In 1949, the Soviet Union tested their first atomic bomb, and in 1953 both superpowers demonstrated their new hydrogen bombs. Strategically, the nuclearization of warfare polarized the world. Countries without nuclear weapons found it difficult to avoid joining either the Soviet or American military pacts. Over time countries split into two groups: the superpowers with enormous military budgets and those countries that relied on agreements and international law. The nuclearization of warfare also encouraged "proxy wars" between clients of superpowers. Culturally, the hydrogen bomb came to symbolize the age and both humanity's power and vulnerability.

**Augustine of Hippo** (c. 354–397) One of the most influential theologians of all time, Augustine described his conversion to Christianity in his autobiographical *Confessions* and articulated a new Christian worldview in *The City of God*, among other works.

**Augustus** (63 B.C.E.–14 C.E.) Born Gaius Octavius, this grandnephew and adopted son of Julius Caesar came to power in 27 B.C.E. His reign signals the end of the Roman Republic and the beginning of the Principate, the period when Rome was dominated by autocratic emperors.

**Auschwitz-Birkenau** The Nazi concentration camp in Poland that was designed to systematically murder Jews and gypsies. Between 1942 and 1944 over one million people were killed in Auschwitz-Birkenau.

**Austro-Hungarian Empire** The dual monarchy established by the Habsburg family in 1867; it collapsed at the end of the First World War.

**authoritarianism** A centralized and dictatorial form of government, proclaimed by its adherents to be superior to parliamentary democracy. Authoritarian governments claim to be above the law, do not respect individual rights, and do not tolerate political opposition. Authoritarian regimes that have developed a central ideology such as fascism or communism are sometimes termed "totalitarian."

**Avignon** A city in southeastern France that became the seat of the papacy between 1305 and 1377, a period known as the "Babylonian Captivity" of the Roman Church.

**Aztecs** An indigenous people of central Mexico; their empire was conquered by Spanish conquistadors in the sixteenth century.

**baby boom** (1950s) The post–Second World War upswing in U.S. birth rates; it reversed a century of decline.

**Babylon** An ancient city between the Tigris and Euphrates rivers, which became the capital of Hammurabi's empire in the eighteenth century B.C.E. and continued to be an important administrative and commercial capital under many subsequent imperial powers, including the Neo-Assyrians, Chaldeans, Persians, and Romans. It was here that Alexander the Great died in 323 B.C.E.

**Francis Bacon** (1561–1626) British philosopher and scientist who pioneered the scientific method and inductive reasoning. In other words, he argued that thinkers should amass many observations and then draw general conclusions or propose theories on the basis of this data.

**Balfour Declaration** A letter dated November 2, 1917, by Lord Arthur J. Balfour, British Foreign Secretary, that promised a homeland for the Jews in Palestine.

**Laura Bassi** (1711–1778) She was accepted into the Academy of Science in Bologna for her work in mathematics, which made her one of the few women to be accepted into a scientific academy in the seventeenth century.

**Bastille** The Bastille was a royal fortress and prison in Paris. In June of 1789, a revolutionary crowd attacked the Bastille to show support for the newly created National Assembly. The fall of the Bastille was the first instance of the people's role in revolutionary change in France.

**Bay of Pigs** (1961) The unsuccessful invasion of Cuba by Cuban exiles, supported by the U.S. government. The rebels intended to incite an insurrection in Cuba and overthrow the communist regime of Fidel Castro.

**Cesare Beccaria** (1738–1794) An influential writer during the Enlightenment who advocated for legal reforms. He believed that the only legitimate rationale for punishments was to maintain social order and to prevent other crimes. He argued for the greatest possible leniency compatible with deterrence and opposed torture and the death penalty.

**Beer Hall Putsch** (1923) An early attempt by the Nazi party to seize power in Munich; Adolf Hitler was imprisoned for a year after the incident.

**Benedict of Nursia** (c. 480–c. 547) Benedict's rule for monks formed the basis of western monasticism and is still observed in monasteries all over the world.

**Benedictine Monasticism** This form of monasticism was developed by Benedict of Nursia. Its followers adhere to a defined cycle of daily prayers, lessons, communal worship, and manual labor.

**Berlin airlift** (1948) The transport of vital supplies to West Berlin by air, primarily under U.S. auspices, in response to a blockade of the city that had been instituted by the Soviet Union to force the Allies to abandon West Berlin.

**Berlin Conference** (1884) At this conference, the leading colonial powers met and established ground rules for the partition of Africa by European nations. By 1914, 90 percent of African territory was under European control. The Berlin Conference ceded control of the Congo region to a private company run by King Leopold II of Belgium. They agreed to make the Congo valleys open to free trade and commerce, to end the slave trade in the region, and to establish a Congo Free State. In reality, King Leopold II's company established a regime that was so brutal in its treatment of local populations that an international scandal forced the Belgian state to take over the colony in 1908.

**Berlin wall** The wall built in 1961 by East German Communists to prevent citizens of East Germany from fleeing to West Germany; it was torn down in 1989.

**birth control pill** This oral contraceptive became widely available in the mid-1960s. For the first time, women had a simple method of birth control that they could take themselves.

**Otto von Bismarck** (1815–1898) The prime minister of Prussia and later the first chancellor of a unified Germany, Bismarck was the architect of German unification and helped to consolidate the new nation's economic and military power.

**Black Death** The epidemic of bubonic plague that ravaged Europe, Asia, and North Africa in the fourteenth century, killing one third to one half of the population.

**Black Jacobins** A nickname for the rebels in Saint Domingue, including Toussaint L'Ouverture, a former slave who in 1791 led the slaves of this French colony in the largest and most successful slave insurrection.

**Black Panthers** A radical African American group that came together in the 1960s; the Black Panthers advocated black separatism and pan-Africanism.

**Blackshirts** The troops of Mussolini's fascist regime; the squads received money from Italian landowners to attack socialist leaders.

**Black Tuesday** (October 29, 1929) The day on which the U.S. stock market crashed, plunging U.S. and international trading systems into crisis and leading the world into the "Great Depression."

**William Blake** (1757–1827) Romantic writer who criticized industrial society and factories. He championed the imagination and poetic vision, seeing both as transcending the limits of the material world.

***Blitzkrieg*** The German "lightning war" strategy used during the Second World War; the Germans invaded Poland, France, Russia, and other countries with fast-moving and well-coordinated attacks using aircraft, tanks and other armored vehicles, followed by infantry.

**Bloody Sunday** On January 22, 1905, the Russian tsar's guards killed 130 demonstrators who were protesting the tsar's mistreatment of workers and the middle class.

**Jean Bodin** (1530–1596) A French political philosopher whose *Six Books of the Commonwealth* advanced a theory of absolute sovereignty, on the grounds that the state's paramount duty is to maintain order and that monarchs should therefore exercise unlimited power.

**Boer War** (1898–1902) Conflict between British and ethnically European Afrikaners in South Africa, with terrible casualties on both sides.

**Boethius** (c. 480–524) Member of a prominent Roman family, he sought to preserve aspects of ancient learning by compiling a series of handbooks and anthologies appropriate for Christian readers. His translations of Greek philosophy provided a crucial link between classical Greek thought and the early intellectual culture of Christianity.

**Simon de Bolivar** (1783–1830) Venezuelan-born general called "The Liberator" for his assistance in helping Bolivia, Panama, Colombia, Ecuador, Peru, and Venezuela win independence from Spain.

**Bolsheviks** Former members of the Russian Social Democratic Party who advocated the destruction of capitalist political and economic institutions and started the Russian Revolution. In 1918 the Bolsheviks changed their name to the Russian Communist Party. Prominent Bolsheviks included Vladimir Lenin and Josef Stalin. Leon Trotsky joined the Bolsheviks late but became a prominent leader in the early years of the Russian Revolution.

**Napoleon Bonaparte** (1769–1821) Corsican-born French general who seized power and ruled as dictator from 1799 to 1814. After the successful conquest of much of Europe, he was defeated by Russian and Prussian forces and died in exile.

**Sandro Botticelli** (1445–1510) An Italian painter devoted to the blending of classical and Christian motifs by using ideas associated with the pagan past to illuminate sacred stories.

**bourgeoisie** Term for the middle class, derived from the French word for a town-dweller, *bourgeois.*

**Boxer Rebellion** (1899–1900) Chinese peasant movement that opposed foreign influence, especially that of Christian missionaries; it was finally put down after the Boxers were defeated by a foreign army composed mostly of Japanese, Russian, British, French, and American soldiers.

**Tycho Brahe** (1546–1601) Danish astronomer who believed that the careful study of the heavens would unlock the secrets of the universe. For over twenty years, he charted the movements of significant objects in the night sky, compiling the finest set of astronomical data in Europe.

**British Commonwealth of Nations** Formed in 1926, the Commonwealth conferred "dominion status" on Britain's white settler colonies in Canada, Australia, and New Zealand.

**Bronze Age** (3200–1200 B.C.E.) The name given to the era characterized by the discovery of techniques for smelting bronze (an alloy of copper and tin), which was then the strongest known metal.

**Brownshirts** Troops of young German men who dedicated themselves to the Nazi cause in the early 1930s by holding street marches, mass rallies, and confrontations. They engaged in beatings of Jews and anyone who opposed the Nazis.

**Lord Byron** (1788–1824) Writer and poet whose life helped give the Romantics their reputation as rebels against conformity. He was known for his love affairs, his defense of working-class movements, and his passionate engagement in politics, which led to his death in the war for Greek independence.

**Byzantium** The name of a small settlement located at the mouth of the Black Sea and at the crossroads between Europe and Asia, it was chosen by Constantine as the site for his new imperial capital of Constantinople in 324 C.E. Modern historians use this name to refer to the eastern Roman Empire that persisted in this region until 1453, but the inhabitants of that empire referred to themselves as Romans.

**Julius Caesar** (100–44 B.C.E.) The Roman general who conquered the Gauls, invaded Britain, and expanded Rome's territory in Asia Minor. He became the dictator of Rome in 46 B.C.E. His assassination led to the rise of his grandnephew and adopted son, Gaius Octavius Caesar, who ruled the Roman Empire as Caesar Augustus.

**caliphs** Islamic rulers who claim descent from the prophet Muhammad.

**John Calvin** (1509–1564) French-born theologian and reformer whose radical form of Protestantism was adopted in many Swiss cities, notably Geneva.

**Canary Islands** Islands off the western coast of Africa that were colonized by Portugal and Spain in the mid-fifteenth century, after which they became bases for further expeditions around the African coast and across the Atlantic.

**Carbonari** An underground organization that opposed the Concert of Europe's restoration of monarchies. They held influence in southern Europe during the 1820s, especially in Italy.

**Carolingian** Derived from the Latin name Carolus (Charles), this term refers to the Frankish dynasty that began with the rise to power of Charlemagne's grandfather, Charles Martel (688–741). At its height under Charlemagne (Charles the Great), the dynasty controlled what is now France, Germany, northern Italy, Catalonia and portions of central Europe. The Carolingian Empire collapsed under the combined weight of Viking raids, economic disintegration, and the growing power of local lords.

**Carolingian Renaissance** A cultural and intellectual flowering that took place around the court of Charlemagne in the late eighth and early ninth centuries.

**Carthage** The great maritime empire that grew out of Phoenician trading colonies in North Africa and rivaled the power of Rome. Its wars with Rome, collectively known as the Punic Wars, ended in its destruction in 146 B.C.E.

**Cassidorus** (c. 490–c. 583) Member of an old senatorial family, he was largely responsible for introducing classical learning into the monastic curriculum and for turning monasteries into centers for the collection, preservation, and transmission of knowledge. His *Institutes*, an influential handbook of classical literature for Christian readers, was intended as a preface to more intensive study of theology and the Bible.

**Catholic Church** The "universal" (catholic) church based in Rome, which was redefined in the sixteenth century, when the Counter-Reformation resulted in the rebirth of the Catholic faith at the Council of Trent.

**Margaret Cavendish** (1623–1673) English natural philosopher who developed her own speculative natural philosophy. She used this philosophy to critique those who excluded her from scientific debate.

**Camillo Benso di Cavour** (1810–1861) Prime minister of Piedmont-Sardinia and founder of the Italian Liberal Party; he played a key role in the movement for Italian unification under the Piedmontese king, Victor Emmanuel II.

**Central Powers** The First World War alliance between Germany, Austria-Hungary, Bulgaria, and Turkey.

**Charlemagne** (742–814) As king of the Franks (767–813), Charles "the Great" consolidated much of western Europe under his rule. In 800 he was crowned emperor by the pope in Rome, establishing a problematic precedent that would have wide-ranging consequences for western Europe's relationship with the eastern Roman Empire in Byzantium and for the relationship between the papacy and secular rulers.

**Charles I** (1625–1649) The second Stuart king of England, Charles attempted to rule without the support of Parliament, sparking a controversy that erupted into civil war in 1642. The king's forces were ultimately defeated and Charles himself was executed by act of Parliament, the first time in history that a reigning king was legally deposed and executed by his own government.

**Chartists** A working-class movement in Britain which called for reform of the political system in Britain during the 1840s. They were supporters of the "People's Charter," which had six demands: universal white male suffrage, secret ballots, an end to property qualifications as a condition of public office, annual parliamentary elections, salaries for members of the House of Commons, and equal electoral districts.

**Chernobyl** (1986) Site of the world's worst nuclear power accident; in Ukraine, formerly part of the Soviet Union.

**Christine de Pisan** (c. 1364–c. 1431) Born in Italy, Christine spent her adult life attached to the French court and, after her husband's death, became the first lay woman to earn her living by writing. She is the author of treatises in warfare and chivalry, as well as of books and pamphlets that challenge longstanding misogynistic claims.

**Church of England** Founded by Henry VIII in the 1530s, as a consequence of his break with the authority of the Roman pope.

**Winston Churchill** (1874–1965) British prime minister who led the country during the Second World War. He also coined the phrase "Iron Curtain" in a speech at Westminster College in 1946.

**Cicero** (106–43 B.C.E.) Influential Roman senator, orator, Stoic philosopher, and prose stylist. His published writings still form the basis of the instruction in classical Latin grammar and usage.

**Cincinnatus** (519–c. 430 B.C.E.) A legendary citizen-farmer of Rome who reluctantly accepted an appointment as dictator. After defeating Rome's enemies, he allegedly left his political office and returned to his farm.

**Civil Constitution of the Clergy** Issued by the French National Assembly in 1790, the Civil Constitution of the Clergy decreed that all bishops and priests should be subject to the authority of the state. Their salaries were to be paid out of the public treasury, and they were required to swear allegiance to the new state, making it clear they served France rather than Rome. The Assembly's aim was to make the Catholic Church of France a truly national and civil institution.

**civilizing mission** An argument made by Europeans to justify colonial expansion in the nineteenth century. Supporters of this idea believed that Europeans had a duty to impose western ideas of economic and political progress on the indigenous peoples they ruled over in their colonies. In practice, the colonial powers often found that ambitious plans to impose European practices on colonial subjects led to unrest that threatened the stability of colonial rule, and by the early twentieth century most colonial powers were more cautious in their plans for political or cultural transformation.

**Civil Rights Movement** The Second World War increased African American migration from the American South to northern cities, intensifying a drive for rights, dignity, and independence. By 1960, civil rights groups had started organizing boycotts and demonstrations directed at discrimination against blacks in the South. During the 1960s, civil rights laws passed under President Lyndon B. Johnson did bring African Americans some equality with regard to voting rights and, to a much lesser degree, school desegregation. However, racism continued in areas such as housing, job opportunities, and the economic development of African American communities.

**Civil War** (1861–1865) Conflict between the northern and southern states of America that cost over 600,000 lives; this struggle led to the abolition of slavery in the United States.

**Classical learning** The study of ancient Greek and Latin texts. After Christianity became the only legal religion of the Roman Empire, scholars needed to find a way to make classical learning applicable to a Christian way of life. Christian monks played a significant role in resolving this problem by reinterpreting the classics for a Christian audience.

**Cluny** A powerful Benedictine monastery founded in 910 whose enormous wealth and prestige would derive from its independence from secular authorities, as well as from its wide network of daughter houses (priories).

**Cold War** (1945–1991) Ideological, political, and economic conflict in which the USSR and Eastern Europe opposed the United States and Western Europe in the decades after the Second World War. The Cold War's origins lay in the breakup of the wartime alliance between the United States and the Soviet Union in 1945, and resulted in a division of Europe into two spheres: the West, commited to market capitalism, and the East, which sought to build Socialist republics in areas under Soviet Control. The Cold War ended with the collapse of the Soviet Union in 1991.

**collectivization** Stalin's plan for nationalizing agricultural production, begun in 1929. 25 million peasants were forced to give up their land and join 250,000 large collective farms. Many who resisted were deported to labor camps in the Far East, and Stalin's government cut off food rations to those areas most marked by resistance to collectivization. In the ensuing man-made famines, millions of people starved to death.

**Christopher Columbus** (1451–1506) A Genoese sailor who persuaded King Ferdinand and Queen Isabella of Spain to fund his expedition across the Atlantic, with the purpose of discovering a new trade route to Asia. His miscalculations landed him in the Bahamas and the island of Hispaniola in 1492.

**Committee of Public Safety** Political body during the French Revolution that was controlled by the Jacobins, who defended the revolution by executing thousands during the Reign of Terror (September 1793–July 1794).

**commune** A community of individuals who have banded together in a sworn association, with the aim of establishing their independence and setting up their own form of representative government. Many medieval towns originally founded by lords or monasteries gained their independence through such methods.

***The Communist Manifesto*** Radical pamphlet by Karl Marx (1818–1883) that predicted the downfall of the capitalist system and its replacement by a classless egalitarian society. Marx believed that this revolution would be accomplished by workers (the proletariat).

**Compromise of 1867** Agreement between the Habsburgs and the peoples living in Hungarian parts of the empire that the Habsburg state would be officially known as the Austro-Hungarian Empire.

**Concert of Europe** (1814–1815) The body of diplomatic agreements designed primarily by Austrian minister Klemens von Metternich between 1814 and 1848, and supported by other European powers until 1914. Its goal was to maintain a balance of power on the Continent and to prevent destabilizing social and political change in Europe.

**Congress of Vienna** (1814–1815) **and Restoration** International conference to reorganize Europe after the downfall of Napoleon and the French Revolution. European monarchies restored the Bourbon family to the French throne, agreed to respect each other's borders and to cooperate in guarding against future revolutions and war.

**conquistador** Spanish term for "conqueror," applied to the mercenaries and adventurers who campaigned against indigenous peoples in central and southern America.

**Conservatism** In the nineteenth century, conservatives aimed to legitimize and solidify the monarchy's authority and the hierarchical social order. They believed that change had to be slow, incremental, and managed so that the structures of authority were strengthened and not weakened.

**Constantine** (275–337) The first emperor of Rome to convert to Christianity, Constantine came to power in 312. In 324, he founded a new imperial capital, Constantinople, on the site of a maritime settlement known as Byzantium.

**Constantinople** Founded by the emperor Constantine on the site of a village called Byzantium, Constantinople became the new capital of the Roman Empire in 324 and continued to be the seat of imperial power after its capture by the Ottoman Turks in 1453. It is now known as Istanbul.

**Nicholas Copernicus** (1473–1543) Polish astronomer who advanced the idea that the earth moved around the sun.

**cosmopolitanism** Stemming from the Greek word meaning "universal city," the culture characteristic of the Hellenistic world challenged and transformed the more narrow worldview of the Greek polis.

**cotton gin** Invented by Eli Whitney in 1793, this device mechanized the process of separating cotton seeds from the cotton fiber, which sped up the production of cotton and reduced its price. This change made slavery profitable in the United States.

**Council of Constance** (1417–1420) A meeting of clergy and theologians in an effort to resolve the Great Schism within the Roman Church. The council deposed all rival papal candidates and elected a new pope, Martin V, but it also adopted the doctrine of conciliarism, which holds that the supreme authority within the Church rests with a representative general council and not with the pope. However, Martin V himself was an opponent of this doctrine, and refused to be bound by it.

**Council of Trent** The name given to a series of meetings held in the Italian city of Trent (Trento) between 1545 and 1563, when leaders of the Roman Church reaffirmed Catholic doctrine and instituted internal reforms.

**Counter-Reformation** The movement to counter the Protestant Reformation, initiated by the Catholic Church at the Council of Trent in 1545.

**coup d'état** French term for the overthrow of an established government by a group of conspirators, usually with military support.

**Crimean War** (1854–1856) War waged by Russia against Great Britain and France. Spurred by Russia's encroachment on Ottoman territories, the conflict revealed Russia's military weakness when Russian forces fell to British and French troops.

**Cuban missile crisis** (1962) Diplomatic standoff between the United States and the Soviet Union that was provoked by the Soviet Union's attempt to base nuclear missiles in Cuba; it brought the world closer to nuclear war than ever before or since.

***Cuius regio, eius religio*** A Latin phrase meaning "as the ruler, so the religion." Adopted as a part of the settlement of the Peace of Augsburg in 1555, it meant that those principalities ruled by Lutherans would have Lutheranism as their official religion and those ruled by Catholics must practice Catholicism.

**cult of domesticity** Concept associated with Victorian England that idealized women as nurturing wives and mothers.

**cult of the Virgin** The beliefs and practices associated with the veneration of Mary the mother of Jesus, which became increasingly popular in the twelfth century.

**cuneiform** An early writing system that began to develop in Mesopotamia in the fourth millennium B.C.E. By 3100 B.C.E., its distinctive markings were impressed on clay tablets using a wedge-shaped stylus.

**Cyrus the Great** (c. 585–529 B.C.E.) As architect of the Persian Empire, Cyrus extended his dominion over a vast territory stretching from the Persian Gulf to the Mediterranean and incorporating the ancient civilizations of Mesopotamia. His successors ruled this Persian Empire as "Great Kings."

**Darius** (521–486 B.C.E.) The Persian emperor whose conflict with Aristagoras, the Greek ruler of Miletus, ignited the Persian Wars. In 490 B.C.E., Darius sent a large army to punish the Athenians for their intervention in Persian imperial affairs, but this force was defeated by Athenian hoplites on the plain of Marathon.

**Charles Darwin** (1809–1882) British naturalist who wrote *On the Origin of Species* and developed the theory of natural selection to explain the evolution of organisms.

**D-Day** (June 6, 1944) Date of the Allied invasion of Normandy, under General Dwight Eisenhower, to liberate Western Europe from German occupation.

**Decembrists** Russian army officers who were influenced by events in France and formed secret societies that espoused liberal governance. They were put down by Nicholas I in December 1825.

**Declaration of Independence** (1776) Historic document stating the principles of government on which the United States was founded.

**Declaration of the Rights of Man and of the Citizen** (1789) French charter of liberties formulated by the National Assembly during the French Revolution. The seventeen articles later became the preamble to the new constitution, which the Assembly finished in 1791.

**democracy** In ancient Greece, this form of government allowed a class of propertied male citizens to participate in the governance of their polis; but excluded women, slaves, and citizens without property from the political process. As a result, the ruling class amounted to only a small percentage of the entire population.

**René Descartes** (1596–1650) French philosopher and mathematician who emphasized the use of deductive reasoning.

**Denis Diderot** (1713–1784) French *philosophe* and author who was the guiding force behind the publication of the first encyclopedia. The encyclopedia showed how reason could be applied to nearly all realms of thought, and aimed to be a compendium of all human knowledge.

**Dien Bien Phu** (1954) Defining battle in the war between French colonialists and the Viet Minh that secured North Vietnam for Ho Chi Minh and his army and left the south to form its own government, to be supported by France and the United States.

**Diet of Worms** The select council of the Church that convened in the German city of Worms and condemned Martin Luther on a charge of heresy in 1521.

**Diocletian** (245–316) As emperor of Rome from 284 to 305, Diocletian recognized that the empire could not be governed by one man in one place. His solution was to divide the empire into four parts, each with its own imperial ruler, but he himself remained the dominant ruler of the resulting tetrarchy (rule of four). He also initiated the Great Persecution, a time when many Christians became martyrs to their faith.

**Directory** (1795–1799) Executive committee that governed after the fall of Robespierre and held control until the coup of Napoleon Bonaparte.

***Discourse on Method*** Philosophical treatise by René Descartes (1596–1650) proposing that the path to knowledge was through logical deduction, beginning with one's own self: "I think, therefore I am."

**Dominican Order** Also called the Order of Preachers, it was founded by Dominic of Osma (1170–1221), a Castilian preacher and theologian, and approved by Innocent III in 1216. The order was dedicated to the rooting out of heresy and the conversion of Jews and Muslims. Many of its members held teaching positions in European universities and contributed to the development of medieval philosophy and theology. Others became the leading administrators of the Inquisition.

**Dominion in the British Commonwealth** Canadian promise to maintain their fealty to the British crown, even after their independence in 1867. Later applied to Australia and New Zealand.

**Dreyfus Affair** The 1894 French scandal surrounding accusations that a Jewish captain, Alfred Dreyfus, sold military secrets to the Germans. Convicted, Dreyfus was sentenced to solitary confinement for life. However, after public outcry, it was revealed that the trial documents were forgeries, and Dreyfus was pardoned after a second trial in 1899. In 1906 he was fully exonerated and reinstated in the army. The affair revealed the depths of popular anti-Semitism in France.

**Alexander Dubček** (1921–1992) Communist leader of the Czechoslovakian government who advocated for "socialism with a human face." He encouraged debate within the party, academic and artistic freedom, and less censorship, which led to the "Prague spring" of 1968. People in other parts of Eastern Europe began to demonstrate in support of Dubček and demand their own reforms. When Dubček tried to democratize the Communist party and did not attend a meeting of the Warsaw Pact, the Soviets sent tanks and troops into Prague and ousted Dubček and his allies.

**Duma** The Russian parliament, created in response to the revolution of 1905.

**Dunkirk** The French port on the English Channel where the British and French forces retreated after sustaining heavy losses against the German military. Between May 27 and June 4, 1940, the Royal Navy evacuated over three hundred thousand troops using commercial and pleasure boats.

**Earth Summit** (1992) Meeting in Rio de Janeiro between many of the world's governments in an effort to address international environmental problems.

**Eastern Front** Battlefront between Berlin and Moscow during the First and Second World Wars..

**East India Company** (1600–1858) British charter company created to outperform Portuguese and Spanish traders in the Far East; in the eighteenth century the company became, in effect, the ruler of a large part of India. There was also a Dutch East India Company.

**Edict of Nantes** (1598) Issued by Henry IV of France in an effort to end religious violence. The edict declared France to be a Catholic country, but tolerated some forms of Protestant worship.

**Eleanor of Aquitaine** (1122–1204) Ruler of the wealthy province of Aquitaine and wife of Louis VII of France, Eleanor had her marriage annulled in order to marry the young count of Anjou, Henry Plantagenet, who became King Henry of England a year later. Mother of two future kings of England, she was an important patron of the arts.

**Elizabeth I** (1533–1603) Protestant daughter of Henry VIII and his second wife, Anne Boleyn, Elizabeth succeeded her sister Mary as the second queen regnant of England (1558–1603).

**emancipation of the serfs** (1861) The abolition of serfdom was central to Tsar Alexander II's program of modernization and reform, but it produced a limited amount of change. Former serfs now had legal rights. However, farm land was granted to the village communes instead of to individuals. The land was of poor quality and the former serfs had to pay for it in installments to the village commune.

**emperor** Originally the term for any conquering commander of the Roman army whose victories merited celebration in an official triumph. After Augustus seized power in 27 B.C.E., it was the title born by the sole ruler of the Roman Empire.

**empire** A centralized political entity consolidated through the conquest and colonization of other nations or peoples in order to benefit the ruler and/or his homeland.

**Enabling Act** (1933) Emergency act passed by the Reichstag (German parliament) that helped transform Hitler from Germany's chancellor, or prime minister, into a dictator, following the suspicious burning of the Reichstag building and a suspension of civil liberties.

**enclosure** Long process of privatizing what had been public agricultural land in eighteenth-century Britain; it helped to stimulate the development of commercial agriculture and forced many people in rural areas to seek work in cities during the early stages of industrialization.

***The Encyclopedia*** Joint venture of French *philosophe* writers, led by Denis Diderot (1713–1784), which proposed to summarize all modern knowledge in a multivolume illustrated work with over 70,000 articles.

**Friedrich Engels** (1820–1895) German social and political philosopher who collaborated with Karl Marx on many publications.

**English Civil War** (1642–1649) Conflicts between the English Parliament and King Charles I erupted into civil war, which ended in the defeat of the royalists and the execution of Charles on charges of treason against the crown. A short time later, Parliament's hereditary House of Lords was abolished and England was declared a Commonwealth.

**English Navigation Act of 1651** Act stipulating that only English ships could carry goods between the mother country and its colonies.

**Enlightenment** Intellectual movement in eighteenth-century Europe, that believed in human betterment through the application of reason to solve social, economic, and political problems.

**Epicureanism** A philosophical position articulated by Epicurus of Athens (c. 342–270 B.C.E.), who rejected the idea of an ordered universe governed by divine forces; instead, he emphasized individual agency and proposed that the highest good is the pursuit of pleasure.

**Desiderius Erasmus** (c. 1469–1536) Dutch-born scholar, social commentator, and Catholic humanist whose new translation of the Bible influenced the theology of Martin Luther.

**Estates-General** The representative body of the three estates in France. In 1789, King Louis XVI summoned the Estates-General to meet for the first time since 1614 because it seemed to be the only solution to France's worsening economic crisis and financial chaos.

**Etruscans** Settlers of the Italian peninsula who dominated the region from the late Bronze Age until the rise of the Roman Republic in the sixth century B.C.E.

**Euclid** Hellenistic mathematician whose *Elements of Geometry* forms the basis of modern geometry.

**eugenics** A Greek term, meaning "good birth," referring to the project of "breeding" a superior human race. It was popularly championed by scientists, politicians, and social critics in the late nineteenth and early twentieth centuries.

**European Common Market** (1957) The Treaty of Rome created the European Economic Community (EEC) or Common Market. The original members were France, West Germany, Italy, Belgium, Holland, and Luxembourg. The EEC sought to abolish trade barriers between its members and it pledged itself to common external tariffs, the free movement of labor and capital among the member nations, and uniform wage structures and social security systems to create similar working conditions in all member countries.

**European Union (EU)** Successor organization to the European Economic Community or European Common Market, formed by the Maastricht Treaty, which took effect in 1993. Currently 27 member states compose the EU, which has a governing council, an international court, and a parliament. Over time, member states of the EU have relinquished some of their sovereignty, and cooperation has evolved into a community with a single currency, the euro.

**Exclusion Act of 1882** U.S. congressional act prohibiting nearly all immigration from China to the United States; fueled by animosity toward Chinese workers in the American West.

**existentialism** Philosophical movement that arose out of the Second World War and emphasized the absurdity of human condition. Led by Jean-Paul Sartre and Albert Camus, existentialists encouraged humans to take responsibility for their own decisions and dilemmas.

**fascism** The doctrine founded by Benito Mussolini, which emphasized three main ideas: statism ("nothing above the state, nothing outside the state, nothing against the state"), nationalism, and militarism. Its name derives from the Latin *fasces*, a symbol of Roman imperial power adopted by Mussolini.

**Fashoda Incident** (1898) Disagreements between the French and the British over land claims in North Africa led to a standoff between armies of the two nations at the Sudanese town of Fashoda. The crisis was solved diplomatically. France ceded southern Sudan to Britain in exchange for a stop to further expansion by the British.

***The Feminine Mystique*** Groundbreaking book by feminist Betty Friedan (b. 1921), which tried to define "femininity" and explored how women internalized those definitions.

**Franz Ferdinand** (1863–1914) Archduke of Austria and heir to the Austro-Hungarian Empire; his assassination led to the beginning of the First World War.

**Ferdinand** (1452–1516) **and Isabella** (1451–1504) In 1469, Ferdinand of Aragon married the heiress to Castile, Isabella. Their union allowed them to pursue several ambitious policies, including the conquest of Granada, the last Muslim principality in Spain, and the expulsion of Spain's large Jewish community. In 1492, Isabella granted three ships to Christopher Columbus of Genoa (Italy), who went on to claim portions of the New World for Spain.

**Fertile Crescent** An area of fertile land in what is now Syria, Israel, Turkey, eastern Iraq, and western Iran that was able to sustain settlements due to its wetter climate and abundant natural food resources. Some of the earliest known civilizations emerged there between 9000 and 4500 B.C.E.

**feudalism** A problematic modern term that attempts to explain the diffusion of power in medieval Europe, and the many different kinds of political, social, and economic relationships that were forged through the giving and receiving of fiefs (*feoda*). But because it is anachronistic and inadequate, this term has been rejected by most historians of the medieval period.

**First Crusade** (1095–1099) Launched by Pope Urban II in response to a request from the Byzantine emperor Alexius Comnenus, who had asked for a small contingent of knights to assist him in fighting Turkish forces in Anatolia; Urban instead directed the crusaders' energies toward the Holy Land and the recapture of Jerusalem, promising those who took the cross (*crux*) that they would merit eternal salvation if they died in the attempt. This crusade prompted attacks against Jews throughout Europe and resulted in six subsequent—and unsuccessful—military campaigns.

**First World War** A total war from August 1914 to November 1918, involving the armies of Britain, France, and Russia (the Allies) against Germany, Austria-Hungary, and the Ottoman Empire (the Central Powers). Italy joined the Allies in 1915, and the United States joined them in 1917, helping to tip the balance in favor of the Allies, who also drew upon the populations and raw materials of their colonial possessions. Also known as the Great War.

**Five Pillars of Islam** The Muslim teaching that salvation is only assured through observance of five basic precepts: submission to God's will as described in the teachings of Muhammad, frequent prayer, ritual fasting, the giving of alms, and an annual pilgrimage to Mecca (the Hajj).

**Five-Year Plan** Soviet effort launched under Stalin in 1928 to replace the market with a state-owned and state-managed economy in order to promote rapid economic development over a five-year period and thereby "catch and overtake" the leading capitalist countries. The First Five-Year Plan was followed by the Second Five-Year Plan (1933–1937) and so on, until the collapse of the Soviet Union in 1991.

**fly shuttle** Invented by John Kay in 1733, this device sped up the process of weaving.

**Fourteen Points** President Woodrow Wilson proposed these points as the foundation on which to build peace in the world after the First World War. They called for an end to secret treaties, "open covenants, openly arrived at," freedom of the seas, the removal of international tariffs, the reduction of arms, the "self-determination of peoples," and the establishment of a League of Nations to settle international conflicts.

**Franciscan Order** Also known as the Order of the Friars Minor. The earliest Franciscans were followers of Francis of Assisi (1182–1226) and strove, like him, to imitate the life and example of Jesus. The order was formally established by Pope Innocent III in 1209. Its special mission was the care and instruction of the urban poor.

**Frankfurt Parliament** (1848–1849) Failed attempt to create a unified Germany under constitutional principles. In 1849, the assembly offered the crown of the new German nation to Frederick William IV of Prussia, but he refused the offer and suppressed a brief protest. The delegates went home disillusioned.

**Frederick the Great** (1712–1786) Prussian ruler (1740–1786) who engaged the nobility in maintaining a strong military and bureaucracy, and led Prussian armies to notable military victories. He also encouraged Enlightenment rationalism and artistic endeavors.

**French Revolution of 1789** In 1788, a severe financial crisis forced the French monarchy to convene an assembly known as the Estates General, representing the three estates of the realm: the clergy, the nobility, and the commons (known as the Third Estate). When the Estates General met in 1789, representatives of the Third Estate demanded major constitutional changes, and when the King and his government proved uncooperative, the Third Estate broke with the other two estates and renamed themselves the National Assembly, demanding a written constitution. The position of the National Assembly was confirmed by a popular uprising in Paris and the King was forced to accept the transformation of France into a constitutional monarchy. This constitutional phase of the revolution lasted until 1972, when the pressures of foreign invasion and the emergence of a more radical revolutionary movement caused the collapse of the monarchy and the establishment of a Republic in France.

**French Revolution of 1830** The French popular revolt against Charles X's July Ordinances of 1830, which dissolved the French Chamber of Deputies and restricted suffrage to exclude almost everyone except the nobility. After several days of violence, Charles abdicated the throne and was replaced by a constitutional monarch, Louis Philippe.

**French Revolution of 1848** Revolution overthrowing Louis Philippe in February, 1848, leading to the formation of the Second Republic (1848–1852). Initially enjoying broad support from both the middle classes and laborers in Paris, the new government became more conservative after elections in which the French peasantry participated for the first time. A workers' revolt was violently repressed in June, 1848, and in December 1848, Napoleon Bonaparte's nephew, Louis-Napoleon Bonaparte, was elected president. In 1852, Louis-Napoleon declared himself emperor and abolished the republic.

**Sigmund Freud** (1856–1939) The Austrian physician who founded the discipline of psychoanalysis and suggested that human behavior was largely motivated by unconscious and irrational forces.

**Galileo Galilei** (1564–1642) Italian physicist and inventor; the implications of his ideas raised the ire of the Catholic Church, and he was forced to retract most of his findings.

**Gallipoli** (1915) In the First World War, a combined force of French, British, Australian and New Zealand troops tried to invade the Gallipoli peninsula, in the first large-scale amphibious attack in history, and seize it from the Turks. After seven months of fighting, the Allies had lost 200,000 soldiers. Defeated, they withdrew.

**Mohandas K. (Mahatma) Gandhi** (1869–1948) The Indian leader who advocated nonviolent noncooperation to protest colonial rule and helped win home rule for India in 1947.

**Giuseppe Garibaldi** (1807–1882) Italian revolutionary leader who led the fight to free Sicily and Naples from the Habsburg Empire; the lands were then peaceably annexed by Sardinia to produce a unified Italy.

**Gaul** The region of the Roman Empire that was home to the Celtic people of that name, comprising modern France, Belgium, and western Germany.

**Geneva Peace Conference** (1954) International conference to restore peace in Korea and Indochina. The chief participants were the United States, the Soviet Union, Great Britain, France, the People's Republic of China, North Korea, South Korea, Vietnam, the Viet Minh party, Laos, and Cambodia. The conference resulted in the division of North and South Vietnam.

**Genoese** Inhabitants of the maritime city on Italy's northwestern coast, the Genoese were active in trading ventures along the Silk Road and in the establishment of trading colonies in the Mediterranean. They were also involved in the world of finance and backed the commercial ventures of other powers, especially Spain's.

**German Democratic Republic** Nation founded from the Soviet zone of occupation of Germany after the Second World War; also known as East Germany.

**German Social Democratic Party** Founded in 1875, it was the most powerful socialist party in Europe before 1917.

**Gilgamesh** Sumerian ruler of the city of Uruk around 2700 B.C.E., Gilgamesh became the hero of one of the world's oldest epics, which circulated orally for nearly a millennium before being written down.

**globalization** The term used to describe political, social, and economic networks that span the globe. These global exchanges are not limited by nation-states and in recent decades are associated with new technologies, such as the Internet. Globalization is not new, however, as human cultures and economies have been in contact with one another for centuries.

**Gold Coast** Name that European mariners and merchants gave to that part of West Equatorial Africa from which gold and slaves were exported. Originally controlled by the Portuguese, this area later became the British colony of the Gold Coast.

**Mikhail Gorbachev** (1931–) Soviet leader who attempted to reform the Soviet Union through his programs of *glasnost* and *perestroika* in the late 1980s. He encouraged open discussions in other countries in the Soviet bloc, which helped inspire the velvet revolutions throughout Eastern Europe. Eventually the political, social, and economic upheaval he had unleashed would lead to the breakup of the Soviet Union.

**Gothic style** A type of graceful architecture emerging in twelfth- and thirteenth-century England and France. The style is characterized by pointed arches, delicate decoration, and large windows.

**Olympe de Gouges** (1748–1793) French political radical and feminist whose *Declaration of the Rights of Woman* demanded an equal place for women in France.

**Great Depression** Global economic crisis following the U.S. stock market crash on October 29, 1929, and ending with the onset of the Second World War.

**Great Fear** (1789) Following the outbreak of revolution in Paris, fear spread throughout the French countryside, as rumors circulated that armies of brigands or royal troops were coming. The peasants and villagers organized into militias, while others attacked and burned the manor houses in order to destroy the records of manorial dues.

**Great Schism** (1378–1417) Also known as the Great Western Schism, to distinguish it from the longstanding rupture between the Greek East and Latin West. During the schism, the Roman Church was divided between two (and, ultimately, three) competing popes. Each pope claimed to be legitimate and each denounced the heresy of the others.

**Great Terror** (1936–1938) The systematic murder of nearly a million people and the deportation of another million and a half to labor camps by Stalin's regime in an attempt to consolidate power and remove perceived enemies.

**Greek East** After the founding of Constantinople, the eastern Greek-speaking half of the Roman Empire grew more populous, prosperous and central to imperial policy. Its inhabitants considered themselves to be the true heirs of Rome, and their own Orthodox Church to be the true manifestation of Jesus' ministry.

**Greek Independence** Nationalists in Greece revolted against the Ottoman Empire and fought a war that ended in Greek independence in 1827. They received crucial help from British, French, and Russian troops as well as widespread sympathy throughout Europe.

**Pope Gregory I** (r. 590–604) Also known as Gregory the Great, he was the first bishop of Rome to successfully negotiate a more universal role for the papacy. His political and theological agenda widened the rift between the western Latin (Catholic) Church and the eastern Greek (Orthodox) Church in Byzantium. He also articulated the Church's official position on the status of Jews, promoted affective approaches to religious worship, encouraged the Benedictine monastic movement, and sponsored missionary expeditions.

**Guernica** The Basque town bombed by German planes in April 1937 during the Spanish Civil War. It is also the subject of Pablo Picasso's famous painting from the same year.

**guilds** Professional organizations in commercial towns that regulated business and safeguarded the privileges of those practicing a particular craft. Often identical to confraternities ("brotherhoods").

**Gulag** The vast system of forced labor camps under the Soviet regime; it originated in 1919 in a small monastery near the Arctic Circle and spread throughout the Soviet Union. Penal labor was required of both ordinary criminals and those accused of political crimes. Tens of millions of people were sent to the camps between 1928 and 1953; the exact figure is unknown.

**Gulf War** (1991) Armed conflict between Iraq and a coalition of thirty-two nations, including the United States, Britain, Egypt, France, and Saudi Arabia. The seeds of the war were planted with Iraq's invasion of Kuwait on August 2, 1990.

**Habsburg Empire** Ruling house of Austria, which once ruled the Netherlands, Spain, and central Europe but came to settle in lands along the Danube River. It played a prominent role in European affairs for many centuries. In 1867, the Habsburg Empire was reorganized into the Austro-Hungarian Dual Monarchy, and in 1918 it collapsed.

**Hagia Sophia** The enormous church dedicated to "Holy Wisdom," built in Constantinople at the behest of the emperor Justinian in the sixth century C.E. When Constantinople fell to Ottoman forces in 1453, it became an important mosque.

**Haitian Revolution** (1802–1804) In 1802, Napoleon sought to reassert French control of Saint-Domingue, but stiff resistance and yellow fever crushed the French army. In 1804, Jean-Jacques Dessalines, a general in the army of former slaves, declared the independent state of Haiti. (See **slave revolt in Saint-Domingue**)

**Hajj** The annual pilgrimage to Mecca; an obligation for Muslims.

**Hammurabi** Ruler of Babylon from 1792 to 1750 B.C.E., Hammurabi issued a collection of laws that were greatly influential in the Near East and which constitute the world's oldest surviving law code.

**Harlem Renaissance** Cultural movement in the 1920s that was based in Harlem, a part of New York City with a large African American population. The movement gave voice to black novelists, poets, painters, and musicians, many of whom used their art to protest racial subordination.

**Hatshepsut** (1479–1458 C.E.) As a pharaoh during the New Kingdom, she launched several successful military campaigns and extended trade and diplomacy. She was an ambitious builder who probably constructed the first tomb in the Valley of the Kings. Though she never pretended to be a man, she was routinely portrayed with a masculine figure and a ceremonial beard.

**Hebrews** Originally a pastoral people divided among several tribes, they were briefly united under the rule of David and his son, Solomon, who promoted the worship of a single god, Yahweh, and constructed the first temple at the new capital city of Jerusalem. After Solomon's death, the Hebrew tribes were divided between the two kingdoms of Israel and Judah, which were eventually conquered by the Neo-Assyrian and Chaldean empires. It was in captivity that the Hebrews came to define themselves through worship of Yahweh, and to develop a religion, Judaism, that could exist outside of Judea. They were liberated by the Persian king Cyrus the Great in 539 B.C.E.

**Hellenistic art** The art of the Hellenistic period bridged the tastes, ideals, and customs of classical Greece and those that would be more characteristic of Rome. The Romans strove to emulate Hellenistic city planning and civic culture, and thereby exported Hellenistic culture to their own far-flung colonies in western Europe.

**Hellenistic culture** The "Greek-like" culture that dominated the ancient world in the wake of Alexander's conquests.

**Hellenistic kingdoms** Following the death of Alexander the Great, his vast empire was divided into three separate states: Ptolemaic Egypt (under the rule of the general Ptolemy and his successors), Seleucid Asia (ruled by the general Seleucus and his heirs) and Antigonid Greece (governed by Antigonus of Macedonia). Each state maintained its independence, but the shared characteristics of Greco-Macedonian rule and a shared Greek culture and heritage bound them together in a united cosmopolitan world.

**Hellenistic world** The various western civilizations of antiquity that were loosely united by shared Greek language and culture, especially around the eastern Mediterranean.

**Heloise** (c. 1090–1164) One of the foremost scholars of her time, she became the pupil and the wife of the philosopher and teacher Peter Abelard. In later life, she was the founder of a new religious order for women.

**Henry VIII** (1491–1547) King of England from 1509 until his death, Henry rejected the authority of the Roman Church in 1534 when the pope refused to annul his marriage to his queen, Catherine of Aragon; he became the founder of the Church of England.

**Henry of Navarre** (1553–1610) Crowned King Henry IV of France, he renounced his Protestantism but granted limited toleration for Huguenots (French Protestants) by the Edict of Nantes in 1598.

**Prince Henry the Navigator** (1394–1460) A member of the Portuguese royal family, Henry encouraged the exploration and conquest of western Africa and the trade in gold and slaves.

**hieroglyphs** The writing system of ancient Egypt, based on a complicated series of pictorial symbols. It fell out of use when Egypt was absorbed into the Roman Empire, and was only deciphered after the discovery of the Rosetta Stone in the early nineteenth century.

**Hildegard of Bingen** (1098–1179) A powerful abbess, theologian, scientist, musician, and visionary who claimed to receive regular revelations from God. Although highly influential in her own day, she was never officially canonized by the Church, in part because her strong personality no longer matched the changing ideal of female piety.

**Hiroshima** Japanese port devastated by an atomic bomb on August 6, 1945.

**Adolf Hitler** (1889–1945) The author of *Mein Kampf* and leader of the Nazis who became chancellor of Germany in 1933. Hitler and his Nazi regime started the Second World War and orchestrated the systematic murder of over five million Jews.

**Hitler-Stalin Pact** (1939) Treaty between Stalin and Hitler, which promised Stalin a share of Poland, Finland, the Baltic States, and Bessarabia in the event of a German invasion of Poland, which began shortly thereafter, on September 1, 1939.

**HIV epidemic** The first cases of HIV-AIDS appeared in the late 1970s. As HIV-AIDS became a global crisis, international organizations recognized the need for an early, swift, and comprehensive response to future outbreaks of disease.

**Thomas Hobbes** (1588–1679) English political philosopher whose *Leviathan* argued that any form of government capable of protecting its subjects' lives and property might act as an all-powerful sovereign. This government should be allowed to trample over both liberty and property for the sake of its own survival and that of his subjects. For in his natural state, Hobbes argued, man was like "a wolf" toward other men.

**Holy Roman Empire** The loosely allied collection of lands in central and western Europe ruled by the kings of Germany (and later Austria) from the twelfth century until 1806. Its origins are usually identified with the empire of Charlemagne, the Frankish king who was crowned emperor of Rome by the pope in 800.

**homage** A ceremony in which an individual becomes the "man" (French: *homme*) of a lord.

**Homer** (fl. 8th c. B.C.E.) A Greek rhapsode ("weaver" of stories) credited with merging centuries of poetic tradition in the epics known as the *Iliad* and the *Odyssey*.

**hoplite** A Greek foot-soldier armed with a spear or short sword and protected by a large round shield (*hoplon*). In battle, hoplites stood shoulder to shoulder in a close formation called a phalanx.

**Huguenots** French Protestants who endured severe persecution in the sixteenth and seventeenth centuries.

**humanism** A program of study associated with the movement known as the Renaissance, humanism aimed to replace the scholastic emphasis on logic and philosophy with the study of ancient languages, literature, history, and ethics.

**human rights** The belief that all people have the right to legal equality, freedom of religion and speech, and the right to participate in government. Human rights laws prohibit torture, cruel punishment, and slavery.

**David Hume** (1711–1776) Scottish writer who applied Newton's method of scientific inquiry and skepticism to the study of morality, the mind, and government.

**Hundred Years' War** (1337–1453) A series of wars between England and France, fought mostly on French soil and prompted by the territorial and political claims of English monarchs.

**Jan Hus** (c. 1373–1415) A Czech reformer who adopted many of the teachings of the English theolojan John Wyclif, and who also demanded that the laity be allowed to receive both the consecrated bread and wine of the Eucharist. The Council of Constance burned him at the stake for heresy. In response, his supporters, the Hussites, revolted against the Church.

**Saddam Hussein** (1937–2006) The former dictator of Iraq who invaded Iran in 1980 and started the eight-year-long Iran-Iraq War; invaded Kuwait in 1990, which led to the Gulf War of 1991; and was overthrown when the United States invaded Iraq in 2003. Involved in Iraqi politics since the mid-1960s, Hussein became the official head of state in 1979.

**Iconoclast Controversy** (717–787) A serious and often violent theological debate that raged in Byzantium after Emperor Leo III ordered the destruction of religious art on the grounds that any image representing a divine or holy personage is prone to promote idol worship and blasphemy. Iconoclast means "breaker of icons." Those who supported the veneration of icons were called "iconodules," "adherents of icons."

**Il-khanate** Mongol-founded dynasty in thirteenth-century Persia.

**Indian National Congress** Formed in 1885, this Indian political party worked to achieve Indian independence from British colonial control. The Congress was led by Ghandi in the 1920s and 1930s.

**Indian Rebellion of 1857** The uprising began near Delhi, when the military disciplined a regiment of Indian soldiers employed by the British for refusing to use rifle cartridges greased with pork fat—unacceptable to either Hindus or Muslims. Rebels attacked law courts and burned tax rolls, protesting debt and corruption. The mutiny spread through large areas of northwest India before being violently suppressed by British troops.

**Indo-Europeans** A group of people speaking variations of the same language who moved into the Near East and Mediterranean region shortly after 2000 B.C.E.

**indulgences** Grants exempting Catholic Christians from the performance of penance, either in life or after death. The abusive trade in indulgences was a major catalyst of the Protestant Reformation.

**Inkas** The highly centralized South American empire that was toppled by the Spanish conquistador Francisco Pizarro in 1533.

**Innocent III** (1160/61–1216) As pope, he wanted to unify all of Christendom under papal hegemony. He furthered this goal at the Fourth Lateran Council of 1215, which defined one of the Church's dogmas as the acknowledgement of papal supremacy. The council also took an unprecedented interest in the religious education and habits of every Christian.

**Inquisition** Tribunal of the Roman Church that aims to enforce religious orthodoxy and conformity.

**International Monetary Fund (IMF)** Established in 1945 to ensure international cooperation regarding currency exchange and monetary policy, the IMF is a specialized agency of the United Nations.

**Investiture Conflict** The name given to a series of debates over the limitations of spiritual and secular power in Europe during the eleventh and early twelfth century, it came to a head when Pope Gregory VII and Emperor Henry IV of Germany both claimed the right to appoint and invest bishops with the regalia of office. After years of diplomatic and military hostility, it was partially settled by the Concordat of Worms in 1122.

**Irish potato famine** Period of agricultural blight from 1845 to 1849 whose devastating results produced widespread starvation and led to mass emigration to America.

**Iron Curtain** Term coined by Winston Churchill in 1946 to refer to the borders of Eastern European nations that lay within the zone of Soviet control.

**Italian invasion of Ethiopia** (1896) Italy invaded Ethiopia, which was the last major independent African kingdom. Menelik II, the Ethiopian emperor, soundly defeated them.

**Ivan the Great** (1440–1505) Russian ruler who annexed neighboring territories and consolidated his empire's position as a European power.

**Jacobins** Radical French political group during the French Revolution that took power after 1792, executed the French king, and sought to remake French culture.

**Jacquerie** Violent 1358 peasant uprising in northern France, incited by disease, war, and taxes.

**James I** (1566–1625) Monarch who ruled Scotland as James VI, and who succeeded Elizabeth I as king of England in 1603. He oversaw the English vernacular translation of the Bible known by his name.

**Janissaries** Corps of enslaved soldiers recruited as children from the Christian provinces of the Ottoman Empire and brought up to display intense personal loyalty to the Ottoman sultan, who used these forces to curb local autonomy and as his personal bodyguards.

**Jerome** (c. 340–420) One of the early "fathers" of the Church, he translated the Bible from Hebrew and Greek into a popular form of Latin—hence the name by which this translation is known: the Vulgate, or "vulgar" (popular), Bible.

**Jesuits** The religious order formally known as the Society of Jesus, founded in 1540 by Ignatius Loyola to combat the spread of Protestantism. The Jesuits would become active in politics, education, and missionary work.

**Jesus** (c. 4 B.C.E.–c. 30 C.E.) A Jewish preacher and teacher in the rural areas of Galilee and Judea who was arrested for seditious political activity, tried, and crucified by the Romans. After his execution, his followers claimed that he had been resurrected from the dead and taken up into heaven. They began to teach that Jesus had been the divine representative of God, the Messiah foretold by ancient Hebrew prophets, and that he had suffered for the sins of humanity and would return to judge all the world's inhabitants at the end of time.

**Joan of Arc** (c. 1412–1431) A peasant girl from the province of Lorraine who claimed to have been commanded by God to lead French forces against the English occupying army during the Hundred Years' War. Successful in her efforts, she was betrayed by the French king and handed over to the English, who condemned her to death for heresy. Her reputation underwent a process of rehabilitation, but she was not officially canonized as a saint until 1920.

**Judaism** The religion of the Hebrews as it developed in the centuries after the establishment of the Hebrew kingdoms under David and Solomon, especially during the period of Babylonian Captivity.

**Justinian** (527–565) Emperor of Rome who unsuccessfully attempted to reunite the eastern and western portions of the empire. Also known for his important codification of Roman law, in the *Corpus Juris Civilis*.

**Justinian's Code of Roman Law** Formally known as the *Corpus Juris Civilis* or "body of civil law," this compendium consisted of a systematic compilation of imperial statutes, the writings of Rome's great legal authorities, a textbook of legal principles, and the legislation of Justinian and his immediate successors. As the most authoritative collection of Roman law, it formed the basis of canon law (the legal system of the Roman Church) and became essential to the developing legal traditions of every European state, as well as of many countries around the world.

***Das Kapital*** (Capital) The 1867 book by Karl Marx that outlined the theory behind historical materialism and attacked the socioeconomic inequities of capitalism.

**Johannes Kepler** (1571–1630) Mathematician and astronomer who elaborated on and corrected Copernicus's theory and is chiefly remembered for his discovery of the three laws of planetary motion that bear his name.

**Keynesian Revolution** Post-depression economic ideas developed by the British economist John Maynard Keynes, wherein the state took a greater role in managing the economy, stimulating it by increasing the money supply and creating jobs.

**KGB** Soviet political police and spy agency, first formed as the Cheka not long after the Bolshevik coup in October 1917. It grew to more than 750,000 operatives with military rank by the 1980s.

**Chingiz Khan** (c. 1167–1227) "Oceanic Ruler," the title adopted by the Mongol chieftain Temujin, founder of a dynasty that conquered much of southern Asia.

**Khanate** The major political unit of the vast Mongol Empire. There were four Khanates, including the Yuan Empire in China, forged by Chingiz Khan's grandson Kubilai in the thirteenth century.

**Ruhollah Khomeini** (1902–1989) Iranian Shi'ite religious leader who led the revolution in Iran after the abdication of the Shah in 1979. His government allowed some limited economic and political populism combined with strict constructions of Islamic law, restrictions on women's public life, and the prohibition of ideas or activities linked to Western influence.

**Nikita Khrushchev** (1894–1971) Leader of the Soviet Union during the Cuban missile crisis, Khrushchev came to power after Stalin's death in 1953. His reforms and criticisms of the excesses of the Stalin regime led to his fall from power in 1964.

**Kremlin** Once synonymous with the Soviet government, it refers to Moscow's walled city center and the palace originally built by Ivan the Great.

**Kristallnacht** Organized attack by Nazis and their supporters on the Jews of Germany following the assassination of a German embassy official by a Jewish man in Paris. Throughout Germany, thousands of stores, schools, cemeteries and synagogues were attacked on November 9, 1938. Dozens of people were killed, and tens of thousands of Jews were arrested and held in camps, where many were tortured and killed in the ensuing months.

**Labour party** Founded in Britain in 1900, this party represented workers and was based on socialist principles.

**Latin West** After the founding of Constantinople, the western Latin-speaking half of the Roman Empire became poorer and more peripheral, but it also fostered the emergence of new barbarian kingdoms. At the same time, the Roman pope claimed to have inherited both the authority of Jesus and the essential elements of Roman imperial authority.

**League of Nations** International organization founded after the First World War to solve international disputes through arbitration; it was dissolved in 1946 and its assets were transferred to the United Nations.

**Vladimir Lenin** (1870–1924) Leader of the Bolshevik Revolution in Russia (1917) and the first leader of the Soviet Union.

**Leviathan** A book by Thomas Hobbes (1588–1679) that recommended a ruler have unrestricted power.

**liberalism** Political and social theory that judges the effectiveness of a government in terms of its ability to protect individual rights. Liberals support representative forms of government, free trade, and freedom of speech and religion. In the economic realm, liberals believe that individuals should be free to engage in commercial or business activities without interference from the state or their community.

**lithograph** Art form that involves putting writing or design on stone and producing printed impressions.

**John Locke** (1632–1704) English philosopher and political theorist known for his contributions to liberalism. Locke had great faith in human reason, and believed that just societies were those which infringed the least on the natural rights and freedoms of individuals. This led him to assert that a government's legitimacy depended on the consent of the governed, a view that had a profound effect on the authors of the United States' Declaration of Independence.

**Louis XIV** (1638–1715) Called the "Sun King," he was known for his success at strengthening the institutions of the French absolutist state.

**Louis XVI** (1754–1793) Well-meaning but ineffectual king of France, finally deposed and executed during the French Revolution.

**Ignatius Loyola** (1491–1556) Founder of the Society of Jesus (commonly known as the Jesuits), whose members vowed to serve God through poverty, chastity, and missionary work. He abandoned his first career as a mercenary after reading an account of Christ's life written in his native Spanish.

**Lucretia** According to Roman legend, Lucretia was a virtuous Roman wife who was raped by the son of Rome's last king and who virtuously committed suicide in order to avoid bringing shame on her family.

**Luftwaffe** Literally "air weapon," this is the name of the German air force, which was founded during the First World War, disbanded in 1945, and reestablished when West Germany joined NATO in 1950.

***Lusitania*** The British passenger liner that was sunk by a German U-boat (submarine) on May 7, 1915. Public outrage over the sinking contibuted to the U.S. decision to enter the First World War.

**Martin Luther** (1483–1546) A German monk and professor of theology whose critique of the papacy launched the Protestant Reformation.

**ma'at** The Egyptian term for the serene order of the universe, with which the individual soul (*ka*) must remain in harmony. The power of the pharaoh was linked to ma'at, insofar as it ensured the prosperity of the kingdom. After the upheavals of the First Intermediate Period, the perception of the pharaoh's relationship with ma'at was revealed to be conditional, something that had to be earned.

**Niccolo Machiavelli** (1469–1527) As the author of *The Prince* and the *Discourses on Livy*, he looked to the Roman past for paradigms of greatness, while at the same time hoping to win the patronage of contemporary rulers who would restore Italy's political independence.

**Magna Carta** The "Great Charter" of 1215, enacted during the reign of King John of England and designed to limit his powers. Regarded now as a landmark in the development of constitutional government. In its own time, its purpose was to restore the power of great lords.

**Magyar nationalism** Lajos Kossuth led this national movement in the Hungarian region of the Habsburg Empire, calling for national independence for Hungary in 1848. With the support of Russia, the Habsburg army crushed the movement and all other revolutionary activities in the empire. Kossuth fled into exile.

**Moses Maimonides** (c. 1137–1204) Jewish scholar, physician, and scriptural commentator whose *Mishneh Torah* is a fundamental exposition of Jewish law.

**Thomas Malthus** (1766–1834) British political economist who believed that populations inevitably grew faster than the available food supply. Societies that could not control their population growth would be checked only by famine, disease, poverty, and infant malnutrition. He argued that governments could not alleviate poverty. Instead, the poor had to exercise "moral restraint," postpone marriage, and have fewer children.

**Nelson Mandela** (b. 1918) The South African opponent of apartheid who led the African National Congress and was imprisoned from 1962 until 1990. After his release from prison, he worked with Prime Minister Frederik Willem De Klerk to establish majority rule. Mandela became the first black president of South Africa in 1994.

**Manhattan Project** The secret U.S. government research project to develop the first nuclear bomb. The vast project involved dozens of sites across the United States, including New Mexico, Tennessee, Illinois, California, Utah, and Washington. The first test of a nuclear bomb was near Alamogordo, New Mexico on July 16, 1945.

**manors** Common farmland worked collectively by the inhabitants of entire villages, sometimes on their own initiative, sometimes at the behest of a lord.

**Mao Zedong** (1893–1976) The leader of the Chinese Revolution who defeated the Nationalists in 1949 and established the Communist regime in China.

**Marne** A major battle of the First World War in September 1914, which halted the German invasion of France and led to protracted trench warfare on the Western Front.

**Marshall Plan** Economic aid package given to Europe by the United States after the Second World War to promote reconstruction and economic development and to secure the countries from a feared communist takeover.

**Karl Marx** (1818–1883) German philosopher and economist who believed that a revolution of the working classes would overthrow the capitalist order and create a classless society. Author of *Das Kapital* and *The Communist Manifesto*.

**Marxists** Followers of the socialist political economist Karl Marx who called for workers everywhere to unite and create an independent political force. Marxists believed that industrialization produced an inevitable struggle between laborers and the class of capitalist property owners, and that this struggle would culminate in a revolution that would abolish private property and establish a society committed to social equality.

**Mary**; see **cult of the Virgin**.

**Mary I** (1516–1558) Catholic daughter of Henry VIII and his first wife, Catherine of Aragon, Mary Tudor was the first queen regnant of England. Her attempts to reinstitute Catholicism in England met with limited success, and after her early death she was labeled "Bloody Mary" by the Protestant supporters of her half sister and successor, Elizabeth I.

**mass culture** The spread of literacy and public education in the nineteenth century created a new audience for print entertainment and a new class of entrepreneurs in the media to cater to this audience. The invention of radio, film, and television in the twentieth century carried this development to another level, as millions of consumers were now accessible to the producers of news, information, and entertainment. The rise of this "mass culture" has been celebrated as an expression of popular tastes but also criticized as a vehicle for the manipulation of populations through clever and seductive propaganda.

**Mayans** Native American peoples whose culturally and politically sophisticated empire encompassed lands in present-day Mexico and Guatemala.

**Giuseppe Mazzini** (1805–1872) Founder of Young Italy and an ideological leader of the Italian nationalist movement.

**Mecca** Center of an important commercial network of the Arabian Peninsula and birthplace of the prophet Muhammad. It is now considered the holiest site in the Islamic world.

**Medici** A powerful dynasty of Florentine bankers and politicians whose ancestors were originally apothecaries ("medics").

**Meiji Empire** Empire created under the leadership of Mutsuhito, emperor of Japan from 1868 until 1912. During the Meiji period Japan became a world industrial and naval power.

**Mensheviks** Within the Russian Social Democratic Party, the Mensheviks advocated slow changes and a gradual move toward socialism, in contrast with the Bolsheviks, who wanted to push for a proletarian revolution. Mensheviks believed that a proletarian revolution in Russia was premature and that the country needed to complete its capitalist development first.

**mercantilism** A theory and policy for directing the economy of monarchical states between 1600 and 1800 based on the assumption that wealth and power depended on a favorable balance of trade (more exports and fewer imports) and the accumulation of precious metals. Mercantilists advocated forms of economic protectionism to promote domestic production.

**Maria Sybilla Merian** (1647–1717) A scientific illustrator and an important early entomologist. She conducted research on two continents and published the well-received *Metamorphosis of the Insects of Surinam*.

**Merovingian** A Frankish dynasty that claimed descent from a legendary ancestor called Merovic, the Merovingians were the only powerful family to establish a lasting kingdom in western Europe during the fifth and sixth centuries.

**Mesopotamia** The "land between the Tigris and the Euphrates rivers," Tigris and Euphrates where the civilization of Sumer, the first urban society, flourished.

**Klemens von Metternich** (1773–1859) Austrian foreign minister whose primary goals were to bolster the legitimacy of monarchies and, after the defeat of Napoleon, to prevent another large-scale war in Europe. At the Congress of Vienna, he opposed social and political change and wanted to check Russian and French expansion.

**Michelangelo Buonarroti** (1475–1564) A virtuoso Florentine sculptor, painter, and poet who spent much of his career in the service of the papacy. He is best known for the decoration of the Sistine Chapel and for his monumental sculptures.

**Middle Kingdom of Egypt** (2055–1650 B.C.E.) The period following the First Intermediate Period of dynastic warfare, which ended with the reassertion of pharonic rule under Mentuhotep II.

**Miletus** A Greek polis and Persian colony on the Ionian coast of Asia Minor. Influenced by the cultures of Mesopotamia, Egypt, and Lydia, it produced several of the ancient world's first scientists and sophists. Thereafter, a political conflict between the ruler of Miletus, Aristagoras, and the Persian Emperor, Darius, sparked the Persian Wars with Greece.

**John Stuart Mill** (1806–1873) English liberal philosopher whose faith in human reason led him to support a broad variety of civic and political freedoms for men and women, including the right to vote and the right to free speech.

**Slobodan Milosevic** (1941–2006) The Serbian nationalist politician who became president of Serbia and whose policies during the Balkan wars of the early 1990s led to the deaths of thousands of Croatians, Bosnian Muslims, Albanians, and Kosovars. After leaving office in 2000 he was arrested and tried for war crimes at the International Court in The Hague. The trial ended before a verdict with his death in 2006.

**Minoan Crete** A sea empire based at Knossos on the Greek island of Crete and named for the legendary King Minos. The Minoans dominated the Aegean for much of the second millennium B.C.E.

**Modernism** There were several different modernist movements in art and literature, but they shared three key characteristics. First, they had a sense that the world had radically changed and that this change should be embraced. Second, they believed that traditional aesthetic values and assumptions about creativity were ill-suited to the present. Third, they developed a new conception of what art could do that emphasized expression over representation and insisted on the value of novelty, experimentation, and creative freedom.

**Mongols** A nomadic people from the steppes of Central Asia who were united under the ruler Chingiz Khan. His conquest of China was continued by his grandson Kubilai and his great-grandson son Ogedei, whose army also seized southern Russia and then moved through Hungary and through Poland toward eastern Germany. The Mongol armies withdrew from Eastern Europe after the death of Ogedei, but his descendents continued to rule his vast empire for another half century.

**Michel de Montaigne** (1533–1592) French philosopher and social commentator, best known for his *Essays*.

**Montesquieu** (1689–1755) An Enlightenment *philosophe* whose most influential work was *The Spirit of Laws*. In this work he analyzed the structures that shaped law and categorized governments into three types: republics, monarchies, and despotisms. His ideas about the separation of powers between the executive, the legislative, and the judicial branches of government influenced the authors of the United States Constitution.

**Thomas More** (1478–1535) Christian humanist, English statesman, and author of *Utopia*. In 1529, he was appointed Lord Chancellor of England but resigned because he opposed King Henry VIII's plans to establish a national church under royal control. He was eventually executed for refusing to take an oath acknowledging Henry to be the head of the Church of England, and has since been canonized by the Catholic Church.

***mos maiorum*** Literally translated as "the code of the elders" or "the custom of ancestors." This unwritten code governed the lives of Romans under the Republic and stressed the importance of showing reverence to ancestral tradition. It was sacrosanct and essential to Roman identity, and an important influence on Roman culture, law, and religion.

**Wolfgang Amadeus Mozart** (1756–1791) Austrian composer, famous at a young age as a concert musician and later celebrated as a prolific composer of instrumental music and operas that are seen as the apogee of the Classical style in music.

**Muhammad** (570–632 C.E.) The founder of Islam, regarded as God's last and greatest prophet by his followers.

**Munich Conference** (1938) Hitler met with the leaders of Britain, France, and Italy and negotiated an agreement that gave Germany a major slice of Czechoslovakia. British prime minister Chamberlain believed that the agreement would bring peace to Europe. Instead, Germany invaded and seized the rest of Czechoslovakia.

**Muscovy** The duchy centered on Moscow whose dukes saw themselves as heirs to the Roman Empire. In the early fourteenth century, Moscow was under the control of the Mongol Khanate. After the collapse of the Khanate, the Muscovite grand duke, Ivan III, conquered all the Russian principalities between Moscow and the border of Poland-Lithuania, and then Lithuania itself. By the time of his death, Ivan had established Muscovy as a dominant power.

**Muslim learning and culture** The Crusades brought the Latin West in contact with the Islamic world, which impacted European culture in myriad ways. Europeans adapted Arabic numerals and mathematical concepts as well as Arabic and Persian words. Through Arabic translations, western scholars gained access to Greek learning, which had a profound influence on Christian theology. European scholars also learned from the Islamic world's accomplishments in medicine and science.

**Benito Mussolini** (1883–1945) The Italian founder of the Fascist party who came to power in Italy in 1922 and allied himself with Hitler and the Nazis during the Second World War.

**Mycenaean Greece** (1600–1200 B.C.E.) The term used to describe the civilization of Greece in the late Bronze Age, when territorial kingdoms like Mycenae formed around a king, a warrior caste, and a palace bureaucracy.

**Nagasaki** Second Japanese city on which the United States dropped an atomic bomb. The attack took place on August 9, 1945; the Japanese surrendered shortly thereafter, ending the Second World War.

**Napoleon III** (1808–1873) Nephew of Napoleon Bonaparte, Napoleon III was elected president of the French Second Republic in 1848 and made himself emperor of France in 1852. During his reign (1852–70), he rebuilt the French capital of Paris. Defeated in the France-Prussian War of 1870, he went into exile.

**Napoleonic Code** Legal code drafted by Napoleon in 1804 and based on Justinian's *Corpus Iuris Civilis*. It distilled different legal traditions to create one uniform law. The code confirmed the abolition of feudal privileges of all kinds and set the conditions for exercising property rights.

**Napoleon's military campaigns** In 1805, the Russians, Prussians, Austrians, Swedes, and British attempted to contain Napoleon, but he defeated them. Out of his victories, Napoleon created a new empire and affiliated states. In 1808, he invaded Spain, but fierce resistance prevented Napoleon from achieving a complete victory. In 1812, Napoleon invaded Russia, and his army was decimated as it retreated from Moscow during the winter. After the Russian campaign, the united European powers defeated Napoleon and forced him into exile. He escaped and reassumed command of his army, but the European powers defeated him for the final time at the Battle of Waterloo.

**Gamal Abdel Nasser** (1918–1970) Former president of Egypt and the most prominent spokesman for secular pan-Arabism. He became a target for Islamist critics, such as Sayyid Qutb and the Muslim Brotherhood, angered by the Western-influenced policies of his regime.

**National Assembly of France** Governing body of France that succeeded the Estates-General in 1789 during the French Revolution. It was composed of, and defined by, the delegates of the Third Estate.

**National Association for the Advancement of Colored People (NAACP)** Founded in 1910, this U.S. civil rights organization was dedicated to ending inequality and segregation for black Americans.

**National Convention** The governing body of France from September 1792 to October 1795. It declared France a republic and then tried and executed the French king. The Convention also confiscated the property of the enemies of the revolution, instituted a policy of de-Christianization, changed marriage and inheritance laws, abolished slavery in its colonies, placed a cap on the price of necessities, and ended the compensation of nobles for their lost privileges.

**nationalism** Movement to unify a country under one government based on perceptions of the population's common history, customs, and social traditions.

**nationalism in Yugoslavia** In the 1990s, Slobodan Milosevic and his allies reignited Serbian nationalism in the former Yugoslavia, which led non-Serb republics in Croatia and Slovenia to seek independence. The country erupted into war, with the worst violence taking place in Bosnia, a multi-ethnic region with Serb, Croatian and Bosnian Muslim populations. European diplomats proved powerless to stop attempts by Croatian and Serbian military and paramilitary forces to claim territory through ethnic cleansing and violent intimidation. Atrocities were committed on all sides, but pro-Serb forces were responsible for the most deaths.

**NATO** The North Atlantic Treaty Organization, a 1949 military agreement between the United States, Canada, Great Britain, and eight Western European nations, which declared that an armed attack against any one of the members would be regarded as an attack against all. Created during the Cold War in the face of the Soviet Union's control of Eastern Europe, NATO continues to exist today and the membership of twenty-eight states includes former members of the Warsaw Pact as well as Albania and Turkey.

**Nazi party** Founded in the early 1920s, the National Socialist German Workers' Party (NSDAP) gained control over Germany under the leadership of Adolf Hitler in 1933 and continued in power until Germany was defeated in 1945.

**Nazism** The political movement in Germany led by Adolf Hitler, which advocated a violent anti-Semitic, anti-Marxist, pan-German ideology.

**Neo-Assyrian Empire** (883–859 B.C.E.–612–605 B.C.E.) Assurnasirpal II laid the foundations of the Neo-Assyrian Empire through military campaigns against neighboring peoples. Eventually, the empire stretched from the Mediterranean Sea to Western Iran. A military dictatorship governed the empire through its army, which it used to frighten and oppress both its subjects and its enemies. The empire's ideology was based on waging holy war in the name of its principal god, Assur, and the exaction of tribute through terror.

**Neoliberalism** Neoliberals believe that free markets, profit incentives, and restraints on both budget deficits and social welfare programs are the best guarantee of individual liberties. Beginning in the 1980s, neoliberal theory was used to structure the policy of financial institutions like the International Monetary Fund and the World Bank, which turned away from interventionist policies in favor of market-driven models of economic development.

**Neolithic Revolution** The "New" Stone Age, which began around 11,000 B.C.E., saw new technological and social developments, including managed food production, the beginnings of permanent settlements, and the rapid intensification of trade.

**Neoplatonism** A school of thought based on the teachings of Plato and prevalent in the Roman Empire, which had a profound effect on the formation of Christian theology. Neoplatonists argued that nature is a book written by its creator to reveal the ways of God to humanity. Convinced that God's perfection must be reflected in nature, neoplatonists searched for the ideal and perfect structures that they believed must lie behind the "shadows" of the everyday world.

**New Deal** President Franklin Delano Roosevelt's package of government reforms that were enacted during the depression of the 1930s to provide jobs for the unemployed, social welfare programs for the poor, and security to the financial markets.

**New Economic Policy** In 1921, the Bolsheviks abandoned war communism in favor of the New Economic Policy (NEP). Under NEP, the state still controlled all major industry and financial concerns, while individuals could own private property, trade freely within limits, and farm their own land for their own benefit. Fixed taxes replaced grain requisition. The policy successfully helped Soviet agriculture recover from the civil war, but was later abandoned in favor of collectivization.

**Isaac Newton** (1642–1727) One of the foremost scientists of all time, Newton was an English mathematician and physicist; he is noted for his development of calculus, work on the properties of light, and theory of gravitation.

**Tsar Nicholas II** (1868–1918) The last Russian tsar, who abdicated the throne in 1917. He and his family were executed by the Bolsheviks on July 17, 1918.

**Friedrich Nietzsche** (1844–1900) The German philosopher who denied the possibility of knowing absolute "truth" or "reality," since all knowledge comes filtered through linguistic, scientific, or artistic systems of representation. He also criticized Judeo-Christian morality for instilling a repressive conformity that drained civilization of its vitality.

**nongovernmental organizations (NGOs)** Private organizations like the Red Cross that play a large role in international affairs.

**North American Free Trade Agreement (NAFTA)** Treaty negotiated in the early 1990s to promote free trade among Canada, the United States, and Mexico.

***Novum Organum*** Work by English statesman and scientist Francis Bacon (1561–1626) that advanced a philosophy of study through observation.

**October Days** (1789) The high price of bread and the rumor that the king was unwilling to cooperate with the assembly caused the women who worked in Paris's large central market to march to Versailles along with their supporters to address the king. Not satisfied with their initial reception, they broke through the palace gates and called for the king to return to Paris from Versailles, which he did the following day.

**Old Kingdom of Egypt** (c. 2686–2160 B.C.E.) During this time, the pharaohs controlled a powerful and centralized bureaucratic state whose vast human and material resources are exemplified by the pyramids of Giza. This period came to an end as the pharaoh's authority collapsed, leading to a period of dynastic warfare and localized rule.

**OPEC (Organization of the Petroleum Exporting Countries)** Organization created in 1960 by oil-producing countries in the Middle East, South America, and Africa to regulate the production and pricing of crude oil.

**Operation Barbarossa** The codename for Hitler's invasion of the Soviet Union in 1941.

**Opium Wars** (1839–1842) War fought between the British and Qing China to protect British trade in opium; resulted in the ceding of Hong Kong to the British.

**Oracle at Delphi** The most important shrine in ancient Greece. The priestess of Apollo who attended the shrine was believed to have the power to predict the future.

**Ottoman Empire** (c.1300–1923) During the thirteenth century, the Ottoman dynasty established itself as leader of the Turks. From the fourteenth to sixteenth centuries, they conquered Anatolia, Armenia, Syria, and North Africa as well as parts of southeastern Europe, the Crimea, and areas along the Red Sea. Portions of the Ottoman Empire persisted up to the time of the First World War, but it was dismantled in the years following it.

**Reza Pahlavi** (1919–1980) The Western-friendly Shah of Iran who was installed during a 1953 coup supported by Britain and the United States. After a lengthy economic downturn, public unrest, and personal illness, he retired from public life under popular pressure in 1979.

**Pan-African Conference** 1900 assembly in London that sought to draw attention to the sovereignty of African people and their mistreatment by colonial powers.

**Panhellenism** The "all Greek" culture that allowed ancient Greek colonies to maintain a connection to their homeland and to each other through their shared language and heritage. These colonies also exported their culture into new areas and created new Greek-speaking enclaves, which permanently changed the cultural geography of the Mediterranean world.

**pan-Slavism** Cultural movement that sought to unite native Slavic peoples within the Russian and Habsburg empires under Russian leadership.

**Partition of India** (1947) At independence, British India was partitioned into the nations of India and Pakistan. The majority of the population in India was Hindu and the majority of the population in Pakistan was Muslim. The process of partition brought brutal religious and ethnic warfare. More than one million Hindus and Muslims died and twelve million became refugees.

**Blaise Pascal** (1623–1662) A Catholic philosopher who wanted to establish the truth of Christianity by appealing simultaneously to intellect and emotion. In his *Pensées*, he argued that faith alone can resolve the world's contradictions and that his own awe in the face of evil and uncertainty must be evidence of God's existence.

**Paul of Tarsus** Originally known as Saul, Paul was a Greek-speaking Jew and Roman citizen who underwent a miraculous conversion experience and became the most important proponent of Christianity in the 50s and 60s C.E.

**Pax Romana** (27 B.C.E.–180 C.E.) Literally translated as "the Roman Peace." During this time, the Roman world enjoyed an unprecedented period of peace and political stability.

**Peace of Augsburg** A settlement negotiated in 1555 among factions within the Holy Roman Empire, it formulated the principle *cuius regio, eius religio,* "he who rules, his religion": meaning that the inhabitants of any given territory should follow the religion of its ruler, whether Catholic or Protestant.

**Peace of Paris** The 1919 Paris Peace Conference established the terms to end the First World War. Great Britain, France, Italy, and the United States signed five treaties with each of the defeated nations: Germany, Austria, Hungary, Turkey, and Bulgaria. The settlement is notable for the territory that Germany had to give up, including large parts of Prussia to the new state of Poland, and Alsace and Lorraine to France; the disarming of Germany; and the "war guilt" provision, which required Germany and its allies to pay massive reparations to the victors.

**Peace of Westphalia** (1648) An agreement reached at the end of the Thirty Years' War that altered the political map of Europe. France emerged as the predominant power on the Continent, while the Austrian Habsburgs had to surrender all the territories they had gained and could no longer use the office of the Holy Roman Emperor to dominate central Europe. Spain was marginalized and Germany became a volatile combination of Protestant and Catholic principalities.

**Pearl Harbor** The American naval base in Hawaii that was bombed by the Japanese on December 7, 1941, bringing the United States into the Second World War.

**peasantry** Term used in continental Europe to refer to rural populations that lived from agriculture. Some peasants were free, and could own land. Serfs were peasants who were legally bound to the land, and subject to the authority of the local lord.

**Peloponnesian War** The name given to the series of wars fought between Sparta (on the Greek Peloponnesus) and Athens from 431 B.C.E. to 404 B.C.E., and which ended in the defeat of Athens and the loss of her imperial power.

**perestroika** Introduced by Soviet leader Mikhail Gorbachev in June 1987, perestroika was the name given to economic and political reforms begun earlier in his tenure. It restructured the state bureaucracy, reduced the privileges of the political elite, and instituted a shift from the centrally planned economy to a mixed economy, combining planning with the operation of market forces.

**Periclean Athens** Following his election as *strategos* in 461 B.C.E., Pericles pushed through political reforms in Athens, which gave poorer citizens greater influence in politics. He promoted Athenians' sense of superiority through ambitious public works projects and lavish festivals to honor the gods, thus ensuring his continual reelection. But eventually, Athens' growing arrogance and aggression alienated it from the rest of the Greek world.

**Pericles** (c. 495–429) Athenian politician who occupied the office of strategos for thirty years and who presided over a series of civic reforms, building campaigns, and imperialist initiatives.

**Persian Empire** Consolidated by Cyrus the Great in 559, this empire eventually stretched from the Persian Gulf to the Mediterranean, and also encompassed Egypt. Persian rulers were able to hold this empire together through a policy of tolerance and a mixture of local and centralized governance. This imperial model of government would be adopted by many future empires.

**Persian Wars** (490–479 B.C.E.) In 501 B.C.E., a political conflict between the Greek ruler of Miletus, Aristagoras, and the Persian Emperor, Darius, sparked the first of the Persian Wars when Darius sent an army to punish Athens for its intervention on the side of the Greeks. Despite being heavily outnumbered, Athenian hoplites defeated the Persian army at the plain of Marathon. In 480 B.C.E., Darius' son Xerxes invaded Greece but was defeated at sea and on land by combined Greek forces under the leadership of Athens and Sparta.

**Peter the Great** (1672–1725) Energetic tsar who transformed Russia into a leading European country by centralizing government, modernizing the army, creating a navy, and reforming education and the economy.

**Francesco Petrarca (Petrarch)** (1304–1374) Italian scholar who revived interest in classical writing styles and was famed for his vernacular love sonnets.

**pharaoh** A term meaning "household" which became the title borne by the rulers of ancient Egypt. The pharaoh was regarded as the divine representative of the gods and the embodiment of Egypt itself. The powerful and centralized bureaucratic state ruled by the pharaohs was more stable and long-lived than any another civilization in world history, lasting (with few interruptions) for approximately three thousand years.

**Pharisees** A group of Jewish teachers and preachers that emerged in the third century B.C.E. They insisted that all of Yahweh's (God's) commandments were binding on all Jews.

**Philip II** (382–336 B.C.E.) King of Macedonia and father of Alexander, he consolidated the southern Balkans and the Greek city-states under Macedonian domination.

**Philip II Augustus** (1165–1223) The first French ruler to use the title "king of France" rather than "king of the French." After he captured Normandy and its adjacent territories from the English, he built an effective system of local administration, which recognized regional diversity while promoting centralized royal control. This administrative pattern would characterize French government until the French Revolution.

**Philistines** Descendants of the Sea Peoples who fled to the region that now bears their name, Palestine, after their defeat at the hands of the pharaoh Ramses III. They dominated their neighbors, the Hebrews, who used writing as an effective means of discrediting them (the Philistines themselves did not leave a written record to contest the Hebrews' views).

**philosophe** During the Enlightenment, this word referred to a person whose reflections were unhampered by the constraints of religion or dogma.

**Phoenicians** A Semitic people known for their trade in exotic purple dyes and other luxury goods, they originally settled in present-day Lebanon around 1200 B.C.E. and from there established commercial colonies throughout the Mediterranean, notably Carthage.

**Plato** (429–349 B.C.E.) A student of Socrates, Plato dedicated his life to transmitting his teacher's legacy through the writing of dialogues on philosophical subjects, in which Socrates himself plays the major role. The longest and most famous of these, known as the *Republic*, describes an idealized polis governed by a superior group of individuals chosen for their natural attributes of intelligence and character, who rule as "philosopher-kings."

**Plotinus** (204–270 C.E.) A Neoplatonist philosopher who taught that everything in existence has its ultimate source in the divine, and that the highest goal of life should be the mystic reunion of the soul with this divine source, something that can be achieved through contemplation and asceticism. This outlook blended with that of early Christianity and was instrumental in the spread of that religion within the Roman Empire.

**poleis** One of the major political innovations of the ancient Greeks was the *polis*, or city-state (plural *poleis*). These independent social and political entities began to emerge in the ninth century B.C.E., organized around an urban center and fostering markets, meeting places, and religious worship; frequently, poleis also controlled some surrounding territory.

**Marco Polo** (1254–1324) Venetian merchant who traveled through Asia for twenty years and published his observations in a widely read memoir.

**population growth** In the nineteenth century, Europe experienced a dramatic population growth. During this period, the spread of rural manufacturing allowed men and women to begin marrying younger and raising families earlier, which increased the size of the average family. As the population grew, the portion of young and fertile people also increased, which reinforced the population growth. By 1900, population growth was strongest in Britain and Germany, and slower in France.

**Potsdam** (1945) At this conference, Truman, Churchill and Stalin met to discuss their options at the conclusion of the Second World War, including making territorial changes to Germany and its allies and the question of war reparations.

**Prague spring** A period of political liberalization in Czechoslovakia between January and August 1968 that was initiated by Alexander Dubček, the Czech leader. This period of expanding freedom and openness in this Eastern bloc nation ended on August 20, when the USSR and Warsaw Pact countries invaded with 200,000 troops and 5,000 tanks.

**pre-Socratics** A group of philosophers in the Greek city of Miletus, who raised questions about humans' relationship with the natural world and the gods, and who formulated rational theories to explain the physical universe they observed. Their name reflects the fact that they flourished prior to the lifetime of Socrates.

**Price Revolution** An unprecedented inflation in prices in the latter half of the sixteenth century, resulting in part from the enormous influx of silver bullion from Spanish America.

**Principate** Modern term for the centuries of autocratic rule by the successors of Augustus, who seized power in 27 B.C.E. and styled himself *princeps* or Rome's "first man." See **Roman Republic**.

**Protestantism** The name given to the many dissenting varieties of Christianity that emerged during the Reformation in sixteenth-century western Europe. While Protestant beliefs and practices differed widely, all were united in their rejection of papal authority and the dogmas of the Roman Catholic Church.

**Provisional Government** After the collapse of the Russian monarchy, leaders in the Duma organized this government and hoped to establish a democratic system under constitutional rule. They also refused to concede military defeat, and it was impossible to institute domestic reforms and fight a war at the same time. As conditions worsened, the Bolsheviks gained support. In October 1917, they attacked the provisional government and seized control.

**Claudius Ptolomeus, called Ptolemy** (c. 85–165 C.E.) A Greek-speaking geographer and astronomer active in Roman Alexandria, he rejected the findings of previous Hellenistic scientists in favor of the erroneous theories of Aristotle, publishing highly influential treatises that promulgated these errors and suppressed (for example) the accurate findings of Aristarchus (who had discovered the Heliocentric universe) and Erathosthenes (who had calculated the circumference of the earth).

**Ptolemaic system** Ptolemy of Alexandria promoted Aristotle's understanding of cosmology. In this system, the heavens orbit the earth in an organized hierarchy of spheres, and the earth and the heavens are made of different matter and subject to different laws of motion. A prime mover produces the motion of the celestial bodies.

**Ptolemy** (c. 367–c. 284 B.C.E.) One of Alexander the Great's trusted generals (and possibly his half brother), he became pharaoh of Egypt and founded a new dynasty that lasted until that kingdom's absorption into the Roman Empire in 30 B.C.E.

**Punic Wars** (264–146 B.C.E.) Three periods of warfare between Rome and Carthage, two maritime empires who struggled for dominance of the Mediterranean. Rome emerged as the victor, destroyed the city of Carthage and took control of Sicily, North Africa and Hispania (Spain).

**pyramid** Constructed during the third millennium B.C.E., these structures were monuments to the power and divinity of the pharaohs entombed inside them.

**Qu'ran (often Koran)** Islam's holy scriptures, comprised of the prophecies revealed to Muhammad and redacted during and after his death.

**Raphael (Raffaelo Sarazio)** (1483–1520) Italian painter active in Rome, his works include *The School of Athens*.

**realism** Artistic and literary style which sought to portray common situations as they would appear in reality.

**Realpolitik** Political strategy based on advancing power for its own sake.

**reason** The human capacity to solve problems and discover truth in ways that can be verified intellectually. Philosophers distinguish the knowledge gained from reason from the teachings of instinct, imagination, and faith, which are verified according to different criteria.

**Reformation** Religious and political movement in sixteenth-century Europe that led to a break between dissenting forms of Christianity and the Roman Catholic Church; notable figures include Martin Luther and John Calvin.

**Reich** A term for the German state. The First Reich corresponded to the Holy Roman Empire (9th c.–1806), the Second Reich was from 1871 to 1919, and the Third Reich lasted from 1933 through May 1945.

**Renaissance** From the French word "rebirth," this term came to be used in the nineteenth century to describe the artistic, intellectual, and cultural movement that emerged in Italy after 1300, and which sought to recover and emulate the heritage of the classical past.

**Restoration period** (1815–1848) European movement after the defeat of Napoleon to restore Europe to its pre–French Revolution status and to prevent the spread of revolutionary or liberal political movements.

**Cardinal Richelieu** (1585–1642) First minister to King Louis XIII, he is considered by many to have ruled France in all but name, centralizing political power and suppressing dissent.

**Roman army** Under the Republic, the Roman army was made up of citizen-soldiers who were required to serve in wartime. As Rome's empire grew, the need for more fighting men led to the extension of citizenship rights and, eventually, to the development of a vast, professional, standing army that numbered as many as 300,000 by the middle of the third century B.C.E. By that time, however, citizens were not themselves required to serve, and many legions were made up of paid conscripts and foreign mercenaries.

**Roman citizenship** The rights and responsibilities of Rome's citizens were gradually extended to the free (male) inhabitants of other Italian provinces and later to most provinces in the Roman world. In contrast to slaves and non-Romans, Romans had the right to be tried in an imperial court and could not be legally subjected to torture.

**Roman Republic** The Romans traced the founding of their republic to the overthrow of their last king and the establishment of a unique form of constitutional government, in which the power of the aristocracy (embodied by the Senate) was checked by the executive rule of two elected consuls and the collective will of the people. For hundreds of years, this balance of power provided the Republic with a measure of political stability and prevented any single individual or clique from gaining too much power.

**Romanticism** Beginning in Germany and England in the late eighteenth century and continuing up to the end of the nineteenth century, Romanticism was a movement in art, music, and literature that countered the rationalism of the Enlightenment by placing greater value on human emotions and the power of nature to stimulate creativity.

**Jean-Jacques Rousseau** (1712–1778) Philosopher and radical political theorist whose *Social Contract* attacked privilege and inequality. One of the primary principles of Rousseau's political philosophy is that politics and morality should not be separated.

**Royal Society** This British society's goal was to pursue collective research. Members would conduct experiments, record the results, and share them with their peers, who would study the methods, reproduce the experiment, and assess the results. The arrangement gave English scientists a sense of common purpose as well as a system to reach a consensus on facts.

**Russian Revolution of 1905** After Russia's defeat in the Russo-Japanese War, Russians began clamoring for political reforms. Protests grew over the course of 1905, and the autocracy lost control of entire towns and regions as workers went on strike, soldiers mutinied, and peasants revolted. Forced to yield, Tsar Nicholas II issued the October Manifesto, which pledged individual liberties and provided for the election of a parliament (called the Duma). The most radical of the revolutionary groups were put down with force, and the pace of political change remained very slow in the aftermath of the revolution.

**Russo-Japanese War** (1904–1905) Japanese and Russian expansion collided in Mongolia and Manchuria. Russia was humiliated after the Japanese navy sunk its fleet, which helped provoke a revolt in Russia and led to an American-brokered peace treaty.

**Saint Bartholomew's Day Massacre** The mass murder of French Protestants (Huguenots) instigated by Queen Catherine de' Medici of France and carried out by Catholics. It began in Paris on 24 August 1572 and spread to other parts of France, continuing into October of that year. More than 70,000 people were killed.

**salons** Informal gatherings of intellectuals and aristocrats that allowed discourse about Enlightenment ideas.

**Sappho** (c. 620–c. 550 B.C.E.) One of the most celebrated Greek poets, she was revered as "the Tenth Muse" and emulated by many male poets. Ironically, though, only two of her poems survive intact, and the rest must be pieced together from fragments quoted by later poets.

**Sargon the Great** (r. 2334–2279 B.C.E.) The Akkadian ruler who consolidated power in Mesopotamia.

**SARS epidemic** (2003) The successful containment of severe acute respiratory syndrome (SARS) is an example of how international health organizations can effectively work together to recognize and respond to a disease outbreak. The disease itself, however, is a reminder of the dangers that exist in a globalized economy with a high degree of mobility in both populations and goods.

**Schlieffen Plan** Devised by German general Alfred von Schlieffen in 1905 to avoid the dilemma of a two-front war against France and Russia. The Schlieffen Plan required that Germany attack France first through Belgium and secure a quick victory before wheeling to the east to meet the slower armies of the Russians on the Eastern Front. The Schlieffen Plan was put into operation on August 2, 1914, at the outset of the First World War.

**Scientific Revolution of Antiquity** The Hellenistic period was the most brilliant age in the history of science before the seventeenth century C.E. Aristarchus of Samos posited the existence of a heliocentric universe. Eratosthenes of Alexandria accurately calculated the circumference of the earth. Archimedes turned physics into its own branch of experimental science. Hellenistic anatomists became the first to practice human dissection, which improved their understanding of human physiology. Ironically, most of these discoveries were suppressed by pseudo-scientists who flourished under the Roman Empire during the second century C.E., notably Claudus Ptolomeus Ptolemy) and Aelius Galenus (Galen).

**second industrial revolution** The technological developments in the last third of the nineteenth century, which included new techniques for refining and producing steel; increased availability of electricity for industrial, commercial, and domestic use; advances in chemical manufacturing; and the creation of the internal combustion engine.

**Second World War** Worldwide war that began in September 1939 in Europe, and even earlier in Asia (the Japanese invasion of Manchuria began in 1931), pitting Britain, the United States, and the Soviet Union (the Allies) against Nazi Germany, Italy, and Japan (the Axis). The war ended in 1945 with Germany and Japan's defeat.

**Seleucus** (d. 280 B.C.E.) The Macedonian general who ruled the Persian heartland of Alexander the Great's empire.

**Semitic** The Semitic language family has the longest recorded history of any linguistic group and is the root for most languages of the Middle and Near East. Ancient Semitic languages include those of the ancient Babylonians and Assyrians, Phoenician, the classical form of Hebrew, early dialects of Aramaic, and the classical Arabic of the Qu'ran.

**Sepoy Mutiny of 1857** See **Indian Rebellion of 1857**.

**serf** An unfree peasant laborer. Unlike slaves, serfs are "attached" to the land they work, and are not supposed to be sold apart from that land.

**William Shakespeare** (1564–1616) An English playwright who flourished during the reigns of Elizabeth I and James I, Shakespeare received a basic education in his hometown of Stratford-upon-Avon and worked in London as an actor before achieving success as a dramatist and poet.

**Shi'ites** An often-persecuted minority within Islam, Shi'ites believe that only descendants of Muhammad's successor Ali and his wife Fatimah (Muhammad's daughter) can have any authority over the Muslim community. Today, Shi'ites constitute the ruling party in Iran and are numerous in Iraq, but otherwise comprise only 10 percent of Muslims worldwide.

**Abbé Sieyès** (1748–1836) In 1789, he wrote the pamphlet "What is the Third Estate?" in which he posed fundamental questions about the rights of the Third Estate and helped provoke its secession from the Estates-General. He was a leader at the Tennis Court Oath, but he later helped Napoleon seize power.

**Sinn Féin** The Irish revolutionary organization that formed in 1900 to fight for Irish independence.

**Sino-Japanese War** (1894–1895) Conflict over the control of Korea in which China was forced to cede the province of Taiwan to Japan.

**slave revolt in Saint-Domingue** (1791–1804) In September of 1791, the largest slave rebellion in history broke out in Saint-Domingue, an important French colony in the Caribbean. In 1794, the revolutionary government in France abolished slavery in the colonies, though this act was essentially only recognizing the liberty that the slaves had seized by their own actions. Napoleon reestablished slavery in the French Caribbean in 1802, but failed in his attempt to reconquer Saint-Domingue. Armies commanded by former slaves succeeded in winning independence for a new nation, Haiti, in 1804, making the revolt in Saint-Domingue the first successful slave revolt in history.

**slavery** The practice of subjugating people to a life of bondage, and of selling or trading these unfree people. For most of human history, slavery had no racial or ethnic basis, and was widely practiced by all cultures and civilizations. Anyone could become a slave, for example, by being captured in war or by being sold for the payment of a debt. It was only in the fifteenth century, with the growth of the African slave trade, that slavery came to be associated with particular races and peoples.

**Adam Smith** (1723–1790) Scottish economist and liberal philosopher who proposed that competition between self-interested individuals led naturally to a healthy economy. He became famous for his influential book, *The Wealth of Nations* (1776).

**Social Darwinism** Belief that Charles Darwin's theory of natural selection (evolution) was applicable to human societies and justified the right of the ruling classes or countries to dominate the weak.

**social democracy** The belief that democracy and social welfare go hand in hand, and that diminishing the sharp inequalities of class society is crucial to fortifying democratic culture.

**socialism** Political ideology that calls for a classless society with collective ownership of all property.

**Society of Jesus**; see **Jesuits**.

**Socrates** (469–399 B.C.E.) The Athenian philosopher and teacher who promoted the careful examination of all inherited opinions and assumptions on the grounds that "the unexamined life is not worth living." A veteran of the Peloponnesian War, he was tried and condemned by his fellow citizens for engaging in allegedly seditious activities, and was executed in 399 B.C.E. His most influential pupils were the philosopher Plato and the historian and social commentator Xenophon.

**Solon** (d. 559 B.C.E.) Elected archon in 594 B.C.E., this Athenian aristocrat enacted a series of political and economic reforms that formed the basis of Athenian democracy.

**Somme** (1916) During this battle of the First World War, Allied forces attempted to take entrenched German positions from July to mid-November of 1916. Neither side was able to make any real gains despite massive casualties: 500,000 Germans, 400,000 British, and 200,000 French.

**Soviet bloc** International alliance that included the East European countries of the Warsaw Pact as well as the Soviet Union; it also came to include Cuba.

**soviets** Local councils elected by workers and soldiers in Russia. Socialists started organizing these councils in 1905, and the Petrograd soviet in the capital emerged as one of the centers of power after the Russian monarchy collapsed in 1917 in the midst of World War I. The soviets became increasingly powerful and pressed for social reform, the redistribution of land, and called for Russian withdrawal from the war effort.

**Spanish-American War** (1898) War between the United States and Spain in Cuba, Puerto Rico, and the Philippines. It ended with a treaty in which the United States took over the Philippines, Guam, and Puerto Rico; Cuba won partial independence.

**Spanish Armada** Supposedly invincible fleet of warships sent against England by Philip II of Spain in 1588 but vanquished by the English fleet and bad weather in the English Channel.

**Sparta** Around 650 B.C.E., after the suppression of a slave revolt, Spartan rulers militarized their society in order to prevent future rebellions and to protect Sparta's superior position in Greece, orienting their society toward the maintenance of their army. Sparta briefly joined forces with Athens and other poleis in the second war with Persia in 480–479 B.C.E., but these two rivals ultimately fell out again in 431 B.C.E., when Sparta and her Peloponnesian allies went to war against Athens and her allies. This bloody conflict lasted until Athens was defeated in 404 B.C.E., after Sparta received military aid from the Persians.

**Spartiate** A full citizen of Sparta, hence a professional soldier of the hoplite phalanx.

**spinning jenny** Invention of James Hargreaves (c. 1720–1774) that revolutionized the British textile industry by allowing a worker to spin much more thread than was possible on a hand spinner.

**SS (Schutzstaffel)** Formed in 1925 to serve as Hitler's personal security force and to guard Nazi party (NSDAP) meetings, the SS grew into a large militarized organization that became notorious for their participation in carrying out Nazi policies.

**Joseph Stalin** (1879–1953) The Bolshevik leader who succeeded Lenin as the leader of the Soviet Union and ruled until his death in 1953.

**Stalingrad** (1942–1943) The turning point on the Eastern Front during the Second World War came when the German army tried to take the city of Stalingrad in an effort to break the back of Soviet industry. The German and Soviet armies fought a bitter battle, in which more than half a million German, Italian, and Romanian soldiers were killed and the Soviets suffered over a million casualties. The German army surrendered after over five months of fighting. After Stalingrad, the Soviet army launched a series of attacks that pushed the Germans back.

**Stoicism** An ancient philosophy derived from the teachings of Zeno of Athens (fl. c. 300) and widely influential within the Roman Empire; it also impacted the development of Christianity. Stoics believe in the essential orderliness of the cosmos, and that everything that occurs happens for the best. Since everything is determined in accordance with rational purpose, no individual is master of his or her fate, and the only agency that human beings have consists in their responses to good fortune or adversity.

**Sumerians** The ancient inhabitants of southern Mesopotamia (modern Iraq and Kuwait) whose sophisticated civilization emerged around 4000 B.C.E.

**Sunnis** Proponents of Islam's customary religious practices (*sunna*) as they developed under the first two caliphs to succeed Muhammad, his father-in-law Abu-Bakr and his disciple Umar. Sunni orthodoxy is dominant within Islam, but is opposed by the Shi'ites (from the Arabic word *shi'a*, "faction").

**Syndicalists** A nineteenth century political movement that embraced a strategy of strikes and sabotage by workers. Their hope was that a general strike of all workers would bring down the capitalist state and replace it with workers' syndicates or trade associations. Their refusal to participate in politics limited their ability to command a wide influence.

**tabula rasa** Term used by John Locke (1632–1704) to describe man's mind before he acquired ideas as a result of experience; Latin for "clean slate."

**Tennis Court Oath** (1789) Oath taken by representatives of the Third Estate in June, 1789, in which they pledged to form a National Assembly and write a constitution limiting the powers of the king.

**Reign of Terror** (1793–1794) Campaign at the height of the French Revolution in which violence, including systematic executions of opponents of the revolution, was used to purge France of its "enemies" and to extend the revolution beyond its borders; radicals executed as many as 40,000 persons who were judged enemies of the state.

**Tetrarchy** The result of Diocletian's political reforms of the late third century C.E., which divided the Roman Empire into four quadrants.

**Theban Hegemony** The term describing the period when the polis of Thebes dominated the Greek mainland, which reached its height after 371 B.C.E., under leadership of the Theban general Epaminondas. It was in Thebes that the future King Philip II of Macedon spent his youth, and it was the defeat of Thebes and Athens at the hands of Philip and Alexander—at the Battle of Chaeronea in 338—that Macedonian hegemony was forcefully asserted.

**theory of evolution** Darwin's theory that linked biology to history. Darwin believed that competition between different organisms and struggle with the environment were fundamental and unavoidable facts of life. In this struggle, those individuals who were better adapted to their environment survived, while the weak perished. This produced a "natural selection," or favoring of certain adaptive traits over time, leading to a gradual evolution of different species.

**Third Estate** The population of France under the Old Regime was divided into three estates, corporate bodies that determined an individual's rights or obligations under royal law. The nobility constituted the First Estate, the clergy the Second, and the commoners (the vast bulk of the population) made up the Third Estate.

**Third Reich** The German state from 1933 to 1945 under Adolf Hitler and the Nazi party.

**Third World** Nations—mostly in Asia, Latin America, and Africa—that are not highly industrialized.

**Thirty Years' War** (1618–1648) Beginning as a conflict between Protestants and Catholics in Germany, this series of skirmishes escalated into a general European war fought on German soil by armies from Sweden, France, and the Holy Roman Empire.

**Timur the Lame** (1336–1405) Also known as Tamerlane, he was the last ruler of the Mongol Khans' Asian empire.

**Marshal Tito** (1892–1980) The Yugoslavian communist and resistance leader who became the leader of Yugoslavia and fought to keep his government independent of the Soviet Union. In response, the Soviet Union expelled Yugoslavia from the communist countries' economic and military pacts.

**towns** Centers for markets and administration. Towns existed in a symbiotic relationship with the countryside. They provided markets for surplus food from outlying farms as well as producing manufactured goods. In the Middle Ages, towns tended to grow up around a castle or monastery which afforded protection.

**Treaty of Brest-Litovsk** (1918) Separate peace between imperial Germany and the new Bolshevik regime in Russia. The treaty acknowledged the German victory on the Eastern Front and withdrew Russia from the war.

**Treaty of Utrecht** (1713) Resolution to the War of Spanish Succession that reestablished a balance of power in Europe, to the benefit of Britain and in ways that disadvantaged Spain, Holland, and France.

**Treaty of Versailles** Signed on June 28, 1919, this peace settlement ended the First World War and required Germany to surrender a large part of its most valuable territories and to pay huge reparations to the Allies.

**trench warfare** Weapons such as barbed wire and the machine gun gave tremendous advantage to defensive positions in World War I, leading to prolonged battles between entrenched armies in fixed positions. The trenches eventually consisted of twenty-five thousand miles of holes and ditches that stretched across the Western Front in northern France, from the Atlantic cost to the Swiss border during the First World War, On the eastern front, the large expanse of territories made trench warfare less significant.

**triangular trade** The eighteenth-century commercial Atlantic shipping pattern that took rum from New England to Africa, traded it for slaves taken to the West Indies, and brought sugar back to New England to be processed into rum.

**Triple Entente** Alliance developed before the First World War that eventually included Britain, France, and Russia.

**Truman Doctrine** (1947) Declaration promising U.S. economic and military intervention to counter any attempt by the Soviet Union to expand its influence. Often cited as a key moment in the origins of the Cold War.

**tsar** Russian word for "emperor," derived from the Latin *caesar* and similar to the German *kaiser,* it was the title claimed by the rulers of medieval Muscovy and of the later Russian Empire.

**Ubaid culture** An early civilization that flourished in Mesopotamia between 5500 and 4000 B.C.E., it was characterized by large village settlements and temple complexes: a precursor to the more urban civilization of the Sumerians.

**Umayyad Caliphate** (661–930) The Umayyad family resisted the authority of the first two caliphs who succeeded Muhammad, but eventually placed a member of their own family in that position of power. The Umayyad Caliphate ruled the Islamic world from 661 to 750, modeling their administration on that of the Roman Empire. But after a rebellion led by the rival Abbasid family, the power of the Umayyad Caliphate was confined to their territories in al-Andalus (Spain).

**Universal Declaration of Human Rights** (1948) United Nations declaration that laid out the rights to which all human beings were entitled.

**University of Paris** The reputation of Peter Abelard and his students attracted many intellectuals to Paris in the twelfth century, some of whom began offering instruction to aspiring scholars. By 1200, this loose association of teachers had formed themselves into a UNIVERSITAS, or corporation. They began collaborating in the higher academic study of the liberal arts with a special emphasis on theology.

**Pope Urban II** (1042?–1099) Instigator of the First Crusade (1096–1099), who promised that anyone who fought or died in the service of the Church would receive absolution from sin.

**urban populations** During the nineteenth century, urban populations in Europe increased six fold. For the most part, urban areas had medieval infrastructures, which new populations and industries overwhelmed. As a result, many European cities became overcrowded and unhealthy.

**Utopia** Title of a semi-satirical social critique by the English statesman Sir Thomas More (1478–1535); the word derives from the Greek "best place" or "no place."

**Lorenzo Valla** (1407–1457) One of the first practitioners of scientific philology (the historical study of language), Valla's analysis of the so-called Donation of Constantine showed that the document could not possibly have been written in the fourth century C.E., but must have been forged centuries later.

**vassal** A person who pledges to be loyal and subservient to a lord in exchange for land, income, or protection.

**velvet revolutions** The peaceful political revolutions throughout Eastern Europe in 1989.

**Verdun** (1916) This battle between German and French forces lasted for ten months during the First World War. The Germans saw the battle as a chance to break French morale through a war of attrition, and the French believed the battle to be a symbol of France's strength. In the end, over 400,000 lives were lost and the German offensive failed.

**Versailles Conference** (1919) Peace conference between the victors of the First World War; resulted in the Treaty of Versailles, which forced Germany to pay reparations and to give up its colonies to the victors.

**Queen Victoria** (1819–1901) Influential monarch who reigned from 1837 until her death; she presided over the expansion of the British Empire as well as the evolution of English politics and social and economic reforms.

**Viet Cong** Vietnamese communist group formed in 1954; committed to overthrowing the government of South Vietnam and reunifying North and South Vietnam.

**Vikings** (800–1000) The collapse of the Abbasid Caliphate disrupted Scandinavian commercial networks and turned traders into raiders (the word "viking" describes the activity of raiding). These raids often escalated into invasions that contributed to the collapse of the Carolingian Empire, resulted in the devastation of settled territories, and ended with the establishment of Viking colonies. By the tenth century, Vikings controlled areas of eastern England, Scotland, the islands of Ireland, Iceland, Greenland, and parts of northern France. They had also established the beginnings of the kingdom that became Russia and made exploratory voyages to North America, founding a settlement at Newfoundland (Canada).

**Leonardo da Vinci** (1452–1519) Florentine inventor, sculptor, architect, and painter whose breadth of interests typifies the ideal of "the Renaissance man."

***A Vindication of the Rights of Woman*** Noted work of Mary Wollstonecraft (1759–1797), English republican who applied Enlightenment political ideas to issues of gender.

**Virgil** (70–19 B.C.E.) An influential Roman poet who wrote under the patronage of the emperor Augustus. His *Aeneid* mimicked the ancient Greek epics of Homer, and told the mythical tale of Rome's founding by the Trojan refugee Aeneas.

**Visigoths** The tribes of "west" Goths who sacked Rome in 410 C.E. and later established a kingdom in the Roman province of Hispania (Spain).

**Voltaire** Pseudonym of French philosopher and satirist Francois Marie Arouet (1694–1778), who championed the cause of human dignity against state and church oppression. Noted deist and author of *Candide*.

**Lech Walsea** (1943–) Leader of the Polish labor movement Solidarity, which organized a series of strikes across Poland in 1980. They protested working conditions, shortages, and high prices. Above all, they demanded an independent labor union. Solidarity's leaders were imprisoned and the union banned, but they launched a new series of strikes in 1988, which led to the legalization of Solidarity and open elections.

**war communism** The Russian civil war forced the Bolsheviks to take a more radical economic stance. They requisitioned grain from the peasantry and outlawed private trade in consumer goods as "speculation." They also militarized production facilities and abolished money.

**Wars of the Roses** Fifteenth-century civil conflict between the English dynastic houses of Lancaster and York, each of which was symbolized by the heraldic device of a rose (red and white, respectively). It was ultimately resolved by the accession of the Lancastrian king Henry VII, who married Elizabeth of York.

**Warsaw Pact** (1955–1991) Military alliance between the USSR and other communist states that was established as a response to the creation of the NATO alliance.

***The Wealth of Nations*** 1776 treatise by Adam Smith, whose laissez-faire ideas predicted the economic boom of the Industrial Revolution.

**Weimar Republic** The government of Germany between 1919 and the rise of Hitler and the Nazi party.

**Western Front** Military front that stretched from the English Channel through Belgium and France to the Alps during the First World War.

**Whites** Refers to the "counterrevolutionaries" of the Bolshevik Revolution (1918–1921) who fought the Bolsheviks (the "Reds"); included former supporters of the tsar, Social Democrats, and large independent peasant armies.

**William the Conqueror** (1027–1087) Duke of Normandy who laid claim to the throne of England in 1066, defeating the Anglo-Saxon King Harold at the Battle of Hastings. He and his Norman followers imposed imperial rule in England through a brutal campaign of military conquest, surveillance, and the suppression of the indigenous Anglo-Saxon language.

**William of Ockham** (d. 1349) An English philosopher and Franciscan friar, he denied that human reason could prove fundamental theological truths, such as the existence of God: he argued that there is no necessary connection between the observable laws of nature and the unknowable essence of divinity. His theories, derived from the work of earlier scholastics, form the basis of the scientific method.

**Woodrow Wilson** (1856–1924) U.S. president who requested and received a declaration of war from Congress so that America could enter the First World War. After the war, his prominent role in the Paris Peace Conference signaled the rise of the United States as a world power. He also proposed the Fourteen Points, which influenced the peace negotiations.

**Maria Winkelmann** (1670–1720) German astronomer who worked with her husband in his observatory. Despite discovering a comet and preparing calendars for the Berlin Academy of Sciences, the academy would not let her take her husband's place within the body after he died.

**Witch craze** The rash of persecutions that took place in both Catholic and Protestant countries of early modern Europe and her colonies, facilitated by secular governments and religious authorities.

**women's associations** Because European women were excluded from the workings of parliamentary and mass politics, some women formed organizations to press for political and civil rights. Some groups focused on establishing educational opportunities for women, while others campaigned energetically for the vote.

**William Wordsworth** (1770–1850) Romantic writer whose central themes were nature, simplicity, and feeling. He considered nature to be man's most trustworthy teacher and source of sublime power that nourished the human soul.

**World Bank** International agency established in 1944 to provide economic assistance to war-torn nations and countries in need of economic development.

**John Wyclif** (c. 1330–1384) A professor of theology at the University of Oxford, Wyclif urged the English king to confiscate ecclesiastical wealth and to replace corrupt priests and bishops with men who would live according to the apostolic standards of poverty and piety. He advocated direct access to the Scriptures and promoted an English translation of the Bible. His teachings played an important role in the Peasants' Revolt of 1381 and inspired the still more radical initiatives of a group known as Lollards.

**Xerxes** (519?–465 B.C.E.) Xerxes succeeded his father, Darius, as Great King of Persia. Seeking to avenge his father's shame and eradicate any future threats to Persian hegemony, he launched his own invasion of Greece in 480 B.C.E. An allied Greek army defeated his forces in 479 B.C.E.

**Yalta Accords** Meeting between President Franklin D. Roosevelt, Prime Minister Winston Churchill, and Premier Joseph Stalin that occurred in the Crimea in 1945 shortly before the end of the Second World War to plan for the postwar order.

**Young Turks** The 1908 Turkish reformist movement that aimed to modernize the Ottoman Empire, restore parliamentary rule, and depose Sultan Abdul Hamid II.

**ziggurats** Temples constructed under the Dynasty of Ur in what is now Iraq, beginning around 2100 B.C.E.

**Zionism** A political movement dating to the end of the nineteenth century holding that the Jewish people constitute a nation and are entitled to a national homeland. Zionists rejected a policy of Jewish assimilation, and advocated the reestablishment of a Jewish homeland in Palestine.

**Zollverein** In 1834, Prussia started a customs union, which established free trade among the German states and a uniform tariff against the rest of the world. By the 1840s, the union included almost all of the German states except German Austria. It is considered an important precedent for the political unification of Germany, which was completed in 1870 under Prussian leadership.

**Zoroastrianism** One of the three major universal faiths of the ancient world, alongside Judaism and Christianity, it was derived from the teachings of the Persian Zoroaster around 600 B.C.E. Zoroaster redefined religion as an ethical practice common to all, rather than as a set of rituals and superstitions that cause divisions among people. Zoroastrianism teaches that there is one supreme god in the universe, Ahura-Mazda (Wise Lord), but that his goodness will be constantly assailed by the forces of evil until the arrival of a final "judgment day." Proponents of this faith should therefore help good to triumph over evil by leading a good life, and by performing acts of compassion and charity. Zoroastrianism exercised a profound influence over many early Christians, including Augustine.

**Ulrich Zwingli** (1484–1531) A former priest from the Swiss city of Zurich, Zwingli joined Luther and Calvin in attacking the authority of the Roman Catholic Church.

# Text Credits

**Leon B. Alberti**: "On the Importance of Literature" from *University of Chicago Readings in Western Civilization, Vol. 5*, eds. Cochrane & Krishner. Copyright © 1986 by The University of Chicago. Reprinted by permission of The University of Chicago Press. "On the Family" from *The Family in Renaissance Florence*, trans./ed. by Renée Neu Watkins (University of South Carolina Press, 1969), pp. 208–213. Reprinted by permission of the translator.

**Aristophanes**: 300 words from *Lysistrata and Other Plays* by Aristophanes, translated with an introduction by Alan H. Sommerstein (Penguin Classics, 1973). Copyright © Alan H. Sommerstein, 1973. Reproduced by permission of Penguin Books Ltd.

**Arrian**: 300 words from *The Campaigns of Alexander* by Arrian, translated by Aubrey de Sélincourt, revised with an introduction and notes by J.R. Hamilton (Penguin Classics 1958, Revised edition 1971). Copyright © the Estate of Aubrey de Sélincourt, 1958. Introduction and Notes copyright © J.R. Hamilton, 1971. Reproduced by permission of Penguin Books Ltd.

**Nels Bailkey (ed.)**: From Bailkey, *Readings in Ancient History, 5th Edition*. © 1996 Wadsworth, a part of Cengage Learning, Inc. Reproduced by permission. www.cengage.com/permissions.

**Bernard of Angers**: "Miracles of Saint Foy" from *Readings in Medieval History, 2nd Edition*, edited by Patrick J. Geary (Toronto, Ont: University of Toronto Press, 2003). Copyright © 2003. Reprinted by permission of the publisher.

**Henry Bettenson (ed.)**: "Obedience as a Jesuit Hallmark" from *Documents of the Christian Church*, 2nd Edition. Copyright © 1967, Oxford University Press. Reprinted by permission of Oxford University Press.

**Gabriel Biel**: "Execrabilis." Reprinted by permission of the publisher from *Defensorium Obedientiae Apostolicae Et Alia Documenta* by Gabriel Biel, edited and translated by Heiko A. Oberman, Daniel E. Zerfoss and William J. Courtenay, pp. 224–227, Cambridge, Mass.: The Belknap Press of Harvard University Press, Copyright © 1968 by the President and Fellows of Harvard College.

**Anna Comnena**: 340 words from *The Alexiad of Anna Comnena*, translated by E.R.A. Sewter (Penguin Classics, 1969). Copyright © E.R.A. Sewter, 1969. Reproduced by permission of Penguin Books Ltd.

**Michel de Montaigne**: From *Montaigne: Selections from the Essays*, translated and edited by Donald M. Frame (Harlan Davidson, Inc., 1973), pp. 34–38. Reprinted by permission of Harlan Davidson, Inc.

**Rene Descartes**: From *A Discourse on the Method of Correctly Conducting One's Reason*, trans. Ian Maclean. Copyright © Ian Maclean 2006. Reprinted by permission of Oxford University Press.

**Homer**: *Iliad*, translated by Stanley Lombardo, selections from pp. 115–118. Copyright © 1997 by Hackett Publishing Company, Inc. Reprinted by permission of Hackett Publishing Company, Inc. All rights reserved.

**Rosemary Horrox (ed.)**: From *The Black Death*, by Horrox (Trans., Ed.), 1994, Manchester University Press, Manchester, UK. Reprinted with permission.

**Juvenal**: 224 words from *The Sixteen Satires* by Juvenal, translated by Peter Green (Penguin Classics 1967, Revised edition 1974). Copyright © Peter Green 1967, 1974. Reproduced by permission of Penguin Books Ltd.

**Maureen Gallery Kovacs (trans.)**: Excerpts from *The Epic of Gilgamesh*, with an Introduction and Notes by Kovacs, Maureen Gallery, translator. Copyright © 1985, 1989 by the Board of Trustees of the Leland Stanford Junior University. All rights reserved. Used with the permission of Stanford University Press, www.sup.org.

**Carolyne Larrington**: "The Condemnation of Joan of Arc by the University of Paris" from *Women and Writing in Medieval Europe*, Carolyne Larrington, Copyright © 1995 Routledge. Reproduced by permission of Taylor & Francis Books UK.

**L.R. Loomis (ed. and trans.)**: "Haec Sancta Synodus" and "Frequens" from *The Council of Constance* (New York: Columbia University Press, 1961), pp. 229, 246–247. Copyright © 1962, Columbia University Press. Reprinted by permission of the publisher. We have made diligent efforts to contact the copyright holder to obtain electronic permission to reprint this selection. If you have information that would help us, please write to Permissions Department, W. W. Norton & Company, Inc., 500 Fifth Avenue, New York, NY 10110.

**H.R. Loyn and John Percival**: "Capitulary concerning the parts of Saxony" from *The Reign of Charlemagne: Documents on Carolingian Government and Administration*, H.R. Loyn and John Percival. Copyright © 1976 by the author and reprinted by permission of St. Martin's Press, LLC.

**Jo Ann McNamara and John E. Halborg, E. Gordon Whatley, trans.**: "Here Begins the Life of the Blessed Queen Bathild," in *Sainted Women of the Dark Ages*, pp. 268–270. Copyright, 1992, Duke University Press. All rights reserved. Reprinted by permission of the publisher.

**Konstantin Mihailovic**: *Memoirs of a Janissary*, trans. Benjamin Stolz. Michigan Slavic Translations no. 3 (Ann Arbor: Michigan Slavic Publications, 1975), pp. 157–159. Copyright © 1975, Michigan Slavic Publications. Reprinted by courtesy of Michigan Slavic Publications, Ann Arbor, Mich.

**National Council of the Churches of Christ in the USA**: 1 Maccabees 1, 2 Maccabees 4, 4 Maccabees 6, 1 Samuel 8:4–22, 10:20–25, 1 Samuel 9:1–10:1, Acts of the Apostles 23:31–24:27, Genesis 6:5–9:1 from the New Revised Standard Version of the Bible, copyright © 1989 the National Council of the Churches of Christ in the USA. Used by permission. All rights reserved.

**Denys Page**: "The Tawagalawas Letter" from *History and the Homeric Iliad*, by Denys Page (Berkeley: University of California Press, 1959), pp. 11–12. © 1959 by the Regents of the University of California, renewed 1987 by Denys Page. Reprinted by permission of the University of California Press.

**Phintys**: From Lefkowitz, Mary R., and Maureen B. Fant, eds.. *Women's Life in Greece and Rome*, second edition. pp. 163–164. © 1992 Maureen B. Fant & Mary R. Lefkowitz. Reprinted by permission of Gerald Duckworth & Co. Ltd and The Johns Hopkins University Press.

**E.M. Plass**: From *What Luther Says, Vol. II*, (pgs. 888–889) © 1959, 1987 Concordia Publishing House. Used with permission of CPH. All rights reserved.

**Plato**: 365 words from *The Last Days of Socrates* by Plato, translated with an introduction by Hugh Tredennick (Penguin Classics 1954, Third edition 1969). Copyright © Hugh Tredennick, 1954, 1959, 1969. Reproduced by permission of Penguin Books Ltd.

**Pliny the Younger**, Letters from Book Ten of *Pliny the Younger: Complete Letters*, trans. P.G. Walsh. Copyright © P.G. Walsh 2006. Reprinted by permission of Oxford University Press.

**Plutarch**: From Lefkowitz, Mary R., and Maureen B. Fant, eds.. *Women's Life in Greece and Rome*, second edition. pp. 147–149. © 1992 Maureen B. Fant & Mary R. Lefkowitz. Reprinted by permission of Gerald Duckworth & Co. Ltd and The Johns Hopkins University Press.

**Polybius**: 350 words from *The Rise of the Roman Empire* by Polybius, translated by Ian Scott-Kilvert, selected with an introduction by F.W. Walbank (Penguin Classics, 1979). Copyright © Ian Scott-Kilvert, 1979. Reproduced by permission of Penguin Books Ltd.

**James B. Pritchard (ed.)**: "Cyrus (557–529)." From *Ancient Near Eastern Texts Relating to the Old Testament – Third Edition with Supplement*. © 1950, 1955, 1969, renewed 1978 by Princeton University Press. Reprinted by permission of Princeton University Press.

**Martha T. Roth**: Excerpts from "The Code of Hammurabi" from *Law Collections from Mesopotamia and Asia Minor*, edited by Martha T. Roth (Scholars Press, 1997), pp. 80–82, 84, 91, 100, 105, 108. Reprinted by permission of Society of Biblical Literature.

**Samuel the Nagid**: "A Hebrew Poem in Praise of Wine." Reprinted from *Wine, Women, and Death: Medieval Hebrew Poems on the Good Life*, © 1986, by Raymond P. Scheindlin, published by The Jewish Publication Society with the permission of the publisher.

**Sappho**: "Fragment 16" from *The Poetry of Sappho*, translated and notes by Jim Powell, pp. 6–7. Copyright © 2007 by Jim Powell. Reprinted by permission of Oxford University Press. "Sappho to Her Pupils," translated by Lachlan Mackinnon, *Times Literary Supplement*, July 15, 2005. We have made diligent efforts to contact the copyright holder to obtain permission to reprint this section. If you have information that would help us, please write to Permissions Department, W. W. Norton & Company, Inc., 500 Fifth Avenue, New York, NY 10110.

**Michael Sells (trans.)**: "81: The Overturning" from *Approaching the Qur'an: The Early Revelations*, translated by Michael Sells, pp. 48, 50. Copyright © 1999 by Michael A. Sells. Reprinted by permission of White Cloud Press.

**M.C. Seymour (ed.)**: "The Legend of Prester John" from *Mandeville's Travels*, pp. 195–199. Copyright © 1967, Clarendon Press. Reprinted by permission of Oxford University Press.

**Sidonius**: Reprinted by permission of the publishers and the Trustees of the Loeb Classical Library from *Sidonius: Volume II – Letters*, Loeb Classical Library Volume 420, prepared by W.H. Semple and E.H. Warmington from material left by W.B. Anderson, pp. 127–129, 181–183, Cambridge, Mass.: Harvard University Press, Copyright © 1965 by the President and Fellows of Harvard College. Loeb Classical Library ® is a registered trademark of the President and Fellows of Harvard College.

**William Kelly Simpson (ed.)**: "The Prophecies of Neferty" from *The Literature of Ancient Egypt*, pp. 214–220. Copyright © 2003 by Yale University. All rights reserved. Reprinted by permission of Yale University Press.

**St. Ambrose**: "The Memorial of Symmachus, Prefect of the City" from *A Select Library of Nicene and Post-Nicene Fathers of the Christian Church, Vol. X*, eds. Schaff & Wace (Grand Rapids, MI: Wm. B. Eerdmans Publishing Company, 1955), pp. 414–415.

**St. Francis of Assisi**: Excerpts from *St. Francis of Assisi: Omnibus of Sources, Volume One*, edited by Marion A. Habig, © 2008 by St. Anthony Messenger Press, are used by permission. All rights reserved.

**Tacitus**: 480 words from *The Annals of Imperial Rome* by Tacitus, translated with and introduction by Michael Grant (Penguin Classics 1956, Sixth revised edition 1989). Copyright © Michael Grant Publications Ltd, 1956, 1959, 1971, 1973, 1975, 1977, 1989. Reproduced by permission of Penguin Books Ltd.

**Tyrtaeus**: "Exhortation to the Young Hoplite" from *University of Chicago Readings in Western Civilization, Vol. 1*, eds. Adkins & White, pp. 23–24. Copyright © 1986 by The University of Chicago. Reprinted by permission of The University of Chicago Press.

**Pope Urban II**: "Pope Urban II's Call at Clermont, November 1195" from *The Crusades: A Reader*, edited by S.J. Allen and Emilie Amt. © Broadview Press/UTP Higher Education. Reprinted with permission of the publisher.

**Peter Waldo**: "The Conversion of Peter Waldo" from *The Birth of Popular Heresy*, edited/translated by Robert I. Moore (Edward Arnold, 1975). Copyright © 1975, Edward Arnold Publishers. Reproduced by permission of Edward Arnold (Publishers) Limited.

**Xenophon**: "Book I, The Anabasis" from *The Greek Historians* by M.I. Finley, copyright © 1959 by The Viking Press, Inc., renewed © 1987 by Charles Richard Whittaker. Used by permission of Viking Penguin, a division of Penguin Group (USA) Inc.

# Photo Credits

**Chapter 1: p. 2:** The Louve, Paris. Giraudon/Art Resource, NY; **p. 5:** The Bridgeman Art Library; **p. 7:** Hirmer Fotoarchiv; **p. 9:** Nick Wheeler; **p. 10 (left):** British Museum; **p. 10 (right):** Ashmolean Museum, Oxford; **p. 14:** Bettmann Corbis; **p. 15:** Courtesy of the Oriental Institute of the University of Chicago; **p. 16 (left):** Iraq Museum, Baghdad, Iraq. Photo: Scala/Art Resource, NY; **p. 16 (right):** University of Pennsylvania Museum; **p. 17:** Hirmer Fotoarchiv; **p. 19:** The Louvre, Paris/Herve Lewandowski, Réunion des Musées/Nationaux Art Resource, NY; **p. 21 (left):** Eric Lessing/Art Resource; **p. 21 (right):** Art Resource; **p. 25 (left):** Scala/Art Resource; **p. 25 (right):** Scala/Art Resource; **p. 26 (top):** Ancient Civilizations, 2/E by Scarre/Fagan, (c) 2003. Reprinted by permission of Pearson Education, Inc., Upper Saddle River, NJ; **p. 26 (bottom):** Bettmann/Corbis; **p. 27:** Roger Wood/Corbis; **p. 28:** Charles & Josette Lenars/Corbis; **p. 29:** Archivo Iconografico, S.A./Corbis; **p. 30:** The Metropolitan Museum of Art/Art Resource, NY; **p. 32 (left):** British Museum/HIP/Art Resource, NY; **p. 32 (right):** British Museum/HIP/Art Resource, NY; **p. 34:** The Louvre, Paris/ Bridgeman Art Library.

**Chapter 2: p. 36:** Erich Lessing/Art Resource, NY; **p. 40:** The Trustees of The British Museum/Art Resource, NY; **p. 44:** Jose Fuste Raga/Corbis; **p. 42 (left):** PCL/Alamy; **p. 42 (right):** Ian M Butterfield (P)/Alamy; **p. 43 (left):** Sebastian Bergmann/Flickr/Creative Commons; **p. 43 (right):** Jim Henderson/Alamy; **p. 45 (top):** Erich Lessing/Art Resource, NY; **p. 45: (bottom):** Boltin Picture Library; **p. 47:** Gian Berto Vanni/Corbis; **p. 48:** Erich Lessing/Art Resource, NY; **p. 49 (top):** Gianni Dagli Orti/Corbis; **p. 49 (bottom):** Gianni Dagli Orti/Corbis; **p. 68:** Courtesy of Zev Radovan; **p. 60:** British Museum, London, Great Britain, photo: Erich Lessing/Art Resource, NY; **p. 61:** Gianni Dagli Orti/Corbis; **p. 62:** The Metropolitan Museum of Art/Art Resource, NY; **p. 66:** The Art Gallery Collection/ Alamy; **p. 69:** Bildarchiv Preussischer Kulturbesitz/Art Resource, NY.

**Chapter 3: p. 72:** Erich Lessing/Art Resource, NY; **p. 74:** Nagelestock.com/Alamy; **p. 80:** Wikimedia commons; **p. 81:** Greek Infantry Advancing into Combat (Hirmer Fotoarchiv); **p. 83:** Reunion des Musees Nationaux/Art Resource, NY; **p. 86:** American School of Classical Studies at Athens: Agora Excavations; **p. 85:** Scala/Art Resource, NY; **p. 91:** Photo: Paul Lipke/Trireme Trust, Montague, MA; **p. 93:** National Museums of Scotland/Bridgeman Art Library; **p. 95 (right):** Vanni/Art Resource, NY; **p. 96 (left):** Hartwig Koppermann; **p. 96 (center):** Photo (c) RMN Paris; **p. 96 (right):** Nimatallah/Art Resource, NY; p. 97: Original model by G.P. Stevens; additions by Sylvia Hahn/Royal Ontario Museum; **p. 98:** Bildarchiv Preussischer Kulturbesitz/Art Resource, NY; **p. 101:** Erich Lessing/Art Resource, NY; **p. 104:** Deutschen Archaologischen.

**Chapter 4: p. 106:** Erich Lessing/Art Resource, NY; **p. 108:** The Art Archive/Gianni Dagli Orti; **p. 112 (left):** Marie-Lan Nguyen/ Ludovisi Collection/Wikimedia; **p. 112 (right):** Vanni/Art Resource, NY; **p. 113:** Marie-Lan Nguyen/Wikimedia Commons; **p. 114:** Scala/Art Resource, NY; **p. 117:** Gianni Dagli Orti/Corbis; **p. 118:** Erin Babnik/Alamy; **p. 119 (top):** Erich Lessing/Art Resource, NY; **p. 119 (bottom):** Erich Lessing/Art Resource, NY; **p. 120:** Wikimedia Commons; **p. 122:** www.livius.org; **p. 125 (left):** The Trustees of the British Museum; **p. 125 (right):** Bildarchiv Preussischer Kulturbesitz/Art Resource, NY; **p. 127:** Erich Lessing/Art Resource, NY; **p. 134:** Verulamium Museum, St.Albans, Hertfordshire, UK/The Bridgeman Art Library; **p. 135:** Interfoto/Alamy; **p. 136 (top):** Erdmut Lerner; **p. 136 (bottom):** Scala/Art Resource, NY; **p. 137 (left):** Marie-Lan Nguyen/Wikimedia Commons; **p. 137 (right):** Scala/Art Resource, NY.

**Chapter 5: p. 141:** Scala/Art Resource, NY; **p. 143:** Italic, Etruscan, Late Classical or Early Hellenistic Period, about 330-300 BC; Findspot and Place of Manufacture: Italy, Lazio, Vulci; Marble, 93.3cm high x 117.4 cm width x 213.8 cm length; Museum of Fine Arts, Boston, Gift of Mrs. Gardner Brewer, 86.145a-b. Photograph © 2004 Museum of Fine Arts, Boston; **p. 146:** Statue of Cincinnatus, Cincinnati, OH, 2010, by Rick Dikeman; **p. 147:** WoodyStock/ Alamy; **p. 148:** Scala/Art Resource, NY; **p. 151:** The Trustees of the British Museum; **p. 155:** Scala/Art Resource, NY; **p. 157:** Scala/Art Resource, NY; **p. 158:** Sandro Vannini/Corbis; **p. 159:** The Trustees of the British Museum; **p. 161:** The Granger Collection, New York; **p. 164:** Courtesy of Carol Symes; **p. 165:** Silver Stock/Alamy; **p. 167 (top):** The Trustees of the British Museum; **p. 167 (bottom):** Scala/Art Resource, NY; **p. 169 (top):** Vanni/Art Resource, NY; **p. 169 (bottom):** The Print Collector/Alamy.

**Chapter 6: p. 174:** Alinari/Art Resource, NY; **p. 177:** Erich Lessing/ Art Resource, NY; **p. 178:** AFP Photo/Osservatore Romano/Pontifical Commission for Sacred Archeology; **p. 180:** TopFoto/The Image Works; **p. 181:** Akg-images/Pirozzi; **p. 186:** The Trustees of the British Museum; **p. 185:** Gift of Martin A. Ryerson, 1922.4883. Photograph © 1997, The Art Institute of Chicago; **p. 187:** Warder Collection, NY; **p. 190 (left):** Wikipedia Commons; **p. 190 (right):** Wikipedia Commons; **p. 191:** The Trustees of the British Museum; **p. 194:** The Louvre, Paris. Photo: Herve Lewandowski, Reunion des Musees Nationaux/Art Resource, NY; **p. 198:** Warder Collection;

**p. 202:** By permission of the Houghton Library, Harvard University; **p. 204:** Biblioteca Medicea Laurenziana, Florence.

**Chapter 7: p. 206:** akg-images; **p. 210 (top):** Scala/Art Resource, NY; **p. 210 (bottom):** Scala/Art Resource, NY; **p. 211:** Wikipedia Commons; **p. 213:** Wikipedia Commons; **p. 216:** Vanni/Art Resource, NY; **p. 217:** The Art Archive/Dagli Orti; **p. 219:** Jamal Nasrallah/epa/Corbis; **p. 221:** Frédéric Soltan/Sygma/Corbis; **p. 222:** Bildarchiv Preussischer Kulturbesitz/Art Resource, NY; **p. 226 (left):** Birmingham Museums & Art Gallery; **p. 226 (right):** The Trustees of the British Museum/Art Resource, NY; **p. 227 (top):** The Trustees of the British Museum; **p. 227 (left):** The Trustees of the British Museum; **p. 227 (right):** The Trustees of the British Museum; **p. 228:** Courtesy of Carol Symes; **p. 230 (left):** The Pierpont Morgan Library/Art Resource, NY; **p. 230 (right):** The Granger Collection, New York; **p. 234:** Bibliotheque Nationale, Paris, France/The Bridgeman Art Library; **p. 235:** Vatian Library: MS. Reg. Ret. 762, fol. 82r, written at Tours 800 A.D. (detail).

**Chapter 8: p. 240:** The Granger Collection, New York; **p. 242:** Berig/Wikimedia Commons; **p. 244:** Wikimedia Commons; **p. 245 (left):** Biblioteca Riccardiana, Florence, Manuscript Ricc. 492 c. 18, with the permission of the Ministero per I Beni Culturali e Ambientali; **p. 245 (right):** The Art Archive/Biblioteca Nazionale Marciana Venice/Dagli Orti (A); **p. 247:** From David Nicholas, Urban Europe, 1100-1700 (Palgrave MacMillan, 2003, p.74 fig 3.3); **p. 249:** The Granger Collection, New York; **p. 250:**The Art Archive/British Library/British Library; **p. 251:** Wikimedia Commons; **p. 254 (top):** French School/The Bridgeman Art Library/Getty Images; **p. 254 (bottom):** French School/The Bridgeman Art Library/Getty Images; **p. 255:** The Granger Collection, New York; **p. 256:** Wikimedia Commons; **p. 257:** Treasury, Abbey Ste. Foy, Conques, France. Photo: Giraudon/Art Resource, NY; **p. 262:** HIP/Art Resource, NY; **p. 269:** Triumph of St Thomas Aquinas, detail of figure below the throne, from the Spanish Chapel, c.1365 (fresco), Andrea di Bonaiuto (Andrea da Firenze) (fl.1343–77)/Santa Maria Novella, Florence, Italy/The Bridgeman Art Library; **p. 268:** Giraudon/Art Resource, NY; **p. 270:** The Metropolitan Museum of Art/Art Resource, NY.

**Chapter 9: p. 274:** The Granger Collection, New York; **p. 276:** Giraudon/Art Resource, NY; **p. 277:** The Walters Art Gallery, Baltimore; **p. 282:** Wikimedia Commons; **p. 284:** Benito Ruiz/Newscom; **p. 285 (left):** The Art Archive/Archivo de la Corona de Aragon Barcelona/Laurie Platt Winfrey; **p. 285 (right):** The Granger Collection, New York; **p. 287:** Bibliotheque Sainte-Genevieve, Paris, France/Archives Charmet/The Bridgeman Art Library; **p. 290:** © Otto Muller Verlag, Salzburg, Austria; **p. 291:** The Metropolitan Museum of Art/Art Resource, NY; **p. 292:** Sueddeutsche Zeitung Photo/The Image Works; **p. 296:** Bayerische Staatsbibliothek, München; **p. 297 (left):** Cliché Bibliothèque Nationale de France, Paris; **p. 297 (right):** Cliché Bibliothèque Nationale de France, Paris; **p. 298:** Erich Lessing/Art Resource, NY; **p. 303:** AKG-images; **p. 307 (left):**Richard List/Corbis; **p. 307(right):** Richard List/Corbis.

**Chapter 10: p. 310:** Réunion des Musées Nationaux/Art Resource, NY; **p. 312:** HIP/Art Resource, NY; **p. 317:** Réunion des Musées Nationaux/Art Resource, NY; **p. 318:** Réunion des Musées Nationaux/Art Resource, NY; **p. 319:** Réunion des Musées Nationaux/Art Resource, NY; **p. 324:** Réunion des Musées Nationaux/Art Resource, NY; **p. 325:** Museo del Prado, Madrid; **p. 329:** Vova Pomortzeff/Alamy; **p. 330:** Chris Hellier/Corbis; **p. 334:** The Art Archive; **p. 336:** The Art Archive/British Library; **p. 338:** British Library/Art Resource, NY; **p. 340:** Cameraphoto Arte, Venice/Art Resource, NY; **p. 341 (left):** Scala/Art Resource, NY; **p. 341 (right):** Bildarchiv Preussischer Kulturbesitz/Art Resource, NY; **p. 342:** Bibliothèque Royale Albert I, Brussels; **p. 344:** Bibliothèque Royale Albert I, Brussels, ms. 11209, fol. 3 recto.

**Chapter 11: p. 346:** The Art Archive/Topkapi Museum Istanbul/Gianni Dagli Orti; **p. 350:** Wikimedia Commons; **p. 348:** John Massey Stewart Picture Library; **p. 351:** Bibliotheque Nationale, Paris, France/The Bridgeman Art Library; **p. 354:** Werner Forman Archive/Topkapi Palace Library, Istanbul/Art Resource, NY; **p. 357:** Mansell/TimePix; **p. 358:** Cameraphoto Arte, Venice/Art Resource, NY; **p. 359:** Myriam Thyes/Wikimedia Commons; **p. 361:** Wikimedia Commons; **p. 362:** Royal Armouries Museum; **p. 363:** José Pessoa, Arquivo Nacional de Fotografia, Instituto Português de Museus; **p. 365:** Bibliotheque Nationale, Paris, France/Giraudon/The Bridgeman Art Library; **p. 364:** akg-images; **p. 368:**The Art Archive/Biblioteca Nacional de Madrid/Dagli Orti.

**Chapter 12: p. 372:** Erich Lessing/Art Resource, NY; **p. 378:** Erich Lessing/Art Resource, NY; **p. 380:** Reunion de Musees Nationaux; **p. 383:** Erich Lessing/Art Resource, NY; **p. 384:** Erich Lessing/Art Resource, NY; **p. 385:** Galleria degli Uffizi, Florence, Italy/The Bridgeman Art Library; **p. 386 (bottom):** Scala/Art Resource, NY; **p. 386 (top):** Réunion des Musées Nationaux/Art Resource, NY; **p. 387 (bottom):** Ted Spiegel/Corbis; **p. 387 (top):** Erich Lessing/Art Resource, NY; **p. 388 (bottom):** Vatican Museums and Galleries, Vatican City, Italy/Alinari/The Bridgeman Art Library; **p. 388 (top):** Scala/Art Resource, NY; **p. 389 (center):** Scala/Art Resource, NY; **p. 389 (left):** Nimatallah/Art Resource, NY; **p. 389 (right):** Erich Lessing/Art Resource, NY; **p. 391:** Bildarchiv Preussischer Kulturbesitz/Art Resource, NY; **p. 392:** Sandro Vannini/Corbis; **p. 393:** Louvre, Paris, France/Giraudon/The Bridgeman Art Library; **p. 394:** National Portrait Gallery, London, UK/The Bridgeman Art Library; **p. 395 (bottom):** Bildarchiv Preussischer Kulturbesitz/Art Resource, NY; **p. 395 (top):** Vanni/Art Resource, NY.

**Chapter 13: p. 398:** The Art Archive/Nationalmuseet Copenhagen Denmark/Alfredo Dagli Orti; **p. 400:** Martin Luther, portrait by Louis Cranach (Scala/Art Resource); **p. 401:** Bildarchiv Preussischer Kulturbesitz/Art Resource, NY; **p. 402:** Sandro Vannini/Corbis; **p. 403:** Staatsbibliothek, Bern; **p. 404 (left):** Staatsbibliothek, Bern; **p. 404 (right):** Staatliche Museen zu Berlin-Preußischer Kulturbesitz, Kupferstichkabinett; **p. 405 (left):** By permission of the British Library/Art Resource, NY; **p. 405 (right):** Alinari/Art Resource, NY; **p. 406:** Bayerische Staatsgemäldesammlungen/Alte Pinakothek, Munich; **p. 408:** Wikipedia Commons; **p. 410 (left):** Warder Collection, NY; **p. 410 (right):** Warder Collection, NY; **p. 412 (left):** Erich Lessing/Art Resource, NY; **p. 412 (right):** Warder Collection, NY; **p. 416:** National Trust/Art Resource, NY; **p. 419 (right):** Scala/Art Resource, NY; **p. 419 (right):** Scala/Art Resource, NY; **p. 420:**

Scala/Art Resource, NY; **p. 421:** Kunsthistorisches Museum, Vienna; **p. 423:** Corbis.

**Chapter 14: p. 426:** Woburn Abbey, Bedfordshire, UK/The Bridgeman Art Library International; **p. 429:** Bettmann/Corbis; **p. 430:** Gianni Dagli Orti/Corbis; **p. 431:** Archivo Iconografico, S.A./Corbis; **p. 433:** The New York Public Library: Astor, Lenox, and Tilden Foundations/Art Resource, NY; **p. 434:** Wikimedia Commons; **p. 438**: Archivo Iconografico, S.A./Corbis; **p. 441:** The National Trust Photolibrary/Alamy; **p. 444:** Wikimedia Commons; **p. 445:** Interfoto/Alamy; **p. 446:** Wikimedia Commons; **p. 447:** Bibliothéque des Arts decoratifs, Paris/Bridgeman Art Library; **p. 450:** Scala/Art Resource, NY; **p. 451:** Image copyright © The Metropolitan Museum of Art/Art Resource, NY; **p. 451:** Museo del Prado, Madrid; **p. 452 (left):** © English Heritage Photo Library; **p. 452 (right):** Gift of Mr. and Mrs. Robert Woods Bliss, © 1997 Board of Trustees, National Gallery of Art, Washington, D.C.; **p. 453:** Erich Lessing/Art Resource, NY; **p. 453:** Nimatallah/Art Resrouce, NY.

**Chapter 15: p. 456:** The Royal Collection © 2010 Her Majesty Queen Elizabeth II; **p. 462 (left):** Erich Lessing/Art Resource, NY; **p. 462 (right):** Réunion des Musées Nationaux/Art Resource, NY; **p. 463 (bottom):** Giraudon/Art Resource, NY; **p. 463 (top):** With kind permission of the University of Edinburgh/The Bridgeman Art Library International; **p. 466:** The Royal Collection © 2010 Her Majesty Queen Elizabeth II; **p. 467:** Snark/Art Resource, NY; **p. 468:** Bridgeman Art Library; **p. 469:** The Art Archive/Musee du Chateau de Versailles/Dagli Orti; **p. 470:** Scala/Art Resource, NY; **p. 472:** Interfoto/Alamy; **p. 473:** Bildarchiv Preussischer Kulturbesitz/Art Resource, NY; **p. 474:** Courtesy Dr. Alexander Boguslawski, Professor of Russian Studies, Rollins College; **p. 476:** Giraudon/Art Resource, NY; **p. 477:** Giraudon/Art Resource, NY; **p. 480:** Ali Meyer/Corbis; **p. 482:** Corbis; **p. 484:** John R. Freeman & Co.; **p. 485:** Gianni Dagli Orti/Corbis; **p. 486:** Warder Collection, NY.

# Index

Page numbers in *italics* refer to illustrations, maps, and tables.